THIRD EDITION

UNIX POWER TOOLS

Shelley Powers, Jerry Peek, Tim O'Reilly, and Mike Loukides

with *Steven Champeon, Joe Johnston, and Deborah Hooker*

and other authors of O'Reilly books, including Linda Mui, Dale Dougherty, Larry Wall, Randal Schwarz, and Tom Christiansen

as well as Usenet contributors, including Chris Torek, Jonathan Kamens, and Bruce Barnett

O'REILLY®

Beijing · Cambridge · Farnham · Köln · Paris · Sebastopol · Taipei · Tokyo

Unix Power Tools, Third Edition
by Shelley Powers, Jerry Peek, Tim O'Reilly, Mike Loukides, and other contributors
(A complete list of contributors is given in the Preface.)

Published by O'Reilly Media, Inc., 1005 Gravenstein Highway North, Sebastopol, CA 95472.

O'Reilly & Associates books may be purchased for educational, business, or sales promotional use.
Online editions are also available for most titles (*safari.oreilly.com*). For more information, contact our
corporate/institutional sales department: (800) 998-9938 or *corporate@oreilly.com*.

Editors:	Tim O'Reilly, Laurie Petrycki, and Chuck Toporek
Production Editor:	Jeffrey Holcomb
Cover Designer:	Edie Freedman
Interior Designer:	David Futato

Printing History:

March 1993:	First Edition.
August 1997:	Second Edition.
October 2002:	Third Edition.

ISBN: 0-596-00330-7
[M]
[3/04]

Table of Contents

Part II   Customizing Your Environment

Part V   Processes and the Kernel

Part VII   Extending and Managing Your Environment

How to Use This Book

Dictionary-Style Headers

As in a dictionary, we show the entry that starts or ends each page. On a lefthand page, the first article whose title is visible is shown in the shaded box to the upper left; on a righthand page, the last article is shown in the upper right.

Summary Boxes

You'll see gray shaded summary boxes all through the book. They summarize a topic and point you to articles with examples and further explanation.

Article Number

The first two digits indicate in which chapter the article resides; the last two digits indicate the number of the article within that chapter. The article number is used to refer to this article in all cross-references throughout the book.

Cross-Reference in a Sentence

To find out more about the topic displayed in gray type, see the article referenced by the number in parentheses immediately following the term.

Cross-Reference in a Code Example

When a cross-reference occurs in an example, the cross-referenced text and related article number appear in the left margin.

14.12

We'll also give hints for:

- Deleting unused (or rarely used) files (article 14.12).
- Deleting all the files in a directory, except for one or two (article 14.13).

Most tips for deleting files also work for renaming the files (if you want to keep them): just replace the *rm* command with *mv*.

—ML

14.12 Deleting Stale Files

Sooner or later, a lot of junk collects in your directories: files that you don't really care about and never use. It's possible to write *find* (9.1) commands that will automatically clean these up. If you want to clean up regularly, you can add some *find* commands to your *crontab* file (25.2).

Basically, all you need to do is write a *find* command that locates files based on their last access time (*–atime* (9.9)), and use *–ok* or *–exec* (9.9) to delete them. Such a command might look like this:

```
% find . -atime +60 -ok rm -f {} \;
```

This locates files that haven't been accessed in the last 60 days, asks if you want to delete the file, and then deletes the file. (If you run it from *cron*, make sure you use *–exec* instead of *–ok*; and make *absolutely sure* that the *find* won't delete files that you think are important.)

Of course, you can modify this *find* command to exclude (or select) files with particular names; for example, the command below deletes old core dumps and GNU Emacs backup files (whose names end in ~), but leaves all others alone:

```
% find . \( -name core -o -name "*~" \) -atime +60 -ok rm -f {} \;
```

If you take an automated approach to deleting stale files, here are some things to watch out for:

- There are plenty of files (for example, Unix utilities and log files) that should *never* be removed. Never run any "automatic deletion" script on /usr or / or any other "system" directory.
- On some systems, executing a binary executable doesn't update the last access time. Since there's no reason to read these files, you can expect them to get pretty stale, even if they're used often. You don't want to delete them. If you cook up a complicated enough *find* command, you should be able to handle this automatically. Something like this should (at least partially) do the trick:

```
! 9.6
–perm 9.15          % find . -atime +30 ! -perm -111 ... -exec rm {} \;
```

266   Part Three: Working with the Filesystem

Running Footer

The part title appears in the footer on all lefthand pages; the chapter title appears on all righthand pages (except for the first page of any chapter).

Globe

If you don't want to type this script into a file yourself, or if we're talking about a C program that isn't shown, you can download it from the book's web site. See the *Preface* for full details on the content available for download.

Screw

Be careful with this feature, or you might get screwed.

Pushpin

A note to keep in mind, or a helpful tip.

Bomb

A bomb icon in the margin is a cross-reference to another article that explains the possible trouble you might encounter using the tip or script in the current article. (You can think of the bomb as a cross-referenced screw.)

Author's Initials

The author's full name is listed in the Preface.

join

join can do a lot more than this simple example shows. See your online manual page. The GNU version of *join* is on the CD-ROM.

—JP

21.20 What is (or isn't) Unique?

uniq

uniq reads a file and compares adjacent lines (which means you'll usually want to sort the file first—to be sure identical lines appear next to each other). Here's what *uniq* can do as it watches the input lines stream by:

- With the *-u* option, the output gets only the lines that occur just once (and weren't repeated).
- The *-d* option does the opposite: the output gets a *single* copy of each line that was repeated (no matter how many times it was repeated).

  (The GNU version also has a *-D* option. It's like *-d* except that *all* duplicate lines are output.)
- The default output (with no options) is the union of *-u* and *-d*: only the first occurrence of a line is written to the output file; any adjacent copies of a line (second, third, etc.) are ignored.
- The output with *-c* is like the default, but each line is preceded by a count of how many times it occurred.

Be warned:

```
% uniq file1 file2
```

will *not* print the unique lines from both *file1* and *file2* to standard output. It will *replace* the contents of *file2* with the unique lines from *file1*!

Three more options control how comparisons are done:

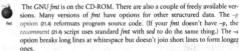
Real World-watching generation fail to realize is that
our American forefathers, under the tutelage of Zog,
the wizened master sage from Zeta-Reticuli, had to fight
not only the godless and effete British for our system of
self-determined government, but also avoid the terrors of
hypno-death from the dark and unclean Draco-Reptillians.

There is one subtlety to *fmt* to be aware of: *fmt* expects sentences to end with either a period, a question mark or an exclaimation point followed by two spaces. If your document isn't marked up according to this convention, *fmt* can't differentiated between sentences and abbreviations. This is a common "gotcha" that appears frequently on Usenet.

On at least one version of Unix, *fmt* is a disk initializer (disk formatter) command. Don't run *that* command accidentally! Check your online manual page and see the *fmt* equivalents below.

There are a few different versions of *fmt*, some fancier than others. In general, the program assumes that:

- Paragraphs have blank lines between them.
- If a line is indented, keep the indentation.
- The output lines should be about 70 characters wide. Some have a command line option to let you set this. For example, fmt -132 (or, on some versions, fmt -1 132) would reformat your file to have lines with no more than 132 characters on each.
- It reads files or standard input. Lines will be written to standard output.

fmt

The GNU *fmt* is on the CD-ROM. There are also a couple of freely available versions. Many versions of *fmt* have options for other structured data. The *-p* option (21.4) reformats program source code. (If your *fmt* doesn't have *-p*, the *recomment* (21.4) script uses standard *fmt* with *sed* to do the same thing.) The *-s* option breaks long lines at whitespace but doesn't join short lines to form longer ones.

Alternatively, you can make your own (21.3) simple (and a little slower) version with *sed* and *nroff*. If you want to get fancy (and use some *nroff* and/or *tbl* coding), this will let you do automatically formatted text tables, bulleted lists, and much more.

—JP, TOR, and JJ

21.3 Alternatives to fmt

fmt (21.2) is hard to do without once you've learned about it. Unfortunately, it's not available in some versions of Unix. You can get the GNU version from the

Preface

A Book for Browsing

Technical books can be boring. But this is not an ordinary technical book! This book is like an almanac, a news magazine, and a hypertext database all rolled into one. Instead of trying to put the topics in perfect order—and expecting you to start at the beginning, then read through to the end—we hope that you'll browse. Start anywhere. Read what you want. (That's not quite true. First, you should read this Preface and the pages before it titled *How to Use This Book*. They will help you get the most out of your time with this book. Next, you may want to skim through the Unix fundamentals in Chapter 1. *Then* read what you want.)

Like an Almanac

The book is full of practical information. The main purpose isn't to teach you concepts (though they're in here). We've picked a lot of common problems, and we'll show you how to solve them.

Even though it's not designed to be read in strict order, the book is organized into chapters with related subject matter. If you want to find a specific subject, the table of contents is still a good place to start. In addition, several of the chapters contain **shaded boxes**. These are like small tables of contents on a particular subject, which might be even more limited than the scope of the chapter itself. Use the **Index** when you're trying to find a specific piece of information instead of a general group of articles about a topic.

Like a News Magazine

This book has **short articles**. Most show a problem and a solution—in one page or less. The articles are numbered within each chapter. Not all articles are "how-to" tips. Some articles have background information and concepts.

Like a Hypertext Database

Each article doesn't define all the concepts and words used. Instead, it gives you "links" that let you get more information *if you need it*. It's easy to get more information when you need it, but just skip the link if you don't. *Unix Power Tools* uses two kinds of links: those in a sentence and those in the margin. For examples, see the pages before this Preface titled *How to Use This Book*.

Programs on the Web

 The book describes scripts and freely available programs that are available on the web site. An article about a program or file that's on the web site will have a globe icon next to it, like this. To get one of these programs, visit the web site:

http://www.oreilly.com/catalog/upt3/

About Unix Versions

There are lots of similarities between different versions of Unix. But it's almost impossible to write a book that covers every detail of every version correctly. Where we know there might be big differences or problems, we'll print a note in the text. Other places, we're forced to use "weasel words" like "Some versions of XXX will do...," without telling you exactly *which* versions. When you see those weasel words, what can you do?

- If the command or feature won't destroy anything when it doesn't work, try it! For instance, don't experiment with *rm*, the command that removes files. But *cat*, a command that shows files, probably won't hurt anything if some feature doesn't work with your version.

- Look at the *online* manual or check your *vendor's* latest printed manuals. However, even these can be wrong. For instance, your system administrator may have installed a local version of a command that works differently—but not updated the online documentation. Be careful with "generic" manuals, the kind you buy at a bookstore; there are lots of versions of Unix, and the manual may not match your version closely enough.

- Ask your system administrator or another "guru" for help before you use a command that might be dangerous.

Cross-References

If a cross-reference is to a single word—for example, a command name like this: *tar*—the cross reference is probably to an article that introduces that command. Cross references to phrases—like this: from a parent process to child process—are to an article that explains more about the concept or problem printed in gray.

Cross references don't necessarily give a complete list of all articles about a topic. We've tried to pick one or a few articles that give the best information. For a more complete list, use the Index.

What's New in the Third Edition

There have been some big changes in Unix since we wrote the first edition in the early 1990s, and there's been a surprising number of changes since the second edition, released in the late 1990s. Well over half of the articles have been revised, and we've expanded our coverage of the so-called small Unix flavors: Linux, FreeBSD, Mac OS X's Darwin, and so on.

A major change to this edition was the addition of several new topics relevant to today's connected world, including protecting your machine from attack and several articles related to Internet protocols. We've also added chapters with coverage of two of the more popular languages used in Unix: Perl and Python.

Typefaces and Other Conventions

Italic

> Is used for the names of all Unix utilities, switches, directories, and filenames and to emphasize new terms and concepts when they are first introduced. It's also used in programs and examples to explain what's happening or what's been left out at the ... marks.

Bold

> Is used occasionally within text to make words easy to find—just like movie stars' names in the People section of your local newspaper.

`Constant width`

> Is used for sample code fragments and examples. A reference in text to a word or item used in an example or code fragment is also shown in constant width font.

`Constant width bold`

> Is used in examples to show commands or text that would be typed in literally by the user.

*Constant width italic, **bold italic***

> Are used in code fragments and examples to show variables for which a context-specific substitution should be made. (The variable *filename*, for example, would be replaced by some actual filename.)

function(n)

> Is a reference to a manual page in Section *n* of the Unix programmer's manual. For example, *getopt(3)* refers to a page called *getopt* in Section 3.

%   Is the C-shell prompt.

$ Is the Bourne-shell prompt.

:-)

> Is a "smiley face" that means "don't take this seriously." The idea started on *Usenet* and spread.

&·...

> Stands for text (usually computer output) that's been omitted for clarity or to save space.

CTRL

> Starts a control character. To create CTRL-d, for example, hold down the "control" key and press the "d" key. Control characters are not case sensitive; "d" refers to both the upper- and lowercase letter. The notation ^D also means CTRL-d. Also, you'll sometimes see the key sequence in bold (for example, **CTRL-d** is used when we want to make it clear exactly what you should type.

˘   Is used in some examples to represent a space chara.cter.

TAB

> Is used in some examples to represent a TAB character.

The Authors

This book is the effort of several authors who have contributed to one edition or another since the first edition was released. Much of the material for the first and second edition came from three authors: Jerry Peek, Tim O'Reilly, and Mike Loukides. Their work is still present, though edited for current times. This third edition brought in four new authors, who edited the previous material, in addition to contributing new articles: Shelley Powers, Steven Champeon, Deborah Hooker, and Joe Johnston.

In addition, we also had several other authors contribute to all three editions—either people who originally posted a good tip to Usenet, authors of Nutshell Handbooks who let us take material from their books, or authors of software packages who let us take a few paragraphs from README files or other documentation.

Here's a list of authors and their initials:

AD	Angus Duggan		JIK	Jonathan I. Kamens
AF	AEleen Frisch		JM	Jeff Moskow
AN	Adrian Nye		JP	Jerry Peek
BA	Brandon S. Allbery		JJ	Joe Johnston
BB	Bruce Barnett		JS	John Strang
BR	Bill Rosenblatt		LK	Lar Kaufman
CT	Chris Torek		LL	Linda Lamb
DC	Debra Cameron		LM	Linda Mui
DD	Dale Dougherty		LW	Larry Wall
DG	Daniel Gilly		MAL	Maarten Litmaath
DH	Dave Hitz		ML	Mike Loukides
DJPH	Deborah Hooker		MS	Mike Stansbery
DL	Don Libes		RS	Randal Schwartz
DR	Daniel Romike		SP	Shelley Powers
DS	Daniel Smith		SG	Simson Garfinkel
EK	Eileen Kramer		SC	Steve Champeon
EP	Eric Pearce		SW	Sun Wu
GS	Gene Spafford		TC	Tom Christiansen
GU	Greg Ubben		TOR	Tim O'Reilly
HS	Henry Spencer		UM	Udi Manber

The Fine Print

Where we show an article from an author on Usenet, that person may not have thought of the idea originally, but may just be passing on something he or she learned. We attribute everything we can.

Request for Comments

Please tell us about any errors you find in this book or ways you think it could be improved. Our U.S. mail address, phone numbers, and electronic mail address are as follows:

O'Reilly & Associates, Inc.
1005 Gravenstein Highway North
Sebastopol, CA 95472
(800) 998-9938 (in the United States or Canada)
(707) 829-0515 (international/local)
(707) 829-0104 (fax)
bookquestions@oreilly.com (email)

Acknowledgments for the First Edition

This book wouldn't exist without Ron Petrusha. As the technical book buyer at Golden-Lee, a major book distributor, he discovered us soon after we started publishing Nutshell Handbooks in the mid-1980s. He was one of our early boosters, and we owed him one. So when he became an editor at Bantam (whose computer-book publishing operations were later acquired by Random House), we took him seriously when he started asking if there was anything we could do together.

At first nothing seemed to fit, since by that time we were doing pretty well as a publisher. We needed to find something that we could do together that might sell better than something that either company might do alone. Eventually, Ron suggested that we copublish a Unix book for Bantam's "Power Tools" series. This made sense for both of us. It gave Bantam access to our Unix expertise and reputation, and it gave us a chance to learn from Bantam about the mass market bookstore trade, as well as build on their successful "Power Tools" series.

But what would the book contain? There were two features of Bantam's original *DOS Power Tools* that we decided to emulate: its in-depth treatment of under-documented system features and its large collection of freely available scripts and utilities. However, we didn't want to write yet another book that duplicated the format of many others on the market, in which chapters on each of the major Unix tools follow one another in predictable succession. Our goal was certainly to provide essential technical information on Unix utilities, but more importantly, to show how the utilities can be combined and used to solve common (and uncommon) problems.

Similarly, because we were weary of the multitude of endless tutorial books about Unix utilities, we wanted to keep the tone brisk and to the point. The solution I came up with, a kind of "hypertext in print," actually owes a lot to Dale Dougherty. Dale has been working for several years on hypertext and online information delivery, and I was trying to get him to work with me on this project. So I tried to imagine the kind of book that he might like to create. (We have a kind of friendly rivalry, in which we try to leapfrog each other with ideas for new and better books!) Dale's involvement never went far beyond the early brainstorming stage, but the book still bears his indirect stamp. In some of the first books he wrote for me, he introduced the idea that sidebars—asides that illuminate and expand on the topic under discussion—could be used effectively in a technical book. Well, Dale, here's a book that's nothing but sidebars!

Dale, Mike Loukides, and I worked out the basic outline for the book in a week or two of brainstorming and mail exchanges. We thought we could throw it together pretty quickly by mining many of our existing books for the tips and tricks buried in them. Unfortunately, none of us was ever able to find enough time, and the book looked to be dying a slow death. (Mike was the only one who got any writing done.) Steve Talbott rescued the project by insisting that it was just too good an idea to let go; he recruited Jerry Peek, who had just joined the company as a writer and Unix consultant/tools developer for our production department.

Production lost the resulting tug of war, and Jerry plunged in. Jerry has forgotten more Unix tips and tricks than Mike, Dale, or I ever knew; he fleshed out our outline and spent a solid year writing and collecting the bulk of the book. I sat back in amazement and delight as Jerry made my ideas take shape. Finally, though, Jerry had had enough. The book was just too big, and he'd never signed on to do it all alone! (It was about 1,000 pages at that point, and only half done.) Jerry, Mike, and I spent a week locked up in our conference room, refining the outline, writing and cutting articles, and generally trying to make Jerry feel a little less like Sisyphus.

From that point on, Jerry continued to carry the ball, but not quite alone, with Mike and I playing "tag team," writing and editing to fill in gaps. I'm especially grateful to Mike for pitching in, since he had many other books to edit and this was supposed to be "my" project. I am continually amazed by the breadth of Mike's knowledge and his knack for putting important concepts in perspective.

Toward the end of the project, Linda Mui finished up another book she was working on and joined the project, documenting many of the freely available utilities that we'd planned to include but hadn't gotten around to writing up. Linda, you really saved us at the end!

Thanks also to all the other authors, who allowed us to use (and sometimes abuse!) their material. In particular, we're grateful to Bruce Barnett, who let us use so much of what he's written, even though we haven't yet published his book, and Chris Torek, who let us use many of the gems he's posted to the Net over the years. (Chris didn't keep copies of most of these articles; they were saved and sent in by Usenet readers, including Dan Duval, Kurt J. Lidl, and Jarkko Hietaniemi.)

Jonathan Kamens and Tom Christiansen not only contributed articles but read parts of the book with learned and critical eyes. They saved us from many a "power goof." If we'd been able to give them enough time to read the whole thing, we wouldn't have to issue the standard disclaimer that any errors that remain are our own. H. Milton Peek provided technical review and proofreading. Four sharp-eyed Usenet readers helped with debugging: Casper Dik of the University of Amsterdam, Byron Ratzikis of Network Appliance Corporation, Dave Barr of the Population Research Institute, and Duncan Sinclair.

In addition to all the acknowledged contributors, there are many unacknowledged ones—people who have posted questions or answers to the Net over the years and who have helped to build the rich texture of the Unix culture that we've tried to reflect in this book. Jerry also singles out one major contributor to his own mastery of Unix. He says: "Daniel Romike of Tektronix, Inc. (who wrote articles 28.5 and 30.8 in the early 1980s, by the way) led the first Unix workshop I attended. He took the time to answer a ton of questions as I taught myself Unix in the early 1980s. I'm sure some of the insights and neat tricks that I thought I've figured out myself actually came from Dan instead."

James Revell and Bryan Buus scoured "the Net" for useful and interesting free software that we weren't aware of. Bryan also compiled most of the software he collected so we could try it out and gradually winnow down the list.

Thanks also to all of the authors of the software packages we wrote about and included on the CD! Without their efforts, we wouldn't have had anything to write about; without their generosity in making their software free in the first place, we wouldn't be able to distribute hundreds of megabytes of software for the price of a book.

Jeff Moskow of Ready-to-Run Software solved the problem we had been putting off to the end: that of packaging up all the software for the original disk, porting it to the major Unix platforms, and making it easy to install. This was a much bigger job than we'd anticipated, and we could never have done it without Jeff and the RTR staff. We might have been able to distribute source code and binaries for a few platforms, but without their porting expertise, we could never have ported all these programs to every supported platform. Eric Pearce worked with RTR to pre-master the software for CD-ROM duplication, wrote the installation instructions, and made sure that everything came together at the end! (Eric, thanks for pitching in at the last minute. You were right that there were a lot of details that might fall through the cracks.)

Edie Freedman worked with us to design the format of the book—quite an achievement considering everything we wanted the format to do! She met the challenge of presenting thousands of inline cross-references without distracting the reader or creating a visual monstrosity. What she created is as attractive as it is useful—a real breakthrough in technical book design, and one that we plan to use again and again!

Lenny Muellner was given the frightful task of implementing all of our ideas in *troff*—no mean feat, and one that added to his store of grey hair.

Eileen Kramer was the copyeditor, proofreader, and critic who made sure that everything came together. For a thousand-plus page book with multiple authors, it's hard to imagine just how much work that was.

Ellie Cutler wrote the index; Chris Reilley created the illustrations. Additional administrative support was provided by Bonnie Hyland, Donna Woonteiler, and Jane Appleyard.

—*Tim O'Reilly*

Acknowledgments for the Second Edition

After teaching myself about Unix for the past 15 years, I'm off to graduate school in Computer Science. Frank Willison, O'Reilly's Editor-in-Chief, fit this project into the summer between leaving my position at ORA and starting school. Frank didn't just give me something to do in the summer: the royalties should help to pay for my coursework. (So, buy this book and support a student! ;-)) Gigi Estabrook edited this edition and fielded my zillions of questions along the way. Many thanks to Gigi, Frank, and ORA's Production staff. Clairemarie Fisher O'Leary and Nancy Wolfe Kotary shared the jobs of production editor and project manager. Madeleine Newell and Kismet McDonough-Chan provided production support. Sheryl Avruch, Nicole Gipson Arigo, and Danny Marcus provided quality control checks. Lenny Muellner provided extensive *troff* assistance and technical support. Chris Reilley created the technical illustrations.

When time was short, I got expert advice from Arnold Robbins, the maintainer of the GNU *gawk* utility, and coauthor of O'Reilly's *sed & awk*, Second Edition. He reviewed parts of the book and gave me thorough comments.

I'd also like to thank all the readers who took a moment to send us comments and corrections. I read every message, and the ideas in them made a big difference in this second edition. Three peoples' comments were extensive enough to mention specially. Ted Timar spotted problems that showed his deep knowledge of Unix. I'm glad he still found the book useful enough to read it—and to spot goofs in some of our hairier tips. Andrew T. Young sent two long email messages: one a few years ago and another after I contacted him. He caught plenty of techno-goofs and also sent fixes for them. Andy doesn't know just Unix: his background in English helped to sharpen a few rough spots in our folksy writing style. Finally, Greg Ubben sent a 15-page (!) email message that took me most of a week to work through. When I tracked him down, three years after writing his message, he was even more helpful. Greg wrote enough to make into a small book—and, in fact, agreed to write a few new articles, too. He's an expert in *sed* and regular expressions (and Unix) who taught me a lot in our month of email messages back and forth. I deeply appreciate all that he's given to this book's readers.

—*Jerry Peek, jpeek@jpeek.com*

Acknowledgments for the Third Edition

Though much of this book is new material or has been newly updated for changes in Unix, there is a core that remains from previous editions. The fact that this material has continued to be fresh, useful, and relevant through the years is a testament to the abilities—technical and writing—of the original authors. These include Tim O'Reilly and Jerry Peek, among others previously mentioned, who contributed to past editions. We, the authors of this current edition, thank you. We had a number of terrific reviewers comment on this version of the text. We appreciate the work of Dave Carrano, Chris DiBona, Schuyler Erle, Jeff Kawski, Werner Klauser, Adam Langley, Arnold Robbins, Jaron Rubenstein, Kevin Schmidt, Jay Sekora, Joe Sloan, Nat Torkington, and Jay Ts.

In addition, I would like to thank those who contribute their time and efforts on Unix systems, particularly the open source versions of Unix such as FreeBSD, Linux, and now Darwin.

—*Shelley Powers*

I'd just like to thank you all for inviting me to contribute to a book that helped me learn Unix a long time ago. It's nice to be able to give something back, given how much the book helped me back in 1994 when I was just another Unix newbie.

—*Steven Champeon*

Thank you, Amy and Joel, for the input and review and just for putting up with me through it, and Jasper, for being my strength when I needed it.

—*Deborah Hooker*

Basic Unix Environment

Part I contains the following chapters:

1

Introduction

1.1 What's Special About Unix?

If we were writing about any other operating system, "power tools" might mean "nifty add-on utilities to extend the power of your operating system." That sounds suspiciously like a definition of Unix: an operating system loaded with decades' worth of nifty add-on utilities.

Unix is unique in that it wasn't designed as a commercial operating system meant to run application programs, but as a hacker's toolset, by and for programmers. In fact, an early release of the operating system went by the name PWB (Programmer's Work Bench).

When Ken Thompson and Dennis Ritchie first wrote Unix at AT&T Bell Labs, it was for their own use and for their friends and coworkers. Utility programs were added by various people as they had problems to solve. Because Bell Labs wasn't in the computer business, source code was given out to universities for a nominal fee. Brilliant researchers wrote their own software and added it to Unix in a spree of creative anarchy, which has been equaled only with Linux, in the introduction of the X Window System (1.22), and especially the blend of Mac and Unix with Darwin included in the Mac OS X.

Unlike most other operating systems, where free software remains an unsupported add-on, Unix has taken as its own the work of thousands of independent programmers. During the commercialization of Unix within the past several years, this incorporation of outside software has slowed down for larger Unix installations, such as Sun's Solaris and HP's hp-ux, but not stopped entirely. This is especially true with the newer lighter versions of Unix, such as the various flavors of Linux and Darwin.

Therefore, a book on Unix inevitably *has* to focus not just on add-on utilities (though we do include many of those), but on how to use clever features of the many utilities that have been made part of Unix over the years.

Unix is also important to power users because it's one of the last popular operating systems that doesn't force you to work behind an interface of menus, windows, and mouse with a "one-size(-doesn't)-fit-all" programming interface. Yes, you can use Unix interfaces with windows and menus—and they can be great time savers in a lot of cases. But Unix also gives you building blocks that, with some training and practice, will give you many more choices than any software designer can cram onto a set of menus. If you learn to use Unix and its utilities from the command line, you don't have to be a programmer to do very powerful things with a few keystrokes.

So, it's also essential that this book teach you some of the underlying principles that make Unix such a tinkerer's paradise.

In the body of this book, we assume that you are already moderately familiar with Unix—a journeyman hacker wanting to become a master. But at the same time, we don't want to leave beginners entirely at sea; so in this chapter, we include some fundamental concepts. We've tried to intersperse some simple tips and tricks to keep things interesting, but the ratio of concept articles to tips is much higher than in any other part of the book. The concepts covered are also much more basic. If you aren't a beginner, you can safely skip this chapter, though we may bounce you back here if you don't understand something later in the book.

Don't expect a complete introduction to Unix—if you need that, buy an introductory book. What you'll find here is a selection of key concepts that you'll need to understand to progress beyond the beginner stage, as well as answers to frequently asked questions and problems. In some ways, consider this introduction a teaser. If you are a beginner, we want to show you enough of Unix to whet your appetite for more.

Also, don't expect everything to be in order. Because we don't want you to get in the habit of reading through each chapter from beginning to end, as in most books, the articles in this chapter are in loose order. We've tried not to make you jump around too much, but we've also avoided a lot of the transitional material that makes reading most books a chore.

—TOR, JP, and SP

1.2 Power Grows on You

It has been said that Unix is not an operating system as much as it is a way of thinking. In *The UNIX Programming Environment*, Kernighan and Pike write that at the heart of the Unix philosophy "is the idea that the power of a system comes more from the relationships among programs than from the programs themselves."

Most of the nongraphical utility programs that have run under Unix since the beginning, some 30 years ago, share the same user interface. It's a minimal interface, to be sure—but one that allows programs to be strung together in pipelines to do jobs that no single program could do alone.

Most operating systems—including modern Unix and Linux systems—have graphical interfaces that are powerful and a pleasure to use. But none of them are so powerful or exciting to use as classic Unix pipes and filters, and the programming power of the shell.

A new user starts by stringing together simple pipelines and, when they get long enough, saving them for later execution in a file (1.8), alias (29.2), or function (29.11). Gradually, if the user has the right temperament, he gets the idea that the computer can do more of the boring part of many jobs. Perhaps he starts out with a *for* loop (28.9) to apply the same editing script to a series of files. Conditions and cases soon follow and before long, he finds himself programming.

On most systems, you need to learn consciously how to program. You must take up the study of one or more programming languages and expend a fair amount of concentrated effort before you can do anything productive. Unix, on the other hand, teaches programming imperceptibly—it is a slow but steady extension of the work you do simply by interacting with the computer.

Before long, you can step outside the bounds of the tools that have already been provided by the designers of the system and solve problems that don't quite fit the mold. This is sometimes called hacking; in other contexts, it is called "engineering." In essence, it is the ability to build a tool when the right one is not already on hand.

No single program, however well thought out, will solve every problem. There is always a special case, a special need, a situation that runs counter to the expected. But Unix is not a single program. It is a collection of hundreds of them, and with these basic tools, a clever or dedicated person can meet just about any computing problem.

Like the fruits of any advanced system, these capabilities don't fall unbidden into the hands of new users. But they are there for the reaching. And over time, even those users who want a system they don't have to think about will gradually reach out for these capabilities. Faced with a choice between an hour spent on a boring, repetitive task and an hour putting together a tool that will do the task in a flash, most of us will choose the latter.

—*TOR*

1.3 The Core of Unix

In recent times, more attention has been paid on the newer and more light-weight varieties of Unix: FreeBSD, Linux, and now Darwin—the version of BSD Unix that Apple used as the platform for the new Mac OS X. If you've worked with the larger Unix versions, you might be curious to see how it differs within these new environments.

For the most part, basic Unix functionality differs very little between implementations. For instance, I've not worked with a Unix box that doesn't have *vi* (21.7) installed. Additionally, I've also not found any Unix system that doesn't have basic functionality, such as traversing directories with *cd* (1.16) or getting additional help with *man* (2.1).

However, what can differ between flavors of Unix is the behavior of some of the utilities and built-in commands, as well as the options. Even within a specific Unix flavor, such as FreeBSD, installations can differ because one installation uses the built-in version of a utility such as *make* (40.3) and another installation has a GNU version of the same application.

An attempt was made to create some form of standardization with the POSIX effort. POSIX, which stands for *Portable Operating System Interface*, is an IEEE standard to work towards application interoperability. With this, C programs written on one flavor of Unix should work, with minimum modification, on another flavor of Unix.

Unfortunately, though the POSIX effort has had some impact on interoperability, there still are significant differences between Unix versions. In particular, something such as System V Unix can differ considerably from something such as Darwin.

However, there is stability in this seeming chaos: for the most part, the basic Unix utilities and commands behave the same in all Unix flavors, and aside from some optional differences, how a command works within one environment is exactly the same as in another environment. And if there are differences, using the facilities described in Chapter 2 should help you resolve these quickly.

—SP

1.4 Communication with Unix

Probably the single most important concept for would-be power users to grasp is that you don't "talk" directly to the Unix operating system. Instead, you talk to a *program*—and that program either talks to Unix itself or it talks to *another* program that talks to Unix. (When we say "talk" here, we mean communication using a keyboard and a mouse.)

There are three general kinds of programs you'll probably "talk" to:

- The program called the *shell* (27.1). A shell is a *command interpreter*. Its main job is to interpret the commands you type and to run the programs you specify in your command lines. By default, the shell reads commands from your *tty* and arranges for other programs to write their results there. The shell protects Unix from the user (and the user from Unix). It's the main focus of this book (and the rest of this article).

- An *interactive command*, running "inside" a *tty*, that reads what you type directly. These take input directly from the user, without intervention from the shell. The shell's only job is to start them up. A text editor, a mail program, or almost any application program (such as word processing) includes its own command interpreter with its own rules. This book covers a few interactive commands—such as the *vi* editor—but its main focus is the shell and "noninteractive" utilities that the shell coordinates to do what needs doing.

- A Graphical User Interface (GUI) with a desktop, windows, and so on. On Unix, a GUI is implemented with a set of running programs (all of which talk to Unix for you).

  Unix was around long before GUIs were common, and there's no need to use a GUI to use Unix. In fact, Unix started in the days of teletypes, those clattering printing devices used to send telegrams. Unix terminals are still referred to as teletypes or *ttys* (2.7).

The core of the Unix operating system is referred to as the kernel (1.10). Usually, only programs talk to the kernel (through system calls). Users talk to one of the three previous types of programs, which interprets their commands and either executes them directly or passes them on to other programs. These programs may, in turn, request lower-level services from the kernel.

Let's look at a specific example of using the shell. When you type a command to display files whose four-character filenames start with the letter "m":

??? 1.13

```
% cat m???
```

it is the shell that finds the filenames, makes a complete list of them, and calls the *cat* (12.2) command to print the expanded list. The *cat* command calls on the kernel to find each file on the disk and print its contents as a stream of characters on the display.

Why is this important? First of all, you can choose between several different shells (1.6), each of which may have different rules for interpreting command lines.

Second, the shell has to interpret the command line you type and package it up for the command you are calling. Because the shell reads the command line first, it's important to understand just how the shell changes what it reads.

For example, one basic rule is that the shell uses "whitespace" (spaces or tabs) to separate each "argument" of a command. But sometimes, you want the shell to interpret its arguments differently. For example, if you are calling *grep* (13.1), a program for searching through files for a matching line of text, you might want to supply an entire phrase as a single argument. The shell lets you do this by quoting (27.12) arguments. For example:

```
% grep "Power Tools" articles/*
```

Understanding how the shell interprets the command line, and when to keep it from doing so, can be very important in a lot of special cases, especially when dealing with wildcards (1.13), like the * (asterisk) in the previous example.

You can think of the relationship of the kernel, the shell, and various Unix utilities and applications as looking like Figure 1-1.

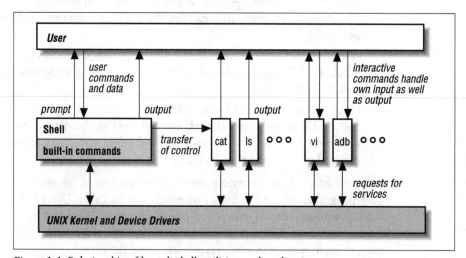

Figure 1-1. Relationship of kernel, shell, utilities, and applications

Figure 1-1 shows that a user can interact with the shell, as well as directly with interactive commands like *cat* and *ls*. The shell transfers control to the commands it starts for you—then those commands may write the output you see. The shell also has some built-in commands (1.9) that run directly within the shell itself. All of the commands shown in Figure 1-1 interact directly with Unix itself.

—*TOR and JP*

1.5 Programs Are Designed to Work Together

As pointed out by Kernighan and Pike in *The UNIX Programming Environment*, there are a number of principles that distinguish the Unix environment. One key concept is that programs are tools. Like all good tools, they should be specific in function, but usable for many different purposes.

In order for programs to become general-purpose tools, they must be data independent. This means three things:

1. Within limits, the output of any program should be usable as the input to another.

2. All of the information needed by a program should be either contained in the data stream passed to it or specified on the command line. A program should not prompt for input or do unnecessary formatting of output. In most cases, this means that Unix programs work with plain text files that don't contain "nonprintable" or "control" characters.

3. If no arguments are given, a program should read the standard input (usually the terminal keyboard) and write the standard output (usually the terminal screen).

Programs that can be used in this way are often called *filters*.

One of the most important consequences of these guidelines is that programs can be strung together in "pipelines" in which the output of one program is used as the input of another. A vertical bar (|) represents *pipe* and means "take the output of the program on the left and feed it into the program on the right."

For example, you can pipe the output of a search program to another program that sorts the output, and then pipe the result to the printer program or redirect it to a file (43.1).

Not all Unix programs work together in this way. An interactive program like the Emacs editor (19.1) generally doesn't read from or write to pipes you'd create on the command line. Instead, once the shell has started Emacs, the editor works independently of the shell (1.4), reading its input and output directly from the terminal. And there are even exceptions to this exception. A program like *less* (12.3) can read its standard input from a pipe and still interact with you at the keyboard. It does that by reading directly from your *tty* (2.7).

—TOR

1.6 There Are Many Shells

With most operating systems, the command intepreter is built in; it is an integral part of the operating system. With Unix, your command interpreter is just another program. Traditionally, a command interpreter is called a "shell," perhaps because it protects you from the underlying kernel—or because it protects the kernel from you!

In the early 1980s, the most common shells were the Bourne shell (*sh*) and the C shell (*csh*). The Bourne shell (3.3) (named after its creator, Steve Bourne) came first. It was excellent for shell programming (1.8). But many Unix users (who were also writing programs in the C language) wanted a more familiar programming syntax—as well as more features for interactive use. So the C shell came from Berkeley as part of their Unix implementation. Soon (on systems that gave you the choice, at least) *csh* was much more popular for interactive use than *sh*. The C shell had a lot of nice features that weren't available in the original Bourne shell, including job control (23.1) and history (30.2). However, it wasn't hard for a shell programmer or an advanced user to push the C shell to its limits.

The Korn shell (also named after its creator, David Korn) arrived in the mid-1980s. The *ksh* is compatible with the Bourne shell, but has most of the C shell's features plus features like history editing (30.14), often called *command-line editing*. The Korn shell was available only with a proprietary version of Unix, System V—but now a public-domain version named *pdksh* is widely available.

These days, most original C shell users have probably switched to *tcsh* (pronounced "T-shell"). It has all the features of *csh* and more—as well as fewer mis-features and outright bugs.

The "Bourne-again" shell, *bash*, is from the Free Software Foundation. It's fairly similar to the Korn shell. It has most of the C shell's features, plus command-line editing and a built-in help command. The programming syntax, though, is much more like the original Bourne shell—and many systems (including Linux) use *bash* in place of the original Bourne shell (but still call it *sh*).

The Z shell, *zsh*, is an interesting hybrid. It tries to be compatible with most features of all the other shells, with compatibility modes and a slew of options that turn off conflicting features. In its soul, though, *zsh* has a different way of doing some things. It's been accused of feature creep. But *zsh* users love its flexibility.

There are other shells. If you're a fan of the Bell Labs research operating system named *Plan 9* (actually, *Plan 9 from Outer Space*), you'll be happy to know that its shell, *rc*, has been ported to Unix. If you program in Tcl, you'll probably be familiar with *tclsh*, which lets you intermix Unix commands with Tcl commands. (And we can't forget *wish*, the shell that's a superset of *tclsh*: it uses Tcl/Tk commands to let you build graphical interfaces as you go.) Least—but certainly not last—if you're a minimalist who needs the original *sh*, a newer shell named *ash* emulates the late-1980s Bourne shell.

In this book, we try to be as generic as we can. Where we need to get specific, many examples are shown in the style of both the Bourne shell and the C shell—for instance, we'll often show Bourne-shell functions side-by-side with C-shell aliases. Because *bash* and *ksh* can read scripts written for the original Bourne shell, we use original *sh* syntax to make our shell programming as portable as possible.

Where we talk about "the Bourne shell" or *sh*, it's usually a safe bet that the information applies to *bash* and *ksh* too. In the same way, "the C shell" generally also means *tcsh*.

—*JP and ML*

1.7 Which Shell Am I Running?

You can usually tell which family your shell belongs to by a character in the prompt it displays. Bourne-type shells, such as *bash*, usually have $ in the prompt. The C shell uses % (but *tcsh* users often use >).

If your shell has superuser (1.18) privileges, though, the prompt typically ends with a hash, #.

To check the shell that runs automatically when you log in to Unix, type one of these commands (the second is for systems that use NIS, Sun's Network Information Service, to manage network-wide files):

```
% grep yourloginname /etc/passwd
% ypmatch yourloginname passwd
```

You should get back the contents of your entry in the system password file. For example:

```
shelleyp:*:1006:1006:Shelley Powers:/usr/home/shelleyp:/usr/local/bin/bash
```

The fields are separated by colons, and the default shell is usually specified in the last field.

Note that in Mac OS X, passwords are managed and stored in Netinfo by default. To store the passwords in */etc/passwd*, you'll need to configure this using Netinfo.

—*TOR and SP*

1.8 Anyone Can Program the Shell

One of the really wonderful things about the shell is that it doesn't just read and execute the commands you type at a prompt. The shell is a complete programming language.

The ease of shell programming is one of the real highlights of Unix for novices. A shell program need be no more than a single complex command line saved in a file—or a series of commands.

For example, let's say that you occasionally need to convert a Macintosh Microsoft Word file for use on your Unix system. Word lets you save the file in ASCII format. But there's a catch: the Mac uses a carriage return ASCII character 015 to mark the end of each line, while Unix uses a linefeed (ASCII 012). As a result, with Unix, the file looks like one long paragraph, with no end in sight.

That's easy to fix: the Unix *tr* (21.11) command can convert every occurrence of one character in a file to another:

```
bash-2.04$ tr '\015' '\012' < file.mac > file.unix
```

But you're a novice, and you don't want to remember this particular piece of magic. Fine. Save the first part of this command line in a file called *mac2unix* in your personal *bin* directory (7.4):

```
tr '\015' '\012'
```

Make the file executable with *chmod* (50.5):

```
bash-2.04$ chmod +x mac2unix
```

Now you can say:

```
bash-2.04$ mac2unix < file.mac > file.unix
```

But why settle for that? What if you want to convert a bunch of files at once? Easy. The shell includes a general way of referring to arguments passed to a script and a number of looping constructs. The script:

for **35.21**

$x **35.9**

```
for x
do
    echo "Converting $x"
    tr '\015' '\012' < "$x" > "tmp.$x"
    mv "tmp.$x" "$x"
done
```

will convert any number of files with one command, replacing each original with the converted version:

```
bash-2.04$ mac2unix file1 file2 file3 ...
```

As you become more familiar with Unix, it quickly becomes apparent that doing just a little homework can save hours of tedium. This script incorporates only two simple programming constructs: the *for* loop and variable substitution (35.9, 35.3).* As a new user with no programming experience, I learned these two constructs by example: I saved a skeleton *for* loop in a file and simply filled in the blanks with whatever commands I wanted to repeat. Article 35.2 has more about shell programming.

In short, Unix is sometimes difficult because it is so rich and complex. The user who doesn't want to learn the complexity doesn't have to—the basic housekeeping commands are simple and straightforward. But the user who wants to take the time to investigate the possibilities can uncover a wealth of useful tools.

—*TOR*

---

* [Tim is keeping this article simple, as an illustration of how easy writing a shell program can be. If you're writing this little script for general use, you can make it work like a filter (1.5) by adding four or five more lines of code: a *case* (35.10) or *if* (35.13) statement that tests the number of command-line arguments. With no filename arguments, the script would simply run tr '\015' '\012'. —*JP*]

1.9 Internal and External Commands

Some commands that you type are *internal*, which means they are built into the shell, and it's the shell that performs the action. For example, the *cd* command is built-in. The *ls* command, on the other hand, is an *external* program stored in the file */bin/ls*.

The shell doesn't start a separate process to run internal commands. External commands require the shell to *fork* and *exec* (27.2) a new subprocess (24.3); this takes some time, especially on a busy system.

When you type the name of a command, the shell first checks to see if it is a built-in command and, if so, executes it. If the command name is an absolute pathname (1.16) beginning with /, like */bin/ls*, there is no problem: the command is likewise executed. If the command is neither built-in nor specified with an absolute pathname, most shells (except the original Bourne shell) will check for aliases (29.2) or shell functions (29.11), which may have been defined by the user—often in a shell setup file (3.3) that was read when the shell started. Most shells also "remember" the location of external commands (27.6); this saves a long hunt down the search path. Finally, all shells look in the search path for an executable program or script with the given name.

The search path is exactly what its name implies: a list of directories that the shell should look through for a command whose name matches what is typed.

The search path isn't built into the shell; it's something you specify in your shell setup files.

By tradition, Unix system programs are kept in directories called */bin* and */usr/ bin*, with additional programs usually used only by system administrators in either */etc* and */usr/etc* or */sbin* and */usr/sbin*. Many versions of Unix also have programs stored in */usr/ucb* (named after the University of California at Berkeley, where many Unix programs were written). There may be other directories containing programs. For example, the programs that make up the X Window System (1.22) are stored in */usr/bin/X11*. Users or sites often also have their own directories where custom commands and scripts are kept, such as */usr/local/bin* or */opt*.

The search path is stored in an environment variable (35.3) called *PATH* (35.6). A typical *PATH* setting might look something like this:

```
PATH=/bin:/usr/bin:/usr/bin/X11:/usr/ucb:/home/tim/bin:
```

The path is searched in order, so if there are two commands with the same name, the one that is found first in the path will be executed. For example, your system certainly has the *ls* command we mentioned earlier—and it's probably in */bin/ls*.

You can add new directories to your search path on the fly, but the path is usually set in shell setup files.

—*TOR*

1.10 The Kernel and Daemons

If you have arrived at Unix via Windows 2000 or some other personal computer operating system, you will notice some big differences. Unix was, is, and always will be a multiuser operating system. It is a multiuser operating system even when you're the only person using it; it is a multiuser operating system even when it is running on a PC with a single keyboard; and this fact has important ramifications for everything that you do.

Why does this make a difference? Well, for one thing, you're never the only one using the system, even when you think you are. Don't bother to look under your desk to see if there's an extra terminal hidden down there. There isn't. But Unix is always doing things "behind your back," running programs of its own, whether you are aware of it or not. The most important of these programs, the *kernel*, is the heart of the Unix operating system itself. The kernel assigns memory to each of the programs that are running, partitions time fairly so that each program can get its job done, handles all I/O (input/output) operations, and so on. Another important group of programs, called *daemons*, are the system's "helpers." They run continuously—or from time to time—performing small but important tasks like handling mail, running network communications, feeding data to your printer, keeping track of the time, and so on.

Not only are you sharing the computer with the kernel and some mysterious daemons, you're also sharing it with yourself. You can issue the *ps x* (24.5) command to get a list of all processes running on your system. For example:

```
  PID TTY   STAT  TIME COMMAND
18034 tty2  S     0:00 -zsh
18059 ?     S     0:01 ssh-agent
18088 tty2  S     0:00 sh /usr/X11R6/bin/startx
18096 tty2  S     0:00 xinit /etc/X11/xinit/xinitrc -- :0 -auth /home/jpeek/
18101 tty2  S     0:00 /usr/bin/gnome-session
18123 tty2  S     0:33 enlightenment -clientId default2
18127 tty2  S     0:01 magicdev --sm-client-id=default12
18141 tty2  S     0:03 panel --sm-client-id default8
18145 tty2  S     0:01 gmc --sm-client-id default10
18166 ?     S     1:20 gnomepager_applet --activate-goad-server gnomepager_a
18172 tty2  S     0:01 gnome-terminal
18174 tty2  S     0:00 gnome-pty-helper
18175 pts/0 S     0:00 zsh
18202 tty2  S     0:49 gnome-terminal
18203 tty2  S     0:00 gnome-pty-helper
18204 pts/1 S     0:01 zsh
18427 pts/1 T     0:00 man zshjp
```

```
18428 pts/1  T     0:00 sh -c /bin/gunzip -c /home/jpeek/.man/cat1/zshjp.1.gz
18430 pts/1  T     0:03 /usr/bin/less -is
18914 pts/1  T     0:02 vi upt3_changes.html
 1263 pts/1  T     0:00 vi urls.html
 1511 pts/1  T     0:00 less coding
 3363 pts/1  S     0:00 vi 1007.sgm
 4844 tty2   S     0:24 /usr/lib/netscape/netscape-communicator -irix-session
 4860 tty2   S     0:00 (dns helper)
 5055 pts/1  R     0:00 ps x
```

This output tells us that the user has only three windows open. You may think that they're only running four or five programs, but the computer is actually doing a lot more. (And, to keep this brief, we aren't showing all the lines of output!) The user logged into his Linux system on virtual console (23.12) 2, which shows as tty2 in the TTY column; a lot of programs are running there, including the X Window System (1.22) (which actually runs itself as another user—*root*—so its process isn't listed here). The user is also running Gnome and Enlightenment, which keep track of the workstation's display. Two of the windows are Gnome terminals, which are windows that act like separate terminals; each has its own *tty*, pts/0 and pts/1. And the list continues.

If you are running a different window system (or no window system at all) or different utility programs, you will see something different. But we guarantee that you're running at least two programs, and quite likely many more. If you want to see everything that's running, including the daemons, type the command ps aux (Berkeley-style *ps*) or ps -el (for many other flavors of *ps*). You'll be impressed.

Because there is so much going on at once, Unix requires a different way of thinking. The Unix kernel is a traffic cop that mediates different demands for time, memory, disks, and so on. Not only does the kernel need to run your programs, but it also needs to run the daemons, any programs that other users might want to start, or any programs that you may have scheduled to run automatically, as discussed in Chapter 23. When it runs a program, the kernel allocates a small slice of time—up to a second—and lets the program run until that slice is used up or until the program decides to take a rest of its own accord (this is called "sleeping"). At this point, regardless of whether the program is finished, the kernel finds some other program to run. The Unix kernel never takes a vacation: it is always watching over the system.

Once you understand that the kernel is a manager that schedules many different kinds of activity, you understand a lot about how Unix works. For example, if you have used any computer system previously, you know that it's a bad idea to turn the computer off while it is writing something to disk. You will probably destroy the disk, and you could conceivably damage the disk drive. The same is true for Unix—but with an important complication. Any of the programs that are running can start doing something to the disk at any time. One of the daemons makes a point of accessing the disk drive every 30 seconds or so, just to stay in touch. Therefore, you can't just turn a Unix computer off. You might do all sorts of damage to the system's files—and not just your own, but conceivably files belonging to many other users. To turn a Unix system off, you must first run a program called *shutdown*, which kicks everyone off the system, makes sure that a daemon won't try to play with a disk drive when you aren't looking, and runs a program named *sync* to make sure that the disks have the latest version of everything. Only then is it safe to pull the switch. When you start up a Unix system, it automatically runs a program called *fsck*, which stands for "filesystem check"; its job is to find out if you shut down the system correctly and try to fix any damage that might have happened if you didn't.

—ML and JP

1.11 Filenames

Like all operating systems, Unix files have names. (Unix directories, devices, and so on also have filenames—and are treated like files (1.19).) The names are words (sequences of characters) that let you identify a file. Older versions of Unix had some restrictions on the length of a filename (14 characters), but modern versions have removed these restrictions for all practical purposes. Sooner or later you will run into a limit, but if so, you are probably being unnecessarily verbose.

Technically, a filename can be made from almost any group of characters (including nonprinting characters and numbers) except a slash (/). However, you should avoid filenames containing most punctuation marks and all nonprinting characters. To be safe, limit your filenames to the following characters:

Upper- and lowercase characters
> Unix filenames are *always* case sensitive. That is, upper- and lowercase letters are always different (unlike Microsoft Windows and others that consider upper- and lowercase letters the same). Therefore, *myfile* and *Myfile* are different files. It is usually a bad idea to have files whose names differ only in their capitalization, but that's your decision.

Underscores (_)
> Underscores are handy for separating "words" in a filename to make them more readable. For example, *my_long_filename* is easier to read than *mylongfilename*.

Periods (.)
> Periods are used by some programs (such as the C compiler) to separate filenames from filename extensions (1.12). Extensions are used by these programs to recognize the type of file to be processed, but they are not treated specially by the shell, the kernel, or other Unix programs.

Filenames that begin with a period are treated specially by the shell: wildcards won't match (1.13) them unless you include the period (like .*). The *ls* command, which lists your files, ignores files whose names begin with a period unless you give it a special option (*ls –a* (8.9)). Special configuration files are often "hidden" in directories by beginning their names with a period.

Certain other punctuation
About the only other punctuation mark that is always safe is the comma (,), although it isn't part of the POSIX-portable character set.

I'm so dead-set against using weird, nonprinting characters in filenames that I won't even tell you how to do it. I will give you some special techniques for deleting files with weird names (14.11), though, in case you create some by accident.

Some things to be aware of:

- Unix does not have any concept of a file *version*. There are some revision control programs (39.4) that implement their own notion of a version, but there is nothing built into the operating system that handles this for you. If you are editing a file, don't count on Unix to save your previous versions—you can program this (35.16, 18.14) though, if you want to; the GNU Emacs editor also makes backups (19.4).

- Once you delete a file in Unix, it is gone forever (14.3). You can't get it back without restoring it from a backup. So be careful when you delete files. Later, we'll show you programs that will give you a "grace period" between the time you delete a file and the time it actually disappears.

—*ML*

1.12 Filename Extensions

In Microsoft Windows and some other operating systems, filenames often have the form *name.extension*. For example, plain text files have extensions such as *.txt*. The operating system treats the extension as separate from the filename and has rules about how long it must be, and so forth.

Unix doesn't have any special rules about extensions. The dot has no special meaning as a separator, and extensions can be any length. However, a number of programs (especially compilers) make use of extensions to recognize the different types of files they work with. In addition, there are a number of conventions that users have adopted to make clear the contents of their files. For example, you might name a text file containing some design notes *notes.txt*.

Table 1-1 lists some of the filename extensions you might see and a brief description of the programs that recognize them.

Table 1-1. Filename extensions that programs expect

Extension	Description
.a	Archive file (library)
.c	C program source file
.f	FORTRAN program source file
.F	FORTRAN program source file to preprocess
.gz	*gzip*ped file (15.6)
.h	C program header file
.html or .htm	HTML file for web servers
.xhtml	XHTML file for web servers
.o	Object file (compiled and assembled code)
.s	Assembly language code
.z	Packed file
.Z	Compressed file (15.6)
.1 to .8	Online manual (2.1) source file
~	Emacs editor backup file (19.4)

In Table 1-2 are some extensions often used by users to signal the contents of a file, but are not actually recognized by the programs themselves.

Table 1-2. Filename extensions for user's benefit

Extension	Description
.tar	*tar* archive (39.2)
.tar.gz or .tgz	*gzip*ped (15.6) *tar* archive (39.2)
.shar	Shell archive
.sh	Bourne shell script (1.8)
.csh	C shell script
.mm	Text file containing *troff*'s *mm* macros
.ms	Text file containing *troff*'s *ms* macros
.ps	PostScript source file
.pdf	Adobe Portable Document Format

—*ML and TOR*

1.13 Wildcards

The shells provide a number of *wildcards* that you can use to abbreviate filenames or refer to groups of files. For example, let's say you want to delete all filenames ending in *.txt* in the current directory (1.16). You could delete these files one by one, but that would be boring if there were only 5 and *very* boring if there were 100. Instead, you can use a wildcarded name to say, "I want all files whose names end with *.txt*, regardless of what the first part is." The wildcard is the "regardless" part. Like a wildcard in a poker game, a wildcard in a filename can have any value.

The wildcard you see most often is * (an asterisk), but we'll start with something simpler: ? (a question mark). When it appears in a filename, the ? matches any single character. For example, letter? refers to any filename that begins with *letter* and has exactly one character after that. This would include *letterA*, *letter1*, as well as filenames with a nonprinting character as their last letter, such as *letter^C*.

The * wildcard matches any character or group of zero or more characters. For example, *.txt matches all files whose names end with *.txt*; c* matches all files whose names start with *c*; c*b* matches names starting with *c* and containing at least one *b*; and so on.

The * and ? wildcards are sufficient for 90 percent of the situations that you will find. However, there are some situations that they can't handle. For example, you may want to list files whose names end with *.txt*, *mail*, or *let*. There's no way to do this with a single *; it won't let you exclude the files you don't want. In this situation, use a separate * with each filename ending:

```
*.txt *mail *let
```

Sometimes you need to match a particular group of characters. For example, you may want to list all filenames that begin with digits or all filenames that begin with uppercase letters. Let's assume that you want to work with the files program.*n*, where *n* is a single-digit number. Use the filename:

```
program.[0123456789]
```

In other words, the wildcard [character-list] matches any single character that appears in the list. The character list can be any group of ASCII characters; however, if they are consecutive (e.g., A–Z, a–z, 0–9, or 3–5, for that matter), you can use a hyphen as shorthand for the range. For example, [a-zA-Z] means any alphabetic English character.

There is one exception to these wildcarding rules. Wildcards never match /, which is both the name of the filesystem root (1.14) and the character used to separate directory names in a path (1.16). The only way to match on this character is to *escape it* using the backslash character (\). However, you'll find it difficult to use the forward slash within a filename anyway (the system will keep trying to use it as a directory command).

If you are new to computers, you probably will catch on to Unix wildcarding quickly. If you have used any other computer system, you have to watch out for one important detail. Virtually all computer systems except for Unix consider a period (.) a special character within a filename. Many operating systems even require a filename to have a period in it. With these operating systems, a * does not match a period; you have to say *.*. Therefore, the equivalent of rm * does virtually nothing on some operating systems. Under Unix, it is dangerous: it means "delete all the files in the current directory, regardless of their name." You only want to give this command when you really mean it.

But here's the exception to the exception. The shells and the *ls* command consider a . special if it is the first character of a filename. This is often used to hide initialization files and other files with which you aren't normally concerned; the *ls* command doesn't show these files unless you ask (8.9) for them. If a file's name begins with ., you always have to type the . explicitly. For example, .*rc matches all files whose names begin with . and end with *rc*. This is a common convention for the names of Unix initialization files.

Table 1-3 has a summary of common wildcards.

Table 1-3. Common shell wildcards

Wildcard	Matches
?	Any single character
*	Any group of zero or more characters
[ab]	Either a or b
[a-z]	Any character between a and z, inclusive

Wildcards can be used at any point or points within a path. Remember, wildcards only match names that already exist. You can't use them to create new files (28.3)—though many shells have curly braces ({}) for doing that. Article 33.3 explains how wildcards are handled, and article 33.2 has more about wildcards, including specialized wildcards in each of the shells.

—*ML*

1.14 The Tree Structure of the Filesystem

A multiuser system needs a way to let different users have different files with the same name. It also needs a way to keep files in logical groups. With thousands of system files and hundreds of files per user, it would be disastrous to have all of the files in one big heap. Even single-user operating systems have found it necessary to go beyond "flat" filesystem structures.

Almost every operating system solved this problem by implementing a tree-structured, or *hierarchical*, filesystem. Unix is no exception. A hierarchical filesystem is not much different from a set of filing cabinets at the office. Your set of cabinets consists of many individual cabinets. Each individual cabinet has several drawers; each drawer may have several partitions in it; each partition may have several hanging (Pendaflex) folders; and each hanging folder may have several files. You can specify an individual file by naming the filing cabinet, the drawer, the partition, the group of folders, and the individual folder. For example, you might say to someone: "Get me the 'meeting of July 9' file from the Kaiser folder in the Medical Insurance Plans partition in the Benefits drawer of the Personnel file cabinet." This is backwards from the way you'd specify a filename, because it starts with the mfost specific part, but the idea is essentially the same.

You could give a complete path like this to any file in any of your cabinets, as shown in Figure 1-2. The concept of a "path" lets you distinguish your July 9 meeting with Kaiser from your July 9 interview with a job applicant or your July 9 policy-planning meeting. It also lets you keep related topics together: it's easy to browse through the "Medical Insurance" section of one drawer or to scan all your literature and notes about the Kaiser plan. The Unix filesystem works in exactly the same way (as do most other hierarchical filesystems). Rather than having a heap of assorted files, files are organized into *directories*. A directory is really nothing more than a special kind of file that lists a bunch of other files (see article 10.2). A directory can contain any number of files (although for performance reasons, it's a good idea to keep the number of files in one directory relatively small—under 100, when you can). A directory can also contain other directories. Because a directory is nothing more than a special kind of file, directories also have names. At the top (the filesystem "tree" is really upside down) is a directory called the "root," which has the special name / (pronounced "slash," but never spelled out).

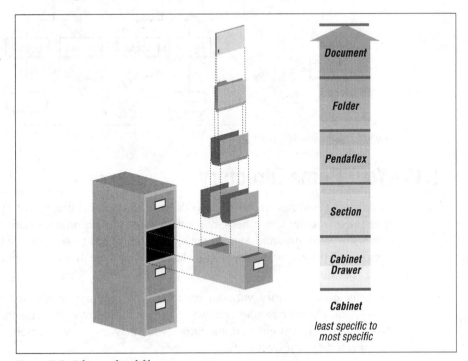

Figure 1-2. A hierarchical filesystem

To locate any file, we can give a sequence of names, starting from the filesystem's root, that shows the file's exact position in the filesystem: we start with the root and then list the directories you go through to find the file, separating them by slashes. This is called a *path*. For examples, let's look at the simple filesystem represented by Figure 1-3. The names */home/mkl/mystuff/stuff* and */home/hun/publick/stuff* both refer to files named *stuff*. However, these files are in different directories, so they are different files. The names *home*, *hun*, and so on are all names of directories. Complete paths like these are called "absolute paths." There are shorter ways to refer to a file: relative paths (1.16).

—*ML*

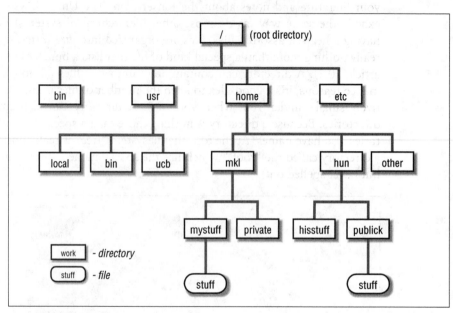

Figure 1-3. A Unix filesystem tree

1.15 Your Home Directory

Microsoft Windows and the Mac OS have hierarchical filesystems (1.14), much like those in Unix and other large systems. But there is an important difference. On many Windows and Mac systems, you start right at the "root" of the filesystem tree. In effect, you start with a blank slate and create subdirectories to organize your files.

A Unix system comes with an enormous filesystem tree already developed. When you log in, you start somewhere down in that tree, in a directory created for you by the system administrator (who may even be yourself, if you are administering your own system).

This directory—the one place in the filesystem that is your very own, to store your files (especially the shell setup files (3.3) and rc files (3.20) that you use to customize the rest of your environment)—is called your *home directory*.

Home directories were originally stored in a directory called */usr* (and still are on some systems), but are now often stored in other directories, such as */home*. Within the Linux Filesystem Hierarchy Standard (FHS), the home directory is always at */home*, as configuration files are always in */etc* and so on.

To change your current directory (1.16) to your home, type cd with no pathname; the shell will assume you mean your home directory.

Within the Mac OS X environment, *home* is in the */Users/username* directory by default.

—*TOR*

1.16 Making Pathnames

Pathnames locate a file (or directory, or any other object) in the Unix filesystem. As you read this article, refer to Figure 1-4. It's a diagram of a (very) small part of a Unix filesystem.

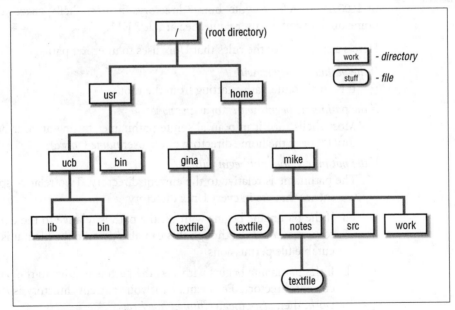

Figure 1-4. Part of a Unix filesystem tree

Whenever you are using Unix, you have a *current directory*. By default, Unix looks for any mentioned files or directories within the current directory. That is, if you don't give an absolute pathname (1.14) (starting from the root, /), Unix tries to look up files *relative* to the current directory. When you first log in, your current directory is your home directory (1.15), which the system administrator will assign to you. It typically has a name like */u/mike* or */home/mike*. You can change your current directory by giving the *cd* command, followed by the name of a new directory (for example, cd /usr/bin). You can find out your current directory by giving the *pwd* ("print working directory") command.

If your current directory is */home/mike* and you give the command cat textfile, you are asking Unix to locate the file *textfile* within the directory */home/mike*. This is equivalent to the absolute path */home/mike/textfile*. If you give the command cat notes/textfile, you are asking Unix to locate the file *textfile* within the directory *notes*, within the current directory */home/mike*.

A number of abbreviations help you to form relative pathnames more conveniently. You can use the abbreviation . (dot) to refer to the current working directory. You can use .. (dot dot) to refer to the parent of the current working directory. For example, if your current directory is */home/mike*, *./textfile* is the same as *textfile*, which is the same as */home/mike/textfile*. The relative path *../gina/textfile* is the same as */home/gina/textfile*; .. moves up one level from */home/mike* (to */home*) and then searches for the directory *gina* and the file *textfile*.

You can use either the abbreviation ~ (tilde) or the environment variables $HOME or $LOGDIR, to refer to your home directory. In most shells, *~name* refers to the home directory of the user *name*. See article 31.11.

Here's a summary of the rules that Unix uses to interpret paths:

If the pathname begins with /
> It is an absolute path, starting from the root.

If the pathname begins with ~ or with ~name
> Most shells turn it into an absolute pathname starting at your home directory (~) or at the home directory of the user *name* (~name).

If the pathname does not begin with a /
> The pathname is relative to the current directory. Two relative special cases use entries that are in every Unix directory:
>
> a. If the pathname begins with ./, the path is relative to the current directory, e.g., *./textfile*, though this can also execute the file if it is given executable file permissions.
>
> b. If the pathname begins with ../, the path is relative to the parent of the current directory. For example, if your current directory is */home/mike/work*, then *../src* means */home/mike/src*.

Article 10.2 explains where . and .. come from.

The . and .. may appear at any point within a path. They mean "the current directory at this point in the path" and "the parent of the current directory at this point in the path." You commonly see paths starting with ../../ (or more) to refer to the grandparent or great-grandparent of the current directory. However, they can appear at other places in a pathname as well. For example, /usr/ucb/./bin is the same as /usr/ucb/bin, and /usr/ucb/bin/../lib is the same as /usr/ucb/lib. Placing . or .. in the middle of a path may be helpful in building paths within shell scripts, but I have never seen them used in any other useful way.

—ML and JP

1.17 File Access Permissions

Under Unix, access to files is based on the concept of users and groups.

Every "user" on a system has a unique account with a unique login name and a unique UID (24.3) (user ID number). It is possible, and sometimes convenient, to create accounts that are shared by groups of people. For example, in a transaction-processing application, all of the order-entry personnel might be assigned a common login name (as far as Unix is concerned, they only count as one user). In a research and development environment, certain administrative operations might be easier if members of a team shared the same account, in addition to having their own accounts. However, in most situations each person using the system has one and only one user ID, and vice versa.

Every user may be a member of one or more "groups."* The user's entry in the master password file (/etc/passwd (22.3)) defines his "primary group membership." The /etc/group (49.6) file defines the groups that are available and can also assign other users to these groups as needed. For example, I am a member of three groups: *staff*, *editors*, and *research*. My primary group is *staff*; the *group* file says that I am also a member of the *editors* and *research* groups. We call *editors* and *research* my "secondary groups." The system administrator is responsible for maintaining the *group* and *passwd* files. You don't need to worry about them unless you're administering your own system.

Every file belongs to one user and one group. When a file is first created, its owner is the user who created it; its group is the user's primary group or the group of the directory in which it's created. For example, all files I create are owned by the user *mikel* and the group *staff*. As the file's owner, I am allowed to

---

* In most newer Unix systems, users have the access privileges of all groups to which they belong, all at the same time. In other Unix systems, you use a command like *newgrp* (49.6) to change the group to which you currently belong. Your system may even support both methods.

use the *chgrp* command to change the file's group. On filesystems that don't have quotas (15.11), I can also use the *chown* command to change the file's owner. (To change ownership on systems with quotas, see article 50.15.) For example, to change the file *data* so that it is owned by the user *george* and the group *others*, I give the commands:

```
% chgrp others data
% chown george data
```

 If you need to change both owner and group, change the group first! You won't have permission to change the group after you aren't the owner.

Some versions of *chown* can change both owner and group at the same time:

```
% chown george.others data
```

File access is based on a file's user and group ownership and a set of access bits (commonly called the *mode bits*). When you try to access a file, you are put into one of three classes. You are either the file's owner, a member of the file's group, or an "other." Three bits then determine whether you are allowed to read, write, or execute the file. So, as Figure 1-1 shows, there are a total of nine mode bits (three for each class) that set the basic access permissions.

—*ML*

1.18 The Superuser (Root)

In general, a *process* (24.1) is a program that's running: a shell, the *ls* command, the *vi* editor, and so on. In order to kill a process (24.12), change its priority (26.5), or manipulate it in any other way, you have to be the process' owner (i.e., the user who started it). In order to delete a job from a print queue (45.1), you must be the user who started it.

As you might guess, there needs to be a way to circumvent all of this security. Someone has to be able to kill runaway programs, modify the system's files, and so on. Under Unix, a special user known as *root* (and commonly called the "superuser") is allowed to do anything.

To become the superuser, you can either log in as *root* or use the *su* (49.9) command. In this book, though, we'll assume that you don't have the superuser password. Almost all of what we describe can be done without becoming superuser.

—*ML*

1.19 When Is a File Not a File?

Unix differs from most operating systems in that it is file oriented. The designers of Unix decided that they could make the operating system much simpler if they treated everything as if it were a file. As far as Unix is concerned, disk drives, terminals, modems, network connections, etc. are all just files. Recent versions of Unix (such as Linux) have gone further: files can be pipes (FIFOs) (43.11) and processes are files (24.9). Like waves and particles in quantum physics, the boundary between files and the rest of the world can be extremely fine: whether you consider a disk a piece of hardware or a special kind of file depends primarily on your perspective and what you want to do with it.

Therefore, to understand Unix, you have to understand what files are. A file is nothing more than a stream of bytes—that is, an arbitrarily long string of bytes with no special structure. There are no special file structures and only a few special file types (for keeping track of disks and a few other purposes). The structure of any file is defined by the programs that use it, not by the Unix operating system.* You may hear users talk about file headers and so on, but these are defined by the applications that use the files, not by the Unix filesystem itself.

Unix programs do abide by one convention, however. Text files use a single newline character (linefeed) between lines of text, rather than the carriage return-linefeed combination used in Microsoft Windows or the carriage returns used in the Macintosh. This difference may cause problems when you bring files from other operating systems over to Unix. Windows files will often be littered with carriage returns (Ctrl-M), which are necessary for that operating system but superfluous for Unix. These carriage returns will look ugly if you try to edit or print the file and may confuse some Unix programs. Mac text files will appear to be one long line with no breaks. Of course, you can use Unix utilities to convert Mac and Windows files for Unix.

—ML

1.20 Scripting

Scripting languages and scripting applications differ from compiled languages and applications in that the application is interpreted as run rather than compiled into a machine-understandable format. You can use shell scripting for many of your scripting needs, but there are times when you'll want to use something more sophisticated. Though not directly a part of a Unix system, most Unix installations come with the tools you need for this more complex scripting—Perl (Chapter 41), Python (Chapter 42), and Tcl.

---

* Many executable files—programs—begin with a *magic number*. This is a special two-byte-long sequence that tells the kernel how to execute the file.

These three scripting languages seem so prevelant within the Unix world that I think of them as the Unix Scripting language triumvirate.

Perl is probably the granddaddy of scripting. Created by Larry Wall, this language is probably used more than any other for creating complex scripts to perform sophisticated functionality with Unix and other operating systems. The language is particularly noted for its ability to handle regular expressions, as well as working with files and other forms of I/O.

Python isn't as widespread as Perl, but its popularity is growing. One reason it's gaining popularity is that as a language, Python is more structured and a little more verbose than Perl, and therefore a little easier to read. In addition, according to its fans, Python has more object-oriented and data-manipulation features than the file-manipulation and regular-expression manipulation of Perl.

Tcl is particularly prevalant within Linux systems, though its use is widespread throughout all Unix systems. It's popular because it's simpler to learn than Perl and allows scripters to get up to speed more quickly than you can with Perl or Python. In addition, the language also has access to a very popular graphical user interface library called the Tk toolkit. You'll rarely hear about Tcl without the associated Tk.

—*TOR and SP*

1.21 Unix Networking and Communications

Generally speaking, a network lets two or more computers communicate and work together. Partly because of the open design of Unix, a lot of networking development has been done in this operating system. Just as there are different versions of Unix, there are different ways and programs to use networks from Unix.

There's an entire chapter devoted to Connectivity (Chapter 46), but for now, here's a quick review of the major networking components.

The Internet

> The Internet is a worldwide network of computers. Internet users can transfer files, log into other computers, and use a wide range of programs and services.

WWW

> The World Wide Web is a set of information servers on the Internet. The servers are linked into a hypertext web of documents, graphics, sound, and more. Point-and-click *browser* programs turn that hypertext into an easy-to-use Internet interface. (For many people, the Web *is* the Internet. But Unix lets you do much more.)

mail

A Unix facility that's been around for years, long before networking was common, is electronic mail. Users can send electronic memos, usually called *email messages*, between themselves. When you send email, your message waits for the other user to start his own mail program. System programs can send you mail to tell you about problems or give you information. You can send mail to programs, asking them for information. Worldwide mailing lists connect users into discussion groups.

ftp

The *ftp* program is one way to transfer files between your computer and another computer with TCP/IP, often over the Internet network, using the File Transfer Protocol (FTP).

UUCP

Unix-to-Unix Copy is a family of programs (*uucp*, *uux*, *uulog*, and others) for transferring files and email between computers. UUCP is usually used with modems over telephone lines and has been mostly superceded by Internet-type connections.

Usenet

Usenet isn't exactly a network. It's a collection of hundreds of thousands (millions?) of computers worldwide that exchange files called *news articles*. This "net news" system has thousands of interactive discussion groups—electronic bulletin boards—for discussing everything from technical topics to erotic art.

telnet

This utility logs you into a remote computer over a network (such as the Internet) using TCP/IP. You can work on the remote computer as if it were your local computer. The *telnet* program is available on many operating systems; *telnet* can log you into other operating systems from your Unix host and vice versa.

rsh

This starts a "remote *shell*" to run a command on a remote system without needing to log in interactively. If you don't give a command, *rsh* acts like *rlogin*. This is often used to start remote X Window System (1.22) programs whose display opens on your local system. Article 6.10 has examples—as well as details on problems you can have running *rsh* for *any* application.

ssh

ssh acts like *rsh* (and *rlogin*), but it makes a secure encrypted connection to the remote computer. It also can encrypt X Window System (1.22) connections, as well as other types of connections, between hosts. The utility *ssh-agent* allows remote logins without typing a passphrase. We've included an entire chapter on *ssh* (Chapter 51).

rcp

> This is a "*remote cp*" program for copying files between computers. It has the same command-line syntax as *cp* except that hostnames are added to the remote pathnames.

scp

> This is a secure version of *rcp* that uses the ssh protocol. *ssh-agent* works here, too.

NFS

> NFS isn't a user utility. The Network FileSystem and related packages like NIS (the Network Information Service) let your system administrator mount remote computers' filesystems onto your local computer. You can use the remote filesystem as easily as if it were on your local computer.

write

> This sends messsages to another user's screen. Two users can have a discussion with *write*.

talk

> A more sophisticated program than *write*, *talk* splits the screen into two pieces and lets users type at the same time if they wish. *talk* can be used over networks, though not all versions of *talk* can talk to one another.

irc

> Internet Relay Chat allows multiple users to carry on multiple discussions across the Internet and other networks. One popular IRC client is *irc*.

—*JP*

1.22 The X Window System

In 1988, an organization called the MIT (Massachusetts Institute of Technology) X Consortium was formed to promote and develop a vendor-neutral windowing system called the X Window System. (It was called "X" because it was a follow-on to a window system called "W" that was developed at Stanford University.) The organization eventually moved away from MIT and became known as the X Consortium. The XFree86 Project, Inc. is another major group developing X; they produce a freely redistributable version that's used on Linux and other Unix-like systems such as Darwin.

A window system is a way of dividing up the large screen of a workstation into multiple virtual terminals, or windows. Each window can interact with a separate application program—or a single application can have many windows. While the "big win" is to have applications with point-and-click mouse-driven user interfaces, one of the most common applications is still a simple terminal emulator (*xterm* (5.9)). X thus allows a workstation to display multiple simultaneous terminal sessions—which makes many of the standard Unix multitasking features such as job control less important because programs can all be running in the foreground in separate windows. X also runs on many kinds of hardware, and it lets you run a program on a remote computer (across a network) while the program's windows are displayed on your local system. Because Unix systems also run on many kinds of hardware, this makes X a good match for Unix.

Unix boxes are, by default, characters-based systems. GUI systems are added to facilitate ease of use, as well as to provide access to a great number of sophisticated applications. The Mac OS X, though, is already a GUI, built on the BSD-based Unix environment, Darwin.

Though Darwin doesn't come with X Windows, you can download and install this, as well as X Windows–based GUIs, such as XDarwin (accessible at *http://www.xdarwin.org*) and OroborOSX (available at the Apple web site at *http://www.apple.com*).

—TOR and JP

2

Getting Help

2.1 The man Command

The Unix operating system was one of the first to include online documentation. It's not the best in the world—most users who haven't internalized the manual set curse it once a week—but it has proven surprisingly resilient. What's particularly interesting about Unix's online documentation is that, unlike other early help systems, it isn't an adjunct to another set of printed documentation that contains the "real" truth. The online manual is complete, authoritative, and usually more current than any printed documentation.

The basis for Unix's online documentation is the *man* command. Most simply, you use it as follows:

```
% man topic
```

where *topic* is usually the name of some command; but it can also be the name of a system call, a library routine, an I/O device, or an administrative file (or file type). The output from *man* is usually sent to a pager like *more*, which allows you to page through the results.

There are several command-line options for the *man* command that can differ based on system. For instance, to look at a command within a specific section, on a System V machine use the *-s* "section" option, with the following format:

```
% man section topic
% man -s section topic
```

For example, if you want to read documentation about the */etc/passwd* file (rather than the *passwd* command) on a System V machine, give the command:

```
% man -s 4 passwd
```

This is an easy way to distinguish between topics with the same name, but in different sections. For other Unix systems, such as FreeBSD, the option to search a section could be something different, such as *-S*.

Another useful command-line option is the *–k* option, which is equivalent to the *apropos* command. This option searches database files for matches of a given keyword, returning the results. This is particularly helpful in finding commands that contain a specific keyword if you're not quite sure what the command is.

Your system may have a configuration file for *man* named */etc/man.config*. If it does, reading it will show you the directories in which manpages are stored, the order in which manpages are searched by default, and more. Even if you don't have an */etc/man.config* file, your *man* command may understand the *MAN-PATH* (3.21) environment variable, a list of where *man* should search. You can set your own *MANPATH*, for example, to show manpages for local versions of commands before standard versions with the same name.

Your system may also have a different manual page system: *info* (2.9).

—*ML and JP*

2.2 whatis: One-Line Command Summaries

whatis is almost identical to *apropos* or the use of *man –k* (2.1), but it requires a command name as an argument—rather than an arbitrary string. Why is this useful? Well, let's say you forget what *cat* (12.2) does. On my system, *apropos cat* gives you several screenfuls of output. You may not want to read the entire manual page. But *whatis cat* gives you a nice one-line summary:

```
% whatis cat
cat (1V)     - concatenate and display
```

The *whatis* command is equivalent to *man –f* on most systems.

Before running *whatis* the first time on your system—particularly if you're running a standalone machine using FreeBSD, Linux, or Darwin—you'll want to run the *makewhatis* at */usr/libexec/makewhatis*, which creates the whatis database by scanning the command names from the existing manpages.

—*ML*

2.3 whereis: Finding Where a Command Is Located

The *whereis* command helps you to locate the executable file, source code, and manual pages for a program. I use it primarily as a sanity check; if I type cat useless.txt and get the message "cat: command not found," I immediately try whereis cat. This gives me a lot of information about what went wrong: someone may have removed *cat* (12.2) from the system, or my *PATH* (35.6) environment variable may be set incorrectly, etc.

Output from *whereis* typically looks like this:

```
% whereis more
cat: /bin/cat /usr/share/man/man1/cat.1.gz
```

This says that the executable file is */bin/cat* and the manual page is */usr/share/man/man1/cat.1.gz*.

whereis has a few options worth mentioning:

–b Only report the executable name

–m Only report the location of the manual page

–s Only search for source files

–u Only issue a report if any of the requested information (executable, manual page, source) is missing

There are other options for modifying the list of directories through which *whereis* searches; if you need these, check your manual pages. In addition, the functionality and flags for *whereis* can differ between versions of Unix. For instance, much of the basic functionality of the command was removed in version 4.4 of FreeBSD as well as Darwin. Again, the manual pages will show you this information.

—*ML and SP*

2.4 Searching Online Manual Pages

When the other techniques in this chapter don't find the information you want, you can try searching the online manual page (2.1) files. You'll probably have to wade through a lot of stuff that you don't want to see, but this method can work when nothing else does. As an example, you remember that there's some command for chopping columns out of a file. You try *man –k* or *apropos*, but it only mentions *colrm* and *pr*, and those aren't what you want. You'll usually be able to narrow your search to one or two manual page sections (2.1); here, you know that user commands are in section 1. So you go to the manual pages and do a case-insensitive search through all the files for "column" or "chop":

```
% cd /usr/man/man1
% egrep -i 'column|chop' *
awk.1:Add up first column, print sum and average:
colrm.1:colrm \- remove characters from specified columns within each line
  ...
cut.1:.IX  cut  ""  "\fIcut\fP \(em remove columns from file"
  ...
```

It's *cut*! Notice that *awk* also handles columns, but *apropos* doesn't say so.

(I cheated on that example: there were other ways to find *cut*—using the synonym *apropos field* instead of *apropos column*, for instance. But this method does work in tougher cases.) To search the manual page files, you'll need to know where they're stored. There are lots of possibilities. If your system has an */etc/man.config* file, it'll probably tell you. Otherwise, the directories */usr/man* or */usr/share/man* are good places to look. If the command is local, try */usr/local/man* and maybe */opt* (a big tree where *find* (9.4) can help). If your system has fast *find* or *locate* (9.18), try searching for man or */man*.

Your manpage files may be compressed (15.6). In that case, use *grep* (13.2) with the –Z option, grep -Z.

You'll probably find subdirectories with names like *man1*, *man2*,…and/or *cat1*, *cat2*,… Directory names like *manN* will have unformatted source files for section *N*; the *catN* directories have formatted source files. Or you may just find files named *command.N*, where *N* is *1* for section 1, *2* for section 2, and so on.

There are two types of manpage files: unformatted (shown in article 3.22) and formatted. The unformatted pages are easier to search because none of the words will have embedded backspace characters. The previous example shows how. The unformatted pages have *nroff* commands and macros in them, though, which can make searching and reading tougher.

To search formatted pages, you'll want to strip the embedded backspace characters. Otherwise, *grep* might miss the word you want because it was boldfaced or underlined—with backspaces in it. In the following example, a shell loop (28.9) applies a series of commands to each file. First, *col –b* removes the overstriking. *grep* does a search (case insensitive, as before). Because *grep* is reading its standard input, it doesn't know the filename, so a little *sed* command adds the name to the start of every line *grep* outputs.

* 1.13
```
$ cd /usr/man/cat1
$ for file in *
> do col -b < $file | grep -i column | sed "s/^/${file}:/"
> done
awk.1:   Add up first column, print    sum and average:
  ...
cut.1:   Use cut to cut out columns from a table or fields from each
  ...
```

If your manpage files are compressed, replace col -b < $file with:

```
zcat $file | col -b
```

In Bourne shells, you can pipe the output of the loop to a pager (like *less* (12.3)) to see the output a screenful at a time and quit (with q) when you're done. To do that, change the last line of the *for* loop to:

```
done | less
```

—*JP*

2.5 How Unix Systems Remember Their Names

Each computer on a network needs a name. On many Unix versions, the *uname –n* command shows you this name. On some systems, the command *hostname* or *uuname –l* (two *us*, lowercase *L*) may be what you want. If you use more than one system, the hostname is great to use in a shell prompt—or any time you forget where you're logged in.

—JP

2.6 Which Version Am I Using?

Your system may have several versions of a particular command—for instance, a BSD-compatible version in one directory and a System V–compatible version somewhere else (and you might have added a private version in your own *bin* directory (7.4)). Which command you'll get depends on your *PATH* (35.6) environment variable. It's often essential to know which version you're using. For example:

```
$ type sort
sort is /bin/sort
```

tells me exactly which version of the *sort* program I'm using. (On one system I've used, there were two *sorts*; I had also defined an alias for *sort*.) If I want to see all versions, *bash* supports a *–all* option:

```
$ type -all sort
sort is aliased to `TMPDIR=/var/tmp /bin/sort'
sort is /bin/sort
sort is /usr/5bin/sort
```

A similar command is *whence*.

But *type* and *whence* are built into shells and are also Unix-version dependent (not all Unix systems have them), so they won't work everywhere. The *which* command is usually external (1.9), so it works everywhere—although, because it isn't built into the shells, it can't always find out about aliases defined in your current shell. For example:

```
% which sort
/usr/bin/sort
```

You'll find that *which* comes in handy in lots of other situations. I find that I'm always using *which* inside of backquotes to get a precise path. (*whence* and *type* may print extra text.) For example, when I was writing these articles, I started wondering whether or not *man*, *apropos*, and *whatis* were really the same executable. It's a simple question, but one I had never bothered to think about. There's one good way to find out:

```
% ls -li `which man` `which apropos` `which whatis`
102352 -rwxr-xr-x  3 root        24576 Feb  8  2001 /usr/ucb/apropos
102352 -rwxr-xr-x  3 root        24576 Feb  8  2001 /usr/ucb/man
102352 -rwxr-xr-x  3 root        24576 Feb  8  2001 /usr/ucb/whatis
```

What does this tell us? Well, within this system the three commands have the same file size, which means that they're likely to be identical; furthermore, each file has three links, meaning that each file has three names. The *–i* option confirms it; all three files have the same i-number. So, *apropos*, *man*, and *whatis* are just one executable file that has three hard links.

However, running the same command in another environment, such as in Darwin, results in a different output:

```
117804 -r-xr-xr-x  1 root   wheel  14332 sep  2  2001  /usr/bin/apropos
117807 -r-xr-xr-x  1 root   wheel  19020 sep  2  2001  /usr/bin/man
117808 -r-xr-xr-x  1 root   wheel  14336 sep  2  2001  /usr/bin/whatis
```

In Darwin, the commands are separate entities.

A few System V implementations don't have a *which* command.

—*ML, JP, MAL, and SP*

2.7 What tty Am I On?

Each login session has its own *tty* (24.6)—a Unix device file that handles input and output for your terminal, window, etc. Each tty has its own filename. If you're logged on more than once and other users want to *write* or *talk* (1.21) to you, they need to know which tty to use. If you have processes running on several ttys, you can tell which process is where.

To do that, run the *tty* command at a shell prompt in the window:

```
% tty
/dev/tty07
```

You can tell other users to type write *your-username* tty07.

Most systems have different kinds of ttys: a few dialup terminals, some network ports for *rlogin* and *telnet*, etc. (1.21). A system file like */etc/ttys* lists which ttys are used for what. You can use this to make your login setup more automatic. For example, most network terminals on our computers have names like */dev/ttypx* or */dev/pts/x*, where *x* is a single digit or letter. I have a test in my *.logout* file (4.17) that clears the screen on all ttys except network:

`28.14`
```
# Clear screen non-network ttys:
if ("`tty`" !~ /dev/ttyp?) then
    clear
endif
```

(Of course, you don't need to clear the terminal screen if you're using an *xterm* window that you close when you log out.)

—*JP*

2.8 Who's On?

The *who* command lists the users logged on to the system now. Here's an example of the output on my system:

```
% who
naylor    ttyZ1    Nov  6 08:25
hal       ttyp0    Oct 20 16:04    (zebra.ora.com:0.)
pmui      ttyp1    Nov  4 17:21    (dud.ora.com:0.0)
jpeek     ttyp2    Nov  5 23:08    (jpeek.com)
hal       ttyp3    Oct 28 15:43    (zebra.ora.com:0.)
  ...
```

Each line shows a different terminal or window. The columns show the username logged on, the *tty* (2.7) number, the login time, and, if the user is coming in via a network (1.21), you'll see their location (in parentheses). The user *hal* is logged on twice, for instance.

It's handy to search the output of *who* with *grep* (13.1)—especially on systems with a lot of users. For example:

```
% who | grep "^hal "          ...where is hal logged on?
% who | grep "Nov  6"         ...who logged on today?
```
–v 13.3
```
% who | grep -v "Nov  6"      ...who logged on before today?
  ...
```

The GNU *who*, on the CD-ROM, has more features than some other versions.

—*JP*

2.9 The info Command

An information system gaining popularity on the more lightweight Unix-based systems is info. It's particularly relevant for finding information within Linux and FreeBSD.

Unlike man—which displays all information on a topic at once, usually routed through some form of paging system such as cat—info is based on a hypertext like linkage between topic components. You connect to each of the subtopics using character-based commands and typing part or all of the subtopic title—at least enough to distinguish one subtopic from another.

To use info, you type the command *info* followed by the Unix command about which you're trying to find information. For instance, to find out more about info itself, you would use the following command line:

```
info info
```

This will return the main info introduction page and a menu of subtopics such as:

```
Getting Started
Advanced Info
Creating an Info File
```

To access the subtopic, you type the letter m for menu, and then in the prompt that opens at the bottom of the screen, type enough of the letters to distinguish the subtopic menu item from any other. You don't have to complete the command: you can just type enough of the letters followed by a TAB to fill in the rest. Once the subtopic menu item has been filled in, hitting ENTER sends you to the information.

To learn more about using info, you can type the letter h when you're in info and no command line buffer is showing. This brings up basic information about the *info* command, including the commands you use within info to use the application. These letters are summarized in Table 2-1.

Table 2-1. info commands

Command	Action
h	To get help on using info
m	To access a subtopic menu item
n	To get to next related subtopic
p	To get to the previous related subtopic
space	To move forward in the display if it exceeds page size
delete	To move backward in the display if it exceeds page size
Ctrl-l	To clean up the display if it gets mangled
b	To get to the first page of the display
?	To get a list of info commands
q	To quit info
d	To return to highest level of info topics
mEmacs*return*	To access the Emacs manual
s	To search for string within current node

Note that the letter commands are case insensitive: *U* works the same as *u*.

Use the *d* command to pull up the Directory node, the menu of info major topics. In fact, this is a good way to become familiar with info and its contained subtopics—type *d* and then use the menu commands to explore each of the major subtopic areas.

For instance, from the Directory Node, typing m followed by typing strings into the command buffer pulls up the strings info node.

When using the *info* command, if the information doesn't fit within a page, header and footer information will provide you some details about the subtopic, such as the info file, node, and the next nodes within the hierarchy. For instance, when accessing information about *man*, depending on your system the header reads as follows:

```
File: *manpages*, Node:man, Up: (dir)
```

This translates to the info file manpages and the node for man. Typing the *u* will move you up to the dir info page. Within Emacs, use mouse button two to click on and access a subtopic.

The footer provides a summary of the header information and also provides the number of lines for the topic if the topic page extends past the current screen. To see more information, type the *space* to page through the topic, just as you do with *man*.

Much of the help information within info is pulled over as is from manpages and hasn't been converted to the hypertext format of info. Because of this, the use of the *m* command won't pull up any subtopic. You'll need to use the space key to access the additional information.

To search within an info node/page, type *s* and then type the search string into the command buffer. The cursor is moved to the first occurance of the string.

—*SP*

Part II

Customizing Your Environment

Part II contains the following chapters:

3

Setting Up Your Unix Shell

3.1 What Happens When You Log In

When you first log in to a Unix system, the *login* program performs various security measures. These vary slightly from Unix variant to Unix variant, but they are largely the same.

First, *login* checks to see if you are not the root user and whether the file */etc/nologin* exists (it is created by the *shutdown* command to indicate that the system is being brought down for maintenance). If both of these conditions are true, the *login* program prints the contents of that file to the terminal, and the login fails. If you are the root user, however, you will be allowed to log in.

Second, *login* checks to see if there are any special conditions on your login attempt (which may be defined in */etc/usertty* or */etc/securetty*), such as on which tty you're coming in. Linux systems do this, for example. Some systems (such as Darwin and other BSD-based systems) also check */etc/fbtab* and may restrict your access to any devices listed in that file. These systems may also log failed login attempts to a file, such as */var/log/failedlogin*, if it exists.

login may also record the time of login in the file */var/log/lastlog*, make an entry in the file */var/run/utmp*, showing that you are successfully logged in (it is removed once you log out), and append the *utmp* entry to the file */var/log/wtmp*, showing that you logged in. This *wtmp* record will be updated on logout, showing the duration of your login session.

If the file *.hushlogin* exists in the user's home directory, the login will be quiet; otherwise, the following sequence of events will occur. If the system has any special copyright information to display, it will be printed to the terminal, followed by the message of the day (usually stored in */etc/motd*), and the user's last login time and system of origin (from the *wtmp* file, as discussed in the previous paragraph). If you want your login to be quiet, simply *touch ~/.hushlogin*. If you want it to be noisy, remove the file.

Finally, if all other checks have passed and restrictions have been performed, *login* starts a shell for you. Which shell depends on what is set in your user database entry (*/etc/passwd*, NIS, or possibly NetInfo under Darwin). If the shell specified for you is not interactive (3.4), you may well be denied a command line. This is common for POP and ftp-only user accounts, where */bin/true* and */bin/false* are often specified as shells to disallow shell logins from those accounts.

—*JP and SJC*

3.2 The Mac OS X Terminal Application

Throughout the book, we will refer to terminals, terminal emulators, and other software that allows you, the end user, to interact with the computer via some character-driven screen. In the old days, most terminals were separate hardware, but nowadays they're usually software. Mac OS X is no exception: its Terminal application, found in the Utilities folder of your Applications folder, is a terminal emulator.

You can launch Terminal by double-clicking on the icon in the Finder, or if you have the Terminal icon in your Dock, by single-clicking on that icon.

Once launched, Terminal may be configured as most Mac applications can: by setting preferences in the Preferences dialog and choosing a font family and size from the Font menu.

One big difference between Terminal and other, X-specific applications is that instead of running individual instances of *xterm*, you run one instance of Terminal and may have multiple windows, known as "shells," which may have saved settings (such as color, size, font choice, and various other settings). You can't run a shell in Mac OS X without running Terminal.

—*SJC*

3.3 Shell Setup Files—Which, Where, and Why

To understand setup files, you need to understand that a shell can act like a *login shell* or a *nonlogin shell* (3.4). There are different setup files for nonlogin and login shells.

When you log in to a Unix system—but not under a window system—the *login* program starts a shell for you. The *login* program sets a special flag (3.19) to tell a shell that it's a login shell. If the shell doesn't have that flag set, it won't act like a login shell. Opening a new window in a window system may or may not set the "login shell" flag—that depends on the configuration. (For example, the command *xterm –ls* starts a login shell in an *xterm* window (24.20); *xterm +ls* starts a nonlogin shell.) When you connect to a system with programs like *ftp* and *scp*, that usually starts a nonlogin shell. And a subshell (24.4) is never a login shell (unless you set a command-line option to force a login shell, like bash -l).

How can you tell whether your shell is a login shell? The answer is "it depends." When you first log in to a system, you want a login shell that sets things like the terminal type (5.2, 5.3). Other shells on the same terminal should be nonlogin shells—to avoid redoing those one-time-only setup commands. Different shells have their own methods for handling first-time shell invocations versus later invocations, and that's what the rest of this article is about.

Parenthesis operators (43.7) don't read any setup file. Instead, they start another instance of your current shell. Parentheses are called "subshell operators," but the subshell they start doesn't print a prompt and usually has a short lifetime.

Next, let's look at the setup files—login and nonlogin—for the major shells. I recommend that you read about all of them. Then experiment with your shell's setup files until you get things working the way you want them.

System-wide setup

Your *login*(1) command probably sets some environment variables (35.3) like HOME, PATH, SHELL, TERM, MAIL, and LOGNAME or USER; check its manual page. Your system may set some environment variables or other parameters that apply to all shells or to all shells of a particular type (all *bash* shells, *zsh* shells, etc.). All of these will be passed through the environment, from parent process to child process (35.4), to all of your shells, login and nonlogin.

Once *login* or your window system starts your individual shell, it may also read its own system-wide setup files. These files, if any, will be read before your personal setup files. Check your shell's manual page and the */etc* directory for files like *csh.login*, *bashrc*, *zshrc*, and so on. On Red Hat systems, for example, there is a directory named */etc/profile.d* containing package-specific C and Bash shell config files that are sourced (read into the current shell) on startup of a shell. On Mac OS X, when you use Terminal (3.2), your shell (which is *tcsh* by default) reads */private/etc/csh.cshrc*, as well as any user-specific files (e.g., ~/.tcshrc).

Bourne shell

The original Bourne shell has one file that it reads when you log in: it's called *.profile* and is in your home directory. Put all your setup commands there. Later versions of the Bourne shell may also read */etc/profile* before your local setup file is read and may also read the contents of whatever file is named in the ENV environment variable (35.3) (but only for interactive shells). You may set this variable from your own *.profile*:

```
ENV=$HOME/.mystartup; export ENV
```

The Bourne shell doesn't read *.profile* when you start a nonlogin shell or subshell (43.7), though. Subshells are set up through inheritance of environment variables (35.3) that were set when you first logged in (in system-wide setup files or *.profile*) or from commands you typed since.

C shell

C shell users have several shell setup files available:

- The *.cshrc* file is read any time a C shell starts—that includes shell escapes and shell scripts.* This is the place to put commands that should run every time you start a shell. For instance, shell variables like *cdpath* (31.5) and *prompt* should be set here. Aliases (29.2) should, too. Those things aren't passed to subshells through the environment, so they belong in *.cshrc* (or *.tcshrc*). See the upcoming section on *tcsh* for more details.

  Alternately, you can put aliases into a separate file and use the *source* command to read the file into the current shell from your *.cshrc/ .tcshrc*—if you're the sort who likes to have custom init files for every host you log in to, but like your aliases to be common wherever you go. This provides a quick and easy way for you to copy your *.csh.aliases* (or whatever name you give it, being careful to distinguish between it and the slightly different format required by *bash* aliases) from host to host without clobbering your custom, localized init files.

- When *csh* starts up, on recent systems it may read a system-wide setup file, such as */etc/csh.cshrc*,† and for login shells, */etc/csh.login*.

- Your *.login* file is read when you start a login shell. You should set several things here. Set environment variables (35.3) (which Unix will pass to subshells automatically). Run commands like *tset* (5.3) and *stty* (5.7, 5.8) that set up your terminal. Finally, include commands you want to run every time you log in—checking for mail and news (1.21), running *fortune*, checking your calendar for the day, etc.

  Note that *.cshrc* is read before *.login*, by *csh*, but that tcsh may be compiled such that the order is reversed, and *.tcshrc* may be read *after .login* in some environments. Check the *version* shell variable to find out how your environment is set up.

- The shell reads *.logout* when you end a login shell. Article 3.8 has tips for reading *.logout* from nonlogin shells.

---

* If you write a *csh* (or *tcsh*) script, you probably should use the *–f* option to keep scripts from reading *.cshrc* (or *.tcshrc*). However, you probably shouldn't use *csh* or *tcsh* for scripts.

† On Mac OS X, */etc* is a symbolic link to */private/etc*. The actual initialization files for *tcsh* are in */usr/ share/init/tcsh*.

Korn shell

The Korn shell is a lot like the Bourne shell. A login Korn shell (3.4) will read the *.profile* first; recent versions do so only after reading */etc/profile*, if present. The *.profile* can set the *ENV* (35.5) environment variable to the pathname of a file (typically *$HOME/.kshrc*). Any child Korn shell started by that login shell—including all subshells—will read the file named by $ENV as it starts up, before printing a prompt or running other commands.

The public domain Korn shell often found on Linux may also be further restricted when invoked as a "privileged" shell, using a pattern that matches r*sh, in which case neither the *~/.profile* nor the file named by the *ENV* environment variable will be read. Instead, the shell will be initialized using */etc/suid_profile*, if present.

bash

bash is something of a cross between the Bourne and C shells. A login *bash* will read *.bash_profile*, *.bash_login*, or *.profile*. A noninteractive *bash* will read a file named *.bashrc* in your home directory. The shell reads *.bash_logout* when you end a login shell; you can set a *trap* (4.18) to handle nonlogin shells.

bash also uses GNU Readline for reading and editing text you enter at a shell prompt. The *.inputrc* file configures Readline for a given user; */etc/inputrc* is for global configuration.

tcsh

tcsh is like the C shell but more flexible. If a *tcsh* shell is run, it first tries to read *.tcshrc* and, if not found, then tries *.cshrc*. In addition, *tcsh* will also load either *.history* or the value of the *histfile* variable, if set; then it may try to read *.cshdirs* or the value of the *dirsfile* variable.

zsh

As always, *zsh* is very flexible. Startup files are read from the directory named in the *ZDOTDIR* environment variable, if any;* otherwise, from *HOME*. All shells read the global */etc/zshenv* and your *.zshenv* files. If the shell is a login shell, commands are read from */etc/zprofile* and then your *.zprofile*. Then, if the shell is interactive, commands are read from */etc/zshrc* and your *.zshrc*. Finally, if the shell is a login shell, */etc/zlogin* and your *.zlogin* files are read.

—*JP and SJC*

---

* *ZDOTDIR* may be hard to set on your first login—when your *zsh* is a login shell—because it's hard to set an environment variable before your first shell starts. (The system program that starts your shell, like *login*(1), could do the job, I guess.)

3.4 Login Shells, Interactive Shells

Each Unix shell (*sh*, *csh*, etc.) can be in *interactive* mode or *noninteractive* mode. A shell also can act as a *login* shell or a *nonlogin* shell. A shell is a shell is a shell—e.g., a login *bash* shell is the same program (like */bin/bash*) as a nonlogin *bash* shell. The difference is in the way that the shell acts: which setup files it reads, whether it sets a shell prompt, and so on.

Login Shells

When you first log in to a Unix system from a terminal, the system normally starts a *login shell*. (3.4) A login shell is typcally the top-level shell in the "tree" of processes that starts with the *init* (24.2) process. Many characteristics of processes are passed from parent to child process down this "tree"—especially environment variables (35.3), such as the search path (35.6). The changes you make in a login shell will affect all the other processes that the top-level shell starts—including any subshells (24.4).

So, a login shell is where you do general setup that's done only the first time you log in—initialize your terminal, set environment variables, and so on. A shell "knows" (3.19) when it's a login shell—and, if it is, the shell reads special setup files (3.3) for login shells. For instance, login C shells read your *.login* file, and Bourne-type login shells read *.profile*. Bash may also read */etc/profile*, and *~/.bash_profile* or *~/.bash_login* or *~/.profile*, depending on whether those files exist and whether the *–noprofile* option has been passed (which would disable reading of any startup files).

Nonlogin shells are either subshells (started from the login shell), shells started by your window system (24.20), or "disconnected" shells started by *at* (25.5), *rsh* (1.21), etc. These shells don't read *.login* or *.profile*. In addition, *bash* allows a nonlogin shell to read *~/.bashrc* or not, depending on whether the *–norc* or *–rcfile* options have been passed as arguments during invocation. The former simply disables reading of the file, and the latter allows a substitute file to be specified as an argument.

Some shells make it easy to know if a particular invocation is a login shell. For instance, *tcsh* sets the variable *loginsh*. Check your shell's manual page for details. Article 4.12 shows another solution: the *SHLVL* variable that's set in most modern shells. Or you can add the following line to the beginning of a setup file that's only read by login shells (3.3). The line sets a shell variable (35.9) named *loginshell*:

```
set loginsh=yes   ...csh

loginshell=yes    ...bash and other sh-type shells
```

Now wherever you need to know the type of shell, use tests like:

if **35.13**

```
if ($?loginsh)    ...csh-type shells
```

```
if [ -n "$loginshell" ]    ...sh-type shells (including bash)
```

This works because the flag variable will only be defined if a shell has read a setup file for login shells. Note that none of the variable declarations use the "export" keyword—this is so that the variable is not passed on to subsequent shells, thereby ruining its purpose as a flag specific to login shells.

Interactive Shells

In general, shells are used for two jobs. Sometimes, a shell handles commands that you type at a prompt. These are *interactive shells*. Other times, a shell reads commands from a file—a shell script (35.2). In this case, the shell doesn't need to print a prompt, to handle command-line editing, and so on. These shells can be *noninteractive shells*. (There's no rule that only noninteractive shells can read shell scripts or that only interactive shells can read commands from a terminal. But this is generally true.)

One other difference between interactive and noninteractive shells is that interactive shells tie STDOUT and STDERR to the current terminal, unless otherwise specified.

It's usually easy to see whether a particular invocation of your shell is interactive. In C shells, the *prompt* variable will be set. In the Korn shell and *bash*, the –i flag is set. Your current flags may be displayed using the $– variable:

```
prompt$ echo $-
imH
```

The previous example, from an interactive bash shell, shows that the flags for an interactive shell (i), monitor mode (m), and history substitution (H) have been set.

—*JP and SJC*

3.5 What Goes in Shell Setup Files?

Setup files for login shells (3.4)—such as *.login* and *.profile*—typically do at least the following:

- Set the search path (27.6) if the system default path isn't what you want.
- Set the terminal type (5.3) and make various terminal settings (5.7, 5.8) if the system might not know your terminal (if you log in from various terminals over a dialup line or from a terminal emulator on a desktop machine, for instance).

- Set environment variables (35.3) that might be needed by programs or scripts that you typically run.

- Run one or more commands that you want to run whenever you log in. For example, if your system *login* program doesn't show the message of the day, your setup file can. Many people also like to print an amusing or instructive fortune. You also might want to run *who* (2.8) or *uptime* (26.4) or *w* (a combination of the other two, but not found on all systems) for information about the system.

In the C shell, the *.cshrc* file is used to establish settings that will apply to every instance of the C shell, not just login shells. For example, you typically want aliases (29.2) available in every interactive shell you run—but these aren't passed through the environment, so a setup file has to do the job. You may wish to put all of your aliases into another file, such as *.aliases*, or qualify the name with the shell's name, such as *.csh.aliases*, to allow for different alias formats between shells, and then you can use the *source* command to read in that file on startup from *.cshrc*.

Even novices can write simple setup files. The trick is to make these setup scripts really work for you. Here are some of the things you might want to try:

- Creating a custom prompt.
- Coordinating custom setup files on different machines (article 3.18).
- Making different terminal settings depending on which terminal you're using (article 3.10 and others).
- Seeing the message of the day only when it changes.
- Doing all of the above without making your login take forever.

—*TOR and SJC*

3.6 Tip for Changing Account Setup: Keep a Shell Ready

The shell is your interface to Unix. If you make a bad mistake when you change your setup file (3.3) or your password, it can be tough to log in and fix things.

Before you change your setup, it's a good idea to start a login session to the same account from somewhere else. Use that session for making your changes. Log in again elsewhere to test your changes.

Don't have a terminal with multiple windows or another terminal close to your desk? You can get the same result by using *rlogin* or *telnet* (1.21) to log in to your host again from the same terminal. What I mean is:

```
somehost% vi .cshrc
    ...Make edits to the file...
somehost% rlogin localhost
    ...Logs you in to your same account...
An error message
somehost% logout
Connection closed.
somehost% vi .cshrc
    ...Edit to fix mistake...
```

If you don't have *rlogin* or *telnet*, the command su - *username,* where *username* is your username, will do almost the same thing. Or, if you're testing your login shell configuration, *login* will do as well.

—JP and SJC

3.7 Use Absolute Pathnames in Shell Setup Files

One common mistake in shell setup files (3.3) is lines like these:

```
source .aliases
```

$$ 27.17
`...` 28.14
```
echo "Shell PID $$ started at `date`" >> login.log
```

What's wrong with those lines? Both use relative pathnames (1.16) for the files (*.aliases, login.log*), assuming the files are in the home directory. Those lines won't work when you start a subshell (24.4) from somewhere besides your home directory because your setup files for nonlogin shells (like *.cshrc*) are read whenever a shell starts. If you ever use the *source* or . commands (35.29) to read the setup files from outside your home directory, you'll have the same problem.

Use absolute pathnames instead. As article 31.11 explains, the pathname of your home directory is in the tilde (~) operator or the $HOME or $LOGDIR environment variable:

```
source ~/.aliases
echo "Shell PID $$ started at `date`" >> ~/login.log
```

—JP

3.8 Setup Files Aren't Read When You Want?

The C shell reads its *.cshrc*, *.login*, and *.logout* setup files at particular times (3.3). Only "login" C shells (3.4) will read the *.login* and *.logout* files. Back when *csh* was designed, this restriction worked fine. The shell that started as you logged in was flagged as a login shell, and it read all three files. You started other shells (shell escapes, shell scripts, etc.) from that login shell, and they would read only

.cshrc. The same can be said of other shell variants, such as *tcsh*, though they may have multiple startup files—the problem of distinguishing between login and nonlogin shell startup is the same.

Now, Unix has interactive shells started by window systems (like *xterm* (24.20)), remote shells (like *rsh* (1.21) or *ssh*), and other shells that might need some things set from the *.login* or *.logout* files. Depending on how these shells are invoked, these might not be login shells—so they might read only *.cshrc* (or *.tcshrc*, etc.). How can you handle that? Putting all your setup commands in *.cshrc* isn't a good idea because all subshells (24.4) read it…you definitely don't want to run terminal-setting commands like *tset* (5.3) during shell escapes!

Most other shells have the same problem. Some, like *zsh* and *bash*, have several setup files that are read at different times—and probably can be set up to do what you want. For other shells, though, you'll probably need to do some tweaking.

To handle problems at login time, put almost all of your setup commands in a file that's read by all instances of your shell, login or nonlogin. (In the C shell, use *.cshrc* instead of *.login*.) After the "login-only" commands have been read from the setup file, set the *ENV_SET* environment variable (35.3) as a flag. (There's nothing special about this name. You can pick any name you want.) You can then use this variable to test whether the login-only commands have already been run and skip running them again in nonlogin shells.

Because the environment variables from a parent process are passed to any child processes it starts, the shell will copy the "flag" variable to subshells, and the *.cshrc* can test for it. If the variable exists, the login-only commands are skipped. That'll keep the commands from being read again in a child shell.

Here are parts of a *.cshrc* that show the idea:

```
...Normal .cshrc stuff...
if ($?prompt && ! $?ENV_SET) then
    # Do commands that used to go in .login file:
    setenv EDITOR /usr/ucb/vi
    tset
        ...
    setenv ENV_SET done
endif
```

You might put a comment in the file you've bypassed—the *csh .login* file, the *ksh .profile* file, etc.—to explain what you've done.

The file that runs when you log out (in the C shell, that's *.logout*) should probably be read only once—when your last ("top-level") shell exits. If your top-level shell isn't a login shell, you can make it read the logout file anyway. Here's how: first, along with the previous fixes to your *.cshrc*-type file, add an alias that will read your logout file when you use the *exit* command. Also set your shell to force you to use the *exit* command (35.12) to log out—in *csh*, for example, use *set ignoreeof*. Here's what the chunk of your *.bashrc* will look like:

```
  case 35.10        case "$-/${ENV_SET:-no}" in
     / 36.25        *i*/no)
                        # This is an interactive shell / $ENV_SET was not set earlier.
                        # Make all top-level interactive shells read .bash_logout file:
                        set -o ignoreeof
 function 29.11          function exit {
     . 35.29                 . ~/.bash_logout
                            builtin exit
                        }
                        ;;
                    esac
```

The builtin exit (27.9) prevents a loop; it makes sure *bash* uses its internal *exit* command instead of the *exit* function you've just defined. In the C shell, use ""exit (27.10) instead. This isn't needed on all shells though. If you can't tell from your manual page, test with another shell (3.6) and be ready to *kill* (24.12) a looping shell.

—JP and SJC

3.9 Gotchas in set prompt Test

Lots of users add an if (! $?prompt) exit test to their *.cshrc* files. It's gotten so common that some vendors add a workaround to defeat the test. For instance, some versions of the *which* command (2.6) set the *prompt* variable so that it can see your aliases "hidden" inside the $?prompt test. I've also seen a version of *at* that starts an interactive shell to run jobs.

If you've buried commands after if (! $?prompt) that should only be run on interactive shells or at login time, then you may have trouble.

There are workarounds. What you'll need depends on the problem you're trying to work around.

- The version of *which* on the CD-ROM works without reading your *.cshrc* file, so there's no problem there.

- Here's a way to stop the standard *which* from reading parts of your *.cshrc* that you don't want it to read. The first time you log in, this scheme sets a *CSHRC_READ* environment variable (35.3). The variable will be copied into all subshells (24.4) (like the one that *which* starts). In subshells, the test if ($?CSHRC_READ) will branch to the end of your *.cshrc* file:

```
if (! $?prompt) goto cshrc_end

# COMMANDS BELOW HERE ARE READ ONLY BY INTERACTIVE SHELLS:
alias foo bar
   ...

if ($?CSHRC_READ) goto cshrc_end
```

```
# COMMANDS BELOW HERE ARE READ ONLY AT LOGIN TIME:
setenv CSHRC_READ yes
   ...

cshrc_end:
```

- If you have a buggy version of *at* (25.5) that runs jobs from interactive shells, make your own frontend to *at* (29.1) that sets an environment variable named *AT* temporarily before it submits the *at* job. Add a test to your *.cshrc* that quits if *AT* is set:

```
# at JOBS RUN INTERACTIVE SHELLS ON MY BUGGY VERSION OF UNIX.
# WORKAROUND IS HERE AND IN THE at ALIAS BELOW:
if ($?AT) goto cshrc_end

   ...
alias at '(setenv AT yes; \at \!*)'
   ...

cshrc_end:
```

( ) **43.7**
\at **29.8**

Most modern versions of *at* save a copy of your environment when you submit the job and use it when the *at* job is run. At that time, the *AT* environment variable will be set; the C shell will skip the parts of your *.cshrc* that you want it to. It's ugly, but it works.

Those workarounds probably won't solve all the problems on your version of Unix, but I hope they'll give you some ideas.

—JP and SJC

3.10 Automatic Setups for Different Terminals

If you work at several kinds of terminals or terminal emulators, terminal setup can be tough. For instance, my X terminal sends a backspace character when I push the upper-right key, but the same key on another terminal sends a delete character—I want *stty erase* (5.8) to set the correct erase character automatically.* Maybe you want a full set of calendar programs started when you log in to the terminal at your desk, but not when you make a quick login from somewhere else.

The next seven articles have ideas for changing your login sequence automatically. Some examples are for the C shell and use that shell's *switch* and *if*. Examples for Bourne-type shells use *case* (35.10) and *if* (35.13). If you use the other type of shell, the idea still applies; just swap the syntax.

---

* Of course, it is all arbitrary and contingent on your keyboard layout and configuration.

- If you use several kinds of terminals or terminal emulators, try testing the *TERM* environment variable (3.11). Testing other environment variables (3.14) can identify the frontend system (like a window system) you're using.

- Test the output of *who am i* (3.12) to find out about the remote system from which you've logged in.

- If you log into different kinds of ports—network, hardwired, and so on— search for the port type (3.15) in a table like */etc/ttys* (in BSD derivatives) or */etc/inittab* (in some other variants). Testing the port name (3.13) may also work.

- In the X Window System, you can test the window size (3.16) and make various settings based on that. Naming windows (3.17) lets you identify a particular window by reading its environment.

- You can also handle some of these cases using the venerable but obscure *tset* (5.3) program to select and initialize the correct terminal type. Another program that sets the terminal type is *qterm* (5.4).

Because your terminal type doesn't change after you've logged in, many of these tests probably belong in your *.profile* or *.login* file. Those setup files are read when you first log in to a *tty*. Other tests, especially ones that involve windows, will probably fit better in a per-shell setup file such as *.bashrc* or *.cshrc*. Article 3.3 can help you choose.

—*JP and SJC*

3.11 Terminal Setup: Testing TERM

If you use several different kinds of terminals (or, as is far more common these days, terminal emulators) and your TERM environment variable is set differently on each terminal, you can add a test like this to your C shell *.login* file:

```
switch ($TERM)
case vt100:
    ...do commands for vt100
    breaksw
case xxx:
    ...do commands for xxx
    breaksw
default:
    ...do commands for other terminals
    breaksw
endsw
```

If you have a Bourne-type shell, use a *case* statement (35.10) in your *.profile* instead:

```
case "$TERM" in
vt100)
       ...do commands for vt100
       ;;
   xterm)
       ...do commands for xterm
       ;;
  *)
       ...do commands for other terminals
       ;;
esac
```

—*JP and SJC*

3.12 Terminal Setup: Testing Remote Hostname and X Display

If you log in from other hosts (1.21) or from hosts running the X Window System (24.20), the *who am i* command will probably show a hostname and/or window information in parentheses:

```
schampeo@fugazi:1002 $ who am i
schampeo ttyp7    Jun 19 03:28 (fugazi:0.0)
```

(Long hostnames may be truncated. Also, note that some versions of *who am i* prepend the name of the local host to the username and don't include the remote hostname at all in their output. Check yours before you write this test.) The information in parentheses can help you configure your terminal based on where you've logged in from and/or which display you're using. To test it, add commands such as the following to your *.profile* file. (In C-type shells, use a *switch* statement in *.login* instead.)

case **35.10**
\(..\) \1
34.11

```
case "`who am i | sed -n 's/.*(\(.*\))/\1/p'`" in
*0.0)    ...do commands for X display 0 ;;
mac2*)   ...do commands for the host mac2.foo.com ;;
"")      ...no output (probably not a remote login) ;;
*)       ...do commands for other situations ;;
esac
```

That uses *sed* (34.1) to give the text between the parentheses for that remote host to the case. This *0.0 case matches lines ending with 0.0; the mac2 case matches lines that start with mac2; an empty string means *sed* probably didn't find any parentheses; and the * case catches everything else.

—*JP and SJC*

---

* Also try *"who mom likes"* or maybe *"who is responsible?"*—the *who* doesn't really care, as long as there are only two arguments. So, *"who let the dogs out?"*, as you might expect, causes an error.

3.13 Terminal Setup: Testing Port

If you know that certain port (tty) numbers are used for certain kinds of logins, you can test that and change your terminal setup based on the *tty* you're currently using. For example, some systems use *ttyp0*, *ttyq1*, etc. as network ports for *rlogin* and *ssh* (1.21), while others use *pty0*, etc. This Bourne-type *case* statement branches on the port name:

tty **2.7**
```
case "`tty`" in
/dev/tty[pqrs]?)
    # rlogin, telnet:
    ...
/dev/tty02)
    # terminal on my desk:
    ...
"not a tty") ;;   ...not a terminal login session; do nothing
esac
```

In C-type shells, try a *switch* or *if* statement instead.

On Linux, you may need to look for patterns to match */dev/pts/0*, */dev/pts/1*, etc.

—JP and SJC

3.14 Terminal Setup: Testing Environment Variables

Certain systems set certain environment variables. For example, the X Window System sets a *DISPLAY* environment variable (35.5). If you've logged in from a remote system using *ssh* (1.21), look for variables like *SSH_CLIENT* and *SSH_TTY* or *SSH_AUTH_SOCK* on the system you log in to. (If you aren't sure about your system, use the *env* or *printenv* command (35.3) to look for changes in your environment at different systems.)

Your shell setup file (3.3) makes decisions based on the environment variables that have been set. Here are examples for both C-type and Bourne-type shells:

[ ] **35.26**
```
if ($?DISPLAY) then              if [ -n "$DISPLAY" ]; then
    # on X window system             # on X window system
    ...                              ...
else if ($?XDARWIN_VERSION) then elif [ -n "$XDARWIN_VERSION" ]; then
    # on MacOS X system              # on MacOS X system
    ...                              ...
else                             else
    ...                              ...
endif                            fi
```

—JP and SJC

3.15 Terminal Setup: Searching Terminal Table

Your system may have an */etc/ttytab* or */etc/ttys* file that lists the type of each terminal port (*tty* (24.6)).* Here are lines from */etc/ttys* on a NetBSD system I use:

```
console  "/usr/libexec/getty std.9600"  vt100      on  local
tty00    "/usr/libexec/getty std.9600"  dialup     off local
tty01    "/usr/libexec/getty std.9600"  plugboard  off local
  ...
ttyp0    none                           network    off
  ...
```

For example, port *ttyp0* is *network*, the type used by *xterm* (24.20), *telnet* (1.21), etc.

To change your account configuration based on the tty port type, match the first column of that file to the output of the *tty* (2.7) command, which shows your current tty pathname. The output of *tty* starts with */dev* or */dev/pts*. So, to match your current tty to the file, you need to strip the name to its tail. For example, in *bash* and *ksh*, these three lines would put the terminal port type (vt100, plugboard, etc.) into the *ttykind* shell variable:

awk 20.10

```
tty=`tty`
ttytail=${tty#/dev/}
ttykind=`awk '$1 == "'$ttytail'" {print $3}' /etc/ttys`
```

Then you can test the value with *case* (35.10) or *if* (35.13). In C shells, you can set *ttytail* by using the :t string modifier (28.5) and test its value with *switch* or *if*.

—JP and SJC

3.16 Terminal Setup: Testing Window Size

I use several terminal windows of different sizes. I don't stretch the windows after I open them; instead, I set the size as I start each *xterm*. Here's an excerpt from my X setup file (3.20) that opens the windows:

-e 5.22

```
xterm -title SETI -geometry 80x9+768+1 -e setiathome -verbose -nice 10 &
xterm -title "work xterm" -geometry 80x74+329-81 &
```

The first window has 9 rows (80x9) and the second has 74 rows (80x74).† I'd like the *less* (12.3) pager to use different jump-target lines in larger windows. If the window has more than 24 lines, I want *less* to use its option *–j3* to show search-matches on the third line of the window instead of the first.

---

* Then again, it may not. The RedHat Linux system I tested this on did not; the MacOS X 10.1.5 box I tested it on did.

† Both windows have 80 columns. This is a Unix custom that comes from "the old days" when terminals all were 80 columns wide. But it's still a common width today—and a good default when you don't need a wider window. Some people are even sort of weird about it, especially for reading email.

On many systems, the command *stty size* gives the number of rows and columns in the current window, like this:

```
$ stty size
74 80
```

Your system might need the command *stty –a* instead—or it could have environment variables named *LINES* and *COLUMNS*. We'll use *stty size* in the following Bourne shell setup file. The *set* (35.25) command puts the number of rows into the $2 shell parameter. (Using *set* this way is portable to all shells, but it's a clumsy way to split *stty*'s output into words. If you have a newer shell with array support, it'll be easier.) Then a series of *if* (35.13)/*then* (35.26) tests handle different window sizes:

```
LESS=emqc; export LESS
# Put number of rows into $2, configure session based on that:
set x `stty size`
if [ -z "$2" -o "$2" -lt 1 ]
then echo ".profile: bogus number of rows ($2) in window!?" 1>&2
elif [ "$2" -gt 24 ]
then LESS=j3$LESS
    ...
fi
```

Additionally, you may be able to run *resize* on machines with the X Window System installed; it may output something like this:

```
schampeo@fugazi:1046 $ resize
COLUMNS=80;
LINES=37;
export COLUMNS LINES;
```

You may then capture the output and read it for the current setting or simply check the COLUMNS or LINES environment variables.

—JP and SJC

3.17 Terminal Setup: Setting and Testing Window Name

I use several *xterm* windows. Here's an excerpt from my X setup file (3.20):

```
WINNAME=console xterm -C -title Console -geometry 80x9+0+0 &
WINNAME=work xterm -title "work xterm" -geometry 80x74+329-81 &
```

The WINNAME=*name* sets an environment variable named *WINNAME* for the particular command line it's on. This is passed through the environment, through the *xterm* process, to the shell running inside the window. So the shell's setup file can test for this variable—and, by knowing the window name stored in that variable, do specific setup for just that window. For example, in *tcsh*:

```
if ($?WINNAME) then
    switch ($WINNAME)
```

```
                        case console:
                            # Watch logs:
-f 12.10                    tail -f /var/log/{messages,maillog,secure} ~/tmp/startx.log &
{ } 28.4                    breaksw
                        case work:
                            /usr/games/fortune
                            fetchmail
                            breaksw
                        endsw
                    endif
```

On the console terminal, this *.tcshrc* file starts a job in the background (23.2) to watch log files. On the work *xterm*, I get a fortune and grab email from the POP server.

—*JP and SJC*

3.18 A .cshrc.$HOST File for Per Host Setup

I work with different types of machines every day. It is often necessary to set things up differently for, say, a Linux box than a SPARCstation or a MacOS X box. Going beyond that, you may want to set things up differently on a per-host basis.

I have this test in my *.cshrc* file:

```
setenv 35.3        setenv HOST "`uname -n`"
~ 31.11            if (-e ~/lib/cshrc.hosts/cshrc.$HOST) then
                       source ~/lib/cshrc.hosts/cshrc.$HOST
                   endif
```

So, if I log in to a machine named (2.5) *bosco*, and I have a file called *~/lib/cshrc.hosts/cshrc.bosco*, I can *source* (35.29) it to customize my environment for that one machine. These are examples of things you would put in a *.cshrc.$HOST* file:

Search path (27.6)

Some machines have */usr/local/bin*, and some have */opt*. The same goes for *cdpath* (31.5).

Terminal settings (5.8)

I always like to reach for the upper-right part of a keyboard to erase characters. Sometimes this is the location for the BACKSPACE key, and sometimes it is the DELETE key. I set things up so that I can consistently get "erase" behavior from whatever key is there.

Other shell variables (35.9) *and environment variables* (35.3)

These may be different. You may run a package on a certain machine that relies on a few environment variables. No need to always set them and use up a little bit of memory if you only use them in one place!

In general, this idea allows you to group together whatever exceptions you want for a machine, rather than having to write a series of *switch* or *if* statements throughout your *.cshrc* and *.login* files. The principle carries over directly to the newer shells as well.

—DS and SJC

3.19 Making a "Login" Shell

When you log in to most Unix systems, your shell is a *login shell*. When a shell is a login shell, it acts differently (3.4).

Sometimes, when you're testing an account or using a window system, you want to start a login shell without logging in. Unix shells act like login shells when they are executed with a name that starts with a dash (-).* This is easy to do if you're using a system call in the *exec*(3) family. These system calls let a C-language programmer give both the filename of an executable file, like *sh* or */bin/sh*, as well as the name that should be used to identify the process (in a *ps* (24.5) listing, for example), like *–sh*.

If you're currently using *zsh*, you can invoke another shell this way by typing a dash and a space before the shell's name:

```
zsh% - csh
   ...C shell starts, acting like a login shell...
%
```

C programmers can write a little program that runs the actual shell but tells the shell that its name starts with a dash. This is how the Unix *login* process does it:

```
run_login_csh()
{
    execl("/bin/csh", "-csh", 0);
}
```

A more general solution is to make a link (10.4) to the shell and give the link a filename starting with a dash. If your own *bin* subdirectory is on the same filesystem as */bin* (or wherever the executable shell file is), you can use a hard link. Otherwise, make a symbolic link, as shown here:

bin 7.4
./– 14.13
```
$ cd $HOME/bin
$ ln -s /bin/csh ./-csh
```

---

* *bash* also has a command-line option, *–login*, that makes it act like a login shell. *zsh –l* (lowercase L) does the same for *zsh*.

Then you can execute your new shell by typing its name:

```
$ -csh
    ...normal C shell login process...
%   ...run whatever commands you want...
% logout
$   ...back to original shell
```

—JP and SJC

3.20 RC Files

One way to set defaults for your applications is with environment variables (35.3) that the applications might read. This can get messy, though, if your environment has tens or hundreds of variables in it. A lot of applications have a different way to choose defaults: setup files, similar to shell setup files (3.3). Most of these filenames end with *rc*, so they're often called *RC files*.* Today's more-complex applications also use their own setup subdirectories. Almost all of these files and directories are hidden (8.9) in your home directory; you'll need *ls –A* to see them.

This article describes some of the most common setup files. For a more complete list, check your application's manpage:

.emacs
> For the Emacs editor. See article 19.3.

.exrc
> For the *vi* (actually, *ex*) editor. See article 17.5.

.inputrc
> For the GNU Readline library and applications that use it, such as the *bash* shell.

.mailrc
> For the *mail* (1.21) program and others like it. This can be handy if you use *mail* from the command line to send quick messages. For example:
> ```
> # If I send mail to "bookquestions", send it to myself too:
> alias bookquestions bookquestions@oreilly.com, jerry
> # When I send a message, prompt me for "cc:" addresses:
> set askcc
> ```

.mh_profile
> For the MH email system.

---

* Don't ask me why. It's one of those acronyms, like spool (45.2), that's open to interpretation, though one theory is that it is derived from "runcom files," (possibly short for "run commands") on the Compatible Time-Sharing System, c.1962-63 (source: The Jargon File).

.netrc

A listing of hostnames, accounts—and possibly passwords—used for connecting to remote hosts with *ftp* and some other programs. Should have file access mode (50.2) 600 or 400 for security, but this may not be enough protection for passwords! Best used for *Anonymous ftp*.

.newsrc

For news readers (1.21). (Some newer news readers have more complex files.) A list of newsgroups in the order you want to see them. For example:

```
comp.security.announce: 1-118
news.announce.important: 1
comp.org.usenix: 1-1745
comp.sys.palmtops! 1-55069,55071
   ...
```

A newsgroup name ending with a colon (:) means you want to read that newsgroup; an exclamation point (!) means you don't. After each name is a list of the article numbers you've read in that newsgroup; a range like 1-55069 means you've read all articles between number 1 and number 55069.

.rhosts

A list of remote hostnames that are allowed to access your local machine with clients like *rsh* and *rlogin* (1.21). Remote usernames are assumed the same as your local username unless the remote username is listed after the hostname. This file can be a security hole; make its file access mode (50.2) 600 or 400. We suggest you only use it if your system or network administrator approves. For example:

```
rodan          Allow a user with same username from host rodan
foo.bar.com joe   Allow username joe from host foo.bar.com
```

.Xauthority

For *xauth*, a program that handles authorization information used in connecting to the X Window System server.

.Xdefaults

A resource file (6.5) for the X Window System. Sometimes also called *.xrdb*.

.xinitrc

A shell script (35.2) that runs as you log in to an X Window System session using *xinit*. (Also see *.xsession*, later in this list.)

All commands *except the last* typically end with an ampersand (&), which makes those clients run in the background. The last command becomes the *controlling process*; when that process exits (for instance, you use the window manager's "quit" command), the window system shuts down. For example:

$Id 39.5

```
#! /bin/sh
# $Id: ch03,v 1.36 2002/10/13 03:50:27 troutman Exp troutman $
# Usage: .xinitrc [DISPLAY]

wm=fvwm2     # window manager
```

```
                     # Put all output into log that you can watch from a window (tail -f):
                     mv -f $HOME/tmp/startx.log $HOME/tmp/,startx.log
 exec > 36.5         exec > $HOME/tmp/startx.log 2>&1
     -v 35.25        set -v

                     # Set DISPLAY from $1 if the X server isn't on same host as client:
                     if [ $# -gt 0 ]
                     then
                         if [ $# -ne 1 ]
                         then
                             echo "Usage: .xintirc [DISPLAY]" 1>&2
                             exit 1
                         else
                             DISPLAY=$1
                         fi
                     else
 uname -n 2.5            host=`uname -n`
${..:=..} 36.7          DISPLAY=${DISPLAY:=$host:0.0}
                     fi
 export 35.3         export DISPLAY

    xrdb 6.8         xrdb -load $HOME/.xrdb

                     #
                     # Clients
                     #
                     xterm -C -geometry 80x9+0+0 -sl 2000 &
                     oclock -geometry -1+1 &
                     xterm -title "SETI console" -bg blue -fg white -geometry 80x9+768+1 -e \
  sh -c 24.21            sh -c 'cd /var/cache/seti && exec ./setiathome -nice 5 -verbose' &
   exec 36.5         # Don't use -e because Mozilla crashes; start by hand from prompt:
                     xterm -title "Mozilla console" -bg orange -geometry 80x9-0+1 &
                     xterm -geometry 80x74+329-81 &

                     #
                     # Start window manager
                     #
                     exec $wm
```

.xsession

An executable file (generally a shell script (35.2), but it can be any executable) that runs as you log into an X Window System session using *xdm*. See *.xinitrc*, earlier in this list.

/etc/rc*

Last but not least, your system probably has a lot of setup files in its */etc* directory. Look for subdirectory or filenames starting with *rc*. These are read when your system reboots or changes its runlevel (for example, from single-user mode to multiuser mode). These files are basically shell scripts (35.2). If you know a little about shell programming, you can learn a lot about your system by looking around these files.

—*JP and SJC*

3.21 Make Your Own Manpages Without Learning troff

We strongly suggest that you write a manual page for each command that you place in your *bin* directory. Unix manual pages typically have the following format, which we suggest you follow:

NAME
> The program's name; one line summary of what it does.

SYNOPSIS
> How to invoke the program, including all arguments and
> command-line options. (Optional arguments are placed in
> square brackets.)

DESCRIPTION
> A description of what the program does—as long as
> is necessary.

OPTIONS
> An explanation of each option.

EXAMPLES
> One or more examples of how to use the program.

ENVIRONMENT
> Any environment variables that control the program's behavior.

FILES
> Files the program internals will read or write. May include
> temporary files; doesn't include files on the command line.

BUGS
> Any known bugs. The standard manual pages don't take
> bug recording seriously, but this can be very helpful.

AUTHOR
> Who wrote the program.

To see how a "real" manual page looks, type man ls.

Feel free to add any other sections that you think are necessary. You can use the *nroff –man* macros (3.22) if you want a nicely formatted manual page. However, *nroff* is fairly complicated and, for this purpose, not really necessary. Just create a text file that looks like the one we showed previously. If you are using a BSD system and want your manual pages formatted with *nroff*, look at any of the files in */usr/man/man1*, and copy it.

If you insist on formatting your manual page properly, using the *troff* or *groff* "man" macros, you can use *nroff* to preview the file.

The *man* (2.1) command is essentially the same as this:

-s 12.7

```
% nroff -e -man filename | more -s
```

gnroff
awf

You can safely omit the *-e* option to *nroff* and the *-s* option to *more*, or even substitute in your favorite pager, such as *less*. And remember that *nroff* may not be available on all systems, but the web site has *gnroff* and *awf*. In fact, on some systems, *nroff* is simply a script that emulates the real *nroff* using *groff*.

Now, you want to make this manual page "readable" by the standard *man* command. There are a few ways to do this, depending on your system. Create the directory *man* in your home directory; create the directory *cat1* as a subdirectory of *man*; then copy your manual entry into *cat1*, with the name *program.1* (where *program* is the name of your special command). When you want to read the manual page, try the command:

~ 31.11

```
% man -M ~/man program
```

We like to be more strict about naming things properly, but you can omit the *man* directory and just put the *cat1* directory into your home directory. In this case, the command would be as follows:

```
% man -M ~ program
```

Some systems have a *MANPATH* environment variable (35.3), a colon-separated list of directories where the *man* command should look. For example, my *MANPATH* contains:

```
/home/mike/man:/usr/local/man:/usr/man
```

MANPATH can be more convenient than the *-M* option.

We are telling you to put the manual page into the *cat1* directory rather than the *man1* directory because the *man* program assumes that files in *cat1* are already formatted.

If you are sharing your program with other people on the system, you should put your manual entry in a public place. Become superuser and copy your documentation into */usr/local/man/cat1*, giving it the name *program.l* (the "l" stands for "local"). You may need to create */usr/local* and */usr/local/man* first. If you can't become superuser, get the system administrator to do it for you. Make sure that everyone can read the manual page; the permissions should be something like this:

```
% ls -l /usr/local/man/cat1
-r--r--r--  1 root        468 Aug  5 09:21 program.1
```

Then give the command man *program* to read your documentation.

If you are working on some other systems, the rules are a little different. The organization of the manual pages and the *man* command itself are slightly different—and really, not as good. Write your manual entry, and place it in your *doc* directory. Then create the following C shell alias (29.3):

less **12.3**

```
alias myman "(cd ~/doc; man -d \!$ | less)"
```

or shell function (29.11):

```
myman() { (cd $HOME/doc; man -d "$1" | less); }
```

Now the command *myman docfilename* will retrieve your manual page. Note that if you use a section-number extension like .1, you have to give the entire filename (e.g., *program.1*), not just the program's name.

If you want to make your manual page publicly available, copy the file into the system manual page directory for section 1; you may have to become superuser to do so. Make sure that anyone on the system can read your file. If the entry is extremely long and you want to save space in your filesystem, you can use the *gzip* (15.6) utility on your documentation file. The resulting file will have the name *program.1.gz*; newer versions of the *man* command will automatically uncompress the file on-the-fly.

—*ML and SJC*

3.22 Writing a Simple Manpage with the –man Macros

If you're not satisfied with the simple manual pages we discussed in article 3.21, here's how to go all the way and create a "real" manual page. As we said, the best way to create a manual page is to copy one that already exists. So here's a sample for you to copy. Rather than discuss it blow by blow, I'll include lots of comments (these start with .\" or \").

1 **2.1**

```
.\" Title: Program name, manual section, and date
.TH GRIND 1
.\" Section heading: NAME, followed by command name and one line summary
.\" It's important to copy this exactly; the "whatis" database (used
.\" for apropos) looks for the summary line.
.SH NAME
grind \- create output from input
.\" Section heading: SYNOPSIS, followed by syntax summary
.SH SYNOPSIS
.B grind            \" .B: bold font; use it for the command name.
```

```
[ -b ] [ -c ] [ -d ]  \" Put optional arguments in square brackets.
[ input [ output ]]   \" Arguments can be spread across several lines.
.br                           \" End the synopsis with an explicit line break (.br)
.\" A new section: DESCRIPTION, followed by what the command does
.SH DESCRIPTION
.I Grind          \" .I: Italic font for the word "Grind"
performs lots of computations. Input to
.IR grind ,       \" .IR: One word italic, next word roman, no space between.
is taken from the file
.IR input ,
and output is sent to the file
.IR output ,
which default to standard input and standard output if not specified.
.\" Another section: now we're going to discuss the -b, -c, and -d options
.SH OPTIONS
.\" The .TP macro precedes each option
.TP
.B \-b  \" print the -b option in bold.
Print output in binary.
.TP
.B \-c  \" \- requests a minus sign, which is preferable to a hyphen (-)
Eliminate ASCII characters from input before processing.
.TP
.B \-d
Cause daemons to overrun your computer.
.\" OK, we're done with the description and the options; now mention
.\" other requirements (like environment and files needed) as well as
.\" what can go wrong. You can add any other sections you want.
.SH FILES
.PD 0
.TP 20
.B /dev/null
data file
.TP
.B /tmp/grind*
temporary file (typically 314.159 Gigabytes)
.PD
.SH BUGS
In order to optimize computational speed, this program always produces
the same result, independent of the input.
.\" Use .LP between paragraphs
.LP
If the moon is full,
.I grind
may destroy your input file. To say nothing of your sex life.
.\" Good manual pages end by stating who wrote the program.
.SH AUTHOR
I wouldn't admit to this hack if my life depended on it.
```

After all that, you should have noticed that there are four important macros (listed in Table 3-1) to know about.

Table 3-1. Important –man macros

Macro	Meaning
.TH	Title of the manual page.
.SH	Section heading; one for each section.
.TP	Formats options correctly (sets up the "hanging indent").
.LP	Used between paragraphs in a section.

For some arcane reason, all manual pages use the silly .B, .BI, etc. macros to make font changes. I've adhered to this style in the example, but it's much easier to use inline font changes: \fI for *italic*, \fB for **bold**, and \fR for roman. There may be some systems on which this doesn't work properly, but I've never seen any.

—ML and SJC

4

Interacting with Your Environment

4.1 Basics of Setting the Prompt

The prompt displayed by your shell is contained in a shell variable (35.9) called *prompt* in C-type shells and *PS1* in Bourne-type shells. As such, it can be set like any other shell variable.

There are two or three ways to set a prompt. One is a *static prompt* (4.2) that doesn't change during your login session (as you change directories, as the time of day changes, etc.). Some shells let you set a *dynamic prompt* (4.3) string that is interpreted by the shell before each prompt is printed. Even on shells that don't interpret prompt strings dynamically, you can simulate a dynamic prompt (4.4) by changing the prompt string automatically.*

Depending on your shell's capabilties, you can use or combine those three techniques—and those found in the rest of this chapter—to do a lot. But, of course, you don't want to type that prompt-setting command every time you log in. So after you've perfected your prompt on the command line, store it in the correct shell setup file (3.3): use the file that's read by interactive shells or add an interactive shell test to your setup file. (Setting the prompt in noninteractive shells is pointless—and it can even cause problems (4.5).)

—JP, TOR, and SJC

4.2 Static Prompts

As article 4.1 explains, the simplest prompts—which I call *static prompts*—are prompts whose value are set once. The prompt doesn't change (until you reset the prompt variable, of course).

---

* I haven't seen prompts described this way before. I invented the terms *static prompt* and *dynamic prompt* to make them easier to talk about.

The default *bash* prompt is a good example of a static prompt. It's "bash$ " (with a space at the end, to make the command you type stand out from the rest of the prompt). You could set that prompt with the simple command:

```
PS1='bash$ '.
```

Notice the single quotes (12.3) around the value; this is a good idea unless you want special characters in the prompt value to be interpreted before it's set. You can try it now: type that command on a command line, just as you would to set any other shell variable. Experiment a bit. The same prompt works on *ksh* and *sh*.

If you use *csh* or *tcsh*, try one of these, then experiment:

```
set prompt='csh% '
set prompt='tcsh> '
```

(*zsh* users: you can use any of the previous styles, but omit the *set* from the set prompt style.) Those prompts are fairly useless, right? If you log in to more than one machine, on more than one account, it's nice to have your hostname and username in the prompt. So try one of the following prompts. (From here on, I won't show a separate *tcsh* version with a > instead of a %. You can do that yourself, though, if you like.) If your system doesn't have *uname*, try *hostname* instead:

```
PS1="$USER@`uname -n`$ "
set prompt="$user@`uname -n`% "
```

Notice that I've used double quotes (12.3) around the values, which lets the shell expand the values inside the prompt string *before the prompt is stored*. The shell interprets the variable $USER or $user—and it runs the command substitution (28.14) that gives the hostname—*once, before* the prompt is set. Using double quotes is more efficient if your prompt won't change as you move around the system.

—*JP and SJC*

4.3 Dynamic Prompts

Many shells can interpret the stored prompt string *as each prompt is printed*. As article 4.1 explains, I call these *dynamic prompts*.

Special character sequences in the prompt let you include the current directory, date and time, username, hostname, and much more. Your shell's manual page should list these at the *PS1* or *prompt* variable. (If you use the Korn shell or the original C shell, you don't have these special sequences. Article 4.4 has a technique that should work for you.)

It's simplest to put single quotes around the prompt string to prevent interpretation (27.1) as the prompt is stored. For example, the following prompt shows the date and time, separated by spaces. It also has a special sequence at the end (\\$ in *bash*, %# in *tcsh* and *zsh*) that's printed as a hash mark (#) if you're the superuser, or the usual prompt character for that shell otherwise. The first command in the following code listing works only in *bash*; the second only in *tcsh*:

```
PS1='\d \t \$ '                ...bash
set prompt='%w %D %Y %P %# '   ...tcsh
PS1='%W %* %# '                ...zsh
```

Having the history number in your prompt, as article 4.14 shows, makes it easy to use history (30.8) to repeat or modify a previous command. You can glance up your screen to the prompt where you ran the command, spot the history number (for example, 27), and type !27 to repeat it, !27:$ to grab the filename off the end of the line, and much more. In *csh*, *tcsh*, and *bash* prompts, use \\! to get the history number. In *zsh*, use %! instead.

—*JP, TOR, and SJC*

4.4 Simulating Dynamic Prompts

Some shells don't have the special "dynamic" prompt-setting sequences shown in article 4.3. If you still want a dynamic prompt, you probably can simulate one. Both *ksh* and *bash* will expand variables (like $PWD), do command substitution (to run a command like 'date'), and do arithmetic as they print the prompt. So, for example, you can put single quotes around the prompt string to prevent interpretation of these items as the prompt is stored. When the prompt string is interpreted, the current values will be put into *each* prompt. (*zsh* gives control over whether this happens as a prompt is printed. If you want it to happen, put the command *setopt prompt_subst* (28.14) in your *.zshrc* file (3.3).)

The following prompt stores the $PWD parameter to give the current directory, followed by a backquoted *date* command. The argument to *date* is a format string; because the format string is inside single quotes, I've used nested double quotes around it. Because it's in single quotes, it's stored verbatim—and the shell gets the latest values from *date* and $PWD each time a prompt is printed. Try this prompt, then *cd* around the filesystem a bit:

```
PS1='`date "+%D %T"` $PWD $ '
```

That prompt prints a lot of text. If you want all of it, think about a multiline prompt (4.7). Or you could write a simple shell function (29.11) named, say, *do_prompt*:

```
# for bash
function do_prompt {
    date=`date '+%D %T'`
    dir=`echo $PWD | sed "s@$HOME@~@"`
    echo "$date $dir"
    unset date dir
```

```
    }
    # for ksh
    do_prompt() {
        date=`date '+%D %T'`
        dir=`echo $PWD | sed "s@$HOME@~@"`
        echo "$date $dir"
        unset date dir
    }
```

and use its output in your prompt:

```
    PS1='`do_prompt` $ '    ...for sh-type shells
```

The original C shell does almost no interpretation inside its *prompt* variable. You can work around this by writing a shell alias (29.2) named something like *set-prompt* (4.14) that resets the *prompt* variable after you do something like changing your current directory. Then, every time *csh* needs to print a prompt, it uses the latest value of *prompt*, as stored by the most recent run of *setprompt*. (Original Bourne shell users, see article 4.15 for a similar trick.)

—JP, TOR, and SJC

4.5 C-Shell Prompt Causes Problems in vi, rsh, etc.

Stray prompts can cause trouble for many commands that start a noninteractive shell. This problem may have (and probably has) been fixed in your C shell, but some of the following tricks will speed up your *.cshrc*, so keep reading.

If you *set prompt* in your *.cshrc* file without carefully checking first whether *prompt* was already set (4.1), many older versions of the C shell will cheerfully print prompts into the pipe *vi* uses to expand glob characters, such as filename wildcards (*, ?, [ ]) (1.13) and the tilde (~) (31.11).

When you type :r abc*, *vi* opens a pipe to the C shell, writes the command echo abc* down the pipe, then reads the response. If the response contains spaces or newlines, *vi* gets confused. If you set your prompt to (n) in your *.cshrc* [i.e., if you show the history number in parentheses as the prompt—TOR], *vi* tends to get:

```
    (1) abc.file (2)
```

back from the C shell, instead of just abc.file.

The solution is to kludge your *.cshrc* like this:

```
    if ($?prompt) then
        # things to do for an interactive shell, like:
        set prompt='(\!) '
    endif
```

This works because a noninteractive shell has no initial prompt, while an interactive shell has it set to % .

If you have a large *.cshrc*, this can speed things up quite a bit when programs run other programs with csh -c 'command', if you put all of it inside that test.

—CT

4.6 Faster Prompt Setting with Built-ins

To set your prompt, you execute a command (on most shells, that command sets a shell variable). Before setting the prompt, you may run other commands to get information for it: the current directory name, for example. A shell can run two kinds of commands: built-in and external (1.9). Built-in commands usually run faster than external commands. On a slow computer, the difference may be important—waiting a few seconds for your prompt to reset can get irritating (though the computer would have to be quite slow nowadays for it to matter that much). Creative use of your shell's built-in commands might pay off there, and they are still quite useful for those trying to squeeze the most performance out of their system. Let's look at some examples:

- Article 4.3 has examples of some shells' special characters, such as %D to give the current date. Check your shell's manual page; if it has these features, using them won't slow you down the way an external command in backquotes (28.14), like 'date', might.

- If you're putting your current directory in your prompt, you may only want the tail of the pathname (the name past the last slash). How can you edit a pathname? You might think of using *basename* (36.13) or *sed* (34.1) with the current directory from $cwd—as in the first command in the following code listing, and probably in an alias like setprompt (4.7) to make sure the prompt is updated whenever you change directories. The faster way is with the second command, using the C shell's built-in "tail" operator, :t:

{} 35.9
```
set prompt="`basename $cwd`% "
set prompt="${cwd:t}% "
```

If your current directory is */usr/users/hanna/projects*, either of those prompts would look like "projects% " (with a space after the percent sign).

The C shell has several of these built-in string operators (28.5) like :t; the Korn Shell, *zsh*, and *bash* have more-powerful string operators (28.5).

- If your prompt gets complex, you can use a shell function (29.11) to access other built-in commands and edit the prompt. This can be faster than using an external shell or Perl script because functions run within the shell instead of in an external process. Here's an example from my *.zshrc* file:

```
# Change "script" prompt automatically so I remember I'm in one.
alias script='SCRIPT=yes /usr/bin/script'
```

```
#
# Functions:
#
setprompt() {
        case "${TTY##*/}" in
        tty[1-9]) xpi=':tty%l' ;;  # Virtual console
        *) xpi= ;;
        esac

        PS1="
$USER@%m$xpi $(dirs)
%* \$(folder -list)
${SCRIPT+SCRIPT-}%!%# "
}
```

$(...) **28.14**

${+} **36.7**

Before the function, I set an alias that temporarily sets an environment variable named *SCRIPT* while the *script* (37.7) program is running. The *setprompt* function, running in the child shell under *script*, sees that this environment variable has been set and adds the string SCRIPT- before the prompt. This reminds me that I'm logging to a script file. (If this is hard to visualize, articles 24.3 and 35.3 have some background.)

The *setprompt* function itself has two parts. The first is a *case* statement (35.11) that tests $TTY, the name of the *tty* (2.7) I'm currently using. If the name ends in *tty1*, *tty2*, etc., it's one of my Linux virtual consoles (23.12). In that case, I want to add the console name (*tty1*, etc.) to my prompt—so I store the name in the *xpi* (*extra prompt info*) shell variable. This variable's value—if it's been set—is expanded when the prompt is printed. The second part sets the prompt variable *PS1*. The whole prompt looks like this:

```
jpeek@kludge:tty1 ~/pt/art
15:38:30 inbox pt
501%
```

The first line shows my username, hostname, the virtual console name (if any), and the current directory (in this example, there was nothing else on the directory stack (31.7)). The second line has the time—and my email folder stack, from the MH *folder –list* command, which is the only nonbuilt-in command used in the prompt. And here's a subtle point that's worth perusing. The whole prompt string is inside double quotes (27.12) so that variable and command substitution will happen whenever *setprompt* is run. But, the way my prompt is set, the MH folder stack may change between the times that *setprompt* resets the prompt. So I escape the $ in \$(folder -list). This stores the command substitution without executing *folder*! So, when *every* prompt is about to be printed, the shell will evaulate the prompt string and expand the $(...) operators into the current folder stack. The third line sets the end of the prompt string: the *zsh* prompt substitution at %m, %*, %! and %#.

On a slow machine, I'd try hard to find a way to eliminate the external *folder –list* command. But my Linux box is fast enough so that I don't notice any delay before a prompt. To make this work, I needed a good understanding of what's evaluated when. It's this sort of subtlety that makes prompt setting a challenge—and a pleasure, too, when you get it working just right.

As another example, article 4.14 shows more about using *dirs* in a shell prompt.

—JP and SJC

4.7 Multiline Shell Prompts

Lots of people like lots of information in their prompts: hostname, directory name, history number, and maybe username. Lots of people have spent lots of time trying to make their prompts short enough to fit across the screen and still leave room for typing a command longer than *ls*:

```
<elaineq@applefarm> [/usr/elaineq/projects/april/week4] 23 % ls
```

Even with fairly short prompts, if you look back at a screen after running a few commands, telling the data from the prompts can be a little tough (real terminals don't show user input in boldface, so I won't do it here either):

```
+<elaineq@applefarm> [~] 56% cd beta
<elaineq@applefarm> [~/beta] 57% which prog
/usr/tst/applefarm/bin/beta/prog
<elaineq@applefarm> [~/beta] 58% prog
61,102 units inventoried; 3142 to do
<elaineq@applefarm> [~/beta] 59%
```

mlprompt.csh
mlprompt.sh

One nice answer is to make a prompt that has more than one line. Here's part of a *.cshrc* file that sets a three-line prompt: one blank line, one line with the hostname and current directory, and a third line with the history number and a percent sign. (If this were a *tcsh*, I could have gotten the hostname with %m.) The C shell quoting (27.13) is ugly—doubly ugly because the prompt is set inside an alias—but otherwise it's straightforward:

uname -n 2.5

{..} 35.9

```
set hostname=`uname -n`
alias setprompt 'set prompt="\\
${hostname}:${cwd}\\
\! % "'
alias cd 'chdir \!* && setprompt'
alias pushd 'pushd \!* && setprompt'
alias popd 'popd \!* && setprompt'
setprompt                # to set the initial prompt
```

(There's a version on the Web for Bourne-type shells.) The prompts look like this:

```
applefarm:/usr/elaineq/projects/april/week4
23 % prog | tee /dev/tty | mail -s "prog results" bigboss@corpoffice
61,102 units inventoried; 3142 to do
```

```
applefarm:/usr/elaineq/projects/april/week4
24 % cd ~/beta

applefarm:/usr/elaineq/beta
25 % prog | mail joanne
```

The blank lines separate each command—though you may want to save space by omitting them. For example, Mike Sierra of O'Reilly & Associates has used a row of asterisks:

```
***** 23 *** <mike@mymac> *** ~/calendar *****
% cd Sep*
***** 24 *** <mike@mymac> *** ~/calendar/September *****
%
```

Other shells have different syntax, but the idea is the same: embed newlines to get multiline prompts. In Bourne-type shells you'll need zero or one backslash before each newline; article 27.12 explains. In *bash*, put a \n (which stands for a newline character) anywhere you want the prompt to break to a new line.

What I like best about multiline prompts is that you get a lot of information but have the whole screen width for typing. Of course, you can put different information in the prompt than I've shown here. The important idea is that if you want more information and need room to type, try a multiline prompt.

—*JP and SJC*

4.8 Session Info in Window Title or Status Line

Some people don't like to put the current directory, hostname, etc. into their prompts because it makes the screen look cluttered to them. Here's another idea. If your terminal or window system has a status line or titlebar, you might be able to put the information there. That's nice because you can see the information while you run programs. The down side is that the information can get out of date if you use a command that takes you to another host or directory without updating the status line. The latest *bash* and *zsh* shells do this by default when you're using an *xterm* window. For the rest of you, here's how to do it yourself. Because neither *csh* or *tcsh* do this by default, I'll show C-shell-type syntax. But you can do the same thing in Bourne-type shells with a shell function and *case* (35.10) statement; there's a ready-to-use version on the web site.

When you use *cd*, *pushd*, or *popd*, an alias uses the *echo* command to write special escape sequences to the terminal or window.

Here are *cd* aliases and other commands for your *.cshrc* or *.tcshrc* file. If I were logged in to *www.jpeek.com* in the directory */home/jpeek*, this alias would put:

```
www:/home/jpeek
```

in the status area or window title, depending on which terminal type I'm using. Of course, you can change the format of the status line. Change the following command string, ${host:h}:${cwd}, to do what you need; see your shell's manual page for a list of variables, or create your own custom information.

stattitle.csh
stattitle.sh

:h **28.5**

&& **35.14**

```
set e=`echo x | tr x '\033'`    # Make an ESCape character

set g=`echo x | tr x '\07'`     # And a Ctrl-g
set host=`uname -n`
# Puts $host and $cwd in VT102 status line. Escape sequences are:
# ${e}7 = save cursor position, ${e}[25;1f = go to start of status
# line (line 25), ${e}[0K = erase line, ${e}8 = restore cursor
alias setstatline 'echo -n "${e}7${e}[25;1f${e}[0K    ${host:h}:${cwd}${e}8"'
alias settitle 'echo -n "${e}]2;${host:h}:${cwd}${g}"'
switch ($TERM)
case vt10?:
  alias cd 'cd \!* && setstatline'
  alias pushd 'pushd \!* && setstatline'
  alias popd 'popd \!* && setstatline'
  breaksw
case xterm*:
  alias cd 'cd \!* && settitle'
  alias pushd 'pushd \!* && settitle'
  alias popd 'popd \!* && settitle'
  breaksw
endsw
```

(Article 5.15 has more about how this works in *xterms*.)

The ESC and CTRL-g characters are stored with a trick that should work on all Unix shells. Most modern *echos* will let you make a nonprintable character directly, like this: g=`echo '\07'`.

If you always use a VT102-type terminal (and many people do), the *setstatline* alias will work fine. If you use a different terminal, try it anyway! Otherwise, read the terminal manual or its *termcap/terminfo* entry and find the escape sequences that work for it; then add a new case to the *switch* statement.

Note that you might have some trouble here: if this code is in your *.cshrc* file but your terminal type is set in your *.login* file, the terminal type may not be set until after the alias has been read. There are workarounds (3.8).

The status line or titlebar can also get out of sync with reality if you use remote logins (1.21), subshells (24.4), etc. These might make a new status line or titlebar but not reset the original one when needed. To fix this, just type *setstatline* or *settitle* at a shell prompt. Or, if you don't want to bother to think of the name of the alias, use the following command to change to the current directory (.), which will use the correct alias and reset the status or title:

```
% cd .
```

If you're using *tcsh*, its special alias *cwdcmd* will be run every time you change the shell's current directory. So, in *tcsh*, you can replace the three aliases for *cd*, *pushd*, and *popd* with something like this:

```
alias cwdcmd settitle
```

—JP and SJC

4.9 A "Menu Prompt" for Naive Users

Some people don't want to be faced with a Unix % or $ shell prompt. If you (or, if you're a sys admin on a multiuser system, your users) usually run only a few particular Unix commands, you can put those command names in the shell prompt. Here's a simple one-line Bourne-shell prompt for a *.profile*:

```
PS1='Type "rn", "mailx", "wp", or "logout": '
```

Next, a multiline prompt (4.7) for the C shell *.cshrc* or *.tcshrc* file:

```
if ($?prompt) then
set prompt='\\
Type "pine" to read the news,\\
type "mutt" to read and send mail,\\
type "wp" for word processing, or\\
type "logout" to log out.\\
YES, MASTER? '
endif
```

You get the idea.

—JP and SJC

4.10 Highlighting and Color in Shell Prompts

If your prompt has some information that you want to stand out—or if you want your whole prompt to stand out from the rest of the text on the screen—you might be able to make it in enhanced characters or colors. If your terminal has special escape sequences for enhancing the characters (and most do), you can use them to make part or all of your prompt stand out. Newer versions of *xterm* also have color capability, as does the Mac OS X Terminal program, though Terminal may not properly support the escape sequences we discuss later. (The GNU *dircolors* (8.6) command sets up a color-capable terminal.)

Let's say that you want to make sure people notice that they're logged in as root (the superuser) by making part of the root prompt flash. Here are lines for the root *.cshrc*:

blink-
prompt.csh
blink-
prompt.sh

uname -n **2.5**

```
# Put ESCape character in $e.  Use to start blinking mode (${e}[5m)
# and go back to normal mode (${e}[0m) on VT100-series terminals:
set e="`echo x | tr x '\033'`"
set prompt="${e}[5mroot${e}[0m@`uname -n`# "
```

That prompt might look like this, with the word root flashing:

```
root@www.jpeek.com#
```

 Shells with command-line editing need to calculate the width of your prompt string. When you put nonprinting escape sequences in a prompt (as we're doing here), in *zsh* and *tcsh* you have to delimit them with %{ and %}. In *bash*, bracket nonprinting characters with \[and \]. In the Korn shell, prefix your prompt with a nonprinting character (such as CTRL-a) followed by a RETURN, and delimit the escape codes with this same nonprinting character. As the *pdksh* manual page says, "Don't blame me for this hack; it's in the original *ksh*."

The prompt is set inside double quotes ("), so the uname, -n command is run once, when the *PS1* string is first stored. In some shells, like *bash* and *pdksh*, you can put single quotes (') around the *PS1* string; this stores the backquotes (`) in the string, and the shell will interpret them before it prints each prompt. (In this case, that's useless because the output of uname -n will always be the same in a particular invocation of a shell. But if you want constantly updated information in your prompt, it's very handy.) Articles 4.6 and 27.12 have more info.

Because the same escape sequences won't work on all terminals, it's probably a good idea to add an *if* test that only sets the prompt if the terminal type *$TERM* is in the Digital Equipment Corporation VT100 series (or one that emulates it). Table 4-1 shows a few escape sequences for VT100 and compatible terminals. (The ESC in each sequence stands for an ESCape character.)

Table 4-1. VT100 escape sequences for highlighting

Sequence	What it does
ESC[1m	Bold, intensify foreground
ESC[4m	Underscore
ESC[5m	Blink
ESC[7m	Reverse video
ESC[0m	All attributes off

Of course, you can use different escape sequences if your terminal needs them. Better, read your terminal's *terminfo* or *termcap* database with a program like *tput* or *tcap* to get the correct escape sequences for your terminal. Store the escape sequences in shell variables (35.9).

bash interprets octal character codes (like \033) in the prompt. It also has special-backslashed special-prompt characters—for instance, *bash* Version 2 has \e, which outputs an ESCape character, and \H, which gives the complete hostname.

The string \$ is replaced by a dollar sign ($) on non-*root* shells and a hash mark
(#) if you're currently *root*. So, on *bash*, you can make the previous *csh* prompt
this way:

```
PS1='\[\e[5m\]root\[\e[0m\]@\H\$ '
```

(The delimiters for nonprinting characters, \[and \], might make it look complicated. Try spotting them first, as you look at the prompt string, so you can see
what's left.)

Eight-bit-clean versions of *tcsh* can put standout, boldface, and underline—and
any other terminal escape sequence, too—into your shell prompt. For instance,
%S starts standout mode and %s ends it; the *tcsh* manpage has details for your version. The next example shows how to make the same prompt as earlier with the
word root in standout mode. (*tcsh* puts the hostname into %m.) Because *tcsh*
"knows" the width of its special %S and %s formatting sequences, they don't need
to be delimited with %{ or %}:

```
set prompt = '%Sroot%s@%m# '
```

You also can add color to your prompt! For instance, make the previous prompt
for *bash* using bright red (1;31) on a blue background (44):

```
PS1='\[\e[1;31;44m\]root\[\e[0m\]@\H# '
```

—*JP and SJC*

4.11 Right-Side Prompts

Both *zsh* and *tcsh* have an optional prompt at the right side of the screen. Unlike
the normal left-side prompt, the cursor doesn't sit next to the right-side prompt
(though the right prompt disappears if you type a long command line and the
cursor passes over it). It's stored in the *zsh* RPROMPT variable and in *tcsh*
rprompt.

What can you do with a right-hand prompt? Anything you want to! (You'll
probably want to keep it fairly short, though.) Put the time of day on the right-
hand side, for instance; on *tcsh*, it's this easy:

```
[jpeek@ruby ~]% set rprompt='%t'
[jpeek@ruby ~]% users                                    3:44pm
jpeek ollie
[jpeek@ruby ~]%                                          3:45pm
```

As another idea, you could use *sched* to remind you of an important meeting by
setting the right-hand prompt. Here's a shell function for *zsh* that sets the right
prompt to "LEAVE NOW" at a particular time. You can give it one argument to
set the time to remind you. Or, with no argument, it removes the right-hand
prompt:

```
leave() {
    case "$#" in
```

```
        0) unset RPROMPT ;;
        1) sched "$1" "RPROMPT='LEAVE NOW'" ;;
        *) echo "Usage: leave [time]" 1>&2 ;;
        esac
    }
```

Here's an example:

```
jpeek$ date
Fri May 12 15:48:49 MST 2000
jpeek$ leave 15:55
    ...do some work...
jpeek$ pwd
/u/jpeek/pt
jpeek$ date                                             LEAVE NOW
Fri May 12 15:55:22 MST 2000
jpeek$ lpr report                                       LEAVE NOW
jpeek$ leave                                            LEAVE NOW
jpeek$
```

—JP and SJC

4.12 Show Subshell Level with $SHLVL

If you're like me, when you start a shell escape (17.21) or any subshell (24.4), you can forget that you aren't in your login shell. Your shell history (30.1) might get confused, shell variables (35.9) may not be set, and other problems may come up. *zsh* and *bash* have a built-in *SHLVL* environment variable (35.3) that lets you track how many subshells deep your current shell is. *tcsh* has a *shlvl* shell variable that's automatically set from (and sets) *SHLVL*. So, all three shells cooperate with each other to set the right value, even if you start one shell from another. (For other shells that don't have SHLVL—*ksh* and *csh*—you can set up something similar with a bit of arithmetic in the *ENV* (35.5) file or the *.cshrc* file, respectively.)

In your top-level shell, the value of $shlvl is 1 (one). In the first subshell, it's 2; in a sub-subshell, it's 3; and so on. You can use this to control your shell startup files—for example, have some commands in your *.cshrc* that run when you first log in (and $shlvl is 1), but don't run in subshells. You can also put $shlvl in your prompt (but only during subshells, if you'd like—as a reminder that you aren't in your top-level shell). You can set your prompt to mike% in top-level shells, (1) mike% in a first-level subshell, (2) mike% in a second-level subshell, and so on. Here's some sample prompt-setting code for your *.tcshrc*:

```
# If this is a subshell, put shell level in prompt:
if ($shlvl == 1) then
    set prompt="${USER}% "
else
    set prompt="($SHLVL) ${USER}% "
endif
```

bash doesn't need an *if* because login shells read your *.bash_profile* (or *.profile*) and subshells read your *.bashrc*. Here are commands to set the prompts I mentioned earlier:

```
PS1='\u\$ '            ...for the .bash_profile
PS1='($SHLVL) \u\$ '   ...for the .bashrc
```

Does your account run a windowing system that's started from your top-level shell startup file (like *.login*)? If it does, lines like the following examples (these are for *.login*) will reset *SHLVL* so that the shell in the window will start at a *SHLVL* of 1—and act like a top-level shell. This code assumes that your first login shell starts on a *tty* named */dev/tty1* through */dev/tty6* (which are the Linux virtual consoles (23.12)) and that the windows that open won't have a tty with the same name (which is true on Linux). (If you aren't sure, check *who* (2.8).) You may need to adapt this. The trick is to make *SHLVL* 0 (zero) before you start the windowing system. When the windows' shells start, they'll raise *SHLVL* to 1:

```
# If on a virtual console, bury this shell and start X right away:
if ("`tty`" =~ /dev/tty[1-6]) then
    setenv SHLVL 0
    startx
endif
```

Getting this to work right in every situation (*rsh* (1.21), *ssh*, *su*, shell escapes (17.21)—both interactive and noninteractive (3.4)—subshells, window systems, *at* jobs (25.5), and so on) can be a challenge (3.8)! It takes a little planning. Sit down and think about all the ways you start subshells—which subshells are interactive and which aren't—and whether they'll get *SHLVL* passed from their parent process. (If you aren't sure, test that with an *env* or *printenv* command (35.3).) Then plan which kind of shell needs which *SHLVL* settings. If it gets too complicated, make it work in most cases! If you use many subshells, this system can be too handy to ignore.

—JP and SJC

4.13 What Good Is a Blank Shell Prompt?

This tip is also great if you use a mouse to copy and paste command lines in your window.

Some terminals I've used (like old Hewlett-Packard and Tektronix terminals) had local editing. You could move your cursor up the screen to a previous command line, maybe make some edits to it, then press a SEND LINE key to resend that line to the host. This didn't have anything to do with sophisticated command-line editing (30.14) that modern Unix shells have, though. Maybe your terminal can do that, too. Depending on how your *emacs* editor is configured, *shell-mode* may work that way, as well.

The problem was that unless I erased the shell prompt (%) on my screen, it would be sent back to the shell and give the error "%: Command not found." So I set my shell prompt to this:

```
set prompt='    '
```

That's right: four spaces. Most Unix commands start their output at column 1, so my command lines were easy to find because they were indented. The shell didn't care if I sent four spaces before the command line. So everything was fine until I got my new terminal without a SEND LINE key...

If you want some information in your prompt, too, make a multiline prompt (4.7) with four spaces in the last line.

—JP and SJC

4.14 dirs in Your Prompt: Better Than $cwd

Many people use the current directory in their prompts. If you use the *pushd* and *popd* (31.7) commands, you may not always remember exactly what's in your directory stack (I don't, at least). Here's how: run the *dirs* command, and use its output in your prompt. A simple *csh* and *tcsh* alias looks like this:

```
alias cd 'chdir \!* && set prompt="`dirs`% "'
```

and the prompts look like:

```
/work/project % cd
~ % cd bin
~/bin %
```

Here's what to put in *.cshrc* or *.tcshrc* to make a multiline prompt (4.7) that shows the directory stack:

uname -n **2.5**
expr **36.21**

dirs-
prompt.csh
dirs-
prompt.sh

```
# PUT hostname.domain.name IN $hostname AND hostname IN $HOST:
set hostname=`uname -n`
setenv HOST `expr $hostname : '\([^.]*\).*'`
alias setprompt 'set prompt="\\

${USER}@${HOST} `dirs`\\
\! % "'
alias cd     'chdir \!* && setprompt'
alias pushd  'pushd \!* && setprompt'
alias popd   'popd \!* && setprompt'
setprompt    # SET THE INITIAL PROMPT
```

Because *bash* can run a command each time it sets its prompt, and because it has built-in prompt operators (4.3) like \u, the *bash* version of all the previous stuff fits on one line:

$(...) **28.14**

```
PS1='\n\u@\h $(dirs)\n\! \$ '
```

That makes a blank line before each prompt; if you don't want that, join the first and second lines of the *setprompt* alias or remove the first \n. Let's push a couple of directories and watch the prompt:

```
jerry@ora ~
1 % pushd /work/src/perl
/work/src/perl ~

jerry@ora /work/src/perl ~
2 % cd ../cnews

jerry@ora /work/src/cnews ~
3 % pushd ~/bin
~/bin /work/src/cnews ~

jerry@ora ~/bin /work/src/cnews ~
4 %
```

Of course, the prompt looks a little redundant here because each *pushd* command also shows the *dirs* output. A few commands later, though, having your directory stack in the prompt will be handy. If your directory stack has a lot of entries, the first line of the prompt can get wider than the screen. In that case, store the *dirs* output in a shell array, and edit it with a command like *sed* or with the built-in *csh* string editing (28.5).

For example, to show just the tail of each path in the *dirs* output, use the following alias; the C shell operator :gt globally edits all words, to the tail of each pathname:

**dirstail-
prompt.csh**

```
alias setprompt 'set dirs=(`dirs`); set prompt="\\
${USER}@${HOST} $dirs:gt\\
\! % "'
```

Watch the prompt. If you forget what the names in the prompt mean, just type dirs:

```
jerry@ora bin cnews jerry
5 % pushd ~/tmp/test
~/tmp/test ~/bin /work/src/cnews ~
   ...
jerry@ora test bin cnews jerry
12 % dirs
~/tmp/test ~/bin /work/src/cnews ~
```

—*JP and SJC*

4.15 External Commands Send Signals to Set Variables

The Bourne shell's *trap* (35.17) will run one or more commands when the shell gets a signal (24.10) (usually, from the *kill* command). The shell will run any command, including commands that set shell variables. For instance, the shell could reread a configuration file; article 24.13 shows that. Or it could set a new *PS1* prompt variable that's updated any time an external command (like another shell script or a *cron* job (25.2)) sends the shell a signal. There are lots of possibilities.

This trick takes over signal 5 (SIGTRAP), which usually isn't used. When the shell gets signal 5, a *trap* runs a command to get the date and time, then resets the prompt. A background (23.2) job springs this trap once a minute. So, every minute, after you type any command, your prompt will change.

You can use any command's output in your prompt (possibly with some editing, probably with *sed* (34.1) or *expr* (36.21)): count the number of users, show the load average (26.4), whatever. Newer shells, like *bash*, can run a command in backquotes (28.14) each time the prompt is displayed—article 4.10 has an example. But, to have an external command update a shell variable at any random time, this *trap* trick is still the best.

date-prompt.sh

: 36.6

Now on to the specific example of putting date and time in the old Bourne shell's prompt. If your system's *date* command doesn't understand date formats (like +%a), get one that does. Put these lines in your *.profile* file (or just type them in at a Bourne shell prompt):

```
# Put date and time in prompt; update every 60 seconds:
trap 'PS1=`date "+%a %D %H:%M%n"`\
$\ ' 5
while :
do
      sleep 60
      kill -5 $$
done &
promptpid=$!
```

Now, every minute after you type a command, your prompt will change:

```
Thu 06/20/02 02:33
$ cc bigprog.c
undefined symbol                    first referenced in file
xputc                                      bigprog.o
ld fatal: Symbol referencing errors.
Thu 06/20/02 02:34
$ ls
bigprog.c
bigprog.o
Thu 06/20/02 02:35
$
```

The prompt format is up to you. This example makes a two-line prompt (4.7) with backslashes (\) to protect the newline and space from the *trap*; a single-line prompt might be easier to design. The manual page for *date* lists what you can put in the prompt.

This setup starts a *while* loop (35.15) in the background. The *promptpid* variable holds the process ID number (24.3) of the background shell. Before you log out, you should *kill* (24.12) the loop. You can type the command:

```
kill $promptpid
```

at a prompt or put it in a file that's executed when you log out (4.18).

—*JP and SJC*

4.16 Preprompt, Pre-execution, and Periodic Commands

bash, *tcsh*, and *zsh* can run a Unix command, or multiple commands, before printing each prompt. *tcsh* and *zsh* also can do something you specify before executing the command you've typed at a prompt. Finally, *tcsh* and *zsh* can do something periodically (every *n* seconds) before whatever prompt comes next. (Article 4.15 shows how to execute commands periodically in the original Bourne shell.) These commands don't have anything to do with setting the prompt itself, though they can. The command could do some system checking, reset shell variables, or almost anything that you could type at a shell prompt. If the commands run slowly, they'll delay whatever else you're doing, so keep that in mind.

Let's start with *precmd*, the *tcsh* alias that's run after your command line is read and before the command is executed. In *zsh*, the same thing is done by the shell function named *preexec*. Shell history is available, so you can use history substitution (30.8) inside the alias or function. Here's a nice example adapted from the *tcsh* manual page: showing the command line you're running in your *xterm* window titlebar. It's ugly because it has ESC and CTRL-g characters embedded directly in the alias; I'd rather store the escape sequences in shell variables, as shown in the *xterm* titlebar article (4.8). The *if* sets the alias only if you're using an *xterm* terminal:

```
# Show each command line in xterm title bar:
if ($TERM == xterm) alias postcmd 'echo -n "^[]2;\!#^G"'
```

Next, let's look at running a command periodically. You'd like to watch the load average by running *uptime* (26.4) every minute, before a prompt. Here's how to do it in *zsh*: put code like this in your *.zshrc* file (3.3) (or just type it at a prompt to try it). The *PERIOD* shell variable is the interval, in seconds, between runs of the *periodic* function as shown in the following code:

```
# Run "uptime" every 60 seconds; put blank line before:
periodic() {echo "\n==> $(uptime) <==";}
PERIOD=60
```

Here's how it looks:

```
jpeek@ruby$ pwd
/u/jpeek/pt


==>   5:16pm  up  4:07,  6 users,  load average: 0.22, 0.15, 0.08 <==
jpeek@ruby$ lpr xrefs
jpeek@ruby$ mail -s "xrefs list" jan < xrefs


==>   5:17pm  up  4:08,  7 users,  load average: 1.29, 0.55, 0.23 <==
jpeek@ruby$
```

Finally, here's how to set prepompt commands. These are run before each shell prompt is printed. In *tcsh*, define a *precmd* alias. In *zsh*, define a *precmd* function. In *bash*, store the command(s) in the *PROMPT_COMMAND* shell variable. Let's look at *bash* this time. Here's a silly example that I used to have in my *bash* setup file (3.3):

IFS 36.23

set 35.25

shift $# 36.10

```
PROMPT_COMMAND='
# Save old $IFS; set IFS to tab:
OIFS="$IFS"; IFS="    "
# Put x in $1, face in $2, explanation[s] in $3[, $4, ...]:
set x `smiley`
# Put face into $face and explanation(s) into $explan:
face="$2"; shift 2; explan="$*"
# Restore shell environment:
shift $#; IFS="$OIFS"'

# Prompt I use (includes the latest $face):
PS1='\u@\h $face '
```

The first part is a series of shell commands that are stored in the *PROMPT_COMMAND* variable; they're surrounded by a pair of single quotes (', '), one on the first line (after the =) and the other after IFS is reset. That series of commands is executed before every prompt. It sets two shell variables, $face and $explan, with new values before each prompt is set. The prompt is set on the last line; it includes the value of $face.

Here's what my screen looked like with this ridiculous setup. Notice that the prompt keeps changing as the *PROMPT_COMMAND* resets $face and $explan. If I wanted the explanation of a face I saw as I went along, I could type echo <"> $explan<">:

```
jerry@ruby :-{) echo "$explan"
normal smiling face with a moustache
jerry@ruby +<||-) vi proj.cc
    ...
jerry@ruby :-O echo "$explan"
Mr. Bill
```

```
          Wow!
          ohh, big mouth, Mick Jagger
          uh oh
   jerry@ruby :-)    < g++ -Wall proj.cc
     ...
```

(It was even more useless than psychoanalyze-pinhead (19.13), but it was fun while it lasted.) Seriously now, I'll say again: preprompt commands do *not* have to be used to set a prompt. You can use them to do anything. If the commands in *PROMPT_COMMAND*—or any of the other functions or aliases we've covered—write to standard output or standard error, you'll see that text on your screen, before or after the prompt, at the point where the commands are executed.

—*JP and SJC*

4.17 Running Commands When You Log Out

Is there something you want to do every time you log out: run a program that deletes temporary files, asks you a question, or prints a fortune to your screen? If you use the C shell, make a file named *.logout* (3.3) in your home directory and put the commands there. Before a login C shell exits, it will read that file. A login *bash* reads *.bash_logout*, and *zsh* reads *.zlogout*. But not all shells are login shells; you might want these shells to read your logout-type file, too. Article 4.18 shows a fix for the Bourne and Korn shells; articles 3.8 and 3.4 have background information.

Some ideas for your logout file are:

- A command like *fortune* to give you something fun to think about when you log out.

- A command to list a "reminder" file—for example, work to take home.

- A script that prompts you for the hours you've worked on projects so you can make a timesheet later.

- The command *clear* to erase your screen. This keeps the next user from reading what you did.[*] In the Mac OS X Terminal application, **command–k** will delete the scrollback buffer. It also helps to stop "burn-in" damage to old, monochrome monitors caused by characters left over from your login session (though this is hardly a concern nowadays; most of us have moved

---

[*] Some terminals and windows have "scroll back" memory of previous screens. *clear* usually doesn't erase all of that. To set scrollback in *xterm*, use the *–sb* and *–sl* options. Most other terminal emulators have similar mechanisms to set the number of lines to keep in the scrollback buffer.

on to color screens that are not subject to burn-in). (Some Unixes clear the screen before printing the login: prompt. Of course, this won't help users who connect with a data switch or port manager because the connection will be broken before the next login prompt.)

If you connect to this host over a network, with a slow modem or on a data switch—and you don't see all the logout commands run before your connection closes—try putting the command sleep 2 (25.9) at the end of the file. That makes the shell wait two seconds before it exits, which gives output more time to get to your screen.

—*JP and SJC*

4.18 Running Commands at Bourne/Korn Shell Logout

Article 4.17 describes logout files. Commands in those files are run when you log out. The Bourne and Korn shells don't have a logout file, though. Here's how to make one:

1. In your *.profile* file, add the line:

trap **35.17**
. **35.29**
```
    trap '. $HOME/.sh_logout; exit' 0
```
(Some systems may need $LOGDIR instead of $HOME.)

2. Make a file in your home directory named *.sh_logout*. Put in the commands you want to be run when you log out. For example:

if **35.13**
[-f **35.26**
```
    clear
    if [ -f $HOME/todo.tomorrow ]
    then
        echo "=========== STUFF TO DO TOMORROW: ============"
        cat $HOME/todo.tomorrow
    fi
```

The *trap* will read the *.sh_logout* file when the shell exits.

—*JP and SJC*

4.19 Stop Accidental Bourne-Shell Logouts

It's pretty easy to type one too many CTRL-d characters and log out of a Bourne shell without meaning to. The C shell has an *ignoreeof* shell variable that won't let you log out with CTRL-d. So do the Korn shell and *bash*; use set -o ignoreeof.

Here's a different sort of solution for the Bourne shell. When you end the shell, it asks if you're sure. If you don't answer yes, a new shell is started to replace your old one.

First, make a file like the C shell's *.logout* that will be read when your Bourne shell exits (4.18). Save your tty (2.7) name in an environment variable (35.3), too—you'll need it later:

```
TTY=`tty`; export TTY
trap '. $HOME/.sh_logout; exit' 0
```

trap **35.17**

(Your system may need $LOGDIR instead of $HOME.) Put the following lines in your new *.sh_logout* file:

exec < **36.15**

case **35.11**

exec **24.2**
-sh **3.19**

```
exec < $TTY
echo "Do you really want to log out? \c"
read ans
case "$ans" in
[Yy]*) ;;
*)  exec $HOME/bin/-sh ;;
esac
```

The last line uses some trickery to start a new login shell (3.19). The shell closes your tty (36.15) before reading your *.sh_logout* file; the exec < $TTY reconnects the shell's standard input to your terminal.

Note that if your system is *very* slow, you may not get the reminder message for a couple of seconds—consequently, you might forget that it's coming and walk away. That hasn't been a problem where I've tested this. If it is for you, though, replace the read ans with a program like *grabchars* that times out and gives a default answer after a while. There may be some Bourne shells that need other tricks—and others that don't need these tricks—but this should give you an idea of what to do.

—JP and SJC

5

Getting the Most out of Terminals, xterm, and X Windows

5.1 There's a Lot to Know About Terminals

This chapter covers most of what you need to know to set up your terminal or terminal emulator from your shell setup files (3.3).

In the latter half of the chapter, we cover the ins and outs of working with some of the most popular terminal-emulator software for the X Window System, including *xterm*, *rxvt*, and others, where applicable. The list of terminals and emulators you might come into contact with is long and getting longer, though, so the advice we give in the first section of the chapter regarding how to configure your terminal will be helpful. As you find yourself suddenly confronted with the prospect of configuring the terminal emulator on your cell phone or tablet computer, remember: you can usually make it work, with enough time and effort.

It is important to remember, however, that the tricks and tips we discuss in this chapter, if implemented incorrectly, may cause your terminal to hang. One way around a hung terminal is always to keep at least one other terminal emulator window, with sane settings, open all the time you're modifying the setup of the other. That way, if you hang up the terminal you're actively modifying, you can always go back to the other and save yourself. On systems that support virtual consoles, such as Linux, you can also use command keys (e.g., ALT and the first five function keys) to switch between various virtual consoles, just as you might with a terminal emulator. Don't just reach for the power switch!

—*TOR and SJC*

5.2 The Idea of a Terminal Database

In the past few years, terminals have been standardized to a few types. In fact, most terminals nowadays are terminal *emulators* (like *xterm*) that simulate a terminal on a graphical display. Years ago, though, terminals differed widely. Rather than simply being implemented in software, they were hardware—keyboards and monitors or even teletypes, with which the user interacted to communicate with an often faraway mainframe or other big iron. All were specialized, and differences between them often came down to how much you paid and to what manufacturer. This lets you take advantage of other features of the manufacturer's primary hardware—the big computers they considered their main product. Manufacturers produced a variety of terminals, each one including a particular set of features for a certain price. There were smart terminals and dumb ones, terminals with big screens and terminals with small screens, printing terminals and video displays, and terminals with all sorts of special features.

Differences between terminals do not matter much to programs like *cat* (12.2) or *who* (2.8) that use the terminal screen as a sort of typewriter with an endless scroll of paper. These programs produce sequential output and do not make use of the terminal's special features; they do not need to know much to do their job. Only programs such as screen editors, which make use of screen-handling features, need to know a lot about differences between terminals.

However, even today, we find a wide variety of terminal emulators across a multitude of platforms. My new Kyocera Smartphone, for example, is a Palm device integrated with a PCS telephone; one of the main reasons I bought it was for remote, emergency *ssh* access to my servers, using a tiny terminal emulator that runs on the PalmOS. Many Unix programs assume a basic environment that this terminal emulator does not provide—an 80-column screen—so even simple commands such as *w*, which prints a list of who is logged in, where they logged in from, and what they're currently running, become impossible to run. But let's go back to the early days and revisit some of the old problems that plagued early Unix developers, so that we might better understand how to deal with today's problems.

In the late 1970s, Bill Joy created the *vi* (17.2) text editor at UC Berkeley. Like all screen-oriented editors, *vi* uses the terminal screen nonsequentially (in stark contrast to earlier editors such as *ed*, which were designed for a teletype, and so use even more terse commands and feature even more terse output). A program performing nonsequential output does not just print character after character, but must manipulate the text that was sent before, scroll the page, move the cursor, delete lines, insert characters, and more. While it would be possible to keep redrawing the screen in its entirety, many features are provided in hardware or firmware by the terminal itself, saving too much time and trouble to be ignored.

The first version of *vi* was written specifically for Lear Siegler ADM3a terminals. *vi* was such an improvement over line-oriented editors that there was great demand to port *vi* to other brands of terminals. The problem was that each terminal had different features and used different control codes to manipulate the features that they did have in common.

Rather than write separate terminal drivers for each terminal type, Bill Joy did something very clever, which all Unix users now take for granted. He wrote a version of *vi* with generic commands to manipulate the screen instead of hard-coding the control codes and dimensions for a particular terminal.*

Joy came up with a generic terminal-handling mechanism that had two parts: a database describing the capabilities of each of the terminals to be supported and a subroutine library that allows programs to query that database and make use of the capability values it contains. Both the library and the database were given the name *termcap*, which is short for *term*inal *cap*abilities.

At this point, users take for granted that you can use just about any terminal with a Unix system and use screen-oriented programs like *vi* without any problem. But this is really quite remarkable!

The *termcap* database is contained in a single text file, which grew quite large over the years to include descriptions of hundreds of different terminals. To improve performance, AT&T later introduced a database called *terminfo*, which stores terminal descriptions in compiled form in a separate file for each terminal.

If a program is designed to use *termcap* or *terminfo*, it queries an environment variable called *TERM* to determine the terminal type (or terminal type being emulated), then looks up the entry for that terminal in the terminal database, and reads the definition of any capabilities it plans to use as external variables. Programs that use *termcap* or *terminfo* range from screen editors like *vi* and *emacs* (19.1), which use the complete terminal description, to a program like *clear*, which needs to know only one capability (the escape sequence to clear the screen). Other programs include *more*, *pg*, *rogue*, *tset* (5.3), *ul*, and *nroff*.

—*JS and SJC*

---

* When we refer to *terminals* throughout this and other chapters, understand that we mean, more often than not, the set of standard terminal-emulation control codes implemented by terminal emulators, such as *vt100* or *ANSI color*. So, though we may refer to a vt100 terminal, we're more likely referring to any terminal-emulator software that can understand and react to that set of control codes.

5.3 Setting the Terminal Type When You Log In

If you always work at the same terminal or use the same terminal emulator, there's no problem with setting the terminal type explicitly in your shell setup file (3.3)—like *.login* or *.profile*. Just set the *TERM* environment variable (35.3):

```
setenv TERM vt100          ...csh, tcsh
TERM=vt100; export TERM    ...sh, ksh, zsh
export TERM=vt100          ...pdksh, bash, zsh
```

In fact, on a hardwired terminal, your terminal type may already have been set in a system file like */etc/ttys* or */etc/ttytype* (3.15). But if, like many Unix users, you might log in from time to time at different terminals, from home, or on different systems over a network, you may need some more intelligent method for setting the terminal type. To find out, try logging in at each place and starting a screen-oriented program like *vi*. Do various operations: scrolling up, inserting text that wraps onto another line, deleting lines. If the screen scrambles or the cursor gets "out of sync," your terminal type may need to be set.

It's possible to set up various tests (3.10) in your shell setup files to do this. But you can also do a surprising amount of terminal type testing with *tset*, even though it was nominally designed for initializing the terminal:

- If no arguments (1.4) are specified and *TERM* is already set, *tset* uses the value of *TERM* to determine the terminal type.

- If no arguments are specified and *TERM* is *not* set, then *tset* uses the value specified in the system file */etc/ttytype* or */etc/ttys* (BSD 4.3 and later and its derivatives only). On Linux systems, the terminal type is determined by *getty*, based on a similar process but using the */etc/inittab* file or other configuration files used by *getty* during initialization. On SVR4 systems, a similar process is managed by *ttymon* and *listen*.[*]

- If a terminal type is specified as an argument, that argument is used as the terminal type, regardless of the value of *TERM*.

- The *−m* (map) option allows a fine degree of control in cases where the terminal type may be ambiguous. For example, if you sometimes log in on a dialup line, sometimes over a local area network, and sometimes on a hardwired line, the *−m* option can be specified to determine which login is currently being used, and the terminal type can be set accordingly.

---

[*] *getty* is spawned by the *init* at multiuser system startup, and it sets up all ttys, handles the initial login prompt, and then hands successful logins over to *login* to complete.

In Bourne-type shells, *tset* can be used to set the value of *TERM* as follows:

```
export TERM=`tset - -Q options`          ...newer shells
TERM=`tset - -Q options`; export TERM    ...all shells
```

(Given the – option, *tset* prints the value determined for the terminal type to standard output (43.1). Otherwise, it initializes the terminal (5.3), but keeps the terminal type to itself. The –*Q* (quiet) option causes *tset* to suppress printing a message it normally prints regarding the values set for the erase and kill characters—a job it does in its alternate role as terminal initializer. The backquotes (28.14) surrounding the *tset* command interpolate its output into the command line.)

In the C shell, you should use the *eval* (27.8) command to capture the output of *tset*; this will also allow you to set the *TERMCAP* variable (35.5). (You must also issue the command set noglob.) To simplify the rest of this article, we'll show examples for the C shell; if you don't use a C-type shell, please translate to Bourne-shell syntax (as shown earlier).

To see what *tset* can do, consider a case where the terminal's serial line is connected to a dialup modem, through which several different users might be connected, each using a different type of terminal. Accordingly, the default terminal type in */etc/ttytype* or */etc/ttys* should be set to *dialup*. The *tset* command could then be used in the *.login* file as follows, with the appropriate terminal type set for each user:

```
set noglob
eval `tset -s -Q -m 'dialup:vt100'`
```

This means that if *ttytype* says *dialup*, use *vt100* as the terminal type. A colon separates the *ttytype* value and the value to which it is to be mapped. If a user wants to be prompted to be sure, place a question mark after the colon and before the mapped terminal type:

```
set noglob
eval `tset -s -Q -m 'dialup:?vt100'`
```

The prompt will look like this:

```
TERM = (vt100)
```

If the user presses RETURN, the preferred terminal type will be used. Alternately, another terminal type could be entered at that time.

You can cause *tset* to prompt for a terminal type even without testing a generic entry like *dialup*. Just specify the desired terminal type, preceded by a question mark, after the –*m* option. For example:

```
set noglob
eval `tset -s -Q -m '?vt100'`
```

It is also possible to specify different terminal types for different line speeds. For example, say that you normally used a Wyse-50 with a 9600-bps modem when dialing in from home, but used a portable PC with a VT100 terminal emulator and 2400-bps modem on the road.* You might then use a *tset* command like this:

```
set noglob
eval `tset -s -Q -m 'dialup@2400:vt100' wy50`
```

Assuming that the type is set in */etc/ttys* or */etc/ttytype* as *dialup*, *tset* will use the type *vt100* if at 2400 bps and, if not, will use the type *wy50*. See the *tset*(1) manual page for more choices. Watch out for the line-speed switches. They don't work on a lot of networked systems—usually, the line speed at the computer's port is higher than the speed at the terminal. The same problem occurs with dialup modems that use data compression. The *stty* command will tell you what data rate the system believes you're using.

Multiple *–m* options can be specified; the first map to be satisfied will be used. If no match is found, a final value specified on the line without a *–m* option (as in the previous example) will be used. If no value is specified, the type in */etc/ttytype* or */etc/ttys* will be used.

—TOR and SJC

5.4 Querying Your Terminal Type: qterm

tset (5.3) is a powerful tool to use if you often log in at different terminals. You can use *tset* to prompt you with a default terminal type, giving you the opportunity to specify a new terminal type when you log in:

```
TERM = (vt100)
```

However, *tset* requires you to know your terminal type. You might log in at a new terminal and have no idea what to set the terminal type to. Or your terminal might be configured to emulate another terminal type without your knowledge. New users in particular are confused by the *tset* prompt. In some respects, this is not a surprise, as the prompt itself can be confusing without a bit of context.

qterm

As an alternative, try Michael Cooper's *qterm* program on our CD-ROM. *qterm* sends the terminal a test string and determines what sort of terminal you're using based on how the terminal responds. Using *qterm*, you can make sure you always use the correct terminal type by placing the following line in your *.login*:

'...' 28.14

```
setenv TERM `qterm`
```

or in *.profile*:

```
TERM=`qterm`;export TERM
```

---

* Sure, you don't have to worry about whether there is a local TYMNET dialup nowadays, but back in the day...

The advantage of *qterm* is that it sets the terminal type without your intervention. You don't need to know your terminal type; it gets set automatically.

qterm works by sending the terminal a query string and returning the terminal type depending on the terminal's response. *qterm* is configured using a listing of responses and the terminals to which they correspond. By default, *qterm* looks for the listings in a system-wide location such as */usr/local/lib/qtermtab*. In addition, you can call *qterm* with the *+usrtab* option, so that it will look for a file called *.qtermtab* in your home directory.

The string used to query the terminal is usually ESC Z. The sample *qtermtab* file distributed with *qterm* defines the responses several different terminals give for that string:

```
#
# QtermTab - Query terminal table for qterm.
#
#SendStr ReceiveStr      TermName      FullTermName
#
^[Z      ^[[?1;0c        vt100         Base vt100
^[Z      ^[[?1;1c        vt100         vt100 with STP
^[Z      ^[[?1;2c        vt100         ANSI/VT100 Clone
   ...
^[Z      ^[/K            h29           Zenith z29 in zenith mode
^[Z      ^[/Z            vt52          Generic vt52
^[Z      ^[[0n           vt100         AT&T Unix PC 7300
```

If your terminal isn't listed here, you can just add it. To find out your terminal's response to the query string, just echo ESC Z to your terminal and see what the response is. For example, I logged in from my Macintosh terminal emulator at home and found that *qterm* didn't recognize my terminal type:

```
% qterm
Terminal NOT recognized - defaults to "vt100".
vt100
```

qterm defaults to the right terminal description, but I'd still rather define my own entry. I find out my terminal's response to the ESC Z string:

```
% echo "^[Z"
^[[E;Y|
```

(Note that ESC prints as ^[.) Then I add the entry to my *qterm* description file:

```
^[Z        ^[[E;Y|        vt100        Macintosh terminal emulator
```

Now when I run *qterm*, the terminal is recognized:

```
% qterm
Terminal recognized as vt100 (Macintosh terminal emulator)
vt100
```

The string Terminal recognized as ... is sent to standard error (43.1); only the terminal type itself is sent to standard output (43.1). So if you use the following command line:

```
% setenv TERM `qterm`
Terminal recognized as vt100 (Macintosh terminal emulator)
```

the TERM variable is set correctly:

```
% echo $TERM
vt100
```

Now for the caveat: *qterm*'s results are only as accurate as the *qtermtab* file. Not all terminals respond to the ESC Z string, and you may not find a string to which it responds uniquely. And some terminals do uncanny imitations of others. For example, I'm currently using an *xterm* (24.20) window, but *qterm* thinks I'm using a *vt100*:

```
% echo $TERM
xterm
% qterm
Terminal recognized as vt100 (ANSI/VT100 Clone)
vt100
```

As a hack, you can just edit your *.qtermtab* file. For example, I could comment out the old *vt100* entry and map ^[[?1;2c to *xterm* instead:

```
#^[Z    ^[[?1;2c         vt100       ANSI/VT100 Clone
^[Z     ^[[?1;2c         xterm       xterm window
```

and then call *qterm* with the *+usrtab* command-line option:

```
setenv TERM `qterm +usrtab`
```

—*LM and SJC*

5.5 Querying Your xterm Size: resize

When the *xterm* client is called, it not only sets the *TERM* environment variable, but it also adjusts the terminal definition for the size of the window being created. The size of *xterm* windows, however, can be changed later on by using the window manager. If the window is resized, then the user's shell may need to be passed the new size information as well, or programs that use termcap and terminfo won't work correctly. The *resize* client is provided for redefining the number of lines and columns for the terminal database used in an *xterm* window. Note that *resize* cannot be used for terminal emulators other than *xterm* (except for those, like *rxvt*, that emulate *xterm*) because it depends on *xterm*'s escape sequences.

Some systems can send a "window size changed" signal (*SIGWINCH*) to programs and do not require *resize* to be run for a resized *xterm* window. We recommend using *resize* only if terminal-based programs start to have problems with your window size. A typical terminal-based program that is having problems with the window size will fill only some of the lines in the window—or may scroll lines down the window when it shouldn't.

The *resize* client is typically used immediately after the dimensions of an *xterm* window are changed. A peculiarity of the *resize* client is that it does not access the shell itself, but simply returns the shell commands that would be needed; to have those commands read by the shell, you either save its output in a file and read the file with the shell commands *source* or . (35.29), or evaluate *resize* output using the shell command *eval* (27.8). For example, after resizing a window, you would type in that shell:

`...` 28.14   `% eval \`resize\``

When you call the *resize* command under a termcap system, it produces the commands for resetting the TERMCAP environment variable with the *li#* and *co#* capabilities reflecting the current dimensions. When you call the *resize* command under a terminfo system, it produces the commands for resetting the *LINES* and *COLUMNS* environment variables.

The *resize* command consults the value of your *SHELL* environment variable and generates the commands for setting variables within that shell. If you're using a nonstandard shell, *resize* may still recognize your shell; as of X Release 5, *resize* recognizes *tcsh*, *jcsh*, *ksh*, *bash*, and *jsh*. But if *resize* does not recognize your shell, try using the *-c* or *-u* options to force *resize* to use C- or Bourne-shell syntax (respectively), depending on which syntax is appropriate for your shell.

—LM, EP, and SJC

5.6 Checklist: Terminal Hangs When I Log In

If your terminal seems to "hang" (freeze, lock up) when you log in, here are some things to try:

- Have another user look at your shell's setup files (3.3). There could be some obvious mistakes that you didn't catch.

- Log in to another account and use the *su stucklogin* command (if the stuck account uses Bourne-type shells) or the *su -f stucklogin* command (if the stuck account uses *csh* or *tcsh*). Change (*cd*) to the home directory. Rename the account's setup files so the shell won't see them as you log in. (If you have superuser access (1.18), you also can use it to rename the file.)*

---

* Note that there is no user named *stucklogin*; you're expected to supply the actual login username as an argument to *su*.

If you can log in after that, you know that the problem is with the account's setup files.

- Set shell debugging (27.15) on the stuck account's setup files. From another account or as the superuser, start an editor and put the following line at the top of an *sh*-like setup file (such as *.profile*). It'll tell you whether *.profile* is being read at all and where it hangs:

      set -xv

  You'll see each line read from the *.profile* and the commands executed on the screen. If you don't see anything, then the shell probably didn't read *.profile*. Bash users would want to check *.bashrc* or *.bash_profile*.

  C-shell users should put this command at the top of *.cshrc* (or *.tcshrc*, for *tcsh*) instead:

      set echo verbose

  Note that on many Unix systems, the shell won't read its startup files if the files aren't owned by you. You might use *ls –l* (50.2) to check.

- Look at the entry in the */etc/passwd* file (22.3) for this user. Be sure it has the correct number of fields (separated by :). Also, see if there's another user with the same login name. (If your system has commands like *useradd*, *linuxconf*, or *vipw*(8) and *pwck*(8), using them to edit and check the *passwd* file will avoid many of these problems, as those programs perform sanity checks on any modifications you make before taking them live.)

- Does your account use any directories remotely mounted (by NFS) (1.21)? If the remote host or network is down and any command in your startup files (especially *set path*) tries to access those directories, the shell may hang there.

  To fix that problem, *su* to the account as explained earlier, and take the command or directory name out of your startup file. Or, if this problem happens a lot, the system administrator can mount an NFS filesystem "soft" (instead of "hard," the default) and limit the number of retrys.

- What looks like a "hang" might also be that you just aren't getting any output to the terminal, for some very weird reason. Then the *set –xv* wouldn't help you. In that case, try adding this line to the start of the *.profile*:

      exec > /tmp/sh.out.$$ 2>&1

  If the Bourne shell starts reading *.profile*, it'll make a file in */tmp* called `sh.out.nnn` with output from the commands and the shell's *set –xv*.

  There's no command like that for the C shell or *tcsh*.

Here are a few more tips for dealing with stuck terminals.

Output Stopped?

If your terminal has a HOLD SCREEN or SCROLL LOCK button, did you accidentally press it? Try pressing it and see if things start working again. If pressing the button once doesn't fix the problem, you should probably press it once more to undo the screen hold. Otherwise, you may lock up your session worse than it was before!

Another way to stop output is by pressing CTRL-s. The way to restart stopped output is with CTRL-q—try pressing that now. (Unlike a SCROLL LOCK button, though, if CTRL-q doesn't help, you don't need to undo it.)

Job Stopped?

If you're at a shell prompt instead of in the program you thought you were running—and if your Unix has job control—you may have stopped a job. Try the *jobs* command (23.1); if the job is stopped, restart it.

Program Waiting for Input?

The program may be waiting for you to answer a question or type text to its standard input.

If the program you were running does something that's hard to undo—like removing files—*don't* try this step unless you've thought about it carefully.

If your system has job control, you can find out by putting the job in the background with CTRL-z and *bg*. If the job was waiting for input, you'll see the message:

```
[1]  + Stopped (tty input)  grep pat
```

You can bring the job back into the foreground and answer its question, if you know what that question is. Otherwise, now that the job is stopped, you can kill it. See the following directions.

On systems without job control, you might satisfy the program by pressing RETURN or some other key that the program is expecting, like *y* or *n*. You could also try pressing CTRL-d or whatever your "end of input" character is set to. That might log you out, though, unless you've set the *ignoreeof* variable.

Stalled Data Connection?

Be sure that the wires haven't come loose.

If you're using a modem and the modem has function lights, try pressing keys to see if the Send Data (SD) light flashes. If it does, your terminal is sending data to the host computer. If the Receive Data (RD) light flashes, the computer is sending data to your terminal. If you don't see anything, there might be something wrong on your terminal.

If you're connected with *rlogin* or *telnet* or *ssh* (1.21), the network to the remote computer might be down or really slow. Try opening another connection to the same remote host—if you get a response like Connection timed out, you have two choices:

1. Wait for your original connection to unfreeze. The connection may come back and let you keep working where you left off. Or the connection may end when *rlogin, telnet,* or *ssh* notices the network problem.

2. Quit the session, and try again later.

Aborting Programs

To abort a program, most users press CTRL-c. Your account may be set up to use a different interrupt character, such as DELETE. If this doesn't work, try CTRL-\ (CTRL-backslash). Under most circumstances, this will force the program to terminate. Otherwise, do the following:

1. Log in at another terminal or window.

2. Enter the command ps x, or, if that doesn't work, use ps -u *yourname*, where *yourname* is your Unix username. This displays a list of the programs you are running, something like this:

```
% ps x
PID     TTY     STAT    TIME    COMMAND
163     i26     I       0:41    -csh (csh)
8532    i26     TW      2:17    vi ts.ms
22202   i26     S       12:50   vi UNIXintro.ms
8963    pb      R       0:00    ps -x
24077   pb      S       0:05    -bin/csh (csh)
%
```

3. Search through this list to find the command that has backfired. Note the process identification (PID) number for this command.

4. Enter the command kill *PID* (24.12), where *PID* is the identification number from the previous step. If that doesn't work, try kill -1 *PID* to send a HUP signal. You can also try various other signals, including -2 or -15. If none of them work, you may need *kill –9*, but try the other *kill*s first.

5. If the Unix shell prompt (such as % or $) has appeared at your original terminal, things are probably back to normal. You may still have to take the terminal out of a strange mode though.

   If the shell prompt hasn't come back, find the shell associated with your terminal (identified by a tty number), and *kill* it. The command name for the C shell is *csh*. For the Bourne shell, it is *sh*. In most cases, this will destroy any other commands running from your terminal. Be sure to *kill* the shell on your own terminal, not the terminal you borrowed to enter these commands. The tty you borrowed is the one running *ps*; look at the previous example and check the TTY column. In this case, the borrowed terminal is TTY pb.

Check *ps* to ensure that your shell has died. If it is still there, take more drastic action with the command `kill -9`*PID*.

6. Run `ps x` or `ps -u` *yourname* again to be sure that all processes on the other tty have died. (In some cases, processes will remain.) If there are still processes on the other tty, kill them.

7. At this point, you should be able to log in again from your own terminal.

The *ps* (24.5) command, which lists some or all of the programs you are running, also gives you useful information about the status of each program and the amount of CPU time it has consumed.

—*JP and SJC*

5.7 Find Out Terminal Settings with stty

stty

It may hardly seem appropriate to follow Chris Torek's learned article about how *stty* works with some basics, but this book is designed for beginners as well as those who already know everything. :-) [Good idea, Tim. This is also a handy place to put the globe icon for the GNU version. ;^) —*JP*]

So, to find out what settings your terminal line currently has, type:

    % stty

For a more complete listing, type:

    % stty -a

On older BSD-style systems, use `stty everything` instead. On most newer BSD-derived systems, `stty everything` and `stty -a` are both supported, but with slightly different output formats. The former prints a tabular layout, while the latter prints each control character setting in a *name* = *value* format.

As Jerry Peek said in an editorial aside to Chris's article, be sure to have your *stty* manual page handy!

—*TOR and SJC*

5.8 Setting Your Erase, Kill, and Interrupt Characters

Have you ever sat down at a terminal where the "erase" key (the character that deletes the last thing you typed) wasn't where you thought it would be? If you have, you know how disorienting this can be! On Linux, there's *loadkeys*. If you're using the X Window System, check into the *xmodmap* (6.1) command. Newer shells, like *bash* and *zsh*, tend to do their own handling of these special characters—especially during their built-in command-line editing (30.14). Check your shell's manual page about *readline*. The most portable method is with the *stty* (5.7) command. All of these give you a way of changing the erase character (along with several others) so you can restore some order to your world.

stty takes two kinds of input. If you want to give the command interactively, type stty erase *char*, where *char* is the key you normally use for erase—BACK-SPACE, DELETE, whatever—followed by RETURN. This will do the trick, provided that the character you type isn't already used for something. If the character is in use or if you're putting *stty* commands into your *.login*, *.profile*, or *.bash_profile* file, it's better to "spell these characters out." "Control" characters in *.login* are allowed, but they aren't a great idea. If you like to use the BACK-SPACE key as the erase key, add the following line:

    stty erase ^h

If you want to use the DELETE key, quote the ? character so the shell won't treat it as a wildcard (1.13):

    stty erase ^\?

That is, *stty* lets you represent a control key with the two-character combination ^*x*, where ^ is the literal key ^ (caret) and *x* is any single character. You may need to put a \ before the *x* to prevent the shell from interpreting it as a wildcard [and a \ before the ^ to prevent old Bourne shells from interpreting it as a pipe!—*JP*].

Of course, you're not limited to the BACKSPACE or DELETE keys; you can choose any other key you want. If you want to use "Z" as your DELETE key, type stty erase Z. Just make sure you never want to type a real Z!

Table 5-1 lists functions that *stty* can change.

Table 5-1. Keys to set with stty

Character	Function	Good setting	See article
erase	Erases the previous character.	^\? (DELETE)	5.8
kill	Erases the entire line.	^u (CTRL-u)	5.8
werase	Erases the previous word.	^w (CTRL-w)	5.8
intr	Terminates the current job.	^c (CTRL-c)	24.11
quit	Terminates the current job; makes a core file.	^\ (CTRL-\)	24.11
susp	Stops the current job (so you can put it in the background).	^z (CTRL-z)	23.3
rprnt	Redisplays the current line.	^r (CTRL-r)	28.2

The command *stty everything* (BSD derivatives) or *stty –a* (Linux and System V derivatives) shows all your current terminal settings. The *werase* and *rprnt* characters aren't implemented on some older versions of Unix, though they are on Linux and Darwin and most other modern Unix variants.

It's amazing how often you'll see even moderately experienced Unix users holding down the BACKSPACE or DELETE key to delete a partially completed command line that contains an error.

It's usually easier to use the line-kill characters—typically CTRL-u or CTRL-x. (The command *stty –a* or *stty everything* (41.3) will tell you which. Article 5.7 shows how to change them.) The line-kill character will work on a command line (at a shell prompt (4.1)) and in other places where the terminal is in cooked mode. Some Unix programs that don't run in cooked mode, like *vi*, understand the line-kill character, too.

Even better, many stystems have a "word-erase" character, usually CTRL-2, which deletes only back to the previous whitespce. There's no need to delete the entire command line if you want to change only part of it!

As a historical note, the erase character was originally #, and the kill character was originally @. These assignments go back to the olden days, when terminals printed with real ink on real paper and made lots of noise. However, I'm told that there are some modern systems on which these settings are still the default.*

 Terminal emulators, editors, and other programs can fool around with all of this stuff. They *should* be well behaved and reset your terminal when you leave them, but that's often not true. So don't expect your settings to work within a terminal emulator; they may, or they may not. And don't expect your settings to be correct after you exit from your terminal emulator. Again, they may, or they may not. This is primarily due to the fact that some terminal-emulator programs lie about the extent to which they support a given set of control codes.

The *tset* program also fools around (5.3) with key settings. Therefore, in your shell setup files (3.3), put *stty* after *tset*.

—*ML, JP, SJC, and TOR*

5.9 Working with xterm and Friends

xterm is by far the most commonly used X client, although more and more people are switching from *xterm* to similar or related programs, such as *rxvt*—which is a lightweight *xterm* derivative without the Tektronix terminal emulation support. Regardless, the most commonly used clients are largely derivatives of *xterm*, so we're devoting the rest of this section to this single client and its family.

* ...for some values of "modern", anyway...—*SJC*

xterm[*] gives you a window containing your standard shell prompt (as specified in your */etc/passwd* entry). You can use this window to run any command-line-oriented Unix program or to start additional X applications.

The uncustomized *xterm* window should be sufficient for many users' needs. Certainly you can do anything in a vanilla *xterm* window that you can from a character-based terminal. But *xterm* also has special features you can use, and since you spend so much time in *xterm*, you might as well use them.

The rest of this chapter gives you a set of tricks and tips about using *xterm*, including the following:

- Specifying and using a scrollbar (article 5.11).
- Copying and pasting text selections (article 5.13).
- Modifying text-selection behavior (article 5.14).
- Printing the current directory in the *xterm* titlebar (article 5.15).
- Dynamically changing fonts and other features (articles 5.17, 5.18).

The articles in this chapter use terms that you may want defined:

- A *pointer*, or pointing device, is a piece of hardware designed for navigating a screen. Most people use a mouse as their pointer, but there are also trackballs, touchpads, and others.
- The best pointer to use with X has three buttons. When we refer to the *first button* or *button 1*, we mean the button you click with your index finger. For right-handed people, this is usually the left button on a mouse. But the X client *xmodmap* (6.1) lets left-handed users swap mouse buttons to make the rightmost button the "first."
- Even though the actual image on the screen is called a cursor, throughout this chapter we refer to "moving the pointer" to avoid confusion with the standard text cursor that can appear in an *xterm* window.

—LM, VQ, and SJC

5.10 Login xterms and rxvts

If you want your *xterm* or *rxvt* to run a login shell (3.4), give it the *–ls* flag, or put a line like one of the following in your X resource file (6.5):

```
xterm*loginShell:  true   ...for xterm
XTerm*loginShell:  true   ...for xterm or rxvt
Rxvt*loginShell:   true   ...for rxvt
```

---

[*] When we refer, throughout the rest of the chapter, to *xterm*, we're often referring to *xterm* proper, as well as *rxvt* and other related terminal programs.

Once you've defined the appropriate resource, you can get a nonlogin shell (which is otherwise the default) with *xterm +ls*.

—*JP and SJC*

5.11 Working with Scrollbars

The scrollbar is a favorite *xterm* feature, particularly among those whose terminals lacked the ability to scroll backwards. Using the scrollbar, you can re-examine the output or error from a command, select previous text to supply in another command line or to paste into a file, or to hide your current screen from a nosy coworker.

There are many ways to start up the scrollbar. You can specify the *–sb* option on the command line:

```
% xterm -sb &
% rxvt -sb &
```

or you can set the scrollBar resource (6.5) to true:

```
XTerm*scrollBar:      true  ...for xterm or rxvt
Rxvt*scrollBar:             true  ...for rxvt
```

or for an *xterm* window that's already running, you can call up the **VT Options** menu (5.17) by holding down the CTRL key and the center mouse button or by selecting **Enable Scrollbar**. These menus are not supported by *rxvt*.

A scrollbar appears on the left side of the *xterm* window, as shown in Figure 5-1.

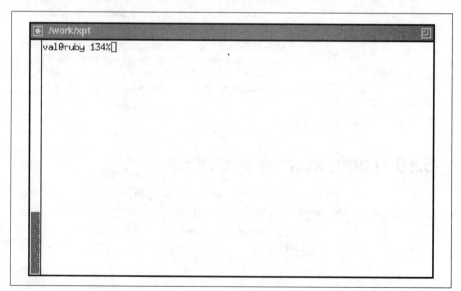

Figure 5-1. xterm window with scrollbar

—*LM and SJC*

5.12 How Many Lines to Save?

If you use the scrollbar in *xterm* (5.11), you'll find that by default the scrollbar retains only 64 previous lines of text. You can change this by using the *–sl* command-line option:

```
% xterm -sb -sl 200 &
% rxvt -sb -sl 200 &
```

or by setting the saveLines resource:

```
XTerm*saveLines: 200
```

You don't want to go crazy with the number of saved lines, though. Too many lines saved may crunch on virtual memory and also make it hard to scroll.

—*LM and SJC*

5.13 Simple Copy and Paste in xterm

You can use the pointer to select text to copy and paste within the same *xterm* window or between *xterm* windows. You don't need to be in a text editor to copy and paste. You can also copy or paste text to and from the command line, between the command line and a file, etc.

There are several ways to select (copy) text; all require you to use the pointer. You can select a passage of text, or you can select text by individual words or lines.

When you select text, it is highlighted and copied into global memory from which you can paste it into any *xterm* window. Regardless of the number of *xterm* windows you're running, you can store only one selection in memory at a time. However, you can paste that selection as many times as you like. When you make another selection, the new text replaces the previous selection in memory.

Table 5-2 summarizes all of the text-selection methods.

Table 5-2. Button combinations to select text for copying

To select	Do this
Passage	Click the first button at the start of the selection and the third button at the end of the selection. Or at the beginning of the selection, hold down the first button; drag the pointer to the end of the desired text; release the button.
Word	Double-click the first button anywhere on the word.
Line	Triple-click the first button anywhere on the line.

To clear the highlighting, move the pointer off the selection, and click the first button anywhere else in the window. Note, however, that the text still remains in memory until you make another selection.

Of the two methods for selecting a passage, the first is generally easier. Hypothetically, you can select a passage of any length; in practice, we've found there to be limitations. The size of the window limits the amount of text you can highlight in one action. You can extend a selection beyond the parameters of a window. Copying an extremely long selection, however, doesn't seem to work reliably. Also, when pasting a long selection, the text can become garbled.

You can paste text into any *xterm* window, either onto the command line or into a text file you're editing. In both cases, move the pointer into the window, and click the second button. The text will be pasted; in other words, it will appear on the screen, just as if you typed it.

 To paste into an open text file, the editing program must be in insert mode. (If not, when pasted, the selection may be interpreted as a stream of editor commands, such as in *vi*. The act of pasting the word "selection" in a *vi* editor not in insert mode would be to ignore everything up until the *i*, which would place *vi* into insert mode, and then the last three letters would be inserted into the buffer.)

—*VQ and SJC*

5.14 Defining What Makes Up a Word for Selection Purposes

You probably already know how to select text (5.13) in an *xterm*, and you've probably discovered that double-clicking (5.13) will select the entire word around the pointer. What you may not know is that it is possible to change what defines a "word."

xterm maintains a table of all the ASCII characters and their *character classes*. Any sequence of adjacent characters of the same class is treated as a word. Numbers, letters, and the underscore are in class 48 (which is the ASCII code for the character 0) and SPACE and TAB are in class 32 (the ASCII code for SPACE). By default, all the other characters are in classes by themselves.

For Unix users, this isn't the most useful default; it would be better if you could select filenames, email addresses, URLs, resource specifications, etc. as single words even though they often contain punctuation characters.

You can modify the character class table with *xterm*'s charClass resource variable (6.3). The value this resource accepts is a comma-separated list; each item on the list is an ASCII character code or range of characters, followed by a colon, followed by the character class to which the character should be added. I set the charClass resource as follows:

```
xterm*charClass: 33:48, 37:48, 42:48, 45-47:48, 63-64:48, 126:48
```

This tells *xterm* to treat !, %, *, -, ., /, ?, @, and ~ as characters of the same class as numbers and letters. You may also want to treat : as a member of this class, for URLs; in that case, use the following charClass string:

```
xterm*charClass: 33:48, 37:48, 42:48, 45-47:48, 58:48, 63-64:48, 126:48
```

—*DJF and SJC*

5.15 Setting the Titlebar and Icon Text

Under most modern window managers, most windows (including *xterm*) are displayed with a titlebar. You can change the text in the titlebar using the following *xterm* escape sequence:

```
^[]2;string^G
```

Note that this sequence has a close bracket (]) following the ESC (Escape, ^[)—not an open bracket. It ends with a CTRL-g character—not a caret followed by a "g".

I use this sequence to display my current working directory and directory stack in the titlebar, where they are visible but unobtrusive. I do this by adding a few lines to my shell setup file (3.3). Article 4.8 explains.

If you change the number "2" in the escape sequence to "1," it will set the text that appears in the *xterm*'s icon instead of its titlebar. If you change it to "0," it will set the text for both the icon and the titlebar. If you use and iconify a number of *xterm*s, you may find these sequences useful.

You may also wish simply to specify an icon name and/or title text for a given window, statically, for those situations where the window is only used to display output from some program, and not for interactive use. Both *xterm* and *rxvt* allow this, using the *–n* option to specify the icon name and the *–T* option to specify the title. You may also use X resources to specify icon name or title.

The Mac OS X Terminal application lets you set the title from the Set Title command on the Shell menu as well.

—*DJF and SJC*

5.16 The Simple Way to Pick a Font

X font names make the Rosetta Stone look like bedtime reading. Those hardy souls who want to experiment with fonts or access fonts on remote machines must take the high road and learn the X font naming conventions anyway. But if you just want to locate some fonts to use with *xterm* and other clients, you can use the predefined aliases for some of the constant-width fonts available on most systems.

Figure 5-2 lists the aliases for some constant-width fonts that should be appropriate for most of the standard clients, including *xterm*. [These "aliases" are basically font *names*. They aren't the same as shell aliases (29.1). Also note that terminals should use constant-width fonts (where every character—thin or wide—occupies the same horizontal width). Constant-width fonts ensure that, for instance, the 54th character in every line of output from *ls –l* is always in the same horizontal position on the screen—so columns will always be straight.—*JP*] To give you an idea of the range of sizes, each alias is written in the font it identifies.

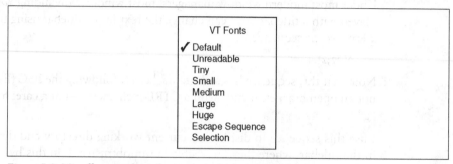

Figure 5-2. Miscellaneous fonts for xterm and other clients

In these cases, the aliases refer to the dimensions in pixels of each character in the font. (For example, "10×20" is the alias for a font with characters 10 pixels wide by 20 pixels high.) Note, however, that an alias can be virtually any character string.

The default font for many applications, including *xterm*, is a 6×13 pixel font that has *two* aliases: "fixed" and "6×13." Many users consider this font to be too small. If you have enough screen space, you might want to use the 10×20 font for *xterm* windows:

```
% xterm -fn 10x20 &
```

You can make this font the default for *xterm* by specifying it as the value for the font resource variable (6.3):

```
XTerm*font: 10x20
```

Another quick way to get a list of fonts that match a given string is to use the *xlsfonts* program, which accepts a variety of options but may be used as simply as this:

```
% xlsfonts -fn \*-10-\*
```

This command will display all of the fonts that are 10 pixels wide. The string *-10-* is a wildcard expression matching any font specification containing -10-. Be sure to escape the * and ? characters when specifying a pattern on the command line, to avoid interpolation by the shell.

—VQ and SJC

5.17 The xterm Menus

xterm has four different menus, each providing items that serve different purposes. You display a menu by placing the pointer on the window and simultaneously pressing the CTRL (keyboard) key and a pointer button. When you're using a window manager that provides a titlebar or frame, the pointer must rest within the window proper and *not* on any window decoration.

Table 5-3 describes the menus and how to display them.

Table 5-3. The xterm menus

Menu title	Display by holding	Use to
Main Options	CTRL, pointer button 1	Enter secure mode; interrupt, stop, etc., the xterm process.
VT Options	CTRL, pointer button 2	Toggle user preferences, including scrollbar, reverse video, margin bell; toggle Tektronix/VT100 mode.
VT Fonts	CTRL, pointer button 3	Select alternative display font.
Tek Options	CTRL, pointer button 2, on Tektronix window	Toggle VT100/Tektronix mode; select display font.

As shown in Table 5-3, three of the four *xterm* menus are divided into sections separated by horizontal lines. The top portion of each divided menu contains various modes that can be toggled. (The one exception is the **Redraw Window** item on the **Main Options** menu, which is a command.) A check mark appears next to a mode that is currently active. Selecting one of these modes toggles its state.

The items on the **VT Fonts** menu change the font in which text is displayed in the *xterm* window. Only one of these fonts can be active at a time. To turn one off, you must activate another. See article 5.18 for information on using the **VT Fonts** menu.

When you display an *xterm* menu, the pointer becomes the arrow pointer and initially appears in the menu's title. Once the menu appears, you can release any keyboard key. The menu will remain visible as long as you continue to hold down the appropriate pointer button. (You can move the pointer off the menu without it disappearing.) To toggle a mode or activate a command, drag the pointer down the menu and release the pointer button on the item you want.

If you decide not to select a menu item after the menu has appeared, move the pointer off the menu and release the button. The menu disappears and no action is taken.

You probably won't use the *xterm* menus too often. You can set most mode entries by using command-line options when invoking *xterm* or by using entries in a resource file (6.5). See the *xterm* manpage for a complete list of options and resource variables.

The various modes on the menus are very helpful if you've set (or failed to set) a particular mode on the command line and then decide you want the opposite characteristic. For instance, say you've run *xterm* without a scrollbar and then decide you want one. You can toggle the scrollbar from the **VT Options** menu.

The sections below the modes portion of each menu contain various commands. Selecting one of these commands performs the indicated function. Many of these functions can be invoked only from the *xterm* menus. However, some functions can be invoked in other ways, which are often more convenient. For example, you can remove the *xterm* window using several of the items on the **Main Options** menu, but it's probably simpler to type exit or logout, or use a window manager menu or button. Of course, the *xterm* menus can be very helpful when other methods fail to invoke a function. And some functions (such as **Secure Keyboard**) are not available in any other way—unless you do a little customizing.

Most people tend to use the mode toggles on the **VT Options** menu (which allow you to turn features like the scrollbar on and off) and the items on the **VT Fonts** menu (which allow you to change the display font once the client is running). If you're concerned about security, you may want to invoke secure keyboard mode from the **Main Options** menu before typing passwords or other sensitive information.

Note that a Release 5 patch (20.9) has eliminated *xterm*'s logging capability for security reasons. If this patch has been applied, your **Main Options** menu will not offer the **Log to File** option.

—VQ and SJC

5.18 Changing Fonts Dynamically

Ideally, you want to set up your environment so that *xterm* windows (and other clients) come up automatically with the characteristics you prefer, including the display font. I use the very large 10×20-pixel font (5.16) for all my *xterm* windows by specifying the resource variable (6.3):

```
XTerm*font: 10x20
```

But if you start an *xterm* and then decide you want a different font, you do have an option.

VT Fonts Menu

The *xterm* **VT Fonts** menu (5.17) allows you to change a window's font on the fly, which is a very handy capability. You can change the font any number of times to accommodate a variety of uses. You might choose to use a large font for text editing; you could then change to a smaller font while a process is running, since you don't need to be reading or typing in that *xterm*. Since *xterm*'s dimensions are determined by the number of characters wide by the number of lines high, changing the font also changes the size of the window.

When the focus is on an *xterm*, you display the menu by pressing CTRL and then the third pointer button. The default menu is shown in Figure 5-3.

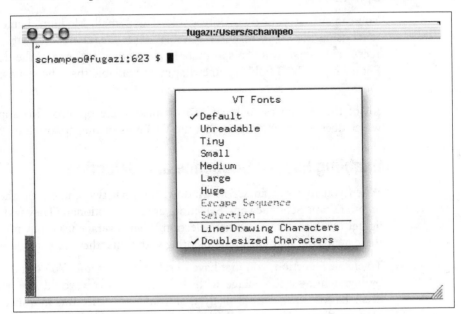

Figure 5-3. xterm's VT Fonts menu lets you change fonts dynamically

The items on the **VT Fonts** menu are toggles, each of which provides a different size display font. If you have not toggled any items on this menu, a check mark will appear next to **Default**, which is the font specified when the *xterm* was run. This font could have been specified on the *xterm* command line or in a resource file. Whatever the case, this font remains the **Default** for the duration of the current *xterm* process.

By default, the **Unreadable**, **Tiny**, **Small**, **Medium**, **Large**, and **Huge** menu choices toggle the constant-width fonts shown in Table 5-4.

Table 5-4. VT Fonts menu defaults

Menu item	Default font
Unreadable	nil2
Tiny	5×7
Small	6×10
Medium	7×13
Large	9×15
Huge	10×20

Bring up the **VT Fonts** menu, and toggle some of these fonts to see what they look like. The first choice is not called **Unreadable** for nothing, but it does have a practical use.

You can specify your own Unreadable, Tiny, Small, Medium, Large, and Huge fonts using the *xterm* resource variables font1, font2, font3, font4, font5, and font6. You might want to specify bold alternatives to some of the default fonts. For example, 7×13 bold is somewhat more readable than the standard **Medium** font.

All of the references to fonts and command-line options also apply to *rxvt*, which does not, however, support the **VT Fonts** menu supported by *xterm*.

Enabling Escape Sequence and Selection

When you first run an *xterm* window, the final two choices on the **VT Fonts** menu, **Escape Sequence** and **Selection**, are not functional. (They will appear in a lighter typeface than the other selections.) The average user may not care about these items, but if you're experimenting with fonts, they are sometimes useful.

To enable **Selection**, you first have to select a font name. You can do this simply by highlighting a font name with the pointer, as you would any text selection (5.13). However, it's more likely that you'll use **Selection** in concert with the *xfontsel* client. [This is a client that does point-and-click selection of X11 font names; see its manpage.—JP] Once you've selected a font name, you can toggle it using the **Selection** menu item. A serious limitation: **Selection** tries to use the last selected text as a font name. If the last selected text was not a valid font name, toggling **Selection** will get you nothing more than a beep. When there is no primary text selection in memory, the menu item is grayed out again.

The **Escape Sequence** item is a little more complicated, but once set up it will be available for the duration of the *xterm* process. To make it available, you first need to change the font by a more primitive method, using a literal escape sequence that you send to the *xterm* using *echo*:

```
val@ruby 181% echo "Esc]50;7x13boldControl-g"
```

These are the literal keys you type to change the font to 7×13bold. But pressing ESC actually generates the symbol ^[, and CTRL-g appears as ^G, so you'll get a line that looks like this:

```
val@ruby 181% echo "^[]50;7x13bold^G"
```

If you *don't* get this string, try typing the CTRL-v character before both the ESC and CTRL-g characters, letting the system know you intend for the following character to be a literal.

I've used a short font name alias (5.16), but you could use a full name or a name with wildcards. Once you've changed the font in this manner, you can toggle it using the **Escape Sequence** menu item. If you change the font again using the literal escape sequence, that font will be available via the menu item. Note that the trick for changing the font discussed earlier also works in *rxvt*, but does not enable any font menus.

—*VQ and SJC*

5.19 Working with xclipboard

The *xclipboard* client does exactly what you might think: it allows you to save multiple text selections (5.13) and copy them to other windows. Text you copy from an *xterm* window can be made the CLIPBOARD selection (and thus automatically appear in the *xclipboard* window). To set this up, you first need to customize *xterm* using resources.*

For text you copy from an *xterm* to be pasted automatically into *xclipboard*, the text must be made the CLIPBOARD selection. You set this up to happen by specifying a few translations (6.4) for *xterm*.† Here are the translations I use to coordinate *xterm* with *xclipboard*:

---

* Since there can be only one CLIPBOARD selection at a time, you can only run one *xclipboard* per display.

† If you're using a terminal emulator other than *xterm*, the program should also allow this sort of customization. See the client manpage for the actions (the equivalents of select-end and insert-selection) to include in the translation table.

```
*VT100.Translations:    #override\
   Button1 <Btn3Down>:  select-end(primary,CUT_BUFFER0,CLIPBOARD)\n\
   !Shift <Btn2Up>:     insert-selection(CLIPBOARD)\n\
   ~Shift ~Ctrl ~Meta <Btn2Up>:  insert-selection(primary,CUT_BUFFER0)
```

To let you store multiple text selections, the seemingly tiny *xclipboard* actually provides multiple screens, each of which can be thought of as a separate buffer. Each time you use the pointer to make text the CLIPBOARD selection, the *xclipboard* advances to a new screen in which it displays and stores the text. If you make a long selection, it might take up more than one screen, but the clipboard still considers it a single buffer. When you make a selection that extends beyond the bounds of the *xclipboard* window (either horizontally, vertically, or both), scrollbars (5.11) will be activated in the window to allow you to view the entire selection.

To the right of the command buttons is a tiny box that displays a number corresponding to the selection currently in the *xclipboard* window. Once you have saved multiple selections, you can click on the client's Next and Prev command buttons to move forward and backward among these screens of text.

If you've coordinated *xterm* with *xclipboard* using the guidelines outlined earlier, you paste the CLIPBOARD selection in an *xterm* window by holding down the Shift key and clicking the second pointer button. When you paste the CLIPBOARD selection, you get the selection that's currently being displayed in the *xclipboard* window. Here's where the client really comes in handy. Suppose you send four selections to *xclipboard* and you want to paste #2. Just go back to selection #2 using the Prev command button; when you use the pointer command to paste the CLIPBOARD selection, selection #2 is pasted. In Figure 5-4, we've pasted selection #2 into a new file. (Notice that the text is too wide for the *xclipboard* window and that a horizontal scrollbar has been provided so we can view the entire selection.)

A selection remains available in *xclipboard* until you Quit the program or use the Delete button to erase the current buffer.

Use the Save command button to save the text in the current buffer to a file. A dialog will ask you to Accept or Cancel the save to a file with the default name *clipboard*. You can change the filename using *Text widget commands* [these are listed in the *xedit*(1) manpage—*JP*]. If you want to save multiple selections, you'll need to change the filename each time, or you'll overwrite the previous save.

You can edit text you send to the *xclipboard* using Text widget commands. When you edit a screenful of text, the *xclipboard* continues to store the edited version until you delete it or exit the program.

—*VQ and SJC*

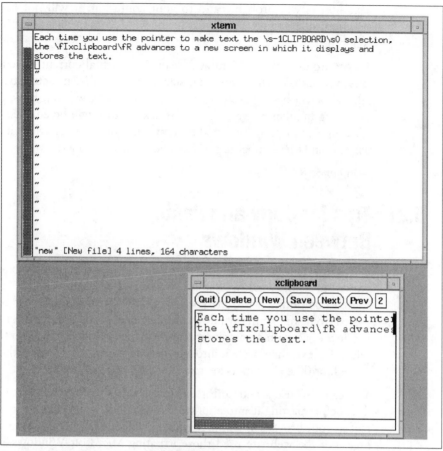

Figure 5-4. Text you copy from an xterm appears in xclipboard

5.20 Problems with Large Selections

If you experiment making large selections with *xclipboard*, you may discover what seems to be a bug in the program. Though making a new selection usually causes the screen to advance and display the new text, this does not happen reliably after a selection that vertically spans more than one screenful. In these cases, the new selection *is* saved in the *xclipboard* (and the number in the small box is incremented to indicate this); however, the *xclipboard* window does not automatically advance to show you the new current selection. Instead, the previous long selection is still displayed. (For example, though the box says "5," indicating that a fifth selection has been saved, the window is still displaying selection #4.) This is a bit of *xclipboard* sleight of hand: the new selection has been successfully made, but the appearance of the window belies this fact. The

Next button will probably add to your confusion; it will not be available for selection, suggesting that the text in the window is the last selection saved. This is not the case.

To get around this problem and display the actual current selection, press the Previous button. The same long selection (which is, in actuality, the Previous selection) will be displayed again. (The small box will flip back to display the preceding number as well.) Then the Next button will be enabled, and you can click on it to display the actual current selection. The selection displayed in the window and the number in the small box will correspond.*

—VQ and SJC

5.21 Tips for Copy and Paste Between Windows

One of my favorite uses for an *xterm* (which may seem natural to people who've grown up using window systems, but was a pleasant surprise for a guy who started computing with teletypes in 1970) is using a window to accept text pasted from some other window. For instance, in writing this book, I'll have one window open with something happening that I want to put into the book. So I select the text, then paste it into another *xterm* window—where there's usually a text editor (like *vi*, with its keymaps for pasting text (18.5)).

You can also use a text editor or Unix utilities to reformat text from one window before pasting it into another. For instance, you'd like to send most of the text in your browser to another window where you're composing an email message. But the web site used those irritating Microsoft Windows–specific quote characters that show up as question marks (?) on any other platform. So you paste the text into an Emacs window, do a quick run of text substitution, and copy the result to paste into the email window.

requote

Another problem with email messages comes when you're sending a reply to someone who's used very long or jagged lines and the quoted text is a mess. But if you cut the messy text into an *xterm* window running the *requote* shell script, you'll get a neatened version. In the following example, the text I paste (cut from a quoted email message) is shown in boldface. Then I press CTRL-d, and the result appears; I can paste it back into the email message:

```
$ requote
> This is a long line of text that runs on and on and wraps to the next
line without a quote character at the start and it goes on and on and on
and well you know
> This is the next line of text
```

---

* By this time, the observant reader will have concluded that *xclipboard* is a nuisance at best.

```
CTRL-d
> This is a long line of text that runs on and on and wraps to the next
> line without a quote character at the start and it goes on and on and
> on and well you know This is the next line of text
```

You can pass a *fmt* width option to tell *requote* how wide to make the output lines. (Different versions of *fmt* have different width options: *–w*, *–l*, etc.) *requote* also works great as a *vi* filter-through (17.18): paste the messy text into *vi*, and run a command like !{requote to requote the text in place.

requote is a simple script that doesn't try to handle multiple levels of quoting (>> > >>, etc.). The main formatting commands are shown here; the temporary file $temp makes sure *fmt* has read all the text before the final *sed* outputs any of it:

${1+"$@"} **36.7**
```
sed 's/^> //' |
fmt ${1+"$@"} > $temp
sed 's/^/> /' $temp
```

Here's another problem like the one *requote* solves. When I copy text from a browser window, my browser usually puts some whitespace before each line. When I paste the text, it's a mess. I could use a text editor to clean up the lines, but a one-line *sed* script can do the job faster.

Let's look at three examples of *dedent*. It removes all space and TAB characters from the start of each line it reads on its standard input, and it writes the result to standard output.

```
$ dedent > order_confirmation
    ...paste text into xterm, press CTRL-d...
$ dedent | fmt > johnson
    ...paste text into xterm, press CTRL-d...
$ dedent | mail -s 'article I mentioned' ali
    ...paste text into xterm, press CTRL-d...
$
```

In the first example, I started *dedent* and pasted text into the *xterm*. After I pressed CTRL-d, *dedent* removed leading whitespace from the pasted text and wrote the result to standard output, which the shell had redirected to a file named *order_confirmation*. In the second example, *dedent*'s output is piped to *fmt* (21.2) to make the lines neat. (Without *dedent*, most versions of *fmt* would indent the reformatted text.) The third example removes leading whitespace, then emails (1.21) the text to *ali*.

One more thing: many of the tricks discussed earlier may be implemented as shell functions or even *emacs* functions or *vi* macro. If you use a mail user agent such as *mutt*, you can specify your favorite editor for email messages and just call the functions or macros while you edit. This is how I requote my replies to others' email, wrap it to a sane width, and so on. In *emacs*, ESC q is mapped to the function `fill-paragraph`, so if I need a paragraph wrapped to a certain width (determined by `default-fill-column`), I just position the cursor inside the paragraph and call the function. If the `fill-prefix` variable is properly set (say, to >) it even knows how to wrap several levels of nested quoting in email.

—*JP and SJC*

5.22 Running a Single Command with xterm –e

The *–e* option to *xterm* is useful for running a single command before exiting. For example, if you just want to run a character-based mail program, type the following:

```
% xterm -e mail
```

When you quit the *mail* program, the *xterm* window exits.

The *–e* option needs to be the last *xterm* option on the command line. The remainder of the command line is assumed to be part of the command to be executed by *xterm*. The new window has the command name in its titlebar by default (unless overridden by other command-line options (5.15)).

One use for *xterm –e* is for running a window with a login session to a remote system, like this:

```
% xterm -e ssh hostname &
```

ssh-agent

The *xterm* process runs on the local system, but immediately logs you into the remote machine. You are prompted for a password in the new *xterm* that pops up—before you can log in to the remote system. This isn't as convenient as putting that command in your X setup file (like *.xinitrc* or *.xsession*)—but it's far more secure because you don't need to put your hostname in your *.rhosts* or *.shosts* file (1.21), which is a potential security hole. (Or, if you use *ssh* for your remote login—and you start *ssh-agent* before you start X—you won't need to type passwords at all during your X session. This is the handiest setup by far.)

You can use *–e* to create a makeshift X display for any character-based programs you like to run. For example, you might want to keep track of messages sent to the console, but you can't run *xterm –C* to get console messages because you aren't actually logged in on the console. You might run something like this:

`tail -f 12.10`

```
% xterm -e tail -f /var/log/messages &
```

Article 24.21 has more about how this works.

—*LM, JP, and SJC*

5.23 Don't Quote Arguments to xterm –e

Being a belt-and-suspenders kind of guy, I've gotten in the habit of quoting arguments to commands. This makes good sense with lots of Unix shell commands, but it can get you in trouble with *xterm –e*. For example, I wanted to set up a job that would open *vi* in a window to edit a file named *.postit*. At first, I used the command:

```
xterm ... -e 'vi .postit' &
```

only to receive the perplexing message in the resulting window:

```
Can't execvp vi .postit
```

The quotes passed the entire string to *xterm* as an argument, which parsed it as a single command name, rather than a command plus argument. Removing the quotes solved the problem.

—TOR and SJC

6

Your X Environment

6.1 Defining Keys and Button Presses with xmodmap

If you have a Linux system, you may want to use *loadkeys* instead of *xmodmap*. *loadkeys* is designed to set the keymap used by the system as a whole, particularly the console, so use your own judgment. Whatever is done in *xmodmap* will affect X but not the system console.

An important piece to the X Window System puzzle is filled by the *xmodmap* client. When the user performs any action—such as typing a key or moving the mouse—the server sends a packet of information to the client called an *event*. These events are then translated into actions by the client. You can use the *xmodmap* utility to effectively change the event that is reported to the client.

Keysym mappings are mappings of keyboard events at the server level, before the event is sent to the client. *Keysyms* are the symbols used for each key on the keyboard.

The X server maintains a *keymap table*, which contains a listing of keys on the keyboard and how they should be interpreted. A client gets the keymap table from the server upon client startup. In most cases, the keymap table is used to interpret keys literally—when you press the letter "a," a key code is sent to the client that corresponds to the letter "a" in the keymap table.

You can use the *xmodmap* client to reassign key codes within the keymap table. *xmodmap* can therefore be used to redefine how the key is interpreted by the client. You probably wouldn't want to translate the alphanumeric keys on the keyboard, but you may want to translate others. For example, you might want to change the BACKSPACE key to DELETE:

```
% xmodmap -e "keysym BackSpace = Delete"
```

Another example is if you mistakenly hit the CAPS LOCK key a bit too often, you can disable it completely. Some people might disable CAPS LOCK the low-tech way (by just removing the key from the keyboard!), but you can also render it harmless with the command:

```
% xmodmap -e "keysym Caps_Lock = "
```

effectively disabling the CAPS LOCK key entirely. Note that the symbol is now gone and can't be redefined without using the hardware key code.

If you are a DVORAK typist, you can use *xmodmap* to translate every key on the keyboard and so your QWERTY keyboard behaves like a DVORAK keyboard.

If it ever seems that keystrokes are not working correctly, you can check current keysym settings by running *xmodmap* with the *–pk* argument. Use the *xev* client to determine exactly which key code a key generates on your display. There is also a public domain client called *xkeycaps* that can be used to display the keysyms for selected keyboards.

You can use *xmodmap* to add or remove keysyms, or even to redefine the key code associated with that keysym. You can also use it to redefine the mouse buttons, using the `pointer` keyword. For example, to have the second and third mouse button switch places, you can enter:

```
% xmodmap -e "pointer = 1 3 2"
```

If you have a large number of keys to remap, you can put the commands in a file that is read when your X session starts. For example, create a file called *.Xmodmap*:

```
! my .Xmodmap file
remove Lock = Caps_Lock
remove Control = Control_L
keysym Control_L = Caps_Lock
keysym Caps_Lock = Control_L
add Lock = Caps_Lock
add Control = Control_L
  ...
```

These commands effectively reverse your CTRL and CAPS LOCK keys. (CTRL and CAPS LOCK are "switched" on PC and Macintosh keyboards, which can be exceedingly frustrating.) This file can then be read automatically in a X startup script:

```
  ...
xset b 10 100 10
xrdb $HOME/.Xdefaults
xmodmap $HOME/.Xmodmap
fvwm &
  ...
```

Alternately, you might want to assign different functions to little-used keys, such as making the tiny "enter" key on Powerbook keyboards into another command key. Remember, too, that some keys may have different names than what you're used to. Sun keyboards, for example, often come with a "meta" key; Macintosh keyboards have an "option" key where PC users expect to find "alt" (though they act the same); and so forth.

On Linux systems, the *loadkeys* command is often used to make system-level changes to key mappings; it's common to see a variety of keytables already defined and a system default chosen from among them. The system default is often found in */etc/sysconfig/keytable* (Red Hat 6 and earlier) or */etc/sysconfig/keyboard* (Red Hat 7) or otherwise defined in a directory such as */usr/share/keymaps* or */usr/lib/kbd/keymaps*. On Debian, the keytable is simply set in */etc/console-tools/default.kmap.gz*.

If you have a physical keyboard on which you've switched certain keys, you may want to modify the system-level key mappings as well, so that they are always loaded properly for those times when you need the console to work without any special user-level configuration. For example, on my Red Hat systems, I always modify my keymap (in 6.* and earlier, found in */usr/lib/kbd/keymaps/i386/qwerty/us.kmap.gz*, and in 7.*, found in */lib/kbd/keymaps/i386/qwerty/us.kmap.gz*) to reflect the fact that the keyboard I carry with me to the co-lo has swapped CAPS LOCK and CTRL keys. Just *gunzip* the file, edit, and then *gzip* it back up again. Alternately, you can create a new file from an existing one, make your edits, and specify the new file in your */etc/sysconfig/keytable* or */etc/syscongig/keyboard* file, as appropriate.

The keymaps directory tree is broken down by the platform (Amiga, Atari, i386, Mac, Sun) and then by the layout type of the keyboard (DVORAK, QWERTY, and various other layouts) and finally by the language or character set. So, there is a U.S. keymap, a U.K. keymap, a Hebrew keymap, and dozens of various others, for all of the systems on which Linux is supported. The files are in a relatively straightforward format:

```
keycode  54 = Shift
keycode  56 = Alt
keycode  57 = space
        control keycode  57 = nul
keycode  58 = Control
keycode  86 = less           greater        bar
keycode  97 = Control
```

First comes the keycode keyword, followed by the numeric value of the keysym generated when the key is pressed, and then a keyword (or several) describing the character to be generated when a given keysym is received. Modifiers may precede the keycode keyword, binding the combination of modifier key and keysym to another character value.

One danger of using *xmodmap* is that anything set with *xmodmap* might remain in effect after you have logged out. This isn't a problem if you use the same X server every day, but be aware that if you use a coworker's X terminal in his absence, he may come back complaining that you broke his CAPS LOCK key. This might happen if you use *xdm*, since the server is not restarted after every X session. On some X terminals, you can fix this problem by toggling "Retain X Settings" on the X terminal setup menu.

—LM, EP, and SJC

6.2 Using xev to Learn Keysym Mappings

The *xev* client is essential for debugging X Window System keysym mappings (6.1). When you start up *xev*, a small "event window" appears. All events that take place within that window are shown on standard output. This means screenfuls of output, but it also means that when you type a key, you can immediately trace the resulting event. For example, if you need to know what keysym is sent when you type the DELETE key on the keyboard, just run *xev* and type the DELETE key in the event window. Typical output might be the following:

```
KeyPress event, serial 13, synthetic NO, window 0x800001,
    root 0x8006d, subw 0x800002, time 1762968270, (50,36),
    root:(190,176), state 0x0, keycode 27 (keysym 0xffff, Delete),
    same_screen YES, XLookupString gives 1 characters: "^?"

KeyRelease event, serial 15, synthetic NO, window 0x800001,
    root 0x8006d, subw 0x800002, time 1762968336, (50,36),
    root:(190,176), state 0x0, keycode 27 (keysym 0xffff, Delete),
    same_screen YES, XLookupString gives 1 characters: "^?"
```

This tells you that the DELETE key (keycode 27) is interpreted as keysym 0xffff, which is Delete and character ^?. If you do an xmodmap -pk (6.1), you should see a line resembling:[*]

```
27      0xffff (Delete)
```

If you redefine the DELETE key as the BACKSPACE key and do the same exercise (run *xev* and press the DELETE key), you should see something like this:

```
% xmodmap -e "keysym Delete = BackSpace"
% xev
    ...
```

[*] The keycode numbers may vary from system to system, depending on how your key mappings are configured. For example, under a Debian 2.2 install running inside VirtualPC on a Powerbook G3, DELETE is keycode 107, whereas under OroborusX on the same machine, the same keypress produces keycode 59, the BACKSPACE character. On both systems, however, the hexadecimal keysym values for DELETE and BACKSPACE are the same: 0xffff and 0xff08, respectively.

```
KeyPress event, serial 13, synthetic NO, window 0x800001,
    root 0x8006d, subw 0x800002, time 1763440073, (44,39),
    root:(240,235), state 0x0, keycode 27 (keysym 0xff08, BackSpace),
    same_screen YES, XLookupString gives 1 characters: "^H"

KeyRelease event, serial 15, synthetic NO, window 0x800001,
    root 0x8006d, subw 0x800002, time 1763440139, (44,39),
    root:(240,235), state 0x0, keycode 27 (keysym 0xff08, BackSpace),
    same_screen YES, XLookupString gives 1 characters: "^H"
```

This tells you that now the DELETE key (still keycode 27) is being interpreted as hexadecimal 0xff08, keysym BackSpace, and generates character "^H." xmodmap -pk should show you the following:

```
27      0xff08 (BackSpace)
```

For more information, see O'Reilly & Associates' *X Window System User's Guide*, Volume 3.

—*LM, EP, and SJC*

6.3 X Resource Syntax

Virtually all X Window System clients are customizable.* You can specify how a client looks on the screen—its size and placement, its border and background color or pattern, whether the window has a scrollbar, and so on. This article introduces X resources and shows their syntax.

Traditional Unix applications rely on command-line options to allow users to customize the way they work. X applications support command-line options too, but often not for all features. Almost every feature of an X program can be controlled by a variable called a *resource*; you can change the behavior or appearance of a program by changing the *value* associated with a resource variable.

Resource variables may be Boolean (such as scrollBar: True) or take a numeric or string value (borderWidth: 2 or foreground: blue). What's more, in applications written with the X Toolkit (or an Xt-based toolkit such as the Motif toolkit), resources may be associated with separate *objects* (or "widgets") within an application. There is a syntax that allows for separate control over both a *class* of objects in the application and an individual *instance* of an object. This is illustrated by these resource specifications for a hypothetical application called *xclient*:

---

* Not to be confused with the extensive customization of window decorations and the like now possible with window managers such as Enlightenment, Afterstep, FVWM, or Sawfish. If you have a difficult time visualizing what is affected by these resource assignments apart from the fancy decoration around the windows themselves, try killing your window manager and viewing just the X clients themselves, in all of their sparse glory.

```
xclient*Buttons.foreground:      blue
xclient*help.foreground:         red
```

The first resource specification makes the foreground color blue for all buttons in the *xclient* application (in the class Buttons); the second resource specification makes the foreground color red for the help button in this application (an instance of the class Buttons). Resource settings can be even simpler than this.

The values of resources can be set as application defaults using a number of different mechanisms, including resource files in your home directory and a program called *xrdb* (X resource database manager). As we'll see, the *xrdb* program stores resources directly in the X server, making them available to all clients, regardless of the machine on which the clients run.[*]

Placing resources in files allows you to set many resources at once without the restrictions encountered when using command-line options. In addition to a primary resource file (often called *.Xdefaults*, *.Xresources*, or *xrdb*) in your home directory, which determines defaults for the clients you yourself run, the system administrator can create system-wide resource files to set defaults for all instances of the application run on this machine. It is also possible to create resource files to set some resources for just the local machine, some for all machines in a network, and some for one or more specific machines.[†]

The various resource files are automatically read in and processed in a certain order within an application by a set of routines called the *resource manager*. The syntax for resource specifications and the rules of precedence by which the resource manager processes them are intended to give you the maximum flexibility in setting resources with the minimum amount of text. You can specify a resource that controls only one feature of a single application, such as the red help button in the hypothetical *xclient* settings listed earlier. You can also specify a resource that controls one feature of multiple objects within multiple applications with a single line.

Command-line options normally take precedence over any prior resource settings; so you can set up the files to control the way you *normally* want your application to work and then use command-line options (in an alias or shell function (29.1), for instance) to specify changes you need for only one or two instances of the application.

---

[*] Remember, in X the client server model is the inverse of what you may be used to; the server is local, and displays clients that may be running remotely.

[†] While this is often okay for applications such as *xterm* that have not been modified much since the early nineties, app-defaults files can be more trouble than they're worth in a rapid application development environment, as they can quickly get out of sync with changes in the application itself from one version to the next.

The basic syntax of a resource definition file is fairly simple. Each client recognizes certain resource variables that can be assigned a value; see the client's manpage for a list.

Toolkits are a mechanism for simplifying the design and coding of applications and making them operate in a consistent way. Toolkits provide a standard set of objects or widgets, such as menus, command buttons, dialog boxes, scrollbars, and so on. If a client was built with the X Toolkit, this should be noted on its manual page. In addition to certain application-specific resource variables, most clients that use the X Toolkit recognize a common set of resource variables.

The most basic line you can have in a resource definition file consists of the name of a client, followed by a dot (.) or an asterisk (*), and the name of a variable. A colon (:) and whitespace separate the client and variable names from the actual value of the resource variable. The following line gives a scrollbar to all instances of the *xterm* client:

```
xterm*scrollBar:        True
```

If the name of the client is omitted, the variable is *global*: it applies to all instances of all clients (in this case, all clients that can have a scrollbar). If the same variable is specified as a global variable and a client-specific variable, the value of the client-specific variable takes precedence for that client. However, if the name of the client is omitted, the line should generally begin with an asterisk.

Be sure not to omit the colon inadvertently at the end of a resource specification. This is an easy mistake to make, and the resource manager provides no error messages. If there is an error in a resource specification (including a syntax error such as the omission of the colon or a misspelling), the specification is ignored. The value you set will simply not take effect.

A line starting with an exclamation point (!) is ignored as a comment. If the last character on a line is a backslash (\), the resource definition on that line is assumed to continue on the next line.

—*VQ and SJC*

6.4 X Event Translations

This article introduces event translations, which are special X Window System resources that control actions of things like mouse clicks. Article 6.3 introduces X resources and shows their syntax. Articles 6.5 through 6.9 explain how to set and check resources—as you log in and after.

We've discussed the basics of resource-naming syntax. From the sample resource settings, it appears that what many resource variables do is self-evident or nearly so. Among the less obvious resource variables, there is one type of specification, an event translation, that can be used with many clients and warrants somewhat closer examination.

User input and several other types of information pass from the server to a client in the form of *events*. An event is a packet of information that gives the client something to act on, such as keyboard input. Moving the pointer or pressing a key causes *input* events to occur. When a program receives a meaningful event, it responds with some sort of action.

For many clients, the resource manager recognizes mappings between certain input events (such as a pointer button click) and some sort of action by the client program (such as selecting text). A mapping between one or more events and an action is called a *translation*. A resource containing a list of translations is called a *translation table*.

Many event translations are programmed into an application and are invisible to the user.* For our purposes we are only concerned with very visible translations of certain input events, primarily the translation of keystrokes and pointer button clicks to particular actions by a client program.

The operation of many clients, notably *xterm*, is partly determined by default input event translations. For example, selecting text with the first pointer button (an event) saves that text into memory (an action).

In this case, the input "event" is actually three separate X events:

1. Pressing the first pointer button.
2. Moving the pointer while holding down the first button.†
3. Releasing the button.

Each of these input events performs a part of the action of selecting text:

1. Unselects any previously selected text and begins selecting new text.
2. Extends the selection.
3. Ends the selection, saving the text into memory (both as the primary selection and CUT_BUFFER0).

The event and action mappings would be expressed in a translation table as follows:

```
<Btn1Down>: select-start()\n\
<Btn1Motion>: select-extend()\n\
<Btn1Up>: select-end(primary,CUT_BUFFER0)
```

---

* For more information on events and translations, see O'Reilly & Associates' *X Window System Guide*, Volume 4.

† Actually, if there is no text to select, motion is recorded as a series of *MotionNotify* events.

where each event is enclosed in angle brackets (<>) and produces the action that follows the colon (:). A space or TAB generally precedes the action, though this is not mandatory:

```
<event>: action
```

A translation table must be a continuous string. To link multiple mappings as a continuous string, each event-action line should be terminated by a newline character (\n), which is in turn followed by a backslash (\) to escape the actual newline.

These are default translations for *xterm*.[*] All of the events are simple, comprised of a single button motion. As we'll see, events can also have modifiers: i.e., additional button motions or keystrokes (often CTRL or Meta) that must be performed with the primary event to produce the action. (Events can also have modifiers that *must not* accompany the primary event if the action is to take place.)

As you can see, the default actions of keysym mappings are hardly intuitive. The client's manpage usually lists the event-action mappings that you can modify.

You can specify nondefault translations using a translation table (a resource containing a list of translations). Since actions are part of the client application and cannot be modified, you are actually specifying alternative events to perform an action.[†] Keep in mind that only applications written with the X Toolkit (or an Xt-based toolkit such as the Motif Toolkit) recognize translation-table syntax as described here.

The basic syntax for specifying a translation table as a resource is as follows:

```
[object*[subobject...]]*translations:   #override\
      [modifier]<event>:   action
```

The first line is basically like any other resource specification with a few exceptions. First, the final *argument* is always translations, indicating that one (or more) of the event-action bindings associated with the [object*[subobject...]] are being modified.

Second, note that #override is not the *value* of the resource; it is literal and indicates that what follows should override any default translations. In effect, #override is no more than a pointer to the true *value* of the resource: a new event-action mapping (on the following line) where the event may take a modifier.

---

[*] They are actually slightly simplified versions of default translations. Before you can understand the actual translations listed in the *xterm* manual page, you must learn more about the syntax of translations. We cover the basics here; for more information, see O'Reilly & Associates' *X Window System Guide,* Volume 3M, Appendix F.

[†] As we'll see, in certain cases you may be able to supply an alternative *argument* (such as a selection name) to an action. These changes *are* interpreted by the resource manager.

A not-so-obvious principle behind overriding translations is that you only literally "override" a default translation when the event(s) of the new translation match the event(s) of a default translation *exactly*. If the new translation does not conflict with any existing translation, it is merely appended to the defaults.

To be specified as a resource, a translation table must be a single string. The #override is followed by a backslash (\) to indicate that the subsequent line should be a continuation of the first.

In the previous basic syntax example, the *value* is a single event-action mapping. The *value* could also be a list of several mappings, linked by the characters \n\ to make the resource a continuous string.

The following *xterm* translation table shows multiple event-action mappings linked in this manner:

```
*VT100.Translations:    #override\
        <Btn1Down>:     select-start()\n\
        <Btn1Motion>:   select-extend()\n\
        <Btn1Up>:       select-end(primary,CUT_BUFFER0)
```

—*VQ and SJC*

6.5 Setting X Resources: Overview

Learning to write resource specifications is a fairly manageable task, once you understand the basic rules of syntax and precedence. In contrast, the multiple ways you can set resources—for a single system, multiple systems, a single user, or for all users—can be confusing. For our purposes, we are primarily concerned with specifying resources for a single user running applications both on the local system and on remote systems in a network.

As we've said, resources are generally specified in files. A resource file can have any name you like. Resources are generally "loaded" into the X server by the *xrdb* (6.8) client, which is normally run from your startup file or run automatically by *xdm* when you log in. Prior to Release 2 of X, there was only one resource file called *.Xdefaults*, placed in the user's home directory. If no resource file is loaded into the server by *xrdb*, the *.Xdefaults* file will still be read.

Remember that X allows clients to run on different machines across a network, not just on the machine that supports the X server. One problem with the older *.Xdefaults* mechanism was that users who were running clients on multiple machines had to maintain multiple *.Xdefaults* files, one on each machine. By contrast, *xrdb* stores the application resources directly in the server, thus making them available to all clients, regardless of the machine on which the clients are running. As we'll see, *xrdb* also allows you to change resources without editing files.

Of course, you may want certain resources to be set on all machines and others to be set only on particular machines. For a complex setup, check the detailed information in O'Reilly & Associates' *X Window System Guide,* Volume 3M, Chapter 11.

In addition to loading resource files, you can specify defaults for a particular instance of an application from the command line using two options: *–xrm* and *–name*.

A sample resources file follows. This file sets the border width for all clients to a default value of two pixels, and it sets other specific variables for *xclock* and *xterm*. The meaning of each variable is obvious from its name. (For example, xterm*scrollBar: True means that *xterm* windows should be created with a scrollbar.)

Note that comments are preceded by an exclamation point (!).

For a detailed description of each variable, see the X client manpages.

```
*borderWidth:           2
!
! xclock resources
!
xclock*borderWidth:     5
xclock*geometry:        64x64
!
! xterm resources
!
xterm*curses:           on
xterm*cursorColor:      skyblue
xterm*pointerShape:     pirate
xterm*jumpScroll:       on
xterm*saveLines:        300
xterm*scrollBar:        True
xterm*scrollKey:        on
xterm*background:       black
xterm*borderColor:      blue
xterm*borderWidth:      3
xterm*foreground:       white
xterm*font:             8x13
```

Article 6.6 takes a look at the use of the *–xrm* command-line option in standard X clients; article 6.7 covers *–name*. Article 6.8 discusses various ways you can load resources using the *xrdb* program. Article 6.9 shows how to list the resources for a client with *appres*.

—VQ and SJC

6.6 Setting Resources with the –xrm Option

The *–xrm* command-line option, which is supported by all X Window System clients written with the X Toolkit, can be useful in specifying from the command line any specification that you would otherwise put into a resources file (6.5). For example:

```
% xterm -xrm 'xterm*Foreground: blue' &
```

Note that a resource specification on the command line must be quoted using the single quotes.

The *–xrm* option only specifies the resource(s) for the current instance of the application. Resources specified in this way do not become part of the resource database.

The *–xrm* option is most useful for setting classes, since most clients have command-line options that correspond to instance variable names. For example, the *–fg* command-line option sets the foreground attribute of a window, but *–xrm* must be used to set Foreground.

Note also that a resource specified with the *–xrm* option will not take effect if a resource that takes precedence has already been loaded with *xrdb*. For example, say you've loaded a resource file that includes the specification:

```
xterm*pointerShape:  pirate
```

The command-line specification of another cursor will fail:

```
% xterm -xrm '*pointerShape:  gumby' &
```

because the resource xterm*pointerShape is more specific than the resource *pointerShape. Instead, you'll get an *xterm* with the previously specified pirate cursor.

To override the resource database (and get the Gumby cursor), you'd need to use a resource equally (or more) specific, such as the following:

```
% xterm -xrm 'xterm*pointerShape:  gumby' &
```

—*VQ and SJC*

6.7 How –name Affects Resources

The command-line option *–name* lets you name one instance of an application; the server identifies the single instance of the application by this name. The name of an application affects how resources are interpreted. This option is supported by all X Window System clients written with the X Toolkit.

For example, the following command sets the *xterm* instance name to bigxterm:

```
% xterm -name bigxterm &
```

When this command is run, the client uses any resources specified for bigxterm rather than for xterm.

The *–name* option allows you to create different instances of the same application, each using different resources. For example, you could put the following entries into a resource file such as *.Xresources*:

```
XTerm*Font:         8x13
smallxterm*Font:    6x10
smallxterm*Geometry: 80x10
bigxterm*Font:      9x15
bigxterm*Geometry:  80x55
```

You could then use these commands to create *xterm*s of different specifications. The command:

```
% xterm &
```

would create an *xterm* with the default specifications, while:

```
% xterm -name bigxterm &
```

would create a big *xterm*, 80 characters across by 55 lines down, displaying in the font 9x15. The command:

```
% xterm -name smallxterm &
```

would create a small *xterm*, 80 characters across by 10 lines down, displaying in the font 6x10.

—VQ and SJC

6.8 Setting Resources with xrdb

The *xrdb* program saves you from maintaining multiple resource files if you run clients on multiple machines. It stores resources on the X server, where they are accessible to all clients using that server. (This property is also called the resource database.)

Place the appropriate *xrdb* command line in your *.xinitrc* file or *.xsession* file to initialize resources at login, although it can also be invoked interactively. It has the following syntax:

```
xrdb [options] [filename]
```

The *xrdb* client takes several options, all of which are documented on its manual page. We'll discuss the most useful options.

The optional *filename* argument specifies the name of a file from which the values of client variables (resources) will be read. If no filename is specified, *xrdb*

---

will expect to read its data from standard input. Note that whatever you type will override the previous contents, so if you inadvertently type *xrdb* without a filename argument and then quit with CTRL-d, you will delete any previous values. (You can append new settings to current ones using the *–merge* option discussed later in this article.)

The resource *filename* can be anything you want. Two commonly used names are *.Xresources* and *.Xdefaults*.

You should load a resource file with the *xrdb –load* option. For example, to load the contents of your *.Xresources* file into the RESOURCE_MANAGER, you would type:

```
% xrdb -load .Xresources
```

Querying the resource database

You can find out what options are currently set by using the *–query* option. For example:

```
% xrdb -query
XTerm*ScrollBar:      True
bigxterm*font:        9x15
bigxterm*Geometry:    80x55
smallxterm*Font:      6x10
smallxterm*Geometry: 80x10
xterm*borderWidth:    3
```

If *xrdb* has not been run, this command will produce no output.

Loading new values into the resource database

By default, *xrdb* reads its input (either a file or standard input) and stores the results into the resource database, replacing the previous values. If you simply want to merge new values with the currently active ones (perhaps by specifying a single value from standard input), you can use the *–merge* option. Only the new values will be changed; variables that were already set will be preserved rather than overwritten with empty values.

For example, let's say you wanted to add new resources listed in the file *new.values*. You could say:

```
% xrdb -merge new.values
```

As another example, if you wanted all subsequently run *xterm* windows to have scrollbars, you could use standard input and enter:

```
% xrdb -merge
xterm*scrollBar:       True
```

and then press CTRL-d to end the standard input. Note that because of precedence rules for resource naming, you may not get what you want automatically. For example, if you specify:

```
xterm*scrollBar:       True
```

and the more specific value:

```
xterm*vt100.scrollBar:  False
```

has already been set, your new, less specific setting will be ignored. The problem isn't that you used the *–merge* option incorrectly—you just got caught by the rules of precedence.

If your specifications don't seem to work, use the *–query* option to list the values in the RESOURCE_MANAGER property, and look for conflicting specifications.

Note also that when you add new specifications, they won't affect any programs already running—only programs started after the new resource specifications are in effect. (This is also true even if you overwrite the existing specifications by loading a new resource file. Only programs run after this point will reflect the new specifications.)

Saving active resource definitions in a file

Assume that you've loaded the RESOURCE_MANAGER property from an *.Xresources* or other file. However, you've dynamically loaded a different value using the *–merge* option, and you'd like to make the new value your default.

You don't need to edit the file manually (although you certainly could.) The *–edit* option allows you to write the current value of the RESOURCE_MANAGER property to a file. If the file already exists, it is overwritten with the new values. However, *xrdb* is smart enough to preserve any comments and preprocessor declarations in the file being overwritten, replacing only the resource definitions. For example:

```
% xrdb -edit ~/.Xresources
```

will save the current contents of the RESOURCE_MANAGER property in the file *.Xresources* in your home directory.

If you want to save a backup copy of an existing file, use the *–backup* option:

```
% xrdb -edit .mydefaults -backup old
```

The string following the *–backup* option is an extension appended to the old filename. In the prior example, the previous copy of *.mydefaults* would be saved as *.mydefaults.old*.

Removing resource definitions

You can delete the definition of the RESOURCE_MANAGER property from the server by calling *xrdb* with the *–remove* option.

There is no way to delete a single resource definition other than to read the current *xrdb* values into a file. For example:

```
% xrdb -query > filename
```

Use an editor to edit the file, deleting the resource definitions you no longer want, and save the file:

    % **vi** *filename*

Then read the edited values back into the RESOURCE_MANAGER with *xrdb* (note that we're replacing the values, not merging them, so we use *–load*):

    % **xrdb -load** *filename*

—*VQ and SJC*

6.9 Listing the Current Resources for a Client: appres

The *appres* (*application resource*) program lists the resources that currently might apply to a client. These resources may be derived from several sources, including the user's *.Xresources* file and a system-wide application defaults file. The directory */usr/lib/X11/app-defaults* contains application-default files for several clients. (Note that it may be in a different place depending on how your X11 is installed; on Mac OS X, which does not come with X by default, you might find it in */usr/X11R6/etc/app-defaults* in one popular install or */usr/local/lib/X11/app-defaults* in another.) The function of these files is discussed in the next section. For now, be aware that all of the resources contained in these files begin with the class name of the application.

Also be aware that *appres* has one serious limitation: it cannot distinguish between valid and invalid resource specifications. It lists all resources that might apply to a client, regardless of whether the resources are correctly specified.

appres lists the resources that apply to a client having the `class_name` and/or `instance_name` you specify. Typically, you would use *appres* before running a client program to find out what resources the client program will access.

For example, say you want to run *xterm*, but you can't remember the latest resources you've specified for it, whether you've loaded them, what some of the application defaults are, etc. You can use the *appres* client to check the current *xterm* resources. If you specify only a class name, as in this command line:[*]

    % **appres XTerm**

appres lists the resources that any *xterm* would load. In the case of *xterm*, this is an extensive list, encompassing all of the system-wide application defaults, as well as any other defaults you have specified in a resource file.

---

[*] The class name of *xterm* starts with *two* uppercase letters; this is contrary to the naming scheme followed by most other application classes.

You can also specify an instance name to list the resources that applies to a particular instance of the client, as in:

    % **appres XTerm bigxterm**

If you omit the class name, *xappres* assumes the class -NoSuchClass-, which has no defaults, and returns only the resources that would be loaded by the particular instance of the client.

Note that the instance can simply be the client name, e.g., xterm. In that case none of the system-wide application defaults would be listed, since all begin with the class name XTerm. For example, the command:

    % **appres xterm**

might return resources settings similar to these:

```
xterm.vt100.scrollBar:   True
xterm*PhonyResource:     youbet
xterm*pointerShape:      gumby
xterm*iconGeometry:      +50+50
*VT100.Translations:     #override\
    Button1 <Btn3Down>:    select-end(CLIPBOARD)\n\
    ~Ctrl ~Meta <Btn2Up>: insert-selection(primary,CLIPBOARD)
```

Most of these resources set obvious features of *xterm*. The translation table sets up *xterm* to use the *xclipboard*. Notice also that *appres* has returned an invalid resource called PhonyResource that we created for demonstration purposes. You can't rely on *appres* to tell you what resources a client will actually load because the *appres* program cannot distinguish a valid resource specification from an invalid one. Still, it can be fairly useful to jog your memory as to the defaults you've specified in your *.Xresources* file, as well as the system-wide application defaults.

—*VQ and SJC*

6.10 Starting Remote X Clients

One of the unique advantages of window systems such as X is that you can run applications remotely and view them on the local display (as opposed to systems that merely allow for the execution of shared applications by the local host, such as Windows and the Mac OS prior to OS X). Even Mac OS X, except insofar as it can run an X server, does not allow for a split between an application's display and its execution. Only X-aware applications may be executed in such a fashion.

Starting Remote X Clients from Interactive Logins

You can try this easily enough by doing an *rlogin* or *telnet** to the remote host, setting the DISPLAY environment variable and starting up an X client. Of course, it helps to have an X server already running on your local machine. In the following example, we start up a new *xload* client running on the host *ruby*:

```
sapphire:joan % rlogin ruby
Password:
Last login: Mon Mar 12 16:27:23 from sapphire.oreilly.com
NetBSD 1.4.2A (ORA-GENERIC) #6: Wed May 31 06:12:46 EEST 2000

TERM = (vt100) xterm

ruby:joan % setenv DISPLAY sapphire:0
ruby:joan % xload &
```

(You must, of course, have an account on the remote system.)

The first thing that might go wrong is that you may run into server access control. If you see the following error:

```
Xlib: connection to "sapphire:0" refused by server
Xlib: Client is not authorized to connect to Server
Error: Can't open display: sapphire:0
```

you can probably fix it by typing xhost +ruby in a *sapphire* window and running the command again on *ruby*.[†]

Once you have networking and access control issues solved, you should be able to display clients from the remote machine. The next issue is how to run remote clients *easily*.

If you have *ssh* (1.21), its X forwarding handles authorization (setting *DISPLAY*) and also encrypts the connection to make it secure. Here's an example using *ssh* for an interactive login:

```
sapphire:joan % ssh ruby
joan's passphrase:
Last login: Mon Mar 12 16:27:23 from sapphire.oreilly.com
NetBSD 1.4.2A (ORA-GENERIC) #6: Wed May 31 06:12:46 EEST 2000

TERM = (vt100) xterm

ruby:joan % xload &
```

---

* Most of the recent distributions of Unix default to the use of *ssh* as a secure replacement for the various r* command, (rsh, rcp, rlogin, et al.), so you may want to skip ahead to Chapter 5.

† The security-conscious may prefer to use the fully qualified domain name on the *xhost* command line (such as xhost +ruby.oreilly.com).

Starting a Remote Client with rsh and ssh

If you have *ssh*, that's the easiest way to start a remote client:

```
sapphire:joan % ssh ruby -n xterm &
```

If you aren't running an SSH agent, you'll need to enter your password before the remote command can run. If you have trouble, try the *ssh –f* option—with no ampersand (&) at the end of the command line.

If you don't have *ssh*, the best way to start a remote client is the same way you'd start any remote command: using the *rsh* command:

```
sapphire:joan % rsh ruby -n xterm -display sapphire:0
```

There are a few issues to be ironed out first, though.

To run *rsh* successfully, make sure that you have permission to run remote shells on the remote machine. This means that the local machine must be listed either in the remote machine's */etc/hosts.equiv* file or in your personal *$HOME/.rhosts* file on the remote machine. For example, an *.rhosts* file might read:

```
sapphire.ora.com
harry.ora.com
```

If the host is properly set up on the remote machine, then *rsh* will execute properly, and *rlogin* will no longer ask for a password when you try to connect to the remote machine. If it is not set up properly, then *rlogin* will prompt for a password, and *rsh* will fail with the message Permission denied.

Using *.rhosts* or */etc/hosts.equiv* for this purpose might be considered a breach of security: it means that if someone breaks into your account on one machine, he can break into your account on all other machines as well. Clearly, you want to be careful what hosts you list in *.rhosts*. For that reason, it's better to use the fully qualified domain name (i.e., *harry.ora.com* instead of just *harry*).

There are a few more rules:

- For security reasons, the *.rhosts* file will be ignored if it is publically writable. Make sure that the *.rhosts* file is writable only by you.
- Make sure that you are running the correct *rsh* command. Some systems have a *restricted* shell, also named *rsh*. If you get the following error:

  ```
  ruby: ruby: No such file or directory
  ```

  or:

  ```
  ruby: ruby: cannot open
  ```

  where ruby is the name of the system that you wanted to run the remote shell on, the problem is probably that you are using the wrong *rsh* command. Use the *which* (2.6) or *whereis* (2.3) command to see which *rsh* you are using:

```
sapphire:joan % which rsh
/bin/rsh
sapphire:joan % echo $path
/bin /usr/bin /usr/bin/X11 /usr/bsd
```

On some System V–derived systems such as IRIX, the restricted shell *rsh* might live in */bin*, while the remote shell *rsh* (the one you want) resides in */usr/bsd*. */bin* often shows up in search paths earlier than */usr/bsd*, so on those systems you need to redefine your path explicitly so that */usr/bsd* is searched before */bin*. Alternately, you can supply the full path to the command when you invoke it.

- You may need to append the *–n* option to *rsh* to avoid a Stopped error message on some machines.

- You need to be sure that the directory containing X binaries is defined in your search path in your shell setup file (3.3) on the remote system.

- If you are using host-based access control, you need to execute the *xhost* client to extend access to the remote host before the *rsh* command is run. Otherwise, clients from the remote host will not have permission to access your display. If you are using user-based access control, you may need to run the *xauth* command to copy your access code to the remote machine.

- You have to use the *–display* option in calling a remote shell, or the Can't Open display error will be returned. (Alternatively, you can have your DISPLAY environment variable hard-coded into your shell setup file (3.3) on the remote machine, but this is a *very bad idea*.) See article 35.8 for more information on setting your display.

- Be careful not to use unix:0.0 or :0.0 as the display name! Otherwise, the client will display the window on the local display of the remote host. If this succeeds, the user on that display could either become very annoyed or take advantage of the sudden access to your account by reading personal files and sending nasty mail to your boss. You would have no warning; all you would know is that your window didn't appear. So, before running *another* client, you may want to log in to the remote system and do a *ps* to ensure that you're not already running the application on the remote display.

ssh expects slightly different files than does *rsh*, although the server may be configured to allow the use of both *.rhosts* and *.shosts*, as well as the system-level */etc/hosts.equiv* and */etc/ssh/shosts.equiv* files. Many administrators have wisely chosen to avoid *rsh* and related commands altogether, even to the point of disallowing fallback to *rsh* from a *ssh* login attempt. More information about the peculiarities of *ssh* may be found in Chapter 51.

—LM, EP, JP, and SJC

Part III

Working with Files and Directories

Part III contains the following chapters:

7

Directory Organization

7.1 What? Me, Organized?

Computers and offices have one thing in common: you lose things in them. If you walk into my office, you'll see stacks of paper on top of other stacks of paper, with a few magazines and business cards in the mix. I can often find things, but I'd be lying if I said that I could *always* find that article I was reading the other day!

When you look at a new computer user's home directory (31.11) , you often see something similar to my office. You see a huge number of unrelated files with obscure names. He hasn't created any subdirectories, aside from those the system administrator told him they needed; and those probably aren't even being used. His home directory probably contains programs for several different projects, personal mail, notes from meetings, a few data files, some half-finished documentation, a spreadsheet for something he started last month but has now forgotten, and so on.

Remember that a computer's filesystem isn't that much different from any other filing system. If you threw all of your papers into one giant filing cabinet without sorting them into different topics and subtopics, the filing cabinet wouldn't do you much good at all: it would just be a mess. On a computer, the solution to this problem is to sort your files into *directories*, which are analogous to the filing cabinets and drawers.

The *Unix filesystem* can help you keep all of your material neatly sorted. Your directories are like filing cabinets, with dividers and folders inside them. In this chapter, we'll give some hints for organizing your computer "office." Of course, things occasionally get misplaced even in the most efficient offices. Later we'll show some scripts that use the *find* (8.3) and *grep* (9.21) commands to help you find files that are misplaced.

—ML

7.2 Many Homes

Various operating systems store users' home directories in many places, and you've probably already noticed evidence of this throughout this book. Home directories may be in */home/username*, */u/username*, */Users/username*, or some other, more esoteric location.

The simplest way to find out where your system believes your home directory to be is to take advantage of the fact that *cd* with no arguments changes to your home directory:

```
% cd
% pwd
/home/users/deb
```

Generally, the $HOME environment variable will point to your home directory:

```
% echo $HOME
/home/users/deb
```

Most shells also expand tilde (~) to a user's home directory as well, so *~/archive* on my machine becomes */home/users/deb/archive* and *~joel/tmp* expands to */home/users/joel/tmp*.

Your home directory is set in your */etc/passwd* entry (or equivalent—Netinfo on Darwin and NIS on Solaris store the same information, for example). There is no actual requirement that all users' home directories be in the same directory. In fact, I've seen systems that have lots of users organize home directories by the first few letters of the username (so my home directory there was */home/d/de/deb*).

If you add user accounts using a tool rather than by using *vipw* and adding them by hand, take a peek at the documentation for your tool. It should tell you both where it wants to put home directories by default and how to change that default should you want to.

—*DJPH*

7.3 Access to Directories

Unix uses the same mode bits (50.2) for directories as for files, but they are interpreted differently. This interpretation will make sense if you remember that a directory is nothing more than a list of files. Creating a file, renaming a file, or deleting a file from a directory requires changing this list: therefore, you need write access to the directory to create or delete a file. Modifying a file's contents does not require you to change the directory; therefore, you can modify files even if you don't have write access to the directory (provided that you have write access to the file).

Reading a directory is relatively straightforward: you need read access to list the contents of a directory (find out what files it contains, etc.). If you don't have read access, you can't list the contents of the directory. However (surprise!), you may still be able to access files in the directory, provided that you already know their names.

Execute access for a directory has no meaning per se, so the designers of Unix have reassigned this. It is called the *search bit*. Search access is needed to perform any operation within a directory and its subdirectories. In other words, if you deny execute access to a directory, you are effectively denying access to the directory and everything beneath it in the directory tree. Note that providing search access to a directory without read access prevents people from listing the directory, but allows them to access files if they know their names. This is particularly useful in situations where you want to allow public access to areas, but only to people who know exactly what files to access; files available via a web server are a good example.

The SUID bit (50.4) is meaningless for directories, but the SGID bit set on a directory affects group ownership of files created in that directory, and the sticky bit prohibits users with write access to the directory from deleting or renaming files that they don't own.

The exception is, of course, that the superuser can do absolutely anything at any time.

—ML

7.4 A bin Directory for Your Programs and Scripts

If you compile programs or write shell scripts, it's good to put them in one directory. This can be a subdirectory of your home directory. Or, if several people want to use these programs, you could pick any other directory—as long as you have write access to it. Usually, the directory's name is something like *bin*—though I name mine *.bin* (with a leading dot) to keep it from cluttering my *ls* listings.

For instance, to make a *bin* under your home directory, type:

```
% cd
% mkdir bin
```

Once you have a directory for storing programs, be sure that the shell can find the programs in it. Type the command *echo $PATH* and look for the directory's pathname. For instance, if your directory is called */u/walt/bin*, you should see:

```
% echo $PATH
...:/u/walt/bin:...
```

If the directory isn't in your *PATH*, add it in your *.profile* or *.cshrc*.

If other people are using your *bin* directory, use a command like *chmod go+rx bin* to give them access. If you're concerned about security, prevent unauthorized users from adding, removing, or renaming files in your directory by making sure that only you have write access; you can do this with a command like *chmod go-w bin*. Also be sure that individual files can't be edited by people who shouldn't have access to the files.

When you add a new program to your *bin* directory, if you use the C shell or a C-shell derivative, you need to use the shell's *rehash* command to update its command search path.

—JP

7.5 Private (Personal) Directories

You might want to create a private directory for your personal files: love letters, financial data, complaints about your boss, off-color jokes, or whatever you want to keep there. While you can set any directory you own to be private, having one in your home directory is convenient to organize all of your private directories together. For simplicity, you can just name it *private*; giving it a less obvious name, however, can make it more difficult for prying eyes to discover.

Once you've created a private directory, you should set its *file access mode* (50.2) to 700; this means that you're the only person allowed to read, write, or even list the files that are in the directory. Here's how:

```
% mkdir private
% chmod 700 private
```

On any Unix system, anyone who knows the root password can become *superuser* (49.9) and read any files he wants. So a private personal directory doesn't give you complete protection by any means—especially on systems where most users know the root password. If you really need security, you can always encrypt your files.

—ML and DJPH

7.6 Naming Files

Let's think about a filing cabinet again. If the files in your filing cabinet were called *letter1*, *letter2*, *letter3*, and so on, you'd never be able to find anything—the names aren't descriptive enough. The same is true on your computer—you should come up with a descriptive name for each file that you create. Unix systems let you have very long filenames. A few older systems have a 14-character limit, but most allow names that are 256 characters long—hopefully, longer than you will ever need.

Generally, a descriptive filename summarizes the contents with a few useful words. *letter* is not a terribly useful summary, unless perhaps you've only ever written one letter and don't expect to write another. The recipient's name (*JohnShmoe*, for example) would only be a useful summary if you expect to send only one letter to that person. Even if you only plan to send one letter, the name doesn't tell you anything about what you sent Mr. Shmoe.

OctoberGoldPriceTrends is a pretty good summary; it's obvious what the contents of that file are, though you might want to know to which year it referred, looking back two years from now. I often start time-specific files with the date, so that *ls* sorts the files in date order. If you do this, I recommend a *YYYYMMDD* format to get proper sorting, so files look like *20021004-GoldPrices*. If you're going to have regular updates to something, you might want to make a directory to hold those things (e.g., *GoldPrices/20021004*, *GoldPrices/20021108*, *GoldPrices/20021206*, and so forth). Note that in this specific example, a filename of nothing but a date makes sense, because you don't have anything else in that directory but information on gold prices.

Bruce Barnett has suggested that, by using long filenames, you can create a simple "relational database." For example, you could find out everything you've recorded about the price of gold with a command like *more *Gold*Price**. Of course, if this starts to get very complex, using an actual database is much simpler.

Similarly, if you're a programmer, the name of each file in your program should describe what the code does. If the code diagonalizes matrices, the file should be called something like *MatrixDiagonalizer.cpp*. If the code reads input from bank tellers, it should be called something like *teller_input.c*. Some programming languages even enforce this by requiring a particular file-naming convention; Java requires files to have only one object per file, and the name of the file and the object within it must be the same. (Of course, if your object names aren't very good, you're right back where you started.)

—*DJPH*

7.7 Make More Directories!

Creating many directories has several advantages:

- First, it is easier to find any particular file if your home directory is well sorted. Imagine a rack of filing cabinets that isn't sorted; people just insert files wherever they fit. You may as well throw your data out; when you need something, you'll never be able to find it.

- Second, Unix can access files much faster when directories are relatively small. Ideally, directories should have at most 60 files in them.

- Third, directories are an important part of Unix file protections. By setting the permissions on the directories themselves, you can use directories to help protect certain groups of files against access by others.

Create new directories liberally! Make a new directory for every new project you start; make subdirectories within these directories for subtopics. Your home directory should ideally contain *nothing* but subdirectories. Following are some recommended conventions.

If you're a programmer, create a new directory for each project. In the project directory, create a directory called *src* for source files, a directory called *doc* or *man* for documentation, a directory called *obj* for object files, a directory called *rel* for the current working version (or almost-working version) of the program, a directory called *test* for test files and results, and so on. If the program is large, your *src* and *obj* directories should also be split into different subdirectories, each containing different parts of the project (or perhaps the subdirectory for each part of the project should have its own *src* and *obj* directories).

Many users save all of their mail in one directory (often called *Mail* or *Maildir*, depending on your mail system), which is then divided into subdirectories by topic. I use a variation of this scheme; I keep general mail in my *Mail* directory, but I save correspondence about particular projects with the project itself. For example, my Power Tools mail is shelved with the source code for this article.

—*ML*

7.8 Making Directories Made Easier

Earlier we told you that you should have lots of directories. Experienced Unix users are creating new directories all the time. How do you make a directory?

It's easy. Use the *mkdir* command, followed by the name of your new directory:

```
% mkdir directory
```

This creates the new directory you want. It doesn't necessarily have to be in your current directory. For example:

```
% cd /home/los/mikel
% mkdir /src/books/power/articles/files
```

The only requirements are:

- The parent of the directory you want to create must exist (in this case, */src/ books/power/articles*).
- You must have write access to the parent directory.

What if the parent directory doesn't already exist? Assume, for example, that */src/books* already exists, but the *power* and *articles* directories do not. You can make these "by hand," or on many Unix systems you can add the *–p* (parents) option:

```
% mkdir -p /src/books/power/articles/files
```

This tells *mkdir* to create all the intermediate directories that are needed. So the previous command creates three directories:

```
/src/books/power
/src/books/power/articles
/src/books/power/articles/files
```

If your *mkdir* doesn't have *–p*, you can use *history substitution*:

```
% mkdir /src/books/power
% !!/articles
mkdir /src/books/power/articles
% !!/files
mkdir /src/books/power/articles/files
```

On some *mkdirs*, you can also supply the *file protection mode* to be assigned to the directory. (By default, the file protection mode is derived from your umask.) To do so, use the *–m* option. For example:

```
% mkdir -m 755 /src/books/power/articles/files
```

This creates the directory with access mode 755, which allows the owner to do anything with the directory. Note that this must be a *numeric* mode.

—*ML*

8

Directories and Files

8.1 Everything but the find Command

A computer isn't that much different from a house or an office; unless you're incredibly orderly, you spend a lot of time looking for things that you've misplaced. Even if you are incredibly orderly, you still spend some time looking for things you need—you just have a better idea of where to find them. After all, librarians don't memorize the location of every book in the stacks, but they do know how to find any book, quickly and efficiently, using whatever tools are available. A key to becoming a proficient user of any system, then, is knowing how to find things.

This chapter is about how to find things. We're excluding the *find* (9.1) utility itself because it's complicated and deserves a chapter of its own. We'll concentrate on simpler ways to find files, beginning with some different ways to use *ls*.

Well, okay, towards the end of the chapter we'll touch on a few simple uses of *find*, but to really get into *find*, take a peek at chapter Chapter 9.

—*ML*

8.2 The Three Unix File Times

When you're talking to experienced Unix users, you often hear the terms "change time" and "modification time" thrown around casually. To most people (and most dictionaries), "change" and "modification" are the same thing. What's the difference here?

The difference between a change and a modification is the difference between altering the label on a package and altering its contents. If someone says *chmod a–w myfile*, that is a change; if someone says *echo foo >> myfile*, that is a modification. A change modifies the file's inode; a modification modifies the contents of the file itself. A file's modification time is also called the *timestamp*.

As long as we're talking about change times and modification times, we might as well mention "access times," too. The access time is the last time the file was read or written. So reading a file updates its access time, but not its change time (information about the file wasn't changed) or its modification time (the file itself wasn't changed).

Incidentally, the change time or "ctime" is incorrectly documented as the "creation time" in many places, including some Unix manuals. Do not believe them.

—CT

8.3 Finding Oldest or Newest Files with ls –t and ls –u

Your directory might have 50, 100, or more files. Which files haven't been used for a while? You might save space by removing them. You read or edited a file yesterday, but you can't remember its name? These commands will help you find it. (If you want a quick review of Unix file times, see article 8.2.)

In this example, I'll show you my *bin* (7.4) directory full of shell scripts and other programs—I want to see which programs I don't use very often. You can use the same technique for directories with text or other files.

The *ls* command has options to change the way it orders files. By default, *ls* lists files alphabetically. For finding old files, use the *–t* option. This sorts files by their *modification time*, or the last time the file was changed. The newest files are listed first. Here's what happens:

```
jerry@ora ~/.bin
60 % ls -t
weather      unshar       scandrafts   rn2mh        recomp
crontab      zloop        tofrom       rmmer        mhprofile
rhyes        showpr       incc         mhadd        append
rhno         rfl          drmm         fixsubj      README
pickthis     maillog      reheader     distprompter rtfm
cgrep        c-w          zrefile      xmhprint     saveart
dirtop       cw           zscan        replf        echoerr
which        cx           zfolders     fols
tcx          showmult     alifile      incs
```

I just added a shell script named *weather* yesterday; you can see it as the first file in the first column. I also made a change to my script named *crontab* last week; it's shown next. The oldest program in here is *echoerr*; it's listed last.*

---

* On some systems, *ls –t* will list the files in one column, with the newest file first. Although that's usually a pain, I actually find that more convenient when I'm interested in the most recent files. If your system does that and you don't like the single-column display, you can use *ls –Ct*. On other systems, if a single-column display would be handy, use *ls –1t*; the "1" option means "one column." You can also use *ls –lt*, since long listings also list one file per line. Throughout this article, we'll assume you're using an *ls* version that makes multicolumn output.

ls –t is also great for file-time comparisons in a script (8.15). *ls –t* is quite useful when I've forgotten whether I've edited a file recently. If I've changed a file, it will be at or near the top of the *ls –t* listing. For example, I might ask, "Have I made the changes to that letter I was going to send?" If I haven't made the changes (but only think I have), my letter will most likely appear somewhere in the middle of the listing.

The *–u* option shows the files' last-access time instead of the last-modification time. The *–u* option doesn't do anything with plain *ls*—you have to use it with another option like *–t* or *–l*. The next listing shows that I've recently used the *rtfm* and *rmmer* files. I haven't read *README* in a long time, though—oops:

```
jerry@ora ~/.bin
62 % ls -tu
rtfm          cx            drmm          saveart       fixsubj
rmmer         c-w           zscan         scandrafts    echoerr
rfl           cw            zrefile       rhno          dirtop
mhprofile     distprompter  xmhprint      rhyes         cgrep
showmult      recomp        zloop         replf         append
tcx           crontab       zfolders      reheader      alifile
tofrom        mhadd         which         incs          README
rn2mh         pickthis      unshar        maillog
weather       incc          showpr        fols
```

(Some Unixes don't update the last-access time of executable files when you run them. Shell scripts are always read, so their last-access times will always be updated.)

The *–c* option shows when the file's inode information was last changed. The inode time tells when the file was created, when you used *chmod* to change the permissions, and so on.

```
jerry@ora ~/.bin
64 % ls -tc
weather       maillog       reheader      recomp        incs
crontab       tcx           rn2mh         fols          cx
cgrep         zscan         tofrom        rmmer         cw
zloop         zrefile       mhadd         fixsubj       c-w
dirtop        rfl           drmm          mhprofile     echoerr
pickthis      showmult      alifile       append        which
rhno          rtfm          showpr        saveart       README
unshar        incc          scandrafts    distprompter
rhyes         zfolders      xmhprint      replf
```

If you're wondering just how long ago a file was modified (or accessed), add the *–l* option for a long listing. As before, adding *–u* shows the last-access time; *–c* shows inode change time. If I look at the access times of a few specific files, I find that I haven't read *README* since 2001.

```
jerry@ora ~/.bin
65 % ls -ltu README alifile maillog
-rwxr-xr-x  1 jerry    ora              59 Feb  2 2002 maillog
-rwxr-xr-x  1 jerry    ora             213 Nov 29 2001 alifile
-rw-r--r--  1 jerry    ora            3654 Nov 27 2001 README
```

—JP

8.4 List All Subdirectories with ls –R

By default, *ls* lists just one directory. If you name one or more directories on the command line, *ls* will list each one. The –R (uppercase R) option lists all subdirectories, recursively. That shows you the whole directory tree starting at the current directory (or the directories you name on the command line).

This list can get pretty long; you might want to pipe the output to a pager program such as *less* (12.3). The *ls* –C option is a good idea, too, to list the output in columns. (When the *ls* output goes to a pipe, many versions of *ls* won't make output in columns automatically.)

—JP

8.5 The ls –d Option

If you give *ls* the pathname of a directory, *ls* lists the entries in the directory:

```
% ls -l /home/joanne
total 554
-rw-r--r--  1 joanne        15329 Oct  5 14:33 catalog
-rw-------  1 joanne        58381 Oct 10 09:08 mail
    ...
```

With the *–d* option, *ls* lists the directory itself:

```
% ls -ld /home/joanne
drwxr-x--x  7 joanne         4608 Oct 10 10:13 /home/joanne
```

The *–d* option is especially handy when you're trying to list the names of some directories that match a wildcard. Compare the listing with and without the *–d* option:

```
% ls -Fd [a-c]*
arc/                    bm/                     ctrl/
atcat.c                 cdecl/
atl.c.Z                 cleanscript.c
% ls -F [a-c]*
atcat.c                 atl.c.Z                 cleanscript.c

arc:
BugsEtc.Z      arcadd.c         arcext.c.Z      arcmisc.c.Z
    ...
```

```
bm:
Execute.c.Z    MakeDesc.c.Z    MkDescVec.c.Z    Search.c.Z
   ...
```

—JP

8.6 Color ls

The GNU *ls* command—which is on a lot of systems, including Linux—can display names in colors. For instance, when I enable color listings on my system, directory names are in dark blue, symbolic links are in sky blue, executable files (scripts, programs, etc.) are in green, and so on.

tcsh's built-in *ls –F* command can display in colors, too. Just *set color* in your *.cshrc* to enable it, and configure it using LS_COLORS as described later in this section. You may also want to look at the section "Another color ls" for another way to configure colors if *––color* doesn't seem to work.

Trying It

GNU ls

Has your system been set up for this? Simply try this command:

```
$ ls --color / /bin
```

If you don't get an error (*ls: no such option --color*, or something similar), you should see colors. If you don't get an error, but you also don't get colors, try one of these commands, and see what you get:

```
$ ls --color=always / /bin | cat -v
^[[00m/:
^[[01;34mbin^[[00m
^[[01;34mboot^[[00m

   ...
^[[01;34mvar^[[00m

/bin:
^[[01;32march^[[00m
^[[01;36mawk^[[00m
^[[01;32mbasename^[[00m

   ...
```

```
$ ls --color=yes / /bin | cat -v
   ...same kind of output...
```

Those extra characters surrounding the filenames, such as ^[[01;34m and ^[[00m, are the escape sequences that (you hope) make the colors. (The *cat –v* (12.4) command makes the sequences visible, if there are any to see.) The ^[is an ESC character; the next [starts a formatting code; the 01 code means "boldface"; the semicolon (;) is a code separator; the 34 means "blue"; and the m ends the escape sequence. ^[[00m is an escape sequence that resets the attributes to normal. If you see the escape sequences when you use cat -v, but you haven't gotten any highlighting effects when you don't use it, there's probably some kind of mismatch between your termcap or terminfo entry (5.2) (which should define the sequences) and the color database (see later in this section). If you don't see the escape sequences at all, take a look at Chapter 8 for another way to configure color *ls*.

Configuring It

How are the colors set? Both GNU *ls* and *tcsh*'s *ls −F* use the LS_COLORS environment variable to decide how to format filenames. Here's a sample (truncated and split onto three lines for printing):

```
$ echo $LS_COLORS
LS_COLORS=no=00:fi=00:di=01;34:ln=01;36:pi=40;33:so=01;35:
bd=40;33;01:cd=40;33;01:or=01;05;37;41:mi=01;05;37;41:ex=01;32:
*.cmd=01;32:*.exe=01;32:*.com=01;32:*.btm=01;32:*.bat=01;32:
  ...
```

The *LS_COLORS* value is a series of *item=attribute* values with a colon (:) between each pair. For instance, fi=00 means that files have the attribute (color) *00*; di=01;34 means that directories have the attributes *01* (bold) and *34* (blue); and *.exe=01;32 means that filenames ending with *.exe* have the attributes *01* (bold) and *32* (green). There can be up to three numbers. The first is an attribute code (bold, underscore, etc.); the second is a foreground color; the third is a background color. So, 01;37;41 indicates boldfaced white foreground (37) text on a red background (41).

The format is fairly obtuse, so you won't want to set *LS_COLORS* directly if you don't have to. The easy way to set it is with the *dircolors* command—typically in a shell setup file (3.3):

eval **27.8**
'...' **28.14**
```
eval `dircolors`
```

There, *dircolors* is reading the default database and outputting a command to set *LS_COLORS*. What if you don't want the default database settings? You can make your own. An easy place to start is with *dircolors −p*, which outputs a copy of the database. You can redirect the output to a file; a good option is to use a *.dircolorsrc* file in your home directory. Then take a look at it:

```
$ dircolors -p > $HOME/.dircolorsrc
$ cat $HOME/.dircolorsrc
   ...
# Below should be one TERM entry for each colorizable termtype
TERM linux
   ...
TERM vt100

# Below are the color init strings for the basic file types. A color
# init string consists of one or more of the following numeric codes:
```

```
# Attribute codes:
# 00=none 01=bold 04=underscore 05=blink 07=reverse 08=concealed
# Text color codes:
# 30=black 31=red 32=green 33=yellow 34=blue 35=magenta 36=cyan 37=white
# Background color codes:
# 40=black 41=red 42=green 43=yellow 44=blue 45=magenta 46=cyan 47=white
NORMAL 00     # global default, although everything should be something.
FILE 00       # normal file
DIR 01;34     # directory
LINK 01;36    # symbolic link
   ...

# List any file extensions like '.gz' or '.tar' that you would like ls
# to colorize below. Put the extension, a space, and the color init string.
# (and any comments you want to add after a '#')
.tar 01;31 # archives or compressed (bright red)
.tgz 01;31
   ...
```

The file starts with a listing of terminal type (5.3) names that understand the color escape sequences listed in this file. Fortunately, the escape sequences are almost universal; there are some old terminals (like my old Tektronix 4106, I think... R.I.P.) that don't understand these, but not many. (If you have a different terminal or an odd terminal emulator, you can select a setup file automatically as you log in (3.10).) The second section has a commented-out list of the attributes that these terminals recognize. You can use that list in the third section—which has standard attributes for files, directories, and so on. The fourth section lets you choose attributes for files by their filename "extensions"—that is, the part of the filename after the final dot (like *.tar*).

If you make your own database, you'll need to use it (again, typically in a shell setup file) to set *LS_COLORS*:

```
eval `dircolors $HOME/.dircolorsrc`
```

The --color Option

For better or for worse, the way to activate color *ls* is by using the --color option on the command line. Because almost no one will want to type those characters every time they run *ls*, most users need to make an alias (29.2, 29.4) for *ls* that runs ls --color. For example, here are the three aliases defined for *bash* on my Linux system:

```
alias l.='ls .[a-zA-Z]* --color=auto'
alias ll='ls -l --color=auto'
alias ls='ls --color=auto'
```

If you're using *tcsh*, setting the color variable to enable *ls –F*'s color also arranges to send *--color=auto* to regular *ls*.

The *--color* option gives you three choices of when the *ls* output should be colored: *--color=never* to never output color, *--color=always* to always output color, and *--color=auto* to only output color escape sequences if the standard output of *ls* is a terminal. I suggest using *--color=auto*, because *--color=always* means that when you pipe the output of *ls* to a printer or redirect it to a file, it will still have the ugly escape sequences you saw earlier in this article.

Another color ls

Some systems have another way to configure and use color *ls*. My FreeBSD systems use this scheme; if none of the configuration techniques described earlier work, use *ls –G* or set the CLICOLOR environment variable. If this works, you'll want to use the LSCOLORS environment variable to configure color information instead of LS_COLORS as described earlier. Spend a little time perusing your *ls(1)* manpage for further details if your *ls* seems to work this way, as configuring it is likely to be completely different from what we described previously.

—JP and DJPH

8.7 Some GNU ls Features

A lot of the GNU utilities came from Unix utilities—but with extra features. The GNU *ls* command is no exception: as its *info* page (2.9) says, "Because *ls* is such a fundamental program, it has accumulated many options over the years." Amen. Let's look at three of the options that aren't covered by other articles on *ls*.

An Emacs editor backup file (19.4) has a name ending in ~ (tilde). If you use Emacs a lot, these files can really clutter your directories. The *ls –B* option ignores Emacs backup files:

```
$ ls
bar.c bar.c~ baz.c baz.c~ foo.c foo.c~
$ ls -B
bar.c baz.c foo.c
```

The option *–I* (uppercase letter *I*) takes *–B* one step further: you can give a wild-card expression (shell wildcard pattern, not *grep*-like expressions) for entries *not* to list. (Remember that—because you want to pass the wildcard pattern to *ls*, and *not* let the shell expand it first—you need to quote (27.12) the pattern.) For instance, to skip all filenames ending in *.a* and *.o*, use the wildcard pattern **.[ao]*, like this:

```
$ ls
bar.a bar.c bar.o baz.a baz.c baz.o foo.a foo.c foo.o
$ ls -I "*.[ao]"
bar.c baz.c foo.c
```

The "minimalist" side of me might argue that both *–B* and *–I* are feeping creatures because you can get basically the same effect by combining plain old *ls* with one of the "not this file" shell wildcard operators. This next option is in the same category. Instead of using *–S* to sort the files by size, you could pipe the output of plain *ls –l* to *sort –n* (22.5) and sort on the size field, then strip off the information you didn't want and…ahem. (Grumble, grumble.) Okay, *–S* really is pretty useful. ;-) I use it a lot when I'm cleaning out directories and want to find the most effective files to remove:

```
$ ls -lS
total 1724
-rw-rw-r--  1 jerry  ora  395927 Sep  9 06:21 SunTran_map.pdf
-rw-------  1 jerry  ora  389120 Oct 31 09:55 core
-rw-r--r--  1 jerry  ora  178844 May  8 16:36 how
-rw-------  1 jerry  ora   77122 Oct 29 08:46 dead.letter
   ...
```

—*JP*

8.8 A csh Alias to List Recently Changed Files

Looking for a recently changed file? Not sure of the name? Trying to do this in a directory with lots of files? Try the *lr* alias:

```
alias lr "ls -lagFqt \!* | head"
```

This alias takes advantage of the *–t* option (8.3) to *ls*, so that recent files can float to the top of the listing. !* is the *csh* syntax for "put all of the arguments to the alias here." (We have to escape the exclamation point to keep it from being interpreted when we set the alias.) *head* (12.12) shows just the first ten lines.

A simple *lr* in my home directory gives me:

```
bermuda:home/dansmith :-) lr
total 1616
-rw-------  1 dansmith staff  445092 Oct  7 20:11 .mush256
-rw-r--r--  1 dansmith staff    1762 Oct  7 20:11 .history
drwxr-xr-x 30 dansmith staff    1024 Oct  7 12:59 text/
-rw-------  1 dansmith staff  201389 Oct  7 12:42 .record
drwxr-xr-x 31 dansmith staff    1024 Oct  4 09:41 src/
-rw-r--r--  1 dansmith staff    4284 Oct  4 09:02 .mushrc
   ...
```

You can also give a wildcarded pattern to narrow the search. For example, here's the command to show me the dot files that have changed lately:

```
bermuda:home/dansmith :-) lr .??*
-rw-------  1 dansmith staff  445092 Oct  7 20:11 .mush256
-rw-r--r--  1 dansmith staff    1762 Oct  7 20:11 .history
```

```
-rw-------  1 dansmith staff    201389 Oct  7 12:42 .record
-rw-r--r--  1 dansmith staff      4284 Oct  4 09:02 .mushrc
   ...
```

—DS

8.9 Showing Hidden Files with ls –A and –a

The *ls* command normally ignores any files whose names begin with a dot (.). This is often very convenient: Unix has lots of small configuration files, scratch files, etc. that you really don't care about and don't want to be bothered about most of the time. However, there are some times when you care very much about these files. If you want to see "hidden" files, use the command *ls –a*. For example:

```
% cd
% ls                                Don't show hidden files
Mail       mail.txt     performance  powertools
% ls -a                             This time, show me EVERYTHING
.          .emacs       Mail         powertools
..         .login       mail.txt
.cshrc     .mailrc      performance
```

With the –*a* option, we see four additional files: two C-shell initialization files, the customization files for the GNU Emacs editor, and *mail*. We also see two "special" entries, . and .., which represent the current directory and the parent of the current directory. All Unix directories contain these two entries (10.2).

If you don't want to be bothered with . and .., many versions of *ls* also have a –*A* option:

```
% ls -A    Show me everything but . and ..
.cshrc     .login       Mail         performance
.emacs     .mailrc      mail.txt     powertools
```

—ML

8.10 Useful ls Aliases

Because *ls* is one of the most commonly used Unix commands and provides numerous options, it's a good idea to create aliases for the display formats that best suit your needs. For example, many users *always* want to know about their "hidden" files. That's reasonable—they're just as important as any other files you have. In some cases, they can grow to take up lots of room (for example, some editors hide backup files), so it's worth being aware of them.

Rather than typing *ls –a* every time, you can create a convenient alias that supplies the *–a* or *–A* option (8.9) automatically:

```
$ alias la="ls -aF"
% alias la ls -aF
```

or:

```
$ alias la="ls -AF"
% alias la ls -AF
```

Two things to note here. First, I recommend using *la* as the name of the alias, rather than just renaming *ls*. I personally think it's dangerous to hide the pure, unadulterated command underneath an alias; it's better to pick a new name and get used to using that name. If you ever need the original *ls* for some reason, you'll be able to get at it without problems.

Second, what's with the *–F* option? I just threw it in to see if you were paying attention. It's actually quite useful; many users add it to their *ls* aliases. The *–F* option shows you the *type* of file in each directory by printing an extra character after each filename. Table 8-1 lists what the extra character can be.

Table 8-1. Filename types listed by ls –F

Character	Definition
(nothing)	The file is a regular file.
*	The file is an executable.
/	The file is a directory.
@	The file is a symbolic link (10.4).
|	The file is a FIFO (named pipe) (43.11).
=	The file is a socket.

For example:

```
% la          Alias includes -F functionality
.cshrc   .login    Mail/        performance/
.emacs   .mailrc   mail.txt     powertools@
```

This says that *Mail* and *performance* are directories. *powertools* is a symbolic link (*ls –l* will show you what it's linked to). There are no executables, FIFOs, or sockets in this directory.

[If you use *tcsh*, it has a built-in *ls* called *ls –F*, which not only prints this extra information, but also supports color (8.6) and caching of filesystem information for speed. I generally put *alias ls ls –F* in my *.cshrc.* —DH]

You may want this version instead:

```
$ alias la="ls -aFC"
% alias la ls -aFC
```

The *–C* option lists the files in multiple columns. This option isn't needed with *ls* versions where multicolumn output is the normal behavior. Note, however, that when piped to another command, *ls* output is single-column unless *–C* is used. For example, use `ls -C | less` to preserve multiple columns with a paged listing.

Finally, if you often need the full listing, use the alias:

```
$ alias ll="ls -l"
% alias ll ls -l
```

This alias may not seem like much of a shortcut until after you've typed it a dozen times. In addition, it's easy to remember as "long listing." Some Unix systems even include *ll* as a regular command.

—DG and ML

8.11 Can't Access a File? Look for Spaces in the Name

What's wrong here?

```
% ls
afile    exefiles   j       toobig
% lpr afile
lpr: afile: No such file or directory
```

Huh? *ls* shows that the file is there, doesn't it? Try using:

```
% ls -l | cat -v -t -e
total 89$
-rw-rw-rw-  1 jerry       28 Mar  7 19:46 afile $
-rw-r--r--  1 root     25179 Mar  4 20:34 exefiles$
-rw-rw-rw-  1 jerry      794 Mar  7 14:23 j$
-rw-r--r--  1 root       100 Mar  5 18:24 toobig$
```

-v **12.4**
-t -e **12.5**

The *cat –e* option marks the ends of lines with a $. Notice that afile has a $ out past the end of the column. Aha...the filename ends with a space. Whitespace characters like TABs have the same problem, though the default *ls –q* (8.12) option (on many Unix versions) shows them as ? if you're using a terminal.

If you have the GNU version of *ls*, try its *–Q* option to put double quotes around each name:

```
$ ls -Q
"afile " "exefiles" "j" "toobig"
```

To rename *afile*, giving it a name without the space, type:

```
% mv "afile " afile
```

The quotes (27.12) tell the shell to include the space as part of the first argument it passes to *mv*. The same quoting works for other Unix commands as well, such as *rm*.

—JP

8.12 Showing Nonprintable Characters in Filenames

From time to time, you may get filenames with nonprinting characters, spaces, and other garbage in them. This is usually the result of some mistake—but it's a pain nevertheless.

If you're using a version of *ls* that uses *–q* by default (and most do these days), the *ls* command gives you some help; it converts all nonprinting characters to a question mark (?), giving you some idea that something funny is there.* For example:

```
% ls
ab??cd
```

This shows that there are two nonprinting characters between ab and cd. To delete (or rename) this file, you can use a wildcard pattern like *ab??cd*.

Be careful: when I was new to Unix, I once accidentally generated a lot of weird filenames. *ls* told me that they all began with ????, so I naively typed rm ????*. That's when my troubles began. See article 14.3 for the rest of the gruesome story. (I spent the next day and night trying to undo the damage.) The moral is: it's always a good idea to use *echo* to test filenames with wildcards in them.

If you're using an *ls* that came from System V Unix, you have a different set of problems. System V's *ls* doesn't convert the nonprinting characters to question marks. In fact, it doesn't do anything at all—it just spits these weird characters at your terminal, which can respond in any number of strange and hostile ways. Most of the nonprinting characters have special meanings—ranging from "don't take any more input" to "clear the screen." [If you don't have a System V *ls*, but you want this behavior for some reason, try GNU *ls* with its *–N* option. *—JP*]

To prevent this, or to see what's actually there instead of just the question marks, use the *–b* option.† This tells *ls* to print the octal value of any nonprinting characters, preceeded by a backslash. For example:

---

* Even in *ls*es that use it, the *–q* option is the default only when *ls*'s standard output is a terminal. If you pipe the output or redirect it to a file, remember to add *–q*.

† On systems that don't support *ls –b*, pipe the *ls –q* output through *cat –v* or *od –c* (12.4) to see what the nonprinting characters are.

```
% ls -b
ab\013\014cd
```

This shows that the nonprinting characters have octal values 13 and 14, respectively. If you look up these values in an ASCII table, you will see that they correspond to CTRL-k and CTRL-l. If you think about what's happening—you'll realize that CTRL-l is a formfeed character, which tells many terminals to clear the screen. That's why the regular *ls* command behaved so strangely.

Once you know what you're dealing with, you can use a wildcard pattern to delete or rename the file.

—*ML*

8.13 Counting Files by Types

I use *awk* (20.10) a lot. One of my favorite features of *awk* is its associative arrays. This means *awk* can use anything as an index into an array. In the next example, I use the output of the *file* (12.6) command as the index into an array to count how many files there are of each type:

xargs **28.17**

```
#!/bin/sh
# usage: count_types [directory ...]
# Counts how many files there are of each type
# Original by Bruce Barnett
# Updated version by yu@math.duke.edu (Yunliang Yu)
find ${*-.} -type f -print | xargs file |
awk '{
        $1=NULL;
        t[$0]++;
}
END {
        for (i in t) printf("%d\t%s\n", t[i], i);
}' | sort -nr    # Sort the result numerically, in reverse
```

The output of this might look like:

```
38   ascii text
32   English text
20   c program text
17   sparc executable not stripped
12   compressed data block compressed 16 bits
8    executable shell script
1    sparc demand paged dynamically linked executable
1    executable /bin/make script
```

—*BB*

8.14 Listing Files by Age and Size

If you find a large directory and most of the files are new, that directory may not be suitable for removal, as it is still being used. Here is a script that lists a summary of file sizes, broken down into the time of last modification. You may remember that *ls –l* will list the month, day, hour, and minute if the file is less than six months old and show the month, day, and year if the file is more than six months old. Using this, the script creates a summary for each of the last six months, as well as a summary for each year for files older than that:

```
#!/bin/sh
# usage: age_files [directory ...]
# lists size of files by age
#
# pick which version of ls you use
#    System V
#LS="ls -ls"
#    Berkeley
LS="ls -lsg"
#
find ${*:-.} -type f -print | xargs $LS | awk  '
# argument 7 is the month; argument 9 is either hh:mm or yyyy
# test if argument is hh:mm or yyyy format
{
    if ($9 !~ /:/) {
        sz[$9]+=$1;
    } else {
        sz[$7]+=$1;
    }
}
END {
    for (i in sz) printf("%d\t%s\n", sz[i], i);
}' | sort -nr
```

xargs 28.17

The program might generate results like this:

```
5715    1991
3434    1992
2929    1989
1738    Dec
1495    1990
1227    Jan
1119    Nov
953     Oct
61      Aug
40      Sep
```

[For the book's third edition, I thought about replacing this venerable ten-year-old script with one written in Perl. Perl, after all, lets you get at a file's inode information directly from the script, without the *ls –awk* kludge. But I changed my mind because this technique—groveling through the output of *ls –l* with a "summarizing" filter script—is really handy sometimes.—*JP*]

—*BB*

8.15 newer: Print the Name of the Newest File

Here's a quick alias that figures out which file in a group is the newest:

-d 8.5

```
alias newer "ls -dt \!* | head -1"
```

If your system doesn't have a *head* (12.12) command, use *sed 1q* instead.

For example, let's say that you have two files named *plan.v1* and *plan.v2*. If you're like me, you (often) edit the wrong version by mistake—and then, a few hours later, can't remember what you did. You can use this alias to figure out which file you changed most recently:

```
% newer plan.v*
plan.v1
```

I could also have used command substitution (28.14) to handle this in one step:

```
% emacs `newer plan.*`
```

—ML

8.16 oldlinks: Find Unconnected Symbolic Links

One problem with symbolic links is that they're relatively "fragile" (10.6). The link and the file itself are different kinds of entities; the link only stores the name of the "real" file. Therefore, if you delete or rename the real file, you can be left with a "dead" or "old" link: a link that points to a file that doesn't exist.

This causes no end of confusion, particularly for new users. For example, you'll see things like this:

```
% ls -l nolink
lrwxrwxrwx   1 mikel     users     12 Nov  2 13:57 nolink -> /u/joe/afile
% cat nolink
cat: nolink: No such file or directory
```

The file's obviously there, but *cat* tells you that it doesn't exist.

There's no real solution to this problem, except to be careful. Try writing a script that checks links to see whether they exist. Here's one such script from Tom Christiansen; it uses *find* to track down all links and then uses *perl* to print the names of links that point to nonexistent files. (If you're a Perl hacker and you'll be using this script often, you could replace the Unix *find* utility with the Perl File::Find module.)

```
#!/bin/sh
find . -type l -print | perl -nle '-e || print'
```

The script only lists "dead" links; it doesn't try to delete them or do anything drastic. If you want to take some other action (such as deleting these links automatically), you can use the output of the script in backquotes (28.14). For example:

```
% rm `oldlinks`
```

—ML

8.17 Picking a Unique Filename Automatically

Shell scripts, aliases, and other programs often need temporary files to hold data to be used later. If the program will be run more than once, or if the temp file needs to stay around after the program is done, you need some way to make a unique filename. Generally these files are stored in */tmp* or */usr/tmp*.

One way is with the shell's process ID number (24.3), available in the *$$* parameter. You might name a file */tmp/myprog$$*; the shell will turn that into something like */tmp/myprog*1234 or */tmp/myprog*28471. If your program needs more than one temporary file, add an informative suffix to the names:

```
% errs=/tmp/myprog-errs$$
% output=/tmp/myprog-output$$
```

You can also use *date*'s + option to get a representation of the date suitable for temporary filenames. For example, to output the *Y*ear, *m*onth, *d*ay, *H*our, *M*inute, and *S*econd:

```
% date
Wed Mar  6 17:04:39 MST 2002
% date +'%Y%m%d%H%M%S'
20020306170515
```

Use a + parameter and backquotes (` `) (28.14) to get a temp file named for the current date and/or time. For instance, on May 31 the following command would store *foo.0531* in the Bourne shell variable *temp*. On December 7, it would store *foo.1207*:

```
% temp=foo.`date +'%m%d'`
```

If you'll be generating a lot of temporary files in close proximity, you can use both the process ID and the date/time:

```
% output=/tmp/myprog$$.`date +'%Y%m%d%H%M%S'`
% echo $output
/tmp/myprog25297.20020306170222
```

—JP and DJPH

9

Finding Files with find

9.1 How to Use find

The utility *find* is one of the most useful and important of the Unix utilities. It finds files that match a given set of parameters, ranging from the file's name to its modification date. In this chapter, we'll be looking at many of the things it can do. As an introduction, here's a quick summary of its features and basic operators:

```
% find path operators
```

where *path* is one or more directories in which *find* will begin to search and *operators* (or, in more customary jargon, *options*) tell *find* which files you're interested in. The *operators* are as follows:

-name *filename*
> Find files with the given *filename*. This is the most commonly used operator. *filename* may include wildcards, but if it does, they must be quoted to prevent the shell from interpreting the wildcards.

-perm *mode*
> Find files with the given access mode. You must give the access mode in octal.

-type *c*
> Find the files of the given type, specified by *c*. *c* is a one-letter code; for example, f for a plain file, b for a block special file, l for a symbolic link, and so forth.

-user *name*
> Find files belonging to user *name*. *name* may also be a user ID number.

-group *name*
> Find files belonging to group *name*. *name* may also be a group ID number.

-size *n*

Find files that are *n* blocks long. A block usually equals 512 bytes. The notation +*n* says "find files that are over *n* blocks long." The notation *nc* says "find files that are *n* characters long." Can you guess what +*nc* means?

-inum *n*

Find files with the inode number *n*.

-atime *n*

Find files that were accessed *n* days ago. +*n* means "find files that were accessed over *n* days ago" (i.e., not accessed in the last *n* days). -*n* means "find files that were accessed less than *n* days ago" (i.e., accessed in the last *n* days).

-mtime *n*

Similar to –*atime*, except that it checks the time the file's contents were modified.

-ctime *n*

Similar to –*atime*, except that it checks the time the inode was last changed. "Changed" means that the file was modified or that one of its attributes (for example, its owner) was changed.

-newer *file*

Find files that have been modified more recently than *file*.

You might want to take some action on files that match several criteria. So we need some way to combine several operators:

operator1 **-a** *operator2*

Find files that match both *operator1* and *operator2*. The -a isn't strictly necessary; when two search parameters are provided, one after the other, *find* assumes you want files that match both conditions.

operator1 **-o** *operator2*

Find files that match either *operator1* or *operator2*.

! *operator*

Find all files that do *not* match the given *operator*. The ! performs a logical NOT operation.

\(*expression* **\)**

Logical precedence; in a complex expression, evaluate this part of the *expression* before the rest.

Another group of operators tells *find* what action to take when it locates a file:

-print

Print the file's name on standard output. On most modern *find*s, this is the default action if no action is given.

-ls

> List the file's name on standard output with a format like ls -l. (Not on older versions.)

-exec *command*

> Execute *command*. To include the pathname of the file that's just been found in *command*, use the special symbol {}. *command* must end with a backslash followed by a semicolon (\;). For example:
>
> ```
> % find . -name "*.o" -exec rm -f {} \;
> ```
>
> tells *find* to delete any files whose names end in .o.

-ok *command*

> Same as **-exec**, except that *find* prompts you for permission before executing *command*. This is a useful way to test *find* commands.

A last word: *find* is one of the tools that vendors frequently fiddle with, adding (or deleting) a few operators that they like (or dislike). The GNU version, in particular, has many more. The operators listed here should be valid on virtually any system. If you check your manual page, you may find others.

—ML

9.2 Delving Through a Deep Directory Tree

The first, most obvious, use of this utility is *find*'s ability to locate old, big, or unused files whose locations you've forgotten. In particular, *find*'s most fundamentally important characteristic is its ability to travel down subdirectories.

Normally the shell provides the argument list to a command. That is, Unix programs are frequently given filenames and not directory names. Only a few programs can be given a directory name and march down the directory searching for subdirectories. The programs *find*, *tar* (38.3), *du*, and *diff* do this. Some versions of *chmod* (50.5), *chgrp*, *ls*, *rm*, and *cp* will, but only if a *–r* or *–R* option is specified.

In general, most commands do not understand directory structures and rely on the shell to expand wildcards to directory names. That is, to delete all files whose names end with a .o in a group of directories, you could type:

```
% rm *.o */*.o */*/*.o
```

Not only is this tedious to type, it may not find all of the files you are searching for. The shell has certain blind spots. It will not match files in directories whose names start with a dot. And, if any files match */*/*/*.o, they would not be deleted.

Another problem is typing the previous command and getting the error "Arguments too long." This means the shell would expand too many arguments from the wildcards you typed.

find is the answer to these problems.

A simple example of *find* is using it to print the names of all the files in the directory and all subdirectories. This is done with the simple command:

```
% find . -print
```

The first arguments to *find* are directory and file pathnames—in the example, a dot (.) is one name for the current directory. The arguments after the pathnames always start with a minus sign (-) and tell *find* what to do once it finds a file; these are the search operators. In this case, the filename is printed.

You can use the tilde (~), as well as particular paths. For example:

```
% find ~ ~barnett /usr/local -print
```

And if you have a very slow day, you can type:

```
% find / -print
```

This command will list every file on the system. This is okay on single-user workstations with their own disks. However, it can tie up disks on multiuser systems enough to make users think of gruesome crimes! If you really need that list and your system has fast *find* or *locate*, try the command find '/*' or locate ' *' instead.

find sends its output to standard output, so once you've "found" a list of filenames, you can pass them to other commands. One way to use this is with command substitution:

```
% ls -l `find . -print`
```

The *find* command is executed, and its output replaces the backquoted string. *ls* sees the output of *find* and doesn't even know *find* was used.

An alternate method uses the *xargs* command. *xargs* and *find* work together beautifully. *xargs* executes its arguments as commands and reads standard input to specify arguments to that command. *xargs* knows the maximum number of arguments each command line can handle and does not exceed that limit. While the command:

```
% ls -ld `find / -print`
```

might generate an error when the command line is too large, the equivalent command using *xargs* will never generate that error:

```
% find / -print | xargs ls -ld
```

—BB and JP

9.3 Don't Forget –print

"Why didn't *find* find my file?" I wondered sometimes. "I know it's there!"

More often than not, I'd forgotten to use *–print*. Without *–print* (or *–ls*, on versions of *find* that have it), *find* may not print any pathnames. For a long time, this quirk of *find* confused new users, so most modern versions of *find* will assume *–print* if you don't supply an action; some will give you an error message instead. If you don't get the output you expected from *find*, check to make sure that you specified the action you meant.

—JP and DJPH

9.4 Looking for Files with Particular Names

You can look for particular files by using an expression with wildcards (28.3) as an argument to the *–name* operator. Because the shell also interprets wildcards, it is necessary to quote them so they are passed to *find* unchanged. Any kind of quoting can be used:

```
% find . -name \*.o -print
% find . -name '*.o' -print
% find . -name "[a-zA-Z]*.o" -print
```

Any directory along the path to the file is not matched with the *–name* operator, merely the name at the end of the path. For example, the previous commands would not match the pathname *./subdir.o/afile*—but they would match *./subdir.o* and *./src/subdir/prog.o*.

Article 9.27 shows a way to match directories in the middle of a path. Here's a simpler "find file" alias that can come in very handy:

```
alias ff "find . -name '*\!{*}*' -ls"
```

Give it a file or directory name; the alias will give a long listing of any file or directory names that contain the argument. For example:

```
% ff ch09
2796156 4 -rw-r--r--  1 deb  deb  628 Feb  2 10:41 ./oreilly/UPT/book/ch09.sgm
```

—BB and JP

9.5 Searching for Old Files

If you want to find a file that is seven days old, use the *–mtime* operator:

```
% find . -mtime 7 -print
```

An alternate way is to specify a range of times:

```
% find . -mtime +6 -mtime -8 -print
```

mtime is the last modified time of a file. If you want to look for files that have not been used, check the access time with the *–atime* argument. Here is a command to list all files that have not been read in 30 days or more:

```
% find . -type f -atime +30 -print
```

It is difficult to find directories that have not been accessed because the *find* command modifies the directory's access time.

There is another time associated with each file, called the *ctime*, the inode change time. Access it with the *–ctime* operator. The *ctime* will have a more recent value if the owner, group, permission, or number of links has changed, while the file itself has not. If you want to search for files with a specific number of links, use the *–links* operator.

Article 8.2 has more information about these three times, and article 9.7 explains how *find* checks them.

—BB

9.6 Be an Expert on find Search Operators

find is admittedly tricky. Once you get a handle on its abilities, you'll learn to appreciate its power. But before thinking about anything remotely tricky, let's look at a simple *find* command:

```
% find . -name "*.c" -print
```

The . tells *find* to start its search in the current directory (.) and to search all subdirectories of the current directory. The -name "*.c" tells *find* to find files whose names end in .c. The -print operator tells *find* how to handle what it finds, i.e., print the names on standard output.

All *find* commands, no matter how complicated, are really just variations on this one. You can specify many different names, look for old files, and so on; no matter how complex, you're really only specifying a starting point, some search parameters, and what to do with the files (or directories or links or…) you find.

The key to using *find* in a more sophisticated way is realizing that search parameters are really "logical expressions" that *find* evaluates. That is, *find*:

- Looks at every file, one at a time.
- Uses the information in the file's inode to evaluate an expression given by the command-line operators.

- Takes the specified action (e.g., printing the file's name) if the expression's value is "true."

So, -name "*.c" is really a logical expression that evaluates to true if the file's name ends in .c.

Once you've gotten used to thinking this way, it's easy to use the AND, OR, NOT, and grouping operators. So let's think about a more complicated *find* command. Let's look for files that end in .o or .tmp AND that are more than five days old, AND let's print their pathnames. We want an expression that evaluates true for files whose names match either *.o OR *.tmp:

```
-name "*.o" -o -name "*.tmp"
```

If either condition is true, we want to check the access time. So we put the previous expression within parentheses (quoted with backslashes so the shell doesn't treat the parentheses as subshell operators). We also add a *-atime* operator:

```
-atime +5 \( -name "*.o" -o -name "*.tmp" \)
```

The parentheses force *find* to evaluate what's inside as a unit. The expression is true if "the access time is more than five days ago and \(either the name ends with .o or the name ends with .tmp \)." If you didn't use parentheses, the expression would mean something different:

```
-atime +5 -name "*.o" -o -name "*.tmp"          Wrong!
```

When *find* sees two operators next to each other with no -o between, that means AND. So the "wrong" expression is true if "either \(the access time is more than five days ago and the name ends with .o \) or the name ends with .tmp." This incorrect expression would be true for any name ending with .tmp, no matter how recently the file was accessed—the -atime doesn't apply. (There's nothing really "wrong" or illegal in this second expression—except that it's not what we want. *find* will accept the expression and do what we asked—it just won't do what we want.)

The following command, which is what we want, lists files in the current directory and subdirectories that match our criteria:

```
% find . -atime +5 \( - name "*.o" -o -name "*.tmp" \) -print
```

What if we wanted to list all files that do *not* match these criteria? All we want is the logical inverse of this expression. The NOT operator is an exclamation point (!). Like the parentheses, in most shells we need to escape ! with a backslash to keep the shell from interpreting it before *find* can get to it. The ! operator applies to the expression on its right. Since we want it to apply to the entire expression, and not just the *-atime* operator, we'll have to group everything from -atime to "*.tmp" within another set of parentheses:

```
% find . \! \( -atime +5 \( - name "*.o" -o -name "*.tmp" \) \) -print
```

For that matter, even *–print* is an expression; it always evaluates to true. So are *–exec* and *–ok*; they evaluate to true when the command they execute returns a zero status. (There are a few situations in which this can be used to good effect.)

But before you try anything too complicated, you need to realize one thing. *find* isn't as sophisticated as you might like it to be. You can't squeeze all the spaces out of expressions, as if it were a real programming language. You need spaces before and after operators like !, (,), and {}, in addition to spaces before and after every other operator. Therefore, a command line like the following won't work:

```
% find . \!\(-atime +5 \(-name "*.o" -o -name "*.tmp"\)\) -print
```

A true power user will realize that *find* is relying on the shell to separate the command line into meaningful chunks, or *tokens*. And the shell, in turn, is assuming that tokens are separated by spaces. When the shell gives *find* a chunk of characters like *.tmp)) (without the double quotes or backslashes—the shell took them away), *find* gets confused; it thinks you're talking about a weird filename pattern that includes a couple of parentheses.

Once you start thinking about expressions, *find*'s syntax ceases to be obscure—in some ways, it's even elegant. It certainly allows you to say what you need to say with reasonable efficiency.

—ML and JP

9.7 The Times That find Finds

The times that go with the *find* operators *–mtime*, *–atime*, and *–ctime* often aren't documented very well. The times are in days:

- A number with no sign, for example, 3 (as in *–mtime 3* or *–atime 3*), means the 24-hour period that *ended* exactly 3 days ago (in other words, between 96 and 72 hours ago).

- A number with a minus sign (–) refers to the period *since* that 24-hour period. For example, -3 (as in *–mtime –3*) is any time between now and 3 days ago (in other words, between 0 and 72 hours ago).

- Naturally, a number with a plus sign (+) refers to the period *before* that 24-hour period. For example, +3 (as in *–mtime +3*) is any time more than 3 days ago (in other words, more than 96 hours ago).

Got that? Then you should see that *–atime –2* and *–atime 1* are both true on files that have been accessed between 48 and 24 hours ago. (*–atime –2* is also true on files accessed 24 hours ago or less.)

For more exact comparisons, use *find –newer* with *touch* (9.8).

—JP

9.8 Exact File-Time Comparisons

One problem with *find*'s time operators (*–atime* and its brethren) is that they don't allow very exact comparisons. They only allow you to specify time to within a day, and sometimes that's just not good enough. You think that your system was corrupted at roughly 4 p.m. yesterday (March 20); you want to find any files that were modified after that point, so you can inspect them. Obviously, you'd like something more precise than "give me all the files that were modified in the last 24 hours."

Some versions of *touch*, and other freely available commands like it, can create a file with an arbitrary timestamp. That is, you can use *touch* to make a file that's backdated to any point in the past (or, for that matter, postdated to some point in the future). This feature, combined with *find*'s *–newer* operator, lets you make comparisons accurate to one minute or less.

For example, to create a file dated 4 p.m., March 20, give the command:

```
% touch -t 03201600 /tmp/4PMyesterday
```

Then to find the files created after this, give the command:

```
% find . -newer /tmp/4PMyesterday -print
```

What about "older" files? Older files are "not newer" files, and *find* has a convenient NOT operator (!) for just this purpose. So let's say that you want to find files that were created between 10:46 a.m. on July 3, 1999 and 9:37 p.m. on June 4, 2001. You could use the following commands:[*]

```
% touch -t 199907031046 /tmp/file1
% touch -t 200106042137 /tmp/file2
% find . -newer /tmp/file1 \! -newer /tmp/file2 -print
% rm /tmp/file[12]
```

—*ML*

9.9 Running Commands on What You Find

Often, when you find a file, you don't just want to see its name; you want to do something, like *grep* (13.2) for a text string. To do this, use the *–exec* operator. This allows you to specify a command that is executed upon each file that is found.

---

[*] Very old versions of *find* have trouble with using multiple *–newer* expressions in one command. If *find* doesn't find files that it should, try using multiple explicit *–mtime* expressions instead. They're not as precise, but they will work even on *find*s with buggy *–newer* handling.

The syntax is peculiar and in many cases, it is simpler just to pipe the output of *find* to *xargs* (28.17). However, there are cases where *-exec* is just the thing, so let's plunge in and explain its peculiarities.

The *-exec* operator allows you to execute any command, including another *find* command. If you consider that for a moment, you realize that *find* needs some way to distinguish the command it's executing from its own arguments. The obvious choice is to use the same end-of-command character as the shell (the semicolon). But since the shell uses the semicolon itself, it is necessary to escape the character with a backslash or quotes.

Therefore, every *-exec* operator ends with the characters \;. There is one more special argument that *find* treats differently: {}. These two characters are used as the variable whose name is the file *find* found. Don't bother rereading that last line: an example will clarify the usage. The following is a trivial case and uses the *-exec* operator with *echo* to mimic the *-print* operator:

```
% find . -exec echo {} \;
```

The C shell (29.1) uses the characters { and }, but doesn't change {} together, which is why it is not necessary to quote these characters. The semicolon must be quoted, however. Quotes can be used instead of a backslash:

```
% find . -exec echo {} ';'
```

as both will sneak the semicolon past the shell and get it to the *find* command. As I said before, *find* can even call *find*. If you wanted to list every symbolic link in every directory owned by a group *staff* under the current directory, you could execute:

```
% find `pwd` -type d -group staff -exec find {} -type l -print \;
```

To search for all files with group-write permission under the current directory and to remove the permission, you can use:

```
% find . -perm -20 -exec chmod g-w {} \;
```

or:

```
% find . -perm -20 -print | xargs chmod g-w
```

The difference between *-exec* and *xargs* is subtle. The first one will execute the program once per file, while *xargs* can handle several files with each process. However, *xargs* may have problems with filenames that contain embedded spaces. (Versions of *xargs* that support the *-0* option can avoid this problem; they expect NUL characters as delimiters instead of spaces, and *find*'s *-print0* option generates output that way.)

Occasionally, people create a strange file that they can't delete. This could be caused by accidentally creating a file with a space or some control character in the name. *find* and *-exec* can delete this file, while *xargs* could not. In this case, use *ls -il* to list the files and i-numbers, and use the *-inum* operator with *-exec* to delete the file:

```
% find . -inum 31246 -exec rm {} ';'
```

If you wish, you can use –*ok*, which does the same as –*exec*, except the program asks you to confirm the action first before executing the command. It is a good idea to be cautious when using *find*, because the program can make a mistake into a disaster. When in doubt, use *echo* as the command. Or send the output to a file, and examine the file before using it as input to *xargs*. This is how I discovered that *find* requires {} to stand alone in the arguments to –*exec*. I wanted to rename some files using -exec mv {} {}.orig, but *find* wouldn't replace the {} in {}.orig. I learned that I have to write a shell script that I tell *find* to execute.

> GNU *find* will replace the {} in {}.orig for you. If you don't have GNU *find*, a little Bourne shell *while* loop with redirected input can handle that too:
>
> ```
> $ find ... -print |
> > while read file
> > do mv "$file" "$file.orig"
> > done
> ```
>
> *find* writes the filenames to its standard output. The *while* loop and its *read* command read the filenames from standard input then make them available as $file, one by one.

Articles 9.12 and 9.27 have more examples of –*exec*.

—*BB*

9.10 Using –exec to Create Custom Tests

Here's something that will really make your head spin. Remember that –*exec* doesn't necessarily evaluate to "true"; it only evaluates to true if the command it executes returns a zero exit status. You can use this to construct custom *find* tests.

Assume that you want to list files that are "beautiful." You have written a program called *beauty* that returns zero if a file is beautiful and nonzero otherwise. (This program can be a shell script, a *perl* script, an executable from a C program, or anything you like.)

Here's an example:

```
% find . -exec beauty {} \; -print
```

In this command, –*exec* is just another *find* operator. The only difference is that we care about its value; we're not assuming that it will always be "true." *find* executes the *beauty* command for every file. Then –*exec* evaluates to true when *find* is looking at a "beautiful" program, causing *find* to print the filename. (Excuse us, causing *find* to evaluate the –*print*. :-))

Of course, this ability is capable of infinite variation. If you're interested in finding beautiful C code, you could use the command:

```
% find . -name "*.[ch]" -exec beauty {} \; -print
```

For performance reasons, it's a good idea to put the *—exec* operator as close to the end as possible. This avoids starting processes unnecessarily; the *—exec* command will execute only when the previous operators evaluate to true.

—JP and ML

9.11 Custom —exec Tests Applied

My favorite reason to use *find*'s *—exec* is for large recursive *grep*s. Let's say I want to search through a large directory with lots of subdirectories to find all of the .cc files that call the method GetRaw( ):

```
% find . -name \*.cc -exec grep -n "GetRaw(" {} \; -print
58:     string Database::GetRaw(const Name &owner) const {
67:     string Database::GetRaw(const Name &owner,
./db/Database.cc
39:         return new Object(owner, _database->GetRaw(owner));
51:     string Object::GetRaw(const Property& property) const {
52:        return _database->GetRaw(_owner, property);
86:         Properties properties(_database->GetRaw(owner));
103:      return _database->GetRaw(_owner);
./db/Object.cc
71:       return new DatabaseObject(owner, GetDatabase().GetRaw(owner));
89:        return Sexp::Parse(GetRaw(property));
92:        SexpPtr parent = Sexp::Parse(GetRaw("_parent"))->Eval(this);
./tlisp/Object.cc
```

This output is from a real source directory for an open source project I'm working on; it shows me each line that matched my *grep* along with its line number, followed by the name of the file where those lines were found. Most versions of *grep* can search recursively (using *—R*), but they search all files; you need *find* to *grep* through only certain files in a large directory tree.

—JP and DJPH

9.12 Finding Many Things with One Command

Running *find* is fairly time consuming, and for good reason: it has to read every inode in the directory tree that it's searching. Therefore, combine as many things as you can into a single *find* command. If you're going to walk the entire tree, you may as well accomplish as much as possible in the process.

Let's work from an example. Assume that you want to write a command (eventually for inclusion in a Chapter 27shell script) that sets file-access modes correctly. You want to give 771 access to all directories, 600 access for all backup files (*.BAK), 755 access for all shell scripts (*.sh), and 644 access for all text files (*.txt). You can do all this with one command:

```
$ find . \( -type d       -a -exec chmod 771 {} \; \) -o \
          \( -name "*.BAK" -a -exec chmod 600 {} \; \) -o \
          \( -name "*.sh"  -a -exec chmod 755 {} \; \) -o \
          \( -name "*.txt" -a -exec chmod 644 {} \; \)
```

Why does this work? Remember that –*exec* is really just another part of the expression; it evaluates to true when the following command is successful. It isn't an independent action that somehow applies to the whole *find* operation. Therefore, –*exec* can be mixed freely with –*type*, –*name*, and so on.

However, there's another important trick here. Look at the first chunk of the command—the first statement, that is, between the first pair of \(and \). It says, "If this file is a directory and the *chmod* command executes successfully…" Wait. Why doesn't the –*exec* execute a *chmod* on every file in the directory to see whether it's successful?

Logical expressions are evaluated from left to right; in any chunk of the expression, evaluation stops once it's clear what the outcome is. Consider the logical expression "'A AND B' is true." If A is false, you know that the result of "'A AND B' is true" will also be false—so there's no need to look the rest of the statement, B.

So in the previous multilayered expression, when *find* is looking at a file, it checks whether the file is a directory. If it is, –*type d* is true, and *find* evaluates the –*exec* (changing the file's mode). If the file is not a directory, *find* knows that the result of the entire statement will be false, so it doesn't bother wasting time with the –*exec*. *find* goes on to the next chunk after the OR operator—because, logically, if one part of an OR expression isn't true, the next part may be—so evaluation of an OR…OR…OR… expression has to continue until either one chunk is found to be true, or they've all been found to be false. In this case having the directory first is important, so that directories named, for example, *blah.BAK* don't lose their execute permissions.

Of course, there's no need for the –*exec*s to run the same kind of command. Some could delete files, some could change modes, some could move them to another directory, and so on.

One final point. Although understanding our multilayered *find* expression was difficult, it really was no different from a "garden variety" command. Think about what the following command means:

```
% find . -name "*.c" -print
```

There are two operators: *–name* (which evaluates to true if the file's name ends in *.c*) and *–print* (which is always true). The two operators are ANDed together; we could stick a *–a* between the two without changing the result at all. If *–name* evaluates to false (i.e., if the file's name doesn't end in *.c*), *find* knows that the entire expression will be false. So it doesn't bother with *–print*. But if *–name* evaluates to true, *find* evaluates *–print*—which, as a side effect, prints the name.

As we said in article 9.6, *find*'s business is evaluating expressions—not locating files. Yes, *find* certainly locates files; but that's really just a side effect. For me, understanding this point was the conceptual breakthrough that made *find* much more useful.

—*ML*

9.13 Searching for Files by Type

If you are only interested in files of a certain type, use the -type argument, followed by one of the characters in Table 9-1. Note, though that some versions of *find* don't have all of these.

Table 9-1. find –type characters

Character	Meaning
b	Block special file ("device file")
c	Character special file ("device file")
d	Directory
f	Plain file
l	Symbolic link
p	Named pipe file
s	Socket

Unless you are a system administrator, the important types are directories, plain files, or symbolic links (i.e., types d, f, or l).

Using the *–type* operator, here is another way to list files recursively:

```
% find . -type f -print | xargs ls -l
```

It can be difficult to keep track of all the symbolic links in a directory. The next command will find all the symbolic links in your home directory and print the files to which your symbolic links point. $NF gives the last field of each line, which holds the name to which a symlink points. If your *find* doesn't have a *–ls* operator, pipe to *xargs ls –l* as previously.

```
% find $HOME -type l -ls | awk '{print $NF}'
```

—*BB*

9.14 Searching for Files by Size

find has several operators that take a decimal integer. One such argument is *–size*. The number after this argument is the size of the files in disk blocks. Unfortunately, this is a vague number. Earlier versions of Unix used disk blocks of 512 bytes. Newer versions allow larger block sizes, so a "block" of 512 bytes is misleading.

This confusion is aggravated when the command *ls –s* is used. The *–s* option supposedly lists the size of the file in blocks. But if your system has a different block size than *ls –s* has been programmed to assume, it can give a misleading answer. You can put a c after the number and specify the size in bytes. To find a file with exactly 1,234 bytes (as in an *ls –l* listing), type:

```
% find . -size 1234c -print
```

To search for files using a range of file sizes, a minus or plus sign can be specified before the number. The minus sign (–) means less than, and the plus sign (+) means greater than. This next example lists all files that are greater than 10,000 bytes, but less than 32,000 bytes:

```
% find . -size +10000c -size -32000c -print
```

When more than one qualifier is given, both must be true.

—BB

9.15 Searching for Files by Permission

find can look for files with specific permissions. It uses an octal number for these permissions. If you aren't comfortable with octal numbers and the way Unix uses them in file permissions, article 1.17 is good background reading.

The string rw-rw-r-- indicates that you and members of your group have read and write permission, while the world has read-only privilege. The same permissions are expressed as an octal number as 664. To find all *.o files with these permissions, use the following:

```
% find . -name \*.o -perm 664 -print
```

To see if you have any directories with write permission for everyone, use this:

```
% find . -type d -perm 777 -print
```

The previous examples only match an exact combination of permissions. If you wanted to find all directories with group write permission, you want to match the pattern ----w----. There are several combinations that can match. You could list each combination, but *find* allows you to specify a pattern that can be bitwise

ANDed with the permissions of the file. Simply put a minus sign (–) before the octal value. The group write permission bit is octal 20, so the following negative value:

```
% find . -perm -20 -print
```

will match the following common permissions:

Permission	Octal value
rwxrwxrwx	777
rwxrwxr-x	775
rw-rw-rw-	666
rw-rw-r--	664
rw-rw----	660

If you wanted to look for files that the owner can execute (i.e., shell scripts or programs), you want to match the pattern --x------ by typing:

```
% find . -perm -100 -print
```

When the -perm argument has a minus sign, all of the permission bits are examined, including the set user ID, set group ID, and sticky bits.

—BB

9.16 Searching by Owner and Group

Often you need to look for a file belonging to a certain user or group. This is done with the *–user* and *–group* search operators. You often need to combine this with a search for particular permissions. To find all files that are set user ID (*setuid*) root, use this:

```
% find . -user root -perm -4000 -print
```

To find all files that are set group ID (*setgid*) staff, use this:

```
% find . -group staff -perm -2000 -print
```

Instead of using a name or group from */etc/passwd* or */etc/group*, you can use the UID or GID number:

```
% find . -user 0 -perm -4000 -print
% find . -group 10 -perm -2000 -print
```

Often, when a user leaves a site, his account is deleted, but his files are still on the computer. Some versions of *find* have *–nouser* or *–nogroup* operators to find files with an unknown user or group ID.

—BB

9.17 Duplicating a Directory Tree

In many versions of *find*, the operator {}, used with the *–exec* operator, only works when it's separated from other arguments by whitespace. So, for example, the following command will *not* do what you thought it would:

```
% find . -type d -exec mkdir /usr/project/{} \;
```

You might have thought this command would make a duplicate set of (empty) directories, from the current directory and down, starting at the directory */usr/ project*. For instance, when the *find* command finds the directory *./adir*, you would have it execute *mkdir /usr/project/./adir* (*mkdir* will ignore the dot; the result is */usr/project/adir*).

That doesn't work because those versions of *find* don't recognize the {} in the pathname. The GNU version *does* expand {} in the middle of a string. On versions that don't, though, the trick is to pass the directory names to *sed*, which substitutes in the leading pathname:

```
% find . -type d -print | sed 's@^@/usr/project/@' | xargs mkdir
% find . -type d -print | sed 's@^@mkdir @' | (cd /usr/project; sh)
```

Let's start with the first example. Given a list of directory names, *sed* substitutes the desired path to that directory at the beginning of the line before passing the completed filenames to *xargs* and *mkdir*. An @ is used as a *sed* delimiter because slashes (/) are needed in the actual text of the substitution. If you don't have *xargs*, try the second example. It uses *sed* to insert the *mkdir* command, then it changes to the target directory in a subshell where the *mkdir* commands will actually be executed.

—JP

9.18 Using "Fast find" Databases

Berkeley added a handy feature to its *find* command—if you give it a single argument, it will search a database for file or directory names that match. For example, if you know there's a file named *MH.eps* somewhere on the computer but you don't know where, type the following:

```
% find MH.eps
/nutshell/graphics/cover/MH.eps
```

That syntax can be confusing to new users: you have to give *find* just one argument. With more arguments, *find* searches the filesystem directly. Maybe that's one reason that GNU has a "fast *find*" utility named *locate*—and its *find* utility always searches, as described in the rest of this chapter. The GNU *slocate* command is a security-enhanced version of *locate*. In the rest of this article, I'll describe *locate*—but *find* with a single argument (as shown previously) works about the same way.

The "fast *find*" database is usually rebuilt every night. So, it's not completely up-to-date, but it's usually close enough. If your system administrator has set this up, the database usually lists all files on the filesystem—although it may not list files in directories that don't have world-access permission. If the database isn't set up at all, you'll get an error like /usr/lib/find/find.codes: No such file or directory. (If that's the case, you can set up a "fast *find*" database yourself. Set up your own private *locate* database, or see article 9.20.)

Unless you use wildcards, *locate* does a simple string search, like *fgrep*, through a list of absolute pathnames. Here's an extreme example:

```
% locate bin
/bin
/bin/ar
    ...
/home/robin
/home/robin/afile
/home/sally/bin
    ...
```

You can cut down this output by piping it through *grep*, *sed*, and so on. But *locate* and "fast *find*" also can use wildcards to limit searches. Article 9.19 explains this in more detail.

locate has an advantage over the "fast *find*" command: you can have multiple file databases and you can search some or all of them. *locate* and *slocate* come with a database-building program.

Because *locate* is so fast, it's worth trying to use whenever you can. Pipe the output to *xargs* and any other Unix command, or run a shell or Perl script to test its output—almost anything will be faster than running a standard *find*. For example, if you want a long listing of the files, here are two *locate* commands to do it:

```
% ls -l `locate whatever`
% locate whatever | xargs ls -ld
```

There's one problem with that trick. The *locate* list may be built by *root*, which can see all the files on the filesystem; your *ls –l* command may not be able to access all files in the list. But *slocate* can be configured not to show you files you don't have permission to see.

> The *locate* database may need to be updated on your machine before you can use *locate*, if it's not already in the system's normal *cron* scripts. Use *locate.updatedb* to do this, and consider having it run weekly or so if you're going to use *locate* regularly.

—*JP*

9.19 Wildcards with "Fast find" Database

locate and all the "fast *find*" commands I've used can match shell wildcards (1.13) (*, ?, [ ]). If you use a wildcard on one end of the pattern, the search pattern is automatically "anchored" to the opposite end of the string (the end where the wildcard isn't). The shell matches filenames in the same way.

The difference between the shell's wildcard matching and *locate* matching is that the shell treats slashes (/) in a special manner: you have to type them as part of the expression. In *locate*, a wildcard matches slashes and any other character. When you use a wildcard, be sure to put quotes around the pattern so the shell won't touch it.

Here are some examples:

- To find any pathname that ends with *bin*:

  ```
  % locate '*bin'
  /bin
  /home/robin
  /home/robin/bin
      ...
  ```

- To find any pathname that ends with */bin* (a good way to find a file or directory named exactly *bin*):

  ```
  % locate '*/bin'
  /bin
  /home/robin/bin
  /usr/bin
      ...
  ```

- Typing locate '*bin*' is the same as typing locate bin.

- To match the files in a directory named *bin*, but not the directory itself, try something like this:

  ```
  % locate '*/bin/*'
  /bin/ar
  /bin/cat
      ...
  /home/robin/bin/prog
  ```

- To find the files in */home* whose names end with a tilde (~) (these are probably backup files from the Emacs editor):

  ```
  % locate '/home/*~'
  /home/testfile~
  /home/allan/.cshrc~
  /home/allan/.login~
  /home/dave/.profile~
      ...
  ```

Notice that the *locate* asterisk matches dot files, unlike shell wildcards.

- The question mark (?) and square brackets ([ ]) operators work, too. They're not quite as useful as they are in the shell because they match the slashes (/) in the pathnames. Here are a couple of quick examples:

```
% locate '????'
/bin
/etc
/lib
/src
/sys
/usr
% locate '/[bel]??'
/bin
/etc
/lib
```

—*JP*

9.20 Finding Files (Much) Faster with a find Database

If you use *find* to search for files, you know that it can take a long time to work, especially when there are lots of directories to search. Here are some ideas for speeding up your *finds*.

 By design, setups like these that build a file database won't have absolutely up-to-date information about all your files.

If your system has "fast *find*" or *locate*, that's probably all you need. It lets you search a list of all pathnames on the system.

Even if you have "fast *find*" or *locate*, it still might not do what you need. For example, those utilities only search for pathnames. To find files by the owner's name, the number of links, the size, and so on, you have to use "slow *find*." In that case—or, when you don't have "fast *find*" or *locate*—you may want to set up your own version.

slocate can build and update its own database (with its –*u* option), as well as search the database. The basic "fast *find*" has two parts. One part is a command, a shell script usually named *updatedb* or *locate.updatedb*, that builds a database of the files on your system—if your system has it, take a look to see a fancy way to build the database. The other part is the *find* or *locate* command itself—it searches the database for pathnames that match the name (regular expression) you type.

To make your own "fast *find*":

- Pick a filename for the database. We'll use *$HOME/.fastfind* (some systems use *$LOGDIR* instead of *$HOME*).

- Design the *find* command you want to use. The command to build a database of all the files in your home directory might look like this:

```
% cd
% find . -print | sed "s@^./@@" > .fastfind.new
% mv -f .fastfind.new .fastfind
```

That doesn't update the database until the new one is finished. It also doesn't compress the database. If you're short on disk space, use this instead:

```
% cd
% find . -print | sed "s@^./@@" | gzip > .fastfind.gz
```

The script starts from your home directory, then uses *sed* (13.9) to strip the start of the pathname (like *./*) from every entry. (If you're building a database of the whole filesystem, don't do that part!) To save more space, you can compress with *bzip2* instead; it's slow, but it saved about 25% of the disk space for my database.

- Set up *cron* (25.3) or *at* to run that *find* as often as you want—usually once a day, early in the morning morning, is fine.

- Finally, make a shell script (I call mine *ffind*) to search the database. If you use *egrep* (13.4), you can search with flexible regular expressions:

```
egrep "$1" $HOME/.fastfind | sed "s@^@$HOME/@"
```

or, for a *gzip*ped database:

```
gzcat $HOME/.fastfind.gz | egrep "$1" | sed "s@^@$HOME/@"
```

The *sed* expressions add your home directory's pathname (like */usr/freddie*) to each line.

To search the database, type:

```
% ffind somefile
/usr/freddie/lib/somefile
% ffind '/(sep|oct)[^/]*$'
/usr/freddie/misc/project/september
/usr/freddie/misc/project/october
```

You can do much more: I'll get you started. If you have room to store more information than just pathnames, you can feed your *find* output to a command like *ls –l*. For example, if you do a lot of work with links, you might want to keep the files' i-numbers as well as their names. You'd build your database with a command like this:

```
% cd
% find . -print | xargs ls -id > .fastfind.new
% mv -f .fastfind.new .fastfind
```

Or, if your version of *find* has the handy *–ls* operator, use the next script. Watch out for really large i-numbers; they might shift the columns and make *cut* give wrong output. The exact column numbers will depend on your system:

```
% cd
% find . -ls | cut -c1-7,67- > .fastfind.new
% mv -f .fastfind.new .fastfind
```

Then, your *ffind* script could search for files by i-number. For instance, if you had a file with i-number 1234 and you wanted to find all its links:

```
% ffind "^1234 "
```

The space at the end of that regular expression prevents matches with i-numbers like 12345. You could search by pathname in the same way. To get a bit fancier, you could make your *ffind* a little *perl* or *awk* script that searches your database by field. For instance, here's how to make *awk* do the previous i-number search; the output is just the matching pathnames:

```
awk '$1 == 1234 {print $2}' $HOME/.fastfind
```

With some information about Unix shell programming and utilities like *awk*, the techniques in this article should let you build and search a sophisticated file database—and get information much faster than with plain old *find*.

—JP

9.21 grepping a Directory Tree

Want to search every file, in some directory and all its subdirectories, to find the file that has a particular word or string in it? That's a job for *find* and one of the *grep* commands.

For example, to search all the files for lines starting with a number and containing the words "SALE PRICE," you could use:

```
% egrep '^[0-9].*SALE PRICE' `find . -type f -print`
./archive/ad.1290: 1.99 a special SALE PRICE
./archive/ad.0191: 2.49 a special SALE PRICE
```

Using the backquotes (``` `` ```) might not work. If *find* finds too many files, *egrep*'s command-line arguments can get too long. Using *xargs* can solve that; it splits long sets of arguments into smaller chunks. There's a problem with that: if the last "chunk" has just one filename and the *grep* command finds a match there, *grep* won't print the filename:

```
% find . -type f -print | xargs fgrep '$12.99'
./old_sales/ad.0489: Get it for only $12.99!
./old_sales/ad.0589: Last chance at $12.99, this month!
Get it for only $12.99 today.
```

The answer is to add the Unix "empty file," */dev/null*. It's a filename that's guaranteed never to match but always to leave *fgrep* with at least two filenames:

```
% find . -type f -print | xargs fgrep '$12.99' /dev/null
```

Then *xargs* will run commands like these:

```
fgrep '$12.99' /dev/null ./afile ./bfile ...
fgrep '$12.99' /dev/null ./archives/ad.0190 ./archives/ad.0290 ...
fgrep '$12.99' /dev/null ./old_sales/ad.1289
```

That trick is also good when you use a wildcard (28.3) and only one file might match it. *grep* won't always print the file's name unless you add */dev/null*:

```
% grep "whatever" /dev/null /x/y/z/a*
```

—*JP*

9.22 lookfor: Which File Has That Word?

The following simple shell script, *lookfor*, uses *find* to look for all files in the specified directory hierarchy that have been modified within a certain time, and it passes the resulting names to *grep* to scan for a particular pattern. For example, the command:

```
% lookfor /work -7 tamale enchilada
```

would search through the entire */work* filesystem and print the names of all files modified within the past week that contain the words "tamale" or "enchilada." (For example, if this article is stored in */work*, *lookfor* should find it.)

The arguments to the script are the pathname of a directory hierarchy to search in ($1), a time ($2), and one or more text patterns (the other arguments). This simple but slow version will search for an (almost) unlimited number of words:

```
#!/bin/sh
temp=/tmp/lookfor$$
trap 'rm -f $temp; exit' 0 1 2 15
find $1 -mtime $2 -print > $temp
shift; shift
for word
do grep -i "$word" `cat $temp` /dev/null
done
```

That version runs *grep* once to search for each word. The –*i* option makes the search find either upper- or lowercase letters. Using */dev/null* makes sure that *grep* will print the filename. Watch out, though: the list of filenames may get too long.

The next version is more limited but faster. It builds a regular expression for *egrep* that finds all the words in one pass through the files. If you use too many words, *egrep* will say Regular expression too long. Also, your *egrep* may not have a *–i* option; you can just omit it. This version also uses *xargs*; though *xargs* has its problems.

```
#!/bin/sh
where="$1"
when="$2"
shift; shift
# Build egrep expression like (word1|word2|...) in $expr
for word
do
    case "$expr" in
    "") expr="($word" ;;
    *) expr="$expr|$word" ;;
    esac
done
expr="$expr)"

find $where -mtime $when -print | xargs egrep -i "$expr" /dev/null
```

—*JP and TOR*

9.23 Using Shell Arrays to Browse Directories

Even a graphical file manager might not be enough to help you step through a complicated directory tree with multiple layers of subdirectories. Which directories have you visited so far, and which are left to go? This article shows a simple way, using shell arrays, to step through a tree directory-by-directory. The technique is also good for stepping through lists of files—or almost any collection of things, over a period of time—of which you don't want to miss any. At the end are a couple of related tips on using arrays.

Using the Stored Lists

Let's start with a quick overview of expanding array values; then we'll look at specifics for each shell. A dollar sign ($) before the name of a shell variable gives you its value. In the C shells and *zsh*, that gives all members of an array. But, in the Korn shell and *bash2*, expanding an array value without the index gives just the first member. To pick out a particular member, put its number in square brackets after the name; in *ksh* and *bash2*, you also need to use curly braces ({}). A hash mark (#) gives the number of members. Finally, you can use range operators to choose several members of an array.

Here's a practical example that you might use, interactively, at a shell prompt. You're cleaning your home directory tree. You store all the directory names in an array named d. When you've cleaned one directory, you go to the next one. This way, you don't miss any directories. (To keep this simple, I'll show an example with just four directories.)

 If you don't want to use shell commands to browse the directories, you could use a command to launch a graphical file browser on each directory in the array. For instance, make the *nextdir* alias launch Midnight Commander with *mc $d[1]*.

Let's start with the C shell:

```
% set d=(`find $home -type d -print`)
% echo $#d directories to search: $d
4 directories to search: /u/ann /u/ann/bin /u/ann/src /u/ann/lib
% alias nextdir 'shift d; cd $d[1]; pwd; ls -l'
% cd $d[1]
   ...clean up first directory...
% nextdir
/u/ann/bin
total 1940
lrwxrwxrwx   1 ann     users      14 Feb  7  2002 ] -> /usr/ucb/reset
-r-xr-xr-x   1 ann     users    1134 Aug 23  2001 addup
   ...clean up bin directory...
% nextdir
/u/ann/src
   ...do other directories, one by one...
% nextdir
d: Subscript out of range.
```

You store the array, list the number of directories, and show their names. You then create a *nextdir* alias that changes to the next directory to clean. First, use the C shell's *shift* command; it "throws away" the first member of an array so that the second member becomes the first member, and so on. Next, *nextdir* changes the current directory to the next member of the array and lists it. (Note that members of a C shell array are indexed starting at 1—unlike the C language, which the C shell emulates, where indexes start at 0. So the alias uses *cd $d[1]*.) At the end of our example, when there's not another array member to *shift* away, the command *cd $d[1]* fails; the rest of the *nextdir* alias isn't executed.

Bourne-type shells have a different array syntax than the C shell. They don't have a *shift* command for arrays, so we'll use a variable named n to hold the array index. Instead of aliases, let's use a more powerful shell function. We'll show *ksh* and *bash2* arrays, which are indexed starting at 0. (By default, the first *zsh* array member is number 1.) The first command that follows, to store the array, is different in *ksh* and *bash2*—but the rest of the example is the same on both shells.

```
bash2$ d=(`find $HOME -type d -print`)
ksh$ set -A d `find $HOME -type d -print`

$ echo ${#d[*]} directories to search: ${d[*]}
4 directories to search: /u/ann /u/ann/bin /u/ann/src /u/ann/lib
$ n=0
$ nextdir() {
>    if [ $((n += 1)) -lt ${#d[*]} ]
>    then cd ${d[$n]}; pwd; ls -l
>    else echo no more directories
>    fi
> }
$ cd ${d[o]}
    ...clean up first directory...
$ nextdir
/u/ann/bin
total 1940
lrwxrwxrwx    1 ann    users      14 Feb  7  2002 ] -> /usr/ucb/reset
-r-xr-xr-x    1 ann    users    1134 Aug 23  2001 addup
    ...do directories, as in C shell example...
$ nextdir
no more directories
```

If you aren't a programmer, this may look intimidating—like something you'd never type interactively at a shell prompt. But this sort of thing starts to happen—without planning, on the spur of the moment—as you learn more about Unix and what the shell can do.

Expanding Ranges

We don't use quite all the array-expanding operators in the previous examples, so here's a quick overview of the rest. To expand a range of members in *ksh* and *bash2*, give the first and last indexes with a dash (-) between them. For instance, to expand the second, third, and fourth members of array arrname, use *${arrname[1-3]}*. In *zsh*, use a comma (,) instead—and remember that the first *zsh* array member is number 1; so you'd use *${arrname[2-4]}* in *zsh*. C shell wants *$arrname[2-4]*. If the last number of a range is omitted (like *${arrname[2-]}* or *$arrname[2-]*), this gives you all members from 2 through the last.

Finally, in all shells except *zsh*, remember that expanded values are split into words at space characters. So if members of an array have spaces in their values, be careful to quote them. For instance, Unix directory names can have spaces in them—so we really should have used cd "$d[1]" in the *newdir* alias and cd "${d[$n]}" in the *newdir* function.* If we hadn't done this, the *cd* command could have gotten multiple argument words. But it would only pay attention to the first argument, so it would probably fail.

---

* We didn't do so because the syntax was already messy enough for people getting started.

To expand a range of members safely, such as ${foo[1-3]} in *bash2* and *ksh*, you need ugly expressions without range operators, such as "${foo[1]}" "${foo[2]}" "${foo[3]}". The C shell has a :q string modifier that says "quote each word," so in *csh* you can safely use $foo[1-3]:q. It's hard to quote array values, though, if you don't know ahead of time how many there are! So, using ${foo[*]} to give all members of the *foo* array suffers from word-splitting in *ksh* and *bash2* (but not in *zsh*, by default). In *ksh* and *bash2*, though, you can use "${foo[@]}", which expands into a quoted list of the members; each member isn't split into separate words. In *csh*, $foo[*]:q does the trick.

—*JP*

9.24 Finding the (Hard) Links to a File

Here is how to find hard links, as well as a brief look at the Unix filesystem from the user's viewpoint. Suppose you are given the following:

```
% ls -li /usr/bin/at
8041 -r-sr-xr-x  4 root  wheel  19540 Apr 21  2001 /usr/bin/at*
```

In other words, there are four links, and */usr/bin/at* is one of four names for inode 8041. You can find the full names of the other three links by using *find*. However, just knowing the inode number does not tell you everything. In particular, inode numbers are only unique to a given filesystem. If you do a *find / –inum 8041 –print*, you may find more than four files, if inode 8041 is also on another filesystem. So how do you tell which ones refer to the same file as */usr/bin/at*?

The simplest way is to figure out the filesystem on which */usr/bin/at* lives by using *df*:

```
% df /usr/bin/at
Filesystem   1K-blocks     Used    Avail Capacity  Mounted on
/dev/ad0s1f   3360437  1644024  1447579    53%     /usr
```

Then start your find at the top of that filesystem, and use *–xdev* to tell it not to search into other filesystems:

```
% find /usr -xdev -inum 8041 -print
/usr/bin/at
/usr/bin/atq
/usr/bin/atrm
/usr/bin/batch
```

Some manpages list *–x* as an alternative to *–xdev*; *–xdev* is generally more portable.

—*DJPH and CT*

9.25 Finding Files with –prune

find has lots of operators for finding some particular kinds of files. But *find* won't stop at your current directory—if there are subdirectories, it looks there too. How can you tell it "only the current directory"? Use *–prune*.

Most *find*s also have a *–maxdepth* option that gives the maximum number of directory levels to descend. For example, *find . –maxdepth 0* operates only on the current directory.

–prune cuts short *find*'s search at the current pathname. So, if the current pathname is a directory, *find* won't descend into that directory for any further searches. The command line looks kind of hairy. Here's one to find all files modified in the last 24 hours from the current directory:

```
% date
Tue Feb 12 19:09:35 MST 2002
% ls -l
total 0
drwxr-xr-x  1 deb  deb  0 Feb 12 12:11 adir
-rw-r--r--  1 deb  deb  0 Feb 12 19:08 afile
-rw-r--r--  1 deb  deb  0 Jan 10 10:37 bfile
-rw-r--r--  1 deb  deb  0 Feb 11 22:43 cfile
% find . \( -type d ! -name . -prune \) -o \( -mtime -1 -print \)
./afile
./cfile
```

Let's try to understand this command: once you see the pattern, you'll understand some important things about *find* that many people don't. Let's follow *find* as it looks at a few pathnames.

find looks at each entry, one by one, in the current directory (.). For each entry, *find* tries to match the expression from left to right. As soon as some parenthesized part matches, it ignores the rest (if any) of the expression.[*]

When *find* is looking at the file named *./afile*, the first part of the expression, (*–type d ! –name . –prune*), doesn't match (*./afile* isn't a directory). So *find* doesn't prune. It tries the other part, after the *–o* (or):

Has *./afile* been modified in the last day? In this (imaginary) case, it has—so the *–print* (which is always true) prints the pathname.

Next, *./bfile*: like the previous step, the first part of the expression won't match. In the second part, (*–mtime –1 –print*), the file's modification time is more than one day ago. So the *–mtime –1* part of the expression is false; *find* doesn't bother with the *–print* operator.

---

[*] That's because if one part of an OR expression is true, you don't need to check the rest. This so-called "short-circuit" logical evaluation by *find* is important to understanding its expressions.

Finally, let's look at *./adir*, a directory: the first part of the expression, (*–type d ! –name . –prune*), matches. That's because *./adir* is a directory (*–type d*), its name is not . (*! –name .*). So *–prune*, which is always true, makes this part of the expression true. *find* skips *./adir* (because *–prune* prunes the search tree at the current pathname). Note that if we didn't use *! –name .*, then the current directory would match immediately and not be searched, and we wouldn't find anything at all.

Article 9.27 shows handy aliases that use *–prune*.

—JP

9.26 Quick finds in the Current Directory

find –prune prunes *find*'s search tree at the current pathname. Here are a couple of aliases that use *–prune* to search for files in the current directory. The first one, named *find.* (with a dot on the end of its name, to remind you of ., the relative pathname for the current directory), simply prints names with *–print*. The second alias gives a listing like *ls –gilds*. You can add other *find* operators to the command lines to narrow your selection of files. The aliases work like this:

```
% find. -mtime -1
./afile
./cfile
% find.ls -mtime -1
43073   0 -r--------  1 jerry    ora       0 Mar 27 18:16 ./afile
43139   2 -r--r--r--  1 jerry    ora    1025 Mar 24 02:33 ./cfile
```

The *find.* alias is handy inside backquotes, feeding a pipe, and other places you need a list of filenames. The second one, *find.ls*, uses *–ls* instead of *–print*:

```
alias find. 'find . \( -type d ! -name . -prune \) -o \( \!* -print \)'
alias find.ls 'find . \( -type d ! -name . -prune \) -o \( \!* -ls \)'
```

If you don't want the *./* at the start of each name, add a pipe through *cut –c3–* or *cut –d'/' –f2–* to the end of the alias definition.

—JP

9.27 Skipping Parts of a Tree in find

Q: *I want to run find across a directory tree, skipping standard directories like /usr/spool and /usr/local/bin. A –name dirname –prune clause won't do it because –name doesn't match the whole pathname—just each part of it, such as spool or local. How can I make find match the whole pathname, like /usr/local/bin/, instead of all directories named bin?*

A: It cannot be done directly. You *can* do this:

```
% find /path -exec test {} = /foo/bar -o {} = /foo/baz \; -prune -o pred
```

This will not perform *pred* on */foo/bar* and */foo/baz*; if you want them done, but not any files within them, try:

```
% find /path \( -exec test test-exprs \; ! -prune \) -o pred
```

The second version is worth close study, keeping the manual for *find* at hand for reference. It shows a great deal about how *find* works.

The *–prune* operator simply says "do not search the current path any deeper" and then succeeds a la *–print*.

Q: *I only want a list of pathnames; the pred I use in your earlier answer will be just –print. I think I could solve my particular problem by piping the find output through a sed or egrep –v filter that deletes the pathnames I don't want to see.*

A: That would probably be fastest. Using *test* runs the *test* program for each file name, which is quite slow. Take a peek at *locate*, described in article 9.18.

There's more about complex *find* expressions in other articles, especially 9.6 and 9.12.

—*CT and JP*

9.28 Keeping find from Searching Networked Filesystem

The most painful aspect of a large NFS environment is avoiding the access of files on NFS servers that are down. *find* is particularly sensitive to this because it is very easy to access dozens of machines with a single command. If *find* tries to explore a file server that happens to be down, it will time out. It is important to understand how to prevent *find* from going too far.

To do this, use *–xdev* or *–prune* with *–fstype*, though, unfortunately, not all *finds* have all of these. *–fstype* tests for filesystem types and expects an argument like nfs, ufs, cd9660, or ext2fs. To limit *find* to files only on a local disk or disks, use the clause *–fstype nfs –prune*, or, if your *find* supports it, *–fstype local*.

To limit the search to one particular disk partition, use *–xdev*. For example, if you need to clear out a congested disk partition, you could look for all files bigger than 10 MB (10*1024*1024) on the disk partition containing */usr*, using this command:

```
% find /usr -size +10485760c -xdev -print
```

—*BB*

10

Linking, Renaming, and Copying Files

10.1 What's So Complicated About Copying Files

At first glance, there doesn't seem to be enough material to fill an entire chapter with information about linking, moving, and copying files. However, there are several things that make the topic more complex (and more interesting) than you might expect:

- In addition to moving and copying files, Unix systems also allow you to link them—to have two filenames, perhaps in different directories or even on different filesystems, that point to the same file. Article 10.3 explores the reasons why you want to do that; Article 10.4 discusses the difference between "hard" and "soft" links; Article 10.5 demonstrates how to create links; and other articles discuss various issues that can come up when using links.

- It's nontrivial to rename a group of files all at once, but Unix provides many ways to circumvent the tedium of renaming files individually. In the chapter you'll see many different ways to do this, exploring the variety in the Unix toolbox along the way.

- In a hierarchical filesystem, you're sometimes faced with the problem of moving not only files but entire directory hierarchies from one place to another. Articles 10.12 and 10.13 demonstrate two techniques you can use to perform this task.

—*TOR*

10.2 What's Really in a Directory?

Before you can understand moving and copying files, you need to know a bit more about how files are represented in directories. What does it mean to say that a file is really "in" a directory? It's easy to imagine that files are actually inside of something (some special chunk of the disk that's called a directory). But that's precisely wrong, and it's one place where the filing cabinet model of a filesystem doesn't apply.

A directory really is just another file, and it really isn't different from any other datafile. If you want to prove this, try the command *od –c* . On some Unix systems, it dumps the current directory to the screen in raw form. The result certainly looks ugly (it's not a text file; it just has lots of binary characters). But, if your system allows it, *od –c* should let you see the names of the files that are in the current directory [and, probably, some names of files that have been deleted! Sorry, they're only the old directory entries; you can't get the files back —*JP*]. If *od –c* . doesn't work (and it won't on current versions of Linux, for example), use *ls –if* instead.

A directory is really just a list of files represented by filenames and inode numbers, as shown in the output in Example 10-1.

Example 10-1. Directory-content visualization

```
The file named     .         is inode 34346
The file named     ..        is inode 987
The file named     mr.ed     is inode 10674
The file named     joe.txt   is inode 8767
The file named     grok      is inode 67871
The file named     otherdir  is inode 2345
```

When you give a filename like *grok*, the kernel looks up *grok* in the current directory and finds out that this file has inode 67871; it then looks up this inode to find out who owns the file, where the data blocks are, and so on.

What's more, some of these "files" may be directories in their own right. In particular, that's true of the first two entries: . and ... These entries are in *every* directory. The current directory is represented by ., while .. refers to the "parent" of the current directory (i.e., the directory that "contains" the current directory). The file *otherdir* is yet another directory that happens to be "within" the current directory. However, there's no way you can tell that from its directory entry—Unix doesn't know it's different until it looks up its inode.

Now that you know what a directory is, think about some basic directory operations. What does it mean to move, or rename, a file? If the file is staying in the same directory, the *mv* command just changes the file's name in the directory; it doesn't touch the data at all.

Moving a file into another directory takes a little more work, but not much. A command like *mv dir1/foo dir2/foo* means "delete *foo*'s entry in *dir1* and create a new entry for *foo* in *dir2*." Again, Unix doesn't have to touch the data blocks or the inode at all.

The only time you actually need to copy data is if you're moving a file into another filesystem. In that case, you have to copy the file to the new filesystem; delete its old directory entry; return the file's data blocks to the "free list," which means that they can be reused; and so on. It's a fairly complicated operation, but (still) relatively rare. (On some old versions of Unix, *mv* wouldn't let you move files between filesystems. You had to copy it and remove the old file by hand.)

How does Unix find out the name of the current directory? In Example 10-1 there's an entry for ., which tells you that the current directory has inode 34346. Is the directory's name part of the inode? Sorry—it isn't. The directory's name is included in the parent directory. The parent directory is .., which is inode 987. So Unix looks up inode 987, finds out where the data is, and starts reading every entry in the parent directory. Sooner or later, it will find one that corresponds to inode 34346. When it does that, it knows that it has found the directory entry for the current directory and can read its name.

Complicated? Yes, but if you understand this, you have a pretty good idea of how Unix directories work.

—ML

10.3 Files with Two or More Names

We've talked about hard links (10.1) and symbolic links in a number of places, but we've not discussed *why* you'd want a file with several names. It was easy to understand what a link would *do*, but why would you want one?

There are many situations that links (and only links) are able to handle. Once you've seen a few of the problems that a link can solve, you'll start seeing even more situations in which they are appropriate.

Consider a company phone list on a system that is shared by several users. Every user might want a copy of the phone list in his home directory. However, you wouldn't want to give each user a different phone list. In addition to wasting disk space, it would be a pain to modify all of the individual lists whenever you made a change. Giving each user a "link" to a master phone list is one way to solve the problem.

Similarly, assume that you use several different systems that share files via NFS. Eventually, you get tired of editing five or six different *.login* and *.cshrc* files whenever you decide to add a new alias or change some element in your startup file; you'd like to have the exact same file appear in each of your home directories. You might also want to give several systems access to the same master database files.

How about this: you have a program or script that performs several related functions. Why not perform them all with the same executable? The script or program just needs to check the name by which it's called and act accordingly.

As another example, assume that you have two versions of a file: a current version, which changes from time to time, and one or more older versions. One good convention would be to name the files *data.date*, where *date* shows when the file was created. For example, you might have the files *data.jul1*, *data.jul2*, *data.jul5*, and so on. However, when you access these files, you don't necessarily want to figure out the date—not unless you have a better chronological sense than I do. To make it easier on yourself, create a link (either symbolic or hard) named *data.cur* that always refers to your most recent file. The following script runs the program *output*, puts the data into a dated file, and resets *data.cur*:

```
#!/bin/sh
curfile=data.`date +%h%d`
linkname=data.cur
output > $curfile
rm -f $linkname
ln -s $curfile $linkname
```

Here's an analogous situation. When writing technical manuals at one company, I had two classes of readers: some insisted on referring to the manuals by name, and the others by part number. Rather than looking up part numbers all the time, I created a set of links so that I could look up a manual online via either its name or its part number. For example, if the manual was named "Programming" and had the part number 046-56-3343, I would create the file */manuals/byname/programming*. I would then create the link */manuals/bynumber/046-56-3343*:

.. 1.16

```
% cd /manuals/bynumber
% ln -s ../byname/programming 046-56-3343
```

Sometimes you simply want to collect an assortment of files in one directory. These files may really belong in other places, but you want to collect them for some temporary purpose: for example, to make a tape. Let's say that you want to make a tape that includes manual pages from */development/doc/man/man1*, a manual from */development/doc/product*, source files from */src/ccode*, and a set of executables from */release/68000/execs*. The following shell script creates links for all of these directories within the */tmp/tape* directory and then creates a *tar* tape that can be sent to a customer or friend. Note that the *tar h* option tells *tar* to follow symbolic links and archive whatever is at the end of the link; otherwise, *tar* makes a copy of just the symbolic link:

```
#!/bin/sh
dir=/tmp/tape.mike
test -d $dir || mkdir $dir
cd $dir
rm -f man1 product ccode execs
```

```
ln -s /development/doc/man/man1
ln -s /development/doc/product
ln -s /src/ccode
ln -s /release/68000/execs
tar ch ./man1 ./product ./ccode ./execs
```

These examples only begin to demonstrate the use of linking in solving day-to-day tasks. Links provide neat solutions to many problems, including source control, filesystem layout, and so forth.

—*ML*

10.4 More About Links

Unix provides two different kinds of links:

Hard links

With a hard link, two filenames (i.e., two directory entries) point to the same inode and the same set of data blocks. All Unix versions support hard links. They have two important limitations: a hard link can't cross a filesystem (i.e., both filenames must be in the same filesystem), and you can't create a hard link to a directory (i.e., a directory can only have one name).* They have two important advantages: the link and the original file are absolutely and always identical, and the extra link takes no disk space (except an occasional extra disk block in the directory file).

Symbolic links (also called soft links *or* symlinks)

With a symbolic link, there really are two different files. One file contains the actual data; the other file just contains the name of the first file and serves as a "pointer." We call the pointer the *link*. The system knows that whenever it opens a symlink, it should read the contents of the link and then access the file that really holds the data you want. Nearly all Unix systems support symbolic links these days. Symbolic links are infinitely more flexible than hard links. They can cross filesystems or even computer systems (if you are using *NFS* or *RFS* (44.9)). You can make a symbolic link to a directory. A symbolic link has its own inode and takes a small amount of disk space to store.

You obviously can't do without copies of files: copies are important whenever users need their own "private version" of some master file. However, links are equally useful. With links, there's only one set of data and many different names that can access it. Article 10.5 shows how to make links.

---

* Actually, every directory has at least two names. See the last section of this article.

Differences Between Hard and Symbolic Links

With a hard link, the two filenames are identical in every way. You can delete one without harming the other. The system deletes the directory entry for one filename and leaves the data blocks (which are shared) untouched. The only thing *rm* does to the inode is decrement its "link count," which (as the name implies) counts the number of hard links to the file. The data blocks are only deleted when the link count goes to zero—meaning that there are no more directory entries that point to this inode. Article 9.24 shows how to find the hard links to a file.

With a symbolic link, the two filenames are really not the same. Deleting the link with *rm* leaves the original file untouched, which is what you'd expect. But deleting or renaming the original file removes both the filename and the data. You are left with a link that doesn't point anywhere. Remember that the link itself doesn't have any data associated with it. Despite this disadvantage, you rarely see hard links on Unix versions that support symbolic links. Symbolic links are so much more versatile that they have become omnipresent.

Let's finish by taking a look at the *ls* listing for a directory. This directory has a file named *file* with another hard link to it named *hardlink*. There's also a symlink to *file* named (are you ready?) *symlink*:

```
$ ls -lai
total 8
 140330 drwxr-xr-x   2 jerry     ora      1024 Aug 18 10:11 .
  85523 drwxr-xr-x   4 jerry     ora      1024 Aug 18 10:47 ..
 140331 -rw-r--r--   2 jerry     ora      2764 Aug 18 10:11 file
 140331 -rw-r--r--   2 jerry     ora      2764 Aug 18 10:11 hardlink
 140332 lrwxrwxrwx   1 jerry     ora         4 Aug 18 10:12 symlink -> file
```

You've seen *ls*'s *–l* option (50.2) and, probably, the *–a* option (8.9) for listing "dot files." The *–i* option lists the i-number (14.2) for each entry in the directory; see the first column. The third column has the *link count*: this is the number of hard links to the file.

When you compare the entries for *file* and *hardlink*, you'll see that they have a link count of 2. In this case, both links are in the same directory. Every other entry (i-number, size, owner, etc.) for *file* and *hardlink* is the same; that's because they both refer to exactly the same file, with two links (names).

A symbolic link has an l at the start of the permissions field. Its i-number isn't the same as the file to which it points because a symbolic link takes a separate inode; so, it also takes disk space (which an extra hard link doesn't). The name has two parts: the name of the link (here, *symlink*) followed by an arrow and the name to which the link points (in this case, *file*). The symlink takes just four characters, which is exactly enough to store the pathname (*file*) to which the link points.

Links to a Directory

While we're at it, here's a section that isn't about linking to files or making symbolic links. Let's look at the first two entries in the previous sample directory in terms of links and link counts. This should help to tie the filesystem together (both literally and in your mind!).

You've seen . and .. in pathnames (1.16); you might also have read an explanation of what's in a directory (10.2). The . entry is a link to the current directory; notice that its link count is 2. Where's the other link? It's in the parent directory:

```
$ ls -li ..
total 2
  140330 drwxr-xr-x   2 jerry    ora      1024 Aug 18 10:11 sub
   85524 drwxr-xr-x   2 jerry    ora      1024 Aug 18 10:47 sub2
```

Look at the i-numbers for the entries in the parent directory. Which entry is for our current directory? The entry for *sub* has the i-number 140330, and so does the . listing in the current directory. So the current directory is named *sub*. Now you should be able see why every directory has at least two links. One link, named ., is to the directory itself. The other link, in its parent, gives the directory its name.

Every directory has a .. entry, which is a link to its parent directory. If you look back at the listing of our current directory, you can see that the parent directory has four links. Where are they?

When a directory has subdirectories, it will also have a hard link named .. in each subdirectory. You can see earlier, in the output from *ls –li ..*, that the parent directory has two subdirectories: *sub* and *sub2*. That's two of the four links. The other two links are the . entry in the parent directory and the entry for the parent directory (which is named *test* in *its* parent directory):

-d 8.5
```
% ls -dli ../. ../../test
   85523 drwxr-xr-x   4 jerry    ora      1024 Aug 18 10:47 ../.
   85523 drwxr-xr-x   4 jerry    ora      1024 Aug 18 10:47 ../../test
```

As they should, all the links have the same i-number: 85523. Make sense? This concept can be a little abstract and hard to follow at first. Understanding it will help you, though—especially if you're a system administrator who has to understand *fsck*'s output because it can't fix something automatically or use strong medicine like *clri*. For more practice, make a subdirectory and experiment in it the way shown in this article.

By the way, directories and their hard links . and .. are added by the *mkdir* (2) system call. That's the only way that normal users can create a directory (and the links to it).

—JP and ML

10.5 Creating and Removing Links

The *ln* command creates both hard and soft (symbolic) links (10.4). If by some strange chance you're using Minix or some other Unix that doesn't have sym-links, then *ln* won't have the *-s* option.

```
% ln filename linkname          ...To create a hard link
% ln -s filename linkname       ...To create a symbolic link
```

If creating a hard link, *filename* must already exist, or you will get an error mes-sage. On many versions of *ln*, *linkname* must not exist—if it does, you will also get an error. On other versions, *linkname* may already exist; if you are allowed to write the file, *ln* destroys its old contents and creates your link. If you don't have write access for *linkname*, *ln* asks whether it is okay to override the file's protec-tion. For example:

```
% ln foo bar
ln: override protection 444 for bar? y
```

Typing y gives *ln* permission to destroy the file *bar* and create the link. Note that this will still fail if you don't have write access to the directory.

You are allowed to omit the *linkname* argument from the *ln* command. In this case, *ln* takes the last component of *filename* (i.e., everything after the last slash) and uses it for *linkname*. Of course, this assumes that *filename* doesn't refer to the current directory. If it does, the command fails because the link already exists. For example, the following commands are the same:

```
% ln -s ../archive/file.c file.c
% ln -s ../archive/file.c
```

.. 1.16

Both create a link from *file.c* in the current directory to *../archive/file.c. ln* also lets you create a group of links with one command, provided that all of the links are in the same directory. Here's how:

```
% ln file1 file2 file3 ... filen directory
```

This command uses the filename from each pathname (after the last slash) as each link's name. It then creates all the links within the given *directory*. For example, the first of the following commands is equivalent to the next two:

. 1.16

```
% ln ../s/f1 ../s/f2 current
% ln ../s/f1 current/f1
% ln ../s/f2 current/f2
```

You can replace this list of files with a wildcard expression (33.2), as in:

```
% ln -s ../newversion/*.[ch]
```

Note that symbolic links can get out-of-date (10.6). Hard links can also be "bro-ken" in some situations. For example, a text editor might rename the link *textfile* to *textfile.bak* then create a new *textfile* during editing. Previous links to *textfile* will now give you *textfile.bak*. To track down this problem, find the links (9.24) to each file.

To remove a link, either hard or symbolic, use the *rm* command.

—*ML*

10.6 Stale Symbolic Links

Symbolic links (10.5) have one problem. Like good bread, they become "stale" fairly easily. What does that mean?

Consider the following commands:

```
% ln -s foo bar
% rm foo
```

What happens if you run these two commands? Remember that the link *bar* is a pointer: it doesn't have any real data of its own. Its data is the name of the file *foo*. After deleting *foo*, the link *bar* still exists, but it points to a nonexistent file. Commands that refer to bar will get a confusing error message:

```
% cat bar
cat: bar: No such file or directory
```

This will drive you crazy if you're not careful. The *ls* command will show you that *bar* still exists. You won't understand what's going on until you realize that *bar* is only a pointer to a file that no longer exists.

The commands *ls –Ll* or *ls –LF* will show an unconnected symbolic link. The *–L* option means "list the file that this link points to instead of the link itself." If the link points nowhere, *ls –L* will still list the link.

There are many innocuous ways of creating invalid symbolic links. For example, you could simply *mv* the data file *foo*. Or you could move *foo*, *bar*, or both to some other part of the filesystem where the pointer wouldn't be valid anymore.

One way to avoid problems with invalid links is to use relative pathnames (1.16) when appropriate. For instance, using relative pathnames will let you move entire directory trees around without invalidating links (provided that both the file and the link are in the same tree). Here's an example: assume that you have the file */home/mars/john/project/datastash/input123.txt*. Assume that you want to link this file to */home/mars/john/test/input.txt*. You create a link by giving the command:

```
% cd /home/mars/john/test
% ln -s ../project/datastash/input123.txt input.txt
```

At some later date, you hand the project over to *mary*, who copies (10.13) the entire *project* and *test* data trees into her home directory. The link between *input.txt* and the real file, *input123.txt*, will still be valid. Although both files' names have changed, the relationship between the two (i.e., the relative path from one directory to the other) is still the same. Alternatively, assume that you are assigned to a different computer named *jupiter* and that you copy your entire home directory when you move. Again, the link remains valid: the relative path from your *test* directory to your *datastash* directory hasn't changed, even though the absolute paths of both directories are different.

On the other hand, there is certainly room for absolute pathnames (31.2). They're useful if you're more likely to move the link than the original file. Assume that you are creating a link from your working directory to a file in a master directory (let's say */corp/masterdata/input345.txt*). It is much more likely that you will rearrange your working directory than that someone will move the master set of files. In this case, you would link as follows:

```
% ln -s /corp/masterdata/input345.txt input.txt
```

Now you can move the link *input.txt* anywhere in the filesystem: it will still be valid, provided that *input345.txt* never moves.

Note that hard links never have this problem. With a hard link, there is no difference at all between the link and the original—in fact, it's unfair to call one file the link and the other the original, since both are just links to the same inode. You can't even tell which one came first.

—*ML*

10.7 Linking Directories

One feature of *symbolic links* (10.5) (a.k.a. *symlinks*) is that unlike hard links, you can use symbolic links to link directories as well as files. Since symbolic links can span between filesystems, this can become enormously useful.

For example, sometimes administrators want to install a package in a directory tree that's not where users and other programs expect it to be. On our site, we like to keep */usr/bin* pure—that is, we like to be sure that all the programs in */usr/bin* came with the operating system. That way, when we install a new OS, we know for sure that we can overwrite the entirety of */usr/bin* and not lose any "local" programs. We install all local programs in */usr/local*.

The X11 package poses a problem, though. Our X windows package (discussed in Chapter 5) expects X11 programs to be installed in */usr/bin/X11*. But X isn't distributed as part of our OS, so we'd prefer not to put it there. Instead, we install X programs in */usr/local/X11/bin* and create a symbolic link named */usr/bin/X11*. We do the same for */usr/include/X11* and */usr/lib/X11*:

```
# ln -s /usr/local/X11/bin /usr/bin/X11
# ln -s /usr/local/X11/lib /usr/lib/X11
# ln -s /usr/local/X11/include /usr/include/X11
```

By using symlinks, we installed the package where we wanted, but we kept it invisible to any users or programs that expected the X programs, libraries, or include files to be in the standard directories.

Directory links can result in some unexpected behavior, however. For example, let's suppose I want to look at files in */usr/bin/X11*. I can just *cd* to */usr/bin/X11*, even though the files are really in */usr/local/X11/bin*:

```
% cd /usr/bin/X11
% ls -F
      mkfontdir*    xcalc*      xinit*      xset*
   ...
```

But when I do a *pwd,** I see that I'm really in */usr/local/X11/bin*. If I didn't know about the symlink, this might be confusing for me:

```
% pwd
/usr/local/X11/bin
```

Now suppose I want to look at files in */usr/bin*. Since I did a *cd* to */usr/bin/X11*, I might think I can just go up a level. But that doesn't work:

-F **8.3**
```
% cd ..
% ls -F
bin/      include/    lib/
% pwd
/usr/local/X11
```

What happened? Remember that a symbolic link is just a *pointer* to another file or directory. So when I went to the */usr/bin/X11* "directory," my current working directory became the directory to which */usr/bin/X11* points, which is */usr/local/X11/bin*.

As a solution to this problem and others, the X distribution provides a program called *lndir*. *lndir* makes symlinks between directories by creating links for each individual file. It's cheesy, but it works. If you have it, you can use *lndir* instead of *ln −s*:

lndir
```
# lndir /usr/local/X11/bin /usr/bin/X11
# ls -F /usr/bin/X11
X@        mkfontdir@    xcalc@      xinit@      xset@
   ...
```

—LM

---

* I mean the standard Unix *pwd* command, an external command that isn't built into your shell. Most shells have an internal version of *pwd* that "keeps track" of you as you change your current directory; it may not give the same answer I show here. You can run the external version by typing */bin/pwd*.

10.8 Showing the Actual Filenames for Symbolic Links

sl

The *sl* program is a *perl* script (see coverage of Perl in Chapter 41) that traverses the pathnames supplied on the command line, and for each one, it tells you if it had to follow any symbolic links to find the actual filename. Symbolic links to absolute pathnames start over at the left margin. Symbolic links to relative pathnames are aligned vertically with the path element they replace. For example:

```
$ sl /usr/lib/libXw.a

/usr/lib/libXw.a:
/usr/lib/libXw.a -> /usr/lib/X11/libXw.a
/usr/lib/X11 -> /X11/lib
/X11 -> /usr/local/X11R4
/usr/local/X11R4/lib/libXw.a

$ sl /bin/rnews

/bin -> /usr/bin
/usr/bin/rnews -> /usr/lib/news/rnews
/usr/lib/news -> ../local/lib/news
        local/lib/news/rnews -> inews
                        inews
```

—*LW and RS*

10.9 Renaming, Copying, or Comparing a Set of Files

If you have a group of files whose names end with *.new* and you want to rename them to end with *.old*, you might try something like the following:

```
% mv *.new *.old      Wrong!
```

However, this won't work because the shell can't match *.old* and because the *mv* command just doesn't work that way. Here's one way to do it that will work with most shells:

-d **8.5**
\(..\)..\1
34.11

```
$ ls -d *.new | sed "s/\(.*\)\.new$/mv '&' '\1.old'/" | sh
% ls -d *.new | sed 's/\(.*\)\.new$/mv "&" "\1.old"/' | sh
```

That outputs a series of *mv* commands, one per file, and pipes them to a shell (**3.4**). The quotes help make sure that special characters (**27.17**) aren't touched by the shell—this isn't always needed, but it's a good idea if you aren't sure what files you'll be renaming. Single quotes around the filenames are "strongest"; we use them in the Bourne-type shell version. Unfortunately, *csh* and *tcsh* don't allow $ inside double quotes unless it's the start of a shell variable name. So the C shell version puts double quotes around the filenames—but the Bourne shell version can use the "stronger" single quotes, like this:

```
mv 'afile.new' 'afile.old'
mv 'bfile.new' 'bfile.old'
...
```

To copy, change *mv* to *cp*. For safety, use *mv −i* or *cp −i* if your versions have the −*i* options (14.15). Using *sh −v* (27.15) will show the commands as the shell executes them.

This method works for any Unix command that takes a pair of filenames. For instance, to compare a set of files in the current directory with the original files in the */usr/local/src* directory, use *diff*:

```
% ls -d *.c *.h | sed 's@.*@diff -c & /usr/local/src/&@' | sh
```

Note that *diff −r* does let you compare entire directories, but you need a trick like this to only compare some of the files.

—*JP and DJPH*

10.10 Renaming a List of Files Interactively

Article 10.9 shows how to rename a set of files, e.g., changing *.new to *.old. Here's a different way, done from inside *vi*. This gives you a chance to review and edit the commands before you run them. Here are the steps:

	`% vi`	*Start vi without a filename*
	`:r !ls *.new`	*Read in the list of files, one filename per line*
&& 34.10	`:%s/.*/mv -i &&/`	*Make mv command lines*
	`:%s/new$/old/`	*Change second filenames; ready to review*
$ 32.5	`:w !sh`	*Run commands by writing them to a shell*
	`:q!`	*Quit vi without saving*

If you've made your own version of *ls* that changes its output format, that can cause trouble here. If your version gives more than a plain list of filenames in a column, use `!/bin/ls` instead of just `!ls`.

—*JP*

10.11 One More Way to Do It

I couldn't resist throwing my hat into this ring. I can imagine an unsophisticated user who might not trust himself to replace one pattern with another, but doesn't want to repeat a long list of *mv −i* commands. (The −*i* option will prompt if a new name would overwrite an existing file.) Here's a simple script (1.8) that takes a list of filenames (perhaps provided by wildcards) as input and prompts the user for a new name for each file:

```
#!/bin/sh
# Usage: newname files
for x
do
```

```
        echo -n "old name is $x, new name is: "
        read newname
        mv -i "$x" "$newname"
    done
```

For example:

```
% touch junk1 junk2 junk3
% newname junk*
old name is junk1, new name is: test1
mv: overwrite test1 with junk1? y
old name is junk2, new name is: test2
old name is junk3, new name is: test3
```

In the first case, *test1* already existed, so *mv –i* prompted.

This script is very simple; I just thought I'd use it to demonstrate that there's more than one way to do it, even if you aren't using Perl.

—TOR

10.12 Copying Directory Trees with cp –r

cp has a *–r* (recursive) flag, which copies all the files in a directory tree—that is, all the files in a directory and its subdirectories.

One of our Unix systems has a *cp* without a *–r* option. But it also has an *rcp* (1.21) command that *does* have *–r*. *rcp* can copy to any machine, not just remote machines. When I need *cp –r* on that host, I use *rcp –r*.

cp –r can be used in two ways. The first is much like normal copies; provide a list of files to copy and an existing directory into which to copy them. The *–r* option just means that source directories will be copied as well as normal files. The second allows you to copy a single directory to another location.

- Here's how to do the copy shown in Figure 10-1. This copies the directory */home/jane*, with all its files and subdirectories, and creates a subdirectory named *jane* in the current directory (.) (1.16):

  ```
  % cd /work/bkup
  % cp -r /home/jane .
  ```

- How can you copy the contents of the subdirectory called *data* and all its files (but not the subdirectory itself) into a duplicate directory named *data.bak*? First make sure that the destination directory doesn't exist. That's because if the last argument to *cp* is a directory that already exists, the source directory will be copied to a subdirectory of the destination directory (i.e., it will become *data.bak/data* rather than just *data.bak*):

  ```
  % cd /home/jane
  % cp -r data data.bak
  ```

- Use this to copy the subdirectories *Aug* and *Sep* and their files from the directory */home/jim/calendar* into the current directory (.):

[..]* **33.2**

```
% cp -r /home/jim/calendar/[AS]* .
```

In many shells, if you wanted the *Oct* directory too, but not the file named *Output*, you can copy just the directories by using the handy curly brace operators (28.4):

```
% cp -r /home/jim/calendar/{Aug,Sep,Oct} .
```

Some gotchas:

- Symbolic and hard links (10.4) are copied as files. That can be a good thing; if a symbolic link were not turned into a file along the way, the new symbolic link would point to the wrong place. It can be bad if the link pointed to a really big file; the copy can take up a lot of disk space that you didn't expect. (In Figure 10-1, notice that the symbolic link in *jane*'s home directory was converted to a file named *.setup* with a copy of the contents of *generic*.) This can be prevented by using the *–d* option, if your *cp* supports it.

- On many Unixes, the copy will be dated at the time you made the copy and may have its permissions set by your *umask*. If you want the copy to have the original modification time and permissions, add the *–p* option.

- *cp –r* may go into an endless loop if you try to copy a directory into itself. For example, let's say you're copying everything from the current directory into an existing subdirectory named *backup*, like this:

```
% cp -r * backup
```

Unless your *cp –r* is smart enough to scan for files before it starts copying, it will create *backup/backup*, and *backup/backup/backup*, and so on. To avoid that, replace the * wildcard with other less-"wild" wildcards.

- *cp –r* doesn't deal well with special files. Most platforms support a *–R* option instead, which correctly handles device files and the like. GNU *cp* has *–a* as a recommended option for normal recursive copying; it combines *–R* with *–d* and *–p*, as described earlier.

Note that directories can be copied to another machine using the same basic syntax with *rcp* and *scp*. The only difference is that remote files have *hostname*: in front of them; note that remote files can be used either as source or destination. Relative pathnames for remote files are always relative to your home directory on the remote machine.

```
% scp -r mydata bigserver:backups
% scp -r bass:/export/src/gold-20020131 .
```

scp and *rcp* use the same syntax; *scp* uses SSH (46.6) to do its copying, while *rcp* uses unencrypted connections.

—*DJPH and JP*

10.13 Copying Directory Trees with tar and Pipes

The *tar* (39.2) command isn't just for tape archives. It can copy files from disk to disk, too. And even if your computer has *cp −r* (10.12), there are advantages to using *tar*.

The obvious way to copy directories with *tar* is to write them onto a tape archive with relative pathnames—then read back the tape and write it somewhere else on the disk. But *tar* can also write to a Unix pipe—and read from a pipe. This looks like:

```
% reading-tar | writing-tar
```

with one trick: the *writing-tar* process has a different current directory (24.3, 24.4) (the place where you want the copy made) than the *reading-tar*. To do that, run the *writing-tar* in a subshell (43.7), or if your *tar* supports it, use the −C option.

The argument(s) to the *reading-tar* can be directories or files. Just be sure to use relative pathnames (31.2) that don't start with a slash—otherwise, the *writing-tar* may write the copies in the same place from where the originals came!

"How about an example," you ask? Figure 10-1 has one. It copies from the directory */home/jane*, with all its files and subdirectories. The copy is made in the directory */work/bkup/jane*:

```
% mkdir /work/bkup/jane
% cd /home/jane
% tar cf - . | (cd /work/bkup/jane && tar xvf -)
```

Or, if you want to use −C:

```
% tar cf - . | tar xvf - -C /work/bkup/jane
```

In the subshell version, the && operator (35.14) tells the shell to start tar xvf - only if the previous command (the cd) succeeded. That prevents *tar* writing files into the same directory from which it's reading—if the destination directory isn't accessible or you flub its pathname. Also, don't use the *v* (verbose) option in both *tars* unless you want to see doubled output; one or the other is plenty. I usually put it in the *writing-tar* to see write progress, as that's more interesting to me than how far ahead the system has cached the read for me.

 At least one *tar* version has a *v* (verbose) option that writes the verbose text to standard output instead of standard error! If your *tar* does that, definitely don't use *v* on the *reading-tar* (the *tar* that feeds the pipe)—use *v* on the *writing-tar* only.

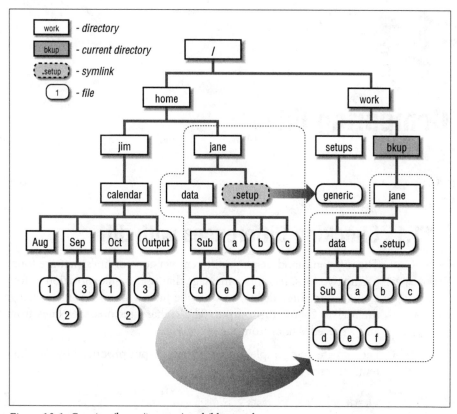

Figure 10-1. Copying /home/jane to /work/bkup with tar

You can use other options that your *tar* might have—such as excluding files or directories—on the *reading-tar*, too. Some gotchas:

- Be aware that symbolic links (10.4) will be copied exactly. If they point to relative pathnames, the copied links might point to locations that don't exist (10.6). You can search for these symbolic links with *find –type l*.

- If your system has *rsh* (1.21) or *ssh*, you can run either the *reading-tar* or the *writing-tar* on a remote system. For example, to copy a directory to the computer named *kumquat*:

  ```
  % ssh kumquat mkdir /work/bkup/jane
  % tar cf - . | ssh kumquat 'cd /work/bkup/jane && tar xvf -'
  ```

—*JP and DJPH*

11

Comparing Files

11.1 Checking Differences with diff

diff

The *diff* command displays different versions of lines that are found when comparing two files. It prints a message that uses *ed*-like notation (*a* for append, *c* for change, and *d* for delete) to describe how a set of lines has changed. The lines themselves follow this output. The < character precedes lines from the first file and > precedes lines from the second file.

Let's create an example to explain the output produced by *diff*. Look at the contents of three sample files:

test1	test2	test3
apples	apples	oranges
oranges	oranges	walnuts
walnuts	grapes	chestnuts

When you run *diff* on *test1* and *test2*, the following output is produced:

```
$ diff test1 test2
3c3
< walnuts
--
> grapes
```

The *diff* command displays the only line that differs between the two files. To understand the report, remember that *diff* is prescriptive, describing what changes need to be made to the first file to make it the same as the second file. This report specifies that only the third line is affected, exchanging walnuts for grapes. This is more apparent if you use the *–e* option, which produces an editing script that can be submitted to *ed*, the Unix line editor. (You must redirect standard output (43.1) to capture this script in a file.)

```
$ diff -e test1 test2
3c
grapes
.
```

This script, if run on *test1*, will bring *test1* into agreement with *test2*. (To do this, feed the script to the standard input of *ed* (20.6) or *ex*; add a *w* command (20.4) at the end of the script to write the changes, if you want to.)

If you compare the first and third files, you find more differences:

```
$ diff test1 test3
1d0
< apples
3a3
> chestnuts
```

To make *test1* the same as *test3*, you'd have to delete the first line (apples) and append the third line from *test3* after the third line in *test1*. Again, this can be seen more clearly in the editing script produced by the *–e* option. Notice that the script specifies editing lines in reverse order; otherwise, changing the first line would alter all subsequent line numbers.

```
$ diff -e test1 test3
3a
chestnuts
.
1d
```

So what's this good for? Here's one example.

When working on a document, it is common practice to make a copy of a file and edit the copy rather than the original. This might be done, for example, if someone other than the writer is inputing edits from a written copy. The *diff* command can be used to compare the two versions of a document. A writer could use it to proof an edited copy against the original.

```
$ diff brochure brochure.edits
49c43,44
< environment for program development and communications,
--
> environment for multiprocessing, program development
> and communications, programmers
56c51
< offering even more power and productivity for commericial
--
> offering even more power and productivity for commercial
76c69
< Languages such as FORTRAN, COBOL, Pascal, and C can be
--
> Additional languages such as FORTRAN, COBOL, Pascal, and
```

Using *diff* in this manner is a simple way for a writer to examine changes without reading the entire document. By redirecting *diff* output to a file, you can keep a record of changes made to any document. In fact, just that technique is used by both RCS and CVS (39.4) to manage multiple revisions of source code and documents.

—DD, *from* Unix Text Processing *(Hayden Books, 1987)*

11.2 Comparing Three Different Versions with diff3

You can use the *diff3* command to look at differences between three files. Here are three sample files, repeated from article 11.1:

test1	test2	test3
apples	apples	oranges
oranges	oranges	walnuts
walnuts	grapes	chestnuts

For each set of differences, *diff3* displays a row of equal signs (====) followed by 1, 2, or 3, indicating which file is different; if no number is specified, then all three files differ. Then, using *ed*-like notation (11.1), the differences are described for each file:

```
$ diff3 test1 test2 test3
====3
1:1c
2:1c
  apples
3:0a
====
1:3c
  walnuts
2:3c
  grapes
3:2,3c
  walnuts
  chestnuts
```

With the output of *diff3*, it is easy to keep track of which file is which; however, the prescription given is a little harder to decipher. To bring these files into agreement, the first range of text (after ====3) shows that you would have to add apples at the beginning of the third file (3:0a). The second range tells you to change line 3 of the second file to line 3 of the first file—change lines 2 and 3 of the third file, effectively dropping the last line.

The *diff3* command also has a *–e* option for creating an editing script for *ed*. It doesn't work quite the way you might think. Basically, it creates a script for building the first file from the second and third files.

```
$ diff3 -e test1 test2 test3
3c
walnuts
chestnuts
.
1d
.
w
q
```

If you reverse the second and third files, a different script is produced:

```
$ diff3 -e test1 test3 test2
3c
grapes
.
w
q
```

As you might guess, this is basically the same output as doing a *diff* on the first and third files.

—DD

11.3 Context diffs

The *diff* examples in articles 11.1 and 11.2 show compact formats with just the differences between the two files. But, in many cases, context *diff* listings are more useful. Context *diffs* show the changed lines and the lines around them. (This can be a headache if you're trying to read the listing on a terminal and there are many changed lines fairly close to one another: the context will make a huge "before" section, with the "after" section several screenfuls ahead. In that case, the more compact *diff* formats can be useful.) A related format, unified *diff*, shows context but doesn't take as much space.

rcs

The *rcsdiff* command shows differences between revisions in an RCS (39.5) file (and will only be available if you have RCS installed). We'll use it here instead of *diff*—but the concepts are the same. Incidentally, these examples would also work with *cvs diff* (39.7), if you have CVS installed.

The *–c* option shows before-and-after versions of each changed section of a file. By itself, *–c* shows three lines above and below each change. Here's an example of a C file before and after some edits; the *-c2* option shows two lines of context. The *–u* option shows changed lines next to each other, not in separate before-and-after sections. Again, an option like *-u2* shows two lines of context around a change instead of the default three lines.

Start of a listing

A *diff –c* listing starts with the two filenames and their last-modified dates ("timestamps"). The first filename (here, *atcat.c* revision 1.1) has three asterisks (***) before it; the second name (*atcat.c* revision 1.2) has three dashes (---). These markers identify the two files in the difference listings below:

```
*** atcat.c 1987/09/19 12:00:44 1.1
--- atcat.c 1987/09/19 12:08:41 1.2
```

A *diff –u* listing also starts with the two filenames and their last-modified dates ("timestamps"). The first filename (here, *atcat.c* revision 1.1) has three minus signs (---) before it, meaning "from" or "before." The second name (*atcat.c* revision 1.2) has three plus signs (+++). Again, these markers identify the two files in the difference listings that follow:

```
--- atcat.c 1987/09/19 12:00:44 1.1
+++ atcat.c 1987/09/19 12:08:41 1.2
```

Start of a section

Each difference section in a *diff –c* listing starts with a row of asterisks:

```
***************
```

In a *diff –u* listing, each difference section starts with a line that has a pair of line numbers and line counts. This one means that the first version of the file (with a - before it) starts at line 14 and contains 5 lines; the second version of the file (with a +) also starts at line 14 and has 5 lines:

```
@@ -14,5 +14,5 @@
```

Changes

In a *diff –c* listing, changed lines that exist in both files are marked with an ! (exclamation point) character in the left margin. So, one of the lines between lines 15–19 was changed. Other lines in the section weren't changed:

```
*** 15, 19 ****
    #ifndef lint
    static char rcsid[] =
!       "$Id: ch11,v 1.33 2002/10/13 03:51:58 troutman Exp troutman $";
    #endif not lint
--- 15,19 ----
    #ifndef lint
    static char rcsid[] =
!       "$Id: ch11,v 1.33 2002/10/13 03:51:58 troutman Exp troutman $";
    #endif not lint
    /* end of Identification */
```

A *diff –u* listing always shows lines that are marked with a minus (-) only in the first version and lines marked with a plus (+) in the second version. Here, one line was changed:

```
@@ -15,5 +15,5 @@
    #ifndef lint
    static char rcsid[] =
-       "$Id: ch11,v 1.33 2002/10/13 03:51:58 troutman Exp troutman $";
```

```
      static char rcsid[] =
  +     "$Id: ch11,v 1.33 2002/10/13 03:51:58 troutman Exp troutman $";
      #endif not lint
      /* end of Identification */
```

Deletions

In a *diff* –*c* listing, a line that exists in the first version but not the second version is marked with a minus sign (-). None of the lines from the second version are shown. So, line 62 in the first version (lines 64–68) was deleted, leaving lines 64–67 in the second version:

```
*** 64,68 ****
    {
        int i;              /* for loop index */
  -     int userid;         /* uid of owner of file */
        int isuname;        /* is a command line argv a user name? */
        int numjobs;        /* # of jobs in spooling area */
--- 64,67 ----
```

A *diff* –*u* listing simply shows the deleted line with a minus (-) sign before it. The section started at line 64 and had 5 lines; after the change, it starts at line 64 and has 4 lines:

```
@@ -64,5 +64,4 @@
    {
        int i;              /* for loop index */
  -     int userid;         /* uid of owner of file */
        int isuname;        /* is a command line argv a user name? */
        int numjobs;        /* # of jobs in spooling area */
```

Additions

In a *diff* –*c* listing, lines that are added are marked with an exclamation point (!) and only appear in the second version. So, one of the lines between lines 111–116 was changed, and two other lines were added, leaving lines 111–118 in the second version:

```
*** 111,116 ****
      * are given, print usage info and exit.
      */
  !     if (allflag && argc)
            usage();

      /*
--- 111,118 ----
      * are given, print usage info and exit.
      */
  !     if (allflag && argc) {
            usage();
  +         exit(1);
  +     }

      /*
```

In a *diff –u* listing, lines that are only in the second version are always marked with a +. Here, one line was changed, and two lines were added. The original version started at line 111 and had 6 lines; the changed version started at line 111 and has 8 lines:

```
@@ -111,6 +111,8 @@
      * are given, print usage info and exit.
      */
-    if (allflag && argc)
+    if (allflag && argc) {
         usage();
+        exit(1);
+    }

     /*
```

Context *diffs* aren't just nice for reading. The *patch* (20.9) program reads context *diff* listings and uses them to update files automatically. For example, if I had the first version of *atcat.c*, someone could send me either of the previous *diff* listings (called a "patch"). From the original and the patch, *patch* could create the second version of *atcat.c*. The advantage of a context *diff* over the formats in articles 11.1 and 11.2 is that context *diffs* let *patch* locate the changed sections even if they've been moved somewhat. In this case, it's probably *not* a good idea to save space by reducing the number of context lines (with -c2 or -u2, as I did here); giving all three lines of context can help *patch* locate the changed sections.

—*JP*

11.4 Side-by-Side diffs: sdiff

After you've used *diff* for a while, the output is easy to read. Sometimes, though, it's just easier to see two files side-by-side. The *sdiff* command does that. Between the files, it prints < to point to lines that are only in the first file, > for lines only in the second file, and | for lines that are in both, but different. By default, *sdiff* shows all the lines in both files. Here's a fairly bogus example that compares two files that contain the output of *who* (2.8) at different times:

```
$ sdiff -w75 who1 who2
jake    vt01      Sep 10 10:37     jake    vt01      Sep 10 10:37
uunmv   ttyi1i    Sep 16 11:43  <
jerry   ttyi1j    Sep 15 22:38     jerry   ttyi1j    Sep 15 22:38
jake    ttyp1     Sep  9 14:55     jake    ttyp1     Sep  9 14:55
jake    ttyp2     Sep  9 15:19  |  ellen   ttyp2     Sep 16 12:07
                                >  carolo  ttyp5     Sep 16 13:03
alison  ttyp8     Sep  9 12:49     alison  ttyp8     Sep  9 12:49
```

To see only lines that are different, use –s (silent):

```
$ sdiff -s -w75 who1 who2
2d1
uunmv    ttyi1i    Sep 16 11:43   <
5c4,5
jake     ttyp2     Sep  9 15:19   |  ellen   ttyp2   Sep 16 12:07
                                  >  carolo  ttyp5   Sep 16 13:03
```

The output lines are usually 130 characters long. That's too long for 80-column-wide screens; if you can put your terminal in 132-column mode or stretch your window, fine. If you can't, use the –w option to set a narrower width, like –w80 for 80-column lines; sdiff will show the first 37 characters from each line (it doesn't write quite all 80 columns). If you can set your printer to compressed type or have a very wide window, use an option like –w170 to get all of each line.

Article 11.5 explains a very useful feature of sdiff: building one file interactively from two files you compare.

—JP

11.5 Choosing Sides with sdiff

One problem you might be tempted to tackle with diff3 (11.2) is sorting out the mess resulting if two people make copies of the same file, and then make changes to their copies. You often find that one version has some things right and another version has other things right. What if you wanted to compile a single version of this document that reflects the changes made to each copy? You want to select which version is correct for each set of differences. An effective way to do this would be to use sdiff (11.4). (Of course, the best thing to do is to prevent the problem in the first place, by using RCS or CVS (39.4).)

One of the most powerful uses of sdiff is to build an output file by choosing between different versions of two files interactively. To do this, specify the –o option and the name of an output file to be created. The sdiff command then displays a % prompt after each set of differences.

You can compare the different versions and select the one that will be sent to the output file. Some of the possible responses are l to choose the left column, r to choose the right column, and q to exit the program.

—TOR and JP

11.6 Problems with diff and Tabstops

The diff (11.1) utility adds extra characters (>, <, +, and so on) to the beginning of lines. That can cause you real grief with tabstops because the extra characters added by *diff* can shift lines enough to make the indentation look wrong. The *diff* –*t* option expands TABs to 8-character tabstops and solves the problem.

If you use nonstandard tabstops, though, piping *diff*'s output through *expand* or *pr* –*e* doesn't help because *diff* has already added the extra characters.

The best answers I've seen are the <( ) process-substitution operator and the ! (exclamation point) script. You can expand TABs before *diff* sees them. For example, to show the differences between two files with 4-column tabstops:

```
$ diff <(expand -4 afile) <(expand -4 bfile)      process substitution
% diff `! expand -4 afile` `! expand -4 bfile`    other shells
```

Of course, nonstandard tabstops cause lots more problems than just with *diff*. If you can, you're better off using 8-space TABs and using spaces instead of tabs for indentation.

—*JP*

11.7 cmp and diff

cmp is another program for comparing files. It's a lot simpler than *diff* (11.1); it tells you whether the files are equivalent and the byte offset at which the first difference occurs. You don't get a detailed analysis of where the two files differ. For this reason, *cmp* is often faster, particularly when you're comparing ASCII files: it doesn't have to generate a long report summarizing the differences. If all you want to know is whether two files are different, it's the right tool for the job.

It's worth noting, though, that *cmp* isn't *always* faster. Some versions of *diff* make some simple checks first, such as comparing file length. If two binary files have different lengths, they are obviously different; some *diff* implementations will tell you so without doing any further processing.

Both *diff* and *cmp* return an exit status (35.12) that shows what they found:

Exit status	Meaning
0	The files were the same.
1	The files differed.
2	An error occurred.

Within a shell script, the exit status from *diff* and *cmp* is often more important than their actual output.

—*ML*

11.8 Comparing Two Files with comm

The *comm* command can tell you what information is common to two lists and what information appears uniquely in one list or the other. For example, let's say you're compiling information on the favorite movies of critics Ebert and Roeper. The movies are listed in separate files (and must be sorted (22.1)). For the sake of illustration, assume each list is short:

```
% cat roeper
Citizen Kane
Halloween VI
Ninja III
Rambo II
Star Trek V
Zelig
% cat ebert
Cat People
Citizen Kane
My Life as a Dog
Q
Z
Zelig
```

To compare the favorite movies of your favorite critics, type:

```
% comm roeper ebert
                Cat People
                                    Citizen Kane
Halloween VI
                My Life as a Dog
Ninja III
                Q
Rambo II
Star Trek V
                Z
                                    Zelig
```

Column 1 shows the movies that only Roeper likes; column 2 shows those that only Ebert likes; and column 3 shows the movies that they both like. You can suppress one or more columns of output by specifying that column as a command-line option. For example, to suppress columns 1 and 2 (displaying only the movies *both* critics like), you would type:

```
% comm -12 roeper ebert
Citizen Kane
Zelig
```

As another example, say you've just received a new software release (Release 4), and it's your job to figure out which library functions have been added so that they can be documented along with the old ones. Let's assume you already have a list of the Release 3 functions (*r3_list*) and a list of the Release 4 functions (*r4_list*). (If you didn't, you could create them by changing to the directory that has the function manual pages, listing the files with *ls*, and saving each list to a file.) In the following lists, we've used letters of the alphabet to represent the functions:

```
% cat r3_list
b
c
d
f
g
h

% cat r4_list
a
b
c
d
e
f
```

You can now use the *comm* command to answer several questions you might have:

- Which functions are new to Release 4? Answer:

  ```
  % comm -13 r3_list r4_list    Show 2nd column, which is "Release 4 only"
  a
  e
  ```

- Which Release 3 functions have been dropped in Release 4? Answer:

  ```
  % comm -23 r3_list r4_list    Show 1st column, which is "Release 3 only"
  g
  h
  ```

- Which Release 3 functions have been retained in Release 4? Answer:

  ```
  % comm -12 r3_list r4_list    Show 3rd column, which is "common functions"
  b
  c
  d
  f
  ```

You can create partial lists by saving the previous output to three separate files.

comm can only compare sorted files. In the GNU version, the option *–l* (lower-case L) means the input files are sorted using the LC_COLLATE collating sequence. If you have non-ASCII characters to sort, check your manual page for details.

—*DG*

11.9 More Friendly comm Output

Article 11.8 didn't show one of my least-favorite *comm* features. The default output (with text in "columns") confuses me if the lines of output have much text (especially text with spaces). For example, if I'm looking at two *who* (2.8) listings to compare who was logged on at particular times, the columns in the *who* output are jumbled:

```
$ comm who1 who2
                root    tty1    Oct 31 03:13
                jpeek   tty2    Oct 31 03:15
    jpeek   pts/0   Oct 31 03:19
                jpeek   pts/1   Oct 31 03:19
                jpeek   pts/2   Oct 31 03:19
    ally    pts/4   Oct 31 03:19
                jpeek   pts/3   Oct 31 03:19
            xena    pts/5   Nov  3 08:41
```

The *commer* script (see later) filters the *comm* output through *sed*. It converts *comm*'s indentation characters (one TAB for lines in "column 2" and two TABs for lines in "column 3") into labels at the start of each output line. The default output looks like this:

```
$ commer who1 who2
BOTH>root    tty1    Oct 31 03:13
BOTH>jpeek   tty2    Oct 31 03:15
 TWO>jpeek   pts/0   Oct 31 03:19
BOTH>jpeek   pts/1   Oct 31 03:19
BOTH>jpeek   pts/2   Oct 31 03:19
 TWO>ally    pts/4   Oct 31 03:19
BOTH>jpeek   pts/3   Oct 31 03:19
 ONE>xena    pts/5   Nov  3 08:41
```

With the *–i* option, the script uses both labels and columns:

```
$ commer -i who1 who2
BOTH>           root    tty1    Oct 31 03:13
BOTH>           jpeek   tty2    Oct 31 03:15
 TWO>jpeek   pts/0   Oct 31 03:19
BOTH>           jpeek   pts/1   Oct 31 03:19
BOTH>           jpeek   pts/2   Oct 31 03:19
 TWO>ally    pts/4   Oct 31 03:19
BOTH>           jpeek   pts/3   Oct 31 03:19
 ONE>   xena    pts/5   Nov  3 08:41
```

commer

Here's the script. The *sed* substitute (s) commands have one or two TABs between the first pair of slashes. Note that the *sed* script is inside double quotes ("), so the shell can substitute the value of $indent with an ampersand (&) into the *sed* script if the *–i* option was used:

```
#!/bin/sh
# commer - label columns in "comm" output
# Usage: commer [-i] file1 file2
#   -i option indents output lines into columns as "comm" does
#
```

```
# Note that script WILL FAIL if any input lines start with a TAB.

case "$1" in
-i) indent='&'; shift ;;
-*|"") echo "Usage: `basename $0` [-i] file1 file2" 1>&2; exit 1 ;;
esac

# In "comm" output, column 1 (lines in file 1) has no leading TAB.
# Column 2 (lines in file 2) has one leading TAB.
# Column 3 (lines in both files) has two leading TABs.
# Search for these tabs and use them to label lines.
# (You could replace ONE and TWO with the filenames $1 and $2)
comm "$1" "$2" |
sed "{
/^                / {s//BOTH>$indent/; b}
/^        / {s// ONE>$indent/; b}
s/^/ TWO>/
}"
```

 The *commer* script will be fooled by lines that already have TAB characters at the start. If this might be a problem, you can modify the script to search the files (grep "^TAB" >/dev/null) before starting *comm*.

—*JP*

11.10 make Isn't Just for Programmers!

The *make* program is a Unix facility for describing dependencies among a group of related files, usually ones that are part of the same project. This facility has enjoyed widespread use in software-development projects. Programmers use *make* to describe how to "make" a program—which source files need to be compiled, which libraries must be included, and which object files need to be linked. By keeping track of these relationships in a single place, individual members of a software-development team can make changes to a single module, run *make*, and be assured that the program reflects the latest changes made by others on the team.

Only by a leap of the imagination do we group *make* with the other commands for keeping track of differences between files. However, although it does not compare two versions of the same source file, it can be used to compare versions of a source file and to the formatted output.

Part of what makes Unix a productive environment for text processing is discovering other uses for standard programs. The *make* utility has many possible applications for a documentation project. One such use is to maintain up-to-date copies of formatted files—which make up a single manual and provide users with a way of obtaining a printed copy of the entire manual without having to know which preprocessors or formatting options (45.13) need to be used.

The basic operation that *make* performs is to compare two sets of files—for example, formatted and unformatted files—and determine if any members of one set, the unformatted files, are more recent than their counterpart in the other set, the formatted files. This is accomplished by simply comparing the last-modification date (8.2) ("timestamp") of pairs of files. If the unformatted source file has been modified since the formatted file was made, *make* executes the specified command to "remake" the formatted file.

To use *make*, you have to write a description file, usually named *Makefile* (or *makefile*), that resides in the working directory for the project. The *Makefile* specifies a hierarchy of dependencies among individual files, called components. At the top of this hierarchy is a target. For our example, you can think of the target as a printed copy of a book; the components are formatted files generated by processing an unformatted file with *nroff* (45.12).

Here's the *Makefile* that reflects these dependencies:

lp **45.2**

```
manual: ch01.fmt ch02.fmt ch03.fmt
        lp ch0[1-3].fmt
ch01.fmt: ch01
        nroff -mm ch01 > ch01.fmt
ch02.fmt: ch02
        tbl ch02 | nroff -mm > ch02.fmt
ch03.fmt: ch03a ch03b ch03c
        nroff -mm ch03[abc] > ch03.fmt
```

This hierarchy is represented in Figure 11-1.

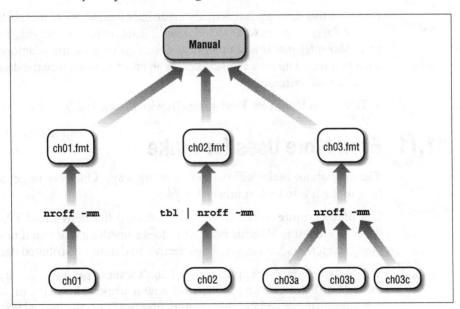

Figure 11-1. What Makefile describes: Files and commands to make manual

The target is *manual*, which is made up of three formatted files whose names appear after the colon. Each of these components has its own dependency line. For instance, *ch01.fmt* is dependent upon a coded file named *ch01*. Underneath the dependency line is the command that generates *ch01.fmt*. Each command line must begin with a TAB.

When you enter the command make, the end result is that the three formatted files are spooled to the printer. However, a sequence of operations is performed before this final action. The dependency line for each component is evaluated, determining if the coded file has been modified since the last time the formatted file was made. The formatting command will be executed only if the coded file is more recent. After all the components are made, the *lp* (45.2) command is executed.

As an example of this process, we'll assume that all the formatted files are up-to-date. Then by editing the source file *ch03a*, we change the modification time. When you execute the *make* command, any output files dependent on *ch03a* are reformatted:

```
$ make
nroff -mm ch03[abc] > ch03.fmt
lp ch0[1-3].fmt
```

Only *ch03.fmt* needs to be remade. As soon as that formatting command finishes, the command underneath the target *manual* is executed, spooling the files to the printer.

Although this example has actually made only limited use of *make*'s facilities, we hope it suggests more ways to use *make* in a documention project. You can keep your *Makefiles* just this simple, or you can go on to learn additional notation, such as internal macros and suffixes, in an effort to generalize the description file for increased usefulness.

—*TOR, from* Unix Text Processing *(Hayden Books, 1987)*

11.11 Even More Uses for make

Thinking about *make* will pay off in many ways. One way to get ideas about how to use it is to look at other *Makefiles*.

One of my favorites is the *Makefile* for NIS (1.21) (formerly called YP, or "Yellow Pages"). I like this *Makefile* because it does something that you'd never think of doing (even though it suits *make* perfectly): updating a distributed database.

The *Makefile* is fairly complicated, so I don't want to get into a line-by-line explication; but I will give you a sketch of how it works. Here's the problem: a system administrator updates one or more files (we'll say the *passwd* file) and wants to get her changes into the NIS database. So you need to check whether the new password file is more recent than the database. Unfortunately, the database isn't represented by a single file, so there's nothing to "check" against. The NIS *Makefile* handles this situation by creating empty files that serve as timestamps. There's a separate timestamp file for every database that NIS serves. When you type *make*, *make* checks every master file against the corresponding timestamp. If a master file is newer than the timestamp, *make* knows that it has to rebuild part of the database. After rebuilding the database, the *Makefile* "touches" the timestamp, so that it reflects the time at which the database was built.

The *Makefile* looks something like this:

```
passwd: passwd.time
passwd.time:  /etc/master/passwd
        @ lots of commands that rebuild the database
        @ touch passwd.time
        @ more commands to distribute the new database

hosts: hosts.time
hosts.time:  similar stuff
```

You may never need to write a *Makefile* this complicated, but you should look for situations in which you can use *make* profitably. It isn't just for programming.

—*ML*

12

Showing What's in a File

12.1 Cracking the Nut

This chapter talks about the many ways of dumping a file to the screen. Most users know the brute force approach provided by *cat* (12.2), but there's more to it than that:

- Pagers such as *more* and *less* (12.3) that give you more control when looking through long files.
- Finding out what type of data a file contains before opening it (article 12.6).
- Looking at just the beginning or end of a file (articles 12.8 through 12.12).
- Numbering lines (article 12.13).

—TOR

12.2 What Good Is a cat?

The *cat* command may well be the first command new users hear about, if only because of its odd name. *cat* stands for con*cat*enate or, as some would say, catenate. Both words mean the same thing: to connect in a series. The *cat* command takes its filename arguments and strings their contents together. Essentially, *cat* takes its input and spits it out again.

cat has many uses, but the four most basic applications are described in the following list. In many ways, they don't illustrate *cat* so much as they illustrate the shell's output redirection (43.1) mechanism.

1. First form:

   ```
   % cat file
   % cat file1 file2 file...
   ```

   Use this form to display one or more files on the screen. The output doesn't pause when the screen is full. As a result, if your files are more than one screenful long, the output will whiz by without giving you a chance to read it. To read output by screenfuls, use a pager such as *less* (12.3).[*]

2. Second form:

   ```
   % cat file(s) > new_file
   ```

   Use this form when you want to combine several smaller files into one large file. Be sure the destination file does not already exist; otherwise, it will be replaced by the new contents (effectively destroying the original). For example, the command:

   ```
   % cat chap1 chap2 chap3 > book
   ```

   creates a new file, *book*, composed of three files, one after the other. The three component files still exist as *chap1*, *chap2*, and *chap3*.

3. Third form:

   ```
   % cat file >> existing_file
   % cat files >> existing_file
   ```

   Use this form to add one or more files to the end of an existing file. For example:

   ```
   % cat note1 note2 > note_list
   % cat note3 >> note_list
   ```

4. Fourth form:

   ```
   % cat > newfile
   ```

   Use this form as a quick-and-dirty way to create a new file. This is useful when you aren't yet familiar with any of the standard text editors. With this command, everything you type at the keyboard goes into the new file. (You won't be able to back up to a previous line.) To finish your input, enter CTRL-d on a line by itself.

Well, that was just in case there are some beginners on board. Articles 12.4, 12.7, and 12.13 give some more useful tips about *cat* options.

—DG

---

[*] You may think this command form is pointless. In truth, this form is rarely used in such a basic way. More often, you'll use this form along with some of *cat*'s display options or connect this command to other Unix commands via a pipe (1.5).

12.3 "less" is More

The most popular pager for Unix systems was once the *more* command, so named because it gave you "one more screen." *more* is ubiquitous, but also somewhat limited in its capability. The *less* command (so named because, of course, "less is more!") is more commonly used. *less* is a full-featured text pager that emulates *more* but offers an extended set of capabilities.

One particularly important feature of *less* is that it does not read all of its input before starting, which makes it faster than an editor for large input. *less* also offers many useful features and is available for almost every operating environment. As an extra bonus, it is installed by default on most free Unixes.

less begins execution by first examining the environment in which it is running. It needs to know some things about the terminal (or window) in which its output will be displayed. Once that's known, *less* formats the text and displays the first screen's output. The last line of the screen is reserved for user interaction with the program. *less* will display a colon (:) on the first column of the last line and leave the cursor there. This colon is a command prompt, awaiting command input from the user. Most commands to *less* are single-character entries, and *less* will act upon them immediately and without a subsequent carriage return (this is known as *cbreak* mode). The most basic command to *less* (and *more*) is a single space, which instructs the pager to move ahead in the text by one screen. Table 12-1 lists commonly used *less* commands.

Table 12-1. Commonly used less commands

Command	Description
Space	Scroll forward one screen.
d	Scroll forward one-half screen.
RETURN	Scroll forward one line.
b	Scroll backward one screen. Unlike *more*, while *less* is reading from pipes (1.5), it can redraw the screen and read previous pages.
u	Scroll backward one-half screen.
y	Scroll backward one line.
g	Go to the beginning of the text (could be slow with large amounts of text).
G	Go to the end of the text (could be slow with large amounts of text).
/pattern	Search forward for *pattern*, which can be a regular expression.
?pattern	Search backward for *pattern*, which can be a regular expression.
n	Search for the next occurance of the last search, in the same direction: forward in the file if the previous search was using / and backwards in the file if the previous search was using ?.
N	Search for the previous occurance of the last search. See earlier.

Table 12-1. Commonly used less commands (continued)

Command	Description
h	Display a help screen.
:n	Display next file from command line (two-character command).
:p	Display previous file from command line (two-character command).

less has a rich command set, and its behavior can be modified as needed for your use. The *lesskey* program lets you make custom key definitions, and you can store your favorite setup options in the *LESS* environment variable (35.3). See the *less* manpage for further details.

One of the big advantages of *less* is that it doesn't require any relearning; *less* does the right thing when you use *more*, *vi* (17.2), or *emacs* (19.1) file-browsing commands. Incidentally, it also protects you from terminal control sequences and other obnoxious things that happen when you try to view a binary file, because it escapes nonprinting characters (12.4).

—JD

12.4 Show Nonprinting Characters with cat –v or od –c

Especially if you use an ASCII-based terminal, files can have characters that your terminal can't display. Some characters will lock up your communications software or hardware, make your screen look strange, or cause other weird problems. So if you'd like to look at a file and you aren't sure what's in there, it's not a good idea to just *cat* the file!

Instead, try *cat –v*. It shows an ASCII ("printable") representation of unprintable and non-ASCII characters. In fact, although most manual pages don't explain how, you can read the output and see what's in the file. Another utility for displaying nonprintable files is *od*. I usually use its –c option when I need to look at a file character by character.

Let's look at a file that's almost guaranteed to be unprintable: a directory file. This example is on a standard V7 (Unix Version 7) filesystem. (Unfortunately, some Unix systems won't let you read a directory. If you want to follow along on one of those systems, try a compressed file (15.6) or an executable program from */bin*.) A directory usually has some long lines, so it's a good idea to pipe *cat*'s output through *fold*:

```
% ls -fa
.
..
comp
```

```
% cat -v . | fold -62
M-^?^N.^@^@^@^@^@^@^@^@^@^@^@^@^@>^G..^@^@^@^@^@^@^@^@^@^@^@^@
M-a
comp^@^@^@^@^@^@^@^@^@^@^@MassAveFood^@^@^@^@^@hist^@^@^
@^@^@^@^@^@^@^@
% od -c .
0000000 377 016   .  \0  \0  \0  \0  \0  \0  \0  \0  \0  \0  \0  \0  \0
0000020   >  007   .   .  \0  \0  \0  \0  \0  \0  \0  \0  \0  \0  \0  \0
0000040 341  \n   c   o   m   p  \0  \0  \0  \0  \0  \0  \0  \0  \0  \0
0000060  \0  \0   M   a   s   s   A   v   e   F   o   o   d  \0  \0  \0
0000100  \0  \0   h   i   s   t  \0  \0  \0  \0  \0  \0  \0  \0  \0  \0
0000120
```

Each entry in a V7-type directory is 16 bytes long (that's also 16 characters, in the ASCII system). The *od –c* command starts each line with the number of bytes, in octal, shown since the start of the file. The first line starts at byte 0. The second line starts at byte 20 octal (that's byte 16 in decimal, the way most people count). And so on. Enough about *od* for now, though. We'll come back to it in a minute. Time to dissect the *cat –v* output:

- You've probably seen sequences like ^N and ^G. Those are control characters. Another character like this is ^@, the character NUL (ASCII 0). There are a lot of NULs in the directory; more about that later. A DEL character (ASCII 177 octal) is shown as ^?. Check an ASCII chart.

- *cat –v* has its own symbol for characters outside the ASCII range with their high bits set, also called metacharacters. *cat –v* prints those as M- followed by another character. There are two of them in the *cat –v* output: M-^? and M-a.

  To get a metacharacter, you add 200 octal. For an example, let's look at M-a. The octal value of the letter a is 141. When *cat –v* prints M-a, it means the character you get by adding 141+200, or 341 octal.

  You can decode that the character *cat* prints as M-^? in the same way. The ^? stands for the DEL character, which is octal 177. Add 200+177 to get 377 octal.

- If a character isn't M-*something* or ^*something*, it's a regular printable character. The entries in the directory (., .., comp, MassAveFood, and hist) are all made of regular ASCII characters.

  If you're wondering where the entries MassAveFood and hist are in the *ls* listing, the answer is that they aren't. Those entries have been deleted from the directory. Unix puts two NUL (ASCII 0, or ^@) bytes in front of the names of deleted V7 directory entries.

cat has two options, *–t* and *–e*, for displaying whitespace in a line. The *–v* option doesn't convert TAB and trailing-space characters to a visible form without those options. See article 12.5.

Next, *od –c*. It's easier to explain than *cat –v*:

- *od –c* shows some characters starting with a backslash (\). It uses the standard Unix and C abbreviations for control characters where it can. For instance, \n stands for a newline character, \t for a tab, etc. There's a newline at the start of the comp entry—see it in the *od –c* output? That explains why the *cat –v* output was broken onto a new line at that place: *cat –v* doesn't translate newlines when it finds them.

  The \0 is a NUL character (ASCII 0). It's used to pad the ends of entries in V7 directories when a name isn't the full 14 characters long.

- *od –c* shows the octal value of other characters as three digits. For instance, the 007 means "the character 7 octal." *cat –v* shows this as ^G (CTRL-g).

  Metacharacters, the ones with octal values 200 and higher, are shown as M-*something* by *cat –v*. In *od –c*, you'll see their octal values—such as 341.

  Each directory entry on a Unix Version 7 filesystem starts with a two-byte "pointer" to its location in the disk's inode table. When you type a filename, Unix uses this pointer to find the actual file information on the disk. The entry for this directory (named .) is 377 016. Its parent (named ..) is at > 007. And *comp*'s entry is 341 \n. Find those in the *cat –v* output, if you want; and compare the two outputs.

- Like *cat –v*, regular printable characters are shown as is by *od –c*.

The *strings* (13.15) program finds printable strings of characters (such as filenames) inside mostly nonprintable files (such as executable binaries).

—JP

12.5 What's in That Whitespace?

The *cat –v* option (12.4) shows an ASCII representation of unprintable and non-ASCII characters. *cat* has two options for displaying whitespace in a line. If you use the *–t* option with *–v*, TAB characters are shown as ^I. The *–e* option combined with *–v* marks the end of each line with a $ character. Some versions of *cat* don't require the *–v* with those options. Let's compare a one-line file without and with the *–t –e* (which may have to be typed separately, by the way; *–te* won't work on some versions):

```
% cat afile
This is a one-line file - boring, eh?
% cat -v -t -e afile
ThiS^Hs is^Ia one-line file^I- boring, eh?        $
```

Although you can't tell it from plain *cat*, there's a backspace (CTRL-h) before the first s, two TABs that take up only one column of whitespace each, and seven spaces at the end of the line. Knowing this can help you debug problems in printing and displaying files. It's also a help for shell programmers who need to parse or sort the output of other programs.

—*JP*

12.6 Finding File Types

Many different kinds of files live on the typical Unix system: database files, executable files, regular text files, files for applications like StarOffice, *tar* files, mail messages, directories, font files, and so on.

You often want to check to make sure you have the right "kind" of file before doing something. For example, you'd like to read the file *tar*. But before typing more `tar`, you'd like to know whether this file is your set of notes on carbon-based sludge or the *tar* executable. If you're wrong, the consequences might be unpleasant. Sending the *tar* executable to your screen might screw up your terminal settings, log you off, or do any number of unpleasant things.

The *file* utility tells you what sort of file something is. It's fairly self-explanatory:

file

```
% file /bin/sh
/bin/sh:        sparc demand paged executable
% file 2650
2650:           [nt]roff, tbl, or eqn input text
% file 0001,v
0001,v:         ascii text
% file foo.sh
foo.sh:         shell commands
```

file is actually quite clever though it isn't always correct—some versions are better than others. It doesn't just tell you if something's binary or text; it looks at the beginning of the file and tries to figure out what it's doing. So, for example, you see that file *2650* is an *nroff* (45.12) file and *foo.sh* is a shell script. It isn't quite clever enough to figure out that *0001,v* is an RCS (39.5) archive, but it does know that it's a plain ASCII text file.

Many versions of *file* can be customized to recognize additional file types. The file */etc/magic* tells *file* how to recognize different kinds of files. [My Linux system has the *file* command from *ftp://ftp.astron.com/pub/file/*, which uses a multiple-database format. It's updated fairly often to understand new file formats. —*JP*] It's capable of a lot (and should be capable of even more), but we'll satisfy ourselves with an introductory explanation. Our goal will be to teach *file* to recognize RCS archives.

/etc/magic has four fields:

```
offset data-type value file-type
```

These are as follows:

`offset`
> The offset into the file at which *magic* will try to find something. If you're looking for something right at the beginning of the file, the offset should be 0. (This is usually what you want.)

`data-type`
> The type of test to make. Use `string` for text comparisons, `byte` for byte comparisons, `short` for two-byte comparisons, and `long` for four-byte comparisons.

`value`
> The value you want to find. For string comparisons, any text string will do; you can use the standard Unix escape sequences (such as \n for newline). For numeric comparisons (byte, short, long), this field should be a number, expressed as a C constant (e.g., 0x77 for the hexadecimal byte 77).

`file-type`
> The string that *file* will print if this test succeeds.

So, we know that RCS archives begin with the word head. This word is right at the beginning of the file (offset 0). Since we obviously want a string comparison, we make the the following addition to */etc/magic*:

```
0     string     head     RCS archive
```

This says, "The file is an RCS archive if you find the string head at an offset of 0 bytes from the beginning of the file." Does it work?

```
% file RCS/0001,v
RCS/0001,v:      RCS archive
```

As I said, the tests can be much more complicated, particularly if you're working with binary files. To recognize simple text files, this is all you need to know.

—*ML*

12.7 Squash Extra Blank Lines

Reading output with lots of empty lines can be a waste of screen space. For instance, some versions of *man* (2.1) show all the blank lines between manual pages. To stop that, read your file or pipe it through *cat* –*s*. (Many versions of *less* (12.3) and *more* have a similar –*s* option.) The –*s* option replaces multiple blank lines with a single blank line. (If your *cat* doesn't have –*s*, see the *sed* alternative at the end.)

cat –s might not always seem to work. The problem is usually that the "empty" lines have SPACE, TAB, or CTRL-m characters on them. The fix is to let *sed* "erase" lines with those invisible characters on them:

```
% sed 's/^[SPACE TAB CTRL-v CTRL-m]*$//' file | cat -s
```

In *vi* (18.6) and many terminal drivers, the CTRL-v character quotes the CTRL-m (RETURN) so that character doesn't end the current line.

If you don't have *cat –s*, then *sed* can do both jobs:

```
% sed -e 's/^[SPACE TAB CTRL-v CTRL-m]*$//' -e '/./,/^$/!d' file
```

—JP

12.8 How to Look at the End of a File: tail

Let's say that you want to look at the end of some large file. For example, you've just sent some mail and want to find out whether it was handled correctly. But when you look at your mail logs, you find out that the log file is 30 or 40 KB long, and you don't care about the whole thing—you certainly don't want to page through it until you get to the end. How do you handle this?

The *tail* command is just what you need in this situation. *tail* reads its input and discards everything except for the last ten lines (by default). Therefore, if you're pretty sure that the information you want is at the end of the file, you can use *tail* to get rid of the junk that you don't want. To see just the end of that mail log (in this case, *qmail*'s log):

```
% tail /var/log/maillog
Feb 19 10:58:45 yyy qmail: 1014141525.474209 delivery 6039: success: did_0+0+1/
Feb 19 10:58:45 yyy qmail: 1014141525.491370 status: local 0/10 remote 0/20
Feb 19 10:58:45 yyy qmail: 1014141525.492211 end msg 111214
Feb 19 11:11:15 yyy qmail: 1014142275.469000 new msg 111214
Feb 19 11:11:15 yyy qmail: 1014142275.469631 info msg 111214: bytes 281 from
<xxx@yyy.zyzzy.com> qp 51342 uid 1000
Feb 19 11:11:15 yyy qmail: 1014142275.562074 starting delivery 6040: msg 111214
to remote xyz@frob.com
Feb 19 11:11:15 yyy qmail: 1014142275.562630 status: local 0/10 remote 1/20
Feb 19 11:11:30 yyy qmail: 1014142290.110546 delivery 6040: success:
64.71.166.115_accepted_message./Remote_host_said:_250_Ok:_queued_as_COEC73E84D/
Feb 19 11:11:30 yyy qmail: 1014142290.127763 status: local 0/10 remote 0/20
Feb 19 11:11:30 yyy qmail: 1014142290.128381 end msg 111214
```

For another common example, to see the latest entries from the BSD or Linux kernel ring buffer:

```
% dmesg | tail
lpt0: <Printer> on ppbus0
lpt0: Interrupt-driven port
ppi0: <Parallel I/O> on ppbus0
IPsec: Initialized Security Association Processing.
```

```
ad0: 19569MB <ST320430A> [39761/16/63] at ata0-master UDMA66
afd0: 239MB <IOMEGA ZIP 250 ATAPI> [239/64/32] at ata0-slave using PIO3
acd0: CDROM <ATAPI CDROM> at ata1-master using PIO4
Mounting root from ufs:/dev/ad0s1a
pid 50882 (fetch), uid 0: exited on signal 10 (core dumped)
pid 88041 (smbd), uid 1000 on /usr: file system full
```

This will give you the last ten lines from the *dmesg* command. If you need more or less than ten lines, look at article 12.9.

Althought the GNU version is better behaved, some older versions of *tail* accept one (and *only* one!) filename:

```
% tail somefile
```

There are many other situations in which *tail* is useful: I've used it to make sure that a job that produces a big output file has finished correctly, to remind me what the last piece of mail in my mailbox was about, and so on. You'll find *tail* important whenever you're interested only in the end of something.

—ML

12.9 Finer Control on tail

What if you need to look at the last 11 lines of the file? The command `tail -n` shows the final *n* lines. The command `tail +n` discards the first *n*–1 lines, giving you line *n* and everything that follows it.

You can also tell *tail* to count the number of characters or the number of 512-byte blocks. To do so, use the *–c* option (count characters) or the *–b* option (count blocks). If you want to state explicitly that you're interested in lines, give the *–l* option.

Your *tail* probably has a *–r* option that shows the file in reverse order, starting from the last line.

Many versions of Unix limit the maximum number of lines that *tail*, especially *tail –r*, can display.

—ML

12.10 How to Look at Files as They Grow

One of the best things that you can do with *tail* is to look at a file as it is growing. For example, I once was debugging a program named *totroff* that converted a manual from a plain text format to *troff*. It was rather slow, so that you didn't want to wait until the program finished before looking at the output. But you didn't want to be typing more every 20 seconds either, to find out whether the part of the file that you were debugging had made it through yet. (*more* quits when you "run out" of file, so it can't really help you look for a part of a file that hasn't been written yet.) The *tail –f* command solves this problem. For example:

§ 23.3
```
% totroff < file.txt > file.ms &
[1] 12345
% tail -f file.ms
.LP
Tail produces output as
the file grows.
...
CTRL-c
```

Now suppose you want to monitor several files at once. Administrators, for example, might want to keep track of several log files, such as */usr/adm/ messages*, */usr/adm/lpd-errs*, UUCP error files, etc. The GNU *tail* program comes in useful for keeping an eye on several administrative log files at once. But it also comes in useful for nonadministrators.

For example, suppose you want to perform several *greps* through many files, saving the output in different files. You can then monitor the files using *tail –f*. For example:

```
% grep Berkeley ch?? > Berkeley.grep &
% grep BSD ch?? > BSD.grep &
% grep "System V" ch?? > SystemV.grep &
% grep SysV ch?? > SysV.grep &
% tail -f Berkeley.grep BSD.grep SystemV.grep SysV.grep
```

When new text appears in the files called with *tail –f*, it also appears on the screen:

```
==> SysV.grep <==
ch01:using a SysV-based UNIX system, you must

==> Berkeley.grep <==
ch01:at the University of California at Berkeley, where

==> BSD.grep <==
ch03:prefer BSD UNIX systems because they are less likely to
ch04:who use a BSD-based UNIX systems must run the

==> SysV.grep <==
ch04:is a SysV derivative sold by Acme Products Inc.
```

(When text is written to a new file, the filename is printed surrounded by ==> and <==.)

What's actually happening here?

When you invoke *tail –f*, *tail* behaves just like it normally does: it reads the file and dumps the last ten (or however many) lines to the screen. But, unlike most applications, *tail* doesn't quit at this point. Instead, *tail* goes into an infinite loop. It sleeps for a second, then wakes up and looks to see if the file is any longer, then sleeps again, and so on. Because this is an infinite loop, you have to enter CTRL-c (or whatever your interrupt key (24.11) is) when you've seen the data you're interested in, or when the file you're watching has been completed. *tail* has no way of knowing when the file has stopped growing.

tail ignores the *–f* option when it is reading from a pipe. For example, *totroff < file.txt | tail –f* wouldn't work.

Article 12.11 shows a useful feature of GNU *tail*: following files by name or file descriptor.

—ML and LM

12.11 GNU tail File Following

I like to keep an *xterm* window open on my Linux system so I can watch various log files. Although there are fancier log-file-monitoring programs (such as *swatch*), *tail –f* (12.10) is perfect for me.

I also run a weekly *cron* (25.2) job to rotate log files (rename the files, compress and archive them). When this job runs, the log files suddenly have new names— *messages* becomes *messages.1*, for instance—so the system logger starts writing to a different *messages* file. Then plain *tail –f* suddenly stops showing the log because it doesn't realize that the same physical file on the disk suddenly has a new name. When this happened, I had to remember to kill and restart *tail* each Sunday morning...until I found the new version of GNU *tail*, that is.

The GNU *tail – –follow* option lets you choose how the files you're watching should be followed. By default, GNU *tail* acts like the standard *tail*: it opens a file for reading and gets a file descriptor (36.15) number, which it constantly watches for changes. But if that file is renamed and a new file with the old name (and a new inode) takes its place, the file descriptor may point to a file that's not in use anymore.

tail

The GNU *tail* options, *– –follow=name* and *– –retry*, tell it to watch the actual file name, not the open file descriptor. Here's what happens Sunday mornings when I'm using this:

{ } 28.4

```
kludge# tail --follow=name --retry ~jerry/tmp/startx.log \
   /var/log/{messages,maillog,secure}
   ...lots of log messages...
tail: `/var/log/secure' has been replaced;  following end of new file
tail: `/var/log/maillog' has been replaced;  following end of new file
tail: `/var/log/messages' has been replaced;  following end of new file
Dec 31 04:02:01 kludge syslogd 1.3-3: restart.
Dec 31 04:02:01 kludge syslogd 1.3-3: restart.
Dec 31 04:02:05 kludge anacron[8397]: Updated timestamp for job
`cron.weekly' to 2000-12-31
```

It's just what I've always needed.

—JP

12.12 Printing the Top of a File

head can be used to print the first few lines of one or more files (the "head" of the file or files). When more than one file is specified, a header is printed at the beginning of each file, and each is listed in succession.

Like *tail* (12.9), *head* supports the *–n* option to control the number of lines displayed and the *–c* option to print characters/bytes instead of lines. GNU *head* also supports an extention to *–c*: *–c n*k prints the first *n* kilobytes of the file, and *–c n*m prints the first *n* megabytes of the file.

—DJPH

12.13 Numbering Lines

There are times when you want to print out a file with the lines numbered—perhaps because you are showing a script or program in documentation and want to refer to individual lines in the course of your discussion.

This is one of the handy things *cat* can do for you with the *–n* option.

cat –n precedes each line with some leading spaces, the line number, and a TAB. How many leading spaces? It depends on how high the line numbers go. The line numbers are right-justified at column 6, which means that a 6-digit number will go all the way back to the margin. I only belabor this point in case you're tempted to trim the leading spaces with something like *cut* (21.14).

nl

If you have a version of *cat* that doesn't support *–n*, try *nl*, the line-numbering program. *nl –ba* acts like *cat –n*. By itself, *nl* numbers only lines with text. The GNU version is on the web site.

You can achieve a similar effect with *pr –t –n*. (The *–t* keeps *pr* from inserting the header and footer (45.6) it normally uses to break its output into pages.) And as long as we're giving you choices, here are five more:

```
less -N filename
grep -n \^ filename
awk '{print NR,$0}' filename
sed = < filename | sed 'N;s/\n/ /'
ex - '+%#\|q' filename
```

—JP and TOR

13

Searching Through Files

13.1 Different Versions of grep

grep is one of Unix's most useful tools. As a result, all users seem to want their own, slightly different version that solves a different piece of the problem. (Maybe this is a problem in itself; there really should be only one *grep*, as the manpage says.) Three versions of *grep* come with every Unix system; in addition, there are six or seven freely available versions that we'll mention here, as well as probably dozens of others that you can find kicking around the Net.

Here are the different versions of *grep* and what they offer. We'll start with the standard versions:

Plain old grep
> Great for searching with regular expressions (article 13.2).

Extended grep (or egrep)
> Handles extended regular expressions. It is also, arguably, the fastest of the standard *greps* (article 13.4).

Fixed grep (or fgrep)
> So named because it matches fixed strings. It is sometimes inaccurately called "fast *grep*"; often it is really the slowest of them all. It is useful to search for patterns with literal backslashes, asterisks, and so on that you'd otherwise have to escape somehow. *fgrep* has the interesting ability to search for multiple strings (article 13.5).

Of course, on many modern Unixes all three are the same executable, just with slightly different behaviors, and so you may not see dramatic speed differences between them. Now for the freeware versions:

agrep, or "approximate grep"
> A tool that finds lines that "more or less" match your search string. A very interesting and useful tool, it's part of the *glimpse* package, which is an indexing and query system for fast searching of huge amounts of text. *agrep* is introduced in article 13.6.

Very fast versions of grep, such as GNU grep/egrep/fgrep
    Most free Unixes use GNU *grep* as their main *grep*.

rcsgrep
    Searches through RCS files (39.5) (article 13.7).

In addition, you can simulate the action of *grep* with *sed*, *awk*, and *perl*. These utilities allow you to write such variations as a *grep* that searches for a pattern that can be split across several lines (13.9) and other context *grep* programs (41.12), which show you a few lines before and after the text you find. (Normal *greps* just show the lines that match.)

—ML

13.2 Searching for Text with grep

There are many well-known benefits provided by *grep* to the user who doesn't remember what his files contain. Even users of non-Unix systems wish they had a utility with its power to search through a set of files for an arbitrary text pattern (known as a regular expression).

The main function of *grep* is to look for strings matching a regular expression and print only the lines found. Use *grep* when you want to look at how a particular word is used in one or more files. For example, here's how to list the lines in the file *ch04* that contain either *run-time* or *run time*:

"..." 27.12
```
$ grep "run[- ]time" ch04
This procedure avoids run-time errors for not-assigned
and a run-time error message is produced.
run-time error message is produced.
program aborts and a run-time error message is produced.
DIMENSION statement in BASIC is executable at run time.
This means that arrays can be redimensioned at run time.
accessible or not open, the program aborts and a run-time
```

Another use might be to look for a specific HTML tag in a file. The following command will list top-level (<H1> or <h1>) and second-level (<H2> or <h2>) headings that have the starting tag at the beginning (^) of the line:

```
$ grep "^<[Hh][12]>" ch0[12].html
ch01.html:<h1>Introduction</h1>
ch01.html:<h1>Windows, Screens, and Images</h1>
ch01.html:<h2>The Standard Screen-stdscr</h2>
ch01.html:<h2>Adding Characters</h2>
ch02.html:<H1>Introduction</H1>
ch02.html:<H1>What Is Terminal Independence?</H1>
ch02.html:<H2>Termcap</H2>
ch02.html:<H2>Terminfo</H2>
```

In effect, it produces a quick outline of the contents of these files.

grep is also often used as a filter (1.5), to select from the output of some other program. For example, you might want to find the process id of your inetd, if you just changed the configuration file and need to HUP inetd to make it reread the configuration file. Using *ps* (24.5) and *grep* together allows you to do this without wading through a bunch of lines of output:

```
% ps -aux | grep inetd
root      321  0.0  0.2  1088  548  ??  Is   12Nov01  0:08.93 inetd -wW
deb     40033  0.0  0.2  1056  556  p5  S+   12:55PM  0:00.00 grep inetd
% kill -HUP 321
```

There are several options commonly used with *grep*. The *–i* option specifies that the search ignore the distinction between upper- and lowercase. The *–c* option tells *grep* to return only a count of the number of lines matched. The *–w* option searches for the pattern "as a word." For example, grep if would match words like *cliff* or *knife*, but grep -w if wouldn't. The *–l* option returns only the name of the file when *grep* finds a match. This can be used to prepare a list of files for another command. The *–v* option (13.3) reverses the normal action, and only prints out lines that don't match the search pattern. In the previous example, you can use the *–v* option to get rid of the extra line of output:

```
% ps -aux | grep inetd | grep -v grep
root      321  0.0  0.2  1088  548  ??  Is   12Nov01  0:08.93 inetd -wW
% kill -HUP 321
```

—DD

13.3 Finding Text That Doesn't Match

The *grep* programs have one very handy feature: they can select lines that don't match a pattern just as they can select the lines that do. Simply use the *–v* option.

I used this most recently when working on this book. We have thousands of separate files under RCS (39.5), and I sometimes forget which ones I've got checked out. Since there's a lot of clutter in the directory and several people working there, a simple *ls* won't do. There are a series of temporary files created by some of our printing scripts that I don't want to see. All of their filenames consist of one or more *x* characters: nothing else. So I use a *findpt* alias to list only the files belonging to me. It's a version of the *find.* alias described in article 9.26, with *–user tim* added to select only my own files and a *grep* pattern to exclude the temporary files. My *findpt* alias executes the following command line:

```
find. | grep -v '^\./xx*$'
```

The leading ./ matches the start of each line of *find.* output, and xx* matches one x followed by zero or more xs. I couldn't use the *find* operators ! -name in that case because *–name* uses shell-like wildcard patterns, and there's no way to say "one or more of the preceding character" (in this case, the character *x*) with shell wildcards.

Obviously, that's as specific and nonreproducible an example as you're likely to find anywhere! But it's precisely these kinds of special cases that call for a rich vocabulary of tips and tricks. You'll never have to use *grep –v* for this particular purpose, but you'll find a use for it someday.

[Note that you could use a slightly simpler regular expression by using *egrep* (13.4), which supports the plus (+) operator to mean "one or more," instead of having to use the basic regular expression *character character zero-or-more* (xx*). The previous regular expression would then become:

```
find. | egrep -v '^\./x+$'
```

The richer regular expression language is the primary advantage of *egrep*. —DJPH]
—*TOR*

13.4 Extended Searching for Text with egrep

The *egrep* command is yet another version of *grep* (13.2), one that extends the syntax of regular expressions. (Versions where *grep* and *egrep* are the same allow you to get *egrep*-like behavior from *grep* by using the *–E* option.) A plus sign (+) following a regular expression matches one or more occurrences of the regular expression; a question mark (?) matches zero or one occurrences. In addition, regular expressions can be nested within parentheses:

```
% egrep "Lab(oratorie)?s" name.list
AT&T Bell Laboratories
AT&T Bell Labs

Symtel Labs of Chicago
```

Parentheses surround a second regular expression and ? modifies this expression. The nesting helps to eliminate unwanted matches; for instance, the word *Labors* or *oratories* would not be matched.

Another special feature of *egrep* is the vertical bar (|), which serves as an *or* operator between two expressions. Lines matching either expression are printed, as in the next example:

```
% egrep "stdscr|curscr" ch03
into the stdscr, a character array.
When stdscr is refreshed, the
stdscr is refreshed.
curscr.
initscr() creates two windows: stdscr
and curscr.
```

Remember to put the expression inside quotation marks to protect the vertical bar from being interpreted by the shell as a pipe symbol. Look at the next example:

```
% egrep "Alcuin (User|Programmer)('s)? Guide" docguide
Alcuin Programmer's Guide is a thorough
refer to the Alcuin User Guide
Alcuin User's Guide introduces new users to
```

You can see the flexibility that *egrep*'s syntax can give you, matching either User or Programmer and matching them regardless of whether they had an 's.

Both *egrep* and *fgrep* can read search patterns from a file using the –*f* option (13.5).

—*DJPD*

13.5 grepping for a List of Patterns

egrep (13.4) lets you look for multiple patterns using its grouping and alternation operators (big words for parentheses and a vertical bar). But sometimes, even that isn't enough.

Both *egrep* and *fgrep* support a –*f* option, which allows you to save a list of patterns (fixed strings in the case of *fgrep*) in a file, one pattern per line, and search for all the items in the list with a single invocation of the program. For example, in writing this book, we've used this feature to check for consistent usage in a list of terms across all articles:

```
% egrep -f terms *
```

(To be more accurate, we used *rcsegrep* (13.7), since the articles are all kept under RCS (39.5), but you get the idea.)

—*TOR*

13.6 Approximate grep: agrep

agrep is one of the nicer additions to the *grep* family. It's not only one of the faster greps around; it also has the unique feature of looking for approximate matches. It's also record oriented rather than line oriented. The three most significant features of *agrep* that are not supported by the *grep* family are as follows:

1. The ability to search for approximate patterns, with a user-definable level of accuracy. For example:

   ```
   % agrep -2 homogenos foo
   ```

   will find "homogeneous," as well as any other word that can be obtained from "homogenos" with at most two substitutions, insertions, or deletions.

   ```
   % agrep -B homogenos foo
   ```

   will generate a message of the form:

   ```
   best match has 2 errors, there are 5 matches, output them? (y/n)
   ```

2. *agrep* is record oriented rather than just line oriented; a record is by default a line, but it can be user-defined with the *–d* option specifying a pattern that will be used as a record delimiter. For example:

```
% agrep -d '^From ' 'pizza' mbox
```

outputs all mail messages (1.21) (delimited by a line beginning with *From* and a space) in the file *mbox* that contain the keyword *pizza*. Another example:

```
% agrep -d '$$' pattern foo
```

will output all paragraphs (separated by an empty line) that contain *pattern*.

3. *agrep* allows multiple patterns with AND (or OR) logic queries. For example:

```
% agrep -d '^From ' 'burger,pizza' mbox
```

outputs all mail messages containing at least one of the two keywords (, stands for OR).

```
% agrep -d '^From ' 'good;pizza' mbox
```

outputs all mail messages containing both keywords.

Putting these options together, one can write queries such as the following:

```
% agrep -d '$$' -2 '<CACM>;TheAuthor;Curriculum;<198[5-9]>' bib
```

which outputs all paragraphs referencing articles in CACM between 1985 and 1989 by *TheAuthor* dealing with Curriculum. Two errors are allowed, but they cannot be in either CACM or the year. (The < > brackets forbid errors in the pattern between them.)

Other *agrep* features include searching for regular expressions (with or without errors), using unlimited wildcards, limiting the errors to only insertions or only substitutions or any combination, allowing each deletion, for example, to be counted as two substitutions or three insertions, restricting parts of the query to be exact and parts to be approximate, and many more.

—JP, SW, and UM

13.7 Search RCS Files with rcsgrep

Storing multiple versions of a file in RCS (39.5) saves space. How can you search a lot of those files at once? You could check out all the files, then run *grep*—but you'll have to remove the files after you're done searching. Or, you could search the RCS files themselves with a command like grep foo RCS/*,v—but that can show you garbage lines from previous revisions, log messages, and other text that isn't in the latest revision of your file. This article has two ways to solve that problem.

rcsgrep, rcsegrep, rcsfgrep

The *rcsgrep* script—and two links to it named *rcsegrep* and *rcsfgrep*—run *grep*, *egrep* (13.4), and *fgrep* on all files in the RCS directory. (You can also choose the files to search.)

The script tests its name to decide whether to act like *grep*, *egrep*, or *fgrep*. Then it checks out each file and pipes it to the version of grep you chose. The output looks just like *grep*'s—although, by default, you'll also see the messages from the *co* command (the *–s* option silences those messages).

By default, *rcsgrep* searches the latest revision of every file. With the *–a* option, *rcsgrep* will search all revisions of every file, from first to last. This is very handy when you're trying to see what was changed in a particular place and to find which revision(s) have some text that was deleted some time ago. (*rcsgrep* uses *rcsrevs* (39.6) to implement *–a*.)

Some *grep* options need special handling to work right in the script: *–e*, *–f*, and *–l*. (For instance, *–e* and *–f* have an argument after them. The script has to pass both the option and its argument.) The script passes any other options you type to the *grep* command. Your *grep* versions may have some other options that need special handling, too. Just edit the script to handle them.

rcsegrep.fast

To search an RCS file, *rcsgrep* and its cousins run several Unix processes: *co*, *grep*, *sed*, and others. Each process takes time to start and run. If your directory has hundreds of RCS files (like our directory for this book does), searching the whole thing can take a lot of time. I could have cut the number of processes by rewriting *rcsgrep* in Perl; Perl has the functionality of *grep*, *sed*, and others built in, so all it would need to do is run hundreds of *co* processes…which would still make it too slow.

rcsegrep.fast

The solution I came up with was to do everything in (basically) one process: a *gawk* (20.11) script. Instead of using the RCS *co* command to extract each file's latest revision, the *rcsegrep.fast* script reads each RCS file directly (The *rcsfile*(5) manpage explains the format of an RCS file.) An RCS file contains the latest revision of its working file as plain text, with one difference: each @ character is changed to @@. *rcsegrep.fast* searches the RCS file until it finds the beginning of the latest revision. Then it applies an *egrep*-like regular expression to each line. Matching lines are written to standard output with the filename first; the *–n* option gives a line number after the filename.

rcsegrep.fast is sort of a kludge because it's accessing RCS files without using RCS tools. There's a chance that it won't work on some versions of RCS or that I've made some other programming goof. But it's worked very well for us. It's much faster than *rcsgrep* and friends. I'd recommend using *rcsegrep.fast* when you need to search the latest revisions of a lot of RCS files; otherwise, stick to the *rcsgrep*s.

—JP

13.8 GNU Context greps

By default, standard *grep* utilities show only the lines of text that match the search pattern. Sometimes, though, you need to see the matching line's context: the lines before or after the matching line. The GNU *greps* (*grep*, *fgrep*, and *egrep*) can do this. There are three context grep options:

- The *–C* option shows two lines of context around each match; you can also give a numeric argument, such as -C 4, to choose how many lines of context (here, four).
- The *–B* option shows context before each match. A numeric argument, such as -B 2 for two lines of context, is required.
- The *–A* option shows context after each match. A numeric argument, such as -A 3 for three lines of context, is required.

Each set of contiguous matching lines is separated by a line of two dashes (--).

Let's look at an example: I'd like to search my system mail log for all messages sent to anyone at *oreilly.com*. But *sendmail* doesn't put all information about a message on the to= log line; some info is in the from= line, which is usually the previous line. So I'll search for all "to" lines and add one line of context before each match. I'll also use the *–n*, which numbers the output lines, to make the context easier to see. This option also puts marker characters after the line number: a line number ends with a colon (:) if this line contains a match, and a dash (-) marks lines before or after a match. Here goes:

```
# grep -n -B 1 'to=<[^@]*@oreilly\.com>' maillog
7-Nov 12 18:57:42 jpeek sendmail[30148]: SAA30148: from=<jpeek@jpeek.com>...
8:Nov 12 18:57:43 jpeek sendmail[30150]: SAA30148: to=<al@oreilly.com>...
9-Nov 12 22:49:51 jpeek sendmail[1901]: WAA01901: from=<jpeek@jpeek.com>...
10:Nov 12 22:49:51 jpeek sendmail[1901]: WAA01901: to=<wfurby@oreilly.com>...
11:Nov 12 22:50:23 jpeek sendmail[2000]: WAA01901: to=<wfurby@oreilly.com>...
--
25-Nov 13 07:42:38 jpeek sendmail[9408]: HAA09408: from=<jpeek@jpeek.com>...
26:Nov 13 07:42:44 jpeek sendmail[9410]: HAA09408: to=<al@oreilly.com>...
27-Nov 13 08:08:36 jpeek sendmail[10004]: IAA10004: from=<jpeek@jpeek.com>...
28:Nov 13 08:08:37 jpeek sendmail[10006]: IAA10004: to=<wfurby@oreilly.com>...
--
32-Nov 13 11:59:46 jpeek sendmail[14473]: LAA14473: from=<jpeek@jpeek.com>...
33:Nov 13 11:59:47 jpeek sendmail[14475]: LAA14473: to=<al@oreilly.com>...
34-Nov 13 15:34:17 jpeek sendmail[18272]: PAA18272: from=<jpeek@jpeek.com>...
35:Nov 13 15:34:19 jpeek sendmail[18274]: PAA18272: to=<al@oreilly.com>...
```

I've truncated each line for printing, but you still can see the matches. A few notes about what's happening here:

- Line 8 matches (so it has a colon after its line number), and line 7 is the line of context before (so it starts with a dash).
- Note that a line is never shown more than once, as you can see in lines 9 through 11: lines 10 and 11 both match, so they both have colons. But because line 10 has already been shown once, it's not repeated as the line "before" line 11.
- There are no matches on line 12, so a line of two dashes is printed as a separator. The next match is on line 26.

—JP

13.9 A Multiline Context grep Using sed

[One weakness of the *grep* family of programs is that they are line oriented. They read only one line at a time, so they can't find patterns (such as phrases) that are split across two lines. *agrep* (13.6) can do multiline searches. One advantage of the *cgrep* script is that it shows how to handle multiple-line patterns in *sed* and can be adapted for work other than searches. —JP]

cgrep

It may surprise you to learn that a fairly decent context *grep* (13.8) program can be built using *sed*. As an example, the following command line:

```
$ cgrep -10 system main.c
```

will find all lines containing the word *system* in the file *main.c* and show ten additional lines of context above and below each match. (The *-context* option must be at least one, and it defaults to two lines.) If several matches occur within the same context, the lines are printed as one large "hunk" rather than repeated smaller hunks. Each new block of context is preceded by the line number of the first occurrence in that hunk. This script, which can also search for patterns that span lines:

```
$ cgrep -3 "awk.*perl"
```

will find all occurrences of the word "awk" where it is followed by the word "perl" somewhere within the next three lines. The pattern can be any simple regular expression, with one notable exception: because you can match across lines, you should use \n in place of the ^ and $ metacharacters.

[While this is a wonderful example of some neat sed techniques, if this is all you're trying to do, use perl. It has features designed to do exactly this sort of thing very efficiently, and it will be much faster. —DH]

—GU

13.10 Compound Searches

You may recall that you can search for lines containing "this" *or* "that" using the *egrep* (13.4) | metacharacter:

```
egrep 'this|that' files
```

But how do you grep for "this" *and* "that"? Conventional regular expressions don't support an *and* operator because it breaks the rule of patterns matching one consecutive string of text. Well, *agrep* (13.6) is one version of *grep* that breaks all the rules. If you're lucky enough to have it installed, just use this:

```
agrep 'cat;dog;bird' files
```

If you don't have *agrep*, a common technique is to filter the text through several *grep*s so that only lines containing all the keywords make it through the pipeline intact:

```
grep cat files | grep dog | grep bird
```

But can it be done in one command? The closest you can come with *grep* is this idea:

```
grep 'cat.*dog.*bird' files
```

which has two limitations—the words must appear in the given order, and they cannot overlap. (The first limitation can be overcome using egrep 'cat.*dog|dog.*cat', but this trick is not really scalable to more than two terms.)

As usual, the problem can also be solved by moving beyond the grep family to the more powerful tools. Here is how to do a line-by-line *and* search using *sed*, *awk*, or *perl*:[*]

```
sed '/cat/!d; /dog/!d; /bird/!d' files
awk '/cat/ && /dog/ && /bird/' files
perl -ne 'print if /cat/ && /dog/ && /bird/' files
```

Okay, but what if you want to find where all the words occur in the same *paragraph*? Just turn on paragraph mode by setting RS="" in *awk* or by giving the –00 option to *perl*:

```
awk '/cat/ && /dog/ && /bird/ {print $0 ORS}' RS= files
perl -n00e 'print "$_\n" if /cat/ && /dog/ && /bird/' files
```

And if you just want a list of the *files* that contain all the words anywhere in them? Well, *perl* can easily slurp in entire files if you have the memory and you use the –0 option to set the record separator to something that won't occur in the file (like *NUL*):

```
perl -ln0e 'print $ARGV if /cat/ && /dog/ && /bird/' files
```

---

[*] Some versions of *nawk* require an explicit $0~ in front of each pattern.

(Notice that as the problem gets harder, the less powerful commands drop out.)

The *grep* filter technique shown earlier also works on this problem. Just add a *–l* option and the *xargs* command (28.17) to make it pass filenames, rather than text lines, through the pipeline:

```
grep -l cat files | xargs grep -l dog | xargs grep -l bird
```

(*xargs* is basically the glue used when one program produces output needed by another program as command-line arguments.)

—*GU*

13.11 Narrowing a Search Quickly

If you're searching a long file to find a particular word or name, or you're running a program like *ls –l* and you want to filter some lines, here's a quick way to narrow down the search. As an example, say your phone file has 20,000 lines like these:

```
Smith, Nancy:MFG:50 Park Place:Huntsville:(205)234-5678
```

and you want to find someone named Nancy. When you see more information, you know you can find which of the Nancys she is:

```
% grep Nancy phones
...150 lines of names...
```

Use the C shell's history mechanism (30.2) and *sed* to cut out lines you don't want. For example, about a third of the Nancys are in Huntsville, and you know she doesn't work there:

```
% !! | sed -e /Huntsville/d
grep Nancy phones | sed -e /Huntsville/d
...100 lines of names...
```

The shell shows the command it's executing: the previous command (!!) piped to *sed*, which deletes lines in the *grep* output that have the word *Huntsville*.

Okay. You know Nancy doesn't work in the MFG or SLS groups, so delete those lines, too:

```
% !! -e /MFG/d -e /SLS/d
grep Nancy phones | sed -e /Huntsville/d -e /MFG/d -e /SLS/d
...20 lines of names...
```

Keep using !! to repeat the previous command line, and keep adding more *sed* expressions until the list gets short enough. The same thing works for other commands. When you're hunting for errors in a BSDish system log, for example, and you want to skip lines from *named* and *sudo*, use the following:

```
% cat /var/log/messages | sed -e /named/d -e /sudo/d
...
```

If the matching pattern has anything but letters and numbers in it, you'll have to understand shell quoting (27.12) and *sed* regular expressions. Most times, though, this quick-and-dirty method works just fine.

[Yes, you can do the exact same thing with multiple *grep –v* (13.3) commands, but using *sed* like this allows multiple matches with only one execution of *sed*. *grep –v* requires a new *grep* process for each condition. —DH]

—JP

13.12 Faking Case-Insensitive Searches

This may be the simplest tip in the book, but it's something that doesn't occur to lots of users.

Some versions of *egrep* don't support the *–i* option, which requests case-insensitive searches. I find that case-insensitive searches are absolutely essential, particularly to writers. You never know whether any particular word will be capitalized.

To fake a case-insensitive search with *egrep*, just eliminate any letters that might be uppercase. Instead of searching for *Example*, just search for *xample*. If the letter that might be capitalized occurs in the middle of a phrase, you can replace the missing letter with a "dot" (single character) wildcard, rather than omitting it.

Sure, you could do this the "right way" with a command like:

```
% egrep '[eE]xample' *
```

but our shortcut is easier.

This tip obviously isn't limited to *egrep*; it applies to any utility that only implements case-sensitive searches, like *more*.

—ML

13.13 Finding a Character in a Column

Here's an idea for finding lines that have a given character in a column. Use the following simple *awk* (20.10) command:

```
% awk 'substr($0,n,1) == "c"' filename
```

where *c* is the character you're searching for, and *n* is the column you care about.

Where would you do this? If you're processing a file with strict formatting, this might be useful; for example, you might have a telephone list with a # in column 2 for "audio" telephone numbers, $ for dialup modems, and % for fax machines.

A script for looking up phone numbers might use an *awk* command like this to prevent you from mistakenly talking to a fax machine.

If your data has any TAB characters, the columns might not be where you expect. In that case, use *expand* on the file, then pipe it to *awk*.

—*JP and ML*

13.14 Fast Searches and Spelling Checks with "look"

Every so often, someone has designed a new, faster *grep*-type program. Public-domain software archives have more than a few of them. One of the fastest search programs has been around for years: *look*. It uses a binary search method that's very fast. But *look* won't solve all your problems: it works only on files that have been sorted (22.1). If you have a big file or database that can be sorted, searching it with *look* will save a lot of time. For example, to search for all lines that start with *Alpha*:

```
% look Alpha filename
Alpha particle
Alphanumeric
```

look

The *look* program can also be used to check the spelling of a word or find a related word; see article 16.3. If you don't have *look* installed on your system, you can get it from the Unix Power Tools web site.

—*JP*

13.15 Finding Words Inside Binary Files

If you try to read binaries on your screen with *cat –v* (12.4), you'll see a lot of non-printable characters. Buried in there somewhere, though, are words and strings of characters that might make some sense. For example, if the code is copy-righted, you can usually find that information in the binary. The pathnames of special files read by the program will probably show up. If you're trying to fig-ure out which program printed an error message, use *strings* on the binaries and look for the error. Some versions of *strings* do a better job of getting just the use-ful information; others may write a lot of junk, too. But what the heck?—pipe the output to a pager (12.3) or *grep* (13.2), redirect it to a file, and ignore the stuff you don't want.

Here's a (shortened) example on FreeBSD:

```
% strings /usr/bin/write
/usr/libexec/ld-elf.so.1
FreeBSD
libc.so.4
```

```
strcpy
...
@(#) Copyright (c) 1989, 1993
        The Regents of the University of California.  All rights reserved.
$FreeBSD: src/usr.bin/write/write.c,v 1.12 1999/08/28 01:07:48 peter Exp $
can't find your tty
can't find your tty's name
you have write permission turned off
/dev/
%s is not logged in on %s
%s has messages disabled on %s
usage: write user [tty]
/var/run/utmp
utmp
%s is not logged in
%s has messages disabled
%s is logged in more than once; writing to %s
%s%s
Message from %s@%s on %s at %s ...
```

The eighth line (*$FreeBSD: ... $*) comes from RCS (39.5)—you can see the version number, the date the code was last modified or released, and so on. The %s is a special pattern that the *printf*(3) function will replace with values like the username, hostname, and time.

By default, *strings* doesn't search all of a binary file: it only reads the initialized and loaded sections. The - (dash) option tells *strings* to search all of the file. Another useful option is -*n*, where *n* is the minimum-length string to print. Setting a higher limit will cut the "noise," but you might also lose what you're looking for.

The *od* command with its option -s*n* command does a similar thing: finds all null-terminated strings that are at least *n* characters long.

—*JP*

13.16 A Highlighting grep

Do you ever *grep* for a word, and when lines scroll down your screen, it's hard to find the word on each line? For example, suppose I'm looking for any mail messages I've saved that say anything about the *perl* programming language. But when I *grep* the file, most of it seems useless:

```
% grep perl ~/Mail/save
> and some of it wouldn't compile properly.  I wonder if
Subject: install script, for perl scripts
 perl itself is installed?
> run but dies with a read error because it isn't properly
> if I can get it installed properly on another machine I
> run but dies with a read error because it isn't properly
> if I can get it installed properly on another machine I
```

Well, as described on its own manual page, here's a program that's "trivial, but cute." *hgrep* runs a *grep* and highlights the string being searched for, to make it easier for us to find what we're looking for.

```
% hgrep perl ~/Mail/save
> and some of it wouldn't compile properly.  I wonder if
Subject: install script, for perl scripts
 perl itself is installed?
> run but dies with a read error because it isn't properly
> if I can get it installed properly on another machine I
> run but dies with a read error because it isn't properly
> if I can get it installed properly on another machine I
```

And now we know why the output looked useless: because most of it is! Luckily, *hgrep* is just a frontend; it simply passes all its arguments to *grep*. So *hgrep* necessarily accepts all of *grep*'s options, and I can just use the *–w* option to pare the output down to what I want:

```
% hgrep -w perl ~/Mail/save
Subject: install script, for perl scripts
 perl itself is installed?
```

The *less* (12.3) pager also automatically highlights matched patterns as you search.

—LM

14

Removing Files

14.1 The Cycle of Creation and Destruction

As a computer user, you spend lots of time creating files. Just as the necessary counterpart of life is death, the other side of file creation is deletion. If you never delete any files, you soon have a computer's equivalent of a population explosion: your disks get full, and you must either spend money (buy and install more disk drives) or figure out which files you don't really need.

In this chapter, we'll talk about ways to get rid of files: how to do it safely, how to get rid of files that don't want to die, and how to find "stale" files—or unused files that have been around for a long time. "Safe" deletion is a particularly interesting topic, because Unix's *rm* command is extreme: once you delete a file, it's gone permanently. There are several solutions for working around this problem, letting you (possibly) reclaim files from the dead.

—*ML*

14.2 How Unix Keeps Track of Files: Inodes

The ability to mumble about *inodes* is the key to social success at a Unix gurus' cocktail party. This may not seem attractive to you, but sooner or later you will need to know what an inode is.

Seriously, inodes are an important part of the Unix filesystem. You don't need to worry about them most of the time, but it does help to know what they are.

An inode is a data structure on the disk that describes a file. It holds most of the important information about the file, including the on-disk address of the file's data blocks (the part of the file that you care about). Each inode has its own identifying number, called an *i-number*.

You really don't care about where a file is physically located on a disk. You usually don't care about the i-number—unless you're trying to find the links (9.24, 10.3) to a file. But you do care about the following information, all of which is stored in a file's inode:

The file's ownership
> The user and the group that own the file

The file's access mode (1.17, 50.2)
> Whether various users and groups are allowed to read, write, or execute the file

The file's timestamps (8.2)
> When the file itself was last modified, when the file was last accessed, and when the inode was last modified

The file's type
> Whether the file is a regular file, a special file, or some other kind of abstraction masquerading (1.19) as a file

Each filesystem has a set number of inodes that are created when the filesystem is first created (usually when the disk is first initialized). This number is therefore the maximum number of files that the filesystem can hold. It cannot be changed without reinitializing the filesystem, which destroys all the data that the filesystem holds. It is possible, though rare, for a filesystem to run out of inodes, just as it is possible to run out of storage space—this can happen on filesystems with many, many small files.

The *ls –l* (50.2) command shows much of this information. The *ls –i* option (10.4) shows a file's i-number. The *stat* command lists almost everything in an inode.

—*ML*

14.3 rm and Its Dangers

Under Unix, you use the *rm* command to delete files. The command is simple enough; you just type rm followed by a list of files. If anything, *rm* is too simple. It's easy to delete more than you want, and once something is gone, it's permanently gone. There are a few hacks that make *rm* somewhat safer, and we'll get to those momentarily. But first, here's a quick look at some of the dangers.

To understand why it's impossible to reclaim deleted files, you need to know a bit about how the Unix filesystem works. The system contains a "free list," which is a list of disk blocks that aren't used. When you delete a file, its directory entry (which gives it its name) is removed. If there are no more links (10.3) to the file (i.e., if the file only had one name), its inode (14.2) is added to the list of free inodes, and its datablocks are added to the free list.

Well, why can't you get the file back from the free list? After all, there are DOS utilities that can reclaim deleted files by doing something similar. Remember, though, Unix is a multitasking operating system. Even if you think your system is a single-user system, there are a lot of things going on "behind your back": daemons are writing to log files, handling network connections, processing electronic mail, and so on. You could theoretically reclaim a file if you could "freeze" the filesystem the instant your file was deleted—but that's not possible. With Unix, everything is always active. By the time you realize you made a mistake, your file's data blocks may well have been reused for something else.

When you're deleting files, it's important to use wildcards carefully. Simple typing errors can have disastrous consequences. Let's say you want to delete all your object (.o) files. You want to type:

```
% rm *.o
```

But because of a nervous twitch, you add an extra space and type:

```
% rm * .o
```

It looks right, and you might not even notice the error. But before you know it, all the files in the current directory will be gone, irretrievably.

If you don't think this can happen to you, here's something that actually did happen to me. At one point, when I was a relatively new Unix user, I was working on my company's business plan. The executives thought, so as to be "secure," that they'd set a business plan's permissions so you had to be *root* (1.18) to modify it. (A mistake in its own right, but that's another story.) I was using a terminal I wasn't familiar with and accidentally created a bunch of files with four control characters at the beginning of their name. To get rid of these, I typed (as *root*):

```
# rm ????*
```

This command took a *long* time to execute. When about two-thirds of the directory was gone, I realized (with horror) what was happening: I was deleting all files with four or more characters in the filename.

The story got worse. They hadn't made a backup in about five months. (By the way, this article should give you plenty of reasons for making regular backups (38.3).) By the time I had restored the files I had deleted (a several-hour process in itself; this was on an ancient version of Unix with a horrible *backup* utility) and checked (by hand) all the files against our printed copy of the business plan, I had resolved to be *very careful* with my *rm* commands.

[Some shells have safeguards that work against Mike's first disastrous example—but not the second one. Automatic safeguards like these can become a crutch, though...when you use another shell temporarily and don't have them, or when you type an expression like Mike's very destructive second example. I agree with his simple advice: check your *rm* commands carefully!—*JP*]

—*ML*

14.4 Tricks for Making rm Safer

Here's a summary of ways to protect yourself from accidentally deleting files:

- Use *rm –i*, possibly as an alias (article 14.8).
- Make *rm –i* less painful (article 14.7).
- Write a "delete" script that moves "deleted" files to a temporary directory (article 14.9).
- *tcsh* has an *rmstar* variable that makes the shell ask for confirmation when you type something like rm *. In *zsh*, this protection is automatic unless you set the RM_STAR_SILENT shell option to stop it.
- Use revision control (article 39.4).
- Make your own backups, as explained in article 38.3.
- Prevent deletion (or renaming or creating) of files by making the *directory* (not necessarily the files in it!) unwritable (article 50.2).

If you want to delete with wild abandon, use *rm –f* (article 14.10).

—ML

14.5 Answer "Yes" or "No" Forever with yes

Some commands—like *rm –i*, *find –ok*, and so on—ask users to answer a "do it or not?" question from the keyboard. For example, you might have a file-deleting program or alias named *del* that asks before deleting each file:

```
% del *
Remove file1? y
Remove file2? y
    ...
```

If you answer y, then the file will be deleted.

What if you want to run a command that will ask you 200 questions and you want to answer y to all of them, but you don't want to type all those ys from the keyboard? Pipe the output of yes to the command; it will answer y for you:

```
% yes | del *
Remove file1?
Remove file2?
    ...
```

If you want to answer n to all the questions, you can do:

```
% yes n | del *
```

 Not all Unix commands read their standard input for answers to prompts. If a command opens your terminal (*/dev/tty* (**36.15**)) directly to read your answer, yes won't work. Try *expect* (**28.18**) instead.

—*JP*

14.6 Remove Some, Leave Some

Most people use *rm –i* for safety: so they're always asked for confirmation before removing a particular file. Mike Loukides told me about another way he uses *rm –i*. When he has several files to remove, but the wildcards (**1.13**) would be too painful to type with a plain *rm*, Mike gives *rm –i* a bigger list of filenames and answers "n" to filenames he doesn't want deleted. For instance:

```
% ls
aberrant     abhorred     abnormal     abominate    acerbic
aberrate     abhorrent    abominable   absurd       acrimonious
...
% rm -i ab*
rm: remove aberrant (y/n)? y
rm: remove aberrate (y/n)? n
rm: remove abhorred (y/n)? y
rm: remove abhorrent (y/n)? n
...
```

—*JP*

14.7 A Faster Way to Remove Files Interactively

The *rm –i* command asks you about each file, separately. The method in this article can give you the safety without the hassle of typing y as much.

Another approach, which I recommend, is that you create a new script or alias, and use that alias whenever you delete files. Call the alias *del* or *Rm*, for instance. This way, if you ever execute your special delete command when it doesn't exist, no harm is done—you just get an error. If you get into this habit, you can start making your delete script smarter. Here is one that asks you about each file if there are three or fewer files specified. For more than three files, it displays them all and asks you once if you wish to delete them all:

```
#!/bin/sh
case $# in
0)     echo "`basename $0`: you didn't say which file(s) to delete"; exit 1;;
[123]) /bin/rm -i "$@" ;;
*)     echo "$*"
       echo do you want to delete these files\?
       read a
       case "$a" in
       [yY]*) /bin/rm "$@" ;;
       esac
       ;;
esac
```

—BB

14.8 Safer File Deletion in Some Directories

Using *noclobber* (43.6) and read-only files only protects you from a few occasional mistakes. A potentially catastrophic error is typing:

```
% rm * .o
```

instead of:

```
% rm *.o
```

In the blink of an eye, all of your files would be gone. A simple, yet effective, preventive measure is to create a file called *–i* in the particular directory in which you want extra protection:

./- **14.13**

```
% touch ./-i
```

In this case, the * is expanded to match all of the filenames in the directory. Because the file *–i* is alphabetically listed before any file except those that start with one of the characters !, #, $, %, &, ', (,), *, +, or ,, the *rm* command sees the *–i* file as a command-line argument. When *rm* is executed with its *–i* option, files will not be deleted unless you verify the action. This still isn't perfect, though. If you have a file that starts with a comma (,) in the directory, it will come before the file starting with a dash, and *rm* will not get the *–i* argument first.

The *–i* file also won't save you from errors like this:

```
% rm [a-z]* .o
```

If lots of users each make a *–i* file in each of their zillions of subdirectories, that could waste a lot of disk inodes (14.2). It might be better to make one *–i* file in your home directory and hard link (15.4) the rest to it, like this:

```
% cd
% touch ./-i
% cd somedir
```
~ **31.11**
```
% ln ~/-i .
    ...
```

Second, to save disk blocks, make sure the *–i* file is zero-length—use the *touch* command, not *vi* or some other command that puts characters in the file.

—BB

14.9 Safe Delete: Pros and Cons

To protect themselves from accidentally deleting files, some users create a "trash" directory somewhere and then write a "safe delete" program that, instead of *rm*ing a file, moves it into the *trash* directory. The implementation can be quite complex, but a simple alias or shell function will do most of what you want:

```
alias del "mv \!* ~/trash/."
```

Or, for Bourne-type shells:

```
del () { mv "$@" $HOME/trash/.; }
```

Of course, now your deleted files collect in your *trash* directory, so you have to clean that out from time to time. You can do this either by hand or automatically, via a *cron* (25.2) entry like this:

&& 35.14
-r 14.16

```
23 2 * * * cd $HOME/trash && rm -rf *
```

This deletes everything in the trash directory at 2:23 a.m. daily. To restore a file that you deleted, you have to look through your trash directory by hand and put the file back in the right place. That may not be much more pleasant than poking through your garbage to find the tax return you threw out by mistake, but (hopefully) you don't make lots of mistakes.

There are plenty of problems with this approach. Obviously, if you delete two files with the same name in the same day, you're going to lose one of them. A shell script could (presumably) handle this problem, though you'd have to generate a new name for the deleted file. There are also lots of nasty side effects and "gotchas," particularly if you want an *rm –r* equivalent, if you want this approach to work on a network of workstations, or if you use it to delete files that are shared by a team of users.

Unfortunately, this is precisely the problem. A "safe delete" that isn't really safe may not be worth the effort. Giving people a safety net with holes in it is only good if you can guarantee in advance that they won't land in one of the holes, believing themselves protected. You can patch some of the holes by replacing this simple alias with a shell script; but you can't fix all of them.

—ML

14.10 Deletion with Prejudice: rm –f

The *–f* option to *rm* is the extreme opposite of *–i*. It says, "Just delete the file; don't ask me any questions." The "f" stands (allegedly) for "force," but this isn't quite right. *rm –f* won't force the deletion of something that you aren't allowed to delete. (To understand what you're allowed to delete, you need to understand directory access permissions (50.2).)

What, then, does *rm –f* do, and why would you want to use it?

- Normally, *rm* asks you for confirmation if you tell it to delete files to which you don't have write access—you'll get a message like Override protection 444 for foo? (The Unix filesystem allows you to delete read-only files, provided you have write access to the directory.) With *–f*, these files will be deleted silently.

- Normally, *rm*'s exit status (35.12) is 0 if it succeeded and 1 if it failed to delete the file. With *–f*, *rm*'s return status is always 0.

I find that I rarely use *rm –f* on the Unix command line, but I almost always use it within shell scripts. In a shell script, you (probably) don't want to be interrupted by lots of prompts should *rm* find a bunch of read-only files.

You probably also don't want to be interrupted if *rm –f* tries to delete files that don't exist because the script never created them. Generally, *rm –f* keeps quiet about files that don't exist; if the desired end result is for the file to be gone, it not existing in the first place is just as good.

—ML

14.11 Deleting Files with Odd Names

A perennial problem is deleting files that have strange characters (or other oddities) in their names. The next few articles contain some hints for the following:

- Deleting files with random control characters in their names (article 14.12).
- Deleting files whose names start with a dash (article 14.13).
- Deleting files with "unprintable" filenames (article 14.14).
- Deleting files by using the inode number (article 14.15).
- Deleting directories and problems that can arise as a result (article 14.16).

We'll also give hints for these:

- Deleting unused (or rarely used) files (article 14.17).
- Deleting all the files in a directory, except for one or two (article 14.18).

Most tips for deleting files also work for renaming the files (if you want to keep them): just replace the *rm* command with *mv*.

—ML

14.12 Using Wildcards to Delete Files with Strange Names

Filenames can be hard to handle if their names include control characters or characters that are special to the shell. Here's a directory with three oddball filenames:

```
% ls
What now
a$file
prog|.c
program.c
```

When you type those filenames on the command line, the shell interprets the special characters (space, dollar sign, and vertical bar) instead of including them as part of the filename. There are several ways (14.11) to handle this problem. One is with wildcards (33.2). Type a part of the filename without the weird characters, and use a wildcard to match the rest. The shell doesn't scan the filenames for other special characters after it interprets the wildcards, so you're (usually) safe if you can get a wildcard to match. For example, here's how to rename *What now* to *Whatnow*, remove *a$file*, and rename *prog|.c* to *prog.c*:

```
% mv What* Whatnow
% rm -i a*
rm: remove a$file? y
% mv prog?.c prog.c
```

Filenames with control characters are just another version of the same problem. Use a wildcard to match the part of the name that's troubling you. The real problem with control characters in filenames is that some control characters do weird things to your screen. Once I accidentally got a file with a CTRL-L in its name. Whenever I ran *ls*, it erased the screen before I could see what the filename was! Article 8.12 explains how, depending on your version of *ls*, you can use the *–q* or *–b* options to spot the offensive file and construct a wildcard expression to rename or delete it. (*ls –q* is the default on most Unix implementations these days, so you will probably never see this particular problem.)

—JP

14.13 Handling a Filename Starting with a Dash (–)

Sometimes you can slip and create a file whose name starts with a dash (–), like –*output* or –*f*. That's a perfectly legal filename. The problem is that Unix command options usually start with a dash. If you try to type that filename on a command line, the command might think you're trying to type a command option.

In almost every case, all you need to do is "hide" the dash from the command. Start the filename with ./ (dot slash). This doesn't change anything as far as the command is concerned; ./ just means "look in the current directory" (1.16). So here's how to remove the file –*f*:

```
% rm ./-f
```

(Most *rm* commands have a special option for dealing with filenames that start with a dash, but this trick should work on *all* Unix commands.)

—*JP*

14.14 Using unlink to Remove a File with a Strange Name

Some versions of Unix have a lot of trouble with eight-bit filenames—that is, filenames that contain non-ASCII characters. The *ls –q* (8.12) command shows the nonASCII characters as question marks (?), but usual tricks like *rm –i* * (14.12) skip right over the file. You can see exactly what the filename is by using *ls –b* (8.12):

```
% ls -q
   ????
afile
bfile
% rm -i *
afile: ? n
bfile: ? n
% ls -b
\t\360\207\005\254
afile
bfile
```

On older Unixes, the –*b* option to *ls* might not be supported, in which case you can use *od –c* (12.4) to dump the current directory, using its relative pathname . (dot) (1.16), character by character. It's messier, and isn't supported on all Unix platforms, but it's worth a try:

```
% od -c .
   ...
00.....   \t 360 207 005 254  \0  \0  \0  \0  ...
```

If you can move all the other files out of the directory, then you'll probably be able to remove the leftover file and directory with *rm –rf* (14.16, 14.10). Moving files and removing the directory is a bad idea, though, if this is an important system directory like */bin*. Otherwise, if you use the escaped name *ls –b* gave you, you might be able to remove it directly by using the system call *unlink*(2) in Perl. Use the same escape characters in Perl that *ls –b* displayed. (Or, if you needed to use *od –c*, find the filename in the *od* listing of the directory—it will probably end with a series of NUL characters, like \0 \0 \0.)

```
perl -e 'unlink("\t\360\207\005\254");'
```

—JP

14.15 Removing a Strange File by its i-number

If wildcards don't work (14.12) to remove a file with a strange name, try getting the file's i-number (14.2). Then use *find*'s *–inum* operator (9.9) to remove the file.

Here's a directory with a weird filename. *ls* (with its default *–q* option (8.12) on most versions) shows that the name has three unusual characters. Running *ls –i* shows each file's i-number. The strange file has i-number 6239. Give the i-number to *find*, and the file is gone:

```
% ls
adir      afile     b???file  bfile     cfile     dfile
% ls -i
  6253 adir        6239 b???file    6249 cfile
  9291 afile       6248 bfile       9245 dfile
% find . -inum 6239 -exec rm {} \;
% ls
adir    afile   bfile   cfile   dfile
```

Instead of deleting the file, I also could have renamed it to *newname* with the command:

```
% find . -inum 6239 -exec mv {} newname \;
```

If the current directory has large subdirectories, you'll probably want to keep *find* from recursing down into them by using the *–maxdepth 1* operator. (*find*s that don't support *–maxdepth* can use *–prune* (9.25) for speed.)

—JP

14.16 Problems Deleting Directories

What if you want to get rid of a directory? The standard—and safest—way to do this is to use the Unix *rmdir* "remove directory" utility:

```
% rmdir files
```

The *rmdir* command often confuses new users. It will *only* remove a directory if it is completely empty; otherwise, you'll get an error message:

```
% rmdir files
rmdir: files: Directory not empty
% ls files
%
```

As in the example, *ls* will often show that the directory is empty. What's going on?

It's common for editors and other programs to create "invisible" files (files with names beginning with a dot). The *ls* command normally doesn't list them; if you want to see them, you have to use *ls –A* (8.9):*

```
% rmdir files
rmdir: files: Directory not empty
% ls -A files
.BAK.textfile2
```

Here, we see that the directory wasn't empty after all: there's a backup file that was left behind by some editor. You may have used rm * to clean the directory out, but that won't work: *rm* also ignores files beginning with dots, unless you explicitly tell it to delete them. We really need a wildcard pattern like .??* or .[a-zA-Z0-9]* to catch normal dotfiles without catching the directories . and ..:

```
% rmdir files
rmdir: files: Directory not empty
% ls -A files
.BAK.textfile2
% rm files/.??*
% rmdir files
%
```

Other pitfalls might be files whose names consist of nonprinting characters or blank spaces—sometimes these get created by accident or by malice (yes, some people think this is funny). Such files will usually give you "suspicious" *ls* output (8.11) (like a blank line).

If you don't want to worry about all these special cases, just use *rm –r*:

```
% rm -r files
```

This command removes the directory and everything that's in it, including other directories. A lot of people warn you about it; it's dangerous because it's easy to delete more than you realize. Personally, I use it all the time, and I've never made a mistake. I *never* bother with *rmdir*.

—ML

---

* If your version of *ls* doesn't have the *–A* option, use *–a* instead. You'll see the two special directory entries . and .. (8.9), which you can ignore.

14.17 Deleting Stale Files

Sooner or later, a lot of junk collects in your directories: files that you don't really care about and never use. It's possible to write *find* (9.1) commands that will automatically clean these up. If you want to clean up regularly, you can add some *find* commands to your *crontab* file (25.2).

Basically, all you need to do is write a *find* command that locates files based on their last access time (*–atime* (9.5)) and use *–ok* or *–exec* (9.9) to delete them. Such a command might look like this:

```
% find . -atime +60 -ok rm -f {} \;
```

This locates files that haven't been accessed in the last 60 days, asks if you want to delete the file, and then deletes the file. (If you run it from *cron*, make sure you use *–exec* instead of *–ok*, and make *absolutely sure* that the *find* won't delete files that you think are important.)

Of course, you can modify this *find* command to exclude (or select) files with particular names; for example, the following command deletes old core dumps and GNU Emacs backup files (whose names end in ~), but leaves all others alone:

```
% find . \( -name core -o -name "*~" \) -atime +60 -ok rm -f {} \;
```

If you take an automated approach to deleting stale files, watch out for these things:

- There are plenty of files (for example, Unix utilities and log files) that should *never* be removed. Never run any "automatic deletion" script on */usr* or / or any other "system" directory.

- On some systems, executing a binary executable doesn't update the last access time. Since there's no reason to read these files, you can expect them to get pretty stale, even if they're used often. But you don't want to delete them. If you cook up a complicated enough *find* command, you should be able to handle this automatically. Something like this should (at least partially) do the trick:

| 9.6
-perm 9.15

```
% find . -atime +30 ! -perm -111 ... -exec rm {} \;
```

- Along the same lines, you'd probably never want to delete C source code, so you might modify your *find* command to look like this:

```
% find . -atime +30 ! -perm -111 ! -name "*.c" ... -exec rm {} \;
```

- I personally find that automatically deleting files is an extreme and bizarre solution. I can't imagine deleting files without knowing exactly what I've deleted or without (somehow) saving the "trash" somewhere just in case I accidentally removed something important. To archive the deleted files on tape, you can use the *find –cpio* operator if your system has it. Otherwise, try a little shell script with GNU *tar*; the following script writes the list of files to a temporary file and then, if that succeeds, reads the list of files, writes them to tape, and removes the files if the tape write succeeds:

if **35.13**
&& **35.14**

```
umask 077
files=/tmp/CLEANUP$$
if find ... -print > $files
then tar -c -T $files --remove && rm $files
else echo "cleanup aborted because find returned nonzero status"
fi
```

Okay, I've said that I don't really think that automated deletion scripts are a good idea. However, I don't have a good comprehensive solution. I spend a reasonable amount of time (maybe an hour a month) going through directories and deleting stale files by hand. I also have a *clean* alias that I type whenever I think about it. It looks like this:

```
alias clean "rm *~ junk *.BAK core #*"
```

That is, this alias deletes all of my Emacs (19.1) backup files, Emacs autosave files (risky, I know), files named *junk*, some other backup files, and core dumps. I'll admit that since I *never* want to save these files, I could probably live with something like this:

```
% find ~ \( -name "*~" -o -name core \) -atime +1 -exec rm {} \;
```

But stil, automated deletion commands make me really nervous, and I'd prefer to live without them.

—*ML*

14.18 Removing Every File but One

One problem with Unix: it's not terribly good at "excluding" things. There's no option to *rm* that says, "Do what you will with everything else, but please don't delete these files." You can sometimes create a wildcard expression (33.2) that does what you want—but sometimes that's a lot of work, or maybe even impossible.

Here's one place where Unix's command substitution (28.14) operators (backquotes) come to the rescue. You can use *ls* to list all the files, pipe the output into a *grep –v* or *egrep –v* (13.3) command, and then use backquotes to give the resulting list to *rm*. Here's what this command would look like:

```
% rm -i `ls -d *.txt | grep -v '^john\.txt$'`
```

This command deletes all files whose names end in *.txt*, except for *john.txt*. I've probably been more careful than necessary about making sure there aren't any extraneous matches; in most cases, *grep –v john* would probably suffice. Using *ls –d* (8.5) makes sure that *ls* doesn't look into any subdirectories and give you those filenames. The *rm –i* asks you before removing each file; if you're sure of yourself, omit the *–i*.

Of course, if you want to exclude two files, you can do that with *egrep*:

```
% rm `ls -d *.txt | egrep -v 'john|mary'`
```

(Don't forget to quote the vertical bar (|), as shown earlier, to prevent the shell from piping *egrep*'s output to *mary*.)

Another solution is the *nom* (33.8) script.

—ML

14.19 Using find to Clear Out Unneeded Files

Do you run *find* on your machine every night? Do you know what it has to go through just to find out if a file is three days old and smaller than ten blocks or owned by "fred" or setuid root? This is why I tried to combine all the things we need done for removal of files into one big *find* script:

cleanup

```
#! /bin/sh
#
# cleanup - find files that should be removed and clean them
# out of the file system.

find / \(        \( -name '#*'                -atime +1 \)  \
        -o  \( -name ',*'                -atime +1 \)  \
        -o  \( -name rogue.sav           -atime +7 \)  \
        -o  \(        \( -name '*.bak'                          \
                       -o -name '*.dvi'                         \
                       -o -name '*.CKP'                         \
                       -o -name '.*.bak'                        \
                       -o -name '.*.CKP' \) -atime +3 \)  \
        -o  \( -name '.emacs_[0-9]*'     -atime +7 \)  \
        -o  \( -name core                          \)  \
        -o  \( -user guest               -atime +9 \)  \
```

2>&1 **36.16**
```
        \) -print -exec rm -f {} \; > /tmp/.cleanup 2>&1
```

This is an example of using a single *find* command to search for files with different names and last-access times (see article 9.5). Doing it all with one *find* is much faster—and less work for the disk—than running a lot of separate *finds*. The parentheses group each part of the expression. The neat indentation makes this big thing easier to read. The -print -exec at the end removes each file and also writes the filenames to standard output, where they're collected into a file named */tmp/.cleanup*—people can read it to see what files were removed. You should probably be aware that printing the names to */tmp/.cleanup* lets everyone see pathnames, such as */home/joe/personal/resume.bak*, which some people might consider sensitive. Another thing to be aware of is that this *find* command starts at the root directory; you can do the same thing for your own directories.

—CT and JP

15

Optimizing Disk Space

15.1 Disk Space Is Cheap

Many of the techniques in this chapter aren't nearly as applicable as they once were. At the time of this writing, EIDE disks are about a dollar a gigabyte; even fast-wide SCSI isn't that expensive. Often the solution to running low on disk space is just to buy more.

That said, many of these techniques illustrate useful things to know about Unix. It's common these days to run Unix on an old, spare machine where it's not worth the trouble of upgrading the disks. You may also be dealing with a Unix box at work or school that uses expensive, highly reliable disks with expensive backup procedures in place, where more disk space just isn't an option. It never hurts to know how to eke the last few bytes out of a partition.

This chapter also has a lot of information about compressing and decompressing files, which is fairly common. (These days, you may well compress files to save network bandwidth rather than disk space, but the same principles apply.) So enjoy exploring!

—DH

15.2 Instead of Removing a File, Empty It

Sometimes you don't want to remove a file completely—you just want to empty it:

- If an active process has the file open (not uncommon for log files), removing the file and creating a new one will not affect the logging program; those messages will just keep going to the file that's no longer linked. Emptying the file doesn't break the association, and so it clears the file without affecting the logging program.

- When you remove a file and create a new one with the same name, the new file will have your default permissions and ownership (50.3). It's better to empty the file now, then add new text later; this won't change the permissions and ownership.

- Completely empty files (ones that *ls* –*l* says have zero characters) don't take any disk space to store (except the few bytes that the directory entry (10.2) uses).

- You can use the empty files as "place markers" to remind you that something was there or belongs there. Some Unix logging programs won't write errors to their log files unless the log files already exist. Empty files work fine for that.

- Empty files hold a "timestamp" (just as files with text do) that shows when the file was last modified. I use empty files in some directories to remind me when I've last done something (backups, printouts, etc.). The *find* –*newer* (9.8) command can compare other files to a timestamp file.

Well, you get the idea by now.

How can you empty a file? Watch out: when some editors say that a file has "no lines," they may still append a newline character when writing the file. Just one character still takes a block of disk space to store. Here are some better ways to get a properly empty file:

- In Bourne-type shells like *sh* and *bash*, the most efficient way is to redirect the output of a null command:

    ```
    $ > afile
    ```

    If the file already exists, that command will truncate the file without needing a subprocess.

- Copy the Unix empty file, */dev/null* (43.12), on top of the file:

    ```
    % cp /dev/null afile
    ```

- Or just *cat* it there:

    ```
    % cat /dev/null > afile
    ```

You can also "almost" empty the file, leaving just a few lines, this way:

tail 12.8
```
% tail afile > tmpfile
% cat tmpfile > afile
% rm tmpfile
```

That's especially good for log files that you never want to delete completely. Use *cat* and *rm*, not *mv*—*mv* will break any other links to the original file (afile) and replace it with the temporary file.

—JP

15.3 Save Space with "Bit Bucket" Log Files and Mailboxes

Some Unix programs—usually background or daemon programs—insist on writing a log file. You might not want the log file itself as much as you want the disk space that the log file takes. Here are a few tips:

- Some programs will write to a log file only if the log file exists. If the program isn't running, try removing the log file.

- If you remove a log file and the program recreates it, look for command-line options or a configuration-file setup that tells the program not to make the log file.

- If you can't get the program to stop writing the log file, try replacing the log file with a symbolic link to *dev/null* (43.12):

  ```
  # rm logfile
  # ln -s /dev/null logfile
  ```

  The program won't complain, because it will happily write its log file to *dev/ null*, which discards everything written to it. (Writing to *dev/null* is also known as "throwing it in the bit bucket," since all the bits just go away.) Watch out for programs that run at reboot or those that run from the system *crontab* (25.2) to truncate and replace the log file. These programs might replace the symbolic link with a small regular file that will start growing again.

- Does a system mailbox for a user like *bin* keep getting mail (1.21) that you want to throw away? You may be able to add a *.forward* file to the account's home directory with this single line:

  ```
  /dev/null
  ```

  Or add an alias in the system mail alias file that does the same thing:

  ```
  bin: /dev/null
  ```

  If your system has a command like *newaliases* to rebuild the alias database, don't forget to use it after you make the change.

—JP

15.4 Save Space with a Link

You might have copies of the same file in several directories for the following reasons:

- Several different users need to read it (a data file, a program setup file, a telephone list, etc.).

- It's a program that more than one person wants to use. For some reason, you don't want to keep one central copy and put its directory in your search path (27.6).

- The file has a strange name or it's in a directory you don't usually use. You want a name that's easier to type, but you can't use *mv*.

Instead of running *cp*, think about *ln*. There are lots of advantages to links (10.3). One big advantage of hard links is that they don't use any disk space.* The bigger the file, the more space you save with a link. A symbolic link always takes some disk space, so a hard link might be better for ekeing the most space out of your disk. Of course, you have to use a symbolic link if you want to link across filesystems, and symbolic links are much more obvious to other people, so a symlink is less likely to confuse people. Generally the clarity is worth the little bit of extra disk space.

—*JP*

15.5 Limiting File Sizes

Here are techniques to keep you from creating large files (which can happen by accident, such as with runaway programs). Your shell may be able to set process limits. If you're writing a program in C or another language that has access to kernel system calls, you can set these limits yourself. And there's one more trick you can use.

These limits are passed to child processes. So, if your shell sets a limit, all programs you start from that shell will inherit the limit from their parent process.

limit and ulimit

Many shells have a built-in command that uses system calls to set resource limits. This is usually done from a shell setup file (3.3), but can also be done from the command line at a shell prompt. To set a maximum file size in C-type shells and *zsh*, use the command limit filesize *max-size*. In the Korn shell and *bash*, use ulimit -f *max-size*. For example, the following *csh* and *ksh* commands keep you from creating any files larger than 2 MB:

```
% limit filesize 2m
$ ulimit -f 2000
```

Similarly, on many systems, you can use *limit* and *ulimit* to restrict the size of core dump files. Core dumps are generally large files, and if you are not actively developing or debugging, they are often not interesting or useful. To set a maximum size for core dumps, execute one of these commands:

```
% limit coredumpsize max-size
$ ulimit -c max-size
```

---

* The link entry takes a few characters in the directory where you make the link. Unless this makes the directory occupy another disk block, the space available on the disk doesn't change.

To eliminate core dumps entirely, use 0 (zero) for *max-size*. Because core dumps are essential for effective debugging, any users who actively debug programs should know the commands unlimit coredumpsize (which removes this restriction in *csh*) and ulimit -c unlimited for *bash* and *ksh*.

Other Ideas

File size limits only apply to processes that are invoked from a shell where the limit is set. For instance, *at* and *cron* jobs might not read the shell setup file (3.3) that sets your limit. One way to fix this is to set the limit explicitly before you start the job. For instance, to keep your *cron* job named *cruncher* from core-dumping, make the *crontab* entry similar to one of these:

; 28.16
```
47 2 * * *   ulimit -c 0; cruncher
47 2 * * *   bash -c 'ulimit -c 0; exec cruncher'
```

If you've written a daemon (1.10) in C that starts as your workstation boots up (so no shell is involved), have your program invoke a system call like *ulimit*(3) or *setrlimit*(2).

If the unwanted files are created in a directory where you can deny write permission to the directory itself—and the files are not created by a process running as *root* (filesystem permissions don't apply to *root*)—simply make the directory unwritable. (If the process needs to write temporary files, have it use */tmp*. An environment variable such as *TMP* or *TMPDIR* may control this.)

You can prevent the files from being created by putting a zero-size unwritable file in the directory where the files are being created. Because the file is zero-length, it doesn't take any disk space to store:

chmod 50.5
```
% touch core
% chmod 000 core
```

If all else fails, try making a symbolic link to */dev/null* (43.12).

—*ML and JP*

15.6 Compressing Files to Save Space

gzip is a fast and efficient compression program distributed by the GNU project. The basic function of *gzip* is to take a file *filename*, compress it, save the compressed version as *filename.gz*, and remove the original, uncompressed file. The original file is removed only if *gzip* is successful; it is very difficult to delete a file accidentally in this manner. Of course, being GNU software, *gzip* has more options than you want to think about, and many aspects of its behavior can be modified using command-line options.

First, let's say that we have a large file named *garbage.txt*:

```
rutabaga% ls -l garbage.txt*
-rw-r--r--  1 mdw      hack       312996 Nov 17 21:44 garbage.txt
```

If we compress this file using *gzip*, it replaces *garbage.txt* with the compressed file *garbage.txt.gz*. We end up with the following:

```
rutabaga% gzip garbage.txt
rutabaga% ls -l garbage.txt*
-rw-r--r--  1 mdw      hack       103441 Nov 17 21:48 garbage.txt.gz
```

Note that *garbage.txt* is removed when *gzip* completes.

You can give *gzip* a list of filenames; it compresses each file in the list, storing each with a .gz extension. (Unlike the *zip* program for Unix and MS-DOS systems, *gzip* will not, by default, compress several files into a single .gz archive. That's what *tar* is for; see article 15.7.)

gzip

How efficiently a file is compressed depends upon its format and contents. For example, many audio and graphics file formats (such as MP3 and JPEG) are already well compressed, and *gzip* will have little or no effect upon such files. Files that compress well usually include plain-text files and binary files such as executables and libraries. You can get information on a *gzip*ped file using *gzip –l*. For example:

```
rutabaga% gzip -l garbage.txt.gz
compressed   uncompr. ratio uncompressed_name
   103115    312996  67.0% garbage.txt
```

To get our original file back from the compressed version, we use *gunzip*, as in:

```
rutabaga% gunzip garbage.txt.gz
rutabaga% ls -l garbage.txt
-rw-r--r--  1 mdw      hack       312996 Nov 17 21:44 garbage.txt
```

which is identical to the original file. Note that when you *gunzip* a file, the compressed version is removed once the uncompression is complete.

gzip stores the name of the original, uncompressed file in the compressed version. This allows the name of the compressed file to be irrelevant; when the file is uncompressed it can be restored to its original splendor. To uncompress a file to its original filename, use the *–N* option with *gunzip*. To see the value of this option, consider the following sequence of commands:

```
rutabaga% gzip garbage.txt
rutabaga% mv garbage.txt.gz rubbish.txt.gz
```

If we were to *gunzip rubbish.txt.gz* at this point, the uncompressed file would be named *rubbish.txt*, after the new (compressed) filename. However, with the *–N* option, we get the following:

```
rutabaga% gunzip -N rubbish.txt.gz
rutabaga% ls -l garbage.txt
-rw-r--r--  1 mdw      hack       312996 Nov 17 21:44 garbage.txt
```

gzip and *gunzip* can also compress or uncompress data from standard input and output. If *gzip* is given no filenames to compress, it attempts to compress data read from standard input. Likewise, if you use the *–c* option with *gunzip*, it writes uncompressed data to standard output. For example, you could pipe the output of a command to *gzip* to compress the output stream and save it to a file in one step, as in:

```
rutabaga% ls -laR $HOME | gzip > filelist.gz
```

This will produce a recursive directory listing of your home directory and save it in the compressed file *filelist.gz*. You can display the contents of this file with the command:

```
rutabaga% gunzip -c filelist.gz | less
```

This will uncompress *filelist.gz* and pipe the output to the *less* (12.3) command. When you use *gunzip –c*, the file on disk remains compressed.

The *gzcat* command is identical to *gunzip –c*. You can think of this as a version of *cat* for compressed files. Some systems, including Linux, even have a version of the pager *less* for compressed files: *zless*.

When compressing files, you can use one of the options *–1*, *–2*, through *–9* to specify the speed and quality of the compression used. *–1* (also *––fast*) specifies the fastest method, which compresses the files less compactly, while *–9* (also *––best*) uses the slowest, but best compression method. If you don't specify one of these options, the default is *–6*. None of these options has any bearing on how you use *gunzip*; *gunzip* can uncompress the file no matter what speed option you use.

bzip
bzip2

Another compression/decompression program has emerged to take the lead from *gzip*. *bzip2* is the new kid on the block and sports even better compression (on the average about 10 to 20% better than *gzip*), at the expense of longer compression times. You cannot use *bunzip2* to uncompress files compressed with *gzip* and vice versa. Since you cannot expect everybody to have *bunzip2* installed on their machine, you might want to confine yourself to *gzip* for the time being if you want to send the compressed file to somebody else (or, as many archives do, provide both *gzip-* and *bzip2*-compressed versions of the file). However, it pays to have *bzip2* installed, because more and more FTP servers now provide *bzip2*-compressed packages to conserve disk space and, more importantly these days, bandwidth. You can recognize *bzip2*-compressed files from their typical *.bz2* file name extension.

While the command-line options of *bzip2* are not exactly the same as those of *gzip*, those that have been described in this section are, except for *––best* and *––fast*, which *bzip2* doesn't have. For more information, see the *bzip2* manual page.

The bottom line is that you should use *gzip/gunzip* or *bzip2/bunzip2* for your compression needs. If you encounter a file with the extension *.Z*, it was probably produced by *compress*, and *gunzip* can uncompress it for you.

[These days, the only real use for *compress*—if you have *gzip* and *bzip2*—is for creating compressed images needed by some embedded hardware, such as older Cisco IOS images. —DJPH]

—MW, MKD, and LK

15.7 Save Space: tar and compress a Directory Tree

In the Unix filesystem, files are stored in blocks. Each nonempty file, no matter how small, takes up at least one block.* A directory tree full of little files can fill up a lot of partly empty blocks. A big file is more efficient because it fills all (except possibly the last) of its blocks completely.

The *tar* (39.2) command can read lots of little files and put them into one big file. Later, when you need one of the little files, you can extract it from the *tar* archive. Seems like a good space-saving idea, doesn't it? But *tar*, which was really designed for magnetic *tape* archives, adds "garbage" characters at the end of each file to make it an even size. So, a big *tar* archive uses about as many blocks as the separate little files do.

Okay, then why am I writing this article? Because the *gzip* (15.6) utility can solve the problems. It squeezes files down—compressing them to get rid of repeated characters. Compressing a *tar* archive typically saves 50% or more. The *bzip2* (15.6) utility can save even more.

 If your compressed archive is corrupted somehow—say, a disk block goes bad—you could lose access to *all* of the files. That's because neither *tar* nor compression utilities recover well from missing data blocks. If you're archiving an important directory, be sure you have good backup copies of the archive.

Making a compressed archive of a directory and all of its subdirectories is easy: *tar* copies the whole tree when you give it the top directory name. Just be sure to save the archive in some directory that won't be copied—so *tar* won't try to archive its own archive! I usually put the archive in the parent directory. For example, to archive my directory named *project*, I'd use the following commands. The *.tar.gz* extension isn't required, but is just a convention; another

---

* Completely empty files (zero characters) don't take a block.

common convention is *.tgz*. I've added the *gzip --best* option for more compression—but it can be a lot slower, so use it only if you need to squeeze out every last byte. *bzip2* is another way to save bytes, so I'll show versions with both *gzip* and *bzip2*. No matter what command you use, watch carefully for errors:

```
% cd project
% tar clf - . | gzip --best > ../project.tar.gz
% gzcat ../project.tar.gz | tar tvf        -Quick verification
% tar clf - . | bzip2 --best > ../project.tar.bz2
% bzcat ../project.tar.bz2 | tar tvf       -Quick verification
% cd ..
% rm -r project
```

.. 1.16

-r 14.16

tar

If you have GNU *tar* or another version with the *z* option, it will run *gzip* for you. This method doesn't use the *gzip --best* option, though—so you may want to use the previous method to squeeze out all you can. Newer GNU *tars* have an *I* option to run *bzip2*. Watch out for other *tar* versions that use –*I* as an "include file" operator—check your manpage or *tar --help*. If you want to be sure that you don't have a problem like this, use the long options (--*gzip* and --*bzip2*) because they're guaranteed not to conflict with something else; if your *tar* doesn't support the particular compression you've asked for, it will fail cleanly rather than do something you don't expect.

Using the short flags to get compression from GNU *tar*, you'd write the previous *tar* command lines as follows:

```
tar czlf ../project.tar.gz .
tar cIlf ../project.tar.bz2 .
```

In any case, the *tar l* (lowercase letter L) option will print messages if any of the files you're archiving have other hard links (10.4). If a lot of your files have other links, archiving the directory may not save much disk space—the other links will keep those files on the disk, even after your *rm –r* command.

Any time you want a list of the files in the archive, use *tar t* or *tar tv*:

less 12.3

```
% gzcat project.tar.gz | tar tvf - | less
rw-r--r--239/100     485 Oct  5 19:03 1991 ./Imakefile
rw-rw-r--239/100    4703 Oct  5 21:17 1991 ./scalefonts.c
rw-rw-r--239/100    3358 Oct  5 21:55 1991 ./xcms.c
rw-rw-r--239/100   12385 Oct  5 22:07 1991 ./io/input.c
rw-rw-r--239/100    7048 Oct  5 21:59 1991 ./io/output.c
   ...
% bzcat project.tar.bz2 | tar tvf - | less
   ...
% tar tzvf project.tar.gz | less
   ...
% tar tIvf project.tar.bz2 | less
   ...
```

To extract all the files from the archive, type one of these *tar* command lines:

```
% mkdir project
% cd project
% gzcat ../project.tar.gz | tar xf -

% mkdir project
% cd project
% bzcat ../project.tar.bz2 | tar xf -

% mkdir project
% cd project
% tar xzf ../project.tar.gz

% mkdir project
% cd project
% tar xIf ../project.tar.bz2
```

Of course, you don't have to extract the files into a directory named *project*. You can read the archive file from other directories, move it to other computers, and so on.

You can also extract just a few files or directories from the archive. Be sure to use the exact name shown by the previous *tar t* command. For instance, to restore the old subdirectory named *project/io* (and everything that was in it), you'd use one of the previous *tar* command lines with the filename at the end. For instance:

```
% mkdir project
% cd project
% gzcat ../project.tar.gz | tar xf - ./io
```

—*JP*

15.8 How Much Disk Space?

Two tools, *df* and *du*, report how much disk space is free and how much is used by any given directory. For each filesystem, *df* tells you the capacity, how much space is in use, and how much is free. By default, it lists both local and remote (i.e., NFS (1.21)) filesystems. Under Linux or BSD Unix, the output from *df* looks like this:

```
% df
Filesystem 1K-blocks      Used    Avail Capacity  Mounted on
/dev/ad0s1a   99183      37480    53769    41%    /
/dev/ad2s1e 3943876    1873453  1754913    52%    /home
/dev/ad0s1f 3360437    1763460  1328143    57%    /usr
/dev/ad0s1e  508143      16925   450567     4%    /var
procfs            4          4        0   100%    /proc
toy:/usr   17383462   15470733   522053    97%    /toy
   ...
```

This report shows information about four local filesystems, the local *procfs* filesystem, and one remote filesystem (from the system *toy*). Note that a normal filesystem that is 100% full really has 5 to 10% free space—but only the superuser (1.18) can use this reserved space, and that usually isn't a good idea. The reserved space is primarily for recovering from the disk filling up for some reason; the superuser can still successfully copy files and the like to free up space. Special filesystems often don't do this sort of block reservation; procfs and ISO-9660 (CD-ROM and CD-R) filesystems don't care.

df can be invoked in several other ways:

- If you already know that you're interested in a particular filesystem, you can use a command such as *df /home* or *df .* (. means "the current directory" (1.16)).

- If your system uses NFS and you are interested only in local (non-NFS) filesystems, use the command *df –t ufs* (most BSDs) or *df –t ext2fs* (most Linuxes). You should always use this command if remote file servers are down. If you have mounted remote disks that are unavailable, *df* will be extremely slow or hang completely.

- If you are interested in inode usage rather than filesystem data capacity, use the command *df –i*. This produces a similar report showing inode statistics.

If you are using the older System V filesystem (for example, on Solaris), the report from *df* will look different. The information it presents, however, is substantially the same. Here is a typical report:

```
% df
/        (/dev/root ):    1758 blocks    3165 i-nodes
/u       (/dev/u    ):     108 blocks   13475 i-nodes
/usr     (/dev/usr  ):   15694 blocks    8810 i-nodes
```

[If you get this sort of output from *df*, you may be able to get the BSDish display by using *df –P* or *df –k*. You may also want to try the GNU *df*. —DH]

There are 1,758 physical blocks (always measured as 512-byte blocks for this sort of *df*, regardless of the filesystem's logical block size) and 3,165 inodes available on the root filesystem. To find out the filesystem's total capacity, use *df –t*. The command *df –l* only reports on your system's local filesystems, omitting filesystems mounted by NFS or RFS.

It is often useful to know how much storage a specific directory requires. This can help you to determine if any users are occupying more than their share of storage. The *du* utility provides such a report. Generally you want to use the *–k* to *du*; by default its reports are in disk blocks and thus somewhat harder to read. *–k* asks *df* to report its numbers in kilobytes. Here's a simple report from *du*:

```
% du -k
107     ./reports
888     ./stuff
```

```
   32    ./howard/private
   33    ./howard/work
  868    ./howard
  258    ./project/code
  769    ./project
 2634    .
```

du shows that the current directory and all of its subdirectories occupy about 2.5 MB (2,634 KB). The biggest directories in this group are *stuff* and *howard*, which have a total of 888 KB and 868 KB, respectively. The total for each directory includes the totals for any subdirectories, as well as files in the directory itself. For instance, the two subdirectories *private* and *work* contribute 65 KB to *howard*; the rest of the 868 KB is from files in *howard* itself. (So, to get the grand total of 2,634, *du* adds 107, 888, 868, and 769, plus files in the top-level directory.) *du* does not show individual files as separate items unless you use its –*a* option.

The –*s* option tells *du* to report the total amount of storage occupied by a directory; it suppresses individual reports for all subdirectories. For example:

```
% du -s
2634    .
```

This is essentially the last line of the previous report. *du* –*s* is particularly useful for showing only the files in the current directory, rather than showing every directory down the tree:

```
% cd /home
% du -sk *
69264     boots
18236     chaos
1337820   deb
...
```

—ML, *from* System Performance Tuning *(O'Reilly, 2002)*

15.9 Compressing a Directory Tree: Fine-Tuning

Here's a quick little command that will compress (15.6) files in the current directory and below. It uses *find* (9.2) to find the files recursively and pick the files it should compress:

^{-size 9.14}
^{xargs 28.17}

```
% find . ! -perm -0100 -size +1 -type f -print | xargs gzip -v
```

This command finds all files that are the following:

- Not executable (! -perm -0100), so we don't compress shell scripts and other program files.

- Bigger than one block, since it won't save any disk space to compress a file that takes one disk block or less. But, depending on your filesystem, the -size +1 may not really match files that are one block long. You may need to use -size +2, -size +1024c, or something else.

- Regular files (-type f) and not directories, named pipes, etc.

The *–v* switch to *gzip* tells you the names of the files and how much they're being compressed. If your system doesn't have *xargs*, use the following:

```
% find . ! -perm -0100 -size +1 -type f -exec gzip -v {} \;
```

Tune the *find* expressions to do what you want. Here are some ideas—for more, read your system's *find* manual page:

! -name *.gz
  Skip any file that's already *gzip*ped (filename ends with *.gz*).

-links 1
  Only compress files that have no other (hard) links.

-user *yourname*
  Only compress files that belong to you.

-atime +60
  Only compress files that haven't been accessed (read, edited, etc.) for more than 60 days.

You might want to put this in a job that's run every month or so by *at* (25.5) or *cron* (25.2).

—JP

15.10 Save Space in Executable Files with strip

After you compile and debug a program, there's a part of the executable binary that you can delete to save disk space. The *strip* command does the job. Note that once you strip a file, you can't use a symbolic debugger like *dbx* or *gdb* on it!

Here's an example. I'll compile a C program and list it. Then I'll strip it and list it again. How much space you save depends on several factors, but you'll almost always save something.

```
% cc -o echoerr echoerr.c
% ls -ls echoerr
   52 -rwxr-xr-x   1 jerry     24706 Nov 18 15:49 echoerr
% strip echoerr
% ls -ls echoerr
   36 -rwxr-xr-x   1 jerry     16656 Nov 18 15:49 echoerr
```

–s 9.14

The GNU *strip* has a number of options to control what symbols and sections are stripped from the binary file. Check the *strip* manpage for specific details of the version you have.

If you know that you want a file stripped when you compile it, your compiler probably has a –s option (which is passed to *ld* after compilation is complete). If you use *ld* directly—say, in a *makefile* (11.10)—use the –s option there.

Here's a shell script named *stripper* that finds all the unstripped executable files in your *bin* directory (7.4) and strips them. It's a quick way to save space on your account. (The same script, searching the whole filesystem, will save even more space for system administrators—but watch out for unusual filenames):

xargs **28.17**

```
#! /bin/sh
skipug="! -perm -4000 ! -perm -2000"  # SKIP SETUID, SETGID FILES
find $HOME/bin -type f \( -perm -0100 $skipug \) -print |
xargs file |
sed -n '/executable .*not stripped/s/: TAB .*//p' |
xargs -rpl strip
```

The *find* (9.2) finds all executable files that aren't setuid or setgid and runs *file* (12.6) to get a description of each. The *sed* command skips shell scripts and other files that can't be stripped. *sed* searches for lines from *file* like the following:

```
/usr/local/bin/xemacs: TAB xxx... executable
xxx... not stripped
```

with the word "executable" followed by "not stripped." *sed* removes the colon, tab, and description, then passes the filename to *strip*.

The final *xargs* command uses the options –r (to not run *strip* if *sed* outputs no names to strip), –p (to be interactive, asking before each *strip*), and –l (to process one filename at a time). None of those options are required; if you don't want them, you might at least use –t so the script will list the files it's stripping.

—*JP*

15.11 Disk Quotas

No matter how much disk space you have, you will eventually run out. One way the system administrator can force users to clean up after themselves is to impose quotas on disk usage. Many Unixes have quota systems available: check your manual pages with a command like apropos quota.

If you're a user, how do quotas affect you? Sooner or later, you may find that you're over your quota. Quotas are maintained on a per-filesystem basis. They may be placed on disk storage (the number of blocks) and on inodes (the number of files). The quota system maintains the concept of *hard* and *soft* limits. When you exceed a soft limit, you'll get a warning (WARNING: disk quota exceeded), but you can continue to accumulate more storage. The warning will be repeated whenever you log in. At some point (i.e., after some number of sessions in which the storage stays above the soft limit), the system loses patience and refuses to allocate any more storage. You'll get a message like OVER DISK QUOTA: NO MORE DISK SPACE. At this point, you must delete files until you're again within the soft limit. Users are never allowed to exceed their hard limit. This design allows you to have large temporary files without penalty, provided that they do not occupy too much disk space long-term.

There may also be a quota on the number of files (i.e., inodes) that you can own per filesystem. It works exactly the same way; you'll get a warning when you exceed the soft limit; if you don't delete some files, the system will eventually refuse to create new files.

The *quota* command shows a user's quota on each filesystem where quotas have been set. With no option, it displays a line for each system where you're over quota. The *–v* option shows a line for each system where you have a quota. The output can be a bit confusing on systems with the automounter running, since it mounts things dynamically and uses symlinks to make things appear where you expect them, so the filesystem names may not match the directory names you're accustomed to:

```
$ quota
Over disk quota on /home/jpeek, remove 228K within 4.0 days
Over file quota on /home/jpeek, remove 13 files within 4.5 days
$ quota -v
Filesystem     usage  quota limit  timeleft  files  quota limit  timeleft
/export/users      0   8000  9000                 0    600   750
/export/home9   8228   8000  9000  4.0 days     613    600   750  4.5 days
```

In this case, the automounter has clearly mounted my home directory on */export/home9*, since that shows the same information that *quota* showed me in the first command.

—*ML and JP*

Part IV

Basic Editing

Part IV contains the following chapters:

16

Spell Checking, Word Counting, and Textual Analysis

16.1 The Unix spell Command

On some Unix systems, the *spell* command reads one or more files and prints a list of words that may be misspelled. You can redirect the output to a file, use *grep* (13.1) to locate each of the words, and then use *vi* or *ex* to make the edits. It's also possible to hack up a shell and *sed* script that interactively displays the misspellings and fixes them on command, but realistically, this is too tedious for most users. (The *ispell* (16.2) program solves many—though not all—of these problems.)

When you run *spell* on a file, the list of words it produces usually includes a number of legitimate words or terms that the program does not recognize. *spell* is case sensitive; it's happy with *Aaron* but complains about *aaron*. You must cull out the proper nouns and other words *spell* doesn't know about to arrive at a list of true misspellings. For instance, look at the results on this sample sentence:

```
$ cat sample
Alcuin uses TranScript to convert ditroff into
PostScript output for the LaserWriter printerr.
$ spell sample
Alcuin
ditroff
printerr
LaserWriter
PostScript
TranScript
```

Only one word in this list is actually misspelled.

On many Unix systems, you can supply a local dictionary file so that *spell* recognizes special words and terms specific to your site or application. After you have run *spell* and looked through the word list, you can create a file containing the words that were not actual misspellings. The *spell* command will check this list after it has gone through its own dictionary. On certain systems, your word-list file must be sorted (22.1).

If you added the special terms in a file named *dict*, you could specify that file on the command line using the + option:

```
$ spell +dict sample
printerr
```

The output is reduced to the single misspelling.

The *spell* command will make some errors based on incorrect derivation of spellings from the root words contained in its dictionary. If you understand how *spell* works (16.4), you may be less surprised by some of these errors.

As stated at the beginning, *spell* isn't on all Unix systems, e.g., Darwin and FreeBSD. In these other environments, check for the existence of alternative spell checking, such as *ispell* (16.2). Or you can download and install the GNU version of *spell* at *http://www.gnu.org/directory/spell.html*.

—DD and SP

16.2 Check Spelling Interactively with ispell

The original Unix spell-checking program, *spell* (16.1), is fine for quick checks of spelling in a short document, but it makes you cry out for a real spellchecker, which not only shows you the misspelled words in context, but offers to change them for you.

ispell

ispell, a very useful program that's been ported to Unix and enhanced over the years, does all this and more. Either it will be preinstalled or you'll need to install it for your Unix version.

Here's the basic usage: just as with *spell*, you spell check a document by giving *ispell* a filename. But there the similarities cease. *ispell* takes over your screen or window, printing two lines of context at the bottom of the screen. If your terminal can do reverse video, the offending word is highlighted. Several alternate possibilities are presented in the upper-left corner of the screen—any word in *ispell*'s dictionary that differs by only one letter, has a missing or extra letter, or transposed letters.

Faced with a highlighted word, you have eight choices:

SPACE

Press the spacebar to accept the current spelling.

A

Type A to accept the current spelling, now and for the rest of this input file.

I

Type I to accept the current spelling now and for the rest of this input file and also to instruct *ispell* to add the word to your private dictionary. By default, the private dictionary is the file *.ispell_words* in your home directory, but it can be changed with the *–p* option or by setting the environment variable (35.3) *WORDLIST* to the name of some other file. If you work with computers, this option will come in handy since we use so much jargon in this business! It makes a lot more sense to "teach" all those words to *ispell* than to keep being offered them for possible correction. (One gotcha: when specifying an alternate file, you must use an absolute pathname (1.14), or *ispell* will look for the file in your home directory.)

0–9

Type the digit corresponding to one of *ispell*'s alternative suggestions to use that spelling instead. For example, if you've typed "hnadle," as I did when writing this article, *ispell* will offer 0: handle in the upper-left corner of your screen. Typing 0 makes the change and moves on to the next misspelling, if any.

R

Type R if none of *ispell*'s offerings do the trick and you want to be prompted for a replacement. Type in the new word, and the replacement is made.

L

Type L if *ispell* didn't make any helpful suggestions and you're at a loss as to how to spell the word correctly. *ispell* will prompt you for a lookup string. You can use * as a wildcard character (it appears to substitute for zero or one characters); *ispell* will print a list of matching words from its dictionary.

Q

Type Q to quit, writing any changes made so far, but ignoring any misspellings later in the input file.

X

Type X to quit without writing any changes.

But that's not all! *ispell* also saves a copy of your original file with a *.bak* extension, just in case you regret any of your changes. If you don't want *ispell* making *.bak* files, invoke it with the *–x* option.

How about this: *ispell* knows about capitalization. It already knows about proper names and a lot of common acronyms—it can even handle words like "TEX" that have oddball capitalization. Speaking of TEX, *ispell* has special modes in which it recognizes TEX constructions.

If *ispell* isn't on your system by default, you should be able to find an installation of it packaged in your system's own unique software-installation packaging, discussed in Chapter 40.

In addition, you can also look for a newer spell-checking utility, *aspell*, based on *ispell* but with improved processing. Though *aspell* is being considered a replacement for *ispell*, the latter is still the most commonly found and used of the two.

—*TOR*

16.3 How Do I Spell That Word?

Are you writing a document and want to check the spelling of a word before you finish (if you aren't using a word processor with automatic spelling correction, that is)? A Unix system gives you several ways to do this.

 Because this is Unix, you can use any of these approaches when you write a script of your own.

1. If you aren't sure which of two possible spellings is right, you can use the *spell* command with no arguments to find out. Type the name of the command, followed by a RETURN, then type the alternative spellings you are considering. Press CTRL-d (on a line by itself) to end the list. The *spell* command will echo back the word(s) in the list that it considers to be in error:

   ```
   $ spell
   misspelling
   mispelling
   CTRL-d
   mispelling
   ```

2. If you're using *ispell* (16.2) or the newer *aspell*, you need to add the *–a* option. The purpose of this option is to let the speller interact with other programs; there are details in the programs' documentation. But, like most Unix filters, you can also let these programs read a word from standard input and write their response on standard output; it will either tell you that the spelling is right or give you a list of suggestions. *aspell* and *ispell* will use their local dictionaries and improved spelling rules.

   As an example, let's check the spelling of *outragous* and *whut* with both *ispell* and *aspell*:

   ```
   $ ispell -a
   @(#) International Ispell Version 3.1.20 10/10/95
   outragous whut
   & outragous 1 0: outrageous
   & whut 5 10: hut, shut, what, whet, whit

   CTRL-d
   $ aspell -a
   @(#) International Ispell Version 3.1.20 (but really Aspell .32.6 alpha)
   outragous whut
   & outragous 3 0: outrageous, outrages, outrage's
   & whut 5 10: what, whet, whit, hut, shut

   CTRL-d
   $
   ```

When these spellers start, they print a version message and wait for input. I type the words I want to check and press RETURN. The speller returns one result line for each word:

- A result of * means the word is spelled correctly.

- A line starting with & means the speller has suggestions. Then it repeats the word, the number of suggestions it has for that word, the character position that the word had on the input line, and finally the suggestions.

  So *ispell* suggested that *outragous* might be *outrageous*. *aspell* also came up with *outrages* and *outrage's*. (I'd say that *outrage's* is barely a word. Be careful with *aspell's* suggestions.) Both spellers had five suggestions for *whut*; the differences are interesting...

- A result of # means there were no suggestions.

  After processing a line, the spellers both print an empty line. Press CTRL-d to end input.

3. Another way to do the same thing is with *look* (13.14). With just one argument, *look* searches the system word file, */usr/dict/words*, for words starting with the characters in that one argument. That's a good way to check spelling or find a related word:

```
% look help
help
helpful
helpmate
```

look uses its *–df* options automatically when it searches the word list. *–d* ignores any character that isn't a letter, number, space or tab; *–f* treats upper- and lowercase letters the same.

—*JP and DD*

16.4 Inside spell

[If you have *ispell* (16.2), there's not a whole lot of reason for using *spell* any more. Not only is *ispell* more powerful, it's a heck of a lot easier to update its spelling dictionaries. Nonetheless, we decided to include this article, because it clarifies the kinds of rules that spellcheckers go through to expand on the words in their dictionaries. —TOR]

On many Unix systems, the directory */usr/lib/spell* contains the main program invoked by the *spell* command along with auxiliary programs and data files.

On some systems, the *spell* command is a shell script that pipes its input through *deroff –w* and *sort –u* (22.6) to remove formatting codes and prepare a sorted word list, one word per line. On other systems, it is a standalone program that does these steps internally. Two separate spelling lists are maintained, one for

American usage and one for British usage (invoked with the *–b* option to *spell*). These lists, *hlista* and *hlistb*, cannot be read or updated directly. They are compressed files, compiled from a list of words represented as nine-digit hash codes. (Hash coding is a special technique used to search for information quickly.)

The main program invoked by *spell* is *spellprog*. It loads the list of hash codes from either *hlista* or *hlistb* into a table, and it looks for the hash code corresponding to each word on the sorted word list. This eliminates all words (or hash codes) actually found in the spelling list. For the remaining words, *spellprog* tries to derive a recognizable word by performing various operations on the word stem based on suffix and prefix rules. A few of these manipulations follow:

–y+iness +ness –y+i+less +less –y+ies –t+ce –t+cy

The new words created as a result of these manipulations will be checked once more against the spell table. However, before the stem-derivative rules are applied, the remaining words are checked against a table of hash codes built from the file *hstop*. The stop list contains typical misspellings that stem-derivative operations might allow to pass. For instance, the misspelled word *thier* would be converted into *thy* using the suffix rule –y+ier. The *hstop* file accounts for as many cases of this type of error as possible.

The final output consists of words not found in the spell list—even after the program tried to search for their stems—and words that were found in the stop list.

You can get a better sense of these rules in action by using the *–v* or *–x* option. The *–v* option eliminates the last look-up in the table and produces a list of words that are not actually in the spelling list, along with possible derivatives. It allows you to see which words were found as a result of stem-derivative operations and prints the rule used. (Refer to the *sample* file in article 16.1.)

```
% spell -v sample
Alcuin
ditroff
LaserWriter
PostScript
printerr
TranScript
+out   output
+s     uses
```

The *–x* option makes *spell* begin at the stem-derivative stage and prints the various attempts it makes to find the stem of each word.

```
% spell -x sample
...
=into
=LaserWriter
=LaserWrite
=LaserWrit
=laserWriter
```

```
=laserWrite
=laserWrit
=output
=put
...
LaserWriter
...
```

The stem is preceded by an equals sign (=). At the end of the output are the words whose stem does not appear in the spell list.

One other file you should know about is *spellhist*. On some systems, each time you run *spell*, the output is appended through *tee* (43.8) into *spellhist*, in effect creating a list of all the misspelled or unrecognized words for your site. The *spellhist* file is something of a "garbage" file that keeps on growing: you will want to reduce it or remove it periodically. To extract useful information from this *spellhist*, you might use the *sort* and *uniq –c* (21.20) commands to compile a list of misspelled words or special terms that occur most frequently. It is possible to add these words back into the basic spelling dictionary, but this is too complex a process to describe here. It's probably easier just to use a local spelling dictionary (16.1). Even better, use *ispell*; not only is it a more powerful spelling program, it is much easier to update the word lists it uses (16.5).

—DD

16.5 Adding Words to ispell's Dictionary

ispell (16.2) uses two lists for spelling verification: a master word list and a supplemental personal word list.

The master word list for *ispell* is normally the file */usr/local/lib/ispell/ispell.hash*, though the location of the file can vary on your system. This is a "hashed" dictionary file. That is, it has been converted to a condensed, program-readable form using the *buildhash* program (which comes with *ispell*) to speed the spell-checking process.

The personal word list is normally a file called *.ispell_english* or *.ispell_words* in your home directory. (You can override this default with either the *–p* command-line option or the *WORDLIST* environment variable (35.3).) This file is simply a list of words, one per line, so you can readily edit it to add, alter, or remove entries. The personal word list is normally used in addition to the master word list, so if a word usage is permitted by either list it is not flagged by *ispell*.

Custom personal word lists are particularly useful for checking documents that use jargon or special technical words that are not in the master word list, and for personal needs such as holding the names of your correspondents. You may choose to keep more than one custom word list to meet various special requirements.

You can add to your personal word list any time you use *ispell*: simply use the *I* command to tell *ispell* that the word it offered as a misspelling is actually correct, and should be added to the dictionary. You can also add a list of words from a file using the *ispell -a* (16.3) option. The words must be one to a line, but need not be sorted. Each word to be added must be preceded with an asterisk. (Why? Because *ispell -a* has other functions as well.) So, for example, we could have added a list of Unix utility names to our personal dictionaries all at once, rather than one-by-one as they were encountered during spell checking.

Obviously, though, in an environment where many people are working with the same set of technical terms, it doesn't make sense for each individual to add the same word list to his own private *.ispell_words* file. It would make far more sense for a group to agree on a common dictionary for specialized terms and always to set *WORDLIST* to point to that common dictionary.

If the private word list gets too long, you can create a "munched" word list. The *munchlist* script that comes with *ispell* reduces the words in a word list to a set of word roots and permitted suffixes according to rules described in the *ispell*(4) reference page that will be installed with *ispell* from the CD-ROM. This creates a more compact but still editable word list.

Another option is to provide an alternative master spelling list using the *-d* option. This has two problems, though:

1. The master spelling list should include spellings that are always valid, regardless of context. You do not want to overload your master word list with terms that might be misspellings in a different context. For example, *perl* is a powerful programming language, but in other contexts, *perl* might be a misspelling of *pearl*. You may want to place *perl* in a supplemental word list when documenting Unix utilities, but you probably wouldn't want it in the master word list unless you were documenting Unix utilities most of the time that you use *ispell*.

2. The *-d* option must point to a hashed dictionary file. What's more, you cannot edit a hashed dictionary; you will have to edit a master word list and use (or have the system administrator use) *buildhash* to hash the new dictionary to optimize spell checker performance.

To build a new hashed word list, provide *buildhash* with a complete list of the words you want included, one per line. (The *buildhash* utility can only process a raw word list, not a munched word list.) The standard system word list, */usr/dict/words* on many systems, can provide a good starting point. This file is writable only by the system administrator and probably shouldn't be changed in any case. So make a copy of this file, and edit or add to the copy. After processing the file with *buildhash*, you can either replace the default *ispell.hash* file or point to your new hashed file with the *-d* option.

—*TOR and LK*

16.6 Counting Lines, Words, and Characters: wc

The *wc* (word count) command counts the number of lines, words, and characters in the files you specify. (Like most Unix utilities, *wc* reads from its standard input if you don't specify a filename.) For example, the file *letter* has 120 lines, 734 words, and 4,297 characters:

```
% wc letter
    120    734    4297 letter
```

You can restrict what is counted by specifying the options *–l* (count lines only), *–w* (count words only), and *–c* (count characters only). For example, you can count the number of lines in a file:

```
% wc -l letter
    120 letter
```

or you can count the number of files in a directory:

```
% cd man_pages
% ls | wc -w
    233
```

The first example uses a file as input; the second example pipes the output of an *ls* command to the input of *wc*. (Be aware that the *–a* option (8.9) makes *ls* list dot files. If your *ls* command is aliased (29.2) to include *–a* or other options that add words to the normal output—such as the line total *nnn* from *ls –l*—then you may not get the results you want.)

The following command will tell you how many more words are in *new.file* than in *old.file*:

```
% expr `wc -w < new.file` - `wc -w < old.file`
```

Many shells have built-in arithmetic commands and don't really need *expr*; however, *expr* works in all shells.

In a programming application, you'll usually want *wc* to read the input files by using a < character, as shown earlier. If instead you say:

```
% expr `wc -w new.file` - `wc -w old.file`
```

the filenames will show up in the expressions and produce a syntax error.*

---

* You could also type cat new.file | wc -w, but this involves two commands, so it's less efficient (43.2).

Taking this concept a step further, here's a simple shell script to calculate the differences in word count between two files:

```
count_1=`wc -w < $1`    # number of words in file 1
count_2=`wc -w < $2`    # number of words in file 2

diff_12=`expr $count_1 - $count_2`    # difference in word count

# if $diff_12 is negative, reverse order and don't show the minus sign:
case "$diff_12" in
-*) echo "$2 has `expr $diff_12 : '-\(.*\)'` more words than $1" ;;
*)  echo "$1 has $diff_12 more words than $2" ;;
esac
```

If this script were called *count.it*, then you could invoke it like this:

```
% count.it draft.2 draft.1
draft.1 has 23 more words than draft.2
```

You could modify this script to count lines or characters.

Unless the counts are very large, the output of *wc* will have leading spaces. This can cause trouble in scripts if you aren't careful. For instance, in the previous script, the command:

```
echo "$1 has $count_1 words"
```

might print:

```
draft.2 has       79 words
```

See the extra spaces? Understanding how the shell handles quoting (27.12) will help here. If you can, let the shell read the *wc* output and remove extra spaces. For example, without quotes, the shell passes four separate words to *echo*—and *echo* adds a single space between each word:

```
echo $1 has $count_1 words
```

that might print:

```
draft.2 has 79 words
```

That's especially important to understand when you use *wc* with *test* or *expr* commands that don't expect spaces in their arguments. If you can't use the shell to strip out the spaces, delete them by piping the *wc* output through tr -d ' ' (21.11).

Finally, two notes about file size:

- *wc –c* isn't an efficient way to count the characters in large numbers of files. *wc* opens and reads each file, which takes time. The fourth or fifth column of output from *ls –l* (depending on your version) gives the character count without opening the file.

- Using character counts (as in the previous item) doesn't give you the total disk space used by files. That's because, in general, each file takes at least one disk block to store. The *du* (15.8) command gives accurate disk usage.

—*JP, DG, and SP*

16.7 Find a a Doubled Word

One type of error that's hard to catch when proofreading is a doubled word. It's hard to miss the double "a" in the title of this article, but you might find yourself from time to time with a "the" on the end of one line and the beginning of another.

We've seen *awk* scripts to catch this, but nothing so simple as this shell function. Here are two versions; the second is for the System V version of *tr* (21.11):

uniq **21.20**

```
ww() { cat $* | tr -cs "a-z'" "\012" | uniq -d; }

ww() { cat $* | tr -cs "[a-z]'" "[\012*]" | uniq -d; }
```

In the script *ww.sh*, the output of the file is piped to *tr* to break the stream into separate words, which is then passed to the *uniq* command for testing of duplicate terms.

—*TOR and JP*

16.8 Looking for Closure

A common problem in text processing is making sure that items that need to occur in pairs actually do so.

Most Unix text editors include support for making sure that elements of C syntax such as parentheses and braces are closed properly. Some editors, such as Emacs (19.1) and *vim* (17.1), also support syntax coloring and checking for text documents—HTML and SGML, for instance. There's much less support in command-line utilities for making sure that textual documents have the proper structure. For example, HTML documents that start a list with <UL> need a closing </UL>.

Unix provides a number of tools that might help you to tackle this problem. Here's a *gawk* script written by Dale Dougherty that makes sure <UL> and </UL> tags macros come in pairs:

gawk **20.11**

```
#! /usr/local/bin/gawk -f
BEGIN {
    IGNORECASE = 1
    inList = 0
    LSlineno = 0
    LElineno = 0
    prevFile = ""
}
# if more than one file, check for unclosed list in first file
FILENAME != prevFile {
    if (inList)
      printf ("%s: found <UL> at line %d without </UL> before end of file\n",
            prevFile, LSlineno)
```

```
            inList = 0
            prevFile = FILENAME
    }
    # match <UL> and see if we are in list
    /^<UL>/ {
        if (inList) {
            printf("%s: nested list starts: line %d and %d\n",
                FILENAME, LSlineno, FNR)
        }
        inList = 1
        LSlineno = FNR
    }
    /^<\/UL>/ {
        if (! inList)
            printf("%s: too many list ends: line %d and %d\n",
                FILENAME, LElineno, FNR)
        else
            inList = 0
        LElineno = FNR
    }
    # this catches end of input
    END {
        if (inList)
            printf ("%s: found <UL> at line %d without </UL> before end of file\n",
                FILENAME, LSlineno)
    }
```

You can adapt this type of script for any place you need to check for a start and finish to an item. Note, though, that not all systems have *gawk* preinstalled. You'll want to look for an installation of the utility for your system to use this script.

A more complete syntax-checking program could be written with the help of a lexical analyzer like *lex. lex* is normally used by experienced C programmers, but it can be used profitably by someone who has mastered *awk* and is just beginning with C, since it combines an *awk*-like pattern-matching process using regular-expression syntax with actions written in the more powerful and flexible C language. (See O'Reilly & Associates' *lex & yacc*.)

Of course, this kind of problem could be very easily tackled with the information in Chapter 41.

—*TOR and SP*

16.9 Just the Words, Please

In various textual-analysis scripts, you sometimes need just the words (16.7).

I know two ways to do this. The *deroff* command was designed to strip out *troff* (45.11) constructs and punctuation from files. The command *deroff –w* will give you a list of just the words in a document; pipe to *sort –u* (22.6) if you want only one of each.

deroff has one major failing, though. It considers a word as just a string of characters beginning with a letter of the alphabet. A single character won't do, which leaves out one-letter words like the indefinite article "A."

A substitute is *tr* (21.11), which can perform various kinds of character-by-character conversions.

To produce a list of all the individual words in a file, type the following:

‹ 43.1
```
% tr -cs A-Za-z '\012' < file
```

The *–c* option "complements" the first string passed to *tr*; *–s* squeezes out repeated characters. This has the effect of saying: "Take any nonalphabetic characters you find (one or more) and convert them to newlines (\012)."

(Wouldn't it be nice if *tr* just recognized standard Unix regular expression syntax (32.4)? Then, instead of -c A-Za-z, you'd say '[^A-Za-z]'. It's no less obscure, but at least it's used by other programs, so there's one less thing to learn.)

The System V version of *tr* (21.11) has slightly different syntax. You'd get the same effect with this:

```
% tr -cs '[A-Z][a-z]' '[\012*]' < file
```

—*TOR*

17

vi Tips and Tricks

17.1 The vi Editor: Why So Much Material?

We're giving a lot of pages to the *vi* editor. People who use another editor, like Emacs, might wonder why. Here's why.

I've watched people (including myself) learn and use *vi* for 20 years. It's the standard editor that comes with almost every Unix system these days, but most people have no idea that *vi* can do so much. People are surprised, over and over, when I show them features that their editor has. Even with its imperfections, *vi* is a power tool. If you work with files, you probably use it constantly. Knowing how to use it well will save you lots of time and work.

But why not give the same coverage to another editor that lots of people use: GNU Emacs (19.1)? That's because GNU Emacs comes with source code and can be extended by writing LISP code. Its commands have descriptive names that you can understand by reading through a list. *vi*'s commands are usually no more than a few characters long; many of the option names are short and not too descriptive either. Lots of Unix systems don't even have *vi* source code these days.

I hope that you *vi* users will learn a lot in this section and that people who don't use *vi* will at least browse through to see some of *vi*'s less obvious features.

If you're looking for additional text-editing power, you can use *vim* instead of the plain vanilla *vi* installed on most systems. All *vi* commands work with *vim*, but with added functionality, power, and more standardized behavior accross flavors of Unix. There should be an installation of *vim* for your Unix.

—*JP and SP*

17.2 What We Cover

The articles in this chapter show you how to get the most for your money from *vi*. If you've been using *vi* for a while, you may already know a lot of these things—but take a quick look at this list of topics to see if there's anything new to you. These articles are almost all based on the "standard" original version of *vi*, not the newer clones like *vim*.

- Travel between files, save text into buffers, and move it around without leaving *vi*: articles 17.3, 17.4, and 17.6.
- Recover deletions from up to nine numbered buffers: article 17.7.
- Do global search and replacement with pattern matching: articles 17.8, 17.13, 17.14, 17.16, and 17.22.
- Save a lot of typing with word abbreviations: articles 17.23, 17.24, and 17.25.
- "Prettify" lines of text that don't fit on the screen as you would like: article 17.28.
- Run other Unix commands without leaving *vi* (called a filter-through): articles 17.18 and 17.21.
- Keep track of functions and included files with *ctags* and *tags*.
- Change your *vi* and *ex* options in your *.exrc* file for all files or just for files in a local directory: article 17.5.

When you type a : (colon) command in *vi*, you're beginning an *ex* command. There's more information about *ex* in a later chapter: articles 20.3, 20.4, and 20.5.

—EK

17.3 Editing Multiple Files with vi

ex commands enable you to switch between multiple files. The advantage is speed. When you are sharing the system with other users, it takes time to exit and re-enter *vi* for each file you want to edit. Staying in the same editing session and traveling between files is not only faster for access, but you also save abbreviations and command sequences that you have defined, and you keep yank buffers (17.4) so that you can copy text from one file to another.

When you first invoke *vi*, you can name more than one file to edit and then use *ex* commands to travel between the files:

```
% vi file1 file2
```

This edits *file1* first. After you have finished editing the first file, the *ex* command :w writes (saves) *file1*, and :n calls in the next file (*file2*). You can type :wn both to save the current file changes and to go to the next file. Typing :q! discards changes and closes the current file. Type vi * to edit all the files in a directory, though this will give you an error in some Unix systems. Type CTRL-g or :f to get the name of your current file; :args lists all filenames from the command line and puts brackets around the [*current*] file.

You can also switch at any time to another file not specified on the command line with the *ex* command :e. If you want to edit another file within *vi*, you first need to save your current file (:w), then you can type the following command:

    :e *filename*

vi "remembers" two filenames at a time as the current and alternate filenames. These can be referred to by the symbols % (current filename) and # (alternate filename).

is particularly useful with :e, since it allows you to switch back and forth between two files easily. The command :e# is always "switch to the other one." With different flavors of Unix, the *vi* command CTRL-^ (control-caret) is a synonym for :e#. This usually seems to work even without pressing the SHIFT key. For instance, if I get a caret by pressing SHIFT-6, I don't need to press CTRL-SHIFT-6 to make *vi* change files: just CTRL-6 is enough.

If you have not first saved the current file, *vi* will not allow you to switch files with :e or :n unless you tell it imperatively to do so by adding an exclamation point after the command.

The command:

    :e!

is also useful. It discards your edits and returns to the last saved version of the current file.

In contrast to the # symbol, % is useful mainly in shell escapes (17.21) and when writing out the contents of the current buffer to a new file. For example, you could save a second version of the file *letter* with the command:

    :w %.new

instead of:

    :w letter.new

—*LL and SP*

17.4 Edits Between Files

When you give a yank buffer (temporary holding buffer) a one-letter name, you have a convenient way to move text from one file to another. Named buffers are not cleared when a new file is loaded into the *vi* buffer with the :e command (17.3). Thus, by yanking (copying) or deleting text from one file (into multiple named buffers if necessary), calling in a new file with :e and putting the named buffer into the new file, you can transfer material between files.

The following table illustrates how to transfer text from one file to another. Type the keystrokes exactly as shown to achieve the stated result.

Keystrokes	Action	Results
"f4yy	Yank four lines into buffer f.	With a screen editor you can scroll the page, move the cursor, delete lines, insert characters, and more, while seeing the results of the edits as you make them
:w	Save the file.	"practice" 6 lines 238 characters
:e letter	Enter the file *letter* with :e. Move cursor to where the copied text will be placed.	Dear Mr. Henshaw: I thought that you would be interested to know that: Yours truly,
"fp	Place yanked text from named buffer f below the cursor.	Dear Mr. Henshaw: I thought that you would be interested to know that: With a screen editor you can scroll the page, move the cursor, delete lines, insert characters, and more, while seeing the results of the edits as you make them Yours truly,

If you yank into a buffer and type the buffer name as an uppercase letter, your new text will be added to the text already in the buffer. For example, you might use "f4yy to yank four lines into the buffer named *f*. If you then move somewhere else and type "F6yy with an uppercase *F*, that will add six more lines to the same *f* buffer—for a total of ten lines. You can yank into the uppercase buffer name over and over. To output all of the yanked text, use the lowercase letter—like "fp. To clear the buffer and start over, use its lowercase name ("fy...) again.

—*LL and JP*

17.5 Local Settings for vi

In addition to reading the *.exrc* file (the vi configuration or startup file) in your home directory, many versions of *vi* will read a file called *.exrc* in the current directory. This allows you to set options that are appropriate to a particular project.

For example, you might want to have one set of options in a directory used mainly for programming:

```
set number lisp autoindent sw=4 terse
set tags=/usr/lib/tags
```

and another set of options in a directory used for text editing:

```
set wrapmargin=15 ignorecase
```

Note that you can set certain options in the *.exrc* file in your home directory (1.15) and unset them (for example, set wrapmargin=0 noignorecase) in a local directory.

Many versions of *vi* don't read *.exrc* files in the current directory unless you first set the exrc option in your home directory's *.exrc* file:

```
set exrc
```

This mechanism makes it harder for other people to place, in your working directory, an *.exrc* file whose commands might jeopardize the security of your system.

You can also define alternate *vi* environments by saving option settings in a file other than *.exrc* and reading in that file with the :so command. For example:

```
:so .progoptions
```

Local *.exrc* files are also useful for defining abbreviations (17.23) and key mappings (18.2). When we write a book or manual, we save all abbreviations to be used in that book in an *.exrc* file in the directory in which the book is being created.

You can also store settings and startup commands for *vi* and *ex* in an environment variable called *EXINIT* (17.27). If there is a conflict between settings in *EXINIT* and an *.exrc* file, *EXINIT* settings take precedence.

You can keep a group of standard *.exrc* files in a central directory and link (10.5) to them from various local directories. For instance, from this book's source-file directory, which is full of SGML files, I made a symlink:

```
% ln -s ~/lib/vi/exrc.sgml .exrc
```

I prefer symbolic links to hard links in a case like this because they make it easy to see to which central file the local *.exrc* link points.

—*TOR*

17.6 Using Buffers to Move or Copy Text

In a *vi* editing session, your last deletion (d or x) or yank (y) is saved in a buffer. You can access the contents of that buffer and put the saved text back in your file with the *put* command (p or P). This is a frequent sequence of commands:

5dd	*delete 5 lines*
	…move somewhere else
p	*put the 5 deleted lines back in a new*
	location, below the current line

Fewer new users are aware that *vi* stores the last nine (17.7) deletions in numbered buffers. You can access any of these numbered buffers to restore any (or all) of the last nine deletions. (Small deletions, of only parts of lines, are not saved in numbered buffers, however.) Small deletions can be recovered only by using the p or P command immediately after you've made the deletion.

vi also allows you to yank (copy) text to "named" buffers identified by letters. You can fill up to 26 (a–z) buffers with yanked text and restore that text with a *put* command at any time in your editing session. This is especially important if you want to transfer data between two files, because all buffers except those that are named are lost when you change files. See article 17.4.

—*TOR*

17.7 Get Back What You Deleted with Numbered Buffers

Being able to delete large blocks of text in a single bound is all very well and good, but what if you mistakenly delete 53 lines that you need? There's a way to recover any of your past *nine* deletions, because they're saved in numbered buffers. The last delete is saved in buffer 1, the second-to-last in buffer 2, and so on.

To recover a deletion, type <"> (the double quote character), identify the buffered text by number, then give the *put* command. To recover your second-to-last deletion from buffer 2, type the following:

```
"2p
```

The deletion in buffer 2 is placed on the line below the cursor.

If you're not sure which buffer contains the deletion you want to restore, you don't have to keep typing <">*n*p over and over again. If you use the *repeat* command (.) with p after u (undo), it automatically increments the buffer number. As a result, you can search through the numbered buffers as follows:

```
"1pu.u.u etc.
```

---

to put the contents of each succeeding buffer in the file one after the other. Each time you type u, the restored text is removed; when you type a dot (.), the contents of the *next* buffer is restored to your file. Keep typing u and . until you've recovered the text you're looking for.

—TOR

17.8 Using Search Patterns and Global Commands

Besides using line numbers and address symbols (., $, %), *ex* (including the *ex* mode of *vi*, of course) can address lines (20.3) using search patterns (32.1). For example:

`:/pattern/d`

Deletes the next line containing *pattern*.

`:/pattern/+d`

Deletes the line *below* the next line containing *pattern*. (You could also use +1 instead of + alone.)

`:/pattern1/,/pattern2/d`

Deletes from the next line (after the current line) that contains *pattern1* through the next following line that contains *pattern2*.

`:.,/pattern/m23`

Takes text from current line (.) through the next line containing *pattern* and puts it after line 23.

Note that patterns are delimited by a slash both *before* and *after*.

If you make deletions by pattern with *vi* and *ex*, there is a difference in the way the two editors operate. Suppose you have in your file named *practice* the following lines:

```
With a screen editor you can scroll the
page, move the cursor, delete lines, insert
characters and more, while seeing results
of your edits as you make them.
```

Key-strokes	Action	Results
d/while	The *vi* delete-to-*pattern* command deletes from the cursor up to the word *while* but leaves the remainder of both lines.	With a screen editor you can scroll the page, move the cursor, while seeing results of your edits as you make them.
:.,/ while/d	The *ex* command deletes the entire range of addressed lines; in this case both the current line and the line containing the pattern. All lines are deleted in their entirety.	With a screen editor you can scroll the of your edits as you make them.

Global Searches

In *vi* you use a / (slash) to search for patterns of characters in your files. By contrast, *ex* has a global command, g, that lets you search for a pattern and display all lines containing the pattern when it finds them. The command :g! does the opposite of :g. Use :g! (or its synonym :v) to search for all lines that do *not* contain *pattern*.

You can use the global command on all lines in the file, or you can use line addresses to limit a global search to specified lines or to a range of lines.

:g/*pattern*/
> Finds (moves to) the last occurrence of *pattern* in the file.

:g/*pattern*/p
> Finds and displays all lines in the file containing *pattern*.

:g!/*pattern*/nu
> Finds and displays all lines in the file that don't contain *pattern*; also displays line number for each line found.

:60,124g/*pattern*/p
> Finds and displays any lines between 60 and 124 containing *pattern*.

g can also be used for global replacements. For example, to search for all lines that begin with WARNING: and change the first word not on those lines to NOT:

> :g/^WARNING:/s/\<not\>/NOT/

—*LL, from* Learning the vi Editor *(O'Reilly, 1998)*

17.9 Confirming Substitutions in vi

It makes sense to be overly careful when using a search-and-replace command. It sometimes happens that what you get is not what you expected. You can undo any search-and-replace command by entering u, provided that the command was intended for the most recent edit you made. But you don't always catch undesired changes until it is too late to undo them. Another way to protect your edited file is to save the file with :w before performing a global replacement. Then at least you can quit the file without saving your edits and go back to where you were before the change was made. You can also read back in the previous version of the buffer with :e! (17.3).

It's wise to be cautious and know exactly what is going to be changed in your file. If you'd like to see what the search turns up and confirm each replacement before it is made, add the c option (for confirm) at the end of the substitute command:

> :1,30s/his/the/gc

The item to be substituted is highlighted so that placement of the cursor on the first character is marked by a series of carets (^^^^).

```
copyists at his school
         ^^^_
```

If you want to make the replacement, you must enter y (for yes) and press RETURN. If you don't want to make a change, simply press RETURN.

The combination of the *vi* commands, n (repeat last search) and dot (.) (repeat last command), is also an extraordinarily useful and quick way to page through a file and make repetitive changes that you may not want to make globally. So, for example, if your editor has told you that you're using *which* when you should be using *that*, you can spot-check every occurrence of *which*, changing only those that are incorrect.

This often turns out to be faster than using a global substitution with confirmation. It also lets you see other lines near the text you're checking, which is hard to do with :s///c in original *vi*. *vi* clones have improved the situation. For instance, in *vim*, :s///c runs in fullscreen mode; it also lets you type CTRL-y and CTRL-e to scroll the screen up or down to see context before you approve or deny each substitution.

—DD, TOR, from Learning the vi Editor (O'Reilly, 1998)

17.10 Keep Your Original File, Write to a New File

You can use :w to save an entire buffer (the copy of the file you are editing) under a new filename.

Suppose you have a file *practice*, containing 600 lines. You open the file and make extensive edits. You want to quit but save *both* the old version of *practice* and your new edits for comparison. To save the edited buffer in a file called *check_me*, give the command:

```
:w check_me
```

Your old version, in the file *practice*, remains unchanged (provided that you didn't previously use :w). You can now quit the old version by typing :q.

—LL, from Learning the vi Editor (O'Reilly, 1998)

17.11 Saving Part of a File

While editing, you will sometimes want to save just part of your file as a separate, new file. For example, you might have entered formatting codes and text that you want to use as a header for several files.

You can combine *ex* line addressing (20.3) with the write command, w, to save part of a file. For example, if you are in the file *practice* and want to save part of practice as the file *newfile*, you could enter:

:230,$w *newfile*
> Saves from line 230 to end-of-file in *newfile*.

:.,600w *newfile*
> Saves from the current line to line 600 in *newfile*.

After *newfile* has been created, you'll need w! instead of w.

—LL, from Learning the vi Editor (O'Reilly, 1998)

17.12 Appending to an Existing File

You can use the Unix redirect and append operator (>>) with w to append all or part of the buffer's contents to an existing file. For example, if you entered:

:1,10w *newfile*

and then:

$ 20.3   :340,$w >>*newfile*

newfile would contain lines 1–10 and line 340 to the end of the buffer.

—TOR, from Learning the vi Editor (O'Reilly, 1998)

17.13 Moving Blocks of Text by Patterns

You can move blocks of text delimited by patterns (17.8). For example, assume you have a 150-page reference manual. All reference pages are organized into three paragraphs with the same three headings: SYNTAX, DESCRIPTION, and PARAMETERS. A sample of one reference page follows:

```
.Rh 0 "Get status of named file" "STAT"
.Rh "SYNTAX"
.nf
integer*4 stat, retval
integer*4 status(11)
character*123 filename
...
retval = stat (filename, status)
.fi
.Rh "DESCRIPTION"
Writes the fields of a system data structure into the
status array.
These fields contain (among other
things) information about the file's location, access
privileges, owner, and time of last modification.
.Rh "PARAMETERS"
```

```
.IP "\fBfilename\fR" 15n
A character string variable or constant containing
the Unix pathname for the file whose status you want
to retrieve.
You can give the ...
```

Suppose that it is decided to move the SYNTAX paragraph below the DESCRIP-TION paragraph. Using pattern matching, you can move blocks of text on all 150 pages with one command!

`:g/SYNTAX/,/DESCRIPTION/-1 mo /PARAMETERS/-1`

This command operates on the block of text between the line containing the word *SYNTAX* and the line just before the word *DESCRIPTION* (`/DESCRIPTION/ -1`). The block is moved (using `mo`) to the line just before *PARAMETERS* (`/PARAMETERS/-1`). Note that *ex* can only place text below the line specified. To tell *ex* to place text above a line, you first have to move up a line with `-1` and then place your text below. In a case like this, one command literally saves hours of work. (This is a real-life example—we once used a pattern match like this to rearrange a reference manual containing hundreds of pages.)

Block definition by patterns can be used equally well with other *ex* commands. For example, if you wanted to delete all DESCRIPTION paragraphs in the reference chapter, you could enter:

`:g/DESCRIPTION/,/PARAMETERS/-1d`

This very powerful kind of change is implicit in *ex*'s line addressing syntax (20.3), but it is not readily apparent even to experienced users. For this reason, whenever you are faced with a complex, repetitive editing task, take the time to analyze the problem and find out if you can apply pattern-matching tools to do the job.

—*TOR, from* Learning the vi Editor *(O'Reilly, 1998)*

17.14 Useful Global Commands (with Pattern Matches)

The best way to learn pattern matching is by example, so here's a short list of pattern-matching examples with explanations. (Article 32.21 has a list of these patterns.) Study the syntax carefully so you understand the principles at work. You should then be able to adapt these examples to your own situation.

1. Change all occurrences of the word *help* (or *Help*) to *HELP*:

‰ 20.3   `:%s/[Hh]elp/HELP/g`

or:

`:%s/[Hh]elp/\U&/g`

The \U changes the pattern that follows to all uppercase. The pattern that follows is the repeated search pattern, which is either *help* or *Help*.

2. Replace one or more spaces following a colon (:) or a period (.) with two spaces (here a space is marked by a ⌄):

   `:%s/\([:.]\)⌄⌄*/\1⌄⌄/g`

   Either of the two characters within brackets can be matched. This character is saved into a hold buffer, using \(and \) (34.11) and restored on the right-hand side by the \1. Note that most metacharacters lose their special meanings inside brackets—so the dot does not need to be escaped with a backslash (\).

3. Delete all blank lines:

   g 20.4

   `:g/^$/d`

   What you are actually matching here is the beginning of the line (^), followed by the end of the line ($), with nothing in between.

4. Delete all blank lines, plus any lines that contain only whitespace:

   `:g/^[⌄tab]*$/d`

   (In the previous line, a TAB character is shown as *tab*.) A line may appear to be blank, but may in fact contain spaces or tabs. The previous numbered example will not delete such a line. This example, like the previous one, searches for the beginning and end of the line. But instead of having nothing in between, the pattern tries to find any number of spaces or tabs. If no spaces or tabs are matched, the line is blank. To delete lines that contain whitespace but that *aren't* blank, you would have to match lines with *at least* one space or tab:

   `:g/^[⌄tab][⌄tab]*$/d`

5. This example and the next both refer to a line in a *troff*-formatted document like this A-level (top-level) heading macro call:

   `.Ah "Budget Projections" "for 2001-2002"`

   To match the first quoted argument of all section header (.Ah) macros and replace each line with this argument:

   `:%s/^\.Ah "\([^"]*\)" .*/\1/`

   this example macro call would be changed to simply:

   `Budget Projections`

   The substitution assumes that the .Ah macro can have more than one argument surrounded by quotes. You want to match everything between quotes, but only up to the *first* closing quote. As article 32.18 explains, using ".*" would be wrong because it would match all arguments on the line. What you do is match a series of characters that *aren't* quotes, [^"]*. The pattern "[^"]*" matches a quote, followed by any number of nonquote characters, followed by a quote. Enclose the first argument in \(and \) so that it can be replayed using \1.

6. Same as previous, except preserve the original lines by copying them:

```
:g/^\.Ah/t$ | s/\.Ah "\([^"]*\)" .*/\1/
```

In *ex*, the vertical bar (|) is a command separator that works like a semi-colon (;) (28.16) on a Unix command line. The first part, `:g/^\.Ah/t$`, matches all lines that begin with a .Ah macro, uses the t command to copy these lines, and places the copies after the last line ($) of the file. The second part is the same as in the previous example, except that the substitutions are performed on copies at the end of the file. The original lines are unchanged.

—*TOR and DG, from* Learning the vi Editor *(O'Reilly, 1998)*

17.15 Counting Occurrences; Stopping Search Wraps

Want to see how many times you used the word *very* in a file? There are a couple of easy ways.

First, tell *vi* to stop searching when you get to the end of the file. Type the command `:set nowrapscan` or put it in your *.exrc* file (17.30).

1. Move to the top of the file with the 1G command. Search for the first *very* with the command /very (HINT: using the word-limiting regular expression /\<very\> (32.12) instead will keep you from matching words like *every*). To find the next *very*, type the n (next) command.

   When *vi* says `Address search hit BOTTOM without matching pattern`, you've found all of the words.

2. Use the command:

   ```
   :g/very/p
   ```

   The matching lines will scroll down your screen.

To find the line numbers, too, type `:set number` before your searches.

—*JP*

17.16 Capitalizing Every Word on a Line

Are you typing the title of an article or something else that needs an uppercase letter at the start of every word? Do you need to capitalize some text that isn't? It can be tedious to press the SHIFT key as you enter the text or to use ~ (tilde) and w commands to change the text. The following command capitalizes the first character of every word.

```
:s/\<./\u&/g
```

(You might be wondering why we didn't use :s/\<[a-z]/\u&/g to match lower-case letters. The <. actually matches the first character of *every* word, but the \u will only affect letters. So, unless you only want to capitalize certain letters, <. is enough.)

The previous example does only the current line. You can add a range of lines after the colon. For example, to edit all lines in the file, type the following:

    :%s/\<./\u&/g

To do the current line and the next five, use this:

    :.,+5s/\<./\u&/g

To make the first character of each word uppercase (with \u) and the rest lower-case (with \L), try:

\(...\)...\1
32.21

    :s/\<\(.\)\([A-Za-z]*\)\>/\u\1\L\2/g

The previous command doesn't convert the back ends of words with hyphens (like *CD-ROM*) or apostrophes (like *O'Reilly*) to lowercase. That's because [A-Za-z]*\> only matches words whose second through last characters are all letters. You can add a hyphen or an apostrophe to make that expression match more words, if you'd like.

Those commands can be a pain to type. If you use one of them a lot, try putting it in a keymap (18.2).

—JP

17.17 Per-File Setups in Separate Files

Do you need to set certain editor options for certain files—but *not* use the same setup for every file you edit? Make a special setup file with the same name and an underscore (_) or an extension like *.vi*, *.ex*, or *.so* at the end. For instance, a file named *report* could have a corresponding setup file named *report_* or *report.so*. (You don't have to use an underscore at the end of the filename. It's convenient, though, because it's not a shell special character (27.17).)

The setup file has the same format as a *.exrc* file (17.5). To make the editor read it, map (18.2) a function key like F1 (or any other key sequence):

source **20.4**
^[**18.6**
    `map #1 :source %_^[`

When you start *vi*, tap that key to read the setup file. (The percent sign stands for the current filename (17.3).)

If you want to use the same setup file for several files in a directory, you might want to make hard links (10.4) between them. That will save disk space. It also means that if you decide to change a setup option, you can edit one of the links to the setup file, and the others will have the same change.

—JP

17.18 Filtering Text Through a Unix Command

When you're editing in *vi*, you can send a block of text as standard input to a Unix command. The output from this command replaces the block of text in the buffer.

In *vi*, you can filter text through a Unix command by typing an exclamation mark (!) followed by any of *vi*'s movement keystrokes that indicate a block of text and then by the Unix command line to be executed. For example:

>   !)*command*

will pass the next sentence through *command*.

There are a couple of unusual features about how *vi* acts when you use this structure:

- First, the exclamation mark doesn't appear on your screen right away. When you type the keystroke(s) for the text object you want to filter, the exclamation mark appears at the bottom of the screen, *but the character you type to reference the object does not.*

- Second, text blocks must be more than one line, so you can use only the keystrokes that would move more than one line (G, { }, ( ), [[ ]], +, -). To repeat the effect, a number may precede either the exclamation mark or the text object. (For example, both !10+ and 10!+ would indicate the next ten lines.) Objects such as w do not work unless enough of them are specified so as to exceed a single line. You can also use a slash (/) followed by a *pattern* and a carriage return to specify the object. This takes the text up to the pattern as input to the command.

- Third, there is a special text object that can be used only with this command syntax; you can specify the current line by entering a second exclamation mark:

>   !!*command*

Remember that either the entire sequence or the text object can be preceded by a number to repeat the effect. For instance, to change lines 96 through 99 as in the previous example, you could position the cursor on line 96 and enter either:

>   4!!sort

or:

>   !4!sort

As another example, assume you have a portion of text in a message that you'd like to convert to all uppercase letters. *ex* has operators to convert case (17.16), but it's also easy to convert case with the *tr* (21.11) command. In this example, the second sentence is the block of text that will be filtered to the command:

```
One sentence before.
With a screen editor you can scroll the page
move the cursor, delete lines, insert characters,
and more, while seeing the results of your edits
as you make them.
One sentence after.
```

Keystrokes	Action	Results
!)	An exclamation mark appears on the last line to prompt you for the Unix command.	One sentence after. ~ ~ ~ !_
tr '[a-z]' '[A-Z]'	Enter the Unix command, and press RETURN. The input is replaced by the output.	One sentence before. WITH A SCREEN EDITOR YOU CAN SCROLL THE PAGE MOVE THE CURSOR, DELETE LINES, INSERT CHARACTERS, AND MORE, WHILE seeING THE RESULTS OF YOUR EDITS AS YOU MAKE THEM. One sentence after.

To repeat the previous command, the syntax is as follows:

```
! object !
```

It is sometimes useful to send sections of a coded document to *nroff* to be replaced by formatted output. Remember that the "original" input is replaced by the output. Fortunately, if there is a mistake, such as an error message being sent instead of the expected output, you can undo the command and restore the lines.

Sometimes a filter-through on old, buggy versions of *vi* can completely scramble and trash your text. Things can be so bad that the *u* (undo) command won't work. If you've been burned this way before, you'll want to write your buffer (with :w) before filter-throughs. This doesn't seem to be a problem with modern versions, but be aware of it.

—*TOR*

17.19 vi File Recovery Versus Networked Filesystems

Have you ever used the *vi −r* command to recover a file? It lets you get a file back that you were editing when the system crashed or something else killed your editor before you could save. The system may send you an email message something like this:

```
Date: Thu, 19 Nov 1999 09:59:00 EST
To: jerry

A copy of an editor buffer of your file "afile"
was saved when the system went down.
This buffer can be retrieved using the "recover" command of the editor.
An easy way to do this is to give the command "vi -r afile".
This works for "edit" and "ex" also.
```

17.20

Your files are saved under a directory named something like */usr/preserve*. Follow the instructions and you'll get back your file, more or less the way it was when you lost it.

If your computers have networked filesystems, such as NFS, there's a wrinkle in the way that *vi −r* works. It may only work right on the specific computer where you were editing a file. For example, if you're editing the file *foo* on the host named *artemis* and it crashes, you may not be able to log on to another host and do *vi −r foo* to recover that file. That's because, on many hosts, temporary files (like editor buffers) are stored on a local filesystem instead of on the networked (shared) filesystems. On this kind of system, you may need to log on to *artemis* to recover your lost editor buffer.

If you don't remember which computer you were using when the file was lost, check the "Received:" lines in the email message header;* they'll often show from which machine the message originally came. Also, if you don't remember what files are saved on a machine, you can usually get a list of your saved files by typing *vi −r* without a filename:

```
% vi -r
/var/preserve/jerry:
On Wed Jul 17 at 08:02 saved 15 lines of file "/u/jerry/Mail/drafts/1"
On Sun Aug 25 at 18:42 saved 157 lines of file "doit"
/tmp:
No files saved.
```

Don't wait too long. Many Unix systems remove these saved editor buffers every month, week, or sooner.

—*JP*

---

* Many email programs hide these header lines from you. You might need to set a "show all header fields" option first.

17.20 Be Careful with vi –r Recovered Buffers

Usually, when you're editing a file with *vi*, if you type the command ZZ, it saves your file. But if you recover a file with *vi –r* (17.19), typing ZZ may not save your edits!

That might be a good thing. When you recover a buffer, you need to decide whether the recovered buffer is really what you want. Maybe you've made other changes to the file since then. Maybe something went wrong as the buffer was being saved (say, the system crashed). You shouldn't just save without checking first.

You can use the :w! command to write the recovered version after you're sure that you want it. Use the :q! command if you don't want the recovered version.

Another good choice is to write the recovered buffer using a different filename, then compare the recovered buffer to the original file. For example, here I recover a draft MH email message and immediately write it to a file named *recovered-9* in my *tmp* directory. Then I use a shell escape (17.21) to run *diff* (11.1) and compare the draft file on disk (*/home/jerry/Mail/drafts/9*) with the copy of the recovered buffer that I just wrote (*/home/jerry/tmp/recovered-9*); the *vi* current filename % and alternate filename # shortcuts (17.3) are handy here. Oops: *diff* shows that the recovered version has replaced the last three lines of the message on disk, in the recovered version, with more than 2,000 lines of junk!

```
% vi -r /home/jerry/Mail/drafts/9
    ...recovered file appears...
:w ~/tmp/recovered-9
/home/jerry/tmp/recovered-9: 55 lines, 168767 characters.
```
less 12.3
```
:!diff % # | less
!diff /home/jerry/Mail/drafts/9 /home/jerry/tmp/recovered-9 | less
5c5
< Subject: Re: Two more Unix Power Tools questions
---
> Subject: Next UPT (was: Re: Two more Unix Power Tools questions)
146,148c146,2182
< Yes, you mentioned it once.  Thanks for pointing that out, Greg.
< I think the next job is to review all the articles in that chapter
< to be sure which items should be included -- just the articles, or
---
> Yes, you^@^@^@^@^@^@^@^@^@^@^@^@^@^@^@^@^@^@^@^@^@^@^@^@^@^@^@^@^@
> ^@^@^@^@^@^@^@^@^@^@^@^@^@^@^@^@^@^@^@^@^@^@^@^@^@^@^@^@^@^@^@^@^@
> ^@^@^@^@^@^@^@^@^@^@^@^@^@^@^@^@^@^@^@^@^@^@^@^@^@^@^@^@^@^@^@^@^@
    ...zillions of lines of junk...
```

At this point, the best thing to do is to quit *vi* immediately (with :q!). Then fix up the original file by copying and pasting the good text from the copy of the recovered buffer that I just wrote. (You might want to rerun *diff*, outside of *vi*, to remind yourself which parts of the recovered file you want to transfer to the original file.) Starting a new *vi* session with the filenames of both the original file and the (mostly trashed) recovered buffer, as article 17.4 explains, can make the recovery job easier.

—*JP*

17.21 Shell Escapes: Running One Unix Command While Using Another

Some Unix commands (usually interactive commands like *vi*) let you run another Unix command temporarily. To do that, you type a special command character—usually an exclamation point (!)—then type the Unix command line you want to run. In this article, I'll show examples for the *vi* editor. To see if this works on another utility, check its documentation or just try typing !*Unixcommand* when the utility is waiting for you to type a command.

You can run any Unix command without quitting *vi*. That's handy, for example, if you want to read your mail or look at some other file…, then go back to the file you were editing without losing your place. It's called a "shell escape." (By the way, there's a another way to do this, job control (23.3), that works on most Unix systems. Job control is often more convenient and flexible than shell escapes.)

Let's say you're editing the file named *foo* and you need to run *grep* to get someone's phone number from your phone file. The steps are as follows:

1. Be sure you're in command mode (press the ESC key if you aren't sure).

2. If you want to run a command that needs the file you're editing, remember to write out your *vi* buffer with the :w command. (So you probably wouldn't need to write anything before the following *grep* command.) Type :! followed by the Unix command, then press RETURN. For example:

   `:!grep tim ~/phone`

3. The *grep* program will run. When it finishes, *vi* will say:

   `[Hit return to continue]`

   After you press RETURN, you'll be right back where you were.

Other examples:

`:!less afile`
> Page through *afile* on your screen.

`:!rcsdiff %`
> Give this file to the *rcsdiff* (11.3) program to see what you've changed since the file was checked out of the archive. *vi* replaces % with the name of the file you're editing now (17.3).

```
:!mail
```
> Read your mail. Be careful about this if you were already running the *mail* program and you used the command ~v to edit a message with *vi* from inside the *mail* program. This shell escape starts a subshell (24.4); it will *not* take you back to the same *mail* session before you started editing!

```
:sh
```
> Start a completely new shell. (If you are using a shell with job control, you'll almost always want to use job control to suspend *vi* temporarily instead (23.6). Press CTRL-z, or use the *ex* command :suspend.)

Basically, anything you can do at a shell prompt, you can do with a shell escape. You'll be in a subshell though, not your original login shell. So commands like *cd* won't affect the program where you started the subshell or any other shell. On the bright side, changing directories or resetting anything in your environment won't affect *vi* or the shell where you started *vi*. Terminating the program you're running in the subshell will bring you right back where you were.

—*JP*

17.22 vi Compound Searches

You probably know that you can search for a word or phrase with the *vi* / (slash) command:

```
/treasure
```

If you have a file that uses the same word over and over again, you might want to find one particular place that the word is used. You can repeat the search with the *n* command until you find the place you want. That can take time and effort, though.

For example, suppose you want to find the word "treasure" in the sentence that has words like "Los Alamos residents…treasure," but you can't remember exactly how the sentence is written. You could use wildcards in your regular expression:

```
/Los Alamos.*treasure
```

but then the phrases "Los Alamos" and "treasure" have to be on the same line of the file you're searching—and they won't always be. Also, you want your cursor on the word *treasure*, but that search would put the cursor on *Los* instead.

"Hmmm," you say, "How about two separate searches, like this?"

```
/Los Alamos
/treasure
```

The problem there is that the file might have the phrase "Los Alamos" all throughout it; you might have to type *n* over and over until you get to the sentence with *treasure*.

Here's the easy way: a compound search. Say your cursor is on line 1 of the following file:

```
Before the second World War, there was a treasured boys' school in
what was to become the city of Los Alamos, New Mexico. The school at
Los Alamos changed the lives and made a lifelong impression on most boys
who attended. One of the boys who attended the Los Alamos school went on
to propose that remote set of mesas as a site for the U.S. Government's
    ...
Since the war ended, most of the boys' school ranch buildings have been torn
down or replaced. But there's one building that Los Alamos residents still
use and treasure. It's The Lodge, a log building on the edge of what's now
    ...
```

Type the command:

```
/Los Alamos/;/treasure/
```

That means "find the first occurrence of *treasure* just after *Los Alamos*." Starting at the top of the previous example, that search will skip past all the *treasure* and *Los Alamos* words until it finds the word *treasure* on the last line shown. (It's probably smarter to type just /Alamos/;/treasure/ in case *Los Alamos* is split across two lines of the file.)

Another example: a C programmer wants to find the *printf* function call just after the line where *i* is incremented by two (i += 2). She could type:

```
/i += 2/;/printf/
```

^M 18.6

You can't repeat a compound search by typing n. The easiest way is to define the search as a key map (18.2):

```
:map #3 /Los Alamos/;/treasure/^M
```

and repeat the search with (in this case) your F3 function key.

—*JP*

17.23 vi Word Abbreviation

You can define abbreviations that *vi* will automatically expand into the full text whenever it's typed during text-input mode. To define an abbreviation, use the *ex* command:

```
:ab abbr phrase
```

abbr is an abbreviation for the specified *phrase*. The sequence of characters that make up the abbreviation will be expanded during text-input mode only if you type it as a full word; *abbr* will not be expanded within a word. [I abbreviate *Covnex* to *Convex*, my company's name, because I have dyslexic fingers. —TC]

Suppose you want to enter text that contains a frequently occuring phrase, such as a difficult product or company name. The command:

`:ab ns the Nutshell Handbook`

abbreviates *the Nutshell Handbook* to the initials *ns*. Now whenever you type *ns* as a separate word during text-input mode, *ns* expands to the full text.

Abbreviations expand as soon as you press a nonalphanumeric character (e.g., punctuation), a carriage return, or ESC (returning to command mode).* When you are choosing abbreviations, choose combinations of characters that don't ordinarily occur while you are typing text. If you create an abbreviation that ends up expanding in places where you don't want it to, you can disable the abbreviation by typing:

`:unab abbr`

To list your currently defined abbreviations, type:

`:ab`

The characters that compose your abbreviation cannot appear at the end of your phrase. For example, if you issue the command:

`:ab PG This movie is rated PG`

you'll get the message `No tail recursion`, and the abbreviation won't be set. The message means that you have tried to define something that will expand itself repeatedly, creating an infinite loop. If you issue the command:

`:ab PG the PG rating system`

you may or may not produce an infinite loop, but in either case you won't get a warning message. For example, when the previous command was tested on a System V version of Unix, the expansion worked. On a Berkeley version, though, the abbreviation expanded repeatedly, like this:

`the the the the the ...`

until a memory error occurred and *vi* quit. We recommend that you avoid repeating your abbreviation as part of the defined phrase.

—DD and DG, from Learning the vi Editor (O'Reilly, 1998)

---

* An abbreviation won't expand when you type an underscore (_); it's treated as part of the abbreviation.

17.24 Using vi Abbreviations as Commands (Cut and Paste Between vi's)

The *vi* command ab (17.23) is for abbreviating words. But it's also good for abbreviating *ex*-mode commands that you type over and over. In fact, for *ex*-mode commands (commands that start with a colon (:)), abbreviations can be better than keymaps (18.2). That's because you can choose almost any command name; you don't have to worry about conflicts with existing *vi* commands.

Here's an example. If you have a windowing terminal or more than one terminal, you might have *vi* sessions running in more than one place. Your system might have a way to transfer text between windows, but it can be easier to use files in */tmp*—especially for handling lots of text. (If your text is confidential and your umask (49.4) isn't set to make new files unreadable by other users, try using a more private directory.) Here are some abbreviations from my *.exrc* (17.30) file:

exrc

```
ab aW w! /tmp/jerry.temp.a
ab aR r /tmp/jerry.temp.a
ab bW w! /tmp/jerry.temp.b
ab bR r /tmp/jerry.temp.b
...
```

I use those abbreviations this way. To write the current and next 45 lines to temporary file *a*, I type this command in one *vi* session:

```
:.,+45 aW
```

To read those saved lines into another *vi* session, I use:

```
:aR
```

You can do the same thing in a single *vi* session by using named buffers (17.4), but temporary files are the only method that works between two separate *vi* sessions.

—JP

17.25 Fixing Typos with vi Abbreviations

Abbreviations (17.23) are a handy way to fix common typos. Try a few abbreviations like this:

```
ab teh the
ab taht that
```

in your *.exrc* (17.5) file.

Any time you find yourself transposing letters or saying, "Darn, I always misspell that word," add an abbreviation to *.exrc*. (Of course, you do have to worry about performance if the file gets too big.)

You may be able to enforce conventions this way. For example, command names should be surrounded by <command> tags, so creating a list of abbreviations like this:

```
ab vi <command>vi</command>
```

saves us from having to type lots of SGML codes.

(Depending on your version of *vi*, this abbreviation may be recursive (17.23) because the vi is sandwiched between other nonalphanumeric characters. *nvi* repeated the <command>) quite a few times and quit, but *vim* did what we wanted.)

—*TOR and JP*

17.26 vi Line Commands Versus Character Commands

[Quite a few *vi* users understand how to build *vi* commands with the *(number)(command)(text object)* model. But not too many people understand the difference between line commands and character commands. This article explains that and gives some examples. —JP]

The _ (underscore) command is very similar to the ^ (caret) command in that it moves to the first nonblank character of the current line. The key difference is that _ is a *line* command while ^ is a *character* command. This is important for all functions that read an "address"—for example, d, y, and c.

In fact, delete, yank, and so on all call a common internal routine in *vi* to get an "address." If the address is of a particular character, *vi* does a character-mode delete or yank or whatever. If it is a line address, *vi* does a line-mode operation. The "address" command may be any of the regular positioning commands (e.g., W, b, $, or /pattern/) or the original character repeated (as in dd or yy).

Some examples are found in Table 17-1.

Table 17-1. Examples of vi character and line commands

Keystrokes	Results
dd	Deletes the current line.
d'a	Deletes all lines between the current line and the line containing mark a, inclusive.
d'a	Deletes all characters between the current character and the character at mark a. This works much like an Emacs W in that the two endpoints are considered to be between two characters. Note that a character-oriented delete may delete newlines.
c/accord/	Changes all characters (*not* lines!) between the current character up to but not including the a in accord. (However, see the following Note.)
c?accord?	Changes all characters between the current character and the accord, including the word accord.

Table 17-1. Examples of vi character and line commands (continued)

Keystrokes	Results
yj	Yanks two lines: the current line and the one below.
yH	Yanks all the lines from the top of the screen to the current line, inclusive.
<G	Unindents or "dedents" the lines between the current line and the last line, inclusive. (The variable *shiftwidth* determines the amount of dedenting.) Note that this command turns character addresses into line addresses (so does >).
!}fmt	Runs the lines between the current line and the end of the paragraph through the program *fmt* (17.28).

If you have *wrapscan* set, a search like c?accord? may wrap from the beginning of the file to the end. This can cause unexpected results and is one reason why I have set nows in my *.exrc*. Unfortunately, turning off *wrapscan* breaks *tags* in many versions of *vi*.

vi combines the repeat count on the command character with the repeat count on the motion command, so that 2y2j yanks five lines. Interestingly, 2y2_ yanks 4 lines (so does 2y2y) since the _ command moves down (repeat count minus 1) lines. Beware, however, of using repeat counts on all of the motion commands; they're not all implemented in the same way. 4$ moves to the end of the third line below the current; 4 merely moves to the first nonblank character of the current line. | (vertical bar) is a synonym for 0 (zero); given a repeat count, it goes that many characters to the right of the beginning of the line (as if you had typed | (*rept–1*) 1). (Exercise for the reader: why can't you give a repeat count to 0?)

Uppercase letters do different things depending on the command. The exact actions may not always seem sensible, but typically they affect the "current line": D acts like d$; C acts like c$; Y acts like yy. The list must merely be memorized, or you can use a good *vi* reference guide.

—CT

17.27 Out of Temporary Space? Use Another Directory

vi keeps its temporary copy of the file you're editing in a temporary-file directory—usually */tmp*, */usr/tmp*, or */var/tmp*. If you're editing a big file or if the temporary filesystem runs out of space, *vi* may not be able to make your temporary file. When that happens, you can use *vi*'s set directory command to set the pathname of a different temporary directory. (If this happens a lot though, you should talk to the system administrator and see if the standard area can be cleaned up or made bigger.)

First, you'll need the absolute pathname (3.7) of a directory on a filesystem with enough room. Use an existing directory, or make a new one.

The *vi* command is set directory. For example:

```
set directory=/usr1/jim/vitemp
```

You have to type that command before giving *vi* a filename to edit—after that, *vi* has made the temporary file, and you'll be too late. But if you type that command while using *vi* and then use the :e command (17.3), all files from then on will use the new temporary directory (in the versions I tried, at least).

To set the directory temporarily, it's probably easiest to add that command to the *EXINIT* environment variable:

```
setenv EXINIT 'set directory=/usr1/jim/vitemp'
```

If you already have a *.exrc* file (17.5), setting *EXINIT* will make *vi* ignore your *.exrc* file. To make the temporary set directory work, too, use a command with a vertical bar (|), like this:

```
setenv EXINIT 'source /usr1/jim/.exrc|set directory=/usr1/jim/vitemp'
```

—*JP*

17.28 Neatening Lines

Have you made edits that left some of your lines too short or long? The *fmt* (21.2) utility can clean that up. Here's an example. Let's say you're editing a file (email message, whatever) in *vi* and the lines aren't even. They look like this:

```
This file is a mess
with some short lines
and some lines that are too long -- like this one, which goes on and on for quite
a while and etc.

Let's see what 'fmt' does with it.
```

You put your cursor on the first line and type (in command mode):

5!! 17.18   **5!!fmt**

which means "filter (17.18) 5 lines through *fmt*." Then the lines will look like this:

```
This file is a mess with some short lines and some lines that are too
long -- like this one, which goes on and on for quite a while and etc.

Let's see what 'fmt' does with it.
```

This is handiest for formatting paragraphs. Put your cursor on the first line of the paragraph and type (in command mode):

!}fmt

If you don't have any text in your file that needs to be kept as is, you can neaten the whole file at once by typing:

% 20.3

:%!fmt

There are a few different versions of *fmt*, some fancier than others. Most of the articles in Chapter 21 about editing-related tools can be handy too. For example, *recomment* reformats program comment blocks. *cut* (21.14) can remove columns, fields, or shorten lines; *tr* (21.11) can do other transformations. To neaten columns, try filtering through with the setup in article 21.17. In general, if the utility will read its standard input and write converted text to its standard output, you can use the utility as a *vi* filter.

—*JP*

17.29 Finding Your Place with Undo

Often, you're editing one part of a file and need to go to another point to look at something. How do you get back?

You can mark your place with the m command. In command mode, type m followed by any letter. (We'll use x in the example.) Here are the commands to do the job:

mx Marks current position with *x* (*x* can be any letter).

'x Moves cursor to first character of line marked by *x*.

`x Moves cursor to character marked by *x*.

`` Returns to exact position of previous mark or context after a move.

'' Returns to the beginning of the line of the previous mark or context.

I often find it just as easy to type u to undo my last edit. That pops me right back to the place where I was editing. Then I type u again to restore the edit. Watch out for the new multilevel undo feature in *vi* clones: typing u twice will undo *two* edits! (I still use m if I want to mark more than one place.)

—*TOR*

17.30 Setting Up vi with the .exrc File

You can store commands and settings to be executed any time you start the *vi* or *ex* editors (17.2) in *.exrc* in your home directory. You can modify the *.exrc* file with the *vi* editor, just as you can any other text file.

If you don't yet have an *.exrc* file, simply use *vi* to create one. Enter into this file the *set*, *ab* (17.23), and *map* (18.2) commands that you want to have in effect whenever you use *vi* or *ex*. A sample *.exrc* file looks like this:

```
set nowrapscan wrapmargin=7
set sections=SeAhBhChDh nomesg
map q :w^M:n^M
" To swap two words, put cursor at start of first word and type v:
map v dwElp
ab ORA O'Reilly & Associates, Inc.
```

The ^M characters are RETURNs. Make them by pressing CTRL-v, then RETURN (18.6). Lines that start with a double quote (") are comments. Since the file is actually read by *ex* before it enters *vi*, commands in *.exrc* should not have a preceding colon (:).

In addition to reading the *.exrc* file in your home directory, *vi* will read the *.exrc* file in the current directory. This allows you to set options that are appropriate to a particular project (17.5).

If your *.exrc* file doesn't seem to be working, watch carefully for error messages just as *vi* starts, before it clears your screen. If you can't read them quickly enough, start *ex* instead of *vi*. The *q!* command quits *ex*:

```
% ex
No tail recursion
:q!
```

—*TOR*

18

Creating Custom Commands in vi

18.1 Why Type More Than You Have To?

Keymapping—storing complex command sequences so that they can be executed with a single keystroke—is one of my favorite timesavers. There's nothing like typing one key and watching a whole string of work take place. For repetitive edits (e.g., font changes) it's a real wrist-saver, too. In this chapter we show you how to:

- Save time by mapping keys: articles 18.2, 18.4, 18.7, and 18.8.
- Know when to map a key and when not to: article 18.3.
- Map keys like ESC and RETURN: article 18.6.
- Move around the file without leaving text-input mode: articles 18.11
- Protect the text you're pasting in from another window: article 18.5.
- Put custom commands in your *.exrc* file: articles 18.9 and 18.12.
- Break long lines of text: article 18.13.

—EK

18.2 Save Time and Typing with the vi map Commands

While you're editing, you may find that you are using a command sequence frequently, or you may occasionally use a very complex command sequence. To save yourself keystrokes—or the time it takes to remember the sequence—assign the sequence to an unused key by using the map and map! commands.

Command Mode Maps

The map command acts a lot like ab (17.23) except that you define a macro for command mode instead of text-input mode. The map! command works during text-input mode; see the following list.

map *x sequence*
> Define *x* as a *sequence* of editing commands.

unmap *x*
> Disable the *x* definition.

map
> List the characters that are currently mapped.

As with other *ex*-mode commands, these map commands can be saved in your *.exrc* file (17.30) or typed in after a colon (:). If you want a keymap to use just during this editing session, you might find that *vi* @-functions (18.4) are easier to create and use. The map commands are best for keymaps that you save in your *.exrc* file and use during many editing sessions.

Before you can start creating your own maps, you need to know the keys not used in command mode that are available for user-defined commands. Here's a list of the unused keys in original *vi*:

Letters
> g K q V v

Control keys
> ^A ^K ^O ^T ^W ^X

Symbols
> _ * \ =

> The = is used by *vi* if Lisp mode is set. In addition, other letters such as v may already be used in other systems.

With maps you can create simple or complex command sequences. As a simple example, you could define a command to reverse the order of words. In *vi*, with the cursor as shown:

    you can the scroll page

the sequence to put *the* after *scroll* would be dwwP: (delete word), dw; (move to the next word), w; (put the deleted word before that word), P. (You can also use W instead of w.) Saving this sequence:

    map v dwwP

enables you to reverse the order of two words at any time in the editing session with the single keystroke v.

You can also map certain multiple-character sequences. Start the map with one of the symbols in the previous list. For example, to map the keystrokes *s to put single quotes around a word ('*word*') and *d to use double quotes ("*word*"):

^[**18.6**

```
map *s Ea'^[Bi'^[
map *d Ea"^[Bi"^[
```

Now you'll be able to make hundreds of keymaps (though your version of *vi* probably has a limit).

You may also be able to associate map sequences with your terminal's function keys if your *termcap* or *terminfo* entry (5.2) defines those keys. For example, to make function key F1 transpose words:

```
map #1 dwelp
```

 Map assignments are not really limited to unused keys. You can map keys that are defined as other *vi* commands, but then the key's original meaning is inaccessible. This is probably okay if the key is tied to a command that you rarely use. There's more information in article 18.12 about the *noremap* option.

Text-Input Mode Maps

The map! command works like map, but map! works during text-input mode. You actually set the map! during command mode, in the same way as a plain map: at a colon (:) prompt. Type map! followed by a space and the key(s) that activate the map; then type a space and the text for which the text-input mode map stands. These text-input mode maps are a lot like abbreviations (17.23); the difference is that map! lets your keymap switch from text-input mode to command mode, execute commands, then go back to text-input mode. To go to command mode during a map!, put an ESC key in the value of the map by typing CTRL-v and then ESC (18.6). After your map! does whatever it does in command mode, it can re-enter text-input mode with the usual commands: a, i, and so on.

Let's say you normally never type the caret (^) key during input mode. When you're typing along, as you realize that what you're typing is important, you want to press the caret key. Then, *vi* should open a line above and insert the phrase "THIS IS IMPORTANT:". Finally, *vi* should return you to text-input mode at the end of the line where you pressed the caret key. To do that, go to command mode and enter the following map! command. The first ^ comes from pressing the caret key. Then you'll see two places with ^[; that are made by pressing CTRL-v followed by the ESC key. Finish the map by pressing RETURN:

```
:map! ^ ^[OTHIS IS IMPORTANT:^[jA
```

What does that do? It executes the same *vi* commands you'd use to add those three words yourself, manually. During text-input mode, typing a caret (^) will:

1. Do ESC to go to command mode.
2. Use 0 to open a new line above (in text-input mode).
3. Enter the text THIS IS IMPORTANT:.
4. Do another ESC to go back to command mode.
5. Do j to go down a line (to the line where you started).
6. Do A to put you at the end of the line, in text-input mode.

The trick is to use map! only to redefine keys you'll never use for anything else during text-input mode. To disable a text-input mode map temporarily, press CTRL-v before the key. For example, to put a real caret into your file, type **CTRL-v ^**. To disable an input-mode map for the rest of your *vi* session, type :unmap! followed by the character(s) that activate the map.

A more common example is mapping your keyboard's arrow or function keys to do something during text-input mode. These keys send a special series of characters. Normally, without a map! defined for these keys, the characters they send will be put into your editor buffer—just as if you'd typed the characters they make yourself, one by one. For instance, my left-arrow key sends the characters ESC, then [(left bracket), then D. Without a text-input mode map! defined for that three-character sequence, *vi* will be hopelessly confused if I press that arrow key.* Many Unix developers have added text-input mode maps for arrow keys. You can see them when you list all your text-input mode maps by typing :map! by itself, with nothing after:

```
up      ^[[A    ^[ka
down    ^[[B    ^[ja
left    ^[[D    ^[hi
right   ^[[C    ^[la
^       ^       ^[0THIS IS IMPORTANT:^[jA
```

Article 18.3 lists some problems with map!.

—*JP, DG, and LL*

18.3 What You Lose When You Use map!

Back in the old days, a terminal's arrow keys didn't work during *vi* text-input mode. To move around in the file, you pressed ESC and used command-mode commands like *5k* and *4w*. Since then, lots of vendors and users have modified *vi*

---

* Actually, the ESC will switch *vi* back to command mode. The first [will make *vi* think you're about to type the section-motion command [[, so the following D will make *vi* beep. Ugly, eh?

so that you can use arrow keys during text-input mode. These days, most people think the new-fangled way that *vi* works is the right way. Here are some reasons to leave the arrow keys alone and do it the old way instead:

- In most cases, the u (undo) command will be useless after text-input mode because the arrow keymap does several hidden commands—and u can only undo the single previous command. The only "undo" command that will do much good is U—it undoes all changes on the current line, and it probably won't work if you've moved off the line since you made the change you want to undo.

- Beginners can get confused by this. They need to learn that *vi* is a moded editor—that you enter text in text-input mode and make changes in command mode. Movement through the file is with commands.

  When people start using *vi* and they find that some motion commands (the cursor keys) work in text-input mode, *vi* seems inconsistent.

- If your map! runs commands that start with an ESC (and it almost always will), your ESC key may work more slowly. That's because every time you press the ESC key, *vi* will wait one second (or so) to be sure that the ESC is just an ESC alone and not the beginning of a map! sequence. Some versions have changed this, though.

  The fast alternative is to press ESC twice. That rings the terminal bell, though.

  —*JP*

18.4 vi @-Functions

The *vi map* command (18.2) lets you define keymaps: short names for a series of one or more commands. You can enter :map to define a keymap while you're editing a file with *vi*. But if you make a mistake, you usually have to re-enter the whole :map command to correct the problem.

@-functions (pronounced "at-functions") give you another way to define complex commands. You can define 26 @-functions named @a through @z. They're stored in named buffers (17.4). So if you're also using named buffers for copying and pasting text, you'll need to share them with your @-functions.

Defining and Using Simple @-Functions

To define an @-function:

1. Enter the command(s) you want to execute onto one or more lines of the file you're editing.

2. Yank or delete the line(s) into a named buffer with a command like `"ay$` or `"bD`.

3. To use the function, type a command like `@a` or `@b`. You can repeat the function by typing `@@` or a dot (.). Use `u` or `U` to undo the effects of the @-function.

Here's an example. You're editing a long HTML file with lines like these:

```
<STRONG>Some heading here</STRONG>
<STRONG>Another heading here</STRONG>
```

When you see one of those lines, you need to change the STRONGs to either H3 or H4. A global substitution with `:%s` won't do the job because some lines need H3 and others need H4; you have to decide line-by-line as you work through the file. So you define the function `@a` to change a line to H3, and `@b` to change to H4.

To design an @-function, start by thinking how you'd make the changes by hand. You'd probably move to the start of the line with `0`, move to the right one character with `l`, type `cw` to change the word STRONG, and type in H3 (or H4). Then you'd press ESC to return to command mode. After going to the end of the line with `$`, you'd move to the character after the slash with `T/`, then change the second STRONG the way you fixed the first one.

To define the function, open a new empty line of your file (first go into text-input mode). Then type the keystrokes that will make the H3 changes; type CTRL-v before each ESC or RETURN (18.6). When you're done, press ESC again to go to command mode. Because the commands for the H4 change are similar, the easiest way to make them is by copying and pasting the line for H3 (by typing `yy` and `p`) and then editing the copy. The pair of command lines should look like this (where `^[` stands for the CTRL-v ESC keys):

```
0lcwH3^[$T/cwH3^[
0lcwH4^[$T/cwH4^[
```

Move to the start of the first line, and delete it into the *a* buffer by typing `"aD`. Go to the next line, and type `"bD`. (This will leave two empty lines; delete them with `dd` if you'd like.) Now, when you type `@a`, it will execute the commands to change a line to H3; typing `@b` on a line will change it to have H4. Move through your file (maybe with a search: `/STRONG ... n ...`), typing `@a` or `@b` as you go. Or use `@@` to make the same change you made on a previous line.

Combining @-Functions

An @-function can execute other @-functions. For example, here are four lines ready for storing as `@a` through `@d`:

```
0l@c$T/@c     ...becomes @a
0l@d$T/@d     ...becomes @b
cwH3^[        ...becomes @c
cwH4^[        ...becomes @d
```

See that the definition of @a has @c in it twice? When you execute @a, it will do 0l to move to the second character on the line, then do @c to change the word to H3, move to the end of the line, and use @c again. Calling one @-function from another can save you from retyping repetitive commands.

A disadvantage is that @@ won't always work as you might expect. If you type @a to make a change in one place, then move somewhere else and type @@, the @@ will do what @c does (instead of what you might have wanted, @a). That's because the @a function finishes by doing @c.

Reusing a Definition

You don't have to delete the definition line into a buffer with dd. If you think you might need to fine-tune the command, you can yank (copy) it into a buffer with a command like "ay$. Then, if you need to revise the command, re-edit the line and type "ay$ to put the revised version into the buffer. Or use "by$ to copy the revised line into another buffer.

Newlines in an @-Function

Stored @-functions can span multiple lines. For example, if you delete the following four lines with "z4dd, typing @z will open a newline below (o) and insert four newlines of text:

```
oThis is the newline one.
This is the newline two.
This is the third line.
This is the fourth.^[
```

After you execute the function with @z, your cursor will move to the line below the new fourth line. Why? Because you included the newlines (RETURNs) in the buffer; each RETURN moves down a line—including the RETURN after the last ESC.

If you don't want that, there are two ways to fix it:

- Delete the first three lines, including the newlines, into the buffer by typing "z3dd. Delete the fourth line, without its newline, and *append* it to the buffer by typing "ZD. (An uppercase letter like Z appends to a named buffer. D deletes all of a line except the newline.)

    Some versions of *vi* will delete four lines, without the last newline, when you use "z4D.

- Type all of the text onto a single line; embed the newlines in that line by typing CTRL-v RETURN between each finished line. It'll look like this:

    ```
    oThis is the new line one.^MThis is the new line two.^MThis is the new...
    ```

Delete that long line into your buffer with "zD. Because D doesn't delete the final newline, your cursor will stay at the end of the fourth newline after you execute the @z.

—JP

18.5 Keymaps for Pasting into a Window Running vi

I usually run *vi* inside windows on a system like X or the Macintosh. The window systems can copy and paste text between windows. Pasting into a *vi* window may be tricky if you use *vi* options like *wrapmargin* or *autoindent* because the text you paste can be rearranged or indented in weird ways.

I've fixed that with the upcoming keymaps. If I'm pasting in text that should be copied exactly with no changes, I go into text-input mode and type CTRL-x. That shuts off autoindent (noai) and the wrapmargin (wm=0). When I'm done pasting, I type CTRL-n while I'm still in text-input mode.

A different kind of "pasted" input is with CTRL-r. It starts the *fmt* (21.2) utility to reformat and clean up lines while I'm pasting them. To use it, go to text-input mode and type CTRL-r. Then paste the text—*fmt* will read it but not display it. Press RETURN, then CTRL-d to end the standard input to *fmt*. The reformatted text will be read into your *vi* buffer.

```
                  " Set 'exact' input mode for pasting exactly what is entered:
^[ 18.6           map! ^X ^[:se noai wm=0^Ma
                  " Set 'normal' input mode with usual autoindent and wrapmargin:

                  map! ^N ^[:se ai wm=8^Ma
                  " Read pasted text, clean up lines with fmt. Type CTRL-d when done:
                  map! ^R ^[:r!fmt^M
```

exrc

Note that some window systems convert TAB characters to spaces when you copy and paste. If you want the TABs back, try a filter-through (17.18) with *unexpand*.

—JP

18.6 Protecting Keys from Interpretation by ex

Note that when defining a map, you cannot simply type certain keys—such as RETURN, ESC, BACKSPACE, and DELETE—as part of the command to be mapped, because these keys already have meaning within *ex*. If you want to include one of these keys as part of the command sequence, you must escape the normal meaning by preceding the key with ^V (CTRL-v). After CTRL-v, a carriage return appears as ^M, escape as ^[, backspace as ^H, and so on.

On the other hand, if you want to map a control character, in most cases you can just hold down the CTRL key and press the letter key at the same time. For example, to map ^A (CTRL-a), simply type:

```
:map CTRL-a sequence
```

There are, however, a few other control characters that must be escaped with a ^V. One is ^T. The others are as follows:

- The characters that your account uses for erasing parts of the input you type at a command line: ^W for erasing words and ^U for erasing lines.
- The characters for interrupting jobs (24.11) and stopping jobs (23.1).

So, if you want to map ^T, you must type:

```
:map CTRL-v CTRL-t sequence
```

The use of CTRL-v applies to any *ex* command, not just a map command. This means that you can type a carriage return in an abbreviation (17.23) or a substitution command. For example, the abbreviation:

```
:ab 123 one^Mtwo^Mthree
```

expands to this:

```
one
two
three
```

(The sequence CTRL-v RETURN is shown as it appears on your screen, ^M.)

You can also add lines globally at certain locations. The command:

```
:g/^Section/s//As you recall, in^M&/
```

inserts a phrase on a separate line before any line beginning with the word *Section*. The & restores the search pattern.

The vertical bar (|) is used to separate multiple *ex* commands; it's especially difficult to quote. Because a map is interpreted when it's stored and again when it's used, you need enough CTRL-v characters to protect the vertical bar from each interpretation. You also need to protect stored CTRL-v characters by adding a CTRL-v before each one! The worst case is a text-input mode map (map! (18.2))— it needs three CTRL-v characters, which means you need to type *six* CTRL-v characters before you type the vertical bar. For example, the following map will make your function key F1 (18.2) insert the string {x|y}:

```
map! #1 {x^V^V^V|y}
```

If you ask for a list of text-input mode maps, you should see a single stored CTRL-v:

```
:map!
f1  ^[OP   {x^V|y}
```

—*LL, DG, and JP, from* Learning the vi Editor *(O'Reilly, 1998)*

18.7 Maps for Repeated Edits

Another way to do this is with @-functions (18.4).

Not every keymap is something you want to save in your *.exrc* file. Some maps are handy just because you have to do a repetitive series of edits. Developing a complex map to repeat your edits can save more time than it takes. For example, assume that you have a glossary with entries like this, separated by blank lines:

```
map - an ex command which allows you to associate
a complex command sequence with a single key.
```

You want to convert this glossary list to HTML format, so that it looks like:

```
<DT>map</DT>
<DD>
An ex command which allows you to associate
a complex command sequence with a single key.
</DD>
```

The best way to define a complex map is to do the edit once manually, writing down each keystroke that you must type. Then recreate these keystrokes as a map.

1. Use I to insert the tag for an data list term (<DT>) at the beginning of the line.

2. Press ESC to terminate text-input mode. Move just before the dash (t-). Use 3s to replace the dash and space after it with the closing term tag (</DT>).

3. Still in text-input mode, press RETURN to insert a new line. (This moves the definition to a newline underneath the <DT> tags.) Enter the opening data list definition (<DD>) tag, and press RETURN again. (The definition moves to yet another newline underneath the <DD> tag.)

4. Press ESC to terminate text-input mode. Your cursor is at the start of the definition. Capitalize the first word of the definition (~).

5. Go to the blank line after the definition (}), open a newline above (0), and insert the closing data list definition (</DD>) tag. Press ESC to end text-input mode.

6. Press RETURN to end the keymap definiton.

That's quite an editing chore if you have to repeat it more than a few times. With map you can save the entire sequence so that it can be re-executed with a single keystroke:

```
map g I<DT>^[t-3s</DT>^M<DD>^M^[~}0</DD>^[
```

(To store a map during a *vi* session, type a colon (:) first.) Note that you have to "quote" both the ESC and RETURN characters with CTRL-v (18.6). ^[is the sequence that appears when you type **CTRL-v** followed by **ESC**. ^M is the sequence shown when you type **CTRL-v RETURN**.

Now, simply typing g will perform the entire series of edits. At a slow data rate you can actually see the edits happening individually. At a fast data rate it will seem to happen by magic.

Don't be discouraged if your first attempt at keymapping fails. A small error in defining the map can give very different results from the ones you expect. You can probably type u to undo the edit and try again. It's safer to write the file (:w) before you use the keymap—in case your version of *vi* can't undo complex keymaps.

If the keymap is complex, or if you're defining several maps at once, you can make a temporary keymap file and edit the maps there until you've worked out the bugs. For instance, write your buffer and type :e temp to open a temporary file *temp*. Make the keymaps, one per line—without a colon (:) first. Write this map file (:w), then read it in to the editor (:so %). If there's no error, switch to the original file (:e # or CTRL-^), and try the map. (Article 17.3 explains % and #.) Then, if there are problems, go back to the map file (:e! #, where the ! tells *vi* not to write the mistakes out to the file), fix the keymap, and repeat the process until you get what you wanted.

In this case, for instance, maybe the next glossary definition starts with an uppercase letter, but the ~ in the keymap is changing that letter to lowercase. You need to change the ~ to an *ex* substitution command that converts a lowercase letter to uppercase (17.16). If you've saved the keymap in a temporary file, just type :e# and change it:

```
map g I<DT>^[t-3s</DT>^M<DD>^M^[:s/^./\u&/^M}0</DD>^[
```

We've changed ~ to :s/^./\u&/^M. As you can see, complex keymaps can be tough to decipher after you've written them, which makes the notes you've written even more useful.

—*TOR and JP, from* Learning the vi Editor *(O'Reilly, 1998)*

18.8 More Examples of Mapping Keys in vi

The examples that follow will give you an idea of the clever shortcuts possible when defining keyboard maps:

1. Add text whenever you move to the end of a word:

   ```
   map e ea
   ```

   Most of the time, the only reason you want to move to the end of a word is to add text. This map sequence puts you in text-input mode automatically. Note that the mapped key, e, has meaning in *vi*. You're allowed to map a key that is already used by *vi*, but the key's normal function will be unavailable as long as the map is in effect. This isn't so bad in this case, since the E command is often identical to e.

   In the remaining examples, we assume that e has been mapped to ea.

2. Save a file and edit the next one in a series (17.3):

   ```
   map q :w^M:n^M
   ```

   Notice that you can map keys to *ex* commands, but be sure to finish each *ex* command with a RETURN. This sequence makes it easy to move from one file to the next, and it's useful when you've opened many short files with one *vi* command. Mapping the letter q helps you remember that the sequence is similar to a "quit."

3. Put HTML emboldening codes (<STRONG> and </STRONG>) around a word:

   ```
   map v i<STRONG>^[e</STRONG>^[
   ```

   This sequence assumes that the cursor is at the beginning of the word. First, you enter text-input mode, then you type the code for bold font. Next, you return to command mode by typing a "quoted" (18.6) ESC. Finally, you append the closing HTML tag at the end of the word, and you return to command mode. Of course, the map is not limited to HTML font tags. You can use it to enclose a word in parentheses or C comment characters, to name just a few applications.

   This example shows you that map sequences are allowed to contain other map commands (the e is already mapped to ea). The ability to use nested map sequences is controlled by *vi*'s remap option (18.12), which is normally enabled.

4. Put HTML emboldening tags around a word, even when the cursor is not at the beginning of the word:

   ```
   map V lbi<STRONG>^[e</STRONG>^[
   ```

   This sequence is the same as the previous one, except that it uses lb to handle the additional task of positioning the cursor at the beginning of the word. The cursor might be in the middle of the word, so you'll want to move to the beginning with the b command.

But if the cursor were already at the beginning of the word, the b command would move the cursor to the previous word instead. To guard against that case, type an l before moving back with b so that the cursor never starts on the first letter of the word. You can define variations of this sequence by replacing the b with B and the e with Ea. In all cases though, the l command prevents this sequence from working if the cursor is at the end of a line. (To get around this, you could add a space to the end of the word before typing the keymap.)

—DG, from Learning the vi Editor (O'Reilly, 1998)

18.9 Repeating a vi Keymap

The *vi* (actually, *ex*) command *map* (18.2) lets you build custom *vi* commands. For example, the following keymap redefines the -key to run the *vi* commands o (open a newline below), *ESCAPE*, 72a– (add 72 dashes), and *ESCAPE* again:

```
:map - o^[72a-^[
```

So typing – draws a row of dashes below the current line. The problem is that on versions of *vi* I've tried, you can't add a repetition number—that is, you can't type the command 10- to add 10 dashed lines.

The workaround is to define another macro that calls the first macro ten times. For example, to make the v key draw ten rows of dashes:

```
:map v ----------
```

(Ugly, eh? But it works.) You might want to put the - map in your *.exrc* file and define "multimaps" like *v* while you're running *vi*.

—JP

18.10 Typing in Uppercase Without CAPS LOCK

You may want to input text in all uppercase letters. Using CAPS LOCK in *vi* can be a pain because you have to release CAPS LOCK almost every time you want to type a *vi* command. Here's a nice way to type lowercase letters during input and *ex* modes; they'll be mapped to uppercase automatically.

Try putting this in your *.exrc* (17.5) file:

```
map! a A
map! b B
map! c C
...
map! z Z
```

Anytime you type (during text-input mode) an a, the editor will map it into A. What's that you say...you don't want this all the time? Just put it in a file called .f (for FORTRAN), and type:

```
:source .f
```

when you want FORTRAN mode. Of course, you can define a function key (18.2) to :source this.

[After that, anywhere you want a lowercase letter, type CTRL–v first to cancel the map temporarily. For example, to type the command :w, type :**CTRL-v w**.

You can also go into the *ex* command mode by typing the *vi* command Q. That takes you to the *ex* colon (:) prompt—where the *map!* macros won't affect what you type. To return to *vi* mode from *ex* command mode, type :vi. —*JP*]

—BB, *in* net.unix *on Usenet, 9 October 1986*

18.11 Text-Input Mode Cursor Motion with No Arrow Keys

Some people don't like to press ESC first to move the cursor while they're using *vi*. These keymaps change CTRL-h, CTRL-j, CTRL-k, and CTRL-l to do the same things during input mode as the commands h, j, k, and l do in command mode.

Is your erase character set to CTRL-h (5.8) outside *vi*? If it is, mapping CTRL-h (usually labeled BACKSPACE on your keyboard) will change the way CTRL-h works during text-input mode: instead of erasing the characters you've typed since you entered text-input mode, now CTRL-h will move backwards over what you type without erasing it. One workaround is to change your Unix erase character to the DELETE or RUBOUT key by typing the command stty erase '^?' before you start *vi*. Then your DELETE key will erase what you type, and the BACKSPACE key will jump back over it without deleting.

exrc

The lines for your *.exrc* file (17.30) are as follows:

```
map! ^H ^[i
map! ^K ^[ka
map! ^L ^[la
map! ^V
^[ja
" Note: the two lines above map ^J (LINEFEED)
```

That last map takes two lines; it's tricky and may not work right on all versions of *vi*. No, it isn't a map for CTRL-v, though that's what it looks like. It maps ^J, the LINEFEED key. The ^V comes at the very end of its line. When you're entering that keymap, type CTRL-v and then press LINEFEED or CTRL-j. The cursor will move to the start of the next line; type a SPACE and the rest of the macro. It's a good idea to add the reminder comment (starting with the comment character, a double quote (")), on the line below the map.

 This map for CTRL-j is obviously something for which the people who wrote my version of *vi* didn't plan. For example, look at the mess it makes when I ask for a list of my text-input keymaps:

```
:map!
^H        ^H        ^[i
^K        ^K        ^[ka
^L        ^L        ^[la

          ^[ja
```

Before you use this map on important files, you probably should test it carefully.

—JP

18.12 Don't Lose Important Functions with vi Maps: Use noremap

For years, I assumed that I could map (18.2) only a few keys in *vi*—the characters like *v* and ^A that aren't used. For instance, if I mapped ^F to do something else, I thought I'd lose that handy "forward one screen" command. You thought the same thing? Then we're both wrong!

Just use the *noremap* option. Here's a simple example. You can make ^F the "show file information" (normally ^G) command. Then, make ^A take over the "forward (ahead) one screen" function. Put these lines in your *.exrc* file (17.5):

```
set noremap
map ^F ^G
map ^A ^F
```

—JP

18.13 vi Macro for Splitting Long Lines

When you add text to the start of a line and make the line longer than your screen's width, *vi* won't break ("wrap") the line unless your cursor crosses the *wrapmargin* point near the righthand edge of the screen. You can get lines that are too long.

exrc

Here are two macros that cut (Kut) the current line:

```
map K 78^V|lBhr^M
map K 0781F r^M
```

The first macro doesn't seem to work on some versions of *vi*. It's the better one though, because it uses the | (vertical bar) command to move to column 78, even if there are TABs in the line. Then it moves one more character to the right (if it can), moves back to the start of the word, moves back one more character onto the blank or TAB before the word, and replaces that character with a RETURN.

The second macro counts TABs as single characters, but it works on every version of *vi* I've tried. It moves to the left edge, then to the 79th character, then back to the previous space. Finally, it replaces that space with a carriage return.

You might try adding a J to the start of either macro. That'll join the next line to the current one before cutting; it might make a nicer "wrap." Another way to do this is with a filter-through (17.18) and the *fmt* (17.28) command:

```
!!fmt
```

That will break the current line neatly, though it also might change the spacing after periods (.) or replace leading TABs with spaces.

—JP

18.14 File-Backup Macros

Emacs automatically keeps backup copies of the file you're editing. If you have editing problems (or just change your mind), you can get the previous file version by recovering from a backup file. I like this idea, but I don't like the way that backups are done automatically. Instead, I want to choose when *vi* makes a backup "snapshot." This macro, CTRL-w, lets me do that: it writes a copy of the current *filename* as *filename~*. (The trailing tilde (~) is an Emacs convention. Article 14.17 shows ways to remove these backup files.) Whenever I want to save a snapshot of the editing buffer, I just type CTRL-w.

^M 18.6

```
map ^W :w! %~^M
```

The w! writes without questions, overwriting any previous backup with that name. *vi* replaces % (percent sign) with the filename (or pathname) you're currently editing.

If you want an Emacs-style backup to be made every time you write the file (except the first time), you could try something like this:

```
map ^W :!cp -pf % %~^M:w^M
```

The first command uses *cp –p* (10.12) to make a backup of the previously written file; the *cp –f* option forces the write. (*vi* may warn you File modified since last write, but the versions I've checked will run *cp* anyway.) The next command writes the current editing buffer into the file.

—JP

GNU Emacs

19.1 Emacs: The Other Editor

The "other" interactive editor that's commonly used is Emacs. Emacs actually refers to a family of editors; versions of Emacs run under most operating systems available. However, the most important (and most commonly used) version of Emacs is "GNU Emacs," developed by the Free Software Foundation.

emacs

GNU Emacs is popular because it's the most powerful editor in the Emacs family; it is also freely available under the terms of the FSF's General Public License. Although there are certainly strong differences of opinion between Emacs and *vi* users, most people agree that Emacs provides a much more powerful and richer working environment.

What's so good about Emacs, aside from the fact that it's free? There are any number of individual features that I could mention. (I'll give a list of favorite features in article 19.2.) Emacs' best feature is the extent to which it interacts with other Unix features. For example, it has a built-in email system so you can send and receive mail without leaving the editor. It has tools for "editing" (deleting, copying, renaming) files, for running a Unix shell within Emacs, and so on. The C shell has a rather awkward command-history mechanism; the Korn shell has something more elaborate. But imagine being able to recall and edit your commands as easily as you edit a letter! That's far beyond the abilities of any shell, but it's simple when you run a shell inside your editor.

In this book, we can't give anywhere near as much attention to Emacs as we can to *vi* (17.1), but we will point out some of its best features and a few tricks that will help you get the most out of it. For the impatient, here's a very brief survival guide to Emacs.

Starting Emacs

Like *vi*, Emacs can be started from the shell prompt by typing its name, emacs. Once started, emacs will present you with a helpful screen of commands. A word of advice: take the tutorial (CTRL-h t). If you want to edit an existing file, simply type emacs with the desired filename after it. While editing your file, you may save your work to disk with CTRL-x CTRL-s.

Exiting Emacs

To exit emacs, type CTRL-x CTRL-c. If you haven't saved your work yet, you will have the opportunity to do so before Emacs quits.

Moving around

Unlike *vi*, Emacs doesn't have a command mode. Like many more modern editors, Emacs allows the user to begin typing his document immediately. Terminal emulation willing, the arrow keys work as expected to move your cursor in and around lines of text. For long documents, you can move by pages rather than lines. Pressing CTRL-v moves the cursor lower in the document, while ESC-v moves the cursor towards the begining.

Deleting characters and lines

The BACKSPACE key normally erases one character to the left of the cursor, and the DELETE key erases the charater under the cursor. Entire lines of text may be removed using CTRL-k, which removes all text from the cursor to the end of the line. You can paste back the most recent cut with CTRL-y.

Undo

To undo your last action, type CTRL-x u. You can cancel out of a command sequence with CTRL-g. This is helpful when you're experiencing key lag and type a few extra CTRL-c's.

One last tip before moving on. The Emacs online help descibes key bindings using different abbreviations than used in this book. In the Emacs documentation, C-x is our CTRL-x. Their M-x is our ESC-x. The M stands for META key, which is mapped to the ESCAPE key and usually to the ALT key as well. For consistency, this chapter always refers to the ESCAPE key.

—*ML, BR, DC, and JJ*

19.2 Emacs Features: A Laundry List

Here's the list we promised—a list of our favorite features:

Windows

Emacs is a "windowed editor." Before anyone heard of the X Window System or the Macintosh, Emacs had the ability to divide a terminal's screen into several "windows," allowing you to do different things in each one. You can edit a different file in each window or read mail in one window, answer mail in another, issue shell commands in a third, and so on.

Now that we all have nice workstations with mice and other crawly things for navigating around a bitmapped screen, why do you care? First, you may not have a bitmapped screen, and even if you have one in the office, you may not at home. Second, I still find Emacs preferable to most "modern" window systems because I don't have to use a mouse. If I want to create another window, I just type CTRL-x 2 (which splits the current window, whatever it is, into two); if I want to work in another window, I just type CTRL-x o; if I want to delete a window, I type CTRL-x 0. Is this faster than reaching for my mouse and moving it around? You bet. Particularly since my mouse is hidden under a pile of paper. (Of course, it's hidden because I hardly ever need it.) Once you've created a window, it's just as easy to start editing a new file, initiate a shell session, and so on. Third, even though you're using a windowing system, you may not have a lot of screen real estate available. By having a split Emacs screen, all editing can be done in one window, leaving enough room for other applications, such as the Mozilla web browser, to be open. Whether you're developing web pages or just reading Slashdot while "working," you'll appreciate the free space on the screen. It isn't uncommon for Emacs users to always have Emacs open on their desktops.

Shells

You can start an interactive shell within any Emacs window; just type ESC-x shell, and you'll see your familiar shell prompt. It's easy to see why this is so useful. It's trivial to return to earlier comands, copy them, and edit them. Even more important, you can easily take the output of a command and copy it into a text file that you're editing—obviously an extremely useful feature when you're writing a book like this. Emacs also lets you issue commands that operate on the contents of a window or a selected region within a window. Another benefit to doing shell work directly in Emacs is that every word that appears in that shell buffer is available for command completions (19.6). So if you're creating a small shell script that has to reference a long directory name, being able to autocomplete that name is an invaluable feature.

In fact, there are many filesystem maintenance tasks with which Emacs can help you. You can view and manipulate directories and files with Dired mode, which can be activated by typing ESC-x dired. You'll be asked which directory you want to view (the current directory is the default). Do you want to remove a file that starts with a hyphen, but *rm* complains that your file is not a valid option? Start Emacs in Dired mode, select the file, and type D. Emacs will ask you for confirmation about the proposed deletion. Want to delete a bunch of files that can't be easily described with wildcards? In dired mode, select each file with d, then remove them all with ESC-x dired-do-flagged-delete.

Keyboard macros and advanced editing features

Emacs lets you define "keyboard macros"—and sequences of commands that can be executed automatically. This is similar to *vi*'s *map* (18.2) facility, with one extra twist: Emacs actually executes the commands while you're defining the macro; *vi* expects you to figure out what you need to do, type it in without any feedback, and hope that the macro doesn't do anything hostile when you edit it. With Emacs, it's much easier to get the macro right. You can see what it's going to do as you're defining it, and if you make a mistake, you can correct it immediately.

To create a macro, you first need to tell Emacs that it needs to remember the next sequence of keystrokes by typing CTRL-x (. Now perform the desired actions. To end the macro recording, type CTRL-x). To execute the most recently defined macro, type CTRL-x e. If you make a mistake when recording the marco, type CTRL-g to cancel out of the entire operation, and begin recording the macro again.

Even if you don't create your own macros, Emacs provides a rich set of text-editing features that often *do what you mean*. For instance, Emacs allows users to make rectangluar text cuts. This is very useful for removing leading whitespace from a series of lines. To make the cut, you must first define the starting point of the rectangle to be cut. Position the cursor in Emacs to the upper-left corner of the area to be excised. Then mark the area with CTRL-SPACE. Move the cursor down to the last line of the area to be removed and then over to right as far as is desired. This is the lowest and rightmost corner of the rectangle. Now remove the area with the key sequence CTRL-x r k.

Editing modes

Emacs has a large number of special editing modes that provide context-sensitive help while you're writing. For example, if you're writing a C program, the C mode will help you to observe conventions for indentation and commenting. It automatically lines up braces for you and tells you when parentheses are unbalanced. In X Windows, Emacs will even do syntax highlighting for you. Perl programmers get two editing modes to choose from, perl-mode and cperl-mode. Based on the file extension, Emacs will figure out which mode you want. (The default and simplest mode is called Fundamental.) You can enter a new mode by typing ESC-x and then the name of the mode. Emacs also integrates well with the perl debugger (ESC-x perldb) so that you can step through your running code in the editor. Emacs also supports many version-control systems including RCS and CVS. Checking out a file from RCS is as simple as typing CTRL-x v v. After you have made your edits, check in the file with CTRL-x v v. That's not a typo; Emacs can figure out the *right thing to do* with your file because it remembers the last version-control state. Pretty cool. There are special modes for virtually every programming language I've ever heard of. There are also special modes for HTML, *troff*, TEX, outlines, stick figures, etc. For any kind of programming, Emacs is the Integrated Development Environment of choice for many users.

Mail, news, FTP, and HTTP

Although I often use Emacs' mail facility as an example, I'm not personally fond of it. However, if you really like working within the Emacs environment, you should try it. Sending mail from Emacs (ESC-x mail) is convenient if you are already editing the file you wish to send. You can simply copy and paste your work into the mail buffer and send it along with CTRL-c CTRL-c. You can even add Cc: and Reply-to: fields to the message just by adding them to the mail buffer directly under the To: field.

Emacs also has a Usenet client called GNUS (ESC-x gnus) that has quite a following. What editor would be complete without an integrated FTP client? Certainly not Emacs. There are two ways to access FTP in Emacs. The first is to type ESC-x ftp. This gives you a shell-like ftp client. While this is nice, Emacs provides an even slicker way to FTP files. Ange-ftp mode allows Emacs users to open remote files almost as if they were local. To open a remote file or directory, simple type CTRL-x CTRL-f. However, you must specify the filename with a leading slash and your remote username followed by @ and followed again by the ftp hostname, a colon, and the full path you wish to retrieve. For example, if I wished to edit the file *index.html* as user edit on my web server, I would use the filename */edit@www.nowhere.com:/home/html/ htdocs/index.html*.

To extend the last example a bit, Emacs even has a web-browser mode so that you could look at the web page you just edited! In truth, lynx is still king of the ASCII web browsers, but the Emacs W3 mode is coming along. It doesn't normally come with Emacs, so you're going to have to look on the Web for it. It has very good integration with XEmacs (neè Lucent Emacs) and can even display images. Speaking of the Web, there's a nice Emacs feature called webjump (ESC-x webjumb) that will make a currently opened Web browser such as Netscape go to a new URL. Webjump comes with a list a predefined URLs, which can be expanded, of course. One of those URLs is Yahoo. When that site is selected, webjump will ask you for a query term to submit. After hitting return, the Yahoo search results will appear in a browser window. Again, it's a nice shortcut.

Customization

Emacs is the most customizable tool I've ever seen. Customization is based on the LISP programming language, so you need to learn some LISP before you can work with it much. However, once you know LISP, you can do virtually anything. For example, you could write a complete spreadsheet program within Emacs—which means that you could use your normal Emacs commands to edit the spreadsheet and incorporate it (in whole or in part) into your documents. In fact, several Emacs spreadsheet modes exist, but their quality and functionality vary wildly. And, because of the FSF's General Public License, virtually all special-purpose packages are available for free.

—ML and JJ

19.3 Customizations and How to Avoid Them

Emacs customizations are usually stored in a file called *.emacs* in your home directory. In article 19.7, we've given a few customizations that I personally find convenient; if you're like most people, you'll add customizations over time. You'll end up doing this even if you're not a LISP programmer; if you know any other Emacs users, you'll soon be borrowing their shortcuts. The best way to customize Emacs to your taste is to find out what works for others...and then steal it. For that matter, many—if not most—of the customizations in my file were stolen from other users over the years. I hope I've gotten this process off to a good start.

However, you should also be aware of the "dark side" of customization. What happens if you sit down at someone else's system, start Emacs, and find out that he's customized it so extensively that it's unrecognizable? Or that a "helpful" administrator has installed some system-wide hacks that are getting in your way? Here's what will help. First, start *emacs* with the option *–q*; that tells Emacs not to load any *.emacs* initialization file. (If you want to load your initialization file instead of someone else's, try the option *–u username*).

That still doesn't solve the problem of system-wide customizations. To keep those from getting in the way, put the following line at the beginning of your *.emacs* file:

```
(setq inhibit-default-init t)
```

This turns off all "global" initializations. (If you're sharing someone else's system, you may still need the *–u* option to force Emacs to read your initialization file.)

—ML, DC, and BR

19.4 Backup and Auto-Save Files

If you're like most people, you often spend a few hours editing a file, only to decide that you liked your original version better. Or you press some strange sequence of keys that makes Emacs do something extremely weird and that you can't "undo." Emacs provides several ways to get out of these tight spots.

First, try the command ESC-x `revert-buffer`. Emacs will ask one of two questions: either "Buffer has been auto-saved recently. Revert from auto-save file? (y or n)" or "Revert buffer from file *your-filename*? (yes or no)".

Before deciding what to do, it's important to understand the difference between these two questions. Emacs creates an auto-save[*] file every 300 keystrokes you type. So, if you're reverting to the auto-save file, you'll at most lose your last 300 keystrokes. Maybe this is what you want—but maybe you made the mistake a long time ago. In that case, you don't want to use the auto-save file; type n, and you'll see the second question, asking if you want to revert to the last copy of the file that you saved. Type yes to go back to your most recent saved version.

It's possible that you'll only see the second question ("Revert buffer from file..."). This means that you have saved the file sometime within the last 300 keystrokes. As soon as you save a file, Emacs deletes the auto-save file. It will create a new one every 300 keystrokes.

It's worth noting that Emacs is *very* picky about what you type. If it asks for a y or an n, you've got to type y or n. If it asks for yes or no, you've got to type yes or no. In situations like this, where the two styles are mixed up, you've got to get it right.

If you're in real trouble and you want to go back to your *original file*—the way it was when you started editing—you need to recover Emacs' *backup file*. If you're editing a file that already exists, Emacs will create a backup file as soon as it starts. If you're editing a new file, Emacs will create a backup the *second* time you save the file. Once it's created, the backup file is never touched; it stays there until the next time you start Emacs, at which point you'll get a new backup, reflecting the file's contents at the start of your editing session.

Now that we're over the preliminaries, how do you recover the backup file? Emacs doesn't have any special command for doing this; you have to do it by hand. The backup file's name is the same as your original filename, with a tilde (~) added to it. So quit Emacs (or start a shell), and type:

```
% mv your-filename~ your-filename
```

Note that Emacs has the ability to save "numbered" backup files, like the VAX/VMS operating system. We've never played with this feature and don't think it's a particularly good idea. But it's there if you want it.

—*ML and DC*

---

[*] For reference, the name of the auto-save file is #*your-filename*#; that is, it sticks a hash mark (#) before and after the file's "regular" name.

19.5 Putting Emacs in Overwrite Mode

Many users are used to editors that are normally in *overwrite mode*: when you backspace and start typing, you type over the character that is underneath the cursor.* By default, Emacs works in *insertion mode*, where new characters are inserted just before the cursor's position.

If you prefer overwrite mode, just give the command ESC-x overwrite-mode. You can use command abbreviation (19.6) to shorten this to ESC-x ov. On many keyboards, pressing INSERT also turns on overwrite mode. If you get tired of overwrite mode, use the same command to turn it off.

If you *always* want to use overwrite mode, create a file named *.emacs* in your home directory, and put the following line in it:

```
(setq-default overwrite-mode t)
```

This is a simple Emacs customization; for a lot more about customization, see O'Reilly & Associates' *Learning GNU Emacs*, by Bill Rosenblatt, Eric Raymond, and Debra Cameron.

—ML and DC

19.6 Command Completion

Emacs has a great feature called *command completion*. Basically, command completion means that Emacs will let you type the absolute minimum and it will fill in the rest. You can use command completion whenever you're typing a filename, buffer name, command name, or variable name. Simply type enough of the name to be "unique" (usually the first few letters), followed by a TAB. Emacs will fill in the rest of the name for you. If the name isn't unique—that is, if there are other filenames that start with the same letters—Emacs will show you the alternatives. Type a few more letters to select the file you want, then press TAB again.

For example, if I'm trying to load the file *outline.txt*, I can simply give the command CTRL-x CTRL-f out TAB. Providing that there are no other filenames beginning with the letters *out*, Emacs will fill in the rest of the filename. When I see that it's correct, I press RETURN, and I'm done.

When you use command completion, always make sure that Emacs has successfully found the file you want. If you don't, the results may be strange: you may end up with a partial filename or the wrong file.

---

* This includes some mainframe editors, like XEDIT, and (in my memory) a lot of older tools for word processing and general editing.

Along the same lines as command completion is a feature called *dynamic expansion*. After typing the first few letters of a word, you can have Emacs search all open buffers for completions of that word. Simply type ESC-/, and emacs will complete the partial word with one you've already typed. You can cycle through all the choices by repeating the keystroke. Warning: this feature is addictive.

—*ML and BR*

19.7 Mike's Favorite Timesavers

I'm a very fast typist—which means that I hate using special function keys, arrow keys, and especially mice. I deeply resent anything that moves me away from the basic alphanumeric keyboard. Even BACKSPACE and DELETE are obnoxious, since they force me to shift my hand position.

With this in mind, I've customized Emacs so that I can do virtually anything with the basic alphabetic keys, plus the CONTROL key. Here are some extracts from my *.emacs* file:

.emacs_ml

```
;; Make CTRL-h delete the previous character. Normally, this gets
;; you into the "help" system.
 (define-key global-map "\C-h" 'backward-delete-char)
;; make sure CTRL-h works in searches, too
 (setq search-delete-char (string-to-char "\C-h"))
;; bind the "help" facility somewhere else (CTRL-underscore).
;; NOTE: CTRL-underscore is not defined on some terminals.
 (define-key global-map "\C-_" 'help-command) ;; replacement
 (setq help-char (string-to-char "\C-_"))
;; Make ESC-h delete the previous word.
 (define-key global-map "\M-h" 'backward-kill-word)
;; Make CTRL-x CTRL-u the "undo" command; this is better than "CTRL-x u"
;; because you don't have to release the CTRL key.
 (define-key global-map "\C-x\C-u" 'undo)
;; scroll the screen "up" or "down" one line with CTRL-z and ESC z
 (defun scroll-up-one () "Scroll up 1 line." (interactive)
    (scroll-up (prefix-numeric-value current-prefix-arg)))
 (defun scroll-down-one () "Scroll down 1 line." (interactive)
    (scroll-down (prefix-numeric-value current-prefix-arg)))
 (define-key global-map "\C-z" 'scroll-up-one)
 (define-key global-map "\M-z" 'scroll-down-one)
;; Use CTRL-x CTRL-v to "visit" a new file, keeping the current file
;; on the screen
 (define-key global-map "\C-x\C-v" 'find-file-other-window)
```

The comments (lines beginning with two semicolons) should adequately explain what these commands do. Figure out which you need, and add them to your *.emacs* file. The most important commands are at the *top* of the file.

—*ML*

19.8 Rational Searches

Emacs has, oh, a hundred or so different search commands. (Well, the number's probably more like 32, but who's counting?) There are searches of absolutely every flavor you could ever imagine: incremental searches, word searches,[*] regular-expression searches, and so on.

However, when it comes to your plain old garden-variety search, Emacs is strangely deficient. There is a simple search that just looks for some arbitrary sequence of characters, but it's rather well hidden. In addition, it lacks one very important feature: you can't search for the same string repeatedly. That is, you can't say "Okay, you found the right sequence of letters; give me the next occurrence"; you have to retype your search string every time.

search.el

I thought this was an incredible pain until a friend of mine wrote a special search command. It's in the file *search.el*. Just stick this into your directory for Emacs hacks (19.12), and add something like the following to your *.emacs* file:

```
;; real searches, courtesy of Chris Genly
;; substitute your own Emacs hack directory for /home/los/mikel/emacs
(load-file "/home/los/mikel/emacs/search.el")
```

Now you can type CTRL-s to search forward and CTRL-r to search back. Emacs will prompt you for a search string and start searching when you press RETURN. Typing another CTRL-s or CTRL-r repeats your previous search. When you try this, you'll see one other useful feature: unlike the other Emacs searches, this kind of search displays the "default" (i.e., most recent) search string in the minibuffer. It's exactly the kind of search I want.

It's conceivable that you'll occasionally want incremental searches. You'll have to "rebind" them, though, to use them conveniently. Here are the key bindings that I use:

```
;; rebind incremental search as ESC-s and ESC-r
(define-key global-map "\M-s" 'isearch-forward)
(define-key global-map "\M-r" 'isearch-backward)
;; have to rebind ESC s separately for text-mode. It's normally
;; bound to 'center-line'.
(define-key text-mode-map "\M-s" 'isearch-forward)
```

That is, ESC-s and ESC-r now give you forward and reverse incremental searches. And once you've started an incremental search, CTRL-s and CTRL-r still repeat the previous incremental search, just as they're supposed to.

---

[*] These are especially nice because they can search for phrases that cross line breaks; most searches assume that all the text you want will all be on the same line. However, you can only search for whole words, and if you use *troff* or TEX, Emacs may be confused by your "markup."

Of course, now you'll have to rebind the "center-line" command if you're fond of it. In my opinion, it's not worth the trouble. The game of "musical key-bindings" stops here.

—ML

19.9 Unset PWD Before Using Emacs

I've seen a number of strange situations in which Emacs can't find files unless you type a complete ("absolute") pathname (1.16), starting from the root (/). When you try to visit a file, you'll get the message File not found and directory doesn't exist.

In my experience, this usually means that the C shell's *PWD* environment variable (35.5) has been incorrectly set. There are a few (relatively pathological) ways of tricking the C shell into making a mistake. More commonly, though, I've seen a few systems on which the C shell sticks an extra slash into *PWD*: that is, its value will be something like */home/mike//Mail* rather than */home/mike/Mail*. Unix doesn't care; it lets you stack up extra slashes without any trouble. But Emacs interprets // as the root directory—that is, it discards everything to the left of the double slash. So if you're trying to edit the file */home/mike//Mail/output.txt*, Emacs will look for */Mail/output.txt*. Even if this file exists, it's not what you want. [This also happens when Emacs is called from a (Bourne) shell script that has changed its current directory without changing *PWD*. —*JP*]

This problem is particularly annoying because the shell will automatically reset *PWD* every time you change directories. The obvious solution, sticking unsetenv PWD in your *.cshrc* file, doesn't do any good.

What will work is defining an alias (29.1):

(..) **43.7**
```
alias gmacs "(unsetenv PWD; emacs \!*)"
```

A better solution might be to switch to another shell that doesn't have this problem. The Bourne shell (*sh*) obviously doesn't, since it doesn't keep track of your current directory.

—ML

19.10 Inserting Binary Characters into Files

I remember being driven absolutely crazy by a guy (who hopefully won't be reading this) who called me every other week and asked me how to stick a page break into some text file he was writing. He was only printing on a garden-variety printer, for which inserting a page break is a simple matter: just add a formfeed character, CTRL-l. But CTRL-l already means something to Emacs ("redraw the screen"). How do you get the character into your file, without Emacs thinking that you're typing a command?

Simple. Precede CTRL-l with the "quoting" command, CTRL-q. CTRL-q tells Emacs that the next character you type is text, not a part of some command. So the sequence CTRL-q CTRL-l inserts the character CTRL-l into your file; you'll see ^L on your screen. (Note that this represents a single character, instead of two characters.) In turn, when you print the file on many printers, the CTRL-l will cause a page eject at the appropriate point.

You can use this technique to get any "control character" into an Emacs file. In fact, under pressure I've done some pretty bizarre binary editing—not a task I'd recommend, but certainly one that's possible.

—ML

19.11 Using Word-Abbreviation Mode

Like *vi*, Emacs provides an "abbreviation" facility. Its traditional usage lets you define abbreviations for long words or phrases so you don't have to type them in their entirety. For example, let's say you are writing a contract that repeatedly references the National Institute of Standards and Technology. Rather than typing the full name, you can define the abbreviation nist. Emacs inserts the full name whenever you type nist, followed by a space or punctuation mark. Emacs watches for you to type an abbreviation, then expands it automatically as soon as you press the spacebar or type a punctuation mark (such as ., ,, !, ?, ;, or :).

One use for word-abbreviation mode is to correct misspellings as you type. Almost everyone has a dozen or so words that he habitually types incorrectly, due to some worn neural pathways. You can simply tell Emacs that these misspellings are "abbreviations" for the correct versions, and Emacs fixes the misspellings every time you type them. If you take time to define your common typos as abbreviations, you'll never be bothered with teh, adn, and recieve when you run the spellchecker. Emacs sweeps up after your typos and corrects them. For example, let's say that you define teh as an abbreviation for the. When you press the spacebar after you type teh, Emacs fixes it immediately, and you continue happily typing. You may not even notice that you typed the word wrong before Emacs fixes it.

Trying Word Abbreviations for One Session

Usually, if you go to the trouble of defining a word abbreviation, you will use it in more than one Emacs session. But if you'd like to try out abbreviation mode to see if you want to make it part of your startup, use the following procedure to define word abbreviations for this session:

1. Enter word-abbreviation mode by typing ESC-x `abbrev-mode`. abbrev appears on the mode line.

2. Type the abbreviation you want to use, and press CTRL-x a. Emacs then asks you for the expansion.

3. Type the definition for the abbreviation, and press RETURN. Emacs then expands the abbreviation; it will do so each time you type it followed by a space or punctuation mark. The abbreviations you've defined will work only during this Emacs session.

If you find that you like using word-abbreviation mode, you may want to make it part of your startup, as described in the following section.

Making Word Abbreviations Part of Your Startup

Once you become hooked on abbreviation mode, make it part of your *.emacs* file so that you enter abbreviation mode and load your word-abbreviations file automatically. To define word abbreviations and make them part of your startup:

1. Add these lines to your *.emacs* file:

   ```
   (setq-default abbrev-mode t)
   (read-abbrev-file "~/.abbrev_defs")
   (setq save-abbrevs t)
   ```

2. Save the *.emacs* file, and re-enter Emacs. Abbrev appears on the mode line. (You'll get an error at this point; ignore it—it won't happen again.)

3. Type an abbreviation you want to use, and then type CTRL-x a following the abbreviation. Emacs asks you for the expansion.

4. Type the definition for the abbreviation, and press RETURN. Emacs expands the abbreviation and will do so each time you type it followed by a space or punctuation mark. You can define as many abbreviations as you wish by repeating Steps 3 and 4.

5. Type ESC-x `write-abbrev-file` to save your abbreviations file. Emacs asks for the filename.

6. Type ~/.abbrev_defs. Emacs then writes the file. You need only take this step the first time you define abbreviations using this procedure. After this file exists, the lines in your *.emacs* file load the abbreviations file automatically.

After you've followed this procedure the first time, you only need to use Steps 3 and 4 to define more abbreviations. When you add word abbreviations in subsequent sessions, Emacs asks whether you want to save the abbreviations file. Respond with a y to save the new abbreviations you've defined and have them take effect automatically. If you define an abbreviation and later regret it, use ESC–x `edit-word-abbrevs` to delete it.

—DC

19.12 Directories for Emacs Hacks

If you use any Emacs editor (GNU Emacs or any of the commercial alternatives), you may have written lots of handy LISP programs to use while you're editing. It's convenient to create a separate directory for these; a good name for this directory is (obviously) *emacs*; it's usually located in your home directory.

If you use GNU Emacs, you should put the following line in the *.emacs* file:

```
(setq load-path (append load-path '("your-emacs-directory")))
```

This tells Emacs that it should look in your personal Emacs directory to find your programs. (It's similar to the *PATH* (35.6) environment variable.)

—*ML*

19.13 An Absurd Amusement

If you have time to waste (and I mean *really* waste), Emacs has things to keep you occupied. There are lots of interesting special effects, such as "disassociated text." My favorite is a command called "psychoanalyze-pinhead." It's based on "doctor," which is a variation of the classic artificial-intelligence demonstration called "Eliza": the computer plays psychotherapist and asks you questions; you reply, and your answers are the basis for new questions. Nothing new, really; I remember it from my high school days, in the early 1970s. If you think you might be in need of a psychotherapist, save your money and try ESC-x doctor RETURN.

If you want to see something really interesting, try ESC-x psychoanalyze-pinhead. This takes the built-in "doctor" program and feeds it with quotations from the cult comic strip *Zippy the Pinhead*. The result is indeed bizarre. Here's some typical output:

```
I am the psychotherapist.  Please, describe your problems.  Each time
you are finished talking, type RET twice.

YOU PICKED KARL MALDEN'S NOSE!!

Why do you say I picked karl malden's nose?

Am I SHOPLIFTING?

Is it because of your plans that you say are you shoplifting?

Are you selling NYLON OIL WELLS??  If so, we can use TWO DOZEN!!
```

Press CTRL-c when you've had enough.

—*ML*

20

Batch Editing

20.1 Why Line Editors Aren't Dinosaurs

In the "old days," when programmers worked on printing terminals, editing was done one line at a time. Editors that let you move a cursor around the screen to select text to edit hadn't yet been invented, because there weren't any screens to look at text on!

With ever more advanced WYSIWYG (What You See Is What You Get) word processors and editing programs, it's easy for novices to think of line editors as a bizarre relic. Perhaps they are—but if so, they are a relic of extraordinary power.

You see, line editors lend themselves to *scripting*—the ability to write what in effect are editing programs that can be applied over and over to different files.

When we talk about "batch editing" or scripts, here are some of the programs you might use:

- *ed* is the original Unix line editor.
- *ex* supports a superset of *ed* commands; it is widely used from within *vi*, which is the *ex* "visual" or "screen" mode.
- *sed* (34.1) is an editor that can *only* be run with scripts or by entering a few short commands as command-line arguments; while it has many similar commands, it has some important differences (34.2) from *ed* and *ex*.
- *awk* (20.10) is a great way to pull apart a line of text into a sequence of elements. Used frequently with *sed*.
- *patch* (20.9) is a specialized editor designed to apply editing scripts created with *diff* (11.1). You can do this with *ed* or *ex* as well, but *patch* is especially clever at it.

Of course, editing is a continuum, and beyond *sed* and *awk* (20.10) lie more complete programming languages like *perl* (41.1) and *python* (42.1) that are very adept at manipulating text.

—*TOR*

20.2 Writing Editing Scripts

When you write a script that contains a series of editing actions and then run the script on an input file, you take what would be a hands-on procedure in an editor such as *vi* and transform it into a look-no-hands procedure.

When performing edits manually, you get to trust the cause-and-effect relationship of entering an editing command and seeing the immediate result. There is usually an "undo" command that allows you to reverse the effect of a command and return the text file to its previous state. Once you learn an interactive text editor, you have the feeling of making changes in a safe and controlled manner, one step at a time.

Most people new to "power editing" will feel there is greater risk in writing a script to perform a series of edits than in making those changes manually. The fear is that by automating the task, something will happen that cannot be reversed. The object of learning scripting with *ex* or *sed* is to understand the commands well enough to see that your results are predictable. In other words, you come to understand the cause-and-effect relationship between your editing script and the output you get.

This requires using the editor in a controlled, methodical way. Gradually, you will develop methods for creating and testing editing scripts. You will come to rely upon these methods and gain confidence that you know what your script is doing and why.

Here are a few tips:

1. Carefully examine your input file, using *grep*, before designing your script.

2. Start with a small sample of occurrences in a test file. Run your script on the sample and make sure the script is working. Remember, it's just as important to make sure the script *doesn't* work where you *don't* want it to. Then increase the size of the sample. Try to increase the complexity of the input.

3. Work carefully, testing each command that you add to a script. Compare the output against the input file to see what has changed. Prove to yourself that your script is complete. Your script may work perfectly based on your assumptions of what is in the input file, but your assumptions may be wrong.

4. *Be pragmatic!* Try to accomplish what you can with your script, but understand that it doesn't have to do 100 percent of the job. If you encounter difficult situations, check to see how frequently they occur. Sometimes it's better to do a few remaining edits manually.

If you can add to these tips with your experience, tack them on.

One additional suggestion is to use a revision control system (39.4) to preserve previous versions. That makes it easy to undo your edits.

—DD

20.3 Line Addressing

The key to making line editors work for you is understanding how to select (or "address") the lines that will be affected by the commands in your script.

In *ed* and *ex*, a command affects only the "current" line—the first line of the file to begin with, and later the site of the last edit or movement command—unless you precede the command with an address to indicate some other line or lines. In *sed*, most commands apply to every line unless you give an address.

Most line editors address lines in three ways:

* with line numbers
* with regular expression patterns
* with special symbols

It's possible to address single lines or a range of lines.

Table 20-1 describes the addresses you can use with *ex*.

Table 20-1. Line addressing in the ex editor

Address	Description
1,$	All lines in the file.
%	All lines; same as 1,$.
x,y	Lines *x* through *y*.
x;y	Lines *x* through *y*, with current line reset to *x*.
1	Top of file.
0	"Before the top" of file. Used to add text above top line: 0r, xm0, etc.
.	Current line.
n	Absolute line number *n*.
$	Last line.
x-n	*n* lines before *x*.
x+n	*n* lines after *x*.
-n	*n* lines previous.
-	Previous line.
+n	*n* lines ahead.

If the address specifies a range of lines, the format is:

x,y

where *x* and *y* are the first and last addressed lines. *x* must precede *y* in the file.

—TOR, DG, and JP

20.4 Useful ex Commands

Many line editor commands are not particularly useful in scripts. The two commands that you will use far and away the most often are s (substitute), to replace one pattern with another, and d (delete), to delete one or more lines. On occasion, though, you'll want to insert text from a script. (Editing scripts built by *diff* (20.6) make heavy use of insert, append, delete, and change commands.) And of course, you need commands to write the file and quit the editor.

Here's the syntax of most of the commands you may encounter in *ex* editing scripts. (The *ed* editor understands the abbreviated versions of some, but not all, of these commands.) Elements in [brackets] are optional; don't type the [or]. The leading colon (:) shown in examples is the *ex* command character used to issue an *ex* command from *vi*; in a script, the colon would be omitted. The autoindent feature referred to below aids anyone writing structured text. Your editor can ease the burden of creating outlines and source code by positioning the cursor beneath the first character of the previous line.

append
> [*address*] a[!] *text* .
>
> Append *text* at specified *address*, or at present address if none is specified. Add a ! to switch the autoindent setting that will be used during input. For example, if autoindent was enabled, ! disables it.

change
> [*address*] c[!] *text* .
>
> Replace the specified lines with *text*. Add a ! to switch the autoindent setting during input of *text*.

copy
> [*address*] co *destination* [*address*] t *destination*
>
> Copy* the lines included in *address* to the specified *destination* address.
>> :1,10 co 50
>> :1,10t50

---

* Note that "t" is short for "to." The ed editor only has one-letter commands and since "c" was already taken for "change," they used "t" for "copy TO."

delete

    [address] d *[buffer]*

Delete the lines included in *address*. If *buffer* is specified, save or append the text to the named buffer.

    :/Part I/,/Part II/-1d   *Delete to line above "Part II"*
    :/main/+d   *Delete line below "main"*
    :.,$d   *Delete from this line to last line*

global

    [address] g[!]/pattern/*[commands]*

Execute *commands* on all lines that contain *pattern*, or if *address* is specified, on all lines within that range. If *commands* are not specified, print all such lines. (Exception: doesn't print when you use it from *vi* by typing : first. You'll need to add a *p*, as in the second example below). If ! is used, execute *commands* on all lines that *don't* contain *pattern*.

    :g/Unix/
    :g/Unix/p
    :g/Name:/s/tom/Tom/

insert

    [address] i[!] *text* .

Insert *text* at line before the specified *address*, or at present address if none is specified. Add a ! to switch the autoindent setting during input of *text*.

move

    [address] m *destination*

Move the lines specified by *address* to the *destination* address.

    :.,/Note/m /END/   *Move block after line containing "END"*

print

    [address] p *[count]*

Print the lines specified by *address*. *count* specifies the number of lines to print, starting with *address*.

    :100;+5p   *Show line 100 and the next five lines*

quit

    q[!]

Terminate current editing session. Use ! to discard changes made since the last save. If the editing session includes additional files in the argument list that were never accessed, quit by typing q! or by typing q twice.

read

    [address] r *file*

Copy in the text from *file* on the line below the specified *address*. If *file* is not specified, the current filename is used.

    :0r $HOME/data   *Read file in at top of current file*

read

> [*address*] r !*command*

Read the output of Unix *command* into the text after the line specified by *address*.

> :$r !cal   *Place a calendar at end of file*

source

> so *file*

Read and execute *ex* commands from *file*.

> :so $HOME/.exrc

substitute

> [*address*] s [/*pattern*/*replacement*/] [*options*] [*count*]

Replace first instance of *pattern* on each of the specified lines with *replacement*. If *pattern* and *replacement* are omitted, repeat last substitution. *count* specifies the number of lines on which to substitute, starting with *address*. The following can be used as *options*:

c   Prompt for confirmation before each change.

g   Substitute all instances of *pattern* on each line.

p   Print the last line on which a substitution was made.

<table>
<tr><td>c 17.9</td><td>:1,10s/yes/no/g</td><td>*Substitute on first 10 lines*</td></tr>
<tr><td>\u 17.14</td><td>:%s/[Hh]ello/Hi/gc</td><td>*Confirm global substitutions*</td></tr>
<tr><td></td><td>:s/Fortran/\U&/ 3</td><td>*Uppercase "Fortran" on next 3 lines*</td></tr>
</table>

write

> [*address*] w[!] [>>] *file*]

Write lines specified by *address* to *file*, or write full contents of buffer if *address* is not specified. If *file* is also omitted, save the contents of the buffer to the current filename. If >> *file* is used, write contents to the end of an existing *file*. The ! flag forces the editor to write over any current contents of *file*.

> :1,10w name_list   *Copy first 10 lines to name_list*
> :50w >> name_list   *Now append line 50*

write

> [*address*] w !*command*

Write lines specified by *address*, or write full contents of buffer if *address* is not specified, to the standard input (43.1) of *command*.

> :1,10w !spell   *Send first 10 lines to the spell command*
> :w !lpr   *Print entire buffer with lpr command*

—TOR and DG

20.5 Running Editing Scripts Within vi

Because *vi* is built on top of the *ex* line editor, you get all the power of a line editor as well. Any experienced *vi* user issues *ex* commands all the time—but usually one by one, at the colon (:) prompt.

The one exception is the *.exrc* file (17.5), which is, at bottom, a list of commands for *ex* to run on startup—in short, an editor script.

What many beginners don't know is that you can save a sequence of *ex* commands in any file and execute it with the :so command (20.4). For example, Bruce Barnett uses this trick to set himself up specially for editing FORTRAN programs (18.10).

In general, *sed* (34.1) is better for general-purpose batch editing—such as making a set of global substitutions over and over again on multiple files—therefore, :so is most often used for reading in setup commands. Keep in mind, though, any time you find yourself issuing the same commands over and over again, *think script!*

—*TOR*

20.6 Change Many Files by Editing Just One

diff

20.8

The *diff* command can make an editing script that you give to the *ex* or *ed* editors or the *patch* (20.9) program. They'll apply your same edits to other copies of the same file. This is handy if you have a lot of copies of a big file, spread around a network or on a lot of disks, and you want to make the same changes to all the files. In fact, this is how the Concurrent Version Control (CVS) system works. Instead of sending new copies of the whole file, just have *diff* make a script—and use that little script to update all the big files.

Here's a demo. I'm going to modify a program called pqs.c. Then I'll use diff and ed to apply the same changes to a copy of the file named remote–pqs.c (which might be at a remote computer):

```
1% cp pqs.c remote-pqs.c
2% cp pqs.c pqs.c.new
3% vi pqs.c.new
4% diff pqs.c pqs.c.new
106,107c106
<       fprintf(stderr,
<           "%s: quitting: not able to %s your .pq_profile file.\n",
--
>       fprintf(stderr, "%s: quitting: can't %s your .pq_profile file.\n",
390a390
>               "WARNING:",
```

```
5% diff -e pqs.c pqs.c.new > edscr
6% cat edscr
390a
                    "WARNING:",
.
106,107c
            fprintf(stderr, "%s: quitting: can't %s your .pq_profile file.\n",
.
```

>> 43.1

```
7% echo w >> edscr
8% ed remote-pqs.c < edscr
19176
19184
9% diff pqs.c.new remote-pqs.c
10%
```

At prompt 1%, I make the simulated "remote" copy of the *pqs.c* file. At prompt 2%, I make another copy of it; at prompt 3%, I edit the copy. Prompt 4% has a *diff* that shows the changes I made. Then, at prompt 5%, I run diff -e (11.1); I save the result in *edscr*, which I show at prompt 6%.

Prompt 7% is important because *diff –e* doesn't add a w command to the script file. That tells *ed* to write its changes to the file. I use echo w (27.5) to add the command.

In prompt 8%, I give *ed* the name of the "remote" file to edit as a command-line argument and give it the script file on its standard input. At prompt 9%, I do a *diff* that shows the changes have been made and the two versions are the same.

If you find yourself needing to keep multiple copies of the same set of files in sync with each other, you might want to consider using CVS. Not only is it a client/server system ready for network use, it is also designed for multiple users. Every check-in is logged, and updating a whole set of files (called "projects") can be done with the command cvs update. This can be a great timesaver for webmasters maintaining multiple web servers with static (or even dynamic) content.

Another great tool for synchronizing many filesystems is *rsync*. This program can be used to update a remote filesystem, say a web directory, with more current version of existing files or add new ones. The synchronization can go both ways. *rsync* even has built-in support for SSH. Here's an example of using *rsync* to publish new web documents to a live server:

```
$ rsync -urz -e /path/to/ssh local_dir hostname:/path/to/web/docs
```

The -u flag tells rsync to update the remote filesystem with newer files on the local system. The -r flag tells *rsync* to recurse into subdirectories. The -z allows the files to be gzipped during transfer (good for slow modem links). While it can be a client/server system, *rsync* can work just fine as a peer-to-peer system where it will need to run some commands on the remote machine. The -e flag provides the path to the *rsh* or *ssh* program that you to have rsync use. The next argument is the directory on the local machine *rsync* is to copy, and the last argument is the hostname and target directory to be updated. *rsync* is a very handy tool, and the manpage illustrates its flexibility.

—JP

20.7 ed/ex Batch Edits: A Typical Example

What *ed* and *ex* lack in intutitive interface design, they make up for when used in batch editing shell scripts. For example, you might be maintaining a web site with a lot of static content all stored in traditional HTML files. One such file might look like this:

```
<html>
<body>
<h1>Hello, world!</h1>
<p>Glad you could make it
<img src="/graphics/smiley.gif" alt="[:-)]">.
<p>Here's a picture of my house:
<img src="/graphics/house.gif" alt="[my house]">
</body>
</html>
```

One day, you get an email that all the images will now be served out of the directory */img* instead of */graphics*. Also, all existing *gif* files have been replaced with png files. Although these changes don't sound like much, making these modifications to a large number of files quickly becomes tedious. By writing a shell script that calls either *ed* or *ex*, you will not only solve today's problem, but you'll also be ready to make new changes to the files whenever that becomes necessary. A Bourne shell script that makes these changes looks like the following:

```
#!/bin/sh
# Convert some of the hard coded values in HTML
# into the new site schema

# Patterns to be replaced
old_graphics_dir="graphics"
old_graphics_ext="gif"

# new values
new_graphics_dir="img"
new_graphics_ext="png"

# Make the changes
for file in *html;
do
    ed $file <<EOF
1,\$s/$old_graphics_dir/$new_graphics_dir/g
1,\$s/$old_graphics_ext/$new_graphics_ext/g
w
EOF
done
```

The script is fairly simple. It defines a few variables to hold the patterns to be found and replaced. The replacement values are defined next. This script is meant to be run in the directory containing all the HTML files. The list of all files ending in "html" is iterated over in a for loop in which *ed* is fed commands from a here document. Recall that $ is a special character for Bourne shell and must be escaped in the line-addressing part of the *ed* command. After the search and replace operations finish, the *ed* buffers need to be written back to disk with the w command. This script works with both *ed* and *ex*.

In older versions of *ed*, you may find that if the first pattern doesn't match, *ed* doesn't even try the second pattern. If your version does this, one workaround suggested by Chris Torek is to use the global command g like this:

```
ed - $i << end
g/$old_graphics_dir/s//$new_graphics_dir/g
g/$old_graphics_ext/s//$new_graphics_ext/g
w
end
```

The addition of the - suppresses the two numbers that *ed* normally prints.

—*CT and JJ*

20.8 Batch Editing Gotcha: Editors Fail on Big Files

People use the *ed* editor with script files to make global edits. But many versions of *ed* can't edit large files. The *ex* editor is usually better, but it has limits, too. How large is "large"? That depends on your version. Most *ed*s I've seen can't handle more than about 100,000 characters.

There are no limits on *sed* (34.1), although you'll need to save its output somehow (34.4), and your editing script may have to be changed to work with *sed*.[*] Here's what you'll see when *ed* fails:

```
% cat edscr
s/Unix/UNIX/g
w
% ed - words < edscr
?
%
```

The ? is *ed*'s "verbose" way of telling you that something's wrong. This obscure message is especially bad if you write a shell script that edits multiple files in a loop; you may not notice the error or be able to tell which file had the problem. Be sure your script checks for errors!

---

[*] By default, *ed* commands apply to the current line. *sed* commands are global. Also, relative line addresses like -5 don't work in *sed*.

Unfortunately for programmers, *ed* may not return an error status that you can test. There are workarounds, though. When the ed - command succeeds, it doesn't display anything. The simplest way to find errors is to check for any output on *stdout* or *stderr*. This chunk of a Bourne shell script shows how (your filename is in the shell variable $filename (35.9)):

```
2>&1 36.16        edout="`ed - $filename < edscr 2>&1`"
  [ ] 35.26       if [ -n "$edout" -o $? -ne 0 ]
                  then
   $? 35.12           echo "$edout" 1>&2
                      echo "QUITTING: 'ed - $filename < edscr' failed?!?" 1>&2
                      exit 1
                  fi
```

—JP

20.9 patch: Generalized Updating of Files That Differ

patch

Like all of Larry Wall's widely used programs (including *perl* (41.1), a software configuration script called *Configure*, and the *rn* news reader), *patch* betrays a whimsical intelligence of its own. Feed it any kind of *diff* listing (11.1) (not just an editing script produced with the *–e* option—the typical way before *patch* came around). *patch* figures out what it needs to do to apply the diff, and updates the file, supplying all the while a breezy commentary on what it's doing:

```
% patch < testfile.diff
Hmm...  Looks like a normal diff to me...
File to patch: testfile
Patching file testfile using Plan A...
Hunk #1 succeeded at 2.
done
```

As Larry once noted, *patch* has done an awful lot to "change the culture of computing." Almost all free software is now updated by means of patches rather than complete new releases. *patch* is smart enough to discard any leading or trailing garbage (such as mail headers or signatures), so a program source file can be updated by piping a mail message containing a diff listing between old and new versions directly to *patch*.

Here are a few of the other things *patch* is smart enough to do:

- Figure out the name of the file to be updated and do it without asking (usually only if the diff file is a context diff (11.3) produced with the *–c* option).

- Look for a suitable RCS or CVS (39.4) file and check it out, if the filename itself can't be found.

- Handle diff listings that don't quite match. This makes it possible for *patch* to update a file that the recipient has already changed from the one that the diff was based on.

- Save any pieces of the diff file that don't end up being used, in a file named by adding the suffix *.rej* (reject) to the name of the file being patched.

- Back up the file that is being patched, appending the suffix *.orig* to the name of the file being patched.

- Recognize that its input may actually apply to several files, and patch each of them separately. For example, a whole directory might be updated by a "patch" file that contained diff listings for each of the files in the directory. (By the way, the *-d* option to *patch* tells it to *cd* to a specified directory before starting work.)

- Recognize (or at least speculate) that a patch might have been created incorrectly, with the old and new files swapped. Larry says, "Yes, I'm afraid that does happen occasionally, human nature being what it is." *patch*'s *-R* option will force *patch* to reverse the sense of the patch; what's really amusing is to see *patch* suggest that this might be the thing to do, when things seem out of sync.

If you are a programmer, *patch* is worth studying just to see how much a program can do to anticipate errors, deal with fuzzy input, and in general "make the computer do the dirty work." But if you're a programmer, you doubtless already know about *patch*.

One last note: *patch* is so useful that it's been added to many Unix systems. Check to see if your system has it before installing the program. Some versions of *patch* we've seen are limted versions or buggy when they come from software vendors, though. The one on the book's website is worth comparing to yours.

—*TOR*

20.10 Quick Reference: awk

Up to this point, we've shown you tools to do basic batch editing of text files. These tools, although powerful, have limitations. Although you can script *ex* commands, the range of text manipulation is quite limited. If you need more powerful and flexible batch editing tools, you need to look at programming languages that are designed for text manipulation. One of the earliest Unix languages to do this is *awk*, created by Al Aho, Peter Weinberger, and Brian Kernighan. Even if you've never programmed before, there are some simple but powerful ways that you can use *awk*. Whenever you have a text file that's arranged in columns from which you need to extract data, *awk* should come to mind.

For example, every Red Hat Linux system stores its version number in */etc/ redhat-release*. On my system, it looks like this:

```
Red Hat Linux release 7.1 (Seawolf)
```

When applying new RPM files to your system, it is often helpful to know which Red Hat version you're using. On the command line, you can retrieve just that number with:

```
awk '{print $5}' /etc/redhat-release
```

What's going on here? By default, *awk* splits each line read from standard input on whitespace, as is explained below. In effect, it's like you are looking at one row of a spreadsheet. In spreadsheets, columns are usually named with letters. In *awk*, columns are numbered and you only can see one row (that is, one line of input) at a time. The Red Hat version number is in the fifth column. Similar to the way shells use $ for variable interpolation, the values of columns in *awk* are retrieved using variables that start with $ and are followed by an integer.

As you can guess, this is a fairly simple demostration of *awk*, which includes support for regular expressions, branching and looping, and subroutines. For a more complete reference on using *awk*, see *Effective awk Programming* or *sed & awk Pocket Reference*, both published by O'Reilly.

Since there are many flavor of *awk*, such as *nawk* and *gawk* (20.11), this article tries to provide a usable reference for the most common elements of the language. Dialect differences, when they occur, are noted. With the exception of array subscripts, values in [brackets] are optional; don't type the [or].

Command-Line Syntax

awk can be invoked in one of two ways:

```
awk [options] 'script' [var=value] [file(s)]
awk [options] -f scriptfile [var=value] [file(s)]
```

You can specify a *script* directly on the command line, or you can store a script in a *scriptfile* and specify it with *–f*. In most versions, the *–f* option can be used multiple times. The variable *var* can be assigned a value on the command line. The value can be a literal, a shell variable (*$name*), or a command substitution (`'cmd'`), but the value is available only after a line of input is read (i.e., after the BEGIN statement). *awk* operates on one or more *file(s)*. If none are specified (or if - is specified), *awk* reads from the standard input (43.1).

The other recognized *options* are:

-Fc

   Set the field separator to character *c*. This is the same as setting the system variable *FS*. *nawk* allows *c* to be a regular expression (32.4). Each record (by default, one input line) is divided into fields by whitespace (blanks or tabs) or by some other user-definable field separator. Fields are referred to by the variables $1, $2,...$n. $0 refers to the entire record. For example, to print the first three (colon-separated) fields on separate lines:

```
% awk -F: '{print $1; print $2; print $3}' /etc/passwd
```

-v *var=value*

Assign a *value* to variable *var*. This allows assignment before the script begins execution. (Available in *nawk* only.)

Patterns and Procedures

awk scripts consist of patterns and procedures:

pattern {procedure}

Both are optional. If *pattern* is missing, {*procedure*} is applied to all records. If {*procedure*} is missing, the matched record is written to the standard output.

Patterns

pattern can be any of the following:

```
/regular expression/
relational expression
pattern-matching expression
BEGIN
END
```

- Expressions can be composed of quoted strings, numbers, operators, functions, defined variables, and any of the predefined variables described later in the section "awk System Variables."

- Regular expressions use the extended set of metacharacters, as described in article 32.15. In addition, ^ and $ (32.5) can be used to refer to the beginning and end of a field, respectively, rather than the beginning and end of a record (line).

- Relational expressions use the relational operators listed in the section "Operators," later in this article. Comparisons can be either string or numeric. For example, $2 > $1 selects records for which the second field is greater than the first.

- Pattern-matching expressions use the operators ~ (match) and !~ (don't match). See the section "Operators" later in this article.

- The BEGIN pattern lets you specify procedures that will take place *before* the first input record is processed. (Generally, you set global variables here.)

- The END pattern lets you specify procedures that will take place *after* the last input record is read.

Except for BEGIN and END, patterns can be combined with the Boolean operators || (OR), && (AND), and ! (NOT). A range of lines can also be specified using comma-separated patterns:

    pattern,pattern

Procedures

procedure can consist of one or more commands, functions, or variable assignments, separated by newlines or semicolons (;), and contained within curly braces ({}). Commands fall into four groups:

- Variable or array assignments
- Printing commands
- Built-in functions
- Control-flow commands

Simple pattern-procedure examples

- Print the first field of each line:

      { print $1 }

- Print all lines that contain pattern:

      /pattern/

- Print first field of lines that contain pattern:

      /pattern/{ print $1 }

- Print records containing more than two fields:

      NF > 2

- Interpret input records as a group of lines up to a blank line:

      BEGIN { FS = "\n"; RS = "" }
      { ...process records... }

- Print fields 2 and 3 in switched order, but only on lines whose first field matches the string URGENT:

      $1 ~ /URGENT/ { print $3, $2 }

- Count and print the number of pattern found:

      /pattern/ { ++x }
      END { print x }

- Add numbers in second column and print total:

      {total += $2 };
      END { print "column total is", total}

- Print lines that contain fewer than 20 characters:

      length($0) < 20

- Print each line that begins with Name: and that contains exactly seven fields:

      NF == 7 && /^Name:/

awk System Variables

nawk supports all *awk* variables. *gawk* supports both *nawk* and *awk*.

Version	Variable	Description
awk	*FILENAME*	Current filename
	FS	Field separator (default is whitespace)
	NF	Number of fields in current record
	NR	Number of the current record
	OFMT	Output format for numbers (default is %.6g)
	OFS	Output field separator (default is a blank)
	ORS	Output record separator (default is a newline)
	RS	Record separator (default is a newline)
	$0	Entire input record
	$n	*n*th field in current record; fields are separated by *FS*
nawk	*ARGC*	Number of arguments on command line
	ARGV	An array containing the command-line arguments
	ENVIRON	An associative array of environment variables
	FNR	Like *NR*, but relative to the current file
	RSTART	First position in the string matched by *match* function
	RLENGTH	Length of the string matched by *match* function
	SUBSEP	Separator character for array subscripts (default is \034)

Operators

This table lists the operators, in increasing precedence, that are available in *awk*.

Symbol	Meaning
= += -= *= /= %= ^=	Assignment (^= only in *nawk* and *gawk*)
?:	C conditional expression (*nawk* and *gawk*)
||	Logical OR
&&	Logical AND
~ !~	Match regular expression and negation
< <= > >= != ==	Relational operators
(blank)	Concatenation
+ -	Addition, subtraction
* / %	Multiplication, division, and modulus
+ - !	Unary plus and minus, and logical negation
^	Exponentiation (*nawk* and *gawk*)
++ --	Increment and decrement, either prefix or postfix
$	Field reference

Variables and Array Assignments

Variables can be assigned a value with an equal sign (=). For example:

```
FS = ","
```

Expressions using the operators +, -, *, /, and % (modulus) can be assigned to variables.

Arrays can be created with the *split* function (see below), or they can simply be named in an assignment statement. Array elements can be subscripted with numbers (*array*[1],...,*array*[*n*]) or with names (as associative arrays). For example, to count the number of occurrences of a pattern, you could use the following script:

```
/pattern/ { array["pattern"]++ }
END { print array["pattern"] }
```

Group Listing of awk Commands

awk commands may be classified as follows:

Arithmetic functions	String functions	Control flow statements	Input/Output processing
atan2[a]	gsub[a]	break	close[a]
cos[a]	index	continue	delete[a]
exp	length	do/while[a]	getline[a]
int	match[a]	exit	next
log	split	for	print
rand[a]	sub[a]	if	printf
sin[a]	substr	return[a]	sprintf
sqrt	tolower[a]	while	system[a]
srand[a]	toupper[a]		

[a] Not in original awk.

Alphabetical Summary of Commands

The following alphabetical list of statements and functions includes all that are available in *awk*, *nawk*, or *gawk*. Unless otherwise mentioned, the statement or function is found in all versions. New statements and functions introduced with *nawk* are also found in *gawk*.

atan2

    atan2(*y*,*x*)

    Returns the arctangent of *y*/*x* in radians. (*nawk*)

break

Exit from a *while*, *for*, or *do* loop.

close

close(*filename-expr*)
close(*command-expr*)

In some implementations of *awk*, you can have only ten files open simultaneously and one pipe; modern versions allow more than one pipe open. Therefore, *nawk* provides a *close* statement that allows you to close a file or a pipe. *close* takes as an argument the same expression that opened the pipe or file. (*nawk*)

continue

Begin next iteration of *while*, *for*, or *do* loop immediately.

cos

cos(*x*)

Return cosine of *x* (in radians). (*nawk*)

delete

delete *array*[*element*]

Delete *element* of *array*. (*nawk*)

do

do *body* while (*expr*)

Looping statement. Execute statements in *body*, then evaluate *expr*. If *expr* is true, execute *body* again. More than one *command* must be put inside braces ({}). (*nawk*)

exit

exit[*expr*]

Do not execute remaining instructions and do not read new input. END procedure, if any, will be executed. The *expr*, if any, becomes *awk*'s exit status (35.12).

exp

exp(*arg*)

Return the natural exponent of *arg*.

for

for ([*init-expr*]; [*test-expr*]; [*incr-expr*])   *command*

C-language-style looping construct. Typically, *init-expr* assigns the initial value of a counter variable. *test-expr* is a relational expression that is evaluated each time before executing the *command*. When *test-expr* is false, the loop is exited. *incr-expr* is used to increment the counter variable after each pass. A series of *commands* must be put within braces ({}). For example:

```
for (i = 1; i <= 10; i++)
    printf "Element %d is %s.\n", i, array[i]
```

for

```
for (item in array)    command
```

For each *item* in an associative *array*, do *command*. More than one *command* must be put inside braces ({}). Refer to each element of the array as *array*[*item*].

getline

```
getline [var][<file] or command | getline [var]
```

Read next line of input. Original *awk* does not support the syntax to open multiple input streams. The first form reads input from *file*, and the second form reads the standard output of a Unix *command*. Both forms read one line at a time, and each time the statement is executed, it gets the next line of input. The line of input is assigned to $0, and it is parsed into fields, setting *NF*, *NR*, and *FNR*. If *var* is specified, the result is assigned to *var* and the $0 is not changed. Thus, if the result is assigned to a variable, the current line does not change. *getline* is actually a function, and it returns 1 if it reads a record successfully, 0 if end-of-file is encountered, and –1 if for some reason it is otherwise unsuccessful. (*nawk*)

gsub

```
gsub(r,s[,t])
```

Globally substitute *s* for each match of the regular expression *r* in the string *t*. Return the number of substitutions. If *t* is not supplied, defaults to $0. (*nawk*)

if

```
if (condition) command [else command]
```

If *condition* is true, do *command(s)*, otherwise do *command(s)* in *else* clause (if any). *condition* can be an expression that uses any of the relational operators <, <=, ==, !=, >=, or >, as well as the pattern-matching operators ~ or !~ (e.g., if ($1 ~ /[Aa].*[Zz]/)). A series of *commands* must be put within braces ({}).

index

```
index(str,substr)
```

Return position of first substring *substr* in string *str* or 0 if not found.

int

```
int(arg)
```

Return integer value of *arg*.

length

```
length(arg)
```

Return the length of *arg*.

log

> log(*arg*)

> Return the natural logarithm of *arg*.

match

> match(s,r)

> Function that matches the pattern, specified by the regular expression *r*, in the string *s* and returns either the position in *s* where the match begins or 0 if no occurrences are found. Sets the values of *RSTART* and *RLENGTH*. (*nawk*)

next

> Read next input line and start new cycle through pattern/procedures statements.

print

> print [*args*] [*destination*]

> Print *args* on output, followed by a newline. *args* is usually one or more fields, but it may also be one or more of the predefined variables—or arbitrary expressions. If no *args* are given, prints $0 (the current input record). Literal strings must be quoted. Fields are printed in the order they are listed. If separated by commas (,) in the argument list, they are separated in the output by the *OFS* character. If separated by spaces, they are concatenated in the output. *destination* is a Unix redirection or pipe expression (e.g., > *file*) that redirects the default standard output.

printf

> printf *format* [, *expression(s)*] [*destination*]

> Formatted print statement. Fields or variables can be formatted according to instructions in the *format* argument. The number of *expressions* must correspond to the number specified in the format sections. *format* follows the conventions of the C-language *printf* statement. Here are a few of the most common formats:

> %s

>> A string.

> %d

>> A decimal number.

> %n.mf

>> A floating-point number, where *n* is the total number of digits and *m* is the number of digits after the decimal point.

> %[-]nc

>> *n* specifies minimum field length for format type *c*, while - left-justifies value in field; otherwise value is right-justified.

format can also contain embedded escape sequences: \n (newline) or \t (tab) are the most common. *destination* is a Unix redirection or pipe expression (e.g., > *file*) that redirects the default standard output.

For example, using the following script:

```
{printf "The sum on line %s is %d.\n", NR, $1+$2}
```

and the following input line:

```
5   5
```

produces this output, followed by a newline:

```
The sum on line 1 is 10.
```

rand

```
rand( )
```

Generate a random number between 0 and 1. This function returns the same series of numbers each time the script is executed, unless the random number generator is seeded using the *srand()* function. (*nawk*)

return

```
return [expr]
```

Used at end of user-defined functions to exit the function, returning value of expression *expr*, if any. (*nawk*)

sin

```
sin(x)
```

Return sine of *x* (in radians). (*nawk*)

split

```
split(string,array[,sep])
```

Split *string* into elements of *array* array[1],...,array[*n*]. *string* is split at each occurrence of separator *sep*. (In *nawk*, the separator may be a regular expression.) If *sep* is not specified, *FS* is used. The number of array elements created is returned.

sprintf

```
sprintf (format [, expression(s)])
```

Return the value of *expression(s)*, using the specified *format* (see *printf*). Data is formatted but not printed.

sqrt

```
sqrt(arg)
```

Return square root of *arg*.

srand

```
srand(expr)
```

Use *expr* to set a new seed for random number generator. Default is time of day. Returns the old seed. (*nawk*)

sub
```
sub(r,s[,t])
```
Substitute *s* for first match of the regular expression *r* in the string *t*. Return 1 if successful; 0 otherwise. If *t* is not supplied, defaults to $0. (*nawk*)

substr
```
substr(string,m[,n])
```
Return substring of *string*, beginning at character position *m* and consisting of the next *n* characters. If *n* is omitted, include all characters to the end of string.

system
```
system(command)
```
Function that executes the specified Unix *command* and returns its status (35.12). The status of the command that is executed typically indicates its success (0) or failure (nonzero). The output of the command is not available for processing within the *nawk* script. Use *command* | getline to read the output of the command into the script. (*nawk*)

tolower
```
tolower(str)
```
Translate all uppercase characters in *str* to lowercase and return the new string. (*nawk*)

toupper
```
toupper(str)
```
Translate all lowercase characters in *str* to uppercase and return the new string. (*nawk*)

while
```
while (condition) command
```
Do *command* while *condition* is true (see *if* for a description of allowable conditions). A series of commands must be put within braces ({}).

—DG

20.11 Versions of awk

awk was introduced as part of Unix's seventh edition and has been part of the standard distribution ever since.

In 1985, the authors of *awk* extended the language, adding many useful features. Unfortunately, this new version remained inside AT&T for several years. It became a regular part of AT&T's System V as of Release 3.1. It can be found under the name of *nawk* (for "new *awk*"); the older version still exists under its original name.

gawk
Unfortunately, *nawk* is not available on all systems. The good news is that the Free Software Foundation GNU project's version of *awk*, called *gawk*, implements all the features of the new *awk*.

In general, you can assume that what is true for *nawk* is true for *gawk*, unless *gawk* is explicitly called out. Scripts written for *nawk* are 100 percent compatible with *gawk*. If you want to use one of the *nawk* scripts and don't have *nawk* on your system, simply change the script to invoke *gawk* instead.

There are a few areas where *gawk* has introduced *gawk*-specific features; however, recent versions of *nawk* support many of these features, suggesting that the remaining differences are really very minor. This shouldn't matter in any case, since we do supply *gawk* on the disc.

This book doesn't cover any of the *awk*s in detail. The recent *awk*s, especially, have quite a few features in common—so documentation for any one of them should help you learn the others.

In this book, we show scripts for *awk* as well as scripts that work only on *nawk* and *gawk*. But we barely scratch the surface of all the *awk*s' features. The completely revised second edition of O'Reilly & Associates' *sed & awk* has detailed information on all of them.* There's also lots of documentation on the CD-ROM. Take your pick.

—*JP and DD, TOR*

---

* And thanks to Arnold Robbins, coauthor of the second edition, for his help with this section and other *awk* material in this book.

21

You Can't Quite Call This Editing

21.1 And Why Not?

There are many specialized forms of editing that happen frequently enough that they sometimes want to be saved into a script. Examples of this kind of thing include:

- *fmt* (21.2) and related scripts (21.3) for reformatting jagged lines into neat paragraphs
- *recomment* (21.4), a script for reformatting comment blocks within programs and scripts
- *behead* (21.5), a script for removing the headers from mail and news messages
- *center* (21.8), a script for centering lines of text in a file

In addition, there are a number of programs that provide some useful ways of modifying files but that you don't normally think of as editors:

- *split* (21.9) and *csplit* (21.10) let you split a big file into smaller pieces.
- *tr* (21.11) lets you substitute one character for another—including non-printing characters that you specify by their octal values.
- *dd* (21.6, 21.13) lets you perform various data conversions on a file.
- *cut* (21.14) lets you cut columns or fields out of a file, and *paste* (21.18) lets you put them back, perhaps in a different order.

This chapter covers all that and more.

—*TOR*

21.2 Neatening Text with fmt

One of the problems with *fold* is that it breaks text at an arbitrary column position—even if that position happens to be in the middle of a word. It's a pretty primitive utility, designed to keep long lines from printing off the edge of a line printer page, and not much more.

fmt can do a better job because it thinks in terms of language constructs like paragraphs. *fmt* wraps lines continuously, rather than just folding the long ones. It assumes that paragraphs end at blank lines.

You can use *fmt* for things like neatening lines of a mail message or a file that you're editing with *vi* (17.28). (Emacs has its own built-in line-neatener.) It's also great for shell programming and almost any place you have lines that are too long or too short for your screen.

To make this discussion more concrete, let's imagine that you have the following paragraph:

```
     Most people take their  Emo Phillips  for granted.  They figure, and not
  without some truth, that he is a God-given right and any government that
  considers   itself a democracy would naturally provide
  its citizens with this
  sort of access.  But what too many of this  Gap-wearing,
  Real World-watching generation  fail to realize
  is that our American
  forefathers, under  the  tutelage of Zog, the wizened master sage from
  Zeta-Reticuli, had to fight  not only   the godless and    effete British
  for our system of  self-determined government, but also  avoid the  terrors
  of hynpo-death  from the dark and
  unclean Draco-Repitilians.
```

To prepare this text for printing, you'd like to have all the lines be about 60 characters wide and remove the extra space in the lines. Although you could format this text by hand, GNU *fmt* can do this for you with the following command line:

```
% fmt -tuw 60 my_file
```

The -t option, short for --tagged-paragraph mode, tells *fmt* to preserve the paragraph's initial indent but align the rest of the lines with the left margin of the second line. The -u option, short for --uniform-spacing, squashes all the inappropriate whitespace in the lines. The final option, -w, sets the width of the output in characters. Like most UNIX commands, *fmt* sends its output to *stdout*. For our test paragraph, *fmt* did this:

```
     Most people take their Emo Phillips for granted.
  They figure, and not without some truth, that he is a
  God-given right and any government that considers itself a
  democracy would naturally provide its citizens with this
  sort of access.  But what too many of this Gap-wearing,
```

```
Real World-watching generation fail to realize is that
our American forefathers, under the tutelage of Zog,
the wizened master sage from Zeta-Reticuli, had to fight
not only the godless and effete British for our system of
self-determined government, but also avoid the terrors of
hynpo-death from the dark and unclean Draco-Repitilians.
```

There is one subtlety to *fmt* to be aware of: *fmt* expects sentences to end with a period, question mark, or exclamation point followed by two spaces. If your document isn't marked up according to this convention, *fmt* can't differentiate between sentences and abbreviations. This is a common "gotcha" that appears frequently on Usenet.

 On at least one version of Unix, *fmt* is a disk initializer (disk formatter) command. Don't run *that* command accidentally! Check your online manual page and see the *fmt* equivalents that follow.

There are a few different versions of *fmt*, some fancier than others. In general, the program assumes the following:

- Paragraphs have blank lines between them.

- If a line is indented, the indentation should be preserved.

- The output lines should be about 70 characters wide. Some have a command-line option to let you set this. For example, fmt -132 (or on some versions, fmt -l 132) would reformat your file to have lines with no more than 132 characters on each.

- It reads files or standard input. Lines will be written to standard output.

fmt

The GNU *fmt* is on the CD-ROM. There are also a couple of free versions available. Many versions of *fmt* have options for other structured data. The *–p* option (21.4) reformats program source code. (If your *fmt* doesn't have *–p*, the *recomment* (21.4) script uses standard *fmt* with *sed* to do the same thing.) The *–s* option breaks long lines at whitespace but doesn't join short lines to form longer ones.

Alternatively, you can make your own (21.3) simple (and a little slower) version with *sed* and *nroff*. If you want to get fancy (and use some *nroff* and/or *tbl* coding), this will let you do automatically formatted text tables, bulleted lists, and much more.

—*JP, TOR, and JJ*

21.3 Alternatives to fmt

fmt (21.2) is hard to do without once you've learned about it. Unfortunately, it's not available in some versions of Unix. You can get the GNU version from the CD-ROM, but it's also relatively easy to emulate with *sed* (37.4) and *nroff*. Using those two utilities also lets you take advantage of the more sophisticated formatting and flexibility that *sed* and *nroff* macros can give you. (If you're doing anything really fancy, like tables with *tbl*,* you might need *col* or *colcrt* to clean up *nroff*'s output.)

Here's the script:

fmt.sh

```
#!/bin/sh
sed '1i\
.ll 72\
.na\
.hy 0\
.pl 1' $* | nroff
```

The reason this is so complicated is that, by default, *nroff* makes some assumptions you need to change. For example, it assumes an 11-inch page (66 lines) and will add blank lines to a short file (or the end of a long file). The quick-and-dirty workaround to this is to manually put the *nroff* request *.pl 1* (page length 1 line) at the top of the text you want to reformat. *nroff* also tends to justify lines; you want to turn this off with the .na request. You also want to turn off hyphenation (.hy 0), and you may want to set the line length to 72 instead of *nroff*'s default 65, if only for consistency with the real *fmt* program. All these *nroff* requests get inserted before the first line of input by the *sed* 1i command.

A fancier script would take a *–nn* line-length option and turn it into a *.ll* request for *nroff*, etc.

Another solution to consider is Damian Conway's Text::Autoformat Perl module. It has some very sophisticated heurestics to try to figure out how text should be formatted, including bulleted and numbered lists. In its simplest form, it can be used to read from *stdin* and write to *stdout*, just as a standard Unix utility would do. You can invoke this module from the command line like this:

```
% perl -MText::Autoformat -e 'autoformat' < your_file_here
```

By default, *autoformat* formats only one paragraph at a time. This behavior can be changed by altering the invocation slightly:

```
% perl -MText::Autoformat -e 'autoformat({all =>1})'
```

The manpage for this module even suggests a way into integrate this into *vi*:

```
map f !Gperl -MText::Autoformat -e'autoformat'
```

—TOR and JJ

---

* [The combination of *tbl*, *nroff*, and *col* can make ASCII tables in a few quick steps. The tables aren't sexy, but they can be quite complex. They can be emailed or printed anywhere and, because they're plain text, don't require sophisticated viewing software or equipment. *tbl* is a powerful way to describe tables without worrying about balancing columns or wrapping text in them. And if you want nicer-looking output, you can feed the same *tbl* file to *groff*. —JP]

21.4 Clean Up Program Comment Blocks

Lines in a program's comment block usually start with one or more special characters, like this:

```
# line 1 of the comment
# line 2 of the comment
# line 3 of the comment
   ...
```

It can be a hassle to add more text to one of the comment lines in a block, because the line can get too long, which requires you to fold that line onto the next line, which means you have to work around the leading comment character(s).

The *fmt* (21.2) program neatens lines of a text file. But the standard *fmt* won't help you "neaten" blocks of comments in a program: it mixes the comment characters from the starts of lines with the words. (If your *fmt* has the –p option, it handles this problem; there's an example below.) The *recomment* script is *fmt* for comment blocks. It's for people who write shell, *awk*, C, or almost any other kind of program with comment blocks several lines long.

The recomment Script

recomment

recomment reads the lines that you feed its standard input. It looks at the first line and figures out what characters you're using to comment the line (see the $cchars variable for a list—typically SPACEs, TABs, #, or *). *recomment* then strips those comment characters off each line, feeds the remaining block of text to the *fmt* utility, and uses *sed* (34.1) to add the comment characters again.

I usually use *recomment* from inside *vi*, with filter-through (17.18) commands like:

```
!}recomment    reformat to the next blank line
5!!recomment   reformat this line and the next 4
```

Normally, *recomment* lets *fmt* choose the width of the comment block (72 characters, typically). To get another width, you can do one of the following:

- Give the width on the command line, like this:

  ```
  recomment -50
  ```

- Set an environment variable named *CBLKWID*. Give the maximum width, in characters, for the comment text. For example, in the C shell, use:

  ```
  % setenv CBLKWID 50
  ```

recomment isn't perfect, but it's usually much better than nothing! Here's the part of the script that does the work. The first two commands get the comment character(s) and count their length. The next three commands strip the comment characters, clean up the remaining comment text, and add the same comment characters to the start of all reformatted lines:

```
                # Get comment characters used on first line; store in $comment:
-n 34.3         comment=`sed -n "1s/^\([$cchars]*\).*/\1/p" $temp`
                # Count number of characters in comment character string:
expr 36.22      cwidth=`expr "$comment" : '.*'`

                # Re-format the comment block.  If $widopt set, use it:
cut 21.14       cut -c`expr $cwidth + 1`- < $temp |    # Strip off comment leader
                fmt $widopt |                          # Re-format the text, and
                sed "s/^/$comment/"                    # put back comment characters
```

When the *expr* command in backquotes (28.14) is expanded, it makes a command like cut -c4-.

fmt –p

Some versions of *fmt* (like the one on the CD-ROM) have a –p option that does the same thing. Unlike the automatic system in *recomment*, you have to tell *fmt –p* what the prefix characters are—but then it will only reformat lines with that prefix character For example, here's the start of a C++ program. The prefix character is *:

```
% cat load.cc
/*
 * This file, load.cc, reads an input
 * data file.
 * Each input line is added to a new node
 * of type struct Node.
 */
    ...
% fmt -p '*' load.cc
/*
 * This file, load.cc, reads an input data file.  Each input line is
 * added to a new node of type struct Node.
 */
    ...
```

—JP

21.5 Remove Mail/News Headers with behead

When you're saving or resending a Usenet article or mail message, you might want to the remove header lines (*Subject:*, *Received:*, and so on). This little script will handle standard input, one or many files. It writes to standard output. Here are a few examples:

- With saved messages, at a shell prompt:

mail 1.21
```
% behead msg* | mail -s "Did you see these?" fredf
```

- To save an article from a pipe without a header, from a program (here, the old *readnews*) that can't cut off headers itself:

    What now? [ynq] **s- | behead > *filename***

Here's the script, adapted a little from the original by Arthur David Olson:

behead

```
#! /bin/sh
case $# in
0)  exec sed '1,/^$/d' ;;
*)  for i
    do sed '1,/^$/d' "$i"
    done
    ;;
esac
```

The script relies on the fact that news articles and mail messages use a blank line to separate the header from the body of the message. As a result, the script simply deletes the text from the beginning up to the first blank line.

—JP

21.6 Low-Level File Butchery with dd

Want to strip off some arbitrary number of characters from the front of a file?

dd

dd provides an unexpectedly easy answer. Let's say you wanted to delete the first 100 characters in a file. Here's the command that will do the trick (assuming of course that you give *dd* a filename with the *if=* option or data from a pipe):

    % **dd bs=100 skip=1**

Or you could try:

    % **dd bs=1 skip=100**

dd normally reads and writes data in 512-byte blocks; the input block size can be changed with the *ibs=* option, and the output block size with *obs=*. Use *bs=* to set both. *skip=* sets the number of blocks to skip at the start of the file.

Why would you want to do this? Article 21.9 gives an interesting example of reading text from standard input and writing it to a series of smaller files. Article 21.13 shows even more uses for *dd*.

—TOR

21.7 offset: Indent Text

Do you have a printer that starts each line too close to the left margin? You might want to indent text to make it look better on the screen or a printed page. Here's a Perl script that does that. It reads from files or standard input and writes to standard output. The default indentation is 5 spaces. For example, to send a copy of a file named *graph* to the *lp* printer, indented 12 spaces:

```
% offset -12 graph | lp
```

Here's the Perl script that does the job:

offset

```
#!/usr/local/bin/perl

if ($ARGV[0] =~ /-[0-9]+/) {
    ($indent = $ARGV[0]) =~ s/-//;
    shift @ARGV;
} else {
    $indent = 5;
}

while (<>) {
    print " " x $indent, $_;
}
```

If there's an indentation amount in the first command-line argument, the dash is stripped and the value stored, then that argument is shifted away. Then a loop steps through the remaining arguments, if any (otherwise standard input is read) and outputs their text preceded by spaces. The script uses the Perl operator "string" x *n*, which outputs the string (in this case, a single space) *n* times. The Perl $_ operator contains the current input line.

—*JP*

21.8 Centering Lines in a File

Here's an *awk* script, written by Greg Ubben, that centers text across an 80-character line. If your system understands #! (36.3), this script will be passed directly to *awk* without a shell. Otherwise, put this into a Bourne shell wrapper (35.19).

center

```
#!/usr/bin/awk -f
{
    printf "%" int(40+length($0)/2) "s\n", $0
}
```

For each input line, the script builds a *printf* command with a width specification just wide enough to center the line (which *awk* holds in $0). For instance, a line 60 characters wide would give a value of int(40+60/2), which is 70. That makes the following *printf* command:

```
printf %70s\n, $0
```

Because %s prints a string right-justified, that command gives a 10-character indentation (70 minus 60) on an 80-character line. The right end of the line is also 10 characters (80 minus 70) from the right edge of the screen.

In *vi*, you can use a filter-through (17.18) command to center lines while you're editing. Or just use *center* from the command line. For example:

```
% center afile > afile.centered
% sort party_list | center | lp
```

—*JP*

21.9 Splitting Files at Fixed Points: split

Most versions of Unix come with a program called *split* whose purpose is to split large files into smaller files for tasks such as editing them in an editor that cannot handle large files, or mailing them if they are so big that some mailers will refuse to deal with them. For example, let's say you have a really big text file that you want to mail to someone:

```
% ls -l bigfile
-r--r--r--  1 jik        139070 Oct 15 21:02 bigfile
```

Running *split* on that file will (by default, with most versions of *split*) break it up into pieces that are each no more than 1000 lines long:

```
% split bigfile
% ls -l
total 283
-r--r--r--  1 jik        139070 Oct 15 21:02 bigfile
-rw-rw-r--  1 jik         46444 Oct 15 21:04 xaa
-rw-rw-r--  1 jik         51619 Oct 15 21:04 xab
-rw-rw-r--  1 jik         41007 Oct 15 21:04 xac
```

wc 16.6
```
% wc -l x*
   1000 xaa
   1000 xab
    932 xac
   2932 total
```

Note the default naming scheme, which is to append "aa", "ab", "ac", etc., to the letter "x" for each subsequent filename. It is possible to modify the default behavior. For example, you can make *split* create files that are 1500 lines long instead of 1000:

```
% rm x??
% split -1500 bigfile
% ls -l
total 288
-r--r--r--  1 jik        139070 Oct 15 21:02 bigfile
-rw-rw-r--  1 jik         74016 Oct 15 21:06 xaa
-rw-rw-r--  1 jik         65054 Oct 15 21:06 xab
```

You can also get it to use a name prefix other than "x":

```
% rm x??
% split -1500 bigfile bigfile.split.
% ls -l
```

```
total 288
-r--r--r--  1 jik      139070 Oct 15 21:02 bigfile
-rw-rw-r--  1 jik       74016 Oct 15 21:07 bigfile.split.aa
-rw-rw-r--  1 jik       65054 Oct 15 21:07 bigfile.split.ab
```

Although the simple behavior described above tends to be relatively universal, there are differences in the functionality of *split* on different Unix systems. There are four basic variants of *split* as shipped with various implementations of Unix:

1. A *split* that understands only how to deal with splitting text files into chunks of *n* lines or less each.

2. A *split*, usually called *bsplit*, that understands only how to deal with splitting nontext files into *n*-character chunks.

3. A *split* that splits text files into *n*-line chunks, or nontext files into *n*-character chunks, and tries to figure out automatically whether it's working on a text file or a nontext file.

4. A *split* that does either text files or nontext files but needs to be told explicitly when it is working on a nontext file.

The only way to tell which version you've got is to read the manual page for it on your system, which will also tell you the exact syntax for using it.

The problem with the third variant is that although it tries to be smart and automatically do the right thing with both text and nontext files, it sometimes guesses wrong and splits a text file as a nontext file or vice versa, with completely unsatisfactory results. Therefore, if the variant on your system is (3), you probably want to get your hands on one of the many *split* clones out there that is closer to one of the other variants (see below).

Variants (1) and (2) listed above are OK as far as they go, but they aren't adequate if your environment provides only one of them rather than both. If you find yourself needing to split a nontext file when you have only a text *split*, or needing to split a text file when you have only *bsplit*, you need to get one of the clones that will perform the function you need.

split

Variant (4) is the most reliable and versatile of the four listed, and it is therefore what you should go with if you find it necessary to get a clone and install it on your system. There are several such clones in the various source archives, including the free BSD Unix version. GNU *split* is on the CD-ROM. Alternatively, if you have installed *perl* (41.1), it is quite easy to write a simple *split* clone in *perl*, and you don't have to worry about compiling a C program to do it; this is an especially significant advantage if you need to run your *split* on multiple architectures that would need separate binaries. The Perl code for a binary split program follows:

```
#!/usr/bin/perl -w --
# Split text or binary files; jjohn 2/2002
use strict;
use Getopt::Std;
```

```perl
my %opts;
getopts("?b:f:hp:ts:", \%opts);

if( $opts{'?'} || $opts{'h'} || !-e $opts{'f'}){
  print <<USAGE;
$0 - split files in smaller ones

USAGE:
    $0 -b 1500 -f big_file -p part.

OPTIONS:

    -?       print this screen
    -h       print this screen
    -b <INT> split file into given byte size parts
    -f <TXT> the file to be split
    -p <TXT> each new file to begin with given text
    -s <INT> split file into given number of parts
USAGE
    exit;
}

my $infile;
open($infile, $opts{'f'}) or die "No file given to split\n";
binmode($infile);
my $infile_size = (stat $opts{'f'})[7];

my $block_size = 1;
if( $block_size = $opts{'b'} ){
    # chunk file into blocks

}elsif( my $total_parts = $opts{'s'} ){
    # chunk file into N parts
    $block_size = int ( $infile_size / $total_parts) + 1;

}else{
    die "Please indicate how to split file with -b or -s\n";
}

my $outfile_base = $opts{'p'} || 'part.';
my $outfile_ext = "aa";

my $offset = 0;
while( $offset < $infile_size ){
    my $buf;
    $offset += read $infile, $buf, $block_size;
    write_file($outfile_base, $outfile_ext++, \$buf);
}

#--- subs ---#
sub write_file {
  my($fname, $ext, $buf) = @_;
```

```
            my $outfile;
            open($outfile, ">$fname$ext") or die "can't open $fname$ext\n";
            binmode($outfile);
            my $wrote = syswrite $outfile, $$buf;
            my $size  = length($$buf);
            warn "WARN: wrote $wrote bytes instead of $size to $fname$ext\n"
                unless $wrote == $size;
        }
```

Although it may seem somewhat complex at first glance, this small Perl script is cross-platform and has its own small help screen to describe its options. Briefly, it can split files into N-sized blocks (given the -b option) or, with -s, create N new segments of the original file. For a better introduction to Perl, see Chapter 42.

If you need to split a nontext file and don't feel like going to all of the trouble of finding a *split* clone to handle it, one standard Unix tool you can use to do the splitting is *dd* (21.6). For example, if *bigfile* above were a nontext file and you wanted to split it into 20,000-byte pieces, you could do something like this:

<table>
<tr><td></td><td>$ ls -l bigfile</td></tr>
<tr><td></td><td>-r--r--r-- 1 jik   139070 Oct 23 08:58 bigfile</td></tr>
<tr><td>for 35.21</td><td>$ for i in 1 2 3 4 5 6 7   #*</td></tr>
<tr><td>> 28.12</td><td>> do</td></tr>
<tr><td></td><td>>   dd of=x$i bs=20000 count=1 2>/dev/null   #†</td></tr>
<tr><td></td><td>> done < bigfile</td></tr>
<tr><td></td><td>$ ls -l</td></tr>
<tr><td></td><td>total 279</td></tr>
<tr><td></td><td>-r--r--r-- 1 jik   139070 Oct 23 08:58 bigfile</td></tr>
<tr><td></td><td>-rw-rw-r-- 1 jik   20000 Oct 23 09:00 x1</td></tr>
<tr><td></td><td>-rw-rw-r-- 1 jik   20000 Oct 23 09:00 x2</td></tr>
<tr><td></td><td>-rw-rw-r-- 1 jik   20000 Oct 23 09:00 x3</td></tr>
<tr><td></td><td>-rw-rw-r-- 1 jik   20000 Oct 23 09:00 x4</td></tr>
<tr><td></td><td>-rw-rw-r-- 1 jik   20000 Oct 23 09:00 x5</td></tr>
<tr><td></td><td>-rw-rw-r-- 1 jik   20000 Oct 23 09:00 x6</td></tr>
<tr><td></td><td>-rw-rw-r-- 1 jik   19070 Oct 23 09:00 x7</td></tr>
</table>

—JIK and JJ

21.10 Splitting Files by Context: csplit

csplit

Like *split* (21.9), *csplit* lets you break a file into smaller pieces, but *csplit* (context split) also allows the file to be broken into different-sized pieces, according to context. With *csplit*, you give the locations (line numbers or search patterns) at which to break each section. *csplit* comes with System V, but there are also free versions available.

---

* To figure out how many numbers to count up to, divide the total size of the file by the block size you want and add one if there's a remainder. The *jot* program can help here.

† The output file size I want is denoted by the *bs* or "block size" parameter to *dd*. The 2>/dev/null (36.16, 43.12) gets rid of *dd*'s diagnostic output, which isn't useful here and takes up space.

Let's look at search patterns first. Suppose you have an outline consisting of three main sections that start on lines with the Roman numerals I., II., and III.. You could create a separate file for each section by typing:

```
% csplit outline /I./ /II./ /III./
28          number of characters in each file
415              .
372              .
554              .
% ls
outline
xx00        outline title, etc.
xx01        Section I
xx02        Section II
xx03        Section III
```

This command creates four new files (*outline* remains intact). *csplit* displays the character counts for each file. Note that the first file (*xx00*) contains any text up to *but not including* the first pattern, and *xx01* contains the first section, as you'd expect. This is why the naming scheme begins with *00*. (If *outline* had begun immediately with a I., *xx01* would still contain Section I, but in this case *xx00* would be empty.)

If you don't want to save the text that occurs before a specified pattern, use a percent sign as the pattern delimiter:

```
% csplit outline %I.% /II./ /III./
415
372
554
% ls
outline
xx00        Section I
xx01        Section II
xx02        Section III
```

The preliminary text file has been suppressed, and the created files now begin where the actual outline starts (the file numbering is off, however).

Let's make some further refinements. We'll use the *-s* option to suppress the display of the character counts, and we'll use the *-f* option to specify a file prefix other than the conventional *xx*:

```
% csplit -s -f part. outline /I./ /II./ /III./
% ls
outline
part.00
part.01
part.02
part.03
```

There's still a slight problem, though. In search patterns, a period is a metacharacter (32.21) that matches any single character, so the pattern /I./ may inadvertently match words like *Introduction*. We need to escape the period with a backslash; however, the backslash has meaning both to the pattern and to the shell, so in fact, we need either to use a double backslash or to surround the pattern in quotes (27.12). A subtlety, yes, but one that can drive you crazy if you don't remember it. Our command line becomes:

```
% csplit -s -f part. outline "/I\./" /II./ /III./
```

You can also break a file at repeated occurrences of the same pattern. Let's say you have a file that describes 50 ways to cook a chicken, and you want each method stored in a separate file. The sections begin with headings *WAY #1*, *WAY #2*, and so on. To divide the file, use *csplit*'s repeat argument:

```
% csplit -s -f cook. fifty_ways /^WAY/ "{49}"
```

This command splits the file at the first occurrence of *WAY*, and the number in braces tells *csplit* to repeat the split 49 more times. Note that a caret (^) (32.5) is used to match the beginning of the line and the C shell requires quotes around the braces (28.4). The command has created 50 files:

```
% ls cook.*
cook.00
cook.01
  ...
cook.48
cook.49
```

Quite often, when you want to split a file repeatedly, you don't know or don't care how many files will be created; you just want to make sure that the necessary number of splits takes place. In this case, it makes sense to specify a repeat count that is slightly higher than what you need (the maximum is 99). Unfortunately, if you tell *csplit* to create more files than it's able to, this produces an "out of range" error. Furthermore, when *csplit* encounters an error, it exits by removing any files it created along the way. (A bug, if you ask me.) This is where the *–k* option comes in. Specify *–k* to *keep* the files around, even when the "out of range" message occurs.

csplit allows you to break a file at some number of lines above or below a given search pattern. For example, to break a file at the line that is five lines below the one containing *Sincerely*, you could type:

```
% csplit -s -f letter. all_letters /Sincerely/+5
```

This situation might arise if you have a series of business letters strung together in one file. Each letter begins differently, but each one begins five lines after the previous letter's *Sincerely* line. Here's another example, adapted from AT&T's *Unix User's Reference Manual*:

```
% csplit -s -k -f routine. prog.c '%main(%' '/^}/+1' '{99}'
```

The idea is that the file *prog.c* contains a group of C routines, and we want to place each one in a separate file (*routine.00*, *routine.01*, etc.). The first pattern uses % because we want to discard anything before *main*. The next argument says, "Look for a closing brace at the beginning of a line (the conventional end of a routine) and split on the following line (the assumed beginning of the next routine)." Repeat this split up to 99 times, using *–k* to preserve the created files.*

The *csplit* command takes line-number arguments in addition to patterns. You can say:

```
% csplit stuff 50 373 955
```

to create files split at some arbitrary line numbers. In that example, the new file *xx00* will have lines 1-49 (49 lines total), *xx01* will have lines 50-372 (323 lines total), *xx02* will have lines 373-954 (582 lines total), and *xx03* will hold the rest of *stuff*.

csplit works like *split* if you repeat the argument. The command:

```
% csplit top_ten_list 10 "{18}"
```

breaks the list into 19 segments of 10 lines each.†

—DG

21.11 Hacking on Characters with tr

The *tr* command is a character translation filter, reading standard input (43.1) and either deleting specific characters or substituting one character for another.

The most common use of *tr* is to change each character in one string to the corresponding character in a second string. (A string of consecutive ASCII characters can be represented as a hyphen-separated range.)

For example, the command:

‹ 43.1   `$ tr 'A-Z' 'a-z' ‹ file`   *Berkeley version*

will convert all uppercase characters in *file* to the equivalent lowercase characters. The result is printed on standard output.

In fact, a frequent trick I use `tr` for is to convert filenames from all uppercase to all lowercase. This comes up when you're dealing with files from MS-DOS or VMS that you are copying on to a Unix filesystem. To change all the files in the current directory to uppercase, try this from a Bash or Bourne shell prompt:

```
$ for i in `ls`; do mv $i `echo $i | tr [A-Z] [a-z]`; done
```

---

* In this case, the repeat can actually occur only 98 times, since we've already specified two arguments and the maximum number is 100.

† Not really. The first file contains only nine lines (1-9); the rest contain 10. In this case, you're better off saying `split -10 top_ten_list`.

Of course, you need to be careful that there are no files that have the same name regardless of case. The GNU *mv* can be passed the -i flag that will make the program prompt you before overwriting an existing file. If you want to uppercase filenames, simply flip the arguments to *tr*. You can even apply this to an entire branch of a file system by sticking this in a *find* command. First, create a small shell script that can downcase a file and call it downcase:

```
#!/bin/sh
mv $1 `echo $1 | tr [A-Z] [a-z]`
```

Now you can really do some damage with *find*:

```
$ find /directory/to/be/affected -exec 'downcase' '{}' ';'
```

Obviously, running this programming on random directories as root is not recomended, unless you're looking to test your backup system.

tr

In the System V version of *tr*, square brackets must surround any range of characters. That is, you have to say [a-z] instead of simply a-z. And of course, because square brackets are meaningful to the shell, you must protect them from interpretation by putting the string in quotes. The GNU *tr*, on the web site, is basically the System V version.

If you aren't sure which version you have, here's a test. Both *tr* examples below will convert the lowercase letters a through z to an uppercase A, but that's not what we're testing here. The Berkeley version also converts the input [ ] to A characters because [ ] aren't treated as range operators:

```
% echo '[]' | tr '[a-z]' A
AA                              Berkeley version
% echo '[]' | tr '[a-z]' A
[]                              System V version
```

There's one place you don't have to worry about the difference between the two versions: when you're converting one range to another range, and both ranges have the same number of characters. For example, this command works in both versions:

```
$ tr '[A-Z]' '[a-z]' < file       both versions
```

The Berkeley *tr* will convert a [from the first string into the same character [in the second string, and the same for the] characters. The System V version uses the [ ] characters as range operators. In both versions, you get what you want: the range A-Z is converted to the corresponding range a-z. Again, this trick works only when both ranges have the same number of characters.

The System V version also has a nice feature: the syntax [a*n], where *n* is some digit, means that the string should consist of *n* repetitions of character "a." If *n* isn't specified or is 0, it is taken to be some indefinitely large number. This is useful if you don't know how many characters might be included in the first string.

As described in article 17.18, this translation (and the reverse) can be useful from within *vi* for translating a string. You can also delete specific characters. The *–d* option deletes from the input each occurrence of one or more characters specified in a string (special characters should be placed within quotation marks to protect them from the shell). For instance, the following command passes to standard output the contents of *file* with all punctuation deleted (and is a great exercise in shell quoting (27.12)):

```
$ tr -d ",.\!?;:\"\'`" < file
```

The *–s* (*squeeze*) option of *tr* removes multiple consecutive occurrences of the same character in the second argument. For example, the command:

```
$ tr -s " " " " < file
```

will print on standard output a copy of *file* in which multiple spaces in sequence have been replaced with a single space.

We've also found *tr* useful when converting documents created on other systems for use under Unix. For example, as described in article 1.8, *tr* can be used to change the carriage returns at the end of each line in a Macintosh text file into the newline Unix expects. *tr* allows you to specify characters as octal values by preceding the value with a backslash, so the following command does the trick:

```
$ tr '\015' '\012' < file.mac > file.unix
```

The command:

```
$ tr -d '\015' < pc.file
```

will remove the carriage return from the carriage return/newline pair that a PC file uses as a line terminator. (This command is also handy for removing the excess carriage returns from a file created with *script* (37.7).)

—TOR, JP, and JJ

21.12 Encoding "Binary" Files into ASCII

Email transport systems were originally designed to transmit characters with a seven-bit encoding—like ASCII. This meant they could send messages with plain English text but not "binary" text, such as program files or graphics (or non-English text!), that used all of an eight-bit byte. Usenet (1.21), the newsgroup system, was transmitted like email and had its same seven-bit limitations. The solution—which is still used today—is to *encode* eight-bit text into characters that use only the seven low bits.

The first popular solution on Unix-type systems was *uuencoding*. That method is mostly obsolete now (though you'll still find it used sometimes); it's been replaced by MIME encoding. The next two sections cover both of those—though we recommend avoiding *uuencode* like the plague.

uuencoding

The *uuencode* utility encodes eight-bit data into a seven-bit representation for sending via email or on Usenet. The recipient can use *uudecode* to restore the original data. Unfortunately, there are several different and incompatible versions of these two utilities. Also, uuencoded data doesn't travel well through all mail gateways—partly because uuencoding is sensitive to changes in whitespace (space and TAB) characters, and some gateways munge (change or corrupt) whitespace. So if you're encoding text for transmission, use MIME instead of *uuencode* whenever you can.

To create an ASCII version of a binary file, use the *uuencode* utility. For instance, a compressed file (15.6) is definitely eight-bit; it needs encoding.

A uuencoded file (there's an example later in this article) starts with a begin line that gives the file's name; this name comes from the first argument you give the *uuencode* utility as it encodes a file. To make *uuencode* read a file directly, give the filename as the second argument. *uuencode* writes the encoded file to its standard output. For example, to encode the file *emacs.tar.gz* from your *~/tarfiles* directory and store it in a file named *emacs.tar.gz.uu*:

```
% uuencode emacs.tar.gz ~/tarfiles/emacs.tar.gz > emacs.tar.gz.uu
```

You can then insert *emacs.tar.gz.uu* into a mail message and send it to someone. Of course, the ASCII-only encoding takes more space than the original binary format. The encoded file will be about one-third larger.*

If you'd rather, you can combine the steps above into one pipeline. Given only one command-line argument (the name of the file for the begin line), *uuencode* will read its standard input. Instead of creating the *~/tarfiles/emacs.tar.gz*, making a second uuencoded file, then mailing that file, you can give *tar* the "filename" so it writes to its standard output. That feeds the archive down the pipe:†

mail **1.21**
```
% tar cf - emacs | gzip | uuencode emacs.tar.gz | \
    mail -s "uuencoded emacs file" whoever@wherever.com
```

What happens when you receive a uuencoded, compressed *tar* file? The same thing, in reverse. You'll get a mail message that looks something like this:

```
From: you@whichever.ie
To: whoever@wherever.com
Subject: uuencoded emacs file
```

---

* If so, why bother *gzipping*? Why not forget about both *gzip* and *uuencode*? Well, you can't. Remember that *tar* files are binary files to start with, even if every file in the archive is an ASCII text file. You'd need to *uuencode* a file before mailing it, anyway, so you'd still pay the 33 percent size penalty that *uuencode* incurs. Using *gzip* minimizes the damage.

† With GNU *tar*, you can use tar czf - emacs | uuencode .... That's not the point of this example, though. We're just showing how to uuencode some arbitrary data.

```
begin 644 emacs.tar.gz
M+DQO"D%L;"!O9B!T:&5S92!P<F]B;;;&5M<R!C86X@8F4@<V]]L=F5D(&)Y(")L
M:6YK<RPG RPE RY H HoHo! No idea
```

```
begin 644 emacs.tar.gz
M+DQO"D%L;"!O9B!T:&5S92!P<F]B;;;&5M<R!C86X@8F4@<V]]L=F5D(&)Y(")L
M:6YK<RPG RPE RY H HoHo
```

```
begin 644 emacs.tar.gz
M+DQO"D%L;"!O9B!T:&5S92!P<F]B;;;&5M<R!C86X@8F4@<V]]L=F5D(&)Y(")L
M:6YK<RPG
```

So you save the message in a file, complete with headers. Let's say you call this file *mailstuff*. How do you get the original files back? Use the following sequence of commands:

```
% uudecode mailstuff
% gunzip emacs.tar.gz
% tar xf emacs.tar
```

The *uudecode* command searches through the file, skipping From:, etc., until it sees its special begin line; it decodes the rest of the file (until the corresponding end line) and creates the file *emacs.tar.gz*. Then *gunzip* recreates your original *tar* file, and *tar xf* extracts the individual files from the archive.

Again, though, you'll be better off using MIME encoding whenever you can.

MIME Encoding

When MIME (Multipurpose Internet Mail Extensions) was designed in the early 1990s, one main goal was robust email communications. That meant coming up with a mail encoding scheme that would work on all platforms and get through all mail transmission paths.

Some text is "mostly ASCII": for instance, it's in a language like German or French that uses many ASCII characters plus some eight-bit characters (characters with a octal value greater than 177). The MIME standard allows that text to be minimally encoded in a way that it can be read fairly well without decoding: the *quoted-printable* encoding. Other text is full binary—either not designed for humans to read, or so far from ASCII that an ASCII representation would be pointless. In that case, you'll want to use the *base64* encoding.

mimencode
mailto

Most modern email programs automatically MIME-encode files. Unfortunately, some aren't too smart about it. The Metamail utilities come with a utility called *mimencode* (also named *mmencode*) for encoding and decoding MIME formats. Another Metamail utility, *mailto*, encodes and sends MIME messages directly—but let's use *mimencode*, partly because of the extra control it gives you.

By default, *mimencode* reads text from standard input, uses a base64 encoding, and writes the encoded text to standard output. If you add the *–q* option, *mimencode* uses quoted-printable encoding instead.

Unlike uuencoded messages, which contain the filename in the message body, MIME-encoded messages need information in the message header (the lines "To:", "From:", etc.). The *mail* utility (except an older version) doesn't let you make a message header. So let's do it directly: create a mail header with cat > (12.2), create a mail body with *mimencode*, and send it using a common system mail transfer agent, *sendmail*. (You could automate this with a script, of course, but we're just demonstrating.) The MIME standard header formats are still evolving; we'll use a simple set of header fields that should do the job. Here's the setup. Let's do it first in three steps, using temporary files:

```
$ cat > header
From: jpeek@oreilly.com
To: jpeek@jpeek.com
Subject: base64-encoded smallfile
MIME-Version: 1.0
Content-Type: application/octet-stream; name="smallfile.tar.gz"
Content-Transfer-Encoding: base64

CTRL-d
$ tar cf - smallfile | gzip | mimencode > body
$ cat header body | /usr/lib/sendmail -t
```

The cat > command lets me create the *header* file by typing it in at the terminal; I could have used a text editor instead. One important note: *the header must end with a blank line*. The second command creates the *body* file. The third command uses *cat* to output the header, then the body; the message we've built is piped to *sendmail*, whose *–t* option tells it to read the addresses from the message header. You should get a message something like this:

```
Date: Wed, 22 Nov 2000 11:46:53 -0700
Message-Id: <200011221846.LAA18155@oreilly.com>
From: jpeek@oreilly.com
To: jpeek@jpeek.com
Subject: base64-encoded smallfile
MIME-Version: 1.0
Content-Type: application/octet-stream; name="smallfile.tar.gz"
Content-Transfer-Encoding: base64

H4sIACj6GzoAA+1Z21YbRxb1c39FWcvBMIMu3AOIBWxDzMTYDuBgrxU/lKSSVHF3V6erGiGv
rPn22edU3wRIecrMPLgfEGpVV53LPvtcOktcW6au3dnZ2mrZcfTkb7g6G5307vb2k06ns7G3
06HPzt7uDn/Sra1N/L+32dnd29ve3tjD+s3NnaOnovN3CHP/yqyTqRBPfk+U+rpknUnlf0Oc
    ...
```

Your mail client may be able to extract that file directly. You also can use *mimencode –u*. But *mimencode* doesn't know about mail headers, so you should strip off the header first. The *behead* (21.5) script can do that. For instance, if you've saved the mail message in a file *msg*:

```
$ behead msg | mimencode -u > smallfile.tar.gz
```

Extract (39.2) *smallfile.tar.gz* and compare it to your original *smallfile* (maybe with *cmp*). They should be identical.

If you're planning to do this often, it's important to understand how to form an email header and body properly. For more information, see relevant Internet RFCs (standards documents) and O'Reilly's *Programming Internet Email* by David Wood.

—JP and ML

21.13 Text Conversion with dd

Besides the other uses of *dd* (21.6) we've covered, you also can use this versatile utility to convert:

- fixed length to variable-length records (*conv=unblock*), and the reverse (*conv=block*)
- uppercase to lowercase (*conv=lcase*), and the reverse (*conv=ucase*)
- the byte order of every pair of bytes (*conv=swab*)
- ASCII to EBCDIC and the reverse (*conv=ebcdic, conv=ibm*). If you're converting old IBM tapes, you'll need to know the tape's blocking factor. And if the tape has multiple files on it, you'll have to use the tape device name that allows "no rewind on close" (38.5) to read past the first file.

The cbs= option must be used to specify a conversion buffer size when using *block* and *unblock* and when converting between ASCII and EBCDIC. The specified number of characters are put into the conversion buffer. For *ascii* and *unblock* conversion, trailing blanks are trimmed and a newline is added to each buffer before it is output. For *ebcdic*, *ibm*, and *block*, the input is padded with blanks up to the specified conversion buffer size.

—TOR

21.14 Cutting Columns or Fields

A nifty command called *cut* lets you select a list of columns or fields from one or more files.

You must specify either the *−c* option to cut by column or *−f* to cut by fields. (Fields are separated by tabs unless you specify a different field separator with *−d*. Use quotes (27.12) if you want a space or other special character as the delimiter.)

In some versions of *cut*, the column(s) or field(s) to cut must follow the option immediately, without any space. Use a comma between separate values and a hyphen to specify a range (e.g., 1-10,15 or 20,23 or 50-).

The order of the columns and fields is ignored; the characters in each line are always output from first to last, in the order they're read from the input. For example, cut -f1,2,4 produces exactly the same output as cut -f4,2,1. If this isn't what you want, try *perl* (41.1) or *awk* (20.10), which let you output fields in any order.

cut is incredibly handy. Here are some examples:

- Find out who is logged in, but list only login names:

  who 2.8
  ```
  % who | cut -d" " -f1
  ```

- Extract usernames and real names from */etc/passwd* (22.3):

  ```
  % cut -d: -f1,5 /etc/passwd
  ```

- Cut characters in the fourth column of *file*, and paste them back as the first column in the same file:

  ```
  % cut -c4 file | paste - file
  ```

Article 21.18 covers the *cut* counterpart, *paste*.

As was mentioned, you can use *awk* or *perl* to extract columns of text. Given the above task to extract the fifth and first fields fields of /etc/passwd, you can use *awk*:

```
% awk -F: '{print $5, "=>", $1}' /etc/passwd
```

An often forgotten command-line option for *perl* is -a, which puts *perl* in *awk* compatibility mode. In other words, you can get the same field-splitting behavior right from the command line:

```
% perl -F: -lane 'print $F[4], "=>", "$F[0]"' /etc/passwd
```

In the line above, *perl* is told about the field separator in the same way *awk* is, with the -F flag. The next four options are fairly common. The -l option removes newlines from input and adds a newline to all print statements. This is a real space saver for "one-line wonders," like the one above. The -a flag tells *perl* to split each line on the indicated field separator. If no field separator is indicated, the line is split on a space character. Each field is stored in the global array @F. Remember that the first index in a Perl array is zero. The -n option encloses the Perl code indicated by the -e to be wrapped in a loop that reads one line at a time from *stdin*. This little Perl snippet is useful if you need to do some additional processing with the contents of each field.

—*TOR, DG, and JJ*

21.15 Making Text in Columns with pr

The *pr* command (45.6) is famous for printing a file neatly on a page—with margins at top and bottom, filename, date, and page numbers. It can also print text in columns: one file per column or many columns for each file.

The *–t* option takes away the heading and margins at the top and bottom of each page. That's useful when "pasting" data into columns with no interruptions.

One File per Column: –m

The *–m* option reads all files on the command line simultaneously and prints each in its own column, like this:

```
% pr -m -t file1 file2 file3
The lines          The lines          The lines
of file1           of file2           of file3
are here           are here           are here
   ...                ...                ...
```

pr may use TAB characters between columns. If that would be bad, you can pipe *pr*'s output through *expand*. Many versions of *pr* have a -s*X* option that sets the column separator to the single character *X*.

By default, *pr –m* doesn't put filenames in the heading. If you want that, use the *–h* option to make your own heading. Or maybe you'd like to make a more descriptive heading. Here's an example using process substitution to compare a directory with its RCS (39.5) subdirectory:

```
% pr -m -h "working directory compared to RCS directory" <(ls) <(ls RCS)

2000-11-22 23:57   working directory compared to RCS directory   Page    1

0001.sgm                           0001.sgm,v
0002.sgm                           0002.sgm,v
0007.sgm                           0007.sgm,v
0008.sgm                           0008.sgm,v
            ...
```

(The heading comes from the GNU version of *pr*. Later examples in this article use a different version with a different heading format.)

One File, Several Columns: –number

An option that's a number will print a file in that number of columns. For instance, the *–3* option prints a file in three columns. The file is read, line by line, until the first column is full (by default, that takes 56 lines). Next, the second column is filled. Then, the third column is filled. If there's more of the file, the first column of page 2 is filled—and the cycle repeats:

```
% pr -3 file1

Nov  1 19:44 1992  file1  Page 1

Line 1 here        Line 57 here       Line 115 here
Line 2 here        Line 58 here       Line 116 here
Line 3 here        Line 59 here       Line 117 here
   ...                ...                ...
```

The columns aren't balanced—if the file will fit into one column, the other columns aren't used. You can change that by adjusting *–l*, the page length option; see the section below.

Order Lines Across Columns: –l

Do you want to arrange your data across the columns, so that the first three lines print across the top of each column, the next three lines are the second in each column, and so on, like this?

```
% pr -l1 -t -3 file1
Line 1 here       Line 2 here       Line 3 here
Line 4 here       Line 5 here       Line 6 here
Line 7 here       Line 8 here       Line 9 here
   ...               ...               ...
```

Use the *–l1* (page length 1 line) and *–t* (no title) options. Each "page" will be filled by three lines (or however many columns you set). You have to use *–t*; otherwise, *pr* will silently ignore any page lengths that don't leave room for the header and footer. That's just what you want if you want data in columns with no headings.

If you want headings too, pipe the output of *pr* through another *pr*:

```
% pr -l1 -t -3 file1 | pr -h file1

Nov  1 19:48 1992  file1  Page 1

Line 1 here       Line 2 here       Line 3 here
Line 4 here       Line 5 here       Line 6 here
Line 7 here       Line 8 here       Line 9 here
   ...               ...               ...
```

The -h file1 puts the filename into the heading.

Also see *paste* (21.18). Of course, programming languages like *awk* (20.10) and *perl* (41.1) can also make text into columns.

—*JP*

21.16 Make Columns Automatically with column

column

Another column-making program, besides *cols* and *pr* (21.15), is the creatively named utility *column*. It tries to determine the terminal width, which you can override with the *–c* option (-c 132, for example, gives 132 columns: handy for printing on wide line-printer paper.) The *–x* option fills columns before rows—similar to *pr* with its -n option and *cols –d*.

What makes *column* different from the others is its *–t* option. This reads input data that's already in columns and rebalances the columns into a table with variable-width columns. Say what? This is easiest to see with an example, and the *column*(1) manual page has a good one.

If you'd like to add column headings to *ls –l* output, it can be a pain to try to make headings that each take the same number of characters as the data below them. For instance, the first field on each line, the permissions, takes 10 characters, but if you want to use the heading "PERM", which takes only 4 characters, you need to balance it by adding 6 spaces after. Using column -t, you can balance these automatically. Here's an example. The first command is plain *ls –l*. In the second and third examples, I use *sed 1d* **(34.1)** to delete the total *n* line from *ls*, and subshells **(24.4)** to make both commands use the same standard output; this is important only in the third command, where I pipe the combined *stdout* to *column* for balancing:

```
$ ls -lo
total 1644
-r--r--r--    1 jpeek      1559177 Sep 19  1999 ORA_tifs.tgz
-rw-rw-r--    1 jpeek         4106 Oct 21  1999 UPT_Russian.jpg
-rw-rw-r--    1 jpeek       101944 Nov 19 09:30 london_dusk-livesights.xwd.gz
dr-xr-xr-x    2 jpeek         4096 Dec 12  1999 me
```

; 28.16
> 28.12

```
$ (echo "PERM        LINKS OWNER         SIZE MON DY TM/YR NAME"; \
> ls -lo | sed 1d)
PERM        LINKS OWNER         SIZE MON DY TM/YR NAME
-r--r--r--    1 jpeek      1559177 Sep 19  1999 ORA_tifs.tgz
-rw-rw-r--    1 jpeek         4106 Oct 21  1999 UPT_Russian.jpg
-rw-rw-r--    1 jpeek       101944 Nov 19 09:30 london_dusk-livesights.xwd.gz
dr-xr-xr-x    2 jpeek         4096 Dec 12  1999 me

$ (echo PERM LINKS OWNER SIZE MONTH DAY HH:MM/YEAR NAME; \
> ls -lo | sed 1d) | column -t
PERM        LINKS  OWNER  SIZE     MONTH  DAY  HH:MM/YEAR  NAME
-r--r--r--  1      jpeek  1559177  Sep    19   1999        ORA_tifs.tgz
-rw-rw-r--  1      jpeek  4106     Oct    21   1999        UPT_Russian.jpg
-rw-rw-r--  1      jpeek  101944   Nov    19   09:30       london_dusk-
livesights.xwd.gz
dr-xr-xr-x  2      jpeek  4096     Dec    12   1999        me
```

My feeble attempt in the second example took a lot of trial-and-error to get the right spacing, and I still had to cram DY over the tiny sixth column and TM/YR over the seventh. In the third example, *column* automatically adjusted the column width to compensate for the HH:MM/YEAR heading. Unfortunately, the long filename *london_dusk-livesights.xwd.gz* ran off the right edge (past column 80, my window width)—but there was nothing *column* could do in this case because the combined header+columns were just too wide.

—*JP*

21.17 Straightening Jagged Columns

As we were writing this book, I decided to make a list of all the articles and the numbers of lines and characters in each, then combine that with the description, a status code, and the article's title. After a few minutes with *wc –l –c* (16.6), *cut* (21.14), *sort* (22.1), and *join* (21.19), I had a file that looked like this:

```
% cat messfile
2850 2095 51441 ~BB A sed tutorial
3120 868 21259 +BB mail - lots of basics
6480 732 31034 + How to find sources - JIK's periodic posting
    ...900 lines...
5630 14 453 +JP Running Commands on Directory Stacks
1600 12 420 !JP With find, Don't Forget -print
0495 9 399 + Make 'xargs -i' use more than one filename
```

Yuck. It was tough to read: the columns needed to be straightened. The *column* (21.16) command could do it automatically, but I wanted more control over the alignment of each column. A little *awk* (20.10) script turned the mess into this:

```
% cat cleanfile
2850 2095 51441 ~BB  A sed tutorial
3120  868 21259 +BB  mail - lots of basics
6480  732 31034 +    How to find sources - JIK's periodic posting
    ...900 lines...
5630   14   453 +JP  Running Commands on Directory Stacks
1600   12   420 !JP  With find, Don't Forget -print
0495    9   399 +    Make 'xargs -i' use more than one filename
```

Here's the simple script I used and the command I typed to run it:

```
% cat neatcols
{
printf "%4s %4s %6s %-4s %s\n", \
    $1, $2, $3, $4, substr($0, index($0,$5))
}
% awk -f neatcols messfile > cleanfile
```

You can adapt that script for whatever kinds of columns you need to clean up. In case you don't know *awk*, here's a quick summary:

- The first line of the *printf*, between double quotes ("), specifies the field widths and alignments. For example, the first column should be right-aligned in 4 characters (%4s). The fourth column should be 4 characters wide left-adjusted (%-4s). The fifth column is big enough to just fit (%s). I used string (%s) instead of decimal (%d) so *awk* wouldn't strip off the leading zeros in the columns.

- The second line arranges the input data fields onto the output line. Here, input and output are in the same order, but I could have reordered them. The first four columns get the first four fields ($1, $2, $3, $4). The fifth column is a catch-all; it gets everything else. substr($0, index($0,$5)) means "find the fifth input column; print it and everything after it."

—*JP*

21.18 Pasting Things in Columns

cut+paste

Do you ever wish you could paste two (or even three) files side by side? You can, if you have the *paste* program (or the public-domain implementation on the disc).

For example, to create a three-column *file* from files *x*, *y*, and *z*:

```
$ paste x y z > file
```

To make *paste* read standard input, use the – option, and repeat – for every column you want. For example, to make an old *ls* (which lists files in a single column) list files in four columns:

```
$ ls | paste - - - -
```

The "standard input" option is also handy when used with *cut* (21.14). You can cut data from one position on a line and paste it back on another.

The separate data streams being merged are separated by default with a tab, but you can change this with the *–d* option. Unlike the *–d* option to *cut*, you need not specify a single character; instead, you can specify a list of characters, which will be used in a circular fashion.

The characters in the list can be any regular character or the following escape sequences:

\n   newline

\t   tab

\\   backslash

\0   empty string

Use quoting (27.12), if necessary, to protect characters from the shell.

There's also a *–s* option that lets you merge subsequent lines from one file. For example, to merge each pair of lines onto a single line:

```
$ paste -s -d"\t\n" list
```

Let's finish with one nice place to use process substitution, if your shell has it. You can use *cut* to grab certain columns from certain files, then use process substitution to make "files" that *paste* will read. Output those "files" into columns in any order you want. For example, to paste column 1 from *file1* in the first output column, and column 3 from *file2* in the second output column:

```
paste <(cut -f1 file1) <(cut -f3 file2)
```

If none of the shells on your system have process substitution, you can always use a bunch of temporary files, one file per column.

—*TOR, DG, and JP*

21.19 Joining Lines with join

If you've worked with databases, you'll probably know what to do with the Unix *join* command; see your online manual page. If you don't have a database (as far as you know!), you still probably have a use for *join*: combining or "joining" two column-format files. *join* searches certain columns in the files; when it finds columns that match one another, it "glues the lines together" at that column. This is easiest to show with an example.

I needed to summarize the information in thousands of email messages under the MH mail system. MH made that easy: it has one command (*scan*) that gave me almost all the information I wanted about each message and also let me specify the format I needed. But I also had to use *wc –l* (16.6) to count the number of lines in each message. I ended up with two files, one with *scan* output and the other with *wc* output. One field in both lines was the message number; I used *sort* (22.1) to sort the files on that field. I used awk '{print $1 "," $2}' to massage *wc* output into comma-separated fields. Then I used *join* to "glue" the two lines together on the message-number field. (Next I fed the file to a PC running dBASE, but that's another story.)

Here's the file that I told *scan* to output. The columns (message number, email address, comment, name, and date sent) are separated with commas (,):

```
0001,andrewe@isc.uci.edu,,Andy Ernbaum,19901219
0002,bc3170x@cornell.bitnet,,Zoe Doan,19910104
0003,zcode!postman@uunet.uu.net,,Head Honcho,19910105
   ...
```

Here's the file from *wc* and *awk* with the message number and number of lines:

```
0001,11
0002,5
0003,187
   ...
```

The following *join* command then joined the two files at their first columns (-t, tells *join* that the fields are comma-separated):

```
% join -t, scanfile wcfile
```

The output file looked like this:

```
0001,andrewe@isc.uci.edu,,Andy Ernbaum,19901219,11
0002,bc3170x@cornell.bitnet,,Zoe Doan,19910104,5
0003,zcode!postman@uunet.uu.net,,Head Honcho,19910105,187
   ...
```

join

join can do a lot more than this simple example shows. See your online manual page. The GNU version of *join* is on the CD-ROM.

—*JP*

21.20 What Is (or Isn't) Unique?

uniq

uniq reads a file and compares adjacent lines (which means you'll usually want to sort the file first to be sure identical lines appear next to each other). Here's what *uniq* can do as it watches the input lines stream by:

- With the *–u* option, the output gets only the lines that occur just once (and weren't repeated).

- The *–d* option does the opposite: the output gets a *single* copy of each line that was repeated (no matter how many times it was repeated).

  (The GNU version also has a *–D* option. It's like *–d* except that *all* duplicate lines are output.)

- The default output (with no options) is the union of *–u* and *–d*: only the first occurrence of a line is written to the output file; any adjacent copies of a line (second, third, etc.) are ignored.

- The output with *–c* is like the default, but each line is preceded by a count of how many times it occurred.

Be warned:

```
% uniq file1 file2
```

will *not* print the unique lines from both *file1* and *file2* to standard output. It will *replace* the contents of *file2* with the unique lines from *file1*!

Three more options control how comparisons are done:

- *-n* ignores the first *n* fields of a line and all whitespace before each. A field is defined as a string of nonwhitespace characters (separated from its neighbors by whitespace).

- *+n* ignores the first *n* characters. Fields are skipped before characters.

- *-w n* in the GNU version compares no more than *n* characters in each line.

- GNU *uniq* also has *–i* to make comparisons case-insensitive. (Upper- and lowercase letters compare equal.)

uniq is often used as a filter. See also *comm* (11.8), *sort* (22.1), and especially *sort –u* (22.6).

So what can you do with all of this?

To send only one copy of each line from *list* (which is typically sorted) to output file *list.new*:

```
uniq list list.new
```

To show which names appear more than once:

```
sort names | uniq -d
```

To show which lines appear exactly three times, search the output of *uniq –c* for lines that start with spaces before the digit *3* and have a tab after. (This is the way GNU *uniq –c* makes its output lines, at least.) In the example below, the space is marked by ⌴; the TAB is marked by *tab*:

grep **13.1**

```
sort names | uniq -c | grep "^⌴*3tab"
```

The lines don't have to be sorted; they simply have to be adjacent. For example, if you have a log file where the last few fields are repeated, you can have *uniq* "watch" those fields and tell you how many times they were repeated. Here we'll skip the first four fields and get a count of how many times the rest of each line was repeated:

```
$ cat log
Nov 21 17:20:19 powerd: down 2 volts
Nov 21 17:20:27 powerd: down 2 volts
Nov 21 17:21:15 powerd: down 2 volts
Nov 21 17:22:48 powerd: down 2 volts
Nov 21 18:18:02 powerd: up 3 volts
Nov 21 19:55:03 powerd: down 2 volts
Nov 21 19:58:41 powerd: down 2 volts
$ uniq -4 -c log
      4 Nov 21 17:20:19 powerd: down 2 volts
      1 Nov 21 18:18:02 powerd: up 3 volts
      2 Nov 21 19:55:03 powerd: down 2 volts
```

—*JP and DG*

21.21 Rotating Text

Every now and then you come across something and say, "Gee, that might come in handy someday, but I have no idea for what." This might happen to you when you're browsing at a flea market or garage sale; if you're like us, it might happen when you're browsing through public domain software.

rot

Which brings us to the *rot* program. *rot* basically just rotates text columns and rows. For example, the first column below shows an input file. The other three columns show the same file fed through *rot* once, twice, and three times:

$ cat file	$ rot file	$ rot file	rot	$ rot file	rot	rot
abcde	54321	5	e
1	a	4	d
2	b	3	c
3	c	2	b
4	d	1	a
5	e	edcba	12345

Now let's compare combinations of *rot* and *tail –r* (**42.1**):

$ cat file	$ rot file	$ rot file	tail -r	$ tail -r file	rot
abcde	54321	e	12345
1	a	d	a
2	b	c	b
3	c	b	c
4	d	a	d
5	e	54321	e

rot rotates the text 90 degrees. *tail –r* turns the text "upside down" (last line in becomes the first line out, and so forth).

rot can also rotate the output of *banner* to print down a page instead of across. By now, we hope you have an idea of what *rot* can do!

—*JP and LM*

22

Sorting

22.1 Putting Things in Order

Sorting a file under Unix is easy, right? Of course it is, if all you want to do is sort a list of single words, or sort lines starting with the first character in the line. But if you want to do more than that, there's a lot more to the *sort* command than typing sort *filename*:

- Article 22.2 describes how to select individual fields from a line for *sort* to operate on.
- Article 22.3 describes how to change the field delimiter from whitespace to some other character.
- Article 22.4 describes the kinds of problems that you can encounter if fields *are* delimited by whitespace.
- Article 22.5 clarifies the distinctions between alphabetic and numeric sorting.
- Article 22.6 gives miscellaneous hints about useful *sort* options.

But learning the mechanics of *sort* isn't the end of the story. Like most of the other things you'll find in the Unix toolbox, *sort* is even more powerful when it's used with other programs. For example, you can:

- Sort paragraphs or other multiline entries.
- Sort lines by how long they are (article 22.7).
- Sort a list of names by last name, whether or not there's a middle name as well (article 22.8).

—*TOR*

22.2 Sort Fields: How sort Sorts

Unless you tell it otherwise, *sort* divides each line into fields at whitespace (blanks or tabs), and sorts the lines by field, from left to right.

That is, it sorts on the basis of field 0 (leftmost), but when the leftmost fields are the same, it sorts on the basis of field 1, and so on. This is hard to put into words, but it's really just common sense. Suppose your office inventory manager created a file like this:

```
supplies     pencils  148
furniture    chairs   40
kitchen      knives   22
kitchen      forks    20
supplies     pens     236
furniture    couches  10
furniture    tables   7
supplies     paper    29
```

You'd want all the supplies sorted into categories, and within each category, you'd want them sorted alphabetically:

```
% sort supplies
furniture    chairs   40
furniture    couches  10
furniture    tables   7
kitchen      forks    20
kitchen      knives   22
supplies     paper    29
supplies     pencils  148
supplies     pens     236
```

Of course, you don't always want to sort from left to right. The command-line option +*n* tells *sort* to start sorting on field *n*; −*n* tells *sort* to stop sorting on field *n*. Remember (again) that *sort* counts fields from left to right, starting with 0.* Here's an example. We want to sort a list of telephone numbers of authors, presidents, and blues singers:

```
Robert M Johnson     344-0909
Lyndon B Johnson     933-1423
Samuel H Johnson     754-2542
Michael K Loukides   112-2535
Jerry O Peek         267-2345
Timothy F O'Reilly   443-2434
```

According to standard "telephone book rules," we want these names sorted by last name, first name, and middle initial. We don't want the phone number to play a part in the sorting. So we want to start sorting on field 2, stop sorting on

---

* I harp on this because I always get confused and have to look it up in the manual page.

field 3, continue sorting on field 0, sort on field 1, and (just to make sure) stop sorting on field 2 (the last name). We can code this as follows:

```
% sort +2 -3 +0 -2 phonelist
Lyndon B Johnson    933-1423
Robert M Johnson    344-0909
Samuel H Johnson    754-2542
Michael K Loukides  112-2535
Timothy F O'Reilly  443-2434
Jerry O Peek        267-2345
```

A few notes:

- We need the *-3* option to prevent *sort* from sorting on the telephone number after sorting on the last name. Without *-3*, the "Robert Johnson" entry would appear before "Lyndon Johnson" because it has a lower phone number.

- We don't need to state *+1* explicitly. Unless you give an explicit "stop" field, *+1* is implied after *+0*.

- If two names are completely identical, we probably don't care what happens next. However, just to be sure that something unexpected doesn't take place, we end the option list with *-2*, which says, "After sorting on the middle initial, don't do any further sorting."

There are a couple of variations that are worth mentioning. You may never need them unless you're really serious about sorting data files, but it's good to keep them in the back of your mind. First, you can add any "collation" operations (discard blanks, numeric sort, etc.) to the end of a field specifier to describe how you want that field sorted. Using our previous example, let's say that if two names *are* identical, you want them sorted in numeric phone number order. The following command does the trick:

```
% sort +2 -3 +0 -2 +3n phonelist
```

The *+3n* option says "do a numeric sort on the fourth field." If you're worried about initial blanks (perhaps some of the phone numbers have area codes), use *+3nb*.

Second, you can specify individual columns within any field for sorting, using the notation *+n.c*, where *n* is a field number, and *c* is a character position within the field. Likewise, the notation *-n.c* says "stop sorting at the character before character *c*." If you're counting characters, be sure to use the *-b* (ignore whitespace) option—otherwise, it will be very difficult to figure out what character you're counting.

—ML

22.3 Changing the sort Field Delimiter

Article 22.2 explained how *sort* separates a line of input into two or more fields using whitespace (spaces or tabs) as field delimiters. The *–t* option lets you change the field delimiter to some other character.

For example, if you wanted to sort the login names on your system by the login shell they use, you could issue a command like this:

/etc..wd **1.7**

```
% sort -t: +6 /etc/passwd
root:SndEKOs9H7YLm:0:1:Operator:/:/bin/bash
sys:*:2:2::/:/bin/bash
jim:LjKwcUt816kZK:2391:1004:Jim O'Callahan:/u/jim:/bin/bash
   ...
bart:2DPD8rCOKBbUu:2665:1004:Bart Buus:/u/bart:/bin/tcsh
tap:xY7oeuJ8WxyGO:2943:1004:Tap Bronman:/u/tap:/bin/tcsh
```

The option *–t:* tells *sort* to use a colon as a field separator—so, in this example, field 0 is the login name, field 1 is the encoded password, field 2 is the user ID number, field 3 is the group ID number, and so on. By this numbering, the login shell is in the sixth field.

Remember that *sort* numbers fields starting with zero—this will save you lots of grief. Two consecutive colons indicate a "null" field that still must be counted.

—ML and TOR

22.4 Confusion with Whitespace Field Delimiters

One would hope that a simple task like sorting would be relatively unambiguous. Unfortunately, it isn't. The behavior of *sort* can be very puzzling. I'll try to straighten out some of the confusion—at the same time, I'll be leaving myself open to abuse by the real *sort* experts. I hope you appreciate this! Seriously, though: if you know of any other wrinkles to the story, please let us know and we'll add them in the next edition.

The trouble with *sort* is figuring out where one field ends and another begins. It's simplest if you can specify an explicit field delimiter (22.3). This makes it easy to tell where fields end and begin. But by default, *sort* uses whitespace characters (tabs and spaces) to separate fields, and the rules for interpreting whitespace field delimiters are unfortunately complicated. As I see them, they are:

- The first whitespace character you encounter is a "field delimiter"; it marks the end of the old field and the beginning of the next field.

- Any whitespace character following a field delimiter is *part of* the new field. That is, if you have two or more whitespace characters in a row, the first one is used as a field delimiter and isn't sorted. The remainder *are* sorted, as part of the next field.

- Every field has at least one nonwhitespace character, unless you're at the end of the line. (That is, null fields only occur when you've reached the end of a line.)

- All whitespace is not equal. Sorting is done according to the ASCII collating sequence. Therefore, TABs are sorted before spaces.

Here is a silly but instructive example that demonstrates most of the hard cases. We'll sort the file *sortme*, which is:

```
        apple   Fruit shipment
20      beta    beta test sites
5               Something or other
```

All is not as it seems—*cat –t –v* (12.5, 12.4) shows that the file really looks like this:

```
^Iapple^IFruit shipment
20^Ibeta^Ibeta test sites
5^I^ISomething or other
```

^I indicates a tab character. Before showing you what *sort* does with this file, let's break it into fields, being very careful to apply the rules above. In the table, we use quotes to show exactly where each field begins and ends:

	Field 0	Field 1	Field 2	Field 3
Line 1	"^Iapple"	"Fruit"	"shipment"	null (no more data)
Line 2	"20"	"beta"	"beta"	"test"
Line 3	" 5"	"^Isomething"	"or"	"other"

OK, now let's try some *sort* commands; I've added annotations on the right, showing what character the "sort" was based on. First, we'll sort on field zero—that is, the first field in each line:

```
% sort sortme                    ...sort on field zero
        apple   Fruit shipments     field 0, first character: TAB
5               Something or other   field 0, first character: SPACE
20      beta    beta test sites      field 0, first character: 2
```

As I noted earlier, a TAB precedes a space in the collating sequence. Everything is as expected. Now let's try another, this time sorting on field 1 (the second field):

```
+% sort +1 sortme                ...sort on field 1
5               Something or other   field 1, first character: TAB
        apple   Fruit shipments      field 1, first character: F
20      beta    beta test sites      field 1, first character: b
```

Again, the initial TAB causes "something or other" to appear first. "Fruit shipments" preceded "beta" because in the ASCII table, uppercase letters precede lowercase letters. Now, let's sort on the next field:

```
+% sort +2 sortme              ...sort on field 2
   20      beta   beta test sites      field 2, first character: b
    5             Something or other   field 2, first character: o
           apple  Fruit shipments      field 2, first character: s
```

No surprises here. And finally, sort on field 3 (the "fourth" field):

```
+% sort +3 sortme              ...sort on field 3
           apple  Fruit shipments      field 3, NULL
    5             Something or other   field 3, first character: o
   20      beta   beta test sites      field 3, first character: t
```

The only surprise here is that the NULL field gets sorted first. That's really no surprise, though: NULL has the ASCII value zero, so we should expect it to come first.

OK, this was a silly example. But it was a difficult one; a casual understanding of what sort "ought to do" won't explain any of these cases, which leads to another point. If someone tells you to sort some terrible mess of a data file, you could be heading for a nightmare. But often, you're not just sorting; you're also *designing* the data file you want to sort. If you get to design the format for the input data, a little bit of care will save you lots of headaches. If you have a choice, *never* allow TABs in the file. And be careful of leading spaces; a word with an extra space before it will be sorted *before* other words. Therefore, use an explicit delimiter between fields (like a colon), or use the *–b* option (and an explicit sort field), which tells *sort* to ignore initial whitespace.

—ML

22.5 Alphabetic and Numeric Sorting

sort performs two fundamentally different kinds of sorting operations: alphabetic sorts and numeric sorts. An alphabetic sort is performed according to the traditional "dictionary order," using the ASCII collating sequence. Uppercase letters come before lowercase letters (unless you specify the *–f* option, which "folds" uppercase and lowercase together), with numerals and punctuation interspersed. The *–l* (lowercase L) option sorts by the current locale instead of the default US/ASCII order.

This is all fairly trivial and common sense. However, it's worth belaboring the difference, because it's a frequent source of bugs in shell scripts. Say you sort the numbers 1 through 12. A numeric sort gives you these numbers "in order," just like you'd expect. An alphabetic sort gives you:

```
1
11
12
2
...
```

Of course, this is how you'd sort the numbers if you applied dictionary rules to the list. Numeric sorts can handle decimal numbers (for example, numbers like 123.44565778); they can't handle floating-point numbers (for example, 1.2344565778E+02). The GNU *sort* does provide the -g flag for sorting numbers in scientific notation. Unfortunately, it is significantly slower than plain old decimal sorting.

What happens if you include alphabetic characters in a numeric sort? Although the results are predictable, I would prefer to say that they're "undefined." Including alphabetic characters in a numeric sort is a mistake, and there's no guarantee that different versions of *sort* will handle them the same way. As far as I know, there is no provision for sorting hexadecimal numbers.

One final note: your version of numeric sort may treat initial blanks as significant, sorting numbers with additional spaces before them ahead of numbers without the additional spaces. This is an incredibly stupid misfeature. There is a workaround: use the –b (ignore leading blanks) and always specify a sort field.* That is, sort -nb +0 will do what you expect; sort -n won't.

—ML

22.6 Miscellaneous sort Hints

Here is a grab bag of useful, if not exactly interesting, *sort* features. The utility will actually do quite a bit, if you let it.

Dealing with Repeated Lines

sort –u sorts the file and eliminates duplicate lines. It's more powerful than *uniq* (21.20) because:

- It sorts the file for you; *uniq* assumes that the file is already sorted and won't do you any good if it isn't.

- It is much more flexible. *sort –u* considers lines "unique" if the sort fields (22.2) you've selected match. So the lines don't even have to be (strictly speaking) unique; differences outside of the sort fields are ignored.

---

* Stupid misfeature number 2: –b doesn't work unless you specify a sort field explicitly, with a +n option.

In return, there are a few things that *uniq* does that *sort* won't do—such as print only those lines that aren't repeated, or count the number of times each line is repeated. But on the whole, I find *sort –u* more useful.

Here's one idea for using *sort –u*. When I was writing a manual, I often needed to make tables of error messages. The easiest way to do this was to *grep* the source code for *printf* statements, write some Emacs (19.1) macros to eliminate junk that I didn't care about, use *sort –u* to put the messages in order and get rid of duplicates, and write some more Emacs macros to format the error messages into a table. All I had to do then was write the descriptions.

Ignoring Blanks

One important option (that I've mentioned a number of times) is *–b*; this tells *sort* to ignore extra whitespace at the beginning of each field. This is absolutely essential; otherwise, your sorts will have rather strange results. In my opinion, *–b* should be the default. But they didn't ask me.

Another thing to remember about *–b*: it works only if you explicitly specify which fields you want to sort. By itself, *sort –b* is the same as *sort*: whitespace characters are counted. I call this a bug, don't you?

Case-Insensitive Sorts

If you don't care about the difference between uppercase and lowercase letters, invoke *sort* with the *–f* (case-fold) option. This folds lowercase letters into uppercase. In other words, it treats all letters as uppercase.

Dictionary Order

The *–d* option tells *sort* to ignore all characters except for letters, digits, and whitespace. In particular, *sort –d* ignores punctuation.

Month Order

The *–M* option tells *sort* to treat the first three nonblank characters of a field as a three-letter month abbreviation and to sort accordingly. That is, JAN comes before FEB, which comes before MAR. This option isn't available on all versions of Unix.

Reverse Sort

The *–r* option tells *sort* to "reverse" the order of the sort; i.e., Z comes before A, 9 comes before 1, and so on. You'll find that this option is really useful. For example, imagine you have a program running in the background that records the number of free blocks in the filesystem at midnight each night. Your log file might look like this:

```
Jan 1 2001:  108 free blocks
Jan 2 2001:  308 free blocks
Jan 3 2001: 1232 free blocks
Jan 4 2001:   76 free blocks
...
```

The script below finds the smallest and largest number of free blocks in your log file:

head **12.12**

```
#!/bin/sh
echo "Minimum free blocks"
sort -t: +1nb  logfile | head -1

echo "Maximum free blocks"
sort -t: +1nbr logfile | head -1
```

It's not profound, but it's an example of what you can do.

—*ML*

22.7 lensort: Sort Lines by Length

A nice little script to sort lines from shortest to longest can be handy when you're writing and want to find your big words:

deroff **16.9**
uniq **21.20**

```
% deroff -w report | uniq -d | lensort
a
an
   ...
deoxyribonucleic
```

Once I used it to sort a list of pathnames:

find **9.1**

```
% find adir -type f -print | lensort
adir/.x
adir/.temp
   ...
adir/subdir/part1/somefile
adir/subdir/part1/a_test_case
```

The script uses *awk* (20.10) to print each line's length, followed by the original line. Next, *sort* sorts the lengths numerically (22.5). Then *sed* (34.1) strips off the lengths and the spaces and prints the lines:

lensort

```
#! /bin/sh
awk 'BEGIN { FS=RS }
{ print length, $0 }' $* |
# Sort the lines numerically
sort +0n -1 |
# Remove the length and the space and print each line
sed 's/^[0-9][0-9]* //'
```

(Some *awks* require a semicolon after the first curly bracket—that is,
{ FS=RS };.)

Of course, you can also tackle this problem with Perl:

```
$ perl -lne '$l{$_}=length;END{for(sort{$l{$a}<=>$l{$b}}keys %l){print}}' \
            filename
```

This one-line wonder has the side effect of eliminating duplicate lines. If this
seems a bit terse, that's because it's meant to be "write-only," that is, it is a bit of
shell magic that you'd use to accomplish a short-term task. If you foresee needing this same procedure in the future, it's better to capture the magic in script.
Scripts also tend to be easier to understand, debug, and expand. The following
script does the same thing as the one-liner but a bit more clearly:

```
#!/usr/bin/perl

my %lines;
while(my $curr_line = <STDIN>){
  chomp $curr_line;
  $lines{$curr_line} = length $curr_line;
}

for my $line (sort{ $lines{$a} <=> $lines{$b} } keys %lines){
  print $line, "\n";
}
```

This script reads in a line from standard input, removes the newline character
and creates an associative array that maps whole line to its length in characters.
After processing the whole file, the keys of the associative array is sorted in
ascending numerical order by each key's value. It is then a simple matter to print
the key, which is the line itself. More Perl tricks can be found in Chapter 11.

—*JP and JJ*

22.8 Sorting a List of People by Last Name

It's hard to sort any old list of peoples' names because some people have one-
word first and last names like Joe Smith, but other people have multi-part names
like Mary Jo Appleton. This program sorts on the last word in each name. That
won't take care of the way that names are used everywhere in the world, but it
might give you some ideas.

namesort

The script reads from files or its standard input; it writes to standard output.

```
#! /bin/sh
# Print last field (last name), a TAB, then whole name:
awk '{print $NF "\t" $0}' $* |
# sort (by last name: the temporary first field)
sort |
# strip off first field and print the names:
cut -f2-
```

If you want more control over the sorting or you're interested in pulling apart names in general, there's a Perl module you might want to look at called Lingua: :EN::NameParse. Below is a Perl script that also sorts a list of names by surname.

```perl
#!/usr/bin/perl

use Lingua::EN::NameParse;

my $Name_Obj = Lingua::EN::NameParse->new(auto_clean => 1);
my @names = <STDIN>;
for my $line (sort by_lastname @names){
  chomp($line);
  print $line, "\n";
}

sub by_lastname {
  my @names;
  for my $name ($a, $b) {
    chomp($name);
    if( my $err = $Name_Obj->parse($name) ){
      warn "WARN: Unparsable name ($name): $err";
    }
    my %tmp = $Name_Obj->components;
    push @names, \%tmp;
  }
  return lc $names[0]->{surname_1} cmp lc $names[1]->{surname_1};
}
```

The script starts by bringing in the Lingua::EN::NameParse library. Then, all lines from standard input are read in and stored in an array. Perl's sort function is particularly flexible in that it can use a user-defined subroutine to determine the desired collating sequence. Here, the subroutine by_lastname receives the next two items of the list to be sorted in the "magical" global variables $a and $b. These names are then parsed by the global Lingua::EN::NameParse object, and the name components are stored in the array @names. It's then a simple matter to alphabetically compare the lowercased surnames and return that value to sort. Although this script may be a little bit more Perl than you wanted to know, the problem of sorting by last names is complex. Fortunately, the Lingua::EN:: NameParse module available on CPAN was available to do the heavy lifting for us. In fact, one of most the compelling reasons to learn Perl is the large collection of free library modules stored on the Comprehensive Perl Archive Network (CPAN), which is mirrored throughout the world. For more about CPAN, see article 41.11.

—JP and JJ

Processes and the Kernel

Part V contains the following chapters:

23

Job Control

23.1 Job Control in a Nutshell

As has been said many times in this book, Unix is a mutliprocessing system. Unlike some historic systems such as MS-DOS, all flavors of Unix run more than one process at a time. In fact, when Unix boots, the first program executed is called *init*, which is the parent of all future processes. *init* immediately creates a new process in which other programs can run, such as *getty* and the various *rc* setup scripts. At some point when a user logs into the system, the *getty* program creates a new shell for that session. Even when the system is in single-user mode, Unix is still capable of running multiple processes. Multiprocessing is prevasive in Unix.

But multiprocessing isn't just for system daemons. It's also there to make your interactive shell session just a little bit more productive. Often, you will need to execute a program that takes a long time to run. For instance, you might be downloading a file with FTP or Lynx. It is possible to have that task put into the background so that you may execute new commands while the previous ones are running to completion. Just as you may have several piles of work on your desk, you often need to set aside one stack to work on another. A process is said to be in the foreground when it is receiving your keyboard input and is writing to your screen. Using the desk analogy, the foreground process is that pile of work currently in front of you. Only one process can be in the foreground at a time. Putting a process in the background is like putting the current stack of work in front of you on the floor. And if your desk is anything like mine, you can soon find your desk surrounded by piles of work. Unlike the real world, Unix is able to continue working on completing processes in the background. The management and manipulation of foreground and background processes is called *job control*. By understanding job control, you can begin to take better advantage of your Unix system.

One cautionary note on job control: there's no such thing as a free lunch. In other words, while Unix blithely lets you put all the processes you want into the background, they all share the same CPU, RAM, and hard drive resources. If one process dominates one of these resources, the other processes won't get done any faster than they would have had you run them one after the other to completion. So if you've got a process that's CPU-intensive (such as a photomosiac program), there's little point in trying to run more processes on that machine.

From the days of mainframes, when programs were submitted on stacks of cards, comes the term "job control." This chapter is going to go into some depth about using your shell's job control features. For those already familar with the concept, here is the thirty-second version of "Job Control in a Nutshell."

Unless otherwise noted, these commands apply only to the C shell, Korn shell, and *bash*:

command & (23.3)

Run *command* in the background. You can continue to execute jobs in the foreground. This is the most common way to put processes in the background.

CTRL-c (24.11)

Kill the current foreground job by sending the *INTR* signal (24.10).

CTRL-z (23.3, 23.6)

Suspend the current foreground job by sending the *TSTP* signal (24.10).

suspend

Suspend a shell with the *suspend* command.

stop

Suspend a background job with the *stop* command or an alias that does the same thing (23.7).

bg %*num* (23.3)

Let a stopped job (by job number *num*) continue in the background.

fg %*num* (23.3)

Put a background job or a stopped job (by job number *num*) into the foreground.

kill %*num* (23.3)

Kill an arbitrary background job (by job number *num*).

kill *pid* (24.12)

Kill an arbitrary job (by process ID number *num*).

jobs (23.3)

List background and stopped jobs and their job numbers.

set notify (23.8)

Immediate job-state change notices.

stty tostop (23.9)

Automatically stop background processes if they try writing to the screen.

Some systems, like Linux, extend the *kill* to kill processes by name. See Chapter 24 (24.15), which introduces *killall*.

—ML and JJ

23.2 Job Control Basics

If you're coming from a Windows or MacOS desktop, Unix job control may seem a little strange at first, but both of those operating systems support a form of job control too. The Windows' taskbar shows the foreground application as a depressed icon. In the classic Mac interface, the current application's icon is present in the upper righthand corner. Such displays aren't possible on the command line (although there are similar metaphores available in modern X11 desktop environments like Gnome and KDE). This article tries to give you some background into, er, background processes.

How Job Control Works

To get a better feel for how to use job control, a brief look at how Unix handles processes can be helpful. As was mentioned in the opening section, Unix systems normally are running many processes at once. A process is defined as a program that is executing in memory, as opposed to an executable file (i.e., the program) that is sitting on the filesystem. When you log into a Unix system, you are running some shell program (e.g., *tcsh* or *bash*). When you ask the shell to run another program, such as *vi*, a new process starts and takes over the terminal from the shell. That new process is in the foreground by default. When you type commands, it is *vi* that responds, not the shell. When you exit *vi*, that process ends and parent process, the shell, returns. When you run *vi*, the shell itself goes into the background. You've been using background processes all along.

You may have noticed that I slipped in a new concept about processes in the last paragraph. Process are related to each other in hierarchical way by the kernel. When you execute a command from the shell, that new command is a child process of the shell. When a process terminates, the parent process is notified and is given an opportunity to take some action. What happens when you log out? All your shell's child processes are terminated along with the shell process itself, and your system's *getty* daemon waits for a new user to log in. What happens when *getty* dies? The ultimate ancestor for all system processes on a Unix system is *init*. When *init* dies, the system is halted.

Using Job Control from Your Shell

Remember that the shell sits there listening to what you type and calling other programs to do jobs that it doesn't have built-in commands to do.

Normally, when the shell calls another program, it waits for the other program to finish. The ampersand (&) at the end of a command line tells the shell not to wait.

Basically all shells allow background processing. On systems that have job control (23.3), however, most shells will give you a lot of extra capabilities for manipulating background processes.

Here's the tip of the iceberg:

- If you forget to put a job into the background, you can stop it on the fly with a suspend signal (24.1) by typing CTRL-z. Then use the *bg* command to put it into the background and restart it:

  ```
  % find /usr -name tim -print > mine
  CTRL-z
  Stopped
  % bg
  [1]    find /usr -name tim -print > mine &
  ```

- You can bring the current background job (23.5) into the foreground with the *fg* command. This is handy when Unix stops the background job that needs input from your keyboard (you can't type to jobs running in the background).

- If you have a lot of background processes running, you can use the *jobs* command to list them all, then bring a selected job into the foreground by job number. You can also kill jobs by job number rather than by process ID. [Recall that job numbers are per-session numbers that the shell generates, whereas process IDs are generated by the operating system and are visible to all other processes. —*JJ*]

—*TOR and JJ*

23.3 Using jobs Effectively

So far, you've seen how to get processes into and out of the background. That's a pretty good start, but what happens when you put more than one process in the background? How do you remember what's in the background at all? Fortunately the *jobs* command, built into Bourne and C shell derviates, lists all your current session's background jobs. Let's see this in action. In the example below, I started several web browsers:

```
[jjohn@marian jjohn]$ jobs
[1]   Running                 netscape &
[2]-  Stopped                 lynx
[3]+  Stopped                 lynx http://aliensaliensaliens.com
```

Every background process is assigned a job number by your shell. This number is unique only for your current session. It isn't globally unique like a process ID.

In fact, one job number is assigned to processes that are pipelined together. For example, the following line gets only one job number.

```
$ uniq bigfile.dat | sort | wc -l &
```

In the *jobs* example above, the first process was started with an ampersand, so it was immediately backgrounded. Job 2 started as a typical interactive session, but I stopped it with CTRL-z. A stopped process is not the same as a terminated process—it simply doesn't receive any CPU time. It's like a caveman frozen in ice, waiting to be thawed out and come back to life. If you find that a job is becoming a resource hog, consider using CTRL-z to suspend the process until you figure out why it's being so gluttonous. The next job listed is a new instance of *lynx*, which is also put into the background so that the *jobs* command could be run for this listing. The plus sign next to the job number indicates that that job will be in the foreground when *fg* is typed. That job is known as the *current job*. The minus sign indicates the *previous job*, the job that used to be the current job.

Job numbers can be supplied to *fg*. In the given example, the first version of *lynx* can be revived using *fg %2*. You can also kill jobs with the job number. Why have two versions of *lynx* running? The first one can be terminated with *kill %2*. You can also supply signal numbers, as you normally would to *kill*. By default *kill* sends the TERM (15 on Linux) signal, which will stop most processes.

When a backgrounded job is terminated or completes, you will be notified before the next command prompt is printed. For example:

```
[jjohn@marian jjohn]$ kill -9 %3
[jjohn@marian jjohn]$
[3]+  Killed                  xcalc
[jjohn@marian jjohn]$
```

Just as before, the job number is printed with a plus sign, indicating that it was the current job. Because this process exited abnormally (it was sent a KILL signal), the reason is printed next, along with the line that was executed. For a process that runs to completion, the output looks slightly different:

```
[jjohn@marian jjohn]$ ls | uniq | sort | wc -l &
    99
[2] 10501
[2]+  Done                    ls --color=tty | uniq | sort | wc -l
[jjohn@marian jjohn]$
```

Here, the command was put in the background immediately. The shell then reported the job number and process ID. Because the command completed very quickly, the shell reports that job 2 exited normally even before the next command prompt could be printed.

As useful as job numbers are, sometimes you don't want to bother running *jobs*, searching for the desired command, finding its job number, and then running *fg* %*num*. Luckily, the job control mechanism uses a simple pattern-matching scheme so that you can supply only part of the command or job you wish to foreground or kill. Instead of prefixing the job number with simply %, use %?. The string you supply must be enough to disambiguate it from all other jobs. Take this job listing, for example:

```
[1]    Running                netscape &
[2]    Running                xcalc &
[3]-   Stopped                lynx
[4]+   Stopped                lynx http://aliensaliensaliens.com
```

I can put the *xcalc* program in the foreground with fg %?xc, because xc doesn't appear in the other jobs. But I can't refer to either of the *lynx* processes with any substring of "lynx." If I do, I get something like the following.

```
[jjohn@marian jjohn]$ fg %?ly
bash: fg: ambigious job spec: ly
```

Instead, I could refer to the second version with fg %?aliens. In order to get at the first *lynx* job, its job number must be used explicitly.

You may find that your shell attempts to interpret %? as a filename wildcard. This is increasingly rare, but you may need to escape the ?, so that you can foreground a process. That can be done like this: fg %\?*string*.

One final shortcut to job control: you can put jobs in the foreground simply by referring to the job number. For instance, typing %2 alone at the command prompt will put job number 2 in the foreground. You can even put jobs into the background with this notation: %2 &. This seems a little terse, even for Unix, but it will save you some typing.

—JJ

23.4 Some Gotchas with Job Control

1. If you're using Bourne-type shells, you have to watch out for putting a series of commands separated by semicolons (28.16) into the background. These shells put only the last command on the line into the background, but wait for the first.

   An easy way to test this is with the following command line, which waits for 15 seconds, then does an *ls*:

   ```
   $ sleep 15; ls &
   ```

   In Bourne-like shells, you won't get your prompt back until the *sleep* (25.9) command has finished.

   With Bourne-type shells, the proper way to put a series of commands into the background is to group them with parentheses:

( ) 43.7
   ```
   $ (sleep 15; ls)&
   ```

This may strike you as a defect, but in fact, it's a sign of the greater precision of Bourne shell syntax, which makes it somewhat exasperating for interactive use but much better for programming.

2. It doesn't make any sense to run an interactive program such as an editor in the background. For example, if you type this from the C shell:

```
% vi &
[1] 3071
```

you'll get a message like the following:

```
[1]  + Stopped (tty output) vi
```

vi can be active only in the foreground. However, it does make sense to have *vi* stopped (23.1) in the background.

If you are running *vi* or any other interactive program, you can quickly get back to the shell by typing CTRL-z to stop the program. The shell will take control of your terminal and print another shell prompt.

Stopping *vi* (23.6) is more efficient than using its shell escape mechanism (17.21), since it lets you go back to your original shell rather than starting a new one. Simply type fg to get back to where you were in editing.

3. We have had the misfortune to share a system with new users who were overenthusiastic in their use of background processes, rather like the man who loved loving so much he sought many lovers. Because each background process is competing for the same resources, running many of them can be a drain on the system, and everything takes longer for everyone. We knew people who thought that if they ran three *troff* processes at once, they'd get their three files formatted faster than if they did them one after another. Boy, were they mistaken.*

4. If you use the Bourne shell, any background processes you have running will normally be terminated when you log out. To avoid this, use the *nohup* (23.10) command.

5. Not all processes are created equal. Unix maintains a queue of processes ordered by priority. Foreground processes, such as a user typing a command at a prompt, often receive higher priority than background processes. However, you may want to run background processes at an even lower priority, by using *nice* (26.5). This is a relatively painless way of being kind to other users—and making your foreground job run faster—though it will make your background tasks take a little longer.

—*TOR and DD*

---

* In the old days, Unix systems gave all processes to a single CPU. Modern Unix systems can have multiple CPUs. On these systems, you may be able to do several jobs almost as quickly as one.

23.5 The "Current Job" Isn't Always What You Expect

% is the current stopped or background job, but not always the last one. If you've stopped any jobs, the current job is the most recently stopped job. Otherwise, it's the most recent background job. For example, try stopping your editor (like *vi*), then putting another job in the background:

```
% vi afile
CTRL-z
Stopped
% sleep 1000 &
[2] 12345
% fg
```

and notice that the fg brings your editor to the foreground.

—JP

23.6 Job Control and autowrite: Real Timesavers!

I see too many people using a series of commands like the ones that follow. Programmers do this when they write and compile programs. Writers use this when they're making a draft file and running it through the formatter. They're probably wasting a lot of time and effort:

```
% vi somefile
    ...Edit somefile, then quit vi...
% someprog somefile
    ...Process somefile...
% vi somefile
    ...Edit somefile again...
% someprog somefile
    ...Process somefile again...
```

Each time they restart *vi*, they have to reset options and move the cursor to the place they were working before. After they restart, *vi* has forgotten the previous search (the *n* command), the previous action (the . command), the previous regular expression, the named and numbered buffers...

In the same way, why quit any other program (that isn't an editor) if you aren't done with it? The programs lose their state. For instance, quitting a *man* (2.1) or *info* (2.9) command when you're in the middle of a document means that when you start it again, it'll be at the start. It will have forgotten the last term you searched for.

If your system has job control (23.1), that solves all these problems. (If it doesn't, you can still use a shell escape (17.21).) Instead of quitting *vi*, get into command mode and write your buffer with the :w command. Stop the editor with the CTRL-z command. Then process the file. When you're ready to do more editing, bring your *vi* job back into the foreground with *fg*. The editor will be just where it was.

Even better, you can set *vi*'s *autowrite* option. If you've made any changes to the buffer before you press CTRL-z, *vi* will automatically write the buffer. You won't need to remember to type :w before you stop the editor. You can set *autowrite* at a colon (:) prompt, but I set it in my *.exrc* file (17.5) instead.

You don't absolutely have to write your file before suspending *vi*. It's a good piece of advice, but not required by the job control mechanism. Typing CTRL-z will suspend the editor whether you've written out your files or not.

—*JP*

23.7 System Overloaded? Try Stopping Some Jobs

If your computer is barely crawling, you can *kill* (24.12) some processes, but you'll have to start them again later. On many Unix systems, you can *renice* (26.7) the processes, but you won't be able to raise the priority again later, after the system speeds up, unless you're the superuser (1.18).

If you don't need your results right away (and you won't get them, anyway, if the system is crawling!), try stopping some jobs. The best candidates are "CPU-eaters" like formatters, compilers, and any job that runs up a lot of time quickly in the *ps* (24.5) or *time* (26.2) reports. Start them again later, and the jobs will take up where they left off.

If the job is in the foreground, just press CTRL-z (23.3) to stop it. If the job is running in the background and you're running *csh* or *tcsh*, use the shell's *stop* command with a job identifier—for example, stop %3 or stop %cc.

On other shells—even shells without job control (!)—you can use *kill* (24.12) with the *–STOP* signal and either the job number or process ID number. The *csh* and *tcsh* command *stop* does this for you. On other shells, if you'd like, you can add an alias named *stop* to the shell setup file (3.3). Later, when the system speeds up, put the job back into the background with *bg* or into the foreground with *fg*. For example:

```
bash$ alias stop='kill -STOP'
bash$ jobs
[1]+  Running              g++ hugeprog.cc &
bash$ stop %1
```

```
[1]+  Stopped (signal)       g++ hugeprog.cc
      ...later...
bash$ bg %1
[1]+ g++ hugeprog.cc &
```

—JP

23.8 Notification When Jobs Change State

Normally, the shell tells you about changes to your background jobs whenever it prints its prompt. That is, when you do something that makes the shell give you a prompt, you'll get a message like:

```
[1]  + Stopped (tty input)   rm -r
%
```

This message tells you that the *rm –r* command, which you're running in the background, needs input; it has probably asked you whether or not to delete a read-only file, or something similar.

This default behavior is usually what you want. By waiting until it prints a prompt, the shell minimizes "damage" to your screen. If you want to be notified immediately when a job changes state, you should set the variable *notify*:

```
% set notify      ...csh, tcsh
$ set -o notify   ...bash, ksh
$ setopt notify   ...zsh
```

The drawback, of course, is that you may be analyzing a screenful of output that you've laboriously constructed, only to have that screen "destroyed" by a lot of messages from the shell. Therefore, most users prefer to leave *notify* off (unset). To stop all background output, use *stty tostop* (23.9).

—ML

23.9 Stop Background Output with stty tostop

If you put a job in the background and don't redirect (43.1) its output, text that the job writes to its standard output and standard error comes to your screen. Those messages can mess up the screen while you're using another program. You could lose the (maybe important) messages, too—they might scroll off your screen and be lost, or your foreground program may clear the screen and erase them.

Many Unix systems have the command *stty tostop*. Type that command at a prompt, or put it in your *.login* or *.profile* file.* After that, your shell's

---

* This command sets the Unix terminal device driver for all processes started on it. You don't need to set this for subshells (3.3).

---

background jobs that try to write to your terminal will be stopped. When you want to see the background job's output, bring it into the foreground (with *fg*).

How will you know that the background job has been stopped? The shell will print a message like this just before it prints a prompt:

```
[1] + Stopped (tty output)    somejob
%
```

The shell can also interrupt your foreground job with that message as soon as the background job is stopped. To make it do that, set *notify* (23.8).

In C shell, you can turn off this feature and let background jobs write to your terminal any time with the command:

```
% stty -tostop
```

In *bash*, the command is similar:

```
$ stty tostop
```

—JP

23.10 nohup

When Unix first started, even local terminals very often communicated with the system via short-haul modems. (After all, Unix was invented by the phone company.) When someone logged out, the modem hung up the phone—and conversely, if the modem hung up, a "hangup" signal was sent to the login shell, whereupon it terminated, bringing down all its child processes (24.3) with it.

In the C shell, processes that you run in the background are immune to hangups, but in the Bourne shell, a process that you started in the background might be abruptly terminated.

nohup

The *nohup* command ("*no hangup*") allows you to circumvent this. (The GNU version is on the web site.) Simply type:

```
$ nohup command &
```

Any output from *command* that would normally go to the terminal (i.e., has not been redirected) goes to a file named *nohup.out* in the current directory.

Of course, if you want to run jobs at off hours, you might do even better using *at*, *cron*, or *batch*.

nohup is sometimes handy in shell scripts to make them ignore the HUP and TERM signals (24.10), though *trap* (35.17) is more versatile. (In System V, *nohup* causes a command to ignore HUP and QUIT, but not TERM.)

—TOR

23.11 Disowning Processes

Job control isn't always a good thing. For instance, I might want to start a long equipment-monitoring job running when I go home for the night. But if I simply put the job in the background and try to log out, *zsh* says zsh: you have running jobs. If I log out anyway, the shell sends my background job a HUP signal. I could use *nohup* (23.10) to block the hangup signal, but there's a simpler way: tell the shell, "Don't use job control on this job." This is also true of jobs that I know are there—a clock running on my X Window System display, for instance—and that I'll never want to use job control on, so the jobs are just cluttering the *jobs* (23.3) list.

To run a job without job control, the trick in most shells is to start the job in a subshell (43.7), and put the job inside that subshell into the background. This is sometimes called "disowning" the job. Note that the ampersand (&) is *inside* the parentheses:

```
% (myprog -opts &)
```

The job won't appear in the *jobs* list, but *ps* (24.5) should show it running. (You might need to use a "show all jobs" option like *ps –x* or *ps –e*.) If you use *ps –l* for a "long" listing, you'll see that the process' PPID (the process ID number of the parent process (24.3)) is 1; this means that the process is now "owned" by *init* (24.2). On the other hand, if you'd started the job in the background normally (without the subshell trick), you'd see that its PPID was that of the shell you started it from.

The Z shell has a more direct way: its &! and &| background operators. Both of them do the same thing: if you use one of those operators instead of plain &, the job will be disowned immediately; it won't appear in the *jobs* list.

In most shells, once you start a job without the subshell trick, the shell that started the job will continue to be its parent. (Some shells, like the C shells, will give up ownership of a child process and let it keep running when you end the shell—that is, when you log out—and then *init* will "inherit" the process.) In *zsh* and *bash* Version 2, though, you can change your mind after you start a job by using the shell's built-in *disown* command. Give *disown* the job number you want the shell to "forget." For instance, I'll start a background job and then disown it. It disappears from the job table, but giving *ps* its process ID shows that the job is still running:

```
zsh% myprog -opts&
[1] 28954
zsh% jobs
[1]  + running    myprog -opts
zsh% disown %1
zsh% jobs
zsh% ps 28954
```

```
    PID TTY      STAT   TIME COMMAND
  28954 pts/5    S      0:09 myprog -opts
```

If you don't give a job number, *disown* "forgets" the current job. The *bash2* version of *disown* has options that *zsh* doesn't: *disown –a* disowns all jobs, and *disown –r* disowns only running jobs. The *bash2* option *–h* does a different job: instead of removing a job from the job table, the job won't receive any HUP signal sent to the shell. This is similar to what the *nohup* command does.

—JP

23.12 Linux Virtual Consoles

Your Linux workstation display may look like just one terminal. It's actually seven terminals—or even more—in one. Linux has built-in *virtual consoles*, a series of *ttys* (2.7) that you can log into separately: each one can have a login session, with its own shell, working at the same time as the others. You can see only one of these consoles at once; you bring a console into view by pressing a hot-key combination. For instance, I log into the first virtual console as *root* and the second as myself.

What Are They?

If your Linux system comes up after a reboot with a mostly blank screen something like this:

```
Red Hat Linux release 6.2 (Zoot)
Kernel 2.2.14-5.0 on an i686

penguin login:
```

you're seeing one of the virtual consoles—in this case, it's the first one you've seen since the reboot, so it has to be console number 1. On the other hand, if your system boots to an X Window display with a graphical *xdm* or *gdm* login box, you're using a different virtual console, probably console number 7. All of this is configurable. But by default, consoles 1 through 6 are *ttys*, with *getty* (24.2) processes running, ready to manage individual login sessions. Virtual console 7 is an X Window System display.

To switch between the consoles—to bring a differnt console "to the front"—use the hot-key combination CTRL-ALT-n, where *n* is the console number. (Actually, the only time you need the CTRL key is when the X Window console is in front. When you've got a nongraphical console in front, you can switch with just ALT-n. But if you find the difference hard to remember, there's no problem with always using the CTRL key.)

Here's one of the reasons I like to start my window system by typing a command (*startx*) at a shell prompt in a virtual console. The X server, and client applications running under X, will spit error messages onto the standard output (or standard error) at the console where I ran *startx*. So it's easy for me to jump back to the console—by pressing CTRL-ALT-2—to see error messages. Then I can jump back to X with CTRL-ALT-7. (I actually changed this setup, later, to log X errors to a file that I watch from a window, but that's another story.)

When you log out of one of the *tty*-type consoles (by typing *exit* or *logout*), the *getty* process there prints a new `login:` prompt. But not every one of these *ttys* needs a login session. For instance, while the Red Hat Linux installation program is working, it uses the first four virtual consoles as logs that show different information about the installation process—and the fifth has a shell prompt where you can do work during the installation. Another handy example is this tip from Chris Hilts, posted to *www.oreilly.com* as a followup to a Linux feature in the summer of 2000. Add the following line to your */etc/syslog.conf* file:

```
*.* /dev/tty9
```

After the next reboot or restart of *syslog*, all of your system's *syslog* messages will appear on virtual console number 9—where you can see them at any time by pressing CTRL-ALT-9.

Scrolling, Using a Mouse

The *tty*-type virtual consoles have some other nice features. One is a scrolling buffer that lets you scroll back to see previous screens of text. Press SHIFT-PAGE UP to move to previous screenfuls, and SHIFT-PAGE DOWN to move toward the most recent screen.

The *tty*-type consoles also support copy-and-paste with your mouse. To copy an area, point to the first character and hold down the first mouse button; move to the end of the text block and release the button. The selected text should be shown in reverse video. To paste the copied text, click the third mouse button. You also can paste from one console into another with the same steps. You can't paste from a *tty*-type console into the X Windows, or vice-versa, though. To do that, use a temporary file. For example, highlight (copy) an area of text, then use the command:

cat › 12.2
```
% cat > /tmp/paste-me
    ...paste the text...
CTRL-d
```

Then switch to the other console. Either read the file directly into an application, or output the file onto the screen (*cat /tmp/paste-me*) and copy from that redisplayed text.

—*JP*

23.13 Stopping Remote Login Sessions

Once you start *telnet*, *rlogin*, *rsh*, and *ssh* for an interactive login, they basically "take over" your shell. Your keystrokes are sent to the shell running on the remote system. So if you type CTRL-z, it won't stop the *telnet* (or whatever) job: it'll stop the job running on the remote system.

It can be very handy to suspend a connection to a remote system and resume it, sometime later, with *fg*. Most of the remote login utilities let you do that.

To stop a *telnet* session, start by pressing the escape character. By default, this is CTRL-] (Control-right bracket). You should get a *telnet* command prompt. Type *z* to suspend the job, Here's how that looks:

```
myhost$ telnet remhost
Trying 198.59.115.17...
Connected to remhost.
Escape character is '^]'.

SunOS 5.6

login: whoever
   ...
remhost% CTRL]
telnet> z

[1]+  Stopped                 telnet remhost

myhost$
```

You can use other commands at the *telnet* command prompt. For a list, see your manual page or type *help* at the prompt. If you get to that prompt accidentally and don't want to stop the *telnet* session, simply press ENTER once.

Other remote-login utilities don't have a command prompt. Their control commands start with ENTER-tilde (~) and one more control character. The command to stop the session is ENTER, then tilde, then CTRL-z. It won't appear on your screen as you type it (if it does appear, it didn't work...try again). For example:

```
myhost$ ssh remhost
Last login: Fri Dec 22 09:08:31 2000 from myhost
NetBSD 1.4.2A (GENERIC) #6: Wed May 31 06:12:46 EST 2000

remhost%
remhost% ~CTRL-z

[1]+  Stopped                 ssh remhost

myhost$
```

Notice the extra prompt: it shows me pressing ENTER first, before typing the tilde. That isn't necessary if you pressed ENTER to complete the previous command line—but I tend to do it all the time, "just in case" I didn't type that ENTER.

You can stop the remote session in the middle of an interactive job, like using a text editor. But I'd recommend getting to a shell prompt on the remote system first, if you can. (For example, stop the remote job with CTRL-z so you'll get a shell prompt on the remote system.) Otherwise, if you bring the remote session into the foreground while you're in the middle of a full-screen editing job there, for example, the remote system won't know that it's supposed to redraw the screen when you come back online. Worse, if you forget where you were on the remote system, you might type a key that could do something disastrous, like deleting lines of the file you're editing. Stopping and starting from a known point—a shell prompt—is the best way I've found.

—JP

24

Starting, Stopping, and Killing Processes

24.1 What's in This Chapter

We've already talked about so many of the topics in this chapter, here or there, that it may seem like a real hodgepodge. It's a grab-bag of important things to know about processes—which you can think of as programs that are actually running, rather than sitting on the disk somewhere.

The chapter starts out with a couple of conceptual articles. They define some important terms that you're likely to encounter in this chapter.

Then we talk about the *ps* command, which tells you what processes you have running and just what they are up to (articles 24.5, 24.6, 24.8).

The next few articles cover signals, which are one way processes communicate with one another. We cover topics like:

* What are signals (article 24.10)?
* How to send signals from the keyboard (articles 24.11 and 24.12; also see article 5.8).
* How shell programs can "handle" signals (articles 24.13 and 35.17).

We go from there to a more general discussion of ways to kill processes:

* How to kill all your processes (article 24.14).
* How to kill processes by name rather than by process ID (article 24.16).
* How to stop runaway jobs (article 24.17).
* Why some processes don't seem to go away when you kill them (articles 24.18, 24.19).
* How to get rid of a frozen window (article 24.22).
* How to make sure processes *don't* die when you log out (article 23.10).

—*TOR*

24.2 fork and exec

We discuss *fork* and *exec* in article 27.2, but the concept comes up so often in this chapter that we thought we ought to have a closer cross reference.

Put simply, *fork* and *exec* are the Unix system calls (requests for operating system services) that Unix programs use to create new processes. When you start up a Unix system, it starts with only one process, a program called *init*.

How does *init* magically turn into the hundreds or perhaps even thousands of processes that make up a working Unix system? That's where *fork* and *exec* come in.

One process spawns another ("spawn" is another term you should get used to seeing) either by replacing itself when it's done—an *exec*—or, if it needs to stay around, by making a copy of itself—a *fork*. In the latter case, the forked copy commits polite suicide by *exec*ing the desired second program.

A good example of this whole sequence can be seen in the way a Unix system's login procedure for terminals (non-network (1.21) logins) works. The *init* process spawns a series of *getty* processes, each of which monitors a serial port (a *tty*), looking for activity. It's the *getty* program that actually puts up the first login: prompt.

Once someone actually types a login name, *getty*'s job is done; it *exec*s the *login* command. *login* prompts for a password (if the account has one) and, if the password is okay, *exec*s the login shell. Whenever you start another program, the shell *fork*s itself, and the copy *exec*s whatever program you asked to run.

That's why some commands are built into the shell (1.9). There's overhead involved in starting a new process. What's more, because a child process can't affect its parent's environment (24.3), some commands don't make sense as separate processes. For example, *cd* must be built in, or it couldn't change the working directory for the current shell.

There's an *exec* command that you can type at a shell prompt; see article 36.5. Watch out, though: it will replace your shell with whatever command you *exec*, with no going back. This is useful only if you want to replace your shell with some other interactive command interpreter with similar powers, or if you'll be ready to log out when the command you *exec* finishes.

—*TOR*

24.3 Managing Processes: Overall Concepts

As you know, when you log into your Unix account and start typing, you're talking to the *shell* (27.1). The shell you use may be a variant of the Bourne shell (such as a standard *sh*, *ksh*, or the GNU shell *bash*), or perhaps it is a variant of the C shell, *csh* (such as, perhaps, the *tcsh* shell that includes line- and history-editing features). Alternatively, you may be using a somewhat less common shell such as *rc*.

Your shell is a *process*, one of many individual programs running at the same time on the machine. Every process has certain pieces of information associated with it, including the following:

- The *process ID* (PID) is a number assigned to the process when it is started up. Process IDs are unique (that is, they cycle and are eventually reused, but no two processes have the same process ID at the same time).

- The *user ID* (UID) tells who the process belongs to. This determines what files and directories the process is allowed to read from or write to (50.1), as well as who is allowed to *kill* the process (24.12) (tell it to stop running).

- The *group ID* (GID) is similar to the user ID but tells which group the process belongs to. On some systems, this controls the group assigned to files created by the process. See article 50.2.

- The *environment* contains a list of variable names and associated values. For example, when you type echo $HOME at the shell and it prints out the name of your home directory (1.15), it has told you the contents of the *environment variable* (35.3) called *HOME*.

- The *current working directory* (31.3) is the directory that is currently the default. When you specify a filename to a program but do not say explicitly where to look for it with a pathname (31.2), the program will look in the current working directory—if the *PATH* variable contains the current directory (article 35.6 explains).

- *File descriptors* are a record of which files a process has opened for reading or writing, as well as the current position in each file.

- Versions of Unix with job control (23.1) have *process groups*. A process group is used for distribution of signals (24.10, 24.11, 24.14). It's also used to control which process can read from a terminal. A process that has the same process group as the terminal is "in the foreground" and can read from the terminal. Other processes are stopped when they try to read from the terminal.

When you're typing commands at the shell, it is the *controlling process* of your terminal, meaning that it (the shell) is the process that gets the input you type. See article 24.6.

Normally, when you type a command at the shell prompt, that command runs and is allowed by the shell to take over the terminal for its lifetime. For example, if you type more .login to view your *.login* file, the shell starts up the *more* program and then sits around waiting for it to finish; while *more* is running, you can type commands to page through the file and *more* (not the shell) will see them. The command you run is called a *child* or *subprocess* of the shell process, which is its *parent*. All process information (user ID, group ID, etc.) is inherited by the child from its parent, except for the process ID, since the child is assigned a new one. Built-in shell commands (1.9) such as *cd* don't start a child process.

Although the normal behavior is for the shell to wait until any command you run has finished before it becomes active again, there are some situations in which you don't want this to occur. For example, if you're using a window system such as X (1.22) and want to start up a new *xterm* window from your shell, you don't want to type just xterm, because then your original shell will wait until the *xterm* finishes before allowing you to type any more commands. This would mean that you still have only one shell to work in, thus defeating the purpose of starting the new *xterm*.

When you don't want a process to finish before getting back to the shell, you can run it in the *background*. You do this by putting an ampersand (&) character at the end of the command, for example, xterm &. The shell will start the child process and then immediately prompt you for another command. Note that in this situation, the shell retains control of the terminal, and the newly created background process cannot read input. Some shells have additional *job control* (23.1) features (processes that are running in the background are often described as *background jobs* or just jobs) that enable you to do things such as kill jobs or bring a job from the background into the *foreground* so that it becomes the controlling process of the terminal and you can type input at it.

An important thing to remember is that although process information is inherited by children *when they are started*, it is impossible for the parent to affect its child's process information (or vice versa) after that point. For example, if you start up the editor *vi*, suspend it (23.6), and then use the *cd* command in the shell to change directories, *vi* will still have the old working directory when you bring it back into the foreground. Similarly, if you write a shell script that changes some environment variables, those variables will contain their old values in the shell when the shell script exits. This sometimes confuses MS-DOS users, since MS-DOS stores information such as the current directory in a global area that is referenced by all programs. If it is necessary to communicate information from a child back to a parent shell, other methods are needed (24.10, 35.29).

One more useful concept: when a process exits, it returns a numeric exit status (35.12) to its parent process. By convention, a zero status means success; nonzero means some kind of failure.

Just as there are ways to modify the environment and the current working directory of the shell, there are also useful ways to manipulate file descriptors (36.16).

—*JIK*

24.4 Subshells

In Unix, when a program starts another program (more exactly, when a process starts another process), the new process runs as a subprocess (24.3) or child process.* When a shell starts another shell, the new shell is called a *subshell*.†

So what? There are some important things to know about it: the child process gets a copy of its parent's environment, and any changes in the environment of the child process aren't passed to its parent. "Still," I hear you say, "so what??"

- Shell scripts are run in a subshell (unless you use the *source* or . commands (35.29) to start the script). If the script makes changes to the environment of its (sub)shell, the parent shell won't see those changes. If the script uses *cd*, it doesn't change the current directory in the parent shell. If the script changes the value of the *TZ* (or any) environment variable, that won't change *TZ* in the parent shell. The script can set a different *umask* than the parent shell—no problem.

- There are times you might want to start a subshell from your current shell. Maybe you have a special project where you need to work in a different current directory, reset environment variables, set a new home directory, reset some aliases, use a different *PATH* (35.6), whatever. When you end the subshell, the parent shell's environment will be the way it was.

  If your parent shell has job control (23.3), you can stop the subshell and pop back to your parent shell without losing the changes in the subshell. If the child shell has job control, too, the command *suspend* (or kill -STOP $$ (27.17)) will stop it. Otherwise, just type CTRL-z at the subshell's prompt. For example:

prompt **4.1**

```
myprompt% csh
myprompt% set prompt="project% "
project% cd project-directory
project% setenv PRINTER plotter
project% set path=($path some-new-directories)
project% setenv EXINIT "se ts=4 sw=4 aw wm=0"
```

---

* This isn't true when the subprocess is *exec*d from the parent process without a *fork* first. Article 24.2 explains.

† When you use the shell's *exec* (36.5) command, it does not start a subprocess.

```
        ...do some work...
project% suspend

Stopped
        ...back to parent shell...
myprompt%
myprompt% fg %csh
        ...back to subshell...
project%
```

I use *suspend* so much that I've made a CTRL-z–like alias named *z*:

```
alias z suspend      ...csh
alias z=suspend      ...bash, ksh
```

- If you need a different type of shell temporarily, just type that shell's name at a prompt. When you end the shell by typing *exit* or by suspending it (as shown above), you're back to your usual shell. For example, you might normally use *bash* but want to use the *zsh* multiline editing for a few loops you need to run. As another example, I started a lot of different shells while I was writing this book—and suspended them, as above, when I wasn't using them. Very handy.

- A shell escape (17.21) starts a subshell. Do whatever you want to the subshell's environment. When you end the shell escape, the changes go away.

- The *su* command starts a subshell. *cd* anywhere, change environment variables, and so on.

If you use the *exit* command, a subshell (or any shell) will terminate. In a script, when the shell reads the end of file, that does an implicit *exit*. On the command line, an end-of-input character (usually CTRL-d) will do the same thing. Article 35.16 explains how *exit* sets a shell's exit status.

—*JP*

24.5 The ps Command

The *ps* command varies from system to system. (The *ps* on one Red Hat Linux system reads a *PS_PERSONALITY* environment variable with 21 possible settings!) This article describes several different versions. Yours is probably different in some ways, so check your *ps* manual page for details.

The *ps* command produces a report summarizing execution statistics for current processes. The bare *ps* command lists the process ID, the terminal from which the command was started, how much CPU time it has used, and the command itself. The output looks something like this (it differs by system):

```
  PID TT STAT  TIME COMMAND
 1803 p5 IW    0:00 -csh (csh)
 1883 p5 IW    0:04 vi outline
 1811 p6 IW    0:01 -csh (csh)
 5353 p6 TW    0:01 vi 4890
```

By default, *ps* lists only your own processes. There are many times, though, when it's desirable to have a more complete listing with a lot of data about all of the processes currently running on the system. The options required to do this differ between BSD Unix and System V. Under BSD Unix, the command is *ps –aux*, which produces a table of all processes, arranged in order of decreasing CPU usage at the moment when the *ps* command was executed. [The *–a* option gives processes belonging to all users, *–u* gives a more detailed listing, and *–x* includes processes that no longer have a controlling terminal (24.6). —*TOR*] It is often useful to pipe this output to *head* (12.12), which will display the most active processes:

```
% ps -aux | head -5
USER      PID %CPU %MEM   SZ  RSS TTY STAT  TIME COMMAND
martin  12923 74.2 22.5  223  376 p5  R     2:12 f77 -o foo foo.F
chavez  16725 10.9 50.8 1146 1826 p6  R N  56:04 g94 Hg0.dat
ng      17026  3.5  1.2  354  240 co  I     0:19 vi benzene.txt
gull     7997  0.2  0.3  142   46 p3  S     0:04 csh
```

The meanings of the fields in this output (as well as others displayed by the *–l* option to *ps*) are given in Table 24-1.

The first line of this output shows that user *martin* is running a FORTRAN compilation (f77). This process has PID (24.3) 12923 and is currently either running or runnable. User *chavez*'s process (PID 16725), executing the program *g94*, is also running or runnable, though at a lowered priority. From this display, it's obvious who is using most system resources at this instant: *martin* and *chavez* have about 85% of the CPU and 73% of the memory between them. However, although it does display total CPU time, *ps* does not average the %CPU or %MEM values over time in any way.

Table 24-1. ps command output fields

Column[a]	Contents
USER (BSD)	Username of process owner
UID (System V)	User ID (24.3) of process owner
PID	Process ID
%CPU	Estimated fraction of CPU consumed (BSD)
%MEM	Estimated fraction of system memory consumed (BSD)
SZ	Virtual memory used in K (BSD) or pages (System V)
RSS	Real memory used (in same units as SZ)
TT, TTY	Terminal port associated with process
STAT (BSD), S (System V)	Current process state; one (or more under BSD) of:

Table 24-1. ps command output fields (continued)

Column[a]	Contents
	R: Running or runnable
	S: Sleeping
	I: Idle (BSD); intermediate state (System V)
	T: Stopped (23.1)
	Z: Zombie process (24.19)
	D (BSD): Disk wait
	P (BSD): Page wait
	X (System V): Growing, waiting for memory
	K (AIX): Available kernel process
	W (BSD): Swapped out
	N (BSD): Niced (26.5, 26.7), execution priority lowered
	> (BSD): Execution priority artificially raised (26.7)
TIME	Total CPU time used
COMMAND	Command line being executed (may be truncated)
STIME (System V)	Time or date process started
C (System V), CP (BSD)	Short term CPU-use factor; used by scheduler for computing execution priority (PRI below)
F	Flags associated with process (see *ps* manual page)
PPID	Parent's PID
PRI	Actual execution priority (recomputed dynamically)
NI	Process nice number (26.5)
WCHAN	Event process is waiting for

[a] Some vendors add other fields, such as the processor number for multiprocessors and additional or different process states (as in the AIX K field). These codes may differ from vendor to vendor: for example, the O code under Stardent Unix means a process that is actually running (and R means runnable), while O under AIX means a nonexistent process.

A vaguely similar listing is produced by the System V *ps –ef* command:

```
$ ps -ef
    UID   PID  PPID  C    STIME      TTY  TIME CMD
   root     0     0  0 09:36:35        ?  0:00 sched
   root     1     0  0 09:36:35        ?  0:02 /etc/init
   ...
   gull   7997     1 10 09:49:32    ttyp3  0:04 csh
 martin  12923 11324  9 10:19:49    ttyp5 56:12 f77 -o foo foo.F
 chavez  16725 16652 15 17:02:43    ttyp6 10:04 g94 HgO.dat
     ng  17026 17012 14 17:23:12  console  0:19 vi benzene.txt
```

The columns hold the username, process ID, parent's PID (the PID of the process that created it), the current scheduler value, the time the process started, its associated terminal, its accumulated CPU time, and the command it is running. Note that the ordering is by PID, not resource usage.

AIX's version of the *ps* command supports both BSD and System V options. The BSD options are not preceded by a hyphen (which is a legal syntax variation), and the System V options are. Thus, under AIX, ps -au is not the same as ps au. The command is the System V version, however, even if its output is displayed with the BSD column headings. Thus, *ps aux* output is displayed in PID rather than %CPU order.

ps is also useful in pipes; a common use is:

```
% ps -aux | grep chavez
```

to see what user *chavez* has currently running. Under System V, use ps -u chavez.

Another way to view the process information is with the *top* command. Unlike *ps*, *top* is an interactive screen program that updates its information every few seconds. It's a good way to get a quick pulse of your system. Not only is process information displayed, but memory statistics and the system *uptime* are also shown. You can find the full range of available interactive commands by typing h once *top* has started. You can sort processes in a variety of ways including CPU and memory usage, as well as by user. You can even kill processes from within *top*.

—AF, *from* Essential System Administration *(O'Reilly, 2002), and JJ*

24.6 The Controlling Terminal

In article 24.5, we pointed out that the *ps* command needs special options (*–x* for BSD-derived versions and *–e* for System V–type) to list processes without a controlling terminal.

But just what is a controlling terminal? Just what it sounds like: the terminal from which the process was started. In the *ps* listing, this is usually given as a *tty*, or terminal ID. That *ps* entry usually corresponds to a serial port, or a *pty*. A *pty* or "pseudo-terminal" is a construct that makes a window or network login (1.21) look to the operating system just like a terminal.

In the *ps* listing, a tty might appear as t1 for */dev/tty1*, p3 for */dev/ttyp3*, or as some other designation, such as co for */dev/console*, the full-screen display of a workstation before any window system is started. Processes without a controlling terminal show a question mark (?).

How does a process "lose" its controlling terminal? Easy. Some processes, such as system "daemons" (1.10) never had one—they were started by system scripts that weren't started from any terminal, or they disconnected themselves from their controlling terminals. But it's also possible that you started a process running in the background, logged out, and logged back on later or on another terminal to find it still running without a controlling terminal. Disowned processes (23.11) fit this categoty too.

The *tty* command can be used to report which "terminal" you're currently connected to. For example:

```
% tty
/dev/ttyp2
```

Running *tty* without a controlling terminal gives the message not a tty.

—*TOR*

24.7 Tracking Down Processes

ps without arguments lists all processes started from the current terminal or pseudo-terminal. But since *ps* is not a shell command, it doesn't correlate process IDs with the shell's job numbers. It also doesn't help you find the ID of the runaway process in another shell window.

To get this information, use *ps –a* (for "all"); this lists information on a different set of processes, depending on your Unix version.

System V

Instead of listing all that were started under a specific terminal, *ps –a* on System V–derived systems lists all processes associated with any terminal that aren't group leaders. For our purposes, a "group leader" is the parent shell of a terminal or window. Therefore, if you are using a windowing system, *ps –a* lists all jobs started in all windows (by all users), but not their parent shells.

Assume that, in the previous example, you have only one terminal or window. Then *ps –a* will print the same output as plain *ps* except for the first line, since that's the parent shell. This doesn't seem to be very useful.

But consider what happens when you have multiple windows open. Let's say you have three windows, all running terminal emulators such as *xterm* for the X Window System. You start background jobs *alice*, *duchess*, and *hatter* in windows with pseudo-terminal numbers 1, 2, and 3, respectively. This situation is shown in Figure 24-1.

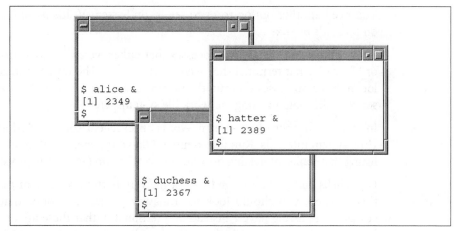

Figure 24-1. Background jobs in multiple windows

Assume you are in the uppermost window. If you type *ps*, you will see something like this:

```
PID TTY       TIME COMD
 146 pts/1   0:03 bash
2349 pts/1   0:03 alice
2390 pts/1   0:00 ps
```

But if you type *ps −a*, you will see this:

```
PID TTY       TIME COMD
 146 pts/1   0:03 bash
2349 pts/1   0:03 alice
2367 pts/2   0:17 duchess
2389 pts/3   0:09 hatter
2390 pts/1   0:00 ps
```

Now you should see how *ps −a* can help you track down and *kill* (24.12) a runaway process. If it's *hatter*, you can type kill 2389. If that doesn't work, try kill -QUIT 2389, or in the worst case, kill -KILL 2389.

BSD

On BSD-derived systems, *ps −a* lists all jobs that were started on any terminal; in other words, it's a bit like concatenating the the results of plain *ps* for every user on the system. Given the above scenario, *ps −a* will show you all processes that the System V version shows, plus the group leaders (parent shells).

Unfortunately, *ps −a* (on any version of Unix) will not report processes that are in certain conditions where they "forget" things such as what shell invoked them and what terminal they belong to. Such processes are known as *zombies* or *orphans* (24.19). If you have a serious runaway process problem, it's possible that the process has entered one of these states.

You need another option to *ps* to see it: on System V, it's *ps –e* ("everything"); on BSD, it's *ps –ax*.

These options tell *ps* to list processes that either weren't started from terminals or "forgot" what terminal they were started from. The former category includes lots of basic processes that run the system and daemons (1.10) that handle system services like mail, printing, network file systems, etc.

In fact, the output of *ps –e* or *ps –ax* is an excellent source of education about Unix system internals. Run the command on your system and, for each line of the listing that looks interesting, invoke *man* (2.1) or *info* (2.9) on the process name.

User shells and processes are listed at the very bottom of *ps –e* or *ps –ax* output; this is where you should look for runaway processes. Notice that many processes in the listing have ? instead of a terminal. Either these aren't supposed to have a terminal (such as the basic daemons), or they're runaways. Therefore it's likely that if *ps –a* doesn't find a process you're trying to kill, *ps –e* or *ps –ax* will list it with ? in the TTY (or TT) column. You can determine which process you want by looking at the COMD (or COMMAND) column.

Article 24.22 shows a similar thing: how to close windows by killing their process.

—CN and BR

24.8 Why ps Prints Some Commands in Parentheses

There is a reason that some versions of *ps*, and thus derivatives such as *w*, sometimes print commands in parentheses:

```
% ps -f -u jerry
      UID   PID PPID  C    STIME TTY     TIME COMMAND
    jerry 29240 29235  0 07:56:19 ttyp1   0:01 sh find_mh_dupes
    jerry 29259 29240 23 07:57:52 ttyp1   0:07 (egrep)
```

The reason is that whoever wrote *ps* liked it that way. The parentheses indicate that the command overwrote its name, or *ps* could not find the name, and that *ps* is printing instead the "accounting name." (The accounting name is the last component of the name given to the *exec* (24.2) system call, and is the name used in the system resource usage accounting file.) Basically, *ps* does this in the C language:

```
if (proc->argv == NULL || strcmp(proc->acct_name, proc->argv[0]) != 0)
    printf("(%s)", proc->acct_name);
```

In the case of a large environment, *ps* is unable to find the argument vector. This is because it reads only the last few stack pages of each process.

Other versions of *ps* use completely different mechanisms for locating the command arguments and may never print parentheses.

—CT, *in* net.unix-wizards *on Usenet, 13 November 1983*

24.9 The /proc Filesystem

In Unix, it seems almost everything can be treated like a file (1.19). On many modern Unix systems, even processes are files—well, sort of. A special filesystem named /proc doesn't actually "contain" processes, but it lets you interact with them. Almost all of the "files" in /proc are plain text, so you can access them from scripts and programs, as well as from the command line. Of the systems I've checked, my Red Hat Linux 6.2 box (kernel version 2.2) seems to have the most in /proc, so I'll cover it. Please check your documentation—a *proc*(5) manual page, for instance—for the story on your system.

All /proc filesystems have one subdirectory for each process currently running on the system. Each of those process subdirectories is named for its PID (24.3). Some versions of /proc also have other named files and subdirectories—and my system has a lot of them. Here's a partial listing of my /proc filesystem at the moment; I've left out a lot of the numbered subdirectories:

−F 8.10
```
$ ls -F /proc
1/       17415/  467/    cmdline      ksyms       pci
1047/    2/      482/    cpuinfo      loadavg     rtc
1052/    3/      5/      devices      locks       scsi/
1057/    345/    553/    dma          mdstat      self@
1287/    370/    593/    fb           meminfo     slabinfo
1289/    379/    594/    filesystems  misc        stat
14288/   393/    595/    fs/          modules     swaps
14289/   4/      596/    ide/         mounts      sys/
17409/   4017/   597/    interrupts   mtrr        tty/
17412/   407/    6/      ioports      net/        uptime
17413/   425/    apm     kcore        partitions  version
17414/   439/    bus/    kmsg
```

Linux system utilities like *ps* and *pidof* use information from /proc. Your programs can use it, too; there are some examples below. But it's also useful when you want to know something about your system. The "files" in /proc are most useful there. Let's look at a series of examples. We'll end with the numbered per-process "directories."

Memory Information

The Linux *free*(1) utility shows your memory status. It simply reads the file /proc/meminfo and reformats the information. If you want an alias (29.2) that simply shows how much memory is free, it's probably simpler to read the *meminfo* file directly. For example:

```
$ cat /proc/meminfo
        total:     used:    free:  shared: buffers:  cached:
Mem:   263929856 253022208 10907648 79675392 30797824 57868288
Swap: 394784768 14585856 380198912
MemTotal:    257744 kB
```

```
MemFree:       10652 kB
MemShared:     77808 kB
Buffers:       30076 kB
Cached:        56512 kB
BigTotal:          0 kB
BigFree:           0 kB
SwapTotal:    385532 kB
SwapFree:     371288 kB
```

grep **13.1**

```
$ alias memfree='grep Free: /proc/meminfo'
$ memfree
MemFree:       10616 kB
BigFree:           0 kB
SwapFree:     371288 kB
```

(The free RAM decreased a bit while I was writing the alias.)

Kernel and System Statistics

The */proc/stat* file has statistics on the kernel and system. As with most of the rest of */proc*, it's updated constantly. For example, we can *grep* for the CPU statistics. The four fields on the cpu line show the number of *jiffies* (hundredths of a second) since the system was last rebooted: time spent in normal-priority user mode, *niced* user mode (26.5), system (kernel) mode, and the idle task, respectively. You might want to use this information from a script that monitors your system's utilization. Here's an example: *grep*ping for the CPU ststistics, then the start of an *awk* (20.10) script that could watch the CPU usage:

```
$ grep cpu /proc/stat
cpu  14693561 48135949 638573 4031301
$ awk '/^cpu/ { print $5 / 100 " seconds idle" }' /proc/stat
40318.7 seconds idle
```

!! **30.8**

```
$ !!
awk '/^cpu/ { print $5 / 100 " seconds idle" }' /proc/stat
40323.8 seconds idle
```

Statistics of the Current Process

The sections below describe per-process subdirectories in */proc*. One special directory is */proc/self*. It has the unusual property of giving a different answer for every process that examines it: information about the current process. (This "directory" is actually a symbolic link (10.4) to the directory numbered for the process' PID.)

For instance, a process can check its */proc/self/fd* directory to see which files its file descriptors (36.15) are currently pointing to. This isn't just what *type* of file (disk file, *tty* (2.7), pipe, etc.) but the actual full pathname of the file. If you're new to Unix, this may not seem too earth-shaking, but it's actually pretty amazing.

For a simple example, here's a shell script that lists its input and outputs. It then redirects its standard input (file descriptor 0) from */dev/null* (43.12) and lists again.

```
$ pwd
/tmp
$ tty
/dev/pts/5
$ cat showfds
#!/bin/sh
cd /proc/self/fd
ls -l
exec 0</dev/null
ls -l
$ ./showfds < somefile
total 0
lr-x------  1 jpeek    jpeek    64 Dec  2 09:03 0 -> /tmp/somefile
lrwx------  1 jpeek    jpeek    64 Dec  2 09:03 1 -> /dev/pts/5
lrwx------  1 jpeek    jpeek    64 Dec  2 09:03 2 -> /dev/pts/5
lr-x------  1 jpeek    jpeek    64 Dec  2 09:03 3 -> /tmp/showfds
total 0
lr-x------  1 jpeek    jpeek    64 Dec  2 09:03 0 -> /dev/null
lrwx------  1 jpeek    jpeek    64 Dec  2 09:03 1 -> /dev/pts/5
lrwx------  1 jpeek    jpeek    64 Dec  2 09:03 2 -> /dev/pts/5
lr-x------  1 jpeek    jpeek    64 Dec  2 09:03 3 -> /tmp/showfds
```

Statistics of Processes by PID

All versions of */proc* that I've seen have subdirectories named for each process currently running on the system. Each subdirectory is named for the process PID (24.3). Here are a series of examples of the useful info on my Linux system:

showenv

- You can use *printenv* or *env* (35.3) to find the environment of your current process. How about the environment of another process? Here's a shell script called *showenv* that works like *printenv*:

```
#!/bin/sh
# showenv - show environment of a process, by PID
# If second argument given, show just that one environment variable.

f=/proc/$1/environ

if [ ! -r "$f" ]; then
    echo "`basename $0`: can't access process $1" 1>&2
    exit 1
fi

case $# in
1) tr '\000' '\012' < $f | sort ;;
2) tr '\000' '\012' < $f | grep "^$2=" ;;
*) echo "Usage: `basename $0` pid [envariable-name]" 1>&2; exit 1 ;;
esac
```

The *tr* (21.11) command translates the NUL-separated entries from the *environ* file into newline-separated lines. With one argument, the whole environment is shown. With two arguments, the script *grep*s for the environment variable named in the second argument. Maybe you'd like to know what the *EXINIT* (17.27) environment variable was set to in a *vi* process with PID 8984:

```
$ showenv 8984
DISPLAY=:0.0
ECIINI=/usr/lib/ViaVoiceTTS/eci.ini
EDITOR=vi
EXINIT=so ~/.lib/vi/exrc8
HISTFILESIZE=1000
  ...
$ showenv 8984 EXINIT
EXINIT=so ~/.lib/vi/exrc8
```

- The *status* file gives status information about the process. A lot of this information is available in *ps* (24.5) output, but it's broken out nicely here. For instance, maybe you're wondering what group access process 918 has, or what process started it (its parent PID (24.3)):

```
% cd /proc/918
% grep PPid status
PPid:    916
% grep Groups status
Groups: 1000 501 103
```

The PPID is 916. The process has the group numbers (can access resources with the group permissions of) GIDs 1000, 501, and 103.

- The command-line arguments of a process are in the *cmdline* file, separated by NUL characters. Hmmm, what files is that *tail –f* job, process 861, watching? Let's see...using *echo* (27.5) to add a final newline:

; 28.16
```
$ tr '\000' ' ' < /proc/861/cmdline; echo
tail -f /var/log/messages /var/log/maillog /u/jerry/tmp/startx.log
```

A Glimpse at Hardware

If you are curious about your system's hardware, a quick look at */proc/cpuinfo*, */proc/interrupts*, and */proc/ioports* will help you size up the system. All the following examples came from a Red Hat Linux box, but you will find these *proc* files on most Linux and BSD systems. For instance, */proc/cpuinfo* looks like this (on my system):

```
processor: 0
vendor_id: GenuineIntel
cpu family: 6
model: 6
model name: Celeron (Mendocino)
stepping: 0
cpu MHz: 400.918
```

```
cache size: 128 KB
fdiv_bug: no
hlt_bug: no
f00f_bug: no
coma_bug: no
fpu: yes
fpu_exception: yes
cpuid level: 2
wp: yes
flags: fpu vme de pse tsc msr pae mce cx8 sep mtrr pat pse36 mmx fxsr
bogomips: 799.53
```

The most important fields to notice are processor, model name, and cpu MHz since these identify how many CPUs are in the system, the model name (although this isn't always so clear in older Pentium models), and the CPU speed of your machine.

The other three *proc* files are important if you are installing hardware or trying to configuring recently installed hardware. */proc/interrupts* lists the hardware interrupt numbers and shows which devices are using which interrupt. On my machine, this looks like:

```
          CPU0
  0:   92887036       XT-PIC  timer
  1:     910141       XT-PIC  keyboard
  2:          0       XT-PIC  cascade
  3:          4       XT-PIC  serial
  5:    4794267       XT-PIC  eth0
  8:   11642728       XT-PIC  rtc
 10:   65248789       XT-PIC  es1371
 11:          0       XT-PIC  usb-uhci
 12:    5109157       XT-PIC  PS/2 Mouse
 14:     560048       XT-PIC  ide0
 15:     408739       XT-PIC  ide1
NMI:          0
ERR:          0
```

/proc/ioports lists the hardware I/O port ranges that all your systems devices use. This is a good file to examine if recently installed hardware can't be found in your drivers. Here's an abbreviated sample of my system's */proc/ioports*.

```
03f6-03f6 : ide0
03f8-03ff : serial(auto)
0cf8-0cff : PCI conf1
4000-403f : Intel Corporation 82371AB PIIX4 ACPI
5000-501f : Intel Corporation 82371AB PIIX4 ACPI
c000-cfff : PCI Bus #01
d000-d01f : Intel Corporation 82371AB PIIX4 USB
d400-d43f : Ensoniq ES1371 [AudioPCI-97]
d800-d807 : Lucent Microelectronics 56k WinModem
dc00-dcff : Lucent Microelectronics 56k WinModem
e000-e0ff : PCI device 1186:1300 (D-Link System Inc)
f000-f00f : Intel Corporation 82371AB PIIX4 IDE
```

This file makes it easy to diagnosis hardware conflicts. However, if your system is working well, you probably won't be looking at any of these files much.

—*JP*

24.10 What Are Signals?

Signals are a simple but important means of interprocess communication. Interprocess communication sounds fancy, but it's really a simple concept: it's the means by which one program sends a message to another program. It's common to think of signals as special messages sent by the Unix kernel (1.10) but, in fact, any program can signal any other program.

What kinds of messages can you send with a signal? Relatively few, in reality. Signals aren't "arbitrary" messages, like letters; they are a small group of predefined messages, each with its own special meaning. System V Unix supports 16 signals, each of which is assigned a number; BSD-derived Unix implementations and SVR4 have 32 signals. Table 24-2 lists some of the more commonly used signals. It also lists keyboard characters that send common signals on BSD systems (these can be changed; see article 5.8).

Table 24-2. Common signals

Signal name	Number	Meaning and typical use
HUP	1	Hangup—stop running. Sent when you log out or disconnect a modem.
INT	2	Interrupt—stop running. Sent when you type CTRL-c.
QUIT	3	Quit—stop running (and dump core). Sent when you type CTRL-\.
KILL	9	Kill—stop unconditionally and immediately; a good "emergency kill."
SEGV	11	Segmentation violation—you have tried to access illegal memory.
TERM	15	Terminate—terminate gracefully, if possible.
STOP	17*	Stop unconditionally and immediately; continue with CONT.
TSTP	18*	Stop—stop executing, ready to continue (in either background or foreground). Sent when you type CTRL-z. *stty* (5.8) calls this *susp*.
CONT	19*	Continue—continue executing after STOP or TSTP.
CHLD	20*	Child—a child process's status has changed.

Note that signal numbers—especially the ones above 15, marked with an asterisk in Table 24-2—vary system-to-system. Use the signal name wherever you can.

While the list in Table 24-2 isn't definitive, it shows you the types of things signals can do. Many signals, like *SIGSEGV*, are warning or error messages. You've probably seen the frustrating "segmentation violation" message. That message came when the kernel detected something wrong and sent your program a *SIG-SEGV* signal; in response, your program quit. Others signals, like *SIGTSTP*, are generated in response to special characters on the keyboard. And a lot of signals just say, "Your time is up, goodbye!"

When a process receives a signal, it can take a number of actions; for example:

- It can take whatever default action is specified for the signal. By default, some signals kill the process that receives them. For some signals, the default action is to stop running and dump core. (*SIGQUIT* is an example of this.) Other signals have no effect by default.

- It can trap (35.17) the signal and run a special "signal handling" function—in which case, it can do whatever it wants. A signal handler often does whatever's necessary to shut the program down nicely: make sure that files are closed and left in a consistent state, and so on.

- It can ignore the signal, in which case nothing happens.

You've probably read that the command *kill –9* is guaranteed to kill a process. Why? Two special signals in Table 24-2 can't be caught or ignored: the *KILL* and *STOP* signals.

The *kill* (24.12) command doesn't kill—it really does nothing more than send signals. As you now know, signals often bring death and destruction, but there's no necessary reason for them to do so.

—*ML*

24.11 Killing Foreground Jobs

You probably know that typing CTRL-c (24.10) will terminate your foreground job. But what actually happens when you type CTRL-c?

When you type CTRL-c, you're sending the *INT* (interrupt) signal (24.10) to the foreground process. Most well-designed programs "catch" the interrupt signal, which means that the program installs some special function (a "signal handler") that is called whenever a signal arrives. The signal handler normally closes all open files, resets your terminal properly (if needed), and does anything else necessary so that the program can depart from this world in peace. Then the program terminates. The *QUIT* signal, sent by CTRL-\, works similarly but also makes a *core* file for debugging.

Of course, it's possible for the signal handler to do something else entirely: the program can decide not to quit, or it can implement some truly bizarre feature. In fact, editors such as *vi* or Emacs almost always ignore most signals. The *trap* (35.17) command handles signals in the Bourne shell.

Whenever you send a signal from the keyboard, it's sent to all processes in the same process group (24.3). This may include the program's child processes, but it may not. And, of course, child processes can choose to ignore signals on their own. But more often than not, killing the parent process kills its children.

Article 5.8 explains how to set the key that sends these and other signals. The *kill* (24.12) command also sends signals.

—ML and JP

24.12 Destroying Processes with kill

Sometimes it's necessary to eliminate a process entirely or to signal a process (24.13); this is the purpose of the *kill* command. You can use the *kill* command with or without a signal id:

```
% kill pid
% kill -signal pid
```

where *pid* is the process' identification number, and *signal* (which is optional) is the signal to send to the process. The default signal is number 15, the *TERM* signal, which tells the process to terminate. On some systems, the signal must be specified numerically; others allow you to use either the signal number or its symbolic name. [Use *kill –l* for a list of signal names; unfortunately, the listing doesn't show the correspondence of names and numbers. However, they are in order, so if you can count, you can figure it out. *—TOR*]

Sometimes, a process may still exist after a *kill* command. If this happens, execute the *kill* command with the *–KILL* or *–9* option. This almost always guarantees that the process will be destroyed. However, it does not allow the dying process to clean up, and therefore may leave the process' files in an inconsistent state.

Occasionally, processes will not die even after being sent the *KILL* signal. The vast majority of such processes fall into one of three categories:

- Zombies. A process in the zombie state (24.19) is displayed as Z status in BSD *ps* (24.5) displays and as *<defunct>* under System V. When a process is exiting, it informs its parent of its imminent death; when it receives an acknowledgment, its PID is removed from the process table. A zombie process is one whose total resources have been freed, but whose parent process' acknowledgment has not occurred. Usually, *init* will step in when the parent is gone, but very occasionally this fails to happen. Zombies are always cleared the next time the system is booted and do not adversely affect system performance.

- Processes waiting for unavailable NFS (1.21) resources (for example, trying to write to a remote file on a system that has crashed) will not die if sent a *KILL* signal. Use the *QUIT* signal (3) or the *INT* (interrupt) signal (2) to kill such processes.

- Processes waiting for a device to complete an operation before exiting. Often this means waiting for a tape to finish rewinding.

Killing a process may also kill all of its children. Child processes may not die if they're blocking or "catching" the signal you use—although, as explained above, the *KILL* signal (9) will usually terminate those processes. Killing a shell can therefore kill all the foreground and stopped background processes initiated from that shell (including other shells). Killing a user's login shell is equivalent to logging the user out. This is a useful (if somewhat painful) way to recover from certain kinds of problems. For example, if a user manages to confuse his editor by mistyping control keys and escape sequences, or enters an infinite loop that he can't terminate by normal means, killing his shell will let him regain control of the situation, possibly at the cost of some work. Use the *ps* command to determine which process is the offending user's shell. Remember that you must be superuser (1.18) to kill someone else's process.

If you're using the X Window System, article 24.20 shows how to find which window has the processes you may need to kill.

—*AF, from* Essential System Adminstration *(O'Reilly, 2002)*

24.13 Printer Queue Watcher: A Restartable Daemon Shell Script

[This article may not appear to have a lot to do with the subject of this chapter, but it illustrates the other side of signal handling—what a program or shell script can do when it receives a signal. Jerry's script uses the *trap* (35.17) command to catch several different signals and act differently depending on whether the signal is a "hangup" (*HUP*, or signal 1) or a *TERM* (signal 15). —TOR]

Unix systems run "daemon" programs such as *cron*(8) and *syslogd*(8) that wait in the background, looking for work to do. Many daemons read configuration files when they start up. System administrators sometimes change the configuration files and want the daemon to reread the file. One way to do that is by terminating and restarting the program—but that's ugly and also means the daemon won't be running for a few seconds until it's restarted. So many daemons are designed to reread their configuration files and/or restart themselves when they get a signal (usually the HUP signal, signal 1). System administrators do this by getting the daemon's process ID number and sending the signal with the *kill* command. Because the daemon "catches" the signal, the daemon isn't actually killed.

You can run a shell script as a daemon by putting it in the background.* Here's a simple example, a shell script named *watchq*. It reads a file full of printer queue names and stores it in a shell variable. Every 30 seconds, it runs *lpq* (45.2) on all printer queues listed. If any queues have an error, the script echoes a message and the output of *lpq* to a particular user with the *write* (1.21) command. (You could change it to write to the system's *syslog* by calling *logger*(1) instead of *write*. Or use *xmessage* (36.26) to pop a notice window onto someone's X Window System console. Etc., etc.)

The script uses numbers (0, 1, 15) instead of signal names (*EXIT, HUP, TERM*). This is for portability to older Unix shells that don't understand names in *trap* commands. But if you write a script like this on a newer system, use signal names if you can.

watchq

/dev/null
43.12

```
#! /bin/sh
# watchq - "daemon" script that watches printer queue(s) for errors
temp=/tmp/WATCHQ$$              # Holds output of lpq
watch=/usr/local/lib/watchqs   # Queue names to watch
writeto=lisa                   # User who gets notices about printer
queues="`cat $watch`"          # Put list of queue names in $queues
trap 'queues="`cat $watch`"' 1 # Reset $queues if we get a SIGHUP
trap 'rm -f $temp; exit' 0 15  # Clean up temp file when killed

# Loop forever (until someone kills script):
while :
do
    for queue in $queues
    do
        lpq -P$queue >$temp
        if egrep '(out of paper|error|warning)' $temp >/dev/null
        then echo "PRINTER QUEUE $queue:" | cat - $temp | write $writeto
        fi
    done
    sleep 30
done
```

Now let's run the script. After the script has run for a while, the printer named *office* goes down. I edit the *watchqs* file and remove that printer so the poor user *lisa* won't keep getting complaints about it. Then I send a signal to have the file reread:

```
% echo office main lobby > /usr/local/lib/watchqs
% watchq &
[1] 4363
    ...
% echo main lobby > /usr/local/lib/watchqs
```

---

* It's usually also a good idea to be sure that the input and outputs are redirected (43.1, 36.16) away from the terminal, maybe to the system console instead. On systems and shells that kill background jobs when you log out, use *nohup* (23.10).

kill 24.12

```
% kill -HUP 4363
...
% kill 4363
[1]    Exit -48              watchq
```

In real life, the *watchq* script might be started from a system file like */etc/rc.local* when the system reboots. Lisa would probably edit the *watchqs* file herself. The username that's notified by *write* might also be resettable with a *kill –HUP* (or *kill –1*).

This isn't foolproof, and you can run into subtle problems. For instance, the *write* command may not work on some Unixes if it's running from a daemon without a controlling tty (24.6). Also, the error messages that *egrep* (13.4) searches for may not catch all problems, and they are system-dependent. If you use *xmessage*, a user who's away from his workstation could come back to tens or hundreds of windows; you might want to make the script pause until the user acknowledges a window. But this script is just a demonstration—to show a great way to write a quick-and-dirty daemon.

—*JP*

24.14 Killing All Your Processes

On many Unix systems, *kill* (24.12) interprets the special "process ID" –1 as a command to signal all your processes (all processes with your user ID), *except* for the process sending the signal. For example, the following command will terminate all your processes:[*]

```
% kill -TERM -1
```

To see if your system supports this feature, type `man 2 kill` (2.1) to read the *kill*(2) manual page.

You can use this to prevent background jobs from continuing after you logout; just stick `kill -TERM -1` into your *.logout* file. There are some good reasons *not* to do this though: if you use several terminals, this will kill *all* your processes when you log out from *any* terminal.

This command is also useful in desperate situations. If processes are spawning out of control, or if your terminal is locked, you can log in from another terminal and kill everything, without having to dig through *ps* (24.5) to find the right process. The *zap* (24.16) script searches process lists and kills processes automatically.

---

[*] Signal 15 is *SIGTERM*, which is the signal *kill* sends by default. In this command, you need to specify it explicitly, for obvious syntactic reasons.

The special –1 process ID is defined differently for the superuser; if you're root, it means "all processes *except* system processes."

If you can't use the –1 process ID, and you use the Bourne shell or another shell without job control, you can use a 0 (zero) process ID. That sends the signal to all members of the process group (that is, processes resulting from the current login). A 0 doesn't work on shells, such as the C shell, that have job control (23.3).

—*ML, JP, and JIK*

24.15 Killing Processes by Name?

This article discusses a particular version of *kill* that has some problems. Your system may have a different *kill* and, possibly, a version of *killall* (24.16) that doesn't seem to have as many problems. But this article is worth reading anyway for what it shows you about process names and the *ps* command. It's good info to keep in mind when you're trying to kill processes in a hurry.

On my Linux system, the *kill*(1) manual page says I can send signals to processes either by PID numbers (as we showed in article 24.12) or by process names. To an old stick-in-the-mud Unix user like me, who's been killing processes by their PIDs for 20 years, this doesn't seem very appealing. But hey, even *I* appreciate some of the new things Unix and Linux can do! ;-) So we're saying that, if my system is slow and I want to temporarily stop the two *gcc* compiles I'm running in the background, I can just type:

```
$ kill -STOP gcc
[2]   Stopped        gcc -c bigprog.c sub1.c sub2.c ...
[4]-  Stopped        gcc -o something something.c
```

Not necessarily. This is not always as simple as it seems. For one, before you kill a process by name, you'd better be sure that there are no other processes by that name, owned by you, running at the same time—unless you want to kill them too. That includes processes on other windows and *ttys* you're logged onto at the time; it also includes *at*, *cron*, or *batch* jobs that are running somewhere else on the system. Second, the process name may not be what you think it is. Third, even if your *kill*(1) manpage says that *kill* can do this, your shell may have a built-in *kill* that doesn't understand how to kill processes by name.

For example, let's say I have a runaway shell script named *cruncher*. I'm running it twice, and I want to kill both instances. Watch:

§ 23.2
```
1$ cruncher & cruncher &
[1] 21451
[2] 21456
2$ kill cruncher
bash2: kill: cruncher: no such pid
3$ type -all kill
```

```
kill is a shell builtin
kill is /bin/kill
4$ /bin/kill cruncher
kill: can't find process "cruncher"
5$ jobs
[1]-  Running                    cruncher &
[2]+  Running                    cruncher &
6$ kill %1
[1]-  Terminated                 cruncher
7$ ps
    ...
21456 pts/1    00:01:25 cruncher
8$ ps x
21456 pts/1    S      1:33 sh /u/jerry/.bin/cruncher
```

In command 1, I put the two jobs in the background. In command 2, I try to kill them by name. But my shell, *bash2*, is complaining "no such pid." Hmmm; it's using the shell's built-in *kill*; the *bash2* manpage seems to say that its *kill* only understands PID numbers. So, in command 3, I run *type –all* and find that the system *kill* is */bin/kill*. In command 4, I give the process name again, but */bin/kill* can't find it. Say what? Typing *jobs*, command 5, shows two *cruncher*s running. And I can kill one of them by using its job number, in command 6. More confusing, running *ps*, in command 7, also shows *cruncher* running.

The story ends at command 8, where I ran the BSD version of *ps* (24.5). It shows me what the default "friendly" System V–style *ps* (in command 7) didn't: the complete command line is actually sh /u/jerry/.bin/cruncher. This is a shell script, so the script filename *cruncher*, with the executable's directory from the *PATH* (35.6) prepended, is passed to a shell as an argument (27.3). So (whew): to kill these shell scripts, I should have typed kill sh. But do I really want to kill all running shells?

Another problem with killing a process by name is that a process can start a subprocess (24.3) with a different name. For instance, if your *make* (11.10) job starts a *gcc* compiler, and you type kill make, will that kill *gcc* too? Maybe—if the signal that *make* gets is passed to its subprocesses (if its subprocesses haven't been disowned (23.11), for instance). But unless all "smart" versions of *kill* are smarter than I think they are, they won't kill subprocesses with different names.

And don't think that you can just write an alias (29.2) to override your shell's *kill* with */bin/kill*: if you do, you won't be able to use job control (23.1) numbers like %1 because the external *kill* doesn't have access to your shell's job table.

My advice? It might be easier to use the old way—running *ps* to find the process(es) and kill by PID number—or use a script like *zap* (24.16) instead.

—*JP*

24.16 Kill Processes Interactively

When you want to kill processes, it's a pain in the neck to run *ps* (24.5), figure out the process ID, and then kill the process—although sometimes you have to do it that way (24.15). We'll look at two easier ways.

killall –i

Many systems have a command named *killall* with a –*i* ("interactive") option. **Be careful**, though, because there are several versions, and the most basic does just what it says: kills all processes on the system (when run as the superuser (1.18)). Check *killall*'s manual page on your system.

The version of *killall* we're talking about here accepts multiple process-name arguments on its command line. Without its –*i* option, the command sends a signal (by default, *TERM*) to any process name that matches. The process name you give has to match completely. Unfortunately, *killall* sends a signal to any process with that name—even processes owned by other users, which you can't kill (unless you're the superuser); you'll get the error `Operation not permitted`. For example:

§ 23.2
[5] 23.3

```
1$ cruncher & sleep 60 &
[5] 2714
[6] 2715
$ killall crunch eep
crunch: no process killed
eep: no process killed
$ killall cruncher sleep
sleep(2708): Operation not permitted
sleep(2710): Operation not permitted
sleep(2712): Operation not permitted
[5]    Terminated              cruncher
[6]    Terminated              sleep 60
```

With –*i*, *cruncher* lists the PID number and gives you a choice of typing *y* to kill a process or *n* to leave it alone:

```
$ cruncher & sleep 60 &
[5] 2732
[6] 2733
$ killall -i cruncher sleep
Kill sleep(2727) ? (y/n) y
sleep(2727): Operation not permitted
Kill cruncher(2732) ? (y/n) y
Kill sleep(2733) ? (y/n) y
Kill sleep(2734) ? (y/n) n
[5]    Terminated              cruncher
[6]    Terminated              sleep 60
```

zap

A more flexible way to kill processes interactively is the *zap* shell script, presented by Brian Kernighan and Rob Pike in their classic book *The UNIX Programming Environment*. The script uses *egrep* (13.4) to pick the processes to kill; you can type extended expressions (32.15) that match more than one process. The expressions can match partial or complete command names, any arguments to the commands, or, actually, any part of the command's line in the *ps* output. For example:

```
% zap 'troff|fmat'
   PID TTY TIME CMD
22117  01 0:02 fmat somefile? n
22126  01 0:15 sqtroff -ms somefile? y
```

We reprint the script by permission of the authors:

zap

```
#! /bin/sh
# zap pattern:  kill all processes matching pattern

PATH=/bin:/usr/bin
IFS='
'                        # just a newline
case $1 in
"")    echo 'Usage: zap [-2] pattern' 1>&2; exit 1 ;;
-*)    SIG=$1; shift
esac

echo '   PID TTY TIME CMD'
```

'…' **36.24**

```
kill $SIG `pick \`ps -ag | egrep "$*"\` | awk '{print $1}'`
```

The ps -ag command displays all processes on the system. Leave off the a to get just your processes. Your version of *ps* may need different options (24.5).

This shell version of *zap* calls another script, *pick*, shown below.[*] *pick* shows each of its command-line arguments and waits for you to type *y*, *q*, or anything else. Answering *y* writes the line to standard output, answering *q* aborts *pick* without showing more lines, and any other answer shows the next input line without printing the current one. *zap* uses *awk* (20.10) to print the first argument (the process ID number) from any *ps* line you've selected with *pick*. The inner set of nested (36.24) backquotes (28.14) in *zap* pass *pick* the output of *ps*, filtered through *egrep*. Because the *zap* script has set the *IFS* variable (36.23) to just a newline, *pick* gets and displays each line of *ps* output as a single argument. The outer set of backquotes passes *kill* (24.12) the output of *pick*, filtered through *awk*.

---

[*] The MH email system also has a command named *pick*. If you use MH, or frontends like *exmh* or mh-e, you could rename this script to something like *choose*.

If you're interested in shell programming and that explanation wasn't detailed enough, take a careful look at the scripts—they're really worth studying. (This book's shell programming chapters, 35 through 37, may help, too.) Here's the *pick* script:

pick

```
#!/bin/sh
# pick:  select arguments

PATH=/bin:/usr/bin

for i
do
    echo -n "$i? " >/dev/tty
    read response
    case $response in
    y*)     echo $i ;;
    q*)     break
    esac
done </dev/tty
```

/dev/tty **36.15**

—JP

24.17 Processes Out of Control? Just STOP Them

Especially if you're a programmer, you can run into a situation where you have processes forking (24.2) out of control—more and more of them. By the time you kill one, fifty more fork.

- On systems with job control (23.3), there's a good answer: use the *STOP* signal to stop the processes:

kill **24.12**

```
kill -STOP ...
```

Stop any process you can so that it can't fork more processes. Stop them all. Then start cleaning up with *kill –9*.

- If your system manager has set a per-user process limit on your computer, the good news is that your processes won't eventually crash the system. But the bad news is, when you try to run any command that isn't built into the shell (1.9) (like *killall* (24.16)), which would be nice to use in this situation, if you have it):

```
% killall -STOP myprog
No more processes.
```

you can't because you're already at your limit.

If that happens, log on to another account or ask someone to run a command that will give a list of your processes. Depending on your system, the command is probably like one of these two:

```
% ps -u yourname        System V
% ps aux | grep yourname   BSD
```

Then go back to your terminal and start stopping :-). If you get the No more processes error, your shell must not have a built-in *kill* command. Many shells do—including *bash* and *csh*. *Carefully* type the next commands to be sure that */bin/bash* exists (assuming your shell has a built-in *echo*, this trick* bypasses the external *ls* command); then, if the shell is there, replace your shell with *bash*. Don't make a mistake (if you do, you may not be able to log in again):

```
$ echo /bin/bas?
/bin/bash
$ exec /bin/bash
bash$ kill ...
```

exec **36.5**

—JP

24.18 Cleaning Up an Unkillable Process

You or another user might have a process that (according to *ps* (24.5)) has been sleeping for several days, waiting for input. If you can't kill (24.12) the process, even with *kill –9*, there may be a bug or some other problem.

- These processes can be unkillable because they've made a request for a hardware device or network resource. Unix has put them to sleep at a very high priority and the event that they are waiting on hasn't happened (because of a network problem, for example). This causes *all* other signals to be held until the hardware event occurs. The signal sent by *kill* doesn't do any good.

- If the problem is with a terminal and you can get to the back of the terminal or the back of the computer, try unplugging the line from the port. Also, try typing CTRL-q on the keyboard—if the user typed CTRL-s while getting a lot of output, this may free the process.

- Ask your vendor if there's a special command to reset the device driver. If there isn't, you may have to reboot the computer.

—JP

---

* This trick uses the shell's built-in wildcard matching (1.13) to show you the shell's name—we hope. If you get an answer like /bin/bas?, or multiple answers that don't include /bin/bash, try another shell name. (Maybe your *bash* is in */usr/local/bin*, for instance.) If you get an answer like No more processes, though, your *echo* command probably isn't built in.

You can't type just echo /bin/bash because that won't do a filesystem search.

24.19 Why You Can't Kill a Zombie

Processes in your *ps* output that are in the <exiting> or Z status are called zombies.

You cannot kill zombies; they are already dead.

"What is a zombie?" I hear you ask. "Why should a dead process stay around?"

Dead processes stick around for two principal reasons. The lesser of these is that they provide a sort of "context" for closing open file descriptors (24.3) and shutting down other resources (memory, swap space, and so forth). This generally happens immediately, and the process remains only for its major purpose: to hold on to its name and exit status (35.12).

A process is named by its *process ID* or PID. Each process also has associated with it a *parent process ID*. The parent PID, or PPID, is the PID of the process that created it via *fork* (24.2); if that particular process has since vanished, the parent PID is 1 (the PID of *init* (24.2)). While the original parent is around, it can remember the PIDs of its children. These PIDs cannot be reused until the parent knows the children are done. The parent can also get a single byte of status (35.12) from each child. The *wait* system call looks for a zombie child, then "collects" it, making its PID available and returning that status. The *init*(8) program is always waiting, so that once a parent exits, *init* will collect all its children as they exit and promptly ignore each status.

So, to get rid of a zombie, you must wait for it. If you have already done so or if the process' PPID is 1, the process is almost certainly stuck in a device driver close routine, and if it remains that way forever, the driver has a bug.

—*CT*

24.20 The Process Chain to Your Window

Almost everything we cover in this book works as well from an old-style, full-screen terminal as it does from an terminal window (like *xterm*) under the X Window System (1.22). Actually, a lot of it works on an old printing teletype, too! In all of those cases, you're interacting with a Unix shell. This article covers things you should know about using a shell from an X window. We'll talk specifically about the X11R6 *xterm* client, but this generally applies to any window with a shell inside of it—like GNOME terminal. This is a guided tour, so it helps to be at a workstation or other X display. If you can't take the tour, please scan through and look for the points I make along the way.

If you don't have an *xterm* window open, open one (by clicking on an icon, choosing a menu entry, or however you usually do it). We'll call this the "first window." Find its *tty* (2.7). Next, in this first window, set an environment variable (35.3) with a unique name and any value you want. You might call it *FAVCOLOR* and set the value to *purple*. Then, in that same window, type cd /tmp to change your current directory to */tmp*. Finally, type xterm -rv -sb (with *no* & after its name); this should open a second *xterm* window. Here's what that first *xterm* should look like (we'll show C shell syntax here):

```
% tty
/dev/pts/1
% setenv FAVCOLOR purple
% cd /tmp
% xterm -rv -sb
```
(cursor sits here; there's no shell prompt)

When your new second *xterm* pops open, it should be in reverse video (swapped foreground/background colors, the *–rv* option) to make it easy to identify, with a scrollbar too. In it, type tty to get its *tty* number, which will be different from the previous *xterm*'s. Run *env* or *printenv* (35.3), and you should see the special environment variable (like *FAVCOLOR*) that you set. Type pwd; the current directory should be */tmp*.[*]

If you've managed to follow this twisty series of steps, you've started a chain of processes (24.3).

You can see that chain of processes by typing the command ps aux or ps -ef (24.5). You should get lines something like these:

```
% tty
/dev/pts/3
% ps -ef
UID         PID  PPID  C STIME TTY        TIME CMD
jpeek       675     1  0 May13 ?      00:00:14 xterm
jpeek       681   675  0 May13 pts/1  00:00:00 zsh
jpeek     14850   681  0 15:58 pts/1  00:00:00 xterm -rv -sb
jpeek     14852 14850  0 15:58 pts/3  00:00:00 zsh
jpeek     14992 14852  0 16:07 pts/3  00:00:00 ps -ef
```

This is the chain of processes that led to the second window. Let's start from the bottom and work up. From the ps -ef command,[†] you'll see that the *ps* command itself had PID (process ID) 14992; its parent's PID (PPID) was 14852. So the process that started the *ps* process is the shell running in that window: in my case, a Z shell, zsh, with PID 14852. Notice that both of these processes are running on the same tty (2.7) named pts/3. That's a way to find all the processes in a particular window: check the tty name. This *zsh* is the shell running in this particular *xterm*. When you exit the shell (by typing CTRL-d or *exit*), the window will close too—but don't try that yet! Instead, find the parent of the shell; it's the

---

[*] If your setup files assume you're in your home directory (3.7), you may have some problems.

[†] Note that, if your system's process ID numbers have "recycled" and started over from 1, the *ps* command may not have the highest number.

---

xterm process, which is running on—are you surprised?—another tty, pts/1. This makes sense, because you started *xterm* from another window, the first window. There's a shell running in the first window too; it's the *zsh* with PID 681. The parent of the first window's shell is, yes, another *xterm*, PID 675. And its parent has PID 1; this is *init* (24.2), the "grandparent" of all processes on your system.

Your window system may not work quite this way. The parent of the top-level *xterm* might not be *init*. Also, an *xterm* could be owned by *root* instead of by you. Still, you should have a "chain" of processes, something like the one I described, on your system.

Why did we go through all this? One reason is so you'll know how to track the processes that lead to an *xterm*—and to know what to look for if you have to *kill* (24.12) a hung window or a process in a window. It's also to show that the environment from a parent window (here, the first window)—the current directory, environment variables, and so on—is passed to the child window (here, the second window). Finally, it's to show what happens when you close a window by exiting the shell: the shell terminates, so its parent *xterm* process terminates too.

So what happens to a shell running in a window if you close the window by clicking the "X" box on the window frame or by choosing the *close* or *destroy* commands in the window manager? The *xterm* gets a signal (24.10), and the system hopes that it dies. But it may *not* die, and the process may stay around. Instead of trusting the window manager to kill a window and the processes in it, I tend to use *ps* so I know for sure that all the processes are gone. Knowing the stuff we've looked at here lets me identify a window and its processes.

But let's not kill things! Instead, in the second window, type *exit* at the prompt. The window should go away. And, in the first window, you should have a new prompt. (If you had started the second *xterm* in the background (23.2), you could have kept working in the first window while the second window ran, too. But watch out for the *zsh* and *ksh* options named *bg_nice* and *bgnice*, respectively, which run background commands at lower priority. You probably don't want your new windows to run at low priority, so be sure that option isn't set.)

—*JP*

24.21 Terminal Windows Without Shells

xterm is an X client that runs a Unix process on a *pty* "inside" a window. By default, this process is a shell: an instance of the same shell you log into the system with. But it can be basically any Unix process. As you saw in article 24.20, when the process exits, the *xterm* window closes because its child process has gone.

To override the default shell process in an *xterm* window, use the −*e* option (5.22), followed by the command line to run the process. This must be the last thing on the *xterm* command line. If you want to open an *xterm* window with no scrollbar (the +*sb* option) and with the *vi* editor in it, to edit the log file named *logfile*, run the command below:

```
% xterm +sb -e vi logfile
%
```

An *xterm* window should open with *vi* running inside it. If you don't know how to use *vi*, the best thing to do is to leave it alone until you've finished this example—then press the ESC key, type :q, and press ENTER to exit *vi*. When *vi* exits, its window should close too, and you'll get another shell prompt.

I chose to have you run *vi* in a window because the *vi* process keeps running until you tell it to quit, and then the window closes. Other Unix processes that don't wait for a "quit" command will terminate as soon as they're done, and the window closes before you can see the process output. For example, let's say you want to display a file in an *xterm* window with a scrollbar. Start by choosing a file and using *wc −l* (16.6) to count the number of lines. Then open an *xterm* and a scrollbar, with the scrolling buffer length set to just the right number of lines:

cat **12.2**
```
% wc -l somefile
    74 somefile
% xterm -sl 74 -sb -e cat somefile
%
```

What happened? Unless your window manager holds it there, the *xterm* window closes just after it opens. Why? Its child *cat* process exited, so the parent *xterm* did too. One easy answer is to use a shell that runs three commands. First is the command you want to run (here, *cat*). Next, echo a prompt. Finally, run the *read* command (35.18) to pause until you give a dummy value—just pressing ENTER will be enough to satisfy *read*, and then the shell will exit. Here's how:

```
% xterm -sl 76 -sb -e \
     sh -c 'cat somefile; echo "Press RETURN to exit..."; read dummy'
```

(First, two notes. The backslash (\) isn't needed if you type the entire command on one line. And we've increased the scroll length to 76 because the *echo* and the newline after it add two lines of text.) Here, *xterm* starts a shell, but it's not the default shell (whatever that happens to be): it's the *sh* shell you specify after the *xterm* −*e* option. The *sh* option −*c* tells the Bourne shell to run the single command line from the following argument and then exit. The command line is in quotes to be sure the shell *inside* the *xterm* interprets it. The three commands are separated by semicolons (;) (28.16). If your command line is really complicated, you might want to change the sh -c '...' to run a little shell script (35.1) instead, like sh $HOME/lib/catter.

—*JP*

24.22 Close a Window by Killing Its Process(es)

In the X Window System, there's a process controlling every window. If the window (or its process) is frozen and you can't get rid of it, the easier way is usually to *kill* (24.12) the process. As article 24.20 explains, there may be a chain of processes running; the window could come from the parent process (as in the case of an *xterm* with a shell running inside of it) or it could be the child (such as when a shell script runs an X client like *xmessage*—as in the *nup* script below). Your job is to use *ps* (24.5) to track down the process(es) behind the window and kill the right one(s). We'll look at two different examples, then look at a shell script that opens a window and, later, closes the window by killing its process.

Example #1: An xterm Window

Let's say you're running *vi* in an *xterm* window, and the window seems to be frozen. Start with some detective work: open up another *xterm* window and run ps alwx or ps -ef. (If you're sure that all the processes in the window are owned by you—and none were set user ID (1.17)—you can use run ps lwx, for example.) You want a listing that shows the chain of process IDs, parent-to-child, in that window. The tty (2.7) of the shell inside the *xterm* will help you find the right one, if you know it. For example, I found vi 0568.sgm running on the tty pts/5, so the shell I want (the parent of *vi*) must also be on pts/5. From the shell's parent ID, I can find the PID of the *xterm* that started the shell. (I'll cut some of the columns in this listing to make it easier to read.)

```
% ps alwx
  UID   PID  PPID STAT TTY    TIME  COMMAND
 1000 11287     1 S    tty2   0:44  xterm -sb -sl 2000
  ...
 1000 11289 11287 S    pts/5  0:04  bash2
  ...
 1000  2621 11289 S    pts/5  0:00  vi 0568.sgm
```

 A Unix system cycles its PIDs. A child process may have a *lower* PID than its parent! (Here, vi's PID is 2621, but its parent's PID is 11289.)

Now you need to decide what process to kill. You could simply kill them all, assuming you own them (on some systems, the *xterm* process may be owned by *root*, so you can't kill it unless you can become superuser). But a little detective work can save trouble. For instance, see whether the *xterm* is still alive by trying to open its menus (5.17). If a menu pops up, the problem is likely with the shell (here, bash2) or its child process (here, vi). Try killing the most junior process (here, vi) first:

```
% kill 2671
% ps 2671
   PID TTY     STAT   TIME COMMAND
  2671 pts/5    S     0:00 vi 0568.sgm
% kill -9 2671
%
```

-9 23.3

In this case, killing the process with a plain *TERM* signal didn't do the job; *ps* showed it was still running. So I had to use kill -9. After this, if there's a shell prompt in the formerly frozen window, you're probably okay—although you may need to reset the terminal modes if it's still acting weird. On the other hand, if the window is still frozen, kill the next-higher process—here, bash2. Continue killing from the bottom up until the window is unfrozen or until the window closes.

Example #2: A Web Browser

The rule I gave in the previous section—killing the lowest child process first—is usually right for *xterm* windows, but not always right. For example, I'm using a development version of the Mozilla browser. It starts a series of child processes. But all the processes are designed to run as a unit, so killing the lowest child may just leave the browser in an unstable state. In cases like this, it's better to kill the top-level process (or one of the top, as I'll explain) and then check to be sure all the children have died.

Start with the long listing of processes. Find the parent and its children. Note that, depending on how they were started, they may not have a tty of their own—in general, a window doesn't need a tty unless it's running a shell-oriented utility. I've cut some lines and columns from the example to make it more readable:

```
% ps lwx
  UID   PID  PPID STAT TTY    TIME COMMAND
 1000  9526   752 S    tty2   0:00 sh /usr/local/mozilla/...
 1000  9536  9526 S    tty2  11:49 /usr/local/mozilla/...
 1000  9538  9536 S    tty2   0:00 /usr/local/mozilla/...
 1000  9539  9538 S    tty2   0:03 /usr/local/mozilla/...
 1000 19843     1 S    tty2   0:00 ./psm
 1000 19846 19843 S    tty2   0:00 ./psm
 1000 19847 19846 S    tty2   0:00 ./psm
 1000 19858  9538 S    tty2   0:00 /usr/local/mozilla/...
 1000 19859 19846 S    tty2   0:00 ./psm
 1000 19866 19846 S    tty2   0:00 ./psm
 1000 32316  9538 S    tty2   0:00 /usr/local/mozilla/...
 1000  5705  9538 S    tty2   0:00 /usr/local/mozilla/...
```

I started Mozilla from a menu on the window system. The window system was started from *tty2* (by typing *startx* in the second virtual console (23.12)). So the processes are "on" *tty2*, too. I happen to know that the ./psm processes are started by Mozilla. Although the parent *psm* is owned by the *init* (24.2) process (PID 1), these were either disowned (23.11) by Mozilla, or somehow the top-level *psm* process "lost" its parent. Finding this sort of disconnected process can be hard. One clue is that its PID is close to other Mozilla processes. Another clue may come when you use an output format like ps ux, which shows the starting time ("wall clock" time—not the CPU TIME column above): you may see that the processes all started near the same time of day.

The first process in the list, the shell script (starting with sh), is what probably started the chain of processes running. Often, on Unix systems, a shell script sets the environment correctly, then starts another library program running. All the other processes here seem to have been started from the process with PID 9536, which has used 11 minutes 49 seconds of CPU time. Just to be safe, I'll kill both top processes at once:

```
% kill 9526 9536
```

The browser window closed, to I'm close to done. I also need to do another *ps* to be sure the other processes have vanished; note that they may need a few seconds to die gracefully on their own. Sometimes you'll get a zombie process (24.19) that can't be killed, but it usually doesn't hurt anything—unless your window's processes have been doing some hardware accesses and the zombie is tying up the hardware. Article 24.18 has some ways to clean up in that case.

Closing a Window from a Shell Script

A shell script that opens windows also may need a way to close them. The simplest way is by killing the window's process. You should be sure that whatever this process does, killing it won't cause it to leave old lock files and other "e-debris" around; it should exit cleanly when it gets a signal.

The *xmessage* client works well in a case like this. It opens a little window with a text message in it. If the user clicks a button in the window, *xmessage* terminates. But, in the example below, I want the shell script to close the window instead. Here's how it works:

**nup
ndown**

The shell script has two links (10.4), or names: *nup* and *ndown*. I use them on my workstation, which no one else (usually) shares. When I run *nup*, the script brings the network up by dialing the modem and making a PPP connection. It also opens a red *xmessage* window with the message "network up" to remind me that my phone line is being tied up. When I'm done online, I run *ndown*. *ndown* disconnects the modem and closes the *xmessage* window by killing its process. Here's the basic script:

```
#!/bin/sh
pidfile=/tmp/.nup-pid

case "$0" in
*nup)
    xmessage -geometry 86x51+645+72 -fg white -bg red 'network up' &
    echo $! > $pidfile
    /sbin/ifup ppp0
    ;;
*ndown)
    pid=`cat $pidfile`
    case "`ps $pid`" in
    *xmessage*)
        kill $pid
        rm -f $pidfile
        ;;
    esac
    /sbin/ifdown ppp0
    ;;
esac
```

$! **27.17**

'...' **28.14**

When the script is invoked as *nup*, it starts *xmessage* in the background (that is, disowned (23.11)) and saves its PID in the temporary file. So *xmessage* will keep running after *nup* exits; its PID will be stored in the temporary file. Later, when the same script is invoked as *ndown*, it reads the temporary file to get the PID into a shell variable, runs *ps* to be sure that the process still exists and that its name still contains *xmessage* (in case another process has replaced *xmessage* in the meantime). If all's well, it kills that process to close the *xmessage* window, then removes the temporary file. Finally it shuts down the network.

The actual script (on the CD-ROM) does more error checking: verifying you're running the X window system before starting *xmessage*, ensuring the temporary file exists, and more. And, of course, this isn't foolproof by any means. For instance, if I click the "OK" button on the *xmessage* window, it will close while the modem is still on. But none of that is the point of this simple example script. It's to demonstrate how to close a window by killing its process. For instance, maybe your script opens an *xclipboard* window and wants to close it later if the user doesn't do so first.

—*JP*

25

Delayed Execution

25.1 Building Software Robots the Easy Way

If you are more familiar with desktop systems than Unix, the concept of delayed execution may be new to you. After all, the prime mover of all activity in the desktop metaphor is the user. In Unix, all kinds of processes start, execute, and report without any users on the system.

There are a few good reasons why you need to know about delayed execution. The first is that long, noninteractive jobs are best run when the fewest users are likely to be on the system. Humans find responsive systems desirable; processes aren't as likely to complain about getting sporadic CPU time. The second situation in which delayed execution is desirable is when a resource you need is only available at certain times. For instance, your group of local workstations create *tar* archives for the day's work, and you need to grab those files and copy them to tape. The third reason for delayed execution is when you need to push or pull information on a regular basis. This is the case with web masters who need to push their updated content to their production environment from their editing machine. The reverse may also hold true: you may need to collect Rich Site Summary files from a variety of web sites for a local cache. In all these cases, you need processes to start without you, like a band of relentless software robots.[*]

This chapter covers the following techniques of delayed execution:

- The venerable *cron* (25.2) system schedules process for regular, periodic execution. It is the most frequently used utility for running programs after hours.

---

[*] Thanks to Jeff Sumler for the phrase "software robots."

- For processes that only need to run once at some future date, the *at* (25.5) command is ideally suited.

- For simple scripts that need to pause before continuing on, the *sleep* (25.9) command is available.

—*JJ*

25.2 Periodic Program Execution: The cron Facility

This article covers two different versions of *cron*. There are other versions around: Vixie *cron*, for instance, has some different features and is common in Linux distributions. A variation called *anacron* doesn't assume (as *cron* does) that the system is running 24 hours a day; it's especially nice on portable computers. Rather than trying to cover every flavor, this article has information on older, basic *cron*s that should show you some of what to expect in whatever version you have.

cron allows you to schedule programs for periodic execution. For example, you can use *cron* to call *rsync* every hour to update your production web site with new articles or to perform any number of other tasks.

With redirection (43.1), *cron* can send program output to a log file or to any username via email.

cron jobs are run by a system program in an environment that's much different from your normal login sessions. The search path (27.6) is usually shorter; you may need to use absolute pathnames for programs that aren't in standard system directories. Be careful about using command aliases, shell functions and variables, and other things that may not be set for you by the system.

Execution Scheduling

The *cron* system is serviced by the *cron* daemon (1.10). What to run and when to run it are specified to *cron* by *crontab* entries, which are stored in the system's *cron* schedule. On older BSD systems, this consists of the files */usr/lib/crontab* and */usr/lib/crontab.local*; either file may be used to store *crontab* entries. Both are ASCII files and may be modified with any text editor. Since usually only *root* has access to these files, all *cron* scheduling must go through the system administrator. This can be either an advantage or a disadvantage, depending on the needs and personality of your site.

Under many other versions of Unix, any user may add entries to the *cron* schedule. *crontab* entries are stored in separate files for each user. The *crontab* files are not edited directly by ordinary users, but are placed there with the *crontab* command (described later in this section). [If your system is using Vixie *cron*, try creating a *crontab* file for yourself by typing crontab -1. This will create a new file with *vi* or the editor you've named in the *EDITOR* environment variable. Each line of this file should contain either a comment or a *crontab* entry (described below). When you save and exit the editor, your file will be added to the *cron* spool directory. —*JJ*] [In my experience, the current directory during these personal *cron* jobs is your home directory. If you read a file or redirect output to a file with a relative pathname (31.2), it will probably be in your home directory. Check your system to be sure. —*JP*]

crontab entries direct *cron* to run commands at regular intervals. Each one-line entry in the *crontab* file has the following format:

```
mins hrs day-of-month month weekday username cmd     (BSD)
mins hrs day-of-month month weekday cmd              (other)
```

Spaces separate the fields. However, the final field, *cmd*, can contain spaces within it (i.e., the *cmd* field consists of everything after the space following *weekday*); the other fields must not contain spaces. The *username* field is used in the original BSD version only and specifies the username under which to run the command. In other versions, commands are run by the user who owns the *crontab* in which they appear (and for whom it is named).

The first five fields specify the times at which *cron* should execute *cmd*. Their meanings are described in Table 25-1.

Table 25-1. crontab entry time fields

Field	Meaning	Range
mins	The minutes after the hour	0–59
hrs	The hour of the day	0–23 (0 = midnight)
day-of-month	The day within a month	1–31
month	The month of the year	1–12
weekday	The day of the week	1–7 (1 = Monday) *BSD*
		0–6 (0 = Sunday) *System V*

These fields can contain a single number, a pair of numbers separated by a dash (indicating a range of numbers), a comma-separated list of numbers and ranges, or an asterisk (*, a wildcard that represents all valid values for that field). Some versions accept strings of letters: for instance, Vixie *cron*, at least, accepts month and day names instead of numbers.

If the first character in an entry is a hash mark (#), *cron* will treat the entry as a comment and ignore it. This is an easy way to temporarily disable an entry without permanently deleting it.

Here are some example *crontab* entries (shown in non-BSD format):

/proc **24.9**

2>&1 **36.16**

\% **25.4**

```
0,15,30,45 * * * *  (echo -n '   '; date; cat /proc/loadavg) >/dev/console
0,10,20,30,40,50 7-18 * * * /usr/lib/atrun
7 0 * * *  find / -name "*.bak" -type f -atime +7 -exec rm {} \;
12 4 * * *  /bin/sh /usr/adm/ckdsk >/usr/adm/disk.log 2>&1
22 2 * * *  /bin/sh /usr/adm/ckpwd 2>&1 | mail root
30 3 * * 1 /bin/csh -f /usr/lib/uucp/uu.weekly >/dev/null 2>&1
12 5 15-21 * * test `date +\%a` = Mon && /usr/local/etc/mtg-notice
#30 2 * * 0,6  /usr/lib/newsbin/news.weekend
```

The first entry displays the date on the console terminal every 15 minutes (on the quarter hour); notice that multiple commands are enclosed in parentheses to redirect their output as a group. (This runs the commands together in a subshell (43.7).) The second entry runs */usr/lib/atrun* every 10 minutes from 7:00 a.m. to 6:50 p.m. daily. The third entry runs a *find* command at 7 minutes after midnight to remove all *.bak* files not accessed in 7 days. To cut wear and tear and load on your disk, try to combine *find* jobs (14.19). Also, as article 25.8 explains, try *not* to schedule your jobs at frequently chosen times like 1:00 a.m., 2:00 a.m., and so on; pick oddball times like 4:12 a.m.

The fourth and fifth lines run a shell script every day, at 4:12 a.m. and 2:22 a.m., respectively. The shell to execute the script is specified explicitly on the command line in both cases; the system default shell, usually the Bourne shell, is used if none is explicitly specified. Both lines' entries redirect standard output and standard error, sending it to a file in one case and mailing it to *root* in the other.

The sixth entry executes a C shell script named *uu.weekly*, stored in */usr/lib/uucp*, at 3:30 a.m. on Monday mornings. Notice that the command format—specifically the output redirection—is for the Bourne shell, even though the script itself will be run under the C shell. The seventh entry runs on the third Monday of every month; there's more explanation below. The final entry would run the command */usr/lib/newsbin/news.weekend* at 2:30 a.m. on Saturday and Sunday mornings were it not disabled with a #. (# can also be used to add comments to your *crontab*.)

The fourth through sixth entries illustrate three output-handling alternatives: redirecting it to a file, piping it through mail, and discarding it to */dev/null* (43.12). If no output redirection is performed, the output is sent via mail to the user who ran the command.

The *cmd* field can be any Unix command or group of commands (properly separated with semicolons). The entire *crontab* entry can be arbitrarily long, but it must be a single physical line in the file.

One problem with the *crontab* syntax is that it lets you specify any day of the month and any day of the week; but it doesn't let you construct cases like "the third Monday of every month." You might think that the *crontab* entry:

```
12 5 15-21 * 1 your-command
```

would do the trick, but it won't; this *crontab* entry runs your command on every Monday, plus the 15th through the 21st of each month.* An answer from Greg Ubben is shown in the seventh entry. He uses the *test* (35.26) and *date* commands to compare the name of today (like Tue) to the day we want the entry to be executed (here, Mon). This entry will be run between the 15th and 21st of each month, but the *mtg-notice* command will run only on the Monday during that period. The shell's && operator (35.14) runs the *mtg-notice* command only when the previous test succeeds. Greg actually writes the entry as shown here, testing for failure of the *test* command:

```
12 5 15-21 * * test `date +\%a` != Mon || /usr/local/etc/mtg-notice
```

He did it that "backwards" way so the *cron* job's exit status would be 0 (success) in the case when it doesn't execute *mtg-notice*. You may need that technique, too.

The *cron* command starts the *cron* program. It has no options. Once started, *cron* never terminates. It is normally started automatically by one of the system initialization scripts. *cron* reads the *crontab* file(s) every minute to see whether there have been changes. Therefore, any change to its schedule will take effect within one minute.

A Little Help, etc.

Some flavors of Unix, notably Red Hat and Debian Linux, have included an easy shortcut to creating periodic processes. In some systems, the */etc* directory will contain the following directories:

> *cron.daily*
> *cron.hourly*
> *cron.monthly*
> *cron.weekly*

By placing programs and scripts in these directories, you can have those chosen processes occur at the interval designated by the extension of the directory name. By sacrificing granularity of when those processes occur, you gain ease of use. Of course, adding several resource-intensive programs to the same directory may bring an underpowered system to its knees. Excerise care.

---

* This strange behavior seems to be a System V peculiarity that somehow infected the rest of the world. Original BSD systems behave the way we explained earlier.

In case you're curious, these directories are really just an extension of the Vixie cron system. Looking inside *etc/crontab*, we begin to see the magic:

```
SHELL=/bin/bash
PATH=/sbin:/bin:/usr/sbin:/usr/bin
MAILTO=root
HOME=/

# run-parts
01 * * * * root run-parts /etc/cron.hourly
02 4 * * * root run-parts /etc/cron.daily
22 4 * * 0 root run-parts /etc/cron.weekly
42 4 1 * * root run-parts /etc/cron.monthly
```

If you want to change when these various *cron* groups execute, this is the place to make your changes. The *run-parts* script is a little be more complicated, but it's worth a brief look.

```
#!/bin/bash

# run-parts - concept taken from Debian

# keep going when something fails
set +e

if [ $# -lt 1 ]; then
        echo "Usage: run-parts <dir>"
        exit 1
fi

if [ ! -d $1 ]; then
        echo "Not a directory: $1"
        exit 1
fi

# Ignore *~ and *, scripts
for i in $1/*[^~,] ; do
        [ -d $i ] && continue
        # Don't run *.{rpmsave,rpmorig,rpmnew,swp} scripts
        [ "${i%.rpmsave}" != "${i}" ] && continue
        [ "${i%.rpmorig}" != "${i}" ] && continue
        [ "${i%.rpmnew}" != "${i}" ] && continue
        [ "${i%.swp}" != "${i}" ] && continue
        [ "${i%,v}" != "${i}" ] && continue

        if [ -x $i ]; then
                $i 2>&1 | awk -v "progname=$i" \
                        'progname {
                            print progname ":\n"
                            progname="";
                        }
                        { print; }'
        fi
done

exit 0
```

The first dozen or so lines of this script are either comments or sanity checks to ensure that it was called with a directory name. The meat of the script is the loop that looks at all the non-tilde files in the given directory. As long as the file isn't a relic from the Red Hat Package Manager or an RCS file, the file is run and its results sent to *awk*, so that a somewhat clean report can be mailed by *cron*. You now have the code to set up this system if your Unix doesn't have it.

—*AF, JP, and JJ*

25.3 Adding crontab Entries

For a good tip on silencing *cron* job mailings, see article 25.6.

Most recent versions of Unix have a special command for maintaining the *crontab* file. To create a new *crontab* file, create a file containing the desired *crontab* entries. Then run the *crontab* command to install the file in the *cron* spool area. For example, if user *chavez* executes the command below, the file *mycron* will be installed as */usr/spool/cron/crontabs/chavez*:

```
$ crontab mycron
```

If *chavez* had previously installed *crontab* entries, they will be *replaced* by those in *mycron*; thus, any current entries that *chavez* wishes to keep must also be present in *mycron*.

The *–l* option to *crontab* lists the current *crontab* entries, and redirecting its output to a file will allow them to be captured and edited:

```
$ crontab -l >mycron
$ vi mycron
$ crontab mycron
```

The *–r* option will remove all current *crontab* entries. Many versions of the *crontab* have an additional *–e* option that lets you directly edit your current *crontab* entries in a single step.

On original BSD-based Unix implementations, there is no separate *crontab* command, nor does each user get a personal *crontab* file. It does distinguish between "global" *crontab* entries (in */usr/lib/crontab*) and "local" entries (in */usr/lib/crontab.local*)—however, you have to edit these files directly, which will probably require you to become superuser. It's a good idea to collect personal and site-specific *crontab* entries in the *crontab.local* file.

—*AF, from* Essential System Administration *(O'Reilly, 2002)*

25.4 Including Standard Input Within a cron Entry

Since *crontab* entries must be a single line long, it's hard to include any standard input with them. Sure, you can use commands like:

```
0 22 * * * echo "It's 10PM; do you know where your children are?" | wall
```

but you can't use "here documents" and other methods of generating multiline input; they intrinsically take several lines.

To solve this problem, *cron* allows you to include standard input directly on the command line. If the command contains a percent sign (%), *cron* uses any text following the sign as standard input for *cmd*. Additional percent signs can be used to subdivide this text into lines. For example, the following *crontab* entry:

```
30 11 31 12 * /etc/wall%Happy New Year!%Let's make next year great!
```

runs the *wall* command at 11:30 a.m. on December 31, using the text:

```
Happy New Year!
Let's make next year great!
```

as standard input. [If you need a literal percent sign in your entry, for a command like date +%a, escape the percent sign with a backslash: \%. —*JP*]

—*AF*

25.5 The at Command

The *at* facility submits a command line (or a script) for execution at an arbitrary later time. It has the form:

```
% at options time < scriptfile
```

This submits *scriptfile* for execution at a later *time*. The redirection (<) isn't required on versions that can read directly from a file. By default, *at* reads the commands from its standard input. So if you don't want to write a script, you can omit the file and type your commands on the terminal, terminated by CTRL-d:

```
% at options time
Command 1
Command 2
...
CTRL-d
```

The *time* is most commonly a four-digit number representing a time on a 24-hour clock. For example, 0130 represents 1:30 a.m. and 1400 represents 2 p.m. You can also use abbreviations such as 1am, 130pm, and so on.

—*ML*

25.6 Making Your at Jobs Quiet

Most modern versions of *at* will mail you any output that your commands make. You might think of using the command line below to throw *at* output into the Unix trash can, */dev/null* (43.12):

>& **43.5**

```
% at sometime... >& /dev/null        ...wrong
```

but that won't work because it throws away the output of the *at* command itself. *at* just saves your job in a file to be run later by a system program. The commands you want quiet are the commands stored in that file. One way to keep *at* quiet, if you use a shell like *csh*, is:

```
% at sometime...
at> some command >& /dev/null
at> another command >& /dev/null
at> ...etc... >& /dev/null
at> CTRL-d
```

Bourne-type shells make it easier:

exec > **36.5**

```
$ at sometime...
at> exec > /dev/null 2>&1
at> some command
at> another command
at> ...etc...
at> CTRL-d
```

Two notes:

- Some versions of *at* have a *-s* option that runs your job with the Bourne shell.

- Not all versions of *at* prompt you with at> as I showed above.

—*JP*

25.7 Checking and Removing Jobs

From time to time, you'll submit an *at* job and realize that there's something wrong with it. How do you get it out of the queue? Two tools help you do this: *atq*, which reports the jobs that are in the queue, and *atrm*, which deletes jobs that are already in the queue.

atq is pretty simple; by default, it reports on all jobs that have been queued. Optionally, you can give it a user name as an argument; in this case it reports all the jobs queued by the given user. The report looks like this:

```
los% atq
Rank     Execution Date      Owner    Job #   Queue   Job Name
 1st   Oct  9, 1996 22:27    mikel    4637      a     stdin
 2nd   Oct 10, 1996 01:08    mikel    4641      a     stdin
 3rd   Oct 10, 1996 02:34    judy     4663      a     stdin
```

Note that *atq* has no objection to telling you about other users' jobs. Although this might seem like a security hole, it's actually useful—see article 25.8. The jobs are ordered according to their execution date. With the *–c* option, *atq* orders jobs according to when they were queued—conceivably a useful feature. (*atq –n* just prints the number of jobs that are queued; I'm not sure when this would be useful.)

Once you've found out the job number, you can delete it with the command *atrm*. You can only delete your own jobs, not someone else's:

```
% atrm 4637
4637: removed
% atrm 4663
4663: permission denied
```

The command *atrm –* removes all the jobs you submitted; it's good for cleaning out your queue completely.

On some versions, use *at –l* to list your jobs (instead of *atq*) and *at –r* to delete your jobs (instead of *atrm*). Other systems may have different commands and options; check your manpage.

Some older BSD-based implementations may not support any of these options. Once you submit a job, you can delete it by finding its filename in the */usr/spool/at* directory and emptying the file (15.2). Or the superuser (1.18) can go to the spool directory and delete the file by hand.

—ML

25.8 Avoiding Other at and cron Jobs

atq and *at –l* (25.7) are more important than they seem. They give you a way to decide when to run your jobs. I suggest that you check *atq* before picking a time to run your job. If you don't, the system may have a dozen huge jobs starting at midnight or 1 a.m. They will bring the system to its knees when there's no one around to help out. Here's an example of what can happen, using the BSD-style *at* commands:

```
% atq
Rank     Execution Date    Owner  Job#   Queue  Job Name
1st      Sep 12, 1996 01:00  mikel  4529   a      trashsys.sh
2nd      Sep 12, 1996 01:00  johnt  4531   a      flame.sh
3rd      Sep 12, 1996 01:00  davek  4532   a      stdin
4th      Sep 12, 1996 01:00  joek   4533   a      troffit
5th      Sep 13, 1996 02:00  bobr   4534   a      stdin
```

Four of the five users happened to pick 1 a.m. as their submission time. There-fore, four big jobs will start in the middle of the night. Will your system survive? Will any of these be done in the morning? These are good questions. Instead of submitting your jobs to run at 1 a.m., midnight, or some other integral number, start them at different times, and make them times like 3:48 a.m. If your system administrator notices lots of jobs running at the same times on your system, she might delete some of them and ask you to reschedule.

If your system has personal *crontab* files (25.2), you won't be able to see other users' *cron* jobs. The best way to cut system load is to pick strange times like 4:37 a.m. for your *cron* jobs.

—*ML*

25.9 Waiting a Little While: sleep

sleep

The *sleep* command waits. That's all it does. (GNU versions are usually loaded with features, but the *sleep* on the CD-ROM doesn't do more than the standard version.) So what good is it?

- A quick-and-dirty reminder service when you don't have *leave*. This will print the message Time to go now.... in 10 minutes (600 seconds):

( ) & 43.7

        % (sleep 600; echo Time to go now....) &

; 28.16

- You can't use *at* (25.5), and you have to run a job later (say, in three hours):

        % (sleep 10800; someprog) &

- To watch a program (usually a shell script) that's running in the back-ground and see what processes it runs:

        % prog &
        [1] 12345
        % sleep 5;ps
          PID TT STAT   TIME COMMAND
        18305 p4 S   0:01 -csh (csh)
        18435 p4 S   0:00 /bin/sh prog
        18437 p4 D   0:00 /bin/sort -r temp
        18438 p4 R   0:00 ps

!! 30.8

        % !!;!!;!!;!!;!!
        sleep 5; ps; sleep 5; ps; sleep 5; ps; sleep 5; ps; sleep 5; ps
          PID TT STAT   TIME COMMAND
            ...
          ...5 seconds pass...
          PID TT STAT   TIME COMMAND
            ...

- When you're running a series of commands that could swamp the com-puter, to give it time to catch up. For instance, the *mail* (1.21) program starts background processes to deliver the mail. If you're sending a bunch of form letters, sleep five or ten seconds after each one:

```
% foreach name (`cat people`)
? formltrprog $name | mail $name
? sleep 10
? end
```

Or, to send print jobs while you're at lunch—but give other people a chance to print between yours:

```
% lp bigfile1;sleep 600;lp bigfile2;sleep 600;lp bigfile3
```

—JP

26

System Performance and Profiling

26.1 Timing Is Everything

Whether you are a system administrator or user, the responsiveness of your Unix system is going to be the primary criterion of evaluating your machine. Of course, "responsiveness" is a loaded word. What about your system is responsive? Responsive to whom? How fast does the system need to be to be responsive? There is no one silver bullet that will slay all system latencies, but there are tools that isolate performance bottlenecks—the most important of which you carry on your shoulders.

This chapter deals with issues that affect system performance generally and how you go about finding and attenuating system bottlenecks. Of course, this chapter cannot be a comprehensive guide to how to maximize *your* system for *your* needs, since that is far too dependent on the flavors of Unix and the machines on which they run. However, there are principles and programs that are widely available that will help you assess how much more performance you can expect from your hardware.

One of the fundamental illusions in a multiuser, multiprocessing operating system like Unix is that every user and every process is made to think that they are alone on the machine. This is by design. At the kernel level, a program called the scheduler attempts to juggle the needs of each user, providing overall decent performance of:

- Keeping interactive sessions responsive
- Processing batch jobs promptly
- Maximizing CPU utilization*
- Cranking through as many processes per hour as possible
- Preventing any particular process for dominating CPU time

---

* This list is modified from Tanenbaum and Woodhull's *Operating Systems: Design and Implementation*, Second Edition (Upper Saddle River: Prentice-Hall, Inc. 1997], 83).

System performance degrades when one of these goals overwhelms the others. These problems are very intuitive: if there are five times the normal number of users logged into your system, chances are that your session will be less responsive than at less busy times.

Performance tuning is a multifaceted problem. At its most basic, performance issues can be looked at as being either *global* or *local* problems. Global problems affect the system as a whole and can generally be fixed only by the system administrator. These problems include insufficient RAM or hard drive space, inadequately powerful CPUs, and scanty network bandwidth. The global problems are really the result of a host of local issues, which all involve how each process on the system consumes resources. Often, it is up to the users to fix the bottlenecks in their own processes.

Global problems are diagnosed with tools that report system-wide statistics. For instance, when a system appears sluggish, most administrators run *uptime* (26.4) to see how many processes were recently trying to run. If these numbers are significantly higher than normal usage, something is amiss (perhaps your web server has been slashdotted).

If *uptime* suggests increased activity, the next tool to use is either *ps* or *top* to see if you can find the set of processes causing the trouble. Because it shows you "live" numbers, *top* can be particularly useful in this situation. I also recommend checking the amount of available free disk space with *df*, since a full filesystem is often an unhappy one, and its misery spreads quickly.

Once particular processes have been isolated as being problematic, it's time to think locally. Process performance suffers when either there isn't more CPU time available to finish a task (this is known as a *CPU-bound* process) or the process is waiting for some I/O resource (i.e., *I/O-bound*), such as the hard drive or network. One strategy for dealing with CPU-bound processes, if you have the source code for them, is to use a profiler like GNU's *gprof*. Profilers give an accounting for how much CPU time is spent in each subroutine of a given program. For instance, if I want to profile one of my programs, I'd first compile it with *gcc* and use the *–pg* compilation flag. Then I'd run the program. This creates the *gmon.out* data file that *gprof* can read. Now I can use *gprof* to give me a report with the following invocation:

```
$ gprof -b executable gmon.out
```

Here's an abbreviated version of the output:

```
Flat profile:

Each sample counts as 0.01 seconds.
 no time accumulated
```

```
 %   cumulative   self              self     total
time    seconds  seconds   calls  Ts/call  Ts/call  name
0.00      0.00     0.00       2     0.00     0.00   die_if_fault_occurred
0.00      0.00     0.00       1     0.00     0.00   get_double
0.00      0.00     0.00       1     0.00     0.00   print_values
```

Here, we see that three subroutines defined in this program (die_if_fault_occurred, get_double, and print_values) were called. In fact, the first subroutine was called twice. Because this program is neither processor- nor I/O-intensive, no significant time is shown to indicate how long each subroutine took to run. If one subroutine took a significantly longer time to run than the others, or one subroutine is called significantly more often than the others, you might want to see how you can make that problem subroutine faster. This is just the tip of the profiling iceberg. Consult your language's profiler documentation for more details.

One less detailed way to look at processes is to get an accounting of how much time a program took to run in user space, in kernel space, and in real time. For this, the *time* (26.2) command exists as part of both C and *bash* shells. As an external program, */bin/time* gives a slightly less detailed report. No special compilation is necessary to use this program, so it's a good tool to use to get a first approximation of the bottlenecks in a particular process.

Resolving I/O-bound issues is difficult for users. Only adminstrators can both tweak the low-level system settings that control system I/O buffering and install new hardware, if needed. CPU-bound processes might be improved by dividing the program into smaller programs that feed data to each other. Ideally, these smaller programs can be spread across several machines. This is the basis of distributed computing.

Sometimes, you want a particular process to hog all the system resources. This is the definition of a dedicated server, like one that hosts the Apache web server or an Oracle database. Often, server software will have configuration switches that help the administrator allocate system resources based on typical usage. This, of course, is far beyond the scope of this book, but do check out *Web Performance Tuning* and *Oracle Performance Tuning* from O'Reilly for more details. For more system-wide tips, pick up *System Performance Tuning*, also from O'Reilly.

As with so many things in life, you can improve performance only so much. In fact, by improving performance in one area, you're likely to see performance degrade in other tasks. Unless you've got a machine that's dedicated to a very specific task, beware the temptation to over-optimize.

—*JJ*

26.2 Timing Programs

Two commands, *time* and */bin/time*, provide simple timings. Their information is highly accurate, because no profiling overhead distorts the program's performance. Neither program provides any analysis on the routine or trace level. They report the total execution time, some other global statistics, and nothing more. You can use them on any program.

time and */bin/time* differ primarily in that *time* is built into many shells, including *bash*. Therefore, it cannot be used in safely portable Bourne shell scripts or in makefiles. It also cannot be used if you prefer the Bourne shell (*sh*). */bin/time* is an independent executable file and therefore can be used in any situation. To get a simple program timing, enter either *time* or */bin/time*, followed by the command you would normally use to execute the program. For example, to time a program named *analyze* (that takes two command-line arguments, an input file and an output file), enter the following command:

```
% time analyze inputdata outputfile
9.0u 6.7s 0:30 18% 23+24k 285+148io 625pf+0w
```

This result (in the default C shell format) indicates that the program spent 9.0 seconds on behalf of the user (user time), 6.7 seconds on behalf of the system (system time, or time spent executing Unix kernel routines on the user's behalf), and a total of 30 seconds elapsed time. Elapsed time is the wall clock time from the moment you enter the command until it terminates, including time spent waiting for other users, I/O time, etc.

By definition, the elapsed time is greater than your total CPU time and can even be several times larger. You can set programs to be timed automatically (without typing *time* first) or change the output format by setting shell variables.

The example above shows the CPU time as a percentage of the elapsed time (18 percent). The remaining data reports virtual memory management and I/O statistics. The meaning varies, depending on your shell; check your online *csh* manual page or article.

In this example, under SunOS 4.1.1, the other fields show the amount of shared memory used, the amount of nonshared memory used (k), the number of block input and output operations (io), and the number of page faults plus the number of swaps (pf and w). The memory management figures are unreliable in many implementations, so take them with a grain of salt.

/bin/time reports only the real time (elapsed time), user time, and system time. For example:

```
% /bin/time analyze inputdata outputfile
        60.8 real       11.4 user       4.6 sys
```

[If you use a shell without a built-in *time* command, you can just type `time`. —*JP*] This reports that the program ran for 60.8 seconds before terminating, using 11.4 seconds of user time and 4.6 seconds of system time, for a total of 16 seconds of CPU time. On Linux and some other systems, that external *time* command is in */usr/bin/time* and may make a more detailed report.

There's a third timer on some systems: *timex*. It can give much more detail if your system has process accounting enabled. Check the *timex*(1) manpage.

—*ML*

26.3 What Commands Are Running and How Long Do They Take?

When your system is sluggish, you will want to see what users are on the system along with the processes they're running. To get a brief snapshot of this information, the tersely named *w* can show you who is logged in, from where, how long they've been idle, and what programs they're running. For instance, when I run *w* on my Red Hat box at home, I get this result:

```
 3:58pm  up 38 days,  4:37,  6 users,  load average: 0.00, 0.07, 0.07
USER     TTY      FROM            LOGIN@   IDLE   JCPU   PCPU  WHAT
jjohn    tty2     -               13Feb02  7:03m  1.32s  0.02s /bin/sh /usr/X
jjohn    pts/1    :0              8:55am   7:02m  0.06s  0.06s bash
jjohn    pts/3    :0              8:55am   0.00s 51.01s  0.05s w
jjohn    pts/0    :0              8:55am   7:02m  0.06s  0.06s bash
jjohn    pts/4    :0              8:55am   2:25m  2:01   0.12s bash
jjohn    pts/2    mp3.daisypark.ne Tue 4pm  3:41m  0.23s  0.23s -bash
```

Originally, I logged in at the console and started X. Most of the sessions are xterminals except for the last, which is an *ssh* session. The JCPU field accounts for the CPU time used by all the processes at that TTY. The PCPU simply accounts for the process named in the WHAT field. This is a quick and simple command to show you the state of your system, and it relies on no special process accounting from the kernel.

When you're debugging a problem with a program, trying to figure out why your CPU usage bill is so high [in the days when CPU cycles were rented —*JJ*], or curious what commands someone (including yourself) is running, the *lastcomm* command on Berkeley-like Unixes can help (if your computer has its process accounting system running, that is). Here's an example that lists the user *lesleys*:

```
% date
Mon Sep  4 16:38:13 EDT 2001
% lastcomm lesleys
emacs          lesleys  ttyp1     1.41 secs Wed Sep  4 16:28
cat          X lesleys  ttyp1     0.06 secs Wed Sep  4 16:37
```

```
stty          lesleys  ttypa    0.02 secs Wed Sep  4 16:36
tset          lesleys  ttypa    0.12 secs Wed Sep  4 16:36
sed           lesleys  ttypa    0.02 secs Wed Sep  4 16:36
hostname      lesleys  ttypa    0.00 secs Wed Sep  4 16:36
quota         lesleys  ttypa    0.16 secs Wed Sep  4 16:35
  ...
```

The processes are listed in the order completed, most recent first. The emacs process on the tty (2.7) ttyp1 started 10 minutes ago and took 1.41 seconds of CPU time. Sometime while *emacs* was on ttyp1, *lesleys* ran *cat* and killed it (the X shows that). Because *emacs* ran on the same terminal as *cat* but finished later, Lesley might have *emacs* (with CTRL-z) stopped (23.3) to run *cat*. The processes on ttypa are the ones run from her *.cshrc* and *.login* files (though you can't tell that from *lastcomm*). You don't see the login shell for ttypa (*csh*) here because it hasn't terminated yet; it will be listed after Lesley logs out of ttypa.

lastcomm can do more. See its manual page.

Here's a hint: on a busy system with lots of users and commands being logged, *lastcomm* is pretty slow. If you pipe the output or redirect it into a file, like this:

```
% lastcomm lesleys > lesley.cmds &
% cat lesley.cmds
    ...nothing...
```

tee **43.8**
```
% lastcomm lesleys | tee lesley.cmds
    ...nothing...
```

the *lastcomm* output may be written to the file or pipe in big chunks instead of line-by-line. That can make it look as if nothing's happening. If you can tie up a terminal while *lastcomm* runs, there are two workarounds. If you're using a window system or terminal emulator with a "log to file" command, use it while *lastcomm* runs. Otherwise, to copy the output to a file, start *script* (37.7) and then run *lastcomm*:

```
% script lesley.cmds
Script started, file is lesley.cmds
% lastcomm lesleys
emacs          lesleys  ttyp1    1.41 secs Wed Sep  4 16:28
cat          X lesleys  ttyp1    0.06 secs Wed Sep  4 16:37
  ...

% exit
Script done, file is lesley.cmds
%
```

A final word: *lastcomm* can't give information on commands that are built into the shell (1.9). Those commands are counted as part of the shell's execution time; they'll be in an entry for *csh*, *sh*, etc. after the shell terminates.

—*JP and JJ*

26.4 Checking System Load: uptime

uptime

The BSD command *uptime*, also available under System V Release 4, AIX, and some System V Release 3 implementations, will give you a rough estimate of the system load:

```
% uptime
3:24pm up 2 days, 2:41, 16 users, load average: 1.90, 1.43, 1.33
```

uptime reports the current time, the amount of time the system has been up, and three load average figures. The load average is a rough measure of CPU use. These three figures report the average number of processes active during the last minute, the last 5 minutes, and the last 15 minutes. High load averages usually mean that the system is being used heavily and the response time is correspondingly slow. Note that the system's load average does not take into account the priorities and *niceness* (26.5) of the processes that are running.

What's high? As usual, that depends on your system. Ideally, you'd like a load average under, say, 3, but that's not always possible given what some systems are required to do. Higher load averages are usually more tolerable on machines with more than one processor. Ultimately, "high" means high enough that you don't need *uptime* to tell you that the system is overloaded—you can tell from its response time.

Furthermore, different systems behave differently under the same load average. For example, on some workstations, running a single CPU-bound background job at the same time as the X Window System (1.22) will bring response to a crawl even though the load average remains quite "low." In the end, load averages are significant only when they differ from whatever is "normal" on your system.

—*AF*

26.5 Know When to Be "nice" to Other Users...and When Not To

The BSD–System V split isn't so obvious in modern Unixes, but the different priority systems still live in various flavors. This article should help you understand the system in whatever version you have.

If you are going to run a CPU-bound (26.1) process that will monopolize the CPU from other processes, you may reduce the urgency of that more intensive process in the eyes of the process scheduler by using *nice* before you run the program. For example:

```
$ nice executable_filename
```

On most systems, no user can directly change a process's priority (only the scheduler does that), and only the administrator can use *nice* to make a process more urgent. In practice, *nice* is rarely used on multiuser systems—the tragedy of the commons—but you may be able to get more processes running simultaneously by judicious use of this program.

If you're not familiar with Unix, you will find its definition of priority confusing—it's the opposite of what you would expect. A process with a high *nice* number runs at low priority, getting relatively little of the processor's attention; similarly, jobs with a low *nice* number run at high priority. This is why the *nice* number is usually called *niceness*: a job with a lot of niceness is very kind to the other users of your system (i.e., it runs at low priority), while a job with little niceness hogs the CPU. The term "niceness" is awkward, like the priority system itself. Unfortunately, it's the only term that is both accurate (*nice* numbers are used to compute priorities but are not the priorities themselves) and avoids horrible circumlocutions ("increasing the priority means lowering the priority...").

Many supposedly experienced users claim that *nice* has virtually no effect. Don't listen to them. As a general rule, reducing the priority of an I/O-bound job (a job that's waiting for I/O a lot of the time) won't change things very much. The system rewards jobs that spend most of their time waiting for I/O by increasing their priority. But reducing the priority of a CPU-bound process can have a significant effect. Compilations, batch typesetting programs (*troff*, TEX, etc.), applications that do a lot of math, and similar programs are good candidates for *nice*. On a moderately loaded system, I have found that *nice* typically makes a CPU-intensive job roughly 30 percent slower and consequently frees that much time for higher priority jobs. You can often significantly improve keyboard response by running CPU-intensive jobs at low priority.

Note that System V Release 4 has a much more complex priority system, including real-time priorities. Priorities are managed with the *priocntl* command. The older *nice* command is available for compatibility. Other Unix implementations (including HP and Concurrent) support real-time scheduling. These implementations have their own tools for managing the scheduler.

The *nice* command sets a job's niceness, which is used to compute its priority. It may be one of the most nonuniform commands in the universe. There are four versions, each slightly different from the others. BSD Unix has one *nice* that is built into the C shell, and another standalone version can be used by other shells. System V also has one *nice* that is built into the C shell and a separate standalone version.

Under BSD Unix, you must also know about the *renice*(8) command (26.7); this lets you change the niceness of a job after it is running. Under System V, you can't modify a job's niceness once it has started, so there is no equivalent.

Think carefully before you *nice* an interactive job like a text editor. See article 26.6.

We'll tackle the different variations of *nice* in order.

BSD C Shell nice

Under BSD Unix, *nice* numbers run from –20 to 20. The –20 designation corresponds to the highest priority; 20 corresponds to the lowest. By default, Unix assigns the *nice* number 0 to user-executed jobs. The lowest *nice* numbers (–20 to –17) are unofficially reserved for system processes. Assigning a user's job to these *nice* numbers can cause problems. Users can always request a higher *nice* number (i.e., a lower priority) for their jobs. Only the superuser (1.18) can raise a job's priority.

To submit a job at a greater niceness, precede it with the modifier *nice*. For example, the following command runs an *awk* command at low priority:

```
% nice awk -f proc.awk datafile > awk.out
```

By default, the *csh* version of *nice* will submit this job with a *nice* level of 4. To submit a job with an arbitrary *nice* number, use *nice* one of these ways, where *n* is an integer between 0 and 20:

```
% nice +n command
% nice -n command
```

The +*n* designation requests a positive *nice* number (low priority); –*n* requests a negative *nice* number. Only a superuser may request a negative *nice* number.

BSD Standalone nice

The standalone version of *nice* differs from C shell *nice* in that it is a separate program, not a command built in to the C shell. You can therefore use the standalone version in any situation: within makefiles (11.10), when you are running the Bourne shell, etc. The principles are the same. *nice* numbers run from –20 to 20, with the default being 0. Only the syntax has been changed to confuse you. For the standalone version, –*n* requests a positive *nice* number (lower priority) and – –*n* requests a negative *nice* number (higher priority—superuser only). Consider these commands:

```
$ nice -6 awk -f proc.awk datafile > awk.out
# nice --6 awk -f proc.awk datafile > awk.out
```

The first command runs *awk* with a high *nice* number (i.e., 6). The second command, which can be issued only by a superuser, runs *awk* with a low *nice* number (i.e., –6). If no level is specified, the default argument is –10.

System V C Shell nice

System V takes a slightly different view of *nice* numbers. *nice* levels run from 0 to 39; the default is 20. The numbers are different but their meanings are the same: 39 corresponds to the lowest possible priority, and 0 is the highest. A few System V implementations support real-time submission via *nice*. Jobs submitted by root with extremely low *nice* numbers (–20 or below) allegedly get all of the CPU's time. Systems on which this works properly are very rare and usually advertise support for real-time processing. In any case, running jobs this way will destroy multiuser performance. This feature is completely different from real-time priorities in System V Release 4.

With these exceptions, the C shell version of *nice* is the same as its BSD cousin. To submit a job at a low priority, use the command:

```
% nice command
```

This increases the command's niceness by the default amount (4, the same as BSD Unix); *command* will run at *nice* level 24. To run a job at an arbitrary priority, use one of the following commands, where *n* is an integer between 0 and 19:

```
% nice +n command
% nice -n command
```

The +*n* entry requests a higher *nice* level (a decreased priority), while –*n* requests a lower *nice* level (a higher priority). Again, this is similar to BSD Unix, with one important difference: *n* is now relative to the default *nice* level. That is, the following command runs *awk* at *nice* level 26:

```
% nice +6 awk -f proc.awk datafile > awk.out
```

System V Standalone nice

Once again, the standalone version of *nice* is useful if you are writing makefiles or shell scripts or if you use the Bourne shell as your interactive shell. It is similar to the C shell version, with these differences:

- With no arguments, standalone *nice* increases the *nice* number by 10 instead of by 4; this is a significantly greater reduction in the program's priority.
- With the argument –*n*, *nice* increases the *nice* number by *n* (reducing priority).
- With the argument – –*n*, *nice* decreases the *nice* number by *n* (increasing priority; superuser only).

Consider these commands:

```
$ nice -6 awk -f proc.awk datafile > awk.out
# nice --6 awk -f proc.awk datafile > awk.out
```

The first command runs *awk* at a higher *nice* level (i.e., 26, which corresponds to a lower priority). The second command, which can be given only by the superuser, runs *awk* at a lower *nice* level (i.e., 14).

—ML

26.6 A nice Gotcha

It's *not* a good idea to *nice* a foreground job (23.3). If the system gets busy, your terminal could "freeze" waiting to get enough CPU time to do something. You may not even be able to kill (24.11) a *nice*'d job on a very busy system because the CPU may never give the process enough CPU time to recognize the signal waiting for it! And, of course, don't *nice* an interactive program like a text editor unless you like to wait... :-)

—JP

26.7 Changing a Running Job's Niceness

On Unix systems with BSD-style priority schemes, once a job is running, you can use the *renice*(8) command to change the job's priority:

```
% /etc/renice priority -p pid
% /etc/renice priority -g pgrp
% /etc/renice priority -u uname
```

where *priority* is the new *nice* level (26.5) for the job. It must be a signed integer between –20 and 20. *pid* is the ID number (24.3) (as shown by *ps* (24.5)) of the process you want to change. *pgrp* is the number of a process group (24.3), as shown by *ps –l*; this version of the command modifies the priority of all commands in a process group. *uname* may be a user's name, as shown in */etc/passwd*; this form of the command modifies the priority of all jobs submitted by the user.

A nice level of 19 is the "nicest": the process will run only when nothing else on the system wants to. Negative values make a process get a greater percentage of the CPU's time than the default niceness (which is 0). Again, only the superuser can lower the *nice* number (raise a process' priority). Users can only raise the *nice* number (lower the priority), and they can modify the priorities of only the jobs they started.

—ML

Part VI

Scripting

Part VI contains the following chapters:

27

Shell Interpretation

27.1 What the Shell Does

As we've said, the shell is just another program. It's responsible for interpreting the commands you type. There are several commonly used shells, primarily based on two or three major families and a wide variety of other projects:

- The Bourne shell (*sh*) and its derivatives and progeny (including *bash*, *ash*, and even the Korn shell *ksh*)
- The C shell (*csh*) and its progeny (including *tcsh*)
- The Korn shell (*ksh*) and variants (including *pdksh* and *zsh**)
- Specialized shells based on languages such as Python, TCL, *perl*, and so on.
- Shells invented to meet specific needs such as restricted command access (*rsh*), recovery after a system failure (*sash*), and downloading, installing, and configuring software libraries.

If you can think of a reason to have a specialized shell, someone probably has already written one to meet that need.

Interpreting your commands might seem simple enough, but a lot of things happen between the time you press RETURN and the time the computer actually does what you want. The process of interpretation is very complex: the shell has to break the command into words and expand aliases (29.2), history operators (30.8), and shell and environment variables (35.3, 35.9). It also sets up standard input and output streams (43.1) and performs a lot of other tasks. Indeed, if a command looks right but doesn't work right, the cause is probably either one of the following:

---

* It's difficult to trace the development of all these shells in a simple manner. Their authors have borrowed ideas and syntax from the others—and sometimes code—and sometimes a shell starts out trying to emulate another but evolves away from its original inspiration (or the inspiration evolves away from the aspirant).

- File permissions are set incorrectly.
- You don't understand how the shell is processing your command line.

I'd say that file permission problems are more common, but it's a close call. File permission problems are usually easy to understand, once you know what to look for, but the rules by which a shell interprets your command line are another thing altogether. Lest I scare you, we'll try to go slow with this material. Although it's difficult, understanding how the shell parses your commands is important to becoming a power user.

In this chapter, we'll look at how a Unix shell interprets commands. Shells have similar interpretation rules. The C shell can be tricky at times, mostly because its behavior isn't as well defined as the others. And *zsh* has some twists that others don't—they're included by design, but they can surprise users of other shells. However, there's nothing "magical" about these rules. Tomorrow morning, you may grab some new shell from the Net and find out that it has a new and different way of interpreting commands. For better or worse, that's what Unix is all about.

As part of this discussion, we'll cover quoting, which is the mechanism by which you can turn off the special meanings that the shell assigns to some characters. Quoting is an integral part of command-line processing; it allows you to control what the shell will do to your commands.

—ML and SJC

27.2 How the Shell Executes Other Commands

When the shell executes an external command (1.9), what happens?

Unix programs are executed through a combination of two system calls (low-level requests to the operating system) called *fork* and *exec*.

The *exec* system call tells the kernel to execute another program. However, the kernel replaces the calling program with the new one being called. This doesn't work too well if you want to return to the original program after the new one has done its job.

To get around this problem, programs that want to stick around first copy themselves with the *fork* system call. Then the copied program *execs* the new program, terminating itself in the process.

You don't really need to know this little tidbit about what goes on behind the scenes, but it sure helps to know about *fork* and *exec* when reading some Unix manuals. Article 24.2 has more information.

—TOR and SJC

27.3 What's a Shell, Anyway?

A *shell* is a program that interprets your command lines and runs other programs. Another name for the shell is "command interpreter." This article covers the two major Unix shell families, including discussion about how shells run, search for programs, and read shell script files.

How Shells Run Other Programs

For each command it runs, a shell performs a series of steps. First, if the shell is reading commands from a terminal (interactively), it prints a prompt (such as % or $) and waits for you to type something. Next, the shell reads the command line (like *cat –v afile bfile > cfile*), interprets it (27.1), and runs the result. When the command finishes running (unless the command is in the background (23.2)), the shell is ready to read another command line.

Interactive Use Versus Shell Scripts

A shell can read command lines from a terminal or it can read them from a file. When you put command lines into a file, that file is called a *shell script* (35.1) or shell program. The shell handles the shell script just as it handles the commands you type from a terminal (though the shell uses its *non-interactive* mode (3.4), which means, basically, that it doesn't print the % or $ prompts, among other things). With this information, you already know how to write simple shell scripts—just put commands in a file and feed them to the shell!

In addition, though, there are a number of programming constructs that make it possible to write shell programs that are much more powerful than just a list of commands.

Types of Shells

There are two main shell families in Unix:

- The *C shell* and its derivatives (*csh*, *tcsh*) are considered very powerful for situations where you are interactively working on a terminal. *csh* will read shell scripts and has some useful features for programmers. Unfortunately, it has some quirks that can make shell programming tough.

- The *Bourne shell* (*sh*) and shells like it are probably used more often for shell programming. (Some newer *sh*-like shells, including *ksh*, *zsh*, and *bash* (1.6), combine handy interactive C shell–like features with Bourne shell syntax.)

Shell Search Paths

As article 27.6 explains, if the shell is trying to run a command, and the command isn't built-in to the shell itself, the shell looks in a list of directories called a *search path*. Unix systems have standard directories with names like /bin and /usr/bin that hold standard Unix programs. Almost everyone's search path includes these directories.

If you do much shell programming, you should make a directory on your account for executable files. Most people name theirs *bin* and put it under their home directory. See article 7.4.

Bourne Shell Used Here

Most serious shell programmers write their scripts for the Bourne shell or its variants, such as *bash* or *ksh*. So do we.

Newer Bourne shells have features—such as shell functions (29.11), an *unset* command for shell variables, and others—that the earlier Version 7 Bourne shell didn't. Most scripts in this book are written to work on all Bourne shells—for the sake of portability, some scripts don't use these new features. It's pretty rare to find such old shells around nowadays, though, so use your own judgment. It is pretty unlikely that if you're writing a shell script for your own use on a new system you will ever need to back-port it to run on a V7 system.

For the rest of these introductory articles, it may be easier if you have a terminal close by so you can try the examples. If your account uses the Bourne shell or one of its relatives (*ksh*, *bash*, etc.), your prompt probably has a dollar sign ($) in it somewhere, unless you've modified the prompt yourself (4.1). If your account isn't running the Bourne shell, start one by typing sh. Your prompt should change to a dollar sign ($). You'll be using the Bourne shell until you type CTRL-d at the start of a line:

```
% sh
$
$ ...Enter commands...
$ CTRL-d
%
```

Default Commands

One more thing to note is that when dealing with shell scripts, which store sequences of commands that you want to be able to run at one time, you will likely need to specify the shell or other program that will run the commands by default. This is normally done using the special #! notation (36.2) in the first line of the script.

```
#!/bin/sh
# everything in this script will be run under the Bourne shell

...

#!/bin/tcsh
# everything in this script will be run under tcsh

...

#!/usr/bin/perl
# everything in this script will be interpreted as a perl command

...
```

—*JP and SJC*

27.4 Command Evaluation and Accidentally Overwriting Files

Before getting into the details of command interpretation, I thought I'd give a very simple example of why it's important. Here's an error that occurs all the time. Let's say you have two files, called *file1* and *file2*. You want to create a new version of *file1* that has *file2* added to the end of it. That's what *cat* is all about, so you give the command:

   % **cat file1 file2 > file1**   *...wrong*

This looks like it should work. If you've ever tried it, you know it doesn't; it erases *file1*, and then dumps *file2* into it. Why? The shell (not *cat*) handles standard input and output:

- As the shell is processing the command, it sees that you're redirecting standard output into *file1*, so it opens the file for writing, destroying the data that's already in it.

- Later, after it's finished interpreting the command line, the shell executes *cat*, passing *file1* and *file2* as arguments. But *file1* is already empty.

- *cat* reads *file1* (which is empty) and writes it on standard output (which goes into *file1*).

- *cat* reads *file2* (which also goes into *file1*). At this point, *cat* is finished, so it exits.

file1 and *file2* are identical, which isn't what you wanted. But it's what you got.

Some versions of *cat* give you a warning message in this situation (cat: file1: input file is output file). This might lead you to believe that somehow *cat* was smart and managed to protect you. Sadly, that's not true. By the time *cat* figures out that an input file and an output file are the same, it's too late: *file1* is already gone. This bit of *catty* cleverness does have a function, though: it prevents commands like the following from creating infinitely long files:

```
% cat file1 file2 >> file2
```

—*ML*

27.5 Output Command-Line Arguments One by One

showargs

When you're experimenting with shell quoting, it's nice to be able to see how arguments on a command line are quoted. Here's a demo of a simple *bash* script* named *showargs*; you might want to save it in a file and run it yourself (35.1). The script shows how many arguments were passed to it. Then it lists the arguments, one per line, surrounded by >> << to show leading or trailing spaces.

cat 12.2
&& 35.14
$# 35.20

path 35.7

```
% cat showargs
#!/bin/bash
test $# -ne 1 && s=s
echo "I got $# argument$s:"
for arg
do echo -E ">>$arg<<"
done
% showargs "Start of path:" $path[1-3] "  that's it!  "
I got 5 arguments:
>>Start of path:<<
>>/u/jpeek/bin<<
>>/bin<<
>>/usr/bin<<
>>  that's it!  <<
```

The output from your shell may differ from that shown above, which is the result of running *showargs* in *tcsh*. *bash* doesn't have a $path variable, for example. And *zsh* expects a comma, rather than a hyphen, to separate the range. But as long as the arguments to *showargs* are quoted properly, you should get the result you're looking for, with a little tweaking, of course!

—*JP and SJC*

27.6 Controlling Shell Command Searches

Your search path (35.6, 35.7) controls what directories—and in what order—the shell searches for external (1.9) commands. You can set a search path that takes effect every time you log in by editing your shell setup file (3.3). You might also

---

* The script uses *bash* because, as this article explains later, its built-in *echo* (27.5) command has the –E option to prevent interpretation of special characters.

want to change the path temporarily. Most shells also keep quick-reference lists of command locations that bypass the search path, so you'll want to know how to manage these.

Changing the path set when you log in is simple: just add the new directory to the appropriate line in your shell's startup files (3.3). It's not recommended to redefine the path completely, though, as some packages rely on their *PATH* being set correctly. Usually, it is best simply to add the new directory's absolute path (31.2) to the end of the existing *PATH* variable:

```
PATH=$PATH:$HOME/bin      zsh, sh, ksh, bash
set path=($path ~/bin)    zsh (omit the set), csh, tcsh
```

If you're configuring the superuser (*root*) account, be careful about using a path set by the parent process (through $PATH or $path). This path can be used in *su* shells, giving you part or all the path of the user you *su*'ed from! Also watch out for a path set by a global setup file like */etc/profile*: if it's modified for other users and an insecure version of a system command is added, it could affect the superuser in unexpected ways.

Of course, there's the opposite danger: forgetting to update the superuser's path because you assume that changing the global path will do the job for *root* too. My advice is to think about it and decide what's best for your system.

For Bourne-type shells, load the updated *PATH* by typing a command like:

```
$ . .profile          sh
$ . .bash_profile     bash
```

For the C shell, type one of these commands, depending on which file you changed:

```
% source .cshrc
% source .tcshrc
% source .login
```

Sometimes you'll want to change the path in just your current shell, though, which is as easy as modifying any other shell or environment variable. Let's assume that for the current session, you want to be able to execute commands being tested before deployment, and that those commands are in your *$HOME/someprog/bin* directory. Simply add that directory to the front of your existing path:

```
$ PATH=$HOME/someprog/bin:$PATH           Bourne shells
$ export PATH

$ export PATH=$HOME/someprog/bin:$PATH    bash, ksh

% set path=(~/xxx/alpha-test $path)       C shells
```

Searching the path (27.6) takes time, especially if it's long or if some filesytems are slow or mounted by a slow network link. Most shells have shortcuts to help them remember the locations of commands.

When the C shell starts, it builds a hash table of all the commands in its path: each command name and its absolute pathname. So, after you start a *csh* running, if new programs are added to directories along the path, you need to use the shell's *rehash* command to rebuild its hash table. (The hash table is internal. If you have multiple *csh* shells running—say, in multiple windows—type *rehash* in each one.)

In *bash*, the command location is automatically stored the first time you use it. This means you don't need a *rehash*-type command. If a program is moved to a new directory while *bash* is running, however, you'll need to use the internal command *hash –r* to make *bash* "forget" the old location.

 Running *hash –r* causes *bash* to forget *all* of its hashed commands, but you may also invoke it with the name of a specific command whose hash should be forgotten:

```
$ hash -r command
```

The Korn shell uses tracked aliases to speed up command locating. When it is turned on with set -o trackall, every time that *ksh* finds a new command by doing a path search, it creates an alias for the command name whose value is the full pathname. In *ksh88*, you can turn alias tracking on and off, and you can mark a command to have an alias defined for it the first time it's executed by using:

```
$ alias -t COMMAND
```

In *ksh93*, even though you can run the command set +o trackall, which turns off alias tracking in *ksh88*, the shell ignores the command, and alias tracking is always in effect.

All tracked aliases are cleared when a new value is assigned to the *PATH* variable. If all you wish to do is remove tracked aliases, use PATH=$PATH.

As you can see, shells' command tracking varies! Check your shell's manual page.

—JP and SJC

27.7 Wildcards Inside Aliases

Here's another example in which command-line parsing is important. Consider this shell alias for counting the number of words in all files:

wc 16.6
```
% alias words "wc -w *"     csh, tcsh
$ alias words="wc -w *"     ksh, bash
```

Right away, we can see one effect of command-line parsing. The shell sees the quotation marks and knows not to expand wildcards inside them. Therefore, `words` is aliased to `wc -w *`; the * isn't evaluated when you create the alias. (If wildcards were processed before quotes, this wouldn't work.)

Now, think about what happens when you execute the alias. You type:

```
% words
```

The shell starts working through its steps and eventually performs alias substitution. When this happens, it converts your command into:

```
wc -w *
```

Now, watch carefully. The shell continues working through the process of interpretation (redirection, variable substitution, command substitution) and eventually gets to filename expansion. At this point, the shell sees the * on the command line, expands it, and substitutes the files in the current directory. Seems simple enough. But think: you didn't type this *; the shell put it there when it expanded the wildcard. What would have happened if the shell expanded wildcards before substituting aliases? The * would never have been expanded; by the time the shell put it on the command line, the wildcard expansion stage would be over, and you'd just count the words in a file named * (which probably doesn't exist).

To me, the amazing thing is that all this works—and works well! The workings of the command line are intricate and complex, but the shell almost always does what you want—and without a lot of thought.

—ML

27.8 eval: When You Need Another Chance

If you read the previous article (27.7), you saw that, most of the time, the shell evaluates the command line "in the right order." But what about when it doesn't? Here's a situation that the shell can't handle. It's admittedly contrived, but it's not too different from what you might find in a shell program (1.8):

```
% set b=\$a
% set a=foo
% echo $b
$a
```

When we use the variable $b, we'd like to get the variable $a, read it, and use its value. But that doesn't happen. Variable substitution happens once, and it isn't recursive. The value of $b is $a, and that's it. You don't go any further.

But there's a loophole. The *eval* command says, in essence, "Give me another chance. Re-evaluate this line and execute it." Here's what happens if we stick *eval* before the *echo*:

```
% eval echo $b
foo
```

The shell converts $b into $a; then *eval* runs through the command-line evaluation process again, converting echo $a into echo foo—which is what we wanted in the first place!

Here's a more realistic example; you see code like this fairly often in Bourne shell scripts:

```
...
command='grep $grepopts $searchstring $file'
for opt
do
    case "$opt" in
        file) output=' > $ofile' ;;
        read) output=' | more'   ;;
        sort) postproc=' | sort $sortopts';;
    esac
done
...
eval $command $postproc $output
```

Do you see what's happening? We're constructing a command that will look something like:

```
grep $grepopts $searchstring $file | sort $sortopts > $ofile
```

But the entire command is "hidden" in shell variables, including the I/O redirectors and various options. If the *eval* isn't there, this command will blow up in all sorts of bizarre ways. You'll see messages like | not found, because variable expansion occurs after output redirection. The "nested" variables (like $ofile, which is used inside $output) won't be expanded either, so you'll also see $ofile not found. Putting an *eval* in front of the command forces the shell to process the line again, guaranteeing that the variables will be expanded properly and that I/O redirection will take place.

eval is incredibly useful if you have shell variables that include other shell variables, aliases, I/O redirectors, or all sorts of perversities. It's commonly used within shell scripts to "evaluate" commands that are built during execution. There are more examples of *eval* in article 5.3 and others.

—ML

27.9 Which One Will bash Use?

bash, like all shells, performs a series of steps when evaluating a command line. (Sorry, we don't cover all of the Unix shells; we explain *bash* because it's one of the most common. For other shells, check their manual pages.) This article takes a closer look at how you can control one part of those steps in *bash*: whether the shell will choose a shell function (29.11), a built-in command (1.9), or an external command (1.9).

Let's say that you want to write shell functions named *cd*, *pushd*, and *popd*. They will run the shell's built-in *cd*, *pushd*, or *popd* command, respectively, each using the command-line arguments that were passed (via the $@ array reference). Next they execute another shell function named *setvars* to do some setup in the new directory:

```
cd() {                pushd() {            popd() {
  cd "$@"               pushd "$@"           popd "$@"
  setvars              setvars              setvars
}                     }                    }
```

But which *cd* will *bash* use when you type *cd*: the built-in *cd* or your *cd* function? (The same question goes for *pushd* and *popd*.) Worse, what if the cd <">$@<"> command inside the function makes *bash* call your *cd* function again, and that starts an endless loop? Well, that actually *will* start a loop—and you need to know how to prevent it.

Typing *command* before the name of a command disables shell function lookup. *bash* will execute only a built-in command or an external command with that name. So, you could keep the functions from re-executing themselves by defining them this way:

```
cd() {                  pushd() {              popd() {
  command cd "$@"         command pushd "$@"     command popd "$@"
  setvars                setvars                setvars
}                       }                      }
```

In the same way, if you don't want to run your new *pushd* function for some reason, here's how to use the built-in *pushd* once:

```
bash$ command pushd somewhere
```

The *command* command still allows *bash* to run an external command (from your *PATH* (35.6)) with the name you give. To force *bash* to use a built-in command—but not a shell function or an external command—type *builtin* before the command name. Although *bash* will always choose a built-in command before an external command, you can specify the built-in *echo* unambiguously with:

```
builtin echo -n 'What next? '
```

What if you want the external *echo* command? The easiest way is probably to type its absolute pathname. For example, once I wanted to test four (!) different external versions of *echo* on a System V machine—and not get the built-in *bash* version. So I typed commands like this:

```
bash$ /bin/echo hi \\ there
```

Finally, you can enable or disable specific built-in *bash* commands with the *enable* command. Unlike *command* and *builtin*, the effect of *enable* lasts until you exit the shell. The command *enable –n* disables one or more built-in commands; give the command names as arguments. For example, in my experiments mentioned above, I could have made sure that I'd get an external *echo* every time by typing this first command once:

```
bash$ enable -n echo
bash$ type echo
echo is hashed (/bin/echo)
```

The –n disables the built-in command named as the following argument. The *bash type* command confirms that I'll now be using the external *echo*. You can re-enable a disabled built-in with enable *command-name*. And *enable –a* lists the status of all *bash* built-ins.

—*JP*

27.10 Which One Will the C Shell Use?

[Article 27.9 shows how to control whether *bash* uses a built-in command, a shell function, or an external command. The way you do that in the C shell is a little, errr, different. Chris Torek explains why, for example, \rm disables an alias for *rm* and \cd disables the built-in *cd* command. He starts with a fairly complex explanation, then gives some practical guidelines. At the end is a "review" that's easy to follow and fun too. —JP]

The C shell first breaks each input line into a *word vector*. It then matches against aliases. Since \rm does not match rm, any alias is ignored. Eventually the C shell fully applies any quoting (since an alias can include quotes, some of this work must be deferred; since an alias can include multiple words, more word vector work must be done as well; it all gets rather hairy).

The C shell implements quoting by setting the eighth bit (bit 7) of each byte of a quoted character. Since '*'|0x80 [a character ORed with 80 hex, a.k.a. 10000000 binary—*JP*] is not the same character as '*', this prevents filename expansion, further word breaking, and so on.

Eventually, the shell has a fully "parsed" line. It then compares word[0] [the first word on the command line—*JP*] against all the built-ins. If there is a match, it runs the corresponding built-in command (and it is up to that command to expand any remaining words; for instance, ls * in a directory containing only the file –*l* produces a long listing, but jobs * produces a usage message). If not, the shell performs globbing on the current word list, producing a new word list, and then:

1. Strips the eighth bit of each byte of each word
2. *exec*()s the resulting command.

This means that \cd not only bypasses any alias, but also reaches the built-in scanner as:

```
'c'|0x80, 'd', '\0'
```

which does not match the built-in command:

```
'c', 'd', '\0'
```

and so does not run the *cd* builtin. It is later stripped, and the shell looks for an external program called *cd*.

If you want to avoid alias substitution but not built-in matching, you can replace:

```
\cd foo    or    \rm foo
```

with:

```
''cd foo    or    ""rm foo
```

These do not match the aliases—during alias scanning they have quote pairs in front of them—but they do match any builtin because the quotes have by then been stripped (setting bit 7 of all the characters contained between the two quotes, here none).

Incidentally, since alias expansion occurs early, you can do some peculiar things with it:

```
% [
Missing ].                    ...on some systems, there is a command named [, sometimes standalone,
                              and sometimes symlinked to test.

% alias [ echo foo
% [
foo                           ...alias expansion occurs before globbing

% unalias [
unalias: Missing ].           ...unalias globs its arguments!

% unalias \[
% alias unalias echo foo
unalias: Too dangerous to alias that.          ...the C shell attempts caution...

% alias \unalias echo foo
% alias
unalias    (echo foo)
```

```
% unalias unalias
  foo unalias                    ...but fails!

% ''unalias unalias
% alias
%                                ...Fortunately, there is an exit.
```

On some systems, there is a command named [, sometimes standalone, and sometimes symlinked to *test*.

—CT

27.11 Is It "2>&1 file" or "> file 2>&1"? Why?

One of the common questions about Bourne-type shells is why only the second
command shown below will redirect both *stdout* and *stderr* (43.1) to a file:

```
$ cat food 2>&1 >file
cat: can't open food
$ cat food >file 2>&1
$
```

Although some manual pages don't mention this, the shell processes I/O redirections from left to right:

1. On the first command line, the shell sees 2>&1 first. That means "make the
   standard error (file descriptor 2) go to the same place that the standard output (fd1) is going." There's no effect because both fd2 and fd1 are already
   going to the terminal. Then >file redirects fd1 (*stdout*) to file. But fd2
   (*stderr*) is still going to the terminal.

2. On the second command line, the shell sees >file first and redirects *stdout*
   to file. Next 2>&1 sends fd2 (*stderr*) to the same place fd1 is going—that's
   to the file. And that's what you want.

Article 36.16 has much more about the *m*>&*n* operator.

—JP

27.12 Bourne Shell Quoting

I can't understand why some people see Bourne shell quoting as a scary, mysterious set of many rules. Quoting on Bourne-type shells is simple. (C shell quoting
is slightly more complicated. See article 27.13.)

The overall idea is this: *quoting turns off (disables) the special meaning of characters.* There are three quoting characters: single quote ('), double quote ("), and backslash (\). Note that a backquote (`) is *not* a quoting character—it does command substitution (28.14).

Special Characters

Listed below are the characters that are special to the Bourne shell. You've probably already used some of them. Quoting these characters turns off their special meaning. (Yes, the last three characters are quoting characters. You can quote quoting characters; more on that later.)

```
# & * ? [ ] ( ) = | ^ ; < > ` $ " ' \
```

Space, tab, and newline also have special meaning as argument separators. A slash (/) has special meaning to Unix itself, but not to the shell, so quoting doesn't change the meaning of slashes.

Newer shells have a few other special characters. For instance, *bash* has ! for history substitution (30.8). It's similar to the C shell ! (27.13) except that, in *bash*, ! loses its special meaning inside single quotes. To find particular differences in your Bourne-type shell, see the quoting section of its manual page. In general, though, the rules below apply to all Bourne-type shells.

How Quoting Works

Table 27-1 summarizes the rules; you might want to look back at it while you read the examples.

Table 27-1. Bourne shell quoting characters

Quoting character	Explanation
'*xxx*'	Disable all special characters in *xxx*.
"*xxx*"	Disable all special characters in *xxx* except $, ', and \.
x	Disable the special meaning of character *x*. At end of line, a \ removes the newline character (continues line).

To understand which characters will be quoted, imagine this: the Bourne shell reads what you type at a prompt, or the lines in a shell script, character by character from first to last. (It's actually more complicated than that, but not for the purposes of quoting.)

When the shell reads one of the three quoting characters, it does the following:

- Strips away that quoting character
- Turns off (disables) the special meaning of some or all other character(s) until the end of the quoted section, by the rules in Table 27-1

You also need to know how many characters will be quoted. The next few sections have examples to demonstrate those rules. Try typing the examples at a Bourne shell prompt, if you'd like. (Don't use C shell; it's different (27.13).) If you need to start a Bourne-type shell, type *sh*; type *exit* when you're done.

- A **backslash** (\) turns off the special meaning (if any) of the next character. For example, * is a literal asterisk, not a filename wildcard (1.13). So, the first *expr* (36.21) command gets the three arguments 79 * 45 and multiplies those two numbers:

  ```
  $ expr 79 \* 45
  3555
  $ expr 79 * 45
  expr: syntax error
  ```

  In the second example, without the backslash, the shell expanded * into a list of filenames—which confused *expr*. (If you want to see what I mean, repeat those two examples using *echo* (27.5) instead of *expr*.)

- A **single quote** (') turns off the special meaning of all characters until the next single quote is found. So, in the command line below, the words between the two single quotes are quoted. The quotes themselves are removed by the shell. Although this mess is probably not what you want, it's a good demonstration of what quoting does:

  ```
  $ echo Hey!      What's next?  Mike's #1 friend has $$.
  Hey! Whats next?  Mikes
  ```

  Let's take a close look at what happened. Spaces outside the quotes are treated as argument separators; the shell ignores the multiple spaces. *echo* prints a single space between each argument it gets. Spaces inside the quotes are passed on to *echo* literally. The question mark (?) is quoted; it's given to *echo* as is, not used as a wildcard.

  So, *echo* printed its first argument Hey! and a single space. The second argument to *echo* is Whats next? Mikes; it's all a single argument because the single quotes surrounded the spaces (notice that *echo* prints the two spaces after the question mark: ?   ). The next argument, #1, starts with a hash mark, which is a comment character (35.1). That means the shell will ignore the rest of the string; it isn't passed to *echo*.

  (*zsh* users: The # isn't treated as a comment character at a shell prompt unless you've run setopt interactive_comments first.)

- **Double quotes** (") work almost like single quotes. The difference is that double quoting allows the characters $ (dollar sign), ' (backquote), and \ (backslash) to keep their special meanings. That lets you do variable substitution (35.9, 35.3) and command substitution (28.14) inside double quotes—and also stop that substitution where you need to.

For now, let's repeat the example above. This time, put double quotes around the single quotes (actually, around the whole string):

```
$ echo "Hey!      What's next?  Mike's #1 friend has $$."
Hey!      What's next?  Mike's #1 friend has 18437.
```

The opening double quote isn't matched until the end of the string. So, all the spaces between the double quotes lose their special meaning, and the shell passes the whole string to *echo* as one argument. The single quotes also lose their special meaning because double quotes turn off the special meaning of single quotes! Thus, the single quotes aren't stripped off as they were in the previous example; *echo* prints them.

What else lost its special meaning? The hash mark (#) did; notice that the rest of the string was passed to *echo* this time because it wasn't "commented out." But the dollar sign ($) didn't lose its meaning; the $$ was expanded into the shell's process ID number (24.3) (in this shell, 18437).

In the previous example, what would happen if you put the $ inside the single quotes? (Single quotes turn off the meaning of $, remember.) Would the shell still expand $$ to its value? Yes, it would: the single quotes have lost their special meaning, so they don't affect any characters between them:

```
$ echo "What's next?  How many $$ did Mike's friend bring?"
What's next?  How many 18437 did Mike's friend bring?
```

How can you make both the $$ and the single quotes print literally? The easiest way is with a backslash, which still works inside double quotes:

```
$ echo "What's next?  How many \$\$ did Mike's friend bring?"
What's next?  How many $$ did Mike's friend bring?
```

Here's another way to solve the problem. A careful look at this will show a lot about shell quoting:

```
$ echo "What's next?  How many "'$$'" did Mike's friend bring?"
What's next?  How many $$ did Mike's friend bring?
```

To read that example, remember that a double quote quotes characters until the next double quote is found. The same is true for single quotes. So, the string What's next? How many (including the space at the end) is inside a pair of double quotes. The $$ is inside a pair of single quotes. The rest of the line is inside another pair of double quotes. Both of the double-quoted strings contain a single quote; the double quotes turn off its special meaning and the single quote is printed literally.

Single Quotes Inside Single Quotes?

You can't put single quotes inside single quotes. A single quote turns off *all* special meaning until the next single quote. Use double quotes and backslashes.

Multiline Quoting

Once you type a single quote or double quote, everything is quoted. The quoting can stretch across many lines. (The C shell doesn't work this way.)

For example, in the short script shown in Figure 27-1, you might think that the $1 is inside quotes, but it isn't.

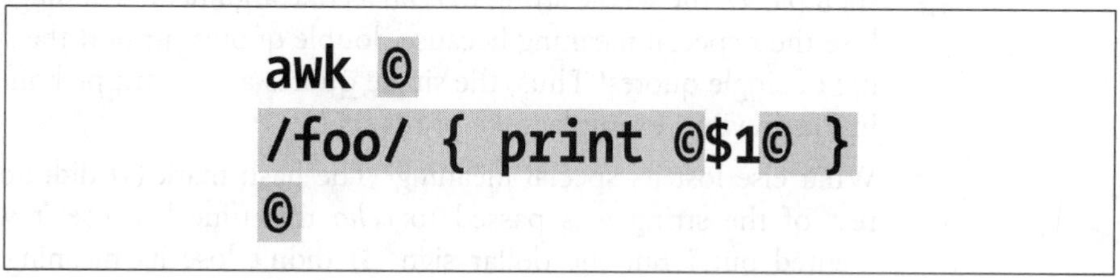

```
awk ©
/foo/ { print ©$1© }
©
```

Figure 27-1. Matching quotes

Actually, all argument text *except* $1 is in quotes. The gray shaded area shows the quoted parts. So $1 is expanded by the Bourne shell, not by *awk*.

Here's another example. Let's store a shell variable (35.9) with a multiline message, the kind that might be used in a shell program. A shell variable must be stored as a single argument; any argument separators (spaces, etc.) must be quoted. Inside double quotes, $ and ' are interpreted (*before* the variable is stored, by the way). The opening double quote isn't closed by the end of the first line; the Bourne shell prints secondary prompts (28.12) (>) until all quotes are closed:

```
$ greeting="Hi, $USER.
> The date and time now
> are:  `date`."
$ echo "$greeting"
Hi, jerry.
The date and time now
are:  Fri Sep  1 13:48:12 EDT 2000.
$ echo $greeting
Hi, jerry. The date and time now are: Fri Sep 1 13:48:12 EDT 2000.
$
```

The first *echo* command line uses double quotes, so the shell variable is expanded, but the shell doesn't use the spaces and newlines in the variable as argument separators. (Look at the extra spaces after the word are:.) The second *echo* doesn't use double quotes. The spaces and newlines are treated as argument separators; the shell passes 14 arguments to *echo*, which prints them with single spaces between.

A backslash has a quirk you should know about. If you use it outside quotes, at the end of a line (just before the newline), the newline will be *deleted*. Inside single quotes, though, a backslash at the end of a line is copied as is. Here are examples. I've numbered the prompts (1$, 2$, and so on):

```
1$ echo "a long long long long long long
> line or two"
a long long long long long long
line or two
2$ echo a long long long long long long\
> line
a long long long long long longline
3$ echo a long long long long long long \
> line
a long long long long long long line
4$ echo "a long long long long long long\
> line"
a long long long long long longline
5$ echo 'a long long long long long long\
> line'
a long long long long long long\
line
```

You've seen an example like example 1 before. The newline is in quotes, so it isn't an argument separator; *echo* prints it with the rest of the (single, two-line) argument. In example 2, the backslash before the newline tells the shell to delete the newline; the words long and line are passed to *echo* as one argument. Example 3 is usually what you want when you're typing long lists of command-line arguments: Type a space (an argument separator) before the backslash and newline. In example 4, the backslash inside the double quotes is ignored (compare to example 1). Inside single quotes, as in example 5, the backslash has no special meaning; it's passed on to *echo*.

—JP

27.13 Differences Between Bourne and C Shell Quoting

This article explains quoting in C-type shells by comparing them to Bourne-type shell quoting. If you haven't read article 27.12 about Bourne shell quoting, please do so now.

As in the Bourne shell, the overall idea of C shell quoting is this: *quoting turns off (disables) the special meaning of characters*. There are three quoting characters: a single quote ('), a double quote ("), and a backslash (\).

Special Characters

The C shell has a few more special characters in addition to the original Bourne shell:

```
! { } ~
```

How Quoting Works

Table 27-2 summarizes the rules; you might want to look back at it while you read the examples.

Table 27-2. C shell quoting characters

Quoting character	Explanation
'xxx'	Disable all special characters in *xxx* except !.
"xxx"	Disable all special characters in *xxx* except $, ', and !.
\x	Disable special meaning of character *x*. At end of line, a \ treats the newline character like a space (continues line).

The major differences between C and Bourne shell quoting are the following:

- The exclamation point (!) character can be quoted only with a backslash. That's true inside and outside single or double quotes. So you can use history substitution (30.8) inside quotes. For example:

  ```
  % grep intelligent engineering file*.txt
  grep: engineering: No such file or directory
  % grep '!:1-2' !:3
  grep 'intelligent engineering' file*.txt
  ...
  ```

- In the Bourne shell, inside double quotes, a backslash (\) stops variable and command substitution (it turns off the special meaning of $ and ').

  In the C shell, you can't disable the special meaning of $ or ' inside double quotes. You'll need a mixture of single and double quotes. For example, searching for the string *use the '–c' switch* takes some work:

  ```
  % fgrep "use the \`-c' switch" *.txt
  Unmatched \`.
  % fgrep 'use the \`-c\' switch' *.txt
  Unmatched '.
  % fgrep "use the "'`-c'"' switch" *.txt
  hints.txt:Be sure to use the `-c' switch.
  ```

  Article 29.10 shows an amazing pair of aliases that automate complicated C shell quoting problems like this.

- In the Bourne shell, single and double quotes include newline characters. Once you open a single or double quote, you can type multiple lines before the closing quote.

  In the C shell, if the quotes on a command line don't match, the shell will print an error unless the line ends with a backslash. In other words, to quote more than one line, type a backslash at the end of each line before the last line. Inside single or double quotes, the backslash-newline becomes a newline. Unquoted, backslash-newline is an argument separator:

```
% echo "one\
? two" three\
? four
one
two three four
```

—*JP*

27.14 Quoting Special Characters in Filenames

If you want to work with files that have spaces or special characters in the filenames, you may have to use quotes. For instance, if you wanted to create a file that has a space in the name, you could use the following:

/dev/null
43.12

```
% cp /dev/null 'a file with spaces in the name'
```

Normally, the shell uses spaces to determine the end of each argument. Quoting (27.12, 27.13) changes that—for example, the *cp* command above has only two arguments. You can also use a backslash (\) before a special character. The example below will rename a file with a space in the name, changing the space to an underscore (_):

```
% mv a\ file a_file
```

Using the same techniques, you can deal with any character in a filename:

```
% mv '$a' a
```

At worst, a space in a filename makes the filename difficult to use as an argument. Other characters are dangerous to use in a filename. In particular, using ? and * in a filename is playing with fire. If you want to delete the file *a?*, you may end up deleting more than the single file.

—*BB*

27.15 Verbose and Echo Settings Show Quoting

C-type shells have two variables that, when set, will help you follow the convoluted trail of variable and metacharacter expansion. This command will echo every command line before shell variables have been evaluated:

set **35.9**

```
% set verbose
```

This command will display each line after the variables and metacharacters have been substituted:

```
% set echo
```

If you wish to turn the options off, use *unset* (35.9) instead of *set*.

Bourne-type shell syntax is different. To turn on the verbose flag, use:

```
$ set -v
```

The command set -x turns on the echo flag. You can also type them together: set -xv.

If your version of Unix understands scripts that start with #!, and nearly all do, here's a convenient way to turn these variables on from the first line of a script:

```
#!/bin/sh -xv
```

It is not necessary to modify the program. You can enable variable tracing in Bourne shell scripts by typing the shell name and options on the command line:

```
$ sh -v script
$ sh -x script
```

Not all Bourne shells let you turn these options off. If yours does (and it probably does), you can do it by using a plus sign instead of a minus sign:

```
set +xv
```

—*BB*

27.16 Here Documents

So far, we've talked about three different kinds of quoting: backslashes (\), single quotes ('), and double quotes ("). The shells support yet one more kind of quoting, called *here documents*. A here document is useful when you need to read something from standard input, but you don't want to create a file to provide that input; you want to put that input right into your shell script (or type it directly on the command line). To do so, use the << operator, followed by a special word:

```
sort >file <<EndOfSort
zygote
abacus
EndOfSort
```

This is very useful because variables (35.9, 35.3) are evaluated during this operation. Here is a way to transfer a file using anonymous *ftp* (1.21)* from a shell script:

---

* You might be better off using *wget* or *curl* for downloads, but this method can be useful for automated uploads.

ftpfile

```
#!/bin/sh
# Usage:
#      ftpfile machine file
# set -x
SOURCE=$1
FILE=$2
GETHOST="uname -n"
BFILE=`basename $FILE`
ftp -n $SOURCE <<EndFTP
ascii
user anonymous $USER@`$GETHOST`
get $FILE /tmp/$BFILE
EndFTP
```

As you can see, variable and command substitutions (28.14) are done. If you don't want those to be done, put a backslash in front of the name of the word:

```
cat >file <<\FunkyStriNG
```

Notice the funky string. This is done because it is very unlikely that I will want to put that particular combination of characters in any file. You should be warned that the C shell expects the matching word (at the end of the list) to be escaped the same way, i.e., \FunkyStriNG, while the Bourne shell does not. See article 36.19.

Most Bourne shells also have the <<- operator. The dash (-) at the end tells the shell to strip any TAB characters from the beginning of each line. Use this in shell scripts to indent a section of text without passing those TABs to the command's standard input.

Other shells, notably *zsh* and later versions of *ksh*, but in the future possibly also *bash*, support a method for taking input from a string:

```
$ tr ... <<< "$xyzzy" | ...
```

—*BB*

27.17 "Special" Characters and Operators

Before you learn about regular expressions (32.1), you should understand how quoting (27.12) works in Unix.

Regular expressions use metacharacters. The shells also have metacharacters. Metacharacters are simply characters that have a special meaning. The problem occurs when you want to use a regular expression in a shell script. Will the shell do something special with the character? Or will it be passed unchanged to the program? The $ character is a good example of a regular expression metacharacter that is also used by the shell, but whose meaning is different depending upon who interprets it, the shell or other programs. It could be the beginning of a variable name or it could be part of a regular expression (32.2). If you need a regular expression, you must know whether any of the characters of the expression are metacharacters, and must know the right way to quote that character so that it is passed to the program without being modified by the shell.

Table 27-3 is a table of special characters and operators in the shells covered by this book. (Because *zsh* acts basically like both C-type and Bourne-type shells, its name would show up in every entry. So we don't list it here unless an entry applies only to *zsh*—or one or two other shells.) The chart also includes several combinations of characters just to be complete. But, to keep things simple, it doesn't include:

- Arithmetic operators like +, -, and so on; see the articles on built-in arithmetic for a list.

- History substitution like !!, !$, and so on; see article 30.8 instead.

As in other parts of this book, the *sh* entries apply to *ksh* and *bash*; the *csh* entries apply to *tcsh*.

Table 27-3. Special characters and their meanings

Character	Where	Meaning	Articles
ESC	csh	Filename completion.	28.6
RETURN	csh, sh	Execute command.	
space	csh, sh	Argument separator.	
TAB	csh, sh	Argument separator.	
TAB	bash	Completion (in interactive shells).	28.6
#	csh, sh	Start a comment.	35.1
`	csh, sh	Command substitution (backquotes).	28.14
"	sh	Weak quotes.	27.12
"	csh	Weak quotes.	27.13
$*var*	csh, sh	Expand variable *var*.	35.3, 35.9
${*var*}	csh, sh	Same as $*var*.	35.9
$*var:mod*	csh	Edit *var* with modifier *mod*	28.5
${*var–default*}	sh	If *var* not set, use *default*.	36.7
${*var:–default*}	bash	If *var* not set or null, use *default*.	36.7

Table 27-3. Special characters and their meanings (continued)

Character	Where	Meaning	Articles
${*var*=*default*}	sh	If *var* not set, set it to *default* and use that value.	36.7
${*var*:=*default*}	bash	If *var* not set or null, set it to *default* and use that value.	36.7
${*var*+*instead*}	sh	If *var* set, use *instead*. Otherwise, null string.	36.7
${*var*:+*instead*}	bash	If *var* set or not null, use *instead*. Otherwise, null string.	36.7
${*var*?*message*}	sh	If *var* set, use its value. Else print *message* (or default) and exit.	36.7
${*var*:?*message*}	bash	If *var* set or not null, use its value. Else print *message* (or default) and exit.	36.7
${*var*#*pat*}	ksh, bash	Value of *var* with smallest *pat* deleted from start.	
${*var*##*pat*}	ksh, bash	Value of *var* with largest *pat* deleted from start.	
${*var*%*pat*}	ksh, bash	Value of *var* with smallest *pat* deleted from end.	
${*var*%%*pat*}	ksh, bash	Value of *var* with largest *pat* deleted from end.	
${^*array*}	zsh	Expand *array* in place, like *rc_expand_param* option.	35.9
${=*spec*}	zsh	Turn on *sh_word_split* option while evaluating *spec*.	35.9
${~*array*}	zsh	Turn on *glob_subst* option while evaluating *spec*.	35.9
|	csh, sh	Pipe standard output.	1.5, 43.1
|&	csh	Pipe standard output and standard error.	43.5
|&	ksh	Coroutine.	24.4
^	sh *only*	Pipe character (obsolete).	
^	csh, bash	Edit previous command line.	30.5
&	csh, sh	Run program in background.	23.2
&!	zsh	Run program in background without job control.	23.11

Table 27-3. Special characters and their meanings (continued)

Character	Where	Meaning	Articles
&|	zsh	Run program in background without job control.	23.11
?	csh, sh	Match one character.	1.13, 33.2
*	csh, sh	Match zero or more characters.	1.13, 33.2
;	csh, sh	Command separator.	
;;	sh	End of *case* element.	35.10
~	csh, ksh, bash	Home directory.	31.11
~*user*	csh, ksh, bash	Home directory of *user*.	31.11
!	csh, bash	Command history.	30.2
!	bash, ksh93, zsh	Toggle exit status.	35.12
-	zsh	Make a login shell.	3.19
=	csh, sh	Assignment.	35.9,
$#	csh, sh	Number of shell arguments or words in an array.	35.20,
"$@"	sh	Original script arguments.	35.20
$*	csh, sh	Original script arguments, broken into words.	35.20
$?	sh	Status of previous command.	35.12
$$	csh, sh	Process identification number.	27.12
$!	sh	Process identification number of last background job.	4.15
$<	csh	Read input from terminal.	28.9
$_	bash, ksh, zsh	Last argument of previous command.	
$*n*	sh	Argument *n*. 1 <= n <= 9 for most shells; bash and ksh93 support ${n} for n >= 10.	
$0	sh	Name of the shell or shell script.	
cmd1 && *cmd2*	csh, sh	Execute *cmd2* if *cmd1* succeeds.	35.14
cmd1 || *cmd2*	csh, sh	Execute *cmd2* if *cmd1* fails.	35.14
$(..)	ksh, bash	Command substitution.	36.24, 28.14
. *file*	sh	Execute commands from *file* in this shell.	35.29
:	sh	Evaluate arguments, return true.	36.6
:	sh	Separate values in paths.	31.5, 35.6

Table 27-3. Special characters and their meanings (continued)

Character	Where	Meaning	Articles
:	csh	Variable modifier.	28.5
[ ]	csh, sh	Match range of characters.	1.13, 33.2
[ ]	sh	Test.	35.26
%*n*	csh, ksh, bash, zsh	Job number *n*.	23.3
(*cmd*;*cmd*)	csh, sh	Run *cmd*;*cmd* in a subshell.	43.7
{ }	csh, bash	In-line expansions.	28.4
>*file*	csh, sh	Redirect standard output.	43.1
>! *file*	csh	Output to *file*, even if *noclobber* set and *file* exists.	43.6
>| *file*	ksh, bash	Output to *file*, even if *noclobber* set and *file* exists.	43.6
>>*file*	csh, sh	Append standard output.	43.1
>>! *file*	csh	Append to *file*, even if *noclobber* set and *file* doesn't exist.	43.6
<*file*	csh, sh	Redirect standard input.	43.1
<<*word*	csh, sh	Read until *word*, do command and variable substitution.	27.16, 28.13
<<*word*	csh, sh	Read until *word*, no substitution.	27.16
<<-*word*	sh	Read until *word*, ignoring leading TABs.	27.16
<> *file*	ksh, bash, zsh	Open *file* for writing and reading.	
>& *file*	csh, bash	Redirect standard output and standard error to *file*.	43.5
m> *file*	sh	Redirect output file descriptor *m* to *file*.	36.16
m>> *file*	sh	Append output file descriptor *m* to *file*.	
m< *file*	sh	Redirect input file descriptor *m* from *file*.	
<&*m*	sh	Take standard input from file descriptor *m*.	
>&*m*	sh	Use file descriptor *m* as standard output.	36.16
>&-	sh	Close standard output.	36.16
m<&-	sh	Close input file descriptor *m*.	36.16
n>&*m*	sh	Connect output file descriptor *n* to file descriptor *m*.	36.16
m>&-	sh	Close output file descriptor *m*.	36.16

—BB and JP

27.18 How Many Backslashes?

The problem with backslashes is that many different programs use them as quoting characters. As a result, it's difficult to figure out how many backslashes you need in any situation.

Here's an example, taken from System V Release 4. (Notice that I'm using the standard System V version of *echo* from */bin/echo*. SVR4 has four versions of *echo*!)

```
% /bin/echo hi \ there
hi  there
% /bin/echo hi \\ there
hi \ there
% /bin/echo hi \\\\ there
hi \ there
```

In the first case, the shell uses the backslash to quote (27.12) the following space character. The space before the backslash is a word separator. So *echo* gets two arguments: "hi" and "⸼there" (without the quotes)—where ⸼ is the space character that was quoted by the backslash. As always, *echo* prints a single space between each argument. The first space you see in the output is echo's argument-separating space, and the second space came along with the second argument (thanks to the backslash).

In the second case, the shell converts \\ to \; the first backslash tells the shell to quote (27.12) (turn off the special meaning of) the second backslash. The *echo* command gets three arguments, "hi", "\", and "there", and it echoes those arguments with a single space between each. (I've heard claims that, on some systems, this command wouldn't print any backslashes, but I wasn't able to reconstruct that situation.)

In the third case, the shell converts each pair of backslashes into a backslash, and runs the command echo hi \\ there. But this is System V, and System V's *echo* interprets backslashes as special characters. So when *echo* sees the remaining two backslashes, it converts them into a single backslash. So you see only a single backslash, even though you typed four. On BSD systems and on Linux, *echo* doesn't do this; you'd see two backslashes. For that matter, if you're using SVR4's C shell, with its built-in *echo* command, you'll see the BSD/Linux behavior. You'll also see the BSD/Linux behavior if you're using SVR4's */usr/ucb/echo*.

The terminal driver is also capable of "eating" backslashes if they appear before special characters. If a backslash precedes the "erase" character (normally CTRL-h) or the "kill" character (normally CTRL-u), the terminal driver will pass the control character to the shell, rather than interpreting it as an editing character. In the process, it "eats" the backslash. So if you type:

```
% echo \CTRL-u
```

The shell receives the line echo CTRL-u. There are certainly system-dependent variations, though. If your system has the *termio*(7) manual page, read it for more information.

What's the point of this article? Well, backslashes are messy. The shell, the terminal driver, *echo* (sometimes), and several other utilities use them. If you think very carefully, you can figure out exactly what's consuming them. If you're not of a rigorous frame of mind, you can just add backslashes until you get what you want. (But, obviously, the nonrigorous approach has pitfalls.) I've seen situations in *troff* (which is another story altogether) where you need eight backslashes in order to have a single backslash left at the point where you want it!

(Extra credit: What happens when you put quotes (" or ') around the strings in the *echo* commands above? Especially, should quotes affect the way \CTRL-u is interpreted?)

—*ML and JP*

28

Saving Time on the Command Line

28.1 What's Special About the Unix Command Line

One of Unix's best features is the shell's command line. Why? Nearly every modern operating system has a command line; we don't use card readers with obscure job setup cards any more. What makes Unix's special?

The Unix shell command line allows lots of shortcuts. Some of these you'll find in other operating systems; some you won't. In this chapter, we'll introduce a lot of these shortcuts. Among other things, we'll discuss:

- How to run commands more than once (28.8).
- Filename completion (28.6, 28.7), which allows you to type the beginning of a filename and let the shell fill in the rest. (This is finally possible on certain Redmond-born OSes as well, but it usually involves a registry hack or two.)
- Command substitution (28.14), which lets you use the output from one command as arguments to another. (Note that this is *different* from pipelining.)
- Process substitution in *bash*, and a script named *!* for other shells, lets you put the output of a command into a temporary file and give that filename to a process.
- The ability to repeat commands with various methods (28.10, 28.11).
- Handling of command lines that become too long (28.17).

Some fundamental command-line features that we aren't discussing in this chapter, but which are discussed elsewhere, are:

- Job control (23.3), which lets you run several commands at the same time.

- Aliases (29.2), or abbreviations, for commands. Shell functions (29.11) are similar.

- Command-line editing (30.14) and history substitution (30.8). These are two different ways (both useful) to "recall" previous commands.

- Quoting (27.12, 27.13), the way you "protect" special characters from the Unix shell.

- Wildcards (33.2).

You don't need to be a command-line virtuoso to use Unix effectively. But you'd be surprised at how much you can do with a few tricks. If all you can do at the command line is type ls or start Mozilla or the Gimp, you're missing out on a lot.

—ML

28.2 Reprinting Your Command Line with CTRL-r

You're logged in from home, running a program and answering a prompt. As you're almost done, modem noise prints xDxD@! on your screen. Where were you? Or you're typing a long command line and a friend interrupts you with *write* (1.21) to say it's time for lunch. Do you have to press CTRL-u and start typing all over again?

If your system understands the *rprnt* character (usually set to CTRL-r), you can ask for the command line to be reprinted as it was. In fact, you can use CTRL-r any time you want to know what the system thinks you've typed on the current line—not just when you're interrupted. But this only works in the normal *cooked* input mode; programs like *vi* that do their own input processing may treat CTRL-r differently. Here's an example:

```
% egrep '(10394|29433|49401)' /work/symtower/

Message from alison@ruby on ttyp2 at 12:02 ...
how about lunch?
EOF
CTRL-r
egrep '(10394|29433|49401)' /work/symtower/logs/*
```

After the interruption, I just pressed CTRL-r. It reprinted the stuff I'd started typing. I finished typing and pressed RETURN to run it.

If you use a shell like the Korn shell that has interactive command editing, you can probably use it to reprint the command line, too. In *bash* and other commands that use the readline file, though, from *vi* editing mode, CTRL-r still seems to start an Emacs-style reverse search. So I added this fix to my *~/.inputrc* file:

```
set editing-mode vi

# By default, in vi text-input mode, ^R does Emacs "reverse-i-search".
# In command mode, you can use the vi command ^L to redraw the line.
# Fix it in text-input mode:
"\C-r": redraw-current-line
```

—*JP*

28.3 Use Wildcards to Create Files?

The shells' [ ] (square bracket) wildcards will match a range of files. For instance, if you have files named *afile*, *bfile*, *cfile*, and *dfile*, you can print the first three by typing:

```
% lpr [a-c]file
```

Now, let's say that you want to *create* some more files called *efile*, *ffile*, *gfile*, and *hfile*. What's wrong with typing the command line below? Try it. Instead of *vi*, you can use your favorite editor or the *touch* (14.8) command:

```
% vi [e-h]file    Doesn't make those four files
% ls
afile    bfile    cfile    dfile
```

Stumped? Take a look at article 1.13 about wildcard matching.

The answer: wildcards can't match names that don't exist yet. That's especially true with a command like touch ?file (14.8) or touch *file—think how many filenames those wildcards could possibly create!

Article 28.4 explains shell { } operators that solve this problem. And, by the way, if you just created one new file named *[e-h]file*, simply quote (27.12) its name to remove it:

```
rm "[e-h]file"
```

—*JP*

28.4 Build Strings with { }

I've been finding more and more uses for the {} pattern-expansion characters in *csh*, *tcsh*, *zsh*, and *bash*. They're similar to *, ?, and [ ] (33.2), but they don't match filenames the way that *, ?, and [ ] do. You can give them arbitrary text (not just filenames) to expand—that "expand-anything" ability is what makes them so useful.

Here are some examples to get you thinking:

- To fix a typo in a filename (change *fixbold5.c fixbold6.c*):

  ```
  % mv fixbold{5,6}.c
  ```

  To see what the shell will do with {}, add *echo* (27.5) before the *mv*:

  ```
  % echo mv fixbold{5,6}.c
  mv fixbold5.c fixbold6.c
  ```

- To copy *filename* to *filename.bak* without retyping *filename*:

  ```
  % cp filename{,.bak}
  ```

- To print files from other directory(s) without retyping the whole pathname:

  ```
  % lpr /usr3/hannah/training/{ed,vi,mail}/lab.{ms,out}
  ```

  That would give *lpr* (45.2) all of these files:

  ```
  /usr3/hannah/training/ed/lab.ms
  /usr3/hannah/training/ed/lab.out
  /usr3/hannah/training/vi/lab.ms
  /usr3/hannah/training/vi/lab.out
  /usr3/hannah/training/mail/lab.ms
  /usr3/hannah/training/mail/lab.out
  ```

  ...in one fell swoop!

- To edit ten new files that don't exist yet:

  ```
  % vi /usr/foo/file{a,b,c,d,e,f,g,h,i,j}
  ```

  That would make */usr/foo/filea*, */usr/foo/fileb*, ... */usr/foo/filej*. Because the files don't exist before the command starts, the wildcard vi /usr/foo/file[a-j] would *not* work (28.3).

- An easy way to step through three-digit numbers 000, 001, ..., 009, 010, 011, ..., 099, 100, 101, ... 299 in the C shell is:

  foreach 28.9

  ```
  foreach n ({0,1,2}{0,1,2,3,4,5,6,7,8,9}{0,1,2,3,4,5,6,7,8,9})
      ...Do whatever with the number $n...
  end
  ```

  Yes, *csh* also has built-in arithmetic, but its @ operator can't make numbers with leading zeros. This nice trick shows that the {} operators are good for more than just filenames.

- In *zsh*, {} also understands .. as an integer-range operator. So you could generate the 300 numbers in the previous example with {000..299}. The leading 00 tells *zsh* to pad all output numbers to three digits with leading zeros.

  If you give the range in reverse order, like {299..0}, *zsh* will output the integers in descending order: 299, 298, and so on, down to 1 and 0.

- To send a *mail* (1.21) message to multiple recipients where a part of each email address is repeated:

  ```
  % mail -s "Link to me" webmaster@{foo,bar,baz}.com < msgfile
  ```

- If you're using a graphical email program (not the command-line *mail* program shown above), and you're sending an email message to lots of people at the same host, it can be a pain to type the same hostname over and over in the "To:" line. Let the shell's {} operators do the dirty work! Use *echo* to output the addresses. (Note the comma (,) after each address.) Then copy all of them—except the final comma—with your mouse, and paste them into the GUI mail program:

  ```
  % echo {jane,joe,jill,john,jean}@foo.org,
  jane@foo.org, joe@foo.org, jill@foo.org, john@foo.org, jean@foo.org,
  ```

- To create sets of subdirectories:

  ```
  % mkdir man
  % mkdir man/{man,cat}{1,2,3,4,5,6,7,8}
  % ls -F man
  cat1/   cat3/   cat5/   cat7/   man1/   man3/   man5/   man7/
  cat2/   cat4/   cat6/   cat8/   man2/   man4/   man6/   man8/
  ```

- Here's how to copy the remote files *file1.c*, *file12.c*, *file45.c*, and *file77.c* from the subdirectory *foo* on the remote host *remulac* to the local system. Your local shell expands the strings (into remulac:foo/file1.c, remulac:foo/file12.c, etc.) and passes them to *scp* (29.14):

  . 1.16
  ```
  % scp remulac:foo/file{1,12,45,77}.c .
  ```

- Here are two ways to print 10 copies of the file *project_report* if your *lpr* (45.2) command doesn't have a *–#10* option. We showed the first way in the first two editions of this book. Dimi Shahbaz sent us the second one: 9 commas give 10 filenames. (Thanks, Dimi!) Both of them work on all the shells I tried:

  ```
  % lpr project_repor{t,t,t,t,t,t,t,t,t,t}
  % lpr project_report{,,,,,,,,,}
  ```

  Of course, this doesn't just work for *lpr* or filenames. Remember that the shell expands the list of strings, so you can use these tricks anywhere you use {}.

In *bash*, the *complete-into-braces* editor command (which is bound to the M-{ key sequence by default in Emacs mode) expands a string into a list of matching filenames in braces. For example:

```
$ ls pr*
prog1.c   prog2.c   program1.c   program2.c
$ cc pr META{
$ cc pr{og1.c,og2.c,ogram1.c,orgram2.c}
```

Then you can edit the brace expression.

—*JP*

28.5 String Editing (Colon) Operators

When the C shells, *zsh*, and *bash* do history substitutions (30.8) they can also edit the substitution. The C shells and *zsh*—but not *bash*—can also edit variable substitutions (35.9). (*bash* has a different syntax, which *zsh* understands, too.) For instance, in the first example below, when !$ contains /a/b/c, adding the "head" operator :h will give just the head of the pathname, /a/b.

For a complete but very terse list of these operators, see the *csh* manual page. We hope the examples below will help you understand these useful operators.

- :h gives the head of a pathname (31.2), as follows:

```
% echo /a/b/c
/a/b/c
% echo !$:h
echo /a/b
/a/b
```

That took off the filename and left the header. This also could be used with C shell variables (35.9) as:

```
% set x = /a/b/c
% echo $x
/a/b/c
% echo $x:h
/a/b
```

- :r returns the root of a filename:

```
% echo xyz.c abc.c
xyz.c abc.c
% echo !$:r
echo abc
abc
```

The :r removed the .c from the last argument, leaving the root name. This could also be used in C shell variable names:

```
% set x = abc.c
% echo $x:r
abc
```

- :g makes the operation global if you have more than one name. For example:

```
% set x = (a.a b.b c.c)
% echo $x:gr
a b c
```

The :gr operator stripped off all dot (.) suffixes. By the way, this use of g does not work with the history commands.

This is the C shell's answer to the *basename* (36.13) command.

- :e returns the extension (the part of the name after a dot). Using *csh* variables:

```
% set x=(abc.c)
% echo $x:e
c
```

No luck using that within history, either.

- :t gives the tail of a pathname—the actual filename without the path:

```
% echo /a/b/c
/a/b/c
% echo !$:t
c
```

With *csh* variables:

```
% set x=(/a/b/c)
% echo $x:t
c
```

And with multiple pathnames, you can do it globally with:

```
% set x=(/a/b/c /d/e/f /g/h/i)
% echo $x:gt
c f i
```

The corresponding heads would be:

```
% set x=(/a/b/c /d/e/f /g/h/i)
% echo $x:gh
/a/b /d/e /g/h
```

- :p prints the command but does not execute it (30.11):

```
% echo *
fn1 fn2 fn3
% !:p
echo fn1 fn2 fn3
```

- :q prevents further filename expansion or prints the command as is:

```
% echo *
fn1 fn2 fn3
% !:q
echo *
*
```

The first command echoed the files in the directory, and when the :q was applied, it echoed only the special character.

- :x is like :q, but it breaks the line into words. That is, when using :q, it is all one word, while :x will break it up into multiple words. :q and :x are more often used with C shell arrays.

[Wait, Dan, what about & on the right-hand side to repeat the previous substitution? And there's more since Dan wrote this article (in 1983!). *tcsh* also has :u to convert the first lowercase letter to uppercase and :l to convert the first uppercase letter to lowercase. In *zsh*, :u converts all letters to uppercase and :l converts all letter to lowercase. *zsh* also has f and F to repeat a substitution until it fails—and even more. Check your shell's manual page. —*JP*]

—*DR*

28.6 Automatic Completion

If you hate typing long filenames, hostnames, command names—or almost anything on a command line—you should know about the shells' "completion" feature.

The basics are pretty simple: just press (in most shells) the TAB key, and the shell should "do the right thing." But how the shell decides what's "right" can be complicated—especially in newer shells, and *especially* in the latest *zsh*, which has incredibly customizable completion. As an example, when you press TAB in *bash*, the shell tries to complete a shell variable if the word begins with $, a username if the word begins with ~, a hostname if the word begins with @, or a command (including aliases and functions). If none of these works, *bash* finally tries filename completion. As another example, the original Korn shell does only simple filename completion, but the public domain Korn shell has more features.

On more-sophisticated shells, completion is actually a function of the shell's built-in customizable command editor. For instance, in *tcsh*, the TAB key is bound to (in other words, it runs) the editor's *complete-word* command. This key binding can be changed. And *tcsh*, like other recent shells, has plenty of other completion-related editor commands.

bash allows for the customization of the different types of completions, as well; you can define a file containing the hostnames to check (in */etc/hosts* format) when the shell is asked to complete a hostname. Just set the environment variable *HOSTFILE* to the name of the file you want. There are extensive built-in functions in *bash*, each associated with a key, to allow for extremely flexible management of completions.

As you can see, completion varies shell to shell, so we'll give an overview here. For more details, see your shell's manpage.

General Example: Filename Completion

Let's look at an example of one type of completion, filename completion. Other types of completion work in generally the same way.

Filename completion is one of the most common types. You can type the initial part of a filename and then press the TAB key. (In the C shell, first enable completion by setting the variable *filec* (30.9) or *complete*, then press ESC.) If the shell can figure out the complete filename from the part that you've typed, it will fill in the rest of the name. If not, it will fill in as much of the name as is unambiguous and then let you type some more. For example:

```
$ ls
alpha.c    alpha.o    beta.c
$ cc b TAB
$ cc beta.c        Shell fills in the filename automatically
```

(With *tcsh* and *csh*, your terminal will beep if more than one file matches the name you've typed. If all this beeping drives you crazy, you can set the *nobeep* shell variable to turn it off.) In this case, only one filename begins with *b*, so the shell can fill in the entire name. This works with pathnames (1.16) too: each time you press TAB, the shell completes the name up to the next slash (/) if it can.

If you type part of a filename and then type CTRL-d (in *bash*, type TAB twice), the shell lists all the files that match whatever you've typed. It then redisplays your command line and lets you continue typing. For example:

```
% cc a CTRL-d
alpha.c    alpha.o
% cc alpha.
```

Two files begin with the letter "a"; the shell lists them. It then redisplays the *cc* command, letting you finish the filename.

Also, be forewarned that filename completion doesn't always work correctly. For example, you can't use filename completion within some older shell applications. You can't mix filename completion with wildcards in any shell except *zsh*. We won't go into detail about these rough edges, but if you're aware that they exist, you won't have trouble.

That last example shows a problem with filename completion: it's matching the ".o file," (1.12) named *alpha.o*. It's a type of file that most users wouldn't want to manipulate from the command line; they'd rather the shell ignore all .o files. Article 28.7 explains the *fignore* list; it solves this problem in most cases. Article 31.10 shows an interesting shortcut to filename completion: *cd*ing to a directory by typing its "initials."

Menu Completion

The filename completion section showed how completion works by default: press TAB, and the shell completes as much as it can and then waits for you either to press TAB again (to see all possible completions) or to type enough of the word to make it unambigious.

Menu completion, supported by *zsh* with the –Y option, works differently. The name might be confusing at first: it doesn't "complete a menu," and it also doesn't pop up a menu of possible completions. Instead, menu completion replaces the word to be completed with a single match from the list of possible completions. Each time you press TAB again, the shell shows you the next possible match, in turn, under your cursor. If you like one of the choices, just keep typing the rest of the command line (or press ENTER to execute it). When the shell has shown all the possible matches, it rings the bell and restores the original text without a match.

Menu completion doesn't work just with filenames. If your shell supports it, menu completion probably works with all completion modes (filenames, hostnames, etc.).

Command-Specific Completion

tcsh and *zsh* let you customize completion even farther: specific completion instructions for each Unix command you define. For instance, the *mail* command wants email addresses on its command line, and you can declare a list of addresses that are available to complete (this could be a list of friends and associates you send a lot of mail to). You might use the *ssh* and *telnet* commands (1.21) to connect to particular remote hosts, and you'd like to be able to complete the hostnames for those particular hosts. (The *bash* hostname completion feature reads hostnames from a file like */etc/hosts*—but it only completes hostnames if the string starts with an @ character or if you use a special editor command for completing hostnames.)

The *tcsh* command *complete* defines these custom completions. The syntax is hairy, so I won't try to explain all of it here. Instead, let's look at an overall example from the MH email system (6.2). You use MH commands directly from a shell prompt instead of first starting an email command interpreter and entering commands at the interpreter's own prompt, as you do with most other email packages. Most MH programs accept a mail folder name as one of their command-line arguments. A mail folder name starts with a + (plus sign)* and can appear anywhere in a command line.

---

* An MH folder name can also start with an @ (at sign), but that use is less common. Besides, this is just an example!

MH mail folders can be stored anywhere on the filesystem—even on a networked filesystem on a remote computer. Here are the four lines that I put in my *.tcshrc* setup file (3.3):

{ } 28.4

```
# Set up MH folder name completion for "folder", "refile", "scan", "show":
folders -fast -recurse | \
    sed -e '/DELETE$/d' -e 's/^/+/' > $HOME/Mail/folderlist
complete {folder,refile,scan,show} 'C@*@`cat $HOME/Mail/folderlist`@'
```

The first command builds a file named *folderlist* with a list of strings (in this case, folder names) to complete. I don't want completion to include folder names I'll never look in, so I filtered the *folder* output with *sed* (34.1) to exclude the names I don't want—in this case, folder names ending with *DELETE*. (This list is also useful in other places, it turns out, not just in *tcsh* completion.) A + is prepended to each folder name because *folders* doesn't add the plus signs, but we need them for *tcsh* matching. So the first few lines of *folderlist* look like this:

```
+drafts
+inbox
+jobs
+jobs/bay-area
+jobs/miscellaneous
    ...
```

The second command, *complete*, starts with a list in braces of the commands that should complete folder names. The next argument is complex and has lots of possible variations; this one matches any pattern included with backquotes (28.14) from the *cat* (12.2) command, which gives us the contents of *folderlist*. There are lots of variations! The bottom line is how this works... here's an example of completing a folder name:

```
tcsh> scan +j TAB
tcsh> scan +jobs/m TAB
tcsh> scan +jobs/miscellaneous last:20
```

After completing the folder name (in two steps), *tcsh* leaves a space; I type the rest of the command line and press ENTER to run it.

Editor Functions for Completion

Some shells have customizable, built-in command-line editors that use key bindings to control how and where completion takes place. For example, in *tcsh*, pressing TAB invokes the *complete-word* function, but you can change TAB to do menu completion (as explained above) by binding the editor function *complete-word-fwd* to TAB key.

In *bash*, TAB does basic completion with the editor's *complete* function. But the *bash* editor has many more bindings than *tcsh* does. For instance, typing M-/ runs *complete-filename*, which treats the text before the cursor as a filename and does filename completion on it. Typing M-$ runs *complete-variable*, which treats the text before the cursor as a shell variable and does variable completion on it. There are plenty of variations—like C-x $, which invokes the *possible-variable-completions* function to list all shell variable names that could be completed. Article 28.4 has an example of M-{, the curly-brace completion function.

For details on your particular shell, check its manual page.

—JP, ML, and SJC

28.7 Don't Match Useless Files in Filename Completion

The shell variable *fignore* in *csh* and *zsh* (*FIGNORE* in *bash* and also *zsh*) lets you tell the shell that you aren't interested in some files when using filename completion (28.6). For example, you may be more likely to refer to C language source files (whose names end with *.c*) than object files (*.o* files); you often need to edit your source files, while you may never need to look at your object modules. Set *fignore* to the suffixes that you want to ignore. For example, to ignore *.o* files in *tcsh* and *csh*, type:

set 35.9
```
% set fignore=(.o)
```

Once you've done this, file completion will ignore your *.o* files when you press the TAB key (ESC in *csh*)—unless a *.o* file is the only match it can find.

Most likely, there's a whole list of suffixes that you don't care about: *.o* (object modules), *.out* (random executables), *.gz* (*gzip*ped files), ~ (Emacs backup files (19.4)), and so on. Article 1.12 has a list of them. Here's how to set *fignore* to a list of filenames:[*]

```
% set fignore=(.o .out .gz \~)      ...tcsh, csh, zsh
$ FIGNORE='.o:.out:.gz:~'           ...bash, zsh
```

fignore has no effect when you press CTRL-d to get a listing of the files that match in *csh* and *tcsh*. Those shells always give you a complete list of all possible completions.

—ML and JP

---

[*] The ~ (for Emacs) has to be quoted (27.13) when it's stored in the *fignore* array. Otherwise, the shell would expand it to your home directory path (31.11).

28.8 Repeating Commands

Let's start with some obvious ways to run commands more than once:

- Type !! (30.8) to repeat the previous command line, or repeat a cycle of commands with !-*n* (30.9)
- Press the up-arrow key (30.14) or a *vi*- or Emacs-style editing command
- Copy and paste the command line with your mouse (28.10)

Whether each of those methods will work depends on the shell you're using and whether you have copy-and-paste built into your interface. All of those methods force you to take some action before each command line repeats—pressing the up-arrow key, for instance. That lets you control exactly when each command runs.

The next four articles show automated ways to repeat a command a certain number of times. You can "mix and match" some parts of different articles—the tips on *read* and *sleep*, for instance. Each article follows on to the one before, so we suggest glancing through all of them:

- In C shells, repeat a single command with the *repeat* command.
- *zsh* can repeat a series of commands with its *repeat* loop.
- Methods for Bourne-type shells use more-general shell features.
- An offbeat method that works with all shells is to output multiple commands using jot.
- The shells' *for* and *foreach* loops (28.9) can vary the commands they run by picking a string (a word, for instance) from a list of strings.
- To repeat a command and display its output in the same place on the screen—so it's easy to spot differences over time—try *vis* (28.11).

Finally, remember that you aren't stuck with the login shell you chose. If you want a feature that your shell doesn't have, you can use another shell temporarily by typing its name (like *csh*), running the commands you need, then typing *exit* to go back to your original shell.

—*JP*

28.9 Repeating and Varying Commands

A foreach Loop

When some people need to repeat a command on several files, the first thing they think of is command line editing (30.14) or—as we show here—history substitution (30.5):

-v **12.4**
less **12.3**

```
% cat -t -v /usr/fran/report | less
  ...
% ^fran/report^rob/file3
cat -t -v /usr/rob/file3 | less
  ...
% ^3^21
cat -t -v /usr/rob/file21 | less
  ...
%
```

The second substitution (changing *3* to *21*) was quick to do, but the first one was longer. If there are lots of related commands like this, it can be easier to list all the variations at once—then let the shell do the dirty work. To do that, use the shell's *foreach* loop in C-type shells—or, in Bourne-type shells, use a *for* loop, shown later in this article. (*zsh* has both *foreach* and *for* loops.) You give the loop a list of the words that will change each time the command line is run. In this example, it's a list of filenames. The loop will step through the words, one by one, storing a word into a shell variable (35.9), then running the command(s). The loop goes on until it has read all the words. For example:

```
% foreach file (/usr/fran/report /usr/rob/file3 /usr/rob/file21)
? cat -t -v $file | less
? end
    ...Shell runs cat -t -v /usr/fran/report | less...
    ...Shell runs cat -t -v /usr/rob/file3 | less...
    ...Shell runs cat -t -v /usr/rob/file21 | less...
%
```

The question marks (?) are secondary prompts (28.12); the shell will keep printing them until you type the command *end*. Then the loop runs.

The list between the parentheses doesn't have to be filenames. Among other things, you can use wildcards (1.13), backquotes (28.14) (command substitution), variables (35.9, 35.3), and the handy curly brace ({}) operators (28.4). For example, you could have typed the above loop this way:

```
% foreach file (/usr/fran/report /usr/rob/file{3,21})
? cat -t -v $file | less
? end
```

If you want the loop to stop before or after running each command, add the C shell operator $<. It reads keyboard input and waits for a RETURN. In this case, you can probably ignore the input; you'll use $< to make the loop wait. For example, to make the previous loop prompt before each command line:

set **35.9**

```
% foreach file (/usr/fran/report /usr/rob/file{3,21})
? echo -n "Press RETURN to see $file--"
? set x="$<"
? cat -t -v $file | less
? end
```

```
Press RETURN to see /usr/fran/report--RETURN
      Shell runs cat -t -v /usr/fran/report | less...
Press RETURN to see /usr/rob/file3--RETURN
      Shell runs cat -t -v /usr/rob/file3 | less...
Press RETURN to see /usr/rob/file21--RETURN
      Shell runs cat -t -v /usr/rob/file21 | less...
```

The loop parameters don't need to be filenames. For instance, you could send a personalized email (1.21) message to five people this way:*

cat - 12.2

```
% foreach person (John Cathy Agnes Brett Elma)
? echo "Dear $person," | cat - formletter | mail $person
? end
```

The first line of the first letter will be "Dear John,"; the second letter "Dear Cathy,"; and so on.

Want to take this idea further? It's a part of shell programming (35.2). I usually don't recommend shell programming with the C shell, but this is a handy technique to use interactively.

A for Loop

The *for* loop in Bourne-type shells is like the *foreach* loop shown earlier: it loops through a list of words, running one or more commands for each word in the list. This saves time when you want to run the same series of commands separately on several files.

Let's repeat an earlier example:

```
$ for file in /usr/fran/report /usr/rob/file2 /usr/rob/file3
> do
> cat -t -v $file | less
> done
      ...Shell runs cat -t -v /usr/fran/report | less...
      ...Shell runs cat -t -v /usr/rob/file2 | less...
      ...Shell runs cat -t -v /usr/rob/file3 | less...
$
```

The greater-than signs (>) are secondary prompts (28.12); the Bourne shell will keep printing them until you type the command *done*. Then it runs the loop. You don't have to press RETURN after the do; you can type the first command on the same line after it.

In a shell script, the loop body (the lines between do and done) is usually indented for clarity.

---

* If you're sending lots of mail messages with a loop, your system mailer may get overloaded. In that case, it's a good idea to put a command like sleep 5 (25.9) on a separate line before the end. That will give the mailer five seconds to send each message.

The list after the in doesn't have to be filenames. Among other things, you can use backquotes (28.14) (command substitution), variables (35.9, 35.3), wildcards (33.1), and, on shells like *bash* that have them, curly brace ({}) operators (28.4). For example, you could have typed the previous loop this way:

```
$ for file in /usr/fran/report /usr/rob/file[23]
> do cat -t -v $file | less
> done
```

If you want the loop to stop before or after running each command, add the shell's *read* command (35.18). It reads keyboard input and waits for a RETURN. In this case, you can ignore the input; you'll use *read* just to make the loop wait. For example, to make the above loop prompt before each command line:

```
$ for file in /usr/fran/report /usr/rob/file[23]
> do
> echo -n "Press RETURN to see $file--"
> read x
> cat -t -v $file | less
> done
Press RETURN to see /usr/fran/report--RETURN
     Shell runs cat -t -v /usr/fran/report | less...
Press RETURN to see /usr/rob/file2--RETURN
     Shell runs cat -t -v /usr/rob/file2 | less...
Press RETURN to see /usr/rob/file3--RETURN
     Shell runs cat -t -v /usr/rob/file3 | less...
```

Article 35.21 has more information about the *for* loop. Article 36.12 shows how to make a *for* loop that varies several parameters at once.

—*JP*

28.10 Repeating a Command with Copy-and-Paste

If you're using an *xterm* window (24.20) or another type of terminal emulator with easy copy-and-paste functionality, that might be the easiest way to repeat all or part of a previous command line. Just select the part you want to copy, and paste it at a new prompt, adding any other text before and after pasting. This can be easier than using the shell's editing commands or history operators: what you see is what you get. Figure 28-1 shows copy-and-paste.*

You can reuse the copied text over and over, if you want; after copying it once, paste as many times and places as you need to. Also, if you've got multiple pieces of text to copy and paste, try using a scratchpad window or *xclipboard* (5.19).

---

* This is Figure 2-3 from O'Reilly & Associates' *Learning the Unix Operating System*, Fourth Edition.

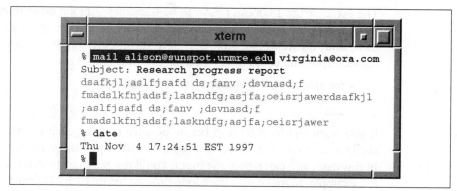

Figure 28-1. Copying and pasting a command

—JP

28.11 Repeating a Time-Varying Command

vis

Sometimes you find yourself repeating the same command over and over again—for example, *ps* (24.5) to monitor the progress of your background processes, or *lpq* (45.2) to know when your printout is finished. Instead of typing the same command repeatedly, or even using shell history (30.2) to repeat it, use the *vis* command. For example:

```
% vis ps
```

The *vis* command takes over your screen and shows the output of the initial *ps* command. Every 15 seconds, the command is executed again and your screen is updated with the new information. If this delay is too long for you, you can get *vis* to use a shorter delay using the *–d* option:

```
% vis -d 2 ps
```

The information will now be updated every 2 seconds. Your screen is cleared and you are shown the output of *ps*. On the top line, *vis* tells you the command being run, how long your delay is (if not the default), and how many times it has been executed. The Exec: line is incremented every time the command is repeated.

```
Command: ps                    Delay: 2          Exec:  1

    PID TT STAT  TIME COMMAND
   2971 p1 S     0:06 -sh (csh)
   6139 p1 S     0:00 vis -d 2 ps
   6145 p1 R     0:00 ps
   3401 q0 IW    0:13 -sh (csh)
   5954 q0 S     0:01 vi ch01
  14019 q5 IW    0:02 -sh (csh)
  29380 r7 IW    0:00 -bin/csh (csh)
  29401 rd IW    0:00 -bin/csh (csh)
```

vis provides a few other command-line options. The –*s* option is particularly neat: using –*s*, any lines that have changed since the last iteration are printed in standout mode.

Note that variations of this command have floated around in the public domain under several different names, such as *display*, *rep*, and *watch*. We found *vis* to be the most useful.

—*LM*

28.12 Multiline Commands, Secondary Prompts

All shells support multiline commands. In Bourne-type shells, a newline following an open quote (' or "), pipe symbol (|), or backslash (\) will not cause the command to be executed. Instead, you'll get a secondary prompt (from the *PS2* shell variable, set to > by default), and you can continue the command on the next line. For example, to send a quick *write* (1.21) message without making the other user wait for you to type the message, try this:

```
$ echo "We're leaving in 10 minutes. See you downstairs." |
> write joanne
```

In the C shells, you can continue a line by typing a backslash (\) before the new-line (27.13). In *tcsh*, you'll see a secondary prompt, a question mark (?), on each continued line. The original *csh* doesn't prompt in this case.

Obviously, this is a convenience if you're typing a long command line. It is a minor feature and one easily overlooked; however, it makes it much easier to use a program like *sed* (34.1) from the command line. For example, if you know you chronically make the typos "mvoe" (for "move") and "thier" (for "their"), you might be inspired to type the following command:

```
$ sed '
> s/mvoe/move/g
> s/thier/their/g' myfile | nroff -ms | lp
```

nroff -ms **3.21**
lp **45.2**

More importantly, the ability to issue multiline commands lets you use the shell's programming features interactively from the command line. In both the Bourne and C shells, multiline programming constructs automatically generate a secondary prompt (> in Bourne shells and ? in C shells) until the construct is completed. This is how our favorite programming constructs for non-programmers, the *for* and *foreach* loops (28.9), work. While a simple loop could be saved into a shell script (1.8), it is often even easier to use it interactively.

Here's an example with *zsh*, which makes secondary prompts that show the names of the construct(s) it's continuing. This *for* loop prints files from the current directory. If a filename ends with *.ps*, it's sent straight to the *ps* printer. Filenames ending with *.tif* are sent through netpbm (45.19) filters, then to the *ps* printer.

case 35.10

echo 27.5

```
zsh% for file in *
for> do case "$file" in
for case> *.ps) lpr -Pps "$file" ;;
for case> *.tif) tifftopnm "$file" | pnmtops | lpr -Pps ;;
for case> *) echo "skipping $file" ;;
for case> esac
for> done
skipping README
...
zsh%
```

zsh's multiline editing makes it easy to go back and edit that multiline nested construct. In other shells, you might consider using a throwaway script or copying and pasting with a mouse if you have one.

—*TOR and JP*

28.13 Here Document Example #1: Unformatted Form Letters

<< **27.16**

The here document operator << (27.16) is often used in shell scripts—but it's also handy at a shell prompt, especially with *zsh* multiline editing or a throwaway script. But you also can just type it in at a Bourne shell prompt (28.12). (If you use *csh* or *tcsh*, you can either use a *foreach* loop (28.9) or start a subshell (24.4).)

The example below shows a *for* loop (28.9) that prints three friendly form letters with the *lpr* (45.2) command. Each letter has a different person's name and the current date at the top. Each line of the loop body starts with a TAB character, which the <<- operator removes before the printer gets the text:

```
for person in "Mary Smith" "Doug Jones" "Alison Eddy"
do
    lpr <<- ENDMSG

    `date`

    Dear $person,

    This is your last notice. Buy me pizza tonight or
    else I'll type "rm -r *" when you're not looking.

    This is not a joak.
```

```
        Signed,
        The midnight skulker
        ENDMSG
    done
```

The shell reads the standard input until it finds the terminator word, which in this case is ENDMSG. The word ENDMSG has to be on a line all by itself. (Some Bourne shells don't have the <<- operator to remove leading TAB characters. In that case, use << and don't indent the loop body.) The backquotes (28.14) run the *date* command and output its date; $person is replaced with the person's name set at the top of the loop. The rest of the text is copied as is to the standard input of the *lpr* command.

—*JP*

28.14 Command Substitution

A pair of backquotes (``) does *command substitution*. This is really useful—it lets you use the standard output from one command as arguments to another command.

Here's an example. Assume you want to edit all files in the current directory that contain the word "error." Type this:

-1 **33.6**
```
$ vi `grep -l error *.c`
3 files to edit
"bar.c" 254 lines, 28338 characters
    ...
$
```

But why does this work? How did we build the incantation above? First, think about how you'd do this without using any special techniques. You'd use *grep* to find out which commands contain the word "error"; then you'd use *vi* to edit this list:

```
$ grep error *.c
bar.c:  error("input too long");
bar.c:  error("input too long");
baz.c:  error("data formatted incorrectly");
foo.c:  error("can't divide by zero"):
foo.c:  error("insufficient memory"):
$ vi bar.c baz.c foo.c
```

Is there any way to compress these into one command? Yes, by using command substitution. First, we need to modify our *grep* command so that it produces only a list of filenames, rather than filenames and text. That's easy; use *grep –l*:

```
$ grep -l error *.c
bar.c
baz.c
foo.c
```

The *–l* option lists each filename only once, even if many lines in the file match. (This makes me think that *grep –l* was designed with precisely this application in mind.) Now, we want to edit these files; so we put the *grep* command inside backquotes, and use it as the argument to *vi*:

```
$ vi `grep -l error *.c`
3 files to edit
"bar.c" 254 lines, 28338 characters
    ...
$
```

You might be wondering about the difference between the "vertical" output from *grep* and the "horizontal" way that people usually type arguments on a command line. The shell handles this with no problems. Inside backquotes, both a newline and a space are argument separators.

The list you use with command substitution doesn't have to be filenames. Let's see how to send a mail message (1.21) to all the users logged on to the system now. You want a command line like this:

```
% mail joe lisa franka mondo bozo harpo ...
```

Getting there takes a little thinking about what Unix commands you need to run to get the output you want. (This is real "Power Tools" stuff!) To get a list of those users, you could use *who* (2.8). The *who* output also lists login time and other information—but you can cut that off with a command like *cut* (21.14):

```
% who | cut -c1-8
joe
lisa
franka
lisa
joe
mondo
joe
...
```

Some users are logged on more than once. To get a unique list, use *sort –u* (22.6). You're done. Just put the name-making command line between backquotes:

```
% mail `who | cut -c1-8 | sort -u`
```

If you aren't sure how this works, replace the command you want to run with *echo* (27.5):

```
% echo `who | cut -c1-8 | sort -u`
bozo franka harpo joe lisa mondo
```

After using Unix for a while, you'll find that this is one of its most useful features. You'll find many situations where you use one command to generate a list of words, then put that command in backquotes and use it as an argument to something else. Sometimes you'll want to nest (36.24) the backquotes—this is where the *bash*, *ksh*, *bash*, and *zsh* $( ) operators (which replace the opening and closing backquote, respectively) come in handy. There are some problems with command substitution, but you usually won't run into them.

This book has many, many examples of command substitution. Here are some of them: making unique filenames (8.17), removing some files from a list (14.18), setting your shell prompt (4.6, 4.8, 4.14), and setting variables (4.8, 36.23).

—*JP*

28.15 Handling Lots of Text with Temporary Files

Sometimes you need to execute a command with a long list of files for arguments. Here's an easy way to create that list without having to type each filename yourself—put the list in a temporary file:

```
% ls > /tmp/mikel
% vi /tmp/mikel
    ...edit out any files you don't want...
% process-the-files `cat /tmp/mikel`
% rm /tmp/mikel
```

'...' 28.14

I added the *vi* step to remind you that you can edit this list; for example, you may want to delete a few files that you don't want to process.

Possible problems: if the list is long enough, you may end up with a command line that's too long for your shell to process. If this happens, use *xargs* (28.17). If your system doesn't have *xargs*, there are other workarounds doesn't that should solve the problem.

—*ML*

28.16 Separating Commands with Semicolons

When the shell sees a semicolon (;) on a command line, it's treated as a command separator—basically like pressing the ENTER key to execute a command. When would you want to use a semicolon instead of pressing ENTER?

- It's nice when you want to execute a series of commands, typing them all at once at a single prompt. You'll see all of them on the same command line and they'll be grouped together in the history list (30.7). This makes it easy to see, later, that you intended this series of commands to be executed one after another. And you can re-execute them all with a simple history command.

As an example, here's a series of commands that puts a listing of the current directory into a temporary file, emails the listing, then overwrites the previous version of the file:

```
$ ll > $tf-1; mail -s backup joe < $tf-1; mv $tf-1 listing
```

I can repeat that same command later by using a history substitution (30.8) like !ll.

- It's useful with *sleep* (25.9) to run a command after a delay. The next example shows a series of commands in a C shell alias that you might use to print a warning and give the user a chance to abort before the last command (*exit*, which ends the current shell) is executed. Be sure to read the important note after this example:

```
alias bye 'echo "Type CTRL-c to abort logout"; sleep 10; exit'
```

Note that, in C-type shells and older Bourne-type shells, pressing your interrupt key (24.10)—like CTRL-c—will stop execution of all jobs on the current command line. The alias above works in shells like that. But in some shells, like *bash2*, interrupting a command in a string of commands separated by semicolons will affect only that single command. So I couldn't rewrite the alias above for *bash2* because, if I pressed CTRL-c while the *sleep* command was executing, that would simply abort *sleep*—and proceed to run *exit*, which would log me out immediately!

- If you're running a series of commands that take some time to complete, you can type all the commands at once and leave them to run unattended. For example, I have little shell scripts named *nup* and *ndown* (24.22) (which run */sbin/ifup* and */sbin/ifdown*, respectively) to start and disable the network. On a system with a dialup modem and a long file transfer to perform, it's nice to be able to type a series of commands that bring up the network, do a couple of file transfers, then bring down the network. I can type this string, go about my business somewhere else, and come back later:

```
$ nup;ptbk;getmail;ndown
```

After *nup* returns, the network is up (the modem has connected). So the shell runs *ptbk* (38.9) to make a backup of my work on this book. Next, *getmail* gets my email (it basically runs *fetchmail*). When *getmail* finishes, *ndown* hangs up the modem. This can take several minutes from start to finish, but the shell manages it all while I do something else. (If I didn't have a windowing system with multiple *xterms*, I could have put that string of commands into a subshell (43.7) in the background (23.2).) This is one place that a GUI interface for network control really loses to command-line utilities and the shell.

Two related operators, && and || (35.14), work like a semicolon, but they only execute the next command if the previous one succeeded or failed, respectively.

—*JP*

28.17 Dealing with Too Many Arguments

Historically, one of the more annoying things about the design of many UNIX tools was their inability to handle large numbers of arguments. For example, if you wanted to print several hundred files using *lpr*, you either had to pass them a few at a time, perhaps using wildcards on the command line to split the list up into shorter groups, or call *lpr* once per file, perhaps using *find* or a loop. One other method, which is still useful today, involves the use of *xargs*.

xargs is one of those Unix utilities that seems pretty useless when you first hear about it—but turns into one of the handiest tools you can have.

xargs

If your system doesn't already have *xargs*, be sure to install it from the web site.

xargs reads a group of arguments from its standard input, then runs a Unix command with that group of arguments. It keeps reading arguments and running the command until it runs out of arguments. The shell's backquotes (28.14) do the same kind of thing, but they give all the arguments to the command at once. This can give you a `Too many arguments` error.

Here are some examples:

- If you want to print most of the files in a large directory, put the output of *ls* into a file. Edit the file to leave just the filenames you want printed. Give the file to *xargs'* standard input:

  ‹ 43.1

  ```
  % ls > allfiles.tmp
  % vi allfiles.tmp
  % xargs lpr < allfiles.tmp
  ```

  What did that do? With lines like these in *allfiles.tmp*:

  ```
  % cat allfiles.tmp
  afile
  application
    ...
  yoyotest
  zapme
  ```

  xargs ran one or more *lpr* commands, each with a group of arguments, until it had read every word in the file:

  ```
  lpr afile application ...
    ...
  lpr ... yoyotest zapme
  ```

  This has another advantage for *lpr*: each print job is fairly short, so you can delete one from the print queue without losing all of them.

- The standard output of *xargs* is the standard output of the commands it runs. So, if you'd created *allfiles.tmp* above, but you wanted to format the files with *pr* (45.6) first, you could type:

  ```
  % xargs pr < allfiles.tmp | lpr
  ```

Then *xargs* would run all of these *pr* commands. The shell would pipe their standard outputs[*] to a single *lpr* command:

```
pr afile application ...
    ...
pr ... yoyotest zapme
```

- In the next example, *find* (9.1) gets a list of all files in the directory tree. Next, we use *xargs* to read those filenames and run *grep –l* (33.6) to find which files contain the word "WARNING". Next, we pipe that to a setup with *pr* and *lpr*, like the one in the previous example:

```
% find . -type f -print | xargs grep -l WARNING | xargs pr | lpr
```

"Huh?" you might say. Just take that step by step. The output of *find* is a list of filenames, like ./afile ./bfile ... ./adir/zfile and so on. The first *xargs* gives those filenames to one or more *grep –l* commands:

```
grep -l WARNING ./afile ./bfile ...
    ...
grep -l WARNING ./adir/zfile ...
```

The standard output of all those *grep*s is a (shortened) list of filenames that match. That's piped to another *xargs*—it runs *pr* commands with the filenames that *grep* found.

Unix is weird and wonderful!

- Sometimes you don't want *xargs* to run its command with as many arguments as it can fit on the command line. The *–n* option sets the maximum number of arguments *xargs* will give to each command. Another handy option, *–p*, prompts you before running each command.

Here's a directory full of files with errors (whose names end with *.bad*) and corrected versions (named *.fixed*). I use *ls* to give the list of files to *xargs*; it reads two filenames at once, then asks whether I want to run *diff –c* to compare those two files. It keeps prompting me and running *diff –c* until it runs out of file pairs:

```
% ls
chap1.bad
chap1.fixed
chap2.bad
chap2.fixed
    ...
chap9.bad
chap9.fixed
% ls | xargs -p -n2 diff -c
diff -c chap1.bad chap1.fixed ?...y
```

---

[*] Actually, the shell is piping the standard output of *xargs*. As I said above, *xargs* sends the standard output of commands it runs to its own standard output.

```
...Output of diff command for chap1...
diff -c chap2.bad chap2.fixed ?...n
diff -c chap3.bad chap3.fixed ?...y
...Output of diff command for chap3...
```

—JP and SJC

28.18 Expect

expect

Expect is a program to control interactive applications such as *telnet* (1.21) and *passwd*. These and many other applications interactively prompt and expect a user to enter keystrokes in response. But you can write simple Expect scripts to automate these interactions. Then the Expect program can run the "interactive" program noninteractively. Expect can also be used to automate only parts of a dialogue, since control can be passed from the script to the keyboard and vice versa. This allows a script to do the drudgery and a user to do the fun stuff.

**tcl
tk**

Expect programs can be written in any language but are almost always written in Tcl. Tcl is an interpreted language that is widely used in many other applications. If you already use a Tcl-based application, you won't have to learn a new language for Expect.

Tcl is a very typical-looking shell-like language. There are commands to set variables (*set*), control flow (*if*, *while*, *foreach*, etc.), and perform the usual math and string operations. Of course, Unix programs can be called, too.

Expect is integrated on top of Tcl and provides additional commands for interacting with programs. Expect is named after the specific command that waits for output from a program. The *expect* command is the heart of the Expect program. It describes a list of patterns to watch for. Each pattern is followed by an action; if the pattern is found, the action is executed.

For example, the following fragment is from a script that involves a login. When executed, the script waits for the strings welcome, failed, or busy, and then it evaluates [(executes)—*JP*] one of the corresponding actions. The action associated with *busy* shows how multiple commands can be evaluated. The *timeout* keyword is a special pattern that matches if no other patterns match in a certain amount of time.

```
expect {
    "welcome" break
    "failed" abort
    timeout  abort
    "busy"   {
        puts "I'll wait - the system is busy!"
        continue
    }
}
```

Dialback

It is surprising how little scripting is necessary to produce something useful. Below is a script that dials a phone. It is used to reverse the charges so that long-distance phone calls are charged to the computer. It is invoked with the phone number as its argument.

```
spawn tip modem
expect "connected"
send "ATD$argv\r"
# modem takes a while to connect
set timeout 60
expect "CONNECT"
```

The first line runs the *tip* program so that the output of a modem can be read by *expect* and its input written by *send*. Once *tip* says it is connected, the modem is told to dial using the command ATD followed by the phone number. The phone number is retrieved from *argv*, which is a variable predefined to contain the original argument with which the script was called.

The fourth line is just a comment noting that the variable being set in the next line controls how long *expect* will wait before giving up. At this point, the script waits for the call to complete. No matter what happens, *expect* terminates. If the call succeeds, the system detects that a user is connected and prompts with login:.

Actual scripts do more error checking, of course. For example, the script could retry if the call fails. But the point here is that it does not take much code to produce useful scripts. This six-line script replaced a 60 KB executable (written in C) that did the same thing!

Automating /bin/passwd

Earlier I mentioned some programs that cannot be automated with the shell. It is difficult to imagine why you might even want to embed some of these programs in shell scripts. Certainly the original authors of the programs did not conceive of this need. As an example, consider *passwd*.

passwd is the command to change a password. The *passwd* program does not take the new password from the command line.* Instead, it interactively prompts for it—twice. Here is what it looks like when run by a system administrator. (When run by users, the interaction is slightly more complex because they are prompted for their old passwords as well.)

---

* Newer versions will accept input from *STDIN*, however.

```
# passwd libes
Changing password for libes on thunder.
New password:
Retype new password:
```

This is fine for a single password. But suppose you have accounts of your own on a number of unrelated computers and you would like them all to have the same password. Or suppose you are a system administrator establishing 1,000 accounts at the beginning of each semester. All of a sudden, an automated *passwd* makes a lot of sense. Here is an Expect script to do just that: automate *passwd* so that it can be called from a shell script.

```
spawn passwd [lindex $argv 0]
set password [lindex $argv 1]
expect "password:"
send "$password\r"
expect "password:"
send "$password\r"
expect eof
```

The first line starts the *passwd* program with the username passed as an argument. The next line saves the password in a variable for convenience. As in shell scripts, variables do not have to be declared in advance.

In the third line, the *expect* command looks for the pattern password:. *expect* waits until the pattern is found before continuing.

After receiving the prompt, the next line sends a password to the current process. The \r indicates a carriage return. (Most of the usual C string conventions are supported.) There are two *expect-send* sequences because *passwd* asks the password to be typed twice as a spelling verification. There is no point to this in a noninteractive *passwd*, but the script has to do it because *passwd* assumes it is interacting with a human who does not type consistently.

The final command expect eof causes the script to wait for the end-of-file character in the output of *passwd*. Similar to *timeout*, *eof* is another keyword pattern. This final *expect* effectively waits for *passwd* to complete execution before returning control to the script.

Take a step back for a moment. Consider that this problem could be solved in a different way. You could edit the source to *passwd* (should you be so lucky as to have it) and modify it so that given an optional flag, it reads its arguments from the command line just the way that the Expect script does. If you lack the source and have to write *passwd* from scratch, of course, then you will have to worry about how to encrypt passwords, lock and write the password database, etc. In fact, even if you only modify the existing code, you may find it surprisingly complicated code to look at. The *passwd* program does some very tricky things. If you do get it to work, pray that nothing changes when your system is upgraded. If the vendor adds NIS, NIS+, Kerberos, shadow passwords, a different encryption function, or some other new feature, you will have to revisit the code.

Expect comes with several example scripts that demonstrate how you can do many things that are impossible with traditional shells. For example, the *passmass* script lets you update your password on many unrelated machines simultaneously. The *rftp* script provides your regular *ftp* client with additional commands to do recursive FTP in either direction. The *cryptdir* script encrypts all the files in a directory. And an amusing script is provided that lets two *chess* processes play each other. Expect has no limit to the number of interactive programs it can drive at the same time. The Unix system may limit Expect, though, by controlling the maximum number of processes or other system resources available.

Testing: A Story

Many people use Expect for testing. You can test interactive programs as easily as you can automate them. And hardware lends itself to testing with Expect, too. For example, we solved a thorny problem when we had to deal with an unreliable bank of modems. We were receiving dozens of calls each week reporting "the modem is hung." No indication of which modem, of course. And it was always too late for us to ask the user to try something to investigate the problem. The connection was gone by then. Our solution was an Expect script that connected to each modem hourly and exercised it. Any problems were recorded so that we had a clear and full history of each modem's behavior. As soon as a defective or hung modem was encountered, the Expect script would send email to the system administrator. With this script in place, reports of modem problems from our users dropped to zero.

Other Problems

These are just a few of the problems that can be solved with Expect. And as with all Expect solutions, recompilation of the original programs is unnecessary. You don't even need the source code! Expect handles many other problems as well. For example, Expect can wrap existing interactive tools with GUI wrappers. This means you can wrap interactive programs with graphic frontends to control applications by buttons, scrollbars, and other graphic elements. And Expect scripts work great as CGI scripts or from *cron* (25.2) or *inetd* [the daemon that controls Internet services provided by a system—*JP*]. Finally, learning Expect may be easier than you think. Expect can watch you interact and then produce an Expect script for you. Interaction automation can't get much easier than this!

More information on Expect is available in *Exploring Expect*, by Don Libes, from O'Reilly & Associates.

—*DL*

Custom Commands

29.1 Creating Custom Commands

- In most shells, aliases are an easy way to shorten a long command line or do a short series of commands. Articles 29.2 through 29.10 cover C shell aliases. Articles 29.4 through 29.14 cover aliases in *bash*, *pdksh*, and *zsh*.

- All except the oldest Bourne-type shells have shell functions (29.11), which are explained in Articles 29.11 through 29.13. These are a cross between aliases and shell scripts. They're good both for shortening command lines and for running a short or long series of commands.

—JP and SJC

29.2 Introduction to Shell Aliases

All shells except the original Bourne shell have an "alias" facility that lets you define abbreviations for commands.

The simplest C shell aliases, which are similar to the alias facility in newer Bourne-type shells, are simply a short name for a command and, often, command options or arguments too. The C shell's aliases can get very complicated. Article 29.3 describes how a C shell alias can use arguments from its command line as it's invoked.

As we've said, aliases in Bourne-type shells (*bash*, *zsh*, and *ksh*) are simpler. Article 29.4 covers some of the differences between those shells and the C shells. Still, the ideas for custom C shell commands are useful in any kind of shell, and if you can't write something in a simple Bourne-type alias, you almost certainly can do it in a shell function (29.11).

You can define aliases from the command line, for use in just your current shell. Any aliases you define can also be placed in your shell setup file (3.3), so they'll be available whenever you're using your shell.

Note that aliases are *not* passed to subprocesses (3.3), so putting them in a setup file that's read only by login shells or top-level shells probably isn't what you want. (One exception is an alias for a command that you want to run *only* in a login shell. For instance, you could define an alias named *X* that starts your X Window System. If that alias isn't defined in subshells, you'll get a message like X: command not found if you try to start the window system from an existing window.)

A common approach is to create separate files for each shell that store your aliases (such as *.bash_aliases* for *bash* or *.aliases.csh* for the C shell), so that you may source them whenever you like.

Here's one last note that applies to all shells. Anytime you want a list of the aliases currently set, just type alias.

—*JP, ML, DG, and SJC*

29.3 C-Shell Aliases with Command-Line Arguments

It's convenient for your aliases to use command-line arguments. For example, let's think about an alias named *phone*:

```
alias phone 'cat ~/phonelist | grep -i'
```

After you define that alias, you could type phone smith. The shell would find the *phone* alias and execute it with the argument (*smith*) at the end (29.2) this way:

```
cat ~/phonelist | grep -i smith
```

Using *cat* and a pipe that way is inefficient (43.2). It might be more sensible to have an alias that worked like this:

```
grep -i name ~/phonelist
```

How do we do this? The C shell's history (30.8) facility lets us use the notation !$ to refer to the last word in the previous command; the notation !* refers to all the arguments of the previous command. Assuming that we only want to look up aliases one at a time, we can use !$ and write our alias like this:

```
alias phone grep -i \!$ ~/phonelist
```

When we use the *phone* command, its final argument will be substituted into the alias. That is, when we type phone bill, the shell executes the command grep -i bill ~/phonelist.

In this example, we needed another kind of quoting. We had to put a backslash before the exclamation point to prevent the shell from replacing !$ with the previous command's last argument. That is, we don't want the shell to expand !$

when we define the alias—that's nonsense. We want the shell to insert the previous argument when we use the alias (in which case, the previous argument is just the argument for the alias itself—clear?).

But why couldn't we just use single quotes or double quotes (27.12)? This isn't the right place for a full explanation, but neither single quotes nor double quotes protect the exclamation point. The backslash does (27.13). If you want to be convinced, experiment with some commands like:

```
% echo '!!'      Print your last command
% echo '\!!'     Print !!
```

The first *echo* command shows that the shell performs history substitution (i.e., replaces !! with your previous command) in spite of the single quotes. The second example shows that the backslash can prevent the shell from interpreting ! as a special character.

Let's look at another alias. We want to pipe the output of *ls –l* into *more*. In this case, we would want all the arguments from the command line instead of merely the last argument (or the only argument). Here's the alias:

```
alias lm 'ls -l \!* | more'
```

This time, we needed both kinds of quoting: a backslash prevents the shell from interpreting the exclamation point immediately. Single quotes protect the pipe symbol and the asterisk (*). If you don't protect them both, and protect only the pipe (with a backslash), look what happens:

```
% alias lm ls -l \!* | more
alias: No match.
```

Because the backslash temporarily stops the special meaning of the !, the shell next tries to find filenames that match the wildcard (1.13) pattern !*. That fails (except in the unusual case when you have a file in the current directory whose name starts with a !).

 Here's a good general rule for quoting aliases. Unless you're trying to do something special with an alias and you understand quoting well, put single quotes (') around the whole definition and put a backslash before every exclamation point (\!).

If you want to pick one argument from the command line, use \!:*n*, where *n* is the number of the argument. Here's a sample alias. It uses *cat* (12.2) to add a header file to the file named in the first argument, then writes them both into the file named in the second argument:

~31.11

```
alias addhead 'cat ~/txt/header \!:1 > \!:2'
```

This alias has two arguments: the file to which you want to add a header and the output file. When you type:

```
% addhead foo bar
```

the C shell substitutes the filename foo for \!:1, and the filename bar for \!:2, executing the command:

```
cat ~/txt/header foo > bar
```

Finally, if you need to append fixed text strings to these arguments, you need to separate the argument text from the fixed text. For instance, here's an alias that tells the Netscape browser to go to a URL *http://info/proj23/xxx1.html*, where *xxx* is a word like *report*, *summary*, etc., that you're typing on the command line (as an argument to the alias). For instance, to go to the page *http://info/proj23/report1.html*, you'd type:

```
% proj report
```

The first alias below shows the wrong way to do this. The second one shows how to quote the argument in curly braces ({}) so the shell doesn't think the 1 after the argument is part of the number (giving you argument 11 instead of what you want: argument 1 with the digit *1* after it):

```
alias proj 'netscape -remote "openURL(http://info/proj23/\!:11.html)"'    ...wrong
alias proj 'netscape -remote "openURL(http://info/proj23/\!{:1}1.html)"'  ...right
```

If you haven't seen this *netscape –remote* technique, by the way, it's very handy. It sends a message to an already-open Netscape browser. You can use it from a command line (shell prompt) or by defining a button or menu item on your window system desktop. Recent Unix versions of Mozilla have also begun to support this API, as well. On the Macintosh, remote control is supported via Apple Events, but not from the command line as of this writing.

—ML, JP, and SJC

29.4 Setting and Unsetting Bourne-Type Aliases

A lot of what we said about aliases in article 29.2 applies to the Korn shell (*ksh*), *zsh*, and *bash*. This article, along with articles 29.5 and 29.6, have an overview of what's different.

One thing that's different from C shells is the syntax of the *alias* command, which is:

```
$ alias name=definition
```

That is, you need an equal sign (no spaces) between the name and the defini-tion. A good guideline is to use single quotes (') around the definition unless you're doing something specialized and you understand how quoting (27.12) works in aliases.

You can't put arguments inside an alias as the C shell's \! operator (29.3) does. To do that, use a shell function (29.11).

As in the C shells, *unalias* removes an alias. To remove all aliases, use *unalias –a* in *ksh* and *bash* or *unhash –a* in *zsh*. *alias* with no arguments lists aliases that are currently defined.

bash aliases are pretty basic; this section covers them. Korn shell and *zsh* aliases do more.

—*JP and SC*

29.5 Korn-Shell Aliases

pdksh (the public domain *ksh*) has three types of aliases. First is the regular com-mand alias covered in article 29.4.

Tracked aliases keep track of the locations of external (1.9) executables. The shell has a default list of commands to track (see the *ksh* manpage). The first time *ksh* searches the PATH for an executable command that's marked as a tracked alias, it saves the full path of that command. This saves the shell the trouble of per-forming the path search each time a command is invoked. The tracked aliases aren't reset unless one becomes invalid or you change the PATH. The command *alias –t* lists and creates tracked aliases. Here's an example with a newly invoked Korn shell:

```
$ alias -t
$ cat somefile > somewhere
$ alias -t
cat=/bin/cat
$ alias -t less
$ alias -t
cat=/bin/cat
less=/usr/bin/less
```

At first, there are no tracked aliases. But the *cat* command is marked for track-ing; as soon as I use it, the shell saves its location, as the next alias -t shows. Next, I add a tracked alias for *less* (12.3) (which isn't one of the default com-mands to track). The Korn shell won't track a command unless it's one of the defaults or you mark it for tracking.

The third kind of alias, directory aliases, set with *alias –d*, let you use a tilde abbreviation like ~*dir* for any directory.

—*JP*

29.6 zsh Aliases

zsh has the regular command alias covered in article 29.4. *zsh* is compatible with the C shell in many ways, but it doesn't accept *csh* alias syntax without an equal sign (=) between the name and value. That's probably because, as in other Bourne-type shells, *zsh* allows you to set multiple aliases with one command, like this:

> zsh$ **alias ri='rm -i' mi='mv -i'**   *...and so on*

In *zsh*, *alias –g* defines a *zsh* global alias: a word that's expanded anywhere (as long as it isn't quoted). These are like a shell variable (35.9) that doesn't need a dollar sign ($) to be expanded. Maybe you have a log file you read and edit often. You could make a global alias named *log*:

> zsh$ **alias -g log=/work/beta/p2/worklog**
>
> zsh$ **less log**
> zsh$ **cp log logtemp**

Global aliases are expanded only when they stand alone and aren't quoted. So if there's a global alias *dir* for a directory, you cannot use emacs `dir/file` to refer to a file in that directory. Also, if you defined the global alias *fserv* for the hostname *fserv.bkk.ac.uk*, you could type telnet `fserv`—but if you type `mail ed@fserv`, the shell wouldn't expand it into a hostname. Named directories and shell variables work better in cases like those.

alias –m lists aliases that match a wildcard-type pattern; alias `-m 'hi*'` shows all alias names that start with *hi* (like *hi*, *hist*, and so on). This matches regular command aliases as well as global aliases. You can use *–m* with *unalias*, too, to remove all aliases matching a pattern.

—*JP*

29.7 Sourceable Scripts

Aliases are a powerful concept in *csh*. Another great capability is shell scripts (1.8). Each has its strengths. An alias is just right for common sequences of commands, calling a command by a different name, and so on. Scripts are great for more flexible processing and batch processing. There are limitations to both, and I will show a way around them.

The limitation to aliases is that you are working pretty much with one command line. Consider this example, which manages various stages of changing directories, updating the prompt, and so forth:

```
alias pp 'set o2=$cwd; popd; set old=$o2; dir_number; record_dir pp; \\
    prompt_set; set cd_attempt=(\!*); if ($#cd_attempt > 0) cd $cd_attempt'
```

Now this works fine for me, and it served me well for a few years and thousands of invocations, but it's at the point where I start thinking that a script is more suited to the job. This brings me to the limitation of scripts.

Shell scripts are great for accomplishing some task that might change a file, start a program, etc. They are limited by the fact that any changes they make to shell or environment variables are not visible (24.3) to the parent shell that started them. In other words, you can write some really cool script that will change directories for you if you don't touch the keyboard for five seconds, but once the script exits, you are still in the same place you started.

The answer is to combine the best of both worlds. Consider this:

```
alias pp 'set cd_attempt=(\!*); source ~/bin/pp_csh'
```

We set up a variable and source a script. The concept is this: put your command-line arguments into a variable and then *source* (35.29) a script to accomplish something. The difference here is that because you are not starting a subshell (24.4) for the script, it can do everything an alias can and more. This is much like Bourne shell functions (29.11).

Some hints on using this technique:

Naming
> I like to name the script that is doing all of the work after the alias, with *_csh* or *.csh* at the end of its name. I put all of the scripts in my *~/bin* (7.4). [Instead of names ending in *.csh*, I put mine in a directory named *~/.lib/csh*. —*JP*]

Feedback
> You don't want to execute the script directly. You want to source it. Here's a good first line that detects this:

```
#! /bin/echo sorry,try:source
```

Usage statement
> Check the variable that you expect to see from the alias. If it isn't there, you can show a usage statement and do a *goto* to the end of the script:

‹‹ 27.16

```
if ($#lg_args == 0) then
    cat << +++
usage: lg [-a][-p] pattern [command]
    -a  lists all (.dot files)
    -p  pipe resulting list into command
+++
    goto lg_end
endif
    ...
lg_end:
```

Alias options

You aren't limited to what an alias can do, since you are sourcing a script. You gain some flexibility here. Here's one way of handling options:

```
unset ls_arg
while (! $?ls_arg)
    switch ("$lg_args[1]")
        case "-a":
            set ls_arg="-a"
            shift lg_args
        case "-p":
            set use_pipe
            shift lg_args
        default:
            set ls_arg
            breaksw
    endsw
end
```

set **35.9**

Have fun with this! You may find yourself tossing some old aliases and rewriting them as sourceable scripts. They're also easier to maintain.

—DS

29.8 Avoiding C-Shell Alias Loops

Article 27.9 has similar information for *bash*.

Here's a situation that came up on the Net a while ago. Someone wanted an *exit* (24.4) alias that would run a *~/.exit* file (31.13) before leaving the shell. The obvious solution is:

```
alias exit "source ~/.exit; exit"
```

This doesn't work; when you use the *exit* alias, the C shell thinks that the alias is trying to execute itself. Recursive aliases aren't allowed on many shells, so the C shell prints an error message (Alias loop) and gives up.

There are many ways to break the loop. Here's the best (in my opinion):

```
alias exit 'source ~/.exit; ""exit'
```

Article 27.10 has the hairy details of what works and why. To summarize, if you need to use the alias's name within a C shell alias, you can use:

`""`*name*

Where *name* is the name of a built-in (1.9) command or any "regular" command.

`\`*name*

Where *name* is the name of any "regular" command, but not a built-in command.

Tempting as this all may sound (and I have to admit, if it didn't sound a bit tempting, I wouldn't be writing this article), I can't really recommend the practice of "redefining" commands with aliases. You should leave the original commands as they are. The original author could have avoided all these problems by calling his alias *quit* rather than *exit*.

If you redefine commands with aliases and then use another account where your alias isn't defined, it's easy for things to go wrong. That's especially true for commands that do something permanent—overwriting or removing files, for example. It also can cause problems if you let someone type a command on your account and the person isn't expecting an aliased version.

Let me give one more example to show you what problems you can have. Let's say you've aliased the *exit* command to *source* a *.exit* file before quitting. Fair enough. But now, let's say that you're not in your login shell, that you've *set ignoreeof*, and that, for no apparent reason, your *.exit* file disappears (maybe it develops a bad block, so the system can't read it; such things happen).

Now you're stuck. If you type exit, the *source* command will fail, and the "real" *exit* command will never be executed. You can't leave the shell. Of course, if you remember what you did, you can always type unalias exit and get the original command back. Or you can type " "exit. Or finally, you could simply write the alias such that it tests for the existence of the file before trying to read it. But if you've foisted this alias on a beginner, he or she might not know that. All of a sudden, you're stuck in some shell that you apparently can't get out of.

The biggest virtue of Unix is that it's infinitely extendable. However, you aren't helping if your extensions hide the basic operations that make everything work. So—extend all you want. But when you write your extensions, give them *new names*. End of sermon.

—ML

29.9 How to Put if-then-else in a C-Shell Alias

The C shell's brain damage keeps you from using an *if* with an *else* in an alias. You have to use a sourceable script (29.7). Or that's what I thought until I saw an article by Lloyd Zusman on *comp.unix.questions* in December 1987. He'd saved an earlier posting on that group (but without its author's name) that showed how. The trick: use enough backslashes (\) and the *eval* (27.8) command.

As an example, here's an alias named *C* for compiling C programs. It needs the *executable* filename (like C prog), not the source filename (like C prog.c). If you type a filename ending in *.c*, it complains and quits. Else, it does the following:

- Renames any old *prog* file to *prog.old*.
- Prints the message *prog* SENT TO cc.
- Compiles *prog.c*.
- And—if there's a *prog* file (if the compile succeeded)—runs *chmod 311 prog* to protect the file from accidental reading with a command like *cat* * or *more* *.

Your alias doesn't need to be as complicated. But this one shows some tricks, such as putting an *if* inside the *if*, that you might want to use. Watch your quoting—remember that the shell strips off one level of quoting when you set the alias (29.3) and another during the first pass of the *eval*. Follow this example and you'll probably be fine:

if-else-
alias.cs

```
# COMPILE AND chmod C PROGRAMS; DON'T USE .c ON END OF FILENAME.
alias C 'eval "if (\!* =~ *.c) then \\
    echo "C quitting: no .c on end of \!* please." \\
else \\
    if (-e \!*) mv \!* \!*.old \\
    echo \!*.c SENT TO cc \\
    cc -s \!*.c -o \!* \\
    if (-e \!*) chmod 311 \!* \\
endif"'
```

—JP

29.10 Fix Quoting in csh Aliases with makealias and quote

Getting quoting right in C shell aliases can be a real problem. Dan Bernstein wrote two aliases called *makealias* and *quote* that take care of this for you.

For example, here I use *makealias* to avoid having to quote ! and *:

```
% makealias mycat
cat `ls | sed '1,/!*/d'` | less
CTRL-d
alias mycat 'cat `ls | sed '\''1,/\!*/d'\''` | less'
```

I typed the makealias mycat command and the line starting with cat, then pressed CTRL-d and got back an alias definition with all the quoting done correctly.

The properly quoted alias definition is sent to the standard output. That line is what you would use to define the alias.*

---

* [The *mycat* alias runs *cat* on all files with names later in the alphabet than the argument you type. The output of *cat* is piped to the *less* (12.3) pager. For example, let's say your current directory has the files *afile*, *count*, *jim*, and *report*. Typing mycat count would display the files *jim* and *report*. —JP]

Here are the *quote* and *makealias* aliases themselves:

makealias.csh

```
alias quote     "/bin/sed -e 's/\\!/\\\\\!/g' \\
  -e 's/'\\\''/'\\\'\\\\\\\\'\\\''/g' \\
  -e 's/^/'\''/' -e 's/"\$/'\''/'"
alias makealias "quote | /bin/sed 's/^/alias \!:1 /' \!:2*"
```

Pretty gross, but they do the job. On Darwin, as on many BSD-derived systems, *sed* is in */usr/bin*, not */bin*. You may wish simply to use the command name without the explicit path, or use the explicit (but correct) path. On Linux, the script above does not work with *tcsh*, which handles multi-line aliases anyway.

—JIK and SJC

29.11 Shell Function Basics

Most shells have aliases (29.2). Almost all Bourne-type shells have functions, which are like aliases, but richer and more flexible. Here are four examples.

Simple Functions: ls with Options

Let's start with two aliases from article 29.2, changed into shell functions: The *la* function includes "hidden" files in *ls* listings. The *lf* function labels the names as directories, executable files, and so on.

```
function la () { ls -a "$@"; }
function lf () { ls -F "$@"; }
```

The spaces and the semicolon (;) are important. You don't need them on some shells, but writing functions this way (or in the multiline format in later examples) is more portable.* The function keyword is not needed in the original Bourne shell but is required in later versions of *bash*. The "$@" (35.20) is replaced by any arguments (other options, or directory and filenames) you pass to the function:

```
$ la -l somedir          ...runs ls -a -l somedir
```

Functions with Loops: Internet Lookup

mx.sh

for 35.21

The *mx* function uses *dig* to look up the DNS MX (mail exchanger) record for a host, then *sed* (34.1) to pull out the "ANSWER SECTION", which has the host-name or hostnames:

```
function mx() {
# Look up mail exchanger for host(s)
for host
do
    echo "==== $host ===="
    dig "$host" mx in |
```

---

* A function is a Bourne shell list construct.

```
        sed -n '/^;; ANSWER SECTION:/,/^$/{
             s/^[^;].* //p
        }'
    done
}
```

mx takes one or more hostname arguments; it runs *dig* and *sed* on each hostname. For example, the mail exchangers for *oreilly.com* are *smtp2.oreilly.com* and *smtp.oreilly.com*. The mail exchanger for *hesketh.com* is *mail.hesketh.com*:

```
$ mx oreilly.com hesketh.com
==== oreilly.com ====
smtp2.oreilly.com.
smtp.oreilly.com.
==== hesketh.com ====
mail.hesketh.com.
```

This example shows how to write a function with more than one line. In that style, with the ending curly brace on its own line, you don't need a semicolon after the last command. (The curly braces in the middle of the function are inside quotes, so they're passed to *sed* as part of its script.)

The *mx* function looks like a little shell program (35.2). Shell functions have the same syntax as a shell script, except for the enclosing function name and curly braces. In fact, a shell function can be defined and used within a shell script (35.30). But, as we've seen, it's also handy for interactive use.

Setting Current Shell Environment: The work Function

Like aliases, functions run in the current shell process—not in a subprocess as shell scripts do. So they can change your shell's current directory, reset shell and environment variables, and do basically anything you could do at a shell prompt. (Article 24.3 has details.)

This next function is for a group of people who are all working on a project. A directory named */work* has symbolic links (10.4) named for each worker—*/work/ ann*, */work/joe*, etc.—and each link points to the directory where that person is working. Each worker makes a function named *work* that, by default, *cds* to her directory and summarizes it. If the person gives an argument to the function— like work todo, for instance—the script edits the file named *.todo* in that directory. This setup also lets people quickly find out where others in the group are working.

Okay, I admit that I made this up as a demonstration for this article, as a way to show a lot of features in a small amount of space. Anyway, here's the function:

work.sh

if **35.13**

```
function work () {
    local status=0
    if [ $# -eq 1 -a "$1" = todo ]
```

```
then
      ${VISUAL-vi} /work/$USER/.todo
      status=$? # return status from editor
elif [ $# -ne 0 ]
then
      echo "Usage: work [todo]" 1>&2
      status=1
else
      cd /work/$USER
      echo "You're in your work directory `pwd`."
      echo "`ls | wc -w` files to edit."
      status=0
fi
return $status
}
```

'...' **28.14**
wc **16.6**

There are three points I should make about this example. First, the *local* command defines a shell variable named *status* that's local to the function—which means its value isn't available outside the function, so it's guaranteed not to conflict with variables set other places in the shell. I've also set the value to 0, but this isn't required. (In the original Korn shell, use the *typeset* command to set a local variable.) Second, when you run a function, the first argument you pass it is stored in $1, the second in $2, and so on (35.20). Shell and environment variables set outside of the function, and nonlocal variables set within the function, are passed to and from the function. Finally, the *return* command returns a status (35.12) to the calling shell. (Without *return*, the function returns the status from the last command in the function.) For a function you use interactively, like this one, you may not care about the status. But you also can use *return* in the middle of a function to end execution and return to the calling shell immediately.

Functions Calling Functions: Factorials

Okay, students, this example is "extra credit" ;-)...You can ignore this ramble unless you want some esoterica. (I'm actually not trying to waste your time. There are some useful bits of info in here about the internal workings of the shells.) Functions can call each other recursively, and local variables are passed to functions they call, but changes in a called function are not passed back to the calling function. When I say "recursion," I've gotta show the classic demonstration: a factorial function.*

---

* Factorial is the product of all integers from some nonnegative number through one. So the factorial of 6, written 6!, is $6 \times 5 \times 4 \times 3 \times 2 \times 1$ or 720. Also, zero factorial (0!) is defined as 1. In recursion, a function typically calls itself to get "the next value," then waits for that value to be returned and returns *its* answer to the function that called it. If you ask a function to calculate 6!, it will call itself and ask for 5!, then call itself and ask for 4!, and so on. This can be confusing if you haven't seen it before, but there's information about it in almost every computer science textbook on basic programming techniques. It is also worth mentioning that recursion is a pretty poor way to calculate factorials in most languages, namely, those that lack support for tail recursion.

The *fac* function calculates the factorial of the number passed in *$1*. It writes the result to standard output, for two reasons. First, doing so lets you type fac *n* at the command line (why you'd need to calculate a factorial very often, though, I'm not sure!). Second, if the shells' *return* command works like the Unix exit statuses (and I haven't checked all versions of all shells), the values are only eight bits—so it's better to return a string, which lets us handle bigger integers. I could put in more error checking, but since this is all theoretical anyway, here's the simple version of *fac*:

fac.sh

```
function fac () {
    if [ "$1" -gt 0 ]
    then echo $(($1 * `fac $(($1 - 1))`))
    else echo 1
    fi
}
```

Then you can play:

```
$ fac 0
1
$ fac 15
2004310016
$ fac 18
-898433024
```

Oops: overflow. Try *zsh* instead of *bash* or *ksh*; *zsh* built-in arithmetic seems to have more capacity:

```
zsh$ fac 18
6402373705728000
```

You can do some simple tracing by typing set -x (27.15) at a shell prompt. Then the shell will display the commands it executes. (This works best in *bash* because it puts one + character at the left edge of each line to show each level of recursion.) You also can add some tracing code that uses a local variable, *level*, to store the depth of recursion. The code *echo*es debugging messages that show the depth of recursion of each call. Note that because the "returned value" of each function is written to its standard output, these debugging messages have to be on the standard error! (To see what happens otherwise, remove the 1>&2 operator (36.16).) Here's *fac* with debugging code:

${..-..} **36.7**

```
fac () {
local level=${level-0}
echo "debug: recursion level is $((level += 1)).  Doing fac of $1" 1>&2
if [ "$1" -gt 0 ]
then echo $(($1 * `fac $(($1 - 1))`))
else echo 1
fi
echo "debug: leaving level $level." 1>&2
}
```

Let's run the code with tracing. Note that changes to the value of *level* at deeper levels doesn't affect the value at higher levels—and that *level* isn't set at all in the top-level shell:

```
$ fac 3
debug: recursion level is 1.  Doing fac of 3
debug: recursion level is 2.  Doing fac of 2
debug: recursion level is 3.  Doing fac of 1
debug: recursion level is 4.  Doing fac of 0
debug: leaving level 4.
debug: leaving level 3.
debug: leaving level 2.
6
debug: leaving level 1.
$ echo $level
$
```

Conclusion

The next two articles cover specifics about functions in particular shells, and article 29.14 shows how to simulate functions in shells that don't have them.

Here's another overall note. Each shell has its own commands for working with functions, but in general, the *typeset –f* command lists the functions you've defined, and *unset –f funcname* deletes the definition of the function named *funcname*.

—*JP and SJC*

29.12 Shell Function Specifics

Article 29.11 introduces shell functions for all Bourne-type shells. This article covers details of functions in specific shells.

Read-only functions

A *bash* and *ksh* function can be made read-only. In *ksh*, that means the function can't be changed. In *bash*, it can't be changed or removed. To make a function read-only, use the *ksh* command *typeset –r funcname* or use *readonly –f funcname* in *bash*, where *funcname* is the name of the function.

A system administrator might want to set read-only functions from a system-wide setup file (3.3) like */etc/profile*. *bash* users can't unset read-only functions, though. So once a function *foo* has been defined, how can you define your own *foo*? As article 27.9 explains, you can type command foo to use a command named *foo* from your search path. Or define an alias named *foo*; aliases are used before functions. Finally, if you'd like to redefine the function, make an alias with the same name, then make the alias invoke a function with a (usually similar) name. For instance, to override a read-only function named *foo*:

```
alias foo=_foo
function _foo() {
    ...your foo function...
}
```

Changing function environment

If a function uses an environment variable—like *VISUAL* or *EDITOR* (35.5), your standard text editor—you can set the value temporarily while the function executes. The syntax is the same for functions, but only in *bash* and *zsh*. For instance, if you usually use *vi*, but you want to use *emacs* as you run the *work* function (29.11):

```
$ VISUAL=emacs work todo
```

Resetting zsh options

There are lots of *zsh* options. You may want to set some of them temporarily during a shell function without needing to reset them to their previous values when the function returns to the calling shell. To make that happen, set the LOCAL_OPTIONS option (run *setopt local_options*) in the function body.

For instance, maybe you use *setopt nounset* to make your interactive shell complain if you try to expand an unset shell variable. During your *func* function, though, you want to use the *unset* option to allow unset variables. Define the function like this:

```
function mullog() {
    setopt unset local_options
        ...do whatever...
}
```

—*JP and SJC*

29.13 Propagating Shell Functions

One easy way to define shell functions that you'll have every time you start a new shell is by defining them in your shell setup files (3.3). Here are two other ways.

Exporting bash Functions

In *bash*, you can export functions to other *bash* subshells (24.4). (The original Korn shell, but not the public-domain version, supposedly does this too, but I haven't had much luck with it.) Just use the command *typeset –fx funcname*, where *funcname* is the name of the function.

How does this work? It stores the function in an environment variable (35.3) whose value starts with ( ). You can see this with *printenv* or *env* (35.3). For example, let's define a simple function named *dir*, export it, start a subshell, run the function, and look for it in the environment:

```
bash$ function dir() { ls -F "$@"; }
bash$ typeset -fx dir          ...export the function
bash$ bash                     ...start subshell
bash$ dir                      ...the function still works
,ptbk.last          ch14.sgm    ch36.ps.gz        fmt/
,xrefs.list         ch15.ps.gz  ch36.sgm          gmatlogs/
bash$ printenv
    ...lots of environment variables...
dir=() {  ls -F "$@"
}
```

FPATH Search Path

Both *ksh* and *zsh* will automatically search for functions in the *PATH* variable (35.6). So you can put a function in a file with the same name as the function (for instance, put the function *foo* in a file named *foo*), and make the file executable (with chmod +x foo (35.1)), and then the shell can find the function.

I don't like to use *PATH* for function-searching, though. One reason is that *PATH* is passed to *all* Unix processes—but if the process isn't a shell and it tries to execute a function file, it'll probably fail in an ugly way.* Also, making a file executable if you don't tell the kernel how to execute it seems to me a recipe for trouble. A better way to help the shell find functions is to set a function search path in the *FPATH* environment variable; it has the same syntax as *PATH*. (In *zsh*, you can also set the *fpath* array—with the same syntax as *path*.) In *FPATH*, list directories that hold function files. In *ksh*, those files don't even need execute permission! Then *ksh* and *zsh* will search the *FPATH* directories if they can't find an executable file in the *PATH*.

Would you like the shells to search *FPATH* before *PATH*, so that a function will be executed before a standard command with the same name? (I would. After all, if I define a function from a shell prompt or shell setup file like *.zshrc*, that function will be run instead of a standard executable.) Here's how to set that up. Tell the shell to *autoload* the function. Autoloading happens automatically *if* there's no match found in *PATH*—because, as I said above, the shell falls back

---

* *zsh* lets you define a function in a function file without the enclosing *funcname*( ) { and } syntax. Then the file could be directly executed in a subshell by some shell that doesn't understand functions. I'm not sure I'd ever use this because running a function this way—as an external command instead of an internal command (1.9)—means the function can't access or modify the environment of the shell that's running it, which is one of the reasons for writing a shell function in the first place! But, like everything in *zsh*, I'm sure someone had a good reason for making this work.

to *FPATH* if it doesn't find a match in *PATH*. But if you want the shell to look for a particular name in *FPATH* before it tries *PATH*, you have to autoload the function. Autoloading a function doesn't actually define the function (read the function body into the shell); it simply declares that the function exists—so the shell will remember that when you eventually want to execute the function.

This has a few twists, so let's look at each shell separately. You might want to do this yourself and follow along: When I first played with *FPATH*, I made two subdirectories of */tmp* named *a* and *b*. Each directory had three simple function files named *func1*, *func2*, and *foo*. The functions *func1* and *func2* simply *echo* a message with their name and location. *foo* invokes a shell script of the same name, but first uses set -xv (37.1) for debugging. *func1* was a single-line function and *func2* was multiline. The files in */tmp/a* weren't executable, and the ones in */tmp/b* were executable. I set the *FPATH* environment variable (set the shell variable and *exported* it) to /tmp/a:/tmp/b—so the shells should try the nonexecutable function files before falling back to the executables. After setting that up, I started a *ksh* subshell and played around. Then I *exited* the *ksh* and started a *zsh*.

Korn shell

Here's what happened in *pdksh*. The standard *ksh* is similar but not as verbose:

```
$ echo $FPATH
/tmp/a:/tmp/b
$ type func1
func1 is a undefined (autoload from /tmp/a/func1) function
$ func1
This is func1 from /tmp/a, a single-line unexecutable function
$ type func1
func1 is a function

$ typeset -f func2
$ type func2
func2 is a undefined (autoload from /tmp/a/func2) function
$ func2
This is func2 from /tmp/a, a multi-line unexecutable function
$ typeset -f func2
func2() {
    echo "This is func2 from /tmp/a, a multi-line unexecutable function"
}

$ type foo
foo is /home/jpeek/.bin/foo
$ autoload foo
$ type foo
foo is a undefined (autoload from /tmp/a/foo) function
$ cat /tmp/a/foo
foo() { sh -xv $HOME/.bin/foo "$@"; }
$ foo
#!/bin/sh
```

```
echo "Welcome to the exciting $0 program..."
+ echo Welcome to the exciting /home/jpeek/.bin/foo program...
Welcome to the exciting /home/jpeek/.bin/foo program...
$ type foo
foo is a function
```

Here's what happened with *func1*, *func2*, and *foo*:

- First, without autoloading, I use *type* (2.6) to see if the shell has found *func1* anywhere. There's no *func1* along the *PATH*, so the shell searches *FPATH*— and finds it. So *func1* is automatically marked for autoloading; note that I didn't have to autoload it myself because there's no *func1* in a *PATH* directory. I run *func1*, then use *type* again; now the shell confirms that it's read the function definition and *func* has been loaded into the shell.

- Next I played with *func2*. *typeset –f* (29.11) shows that the shell doesn't have a definition for the function yet, but *type* shows that the function declaration has been autoloaded. (This isn't just academic. If you edit a function definition file, it's good to know whether the shell has already loaded a copy of a previous definition.) I run the function, then use *typeset* to display the function, which has been loaded (of course!) by now.

- Because there's a program named *foo* in my *PATH*, *type* shows that. But I want the shell to use my front-end *foo* function, so I run *autoload*—and then *type* confirms that the shell looked down *FPATH* and found the function in */tmp/a*. The function definition hasn't been loaded yet, so I use *cat* (12.2) to display the function file. I run the *foo* function; because it set the shell's verbose and echo flags, you can see the contents of the *foo* shell script and the commands that are executed. Finally, *type* shows that the shell will now run the function when I execute *foo*.

If you'd like to be sure that all the functions in your *FPATH* are autoloaded— especially if you add new ones pretty often—here's a way to do it. Put code like this in your *ENV* setup file (3.3):

```
                  # Autoload all functions in FPATH directories.
IFS 36.23         # Temporarily add a colon (:) to IFS to parse FPATH:
                  old_ifs="$IFS"; IFS=":$IFS"
for 28.9          for d in $FPATH
                  do autoload `ls $d`
                  done
                  IFS="$oldifs"; unset old_ifs
```

If a directory in *FPATH* is empty, *autoload* gets no arguments and, in that case, shows the function definitions it has already autoloaded. I only put a directory in my *FPATH* if it has functions to load. If you might have an empty directory in yours, you can avoid seeing the *autoload* output by editing that code to store the output of *ls* in a shell variable and running *autoload* only if the variable isn't empty.

---

zsh

The *zsh* system is mostly like *ksh*. The difference is that *zsh* doesn't automatically search *FPATH*. You have to manually autoload any function that you want *zsh* to search for in *FPATH*.

```
zsh$ echo $FPATH
/tmp/a:/tmp/b
zsh$ type func1
func1 not found
zsh$ func1
zsh: command not found: func1
zsh$ autoload func1
zsh$ type func1
func1 is a shell function
zsh$ func1
This is func1 from /tmp/a, a single-line unexecutable function
zsh$ type func1
func1 is a shell function

zsh$ autoload func2
zsh$ typeset -f func2
undefined func2 () { }
zsh$ func2
This is func2 from /tmp/a, a multi-line unexecutable function
zsh$ typeset -f func2
func2 () {
    echo "This is func2 from /tmp/a, a multi-line unexecutable function"
}

zsh$ type foo
foo is /home/jpeek/.bin/foo
zsh$ autoload foo
zsh$ foo
#!/bin/sh
echo "Welcome to the exciting $0 program..."
+ echo Welcome to the exciting /home/jpeek/.bin/foo program...
Welcome to the exciting /home/jpeek/.bin/foo program...
zsh$ type foo
foo is a shell function
```

I won't repeat all of the explanation from the *ksh* section. Instead, let's just look at the differences:

- The first examples show that *zsh* won't look down *FPATH* for *func1*. Once you autoload the function, *type* doesn't give you a clue whether the function has been defined or just declared.

- In *zsh*, you can see whether a function has been defined by using *typeset –f* (instead of *type*). After autoloading it, *func2* has been declared but not defined. As the example shows, running the function once loads the definition.

If you'd like to be sure that all the functions in your *FPATH* are autoloaded—especially if you add new ones pretty often—here's how to do it in *zsh*. Put code like this in a per-shell setup file (3.3)—typically *.zshrc*:

```
# Autoload all functions in fpath directories:
for d in $fpath
do autoload `ls $d`
done
```

The code is simpler than in *ksh* because we can step through the *fpath* array without parsing it at colon (:) characters. As in *ksh*, though, you'll want to tweak the code if a directory in *fpath* might be empty: store the output of *ls* in an array and run *autoload* only if the array has members.

—*JP*

29.14 Simulated Bourne Shell Functions and Aliases

Until System V Release 2 (circa 1984), the Bourne shell had no way for users to set up their own built-in commands. If you have a Bourne shell with no functions (29.11) or aliases (29.2) and haven't yet turned the host machine into a wet bar, CD/DVD storage case, or some other pragmatic but fun use for a 30-year-old computer, you can do a lot of the same things with shell variables and the *eval* (27.8) command.

Let's look at an example. First, here's a shell function named *cps* (copy safely). If the destination file exists and isn't empty, the function prints an error message instead of copying:

```
cps()
{
    if test ! -s "$2"
    then cp "$1" "$2"
    else echo "cps: cannot copy $1: $2 exists"
    fi
}
```

test **35.26**

If you use the same *cps* twice, the first time you'll make *bfile*. The second time you try, you see the error:

```
$ cps afile bfile
    ...
$ cps afile bfile
cps: cannot copy afile: bfile exists
```

Here's the same *cps*—stored in a shell variable instead of a function:

```
cps='
if test ! -s "$2"
then cp "$1" "$2"
else echo "cps: cannot copy $1: $2 exists"
fi
'
```

Because this fake function uses shell parameters, you have to add an extra step: setting the parameters. Simpler functions are easier to use:

set 35.25

```
$ set afile bfile
$ eval "$cps"
    ...
$ eval "$cps"
cps: cannot copy afile: bfile exists
```

—*JP*

30

The Use of History

30.1 The Lessons of History

It has been said that "the only thing we learn from history is that people don't learn from history."

Fortunately, the original maxim that "history repeats itself" is more appropriate to Unix.

Most shells include a powerful history mechanism that lets you recall and repeat past commands, potentially editing them before execution. This can be a godsend, especially when typing a long or complex command.

All that is needed to set C shell history in motion is a command like this in your *.cshrc* (or *.tcshrc*) file, where *n* is the number of past commands that you want to save:

```
set history=n
```

In *ksh* and *bash*, the variable is *HISTSIZE*, and it's already set for you; the default values are 128 and 500, respectively.

The *history* command (30.7) lists the saved commands, each with an identifying number. (It's also possible to configure the shells to print the history number of each command as part of your prompt (4.3).)

In *tcsh, csh,* and *bash*, you can repeat a past command by typing its number (or its name) preceded by an exclamation point (!). You can also select only parts of the command to be repeated and use various editing operators to modify it. Articles 30.8 and 28.5 give quick tutorial summaries of some of the wonderful things you can do. Most of the rest of the chapter gives a miscellany of tips for using and abusing the shells' history mechanism.

Most shells—except the original Bourne and C shells—also have interactive command-line editing (30.14). Interactive editing might seem to be better than typing !vi or lpr !$. If you learn both systems, though, you'll find plenty of cases where the ! system is faster and more useful than interactive editing.

—TOR

30.2 History in a Nutshell

The C shell and *bash* can save copies of the previous command lines you type. Later, you can ask for a copy of some or all of a previous command line. That can save time and retyping.

This feature is called *history substitution*, and it's done when you type a string that starts with an exclamation point (!*command*). You can think of it like variable substitution ($*varname*) (35.9) or command substitution ('*command*') (28.14): the shell replaces what you type (like !$) with something else (in this case, part or all of a previous command line).

Article 30.1 is an introduction to shell history. These articles show lots of ways to use history substitution:

- We start with favorite uses from several contributors—articles 30.3, 30.4, 30.5, and 30.6.

- Article 30.8 starts with a quick introduction, then covers the full range of history substitutions with a series of examples that show the different kinds of things you can do with history.

  (Back in article 28.5 are examples of *csh/tcsh* and *bash* operators such as :r. Many of these can be used to edit history substitutions.)

- See an easy way to repeat a set of *csh/tcsh* or *bash* commands in article 30.9.

- Each shell saves its own history. To pass a shell's history to another shell, see articles 30.12 and 30.13.

- You don't have to use an exclamation point (!) for history. Article 30.15 shows how to use some other character.

- The Korn shell does history in a different way. Article 30.14 introduces part of that: command-line editing in *ksh* and *bash*.

One last note: putting the history number in your prompt (4.3) makes it easy to reuse commands that haven't scrolled off your screen.

—JP

30.3 My Favorite Is !$

I use !$ so much that it's almost a single character to me. It means "take the last thing on the previous command line." Since most Unix commands have the filename last, you often need to type filenames only once, and then you can use !$ in subsequent lines. Here are some examples of where it comes in handy:

- I get a lot of *tar* archives (39.2). To extract and edit a file from them, I first make a backup for easy comparison after editing:

```
% tar xzf prog.1.05.tar.gz foo.c
% cp -i !$ !$.orig
cp -i foo.c foo.c.orig
```

The same trick is also good when you've edited a file with *vi* and then want to check its spelling:

```
% vi fred.letter.txt
% ispell !$
ispell fred.letter.txt
```

- You often want to move a file to another directory and then *cd* to that directory. The !$ sequence can also be used to refer to a directory:

```
% mv grmacs.tar /usr/lib/tmac
% cd !$
cd /usr/lib/tmac
```

—AN

30.4 My Favorite Is !:n*

I use !$ (30.3) a lot, but my favorite history substitution is !:*n**, where *n* is a number from 0 to 9. It means "take arguments *n* through the last argument on the previous command line." Since I tend to use more than one argument with Unix commands, this lets me type the arguments (usually filenames) only once. For example, to use RCS (39.5) and make an edit to article files named 35.5 and 29.2 for this book, I did:

```
% co -l 1171.sgm 6830.sgm 2340.sgm
RCS/1171.sgm,v  ->  1171.sgm
   ...
RCS/2340.sgm,v  ->  2340.sgm
revision 1.8 (locked)
done
% vi !:2*
vi 1171.sgm 6830.sgm 2340.sgm
3 files to edit
   ...
% ci -m"Changed TERM xref." !*
ci -m"Changed TERM xref." 1171.sgm 6830.sgm 2340.sgm
   ...
```

In the first command line (*co*), I typed the filenames as arguments 2, 3, and 4. In the second command line (*vi*), I used !:2*; which grabbed arguments 2 through the last (in this case, argument 4) from the first command line. The result was a second command line that had those three filenames as its arguments 1, 2, and 3. So, in the third command line (*ci*), I used !* to pick arguments 1 through the last from the previous (second) command line. (!* is shorthand for !:1*.)

You can also grab arguments from previous command lines. For example, !em:2* grabs the second through last arguments on the previous *emacs* command line (command line starting with "em"). There are lots more of these in article 30.8.

If these examples look complicated, they won't be for long. Just learn to count to the first argument you want to grab. It took me years to start using these substitutions—but they've saved me so much typing that I'm sorry I didn't get started earlier!

—*JP*

30.5 My Favorite Is ^^

Well, maybe it's not my favorite, but it's probably the history substitution I use most often. It's especially handy if you have fumble-fingers on a strange keyboard:

```
% cat myflie
cat: myflie: No such file or directory
% ^li^il
cat myfile
```

Obviously, this doesn't save much typing for a short command, but it can sure be handy with a long one. I also use ^^ with :p (30.11) to recall an earlier command so I can change it. For example:

```
% !m:p
more gobbledygook.c
% ^k^k2
more gobbledygook2.c
```

The point is sometimes not to save typing, but to save the effort of remembering, such as, I want to print the file I looked at earlier, but don't remember the exact name.

[My keyboard can repeat characters when I'm not expecting it. I use a single ^ to delete extra characters. For example:

```
% lpr sources/aproggg.c
lpr: sources/aproggg.c: no such file or directory
% ^gg
lpr sources/aprog.c
```

You could type ^gg^, but the second caret isn't required. With a single caret, you don't type a replacement string—just the string to delete. —*JP*]

—*TOR*

30.6 Using !$ for Safety with Wildcards

We all know about using *ls* before a wildcarded *rm* to make sure that we're only deleting what we want. But that doesn't really solve the problem: you can type ls a* and then mistakenly type rm s* with bad consequences—it's just a minor slip of your finger. But what will always work is:

```
% ls a*
a1 a2 a3
% rm !$
```

(ls -d a* (8.5) will make less output if any subdirectory names match the wild-card.)

Using the history mechanism to grab the previous command's arguments is a good way to prevent mistakes.

—*ML*

30.7 History by Number

Most of the history examples we've shown use the first few letters in a com-mand's name: !em to repeat the previous Emacs command, for example. But you also can recall previous commands by their numbered position in the history list. That's useful when you have several command lines that start with the same command. It's also more useful than interactive command-line editing (30.14) when you'd like to see a lot of previous commands at once and then choose one of them by number.

To list previous commands, use the *history* command. For instance, in *bash* and the C shells, *history 20* shows your last 20 commands. In *zsh* and the Korn shell, use a hyphen before the number: *history –20* (also see the discussion of *fc*, later in this article). Here's an example:

```
$ history 8
   15  show last +upt/authors
   16  vi ../todo
   17  co -l 0444.sgm
   18  vi 0444.sgm
   19  ci -u 0444.sgm
   20  rcsdiff -u3.4 0444.sgm > /tmp/0444-diff.txt
   21  scp /tmp/0444-diff.txt webhost:adir/11.03-diff.txt
   22  getmail;ndown
```

```
$ rm !20:$
rm /tmp/0444-diff.txt
$ !16
vi ../todo
```

The number at the start of each line is the history number. So, to remove the temporary file I created in command 20 (the name of which I'd already forgotten!), I can use !20:$ (30.8) to pass that filename as an argument to *rm*. And to repeat command 16 (*vi ../todo*), I can type !16.

This sort of thing is often faster than using arrow keys and editor commands to recall and edit previous commands. It lets me see several commands all at once, which makes it easier to spot the one(s) I want and to remember what I was doing as I worked. I use it so often that I've got a set of aliases that list bigger and bigger chunks of previous commands and an alias that searches history, giving me a chunk of matching command lines. Here they are in C shell syntax:

```
            alias h     history 5       # show last five lines
            alias hi    history 10      # show last ten lines
            alias his   history 20      # show last 20 lines
less 12.3   alias hist  'history 40 | less'     # show last 40; pipe to 'less'
            alias histo 'history 70 | less'     # show last 70; pipe to 'less'
\!* 29.3    alias H     'history -r | fgrep "\!*"'  # find something in history
```

The *history –r* option shows the list in reverse order: most recent first. If you don't give a count of lines to list, you'll see all of them.

 Be careful! In *bash*, *history –r* reads the current history file and uses it as the history from that point onward, trashing any current history for that shell if it has not yet been written to the history file (defined in the environment variable *HISTFILE*).

To avoid typing the *history* command, you can include the history number in your prompt (4.3). Then you can repeat a recent command by glancing up your screen to find the command number from its prompt.

There's another way to see a list of your previous commands in *bash*, *ksh*, and *zsh*: the command *fc –l* (lowercase L, for "list"). (In *ksh*, the command *history* is actually just an alias that executes *fc –l*.) By itself, *fc –l* lists the previous 16 commands:

```
$ fc -l
   ...
19    ls -F
20    less expn.c
21    vi expn.c
22    make
23    expn info@oreilly.com
24    fc -l
```

For an even shorter list, give *fc* the first number or name you want to list. For instance, fc -l vi or fc -l 21 would give the last four lines above. You can also use a second argument that ends the range before the current line. If you type fc -l vi expn or fc -l 21 23, you'll see commands 21 through 23.

tcsh and *zsh* automatically keep timestamps with their history. The *tcsh* command *history* shows the time of day by default. In *zsh*, you can see this info with the options –*d*, which shows the times, –*f*, which shows both dates and times, and –*D*, which shows elapsed times. For example, the *scp* command started running at 12:23 (PM) and took 1 minute 29 seconds to run:

```
% fc -l -f -4
 1003  10/23/2000 12:23  nup
 1004  10/23/2000 12:23  scp ../upt3_changes.html webhost:adir/.
 1005  10/23/2000 12:25  less /etc/hosts
 1006  10/23/2000 12:25  getmail;ndown
% fc -l -D -5
 1003  0:29  nup
 1004  1:29  scp ../upt3_changes.html webhost:adir/.
 1005  0:05  less /etc/hosts
 1006  0:21  getmail;ndown
 1007  0:00  fc -l -f -4
```

zsh also has several related options for *fc* that allow for the history to be written out to a file, read in from a file, et cetera. The other shells allow for even more extended functionality. In *bash*, for example, *fc –e* with appropriate options will start an editor (defined by the *FCEDIT* environment variable) and load up a new file containing the recent history items. Think of it is jump starting a script from a sequence of (hopefully) successfully executed commands. See the other shells' manual pages for more details.

—JP and SJC

30.8 History Substitutions

Although most of the examples here use *echo* to demonstrate clearly just what is going on, you'll normally use history with other Unix commands.

The exclamation point (!) is the default (30.15) history substitution character. This allows you to recall previously entered commands and re-execute them without retyping. To use the ! in a command line, you have several choices. Some of the following examples are more of a headache than they may be worth, but they are also used to select arguments from the command line in aliases (29.3):

- !! repeats the last command.
- !: repeats the last command. This form is used if you want to add a modifier (28.5) like the following:

```
% echo xy
xy
% !:s/xy/yx
echo yx
yx
```

The second ! was left out.

- !so repeats the last command that starts with so.

- !?fn? repeats the last command that has fn anywhere in it. The string could be found in an argument or in the command name. This is opposed to !fn, in which !fn must be in a command name. (The last ? need not be there. Thus !?fn means the same thing.)

- !34 executes command number 34. You can find the appropriate history number when you list your history using the *history* command, or by putting the history number in your prompt (4.3).

- !! & adds an ampersand (&) to the end of the last command, which executes it and places it into the background. You can add anything to the end of a previous command. For example:

```
% cat -v foo
    ...
% !! | more
cat -v foo | more
    ...
```

In this case the shell will repeat the command to be executed and run it, adding the pipe through the *more* pager. Another common usage is:

```
% cat -v foo
    ...
% !! > out
cat -v foo > out
```

which returns the command but redirects the output into a file.

- !:0 selects only the command name, rather than the entire command line.

```
% /usr/bin/grep Ah fn1
    ...
% !:0 Bh fn2
/usr/bin/grep Bh fn2
```

Note that as an operator (28.5), :0 can be appended to these history substitutions as well. For example, !!:0 will give the last command name, and a colon followed by any number will give the corresponding argument. For example, !:3 gives the third argument:

```
% cat fn fn1 fn2
    ...
% more !:3
more fn2
    ...
```

- !:2-4 gives the second through the fourth argument; use any numbers you choose:

```
% echo 1 2 3 4 5
1 2 3 4 5
% echo !:2-4
echo 2 3 4
2 3 4
```

- !:-3 gives zero through the third argument; use any number you wish:

```
% echo 1 2 3 4
1 2 3 4
% echo !:-3
echo echo 1 2 3
echo 1 2 3
```

- !^ gives the first argument of the previous command. This is the same as !:1. Remember that just as the ^ (caret) is the beginning-of-line anchor in regular expressions (32.5), !^ gives the beginning history argument.

```
% cat fn fn1 fn2
   ...
% more !^
more fn
   ...
```

- !$ gives the last argument of the last command. In the same way that $ (dollar sign) is the end-of-line anchor in regular expressions, !$ gives the ending history argument. Thus:

```
% cat fn
   ...
% more !$
more fn
   ...
```

The new command (more) is given the last argument of the previous command. This is also handy for pulling the last argument from earlier commands, which is typically a filename. To get the last argument from the previous *vi* command, for example, you'd use !vi:$. So you could type lpr !vi:$ to print the last file you edited with *vi*.

- !* is shorthand for the first through the last argument. This is used a lot in aliases:

```
% echo 1 2 3 4 5
1 2 3 4 5
% echo !*
echo 1 2 3 4 5
1 2 3 4 5
```

In an alias:

```
alias vcat 'cat -v \!* | more'
```

This alias will pipe the output of *cat –v* (12.4) command through *more*. The backslash (\) has to be there to hide the history character, !, until the alias is used—see article 29.3 for more information.

- !:2* gives the second through the last arguments; use any number you wish:

```
% echo 1 2 3 4 5
1 2 3 4 5
% echo !:2*
echo 2 3 4 5
2 3 4 5
```

- !:2- is like 2* but the last argument is dropped:

```
% echo 1 2 3 4 5
1 2 3 4 5
% echo !:2-
echo 2 3 4
2 3 4
```

- !?fn?% gives the first word found that has fn in it:

```
% sort fn1 fn2 fn3
    . . .
% echo !?fn?%
echo fn1
fn1
```

That found the fn in fn1. You can get wilder with:

```
% echo 1 2 3 4 5
1 2 3 4 5
% echo !?ec?^
echo 1
1
```

That selected the command that had ec in it, and the caret (^) said to give the first argument of that command. You can also do something like this:

```
% echo fn fn1 fn2
fn fn1 fn2
% echo !?fn1?^ !$
echo fn fn2
fn fn2
```

That cryptic command told the shell to look for a command that had fn1 in it (!?fn1?), and gave the first argument of that command (^). Then it gave the last argument (!$).

- ^xy^yx is the shorthand substitution (30.3, 30.5) command. In the case of:

```
% echo xxyyzzxx
xxyyzzxx
% ^xx^ab
echo abyyzzxx
abyyzzxx
```

it replaced the first set of characters xx with ab. This makes editing the previous command much easier.

- !!:s/xx/ab/ is doing the same thing as the previous example, but it is using the substitute command instead of the ^. This works for any previous command, as in:

```
% more afile bfile
    ...
% echo xy
xy
% !m:s/b/c/
more afile cfile
```

You do not have to use the slashes (/); any character can act as a delimiter.

```
% !!:s:xy:yx
```

There we used colons (:), good when the characters you're trying to edit contain a slash. If you want to add more to the replacement, use & to "replay it" and then add on whatever you like:

```
% echo xy
xy
% !!:s/xy/&yx
echo xyyx
xyyx
```

The & in the replacement part said to give what the search part found, which was the xy characters.

The search part, or left side, cannot include metacharacters (32.3). You must type the actual string you are looking for.

Also, the example above replaces only the first occurrence of xy. To replace them all, use g:

```
% echo xy xy xy xy
xy xy xy xy
% !!:s/xy/yx/
echo yx xy xy xy
yx xy xy xy
% !!:gs/xy/yx/
echo yx yx yx yx
yx yx yx yx
```

The g command in this case meant "do all the xys." And oddly enough, the g has to come before the s command. This may seem odd to those of you familiar with vi, so be careful.

Or you could have done this:

```
% echo xy xy xy xy
xy xy xy xy
% !!:s/xy/yx/
echo yx xy xy xy
yx xy xy xy
% !!:g&
echo yx yx yx yx
yx yx yx yx
```

In this example, we told the shell to globally (:g) replace every matched string from the last command with the last substitution (&). Without the g command, the shells would have replaced just one more xy with yx.

—DR

30.9 Repeating a Cycle of Commands

The !! history substitution gives a copy of the previous command. Most people use it to re-execute the previous command line. Sometimes I want to repeat a cycle of two commands, one after the other. To do that, I just type !-2 (second-previous command) over and over:

```
% vi plot
  ...
% vtroff -w plot
  ...
% !-2
vi plot
  ...
% !-2
vtroff -w plot
  ...
```

You can cycle through three commands with !-3, four commands with !-4, and so on. The best part is that if you can count, you never have to remember what to do next. :-)

—JP

30.10 Running a Series of Commands on a File

[There are times when history is not the best way to repeat commands. Here, Jerry gives an example where a few well-chosen aliases can make a sequence of commands, all run on the same file, even easier to execute. —TOR]

While I was writing the articles for this book, I needed to look through a set of files, one by one, and run certain commands on some of those files. I couldn't know which files would need which commands, or in what order. So I typed a few temporary aliases on the C shell command line. (I could have used shell functions (29.11) on sh-like shells.) Most of these aliases run RCS (39.5) commands, but they could run any Unix command (compilers, debuggers, printers, and so on).

```
% alias h 'set f="\!*";co -p -q "$f" | grep NOTE'
% alias o 'co -l "$f"'
% alias v 'vi "$f"'
% alias i 'ci -m"Fixed NOTE." "$f"'
```

The *h* alias stores the filename in a shell variable (35.9). Then it runs a command on that file. What's nice is that, after I use *h* once, I don't need to type the filename again. Other aliases get the filename from $f:

```
% h ch01_summary
NOTE: Shorten this paragraph:
% o
RCS/ch01_summary,v -> ch01_summary
revision 1.3 (locked)
done
% v
"ch01_summary" 23 lines, 1243 characters
    ...
```

Typing a new *h* command stores a new filename.

If you always want to do the same commands on a file, you can store all the commands in one alias:

```
% alias d 'set f="\!*"; co -l "$f" && vi "$f" && ci "$f"'
% d ch01_summary
```

The && (two ampersands) (35.14) means that the following command won't run unless the previous command returns a zero ("success") status. If you don't want that, use ; (semicolon) (28.16) instead of &&.

—JP

30.11 Check Your History First with :p

Here's how to be more sure of your history before you use it. First, remember that the history substitutions !/ and !fra are replaced with the most recent command lines that started with / and fra, respectively.

If your memory is like mine (not very good), you might not be sure that !/ will bring back the command you want. You can test it by adding :p to the end. The shell will print the substitution but won't execute the command line. If you like what you got, type !! to execute it. For example:

```
# !/:p
/usr/sbin/sendmail -qv
# !!
/usr/sbin/sendmail -qv
Running id12345...
```

At the first prompt, the :p meant the command line was only printed. At the second prompt, I didn't use :p and the *sendmail* command was executed. The :p works with all history operators—for instance, !?sendmail?:p.

—JP

30.12 Picking Up Where You Left Off

If you want your command history to be remembered even when you log out, set the C shell's *savehist* shell variable (35.9) to the number of lines of history you want saved. Other shells save history automatically; you don't need to set a variable. (If you want to change the number of lines saved by *bash*, set its *HISTFILE-SIZE* environment variable. In *zsh*, the variable is *SAVEHIST*. In *ksh*, the *HISTSIZE* variable sets the number of commands available to be recalled in your current shell as well the number saved for other shells.)

When you log out, the specified number of lines from the *csh* history list will be saved in a file called *.history* in your home directory. *zsh*, *bash* and *ksh* use the filename given in the *HISTFILE* environment variable. By default, *bash* calls the file *.bash_history*, and the original *ksh* uses *.sh_history*—but note that the new *pdksh* and *zsh* don't save history unless you set *HISTFILE* to a filename. For *zsh*, I chose *$HOME/.zsh_history*, but you can use anything you want.

On modern windowing systems, this isn't as trivial as it sounds. On an old-style terminal, people usually started only one main shell, so they could set the history-saving variable in their *.login* or *.profile* file and have it apply to their login shell.

However, under window systems like X or networked filesystems that share your home directory between several hosts, or on networked servers to which you might login via *ssh*, you may have multiple shells saving into the same history file. Linux systems with multiple virtual consoles (23.12) logged on as the same user will have the same problem. The shells might be overwriting instead of appending, or appending instead of overwriting, or jumbling commands together when you want them separated. The sections below give some possible fixes.

bash, ksh, zsh

Here's the basic way to give a separate history file to each *bash*, *zsh*, or *ksh* shell: customize your setup file (3.3) to set a different *HISTFILE* on each host or each window. Use names like *$HOME/.sh_history.windown* or *~/.bash_history.hostname* to match each file to its window or host. If your setup is always the same each time you log in, that should give each window and/or host the same history it had on the last invocation. (There are related tips in article 3.18 and a series starting at article 3.10.)

If you open random windows, though, you'll have a harder time automatically matching a history file to a shell the next time you log in. Cook up your own scheme.

The simplest fix is to use $$ (27.17)—which will probably expand differently in almost every shell you ever start—as a unique part of the filename. Here are two possibilities:

```
HISTFILE=/tmp/sh_hist.$$
HISTFILE=$HOME/.sh_hist.$$
```

The first example uses the system's temporary-file directory. If your system's /tmp is cleaned out often, you may be able to leave your history files there and let the system remove them; ask the administrator. Note that the history file may be world-readable (50.2) if your umask isn't set to protect your files. If that matters to you, you could make the temporary files in your home directory (or some protected directory), as in the second example shown earlier. Alternately, at the end of each session, you might want to run a command that appends your shell's history file to a global history file that you then read in at startup of a new session (see below).

Two more bits of trivia:

- The original Korn shell maintains the history file constantly, adding a new line to it as soon as you run a command. This means you share history between all your current shells with the same *HISTFILE* name, which can be a benefit or a problem.

- In most other shells, each shell process keeps its own history list in memory. History isn't written to the history file (named by the *HISTFILE* variable in each shell) until the shell exits.

  In *bash*, you can force a write with the command *history –w*. In the same way, if you have an existing history file (or, actually, any file full of command lines), you can read it into your current *bash* with *history –r*. Article 30.13 has another example. Each shell has its own way to do this, so check your manual page carefully and experiment to get it right.

C Shells

In *tcsh*, you can set a history file name in the *histfile* variable; the default filename is *.history* in your home directory. To avoid conflicts between multiple saved *tcsh* histories, use a system like the one described earlier for Bourne shells.

The original C shell has only one possible filename for its automatic history file: *.history*. If you set the C shell variable *savehist* in each of your windows (e.g., by setting it in your *.cshrc* or *.tcshrc*), they will all try to write *.history* at once, leading to trouble. And even if that weren't true, you get the history from every window or host, which might not be what you want.

Of course, you could set *savehist* manually in a single window when you thought you were doing work you might want to pick up later. But there is another way: use the C shell's command *history –h* (which prints the history list without leading numbers, so it can be read back in later) and redirect the output to a file. Then use *source –h* to read it back into your history list when you log in.

Do you want to automate this? First, you'll need to choose a system of filenames, like *~/.history.window* or *~/.history.hostname,* to match each file to its window or host. If each of your C shells is a login shell (3.4),* you can run *history –h* from your *.logout* file and *source –h* from your *.login* file. For nonlogin shells, automation is tougher—try this:

- Set the *ignoreeof* variable to force you to leave the shell with an *exit* (24.4) command.

- Set an alias for *exit* (29.8) that runs *history –h* before exiting.

- Run *source –h* from your *.cshrc* or *.tcshrc* file. Use a $?prompt test to be sure this runs only in interactive shells.

If you choose to run *history –h* and *source –h* by hand occasionally, they will allow you the kind of control you need to write a script (30.13) that saves and restores only what you want.

—JP, TOR, and SJC

30.13 Pass History to Another Shell

Most shells can save a history of the commands you type (30.12). You can add your own commands to some shells' history lists without retyping them. Why would you do that?

- You might have a set of commands that you want to be able to recall and reuse every time you log in. This can be more convenient than aliases because you don't have to think of names for the aliases. It's handier than a shell script if you need to do a series of commands that aren't always in the same order.

- You might have several shells running (say, in several windows) and want to pass the history from one shell to another shell (30.12).

Unfortunately, this isn't easy to do in all shells. For instance, the new *pdksh* saves its history in a file with NUL-separated lines. And the *tcsh* history file has a timestamp-comment before each saved line, like this:

```
#+0972337571
less 1928.sgm
#+0972337575
vi 1928.sgm
#+0972337702
ls -lt | head
```

---

* *xterm –ls* (5.10) runs a login shell in your *xterm* window.

Let's look at an example for two of the shells that make history editing easy. Use the *csh* command *history –h*, or the *bash* command *history –w*, to save the history from a shell to a file. Edit the file to take out commands you don't want:

```
% mail -s "My report" bigboss     $ mail -s "My report" bigboss
   ...                                     ...
% history -h > history.std        $ history -w history.std
% vi history.std                  $ vi history.std
   ...Clean up history...              ...Clean up history...
```

Read that file into another shell's history list with the *csh* command *source –h* or the *bash* command *history –r*:

```
% source -h history.std           $ history -r history.std
% !ma                             $ !ma
mail -s "My report" bigboss       mail -s "My report" bigboss
```

Of course, you can also use *bash* interactive command-line editing (30.14) on the saved commands.

—*JP*

30.14 Shell Command-Line Editing

When Unix started, a lot of people used real teletypes—with a roll or box of paper instead of a glass screen. So there was no way to recall and edit previous commands. (You could see them on the paper, of course, but to reuse them you had to retype them.) The C shell added history substitution operators (30.2) that were great on teletypes—and are still surprisingly useful on "glass teletypes" these days. All shells except the oldest Bourne shells still have history substitution, although it's limited in the Korn shells.

Modern shells also have interactive command-line editing. That's the ability to recall previous command lines and edit them using familiar *vi* or *emacs* commands. Arrow keys—along with Backspace and DELETE keys—generally work, too. So you don't need to know *emacs* or *vi* to edit command lines. But—especially if you're comfortable with Emacs-style commands (meta-*this that*, control-*foo bar*)—you'll find that most shells let you do much more than simply editing command lines. Shells can automatically correct spelling, complete partially-typed filenames (28.6), and much more.

The basic idea of command-line editing is that the previous commands are treated like lines in a plain-text file, with the most recently typed commands at the "end" of the file. By using the editor's "up line" commands (like *k* in *vi* or C-p in Emacs), you can bring copies of earlier commands under your cursor, where you can edit them or simply re-execute them without changes. (It's important to understand that you're not editing the original commands; you're editing *copies* of them. You can recall a previous command as many times as you want to; its original version won't be changed as you edit the copy.) When you've got a command you want to run, you simply press ENTER; your cursor doesn't have to be at the end of the line. You can use CTRL-c (C-c in Emacs jargon) to cancel a command without running it and get a clean shell prompt.

It would be easy for us to fill a chapter with info on command-line editing. (In this book's fourth edition, maybe we should!) Because every shell has its own way to do this, though, we've decided to stick to the basics—with a few of the bells and whistles tossed in as examples. To really dig into this, check your shell's manpage or its Nutshell Handbook.

Another way to do history editing is with your own editor: use the *fc* command.

vi Editing Mode

All shells with command-line editing have support for basic *vi* commands, but it's usually not complete and historically not well documented. For instance, I've used some shells where the . (dot) command wouldn't repeat the previous edit— and other shells where it would—but neither shell's manual page mentioned this useful fact. Macros are limited, and you don't define them with the usual *map* (18.2) command; instead, the shell's built-in key binding command controls which built-in shell editing function is executed when a key is pressed. (The Korn shell doesn't allow any special *vi* bindings, though at least it has complete documentation.) Still, with all those caveats, you'll probably find that *vi* editing is pretty comfortable if you already know *vi*. (If you don't know *vi*, though, I'd recommend Emacs editing. See the next section.)

At a bare shell prompt, you're effectively in *vi* text-input mode: the characters you type appear on the command line. If you want to edit, press ESC to go to command mode. Then you can use typical commands like dw to delete a word and ct. to change all characters to the next dot on the line. Commands like *a*, *i*, and *c* take you to text-input mode. You can execute a command line from either command mode or text-input mode: just press ENTER anywhere on the line.

One difference between the shell's *vi* mode and real *vi* is that the direction of searches is opposite. In real *vi*, the motion command *k* and the search command *?* (question mark) both move to previous commands. In shells, *k* still moves to a previous command, but / (slash) searches for previous commands. By the way, after you specify a search with \, press ENTER to do the search. These differences from real *vi* can be confusing at first, but with practice they soon become natural.

To choose *vi* mode, type set -o vi in Bourne-type shells and bindkey -v in *tcsh*. In *bash*, you may also use *keymap editor*, with a variety of different editor settings (30.14), to set up the editing mode. To make this the default, store the command in your shell's setup file (3.3) (in *bash*, you can also edit your Readline *inputrc* file). You can switch back and forth between the two modes as you work; this is useful because the Emacs mode lets you do things you can't do in *vi*.

Emacs Editing Mode

If you know the Emacs (19.1) editor, you'll feel right at home in the shells. Although the support isn't complete—for instance, you can't write eLisp code (and you can't run psychoanalyze-pinhead (19.13) :-))—the emacs-mode commands act like a natural extension to traditional, simple shell editing commands. So, even if you don't know *emacs*, you'll probably be comfortable with emacs mode. Even many browsers nowadays use the traditional emacs mode commands for moving about in the Location field, so you may already know some of these even if you're not aware that you do.

To move to the beginning of a line, use C-a (that's CTRL-a in Emacs-speak); C-e moves to the end of a line. C-f moves forward a character, and C-b moves backward one character (without deleting). C-n moves forward to the next command, and C-p moves backward to the previous line. Your keyboard's arrow keys probably also work. Your shell has at least one search command; try C-r to start a search and press ENTER to run the search.

Your keyboard's usual delete key (Backspace or DEL) deletes one character backward, and C-d deletes one character forward. C-k deletes ("kills") to the end of the line, and C-w deletes ("wipes") backward to the start of the line.

To choose emacs mode, type set -o emacs in Bourne-type shells and bindkey -e in *tcsh*. In *bash*, use one of the *keymap* editor commands, such as *keymap emacs*. To make this the default, store the command in your shell's setup file (3.3) (in *bash*, you can also edit your Readline *inputrc* file). You can switch back and forth between emacs and vi modes as you work.

tcsh Editing

The *bindkey* command is used to bind keys to built-in editor functions. With no arguments, it gives a list of all key bindings, like this:

```
tcsh> bindkey
Standard key bindings
"^@"           ->   set-mark-command
"^A"           ->   beginning-of-line
"^B"           ->   backward-char
     ...
"¡" to "ŷ"     ->   self-insert-command
Alternative key bindings
Multi-character bindings
"^[[A"         -> up-history
"^[[B"         -> down-history
     ...
```

```
"^X^D"           -> list-choices-raw
Arrow key bindings
down             -> down-history
up               -> up-history
left             -> backward-char
right            -> forward-char
```

In this list, ^ (caret) starts control characters, so ^A means CTRL-a. ^[is an escape character (which is also generated when you press a function key, like F1 or up-arrow, on most keyboards). Thus, ^[[A is the sequence *ESC left-bracket A* (which is also sent by the up-arrow key on VT100-type keyboards). The "alternative key bindings" are used in *vi* command mode, which wasn't enabled in the example above, because I made it while using emacs bindings.

There's a list of some editor functions in the *tcsh* manual page, but that list only includes "interesting" functions. To get a complete list, including "boring" functions like *backward-char* (to move backward one character), type the command *bindkey –l* (lowercase letter L); that lists all the editor functions and describes each one briefly:

```
tcsh> bindkey -l
backward-char
         Move back a character
backward-delete-char
         Delete the character behind cursor
    ...
```

You'll probably want to redirect the output of those *bindkey* commands into a file—or pipe it to a pager such as *less* (12.3) that lets you page through and do searches. (You could probably merge the output of *bindkey* and *bindkey –l* into one list with *perl* (41.1) or *awk* (20.10) and an associative array, but I haven't tried.)

To bind a key to an editor function, use *bindkey* with two arguments: the key to bind and the function name. The key can be the literal key you want to type, but that can be messy when you're trying to put the definition in a shell setup file (which traditionally doesn't have nonprintable characters in it) or when you're trying to bind an arrow key or some other key. So you can represent a control character with two characters: a literal caret (^) followed by the letter—for example, ^A. You can use standard backslash escape sequences, such as \t for a TAB character, but remember to quote (27.13) special characters. And the special option *–k* lets you name an arrow key: for instance, bindkey -k left for the left arrow.

Here's an example of one of my favorite *tcsh* editor functions: *magic-space*. By default, it isn't bound to a key, but it's meant to be bound to the space key. The function expands any history substitutions (30.8) in the command line, then lets you continue editing. In this example, I start by executing an *ls* command. Then I bind the space key. After that, I start a new command line. I type find and a space, but nothing happens yet because there are no history references. Then I type !ls:$, which is the history substitution for the last argument of the previous *ls* command; when I press the space key, that argument is expanded to */usr/local/bin*, and I can type the rest of the command line:

```
tcsh> ls /usr/local/bin
acroread            netscape  rsh-add      ssh
ex                  nex       rsh-agent    ssh-add
lcdctl              nsgmls    rsh-askpass  ssh-add1
   ...
tcsh> bindkey " " magic-space
tcsh> find !ls:$ SPACE
tcsh> find /usr/local/bin -perm  ...
```

You also can bind a key to a Unix command by using *bindkey* with its *−c* option. This is different from simply executing a command at a shell prompt. When a Unix command is bound to a key, the shell will run that command without disturbing the command line you're editing! When the bound command finishes running, the command line you were editing is redisplayed as it was. For example, the binding below makes CTRL-x 1 run the command ls -lt | less:

```
bindkey -c ^Xl 'ls -lt | less'
```

There's much, much more. The *tcsh*(1) manpage is too brief to teach this well (for me, at least). I recommend the O'Reilly book *Using csh & tcsh*; it doesn't cover all of the newest *tcsh*, but it does a complete job on the command-line editor.

ksh Editing

This section covers the public domain Korn shell, *pdksh*. The original Korn shell is similar.

The *bind* command binds keys to built-in Emacs editor functions. (You can't re-bind in *vi* mode.) With no arguments, it gives a list of all key bindings, like this:

```
$ bind
^A = beginning-of-line
^B = backward-char
   ...
^[b = backward-word
^[c = capitalize-word
   ...
^XC = forward-char
^XD = backward-char
```

In that list, ^ (caret) starts control characters, so ^A means CTRL-a. And ^[is an escape character (which is also generated when you press a function key, like F1 or up-arrow, on most keyboards)—so ^[b is the sequence *ESC b*.

There's a complete list of editor functions in the *ksh* manual page. You can also get a list from the command *bind –l* (lowercase letter L):

```
$ bind -l
abort
beginning-of-history
complete-command
    ...
```

To bind a key to an editor function, use *bind* with the string to bind, an equal sign (=), then the binding. The key can be the literal key you want to type, but that can be messy when you're trying to put the definition in a shell setup file (which traditionally doesn't have nonprintable characters in it) or when you're trying to bind an arrow key or some other key. So you can represent a control character with two characters: a literal caret (^) followed by the letter—for example, ^A. The other special prefix supported is the two-character sequence ^[(caret left-square-bracket), which stands for the ESC or Meta key. And remember to quote (27.12) any special characters. So, if you want to make CTRL-r be the traditional Unix *rprnt* (28.2) operation (to reprint the command line), and make META-r search the history (which is bound to CTRL-r by default in *pdksh*), you could use these two bindings:

```
bind '^R'=redraw
bind '^[r'=search-history
```

bash Editing

The most permanent place to customize *bash* editing is in the Readline *inputrc* file. But you also can add temporary bindings from the command line with the *bind* command. These bindings work only in the current shell, until the shell exits. The *bind* syntax is the same as the *inputrc* file, but you have to put quotes (27.12) around the whole binding—so watch out for quoting conflicts. For example, to make CTRL-o output a redirection (43.1) command and pathname:

```
bash$ bind 'Control-o: ">> /usr/local/project/log"'
```

To get a list of all key bindings, use *bind –P* in Version 2 or *bind –v* in original *bash*. In the next example, for instance, you can see that CTRL-m (the ENTER key) and CTRL-j (the LINEFEED key) both accept the command line. Quite a few characters (CTRL-a, CTRL-b, etc.) simply insert themselves into the command line when you type them. If you need a literal control character, you may be able to type CTRL-v and then the character.

less 12.3
```
bash$ bind -P | less
abort is not bound to any keys
accept-line can be found on "\C-j", "\C-m".
    ...
backward-delete-char can be found on "\C-h", "\C-?".
    ...
self-insert can be found on "\C-a", "\C-b", "\C-c", "\C-e", "\C-f", ...
```

There are two *bind* options good for use with *inputrc* type files. To write all the current key bindings out to a file named *inputrc.new*, type `bind -p >  inputrc.new` in *bash2*; use the *–d* option in original *bash*. (You can overwrite your default *.inputrc* file this way, too, if you want.) To read an *inputrc* file into the current shell (if you've just edited it, for instance), use *bind –f* and give the file-name as an argument.

Finally, the *bind* option *–m keymap* chooses the keymap that subsequent bindings apply to. The keymap names that *bash2* understands are *emacs*, *emacs-standard*, *emacs-meta*, *emacs-ctlx*, *vi*, *vi-move*, *vi-command*, and *vi-insert*. (*vi* is the same as *vi-command*, and *emacs* is the same as *emacs-standard*.)

zsh Editing

zsh, as you migh expect by now, has a wide variety of command-line editing capabilities, many similar to or the same as those found in *ksh*, *tcsh*, or *bash*. Emacs mode is the default, but vi mode may also be chosen, and all of the key commands found in either mode may be bound to any character you like using the *bindkey –v* command. See the *zshzle* manual page for a long list of these commands and their default bindings.

—JP and SJC

30.15 Changing History Characters with histchars

The existence of special characters (particularly !) can be a pain; you may often need to type commands that have exclamation points in them, and occasionally need commands with carets (^). These get the C shell confused unless you "quote" them properly. If you use these special characters often, you can choose different ones by setting the *histchars* variable. *histchars* is a two-character string; the first character replaces the exclamation point (the "history" character), and the second character replaces the caret (the "modification" character (30.5)). For example:

```
% set histchars='@#'
% ls file*
file1    file2    file3
% @@                      Repeat previous command (was !!)
ls file*
file1    file2    file3
% #file#data#             Edit previous command (was ^file^data^)
ls data*
data4    data5
```

zsh's *histchars* is like the *csh* and *tcsh* version, but it has three characters. The third is the comment character—by default, #.

An obvious point: you can set *histchars* to any characters you like (provided they are different!), but it's a good idea to choose characters that you aren't likely to use often on command lines. Two good choices might be # (hash mark) and , (comma).*

—ML

30.16 Instead of Changing History Characters

If you need to use ! (or your current history character) for a command (for example, if you still use *uucp* or send mail to someone who does, using the command-line *mail* (1.21) command), you can type a backslash (\) before each history character. You can also drop into the Bourne or Korn shell quickly—assuming that you aren't on a system that has replaced the real Bourne shell with a shell like *bash* that has history substitution built in. (If you're stuck, you can use the command set +H in *bash*; this disables history substitution.) Either of these are probably easier than changing *histchars*. For example:

```
% mail ora\!ishtar\!sally < file1     Quote the !s
% sh                                  Start the Bourne shell
$ mail ora!ishtar!sally < file1       ! not special here
$ exit                                Quit the Bourne shell
%                                     And back to the C shell
```

The original Bourne shell doesn't have any kind of history substitution, so ! doesn't mean anything special; it's just a regular character.

By the way, if you have a window system, you can probably copy and paste the command line (28.10) instead of using shell history.

—ML

---

* In the C shell and *tcsh*, # is a comment character (35.1) only in noninteractive shells. Using it as a history character doesn't conflict because history isn't enabled in noninteractive shells.

31

Moving Around in a Hurry

31.1 Getting Around the Filesystem

How quickly can you move around the Unix filesystem? Can you locate any file or directory on your filesystem with both its absolute and relative pathnames? How can symbolic links help you and hurt you?

A lot of Unix users don't realize how much they'll be helped by completely understanding a few filesystem basics. Here are some of the most important concepts and tricks to know:

- Using relative and absolute pathnames: article 31.2.
- What good is a current directory? article 31.3.
- Saving time and typing when changing directories with *cdpath*: article 31.5.
- Directory stacks keep a list of directories you're using and let you get to them quickly: articles 31.7, 31.8.
- Quick *cd* aliases: article 31.9.
- Using variables and a tilde (~) to help you find directories and files: article 31.11.
- A *mark* alias to mark directory for *cd*'ing back: article 31.12.
- Automatic setup for entering and exiting a directory: article 31.13.

—*JP*

31.2 Using Relative and Absolute Pathnames

Everything in the Unix filesystem—files, directories, devices, named pipes, and so on—has two pathnames: absolute and relative. If you know how to find those names, you'll know the best way to locate the file (or whatever) and use it. Even though pathnames are amazingly simple, they're one of the biggest problems beginners have. Studying this article carefully can save you a lot of time and frustration. See Figure 31-1 for an illustration of the Unix filesystem.

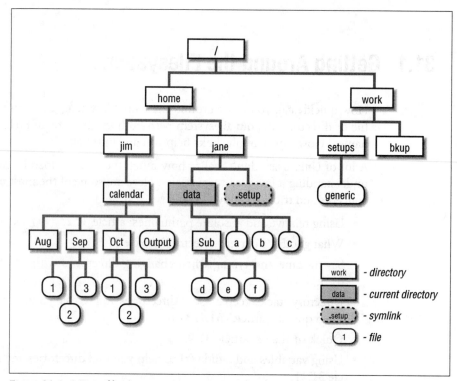

Figure 31-1. A Unix filesystem tree

Table 31-1 describes the two kinds of pathnames.

Table 31-1. Absolute and relative pathnames

Absolute pathnames	Relative pathnames
Start at the root directory.	Start at your current directory (1.16).
Always start with a slash (/).	Never start with a slash.
The absolute pathname to some object (file, etc.) is always the same.	The relative pathname to an object depends on your current directory.

To make an absolute pathname:

- Start at the root directory (/) and work down.
- Put a slash (/) after every directory name—though if the path ends at a directory, the slash after the last name is optional.

For example, to get a listing of the directory highlighted in Figure 31-1, no matter what your current directory is, you'd use an absolute pathname like this:

```
% ls /home/jane/data
Sub   a   b   c
```

To make a relative pathname:

- Start at your current directory.
- As you move down the tree, away from root, add subdirectory names.
- As you move up the tree toward root, add .. (two dots) for each directory.
- Put a slash (/) after every directory name—though if the path is to a directory, the slash after the last name is optional, as it is with absolute pathnames.

For example, if your current directory is the one shown in Figure 31-1, to get a listing of the *Sub* subdirectory, use a relative pathname:

```
% ls Sub
d   e   f
```

Without changing your current directory, you can use a relative pathname to read the file *d* in the *Sub* subdirectory:

```
% cat Sub/d
```

To change the current directory to Jim's home directory, you could use a relative pathname to it:

```
% cd ../../jim
```

Using the absolute pathname, */home/jim*, might be easier there.

The symbolic link (10.4) adds a twist to pathnames. What two absolute pathnames would read the file that the symlink points to? The answer: */home/jane/.setup* or */work/setups/generic*. (The second pathname points directly to the file, so it's a little more efficient.) If your current directory was the one shown in Figure 31-1, what would be the easiest way to read that file with the *more* pager? It's probably through the symlink:

```
% more ../.setup
```

Remember, when you need to use something in the filesystem, you don't always need to use *cd* first. Think about using a relative or absolute pathname with the command; that'll almost always work. If you get an error message, check your pathname carefully; that's usually the problem.

—*JP*

31.3 What Good Is a Current Directory?

People who think the *cd* command is all they need to know about current directories should read this article! Understanding how Unix uses the current directory can save you work.

Each Unix process has its own current directory. For instance, your shell has a current directory. So do *vi*, *ls*, *sed*, and every other Unix process. When your shell starts a process running, that child process starts with the same current directory as its parent. So how does *ls* know which directory to list? It uses the current directory it inherited from its parent process, the shell:

```
% ls
    ...Listing of ls's current directory appears,
            which is the same current directory as the shell.
```

Each process can change its current directory and that won't change the current directory of other processes that are already running. So:

- Your shell script (which runs in a separate process) can *cd* to another directory without affecting the shell that started it. (So, the script doesn't need to *cd* back to the directory where it started before it exits.)

- If you have more than one window or login session to the same computer, they probably run separate processes. So, they have independent current directories.

- When you use a subshell (43.7, 24.4) or a shell escape, you can *cd* anywhere you want. After you exit that shell, the parent shell's current directory won't have changed. For example, if you want to run a command in another directory without *cd*ing there first (and having to *cd* back), do it in a subshell:

```
% pwd
/foo/bar
% (cd baz; somecommand > somefile)
% pwd
/foo/bar
```

When you really get down to it, what good is a current directory? Here it is: relative pathnames start at the current directory. Having a current directory means you can refer to a file by its relative pathname, like *afile*. Programs like *ls* access the current directory through its relative pathname . (dot) (1.16). Without a current directory and relative pathnames, you'd always have to use absolute pathnames (31.2) like */usr/joe/projects/alpha/afile*.

—*JP*

31.4 How Does Unix Find Your Current Directory?

[This article is about the standard Unix *pwd* command, an external (1.9) command that isn't built into your shell. (The external *pwd* is usually stored at */bin/ pwd*.) Most shells have an internal version of *pwd* that "keeps track" of you as you change your current directory; it doesn't have to search the filesystem to find the current directory name. This article describes how the external version finds the pathname of its current directory. This isn't just academic stuff: seeing how *pwd* finds its current directory should help you understand how the filesystem is put together.—JP]

A command like *pwd* inherits the current directory of the process that started it (usually a shell). It could be started from anywhere. How does *pwd* find out where it is in the filesystem? See Figure 31-2 for a picture of the current directory */usr/joe* and its parent directories. The current directory doesn't contain its own name, so that doesn't help *pwd*. But it has an entry named . (dot), which gives the i-number of the directory (10.2).

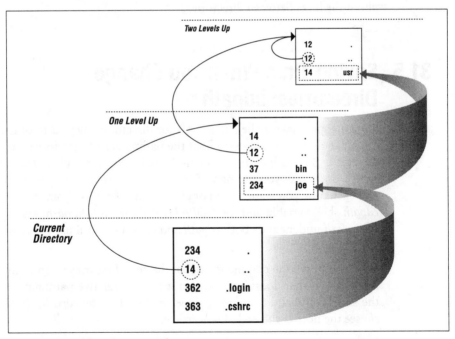

Figure 31-2. Finding the current directory name

The current directory has i-number 234. Next, *pwd* asks Unix to open the parent directory file, the directory one level up, through the relative pathname (..). It's looking for the name that goes with i-number 234. Aha: the current directory is named *joe*, so the end of the pathname must be *joe*.

Next step: *pwd* looks at the . entry in the directory one level up to get its i-number, 14. As always, the name of the one-level-up directory is in its parent (.., i-number 12). To get its name, *pwd* opens the directory two levels up and looks for i-number 14, *usr*. Now *pwd* has the pathname *usr/joe*.

Same steps: look in the parent, i-number 12. What's its name? Hmmm. The i-number of its parent, 12, is the same as its own—and there's only one directory on the filesystem like this: the root directory (/). So *pwd* adds a slash to the start of the pathname and it's done: */usr/joe*.

This explanation is really missing one or two parts: filesystems can be mounted on other filesystems, or they can be mounted across the network from other hosts. So at each step, *pwd* also needs to check the device that the current directory is mounted on. If you're curious, see the *stat*(2) manual page or check a Unix internals book. Also see the last few paragraphs of article 10.4 for more about the links between directories.

—*JP*

31.5 Saving Time When You Change Directories: cdpath

Some people make a shell alias (29.2) for directories they *cd* to often. Other people set shell variables (35.9) to hold the pathnames of directories they don't want to retype. But both of those methods make you remember directory abbreviations—and make you put new aliases or shell variables in your shell startup files (3.3) each time you want to add or change one. There's another way: the C shell's *cdpath* shell variable and the *CDPATH* variable in *ksh*, *bash*, and some versions of *sh*. (*zsh* understands both *cdpath* and *CDPATH*.) I'll use the term "cdpath" to talk about all shells.

When you type the command cd *foo*, the shell first tries to go to the exact pathname *foo*. If that doesn't work, and if *foo* is a relative pathname, the shell tries the same command from every directory listed in the *cdpath*. (If you use *ksh* or *sh*, see the note at the end of this article.)

Let's say that your home directory is */home/lisa* and your current directory is somewhere else. Let's also say that your *cdpath* has the directories */home/lisa*, */home/lisa/projects*, and */books/troff*. If your cd *foo* command doesn't work in your current directory, your shell will try cd /home/lisa/*foo*, cd /home/lisa/projects/*foo*, and cd /books/troff/*foo*, in that order. If the shell finds one, it shows the pathname:

```
% cd foo
/home/lisa/foo
%
```

If there is more than one matching directory, the shell uses the first match; if this isn't what you wanted, you can change the order of the directories in the *cdpath*.

Some Bourne shells don't show the directory name. All shells print an error, though, if they can't find any *foo* directory.

So, set your *cdpath* to a list of the parent directories that contain directories you might want to *cd* to. Don't list the exact directories—list the parent directories (1.16). This list goes in your *.tcshrc*, *.cshrc*, or *.profile* file. For example, *lisa*'s *.tcshrc* could have:

~ 31.11
```
set cdpath=(~ ~/projects /books/troff)
```

A Bourne shell user would have this in his *.profile* file:

```
CDPATH=:$HOME:$HOME/projects:/books/troff
export CDPATH
```

A *bash* user might have it in her *.bashrc* or *.bash_profile*.

(If your system doesn't define $HOME, try $LOGDIR.)

 Note that the Bourne shell *CDPATH* in the above example starts with a colon (:)—which, as in the *PATH* variable, is actually an empty entry (35.6) that stands for "the current directory." Both the *sh* and *ksh* I tested required that. Without an empty entry, neither *sh* or *ksh* would *cd* into the current directory! (*bash* seemed to work like *csh*, though.) You could actually call this a feature. If there's no empty entry in *CDPATH*, a user has to use cd ./*subdirname* to go to a subdirectory of the current directory.

—*JP and SJC*

31.6 Loop Control: break and continue

Normally a *for* loop (35.21) iterates until it has processed all its word arguments. *while* and *until* loops (35.15) iterate until the loop control command returns a certain status. But sometimes—for instance, if there's an error—you want a loop to immediately terminate or jump to the next iteration. That's where you use *break* and *continue*, respectively.

break terminates the loop and takes control to the line after *done*. *continue* skips the rest of the commands in the loop body and starts the next iteration. Here's an example of both. An outer loop is stepping through a list of directories. If we can't *cd* to one of them, we'll abort the loop with *break*. The inner loop steps through all entries in the directory. If one of the entries isn't a file or isn't readable, we skip it and try the next one.

'...' **28.14**

|| **35.14**

* **1.13**

test **35.26**

```
for dir in `find $HOME/projdir -type d -print`
do
        cd "$dir" || break
        echo "Processing $dir"
        for file in *
        do
            test -f "$file" -a -r "$file" || continue
                ...process $dir/$file...
        done
done
```

With nested loops (like the file loop above), which loop is broken or continued? It's the loop being processed at that time. So, the *continue* here restarts the inner (file) loop. The *break* terminates the outer (directory) loop—which means the inner loop is also terminated. Note also that the *–print* argument to *find* is often redundant in the absence of another expression, depending on your version of *find*.

Here we've used *break* and *continue* within *for* loops, after the shell's || operator. But you can use them anywhere within the body of any loop—in an *if* statement within a *while* loop, for instance.

—*JP*

31.7 The Shells' pushd and popd Commands

How often do you need to move to some other directory temporarily, look at some file, and then move back to the directory where you started? If you're like most users, you do this all the time. Most shells have *pushd* and *popd* commands to make this a lot easier. (If you use the original *ksh*, *Learning the Korn Shell*, by Bill Rosenblatt and Arnold Robbins and also published by O'Reilly, shows you shell functions that do the same thing.)

These commands implement a "directory stack." The classical analogy for a stack is one of those spring-loaded plate stackers in a school (or corporate) cafeteria. The last plate put ("pushed") onto the stack is the first plate taken ("popped") from the stack. It's just the same with directories: each time you use *pushd*, the shell adds your current directory to the stack and moves you to the new directory. When you use *popd*, the shell takes the top directory off the stack and moves you to the directory underneath.*

You may as well learn about *pushd* the way I did: by watching. Let's say that I'm in the directory ~/*power*, working on this book. I want to change to my *Mail* directory briefly, to look at some old correspondence. Let's see how. (Note that if you have a cdpath (31.5) that includes your home directory, ~ or $HOME, you won't need to type the ~/ with arguments to *pushd*. In other words, *pushd* looks at your *cdpath*.)

```
los% pushd ~/Mail      current directory becomes ~/Mail
~/Mail ~/power
```

pushd prints the entire stack, giving me some confirmation about where I am and where I can go. When I'm done reading the old mail, I want to move back:

```
los% popd              current directory becomes ~/power
~/power
```

We're back where we started; the *Mail* directory is no longer on the stack.

What if you want to move back and forth repeatedly? *pushd*, with no arguments, just switches the two top directories on the stack, like this:

```
los% pwd               current directory is ~/power
/home/los/mikel/power
los% pushd ~/Mail      current directory becomes ~/Mail
~/Mail ~/power
los% pushd             current directory becomes ~/power
~/power ~/Mail
los% pushd             current directory becomes ~/Mail
~/Mail ~/power
```

And so on.

If you like, you can let your directory stack get really long. In this case, two special commands are useful. *popd +n* deletes the *n* entry in the stack. Entries are counted "down" from the top, starting with zero; that is, your current directory is 0. So *popd +0* and *popd* are the same. If *n* is greater than 0, your current directory does not change. This may seem surprising, but it isn't; after all, you haven't changed the top of the stack.

The command *pushd +n* "rotates" the stack, so that the *n*th directory moves to the top, becoming the current directory. Note that this is a "rotation": the whole stack moves. I don't find the *+n* commands too useful, but you should know about them.

---

* Some people—the *zsh* maintainers, for instance—think of this with a different model. In this other model, the current directory isn't at the top of the stack: it's separate from the stack. The stack is just a list of "remembered" directories. So when you use *pushd*, that first puts the current directory onto the top of the stack, then *cd*s to the directory given. And, when you use *popd*, the top of the stack is popped off to become the new current directory. Maybe you'd like to keep both of the models in mind as you read and experiment with directory stacks—and then decide which seems clearer to you.

The *dirs* command prints the directory stack. It's a good way to find out where you are. (Some people like to put the *dirs* command in their prompt (4.14), but I personally find incredibly long prompts more annoying than helpful.) If you'd like a numbered list of the directories on the stack, most shells support *dirs −v*.

The one drawback to *pushd* and *popd* is that you can easily build up a gigantic directory stack full of useless directories. I suppose this doesn't really hurt anything, but it's needless clutter. One way to clear the stack is to *popd* repeatedly. More to the point, the directories you're most likely to want are at the top of the stack. With seven directories in the stack, you could conceivably do something like this to get rid of the bottom two elements:

```
% pushd +5 ; popd ; popd
```

The *pushd* moves the bottom two elements of a seven-directory stack to the top. A bit inconvenient.

The *zsh* commands *cd +n* and *cd −n* move a directory to the top of the stack and change to the "popped" directory. The + counts from the top (left end) of the stack (starting with zero), and − counts from the bottom. As you do this, remember that in *zsh* terminology, the current directory is *not* on the stack; it's separate from the stack. As the previous footnote explains, this different interpretation of the stack takes some getting used to. Also see the *zshbuiltins*(1) manual page. Whew.

If the stack gets too messy, here's an easy way to start over: In *bash* Version 2 and in *tcsh*, the command *dirs −c* clears the stack. In *csh*, you can use the built-in *repeat* command to clear the stack. For example, if the stack has seven directories, type:

```
% repeat 6 popd
```

—*ML and JP*

31.8 Nice Aliases for pushd

The *pushd* command (31.7) is nice for jumping around the filesystem, but some of the commands you might type a lot, like *pushd +4*, are sort of a pain to type. I saw these aliases (29.2) in Daniel Gilly's setup file. They looked so handy that I decided to steal them for this book. There are C shell versions in the first column and Bourne-type in the second:

```
alias pd pushd              alias pd=pushd
alias pd2 'pushd +2'        alias pd2='pushd +2'
alias pd3 'pushd +3'        alias pd3='pushd +3'
alias pd4 'pushd +4'        alias pd4='pushd +4'
      ...
```

So, for example, to swap the fourth directory on the stack, just type *pd4*.

—*JP*

31.9 Quick cds with Aliases

If you do a lot of work in some particular directories, it can be handy to make aliases (29.2) that take you to each directory quickly. For example, this Korn shell alias lets you type pwr to change to the */books/troff/pwrtools* directory:

```
alias pwr='cd /books/troff/pwrtools'
```

(If your shell doesn't have aliases, you can use a shell function (29.11). A shell script (1.8) won't work, though, because it runs in a subshell (24.4).)

When you pick the alias names, it's a good idea not to conflict with command names that are already on the system. Article 35.27 shows how to pick a new name.

If you have a lot of these directory-changing aliases, you might want to put them in a separate file named something like *.cd_aliases*. Then add these lines to your shell setup file (3.3), like this C shell example for your *.cshrc*:

source **35.29**
~ **31.11**
```
alias setcds source ~/.cd_aliases
setcds
```

That reads your aliases into each shell. If you edit the *.cd_aliases* file, you can read the new file into your shell by typing setcds from any directory.

Finally, if you're in a group of people who all work on the same directories, you could make a central alias file that everyone reads from their shell setup files as they log in. Just adapt the example above.

—JP

31.10 cd by Directory Initials

Here's a handy shell function called *c* for people who *cd* all over the filesystem. (I first saw Marc Brumlik's posting of it on Usenet years ago, as a C shell alias. He and I have both made some changes to it since then.) This function is great for shells that don't have filename completion (28.6). This function works a bit like filename completion, but it's faster because the "initials" match only directories and you don't have to press TAB or ESC after each part of the pathname. Instead, you just type the initials (first letter or more) of each directory in the pathname. Start at the root directory. Put a dot (.) after each part.

Here are three examples. The first one shows that there's no subdirectory of root whose name starts with *q*. The second one matches the directory */usr/include/hsfs* and *cd*s there:

```
$ c q.
c: no match for /q*/.
$ c u.i.h.
/usr/include/hsfs/.
$
```

In the next example, trying to change to *usr/include/pascal* the abbreviations aren't unique the first time. The function shows me all the matches; the second time, I add another letter ("a") to make the name unique:

```
$ c u.i.p.
c: too many matches for u.i.p.:
/usr/include/pascal/. /usr/include/pixrect/. /usr/include/protocols/.
$ c u.i.pa.
/usr/include/pascal/.
$
```

c.csh
c.sh

The Bourne shell function is straightforward; it's shown below.* The C shell alias needs some trickery, and there are two versions of it: one if you already have an alias for *cd* and another if you don't. (The C shell *if* used in the *c* alias won't work with a *cd* alias. Although the *csh* manual page admits it won't work, I'd call that another C shell bug.)

```
function c()
{
    dir="$1"

    # Delete dots.  Surround every letter with "/" and "*".
    # Add a final "/." to be sure this only matches a directory:
    dirpat="`echo $dir | sed 's/\([^.]*\)\./\/\1*/g'`/."

    # In case $dirpat is empty, set dummy "x" then shift it away:
    set x $dirpat; shift

    # Do the cd if we got one match, else print error:
    if [ "$1" = "$dirpat" ]; then
        # pattern didn't match (shell didn't expand it)
        echo "c: no match for $dirpat" 1>&2
    elif [ $# = 1 ]; then
        echo "$1"
        cd "$1"
    else
        echo "c: too many matches for $dir:" 1>&2
        ls -d "$@"
    fi

    unset dir dirpat
}
```

set **35.25**

$# **35.20**

The function starts by building a wildcard pattern to match the directory initials. For example, if you type c u.i.h., *sed* makes the pattern /u*/i*/h*/. in $dirpat. Next, the shell expands the wildcards onto its command-line parameters; the trailing dot makes sure the pattern matches only a directory. If the Bourne shell can't match a wildcard pattern, it leaves the pattern unchanged; the first if test spots that. If there was just one match, there will be one command-

---

* You may need to remove the function keyword in older Bourne shells, but it is required for *bash*.

line parameter left, and the shell *cd*s there. Otherwise, there were too many matches; the function shows them so you can make your pattern longer and more specific.

—JP

31.11 Finding (Anyone's) Home Directory, Quickly

Most shells have a shortcut for the pathname to your home directory: a tilde (~), often called "twiddle" by Unix-heads. You can use ~ in a pathname to the home directory from wherever you are. For example, from any directory, you can list your home directory or edit your *.cshrc* file in it by typing:

```
% ls ~
   ...
% vi ~/.cshrc
```

If you're using a very old Bourne shell, one that does not support the tilde convention, try the $HOME or $LOGDIR variables instead.

You could change your current directory to your home directory by typing cd ~ or cd $HOME, but all shells have a shorter shortcut: typing plain cd with no argument also takes you home.

If your shell understands the tilde, it should also have an abbreviation for other users' home directories: a tilde with the username on the end. For example, the home directory for *mandi*, which might really be */remote/users/m/a/mandi*, could be abbreviated *~mandi*. On your account, if Mandi told you to copy the file named *menu.c* from her *src* directory, you could type:

```
% cp ~mandi/src/menu.c .
```

Don't confuse this with filenames like *report~*. Some programs, like the GNU Emacs (19.4) editor and *vi*, may create temporary filenames that end with a ~ (tilde).

Your version of the Bourne shell might also emulate the special "directory" */u*— if your system administrator hasn't already set up */u*, that is. It's a directory full of symbolic links (10.4) to users' home directories. For instance, */u/jane* could be a link to */home/users/jane*. Many systems are now using */home* for home directories, in favor of the old */usr/users* or */u* conventions. Darwin uses */Users/username* (note the uppercase *U*!), but the tilde works the same there, too.

If all else fails, here's a trick that's probably too ugly to type a lot, but it's useful in Bourne shell scripts, where you don't want to "hardcode" users' home directory pathnames. This command calls the C shell to put *mandi*'s home directory pathname into $*dir*:

```
username=mandi
dir=`csh -fc "echo ~$username"`
```

In fact, using *echo* (27.5) yourself is a good way to see how ~ works. Try echo ~, echo ~/xyz, echo ~xyz, and so on. Note that different shells do different things when *~user* doesn't match any user: some print an error, others return the unmatched string.

—*JP*

31.12 Marking Your Place with a Shell Variable

The following alias stores the current directory name in a variable:

```
alias mark 'set \!:1=$cwd'
```

so as to use a feature of the C shell:

```
% mark here
    ...
% cd here
```

One need not even type $*here*. If a directory does not exist, *csh* tries searching its *cdpath* (31.5), then tries to evaluate the name as a variable.

(I generally use *pushd* and *popd* (31.7) to store directory names; *mark* is more useful with commands that need to look in two different paths, and in that case $*here* is necessary anyway. Ah well.)

[In *bash* and *zsh*, you can do this by setting *cdable_vars*. In your shell setup file (3.3), use cdable_vars=1 for *bash* or setopt cdable_vars or setopt –T for *zsh*.—*JP*]

—*CT*

31.13 Automatic Setup When You Enter/Exit a Directory

If you work in a lot of different directories, here's a way to make the shell do automatic setup when you enter a directory or do cleanup as you leave. We've broken it onto two lines for printing; enter it as one line. On *bash*, make a shell function instead.

csh_init
sh_init

```
alias cd 'if (-o .exit.csh) source .exit.csh; chdir \!*;
    if (-o .enter.csh) source .enter.csh'

function cd() {
   test -r .exit.sh && . .exit.sh
   builtin cd "$1"                    # builtin is a bash command
   test -r .enter.sh && . .enter.sh
}
```

Then create *.enter.csh* and/or *.exit.csh* files in the directories where you want a custom setup. Bourne-type shell users, make *.enter.sh* and/or *.exit.sh* files instead. When you *cd* to a new directory, an *.exit* file is *sourced* (35.29) into your current shell before you leave the old directory. As you enter the new directory, a *.enter* file will be read if it exists. If you use *pushd* and *popd* (31.7), you'll probably want to make the same kind of aliases or functions for them.

The C shell alias tests to be sure you own the files; this helps to stop other users from leaving surprises for you! But if lots of users will be sharing the directory, they may all want to share the same files—in that case, replace the *–o* tests with *–r* (true if the file is readable).

Here's a sample *.enter.csh* file:

.enter.csh
.enter.sh

```
# Save previous umask; reset in .exit.csh:
set prevumask=`umask`

# Let everyone in the group edit my files here:
umask 002
echo ".enter.csh: setting umask to 002"
# Prompt (with blank line before) to keep me awake:
set prompt="\
$cwd - PROJECT DEVELOPMENT DIRECTORY.  EDIT CAREFULLY...\
% "
```

Here's the *.exit.csh* to go with it:

.exit.csh
.exit.sh

```
# .enter.csh file may put old umask in shell variable:
if ($?prevumask) then
    umask $prevumask
    echo ".exit.csh: setting umask to $prevumask"
    unset prevumask
endif
# Reminder to come back here if need to:
echo "If you didn't check in the RCS files, type 'cd $cwd'."
# Set generic prompt (setprompt alias comes from .cshrc file):
setprompt
```

setprompt **4.7**

The *umask* set in the *.enter* file for some directory will also set the permissions for files you create in other directories with commands that use pathnames—like vi */somedir/somefile*.

Can more than one of your directories use the same *.enter* or *.exit* file? If they can, you'll save disk space and redundant editing, as well as the risk of the files getting out of sync, by making hard links (10.4) between the files. If the directories are on different filesystems, you'll have to use a symbolic link (10.4)—though that probably won't save much disk space. If you link the files, you should probably add a comment that reminds you of the links when you make your next edit. When your *.enter* files get really long, you might be able to put a command like this in them:

source **35.29**

```
source ~/.global_enter
```

where the *.global_enter* file in your home directory has a procedure that you want to run from a lot of your *.enter* files. (Same goes for *.exit*, of course.)

One last idea: if a lot of users share the same directory, they can make files with names like *.enter.joanne*, *.exit.allan*, and so on. Your aliases can test for a file named *.enter.$user*.

—JP

32

Regular Expressions (Pattern Matching)

32.1 That's an Expression

When my young daughter is struggling to understand the meaning of an idiomatic expression, such as, "Someone let the cat out of the bag," before I tell her what it means, I have to tell her that it's an *expression*, that she's not to interpret it literally. (As a consequence, she also uses "That's just an expression" to qualify her own remarks, especially when she is unsure about what she has just said.)

An expression, even in computer terminology, is not something to be interpreted literally. It is something that needs to be evaluated.

Many Unix programs use a special "regular expression syntax" for specifying what you could think of as "wildcard searches" through files. Regular expressions describe patterns, or sequences of characters, without necessarily specifying the characters literally. You'll also hear this process referred to as "pattern matching."

In this chapter, we depart a bit from the usual "tips and tricks" style of the book to provide an extended tutorial about regular expressions that starts in article 32.4. We did this because regular expressions are so important to many of the tips and tricks elsewhere in the book, and we wanted to make sure that they are covered thoroughly.

This tutorial article is accompanied by a few snippets of advice (articles 32.16 and 32.18) and a few tools that help you see what your expressions are matching (article 32.17). There's also a quick reference (article 32.21) for those of you who just need a refresher.

For tips, tricks, and tools that rely on an understanding of regular expression syntax, you have only to look at:

- Chapter 13, *Searching Through Files*
- Chapter 17, *vi Tips and Tricks*

- Chapter 20, *Batch Editing*
- Chapter 34, *The sed Stream Editor*
- Chapter 41, *Perl*

O'Reilly's *Mastering Regular Expressions*, by Jeffrey Friedl, is a gold mine of examples and specifics.

—DD and TOR

32.2 Don't Confuse Regular Expressions with Wildcards

Before we even start talking about regular expressions, a word of caution for beginners: regular expressions can be confusing because they look a lot like the file-matching patterns ("wildcards") the shell uses. Both the shell and programs that use regular expressions have special meanings for the asterisk (*), question mark (?), parentheses (( )), square brackets ([ ]), and vertical bar (|, the "pipe").

Some of these characters even act the same way—almost.

Just remember, the shells, *find*, and some others generally use filename-matching patterns and not regular expressions.*

You also have to remember that shell wildcards are expanded before the shell passes the arguments to the program. To prevent this expansion, the special characters in a regular expression must be quoted (27.12) when passed as an argument from the shell.

The command:

```
$ grep [A-Z]*.c chap[12]
```

could, for example, be interpreted by the shell as:

```
grep Array.c Bug.c Comp.c chap1 chap2
```

and so *grep* would then try to find the pattern "Array.c" in files *Bug.c*, *Comp.c*, *chap1*, and *chap2*.

The simplest solution in most cases is to surround the regular expression with single quotes ('). Another is to use the *echo* command to echo your command line to see how the shell will interpret the special characters.

—BB and DG, TOR

---

* Recent versions of many programs, including *find*, now support regex via special command-line options. For example, *find* on my Linux server supports the *–regex* and *–iregex* options, for specifying filenames via a regular expression, case-sensitive and -insensitive, respectively. But the *find* command on my OS X laptop does not.—SJC

32.3 Understanding Expressions

You are probably familiar with the kinds of expressions that a calculator interprets. Look at the following arithmetic expression:

    2 + 4

"Two plus four" consists of several constants or literal values and an operator. A calculator program must recognize, for instance, that 2 is a numeric constant and that the plus sign represents an operator, not to be interpreted as the + character.

An expression tells the computer how to produce a result. Although it is the sum of "two plus four" that we really want, we don't simply tell the computer to return a six. We instruct the computer to evaluate the expression and return a value.

An expression can be more complicated than 2+4; in fact, it might consist of multiple simple expressions, such as the following:

    2 + 3 * 4

A calculator normally evaluates an expression from left to right. However, certain operators have precedence over others: that is, they will be performed first. Thus, the above expression evaluates to 14 and not 20 because multiplication takes precedence over addition. Precedence can be overridden by placing the simple expression in parentheses. Thus, (2+3)*4 or "the sum of two plus three times four" evaluates to 20. The parentheses are symbols that instruct the calculator to change the order in which the expression is evaluated.

A regular expression, by contrast, is descriptive of a pattern or sequence of characters. Concatenation is the basic operation implied in every regular expression. That is, a pattern matches adjacent characters. Look at the following example of a regular expression:

    ABE

Each literal character is a regular expression that matches only that single character. This expression describes "an A followed by a B followed by an E" or simply the string ABE. The term "string" means each character concatenated to the one preceding it. That a regular expression describes a *sequence* of characters can't be emphasized enough. (Novice users are inclined to think in higher-level units such as words, and not individual characters.) Regular expressions are case-sensitive; A does not match a.

Programs such as *grep* (13.2) that accept regular expressions must first evaluate the syntax of the regular expression to produce a pattern. They then read the input, line by line, trying to match the pattern. An input line is a string, and to see if a string matches the pattern, a program compares the first character in the string to the first character of the pattern. If there is a match, it compares the second character in the string to the second character of the pattern. Whenever it fails to make a match, it compares the next character in the string to the first character of the pattern. Figure 32-1 illustrates this process, trying to match the pattern abe on an input line.

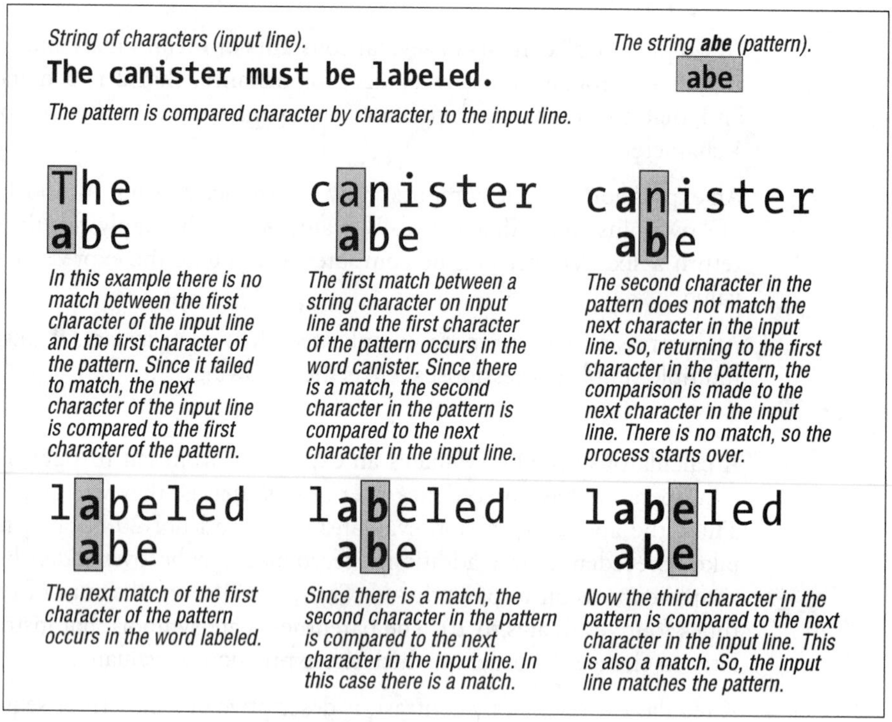

Figure 32-1. Interpreting a regular expression

A regular expression is not limited to literal characters. There is, for instance, a metacharacter—the dot (.)—that can be used as a "wildcard" to match any single character. You can think of this wildcard as analogous to a blank tile in Scrabble™ where it means any letter. Thus, we can specify the regular expression A.E, and it will match ACE, ABE, and ALE. It matches any character in the position following A.

The metacharacter * (the asterisk) is used to match zero or more occurrences of the *preceding* regular expression, which typically is a single character. You may be familiar with * as a *shell* metacharacter, where it also means "zero or more characters." But that meaning is very different from * in a regular expression. By itself, the metacharacter * does not match anything in a regular expression; it modifies what goes before it. The regular expression .* matches any number of characters. The regular expression A.*E matches any string that matches A.E but it also matches any number of characters between A and E: AIRPLANE, A, FINE, AE, A 34-cent S.A.S.E, or A LONG WAY HOME, for example.

If you understand the difference between . and * in regular expressions, you already know about the two basic types of metacharacters: those that can be evaluated to a single character, and those that modify how characters that precede it are evaluated.

It should also be apparent that by use of metacharacters you can expand or limit the possible matches. You have more control over what is matched and what is not. In articles 32.4 and after, Bruce Barnett explains in detail how to use regular expression metacharacters.

—DD

32.4 Using Metacharacters in Regular Expressions

There are three important parts to a regular expression:

Anchors
Specify the position of the pattern in relation to a line of text.

Character sets
Match one or more characters in a single position.

Modifiers
Specify how many times the previous character set is repeated.

The following regular expression demonstrates all three parts:

    ^#*

The caret (^) is an anchor that indicates the beginning of the line. The hash mark is a simple character set that matches the single character #. The asterisk (*) is a modifier. In a regular expression, it specifies that the previous character set can appear any number of times, including zero. As you will see shortly, this is a useless regular expression (except for demonstrating the syntax!).

There are two main types of regular expressions: *simple* (also known as *basic*) regular expressions and *extended* regular expressions. (As we'll see in the next dozen articles, the boundaries between the two types have become blurred as regular expressions have evolved.) A few utilities like *awk* and *egrep* use the extended regular expression. Most use the simple regular expression. From now on, if I talk about a "regular expression" (without specifying simple or extended), I am describing a feature common to both types. For the most part, though, when using modern tools, you'll find that extended regular expressions are the rule rather than the exception; it all depends on who wrote the version of the tool you're using and when, and whether it made sense to worry about supporting extended regular expressions.

[The situation is complicated by the fact that simple regular expressions have evolved over time, so there are versions of "simple regular expressions" that support extensions missing from extended regular expressions! Bruce explains the incompatibility at the end of article 32.15. —*TOR*]

The next eleven articles cover metacharacters and regular expressions:

- The anchor characters ^ and $ (article 32.5)
- Matching a character with a character set (article 32.6)
- Match any character with . (dot) (article 32.7)
- Specifying a range of characters with [...] (article 32.8)
- Exceptions in a character set (article 32.9)
- Repeating character sets with * (article 32.10)
- Matching a specific number of sets with \{ and \} (article 32.11)
- Matching words with \< and \> (article 32.12)
- Remembering patterns with \(, \), and \1 (article 32.13)
- Potential problems (article 32.14)
- Extended regular expressions (article 32.15)

—*BB*

32.5 Regular Expressions: The Anchor Characters ^ and $

Most Unix text facilities are line-oriented. Searching for patterns that span several lines is not easy to do. [But it is possible (13.9, 13.10).—*JP*] You see, the end-of-line character is not included in the block of text that is searched. It is a separator, and regular expressions examine the text between the separators. If you want to search for a pattern that is at one end or the other, you use *anchors*. The caret (^) is the starting anchor, and the dollar sign ($) is the end anchor. The regular expression ^A will match all lines that start with an uppercase A. The expression A$ will match all lines that end with uppercase A. If the anchor characters are not used at the proper end of the pattern, they no longer act as anchors. That is, the ^ is an anchor only if it is the first character in a regular expression. The $ is an anchor only if it is the last character. The expression $1 does not have an anchor. Neither does 1^. If you need to match a ^ at the beginning of the line or a $ at the end of a line, you must *escape* the special character by typing a backslash (\) before it. Table 32-1 has a summary.

Table 32-1. Regular expression anchor character examples

Pattern	Matches
^A	An A at the beginning of a line
A$	An A at the end of a line
A	An A anywhere on a line
$A	A $A anywhere on a line
^\^	A ^ at the beginning of a line
^^	Same as ^\^
\$$	A $ at the end of a line
$$	Same as \$$[a]

[a] Beware! If your regular expression isn't properly quoted, this means "process ID of current process." Always quote your expressions properly.

The use of ^ and $ as indicators of the beginning or end of a line is a convention other utilities use. The *vi* editor uses these two characters as commands to go to the beginning or end of a line. The C shell uses !^ to specify the first argument of the previous line, and !$ is the last argument on the previous line (article 30.8 explains).

It is one of those choices that other utilities go along with to maintain consistency. For instance, $ can refer to the last line of a file when using *ed* and *sed*. *cat –v –e* (12.5, 12.4) marks ends of lines with a $. You might also see it in other programs.

—BB

32.6 Regular Expressions: Matching a Character with a Character Set

The simplest character set is a single character. The regular expression the contains three character sets: t, h, and e. It will match any line that contains the string the, including the word other. To prevent this, put spaces (˛) before and after the pattern: ˛the˛.

You can combine the string with an anchor. The pattern ^From:˛ will match the lines of a mail message (1.21) that identify the sender. Use this pattern with *grep* to print every address in your incoming mailbox. [If your system doesn't define the environment variable MAIL, try */var/spool/mail/$USER* or possibly */usr/spool/mail/$USER*. —*SJC*]

$USER 35.5
```
% grep '^From: ' $MAIL
```

Some characters have a special meaning in regular expressions. If you want to search for such a character as itself, escape it with a backslash (\).

—BB

32.7 Regular Expressions: Match Any Character with . (Dot)

The dot (.) is one of those special metacharacters. By itself it will match any character except the end-of-line character. The pattern that will match a line with any single character is ^.$.

—BB

32.8 Regular Expressions: Specifying a Range of Characters with [...]

If you want to match specific characters, you can use square brackets, [ ], to identify the exact characters you are searching for. The pattern that will match any line of text that contains exactly one digit is ^[0123456789]$. This is longer than it has to be. You can use the hyphen between two characters to specify a range: ^[0-9]$. You can intermix explicit characters with character ranges. This pattern will match a single character that is a letter, digit, or underscore: [A-Za-z0-9_]. Character sets can be combined by placing them next to one another. If you wanted to search for a word that:

- started with an uppercase T,
- was the first word on a line,
- had a lowercase letter as its second letter,
- was three letters long (followed by a space character (.)), and
- had a lowercase vowel as its third letter,

the regular expression would be:

```
^T[a-z][aeiou]⬚
```

To be specific: a range is a contiguous series of characters, from low to high, in the ASCII character set.* For example, [z-a] is *not* a range because it's backwards. The range [A-z] matches both uppercase and lowercase letters, but it also matches the six characters that fall between uppercase and lowercase letters in the ASCII chart: [, \,], ^, _, and '.

—BB

---

* Some languages, notably Java and Perl, do support Unicode regular expressions, but as Unicode generally subsumes the ASCII 7-bit character set, regular expressions written for ASCII will work as well.

32.9 Regular Expressions: Exceptions in a Character Set

You can easily search for all characters except those in square brackets by putting a caret (^) as the first character after the left square bracket ([). To match all characters except lowercase vowels, use [^aeiou].

Like the anchors in places that can't be considered an anchor, the right square bracket (]) and dash (-) do not have a special meaning if they directly follow a [. Table 32-2 has some examples.

Table 32-2. Regular expression character set examples

Regular expression	Matches
[0-9]	Any digit
[^0-9]	Any character other than a digit
[-0-9]	Any digit or a -
[0-9-]	Any digit or a -
[^-0-9]	Any character except a digit or a -
[]0-9]	Any digit or a]
[0-9]]	Any digit followed by a]
[0-99-z]	Any digit or any character between 9 and z
[]0-9-]	Any digit, a -, or a]

Many languages have adopted the Perl regular expression syntax for ranges; for example, \w is equivalent to "any word character" or [A-Za-z0-9_], while \W matches anything *but* a word character. See the *perlre*(1) manual page for more details.

—*BB*

32.10 Regular Expressions: Repeating Character Sets with *

The third part of a regular expression is the modifier. It is used to specify how many times you expect to see the previous character set. The special character * (asterisk) matches *zero or more* copies. That is, the regular expression 0* matches zero or more zeros, while the expression [0-9]* matches zero or more digits.

This explains why the pattern ^#* is useless (32.4), as it matches any number of #s at the beginning of the line, including zero. Therefore, this will match every line, because every line starts with zero or more #s.

At first glance, it might seem that starting the count at zero is stupid. Not so. Looking for an unknown number of characters is very important. Suppose you wanted to look for a digit at the beginning of a line, and there may or may not be spaces before the digit. Just use ^.* to match zero or more spaces at the beginning of the line. If you need to match one or more, just repeat the character set. That is, [0-9]* matches zero or more digits and [0-9][0-9]* matches one or more digits.

—BB

32.11 Regular Expressions: Matching a Specific Number of Sets with \ { and \ }

You cannot specify a maximum number of sets with the * modifier. However, some programs (32.20) recognize a special pattern you can use to specify the minimum and maximum number of repeats. This is done by putting those two numbers between \{ and \}.

Having convinced you that \{ isn't a plot to confuse you, an example is in order. The regular expression to match four, five, six, seven, or eight lowercase letters is:

```
[a-z]\{4,8\}
```

Any numbers between 0 and 255 can be used. The second number may be omitted, which removes the upper limit. If the comma and the second number are omitted, the pattern must be duplicated the exact number of times specified by the first number.

The backslashes deserve a special discussion. Normally a backslash *turns off* the special meaning for a character. For example, a literal period is matched by \. and a literal asterisk is matched by *. However, if a backslash is placed before a <, >, {, }, (, or) or before a digit, the backslash *turns on* a special meaning. This was done because these special functions were added late in the life of regular expressions. Changing the meaning of {, }, (,), <, and > would have broken old expressions. (This is a horrible crime punishable by a year of hard labor writing COBOL programs.) Instead, adding a backslash added functionality without breaking old programs. Rather than complain about the change, view it as evolution.

You must remember that modifiers like * and \{1,5\} act as modifiers only if they follow a character set. If they were at the beginning of a pattern, they would not be modifiers. Table 32-3 is a list of examples and the exceptions.

Table 32-3. Regular expression pattern repetition examples

Regular expression	Matches
*	Any line with a *
*	Any line with a *
\\	Any line with a \
^*	Any line starting with a *
^A*	Any line
^A*	Any line starting with an A*
^AA*	Any line starting with one A
^AA*B	Any line starting with one or more A's followed by a B
^A\{4,8\}B	Any line starting with four, five, six, seven, or eight A's followed by a B
^A\{4,\}B	Any line starting with four or more A's followed by a B
^A\{4\}B	Any line starting with an AAAAB
\{4,8\}	Any line with a {4,8}
A{4,8}	Any line with an A{4,8}

—BB

32.12 Regular Expressions: Matching Words with \ < and \ >

Searching for a word isn't quite as simple as it at first appears. The string the will match the word other. You can put spaces before and after the letters and use this regular expression: ˌtheˌ. However, this does not match words at the beginning or the end of the line. And it does not match the case where there is a punctuation mark after the word.

There is an easy solution—at least in many versions of *ed*, *ex*, *vi*, and *grep*. The characters \< and \> are similar to the ^ and $ anchors, as they don't occupy a position of a character. They *anchor* the expression between to match only if it is on a word boundary. The pattern to search for the words the and The would be: \<[tT]he\>.

Let's define a "word boundary." The character before the t or T must be either a newline character or anything except a letter, digit, or underscore (_). The character after the e must also be a character other than a digit, letter, or underscore, or it could be the end-of-line character.

—BB

32.13 Regular Expressions: Remembering Patterns with \ (, \ ), and \1

Another pattern that requires a special mechanism is searching for repeated words. The expression [a-z][a-z] will match any two lowercase letters. If you wanted to search for lines that had two adjoining identical letters, the above pattern wouldn't help. You need a way to remember what you found and see if the same pattern occurs again. In some programs, you can mark part of a pattern using \(and \). You can recall the remembered pattern with \ followed by a single digit.[*] Therefore, to search for two identical letters, use \([a-z]\)\1. You can have nine different remembered patterns. Each occurrence of \(starts a new pattern. The regular expression to match a five-letter palindrome (e.g., "radar") is: \([a-z]\)\([a-z]\)[a-z]\2\1. [Some versions of some programs can't handle \(\) in the same regular expression as \1, etc. In all versions of *sed*, you're safe if you use \(\) on the pattern side of an *s* command—and \1, etc., on the replacement side (34.11). —*JP*]

—*BB*

32.14 Regular Expressions: Potential Problems

Before I discuss the extensions that extended expressions (32.15) offer, I want to mention two potential problem areas.

The \< and \> characters were introduced in the *vi* editor. The other programs didn't have this ability at that time. Also, the \{*min,max*\} modifier is new, and earlier utilities didn't have this ability. This makes it difficult for the novice user of regular expressions, because it seems as if each utility has a different convention. Sun has retrofitted the newest regular expression library to all of their programs, so they all have the same ability. If you try to use these newer features on other vendors' machines, you might find they don't work the same way.

The other potential point of confusion is the extent of the pattern matches (32.17). Regular expressions match the longest possible pattern. That is, the regular expression A.*B matches AAB as well as AAAABBBBABCCCCBBBAAAB. This doesn't cause many problems using *grep*, because an oversight in a regular expression will just match more lines than desired. If you use *sed*, and your patterns get carried away, you may end up deleting or changing more than you want to. Perl

---

[*] In Perl, you can also use $1 through $9 and even beyond, with the right switches, in addition to the backslash mechanism.

answers this problem by defining a variety of "greedy" and "non-greedy" regular expressions, which allow you to specify which behavior you want. See the *perlre*(1) manual page for details.

—BB

32.15 Extended Regular Expressions

At least two programs use extended regular expressions: *egrep* and *awk*. [*perl* uses expressions that are even more extended. —*JP*] With these extensions, special characters preceded by a backslash no longer have special meaning: \{, \}, \ <, \>, \(, \), as well as \digit. There is a very good reason for this, which I will delay explaining to build up suspense.

The question mark (?) matches zero or one instance of the character set before it, and the plus sign (+) matches one or more copies of the character set. You can't use \{ and \} in extended regular expressions, but if you could, you might consider ? to be the same as \{0,1\} and + to be the same as \{1,\}.

By now, you are wondering why the extended regular expressions are even worth using. Except for two abbreviations, there seem to be no advantages and a lot of disadvantages. Therefore, examples would be useful.

The three important characters in the expanded regular expressions are (, |, and). Parentheses are used to group expressions; the vertical bar acts an an OR operator. Together, they let you match a *choice* of patterns. As an example, you can use *egrep* to print all From: and Subject: lines from your incoming mail [which may also be in */var/spool/mail/$USER*. —*JP*]:

```
% egrep '^(From|Subject): ' /usr/spool/mail/$USER
```

All lines starting with From: or Subject: will be printed. There is no easy way to do this with simple regular expressions. You could try something like ^[FS][ru][ob][mj]e*c*t*: and hope you don't have any lines that start with Sromeet:. Extended expressions don't have the \< and \> characters. You can compensate by using the alternation mechanism. Matching the word "the" in the beginning, middle, or end of a sentence or at the end of a line can be done with the extended regular expression (^|)the([^a-z]|$). There are two choices before the word: a space or the beginning of a line. Following the word, there must be something besides a lowercase letter or else the end of the line. One extra bonus with extended regular expressions is the ability to use the *, +, and ? modifiers after a (...) grouping.

[If you're on a Darwin system and use Apple Mail or one of the many other clients, you can grep through your mail files locally. For Mail, look in your home directory's *Library/Mail/* directory. There should be a subdirectory there, perhaps named something like iTools:example@mail.example.com, with an IMAP directory tree beneath it. IMAP stores messages individually, not in standard Unix mbox format, so there is no way to look for all matches in a single mailbox by grepping a single file, but fortunately, you can use regular expressions to construct a file list to search. :-) —*SJC*]

Here are two ways to match "a simple problem", "an easy problem", as well as "a problem"; the second expression is more exact:

```
% egrep "a[n]? (simple|easy)? ?problem" data
% egrep "a[n]? ((simple|easy) )?problem" data
```

I promised to explain why the backslash characters don't work in extended regular expressions. Well, perhaps the \{...\} and \<...\> could be added to the extended expressions, but it might confuse people if those characters are added and the \(...\) are not. And there is no way to add that functionality to the extended expressions without changing the current usage. Do you see why? It's quite simple. If (has a special meaning, then \(must be the ordinary character. This is the opposite of the simple regular expressions, where (is ordinary and \(is special. The usage of the parentheses is incompatible, and any change could break old programs.

If the extended expression used (...|...) as regular characters, and \(...\|...\) for specifying alternate patterns, then it is possible to have one set of regular expressions that has full functionality. This is exactly what GNU Emacs (19.1) does, by the way—it combines all of the features of regular and extended expressions with one syntax.

—*BB*

32.16 Getting Regular Expressions Right

Writing regular expressions involves more than learning the mechanics. You not only have to learn how to describe patterns, but you also have to recognize the context in which they appear. You have to be able to think through the level of detail that is necessary in a regular expression, based on the context in which the pattern will be applied.

The same thing that makes writing regular expressions difficult is what makes writing them interesting: the variety of occurrences or contexts in which a pattern appears. This complexity is inherent in language itself, just as you can't always understand an expression (32.1) by looking up each word in the dictionary.

The process of writing a regular expression involves three steps:

1. Knowing what you want to match and how it might appear in the text.
2. Writing a pattern to describe what you want to match.
3. Testing the pattern to see what it matches.

This process is virtually the same kind of process that a programmer follows to develop a program. Step 1 might be considered the specification, which should reflect an understanding of the problem to be solved as well as how to solve it. Step 2 is analogous to the actual coding of the program, and step 3 involves running the program and testing it against the specification. Steps 2 and 3 form a loop that is repeated until the program works satisfactorily.

Testing your description of what you want to match ensures that the description works as expected. It usually uncovers a few surprises. Carefully examining the results of a test, comparing the output against the input, will greatly improve your understanding of regular expressions. You might consider evaluating the results of a pattern-matching operation as follows:

Hits
> The lines that I wanted to match.

Misses
> The lines that I didn't want to match.

Misses that should be hits
> The lines that I didn't match but wanted to match.

Hits that should be misses
> The lines that I matched but didn't want to match.

Trying to perfect your description of a pattern is something that you work at from opposite ends: you try to eliminate the "hits that should be misses" by limiting the possible matches, and you try to capture the "misses that should be hits" by expanding the possible matches.

The difficulty is especially apparent when you must describe patterns using fixed strings. Each character you remove from the fixed-string pattern increases the number of possible matches. For instance, while searching for the string what, you determine that you'd like to match What as well. The only fixed-string pattern that will match What and what is hat, the longest string common to both. It is obvious, though, that searching for hat will produce unwanted matches. Each character you add to a fixed-string pattern decreases the number of possible matches. The string them is going to produce fewer matches than the string the.

Using metacharacters in patterns provides greater flexibility in extending or narrowing the range of matches. Metacharacters, used in combination with literals or other metacharacters, can be used to expand the range of matches while still eliminating the matches that you do not want.

—DD

32.17 Just What Does a Regular Expression Match?

One of the toughest things to learn about regular expressions is just what they do match. The problem is that a regular expression tends to find the longest possible match—which can be more than you want.

showmatch

Here's a simple script called *showmatch* that is useful for testing regular expressions, when writing *sed* scripts, etc. Given a regular expression and a filename, it finds lines in the file matching that expression, just like *grep*, but it uses a row of carets (^^^^) to highlight the portion of the line that was actually matched. Depending on your system, you may need to call *nawk* instead of *awk*; most modern systems have an *awk* that supports the syntax introduced by *nawk*, however, ever.

```
#! /bin/sh
# showmatch - mark string that matches pattern
pattern=$1; shift
awk 'match($0,pattern) > 0 {
    s = substr($0,1,RSTART-1)
    m = substr($0,1,RLENGTH)
    gsub (/[^\b- ]/, " ", s)
    gsub (/./,        "^", m)
    printf "%s\n%s%s\n", $0, s, m
}' pattern="$pattern" $*
```

For example:

```
% showmatch 'CD-...' mbox
and CD-ROM publishing. We have recognized
    ^^^^^^
that documentation will be shipped on CD-ROM; however,
                                       ^^^^^^
```

xgrep

xgrep is a related script that simply retrieves only the matched text. This allows you to extract patterned data from a file. For example, you could extract only the numbers from a table containing both text and numbers. It's also great for counting the number of occurrences of some pattern in your file, as shown below. Just be sure that your expression matches only what you want. If you aren't sure, leave off the *wc* command and glance at the output. For example, the regular expression [0-9]* will match numbers like 3.2 *twice*: once for the 3 and again for the 2! You want to include a dot (.) and/or comma (,), depending on how your numbers are written. For example: [0-9][.0-9]* matches a leading digit, possibly followed by more dots and digits.

Remember that an expression like [0-9]* will match zero numbers (because * means "zero or more of the preceding character"). That expression can make *xgrep* run for a very long time! The following expression, which matches one or more digits, is probably what you want instead:

```
xgrep "[0-9][0-9]*" files | wc -l
```

The *xgrep* shell script runs the *sed* commands below, replacing $re with the regular expression from the command line and $x with a CTRL-b character (which is used as a delimiter). We've shown the *sed* commands numbered, like 5>; these are only for reference and aren't part of the script:

```
1> \$x$re$x!d
2> s//$x&$x/g
3> s/[^$x]*$x//
4> s/$x[^$x]*$x/\
   /g
5> s/$x.*//
```

Command 1 deletes all input lines that don't contain a match. On the remaining lines (which do match), command 2 surrounds the matching text with CTRL-b delimiter characters. Command 3 removes all characters (including the first delimiter) before the first match on a line. When there's more than one match on a line, command 4 breaks the multiple matches onto separate lines. Command 5 removes the last delimiter, and any text after it, from every output line.

Greg Ubben revised *showmatch* and wrote *xgrep*.

—*JP, DD, andTOR*

32.18 Limiting the Extent of a Match

A regular expression tries to match the longest string possible, which can cause unexpected problems. For instance, look at the following regular expression, which matches any number of characters inside quotation marks:

```
".*"
```

Let's imagine an HTML table with lots of entries, each of which has two quoted strings, as shown below:

```
<td><a href="#arts"><img src="d_arrow.gif" border=0></a>
```

All the text in each line of the table is the same, except the text inside the quotes. To match the line through the first quoted string, a novice might describe the pattern with the following regular expression:

```
<td><a href=".*">
```

However, the pattern ends up matching almost all of the entry because the second quotation mark in the pattern matches the *last* quotation mark on the line! If you know how many quoted strings there are, you can specify each of them:

```
<td><a href=".*"><img src=".*" border=0></a>
```

Although this works as you'd expect, some line in the file might not have the same number of quoted strings, causing misses that should be hits—you simply want the first argument. Here's a different regular expression that matches the shortest possible extent between two quotation marks:

```
"[^"]*"
```

It matches "a quote, followed by any number of characters that do not match a quote, followed by a quote." Note, however, that it will be fooled by escaped quotes, in strings such as the following:

```
$strExample = "This sentence contains an escaped \" character.";
```

The use of what we might call "negated character classes" like this is one of the things that distinguishes the journeyman regular expression user from the novice.

—DD and JP

32.19 I Never Meta Character I Didn't Like

Once you know regular expression syntax, you can match almost anything. But sometimes, it's a pain to think through how to get what you want. Table 32-4 lists some useful regular expressions that match various kinds of data you might have to deal with in the Unix environment. Some of these examples work in any program that uses regular expressions; others only work with a specific program such as *egrep*. (Article 32.20 lists the metacharacters that each program accepts.) The ⌴ means to use a space as part of the regular expression. Bear in mind that you may also be able to use \< and \> to match on word boundaries.

Note that these regular expressions are only examples. They aren't meant to match (for instance) every occurrence of a city and state in any arbitrary text. But if you can picture what the expression does and why, that should help you write an expression that fits your text.

Table 32-4. Some useful regular expressions

Item	Example	Regular expression
U.S. state abbreviation	(NM)	⌴[A-Z][A-Z]⌴
U.S. city, state	(Portland, OR)	^.*,⌴[A-Z][A-Z]
Month day, year	(JAN 05, 1993); (January 5, 1993)	[A-Z][A-Za-z]\{2,8\}⌴[0-9]\{1,2\},⌴[0-9]\{4\}
U.S. Social Security number	(123-45-6789)	[0-9]\{3\}-[0-9]\{2\}-[0-9]\{4\}=

Table 32-4. Some useful regular expressions (continued)

Item	Example	Regular expression
U.S. telephone number	(547-5800)	`[0-9]\{3\}-[0-9]\{4\}`
Unformatted dollar amounts	($1); ($ 1000000.00)	`\$.*[0-9]+(\.[0-9][0-9])?`
HTML/SGML/XML tags	(<h2>); (<UL COMPACT>)	`<[^>]*>`
troff macro with first argument	(.SH "SEE ALSO")	`^\.[A-Z12]..""[^"]*"`
troff macro with all arguments	(.Ah "Tips for" "ex & vi")	`^\.[A-Z12]..".*"`
Blank lines		`^$`
Entire line		`^.*$`
One or more spaces		`. *`

—DD and JP

32.20 Valid Metacharacters for Different Unix Programs

Some regular expression metacharacters are valid for one program but not for another. Those that are available to a particular Unix program are marked by a bullet (•) in Table 32-5. Quick reference descriptions of each of the characters can be found in article 32.21.

[Unfortunately, even this table doesn't give the whole story. For example, Sun has taken some of the extensions originally developed for *ed*, *ex*, and *vi* (such as the `\<` `\>` and `\{min, max\}` modifiers) and added them to other programs that use regular expressions. So don't be bashful—try things out, but don't be surprised if every possible regular expression feature isn't supported by every program. In addition, there are many programs that recognize regular expressions, such as *perl*, *emacs*, *more*, *dbx*, *expr*, *lex*, *pg*, and *less*, that aren't covered in Daniel's table. —TOR]

Table 32-5. Valid metacharacters for different programs

Symbol	ed	ex	vi	sed	awk	grep	egrep	Action
.	•	•	•	•	•	•	•	Match any character.
*	•	•	•	•	•	•	•	Match zero or more preceding.
^	•	•	•	•	•	•	•	Match beginning of line.
$	•	•	•	•	•	•	•	Match end of line.
\	•	•	•	•	•	•	•	Escape character following.
[ ]	•	•	•	•	•	•	•	Match one from a set.
\(\)	•	•		•				Store pattern for later replay.
\{\}	•			•			•	Match a range of instances.

Table 32-5. Valid metacharacters for different programs (continued)

Symbol	ed	ex	vi	sed	awk	grep	egrep	Action
\<\>	•	•	•					Match word's beginning or end.
+					•		•	Match one or more preceding.
?					•		•	Match zero or one preceding.
|					•		•	Separate choices to match.
( )					•		•	Group expressions to match.

In *ed*, *ex*, and *sed*, note that you specify both a search pattern (on the left) and a replacement pattern (on the right). The metacharacters in Table 32-5 are meaningful only in a search pattern. *ed*, *ex*, and *sed* support the additional metacharacters in Table 32-6 that are valid only in a replacement pattern.

Table 32-6. Valid metacharacters for replacement patterns

Symbol	ex	sed	ed	Action
\	•	•	•	Escape character following.
\n	•	•	•	Reuse pattern stored by \(\) pair number \n.
&	•	•		Reuse previous search pattern.
~	•			Reuse previous replacement pattern.
\u \U	•			Change character(s) to uppercase.
\l \L	•			Change character(s) to lowercase.
\E	•			Turn off previous \U or \L.
\e	•			Turn off previous \u or \l.

—DG

32.21 Pattern Matching Quick Reference with Examples

Article 32.4 gives an introduction to regular expressions. This article is intended for those of you who need just a quick listing of regular expression syntax as a refresher from time to time. It also includes some simple examples. The characters in Table 32-7 have special meaning only in search patterns.

Table 32-7. Special characters in search patterns

Pattern	What does it match?
.	Match any *single* character except newline.
*	Match any number (including none) of the single characters that immediately precede it. The preceding character can also be a regular expression. For example, since . (dot) means any character, .* means "match any number of any character."

Table 32-7. Special characters in search patterns (continued)

Pattern	What does it match?
^	Match the following regular expression at the beginning of the line.
$	Match the preceding regular expression at the end of the line.
[ ]	Match any *one* of the enclosed characters.
	A hyphen (-) indicates a range of consecutive characters. A caret (^) as the first character in the brackets reverses the sense: it matches any one character *not* in the list. A hyphen or a right square bracket (]) as the first character is treated as a member of the list. All other metacharacters are treated as members of the list.
\{*n*,*m*\}	Match a range of occurrences of the single character that immediately precedes it. The preceding character can also be a regular expression. \{*n*\} will match exactly *n* occurrences, \{*n*,\} will match at least *n* occurrences, and \{*n*,*m*\} will match any number of occurrences between *n* and *m*.
\	Turn off the special meaning of the character that follows (except for \{ and \(, etc., where it turns on the special meaning of the character that follows).
\(\)	Save the pattern enclosed between \(and \) into a special holding space. Up to nine patterns can be saved on a single line. They can be "replayed" in substitutions by the escape sequences \1 to \9.
\< \>	Match characters at beginning (\<) or end (\>) of a word.
+	Match one or more instances of preceding regular expression.
?	Match zero or one instances of preceding regular expression.
|	Match the regular expression specified before or after.
(,)	Apply a match to the enclosed group of regular expressions.

The characters in Table 32-8 have special meaning only in replacement patterns.

Table 32-8. Special characters in replacement patterns

Pattern	What does it do?
\	Turn off the special meaning of the character that follows.
n	Restore the *n*th pattern previously saved by \(and \). *n* is a number from 1 to 9, with 1 starting on the left.
&	Reuse the string that matched the search pattern as part of the replacement pattern.
\u	Convert first character of replacement pattern to uppercase.
\U	Convert replacement pattern to uppercase.
\l	Convert first character of replacement pattern to lowercase.
\L	Convert replacement pattern to lowercase.

Note that many programs, especially *perl*, *awk*, and *sed*, implement their own programming languages and often have much more extensive support for regular expressions. As such, their manual pages are the best place to look when you wish to confirm which expressions are supported or whether the program supports more than simple regular expressions. On many systems, notably those with a large complement of GNU tools, the regular expression support is astonishing, and many generations of tools may be implemented by one program (as with *grep*, which also emulates the later *egrep* in the same program, with widely varying support for expression formats based on how the program is invoked). Don't make the mistake of thinking that all of these patterns will work everywhere in every program with regex support, or of thinking that this is all there is.

Examples of Searching

When used with *grep* or *egrep*, regular expressions are surrounded by quotes. (If the pattern contains a $, you must use single quotes from the shell; e.g., `'pattern'`.) When used with *ed*, *ex*, *sed*, and *awk*, regular expressions are usually surrounded by / (although any delimiter works). Table 32-9 has some example patterns.

Table 32-9. Search pattern examples

Pattern	What does it match?
bag	The string bag.
^bag	bag at beginning of line.
bag$	bag at end of line.
^bag$	bag as the only word on line.
[Bb]ag	Bag or bag.
b[aeiou]g	Second letter is a vowel.
b[^aeiou]g	Second letter is a consonant (or uppercase or symbol).
b.g	Second letter is any character.
^...$	Any line containing exactly three characters.
^\.	Any line that begins with a . (dot).
^\.[a-z][a-z]	Same, followed by two lowercase letters (e.g., *troff* requests).
^\.[a-z]\{2\}	Same as previous, *grep* or *sed* only.
^[^.]	Any line that doesn't begin with a . (dot).
bugs*	bug, bugs, bugss, etc.
"word"	A word in quotes.
"*word"*	A word, with or without quotes.
[A-Z][A-Z]*	One or more uppercase letters.
[A-Z]+	Same, extended regular expression format.
[A-Z].*	An uppercase letter, followed by zero or more characters.
[A-Z]*	Zero or more uppercase letters.
[a-zA-Z]	Any letter.

Table 32-9. Search pattern examples (continued)

Pattern	What does it match?
[^0-9A-Za-z]	Any symbol (not a letter or a number).
[567]	One of the numbers 5, 6, or 7.
Extended regular expression patterns	
five|six|seven	One of the words five, six, or seven.
80[23]?86	One of the numbers 8086, 80286, or 80386.
compan(y|ies)	One of the words company or companies.
\<the	Words like theater or the.
the\>	Words like breathe or the.
\<the\>	The word the.
0\{5,\}	Five or more zeros in a row.
[0-9]\{3\}-[0-9]\{2\}-[0-9]\{4\}	U.S. Social Security number (*nnn-nn-nnnn*).

Examples of Searching and Replacing

Table 32-10 shows the metacharacters available to *sed* or *ex*. (*ex* commands begin with a colon.) A space is marked by ⌴; a TAB is marked by *tab*.

Table 32-10. Search and replace commands

Command	Result
s/.*/(&)/	Redo the entire line, but add parentheses.
s/.*/mv & &.old/	Change a word list into *mv* commands.
/^$/d	Delete blank lines.
:g/^$/d	*ex* version of previous.
/^[⌴*tab*]*$/d	Delete blank lines, plus lines containing only spaces or TABs.
:g/^[⌴*tab*]*$/d	*ex* version of previous.
s/⌴⌴*/⌴/g	Turn one or more spaces into one space.
:%s/⌴*/⌴/g	*ex* version of previous.
:s/[0-9]/Item &:/	Turn a number into an item label (on the current line).
:s	Repeat the substitution on the first occurrence.
:&	Same.
:sg	Same, but for all occurrences on the line.
:&g	Same.
:%&g	Repeat the substitution globally.
:.,$s/Fortran/\U&/g	Change word to uppercase, on current line to last line.
:%s/.*/\L&/	Lowercase entire file.

Table 32-10. Search and replace commands (continued)

Command	Result
`:s/\<./\u&/g`	Uppercase first letter of each word on current line (useful for titles).
`:%s/yes/No/g`	Globally change a word to No.
`:%s/Yes/~/g`	Globally change a different word to No (previous replacement).
`s/die or do/do or die/`	Transpose words.
`s/\([Dd]ie\) or \([Dd]o\)/\2 or \1/`	Transpose, using hold buffers to preserve case.

—*DG*

33

Wildcards

33.1 File-Naming Wildcards

Wildcards (1.13) are the shell's way of abbreviating filenames. Just as in poker, where a wildcard is a special card that can match any card in the deck, filename wildcards are capable of matching letters or groups of letters in the alphabet. Rather than typing a long filename or a long chain of filenames, a wildcard lets you provide parts of names and then use some "wildcard characters" for the rest. For example, if you want to delete all files whose names end in *.o*, you can give the following command:

```
% rm *.o
```

You don't have to list every filename.

I'm sure you already know that wildcards are useful in many situations. If not, they are summarized in article 33.2. Here are a few of my favorite wildcard applications:

- If you remember part of a filename, but not the whole name, you can use wildcards to help you find it. If I have a file on genetics saved in a directory with several hundred other files, a command like:

  ```
  % ls *gene*
  ```

  will often find what I want. It's quicker and easier than *find* (9.1).

- Wildcards are a natural when you want to work with groups of files. If I have a general purpose directory that's full of filenames ending in *.c* and *.h*, I can make new subdirectories and use wildcards to move the files easily:

  ```
  % mkdir c h
  % mv *.c c
  % mv *.h h
  ```

- Wildcards often help you to work with files with inconvenient characters in their names. Let's say you have a file named abcxe, where *x* is some unknown control character. You can delete or rename that file by using the wildcarded name abc?e. (When you do this, be careful that your wildcard doesn't match more than you intend, perhaps by running an *ls* using the pattern first.)

- Wildcards can appear in any component of a pathname. This can often be used to your advantage. For example, let's say that you have a directory named /work, split into subdirectories for a dozen different projects. For each project, you have a schedule, in a file called (obviously enough) *schedule.txt*. You can print all the schedules with a command like:

  `% lpr /work/*/schedule.txt`

  (However, you can occasionally run into problems (33.5).)

It's a common misconception, particularly among new users, that application programs and utilities have something to do with wildcards. Given a command like grep ident *.c, many users think that *grep* handles the * and looks to see which files have names that end in *.c*. If you're at all familiar with Unix's workings, you'll realize that this is the wrong picture. The shell interprets wildcards. That is, the shell figures out which files have names ending in *.c*, puts them in a list, puts that list on the command line, and then hands that command line to *grep*. As it processes the command line, the shell turns grep ident *.c into grep ident file1.c file2.c....

Since there are several shells, one might think (or fear!) that there should be several different sets of wildcards. Fortunately, there aren't. The basic wildcards work the same for all shells.

—*ML*

33.2 Filename Wildcards in a Nutshell

This article summarizes the wildcards that are used for filename expansion (see Table 33-1). The shells use the same basic wildcards, though most shells have some extensions. Unless otherwise noted, assume that wildcards are valid for all shells.

Table 33-1. Filename wildcards

Wildcard	Shells	Description
*	All	Match zero or more characters. For example, a* matches the files *a, ab, abc, abc.d*, and so on. (*zsh* users: also see x# and x##, below.)
?	All	Match exactly one character. For example, a? matches *aa, ab, ac*, etc.
[12..a..z]	All	Match any character listed in the brackets. For example, a[ab] matches *aa* or *ab*.
[a-z]	All	Match all characters between a and z, in a case-sensitive manner, based on the characters' value in the ASCII character set. For example, a[0-9] matches *a0, a1*, and so on, up to *a9*.
[!ab..z]	*bash, ksh, zsh,* newer *sh*	Match any character that does *not* appear within the brackets. For example, a[!0-9] doesn't match *a0* but does match *aa*.

Table 33-1. Filename wildcards (continued)

Wildcard	Shells	Description
`[^ab..z]`	*tcsh*, *zsh*	Match any character that does *not* appear within the brackets. For example, `a[^0-9]` doesn't match *a0*, but does match *aa*.
`<m-n>`	*zsh*	Any number in the range *m* to *n*. If *m* is omitted, this matches numbers less than or equal to *n*. If *n* is omitted, it matches numbers greater than or equal to *m*. The pattern `<->` matches all numbers.
`{word1,word2...}`	*bash*, *csh*, *pdksh*, *zsh*	Match *word1*, *word2*, etc. For example, `a_{dog,cat,horse}` matches the filenames *a_dog*, *a_cat*, and *a_horse*. These (28.4) actually aren't filename-matching wildcards. They expand to *all* strings you specify, including filenames that don't exist yet, email addresses, and more. (If you want to match one or more of a group of filenames that already exist, see also the parenthesis operators ( ) below.)
`?(x|y|z)`	*ksh*, *bash2*	Match zero or one instance of any of the specified patterns. For example, `w?(abc)w` matches *ww* or *wabcw*. Also, `?(foo|bar)` matches only *foo*, *bar*, and the empty string. In *bash2*, this works only if you've set the *extglob* option using *shopt*.
`*(x|y|z)`	*ksh*, *bash2*	Match zero or more instances of any of the specified patterns. For example, `w*(abc)w` matches *ww*, *wabcw*, *wabcabcw*, etc. Also, `*(foo|bar)` matches *foo*, *bar*, *foobarfoo*, etc., as well as the empty string. In *bash2*, this works only if you've set the *extglob* option using *shopt*.
`+(x|y|z)`	*ksh*, *bash2*	Match one or more instances of any of the specified patterns. For example, `w+(abc)w` matches *wabcw*, *wabcabcw*, etc. Also, `+(foo|bar)` matches *foo*, *bar*, *foobarfoo*, etc. In *bash2*, this works only if you've set the *extglob* option using *shopt*.
`@(x|y|z)`	*ksh*, *bash2*	Match exactly one of any of the specified patterns. For example, `@(foo|bar)` matches *foo* or *bar*. (See also `{word1,word2...}`.) In *bash2*, this works only if you've set the *extglob* option using *shopt*.
`!(x|y|z)`	*ksh*, *bash2*	Match anything that doesn't contain any of the specified patterns. For example, `w!(abc)w` doesn't match *wabcw* or *wabcabcw*, but it does match practically anything else that begins or ends with *w*. Also, `!(foo|bar)` matches all strings except *foo* and *bar*. In *bash2*, this works only if you've set the *extglob* option using *shopt*. (For other shells, see *nom* (33.8).)
`^pat`	*tcsh*, *zsh*	Match any name that doesn't match *pat*. In *zsh*, this only works if you've set the *EXTENDED_GLOB* option. In *tcsh*, the *pat* must include at least one of the wildcards `*`, `?` and `[ ]`. So, to match all except a single name in *tcsh*, here's a trick: put brackets around one character. For instance, you can match all except *abc* with `^ab[c]`. (For other shells, see *nom* (33.8).)
`(x|y)`	*zsh*	Match either *x* or *y*. The vertical bar (`|`) must be used inside parentheses.
`**`	*zsh*	Search recursively.
`***`	*zsh*	Search recursively, following symbolic links to directories.

Table 33-1. Filename wildcards (continued)

Wildcard	Shells	Description
x#	zsh	Matches zero or more occurrences of the pattern x (like the regular expression (32.2) x*). The pattern can have parentheses ( ) around it. You must have set the *EXTENDED_GLOB* option.
x##	zsh	Matches one or more occurrences of the pattern x (like the regular expression (32.15) x+). The pattern can have parentheses ( ) around it. You must have set the *EXTENDED_GLOB* option.

Note that wildcards *do not* match files whose names begin with a dot (.), like *.cshrc*. This prevents you from deleting (or otherwise mucking around with) these files by accident. The usual way to match those files is to type the dot literally. For example, .[a-z]* matches anything whose name starts with a dot and a lowercase letter. Watch out for plain .*, though; it matches the directory entries . and .. If you're constantly needing to match dot-files, though, you can set the *bash* variable *glob_dot_filenames* and the *zsh* option *GLOB_DOTS* to include dot-files' names in those shells' wildcard expansion.

You can prevent wildcard expansion by quoting (27.12, 27.13), of course. In the C shells, you can stop all wildcard expansion (which is also called *globbing*, by the way) without quoting if you set the *noglob* shell variable. In *bash*, *ksh*, and *zsh*, set the *noglob* option.

And a final note: many operating systems (VAX/VMS and DOS included) consider a file's *name* and *extension* to be different entities; therefore, you can't use a single wildcard to match both. What do we mean? Consider the file *abc.def*. Under DOS or VMS, to match this filename you'd need the wildcard expression *.*. The first * matches the name (the part before the period), and the second matches the extension (the part after the period). Although Unix uses extensions, they aren't considered a separate part of the filename, so a single * will match the entire name.

—JP, ML, and SJC

33.3 Who Handles Wildcards?

Wildcards (1.13) are actually defined by the Unix shells, rather than the Unix filesystem. In theory, a new shell could define new wildcards, and consequently, we should discuss wildcarding when we discuss the shell. In practice, all Unix shells (including *ksh*, *bash*, and other variants (1.6)) honor the same wildcard conventions, and we don't expect to see anyone change the rules. (But most new shells also have extended wildcards (33.2). And different shells do different things when a wildcard doesn't match (33.4).)

You may see different wildcarding if you have a special-purpose shell that emulates another operating system (for example, a shell that looks like the COMMAND.COM in MS-DOS)—in this case, your shell will obey the other operating system's wildcard rules. But even in this case, operating system designers stick to a reasonably similar set of wildcard rules.

The fact that the shell defines wildcards, rather than the filesystem itself or the program you're running, has some important implications for a few commands. Most of the time, a program never sees wildcards. For example, the result of typing:

```
% lpr *
```

is exactly the same as typing:

```
% lpr file1 file2 file3 file4 file5
```

In this case everything works as expected. But there are other situations in which wildcards don't work at all. Assume you want to read some files from a tape, which requires the command *tar x* (38.6), so you type the command tar x *.txt. Will you be happy or disappointed?

You'll be disappointed—unless older versions of the files you want are already in your current directory (1.16). The shell expands the wildcard *.txt, according to what's in the current directory, *before it hands the completed command line over to tar for execution*. All *tar* gets is a list of files. But you're probably not interested in the current directory; you probably want the wildcard * to be expanded on the tape, retrieving any *.txt files that the tape has.

There's a way to pass wildcards to programs, without having them interpreted by the shell. Simply put *.txt in quotes (27.12). The quotes prevent the Unix shell from expanding the wildcard, passing it to the command unchanged. Programs that can be used in this way (like *ssh* and *scp* (46.6)) know how to handle wildcards, obeying the same rules as the shell (in fact, these programs usually start a shell to interpret their arguments). You only need to make sure that the programs see the wildcards, that they aren't stripped by the shell before it passes the command line to the program. As a more general rule, you should be aware of when and why a wildcard gets expanded, and you should know how to make sure that wildcards are expanded at an appropriate time.

 If your shell understands the {} characters (28.4), you can use them because they can generate any string—not just filenames that already exist. You have to type the unique part of each name, but you only have to type the common part once. For example, to extract the files called *project/wk9/summary*, *project/wk14/summary*, and *project/wk15/summary* from a *tar* tape or file, you might use:

```
% tar xv project/wk{9,14,15}/summary
x project/wk9/summary, 3161 bytes, 7 tape blocks
x project/wk14/summary, 878 bytes, 2 tape blocks
x project/wk15/summary, 2268 bytes, 5 tape blocks
```

Some versions of *tar* understand wildcards, but many don't. There is a clever workaround (38.10).

—ML

33.4 What if a Wildcard Doesn't Match?

I ran into a strange situation the other day. I was compiling a program that was core dumping. At some point, I decided to delete the object files and the *core* file, and start over, so I gave the command:

```
% rm *.o core
```

It works as expected most of the time, except when no object files exist. (I don't remember why I did this, but it was probably by using !! (30.8) when I knew there weren't any .o's around.) In this case, you get No match, and the *core* file is not deleted.

It turns out, for C shell users, that if none of the wildcards can be expanded, you get a No match error. It doesn't matter that there's a perfectly good match for other name(s). That's because, when *csh* can't match a wildcard, it aborts and prints an error—it won't run the command. If you create one *.o* file or remove the *.o* from the command line, *core* will disappear happily.

On the other hand, if the Bourne shell can't match a wildcard, it just passes the unmatched wildcard and other filenames:

```
*.o core
```

to the command (in this case, to *rm*) and lets the command decide what to do with it. So, with Bourne shell, what happens will depend on what your *rm* command does when it sees the literal characters *.o.

The Korn shell works like the Bourne shell.

You can make *csh* and *tcsh* act a lot like *sh* (and *ksh*) by setting the shell's *nonomatch* option. Without *nonomatch* set, the shell sees a nonmatching wildcard and never runs *ls* at all. Then I set *nonomatch* and the shell passes the unmatched wildcard on to *ls*, which prints its own error message:

```
% ls a*
ls: No match.
% set nonomatch
% ls a*
ls: a*: No such file or directory
```

In *bash* Version 1, the option *allow_null_glob_expansion* converts nonmatching wildcard patterns into the null string. Otherwise, the wildcard is left as is without expansion. Here's an example with *echo* (27.5), which simply shows the arguments that it gets from the shell. In the directory where I'm running this example, there are no names starting with *a*, but there are two starting with *s*. In the first case below, *allow_null_glob_expansion* isn't set, so the shell passes the unmatched a* to *echo*. After setting *allow_null_glob_expansion*, the shell removes the unmatched a* before it passes the results to *echo*:

```
bash$ echo a* s*
a* sedscr subdir
bash$ allow_null_glob_expansion=1
bash$ echo a* s*
sedscr subdir
```

bash Version 2 leaves nonmatching wildcard patterns as they are unless you've set the shell's *nullglob* option (shopt -s nullglob). The *nullglob* option does the same thing that allow_null_glob_expansion=1 does in *bash* version 1.

zsh gives you all of those choices. See the options *CSH_NULL_GLOB*, *NOMATCH* and *NULL_GLOB*.

—ML and JP

33.5 Maybe You Shouldn't Use Wildcards in Pathnames

Suppose you're giving a command like the one below (not necessarily *rm*—this applies to any Unix command):

```
% rm /somedir/otherdir/*
```

Let's say that matches 100 files. The *rm* command gets 100 complete pathnames from the shell: */somedir/otherdir/afile*, */somedir/otherdir/bfile*, and so on. For each of these files, the Unix kernel has to start at the root directory, then search the *somedir* and *otherdir* directories before it finds the file to remove.

That can make a significant difference, especially if your disk is already busy. It's better to *cd* to the directory first and run the *rm* from there. You can do it in a subshell (with parentheses) (43.7) if you want to, so you won't have to *cd* back to where you started:

&& 35.14
```
% (cd /somedir/otherdir && rm *)
```

There's one more benefit to this second way: you're not as likely to get the error Arguments too long. (Another way to handle long command lines is with the *xargs* (28.17) command.)

—JP

33.6 Getting a List of Matching Files with grep –l

Normally when you run *grep* (13.1) on a group of files, the output lists the filename along with the line containing the search pattern. Sometimes you want to know only the names of the files, and you don't care to know the line (or lines) that match. In this case, use the *–l* (lowercase letter "l") option to list only filenames where matches occur. For example, the following command:

```
% grep -l R6 file1 file2 ... > r6.filelist
```

searches the files for a line containing the string R6, produces a list of those filenames, and stores the list in *r6.filelist*. (This list might represent the files containing Release 6 documentation of a particular product.) Because these Release 6 files can now be referenced by one list, you can treat them as a single entity and run various commands on them all at once:

'...' 28.14
```
% lpr `cat r6.filelist`          Print only the Release 6 files
% grep UNIX `cat r6.filelist`    Search limited to the Release 5 files
```

You don't have to create a file list, though. You can insert the output of a *grep* directly into a command line with command substitution. For example, to edit only the subset of files containing R6, you would type:

```
% vi `grep -l R6 file1 file2 ...`
```

(Of course, you also could use a wildcard like *file** instead of a list of filenames.)

grep –l is also good for shell programs that need to check whether a file contains a particular string. The traditional way to do that test is by throwing away *grep*'s output and checking its exit status:

```
if grep something somefile >/dev/null
then ...
```

If *somefile* is huge, though, *grep* has to search all of it. Adding the *grep –l* option saves time because *grep* can stop searching after it finds the first matching line.

—*DG and JP*

33.7 Getting a List of Nonmatching Files

You can use the *grep* (13.2) option *–c* to tell you how many occurrences of a pattern appear in a given file, so you can also use it to find files that *don't* contain a pattern (i.e., zero occurrences of the pattern). This is a handy technique to package into a shell script.

Using grep –c

Let's say you're indexing a DocBook (SGML) document and you want to make a list of files that don't yet contain indexing tags. What you need to find are files with zero occurrences of the string <indexterm>. (If your tags might be upper-case, you'll also want the –i option (9.22).) The following command:

```
% grep -c "<indexterm>" chapter*
```

might produce the following output:

```
chapter1.sgm:10
chapter2.sgm:27
chapter3.sgm:19
chapter4.sgm:0
chapter5.sgm:39
   ...
```

This is all well and good, but suppose you need to check index entries in hundreds of reference pages. Well, just filter *grep*'s output by piping it through another *grep*. The previous command can be modified as follows:

```
% grep -c "<indexterm>" chapter* | grep :0
```

This results in the following output:

```
chapter4.sgm:0
```

Using *sed* (34.1) to truncate the :0, you can save the output as a list of files. For example, here's a trick for creating a list of files that *don't* contain index macros:

```
% grep -c "<indexterm>" * | sed -n 's/:0$//p' > ../not_indexed.list
```

The *sed* –*n* command prints only the lines that contain :0; it also strips the :0 from the output so that *../not_indexed.list* contains a list of files, one per line. For a bit of extra safety, we've added a $ anchor (32.5) to be sure *sed* matches only 0 at the end of a line—and not, say, in some bizarre filename that contains :0. (We've quoted (27.12) the $ for safety—though it's not really necessary in most shells because $/ can't match shell variables.) The .. pathname (1.16) puts the *not_indexed.list* file into the parent directory—this is one easy way to keep *grep* from searching that file, but it may not be worth the bother.

To edit all files that need index macros added, you could type this:

```
% vi `grep -c "<indexterm>" * | sed -n 's/:0$//p'`
```

This command is more obvious once you start using backquotes a lot.

The vgrep Script

You can put the *grep* –*c* technique into a little script named *vgrep* with a couple of safety features added:

vgrep

```
#!/bin/sh
case $# in
0|1) echo "Usage: `basename $0` pattern file [files...]" 1>&2; exit 2 ;;
2)   # Given a single filename, grep returns a count with no colon or name.
     grep -c -e "$1" "$2" | sed -n "s|^0\$|$2|p"
     ;;
*)   # With more than one filename, grep returns "name:count" for each file.
     pat="$1"; shift
     grep -c -e "$pat" "$@" | sed -n "s|:0\$||p"
     ;;
esac
```

"$@" **35.20**

Now you can type, for example:

```
% vi `vgrep "<indexterm>" *`
```

One of the script's safety features works around a problem that happens if you pass *grep* just one filename. In that case, most versions of *grep* won't print the file's name, just the number of matches. So the first *sed* command substitutes a digit 0 with the filename.

The second safety feature is the *grep* *–e* option. It tells *grep* that the following argument is the search pattern, even if that pattern looks like an option because it starts with a dash (-). This lets you type commands like vgrep -0123 * to find files that don't contain the string *–0123*.

—*DG and JP*

33.8 nom: List Files That Don't Match a Wildcard

nom

The *nom* (no match) script takes filenames (usually expanded by the shell) from its command line. It outputs all filenames in the current directory that *don't* match. As article 33.2 shows, some shells have an operator—! or ^—that works like *nom*, but other shells don't. Here are some examples of *nom*:

- To get the names of all files that *don't* end with *.ms*:

  ```
  % nom *.ms
  ```

- To edit all files whose names don't have any lowercase letters, use command substitution (28.14):

  ```
  % vi `nom *[a-z]*`
  ```

- To copy all files to a subdirectory named *Backup* (except *Backup* itself):

  ```
  % cp `nom Backup` Backup
  ```

Here's the script:

```
#! /bin/sh
temp=/tmp/NOM$$
stat=1      # Error exit status (set to 0 before normal exit)
```

trap **35.17**

```
trap 'rm -f $temp; exit $stat' 0 1 2 15

# Must have at least one argument, and all have to be in current directory:
```
case **35.11**
```
case "$*" in
```
$* **35.20**
```
"")  echo Usage: `basename $0` pattern 1>&2; exit ;;
*/*)    echo "`basename $0` quitting: I can't handle '/'s." 1>&2; exit ;;
esac

# ls gives sorted file list. -d=don't enter directories, -1=one name/line.
ls -d ${1+"$@"} > $temp    # Get filenames we don't want to match
```
comm **11.8**
```
ls -1 | comm -23 - $temp   # Compare to current dir; output names we want
stat=0
```

The *–d* option (8.5) tells *ls* to list the names of any directories, not their contents. The ${1+"$@"} (36.7) works around a problem in some Bourne shells. You can remove the *–1* option on the script's ls command line if your version of *ls* lists one filename per line by default; almost all versions of *ls* do that when they're writing into a pipe. Note that *nom* doesn't know about files whose names begin with a dot (.); you can change that if you'd like by adding the ls -A option (uppercase letter "A", which isn't on all versions of *ls*).

Finally, if you've got a shell with process substitution, such as *bash*, which is what we use below, you can rewrite *nom* without the temporary file and the *trap*:

```
#!/bin/bash
# Must have at least one argument, and all have to be in current directory:
case "$*" in
"")  echo Usage: `basename $0` pattern 1>&2; exit ;;
*/*) echo "`basename $0` quitting: I can't handle '/'s." 1>&2; exit ;;
esac

# ls gives sorted file list. -d=don't enter directories, -1=one name/line.
# Compare current directory with names we don't want; output names we want:
comm -23 <(ls -1) <(ls -d "$@")
```

—JP

34

The sed Stream Editor

34.1 sed Sermon^H^H^H^H^H^HSummary

^H^H^H are ASCII backspace characters. Written printably in email and Usenet messages, they're a tongue-in-cheek way of "erasing" the characters before without actually erasing them. They let you say "I didn't want you to see that" when you actually do.

sed (stream *edit*or) amazes me. Why? It's not just that *sed* can edit data as it streams through a pipe (like all well-behaved Unix filters (1.5) do). *sed* can test and branch and substitute and hold and exchange data as it streams through, but so can almost any scripting language. Maybe it's the minimalist in me that loves a tiny program (by today's standards, at least) with just a few operations—but operations so well-chosen that they make the tool powerful for its size. Sure, sure, Perl probably can do everything that *sed* can—and do each of those things in twenty different ways. Ah, I've got it: when I'm trying to do anything more than a simple substitution on data streaming by, *sed*'s elegant simplicity almost forces me to strip a problem to its basics, to think of what I really need to do. No functions, no libraries, nothing except beautifully simple functionality.

[As someone who learned Perl regular expressions before I learned *sed*, I can relate to what Jerry is saying. One of the things I like about the classic Unix toolbox programs like *sed* is that they really do force you into a sort of Shaker-like elegant simplicity; the best programs, no matter what the language, have a quality like a Shaker chair: pure function, but with a respect for the fact that function doesn't have to be ugly. —*SJC*]

End of sermon. ;-) Even if you aren't into elegance and simplicity, and you just wanna get the job done, what do we cover about *sed* that might be useful?

In this chapter, we start out with the basics: articles 34.2, 34.3, 34.4, 34.5, 34.6, and 34.7 show you how to get started, how to test your scripts, and how to structure more advanced scripts. Articles 34.8 through 34.14 cover regular expressions and complex transformations. Articles 34.15 through 34.24 deal with advanced topics such as multiline matching and deletions, tests, and exiting a script when you're done.

—JP and SJC

34.2 Two Things You Must Know About sed

If you are already familiar with global edits in other editors like *vi* or *ex*, you know most of what you need to know to begin to use *sed*. There are two things, though, that make it very different:

1. It doesn't change the file it edits. It is just what its name says: a "stream *editor*"—designed to take a stream of data from standard input (43.1) or a file, transform it, and pass it to standard output (43.1). If you want to edit a file, you have to write a shell wrapper (34.4) to capture standard output and write it back into your original file.

2. *sed* commands are implicitly global. In an editor like *ex*, the command:

    ```
    s/old/new/
    ```

    will change "old" to "new" only on the current line unless you use the global command or various addressing symbols to apply it to additional lines. In *sed*, exactly the opposite is true. A command like the one above will be applied to all lines in a file. Addressing symbols are used to *limit* the extent of the match. (However, like *ex*, only the first occurrence of a pattern on a given line will be changed unless the g flag is added to the end of the substitution command.)

If all you want to do is make simple substitutions, you're ready to go. If you want to do more than that, *sed* has some unique and powerful commands.

This chapter makes no attempt to cover everything there is to know about *sed*. For the most part, this chapter simply contains advice on working with *sed* and extended explanations of how to use some of its more difficult commands.

—TOR

34.3 Invoking sed

If you were using *sed* on the fly, as a stream editor (34.2), you might execute it as simply as this:

```
% somecommand | sed 's/old/new/' | othercommand
```

Given filenames, *sed* will read them instead of standard input:

```
% sed 's/old/new/' myfile
```

A simple script can go right on the command line. If you want to execute more than one editing command, you can use the *–e* option:

```
% sed -e 's/old/new/' -e '/bad/d' myfile
```

Or you can use semicolons (;), which are a *sed* command separator:

```
% sed 's/old/new/; /bad/d' myfile
```

Or (especially useful in shell scripts (1.8)) you can use the Bourne shell's ability to understand multiline commands:

```
sed '
s/old/new/
/bad/d' myfile
```

Or you can put your commands into a file and tell *sed* to read that file with the *–f* option:

```
% sed -f scriptfile myfile
```

There's only one other command-line option: *–n*. *sed* normally prints every line of its input (except those that have been deleted by the editing script). But there are times when you want only lines that your script has affected or that you explicitly ask for with the *p* command. In these cases, use *–n* to suppress the normal output.

—TOR

34.4 Testing and Using a sed Script: checksed, runsed

All but the simplest *sed* scripts are often invoked from a "shell wrapper," a shell script (35.2) that invokes *sed* and also contains the editing commands that *sed* executes. A shell wrapper is an easy way to turn what could be a complex command line into a single-word command. The fact that *sed* is being used might be transparent to users of the command.

Two shell scripts that you should immediately arm yourself with are described here. Both use a shell *for* loop (35.21) to apply the same edits to any number of files. But the first just shows the changes, so you can make sure that your edits were made correctly. The second writes the edits back into the original file, making them permanent.

checksed

checksed

The shell script *checksed* automates the process of checking the edits that *sed* makes. It expects to find the script file, *sedscr*, in the current directory and applies these instructions to the input files named on the command line. The output is shown by a pager program; the default pager is *more*.

```
#! /bin/sh
script=sedscr

for file
do
        echo "********** < = $file      > = sed output **********"
        sed -f $script "$file" | diff "$file" -
done | ${PAGER-more}
```

For example:

```
$ cat sedscr
s/jpeek@ora\.com/jpeek@jpeek.com/g
$ checksed home.html new.html
********** < = home.html    > = sed output **********
102c102
< <a href="mailto:jpeek@ora.com">Email it</a> or use this form:
--
> <a href="mailto:jpeek@jpeek.com">Email it</a> or use this form:
124c124
< Page created by: <a href="mailto:jpeek@ora.com">jpeek@ora.com</a>>
--
> Page created by: <a href="mailto:jpeek@jpeek.com">jpeek@jpeek.com</a>
********** < = new.html    > = sed output **********
22c22
< <a href="mailto:jpeek@ora.com">Send comments</a> to me!
---
> <a href="mailto:jpeek@jpeek.com">Send comments</a> to me!
```

If you find that your script did not produce the results you expected, perfect the editing script and run *checksed* again.

runsed

runsed

The shell script *runsed* was developed to make changes to a file permanently. It applies your *sedscr* to an input file, creates a temporary file, then copies that file over the original. *runsed* has several safety checks:

- It won't edit the *sed* script file (if you accidentally include *sedscr* on the command line).

- It complains if you try to edit an empty file or something that isn't a file (like a directory).

- If the *sed* script doesn't produce any output, *runsed* aborts instead of emptying your original file.

---

runsed only modifies a file if your *sedscr* made edits. So, the file's timestamp (8.2) won't change if the file's contents weren't changed.

Like *checksed*, *runsed* expects to find a *sed* script named *sedscr* in the directory where you want to make the edits. Supply the name or names of the files to edit on the command line. Of course, shell metacharacters (33.2) can be used to specify a set of files:

```
$ runsed *.html
runsed: editing home.html:
runsed: done with home.html
runsed: editing new.html:
runsed: done with new.html
runsed: all done
```

runsed does not protect you from imperfect editing scripts. You should use *checksed* first to verify your changes before actually making them permanent with *runsed*. (You could also modify *runsed* to keep backup copies of the original versions.)

—DD, JP, and TOR

34.5 sed Addressing Basics

A *sed* command can specify zero, one, or two addresses. An address can be a line number, a line addressing symbol, or a regular expression (32.4) that describes a pattern.

- If no address is specified, the command is applied to each line.
- If there is only one address, the command is applied to any line matching the address.
- If two comma-separated addresses are specified, the command is performed on the first matching line and all succeeding lines up to and including a line matching the second address. This range may match multiple times throughout the input.
- If an address is followed by an exclamation mark (!), the command is applied to all lines that do *not* match the address.

To illustrate how addressing works, let's look at examples using the delete command, *d*. A script consisting of simply the *d* command and no address:

```
d
```

produces no output since it deletes *all* lines.

When a line number is supplied as an address, the command affects only that line. For instance, the following example deletes only the first line:

```
1d
```

The line number refers to an internal line count maintained by *sed*. This counter is not reset for multiple input files. Thus, no matter how many files were specified as input, there is only one line 1 in the input stream.

Similarly, the input stream has only one last line. It can be specified using the addressing symbol, $. The following example deletes the last line of input:

```
$d
```

The $ symbol should not be confused with the $ used in regular expressions, where it means the end of the line.

When a regular expression is supplied as an address, the command affects only the lines matching that pattern. The regular expression must be enclosed by slashes (/). The following delete command:

```
/^$/d
```

deletes only blank lines. All other lines are passed through untouched.

If you supply two addresses, you specify a range of lines over which the command is executed. The following example shows how to delete all lines surrounded by a pair of XHTML tags, in this case, <ul> and </ul>, that mark the start and end of an unordered list:

```
/^<ul>/,/^<\/ul>/d
```

It deletes all lines beginning with the line matched by the first pattern up to and including the line matched by the second pattern. Lines outside this range are not affected. If there is more than one list (another pair of <ul> and </ul> after the first), those lists will also be deleted.

The following command deletes from line 50 to the last line in the file:

```
50,$d
```

You can mix a line address and a pattern address:

```
1,/^$/d
```

This example deletes from the first line up to the first blank line, which, for instance, will delete the header from an email message.

You can think of the first address as enabling the action and the second address as disabling it. *sed* has no way of looking ahead to determine if the second match will be made. The action will be applied to lines once the first match is made. The command will be applied to *all* subsequent lines until the second match is made. In the previous example, if the file did not contain a blank line, then all lines would be deleted.

An exclamation mark following an address reverses the sense of the match. For instance, the following script deletes all lines *except* those inside XHTML unordered lists:

```
/^<ul>/,/^<\/ul>/!d
```

Curly braces ({}) let you give more than one command with an address. For example, to search every line of a list, capitalize the word Caution on any of those lines, and delete any line with <br />:

```
/^<ul>/,/^<\/ul>/{
    s/Caution/CAUTION/g
    /<br \/>/d
}
```

—DD

34.6 Order of Commands in a Script

Combining a series of edits in a script can have unexpected results. You might not think of the consequences one edit can have on another. New users typically think that *sed* applies an individual editing command to all lines of input before applying the next editing command. But the opposite is true. *sed* applies every editing command to the first input line before reading the second input line and applying the editing script to it. Because *sed* is always working with the latest version of the original line, any edit that is made changes the line for subsequent commands. *sed* doesn't retain the original. This means that a pattern that might have matched the original input line may no longer match the line after an edit has been made.

Let's look at an example that uses the substitute command. Suppose someone quickly wrote the following script to change pig to cow and cow to horse:

```
s/pig/cow/
s/cow/horse/
```

The first command would change pig to cow as expected. However, when the second command changed cow to horse on the same line, it also changed the cow that had been a pig. So, where the input file contained pigs and cows, the output file has only horses!

This mistake is simply a problem of the order of the commands in the script. Reversing the order of the commands—changing cow into horse before changing pig into cow—does the trick.

Another way to deal with this effect is to use a pattern you know won't be in the document except when you put it there, as a temporary placeholder. Either way, you know what the "document" looks like after each step in the program.

```
s/pig/cXXXoXXXw/
s/cow/horse/
s/cXXXoXXXw/cow/
```

Some *sed* commands change the flow through the script. For example, the *N* command (34.16) reads another line into the pattern space without removing the current line, so you can test for patterns across multiple lines. Other commands tell *sed* to exit before reaching the bottom of the script or to go to a labeled command. *sed* also maintains a second temporary buffer called the *hold space*. You can copy the contents of the pattern space to the hold space and retrieve it later. The commands that make use of the hold space are discussed in article 34.14 and other articles after it.

—DD

34.7 One Thing at a Time

I find that when I begin to tackle a problem using *sed*, I do best if I make a mental list of all the things I want to do. When I begin coding, I write a script containing a single command that does one thing. I test that it works, then I add another command, repeating this cycle until I've done all that's obvious to do. I say what's obvious because my list is not always complete, and the cycle of implement-and-test often adds other items to the list. Another approach involves actually typing the list of tasks into a file, as comments, and then slowly replacing them with sed commands. If you're one of the rare but highly appreciated breed that actually documents their code, you can just leave the comments in the script or expand on them.

It may seem to be a rather tedious process to work this way, and indeed there are a number of scripts where it's fine to take a crack at writing the whole script in one pass and then begin testing it. However, the one-step-at-a-time method is highly recommended for beginners, because you isolate each command and get to easily see what is working and what is not. When you try to do several commands at once, you might find that when problems arise, you end up recreating the recommended process in reverse; that is, removing or commenting out commands one by one until you locate the problem.

—DD

34.8 Delimiting a Regular Expression

Whether in *sed* or *vi*, when using the substitution command, a delimiter is required to separate the search pattern from the replacement string. The delimiter can be any character except blank or a newline (*vi* seems to be more restrictive than *sed*, although *vim* is extremely flexible). However, the usual practice is to use the slash (/) as a delimiter (for example, s/*search*/*replacement*/).

When either the search pattern or the replacement string contains a slash, it is easier to change the delimiter character than to escape the slash. Thus, if the pattern was attempting to match Unix pathnames, which contain slashes, you could choose another character, such as a colon, as the delimiter:

```
s:/usr/mail:/usr2/mail:
```

Note that the delimiter appears three times and is required after the replacement. Regardless of which delimiter you use, if it does appear in the search pattern or the replacement, put a backslash (\) before it to escape it.

If you don't know what characters the search pattern might have (in a shell program that handles any kind of input, for instance), the safest choice for the delimiter can be a control character.

You can use any delimiter for a pattern address (not just a slash). Put a backslash before the first delimiter. For example, to delete all lines containing */usr/ mail*, using a colon (:) as the delimiter:

```
\:/usr/mail:d
```

—*DD and JP*

34.9 Newlines in a sed Replacement

The backslash (\) in the replacement string of the *sed* substitution command is generally used to escape other metacharacters, but it is also used to include a newline in a replacement string.

Given the following input line where each item is separated by a tab:

```
Column1    Column2    Column3    Column4
```

we can replace the second tab character on each line with a newline character:

```
s/TAB/\
/2
```

₂ **34.12**

Note that no spaces are permitted after the backslash. This script produces the following result:

```
Column1    Column2
Column3    Column4
```

Another example comes from the conversion of a file for *troff* to HTML. It converts the following line for *troff*:

```
.Ah "Major Heading"
```

to a similar line for HTML:

```
<h1>Major Heading</h1>
```

The twist in this problem is that the line needs to be preceded and followed by a blank line. It is an example of writing a multiline replacement string:

```
/^\.Ah/{
s/\.Ah */\
\
<h1>
s/"//g
s/$/<h1>\
/
}
```

The first substitute command replaces .Ah with two newlines and <h1>. Each backslash at the end of the line is necessary to escape the newline. The second substitution removes the quotation marks. The last command matches the end of line in the pattern space (not the embedded newlines) and adds a close h1 tag and a newline after it.

—DD

34.10 Referencing the Search String in a Replacement

As a metacharacter, the ampersand (&) represents the extent of the pattern match, not the line that was matched. For instance, you might use it to match a word and surround it with *troff* requests. The following example surrounds a word with point-size requests:

```
s/UNIX/\\s-2&\\s0/g
```

Because backslashes are also replacement metacharacters, two backslashes are necessary to output a single backslash. The & in the replacement string refers to the string which was originally matched, UNIX. If the input line is:

```
on the UNIX Operating System.
```

the substitute command produces:

```
on the \s-2UNIX\s0 Operating System.
```

The ampersand is particularly useful when the regular expression matches variations of a word. It allows you to specify a variable replacement string that corresponds to what was actually matched. For instance, let's say that you wanted to surround with parentheses any cross reference to a numbered section in a document. In other words, any reference such as See Section 1.4 or See Section 12.9 should appear in parentheses, as (See Section 12.9). A regular expression can match the different combination of numbers, so we use & in the replacement string and surround whatever was matched:

```
s/See Section [1-9][0-9]*\.[1-9][0-9]*/(&)/
```

The ampersand makes it possible to reference the entire match in the replacement string.

In the next example, the backslash is used to escape the ampersand, which appears literally in the replacement section:

```
s/ORA/O'Reilly \& Associates, Inc./g
```

It's easy to forget about the ampersand appearing literally in the replacement string. If we had not escaped it in this example, the output would have been O'Reilly ORA Associates, Inc.

—DD

34.11 Referencing Portions of a Search String

In *sed*, the substitution command provides metacharacters to select any individual portion of a string that is matched and recall it in the replacement string. A pair of escaped parentheses are used in *sed* to enclose any part of a regular expression and save it for recall. Up to nine "saves" are permitted for a single line. \n is used to recall the portion of the match that was saved, where n is a number from 1 to 9 referencing a particular "saved" string in order of use. (Article 32.13 has more information.)

For example, when converting a plain-text document into HTML, we could convert section numbers that appear in a cross-reference into an HTML hyperlink. The following expression is broken onto two lines for printing, but you should type all of it on one line:

```
s/\([sS]ee \)\(Section \)\([1-9][0-9]*\)\.\([1-9][0-9]*\)/
    \1<a href="#SEC-\3_\4">\2\3.\4</a>/
```

Four pairs of escaped parentheses are specified. String 1 captures the word *see* with an upper- or lowercase *s*. String 2 captures the section number (because this is a fixed string, it could have been simply retyped in the replacement string). String 3 captures the part of the section number before the decimal point, and String 4 captures the part of the section number after the decimal point. The replacement string recalls the first saved substring as \1. Next starts a link where the two parts of the section number, \3 and \4, are separated by an underscore (_) and have the string SEC- before them. Finally, the link text replays the section number again—this time with a decimal point between its parts. Note that although a dot (.) is special in the search pattern and has to be quoted with a backslash there, it's not special on the replacement side and can be typed literally. Here's the script run on a short test document, using *checked* (34.4):

```
% checksed testdoc
********** < = testdoc     > = sed output **********
8c8
< See Section 1.2 for details.
---
> See <a href="#SEC-1_2">Section 1.2</a> for details.
19c19
< Be sure to see Section 23.16!
---
> Be sure to see <a href="#SEC-23_16">Section 23.16</a>!
```

We can use a similar technique to match parts of a line and swap them. For instance, let's say there are two parts of a line separated by a colon. We can match each part, putting them within escaped parentheses and swapping them in the replacement:

```
% cat test1
first:second
one:two
% sed 's/\(.*\):\(.*\)/\2:\1/' test1
second:first
two:one
```

The larger point is that you can recall a saved substring in any order and multiple times. If you find that you need more than nine saved matches, or would like to be able to group them into matches and submatches, take a look at Perl.

Articles 43.10, 31.10, 10.9, and 36.23 have examples.

—DD and JP

34.12 Search and Replacement: One Match Among Many

One of the more unusual options of *sed*'s substitution command is the numeric flag that allows you to point to one particular match when there are many possible matches on a particular line. It is used where a pattern repeats itself on a line and the replacement must be made for only one of those occurrences by position. For instance, a line, perhaps containing *tbl* input, might contain multiple tab characters. Let's say that there are three tabs per line, and you'd like to replace the second tab with >. The following substitute command would do it:

```
s/TAB/>/2
```

TAB represents an actual tab character, which is otherwise invisible on the screen. If the input is a one-line file such as the following:

```
Column1TABColumn2TABColumn3TABColumn4
```

the output produced by running the script on this file will be:

```
Column1TABColumn2>Column3TABColumn4
```

Note that without the numeric flag, the substitute command would replace only the first tab. (Therefore, 1 can be considered the default numeric flag.) The range of the allowed numeric value is from 1 to 512, though this may be implementation-dependent.

—DD

34.13 Transformations on Text

The transform command (*y*) is useful for exchanging lowercase letters for uppercase letters on a line. Effectively, it performs a similar function to *tr* (21.11). It replaces any character found in the first string with the equivalent character in the second string. The command:

```
y/abcdefghijklmnopqrstuvwxyz/ABCDEFGHIJKLMNOPQRSTUVWXYZ/
```

will convert any lowercase letter into the corresponding uppercase letter. The following:

```
y/abcdefghijklmnopqrstuvwxyz/nopqrstuvwxyzabcdefghijklm/
```

would perform a *rot13* transformation—a simple form of encryption in which each alphabetic character is replaced by the character halfway through the alphabet. (*rot13* encryption is sometimes used to keep offensive (or comical) news postings (1.21) from being read except by someone who really means to (such as if you have read the joke and now want to read the punch line). Encryption and decryption are automatically supported by most news readers, but it's fun to see how simple the encryption is. By the way, the command above handles only lowercase letters; if we'd shown uppercase as well, the command would have run past the margins!)

—TOR

34.14 Hold Space: The Set-Aside Buffer

The *pattern space* is a buffer that contains the current input line. There is also a set-aside buffer called the *hold space*. The contents of the pattern space can be copied to the hold space, and the contents of the hold space can be copied to the pattern space. A group of commands allows you to move data between the hold space and the pattern space. The hold space is used for temporary storage, and that's it. Individual commands can't address the hold space or alter its contents.

The most frequent use of the hold space is to have it retain a duplicate of the current input line while you change the original in the pattern space. [It's also used as a way to do the "move" and "copy" commands that most editors have—but which *sed* can't do directly because it's designed for editing a stream of input text line-by-line. —GU] The commands that affect the hold space are:

Hold	*h*	Copy contents of pattern space to hold space, replacing previous.
	H	Append newline, then append contents of pattern space, to hold space.
Get	*g*	Copy contents of hold space to pattern space, replacing previous.
	G	Append newline, then append contents of hold space, to pattern space.
Exchange	x	Swap contents of hold space and pattern space.

Each of these commands can take an address that specifies a single line or a range of lines. The hold commands (*h*, *H*) move data into the hold space and the get commands (*g*, *G*) move data from the hold space back into the pattern space. The difference between the lowercase and uppercase versions of the same command is that the lowercase command overwrites the contents of the target buffer, while the uppercase command appends to the existing contents after adding a newline.

The hold command replaces the contents of the hold space with the contents of the pattern space. The get command replaces the contents of the pattern space with the contents of the hold space. The Hold command puts a newline followed by the contents of the pattern space after the contents of the hold space. (The newline is appended to the hold space even if the hold space is empty.) The Get command puts a newline followed by the contents of the hold space after the contents of the pattern space.

The exchange command (*x*) swaps the contents of the two buffers. It has no side effects on either buffer.

Here's an example to illustrate putting lines into the hold space and retrieving them later. We are going to write a script that reads a particular HTML file and copies all headings to the end of the file for a summary. The headings we want start with <h1> or <h2>. For example:

```
...
<body>
<h1>Introduction</h1>
The blah blah blah
<h1>Background of the Project</h1>
    ...
<h2>The First Year</h2>
    ...
<h2>The Second Year</h2>
    ...
</body>
```

The object is to copy those headings into the hold space as *sed* reads them. When *sed* reaches the end of the body (at the </body> tag), output Summary:, then output the saved tags without the heading tags (<h1> or <h2>).

Look at the script:

```
/^<h[12]>/H
/^<\/body>/ {
        i\
<strong>Summary:</strong>
        x
        G
        s/<\/*h[12]>//g
}
```

Any line matching <h1> or <h2> is added to the hold space. (All those lines are also printed; that's the default in *sed* unless lines have been deleted.*) The last part of the script watches for the </body> tag. When it's reached, *sed* inserts the Summary: heading. Then the script uses x to exchange the pattern space (which has the </body> tag) with the saved headers from the hold space. Now the pattern space has the saved headers. Next, G adds the </body> tag to the end of the headers in the pattern space. Finally, a substitute command strips the <h1>, </h1>, <h2>, and </h2> tags. At the end of the script, the pattern space is printed by default.

The sequence of x followed by G is a way to find a matching line—in this case, </body>—and insert the contents of the hold space before the matched line. In other words, it's like an *i* command that inserts the hold space at the current line.

The script could do more cleanup and formatting. For instance, it could make the saved headings into a list with <ul> and <li>. But this example is mostly about the hold space.

Here's the result of running the script on the sample file:

```
% sed -f sedscr report.html
    ...
<body>
<h1>Introduction</h1>
The blah blah blah
<h1>Background of the Project</h1>
    ...
<h2>The First Year</h2>
    ...
<h2>The Second Year</h2>
    ...
<strong>Summary:</strong>

Introduction
Background of the Project
The First Year
The Second Year
</body>
```

---

* Note that this can lead to confusion when the same line is matched by several patterns and then printed, once per match!

For other scripts that use the hold space, see article 34.18. For a fanciful analogy that makes clear how it works, see article 34.17.

—*DD and JP*

34.15 Transforming Part of a Line

The transform command, *y* (34.13), acts on the entire contents of the pattern space. It is something of a chore to do a letter-by-letter transformation of a portion of the line, but it is possible (though convoluted) as the following example demonstrates. [The real importance of this example is probably not the use of the *y* command, but the use of the hold space to isolate and preserve part of the line. —*TOR*]

While working on a programming guide, we found that the names of statements were entered inconsistently. They needed to be uppercase, but some were lowercase while others had an initial capital letter. While the task was simple—to capitalize the name of the statement—there were nearly a hundred statements and it seemed a tedious project to write that many explicit substitutions of the form:

```
s/find the Match statement/find the MATCH statement/g
```

The transform command could do the lowercase-to-uppercase conversion, but it applies the conversion to the entire line. The hold space makes this task possible because we use it to store a copy of the input line while we isolate and convert the statement name in the pattern space. Look at the script first:

```
# capitalize statement names
/the .* statement/{
    h
    s/.*the \(.*\) statement.*/\1/
    y/abcdefghijklmnopqrstuvwxyz/ABCDEFGHIJKLMNOPQRSTUVWXYZ/
    G
    s/\(.*\)\n\(.*the \).*\( statement.*\)/\2\1\3/
}
```

The address limits the procedure to lines that match the `.* statement`. Let's look at what each command does:

`h`

The hold command copies the current input line into the hold space. Using the sample line `find the Match statement`, we'll show what the contents of the pattern space and hold space contain. After the *h* command, the pattern space and hold space are identical.

Pattern space	`find the Match statement`
Hold space	`find the Match statement`

```
s/.*the \(.*\) statement.*/\1/
```

The substitute command extracts the name of the statement from the line and replaces the entire line with it.

Pattern space	Match
Hold space	find the Match statement

```
y/abcdefghijklmnopqrstuvwxyz/ABCDEFGHIJKLMNOPQRSTUVWXYZ/
```

The transform command changes each lowercase letter to an uppercase letter.

Pattern space	MATCH
Hold space	find the Match statement

```
G
```

The Get command appends the line saved in the hold space to the pattern space. The embedded newline from the Get command is shown as \n.

Pattern space	MATCH\nfind the Match statement
Hold space	find the Match statement

```
s/\(.*\)\n\(.*the \).*\( statement.*\)/\2\1\3/
```

The substitute command matches three different parts of the pattern space: (1) all characters up to the embedded newline, (2) all characters following the embedded newline and up to and including the followed by a space, and (3) all characters beginning with a space and followed by statement up to the end of the pattern space. The name of the statement as it appeared in the original line is matched but not saved. The replacement section of this command recalls the saved portions and reassembles them in a different order, putting the capitalized name of the command in between the and statement.

Pattern space	find the MATCH statement
Hold space	find the Match statement

Let's look at a test run. Here's our sample file:

```
find the Match statement
Consult the Get statement.
using the Read statement to retrieve data
```

Running the script on the sample file produces:

```
find the MATCH statement
Consult the GET statement.
using the READ statement to retrieve data
```

As you can see from this script, the hold space can be skillfully used to isolate and manipulate portions of the input line.

—DD

34.16 Making Edits Across Line Boundaries

Most programs that use regular expressions (32.4) are able to match a pattern only on a single line of input. This makes it difficult to find or change a phrase, for instance, because it can start near the end of one line and finish near the beginning of the next line. Other patterns might be significant only when repeated on multiple lines.

sed has the ability to load more than one line into the pattern space. This allows you to match (and change) patterns that extend over multiple lines. In this article, we show how to create a multiline pattern space and manipulate its contents.

The multiline Next command, N, creates a multiline pattern space by reading a new line of input and appending it to the contents of the pattern space. The original contents of the pattern space and the new input line are separated by a newline. The embedded newline character can be matched in patterns by the escape sequence \n. In a multiline pattern space, only the metacharacter ^ matches the newline at the beginning of the pattern space, and $ matches the newline at the end. After the Next command is executed, control is then passed to subsequent commands in the script.

The Next command differs from the next command, n, which outputs the contents of the pattern space and then reads a new line of input. The next command does not create a multiline pattern space.

For our first example, let's suppose that we wanted to change "Owner and Operator Guide" to "Installation Guide", but we found that it appears in the file on two lines, splitting between Operator and Guide. For instance, here are a few lines of sample text:

```
Consult Section 3.1 in the Owner and Operator
Guide for a description of the tape drives
available on your system.
```

The following script looks for Operator at the end of a line, reads the next line of input, and then makes the replacement:

```
/Operator$/{
    N
    s/Owner and Operator\nGuide/Installation Guide/
}
```

In this example, we know where the two lines split and where to specify the embedded newline. When the script is run on the sample file, it produces the two lines of output, one of which combines the first and second lines and is too long to show here. This happens because the substitute command matches the embedded newline but does not replace it. Unfortunately, you cannot use \n to insert a newline in the replacement string. You must either use the backslash to escape the newline, as follows:

```
s/Owner and Operator\nGuide /Installation Guide\
/
```

or use the \(..\) operators (34.11) to keep the newline:

```
s/Owner and Operator\(\n\)Guide /Installation Guide\1/
```

This command restores the newline after Installation Guide. It is also necessary to match a blank space following Guide so the new line won't begin with a space. Now we can show the output:

```
Consult Section 3.1 in the Installation Guide
for a description of the tape drives
available on your system.
```

Remember, you don't have to replace the newline, but if you don't, it can make for some long lines.

What if there are other occurrences of "Owner and Operator Guide" that break over multiple lines in different places? You could change the address to match Owner, the first word in the pattern instead of the last, and then modify the regular expression to look for a space or a newline between words, as shown below:

```
/Owner/{
N
s/Owner *\n*and *\n*Operator *\n*Guide/Installation Guide/
}
```

The asterisk (*) indicates that the space or newline is optional. This seems like hard work though, and indeed there is a more general way. We can read the newline into the pattern space and then use a substitute command to remove the embedded newline, wherever it is:

```
s/Owner and Operator Guide/Installation Guide/
/Owner/{
N
s/ *\n/ /
s/Owner and Operator Guide */Installation Guide\
/
}
```

The first line of the script matches Owner and Operator Guide when it appears on a line by itself. (See the discussion at the end of the article about why this is necessary.) If we match the string Owner, we read the next line into the pattern space and replace the embedded newline with a space. Then we attempt to match the whole pattern and make the replacement followed by a newline. This script will match `Owner` and `Operator Guide` regardless of how it is broken across two lines. Here's our expanded test file:

```
Consult Section 3.1 in the Owner and Operator
Guide for a description of the tape drives
available on your system.

Look in the Owner and Operator Guide shipped with your system.

Two manuals are provided, including the Owner and
Operator Guide and the User Guide.

The Owner and Operator Guide is shipped with your system.
```

Running the above script on the sample file produces the following result:

```
% sed -f sedscr sample
Consult Section 3.1 in the Installation Guide
for a description of the tape drives
available on your system.

Look in the Installation Guide shipped with your system.

Two manuals are provided, including the Installation Guide
and the User Guide.

The Installation Guide is shipped with your system.
```

In this sample script, it might seem redundant to have two substitute commands that match the pattern. The first command matches it when the pattern is found already on one line, and the second matches the pattern after two lines have been read into the pattern space. Why the first command is necessary is perhaps best demonstrated by removing that command from the script and running it on the sample file:

```
% sed -f sedscr2 sample
Consult Section 3.1 in the Installation Guide
for a description of the tape drives
available on your system.

Look in the Installation Guide
shipped with your system.
Two manuals are provided, including the Installation Guide
and the User Guide.
```

Do you see the two problems? The most obvious problem is that the last line did not print. The last line matches `Owner`, and when *N* is executed, there is not another input line to read, so *sed* quits. It does not even output the line. If this is the normal behavior, the Next command should be used as follows to be safe:

```
$!N
```

It excludes the last line ($) from the Next command. As it is in our script, by matching Owner and Operator Guide on the last line, we avoid matching Owner and applying the N command. However, if the word Owner appeared on the last line, we'd have the same problem unless we implement the $!N syntax.

The second problem is a little less conspicuous. It has to do with the occurrence of Owner and Operator Guide in the second paragraph. In the input file, it is found on a line by itself:

    Look in the Owner and Operator Guide shipped with your system.

In the output shown above, the blank line following shipped with your system is missing. The reason for this is that this line matches Owner and the next line, a blank line, is appended to the pattern space. The substitute command removes the embedded newline, and the blank line has in effect vanished. (If the line were not blank, the newline would still be removed but the text would appear on the same line with shipped with your system.) The best solution seems to be to avoid reading the next line when the pattern can be matched on one line. That is why the first instruction attempts to match the case where the string appears all on one line.

—DD

34.17 The Deliberate Scrivener

The operations of *sed*'s most difficult commands—hold (*h* or *H*), get (*g* or *G*), and exchange (*x*)—can be explained, somewhat fancifully, in terms of an extremely deliberate medieval scrivener or amanuensis toiling to make a copy of a manuscript. His work is bound by several spatial restrictions: the original manuscript is displayed in one room; the set of instructions for copying the manuscript are stored in a middle room; and the quill, ink, and folio are set up in yet another room. The original manuscript and the set of instructions are written in stone and cannot be moved about. The dutiful scrivener, being sounder of body than mind, is able to make a copy by going from room to room, working on only one line at a time. Entering the room where the original manuscript is, he removes from his robes a scrap of paper to take down the first line of the manuscript. Then he moves to the room containing the list of editing instructions. He reads each instruction to see if it applies to the single line he has scribbled down.

Each instruction, written in special notation, consists of two parts: a *pattern* and a *procedure*. The scrivener reads the first instruction and checks the pattern against his line. If there is no match, he doesn't have to worry about the procedure, so he goes to the next instruction. If he finds a match, the scrivener follows the action or actions specified in the procedure.

He makes the edit on his piece of paper before trying to match the pattern in the next instruction. Remember, the scrivener has to read through a series of instructions, and he reads all of them, not just the first instruction that matches the pattern. Because he makes his edits as he goes, he is always trying to match the latest version against the next pattern; he doesn't remember the original line.

When he gets to the bottom of the list of instructions, and has made any edits that were necessary on his piece of paper, he goes into the next room to copy out the line. (He doesn't need to be told to print out the line.) After that is done, he returns to the first room and takes down the next line on a new scrap of paper. When he goes to the second room, once again he reads every instruction from first to last before leaving.

This is what he normally does, that is, unless he is told otherwise. For instance, before he starts, he can be told *not* to write out every line (the *–n* option). In this case, he must wait for an instruction that tells him to print (*p*). If he does not get that instruction, he throws away his piece of paper and starts over. By the way, regardless of whether or not he is told to write out the line, he always gets to the last instruction on the list.

Let's look at other kinds of instructions the scrivener has to interpret. First of all, an instruction can have zero, one, or two patterns specified:

- If no pattern is specified, the same procedure is followed for each line.
- If there is only one pattern, he will follow the procedure for any line matching the pattern.
- If a pattern is followed by a !, the procedure is followed for all lines that do *not* match the pattern.
- If two patterns are specified, the actions described in the procedure are performed on the first matching line and all succeeding lines until a line matches the second pattern.

The scrivener can work on only one line at a time, so you might wonder how he handles a range of lines. Each time he goes through the instructions, he tries to match only the first of two patterns. Now, after he has found a line that matches the first pattern, each time through with a new line he tries to match the second pattern. He interprets the second pattern as *pattern*!, so that the procedure is followed only if there is no match. When the second pattern is matched, he starts looking again for the first pattern.

Each procedure contains one or more commands or *actions*. Remember, if a pattern is specified with a procedure, the pattern must be matched before the procedure is executed. We have already shown many of the usual commands that are similar to other editing commands. However, there are several highly unusual commands.

For instance, the N command tells the scrivener to go, right now, and get another line, adding it to the same piece of paper. The scrivener can be instructed to "hold" on to a single piece of scrap paper. The h command tells him to make a copy of the line on another piece of paper and put it in his pocket. The x command tells him to exchange the extra piece of paper in his pocket with the one in his hand. The g command tells him to throw out the paper in his hand and replace it with the one in his pocket. The G command tells him to append the line he is holding to the paper in front of him. If he encounters a d command, he throws out the scrap of paper and begins again at the top of the list of instructions. A D command has effect when he has been instructed to append two lines on his piece of paper. The D command tells him to delete the first of those lines.

If you want the analogy converted back to computers, the first and last rooms in this medieval manor are standard input and standard output. Thus, the original file is never changed. The line on the scrivener's piece of scrap paper is in the *pattern space*; the line on the piece of paper that he holds in his pocket is in the *hold space*. The hold space allows you to retain a duplicate of a line while you change the original in the pattern space.

Article 34.18 shows a practical application of the scrivener's work, a *sed* program that searches for a particular phrase that might be split across two lines.

—DD

34.18 Searching for Patterns Split Across Lines

[Article 13.9 introduced a script called *cgrep*, a general-purpose, *grep*-like program built with *sed*. It allows you to look for one or more words that appear on one line or across several lines. This article explains the *sed* tricks that are necessary to do this kind of thing. It gets into territory that is essential for any advanced applications of this obscure yet wonderful editor. Articles 34.14 through 34.17 have background information.—JP]

Let's review the two examples from article 13.9. The first command below finds all lines containing the word *system* in the file *main.c* and shows 10 additional lines of context above and below each match. The second command finds all occurrences of the word "awk" where it is followed by the word "perl" somewhere within the next 3 lines:

```
cgrep -10 system main.c
cgrep -3 "awk.*perl"
```

Now the script, followed by an explanation of how it works:

```
#!/bin/sh
#  cgrep - multiline context grep using sed
#  Usage: cgrep [-context] pattern [file...]

n=3
case $1 in -[1-9]*)
    n=`expr 1 - "$1"`
    shift
esac
re=${1?}; shift

sed -n "
    1b start
    : top
    \~$re~{
        h; n; p; H; g
        b endif
    }
    N
    : start
    //{ =; p; }
    : endif
    $n,\$D
    b top
" "$@"
```

case **35.11**
expr **36.21**
shift **35.22**
${?} **36.7**
\~..~ **34.8**
"$@" **35.20**

The *sed* script is embedded in a bare-bones shell wrapper (35.19) to parse out the initial arguments because, unlike *awk* and *perl*, *sed* cannot directly access command-line parameters. If the first argument looks like a *–context* option, variable *n* is reset to one more than the number of lines specified, using a little trick—the argument is treated as a negative number and subtracted from 1. The pattern argument is then stored in $re, with the ${1?} syntax causing the shell to abort with an error message if no pattern was given. Any remaining arguments are passed as filenames to the *sed* command.

So that the $re and $n parameters can be embedded, the *sed* script is enclosed in double quotes (27.12). We use the *–n* option because we don't want to print out every line by default, and because we need to use the n command in the script without its side effect of outputting a line.

The *sed* script itself looks rather unstructured (it was actually designed using a flowchart), but the basic algorithm is easy enough to understand. We keep a "window" of *n* lines in the pattern space and scroll this window through the input stream. If an occurrence of the pattern comes into the window, the entire window is printed (providing *n* lines of previous context), and each subsequent line is printed until the pattern scrolls out of view again (providing *n* lines of following context). The *sed* idiom N;D is used to advance the window, with the D not kicking in until the first *n* lines of input have been accumulated.

The core of the script is basically an if-then-else construct that decides whether we are currently "in context." (The regular expression here is delimited by tilde (~) characters because tildes are less likely to occur in the user-supplied pattern than slashes.) **If** we are still in context, **then** the next line of input is read and output, temporarily using the hold space to save the window (and effectively doing an N in the process). **Else** we append the next input line (N) and search for the pattern again (an empty regular expression means to reuse the last pattern). If it's now found, the pattern must have just come into view—so we print the current line number followed by the contents of the window. Subsequent iterations will take the "then" branch until the pattern scrolls out of the window.

—*GU*

34.19 Multiline Delete

The *sed* delete command, *d*, deletes the contents of the pattern space (34.14) and causes a new line of input to be read, with editing resuming at the top of the script. The Delete command, *D*, works slightly differently: it deletes a portion of the pattern space, up to the first embedded newline. It does not cause a new line of input to be read; instead, it returns to the top of the script, applying these instructions to what remains in the pattern space. We can see the difference by writing a script that looks for a series of blank lines and outputs a single blank line. The version below uses the delete command:

```
# reduce multiple blank lines to one; version using d command
/^$/{
    N
    /^\n$/d
}
```

When a blank line is encountered, the next line is appended to the pattern space. Then we try to match the embedded newline. Note that the positional metacharacters, ^ and $, match the beginning and the end of the pattern space, respectively. Here's a test file:

```
This line is followed by 1 blank line.

This line is followed by 2 blank lines.


This line is followed by 3 blank lines.



This line is followed by 4 blank lines.




This is the end.
```

Running the script on the test file produces the following result:

```
% sed -f sed.blank test.blank
This line is followed by 1 blank line.

This line is followed by 2 blank lines.
This line is followed by 3 blank lines.

This line is followed by 4 blank lines.
This is the end.
```

Where there was an even number of blank lines, all the blank lines were removed. Only when there was an odd number of blank lines was a single blank line preserved. That is because the delete command clears the entire pattern space. Once the first blank line is encountered, the next line is read in, and both are deleted. If a third blank line is encountered, and the next line is not blank, the delete command is not applied, and thus a blank line is output. If we use the multiline Delete command, /^\n$/D, we get a different result, and the one that we wanted.

The reason the multiline Delete command gets the job done is that when we encounter two blank lines, the Delete command removes only the first of the two. The next time through the script, the blank line will cause another line to be read into the pattern space. If that line is not blank, both lines are output, thus ensuring that a single blank line will be output. In other words, when there are two blank lines in the pattern space, only the first is deleted. When a blank line is followed by text, the pattern space is output normally.

—*DD*

34.20 Making Edits Everywhere Except...

There are two ways in *sed* to avoid specified portions of a document while making the edits everywhere else. You can use the *!* command to specify that the edit applies only to lines that *do not* match the pattern. Another approach is to use the *b* (branch) command to skip over portions of the editing script. Let's look at an example.

We've used *sed* to preprocess the input to *troff* so that double dashes (--) are converted automatically to em-dashes (—) and straight quotes ("") are converted to curly quotes (""). However, program examples in technical books are usually shown in a constant-width font that clearly shows each character as it appears on the computer screen. When typesetting a document, we don't want *sed* to apply the same editing rules within these examples as it does to the rest of the document. For instance, straight quotes should not be replaced by curly quotes.

Because program examples are set off by a pair of macros (something like .ES and .EE, for "Example Start" and "Example End"), we can use those as the basis for exclusion. Here's some sample text that includes an example:

```
.LP
The \fItrue\fP command returns a zero exit status.
As Joe says, "this is only useful in programming":
.ES
% \fBtrue\fP
% \fBecho "the status was $status"\fP
the status was 0
.EE
```

So you can say:

```
/^\.ES/,/^\.EE/!{
    s/^"/``/
        ...
    s/\\(em"/\\(em``/g
}
```

All of the commands enclosed in braces ({}) will be subject to the initial pattern address.

There is another way to accomplish the same thing. The *b* command allows you to transfer control to another line in the script that is marked with an optional label. Using this feature, you could write the previous script like this:

```
/^\.ES/,/^\.EE/bend
s/^"/``/
    ...
s/\\(em"/\\(em``/g
:end
```

A label consists of a colon (:) followed by up to seven characters. If the label is missing, the *b* command branches to the end of the script. (In the example above, the label end was included just to show how to use one, but a label is not really necessary here.)

The *b* command is designed for flow control within the script. It allows you to create subscripts that will be applied only to lines matching certain patterns and not elsewhere. However, as in this case, it also provides a powerful way to exempt part of the text from the action of a single-level script.

The advantage of *b* over *!* for this application is that you can more easily specify multiple conditions to avoid. The *!* command can be applied to a single command or to the set of commands, enclosed in braces, that immediately follows. On the other hand, *b* gives you almost unlimited control over movement around the script.

—*TOR*

34.21 The sed Test Command

The test command, *t*, branches to a label (or the end of the script) if a successful substitution has been made on the currently addressed line. It implies a conditional branch. Its syntax is as follows:

> [*address*]t[*label*]

If no *label* is supplied, control falls through to the end of the script. If *label* is supplied, execution resumes at the line following the label.

Let's look at a spelling corrector written by Greg Ubben. The script fixes common (in this example, silly) spelling goofs; the *t* command tells about corrections that were made:

```
h
s/seperate/separate/g
s/compooter/computer/g
s/said editor/sed editor/g
s/lable/label/g
t changed
b
: changed
p
g
s/.*/[WAS: &]/
t
```

First, h (34.14) holds a copy of the current input line. Then, if any of the four substitutions succeed, the command t changed branches to the corresponding label (: changed) at the end of the script. Otherwise, if no s succeeded, the b command restarts the script on the next line (as always in *sed*, the input line is printed before the script restarts).

After the label, the script prints the current input line (the line with a spelling error—which, by now, has been corrected). Then g (34.14) gets the original uncorrected line. An s command brackets that line [WAS: *xxx*]. Here's some sample output:

```
$ sed -f sedscr afile
This is a separate test.
[WAS: This is a seperate test.]
I put a label on my computer!
[WAS: I put a lable on my compooter!]
That's all for now.
```

The final t in the script is a work-around for a bug in some versions of *sed*. Greg says, "The *t* flag is supposed to be reset after either the *t* command is executed or a new line of input is read, but some versions of *sed* don't reset it on a new line of input. So I added a do-nothing t to make sure it's reset after the previous always-true s///." Try the script without the extra t; if adding it makes the script work right, your *sed* has the bug and you might try a new version, like GNU *sed*.

—JP and DD

34.22 Uses of the sed Quit Command

The quit command, *q*, causes *sed* to stop reading new input lines (and stop sending them to the output). Its syntax is:

   [*line-address*]q

34.23

It can take only a single-line address. Once the line matching address (*line-address*) is reached, the script will be terminated.

For instance, the following one-liner uses the quit command to print the first ten lines from a file:

```
% sed '10q' myfile
   ...
```

sed prints each line until it gets to line 10 and quits.

The previous version is much more efficient than its functional equivalent:

−n 34.3
```
% sed -n '1,10p' myfile
```

(especially if *myfile* is a long file) because *sed* doesn't need to keep reading its input once the patterns in the script are satisfied.

One possible use of *q* is to quit a script after you've extracted what you want from a file. There is some inefficiency in continuing to scan through a large file after *sed* has found what it is looking for.

—TOR

34.23 Dangers of the sed Quit Command

The *sed* quit command, *q* (34.22), is very useful for getting *sed* to stop processing any more input once you've done what you want.

However, you need to be very careful not to use *q* in any *sed* script that writes its edits back to the original file. After *q* is executed, no further output is produced. It should not be used in any case where you want to edit the front of the file and pass the remainder through unchanged. Using *q* in this case is a dangerous beginner's mistake.

—TOR

34.24 sed Newlines, Quoting, and Backslashes in a Shell Script

Feeding *sed* (34.1) newlines is easy; the real trick is getting them past the C shell and its derivatives (*tcsh* has the same problem, on the systems where we've tested it).

The *sed* documentation says that in order to insert newlines in substitute commands, you should quote them with backslashes. [Surround the commands with single quotes ('), as Chris has. If you use double quotes ("), this script will become s/foo/bar/ because of the way quoting works with backslashes and newlines (27.12). —*JP*]:

```
sed -e 's/foo/b\
a\
r/'
```

Indeed, this works quite well in the Bourne shell and derivatives, such as *bash*, which do what I consider the proper thing (27.12) with this input. The C shell, however, thinks it is smarter than you are and *removes* the trailing backslashes (27.13), and instead you must type:

```
sed -e 's/foo/b\\
a\\
r/'
```

Probably the best solution is to place your *sed* commands in a separate file (34.3) to keep the shell's sticky fingers off them.

—*CT*

35

Shell Programming for the Uninitiated

35.1 Writing a Simple Shell Program

A shell script need be no more than a command line saved in a file. For example, let's assume that you'd like a compact list of all the users who are currently logged in on the system.

A command like this might do the trick:

```
% who | cut -c1-8 | sort -u | pr -l1 -8 -w78 -t
```

A list of logged-in users should come out in columns, looking something like this:

```
abraham  appleton biscuit charlie  charlott fizzie   howard   howie
hstern   jerry    kosmo   linda    ocshner  peterson root     ross
sutton   yuppie
```

We used four Unix commands joined with pipes:

1. who (2.8) gives a list of all users.

2. cut -c1-8 (21.14) outputs columns 1-8 of the *who* output—the usernames.

3. sort -u (22.6) puts names in order and takes out names of users who are logged on more than once.

4. pr -l1 -8 -w78 -t (21.15, 45.6) takes the list of usernames, one per line, and makes it into 8 columns on 78-character-wide lines. (The -l1 is the lower-case letter *L* followed by the digit *1*.)

If you wanted to do this frequently, wouldn't it be better if all you had to do was type something like:

```
% loggedin
```

to get the same result? Here's how:

1. Start a text editor on a new file named *loggedin*.

2. If your system supports the special #! notation (36.2) (and it probably does), the first line of the script file should be:

```
#!/bin/sh
```

Otherwise, leave the first line blank. (When the first line of a script is blank, most shells will start a Bourne shell to read it. Article 36.2 has more information.)

I think that the second line of a shell script should always be a comment to explain what the script does. (Use more than one line, if you want.) A comment starts with a hash mark (#); all characters after it on the line are ignored. Oh, and try to make sure there's a bit of whitespace between the comment character and the actual comment; that's a pet peeve of mine:

```
# loggedin - list logged-in users, once per user, in 8 columns
```

Put this on the third line, just like you did on the command line:

```
who | cut -c1-8 | sort -u | pr -l1 -8 -w78 -t
```

3. Save the file and leave the editor. You've just written a shell script.

4. Next, you need to make the shell script executable. The *chmod* (50.5) (change mode) command is used to change permissions on a file. The plus sign followed by an x (+x) makes the file executable:

```
% chmod +x loggedin
```

5. If your login shell (3.4) is *csh* or *tcsh*, you'll need to reset its command search table. To do that, type:

rehash **27.6**

```
% rehash
```

6. Finally, try the script. Just type its name and it should run:

```
% loggedin
```

If that doesn't run, your current directory may not be in your shell's command search path (35.6, 35.7). In that case, try this:

```
% ./loggedin
```

If it still doesn't work, and you started the first line of your script with #!, be sure that the Bourne shell's pathname on that line (like /bin/sh) is correct. Another common error is to swap the # and !, so check that, too. You should get an error like this, if that is the problem, although the script may itself run as well, depending on your system:

```
!#/bin/sh: No such file or directory
```

7. If you want to run the script from somewhere other than the current directory, or if you want other programs and scripts you write to be able to use it, you need to put it in a directory that's in your search path and/or change your search path (27.6). If you're the only person who plans to use the script, you should put it in your personal *bin* directory (7.4). Otherwise, you might ask your system administrator if there's a systemwide directory for local commands.

—*JP*

35.2 Everyone Should Learn Some Shell Programming

One of the great things about Unix is that it's made up of individual utilities, "building blocks" like *cat* and *grep*, that you run from a shell prompt. Using pipes, redirection, filters, and so on, you can combine those utilities to do an incredible number of things. Shell programming lets you take the same commands you'd type at a shell prompt and put them into a file you can run by just typing its name. You can make new programs that combine Unix programs (and other shell scripts) in your own way to do exactly what you need. If you don't like the way a program works, you can write a shell script to do just what you want.

Because many Unix users use the shell every day, they don't need to learn a whole new language for programming, just some tips and techniques. In fact, this chapter covers a lot of programming techniques that you'll want to use even when you aren't programming. For example, loops and tests are handy on the command line.

(This series of articles does assume that you've written programs in some language before or are generally familiar with programming concepts. If you haven't and aren't, you might start with a more comprehensive shell programming book.)

Unix has plenty of other scripting languages—Perl, Python, and Tcl/Tk are some of the best known. So when should you write a script with the shell and when shouldn't you? That's a personal choice; as you learn more languages and their strengths and weaknesses, you're better able to choose the best one for a situation. My rule of thumb is something like this. I write a shell script if:

- It's a script I developed at the command line, so it's easy to just drop those same commands into a file.

- I know some Unix utility that'll do just what I want.

- It has to be portable to a system that might not have another scripting language I'd rather use.

- The (possibly) slower speed of forking processes to run Unix utilities (especially in loops) doesn't matter.

- The script simply has to make a few decisions—like whether standard input is a *tty* (2.7), checking options and arguments, or something else simple)—before the script ends by running some Unix utility.

- It just feels natural to write a shell script, for whatever reason.

On the other hand, maybe your script needs lots of pipes (|) (1.5) or temporary files, or you have out-of-band data that you have to keep passing in to each Unix utility (maybe because you can't shoehorn multiple types of data into a single chain of pipelines between utilities). In that case, you'll be happier with a scripting language that doesn't depend on Unix utilities and pipes.

Some of the topics you need to learn about as a beginning shell programmer have already been covered in other chapters. Here are the articles you'll probably want to read, in an order that makes sense if you're looking for something of a tutorial:

- To see how to write a simple shell program, article 35.1. To embed scripts from other languages such as *sed* and *awk* in a shell script, article 35.19.

- For explanation of shells in general, article 27.3.

- To read about environment and shell variables, articles 35.3 and 35.9, respectively.

- Shell quoting is explained in article 27.12.

- Stepping through arguments or any list of words with a *for* loop is discussed in article 28.9 (as well as in article 35.21, later in this chapter).

Then, once you've had your refresher, come on back and read the following articles:

- Test strings with a *case* statement, article 35.10. Match patterns in a *case* statement, article 35.11.

- Use the output of one command as arguments to another command with command substitution, article 28.14.

- Find out whether a program worked or failed with its exit status, article 35.12.

- Loop through a set of commands and use another command to control that loop, article 35.15.

- Set exit status of a shell (shell script), article 35.16.

- Handle interrupts (like CTRL-c) and other signals, article 35.17.

- Read input from the keyboard, article 35.18.

- Handle command-line arguments (options, filenames, etc.), article 35.20.

- Test a program's exit status and do different things if it worked or failed, articles 35.13 and 35.14.
- Handle arguments with the *while* and *shift* commands, article 35.22.
- Handle command-line arguments in a more standard and portable way with *getopt*, article 35.24.
- Set shell options and command-line arguments with the *set* command, article 35.25.
- Test files and strings of characters with the *test* command, article 35.26.
- Pick a name for a new command with no conflict, article 35.27.
- Find the name of a program and use it in the script, article 35.28.
- Use "subprograms" that can change the current environment, article 35.29.

This chapter discusses only Bourne shell programming. We don't cover many features from more advanced Bourne-type shells, like *bash* and *zsh*, because those can make your shell scripts nonportable; we stick to concepts that should work almost anywhere. Also, in most cases, the C shell isn't great for shell programming.

A note about command versions: unfortunately, the same commands on different versions of Unix can have different options. Some Bourne shells are a little different from others. For instance, some *test* (35.26) commands have a *–x* option to test for an executable file; others don't. Some *echo* commands use a *–n* option to mean "no newline at the end of this string"; others have you put \c at the end of the string. And so on. Where there are differences, these articles generally use the commands in original Berkeley Unix from the 1980s. If a command doesn't seem to work on your system, check its online manual page or the *sh* manual page.

—JP

35.3 What Environment Variables Are Good For

Many Unix utilities, including the shell, need information about you and what you're doing in order to do a reasonable job.

What kinds of information? Well, to start with, a lot of programs (particularly editors) need to know what kind of terminal you're using. The shell needs to know where any commands you want to use are likely to be found. Lots of Unix programs (like mail programs) include a command to start an editor as a subprocess; they like to know your favorite editor. And so on.

Of course, one could always write programs that made you put all this information on the command line. For example, you might have to type commands like:

```
% mail -editor vi -term aardvark48 -favoritecolor blue_no_red
```

But your favorite editor probably doesn't change every day. (Nor will your favorite color.) The terminal you use may change frequently, but it certainly won't change from the time you log in until the time you log out. And you certainly wouldn't want to type something like this whenever you want to send mail.

Rather than forcing you to type this information with every command, Unix uses *environment variables* to store information you'd rather not worry about. For example, the *TERM* (5.2) environment variable tells programs what kind of terminal you're using. Any programs that care about your terminal type know (or ought to know) that they can read this variable, find out your terminal type, and act accordingly.

Similarly, the directories that store the commands you want to execute are listed in the *PATH* (35.6) variable. When you type a command, your shell looks through each directory in your *PATH* variable to find that command. Presumably, Unix wouldn't need a *PATH* variable if all commands were located in the same directory, but you'll soon be writing your own commands (if you aren't already), and storing them in your own "private" command directories (7.4), and you'll need to tell the shell how to find them (27.6).

Environment variables are managed by your shell. The difference between environment variables and regular shell variables (35.9) is that a shell variable is local to a particular instance of the shell (such as a shell script), while environment variables are "inherited" by any program you start, including another shell (24.4). That is, the new process gets its own copy of these variables, which it can read, modify, and pass on in turn to its own children. In fact, every Unix process (not just the shell) passes its environment variables to its child processes.

You can set environment variables with a command like this:

```
% setenv NAME value          C-type shells
$ NAME=value; export NAME     all Bourne-type shells
$ export NAME=value           newer Bourne-type shells
```

There's nothing particularly special about the *NAME*; you can create environment variables with any names you want. Of course, these don't necessarily do anything for you; variables like *PATH* and *TERM* are important because lots of programs have "agreed" (35.5) that these names are important. But if you want to create an environment variable that holds the name of your lover, that's your business:

```
% setenv LOVER Judy
```

If you're so inclined, you could write a program called *valentine* that reads the *LOVER* environment variable and generates an appropriate message. If you like short-term relationships or tend to forget names, this might even be convenient!

By convention, the names of environment variables use all uppercase letters. There's nothing to enforce this convention—if you're making your own names, you can use any capitalization you please. But there's no advantage to violating the convention, either. The environment variables used by standard Unix programs all have uppercase names. Making shell variable names lowercase so it's easy to tell the difference is helpful.

If you want the C shell to forget that an environment variable ever existed, use the command *unsetenv NAME*. The *tcsh* understands filename wildcard (1.13)-type expressions—for instance, unsetenv VAR* would unset all environment variables whose names start with *VAR*. Most Bourne-type shells, but not all, have a similar command, *unset NAME*, but it doesn't understand wildcards like the *tcsh* version. The *bash* version accepts multiple names as arguments, however, and can also unset functions with the *–f* option.

printenv
env

If you want to list all of your environment variables, use *printenv* or *env*. The *printenv* command also lets you ask about a particular variable. Here's a typical report:

```
% printenv EDITOR
EDITOR=/usr/local/bin/emacs
% printenv
HOME=/home/los/mikel
SHELL=/bin/csh
TERM=sun
USER=mikel
PATH=/usr/local/bin:/usr/ucb:/bin:/usr/bin:.:/home/los/mikel/bin
LOGNAME=mikel
PWD=/home/los/mikel/power/articles
PRINTER=ps
EDITOR=/usr/local/bin/emacs
```

The *set* (35.9) command provides a similar listing of shell variables and functions (in newer Bourne-like shells such as *bash*).

You can also use the *echo* command to show the value of a particular variable by preceding the variable name with a dollar sign (which tells the shell to substitute the value of the variable):

```
% echo $TERM
xterm
```

Or—and this is particularly useful when you want a shell or environment variable's value interpolated into a line—you can surround the variable name with curly brackets:

```
% echo ${TERM}
vt100
% echo ${TERM}-like
vt100-like
```

—*ML*

35.4 Parent-Child Relationships

No, this is not about the psychology of computing. It's just a reminder of one important point.

In the environment variable overview (35.3), we said that each process gets its own copy of its parent's environment variables. We chose those words carefully, and if you think about them, you won't make one common mistake.

Sooner or later, almost everyone writes a shell script that gathers some information, sets a few environment variables, and quits. The writer then wonders why there's no trace of the "new" environment variables to be found. The problem is simple. A Unix process (24.3) cannot change its parent's environment; a Unix process gets its *own* copy of the parent's environment, and any changes it makes it keeps to itself. A process can make changes and pass them to its children, but there's no way of going in reverse.

(You can't teach an old dog new tricks.)

[This is important in window systems, too. Environment variables set in one window (more exactly, in one *process*) probably won't affect any process running in any other window. To affect all windows, set the environment variable before you start the window system. For instance, if you log in and then type *startx* from a shell prompt to start X, you can set environment variables from that prompt or from that shell's setup files (3.3). —*JP*]

—*ML*

35.5 Predefined Environment Variables

We've said that environment variables are used to store information that you'd rather not worry about, and that there are a number of standard environment variables that many Unix programs use. These are often called "predefined" environment variables—not because their values are predefined, but because their names and uses are predefined. Here are some important ones:

PATH (35.6)
> contains your command search path (27.6). This is a list of directories in which the shell looks to find commands. It's usually set in one of your shell setup files (3.3).

EDITOR and VISUAL
> can be loaded with the name of your favorite editor. They're usually set in one of your shell setup files. Some programs distinguish between *EDITOR* (usually set to a line editor (20.1) such as *ed*) and *VISUAL* (set to a full-screen editor like *vi*). Many people don't follow that convention; they set both to the same editor. (The Korn shell checks *VISUAL* and *EDITOR*, in that order, to determine your command editing mode (30.14).)

PRINTER (45.4) *or LPDEST*

> can be loaded with the name of your default printer. This is quite useful at a site with many printers—you don't need to tell *lpr* or *lp* (45.2) which printer to use. (*PRINTER* works on systems that print with *lpr*, and *LPDEST* is for *lp*.) This variable is usually set in one of your shell setup files.

PWD

> may contain the absolute pathname of your current directory. It's set automatically by the cd command in some Unix shells. PWD may be fooled by cding through symbolic links.

HOME (31.11) *(called LOGDIR on some systems)*

> contains the absolute pathname of your home directory. It's set automatically when you log in.

SHELL

> contains the absolute pathname of your login shell. It's set automatically whenever you log in.

USER or LOGNAME

> contains your username. It's set automatically when you log in.

TERM

> contains the name of your terminal type in the *termcap* or *terminfo* database. It's usually set in a shell setup file. On Darwin, in the Terminal program, the *TERM_PROGRAM* variable is also set.

TERMCAP

> is an environment variable that can be loaded with the complete *termcap* database entry for the terminal you are using. This may make some programs start up more quickly, but it's not necessary. It's set (under some conditions) by the *tset* command, which is usually run in your shell setup file.

ENV

> contains the name of an initialization file to be executed whenever a new Korn shell is started. (See article 3.3.) Korn shell only.

BASH_ENV

> contains the name of an initialization file to be executed whenever a new *bash* shell is started. (See article 3.3.) *bash* only. Often set to *.bashrc* by default.

PAGER

> can be set to the name of your favorite page-by-page screen display program like *less* (12.3) or *more*. (Programs like *man* (2.1) use *PAGER* to determine which paging program to use if their output is longer than a single screen.)

PS1

> contains the primary prompt (i.e., interactive command prompt) for Bourne-type shells. You also can set it in a particular shell, as a shell variable with

the same name, but it won't be passed to subshells automatically. (The C shell doesn't store the prompt in an environment variable. It uses a shell variable called *prompt* because the *.cshrc* file (3.3) is read to set up each instance of the shell. See article 4.4.)

PS2 (28.12)

contains the secondary prompt (used within compound commands like *while* and *for*) for Bourne shells. Some Bourne-type shells also use *PS3* and *PS4*. As with *PS1*, these don't have to be stored in the environment.

MANPATH (3.21)

if your *man* (2.1) command supports it, is a colon-separated list of directories to search for manual pages.

TZ

contains the time zone. This is the name of a file in the *zoneinfo* directory that provides time zone information for your locality. It is read by commands such as *date*.

DISPLAY

is used by the X Window System (1.22) to identify the display server (keyboard and screen handling program) that will be used for input and output by X applications. It may be set by *ssh* when you log into a remote system, as well.

INPUTRC

lets you choose a setup filename for the Readline library instead of the default *$HOME/.inputrc*.

LS_COLORS (or *LS_COLOURS*)

lists the colors used by the color *ls* command (8.6).

Because Bourne-type shells don't make as strict a distinction between environment variables and shell variables as the C shell does, we've included a few things here that might not be on other people's lists.

But we haven't even tried to include everything. Here are two good ways to see what's there. One is to look at the end of a command's manual page (2.1) in the ENVIRONMENT section (if there is one). Another is to list your current environment variables (with *env* or *printenv* (35.3)) and make some guesses from the names and corresponding values.

We may have implied that environment variables are relatively constant (like your favorite editor). That's not true. For example, in a windowing environment, the current length of your window might be kept in an environment variable. That can change as often as you resize your window. What is true (fortunately) is exactly what we've said: environment variables store information that you'd rather not have to worry about.

—*ML, JP, and SJC*

35.6 The PATH Environment Variable

Of all the environment variables, the *PATH* and *TERM* variables are the most important. The others are often great conveniences, but *PATH* and *TERM* can make your life miserable if they get screwed up.

The *PATH* variable is just a list of directories separated by colon (:) characters. The shell searches through these directories in order whenever it needs to find a command. So, if you want to execute commands in */bin*, */usr/bin*, */usr/local*, the current directory, and your personal *bin* directory, you would put a line like the one below in your *.login* file. An empty entry (: as the first or last character, or :: in the middle) means "the current directory."

$HOME/bin 7.4

```
setenv PATH /bin:/usr/bin:/usr/local::$HOME/bin
```

Article 27.6 explains more about setting the path.

The most common problem with *PATH* is that, somehow, it gets deleted. This usually happens if you try to change *PATH* and do so incorrectly. When *PATH* is deleted, your shell can find only its built-in commands (1.9) and commands for which you give the complete pathname. Here's a demonstration:

```
% setenv PATH     Set PATH to null accidentally
% ls
ls: Command not found.
```

Needless to say, this can be very frustrating—especially if you can't figure out what's going on. There are a couple of easy fixes. The easiest is just to log out and log back in again. (*logout* is a built-in C shell command, so you won't have trouble finding it. If you get an error message like "Not login shell," try *exit* instead.) Another fix is to read (35.29) whichever initialization file defined your *PATH* variable, usually *.login* for C shell users or *.profile* or *.bash_profile* for Bourne or *bash* shell users, respectively:

```
% source ~/.login
$ . $HOME/.profile
bash$ . $HOME/.bash_profile
```

This will almost certainly give you *some* of your path back; the problem is that a lot of initialization files merely add a few "private" directories to a system-wide default path. In this case, just execute the system-wide initialization files first (if your system has them). Their pathnames vary:

```
+$ source /etc/profile
$ source /etc/profile.d/*.sh
$ source ~/.login
bash$ source ~/.bash_profile
```

Your best bet, if you're unfamiliar with the quirks of your system and how it sets up your shell, is to simply log out and log back in again. Some newer Linux systems, for example, use */etc/profile* for *bash* setup, inheriting the hardwired defaults set by the *login* command, and then go on to read shell-specific files (often in */etc/profile.d*, for example). *tcsh* and *csh* are configured using the */etc/csh.login*, */etc/csh.cshrc*, and other files in */etc/profile.d* in similar fashion to *bash*. This allows package managers to install package specific initialization without modifying (and potentially corrupting) the system's default initialization.

The other common *PATH* problem is that users sometimes can't find the commands they want. This happens most often when someone writes a new shell script with the same name as a standard Unix command—say, *true*. He or she tries to execute it and can't; in fact, all that happens is:

```
% true
%
```

After staring at the script for a long time, the user sometimes gets the right idea: the script is fine; it's the path that's wrong. The *PATH* variable will look something like this:

```
% printenv PATH
/bin:/usr/local/bin:/usr/bin:/sbin::/home/schampeo/bin
```

The shell searches the *PATH* in order; therefore, it finds the system's standard *true* command before seeing the new one. The new command never gets a chance. You *could* fix this problem by putting the current directory and *$HOME/bin* at the head of the search path, in which case commands in the current directory and your private *bin* directory will override the standard commands. However, that's *not* recommended; it's a well-known security hole.

So what is recommended? Nothing much, except that if you write shell scripts or other programs, give them names that are different from the standard Unix utilities (35.27). If you really need an overlapping name, you can use a relative pathname (1.16) to specify "the program called *true* in the current directory":

```
% ./true
```

You can search your *PATH* for a command with *which* (2.6), *findcmd*, and *whereiz*. Article 35.7 explains the pair of *path* variables in *csh* and *zsh*.

—*ML and SJC*

35.7 PATH and path

For *csh* and *zsh*, it's slightly incorrect to say that *PATH* contains the search list for commands. It's a bit more complicated. The *PATH* environment variable is used to set the *path* shell variable; that is, whenever you use *setenv PATH* (35.6) in *csh* or *export PATH* in *zsh*, the shell modifies *path* accordingly. For example:

```
setenv PATH /bin:/usr/bin:/usr/local::$HOME/bin    csh
export PATH=/bin:/usr/bin:/usr/local::$HOME/bin    zsh
```

In *PATH*, an empty entry (::) stands for the current directory. The shells' *path* shell variable (35.9) is the actual search list. Its syntax is slightly different; the list of directories is enclosed in parentheses ([XREF: UPT-ART-0508]), and the directories are separated by spaces. For example:

~31.11

```
set path=(/bin /usr/bin /usr/local . ~/bin)   csh

path=(/bin /usr/bin /usr/local . ~/bin)       zsh
```

If you set the *path* shell variable, the shell will automatically set the *PATH* environment variable. You don't need to set both. Many people set the shell variable instead of the environment variable.

—*ML*

35.8 The DISPLAY Environment Variable

The most important environment variable for X Window System clients is DISPLAY. When a user logs in at an X terminal, the DISPLAY environment variable in each *xterm* window is set to her X terminal's hostname followed by :0.0.

```
ruby:joan % echo $DISPLAY
ncd15.ora.com:0.0
```

When the same user logs in at the console of the workstation named *sapphire* that's running X, the DISPLAY environment variable is defined as just :0.0:*

```
sapphire:joan % echo $DISPLAY
:0.0
```

The DISPLAY environment variable is used by all X clients to determine what X server to display on. Since any X client can connect to any X server that allows it, all X clients need to know what display to connect to upon startup. If DISPLAY is not properly set, the client cannot execute:

```
sapphire:joan % setenv DISPLAY foo:0
sapphire:joan % xterm
xterm Xt error: Can't open display:
```

You can override the value of DISPLAY by using the *–display* command-line option. For example:

```
sapphire:joan % xterm -display sapphire:0.0 &
```

The first part of the display name (up to and including the colon) identifies the type of connection to use and the host that the server is running on. The second part (in most cases, the string 0.0) identifies a *server number* and an optional *screen number*. In most cases, the server and screen numbers will both be 0. You can omit the screen number name if the default (screen 0) is correct.

---

* Before X11 Release 5, the DISPLAY variable might appear as unix:0.0.

Note that we used both :0.0 and sapphire:0.0 to access the local console display of the workstation named *sapphire*. Although both these names will work, they imply different ways of connecting to the X server.

- The : character without an initial hostname specifies that the client should connect using UNIX domain sockets (IPC).

  Since processes can communicate via IPC only if they are running on the same host, you can use a leading colon or the unix keyword in a display name only if both the client and server are running on the same host—that is, for local clients displaying to the local console display of a workstation.

- Using the hostname followed by a colon (e.g., sapphire:) specifies that the client should connect using Internet domain sockets (TCP/IP). You can use TCP/IP connections for displaying clients on any X server on the TCP/IP network, as long as the client has permission to access that server.

Note that like all other environment variables set in your shell environment, the DISPLAY environment variable will propagate (35.3) to all processes you start from that shell.

When you run clients from remote machines, some additional problems with the DISPLAY environment variable need to be addressed. See article 6.10 for more information on running remote clients.

—LM and EP

35.9 Shell Variables

Shell variables are really just the "general case" of environment variables (35.3). If you're a programmer, remember that a Unix shell really runs an interpreted programming language. Shell variables belong to the shell; you can set them, print them, and work with them much as you can in a C program (or a FORTRAN program or a BASIC program). If you're not a programmer, just remember that shell variables are pigeonholes that store information for you or your shell to use.

If you've read the articles on environment variables, you realize that we defined them in exactly the same way. How are shell variables different from environment variables? Whenever you start a new shell or a Unix program, it inherits all of its parent's environment variables. However, it does *not* inherit any shell variables; it starts with a clean slate (except, possibly, variables in some shell setup files (3.3)). If you're a programmer, you can think of environment variables as "global" variables, while shell variables are "local" variables. By convention, shell variables have lowercase names.

Just as some programs use certain environment variables, the shell expects to use certain shell variables. For example, the C shell uses the *history* (30.1) variable to determine how many of your previous commands to remember; if the *noclobber* (43.6) variable is defined, the C shell prevents you from damaging files by making mistakes with standard output. Most users insert code into their *.cshrc* or *.tcshrc* (3.3) files to define these important variables appropriately. Alternatively, they split them up into context-specific files and then read them into their environment (35.29) as needed.

To set a shell variable, use one of these commands:

```
% set name=value    C shell
$ name=value        other shells
```

As a special case, if you omit *value*, the shell variable is set to a "null" value. For example, the following commands are valid:

```
% set name    C shell
$ name=       other shells
```

This is important: giving a variable a null value is not the same as deleting the value. Some programs look at variables to see whether or not they exist; they don't care what the actual value is, and an empty value is as good as anything else.

Most newer shells—but not the original C and Bourne shells—let you prevent accidental changes in a variable by marking it read-only after you've stored its value:

```
% set -r name      tcsh
$ readonly name    other shells
```

(In *zsh*, you can mark a variable read-only as you initialize it: readonly *name=value*.) If you want to make the shell forget that a variable ever existed, use the *unset* command. Note that, in general, you can't unset a read-only variable! Also, older Bourne shells don't have a command like *unset*:

```
% unset name    C shell
$ unset name    others except old Bourne shell
```

If you want to list all of your environment variables, use the command *printenv* or *env* (35.3).[*] If you want to list all of your Bourne or C shell variables, just type set. Here's a typical report in the C shell:

```
% set
argv    ()
cwd     /home/los/mikel/power/articles
history 40
home    /home/los/mikel
noclobber
path    (/home/los/mikel/bin /usr/local/bin /usr/ucb /bin /usr/bin .)
```

---

[*] *printenv* and *env* are external (1.9) commands; they work with any shell.

```
prompt   los%
shell    /bin/csh
status   0
term     sun
user     mikel
```

If you want to print the value of an individual variable, give the command:

% echo "$*variablename*"

(While the example above gives a C shell prompt, this command works in all Unix shells.) The quotes aren't necessary for something as simple as an *echo* statement, but if you want the value captured, for example, so that you can apply it to another variable, they are recommended.

Whenever you need the value of a shell variable—not just with *echo*—you need to put a dollar sign ($) in front of the name. Don't use the dollar sign when you're assigning a new value to a shell variable. You can also stick curly braces ({}) around the name if you want to (e.g., ${*name*}); when you're writing shell programs, this can often make your code much clearer. Curly braces are mostly used when you need to separate the variable name from what comes after it.

But that's getting us out of the range of interactive variable use and into shell programming (35.2).

—*ML and SJC*

35.10 Test String Values with Bourne-Shell case

Each time you type a command line at a shell prompt, you can see what happens and decide what command to run next. But a shell script needs to make decisions like that itself. A *case* statement helps the script make decisions. A *case* statement compares a string (usually taken from a shell or environment variable (35.9, 35.3)) to one or more patterns. The patterns can be simple strings (words, digits, etc.) or they can be *case* wildcard expressions (35.11). When the *case* statement finds a pattern that matches the string, it executes one or more commands.

Here's an example that tests your *TERM* (5.2) environment variable. If you're using a vt100 or tk4023 terminal, it runs a command to send some characters to your terminal. If you aren't on either of those, it prints an error and quits:

```
+case "$TERM" in
vt100 echo 'ea[w' | tr 'eaw' '\033\001\027' ;;
tk4023)  echo "*[p23" ;;
*)  # Not a VT100 or tk4023.  Print error message:
    echo "progname: quitting: you aren't on a VT100 or tk4023." 1>&2
    exit
    ;;
esac
```

exit **35.16**

Here are more details about how this works. The statement compares the string between the words case and in to the strings at the left-hand edge of the lines ending with a) (right parenthesis) character. If it matches the first case (in this example, if it's the vt100), the command up to the ;; is executed. The ;; means "jump to the esac" (*esac* is "case" spelled backwards). You can put as many commands as you want before each ;;, but put each command on a separate line (or separate commands on a line with semicolons (28.16)).

If the first pattern doesn't match, the shell tries the next case—here, *tk4023*. As above, a match runs the command and jumps to the *esac*. No match? The next pattern is the wildcard *. It matches any answer other than *vt100* or *tk4023* (such as *xterm* or an empty string).

You can use as many patterns as you want to. The first one that matches is used. It's okay if none of them match. The style doesn't matter much. Pick one that's readable and be consistent.

—*JP*

35.11 Pattern Matching in case Statements

A *case* statement (35.10) is good at string pattern matching. Its "wildcard" pattern-matching metacharacters work like the filename wildcards (1.13) in the shell, with a few twists. Here are some examples:

?)
  Matches a string with exactly one character like a, 3, !, and so on.
?*)
  Matches a string with one or more characters (a nonempty string).
[yY]|[yY][eE][sS])
  Matches y, Y or yes, YES, YeS, etc. The | means "or."
/*/*[0-9])
  Matches a file pathname, like */xxx/yyy/somedir/file2*, that starts with a slash, contains at least one more slash, and ends with a digit.
'What now?')
  Matches the pattern What now?. The quotes (27.12) tell the shell to treat the string literally: not to break it at the space and not to treat the ? as a wildcard.
"$msgs")
  Matches the contents of the *msgs* variable. The double quotes let the shell substitute the variable's value; the quotes also protect spaces and other special characters from the shell. For example, if *msgs* contains first next, this would match the same string, first next.

To clarify: in *bash*, for example, the *case* statement uses the same pathname expansion rules it uses elsewhere in the shell, to determine how to expand the value. In other shells, such as *ksh*, there are minor differences (such as a relaxation of special treatment for . and / characters). See the manual page for your shell if you have any questions or concerns about what rules your shell will follow.

—*JP and SJC*

35.12 Exit Status of Unix Processes

When a Unix process (command) runs, it can return a numeric status value to the parent process that called (started) it. The status can tell the calling process whether the command succeeded or failed. Many (but not all) Unix commands return a status of zero if everything was okay and nonzero (1, 2, etc.) if something went wrong. A few commands, such as *grep* and *diff*, return a different nonzero status for different kinds of problems; see your online manual pages (or just experiment!) to find out.

The Bourne shell puts the exit status of the previous command in the question mark (?) variable. You can get its value by preceding it with a dollar sign ($), just like any other shell variable. For example, when *cp* copies a file, it sets the status to 0. If something goes wrong, *cp* sets the status to 1:

```
$ cp afile /tmp
$ echo $?
0
$ cp afiel /tmp
cp: afiel: No such file or directory
$ echo $?
1
```

In the C shell, use the *status* variable instead (*tcsh* supports both):

```
% cp afiel /tmp
cp: afiel: No such file or directory
% echo $status
1
tcsh> cp afiel /tmp
cp: afiel: No such file or directory
tcsh> echo $status
1
```

Of course, you usually don't have to display the exit status in this way, because there are several ways (35.13, 35.14, 35.15) to use the exit status of one command as a condition of further execution.

true false

Two simple Unix utilities do nothing but return an exit status. *true* returns a status of 0 (zero); *false* returns 1 (one). There are GNU versions on the web site—and no, they don't have any amazing extra features. ;-)

bash and *zsh* have a handy way to reverse the status of a command line: put an exclamation point (!) before it. Let's look at a simple example (of course, you'd use ! with something besides *true* or *false*):

```
bash$ true
bash$ echo $?
0
bash$ ! true
bash$ echo $?
1
bash$ false
bash$ echo $?
1
bash$ ! false
bash$ echo $?
0
```

tcsh and *zsh* have a handy feature for work with exit statuses. If you set the *tcsh* shell variable *printexitvalue* or the *zsh* shell option *PRINT_EXIT_VALUE*, the shell will print the exit status of any program that doesn't return zero. For example:

```
zsh$ setopt printexitvalue
zsh$ grep '<title>' 0001.sgm
<title>Too Many Arguments for the Command Line</title>
zsh$ grep '<title>' 0000.sgm
grep: 0000.sgm: No such file or directory
zsh: exit 2     grep <title> 0000.sgm
zsh$ grep '<ttle>' 0001.sgm
zsh: exit 1     grep <ttle> 0001.sgm

tcsh% set printexitvalue
tcsh% true
tcsh% false
Exit 1
```

You can't test the exit status of a background job in the Bourne shell unless you use the *wait* command to wait for it (in effect, to bring the job out of the background). Pipelines, however, return the exit status of the last program in the pipeline.

—JP

35.13 Test Exit Status with the if Statement

If you are going to write a shell script of any complexity at all, you need some way to write "conditional expressions." Conditional expressions are nothing more than statements that have a value of "true" or "false", such as "Am I wearing pants today?" or "Is it before 5 p.m.?" or "Does the file *indata* exist?" or "Is the value of $aardvark greater than 60?"

The Unix shell is a complete programming language. Therefore, it allows you to write "if" statements with conditional expressions—just like C, BASIC, Pascal, or any other language. Conditional expressions can also be used in several other situations, but most obviously, they're the basis for any sort of *if* statement. Here's the syntax of an *if* statement for the Bourne shell:

```
+if conditional
then
    # do this if conditional returns a zero ("true") status
    one-or-more-commands
else
    # do this if conditional returns non-zero ("false") status
    one-or-more-commands
fi
```

Depending on how many different ways the command might exit, and thus the varying values its exit status may have, you may want to use either a *case* statement or *elif* (for testing multiple conditionals in a single *if/else* block.)

You can omit the *else* and the block of code following it. However, you can't omit the *then* or the *fi*. If you want to omit the *then* (i.e., if you want to do something special when *condition* is false, but nothing when it is true), write the statement like this:

```
if conditional
then
    :    # do nothing
else
    # do this if conditional returns non-zero ("false") status
    one-or-more-commands
fi
```

Note that this uses a special null command, a colon (:) (36.6). There's another, more useful way of expressing the inverse of a condition (do something if *conditional* is not "true"), the || operator (35.14) (two vertical bars). You can use this to write an *if*-type statement without the *if*!

Don't forget the *fi* terminating the statement. This is a surprisingly common source of bugs (at least for me).

Another common debugging problem: the manual pages that discuss this material imply that you can smash the *if*, *then*, and *else* onto one line. Well, it's true, but it's not always easy. Do yourself a favor: write your *if* statements *exactly* like the one above. You'll rarely be disappointed, and you may even start writing programs that work correctly the first time.

Here's a real-life example, a shell script named *bkedit* that makes a backup copy of a file before editing it. If *cp* returns a zero status, the script edits the file; otherwise, it prints a message. (The $1 is replaced with the first filename from the command line—see article 35.20.)

```
#!/bin/sh
if cp "$1" "$1.bak"
then
      vi "$1"
else
echo "bkedit quitting: can't make backup?" 1>&2
fi
```

You can try typing that shell script in and running it. Or just type in the lines (starting with the if) on a terminal running the Bourne shell; use a real filename instead of $1.

The *if* statement is often used with a command named *test* (35.26). The *test* command does a test and returns an exit status of 0 or 1.

—*ML, JP, and SJC*

35.14 Testing Your Success

The shells let you test for success right on the command line. This gives you a very efficient way to write quick and comprehensible shell scripts.

I'm referring to the || and && operators and in particular, the || operator. *comm1* || *comm2* is typically explained as "execute the command on the right if the command on the left failed." I prefer to explain it as an "either-or" construct: "execute either *comm1* or *comm2*." While this isn't really precise, let's see what it means in context:*

```
cat filea fileb > filec || exit
```

This means "either *cat* the files or *exit*." If you can't *cat* the files (if *cat* returns an exit status of 1), you exit (24.4). If you can *cat* the files, you don't exit. You execute the left side *or* the right side.

I'm stretching normal terminology a bit here, but I think it's necessary to clarify the purpose of ||. By the way, we could give the poor user an error message before flaming out (which, by the way, is a way to write an "inverse *if* (35.13)"):

```
cat filea fileb > filec || {
    echo sorry, no dice 1>&2
    exit 1
}
```

Similarly, *comm1* && *comm2* means "execute *comm1* AND *comm2*," or execute *comm2* if *comm1* succeeds. (But if you can't execute the first, don't do any.) This might be helpful if you want to print a temporary file and delete it immediately.

```
lpr file && rm file
```

---

* Others refer to it as a "short-circuit" operator.

If *lpr* fails for some reason, you want to leave the file around. Again, I want to stress how to read this: print the file and delete it. (Implicitly: if you don't print it, don't delete it.)

—ML

35.15 Loops That Test Exit Status

The Bourne shell has two kinds of loops that run a command and test its exit status. An *until* loop will continue until the command returns a zero status. A *while* loop will continue while the command returns a zero status.

Looping Until a Command Succeeds

The *until* loop runs a command repeatedly until it succeeds. That is, if the command returns a nonzero status, the shell executes the body of the loop and then runs the loop control command again. The shell keeps running the command until it returns a zero status, as shown in the following example:

```
% cat sysmgr
#!/bin/sh
until who | grep "^barb "
do sleep 60
done
echo The system manager just logged on.
% sysmgr &
[1] 2345
        ...time passes...
barb      ttyp7   Jul 15 09:30
The system manager just logged on.
```

The loop runs *who* (2.8) and pipes that output to *grep* (13.1), which searches for any line starting with *barb* and a space. (The space makes sure that usernames like *barbara* don't match.) If *grep* returns a nonzero status (no lines matched), the shell waits 60 seconds. Then the loop repeats, and the script tries the who | grep command again. It keeps doing this until *grep* returns a zero status—then the loop is broken and control goes past the done line. The *echo* command prints a message and the script quits. (I ran this script in the background so I could do something else while I waited for Barb.)

This is also a useful way to get someone with whom you share a machine to turn on their cell phone: just set a loop to wait until they login and then send them a *write* message (in case they don't always check their email, like a few nocturnal system administrators I know).

[A Bourne shell *until* loop is *not* identical to the *until* construction in most programming languages, because the condition is evaluated at the top of the loop. Virtually all languages with an *until* loop evaluate the condition at the bottom. —ML]

Looping Until a Command Fails

catsaway

The *while* loop is the opposite of the *until* loop. A *while* loop runs a command and loops until the command fails (returns a nonzero status). The *catsaway* program below uses a *while* loop to watch the *who* output for the system manager to log off. It's the opposite of the *sysmgr* script.

```
% cat catsaway
#!/bin/sh
while who | grep "^barb " > /dev/null
do sleep 60
done
echo "The cat's away..."
% catsaway &
[1] 4567
    ...time passes...
The cat's away...
```

/dev/null
43.12

—*JP*

35.16 Set Exit Status of a Shell (Script)

Most standard Unix toolbox commands return a status (35.12). Your shell script should, too. This section shows how to set the right exit status for both normal exits and error exits.

To end a shell script and set its exit status, use the *exit* command. Give *exit* the exit status that your script should have. If it has no explicit status, it will exit with the status of the last command run.

bkedit

Here's an example, a rewrite of the *bkedit* script from article 35.13. If the script can make a backup copy, the editor is run and the script returns the exit status from *vi* (usually 0). If something goes wrong with the copy, the script prints an error and returns an exit status of 1. Here's the script:

```
#!/bin/sh
if cp "$1" "$1.bak"
then
    vi "$1"
    exit    # Use status from vi
else
    echo "bkedit quitting: can't make backup?" 1>&2
    exit 1
fi
```

Here's what happens if I run it without a filename:

```
$ bkedit
cp: usage: cp fn1 fn2 or cp fn1 [fn2...] dir
bkedit quitting: can't make backup?
```

And here's what's left in the exit status variable:

```
$ echo $?
1
```

—*JP*

35.17 Trapping Exits Caused by Interrupts

If you're running a shell script and you press your interrupt key (5.8) (like CTRL-c), the shell quits right away. That can be a problem if you use temporary files in your script, because the sudden exit might leave the temporary files there. The *trap* command lets you tell the shell what to do before it exits. A *trap* can be used for a normal exit, too. See Table 35-1.

Table 35-1. Some Unix signal numbers for trap commands

Signal number	Signal name	Explanation
0	EXIT	*exit* command
1	HUP	When session disconnected
2	INT	Interrupt—often CTRL-c
3	QUIT	Quit—often CTRL-\
9	KILL	Kill, often used as a way to stop an errant program (it cannot be caught, so don't bother to trap it)
15	TERM	From *kill* command

Here's a script named *zmore* that uses a temporary file named */tmp/zmore$$* in a system temporary-file directory. The shell will replace $$ with its process ID number (24.3). Because no other process will have the same ID number, that file should have a unique name. The script uncompresses (15.6) the file named on its command line, then starts the *more* file viewer.* The script uses *trap*s, so it will clean up the temporary files, even if the user presses CTRL-c. The script also sets a default exit status of 1 that's reset to 0 if *more* quits on its own (without an interrupt). If you are on a Linux system, you may find that *gzcat* is simply named *zcat*.

```
#!/bin/sh
# zmore - UNCOMPRESS FILE, DISPLAY WITH more
# Usage: zmore file
stat=1  # DEFAULT EXIT STATUS; RESET TO 0 BEFORE NORMAL EXIT
temp=/tmp/zmore$$
trap 'rm -f $temp; exit $stat' 0
trap 'echo "`basename $0`: Ouch! Quitting early." 1>&2' 1 2 15
```

exit 35.16

---

* The script could run gzcat $1 | more directly, but some versions of *more* can't back up when reading from a pipe. You may prefer to use *less*, at any rate.

```
case $# in
1) gzcat "$1" >$temp
   more $temp
   stat=0
   ;;
*) echo "Usage: `basename $0` filename" 1>&2 ;;
esac
```

There are two *traps* in the script:

- The first *trap*, ending with the number 0, is executed for all shell exits—normal or interrupted. It runs the command line between the single quotes. In this example, there are two commands separated with a semicolon (;) (28.16). The first command removes the temporary file (using the *–f* option (14.10), so *rm* won't give an error message if the file doesn't exist yet). The second command exits with the value stored in the *stat* shell variable. Look ahead at the rest of the script—$stat will always be 1 unless the *more* command quit on its own, in which case *stat* will be reset to 0. Therefore, this shell script will always return the right exit status—if it's interrupted before it finishes, it'll return 1; otherwise, 0.*

- The second *trap* has the numbers 1 2 15 at the end. These are signal numbers that correspond to different kinds of interrupts. On newer shells, you can use signal names instead of the numbers. There's a short list in Table 35-1. For a list of all signals, type kill -1 (lowercase "L") or see your online *signal*(3) or *signal*(2) manual page. Alternatively, look for a file named */usr/include/signal.h* or */usr/include/linux/signal.h* (which itself just includes /usr/include/asm/signal.h, which is where the constants themselves are defined).

  This trap is done on an abnormal exit (like CTRL-c). It prints a message, but it could run any list of commands.

Shell scripts don't always have two *traps*. Look at the *nom* (33.8) script for an example.

I usually don't trap signal 3 (QUIT) in scripts that I use myself. That gives me an easy way to abort the script without springing the trap (removing temporary files, etc.). In scripts for general use, though, I usually do trap it.

Also, notice that the *echo* commands in the script have 1>&2 (36.16) at the end. This is the standard way to make error messages. In this particular script, that doesn't matter much because the script is used interactively. But it's a good habit to get into for all of your scripts.

---

* It's important to use single quotes rather than double quotes around the *trap*. That way, the value of $stat won't be interpreted until the trap is actually executed when the script exits.

If your *trap* runs a series of commands, it's probably neater to call a shell function (29.11) than a list of commands:

```
trap funcname 1 2 15
```

—*JP and SJC*

35.18 read: Reading from the Keyboard

The Bourne shell *read* command reads a line of one or more words from the keyboard (or standard input)* and stores the words in one or more shell variables. This is usually what you use to read an answer from the keyboard. For example:

```
echo -n "Type the filename: "
read filename
```

Here is how the *read* command works:

- If you give the name of one shell variable, *read* stores everything from the line into that variable:

    ```
    read varname
    ```

- If you name more than one variable, the first word typed goes into the first variable, the second word into the second variable, and so on. All leftover words go into the last variable. For example, with these commands:

    ```
    echo -n "Enter first and last name: "
    read fn ln
    ```

    if a user types John Smith, the word *John* would be available from $fn and *Smith* would be in $ln. If the user types Jane de Boes, then *Jane* would be in $fn and the two words *de Boes* are in $ln.

Some Bourne shells have a built-in function named *line* that reads a line from standard input and writes it to standard output. Use it with command substitutions (28.14):

```
value=`line`
```

grabchars

The *grabchars* program lets you read from the keyboard without needing to press RETURN.

—*JP*

---

* Some early versions of *read* don't handle < redirection (43.1); they can only read from the terminal.

35.19 Shell Script "Wrappers" for awk, sed, etc.

Although most scripts for most languages can execute directly (36.3) without needing the Bourne shell, it's common to "wrap" other scripts in a shell script to take advantage of the shell's strengths. For instance, *sed* can't accept arbitrary text on its command line, only commands and filenames. So you can let the shell handle the command line (35.20) and pass information to *sed* via shell variables, command substitution, and so on. Simply use correct quoting (27.12) to pass information from the shell into the "wrapped" *sed* script:

<pre>
|| 35.14
</pre>

```
#!/bin/sh
# seder - cd to directory in first command-line argument ($1),
# read all files and substitute $2 with $3, write result to stdout
cd "$1" || exit
sed "s/$2/$3/g" *
```

In *SunExpert* magazine, in his article on *awk* (January, 1991), Peter Collinson suggests a stylization similar to this for *awk* programs in shell scripts (35.2):

```
#!/bin/sh
awkprog='
/foo/{print $3}
/bar/{print $4}'

awk "$awkprog" $*
```

He argues that this is more intelligible in long pipelines because it separates the program from the command. For example:

```
grep foo $input | sed .... | awk "$awkprog" - | ...
```

Not everyone is thrilled by the "advantages" of writing *awk* this way, but it's true that there are disadvantages to writing *awk* the standard way.

Here's an even more complex variation:

<pre>
<<\ 27.16
</pre>

```
#!/bin/sh
temp=/tmp/awk.prog.$$
cat > $temp <<\END
/foo/{print $3}
/bar/{print $4}
END
awk -f $temp $1
rm -f $temp
```

This version makes it a bit easier to create complex programs dynamically. The final *awk* command becomes the equivalent of a shell *eval* (27.8); it executes something that has been built up at runtime. The first strategy (program in shell variable) could also be massaged to work this way.

As another example, a program that I used once was really just one long pipeline, about 200 lines long. Huge *awk* scripts and *sed* scripts intervened in the middle. As a result, it was almost completely unintelligible. But if you start each program with a comment block and end it with a pipe, the result can be fairly easy to read. It's more direct than using big shell variables or temporary files, especially if there are several scripts.

```
#
# READ THE FILE AND DO XXX WITH awk:
#
awk '
    ...the indented awk program...
    ...
    ...
' |
#
# SORT BY THE FIRST FIELD, THEN BY XXX:
#
sort +0n -1 +3r |
#
# MASSAGE THE LINES WITH sed AND XXX:
#
sed '
    ...
```

Multiline pipes like that one are uglier in the C shell because each line has to end with a backslash (\) (27.13). Articles 27.12 and 27.13 have more about quoting.

—*ML and JP*

35.20 Handling Command-Line Arguments in Shell Scripts

To write flexible shell scripts, you usually want to give them command-line arguments. As you've seen in other articles (35.16, 35.17), $1 holds the first command-line argument. The Bourne shell can give you arguments through the ninth, $9. The Korn shell and some other newer Bourne-type shells understand ${10} for the tenth argument, and so on.

With the "$@" Parameter

If you've been reading this series (35.2) of articles in order, you saw the *zmore* (35.17) script that accepted just one command-line argument. If you put "$@" in a script, the shell will replace that string with a quoted (27.12) set of the script's command-line arguments. Then you can pass as many arguments as you want, including pathnames with unusual characters (14.11):

```
% zmore report memo "savearts/What's next?"
```

The third argument has a perfectly legal filename; we see more and more of them on our system—especially filesystems that are networked to computers like the Macintosh, or on systems that use windowing systems to run graphical programs such as FrameMaker, where spaces and other "special" characters in filenames are common. Double-quoting all arguments through the script helps to be sure that the script can handle these unusual but legal pathnames.

In this case, we want the arguments to be passed to the GNU *zcat* command. Let's change the *zmore* script to read:

```
zcat "$@" >$temp
```

When the shell runs the script with the arguments shown above, the command line will become:

```
zcat "report" "memo" "savearts/What's next?" >/tmp/zmore12345
```

On some Bourne shells, if there are no command-line arguments, the "$@" becomes a single empty argument (37.5), as if you'd typed this:

```
zcat "" >/tmp/zmore12345
```

In this case, the *zcat* command would complain that it can't find a file. (Of course, in this script, the *case* would prevent this problem. But not all scripts test the number of arguments.)

On those shells, you can replace "$@" with ${1+"$@"} (36.7). That means that if $1 is defined, "$@" should be used. A not-quite-as-good fix is to replace "$@" with $*. It gives you an unquoted list of command-line arguments; that's usually fine but can cause trouble on pathnames with special characters in them.

With a Loop

A *for* loop (35.21) can step through all command-line arguments, one by one. You can also use a *while* loop (35.15) that tests $# (see below) and removes the arguments one by one with the *shift* command (35.22). The *getopt* and *getopts* (35.24) commands handle arguments in a more standard way.

Counting Arguments with $#

The $# parameter counts the number of command-line arguments. For instance, if there are three arguments, $# will contain 3. This is usually used for error-checking (as in the *zmore* script in article 35.17) with *case* (35.10) or *test* (35.26).

—*JP*

35.21 Handling Command-Line Arguments with a for Loop

Sometimes you want a script that will step through the command-line arguments one by one. (The "$@" parameter (35.20) gives you all of them at once.) The Bourne shell *for* loop can do this. The *for* loop looks like this:

```
for arg in list
do
    ...handle $arg...
done
```

If you omit the in *list*, the loop steps through the command-line arguments. It puts the first command-line argument in *arg* (or whatever else you choose to call the shell variable (35.9)), then executes the commands from do to done. Then it puts the next command-line argument in *arg*, does the loop, and so on, ending the loop after handling all the arguments.

For an example of a *for* loop, let's hack on the *zmore* (35.17) script.

```
#!/bin/sh
# zmore - Uncompress file(s), display with "more"
# Usage: zmore [more options] file [...files]
stat=1  # Default exit status; reset to 0 before normal exit
temp=/tmp/zmore$$
trap 'rm -f $temp; exit $stat' 0
trap 'echo "`basename $0`: Ouch! Quitting early..." 1>&2' 1 2 15

files= switches=
for arg
do
    case "$arg" in
    -*) switches="$switches $arg" ;;
    *)  files="$files $arg" ;;
    esac
done

case "$files" in
"") echo "Usage: `basename $0` [more options] file [files]" 1>&2 ;;
*)  for file in $files
    do
        zcat "$file" | more $switches
    done
    stat=0
    ;;
esac
```

case **35.11**

We added a *for* loop to get and check each command-line argument. For example, let's say that a user typed the following:

```
% zmore -s afile ../bfile
```

The first pass through the *for* loop, $arg is -s. Because the argument starts with a minus sign (-), the *case* treats it as an option. Now the switches variable is replaced by its previous contents (an empty string), a space, and -s. Control goes to the *esac* and the loop repeats with the next argument.

The next argument, afile, doesn't look like an option. So now the files variable will contain a space and afile.

The loop starts over once more with ../bfile in $arg. Again, this looks like a file, so now $files has afile ../bfile. Because ../bfile was the last argument, the loop ends; $switches has the options and $files has all the other arguments.

Next, we added another *for* loop. This one has the word in followed by $files, so the loop steps through the contents of $files. The loop runs *zcat* on each file, piping it to *more* with any switches you gave.

Note that $switches isn't quoted (27.12). This way, if $switches is empty, the shell won't pass an empty argument to *more*. Also, if $switches has more than one switch, the shell will break the switches into separate arguments at the spaces and pass them individually to *more*.

You can use a *for* loop with any space-separated (actually, IFS (36.23)–separated) list of words—not just filenames. You don't have to use a shell variable as the list; you can use command substitution (28.14) (backquotes) or shell wildcards (33.2), or just "hardcode" the list of words:

```
for person in Joe Leslie Edie Allan
do
    echo "Dear $person," | cat - form_letter | lpr
done
```

lpr **45.2**

The *getopt* and *getopts* (35.24) commands handle command-line arguments in a more standard way than *for* loops.

—JP

35.22 Handling Arguments with while and shift

A *for* loop (35.21) is great if you want to handle all of the command-line arguments to a script, one by one. But, as is often the case, some arguments are options that have their own arguments. For example, in the command grep -f *filename*, *filename* is an argument to -f; the option and its argument need to be processed together. One good way to handle this is with a combination of *while* (35.15), *test* (35.26), *case* (35.10), and *shift*. Here's the basic construct:

```
while [ $# -gt 0 ]
do
    case "$1" in
        -a) options="$options $1";;
        ...
```

```
        -f) options="$options $1"
            argfile="$2"
            shift
            ;;
        *) files="$files $1";;
    esac
    shift
done
```

The trick is this: *shift* removes an argument from the script's argument list, shifting all the others over by one ($1 disappears, $2 becomes $1, $3 becomes $2, and so on). To handle an option with its own argument, do another *shift*. The *while* loop uses *test* (35.26) to check that $#—the number of arguments—is greater than zero and keeps going until this is no longer true, which only happens when they have all been used up.

Meanwhile, all the *case* has to do is to test $1 against the desired option strings. In the simple example shown above, we simply assume that anything beginning with a minus sign is an option, which we (presumably) want to pass on to some program that is being invoked by the script. So all we do is build up a shell variable that will eventually contain all the options. It would be quite possible to do something else instead, perhaps setting other shell variables or executing commands.

We assume that anything without a minus sign is a file. This last case could be written more robustly with a *test* to be sure the argument is a file. Here's an example of a simple script that uses this construct to pass an option and some files to *pr* and from there to a program that converts text to PostScript and on to the print spooler (or you could convert SGML or XML files to PDF, whatever):

```
while [ $# -ne 0 ]
do
    case $1 in
        +*) pages="$1" ;;
        *) if [ -f "$1" ]; then
               files="$files $1"
           else
               echo "$0: file $1 not found" 1>&2
           fi;;
    esac
    shift
done
pr $pages $files | psprint | lpr
```

This approach is perhaps obsolete if you have *getopts* (35.24) (it's built into *bash*, for instance), since *getopts* lets you recognize option strings like -abc as being equivalent to -a -b -c, but I still find it handy. [In this example, it's essential. The *pr* option +*page-list* starts with a plus sign. *getopt* and *getopts* don't support those old-style options. —JP]

—TOR and SJC

35.23 Loop Control: break and continue

Normally a *for* loop (35.21) iterates until it has processed all its word arguments. *while* and *until* loops (35.15) iterate until the loop control command returns a certain status. But sometimes—for instance, if there's an error—you want a loop to immediately terminate or jump to the next iteration. That's where you use *break* and *continue*, respectively.

break terminates the loop and takes control to the line after *done*. *continue* skips the rest of the commands in the loop body and starts the next iteration. Here's an example of both. An outer loop is stepping through a list of directories. If we can't *cd* to one of them, we'll abort the loop with *break*. The inner loop steps through all entries in the directory. If one of the entries isn't a file or isn't readable, we skip it and try the next one.

```
          for dir in `find $HOME/projdir -type d -print`
  28.14   do
|| 35.14      cd "$dir" || break
              echo "Processing $dir"

  * 1.13       for file in *
              do
test 35.26        test -f "$file" -a -r "$file" || continue
                      ...process $dir/$file...
              done
          done
```

With nested loops (like the file loop above), which loop is broken or continued? It's the loop being processed at that time. So the *continue* here restarts the inner (file) loop. The *break* terminates the outer (directory) loop, which means the inner loop is also terminated. Note also that the *–print* argument to *find* is often redundant in the absence of another expression, depending on your version of *find*.

Here we've used *break* and *continue* within *for* loops, after the shell's || operator. But you can use them anywhere within the body of any loop—in an *if* statement within a *while* loop, for instance.

—JP

35.24 Standard Command-Line Parsing

Most shell scripts need to handle command-line arguments—options, filenames, and so on. Articles 35.20, 35.21, and 35.22 show how to parse command lines with any Bourne shell. Those methods have two problems. You can't combine arguments with a single dash, e.g., -abc instead of -a -b -c. You also can't specify arguments to options without a space in between, e.g., -barg in addition to -b *arg*.[*]

---

[*] Although most Unix commands allow this, it is actually contrary to the Command Syntax Standard Rules in *intro* of the User's Manual. Check your shell's manual pages for whether it supports *getopts*.

Your Bourne shell may have a built-in command named *getopts.** *getopts* lets you deal with multiple complex options without these constraints. To find out whether your shell has *getopts*, see your online *sh* or *getopts*(1) manual page.

getopt takes two or more arguments. The first is a string that can contain letters and colons (:). Each letter names a valid option; if a letter is followed by a colon, the option requires an argument. The second and following arguments are the original command-line options; you'll usually give "$@" (35.20) to pass all the arguments to *getopt*.

getopt picks each option off the command line, checks to see if the option is valid, and writes the correct option to its standard output. If an option has an argument, *getopt* writes the argument after its option. When *getopt* finds the first nonoption argument (the first argument that doesn't start with a - character), it outputs two dashes (--) and the rest of the arguments. If *getopt* finds an invalid option, or an option that should have an argument but doesn't, it prints an error message and returns a nonzero status (35.12).

Your script can use a loop to parse the *getopt* output. Here's an example script named *opttest* that shows how *getopt* works:

opttest

|| 35.14

: 36.6

```
#!/bin/sh
set -- `getopt "ab:" "$@"` || {
        echo "Usage: `basename $0` [-a] [-b name] [files]" 1>&2
        exit 1
}
echo "Before loop, command line has: $*"
aflag=0  name=NONE
while :
do
        case "$1" in
        -a) aflag=1 ;;
        -b) shift; name="$1" ;;
        --) break ;;
        esac
        shift
done
shift    # REMOVE THE TRAILING --
echo "aflag=$aflag / name=$name / Files are $*"
```

The script has two legal options. The *–a* option sets the variable named *aflag* to 1. The *–b* option takes a single argument; the argument is stored in the variable named *name*. Any other arguments are filenames.

The script starts by running *getopt* inside backquotes (28.14) and using the *set* (35.25) command to replace the command-line arguments with the *getopt* output.

---

* Both *bash* and *ksh* have it. *getopts* replaces the old command *getopt*; it is better integrated into the shell's syntax and runs more efficiently. C programmers will recognize *getopts* as very similar to the standard library routine *getopt*(3).

The first argument to *set*, -- (two dashes) (35.25), is important: it makes sure that *set* passes the script's options to *getopt* instead of treating them as options to the shell itself. An *echo* command shows the output of *getopt*. Then the loop parses the *getopt* output, setting shell variables as it goes. When the loop finds the -- argument from *getopt*, it quits and leaves the remaining filenames (if any) in the command-line arguments. A second *echo* shows what's in the shell variables and on the command line after the loop. Here are a few examples:

```
% opttest
Before loop, command line has: --
aflag=0 / name=NONE / Files are
% opttest -b file1 -a file2 file3
Before loop, command line has: -b file1 -a -- file2 file3
aflag=1 / name=file1 / Files are file2 file3
% opttest -q -b file1
getopt: illegal option -- q
Usage: opttest [-a] [-b name] [files]
% opttest -bfile1
Before loop, command line has: -b file1 --
aflag=0 / name=file1 / Files are
% opttest -ab
getopt: option requires an argument -- b
Usage: opttest [-a] [-b name] [files]
```

Some old Bourne shells have problems with an empty "$@" parameter (37.5). If the *opttest* script doesn't work with an empty command line, as in the first example above, you can change the "$@" in the script to ${1+"$@"}. If you find you're still having some trouble running the script, particularly with *bash*, try setting the *GETOPT_COMPATIBLE* environment variable, which sets GNU *getopt* to emulate the older, less featureful version. Also be sure to read the GNU *getopt*(1) manual page, as it details the support for POSIX-style long options (which let you do things like pass --*longoptions* to programs such as GNU *getopt*.)

The advantages of *getopt* are that it minimizes extra code necessary to process options and fully supports the standard Unix option syntax (as specified in *intro* of the User's Manual).

—*JP and BR*

35.25 The Bourne Shell set Command

[Most of this article, except *IFS* and --, also applies to the C shell. —JP]

You can pass options and arguments to a shell as you start it, as in:

```
sh -v file1 file2
```

and also when a script is invoked with #!. The *set* command lets you set command-line parameters, including most* shell options, after you've started the shell. This simple idea has more uses than you might realize.

Setting Options

The Bourne shell command line can have options like *–e* (exit if any command returns nonzero status). It can also have other arguments; these are passed to shell scripts. You can set new command-line parameters while you're typing interactive commands (at a shell prompt) or in a shell script.

To reset the command-line parameters, just type *set* followed by the new parameters. For example, to ask the shell to show expanded versions of command lines after you type them, set the *–v* (verbose) option (27.15):

```
$ set -v
$ mail $group1 < message
mail andy ellen heather steve wilma < message
$ mail $group2 < message
mail jpeek@jpeek.com randy@xyz.edu yori@mongo.medfly.com < message
$ set +v
```

On many Bourne shells, typing set +v cancels the *v* option. On other (mostly early) shells, there's no + feature. To work around that problem, you could start a subshell (24.4) with sh -v, run the commands there, then exit the subshell to cancel the verbose option.

Setting (and Parsing) Parameters

users

You can put filenames or any other strings in the command-line parameters interactively or from a shell script. That's handy for storing and parsing the output of a Unix command with backquotes (28.14). For example, you can get a list of all logged-in users from the parameters $1, $2, and so on. Use *users* (or *rusers* to find all the logged in users on the local network) if your system has it. Otherwise, use *who* (2.8) and *cut* (21.14) to strip off everything but the usernames:

for 35.21

```
$ set `users`
$ set `who | cut -c1-8`
$ for u
> do
>    ...do something with each user ($u)...
> done
```

You can save the original parameters in another variable and reset them later:

```
oldparms="$*"
set something new
   ...use new settings...
set $oldparms
```

Be sure to watch your quoting (as the next section explains).

---

* Some options for some shells can be set only from the command line as the shell is invoked. Check the shell's manual page.

If the first parameter you *set* starts with a dash, like -e, the shell will treat it as its own option instead of as a string to put into the command-line parameters. To avoid this, use -- (two dashes) as the first argument to *set*. In this example, $1 gets *-e*, and the filenames expanded from the wildcard pattern go into $2, $3, etc.:

```
set -- -e file*
```

(Avoiding?) set with No Arguments

If you type *set* by itself with no arguments, it will show a list of all currently set shell variables. In newer Bourne-type shells, it also shows shell functions (29.11) and other shell settings.

This can cause you grief if you accidentally don't pass arguments to *set* in the middle of a script, and screenfuls of variables spew onto the user's screen. For example, your script runs set 'users' from a *cron* (25.2) job, in the middle of the night when no one is logged on. The *users* command returns an empty string, so *set* gets no arguments, so it outputs a long list of junk.

The standard workaround for this problem is to always use a dummy first parameter—typically, a single x—when you're setting parameters. Then use *shift* (35.22) to shift away the x, leaving the other parameters (possibly none). For example:

```
set x `users`
shift
```

Watch Your Quoting

Because the shell parses and scans the new parameters before it stores them, wildcards (33.2) and other special characters (27.17) will be interpreted, so watch your quoting (27.12). You can take advantage of this to parse lines of text into pieces that aren't separated with the usual spaces and TABs—for instance, a line from a database with colon-separated fields—by setting the *IFS* (36.23) variable before the *set* command.

If you want to save any special quoting on the original command line, be careful: the quoting will be lost unless you're clever. For example, if $1 used to be *John Smith*, it will be split after it's restored: $1 will have *John* and $2 will be *Smith*. A better solution might be to use a subshell (43.7) for the part of the script where you need to reset the command-line parameters:

```
# reset command-line parameters during subshell only:
(set some new parameters
    ...do something with new parameters...
)
# original parameters aren't affected from here on...
```

Can't Set $0

One last note: *set* won't set $0, the name of the script file.

—*JP*

35.26 test: Testing Files and Strings

Unix has a command called *test* that does a lot of useful tests. For instance, *test* can check whether a file is writable before your script tries to write to it. It can treat the string in a shell variable as a number and do comparisons ("Is that number less than 1000?"). You can combine tests, too ("If the file exists *and* it's readable *and* the message number is more than 500..."). Some versions of *test* have more tests than others. For a complete list, read your shell's manual page (if your shell has *test* built in (1.9)) or the online *test*(1) manual page.

The *test* command returns a zero status (35.12) if the test was true and a nonzero status otherwise, so people usually use *test* with *if*, *while*, or *until*. Here's a way your program could check to see if the user has a readable file named *.signature* in the home directory:

$HOME **35.5**

$myname **35.28**

```
if test -r $HOME/.signature
then
    ...Do whatever...
else
    echo "$myname: Can't read your '.signature'.  Quitting." 1>&2
    exit 1
fi
```

The *test* command also lets you test for something that *isn't* true. Add an exclamation point (!) before the condition you're testing. For example, the following test is true if the *.signature* file is *not* readable:

```
if test ! -r $HOME/.signature
then
    echo "$myname: Can't read your '.signature'.  Quitting." 1>&2
    exit 1
fi
```

Unix also has a version of *test* (a link to the same program, actually) named *[*. Yes, that's a left bracket. You can use it interchangeably with the *test* command with one exception: there has to be a matching right bracket (]) at the end of the test. The second example above could be rewritten this way:

```
if [ ! -r $HOME/.signature ]
then
    echo "$myname: Can't read your '.signature'.  Quitting." 1>&2
    exit 1
fi
```

Be sure to leave space between the brackets and other text. There are a couple of other common gotchas caused by empty arguments; articles 37.3 and 37.4 have workarounds.

—JP

35.27 Picking a Name for a New Command

When you write a new program or shell script, you'll probably want to be sure that its name doesn't conflict with any other commands on the system. For instance, you might wonder whether there's a command named *tscan*. You can check by typing one of the commands in the following example. If you get output (besides an error) from one of them, there's probably already a command with the same name. (The *type* command works on *ksh*, *bash*, and many Bourne shells; I've shown it with a dollar sign ($) prompt.)

```
                % man 1 tscan
                No manual entry for tscan in section 1.
    which 2.6   % which tscan
                no tscan in . /xxx/ehuser/bin /usr/bin/X11 /usr/local/bin ...
  whereis 2.3   % whereis tscan
                tscan:
    alias 29.2  % alias tscan
                %
                % whatis tscan
                tscan:
                $ type tscan
                tscan not found
```

—JP

35.28 Finding a Program Name and Giving Your Program Multiple Names

A Unix program should use its name as the first word in error messages it prints. That's important when the program is running in the background or as part of a pipeline—you need to know which program has the problem:

```
someprog: quitting: can't read file xxxxxx
```

It's tempting to use just the program name in the *echo* commands:

```
echo "someprog: quitting: can't read file $file" 1>&2
```

If you ever change the program name, however, it's easy to forget to fix the messages. A better way is to store the program name in a shell variable at the top of the script file and use the variable in all messages:

```
myname=someprog
    ...
echo "$myname: quitting: can't read file $file" 1>&2
```

Even better, use the $0 parameter. The shell automatically puts the script's name there. But $0 can have the absolute pathname of the script, such as */xxx/yyy/bin/ someprog*. The *basename* (36.13) program fixes this: *basename* strips off the head of a pathname—everything but the filename.

For example, if $0 is */u/ehuser/bin/sendit*:

```
myname="`basename $0`"
```

would put *sendit* into the *myname* shell variable.

Just as you can make links (10.3) to give Unix files several names, you can use links to give your program several names (36.8). For instance, see the script named *ll, lf, lg* (...and so on). Use $0 to get the current name of the program.

—JP

35.29 Reading Files with the . and source Commands

As article 35.4 explains, Unix programs can *never, ever* modify the environment of their parents. A program can only modify the environment that later will be passed to its children. This is a common mistake that many new Unix users make: they try to write a program that changes a directory (or does something else involving an environment variable) and attempt to figure out why it doesn't work. You can't do this. If you write a program that executes the *cd* command, that *cd* will be effective within your program—but when the program finishes, you'll be back in your original (parent) shell.

One workaround is to "source" the shell script file (for *csh* and *bash*) or run it as a "dot" script (*sh, ksh,* and *bash,* too). For example, if the file named *change-my-directory* contains:

```
cd /somewhere/else
```

you could use the following commands to change the current directory of the current shell:

```
% source change-my-directory
$ . change-my-directory
```

The *source* and . commands read a script file into the current shell instead of starting a child shell. These commands work only for shell script files (files containing command lines as you'd type them at a shell prompt). You can't use *source* or . to read a binary (directly executable) file into the shell.

If your shell doesn't have shell functions (29.11), you can simulate them (29.14) with the . command. It acts a lot like a subroutine or function in a programming language.

—ML and JP

35.30 Using Shell Functions in Shell Scripts

So far, we have discussed some shell function basics (29.11), using examples such as the mx() function that uses *sed* and *dig* to find out what host accepts mail for a given address. In that example, we simply made a set of complex functionality available as a quick and easy (and short) call from the command line. But you can also define functions and use them within shell scripts, or you can use the . and source commands to include those functions from an external file (35.29).

We've also discussed using functions to automate repetitive tasks (29.11), such as calculating factorials.

For now, let's demonstrate both of these approaches specifically with respect to defining a function to automate a repetitive task and then sharing the function with other shell scripts. Using the mx() function we defined earlier, let's put it into its own file, *mx.sh*, and store it in our personal shell function library directory (in this case, *$HOME/lib*):

```
$ cat > ~/lib/mx.sh
function mx() {
# Look up mail exchanger for host(s)
for host
do
    echo "==== $host ===="
    dig "$host" mx in |
    sed -n '/^;; ANSWER SECTION:/,/^$/{
        s/^[^;].* //p
    }'
done
}
^D
$ more !$
function mx() {
# Look up mail exchanger for host(s)
for host
do
    echo "==== $host ===="
    dig "$host" mx in |
    sed -n '/^;; ANSWER SECTION:/,/^$/{
        s/^[^;].* //p
    }'
done
}
$
```

Now the file *~/lib/mx.sh* contains a function named mx()—fair enough, but let's say we want to be able to pass a list of hosts (determined dynamically on a regular basis, say, from spam-fighting tools that find open SMTP proxies) to a shell script, and have that shell script email a form letter to the postmaster address at that host. We will call the shell script *proxynotify*, and call it as follows:

```
$ proxynotify < proxylist
```

proxylist contains a list of hosts, one per line, in the com domain. We want to iterate over them and mail the postmaster for the domain, rather than mailing directly to an address such as postmaster@[*IP*], on the assumption that maybe the top-level postmaster can fix what may be an unmonitored relay. Just to verify that some other system isn't responsible for delivering the mail, we will check using the mx() shell function. We've also included a quickie shell function named ip() that returns the IP address for a given hostname. As you can see, we use a local variable for the IP address, and we use the -z test for zero length of a string. We also check whether the file is readable, check the script arguments, and use a variety of other tricks.

```
#!/bin/sh
# proxynotify demo

# get our function
. $HOME/lib/mx.sh

function ip() {
    for host
    do
        local ip=`dig in host $host |\
        grep $host |\
        grep "TABATAB" |\
        awk '{print $5}'`
        echo $ip
    done
}

if [ -z "$1" ]
then
    echo "Usage: $0 [file]"
    exit 1
elif [ -r "$1" ]
then
    echo "found a file and it is readable"
else
    echo "file $1 not readable or does not exist"
    exit 1
fi

    for domain in `cat "$1"`
    do
    echo "processing $domain"
    themx=`mx $domain`
    echo "MX for $domain is '$themx'"
    if [ ! -z $themx ]
    then
        cat formletter | mail -s "proxy" postmaster@$themx
    else
```

```
                echo "couldn't find MX for $domain,"
                echo "mailing direct-to-IP instead."
                theip=`ip $domain`
                if [ ! -z $theip ]; then
                    cat formletter | mail -s "proxy" postmaster@$theip
                else
                    echo "giving up, can't find anyone to notify"
                    echo "$domain" >> /tmp/proxybadlist.$$
                    return 1
                fi
        fi
    done
    mail -s "bad proxies" <</tmp/proxybadlist.$$
    rm /tmp/proxybadlist.$$
```

—*SJC*

36

Shell Programming for the Initiated

36.1 Beyond the Basics

This chapter has a bunch of tricks and techniques for programming with the Bourne shell. Some of them are documented but hard to find; others aren't documented at all. Here is a summary of this chapter's articles:

- The first group of articles is about making a file directly executable with #! on the first line. On many versions of Unix, an executable file can start with a first line like this:

      #!/path/to/interpreter

  The kernel will start the program named in that line and give it the file to read. Chris Torek's Usenet classic, article 36.2, explains how #! started. Article 36.3 explains that your "shell scripts" may not need a shell at all.

- The next bunch of articles are about processes and commands. The *exec* command, article 36.5, replaces the shell with another process; it can also be used to change input/output redirection (see below). The : (colon) operator evaluates its arguments and returns a zero status—article 36.6 explains why you should care.

- Next are techniques for handling variables and parameters. Parameter substitution, explained in article 36.7, is a compact way to test, set, and give default values for variables. You can use the $0 parameter and Unix links to give the same script multiple names and make it do multiple things; see article 36.8. Article 36.9 shows the easy way to get the last command-line argument. Article 36.10 has an easy way to remove all the command-line arguments.

- Four articles cover *sh* loops. A *for* loop usually reads a list of single arguments into a single shell variable. Article 36.11 shows how to make the *for* loop read from standard input. Article 36.12 has techniques for making a *for* loop set more than one variable. The *dirname* and *basename* commands can be used to split pathnames with a loop; see article 36.13. A *while* loop can have more than one command line at the start; see article 36.14.

- Next is an assortment of articles about input/output. Article 36.15 introduces open files and file descriptors—there's more to know about standard input/output/error than you might have realized! Article 36.16 has a look at file-descriptor handling in the Bourne shell, swapping standard output and standard error.

- The shell can read commands directly from a shell script file. As article 36.17 points out, a shell can also read commands from its standard input, but that can cause some problems. Article 36.18 shows one place scripts from *stdin* are useful: writing a script that creates another script as it goes.

  Next are two articles about miscellaneous I/O. One gotcha with the here-document operator (for redirecting input from a script file) is that the terminators are different in the Bourne and C shells; article 36.19 explains. Article 36.20 shows how to turn off echoing while your script reads a "secret" answer such as a password.

- Two articles—36.22 and 36.23—show uses for the versatile *expr* expression-handling command. Article 36.21 is a quick reference to *expr*. Article 36.24 covers multiple command substitution (28.14).

  Article 36.25 shows a trick for making one *case* statement (35.10) test two things at once. Finally, article 36.27 has a simple technique for getting exclusive access to a file or other system resource.

—JP

36.2 The Story of : # #!

Once upon a time, there was the Bourne shell. Since there was only "the" shell, there was no trouble deciding how to run a script: run it with *the* shell. It worked, and everyone was happy.

Along came progress and wrote another shell. The people thought this was good, for now they could choose their own shell. So some chose the one, and some the other, and they wrote shell scripts and were happy. But one day someone who used the "other" shell ran a script by someone who used the "other other" shell, and alas! it bombed spectacularly. The people wailed and called upon their Guru for help.

"Well," said the Guru, "I see the problem. The one shell and the other are not compatible. We need to make sure that the shells know which other shell to use to run each script. And lo! the one shell has a 'comment' called :, and the other a true comment called #. I hereby decree that henceforth, the one shell will run scripts that start with :, and the other those that start with #." And it was so, and the people were happy.

But progress was not finished. This time he noticed that only shells ran scripts and thought that if the kernel too could run scripts, this would be good, and the people would be happy. So he wrote more code, and now the kernel could run scripts but only if they began with the magic incantation #!, and if they told the kernel which shell ran the script. And it was so, and the people were confused.

For the #! looked like a "comment." Though the kernel could see the #! and run a shell, it would not do so unless certain magic bits were set. And if the incantation were mispronounced, that too could stop the kernel, which, after all, was not omniscient. And so the people wailed, but alas! the Guru did not respond. And so it was, and still it is today. Anyway, you will get best results from a 4BSD machine by using

```
#! /bin/sh
```

or:

```
#! /bin/csh
```

as the first line of your script. #! /bin/csh -f is also helpful on occasion, and it's usually faster because *csh* won't read your *.cshrc* file (3.3).

—*CT*

36.3 Don't Need a Shell for Your Script? Don't Use One

If your Unix understands files that start with:

```
#!/interpreter/program
```

(and nearly all of them do by now) you don't have to use those lines to start a shell, such as #!/bin/sh. If your script is just starting a program like *awk*, Unix can start the program directly and save execution time. This is especially useful on small or overloaded computers, or when your script has to be called over and over (such as in a loop).

First, here are two scripts. Both scripts print the second word from each line of text files. One uses a shell; the other runs *awk* directly:

```
% cat with_sh
#!/bin/sh
awk '
{ print $2 }
' $*
% cat no_sh
#!/usr/bin/awk -f
{ print $2 }
% cat afile
one two three four five
```

Let's run both commands and *time* (26.2) them. (This is running on a very slow machine. On faster systems, this difference may be harder to measure—though the difference can still add up over time.)

```
% time with_sh afile
two
0.1u 0.2s 0:00 26%
% time no_sh afile
two
0.0u 0.1s 0:00 13%
```

One of the things that's really important to understand here is that when the kernel runs the program on the interpreter line, it is given the script's filename as an argument. If the intepreter program understands a file directly, like */bin/sh* does, nothing special needs to be done. But a program like *awk* or *sed* requires the *–f* option to read its script from a file. This leads to the seemingly odd syntax in the example above, with a call to awk -f with no following filename. The script itself is the input file!

One implication of this usage is that the interpreter program needs to understand # as a comment, or the first interpreter-selection line itself will be acted upon (and probably rejected by) the interpreter. (Fortunately, the shells, Perl, *sed*, and *awk*, among other programs, do recognize this comment character.)

[One last comment: if you have GNU *time* or some other version that has a verbose mode, you can see that the major difference between the two invocations is in terms of the page faults each requires. On a relatively speedy Pentium III/450 running RedHat Linux, the version using a shell as the interpreter required more than twice the major page faults and more than three times as many minor page faults as the version calling *awk* directly. On a system, no matter how fast, that is using a large amount of virtual memory, these differences can be crucial. So opt for performance, and skip the shell when it's not needed. —*SJC*]

—*JP and SJC*

36.4 Making #! Search the PATH

As article 36.3 explains, you can use #!*/path/name* to run a script with the interpreter located at */path/name* in the filesystem. The problem comes if a new version of the interpreter is installed somewhere else or if you run the script on another system that has a different location. It's usually not a problem for Bourne shell programmers: */bin/sh* exists on every Unix-type system I've seen. But some newer shells—and interpreters like Perl—may be lurking almost anywhere (although this is becoming more and more standardized as Perl and other tools like it become part of standard Linux distributions and the like). If the interpreter isn't found, you'll probably get a cryptic message like scriptname: Command not found, where *scriptname* is the name of the script file.

The *env* command will search your *PATH* (35.6) for an interpreter, then execute (*exec* (24.2), replace itself) with the interpreter. If you want to try this, type env ls; *env* will find and run *ls* for you. This is pretty useless when you have a shell around to interpret your commands—because the shell can do the same thing without getting *env* involved. But when the kernel interprets an executable file that starts with #!, there's no shell (yet!). That's where you can use *env*. For instance, to run your script with *zsh*, you could start its file with:

```
#!/usr/bin/env zsh
    ...zsh script here...
```

The kernel *execs* */usr/bin/env*, then *env* finds and *execs* the *zsh* it found. Nice trick, eh? What do you think the problem is? (You have ten seconds... tick, tick, tick...) The catch is: if the *env* command isn't in */usr/bin* on your system, this trick won't work. So it's not as portable as it might be, but it's still handy and probably still better than trying to specify the pathname of a less common interpreter like *zsh*.

Running an interpreter this way can also be a security problem. Someone's *PATH* might be wrong; for instance, it might execute some random command named *zsh* in the user's *bin* directory. An intruder could change the *PATH* to make the script use a completely different interpreter with the same name.

One more problem worth mentioning: you can't specify any options for the interpreter on the first line. Some shell options can be set later, as the script starts, with a command like *set*, *shopt*, and so on—check the shell's manual page.

Finally, understand that using *env* like this pretty much erases any performance gains you may have achieved using the trick in the previous article.

—*JP and SJC*

36.5 The exec Command

The *exec* command executes a command in place of the current shell; that is, it terminates the current shell and starts a new process (24.3) in its place.

Historically, *exec* was often used to execute the last command of a shell script. This would kill the shell slightly earlier; otherwise, the shell would wait until the last command was finished. This practice saved a process and some memory. (Aren't you glad you're using a modern system? This sort of conservation usually isn't necessary any longer unless your system limits the number of processes each user can have.)

exec can be used to replace one shell with another shell:

```
% exec ksh
$
```

without incurring the additional overhead of having an unused shell waiting for the new shell to finish.

exec also manipulates file descriptors (36.16) in the Bourne shell. When you use *exec* to manage file descriptors, it does not replace the current process. For example, the following command makes the standard input of all commands come from the file *formfile* instead of the default place (usually, your terminal):

```
exec < formfile
```

—ML and JP

36.6 The Unappreciated Bourne Shell ":" Operator

Some people think that the Bourne shell's : is a comment character. It isn't, really. It evaluates its arguments and returns a zero exit status (35.12). Here are a few places to use it:

- Replace the Unix *true* command to make an endless *while* loop (35.15). This is more efficient because the shell doesn't have to start a new process each time around the loop (as it does when you use `while true`):

```
while :
do
    commands
done
```

(Of course, one of the *commands* will probably be *break*, to end the loop eventually. This presumes that it is actually a savings to have the *break* test inside the loop body rather than at the top, but it may well be clearer under certain circumstances to do it that way.)

- When you want to use the *else* in an *if* (35.13) but leave the *then* empty, the : makes a nice "do-nothing" place filler:

```
if something
then :
else
    commands
fi
```

- If your Bourne shell doesn't have a true # comment character (but nearly all of them do nowadays), you can use : to "fake it." It's safest to use quotes so the shell won't try to interpret characters like > or | in your "comment":

```
: 'read answer and branch if < 3 or > 6'
```

- Finally, it's useful with parameter substitution (36.7) like ${*var*?} or ${*var=default*}. For instance, using this line in your script will print an error and exit if either the *USER* or *HOME* variables aren't set:

```
: ${USER?} ${HOME?}
```

—JP

36.7 Parameter Substitution

The Bourne shell has a handy set of operators for testing and setting shell variables. They're listed in Table 36-1.

Table 36-1. Bourne shell parameter substitution operators

Operator	Explanation
`${var:-default}`	If *var* is not set or is empty, use *default* instead.
`${var:=default}`	If *var* is not set or is empty, set it to *default* and use that value.
`${var:+instead}`	If *var* is set and is not empty, use *instead*. Otherwise, use nothing (null string).
`${var:?message}`	If *var* is set and is not empty, use its value. Otherwise, print *message*, if any, and exit from the shell. If *message* is missing, print a default message (which depends on your shell).

If you omit the colon (:) from the expressions in Table 36-1, the shell doesn't check for an empty parameter. In other words, the substitution happens whenever the parameter is set. (That's how some early Bourne shells work: they don't understand a colon in parameter substitution.)

To see how parameter substitution works, here's another version of the *bkedit* script (35.13, 35.16):

```
+#!/bin/sh
if cp "$1" "$1.bak"
then
        ${VISUAL:-/usr/ucb/vi} "$1"
        exit   # Use status from editor
else
        echo "`basename $0` quitting: can't make backup?" 1>&2
        exit 1
fi
```

If the *VISUAL* (35.5) environment variable is set and is not empty, its value (such as */usr/local/bin/emacs*) is used and the command line becomes /usr/local/bin/emacs "$1". If *VISUAL* isn't set, the command line defaults to /usr/ucb/vi "$1".

You can use parameter substitution operators in any command line. You'll see them used with the colon (:) operator (36.6), checking or setting default values. There's an example below. The first substitution (${nothing=default}) leaves $nothing empty because the variable has been set. The second substitution sets $nothing to *default* because the variable has been set but is empty. The third substitution leaves $something set to *stuff*:

```
+nothing=
something=stuff
: ${nothing=default}
: ${nothing:=default}
: ${something:=default}
```

Several Bourne-type shells have similar string editing operators, such as
${*var##pattern*}. They're useful in shell programs, as well as on the command
line and in shell setup files. See your shell's manual page for more details.

—*JP*

36.8 Save Disk Space and Programming: Multiple Names for a Program

If you're writing:

- several programs that do the same kinds of things,
- programs that use a lot of the same code (as you're writing the second, third, etc., programs, you copy a lot of lines from the first program), or
- a program with several options that make big changes in the way it works,

you might want to write just one program and make links (10.4, 10.3) to it instead.
The program can find the name you called it with and, through *case* or *test* commands, work in different ways. For instance, the Berkeley Unix commands *ex*,
vi, *view*, *edit*, and others are all links to the same executable file. This takes less
disk space and makes maintenance easier. It's usually sensible only when most
of the code is the same in each program. If the program is full of name tests and
lots of separate code, this technique may be more trouble than it's worth.

Depending on how the script program is called, this name can be a simple relative pathname like prog or ./prog—it can also be an absolute pathname like
/usr/joe/bin/prog (article 31.2 explains pathnames). There are a couple of
ways to handle this in a shell script. If there's just one main piece of code in
the script, as in the *lf* script, a *case* that tests $0 might be best. The asterisk (*)
wildcard at the start of each case (see article 35.11) handles the different
pathnames that might be used to call the script:

```
case "$0" in
*name1)
    ...do this when called as name1...
    ;;
*name2)
    ...do this when called as name2...
    ;;
    ...
*)  ...print error and exit if $0 doesn't match...
    ;;
esac
```

You might also want to use *basename* (36.13) to strip off any leading pathname
and store the cleaned-up $0 in a variable called *myname*. You can test $myname
anywhere in the script and also use it for error messages:

```
myname=`basename $0`
   ...
case "$myname" in
   ...
echo "$myname: aborting; error in xxxxxx" 1>&2
   ...
```

—JP

36.9 Finding the Last Command-Line Argument

Do you need to pick up the last parameter $1, $2 ... from the parameter list on the command line? It looks like eval \$$# would do it:

eval 27.8

```
$ set foo bar baz
$ eval echo \$$#
baz
```

except for a small problem with *sh* argument syntax:

```
$ set m n o p q r s t u v w x
$ echo $11
m1
```

$11 means ${1}1, not ${11}. Trying ${11} directly gives bad substitution. (More recent shells, such as *bash*, do support the ${11} syntax, however, to arbitrary lengths. Our copy of *bash*, for example, allowed at least 10240 command line arguments to set with recall of the last via ${10240}). Your mileage may vary.

The only reliable way to get at the last parameter in the Bourne shell is to use something like this:

```
for i do last="$i"; done
```

The *for* loop assigns each parameter to the shell variable named *last*; after the loop ends, $last will have the last parameter. Also, note that you won't need this trick on all *sh*-like shells. The Korn shell, *zsh*, and *bash* understand ${11}.

—CT

36.10 How to Unset All Command-Line Parameters

The *shift* (35.22) command "shifts away" one command-line parameter. You can shift three times if there are three command-line parameters. Many shells also can take an argument, like *shift 3*, that tells how many times to shift; on those shells, you can shift $# (35.20) to unset all parameters.

The portable way to unset all command-line parameters is probably to set (35.25) a single dummy parameter, then shift it away:

```
+set x
shift
```

Setting the single parameter wipes out whatever other parameters were set before.

—JP

36.11 Standard Input to a for Loop

An obvious place to use a Bourne shell *for* loop (35.21) is to step through a list of arguments—from the command line or a variable. But combine the loop with backquotes (28.14) and *cat* (12.2), and the loop will step through the words on standard input.

Here's an example:

```
for x in `cat`
do
    ...handle $x
done
```

Because this method splits the input into separate words, no matter how many words are on each input line, it can be more convenient than a *while* loop running the *read* command. When you use this script interactively, though, the loop won't start running until you've typed all of the input; using *while read* will run the loop after each line of input.

—JP

36.12 Making a for Loop with Multiple Variables

The normal Bourne shell *for* loop (35.21) lets you take a list of items, store the items one by one in a shell variable, and loop through a set of commands once for each item:

```
for file in prog1 prog2 prog3
do
    ...process $file
done
```

I wanted a *for* loop that stores several different shell variables and makes one pass through the loop for each *set* of variables (instead of one pass for each *item*, as a regular *for* loop does). This loop does the job:

```
       for bunch in "ellie file16" "donna file23" "steve file34"
       do
           # PUT FIRST WORD (USER) IN $1, SECOND (FILE) IN $2...
set 35.25    set $bunch
           mail $1 < $2
       done
```

If you have any command-line arguments and still need them, store them in another variable before you use the *set* command. Or you can make the loop this way:

```
       for bunch in "u=ellie f=file16 s='your files'" \
           "u=donna f=file23 s='a memo'" "u=steve f=file34 s=report"
       do
           # SET $u (USER), $f (FILENAME), $s (SUBJECT):
           eval $bunch
           mail -s "$s" $u < $f
       done
```

This script uses the shell's *eval* (27.8) command to rescan the contents of the *bunch* variable and store it in separate variables. Notice the single quotes, as in s='your files'; this groups the words for *eval*. The shell removes the single quotes before it stores the value into the *s* variable.

—*JP*

36.13 Using basename and dirname

Almost every Unix command can use relative and absolute pathnames (31.2) to find a file or directory. There are times you'll need part of a pathname—the head (everything before the last slash) or the tail (the name after the last slash). The utilities *basename* and *dirname*, available on most Unix systems, handle that.

Introduction to basename and dirname

The *basename* command strips any "path" name components from a filename, leaving you with a "pure" filename. For example:

```
% basename /usr/bin/gigiplot
gigiplot
% basename /home/mikel/bin/bvurns.sh
bvurns.sh
```

basename can also strip a suffix from a filename. For example:

```
% basename /home/mikel/bin/bvurns.sh .sh
bvurns
```

The *dirname* command strips the filename itself, giving you the "directory" part of the pathname:

```
% dirname /usr/bin/screenblank
/usr/bin
% dirname local
.
```

If you give *dirname* a "pure" filename (i.e., a filename with no path, as in the second example), it tells you that the directory is . (the current directory).

dirname and *basename* have a bug in some implementations. They don't recognize the second argument as a filename suffix to strip. Here's a good test:

```
% basename 0.foo .foo
```

If the result is 0, your *basename* implementation is good. If the answer is 0.foo, the implementation is bad. If *basename* doesn't work, *dirname* won't, either.

Use with Loops

Here's an example of *basename* and *dirname*. There's a directory tree with some very large files—over 100,000 characters. You want to find those files, run *split* (21.9) on them, and add *huge.* to the start of the original filename. By default, *split* names the file chunks *xaa*, *xab*, *xac*, and so on; you want to use the original filename and a dot (.) instead of *x*:

```
for path in `find /home/you -type f -size +100000c -print`
do
    cd `dirname $path` || exit
    filename=`basename $path`
    split $filename $filename.
    mv -i $filename huge.$filename
done
```

|| 35.14
exit 35.16

The *find* command will output pathnames like these:

```
/home/you/somefile
/home/you/subdir/anotherfile
```

(The absolute pathnames are important here. The *cd* would fail on the second pass of the loop if you use relative pathnames.) In the loop, the *cd* command uses *dirname* to go to the directory where the file is. The *filename* variable, with the output of *basename*, is used several places—twice on the *split* command line.

If the previous code results in the error `command line too long`, replace the first lines with the two lines below. This makes a redirected-input loop:

```
find /home/you -type f -size +100000c -print |
while read path
```

—*JP and ML*

36.14 A while Loop with Several Loop Control Commands

I used to think that the Bourne shell's *while* loop (35.15) looked like this, with a single command controlling the loop:

```
while command
do
      ...whatever
done
```

But *command* can actually be a *list* of commands. The exit status of the last command controls the loop. This is handy for prompting users and reading answers. When the user types an empty answer, the *read* command returns "false" and the loop ends:

```
while echo -e "Enter command or CTRL-d to quit: \c"
      read command
do
      ...process $command
done
```

You may need a *-e* option to make *echo* treat escaped characters like \c the way you want. In this case, the character rings the terminal bell, however your terminal interprets that (often with a flash of the screen, for instance.)

Here's a loop that runs *who* and does a quick search on its output. If the *grep* returns nonzero status (because it doesn't find $who in $tempfile), the loop quits—otherwise, the loop does lots of processing:

```
while
      who > $tempfile
      grep "$who" $tempfile >/dev/null
do
      ...process $tempfile...
done
```

—*JP and SJC*

36.15 Overview: Open Files and File Descriptors

This introduction is general and simplified. If you're a technical person who needs a complete and exact description, read a book on Unix programming.

Unix shells let you redirect the input and output of programs with operators such as > and |. How does that work? How can you use it better? Here's an overview.

When the Unix kernel starts any process (24.3)—for example, *grep*, *ls*, or a shell—it sets up several places for that process to read from and write to, as shown in Figure 36-1.

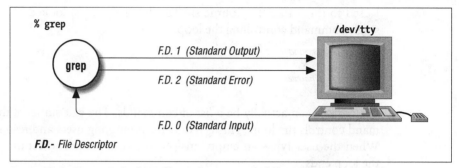

Figure 36-1. Open standard I/O files with no command-line redirection

These places are called *open files*. The kernel gives each file a number called a *file descriptor*. But people usually use names for these places instead of the numbers:

- The *standard input* or *stdin* (File Descriptor (F.D.) number 0) is the place where the process can read text. This might be text from other programs (through a pipe, on the command line) or from your keyboard.

- The *standard output* or *stdout* (F.D. 1) is a place for the process to write its results.

- The *standard error* or *stderr* (F.D. 2) is where the process can send error messages.

By default, as Figure 36-1 shows, the file that's opened for *stdin*, *stdout*, and *stderr* is */dev/tty*—a name for your terminal. This makes life easier for users—and programmers, too. The user doesn't have to tell a program where to read or write because the default is your terminal. A programmer doesn't have to open files to read or write from (in many cases); the programs can just read from *stdin*, write to *stdout*, and send errors to *stderr*.

It gets better. When the shell starts a process (when you type a command at a prompt), you can tell the shell what file to "connect to" any of those file descriptors. For example, Figure 36-2 shows what happens when you run *grep* and make the shell redirect *grep*'s standard output away from the terminal to a file named *grepout*.

Programs can read and write files besides the ones on *stdin*, *stdout*, and *stderr*. For instance, in Figure 36-2, *grep* opened the file *somefile* itself—it didn't use any of the standard file descriptors for *somefile*. A Unix convention is that if you don't name any files on the command line, a program will read from its standard input. Programs that work that way are called *filters*.

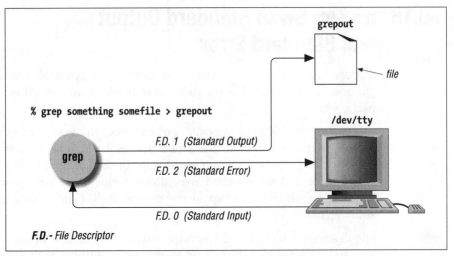

% grep something somefile > grepout

Figure 36-2. Standard output redirected to a file

All shells can do basic redirection with *stdin*, *stdout*, and *stderr*. But as you'll see in article 36.16, the Bourne shell also handles file descriptors 3 through 9 (and *bash* and the other newer shells can handle arbitrary numbers of file descriptiors, up to whatever ulimit -n happens to be set). That's useful sometimes:

- Maybe you have a few data files that you want to keep reading from or writing to. Instead of giving their names, you can use the file descriptor numbers.

- Once you open a file, the kernel remembers what place in the file you last read from or wrote to. Each time you use that file descriptor number while the file is open, you'll be at the same place in the file. That's especially nice when you want to read from or write to the same file with more than one program. For example, the *line* command on some Unix systems reads one line from a file—you can call *line* over and over, whenever you want to read the next line from a file. Once the file has been opened, you can remove its link (name) from the directory; the process can access the file through its descriptor without using the name.

- When Unix starts a new subprocess (24.3), the open file descriptors are given to that process. A subprocess can read or write from file descriptors opened by its parent process. A redirected-I/O loop, as discussed in article 43.6, takes advantage of this.

—*JP*

36.16 n>&m: Swap Standard Output and Standard Error

By default, a command's standard error goes to your terminal. The standard output goes to the terminal or is redirected somewhere (to a file, down a pipe, into backquotes).

Sometimes you want the opposite. For instance, you may need to send a command's standard output to the screen and grab the error messages (standard error) with backquotes. Or you might want to send a command's standard output to a file and the standard error down a pipe to an error-processing command. Here's how to do that in the Bourne shell. (The C shell can't do this, although *tcsh* can.)

File descriptors 0, 1, and 2 are, respectively, the standard input, standard output, and standard error (article 36.15 explains). Without redirection, they're all associated with the terminal file */dev/tty* (36.15). It's easy to redirect any descriptor to any file—if you know the filename. For instance, to redirect file descriptor 2 to *errfile*, type:

```
$ command 2>errfile
```

You know that a pipe and backquotes also redirect the standard output:

```
$ command | ...
$ var=`command`
```

But there's no filename associated with the pipe or backquotes, so you can't use the 2> redirection. You need to rearrange the file descriptors without knowing the file (or whatever) that they're associated with. Here's how. You may find it useful to run this short Perl script, which simply prints "stdout" to standard output, and "stderr" to standard error:

```
#!/usr/bin/perl

print STDOUT "stdout\n";
print STDERR "stderr\n";
```

Let's start slowly. We will combine both standard output and standard error, sending them both as output, to be used as the input to a pipe or as the output of backquotes. The Bourne shell operator *n>&m* rearranges the files and file descriptors. It says, "Make file descriptor *n* point to the same file as file descriptor *m*." Let's use that operator on the previous example. We'll send standard error to the same place standard output is going:

```
$ command 2>&1 | ...
$ var=`command 2>&1`
```

In both those examples, 2>&1 means "send standard error (file descriptor 2) to the same place standard output (file descriptor 1) is going." Simple, eh?

You can use more than one *n>&m* operator. The shell reads them left-to-right before it executes the command.

"Oh!" you might say. "To swap standard output and standard error—make *stderr* go down a pipe and *stdout* go to the screen—I could do this!"

```
$ command 2>&1 1>&2 | ...      wrong...
```

Sorry, Charlie. When the shell sees 2>&1 1>&2, the shell first does 2>&1. You've seen that before—it makes file descriptor 2 (*stderr*) go the same place as file descriptor 1 (*stdout*). Then the shell does 1>&2. It makes *stdout* (1) go the same place as *stderr* (2)... but *stderr* is already going the same place as *stdout*, down the pipe.

This is one place the other file descriptors, 3 through 9 (and higher in *bash*), come in handy. They normally aren't used. You can use one of them as a "holding place," to remember where another file descriptor "pointed." For example, one way to read the operator 3>&2 is "make 3 point the same place as 2." After you use 3>&2 to grab the location of 2, you can make 2 point somewhere else. Then make 1 point where 2 used to (where 3 points now).

We'll take that step-by-step below. The command line you want is one of these:

```
$ command 3>&2 2>&1 1>&3 | ...
$ var=`command 3>&2 2>&1 1>&3`
```

How does it work? Figures 36-3 through 36-6 break the second command line (with the backquotes) into the same steps the shell follows as it rearranges the file descriptors. You can try these on your terminal, if you'd like. Each figure adds another *n>&m* operator and shows the location of each file descriptor after that operator.

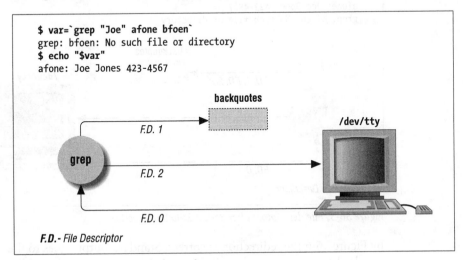

Figure 36-3. File descriptors before redirection

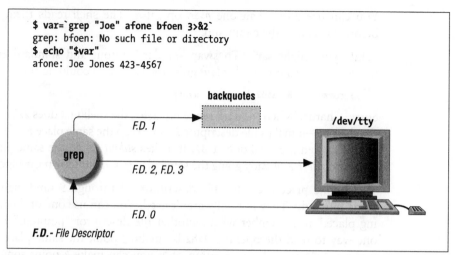

```
$ var=`grep "Joe" afone bfoen 3>&2`
grep: bfoen: No such file or directory
$ echo "$var"
afone: Joe Jones 423-4567
```

Figure 36-4. File descriptors after 3>&2 redirection

The figures use a *grep* command reading two files. *afone* is readable, and *grep* finds one matching line in it; the line is written to the standard output. *bfoen* is misspelled and so is not readable; *grep* writes an error message to the standard error. In each figure, you'll see the terminal output (if any) just after the variable-setting command with the backquotes. The text grabbed by the backquotes goes into the shell variable; the *echo* command shows that text.

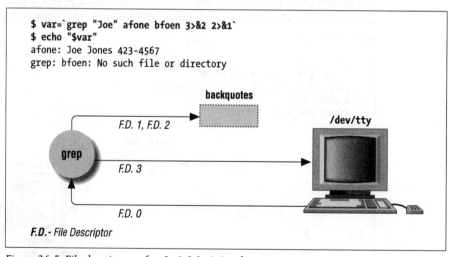

```
$ var=`grep "Joe" afone bfoen 3>&2 2>&1`
$ echo "$var"
afone: Joe Jones 423-4567
grep: bfoen: No such file or directory
```

Figure 36-5. File descriptors after 3>&2 2>&1 redirection

By Figure 36-6 the redirection is correct. Standard output goes to the screen, and standard error is captured by the backquotes.

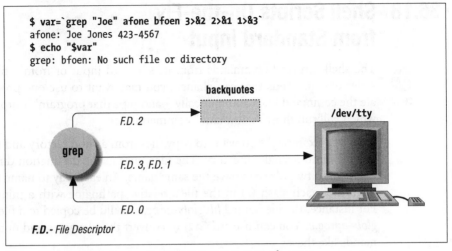

```
$ var=`grep "Joe" afone bfoen 3>&2 2>&1 1>&3`
afone: Joe Jones 423-4567
$ echo "$var"
grep: bfoen: No such file or directory
```

Figure 36-6. File descriptors after 3>&2 2>&1 1>&3 redirection

Open files are automatically closed when a process exits, but it's safer to close the files yourself as soon as you're done with them. That way, if you forget and use the same descriptor later for something else (for instance, use F.D. 3 to redirect some other command, or a subprocess uses F.D. 3), you won't run into conflicts. Use *m*<&- to close input file descriptor *m* and *m*>&- to close output file descriptor *m*. If you need to, you can close standard input with <&- and standard output with >&-.

—JP

36.17 A Shell Can Read a Script from Its Standard Input, but...

Q: *What is the difference between* sh < file *and* sh file?

A: The first way keeps the script from reading anything else from its input. Consider the *stdin-demo* script:

```
while read word
do
    echo $word | sed s/foo/bar/
done
```

If run as sh stdin-demo, it will read from your terminal, replacing foo with bar. If run as sh < stdin-demo, it will exit right away, since after reading the script, there's no input left.

—CT

36.18 Shell Scripts On-the-Fly from Standard Input

36.17

The shell can read commands from its standard input or from a file. To run a series of commands that can change, you may want to use one program to create the command lines automatically—and pipe that program's output to a shell, which will run those "automatic" commands.

Here's an example.* You want to copy files from a subdirectory and all its subdirectories into a single directory. The filenames in the destination directory can't conflict; no two files can have the same name. An easy way to name the copies is to replace each slash (/) in the file's relative pathname with a minus sign (-).† For instance, the file named *lib/glob/aprog.c* would be copied to a file named *lib–glob–aprog.c*. You can use *sed* (34.2) to convert the filenames and output *cp* commands like these:

```
cp from/lib/glob/aprog.c to/lib-glob-aprog.c
cp from/lib/glob/aprog.h to/lib-glob-aprog.h
    ...
```

However, an even better solution can be developed using *nawk* (20.11). The following example uses *find* (9.1) to make a list of pathnames, one per line, in and below the *copyfrom* directory. Next it runs *nawk* to create the destination file pathnames (like *to/lib–glob-aprog.c*) and write the completed command lines to the standard output. The shell reads the command lines from its standard input, through the pipe.

This example is in a script file because it's a little long to type at a prompt. But you can type commands like these at a prompt, too, if you want to:

```
#!/bin/sh
find copyfrom -type f -print |
awk '{
    out = $0
    gsub("/", "-", out)
    sub("^copyfrom-", "copyto/", out)
    print "cp", $0, out
}' |
sh
```

If you change the last line to sh -v, the shell's verbose option (37.1) will show each command line before executing it. If the last line has sh -e, the shell will quit immediately after any command returns a nonzero exit status (35.12)—that

---

* This isn't recommended for systems with a 14-character filename limit. You may also want to watch out on Darwin, which, although it has the typical UNIX filename limits, only displays 31 characters on the Finder Desktop (munging the last few chars or inserting...to provide a unique <32-character filename).

† A replacement like CTRL-a would make unique filenames (legal, but also harder to type).

---

might happen, for instance, if the disk fills up and *cp* can't make the copy. Finally, you may need to use *nawk* rather than *awk*, depending on your system.

—JP

36.19 Quoted hereis Document Terminators: sh Versus csh

When you need to quote your *hereis* document (27.16) terminators, there's an annoying problem: *sh* and *csh* demand different conventions. If you are using *sh*, you *must not* quote the terminator. For example,

```
#! /bin/sh
cat << 'eof'
Hi there.
eof
```

If you are using *csh*, however, you *must* quote the terminator. The following script prints three lines, not one:

```
#! /bin/csh
cat << \eof
Hi.  You might expect this to be the only line, but it's not.
eof
'e'of
\eof
```

—CT

36.20 Turn Off echo for "Secret" Answers

When you type your password, Unix turns off echoing so what you type won't show on the screen. You can do the same thing in shell scripts with stty -echo.

```
                #!/bin/sh
                ...
stty 5.7        trap 'stty echo; exit' 0 1 2 3 15
                # use the right echo for your Unix:
                echo "Enter code name: \c"
                #echo -n "Enter code name: "
                stty -echo
read 35.18      read ans
                stty echo
                ...
```

The response is stored in $ans. The trap (35.17) helps to make sure that, if the user presses CTRL-c to abort the script, characters will be echoed again.

—JP

36.21 Quick Reference: expr

expr is a very handy tool in shell programming, since it provides the ability to evaluate a wide range of arithmetic, logical, and relational expressions. It evaluates its arguments as expressions and prints the result.

Syntax

Here's the syntax. The [brackets] mean "optional"; don't type the brackets:

    expr arg1 operator arg2 [operator arg3 ...]

Arguments and operators must be separated by spaces. In many cases, an argument is an integer, typed literally or represented by a shell variable. There are three types of operators: arithmetic, relational, and logical.

Exit status (35.12) values for *expr* are 0 if the expression evaluates nonzero and non-null, 1 if the expression evaluates to 0 or null, and 2 if the expression is invalid.

Arithmetic operators

Use these to produce mathematical expressions whose results are printed:

+   Add *arg2* to *arg1*.

−   Subtract *arg2* from *arg1*.

*   Multiply the arguments.

/   Divide *arg1* by *arg2*.

%   Take the remainder when *arg1* is divided by *arg2* (modulus).

Addition and subtraction are evaluated last, unless they are grouped inside parentheses. The symbols *, (, and) have meaning to the shell, so they must be escaped (preceded by a backslash or enclosed in quotes).

Relational operators

Use these to compare two arguments. Arguments can also be words, in which case comparisons assume a < z and A < Z. If the comparison statement is true, *expr* writes 1 to standard output (43.1); if false, it writes 0. The symbols > and < must be escaped.

=   Are the arguments equal?

!=   Are the arguments different?

>   Is *arg1* greater than *arg2*?

>=   Is *arg1* greater than or equal to *arg2*?

<   Is *arg1* less than *arg2*?

<=   Is *arg1* less than or equal to *arg2*?

Logical operators

Use these to compare two arguments. Depending on the values, the result written to standard output can be *arg1* (or some portion of it), *arg2*, or 0. The symbols | and & must be escaped.

| Logical OR; if *arg1* has a nonzero (and non-null) value, the output is *arg1*; otherwise, the output is *arg2*.

& Logical AND; if both *arg1* and *arg2* have a nonzero (and non-null) value, the output is *arg1*; otherwise, the output is 0.

: Sort of like *grep* (13.1); *arg2* is a regular expression (32.4) to search for in *arg1*. If the *arg2* pattern is enclosed in \(\), the output is the portion of *arg1* that matches; otherwise, the output is simply the number of characters that match. A pattern match always applies to the beginning of the argument (the ^ symbol (32.5) is assumed by default).

Examples

Division happens first; output is 10:

```
$ expr 5 + 10 / 2
```

Addition happens first; output is 7 (truncated from 7.5):

```
$ expr \( 5 + 10 \) / 2
```

Add 1 to variable *i*; this is how variables are incremented in Bourne shell scripts:

```
i=`expr "$i" + 1`
```

Output 1 (true) if variable *a* is the string "hello":

```
$ expr "$a" = hello
```

Output 1 (true) if variable *b* plus 5 equals 10 or more:

```
$ expr "$b" + 5 \>= 10
```

In the examples below, variable *p* is the string "version.100". This command returns the number of characters in *p*:

```
$ expr "$p" : '.*'
```
        Output is 11

Match all characters and print them:

```
$ expr "$p" : '\(.*\)'
```
        Output is "version.100"

Output the number of lowercase letters matched:

```
$ expr "$p" : '[a-z]*'
```
        Output is 7

Match a string of lowercase letters:

```
$ expr "$p" : '\([a-z]*\)'
```
        Output is "version"

Truncate $x if it contains five or more characters; if not, just output $x. (Logical OR uses the second argument when the first one is 0 or null, i.e., when the match fails.)

```
$ expr "$x" : '\(.....\)'  "$x"
```

—DG

36.22 Testing Characters in a String with expr

The *expr* (36.21) command does a lot of different things with expressions. One expression it handles has three arguments: first, a string; second, a colon (:); third, a regular expression (32.4). The string and regular expression usually need quotes.

expr can count the number of characters that match the regular expression. The regular expression is automatically anchored to the start of the string you're matching, as if you'd typed a ^ at the start of it in *grep*, *sed*, and so on. *expr* is usually run with backquotes (28.14) to save its output:

```
$ part="resistor 321-1234-00"
$ name="Ellen Smith"
   ...
$ expr "$part" : '[a-z ]*[0-9]'       ...character position of first number
10
$ len=`expr "$name" : '[a-zA-Z]*'`
$ echo first name has $len characters
first name has 5 characters
```

When a regular expression matches some character(s), *expr* returns a zero ("true") exit status (35.12). If you want a true/false test like this, throw away the number that *expr* prints and test its exit status:

/dev/null
43.12

```
$ if expr "$part" : '.*[0-9]' > /dev/null
> then echo \$part has a number in it.
> else echo "it doesn't"
> fi
$part has a number in it.
```

—JP

36.23 Grabbing Parts of a String

How can you parse (split, search) a string of text to find the last word, the second column, and so on? There are a lot of different ways. Pick the one that works best for you—or invent another one! (Unix has lots of ways to work with strings of text.)

Matching with expr

The *expr* command (36.21) can grab part of a string with a regular expression. The example below is from a shell script whose last command-line argument is a filename. The two commands below use *expr* to grab the last argument and all arguments except the last one. The "$*" gives *expr* a list of all command-line arguments in a single word. (Using "$@" (35.20) here wouldn't work because it gives individually quoted arguments. *expr* needs all arguments in one word.)

```
last=`expr "$*" : '.* \(.*\)'`      # LAST ARGUMENT
first=`expr "$*" : '\(.*\) .*'`     # ALL BUT LAST ARGUMENT
```

Let's look at the regular expression that gets the last word. The leading part of the expression, .* , matches as many characters as it can, followed by a space. This includes all words up to and including the last space. After that, the end of the expression, \(.*\), matches the last word.

The regular expression that grabs the first words is the same as the previous one—but I've moved the \(\) pair. Now it grabs all words up to but not including the last space. The end of the regular expression, .*, matches the last space and last word—and *expr* ignores them. So the final .* really isn't needed here (though the space is). I've included the final .* because it follows from the first example.

expr is great when you want to split a string into just two parts. The .* also makes *expr* good for skipping a variable number of words when you don't know how many words a string will have. But *expr* is poor at getting, say, the fourth word in a string. And it's almost useless for handling more than one line of text at a time.

Using echo with awk or cut

awk can split lines into words, but it has a lot of overhead and can take some time to execute, especially on a busy system. The *cut* (21.14) command starts more quickly than *awk* but it can't do as much.

Both those utilities are designed to handle multiple lines of text. You can tell *awk* to handle a single line with its pattern-matching operators and its *NR* variable. You can also run those utilities with a single line of text, fed to the standard input through a pipe from *echo*. For example, to get the third field from a colon-separated string:

```
string="this:is:just:a:dummy:string"
field3_awk=`echo "$string" | awk -F: '{print $3}'`
field3_cut=`echo "$string" | cut -d: -f3`
```

Let's combine two *echo* commands. One sends text to *awk* or *cut* through a pipe; the utility ignores all the text from columns 1–24, then prints columns 25 to the end of the variable *text*. The outer *echo* prints *The answer is* and that answer.

Notice that the inner double quotes are escaped with backslashes to keep the Bourne shell from interpreting them before the inner *echo* runs:

```
echo "The answer is `echo \"$text\" | awk '{print substr($0,25)}'`"
echo "The answer is `echo \"$text\" | cut -c25-`"
```

Using set and IFS

The Bourne shell *set* (35.25) command can be used to parse a single-line string and store it in the command-line parameters (35.20) "$@", $*, $1, $2, and so on. Then you can also loop through the words with a *for* loop (35.21) and use everything else the shell has for dealing with command-line parameters. Also, you can set the Bourne shell's *IFS* variable to control how the shell splits the string.

 The formats used by *stty* and the behavior of *IFS* may vary from platform to platform.

By default, the *IFS* (internal field separator) shell variable holds three characters: SPACE, TAB, and NEWLINE. These are the places that the shell parses command lines.

If you have a line of text—say, from a database—and you want to split it into fields, you can put the field separator into *IFS* temporarily, use the shell's *set* (35.25) command to store the fields in command-line parameters, then restore the old *IFS*.

For example, the chunk of a shell script below gets current terminal settings from *stty –g*, which looks like this:

```
2506:5:bf:8a3b:3:1c:8:15:4:0:0:0:11:13:1a:19:12:f:17:16:0:0
```

In the next example, the shell parses the line returned from *stty* by the backquotes (28.14). It stores *x* in $1, which stops errors if *stty* fails for some reason. (Without the *x*, if *stty* made no standard output, the shell's *set* command would print a list of all shell variables.) Then *2506* goes into $2, *5* into $3, and so on. The original Bourne shell can handle only nine parameters (through $9); if your input lines may have more than nine fields, this isn't a good technique. But this script uses the Korn shell, which (along with most other Bourne-type shells) doesn't have that limit.

```
#!/bin/ksh
oldifs="$IFS"
# Change IFS to a colon:
IFS=:
# Put x in $1, stty -g output in $2 thru ${23}:
set x `stty -g`
IFS="$oldifs"
# Window size is in 16th field (not counting the first "x"):
echo "Your window has ${17} rows."
```

Because you don't need a subprocess to parse the output of *stty*, this can be faster than using an external command like *cut* (21.14) or *awk* (20.10).

There are places where *IFS* can't be used because the shell separates command lines at spaces before it splits at *IFS*. It doesn't split the results of variable substitution or command substitution (28.14) at spaces, though. Here's an example— three different ways to parse a line from */etc/passwd*:

```
% cat splitter
#!/bin/sh
IFS=:
line='larry:Vk9skS323kd4q:985:100:Larry Smith:/u/larry:/bin/tcsh'
set x $line
echo "case 1: \$6 is '$6'"
set x `grep larry /etc/passwd`
echo "case 2: \$6 is '$6'"
set x larry:Vk9skS323kd4q:985:100:Larry Smith:/u/larry:/bin/tcsh
echo "case 3: \$6 is '$6'"

% ./splitter
case 1: $6 is 'Larry Smith'
case 2: $6 is 'Larry Smith'
case 3: $6 is 'Larry'
```

Case 1 used variable substitution and case 2 used command substitution; the sixth field contained the space. In case 3, though, with the colons on the command line, the sixth field was split: $6 became *Larry* and $7 was *Smith*. Another problem would have come up if any of the fields had been empty (as in larry:: 985:100:*etc*...)—the shell would "eat" the empty field and $6 would contain */u/ larry*. Using *sed* with its escaped parentheses (34.11) to do the searching and the parsing could solve the last two problems.

Using sed

The Unix *sed* (34.1) utility is good at parsing input that you may or may not otherwise be able to split into words, at finding a single line of text in a group and outputting it, and many other things. In this example, I want to get the percentage-used of the filesystem mounted on */home*. That information is buried in the output of the *df* (15.8) command. On my system,* *df* output looks like:

```
+% df
Filesystem          kbytes    used   avail capacity  Mounted on
  ...
/dev/sd3c          1294854  914230  251139    78%     /work
/dev/sd4c           597759  534123    3861    99%     /home
  ...
```

---

* If you are using something other than GNU *df*, you may need to use the −k switch.

I want the number *99* from the line ending with */home*. The *sed* address / \/home$/ will find that line (including a space before the */home* makes sure the address doesn't match a line ending with */something/home*). The *–n* option keeps *sed* from printing any lines except the line we ask it to print (with its *p* command). I know that the "capacity" is the only word on the line that ends with a percent sign (%). A space after the first .* makes sure that .* doesn't "eat" the first digit of the number that we want to match by [0-9]. The *sed* escaped-parenthesis operators (**34.11**) grab that number:

```
usage=`df | sed -n '/ \/home$/s/.* \([0-9][0-9]*\)%.*/\1/p'`
```

Combining *sed* with *eval* (**27.8**) lets you set several shell variables at once from parts of the same line. Here's a command line that sets two shell variables from the *df* output:

```
eval `df |
sed -n '/ \/home$/s/^[^ ]*  *\([0-9]*\)  *\([0-9]*\).*/kb=\1 u=\2/p'`
```

The left-hand side of that substitution command has a regular expression that uses *sed*'s escaped parenthesis operators. They grab the "kbytes" and "used" columns from the *df* output. The right-hand side outputs the two *df* values with Bourne shell variable-assignment commands to set the *kb* and *u* variables. After *sed* finishes, the resulting command line looks like this:

```
eval kb=597759 u=534123
```

Now $kb gives you *597759*, and $u contains *534123*.

—JP

36.24 Nested Command Substitution

Article 28.14 introduced command substitution with a pair of backquotes (''). Let's review. The shell runs a backquoted string as a command, then replaces the string with its output. Sometimes—though not as often—you'll want to use the results from one backquoted string as arguments to another command, itself also inside backquotes. To do that, you need to nest the backquotes to tell the shell which command (which set of backquotes) should be done first, with its output given to the second command. This is tricky with backquotes; the Korn shell introduced an easier way that you'll see below. Here's a simple example— the first command line uses nested backquotes, and the next two commands show its parts:*

```
$ echo "Next year will be 200`expr \`date +%y\` + 1`."
Next year will be 2002.
$ date +%y
```

---

* True, this won't work after 2008. Also true, most shells have built-in arithmetic, and some can zero-pad results. But this *is* a simple example!

```
01
$ expr 01 + 1
2
```

The command to run first has escaped backquotes (\\'\\') around it. In the example above, that's the date +%y command. date +%y outputs the year—in this case, 01—and that value is passed to the *expr* command. *expr* adds 01 and 1 to get 2. Then that result (from the outer backquotes) is passed to *echo*, on its command line, and *echo* prints the message.

Why does the inner command, inside the escaped backquotes (\\'\\'), run first? It's because the backslash before the backquote turns off the special meaning (27.12) of the backquote. When the shell first evaluates the command line, which backquotes does it see? It sees the unescaped backquotes, the ones around the expr command, and the shell runs the command:

```
expr `date +%y` + 1
```

But when the shell evaluates that command line, it sees the backquotes in it (now unescaped) and runs *that* command—date +%y. The date +%y command outputs 01. Next, the shell can finish the command expr 01 + 1. It outputs 2. Then the *echo* command can print its message.

Whew. Most newer Bourne-type shells have an easier way: the $(*command*) operators. Use $(before the command, where you would use an opening backquote. Put the) after the command, in place of a closing backquote. You don't have to escape these operators when you nest them.

Here's the previous example with $( ), then a more real-life example:

```
$ echo "Next year will be 200$(expr $(date +%y) + 1)."
Next year will be 2002.
```

2>&1 36.16
```
$ tarout=$(tar cf /dev/rst1 $(find . -type f -mtime -1 -print) 2>&1)
    time passes...
$ echo "$tarout"
tar: ./files/145923: Permission denied
```

The inner command—in this case, the *find* (9.1)—is run first. Its output, a list of filenames, is put on the command line of the *tar* (38.2) command. Finally, the output of *tar* (in this case, an error message) is stored in the *tarout* shell variable.

Beginners (and some long-time programmers too) might argue that you should never nest command substitution because it's too confusing. I think there are times nesting is clearer. It's more compact and doesn't need temporary storage. And it's not that hard to understand once you see what's happening. There's another nice example in article 24.16.

—JP

36.25 Testing Two Strings with One case Statement

The shell's *case* statement (35.10) has some advantages over the *test* command (35.26)—for instance, *case* can do pattern matching. But *test* has the −*a* and −*o* "and" and "or" operators; those don't seem easy to do with *case*. And *test* isn't built in to some older shells, so using *case* may be faster.

Here's a way to test two things with one *case* statement. It won't solve all your problems. If you think carefully about the possible values the variables you're testing can have, though, this might do the trick. Use a separator (delimiter) character between the two variables.

In the example below, I've picked a slash (/). You could use almost any character that isn't used in *case* pattern matching (35.11) and that won't be stored in either $# or $1. The *case* below tests the command-line arguments of a script:

```
case "$#/$1" in
1/-f) redodb=yes ;;
0/) ;;
*)   echo "Usage: $0 [-f]" 1>&2; exit 1 ;;
esac
```

If there's one argument ($# is 1) and the argument ($1) is exactly −f, the first pattern matches, and the *redodb* variable is set. If there's no argument, $# will be 0 and $1 will be empty, so the second pattern matches. Otherwise, something is wrong; the third pattern matches, the script prints an error and exits.

Of course, you can do a lot more this way than just testing command-line arguments.

—JP

36.26 Outputting Text to an X Window

Unix has a lot of ways to output text from the command line into the terminal (or window) where a script is running. But there are times you'd like to pop open a new window (under the X Window System (1.22)), give the user a message—and maybe let the user reply too. X comes with a standard client named *xmessage* that does this. It pops open a window like Figure 36-7 with a message, then waits for the user to click a button (possibly one of many) or press RETURN. For details, you can read the *xmessage* manual page. I'll show how I integrated *xmessage* into a shell script.

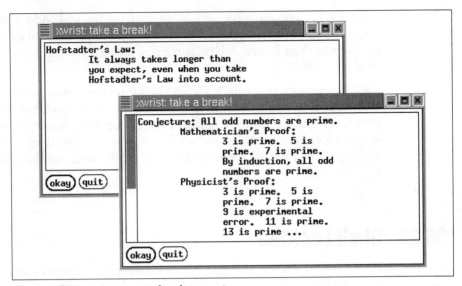

Figure 36-7. An xmessage window from xwrist

xwrist

A good way to prevent wrist injuries (from too much typing) is by taking periodic breaks. The *xwrist* script uses *xmessage* to remind me (every 10 minutes) to take a break—and prints a fortune for me to read while I do.

Let's look at two parts of the script. First, the script checks to see if the X Window System *DISPLAY* environment variable (35.5) is set; if not, it complains (with a message like xwrist: DISPLAY: unset? I only work under the X Window System) and exits:

: **36.6**
${..?..} **36.7**

```
: ${DISPLAY?"unset? I only work under the X Window System"}
```

After checking the command-line arguments and setting some shell variables, the script does its main work with an endless loop:

`...` **28.14**

```
while sleep $delay
do
    if xmessage -nearmouse -geometry $geometry -title "$title" \
        -buttons okay:1,quit:0 -default okay \
        "`/usr/games/fortune | fmt $fmtarg`"
    then exit 0
    fi
done
```

The *while* loop (35.15) is endless because *sleep* normally returns 0 (35.12). As long as the user keeps clicking the *okay* button, a new *xmessage* window will pop up again $delay seconds after the previous one. The *xmessage* command line is split into three pieces. It's run by an *if* statement (35.13). On the second line, -buttons okay:1,quit:0 tells *xmessage* to make the two buttons. If the user clicks the *quit* button, *xmessage* returns 0 status and the *if* runs exit 0 to end the script. Otherwise, *xmessage* returns 1 (because the user clicked *okay* or pressed RETURN; the -default okay sets this up) and the loop repeats.

(Here's a fun enhancement, left as an exercise for you. Add a third button labeled *mail this* that uses *mail*(1) to send you (*$USER*) an email copy of the current fortune. You'll need to change the *if* to a *case* statement (35.10) that tests $? (35.12).)

The last *xmessage* argument is the text to put on the screen. *fmt* (21.2) reformats the output of *fortune* roughly to fit the window. (There's no fancy coding here to be sure that the text fits the window exactly; I just tweak the output width, set in the *fmtarg* variable, to match the window geometry, which is set in the *geometry* variable.) If you set the geometry to make a fairly wide window, you may not need *fmt* at all.

—*JP*

36.27 Shell Lockfile

Here's an efficient and portable way to create a lockfile from a shell script.* It's also an interesting demonstration of the way that Unix umasks and file permissions (50.2) are handled.

A *lockfile* can be used when a particular program might be run more than once at the same time and you need to be sure that only one instance of the program can do something (modify some file, access a printer, etc.). To really do this right, the program needs to both test for the lockfile and create it (if it doesn't exist) in one *atomic* operation. If the test-and-set operation isn't atomic—for instance, if a program tests for the lock file in one command and then creates the lock file in the next command—there's a chance that another user's program could do *its* test at the precise moment between the first program's (non-atomic) test and set operations. The technique in this article lets you make a lockfile atomically from a shell script.

 This technique doesn't work for scripts run as the superuser (*root*). It depends on the fact that a standard user can't write a file without write permisson. But *root* can write *any* file, whether it has write permission or not. If there's a chance that *root* might run your script, you might want to add a test of the UID—by running the *id* command, for instance—and be sure that the UID isn't 0 (the superuser's).

Let's say you have a script called *edmaster*; it edits a master configuration file named *config*. To be sure that two users can't modify the *config* file at the same time, the first *edmaster* checks whether the lockfile exists. If the lockfile doesn't exist, *edmaster* creates it and modifies the *config* file. When it's done editing, it

---

* Greg Ubben sent this idea.

removes the lockfile. If someone tries to run a second *edmaster* process, it sees the lockfile from the first *edmaster*, waits, and checks every few seconds to see if the lockfile is gone. Once the first *edmaster* removes the lockfile, the second *edmaster* can create the lockfile and do its editing of *config*. (Note that some editors—for instance, *nvi-1.79* under Linux—automatically get a write and/or read lock before you to edit a file.)

Here are pieces of a script that check the lock, create it, and (later) remove it:

```
# set name of this program's lockfile:
myname=`basename $0`
LOCKFILE=/tmp/lock.$myname
   ...
# Loop until we get a lock:
until (umask 222; echo $$ >$LOCKFILE) 2>/dev/null    # test & set

do
    # Optional message - show lockfile owner and creation time:
    set x `ls -l $LOCKFILE`
    echo "Waiting for user $4 (working since $7 $8 $9)..."

    sleep 5
done

# Do whatever we need exclusive access to do...
    ...
rm -f $LOCKFILE             # unlock
```

2› **36.16**
/dev/null
43.12

set **35.25**

If another user tried to run *edconfig*, and *jpeek* had run *edconfig* first, she might see:

```
% edconfig
Waiting for user jpeek (working since Aug 23 14:05)...
   ...a 5-second pause
Waiting for user jpeek (working since Aug 23 14:05)...
   another 5-second pause...
   ...then jpeek finishes and she can edit the file.
```

How does it work? Almost all the action is in the first line of the loop. A umask of 222 creates files that are read-only (mode r--r--r--). Because the *umask 222* command is run in a subshell (24.4), it affects only the lockfile that's created in the subshell at the top of the loop. The rest of the shell script keeps its normal umask. And if the redirection fails (because the lock file exists), only the subshell will abort—not the parent shell running the script.

If the lockfile already exists (because another process has created it), the loop executes sleep 5; five seconds later, it tries to create the lock. If the lockfile exists, it will be read-only—so the command echo $$ >$LOCKFILE will return a nonzero status. A nonzero status is what keeps an *until* loop (35.15) running. Once the other process (which has the lock) removes the lockfile, the *echo* command in the subshell writes the shell's process ID number into the lockfile, and the *until* loop terminates.

But if the lockfile is read-only, how can it ever be created? That's the other interesting part of this technique. The umask applies to the file only as it's created; if the file doesn't exist, the umask doesn't apply to it (yet) and the file can be created. In fact, you can create a file with mode 000 by typing:

```
$ (umask 666; echo hi > afile)
$ ls -l afile
---------- 1 jpeek   wheel   3 Aug 23 14:08 afile
$ touch afile
-rw-rw-r-- 1 jpeek   wheel   3 Aug 23 14:10 afile
```

—JP

37

Shell Script Debugging and Gotchas

37.1 Tips for Debugging Shell Scripts

Depending on the Bourne shell version you have, the error messages it gives can be downright useless. For instance, it might say just End of file unexpected. Here are a few tricks to use to get a little more information about what's going on. Remember, it's probably best for you to use one of shells derived from the Bourne shell, rather than the C shell, for scripting.

Use –xv

Start your script like this:

```
#!/bin/sh -xv
```

(If your Unix can't handle #!, use the command set -xv (35.25)). The –xv shows you what's happening as the shell reads your script. The lines of the script will be shown as the shell reads them. The shell shows each command it executes with a plus sign (+) before the command.

Note that the shell reads an entire loop (*for*, *while*, etc.) before it executes any commands in the loop.

If you want to run a script with debugging but you don't want to edit the script file, you can also start the shell explicitly from the command line and give the options there:

```
% sh -xv scrfile
```

Debugging output is usually pretty long, more than a screenful, so I pipe it to a pager like *less*. But the shell sends its debugging output to *stderr*, so I pipe both *stdout* and *stderr* (43.4) to the pager.

```
$ scrfile 2>&1 | less
```

Do you want to save the debugging output in a file and see it on your screen, too? Use *tee* (43.8) to copy the *scrfile* stdout and stderr; add *tee* to the pipeline before the pager.

```
$ scrfile | tee outfile 2>&1 | less
```

If the script is slow, you can run it in the background. Redirect the shell's output and errors (43.5, 27.11) into a temporary file. Use *tail –f* (12.10) to "watch" the log file. If you want to do something else while the script runs, just kill the *tail* command (with CTRL-c or your interrupt key), do something else, then start another *tail –f* when you want to watch again.

Finally, if the script normally writes something to its standard output, you can split the normal and debugging outputs into two files (43.1).

Unmatched Operators

If the shell says End of file unexpected, look for a line in your script that has an opening quote but no closing quote. The shell is probably searching for but never finding the matching quote. Missing parentheses and braces ({}) can cause the same error.

Exit Early

If you're getting an End of file unexpected error, put these two lines near the middle of the script:

```
echo "DEBUG: quitting early..." 1>&2
exit
```

Then run your script. Those lines will print a message and stop the shell where you put them. If you don't get the End of file unexpected error anymore, you know that the problem is somewhere after the exit line, and you can move those two lines farther down and try again. Otherwise, move them up.

Missing or Extra esac, ;;, fi, etc.

A message like line 23: ;; unexpected means that you have an unmatched piece of code somewhere before line 23. You'll also see fi unexpected. Look at all nested *if* and *case* statements, and statements like them, to be sure that they end in the right places.

Line Numbers Reset Inside Redirected Loops

The shell may give you an error that mentions "line 1" or another line number that seems way too small, when there's no error close to the top of your script. Look at any loops or other structures with redirected inputs or outputs (43.6).

Some Bourne shells start a separate shell to run these loops and lose track of the line numbers.

—JP and SJC

37.2 Bourne Shell Debugger Shows a Shell Variable

If you have a shell script that sets several variables and you want to show the value of one of them, you can add a loop that asks you for variable names and displays their values (36.14):

```
% cat myscript
#!/bin/sh
   ...
while echo "Pick a variable; just RETURN quits: \c"
      read var
do
      case "$var" in
      "") break ;;
      *)  eval echo \$$var ;;
      esac
done
```

The loop prompts Pick a variable:, then reads a value; if you type an empty answer, the loop quits. Otherwise, the value of that variable is displayed; the *eval* (27.8) command scans the *echo* command line twice.

This tip isn't just good for debugging. It's good in any shell script where you need to show the value of a variable by typing its name.

—JP

37.3 Stop Syntax Errors in Numeric Tests

The *test* and *[* (square bracket) commands (35.26) can compare two numbers. But it's an error if one of the numbers you test is stored in a shell variable that's empty or doesn't exist. For example, an empty *num* variable here will give you a Syntax error:

```
if [ "$num" -gt 0 ]
then ...
```

To stop syntax errors, add a leading zero, like this:

```
if [ "0$num" -gt 0 ]
then ...
```

In that case, if $num is empty, the test will compare 0 to 0. If $num is 1, the test will be true (because 01 is greater than 0)—and so on, just as it should be.

The zero trick doesn't work with negative numbers, though, so if you expect ever to need to deal with negative numbers, you may want to look into other methods of checking to see if a variable has a value, such as this method from the *bash* shell, which displays an error if the variable is null or unset, or the following method, which assigns a default value:

```
#!/bin/sh
    ...

# check $num first, fail with error
tmp=${num:?"num not set"}

# use a default
default=0
if [ ${num:-default} -gt 0 ]
then
    ...
```

—*JP and SJC*

37.4 Stop Syntax Errors in String Tests

Using the *test* or *[* (square bracket) command (35.26) for a string test can cause errors if the variable starts with a dash (-). For example:

```
if [ "$var" = something ]
then ...
```

If $var starts with -r, the *test* command may think that you want to test for a readable file.

One common fix (that doesn't always work; see below) is to put an extra character at the start of each side of the test. This means the first argument will never start with a dash; it won't look like an option:

```
if [ "X$var" = Xsomething ]
then ...
```

That trick doesn't work if you want the test to fail when the variable is empty or not set. Here's a Bourne shell test that handles empty variables:

```
case "${var+X}" in
X) ...do this if variable is set...
   ;;

*) ...do this if variable is not set...
   ;;
esac
```

If $var is set (even if it has an empty string), the shell replaces ${var+X} (36.7) with just X and the first part of the *case* succeeds. Otherwise the default case, *), is used.

See also article 37.3 for a brief example of *bash* parameter expansion and dealing with unset or null values by reporting an error or by assigning default values.

—JP

37.5 Quoting and Command-Line Parameters

Q: *I need to pass a shell script some arguments with multiple words. I thought that putting quotes (27.12) around command-line arguments would group them. The shell script seems to ignore the quoting, somehow. Here's a simple example:*

```
$ cat script
...
for arg in $*
do
    echo "Argument is $arg"
done
$ script '1 2 3' 4
...
Argument is 1
Argument is 2
Argument is 3
Argument is 4
```

A: **A:** This is the way $* is defined to work. $* expands to:

```
$1 $2
```

[not "$1" "$2" *—JP*] if there are two arguments. Hence the *for* loop reads:

```
for arg in 1 2 3 4
```

Note that the quotes are gone. What you wanted the shell to see was:

```
for arg in '1 2 3' 4
```

You can't get that, but you can get something that is good enough:

"$@" 35.20
```
for arg in "$@"
```

In effect, $@ expands to:

```
$1" "$2
```

Putting ""s around $@, the effect is:

```
for arg in "$1" "$2"
```

Shell quoting is unnecessarily complex. The C shell actually has the right idea (variables can be set to "word lists"; *argv* is such a list), but its defaults and syntax for suppressing them make for an artless programming language:

```
foreach arg ($argv:q)        # colon q ?!?
```

For the special case of iterating a shell variable over the argument list as it stands at the beginning of the iteration, the Bourne shell provides the construct for arg do [i.e., no in *list* —*JP*]:

```
for arg
do echo "Argument is $arg"
done
```

The example produces:

```
Argument is 1 2 3
Argument is 4
```

"$@" is still needed for passing argument lists to other programs. Unfortunately, since $@ is defined as expanding to:

```
"$1" "$2...$n-1" "$n
```

(where *n* is the number of arguments), when there are no arguments, "$@" expands to "", and "" produces a single argument. [Many Unix vendors considered this a bug and changed it so that it produces *no* arguments. —*JP*] The best solution for this is to use, for example:

```
% cat bin/okeeffe
#! /bin/sh
exec rsh okeeffe.berkeley.edu -l torek ${1+"$@"}
%
```

The construct ${1+"$@"} means "expand $1, but if $1 is not defined, use "$@" instead." [You don't need this on Bourne shells with the "bug fix" I mentioned, or on *bash et al.* —*JP*] Hence, if there are no arguments, we get $1 (which is nothing and produces no arguments); otherwise, we get "$@" (which expands as above). ${*var+instead*} is one of several *sh* "expansion shortcuts" (36.7). Another more generally useful one is ${*var-default*}, which expands to $*var*, but if *var* is not set, to *default* instead. All of these can be found in the manual for *sh*, which is worth reading several times, experimenting as you go.

bash has a variety of similar but expanded mechanisms as well, involving a colon before the modifier:

foo=${bar:-baz}	*if bar set and non-null, substitute value, else substitute baz...*
fum=${fee:=foe}	*if fee unset or is null, set it to foe, value then substituted...*
fiend=${jeckyll::=hyde}	*set jeckyll to hyde, then substitute value... (zsh only)*
${required?"error"}	*if required set or non-null, substitute its value, else return "error" and exit...*
man=${fullmoon:+wolfman}	*if fullmoon set and non-null, substitute wolfman, else substitute nothing...*

See the *bash* manual page's section on parameter expansion. *ksh*, *pdksh*, and *zsh* also have support for the same syntax; *zsh* has an entire manual page devoted to just parameter expansions: *zshexpn*(1). Poke around; there's lots of good stuff to explore.

—*CT and SJC*

37.6 How Unix Keeps Time

Like all other operating systems, Unix has a concept of the time. And virtually all Unix systems, even the smallest, include a clock with some sort of battery backup built in.

All Unix systems keep time by counting the number of microseconds since midnight, January 1, 1970, Greenwich Mean Time. This date is commonly called the *epoch*, and it has folk-significance as the begining of the Unix era. Although the first work on Unix began in the late '60s, the first versions of Unix were available (within Bell Laboratories) in the early '70s.

This count gets updated roughly 60 times per second. The exact rate depends on your particular Unix system and is determined by the constant, HZ, defined in the header file */usr/include/sys/param.h:*[*]

```
#define   HZ   60
```

This is the time's "resolution," often referred to as the clock's "tick." Note that it has nothing to do with your system's CPU clock rate. Time measurements are normally no more precise than your system's clock resolution, although some systems have added facilities for more precise timing.

If your Unix system belongs to a network, it is important to keep all the clocks on the network "in sync."[†] Strange things happen if you copy a file from one system to another and its date appears to be some time in the future. Many Unix systems run a *time daemon* (one of those mysterious helper programs (1.10)) to take care of this.[‡]

Unix automatically keeps track of daylight savings time (summer time), leap years, and other chronological trivia. When the system is installed, you have to tell it your time zone and the style of daylight savings time you want to observe. As Unix has become an international standard, the number of time zones (and obscure ways of handling daylight savings time) it can handle correctly has proliferated. In a few cases, you still have to handle these things by hand; for example, in Europe, as of this writing, the beginning and end of Summer Time were set periodically by the European Parliament, and so may change. Care for Libyan Standard Time?

---

[*] It may be in a file included thereby; on Linux, a bit of hunting shows it in */usr/include/asm/param.h*. The value may vary from system to system, as well.

[†] This is particularly true if your system runs public services such as mail or HTTP.

[‡] A popular choice for network time synchronization is *ntp*, available from *http://www.eecis.udel.edu/~ntp/*.

Unix's internal routines compute time in relation to the epoch, but there is no reason for you to worry about it unless you're a C programmer. A library of time routines can convert between this internal representation and more usable representations; see the Unix manual page for *ctime*(3).

—ML

37.7 Copy What You Do with script

Are you typing a complicated set of commands that you need to show someone else or keep "on file" for documentation? Are you debugging a program that goes wrong somewhere—but the error message flashes by so fast that you can't see it? Do you want to show a "prerecorded" demonstration of an interactive program? The *script* program can help with all of these problems.

Versions of *script* on Unix systems without *ptys* aren't as flexible as the version I'm explaining here. For instance, those versions won't let you use job control (23.3) during the script.

To copy everything you do into a file, just type:

```
% script
Script started, file is typescript
%
```

Now you can type any Unix command that you'd use at a shell prompt. Everything you do is copied into a file named *typescript* in the current directory. (To use a different filename, type its pathname (1.16) on the command line, like script *scriptfile*.) When you're done, type CTRL-d or *exit* (24.4) at a shell prompt.

One thing that surprises people is that *everything* will be copied into the script file. That includes escape sequences that programs send to your terminal. This is both good and bad.

The good part is that you can "play back" whatever happened by *cat*ting (12.2) the script to your screen. When things get boring, you can run an interactive program like *vi* inside the script—then quit the script and play it back with *cat typescript*. The cursor will fly across the screen and your file will be re-edited before your eyes. (This is easier to see if the terminal is set to a slow data rate.)

The bad part is that errors you correct and other terminal-control sequences will be in the file, too. If you edit or print the script file, it may be full of "junk" such as ^M (carriage return) and ^H (backspace) characters. (A command like *cat –v* or *od –c* (12.4) will show you these characters.) If the file has just a few of these characters, you can clean it up by hand with your text editor's global substitution commands. You can also automate your "script cleaning" with techniques such as the ones in articles 21.11 and 37.8.

If you're using *xterm*, it may have a built-in logger. Check its menus (5.17).

—*JP*

37.8 Cleaning script Files

As article 37.7 explains, the files made by the *script* program can have stray control characters in them. The shell script called *script.tidy* can clean them up. Dan Bernstein wrote it and posted it to Usenet; I made a few changes. It reads from files or standard input and writes to standard output.

script.tidy

script.tidy uses the *sed* (34.1) substitute command to remove CTRL-m (RETURN) characters from the ends of lines. It uses the *sed* test command (34.21) to repeat a series of commands that delete a character followed by CTRL-h (BACKSPACE). If you use DELETE as your erase character (5.8), change the script to eat DELETE instead of BACKSPACE. *script.tidy* uses a trick with *echo* and *tr* to store the control characters in shell variables. Because the *sed* script has double-quotes (27.12) around it, the shell variables are substituted in the right places before the shell starts *sed*.

```
#!/bin/sh

# Public domain.

# Put CTRL-M in $m and CTRL-H in $b.
# Change \010 to \177 if you use DEL for erasing.
eval `echo m=M b=H | tr 'MH' '\015\010'`
exec sed "s/$m\$//
:x
s/[^$b]$b//
t x" $*
```

eval **27.8**
exec **36.5**

You can also hack the *sed* script in *script.tidy* to delete some of your terminal's escape sequences. (A really automated *script.tidy* would read your *termcap* or *terminfo* entry and look for all those escape sequences in the script file.)

Bear in mind that *script* was designed to emulate a paper terminal; if you've modified your prompt, especially if you are using multiple-line prompts, your *script* output is going to be full of far worse junk than *script.tidy* can fix. If you find that *script* simply doesn't do it for you, you should consider whether you want a complete record of all terminal input and output or just a record of what you typed. If the latter is more to your liking, you should look into the various history editing and printing capabilities provided by modern shells.

—*JP and SJC*

37.9 Making an Arbitrary-Size File for Testing

The *yes* command (14.5) outputs text over and over.* If you need a file of some size for testing, make it with *yes* and *head* (12.12). For example, to make a file 100k (102,400) characters long, with 12,800 8-character lines (7 digits and a newline), type:

```
% yes 1234567 | head -12800 > 100k-file
```

 On some Unix systems, the command may "hang" and need to be killed with CTRL-c because *head* keeps reading input from the pipe. If it hangs on your system, replace head -12800 with sed 12800q.

You might just want to use *perl*, instead:

```
$ perl -e 'print "1234567\n" x 12800' > file
```

For the Unix admin who has everything, here's one more way, this time using the venerated *dd* command:

```
$ yes | dd of=file count=25
```

There are many variations on this theme. The preceding example simply copies 25 blocks of 512 bytes each from standard input (the output of the *yes* command) to the file *file*. You could also specify a number of bytes to read at a time, using the *ibs* option, and then specify the number of records to write out, using *count*:

```
$ yes | dd ibs=1 of=file count=12800
```

There's More Than One Way To Do It. Be careful, though—you can fill up a disk pretty quickly playing around with the *dd* command!

—*JIK, JP, and SJC*

---

* Believe it or not, it does have a purpose; it was originally designed to pipe "y" answers into interactive programs such as *fsck* before those programs provided the option to proceed with implicit approval. The FreeBSD 4.4 manual says of *yes*(1) that it "outputs *expletive*, or, by default, 'y'", forever.

Part VII

Extending and Managing Your Environment

Part VII contains the following chapters:

38

Backing Up Files

38.1 What Is This "Backup" Thing?

Making copies of critical files in case the originals become inaccessible is called backing them up or making backups. Backups are insurance. They are time and effort you spend protecting yourself from things that might never happen. Your hard drive might never crash, but what vital things would you lose if it did?

Exactly what "making a backup" means varies depending on your circumstances. All of the following examples are ways to make backups applicable to some specific environment:

- Copying some files onto another disk on the same machine, so that if one hard drive dies you still have a copy. (A more sophisticated and automatic way of doing this, which you may have heard about, is called *Redundant Array of Inexpensive Disks* or RAID.)

- Making a compressed tar file and copying it to another machine, so that if one machine crashes you still have a copy.

- Writing copies of your files to a Zip drive, CD-RW, or DVD-RW.

- *tar*ring (38.2) files to a tape.

- Nightly automatic backups of everything that's changed that day (called an *incremental backup*) to multiple tapes, with copies of the tapes stored in off-site secure storage.

If you are just trying to protect your files on your personal machine, simply making sure that critical files have copies on multiple physical disks or occasionally copying files onto another machine or removable storage is probably sufficient. If you're administering a machine that has multiple users, regular backups are almost certainly a necessity. If those users are doing business-critical tasks, very regular backups and off-site copies are a requirement to protect the investment of time involved.

—*DJPH*

38.2 tar in a Nutshell

When many Unix users think of file archives, on tape or in an archive file, they think of the *tar* utility. There are other ways to make archives and handle tapes—including *dump* and *dd*. This article summarizes articles about *tar* in this chapter and others.

- Although *tar* is a *tape ar*chiver, one of its common uses is making an archive file on disk (39.2). Because *tar* "pads" its archives with NUL characters, on-disk *tar* archive files can be much bigger than the size of the individual files put together. Both to fix that and generally to save space, *tar* files are often compressed. The GNU *tar* (39.3) can compress files while storing them and uncompress them while reading them, automatically. If you don't have GNU *tar*, you may need to uncompress an archive manually. Note that a compressed *tar* archive can take less disk space (15.7) than compressing individual small files.

  Because *tar* keeps most of a file's inode information, it can make a more complete copy (10.13) of a file or directory tree than utilities such as *cp*.

- Yes, we do have articles about archives on tape. Article 38.3 has enough information to make your own archive, although you might need the details from article 38.5, too. After you've made an archive, you'll probably want to restore it, at least as a test to be sure your archive is okay. Article 38.6 explains how.

  If there isn't a tape drive on your computer, read article 38.7 about using a drive on another computer.

- *tar* copies a directory tree, recursively, from top to bottom. What if you don't want to archive everything? You can back up just some files by combining *ls –lt* and *find*. Some versions of *tar* have options for including or excluding certain files and directories (39.3).

—*JP*

38.3 Make Your Own Backups

As someone who has been an end user and a system administrator, I strongly believe that every user should understand the importance of backups.

 If you have data that is important to you, you should have a known backup.

Accidents and oversights happen. Tapes can be damaged, lost, or mislabeled. Assume that your system administrator is top-notch. The best administrator can recover your lost data 99 percent of the time. There is still a small chance that the files you need might not be recovered. Can you afford to duplicate months of effort 1 percent of the time? No.

An experienced user learns to be pessimistic. Typically, this important perspective is learned the hard way. Perhaps a few hours are lost. Perhaps days. Sometimes months are lost.

Here are some common situations:

- A user works on a file all day. At the end of the day, the file is deleted by accident. The system manager cannot recover the file. A day's work has been lost.

- A programmer tries to clean up a project directory. Instead of typing rm *.o the programmer types rm * .o and the entire directory is lost.

- A user deletes a file by accident. After a few days, the user asks the system administrator to recover the file. The incremental backup system has reused the only tape the missing file was on.

- A large project is archived on a magnetic tape and deleted from the disk. A year later, some of the information is needed. The tape has a bad block at the beginning. The system manager must learn how to recover data from a bad tape. The attempt is often unsuccessful. The information is lost forever, and must be re-created at the cost of months of effort.

- Someone breaks into a computer and alters or deletes crucial information.

- A fire breaks out in the computer room. The disks and *all* of the backup tapes are lost.

Gulp! I scared myself. Excuse me for a few minutes while I load a tape...

Ah! I feel better now. As I was saying, being pessimistic has its advantages.

Making a backup is easy. Get a blank tape and put a label on it. Learn how to load it into the tape drive. Then do the following:

```
% cd
% tar c .
```

Take the tape out. Write-protect the tape (usually, just slide the tab). That's all.

[Well, okay, not exactly. That would back up only your home directory to the default tape device (usually something like */dev/rmt0*). You may want to back up more than just your home directory, the tape drive may not be at the default device, and you may not have permission to write to the tape drive by default. The rest of the chapter talks about variations on the theme. —DJPH]

—BB

38.4 More Ways to Back Up

Article 38.3 explains the minimal basics of using *tar* to make backups, but there are lots of variations that can be very useful.

To create a *tar* archive for copying to another disk or another machine:

```
% tar cvf 20020214-book.tar ./book
```

tar's *c* option stands for *create*, *v* for *verbose*, and the *f* option for *file*. *20020214-book.tar* is the new archive file to create, and *./book* says to archive the directory *book* in the current directory. Once you have an archive, you might want to compress it to save space. *gzip* and *bzip2* are your best bets. (I use *bzip2* here largely because it tends to give better compression, but be aware that *gzip* is more widely available and thus may be safer for backups.) You can compress it once you've made it:

```
% ls -l 20020214-book.tar
-rw-r--r--  1 deb   deb   19415040 Feb 14 23:15 20020214-book.tar
% bzip2 20020214-book.tar
% ls -l 20020214-book.tar.bz2
-rw-r--r--  1 deb   deb    4033775 Feb 14 23:15 20020214-book.tar.bz2
```

Or you can compress it as you make it. GNU *tar* supports *gzip* compression on the fly with the *z* or *--gzip* options and *bzip2* compression on the fly with the *--bzip2* option, or you can pipe into *gzip* or *bzip2*:

```
% tar czvf 20020214-book.tar.gz ./book
```

```
% tar cvf 20020214-book.tar.bz2 --bzip2 ./book
```

```
% tar cvf - ./book | bzip2 > 20020214-book.tar.bz2
```

Articles 39.2 and 39.3 have more information on using *tar*.

You can get more protection from certain kinds of mishaps by using a version control system like RCS (39.5) or CVS (39.7) to save every version of a file you are updating frequently. While it doesn't protect you from disk crashes, a version control system provides the ability to back up to a previous version if something gets changed or deleted incorrectly.

—*DJPH*

38.5 How to Make Backups to a Local Device

This article was written for Linux systems, but the advice applies everywhere. You may need to make some adjustments—in the names of the tape drive devices and some filesystem directories, for instance. If you're making personal backups (of the files on your account, for instance), you can substitute your directory names for the system directories covered here, but the command names and techniques won't change.

What to Back Up

As article 38.3 says, the simplest way to make a backup is to use *tar* to archive all the files on the system or only those files in a set of specific directories. Before you do this, however, you need to decide what files to back up. Do you need to back up every file on the system? This is rarely necessary, especially if you have your original installation disks or CD-ROM. If you have made specific, important changes to the system, but everything else could simply be reinstalled in case of a problem, you could get by archiving only those files you have made changes to. Over time, however, it is difficult to keep track of such changes.

In general, you will be making changes to the system configuration files in */etc*. There are other configuration files as well, and it can't hurt to archive directories such as */usr/local* (where various packages generally get installed) and */usr/X11R6/lib/X11* (which contains the X Window System configuration files). You may want to do filtering on these directories and back up only the configuration files, since binaries in */usr/local* and things like fonts in the X11 distribution can be reinstalled from their original packages easily enough.

You should also back up your kernel sources (if you have patched your kernel sources); these are found in */usr/src/linux* (*/usr/src/sys* on *BSD). At the very least, you'll want to back up your kernel configuration file if you've built your own kernel; it's in */usr/src/linux/.config* (or */usr/src/sys/platform/conf/KERNELNAME* on *BSD).

It's a good idea to keep notes on what features of the system you've changed so you can make intelligent choices when making backups. If you're truly paranoid, go ahead and back up the whole system: that can't hurt, but the cost of backup media might.

Of course, you should also back up the home directories for each user on the system; these are generally found in */home*. If you have your system configured to receive electronic mail, you might want to back up the incoming mail files for each user. Many people tend to keep old and "important" electronic mail in their incoming mail spool, and it's not difficult to accidentally corrupt one of these files through a mailer error or other mistake. These files are usually found in */var/spool/mail*.

Backing Up to Tape

Assuming you know what files or directories to back up, you're ready to roll. The *tar* command can be used directly, as we saw in article 39.2, to make a backup. For example, the command:

```
tar cvf /dev/rft0 /usr/src /etc /home
```

archives all of the files from */usr/src*, */etc*, and */home* to */dev/rft0*. */dev/rft0* is the first "floppy-tape" device—that is, for the type of tape drive that hangs off of the floppy controller. Many popular tape drives for the PC use this interface. If you have a SCSI tape drive, the device names are */dev/st0*, */dev/st1*, and so on, based on the drive number. Those tape drives with another type of interface have their own device names; you can determine these by looking at the documentation for the device driver in the kernel.

You can then read the archive back from the tape using a command such as:

```
tar xvf /dev/rft0
```

This is exactly as if you were dealing with a tar file on disk, as in article 39.2.

When you use the tape drive, the tape is seen as a stream that may be read from or written to in one direction only. Once *tar* is done, the tape device will be closed, and the tape will rewind (if you're using the default tape device; see below on how to prevent this). You don't create a filesystem on a tape, nor do you mount it or attempt to access the data on it as files. You simply treat the tape device itself as a single "file" to create or extract archives from.

Be sure your tapes are formatted before you use them if you are using a tape drive that needs it. This ensures that the beginning-of-tape marker and bad-blocks information has been written to the tape. At the time of this writing, no tools exist for formatting QIC-80 tapes (those used with floppy tape drivers) under Linux; you'll have to format tapes under MS-DOS or use preformatted tapes.

Creating one tar file per tape might be wasteful if the archive requires a fraction of the capacity of the tape. To place more than one file on a tape, you must first prevent the tape from rewinding after each use, and you must have a way to position the tape to the next "file marker," both for tar file creation and for extraction.

The way to do this is to use the nonrewinding tape devices, which are named */dev/nrft0*, */dev/nrft1*, and so on for floppy-tape drivers, and */dev/nrst0*, */dev/nrst1*, and so on for SCSI tapes. When this device is used for reading or writing, the tape will not be rewound when the device is closed (that is, once *tar* has completed). You can then use *tar* again to add another archive to the tape. The two tar files on the tape won't have anything to do with each other. Of course, if you later overwrite the first tar file, you may overwrite the second file or leave an undesirable gap between the first and second files (which may be interpreted as garbage). In general, don't attempt to replace just one file on a tape that has multiple files on it.

Using the nonrewinding tape device, you can add as many files to the tape as space permits. To rewind the tape after use, use the *mt* command. *mt* is a general-purpose command that performs a number of functions with the tape drive. For example, the command:

```
mt /dev/nrft0 rewind
```

rewinds the tape in the first floppy-tape device. (In this case, you can use the corresponding rewinding tape device as well; however, the tape will rewind just as a side effect of the tape device being closed.)

Similarly, the command:

```
mt /dev/nrft0 reten
```

retensions the tape by winding it to the end and then rewinding it.

When reading files on a multiple-file tape, you must use the nonrewinding tape device with *tar* and the *mt* command to position the tape to the appropriate file.

For example, to skip to the next file on the tape, use the command:

```
mt /dev/nrft0 fsf 1
```

This skips over one file on the tape. Similarly, to skip over two files, use:

```
mt /dev/nrft0 fsf 2
```

Be sure to use the appropriate nonrewinding tape device with *mt*. Note that this command does not move to "file number two" on the tape; it skips over the next two files based on the current tape position. Just use *mt* to rewind the tape if you're not sure where the tape is currently positioned. You can also skip back; see the *mt* manual page for a complete list of options.

You need to use *mt* every time you read a multifile tape. Using *tar* twice in succession to read two archive files usually won't work; this is because *tar* doesn't recognize the file marker placed on the tape between files. Once the first *tar* finishes, the tape is positioned at the beginning of the file marker. Using *tar* immediately will give you an error message, because *tar* will attempt to read the file marker. After reading one file from a tape, just use:

```
mt device fsf 1
```

to move to the next file.

Backing Up to Floppies or Zip Disks

Just as we saw in the last section, the command:

```
tar cvf /dev/fd0 /usr/src /etc /home
```

makes a backup of */usr/src*, */etc*, and */home* to */dev/fd0*, the first floppy device. You can then read the backup using a command such as:

```
tar xvf /dev/fd0
```

If we use */dev/hdd* instead of */dev/fd0* (and our Zip drive is the slave drive on the second IDE controller), we'll be writing to and reading from a Zip disk instead of a floppy. (Your device name may vary depending on your OS.) Because floppies and Zip disks have a rather limited storage capacity, GNU *tar* allows you to create a "multivolume" archive. (This feature applies to tapes as well, but it is far more useful in the case of smaller media.) With this feature, *tar* prompts you to insert a new volume after reading or writing each disk. To use this feature, simply provide the *M* option to *tar*, as in:

```
tar cvMf /dev/fd0 /usr/src /etc /home
```

Be sure to label your disks well, and don't get them out of order when attempting to restore the archive.

One caveat of this feature is that it doesn't support the automatic *gzip* compression provided by the *z* option. However, there are various reasons why you may not want to compress your backups created with *tar*, as discussed later. At any rate, you can create your own multivolume backups using *tar* and *gzip* in conjunction with a program that reads and writes data to a sequence of disks (or tapes), prompting for each in succession. One such program is *backflops*, available on several Linux distributions and on the FTP archive sites. A do-it-yourself way to accomplish the same thing would be to write the backup archive to a disk file and use *dd* or a similar command to write the archive as individual chunks to each disk. If you're brave enough to try this, you can figure it out for yourself. [Aw, come on, guys, have a heart! (Psst, readers: look at the end of article 21.9.) —JP]

To gzip, or Not to gzip?

There are good arguments both for and against compression of *tar* archives when making backups. The overall problem is that neither *tar* nor *gzip* is particularly fault-tolerant, no matter how convenient they are. Although compression using *gzip* can greatly reduce the amount of backup media required to store an archive, compressing entire *tar* files as they are written to floppy or tape makes the backup prone to complete loss if one block of the archive is corrupted, say, through a media error (not uncommon in the case of floppies and tapes). Most compression algorithms, *gzip* included, depend on the coherency of data across many bytes to achieve compression. If any data within a compressed archive is corrupt, *gunzip* may not be able to uncompress the file at all, making it completely unreadable to *tar*. The same applies to *bzip2*. It may compress things better than *gzip*, but it has the same lack of fault-tolerance.

This is much worse than if the tar file were uncompressed on the tape. Although *tar* doesn't provide much protection against data corruption within an archive, if there is minimal corruption within a tar file, you can usually recover most of the archived files with little trouble, or at least those files up until the corruption occurs. Although far from perfect, it's better than losing your entire backup.

A better solution would be to use an archiving tool other than *tar* to make backups. There are several options available. *cpio* (38.13) is an archiving utility that packs files together, much like *tar*. However, because of the simpler storage method used by *cpio*, it recovers cleanly from data corruption in an archive. (It still doesn't handle errors well on gzipped files.)

The best solution may be to use a tool such as *afio*. *afio* supports multivolume backups and is similar in some respects to *cpio*. However, *afio* includes compression and is more reliable because each individual file is compressed. This means that if data on an archive is corrupted, the damage can be isolated to individual files, instead of to the entire backup.

These tools should be available with your Linux distribution, as well as from all of the Internet-based Linux archives. A number of other backup utilities, with varying degrees of popularity and usability, have been developed or ported for Linux. If you're serious about backups, you should look into them.*

—*MW, MKD, and LK*

38.6 Restoring Files from Tape with tar

When you create an archive, there are several ways to specify the directory. If the directory is under the current directory, you could type:

```
% tar c project
```

A similar way to specify the same directory is:

```
% tar c ./project
```

If you are currently in the directory you want archived, you can type:

```
% tar c .
```

Another way to archive the current directory is to type:

```
% tar c *
```

---

* Of course, this section was written after the author took the first backup of his Linux system in nearly four years of use!

Here, the shell expands the asterisk (*) to the files in the current directory. However, it does not match files starting with a dot (.), which is why the previous technique is preferred.

This causes a problem when restoring a directory from a *tar* archive. You may not know whether an archive was created using . or the directory name.

I always check the names of the files before restoring an archive:

```
% tar t
```

If the archive loads the files into the current directory, I create a new directory, change to it, and extract the files.

If the archive restores the directory by name, then I restore the files into the current directory.

Restoring a Few Files

If you want to restore a single file, get the pathname of the file as *tar* knows it, using the *t* flag. You must specify the exact filename, because *filename* and *./filename* are not the same to *tar*. You can combine these two steps into one command by using:

```
% tar xvf /dev/rst0 `tar tf /dev/rst0 | grep filename`
```

Note that this may run very slowly, though, as the entire tar file has to be read once (and the tape rewound) before any restoration can happen. Be careful: you may also get a lot more than you expected; for example, if you're looking for *README* using this technique, you'd also get *README.Solaris* and everything in the *doc/READMEs* directory, possibly overwriting files you wanted to keep.

Whenever you use *tar* to restore a directory, you must always specify *some* filename. If none is specified, no files are restored.

There is still the problem of restoring a directory whose pathname starts with a slash (/). Because *tar* restores a file to the pathname specified in the archive, you cannot change *where* the file will be restored. The danger is that either you may overwrite some existing files or you will not be able to restore the files because you don't have permission.

You can ask the system administrator to rename a directory and temporarily create a symbolic link pointing to a directory where you can restore the files. Other solutions exist, including editing the *tar* archive and creating a new directory structure with a C program executing the *chroot*(2) system call. Another solution is to use GNU *tar* (39.3), which allows you to remap pathnames starting with slash (/). It also allows you to create archives that are too large for a single tape, incremental archives, and a dozen other advantages.

But the best solution is never to create an archive of a directory that starts with slash (/) or tilde (~) (31.11) (since the shell will expand ~ into an absolute path that starts with a /).

Remote Restoring

To restore a directory from a remote host, use the following command:

rsh 1.21   `% rsh -n host dd if=/dev/rst0 bs=20b | tar xvBfb - 20 files`

This runs *dd* on the remote host, reading from */dev/rst0* with a blocksize of twenty blocks, and pipes it to a local *tar*. It is difficult to read fixed-size blocks over a network. This is why *tar* uses the B flag to force it to read from the pipe until a block is completely filled. Some versions of *tar*, including GNU *tar*, handle remote drives automatically (38.8).

—*BB*

38.7 Using tar to a Remote Tape Drive

If your computer doesn't have a tape drive connected, creating *tar* (38.2) backup files is slightly more complicated. If you have an account on a machine with a tape drive, and the directory is mounted via NFS (1.21), you can just *rlogin* (1.21) to the other machine and use *tar* to back up your directory.

If the directory is not NFS mounted, or it is mounted but you have permission problems accessing your own files, you can use *tar*, *rsh* (1.21), and *dd* (21.6) to solve this dilemma. The syntax is confusing, but if you forget, you can use *man tar* (2.1) to refresh your memory. The command to dump the current directory to a tape in a remote machine called *zephyrus* is:

`% tar cvfb - 20 . | rsh zephyrus dd of=/dev/rmt0 obs=20b`

Here, the output file of *tar* is -, which *tar* interprets as standard input if *tar* is reading an archive or standard output if *tar* is creating an archive.

The *dd* command copies data from standard input to the device */dev/rmt0*.

This example assumes you can use *rsh* without requiring a password. You can add your current machine's name to the remote *.rhosts* file (1.21) if you get a Password: prompt when you use *rlogin* to access this machine. You also can use *ssh*, which is generally more secure than *rsh*, and the *ssh-agent* utility to allow logins without a password.

—*BB*

38.8 Using GNU tar with a Remote Tape Drive

If you're using GNU *tar*, you can probably ignore the tips in articles 38.7 about using a tape drive on a remote system. GNU *tar* makes it easy to access a remote drive via *rsh* or a similar command like *ssh*.

When referring to a local host, the GNU *tar f* option takes a plain filename like *foo.tar* or a device name like */dev/rmt0*. If you put a colon (:) before that name, though, you can prepend a remote hostname—and, optionally, a username. For example, to get a table of contents of the tape on the drive */dev/rmt8* on the remote host *server2*, logging into *server2* as yourself, type:

```
% tar tf server2:/dev/rmt8
```

To specify a different username than the one on your local host, add it with an @ before the hostname. (This assumes you're allowed to connect to the remote host without a password—because there's a *.rhosts* file on the remote system, for instance.) For example, to connect to *server2* as *heather* and extract the files *reports/products.sgml* and *reports/services.sgml* from */dev/rmt8*:

{ } 28.4

```
% tar xf
heather@server2:/dev/rmt8 reports/{products,services}.sgml
```

By default, GNU *tar* uses *rsh*, *remsh*, or *nsh* to access the remote machine, though that can be changed when *tar* is built and installed on your host. If you want another access command, like *ssh*, you can set that with the *--rsh-command* option. The next example gets the contents of the archive on the drive */dev/rmt8* from the host *capannole.it* using *ssh*. Note that *tar* doesn't check your search path (27.6) for the *rsh-command*; you have to give its absolute pathname (which you can get with a command like *which* (2.6)):

```
% tar -x --file=capannole.it:/dev/rmt8
--rsh-command=/usr/bin/ssh
```

On the other hand, if you need to use a local filename with a colon in it, add the *--force-local* option.

—*JP*

38.9 On-Demand Incremental Backups of a Project

As I was working on this book, I was constantly editing lots of random files all through a directory tree. I archived some of the files in a revision control system (39.4), but those archives, as well as the nonarchived files, still would be vulnerable if my disk crashed. (And naturally, close to a deadline, one hard disk started making whining noises...)

The answer I came up with was easy to use and simple to set up. It's a script named *ptbk*, and this article explains it. To run the script, I just type its name. It searches my directory tree for files that have been modified since the last time I ran *ptbk*. Those files are copied into a dated compressed *tar* archive and copied to a remote system using *scp*. The process looks like this:

```
$ ptbk
upt/upt3_changes.html
upt/BOOKFILES
upt/art/0548.sgm
upt/art/1420.sgm
upt/art/1430.sgm
upt/art/0524.sgm
upt/BOOKIDS
upt/ulpt3_table
Now copying this file to bserver:
-rw-rw-r--   1 jpeek    323740 Jan  3 23:08 /tmp/upt-200101032308.tgz
upt-200101032308.tgz    |    316 KB |  63.2 kB/s | ETA: 00:00:00 | 100%
```

The script actually doesn't copy *all* of the files in my directory tree. I've set up a *tar* exclude file that makes the script skip some files that don't need backing up. For instance, it skips any filename that starts with a comma (,). Here's the file, named *ptbk.exclude*:

```
upt/ptbk.exclude
upt/tarfiles
upt/gmatlogs
upt/drv-jpeek-jpeek.ps
upt/drv-jpeek.31
upt/BOOKFILES~
upt/ch*.ps.gz
upt/ch*.ps
upt/,*
upt/art/,*
```

After the script makes the tar file, it *touch*es a timestamp file named *ptbk.last*. The next time the script runs, it uses *find −newer* (9.8) to get only the files that have been modified since the timestamp file was touched.

The script uses *scp* and *ssh-agent* to copy the archive without asking for a password. You could hack it to use another method. For instance, it could copy using *rcp* (1.21) or simply copy the file to another system with *cp* via an NFS-mounted filesystem (1.21).

This doesn't take the place of regular backups, if only because re-creating days' worth of work from the little individual archives would be tedious. But this system makes it painless to take snapshots, as often as I want, by typing a four-letter command. Here's the *ptbk* script:

```
#!/bin/sh
# ptbk - back up latest UPT changes, scp to $remhost
```

```
                    dirbase=upt
                    dir=$HOME/$dirbase
                    timestamp=$dir/ptbk.last    # the last time this script was run
                    exclude=$dir/ptbk.exclude   # file with (wildcard) pathnames to skip
                    remhost=bserver             # hostname to copy the files to
                    remdir=tmp/upt_bak/.        # remote directory (relative to $HOME)
    || 35.14        cd $dir/.. || exit          # Go to parent directory of $dir
    '...' 28.14     datestr=`date '+%Y%m%d%H%M'`
                    outfile=/tmp/upt-$datestr.tgz

                    # Don't send vim recovery files (.*.swp):
                    tar czvlf $outfile -X $exclude \
                        `find $dirbase -type f -newer $timestamp ! -name '.*.swp' -print`
                    mv -f $timestamp $dir/,ptbk.last
                    echo "Timestamp file for $0.  Don't modify." > $timestamp
                    echo "Now copying this file to $remhost:"
                    ls -l $outfile
                    scp $outfile ${remhost}:${remdir}
```

If the copy fails (because the remote machine is down, for instance), I have to either copy the archive somewhere else or wait and remember to copy the archive later. If you have an unreliable connection, you might want to modify the script to touch the timestamp file only if the copy succeeds—at the possible cost of losing a data file that was modified while the previous archive was (not?) being transferred to the remote host.

—JP

38.10 Using Wildcards with tar

When extracting files from a *tar* archive, it's handy to be able to use wildcards. You have to protect them (27.12) from the shell, so that they are passed directly to *tar*.

Without GNU tar

In general, *tar* can't do wildcard matching on the filenames within an archive. There's a terribly ugly hack that you can use to select the files you want anyway. Try a command like this:

'...' 28.14
```
% tar xvf /dev/rst0 `tar tf /dev/rst0 | egrep 'lib/(foo|bar)'`
```

What you're doing here is using *tar* twice. *tar t* will print the names of all the files on the tape. The pattern supplied to *egrep* (13.4) selects the pathnames containing *lib/foo* or *lib/bar*, and the resulting filenames are passed to the first *tar* command, which actually extracts the files from the archive. Note that these patterns are regular expressions, not wildcards (32.2).

Here's another subtle but important point. Because the regular expression patterns in the example above are not anchored with ^ or $ characters (32.4), they can match anywhere in the file pathnames. So lib/(foo|bar) would match a pathname like *lib/foo* as well as a pathname like */usr/lib/glib/foo.h*.

With GNU tar

GNU tar

One of the many improvements in GNU *tar* is that it understands wildcards in the names of files within an archive. (Remember that because you want *tar*, not the shell, to see these wildcards, you have to quote (27.12) the filename arguments that have wildcards.)

Unlike the examples in the previous section, GNU *tar* uses wildcards, not regular expressions (32.2). Unlike shells, the wildcard expressions in GNU *tar* can match across slashes (/) in pathnames.

Here's a demonstration of using wildcards: we want to extract all subdirectories named *editor*. Command 1 shows how you'd do it in non-GNU *tar*: list the exact pathnames of the subdirectories. Notice that *tar* extracts the directory and any subdirectories too. Command 2 shows the easy way to do the job with GNU *tar*: make a wildcard expression that ends with a slash and the directory name. As before, *tar* extracts the directory and any subdirectories. What if you want to extract anything with the string *editor* in its name—including individual files? Make a wildcard pattern without the slash and a filename surrounded by stars, as in command 3. Finally, command 4 shows an example of how (different than in shells) a wildcard can match across the / characters in pathnames. Command 4 extracts only directories named *editor* somewhere (possibly several layers) underneath a directory named *skin*:

› 28.12

```
1$ tar xvf mozilla.tar package/chrome/en-US/locale/en-US/editor \
> package/chrome/classic/skin/classic/content/editor \
> ...
package/chrome/en-US/locale/en-US/editor/
package/chrome/en-US/locale/en-US/editor/contents.rdf
package/chrome/en-US/locale/en-US/editor/editor.dtd
    ...
package/chrome/classic/skin/classic/editor/
package/chrome/classic/skin/classic/editor/EditModeTabs.css
    ...
package/chrome/classic/skin/classic/editor/images/
package/chrome/classic/skin/classic/editor/images/Map_Copy.gif
    ...
2$ tar xvf mozilla.tar '*/editor'
package/chrome/en-US/locale/en-US/editor/
package/chrome/en-US/locale/en-US/editor/contents.rdf
package/chrome/en-US/locale/en-US/editor/editor.dtd
    ...
```

```
package/chrome/classic/skin/classic/editor/
package/chrome/classic/skin/classic/editor/EditModeTabs.css
    ...
package/chrome/classic/skin/classic/editor/images/
package/chrome/classic/skin/classic/editor/images/Map_Copy.gif
    ...
3$ tar xvf mozilla.tar '*editor*'
package/defaults/pref/editor.js
package/components/editor.xpt
    ...
package/chrome/en-US/locale/en-US/editor/
package/chrome/en-US/locale/en-US/editor/contents.rdf
package/chrome/en-US/locale/en-US/editor/editor.dtd
    ...
package/chrome/comm/content/communicator/editorBindings.xul
package/chrome/comm/content/communicator/search/search-editor.js
    ...
4$ tar xvf mozilla.tar '*/skin/*/editor'
package/chrome/classic/skin/classic/editor/
package/chrome/classic/skin/classic/editor/EditModeTabs.css
    ...
package/chrome/classic/skin/classic/editor/images/
package/chrome/classic/skin/classic/editor/images/Map_Copy.gif
    ...
package/chrome/blue/skin/blue/editor/
package/chrome/blue/skin/blue/editor/contents.rdf
    ...
package/chrome/blue/skin/blue/editor/images/
package/chrome/blue/skin/blue/editor/images/Map_Copy.gif
    ...
package/chrome/modern/skin/modern/editor/
package/chrome/modern/skin/modern/editor/contents.rdf
    ...
```

There's more about wildcard matching in the GNU *tar info* page (but not its *manpage*).

Wildcard Gotchas in GNU tar

One subtle (but sometimes important!) difference between GNU *tar* and other versions comes when you're trying to extract a file whose name contains a wild-card character. You'll probably have to type a backslash (\) before that name. Also, because the shell may also try to interpret that wildcard character—or at least the backslash—you also may need to quote the backslashed expression! (Article 27.18 shows a situation like this one, with multiple layers of backslash interpretation.)

Here's an example. We're archiving the system binary file named *[* (or *test*) (35.26):

```
5$ which [
/usr/bin/[
6$ cd /tmp
7$ tar cvf tartest.tar /usr/bin/[
tar: Removing leading `/' from member names
usr/bin/[
8$ tar xvf tartest.tar usr/bin/[
tar: usr/bin/[: Not found in archive
tar: Error exit delayed from previous errors
9$ tar xvf tartest.tar usr/bin/\[
tar: usr/bin/[: Not found in archive
tar: Error exit delayed from previous errors
10$ tar xvf tartest.tar 'usr/bin/\['
usr/bin/[
```

Storing the file in the archive, in command 7, is simple. The shell doesn't have anything to expand; *tar* simply stores the name as-is because wildcards make sense only when *tar* is *extracting* from an archive. In command 8, though, when we try to extract the file into the current directory, *tar* says it isn't there—because it's now treating [as a wildcard pattern. Adding a single backslash in command 9 doesn't help because the shell strips it off before *tar* sees it. We need to put quotes around the backslash, as in command 10, to make *tar* match the actual name.

—JP and TOR

38.11 Avoid Absolute Paths with tar

One problem with most versions of *tar*: they can't change a file's pathname when restoring. Let's say that you put your home directory in an archive (tape or otherwise) with a command like this:

```
% tar c /home/mike
```

What will these files be named when you restore them, either on your own system or on some other system? They will have *exactly* the same pathnames they had originally. So if */home/mike* already exists, it will be destroyed. There's no way to tell *tar* that it should be careful about overwriting files; there's no way to tell *tar* to put the files in some other directory when it takes them off the tape, etc. If you use absolute pathnames (31.2) when you create a tape, you're stuck. If you use relative paths (31.2) (for example, tar c .), you can restore the files in any directory you want.

This means that you should:

- Avoid using absolute paths when you create an archive (see below).
- Use *tar t* to see what files are on the tape before restoring the archive.
- Use GNU *tar*. It strips the leading / by default when creating archives. (You can give it the *–P* option to make it store absolute pathnames.)

Rather than giving a command like tar c /home/mike, do something like:

```
% cd /
% tar c home/mike
```

Or, even more elegant, use *–C* on the *tar* command line:

```
% tar c -C /home/mike .
```

This command tells *tar* to *cd* to the directory */home/mike* before creating an archive of . (the current directory). If you want to archive several directories, you can use several *–C* options:

```
% tar c -C /home/mike ./docs  -C /home/susan ./test
```

This command archives *mike*'s *docs* directory and *susan*'s *test* directory. [Note that it uses the subdirectory names, as we did in the second-previous example. When the files are extracted, they'll be restored to separate subdirectories, instead of all being mixed into the same . (current) directory. —*JP*]

—*ML*

38.12 Getting tar's Arguments in the Right Order

tar's command line is one of Unix's little mysteries. It's difficult to associate arguments with options. Let's say you want to specify the block size (*b*), the output file (*f*), and an "exclude" file (*X*). Where do you put all this information? It's easy enough to stick the option letters into a lump and put them into a command (**tar cXbf**). But where do you put the block size, the name of the exclude file, and so on?

List any arguments that you need *after* the block of key letters. You must place the arguments in the *same order* as the key letters, as shown in Figure 38-1.

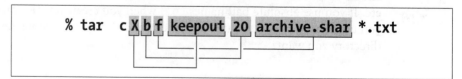

Figure 38-1. tar options and arguments

In this command, **keepout** goes with the *X* option, **20** goes with the *b* option, and **archive.shar** goes with the *f* option. If we put the options in a different order, we also have to put the arguments in a different order (see Figure 38-2).

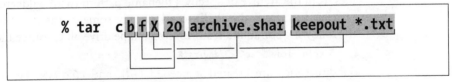

% tar c b f X 20 archive.shar keepout *.txt

Figure 38-2. The same command, rearranged

Note that the files you want to put on the tape (or the files you want to extract from the tape) always go at the *end* of the command. These are not arguments to *c* or *X*; they are part of the command itself.

The *dump* command and a few others work the same way.

GNU *tar* understands this traditional syntax as well as two syntaxes with separate options. For instance, the command line above could also be written in either of the following ways with GNU *tar*:

```
% tar -c -b 20 -X keepout -f archive.tar *.txt
% tar --create --block-size=20 --exclude-from=keepout \
    --file=archive.tar *.txt
```

—ML

38.13 The cpio Tape Archiver

There was a time when people used to debate whether BSD *tar* (38.2, 39.2) (tape archiver) or System V *cpio* (copy in/out) was the better file archive and backup program. At this point, though, no one ships out *cpio* archives over the Net (1.21). *tar* is widespread, and there are free versions available, including GNU *tar* (39.3).

There's still a good reason to use *cpio*: it's better at recovering backups from partially damaged media. If a block of your tape or disk archive goes bad, *cpio* can probably recover all files except the one with the bad block. A *tar* archive may not fare as well. Though we don't give it much air time in this book, here are a few *cpio* basics:

- To write out an archive, use the *–o* option and redirect output either to a tape device or to an archive file. The list of files to be archived is often specified with *find* (9.1), but it can be generated in other ways—*cpio* expects a list of filenames on its standard input. For example:

```
% find . -name "*.old" -print | cpio -ocBv > /dev/rst8
```

or:

```
% find . -print | cpio -ocBv > mydir.cpio
```

- To read an archive in, use the *–i* option and redirect input from the file or tape drive containing the archive. The *–d* option is often important; it tells *cpio* to create directories as needed when copying files in. You can restore all files from the archive or specify a filename pattern (with wildcards quoted to protect them from the shell) to select only some of the files. For example, the following command restores from a tape drive all C source files:

      % cpio -icdv "*.c" < /dev/rst8

  Subdirectories are created if needed (*–d*), and *cpio* will be verbose (*–v*), announcing the name of each file that it successfully reads in.

- To copy an archive to another directory, use the *–p* option, followed by the name of the destination directory. (On some versions of *cpio*, this top-level destination directory must already exist.) For example, you could use the following command to copy the contents of the current directory (including all subdirectories) to another directory:

      % find . -depth -print | cpio -pd newdir

There are lots of other options for things like resetting file access times or ownership or changing the blocking factor on the tape. See your friendly neighborhood manual page for details. Notice that options are typically "squashed together" into an option string rather than written out as separate options.

—TOR and JP

38.14 Industrial Strength Backups

This book mostly focuses on tools like *tar*, because that's what we expect most of you to use most of the time. However, there are other tools that are very important for large-scale backups that it's good to know at least a little about.

dump is an old Unix standby and a complete if somewhat arcane tool for backing up file systems. It is extremely useful for system administrators and personal machines, and it is available as part of the operating system on nearly any Unix. For industrial-strength backups, no simple solution beats *dump*—it is the most reliable tool for ensuring data consistency and stability. It's also a pain to use, so generally system administrators end up writing scripts around it to make it easier, or using a system like Amanda (see below).

The Advanced Maryland Automatic Network Disk Archiver, known as *Amanda*, is a free system for performing regular backups of one or more network-connected machines. Information on Amanda is generally available at *http://www.amanda.org*. Amanda uses *tar* or *dump* to do the actual work of backing up files; its job is to coordinate backups of multiple filesystems to one or more network-accessible tape drives on a regular basis.

Note also that full-scale backup processes need to address things such as tape lifetimes, electronic and physical security of backed-up data, off-site storage, incremental backup schemes and the like. Should you be in a position to need to set up such a process, read one of the good books on the subject—we might recommend O'Reilly's *Unix Backup and Recovery*.

—DJPH

39

Creating and Reading Archives

39.1 Packing Up and Moving

The worst part of living in a nice big house is the headache of moving. The more stuff you've got room for, the more trouble it is to pack it up and take it with you.

The Unix operating system is a little bit like that. One of its real advantages is a filesystem that lets you organize your personal files into a hierarchical directory tree just like the much bigger tree that encompasses the entire filesystem. You can squirrel away all kinds of useful information into neat pigeonholes.

While your personal directory hierarchy is usually only two or three levels deep, for all practical purposes it can have as many levels as you like. And, as is true of any powerful and flexible tool, problems lie in wait for the sorcerer's apprentice. Directories and files grow increasingly complex the longer you use the system, with more forgotten files and more detailed organization.

This chapter will tackle the problems that can arise when you want to move a block of files (in one or many directories) from one place to another.

Maybe you're writing the files to a tape for safety (38.3). In many cases though, this is a "backup and restore" problem. For example, if you were moving your account to another system, you might just ask the system administrator (if there is one) to archive your files to tape or floppy and restore them in the new location. Many new users are less aware that you can use the backup program *tar* (38.2) to create online archives that you can move from one place to another.

This situation is most likely to arise in a networked environment. You might be packaging files to ship as a package to another user. The files might be going to Usenet or an archive site on the Internet, for distribution to many users. Whether you're distributing an archive to lots of people or using it for yourself, though, most of the topics we cover in this chapter will apply.

—*TOR*

39.2 Using tar to Create and Unpack Archives

tar (38.2) is a general-purpose archiving utility capable of packing many files into a single archive file, retaining information such as file permissions and ownership. The name *tar* stands for *tape archive*, because the tool was originally used to archive files as backups on tape. However, use of *tar* is not at all restricted to making tape backups, as we'll see.

The format of the *tar* command is:

    tar *functionoptions files...*

where *function* is a single letter indicating the operation to perform, *options* is a list of (single-letter) options to that function, and *files* is the list of files to pack or unpack in an archive. (Note that *function* is not separated from *options* by any space.)

function can be one of:

c Create a new archive.

x Extract files from an archive.

t List the contents of an archive.

r Append files to the end of an archive.

u Update files that are newer than those in the archive.

d Compare files in the archive to those in the filesystem.

The most commonly used functions are *create*, *extract*, and *table-of-contents*.

The most common *options* are:

v
  Prints verbose information when packing or unpacking archives. This makes *tar* show the files it is archiving or restoring. It is good practice to use this option so that you can see what actually happens, though if you're using *tar* in a shell script you might skip it so as to avoid spamming the user of your script.

k
  Keeps any existing files when extracting—that is, prevents overwriting any existing files contained within the tar file.

f *filename*
  Specifies that the tar file to be read or written is *filename*.

z
  Specifies that the data to be written to the tar file should be compressed or that the data in the tar file is compressed with *gzip*. (Not available on all *tar*s.)

There are other options, which we cover in article 38.5. Article 38.12 has more information about the order of *tar* options, and article 39.3 has a lot more about GNU *tar*.

Although the *tar* syntax might appear complex at first, in practice it's quite simple. For example, say we have a directory named *mt*, containing these files:

```
rutabaga% ls -l mt
total 37
-rw-r--r--   1 root     root           24 Sep 21  1993 Makefile
-rw-r--r--   1 root     root          847 Sep 21  1993 README
-rwxr-xr-x   1 root     root         9220 Nov 16 19:03 mt
-rw-r--r--   1 root     root         2775 Aug  7  1993 mt.1
-rw-r--r--   1 root     root         6421 Aug  7  1993 mt.c
-rw-r--r--   1 root     root         3948 Nov 16 19:02 mt.o
-rw-r--r--   1 root     root        11204 Sep  5  1993 st_info.txt
```

We wish to pack the contents of this directory into a single *tar* archive. To do this, we use the following command:

```
tar cf mt.tar mt
```

The first argument to *tar* is the function (here, c, for create) followed by any options. Here, we use the one option *f mt.tar*, to specify that the resulting tar archive be named *mt.tar*. The last argument is the name of the file or files to archive; in this case, we give the name of a directory, so *tar* packs all files in that directory into the archive.

Note that the first argument to *tar* must be a function letter followed by a list of options. Because of this, there's no reason to use a hyphen (-) to precede the options as many Unix commands require. *tar* allows you to use a hyphen, as in:

```
tar -cf mt.tar mt
```

but it's really not necessary. In some versions of *tar*, the first letter must be the function, as in c, t, or x. In other versions, the order of letters does not matter as long as there is one and only one function given.

The function letters as described here follow the so-called "old option style." There is also a newer "short option style," in which you precede the function options with a hyphen. On some versions of *tar*, a "long option style" is available, in which you use long option names with two hyphens. See the *manpage* or *info* page (2.9) for *tar* for more details if you are interested.

It is often a good idea to use the *v* option with *tar* to list each file as it is archived. For example:

```
rutabaga% tar cvf mt.tar mt
mt/
mt/st_info.txt
mt/README
mt/mt.1
mt/Makefile
mt/mt.c
```

```
mt/mt.o
mt/mt
```

On some *tar*s, if you use *v* multiple times, additional information will be printed, as in:

```
rutabaga% tar cvvf mt.tar mt
drwxr-xr-x root/root        0 Nov 16 19:03 1994 mt/
-rw-r--r-- root/root    11204 Sep  5 13:10 1993 mt/st_info.txt
-rw-r--r-- root/root      847 Sep 21 16:37 1993 mt/README
-rw-r--r-- root/root     2775 Aug  7 09:50 1993 mt/mt.1
-rw-r--r-- root/root       24 Sep 21 16:03 1993 mt/Makefile
-rw-r--r-- root/root     6421 Aug  7 09:50 1993 mt/mt.c
-rw-r--r-- root/root     3948 Nov 16 19:02 1994 mt/mt.o
-rwxr-xr-x root/root     9220 Nov 16 19:03 1994 mt/mt
```

This is especially useful as it lets you verify that *tar* is doing the right thing.

In some versions of *tar*, *f* must be the last letter in the list of options. This is because *tar* expects the *f* option to be followed by a filename—the name of the tar file to read from or write to. If you don't specify *f filename* at all, *tar* uses a default tape device (some versions of *tar* use */dev/rmt0* for historical reasons regardless of the OS; some have a slightly more specific default). Article 38.5 talks about using *tar* in conjunction with a tape drive to make backups.

Now we can give the file *mt.tar* to other people, and they can extract it on their own system. To do this, they would use the command:

```
tar xvf mt.tar
```

This creates the subdirectory *mt* and places all the original files into it, with the same permissions as found on the original system. The new files will be owned by the user running tar xvf (you) unless you are running as *root*, in which case the original owner is generally preserved. Some versions require the *o* option to set ownership. The *x* option stands for "extract." The *v* option is used again here to list each file as it is extracted. This produces:

```
courgette% tar xvf mt.tar
mt/
mt/st_info.txt
mt/README
mt/mt.1
mt/Makefile
mt/mt.c
mt/mt.o
mt/mt
```

We can see that *tar* saves the pathname of each file relative to the location where the tar file was originally created. That is, when we created the archive using tar cf mt.tar mt, the only input filename we specified was *mt*, the name of the directory containing the files. Therefore, *tar* stores the directory itself and all of the files below that directory in the tar file. When we extract the tar file, the directory *mt* is created and the files are placed into it, which is the exact inverse of what was done to create the archive.

If you were to pack up the contents of your /*bin* directory with the command:

```
tar cvf bin.tar /bin
```

you can cause terrible mistakes when extracting the tar file. Extracting a tar file packed as /*bin* could trash the contents of your /*bin* directory when you extract it. If you want to archive /*bin*, you should create the archive from the root directory, /, using the relative pathname (1.16) *bin* (with no leading slash)—and if you really want to overwrite /*bin*, extract the tar file by *cd*ing to / first. Article 38.11 explains and lists workarounds.

Another way to create the tar file *mt.tar* would be to *cd* into the *mt* directory itself, and use a command such as:

```
tar cvf mt.tar *
```

This way the *mt* subdirectory would not be stored in the tar file; when extracted, the files would be placed directly in your current working directory. One fine point of *tar* etiquette is always to pack tar files so that they contain a subdirectory, as we did in the first example with tar cvf mt.tar mt. Therefore, when the archive is extracted, the subdirectory is also created and any files placed there. This way you can ensure that the files won't be placed directly in your current working directory; they will be tucked out of the way and prevent confusion. This also saves the person doing the extraction the trouble of having to create a separate directory (should they wish to do so) to unpack the tar file. Of course, there are plenty of situations where you wouldn't want to do this. So much for etiquette.

When creating archives, you can, of course, give *tar* a list of files or directories to pack into the archive. In the first example, we have given *tar* the single directory *mt*, but in the previous paragraph we used the wildcard *, which the shell expands into the list of filenames in the current directory.

Before extracting a tar file, it's usually a good idea to take a look at its table of contents to determine how it was packed. This way you can determine whether you do need to create a subdirectory yourself where you can unpack the archive. A command such as:

```
tar tvf tarfile
```

lists the table of contents for the named *tarfile*. Note that when using the *t* function, only one *v* is required to get the long file listing, as in this example:

```
courgette% tar tvf mt.tar
drwxr-xr-x root/root         0 Nov 16 19:03 1994 mt/
-rw-r--r-- root/root     11204 Sep  5 13:10 1993 mt/st_info.txt
-rw-r--r-- root/root       847 Sep 21 16:37 1993 mt/README
-rw-r--r-- root/root      2775 Aug  7 09:50 1993 mt/mt.1
-rw-r--r-- root/root        24 Sep 21 16:03 1993 mt/Makefile
-rw-r--r-- root/root      6421 Aug  7 09:50 1993 mt/mt.c
-rw-r--r-- root/root      3948 Nov 16 19:02 1994 mt/mt.o
-rwxr-xr-x root/root      9220 Nov 16 19:03 1994 mt/mt
```

No extraction is being done here; we're just displaying the archive's table of contents. We can see from the filenames that this file was packed with all files in the subdirectory *mt*, so that when we extract the tar file, the directory *mt* will be created, and the files placed there.

You can also extract individual files from a tar archive. To do this, use the command:

```
tar xvf tarfile files
```

where *files* is the list of files to extract. As we've seen, if you don't specify any files, *tar* extracts the entire archive.

When specifying individual files to extract, you must give the full pathname as it is stored in the tar file. For example, if we wanted to grab just the file *mt.c* from the previous archive *mt.tar*, we'd use the command:

```
tar xvf mt.tar mt/mt.c
```

This would create the subdirectory *mt* and place the file *mt.c* within it.

tar has many more options than those mentioned here. These are the features that you're likely to use most of the time, but GNU *tar*, in particular, has extensions that make it ideal for creating backups and the like. See the *tar manpage* or *info* page (2.9) and the following chapter for more information.

—MW, MKD, and LK

39.3 GNU tar Sampler

tar

GNU *tar* has plenty of features; some people would say "too many." I don't agree. GNU *tar* has features I wish I'd had for years in more "standard" versions. This article lists my favorites. For a complete list, check the *info* documentation for *tar*.

- Article 15.7 describes how to compress an archive file you've created. If you're using GNU *tar*, this is even easier, since *tar* itself can do the compression. Simply use the *z* option when writing or reading archives. For example, to make the *gzipped* tar archive *progs.tar.gz* from all ".c" and ".h" files:

  ```
  % tar cvzf progs.tar.gz *.c *.h
  ```

  You can also use the long option *--gzip* to get *gzip* compression, and the long option *--bzip2* to get *bzip2* compression.

- I've made the classic mistake of archiving files with their absolute pathnames (38.11). GNU *tar* saves you from that goof. It always stores absolute pathnames as relative paths unless you add the *--absolute-names* option.

- Often I want to make a tape backup of my most recent work on a big project, but not all the thousands of files in a directory tree. The clumsy way to do that is by using *find −mtime* to make an include-file for the standard *tar −I* option. GNU tar to the rescue: its *−−after-date* option lets me tell it what directories to look in and how recently the files should have been changed.

- When I extract an archive, I may be writing into a directory that has other files. The *−−keep-old-files* option tells GNU *tar* not to overwrite existing files.

One caution about GNU *tar*: it creates ANSI-format *tar* archives. Extracting one of these archives with the old V7 *tar* can cause warning messages like "tar: unexpected EOF." But, of course, GNU *tar* has an option to create old-format archives: *−−old-archive*.

—*JP and TOR*

39.4 Managing and Sharing Files with RCS and CVS

How many times have you wished that you could get a copy of a file the way it looked an hour ago, or yesterday, or last year? That includes times when you just deleted the file—and, especially, when the file is too new for your computer's backup system to have made any copies of it. (You *do* have regular backups of your system, don't you? ;-)) RCS (Revision Control System) and CVS (Concurrent Version System) let you recover a previous version of a file from an archive. Many systems come with either RCS, CVS, or both installed already; if they don't appear to be on your system either install the appropriate package or grab the most current versions from FSF's website (*http://www.fsf.org*).

How does the archive get there? As you work, you periodically put a "snapshot" of the file into the archive. (The archive systems save the *changes*—not the whole file—so this doesn't take as much disk space as it might.) The archive remembers the date and time you store each version. You can enter a log message to describe what's changed since the last time you archived the file. You can do much more, but those are the basics.

When you need a previous version of the file, you read the archive log to decide which version is best (by date and time or by the log message). Then you use one command to get back that version. You don't have to wait for the system manager to load a tape.

Of course, these tools can't protect you from a disk crash or another disaster; that's what reliable backups are for. RCS and CVS are best for protecting you from accidentally deleting or corrupting files. But they're also great for group development projects: controlling who's working on a file, who did what when, and so on. That's especially true of CVS, which was designed to handle software developers from around the world collaborating on a project over a network—as well as a group of developers in the same office. One of my favorite features is the ability to see *diff* (11.1) listings of what's changed between versions.

Once you get started with these tools, you'll wonder how you ever did without them. Article 39.5 explains how to protect your files with RCS. See article 39.7 for an introduction to CVS.

—*JP*

39.5 RCS Basics

The Revision Control System (RCS) is a straightforward, file-based source-control system. It allows you to keep track of multiple snapshots or *revisions* of a file, so that you can back up to any previous version. It also allows you to note particular versions, so that you can do things such as reproduce the version of a file that you gave to someone else or released as part of a software release. Of course, it's useful for more than just software development; any time you want to change a file or set of files, revision control can be useful. To place a file under revision control using RCS:

```
% ci filename
```

The *ci* (checkin) program will prompt you for a short description of the file and commit your changes. It will by default also delete the working copy; if you want to keep a read-only copy, use the *–u* (unlocked) option.

To then get a *working copy* of the file from scratch:

```
% co filename
% co -l filename
```

The *co* (checkout) command will get a read-only copy of the file from RCS. If you want to edit the file, use the *co –l* command (the option is a lowercase L and stands for *lock*). While you have the file checked out and locked, no one else can edit it. When you're done, return the file to RCS (check it in) using *ci* again. If you use the *–l* option to *ci*, it checks in your changes and checks out a new working copy, as if you did *co –l* again. When you check in the file, *ci* asks for a brief description of your changes. These can be very useful, later, to learn the history of revisions and to find a particular revision you might want to recover; the command `rlog filename` gives all of the stored change descriptions.

If you create a subdirectory called *RCS* in the directory where you keep the code or other text files you want to protect, the RCS files will be put there for you, rather than cluttering up your main directory.

It's a good idea (but not required) to add the characters Id somewhere in the file you want to place under RCS. Put this in a comment field. That is, use /
* Id */ in a C program and # Id in a shell or Perl script. RCS will substitute

the revision of the file and other useful information wherever you put Id any time you check the file out; this allows you to look at a file later and know what revision it was.

If you check out a file for editing and later on decide you didn't want to change it, unlock the file using:

```
% rcs -u filename
% rm filename
```

If you want a list of all files currently checked out, use:

```
% rlog -L -R RCS/*
```

(If you don't use RCS often, you may want to store those command lines in aliases or shell functions (29.1) with names like *Checkout*, *Checkedout*, and so on.) That's all there is to it!

If you are not using RCS or CVS, you should. They are an easy, ongoing way to protect yourself and do not require dozens of tapes. It is much easier just to type:

```
% co -r1.12 filename
```

than it is to try to restore that version from backup tapes after you've deleted it. With one command, version 1.12 is restored. If it's not the right one, restore the version before or after the one you just grabbed. (If you would just like to see the file rather than get a copy, you can add the *–p* option to send the file to standard output. Don't forget to pipe the *co –p* output to *less* or something similar, unless it is really short.)

If you are worried that you are keeping 12 versions of the file on the disk and that this will use up a lot of disk space, don't be. RCS stores the differences between versions, not 12 separate copies of the file. It recovers earlier versions of the file on request by starting from a known point and applying patches, rather than just keeping every single revision.

Suppose you delete a file by accident. If the file is just checked out with *co*, it will be retrieved and marked read-only, so trying to delete the file will cause *rm* to ask you for confirmation. If you do delete it, you can just recover it with another *co* command. Suppose, however, you checked out a file with *co –l*, because you planned to change it. If this file gets deleted accidentally, you would lose the most recent changes. This is why you should check your files back into RCS frequently—several times a day or even more. Checking in a version whenever you make significant changes to the file, or if you make changes that would be difficult to remember, is the best insurance. Making hundreds of changes to a file without checking it back into the system is just begging for trouble.

This brief overview left out a lot of features and helpful information. For example, RCS can:

- Merge two or more peoples' work into one with *rcsmerge* and *co –j*.
- Build a tree of revisions with multiple branches and sub-branches. This lets you make and store multiple independent revisions.
- Assign an arbitrary "state" to certain revisions—for example, *alpha*, *released*, *stable*.
- Name some or all revisions and refer to revisions by name instead of number. This is particularly good for naming files that went into a release.
- Keep a list of users who are allowed to manipulate a particular RCS file.

To find out more, see the RCS manual pages. *rcsintro*(1) gives a more complete overview; manpages like *ci*(1) have details on the many other useful features. Finally, O'Reilly & Associates' *Applying RCS and SCCS* is packed with tips and techniques for using revision control in group projects (where you'll need it even more). Articles 13.7 and 39.6 explain tools for searching RCS files.

If you're doing a larger project, take a look at article Chapter 39, which discusses CVS. CVS is much better at large project coordination and provides a whole suite of useful features beyond the simple source control RCS provides.

—*DJPH and BB*

39.6 List RCS Revision Numbers with rcsrevs

rcsrevs

The *rcsrevs* script tells you all the revision numbers that are stored in an RCS (39.5) file. For instance:

```
% rcsrevs myprog
1.3
1.2
1.1
1.2.1.1
```

What good is that? Here are two examples.

1. *rcsgrep –a* (13.7) uses *rcsrevs* when it's searching all revisions of an RCS file. If you want to print all revisions, run a program across all revisions to do some kind of check, and so on, *rcsrevs* can give you the revision numbers to use in a loop (28.9). The shell loop below gets all the revision numbers and stores them in the *revnum* shell variable one by one; it runs *co –p* (39.5) to send each revision to the *pr –h* (45.6) command for formatting with a custom header; the output of the commands in the loop goes to the printer.

'...' 28.14
› 28.12

```
$ for revnum in `rcsrevs somefile`
> do
>   co -p -r$revnum somefile | pr -h "somefile revision #$revnum"
> done | lpr
```

2. You'd like to compare the two most recent revisions of several RCS files to see what the last change was, but the revision numbers in each file are different. (One file's latest revision might be 2.4, another file could be at 1.7, etc.) Use *head* (12.12) to grab the two highest revision numbers from the *rcsrevs* output, *tail –r* (12.9) to reverse the order (put the older revision number first), and *sed* to make the revision numbers into a pair of *–r* options (like -r1.6, -r1.7). Then run *rcsdiff* to do the comparisons and email (1.21) them to *bigboss*:

? 28.12

```
% foreach file (*.cc *.h Makefile)
? set revs=`rcsrevs $f | head -2 | tail -r | sed 's/^/-r/'`
? rcsdiff $revs $f | mail -s "changes to $file" bigboss
? end
```

rcsrevs accepts *rlog* options to control what revisions are shown. So *rcsrevs –r2 somefile* would list only revisions 2.0 and above, *rcsrevs –sbeta* would list the revisions in *beta* state, and so on.

—JP

39.7 CVS Basics

The Concurrent Version System, or CVS, is a version control system designed to support complex project structures or groups of people who are working together on a common set of files. Where RCS (39.5) deals only with individual files, CVS allows you to work with entire projects as a whole. As we have mentioned before, while source control systems were originally developed primarily for use in developing software, they make a great deal of sense any time you want to keep track of changes to files. CVS is good for keeping track of changes to source files for a book or configuration files for *qmail* or *apache*, or for any number of other day-to-day tasks.

CVS stores its archives in a directory called a *cvsroot*. You tell CVS where to find the repository you want to use by setting the *CVSROOT* environment variable or using the *–d* option:

```
% setenv CVSROOT /home/cvsroot
% cvs checkout conf
```

```
% cvs -d /home/deb/cvs checkout book
```

Within a cvsroot are one or more *repositories*. Each repository is associated with a particular project (or in the case of a very complex project, a piece of a project). To work on a project, you much check out its repository to create a *working area* using *cvs checkout*, as in the example above. CVS is helpful and remembers which cvsroot you used for a particular checkout; future commands within that working area automatically use the right repository. For the record, the working area's cvsroot overrides the *CVSROOT* environment variable; the *–d* option overrides them both.

Once you have a working area, you have a writable copy of every file in that project. Edit to your heart's content. To incorporate changes made by other people, or see what you've changed, use *cvs update*:

```
% cd book
% cvs update
cvs update: Updating .
U ch18.sgm
M ch39.sgm
```

CVS update tells you a bit of information about each file that it touched or needs to touch. A U means that it updated your working copy from the repository; if you had also changed that file, it means that CVS successfully merged their changes with yours. A M means that you've modified that file in your working area.

To push your modifications into the repository, you use *cvs commit*. As the name suggests, this commits your changes. Generally you'll want to do this often, so that you aren't set back very far if you delete a file accidentally or make a change you later decide you don't want.

CVS does more, of course. For example, *cvs log* lets you read the log that shows differences between two revisions. *cvs diff* lets you see the differences between two revisions by comparing them with *diff* (11.1). *cvs add* (followed by *cvs commit*) adds a new file or directory to the repository. *cvs remove* removes a file or directory; be sure to remove any local copy first, or use *cvs remove –f* to have CVS remove your local copy for you. *cvs init* initializes a new cvsroot, and *cvs import* creates a new repository. Notifications can be emailed automatically when a file is changed. Part or all of the repository can be made read-only for all but a few users—so you can share files freely but prevent unauthorized changes. O'Reilly's *CVS Pocket Reference* gives a summary of all this and much more about CVS.

—DJPH

39.8 More CVS

Here's a slightly more complex example of how to use CVS. I'm working on this book, via CVS, with my two main coauthors (who are on the east and west coasts of the United States). The repository, which has almost 1,000 files, is on a computer in the O'Reilly office in Massachusetts.

1. From the command line or in a shell setup file (3.3), I need to set an environment variable (35.3) named *CVSROOT* that tells CVS where the repository is and what my username is on that machine. In the C shell, for instance, I'd execute a command that sets my username to *jpeek*, the server hostname to *bserver.east.oreilly.com*, and the repository to */books/cvs*. I'm also using *ssh* for secure access to the server, so I need to set the *CVS_RSH* environment variable and tell CVS to use the "ext" connection method:

   ```
   setenv CVSROOT :ext:jpeek@bserver.east.oreilly.com:/books/cvs
   setenv CVS_RSH ssh
   ```

2. I have a directory where I keep my local copies of the book files. To start, I check out my copy of the *ulpt3* repository from the server:

   ```
   % cd books
   % cvs checkout ulpt3
   cvs checkout: updating ulpt3
   U ulpt3/0001.sgm
   U ulpt3/0007.sgm
   U ulpt3/0023.sgm
        ...more...
   % cd !$
   cd ulpt3
   ```

   !$ **30.3**

3. Now my *ulpt3* subdirectory has the same files that the repository does. I can edit any of them, just as I'd edit files that aren't in CVS—but my changes don't make it back to the repository until I use the CVS command to do that.

   Let's say I edit the file *0123.sgm*. I'd like to write it back to the repository, where the other authors can grab it in case they're printing that part of the book. First I should update my workspace. This brings in any changes by other authors. If another author has updated *0123.sgm* and put it in the archive before I do, CVS will merge the two files and expect me to resolve the differences:

   ```
   % vi 0123.sgm
        ...edit the file...
   % cvs update
   cvs update: updating .
   U ulpt/0075.sgm
   RCS file: /books/cvs/ulpt3/0123.sgm,v
   retrieving revision 3.6
   retrieving revision 3.7
   Merging differences between 3.6 and 3.7 into 0123.sgm
   rcsmerge: warning: conflicts during merge
   cvs update: conflicts found in 0123.sgm
   C 0123.sgm
   %
   ```

   The U line shows that another author changed file *0075.sgm*; CVS is updating my copy of it. As it happens, another author edited *0123.sgm* while I did—and committed his changes to the repository before I got there. CVS sees that the copy in the repository is newer than the one I fetched a while ago, so it merges the two versions. If the changes had been to different parts of the file, CVS wouldn't have complained, just warned me that *0123.sgm* had been merged. As luck would have it (something to do with this being an example, I think ;-)) both changes were in the same place and CVS warned me that the merge failed; there was a conflict.

4. This step only applies if there was a conflict during the update. Edit the file and search for a string of less-than signs (<<<<). You'll see something like this:

```
<para>
<indexterm><primary>serial line modes</primary></indexterm>
<<<<<<< 0123.sgm
    But there is some overlap. For example, a terminal can be unusable
    because a program has left either the serial line modes or the
    terminal itself in an unexpected state. For this reason,
    <link linkend="UPT-ART-0079">terminal initialization</link>,
    as performed by the <command>tset</command> and
=======
    But there is some overlap. For example, a terminal can be unusable
    because a program has left the terminal in an "wedged"
    or unexpected state. The serial modes may be wrong too. This is why
    <link linkend="UPT-ART-0079">terminal initialization</link>,
    as performed by the <command>tset</command> and
>>>>>>> 3.7
    <command>tput</command> programs,
    initializes both the terminal and the serial line interface.
```

The text from your working file is at the top, after the <<<< characters. The conflicting text is after the ==== characters. You decide that your text is better written, so you simply delete the markers and the second chunk of text. [In a slightly less contrived example, there would probably be a process for this. You might use *cvs log* to look at the log message on the conflicting change, talk to the author of the conflicting change or both. Sometimes you might have to look at *cvs log* to figure out who checked in the conflicting change, because there may have been several changes. —DJPH]

5. Things look good. Now tell CVS to put all your changes from your local workspace into the repository by *committing*. You should give a message that describes the changes you made. You can give the message either as an argument to the *–m* option or by typing it into your text editor, like this:

```
% cvs commit
cvs commit: Examining .
   ...your text editor runs...
Checking in 0123.sgm;
/books/cvs/ulpt3/0123.sgm,v <-- 0123.sgm
new revision: 3.8; previous revision: 3.7
done
```

—*JP and DJPH*

40

Software Installation

40.1 /usr/bin and Other Software Directories

The location for certain types of installed files is very important. For instance, on many Unix systems, binary files accessible by users are located in the subdirectory */usr/bin* or */usr/local/bin*. If the applications aren't in these places, they may not be in the *PATH* environment variable and not easily accessible from the command line.

On my FreeBSD system, I've installed a utility called dos2unix, a file-formatting application that converts DOS newline character combinations to the Unix newline character. I used the FreeBSD Ports system to install the application, which automatically placed the program in my application directory, in my case */usr/local/bin*. When I want to execute the application, I can run it from the command line without having to provide the location of the file:

```
dos2unix some.txt > new.txt
```

This command reformats the newline character of the contents of *some.txt*, converting DOS linebreaks to Unix ones.

The */usr/bin* subdirectory differs from the */bin* directory located directly off of the main root directory. The */bin* directory has basic installed binaries built into the Unix operating system, with commands such as *cd* to change directory and so on. When you install an optional software application, it should not install software in the top-level binary subdirectory, but in */usr/bin*, instead.

According to the Filesystem Hierarchy Standard (FHS), subdirectories (Linux- and BSD-specific) shown in Table 40-1 are located directly off the root directory within a standardized directory hierarchy.

Table 40-1. FHS root subdirectories

Subdirectory	Contents
bin	Application binaries
boot	Boot loader static files
dev	Device files
etc	System configuration files
lib	Shared libraries and kernel modules
mnt	Temporary mounting point for filesystems such as CD-ROMs
opt	Larger static software packages
sbin	System binaries
tmp	Temporary files
usr	User hierarchy, which has its own subdirectory with the following entries: • *bin* • *doc* • *etc* • *games* • *include* • *kerberos* • *lib* • *libexec* • *local* • *man* • *sbin* • *share* • *src* • *X11R6*
var	Variable data

If you install an application and the binaries aren't placed into the bin directory, you'll need to add the binary location to your *PATH* environment variable to access the application from the command line.

 For more information about FHS, see the home page at *http://www.pathname.com/fhs/*. Many Unix systems support this hierarchy, including the BSD systems such as FreeBSD and NetBSD, as well as Red Hat Linux and others. However, your own Unix admin may adjust this hierarchy to fit the needs of your enterprise, so you'll want to check subdirectory locations before proceeding with manual software installation.

—SP

40.2 The Challenges of Software Installation on Unix

If you've worked with multiple operating systems such as the Mac OS or Windows along with Unix, then you're aware that software installation on a Unix system—Solaris, Linux, Darwin, and so on—isn't necessarily as easy a task as it is on some of the other systems. The process can be difficult if you're installing open source code that you download from the Internet; many times open source code isn't packaged for ease in installation.

I've worked with Unix for years but still look at the process of installing a new piece of software as one would look at climbing a mountain: be prepared, be brave, and don't look back.

—SP

40.3 Which make?

Many applications and utilities within the Unix environment come as source code that needs to be compiled and installed on your system. Because of this, the make utility is probably the most important utility you have within your Unix toolkit. However, the make utility installed on your system may not necessarily be compatible with the make utility used when the creators tested the software installation.

In fact, one of the problems that can cause the most problems with software installation is that the software compiles cleanly with GNU make but not with other versions of make, because different features of the installation process are supported with GNU make. This happens but not some of the older, more system-specific makes.

For instance, BSD operating systems such as FreeBSD and Darwin, as well as Solaris, have their own version of make in addition to accessibility to GNU make. In some of the systems, such as Darwin, GNU make is installed as the default. In others, such as FreeBSD, BSD make is the default. GNU make is installed but is usually called gmake. This typically isn't a problem because if the compilation fails, try gmake instead:

```
% gmake install
```

—SP

40.4 Simplifying the make Process

One of the problems associated with building and installing software within a Unix environment is ensuring that all the necessary libraries are present, the *makefile* is modified to fit the environment, and so on. The general building process is simplified by two GNU utilities: *autoconf* and *automake*.

The *autoconf* utility takes an input file called *configure.in* containing macros that determine how a configure file is built. The configure file, usually called *Makefile.in*, is then used by automake to create a Makefile that can be used to compile the application.

A README file should provide instructions on building an application, but if one is absent, you know that the application supports autoconf if you see a *configure.in* file, or see a script file called *configure*. If the package creator built a configure script manually, instructions will most likely be included within the README.

As a demonstration, I downloaded a GNU library called *plotutils* that provides graphics capability. After running *gunzip* and *tar* on the package to decompress the files, I looked at the topmost directory and found a configure file. I ran this using the following command:

```
> ./configure
```

The application can actually take a bit of time, and when finished, Makefiles have been generated for the application directories. All that's required at this point is to run make install as root:

```
> make install
```

Once the build was finished, I cleaned up by typing:

```
> make clean
> make distclean
```

The first make cleans up any in-process installation files; the second cleans up the distribution files.

The autoconf and automake utilities have greatly simplified installation of GNU and open source functionality.

—*SP*

40.5 Using Debian's dselect

The *dselect* tool provides an easy-to-use, character-based graphical frontend for accessing *dpkg* (the traditional Debian installation package utility). To launch *dselect*, issue the command:

```
dselect
```

Figure 40-1 shows the screen that appears. The screen presents a simple menu with six items:

Access
Lets you choose the method used to access package files.

Update
Lets you update the list of available packages.

Select
Lets you choose packages for installation or removal.

Install
Initiates installation of selected packages.

Config
Initiates configuration of installed packages.

Remove
Initiates removal of packages selection for removal.

Quit
Exits *dselect*.

The menu items are generally used in the order in which they are presented.

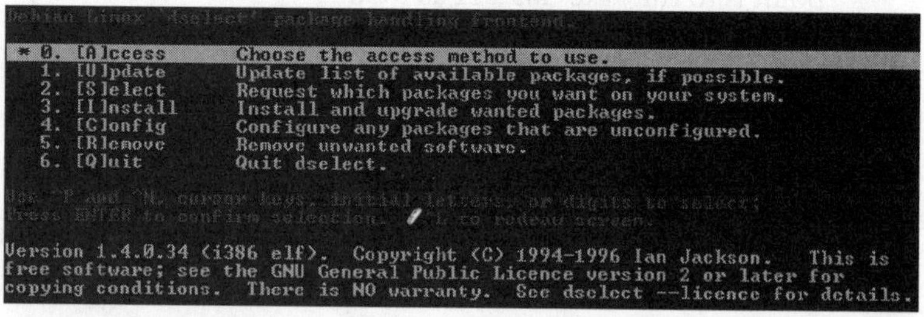

Figure 40-1. The dselect screen

Choosing the Access Method

To choose the access method, use the arrow keys to highlight the Access menu item and press Enter. The screen shown in Figure 40-2 appears.

The most flexible access method—and the method that's generally recommended—is apt. Other available options include:

cdrom
Lets you install packages from a CD-ROM. This access method has been deprecated; you should use *multi_cd* instead.

multi_cd
Lets you install packages from a multivolume set of CD-ROMs.

```
dselect - list of access methods
                      Description
   cdrom       Install from a CD-ROM.
   multi_cd    Install from a CD-ROM set.
   nfs         Install from an NFS server (not yet mounted).
   multi_nfs   Install from an NFS server (using the CD-ROM set) (not yet moun
   harddisk    Install from a hard disk partition (not yet mounted).
   mounted     Install from a filesystem which is already mounted.
   multi_mount Install from a mounted partition with changing contents.
   floppy      Install from a pile of floppy disks.
   ftp         Install using ftp.
   apt              APT Acquisition [file,http,ftp]

Access method 'apt'.
       APT Acquisition [file,http,ftp]

The APT installation method encompasses most other installation methods
under the umbrella of the new Package Acquisition code. This method allows
installation from locations in the filesystem, ftp and http URLs, supports
full installation ordering and dependency checking as well as multiple
sources. See the man pages apt-get(8) and source.list(5)

HTTP proxies can be used by setting http_proxy="http://proxy:port/" before
running DSelect. FTP proxies require special configuration detailed in the
apt.conf(5) man page (see /usr/doc/apt/examples/apt.conf)

Explanation of apt
```

Figure 40-2. Choosing the access method

nfs

Lets you install packages residing on an NFS server. This access method has been deprecated; you should use *multi_nfs* instead.

multi_nfs

Lets you install packages residing on an NFS server that has access to a multivolume set of packages.

harddisk

Lets you install packages residing on a hard disk partition that is not currently mounted. This access method has been deprecated; you should use *apt* or *multi_mount* instead.

mounted

Lets you install packages residing on a currently mounted filesystem. This access method has been deprecated; you should use *apt* or *multi_mount* instead.

multi_mount

Lets you install packages from a multivolume set, one volume of which is currently mounted.

floppy

Lets you install packages from a set of floppy diskettes.

ftp

Lets you install packages residing on an FTP server.

To choose an access method, use the arrow keys to highlight the appropriate menu item and press Enter.

If you selected the *apt* access method, you'll be asked if you want to change the *sources.list* file. If you've previously configured the file, you should respond No.

If you've not configured the file, you can respond Yes, which initiates a dialog that builds a simple configuration. Here's a sample dialog that shows the responses you should give to install packages :

```
I see you already have a source list.
------------------------------------------------------
source list displayed here: contents vary
------------------------------------------------------
Do you wish to change it?[y/N] y
         Set up a list of distribution source locations

Please give the base URL of the debian distribution.
The access schemes I know about are: http ftp file

For example:
              file:/mnt/debian,
              ftp://ftp.debian.org/debian,
              http://ftp.de.debian.org/debian,

URL [http://http.us.debian.org/debian]: file:/cdrom

Please give the distribution tag to get or a path to the
package file ending in a /. The distribution
tags are typically something like: stable unstable frozen non-US

Distribution [stable]: stable

Please give the components to get
The components are typically something like: main contrib non-free

Components [main contrib non-free]: main contrib

Would you like to add another source?[y/N] N
```

The sample dialog assumes that your CD-ROM has been mounted as */cdrom*. If your CD-ROM is mounted differently, you'll need to revise the dialog.

After *dselect* records your choice of access method, the main menu screen re-appears.

Updating Information on Available Packages

After selecting the access method, you should instruct *dselect* to update information on available packages. To do so, use the arrow keys to highlight the Update menu item and press Enter. After a short time, the main menu will re-appear.

Choosing Packages for Installation or Removal

Once you've updated the information on available packages, you're ready to select packages for installation or removal. To do so, use the arrow keys to highlight the Select menu item and press Enter. The screen shown in Figure 40-3 appears.

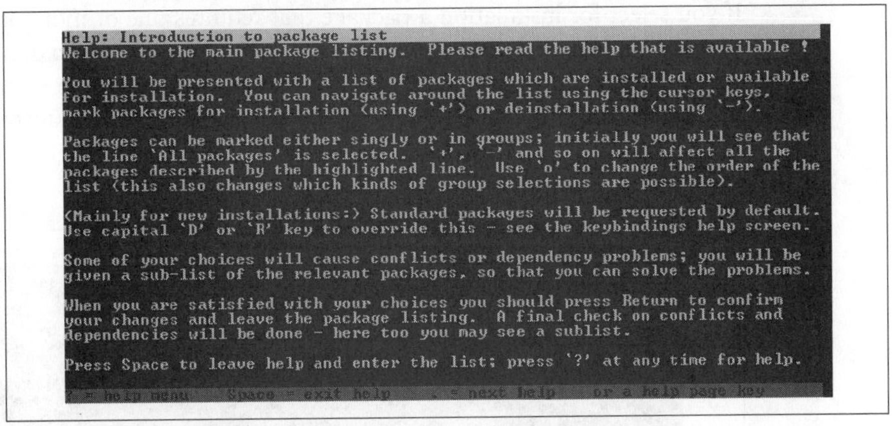

Figure 40-3. The introduction screen

This screen provides an overview of the package selection screens. When you've read its contents, press Space to go to the package selection screen, which is shown in Figure 40-4.

This screen provides an overview of the package selection screens. When you've read its contents, press Space to go to the package selection screen, whih is shown in Figure 40-4 .

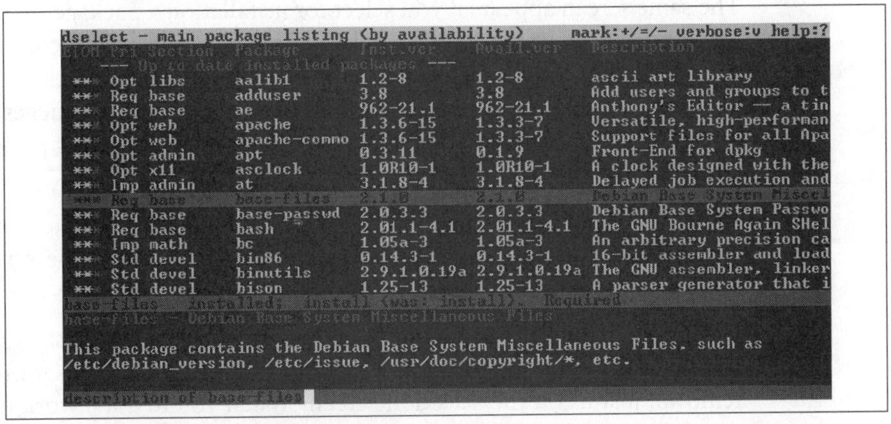

Figure 40-4. The package selection screen

To use the package selection screen, use the arrow keys to highlight a package in the upper part of the screen. The lower part of the screen will display information about the highlighted package. To select the package for installation, press +; to select an installed package for removal, press -.

You can search the package database by typing a slash (/) followed by the string for which you wish to search. To find successive instances of the same string, type a backslash (\). For example, to find the first package that contains the string *gnome* in its name or description, type */gnome* and press Enter.

If you select for installation a package that requires one or more other packages that are not installed, a dependency conflict results. Similarly, a dependency conflict results if you mark for removal a package required by an installed package or if you mark for installation a package that conflicts with an installed package. When *dselect* detects a dependency conflict, it presents the screen shown in Figure 40-5.

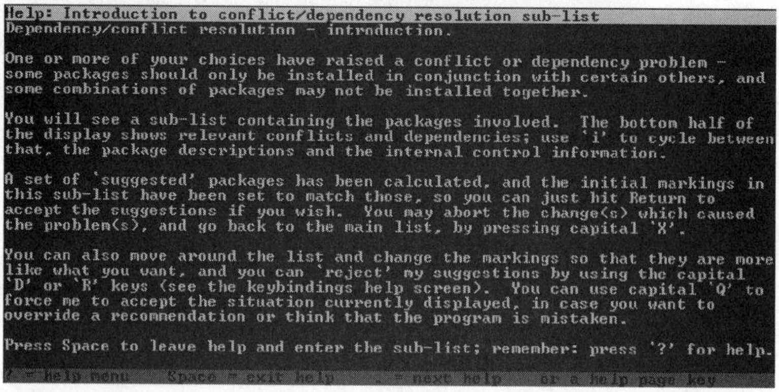

Figure 40-5. The dependency help screen

The same screen appears if you select for installation a package that specifies recommended or suggested packages to be installed with it. A recommended package is one that most users install with the recommending package. A suggested package is one that is related to the suggesting package; suggested packages often extend or complement the functionality of the suggesting package.

When you press Space, you're presented with the conflict resolution screen, shown in Figure 40-6. This screen lets you quickly select for installation or removal the packages involved in a dependency conflict. The screen also presents default choices for recommended and suggested packages.

Using the arrow keys to highlight an entry lets you view a list of dependencies related to the entry. By pressing + or -, you can select packages for installation or removal, just as on the selection screen. When you're done working out dependencies, you can press Space to return to the selection screen.

Exiting the Select Function

You can select the Select function in any of several ways. Pressing Space returns you to the main menu, where you can initiate installation or removal of packages. Pressing x cancels your selections and returns you to the main menu. This feature is useful if you change your mind about installing a package, possibly owing to conflicts associated with the package.

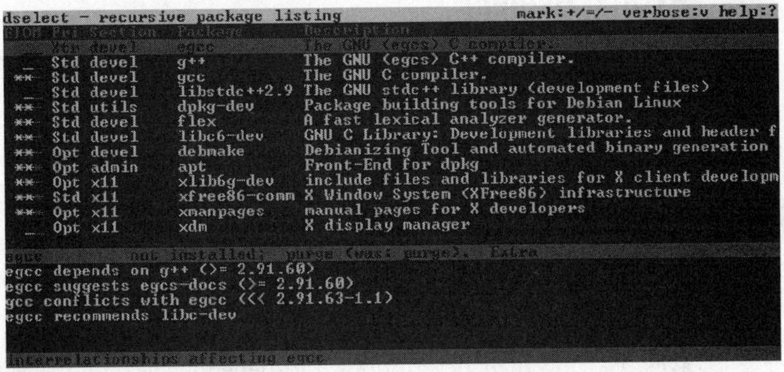

```
dselect - recursive package listing        mark:+/=/- verbose:v help:?
EIOM Pri Section Package        Description
    (Pr devel)        The GNU (egcs) C compiler.
 _  Std devel   g++        The GNU (egcs) C++ compiler.
 ** Std devel   gcc        The GNU C compiler.
 _  Std devel   libstdc++2.9 The GNU stdc++ library (development files)
 ** Std utils   dpkg-dev   Package building tools for Debian Linux
 ** Std devel   flex       A fast lexical analyzer generator.
 ** Std devel   libc6-dev  GNU C Library: Development libraries and header f
 ** Opt devel   debmake    Debianizing Tool and automated binary generation
 ** Opt admin   apt        Front-End for dpkg
 ** Opt x11     xlib6g-dev include files and libraries for X client developm
 ** Std x11     xfree86-comm X Window System (XFree86) infrastructure
 ** Opt x11     xmanpages  manual pages for X developers
 _  Opt x11     xdm        X display manager

     egcs          not installed; purge (was: purge).   Extra
egcc depends on g++ <>= 2.91.60>
egcc suggests egcs-docs <>= 2.91.60>
gcc conflicts with egcc <<< 2.91.63-1.1>
egcc recommends libc-dev

Interrelationships affecting egcc
```

Figure 40-6. The dependency resolution screen

Installing Packages

To begin installing the selected packages, use the arrow keys to highlight the Install menu item and press Enter. As packages are downloaded or installed, you'll see messages on the screen.

If you're using the *apt* access method, selecting Install actually initiates installation, removal, and configuration of packages. You can exit *dselect* after the installation process completes.

If you're using some other access method, *dselect* may not install every selected package in a single operation. When the installation process completes, you should select Install and see if more packages are installed. When you select Install and no more packages are installed, you can proceed to the subsequent steps: configuration and removal.

When the installation process is complete, *dselect* prompts you to press Enter to return to the main menu.

Configuring Packages

To begin configuring the installed packages, use the arrow keys to highlight the Configure menu item and press Enter. Packages that require configuration will prompt you for configuration choices. When the configuration process is complete, *dselect* prompts you to press Enter to return to the main menu.

Removing Packages

To begin removing the packages selected for removal, use the arrow keys to highlight the Remove menu item and press Enter. When the removal process is complete, *dselect* prompts you to press Enter to return to the main menu.

Exiting dselect

To exit *dselect*, use the arrow keys to highlight the Quit menu item and press Enter.

—SP

40.6 Installing Software with Debian's Apt-Get

The *dselect* program is useful, because it lets you browse a list of available packages, viewing their descriptions and dependencies, and selecting desired packages for installation. However, if you know the name of a package you want to install, *apt-get* is often the easiest way to install it. Before using *apt-get*, you must configure the *sources.list* file. This same file is used when you choose the apt access method of *dselect*. Even if you don't plan on using *apt-get*, you'll find the information in the following subsection useful.

Configuring the sources.list File

The *sources.list* file resides in the */etc/apt* directory. Like most other Linux configuration files, it can be revised by using an ordinary text editor, such as *ae*.

The file contains a series of lines, each specifying a source for packages. The lines are consulted serially, so it's usually advantageous to place lines that specify local sources—such as a CD-ROM—ahead of lines that specify remote sources. Doing so can save many minutes of download time.

Each line has the form:

```
deb uri distribution components
```

The *uri* is a universal resource identifier (URI) that specifies the computer on which the packages reside, the location of the packages, and the protocol used for accessing the packages. It has the following form:

```
protocol://host/path
```

Four protocols—sometimes called URI types—are recognized:

cdrom
> A local CD-ROM drive

file
> A directory of the local filesystem

http
> A web server

ftp
> An FTP server

The *host* part of the URI and the preceding pair of slashes (//) are used only for the http and ftp protocols. There, the *host* part of the URI gives the name of the host that contains the packages.

The *path* part of the URI always appears, with the preceding slash (/). It specifies the absolute path of the directory that contains the packages.

Here are some examples of typical URIs:

```
cdrom:/cdrom
cdrom:/mnt/cdrom
file:/mnt
file:/debian
http://www.us.debian.org/debian
http://non-us.debian.org/debian-non-US
ftp://ftp.debian.org/debian
ftp://nonus.debian.org/debian-non-US
```

The distribution part of a *sources.list* line specifies the distribution release that contains the packages. Typical values include:

stable
> The latest stable release; that is, one that is commonly regarded as having sufficiently few serious bugs for everyday use.

unstable
> The latest unstable release. This release sometimes contains serious bugs and should not be installed by users who require high levels of system availability or reliability.

The components part of a *sources.list* line specifies the parts of the distribution that will be accessed. Typical values include:

main
> The main set of packages.

contrib
> Packages not an integral part of the distribution, but which may be useful.

non-free
> Packages that contain software distributed under terms too restrictive to allow inclusion in the distribution, but which may be useful.

A typical *sources.list* file might contain the following entries:

```
deb file:/cdrom stable main contrib
deb http://www.us.debian.org/debian stable main contrib non-free
deb http://non-us.debian.org/debian-non-US stable non-US
```

This configuration allows rapid access to the distribution packages contained on the local CD-ROM. It also allows convenient access via the network to other packages and more recent package versions stored on web servers.

Using apt-get

Once you've configured sources.list, you can use *apt-get* to update information on available packages, install a package, or upgrade installed packages.

Updating information on available packages

To update information on available packages, issue the following command:

```
apt-get update
```

Installing a package

To install a specified package, issue the following command:

```
apt-get install package
```

where *package* specifies the name of the package to be installed.

Upgrading installed packages

To automatically upgrade all installed packages to the latest available version, issue the following command:

```
apt-get upgrade
```

—SP

40.7 Interruptable gets with wget

The GNU utility *wget* can be used to access files through the Internet using HTTP, HTTPS, or FTP. The best thing about the utility is that if the process is interrupted and started again, it continues from where it left off.

wget

The *wget* utility is installed by default in a lot of systems, but if you can't find it, it can be downloaded from GNU, at *http://www.gnu.org/software/wget/wget.html*.

The basic syntax for *wget* is very simple: type wget followed by the URL of the file or files you're trying to download:

```
wget http://www.somefile.com/somefile.htm
wget ftp://www.somefile.com/somefile
```

The file is downloaded and saved and a status is printed out to the screen:

```
--16:51:58--  http://dynamicearth.com:80/index.htm
           => `index.htm'
Connecting to dynamicearth.com:80... connected!
HTTP request sent, awaiting response... 200 OK
Length: 9,144 [text/html]

    OK -> ........                                        [100%]

16:51:58 (496.09 KB/s) - `index.htm' saved [9144/9144]
```

The default use of *wget* downloads the file into your current location. If the download is interrupted, by default *wget* does not resume at the point of interruption. You need to specify an option for this behavior. The *wget* options can be found in Table 40-2. Short and long forms of each option are specified, and options that don't require input can be grouped together:

> wget -drc URL

For those options that do require an input, you don't have to separate the option and the input with whitespace:

> wget -ooutput.file URL

Table 40-2. wget options

Option	Purpose	Examples
-V	Get version of wget	wget -V
-h or --help	Get listing of wget options	wget -help
-b or --background	Got to background after start	wget -b *url*
-e or --execute=*COMMAND*	Execute command	wget -e COMMAND *url*
-o or --output-file=*file*	Log messages to file	wget -o *filename url*
-a or --append-output=*file*	Appends to log file	wget -a *filename url*
-d or --debug	Turn on debug output	wget -d *url*
-q or --quiet	Turn off wget's output	wget -q *url*
-v or --verbose	Turn on verbose output	wget -v *url*
-nv or -non-verbose	Turn off verbose output	wget -nv *url*
-i or --input-file=*file*	Read urls from file	wget -I *inputfile*
-F or --force-html	Force input to be treated as HTML	wget -F *url*
-t or --tries=*number*	Number of re-tries to get file	wget -t 3 *url*
-O or --output-document=*file*	Forces all documents into specified	wget -O *savedfile* -i *inputfile*
-nc or --no-clobber	Don't clobber existing file	wget -nc *url*
-c or --continue	Continue getting file	wget -c *url*
--dot-style=*style*	Retrieval indicator	wget -dot-style=binary *url*
-N or --timestamping	Turn on time-stamping	wget -N *url*
-S or --server-response	Print HTTP headers, FTP responses	wget -S *url*
--spider	Wget behaves as a web spider, doesn't download	wget --spider *url*
-T or --timeout=*seconds*	Set the time out	-wget -T 30 *url*
-w or --wait=*seconds*	Wait specified number of seconds	wget -w 20 *url*
-Y or --proxy=*on/off*	Turn proxy on or off	wget -Y on *url*
-Q or --quota=*quota*	Specify download quota size	wget -Q2M *url*
-nd or --no-directories	Do not create directories in recursive download	wget -nd *url*

Table 40-2. wget options (continued)

Option	Purpose	Examples
-x or --force-directories	Opposite of -nd	`wget -x url`
-nh or --no-host-directories	Disable host-prefixed directories	`wget -nh url`
--cut-dirs=number	Ignore number directories	`wget -cur-dirs=3 url`
-P or --directory-prefix=prefix	Set directory to prefix	`wget -P test url`
--http-user=user --http-passwd=passwd	Set username and password	`wget --http-user=user --http-passwd=password url`

—SP

40.8 The curl Application and One-Step GNU-Darwin Auto-Installer for OS X

curl

The *cURL*, or *curl*, application acts similar to *wget*, except that it works with more protocols, including FTPS, GOPHER, DICT, TELNET, FILE, and LDAP, as well as HTTP, HTTPS, and FTP (40.8). It also supports kerberos, cookies, user authentication, file transfer resume and so on. You can access the application at *http://curl.haxx.se*, though *curl* is installed by default on some systems, including Mac OS X Darwin.

In particular, *curl* is used to download and install the GNU-Darwin auto-installer for OS X, otherwise known as One-Step.

The following command starts the process of installing the basefiles for One-Step. Note that the One-Step installation can take a considerable length of time, and you might get messages about needing to modify certain aspects of the installation, such as adding a font path and so on. Still, the instructions are very clear and once the installation is finished, you'll then be able to use One-Step.

```
# curl http://gnu-darwin.sourceforge.net/one_stop | csh
```

You can CTRL-c at any time during the download portion, and continue the installation at a later time. Use caution, though, with interrupting the installation during the final build portion. You can view the installation script for One-Step at *http://gnu-darwin.sourceforge.net/one_stop/*.

One of the applications installed during the process is *pkg_add*, which you can use to add additional packages at a later time by specifying the command followed by the URL of the package:

```
# pkg_add url
```

—SP

40.9 Installation with FreeBSD Ports

The FreeBSD operating system has a terrific software installation system known as the FreePSD Ports. You can download the entire distribution collection as root giving a specific command within the */usr/ports* directory:

```
# /stand/sysinstall
```

Once the Ports collection is installed, you can then easily install software by changing directory to the specific application and typing make install:

```
# cd /usr/ports
# cd lang
# cd ruby
# make install
# make clean
# make distclean
```

Not only will the Ports application install the application—in this case support for the Ruby programming language—it also pulls in any dependent files that might not exist on the system.

You may have problems downloading the distribution file because your system setup may not allow you to write to the */usr/ports/distfiles* subdirectory for some reason. To install the distribution to a different location, set the *DISTDIR* environment variable to a different location:

```
# make DISTDIR=/local/dir/with/write/permission install
```

To removed an installed application, again change to the ports subdirectory of the application and type:

```
# make deinstall
```

—*SP*

40.10 Installing with FreeBSD Packages

Instead of using the Ports you can install applications individually as packages, using the *pkg_add* utility, similar to that shown in (40.08).

To install using *pkg_add*, download the package by ftp'ing to the FreeBSD FTP server at *ftp2.FreeBSD.org*, and then change to the */pub/ports/packages* directory. At that point, the directory at the FTP server should be similar to the Ports collection directory organization. Change directory to the category (such as "lang"). Get the gzipped tar (15.7) file of the package for your application, using binary transfer. For instance, the Ruby scripting language interpretor is *ruby-1.7.2.2002.05.23.tgz*, which is then downloaded:

```
ftp > get /pub/ports/packages/lang/ruby-1.7.2.2002.05.23.tgz
```

Once the file is downloaded, type `pkg_add` and the package name:

```
# pkg_add ruby-1.7.2.2002.05.23.tgz
```

Instead of downloading the file manually, you can use the *-r* option to have the *pkg_add* application look for the latest build of an application and automatically download necessary dependent files and the target application itself:

```
# pkg_add -r ruby-1.7.2.2002.05.23.tgz
```

Note, though, that the newest versions of an application may not be in the stable build directory. If you want an application not on this tree, you'll have to download the application file manually.

—SP

40.11 Finding and Installing RPM Packaged Software

rpm

A popular tool used to find and install software packages—particularly in Linux —is RPM (at *http://www.rpm.org/*). In addition to working with Linux, RPM also works with Solaris, HP-UX, FreeBSD, NetBSD, and other systems.

To use RPM to install software, just type the following command:

```
rpm -i application.rpm
```

The *-i* option flags RPM to install the package. To uninstall the application, use:

```
rpm -e application.rpm
```

To upgrade a package, use the *-U* option:

```
rpm -U application.rpm
```

—SP

41

Perl

41.1 High-Octane Shell Scripting

Perl* is an ecclectic, interpreted language with deep roots in Unix. It was originally written by Larry Wall, creator of other Unix staples such as *patch* and *rn*, to help with system administration tasks. Because many of its variables are prefixed with $, Perl often looks like an *awk* program or even a Bourne shell script. Like all appearances, this too can be deceiving. Perl is a complete programming language that supports both structured and object oriented programming. Getting started with Perl is easy, since many of the Bourne shell tricks you've seen will work (after a fashion) under Perl. As your knowledge grows, you'll find that Perl will help you scratch increasingly obscure itches. Because Perl has been ported to many different platforms, it brings a Unix-like API to whichever operating system is hosting it. Perl makes cross-platform programming a reality.

The complete guide to Perl is O'Reilly's *Programming Perl*, a book that weighs in at over 1500 pages. Therefore, only the barest of essentials can be presented here to help you identify your Perl installation, tinker with existing scripts, and install new modules. Luckily, Perl always comes with documentation that can be accessed through the *perldoc* (41.10) system.

—*JJ*

41.2 Checking your Perl Installation

perl

Before presenting the details of Perl syntax, it would be prudent to check whether or not Perl is on your system and learn how to install it if it isn't. Perl is an interpreted language whose interpreter is called *perl*. It is this program that reads, compiles and runs Perl source code. Normally, *perl* will be in your shell's

---

* A word on casing: "Perl" refers to the language as an abstract concept; "*perl*" refers to the program installed on your machine.

path. It can often be found lurking in */usr/bin* or */usr/local/bin*. Use your system's *find* or *locate* command to track down *perl* if it doesn't appear in your command path. To see what version of Perl you have, use the -v flag like this:

```
$ perl -v

This is perl, v5.6.1 built for i686-linux

Copyright 1987-2001, Larry Wall

Perl may be copied only under the terms of either the Artistic License or the
GNU General Public License, which may be found in the Perl 5 source kit.

Complete documentation for Perl, including FAQ lists, should be found on
this system using `man perl' or `perldoc perl'.  If you have access to the
Internet, point your browser at http://www.perl.com/, the Perl Home Page.
```

This Perl is the latest stable version, 5.6.1. Perl is under very active development and newer versions may soon be available. As with all software projects, there is an unstable, developer's version of Perl that currently is 5.7.3. The version number scheme follows the pattern:

Revision number

These change only when the language is substantially redefined.

Version number

Even numbers indicate a stable, production-quality release. Odd numbers should only be used by Perl developers and the curious. Version numbers indicate an important change in the language that may affect scripts written to run under a previous version of Perl. Be sure to check out the perldelta manpage for details.

Subversion level

This number is better thought of as the patch level for a given version. Only bug fixes will appear with each new patch level release. of *perl*.

Local configuration information about *perl* can be obtained with the -V flag. A slightly abbreviated version of that command's output appears below.

```
$ perl -V
Summary of my perl5 (revision 5.0 version 6 subversion 1) configuration:
  Platform:
    osname=linux, osvers=2.4.2-2, archname=i686-linux
    uname='linux marian 2.4.2-2 #1 sun apr 8 20:41:30 edt 2001 i686 unknown '
    config_args=''
    hint=recommended, useposix=true, d_sigaction=define
    ...

  Compiler:
    cc='cc', ccflags ='-fno-strict-aliasing ...'
    optimize='-O2',
    cppflags='-fno-strict-aliasing'
    intsize=4, longsize=4, ptrsize=4, doublesize=8, byteorder=1234
    ...
```

```
Characteristics of this binary (from libperl):
  Compile-time options: USE_LARGE_FILES
  Built under linux
  Compiled at Oct  1 2001 16:15:45
  @INC:
    /usr/local/lib/perl5/5.6.1/i686-linux
    /usr/local/lib/perl5/5.6.1
    /usr/local/lib/perl5/site_perl/5.6.1/i686-linux
    /usr/local/lib/perl5/site_perl/5.6.1
    /usr/local/lib/perl5/site_perl
    .
```

The sections followed by ellipses have been truncated. What's important to note here is that the configuration, compiler, and linker options are available (and are used by the *perlbug* program if you need to file a bug report about Perl). Of more practical use is the section beginning with @INC. This lists the directories in which *perl* will look for library modules, described later in article 41.11.

—JJ

41.3 Compiling Perl from Scratch

If you don't have Perl already or you'd like to install the latest version, you have a few options. The first is to get a precompiled version for your platform. This is an option of last resort, since you lose the opportunity to configure Perl for your system. Most Unix systems will compile the Perl source code cleanly.

To compile Perl, you will need to fetch the latest Perl source for the Comprehensive Perl Archive Network (CPAN) (41.11). You can find the gzipped tar archive of the source code at *http://www.cpan.org/src/stable.tar.gz*. The archive is several megabytes, so those on a slow modem link need to plan accordingly. Unpack the archive with the following command:

```
$ gzip -dc stable.tar.gz | tar xvf -
```

You should now have a new subdirectory called *perl-X.Y.Z* (whatever the current version of Perl is). Change into this directory and you will be be ready to configure the build process for *perl*.

Like many Unix utilities, compiling Perl requires configuring a Makefile and then executing *make*. The Perl source comes with a robust *Configure* shell script that will prompt you to confirm information it finds about your system. Often, all the defaults are fine so you can tell the *Configure* not to prompt you for confirmation by passing the -de flag. If all goes well with the configuration stage, you'll want to start compiling the source with *make*. These steps can be effectively combined into to following idiom:

```
$ ./Configure -de && make test
```

Recall that the double ampersand is a kind of flow control operator in the shell that allows the *make* to happen only if the *Configure* succeeds. The Perl source comes with a test suite that attempts to verify that the build went according to plan. Since the test suite needs *perl* to be built, this command is similiar to typing:

```
$ ./Configure -de && make && make test
```

The configuration stage may report missing libraries (like those needed to make NDBM files or read shadowed password files). Generally, these messages are harmless. If an important dependency is missing, the *Configure* script will halt. You will need to read the error message to figure out what's missing from your system that Perl requires. Generally, Perl will configure and compile without much intervention from you.

If the make test command succeeds, you are ready to install your new Perl. Typically, installation requires administrative privileges since you'll be writing files in */usr/local* (the default installation root). One way to do this is to use the *su* command like this:

```
$ su -c 'make install'
```

This will prompt you for root's password. During the installation process, you will be asked if you want Perl installed as */usr/bin/perl*. On a system that didn't have Perl to begin with, you can safely answer yes to this question. On a system that already had Perl, you might wish to answer no here. The new Perl interpreter will still be installed in */usr/local/bin/perl*. You should now have the latest version of Perl on your system. Use */path/to/newly_installed/perl -v* to verify this.

—JJ

41.4 Perl Boot Camp, Part 1: Typical Script Anatomy

It is impossible to present a complete guide to programming Perl in this one small section, but you can glean enough information here to be able to modify existing Perl scripts and evaluate whether you'd like to learn more about this incredibly handy language.

Perl scripts bare a passing resemblence to Bourne shell scripts. Example 41-1 a script called *writewav.pl* that comes with the Perl module Audio::SoundFile. It converts a given sound file into WAV format. The details of what it's doing aren't important, but it does demonstrate some common Perl structures that you should understand at a high level.

Example 41-1. A sample Perl script

```perl
#!/usr/bin/perl -w

=head1 NAME

 writewav - Converts any sound file into .wav format

=cut

use Audio::SoundFile;
use Audio::SoundFile::Header;

my ($buffer, $length, $header, $reader, $writer);
my $BUFFSIZE = 16384;
my $ifile = shift @ARGV || usage();
my $ofile = shift @ARGV || usage();

$reader = Audio::SoundFile::Reader->new($ifile, \$header);
$header->{format} = SF_FORMAT_WAV | SF_FORMAT_PCM;
$writer = Audio::SoundFile::Writer->new($ofile,  $header);

while ($length = $reader->bread_pdl(\$buffer, $BUFFSIZE)) {
    $writer->bwrite_pdl($buffer);
}

$reader->close;
$writer->close;

sub usage {
  print "usage: $0 <infile> <outfile>\n";
  exit(1);
}
```

The first line of Example 41-1 should be familiar to shell hackers; it's the she-bang line. When the first two bytes of a file are the characters #!, the shell uses the rest of that file's first line to determine which program should be used to interpret the rest of the file. In this case, the path to the Perl interpreter is given. Command line arguments can be given to the interpreter. Here -w instructs Perl to print warning messages when it finds code that is likely to be incorrect. This includes such common gaffes as trying to write to a read-only file handle, subroutines that recurse more than 100 times, and attempts to get the value of a scalar variable that hasn't been assigned a value yet. This flag is a new Perl programmer's best friend and should be used in all programs.

All lines that start with = in the left margin are part of Perl's Plain Old Documentation (POD) system. Everything between the directives =head1 and =cut are documentation and do not affect how the script runs. There are Perl tools like *pod2text* and *pod2man* that will format the POD found in a script into the particular output format given in the command's name. There's even a *pod2man* program used during the Perl installation procedure that creates all the Perl manpages on the target system.

The next two lines begin with actual Perl code. To use Perl library files called modules (41.10), scripts invoke the *use module* statement. Perl searches the paths listed in the global variable @INC (41.2) for these modules, which typically have the extension *.pm*.

In Perl, variables don't need to be declared before being used. Although this behavior is convenient for small scripts, larger scripts can benefit from the disciplined approach of declaring variables. Perl 5—that is, Perl revision 5—introduced the my operator as a way of declaring a variable. Declaring variables allows the -w flag to help catch misspelled variable names, which are a common source of bugs in Perl scripts.

A variable that holds a single value is called a *scalar* and is always prefixed with a $ (even in assignments), unlike variables in the Bourne shell. The = is the assignment operator (when it's not appearing as a POD directive). Another kind of variable, called an *array*, can be used to hold many scalar values. Array variables begin with @. One example of a global array variable is @ARGV, which holds the list of command-line arguments passed into the Perl script.

Continuing with Example 41-1, the two variables $ifile and $ofile get values from the command line. The shift operator removes values from the beginning of the @ARGV array. If there aren't enough values on the command line, the user defined subroutine usage( ) is called.

Perl supports object oriented programming (OOP). The hallmark of OOP is that both the data and the subroutines (called *methods* in OOP jargon) for processing that data are accessed through an object. In traditional procedural programming, data structures are stored separately from functions that manipulate them. Fortunately, using object oriented Perl modules is often straightforward. In Example 41-1, the scalar $reader is a new Audio::SoundFile::Reader object. Unlike other OOP languages, Perl's objects are not opaque: the user can set or get values internal to the object. This is what is happening on the next line. The -> dereferencing operator is used both to get at values that are pointed to by references (41.5) and to make method calls. Here, the key format is set to a value that is created by the bitwise or of the values returned by the subroutines SF_FORMAT_WAV and SF_FORMAT_PCM. Another object, $writer, is created on the following line.

The heart of the program is the while loop which, in English, reads, "While reading more chunks of the source file, translate that chunk into WAV data and write it to the outfile." When the loop finishes, those objects are no longer needed, so the close( ) method is called on each of them to release any resources used by those objects. This is the end of the program's execution, but there's a bit more to this script.

Perl allows for user defined subroutines. Although they can be anywhere in the file, subroutine definitions typically come after the main block of code. Here, a subroutine called usage() is defined that simply prints some help to the user and quits. Inside of double quoted strings, Perl interpolates scalar and array values. This is a fancy way of saying that Perl replaces variables with their values. Because Perl tries to do the right thing with interpolation, there may be occasions when Perl's rules surprise you. Take a look at the *perldata* manpage for the definitive rules governing variable interpolation and a peek at the *perltrap* manpage for common interpolation mistakes. You can prevent interpolation by putting a backslash in front of the variable name (e.g. \$foo is $foo) or use single quotes, which never interpolate variables. Finally, the exit(1) function halts the script before the subroutine can return to the caller and returns the value 1 to the operating system.

That's the 50,000-foot view of a Perl script. To confidently modify existing Perl scripts, it is necessary to understand some of the basic components of Perl better.

—JJ

41.5 Perl Boot Camp, Part 2: Variables and Data Types

Data types are the kinds of values Perl supports. Common data types include arbitrarily long strings (e.g., "hi, bob"), intergers (e.g., 42) and floating point numbers (e.g., 3.14). Perl is a *loosely typed* language, which means that Perl works hard to let you forget about what kind of data you're dealing with. For the most part, you will be dealing with strings, which plays to Perl's strengths. To manipulate data, variables are employed. Table 41-1 lists the most common variable types in Perl. For the full story on Perl data types, read the *perldata* manpage.

Table 41-1. Common Perl variables

Name	Example	Description
scalar	$lastname, $PI	Holds single values
array	@people, $peple[0]	Holds an ordered sequence of scalar values
hash	%cgi_params, $cgi_params{'action'}	Holds a set of key-value pairs

Scalars

When you want to store single values, like any of those given in the previous paragraph, you will use a scalar variable. Scalars are labeled with a $ followed by a letter and any sequence of letters, numbers, and underscores. Scalars defined at the top of scripts are often used as constants. You may need to tweak some of them, particularly those containing filesystem paths, to get third-party scripts to run on your system.

Of course, values can be compared to each other or added together. Perl has relational operators that treat values as numbers and other relational operators that treat values as strings. Although Perl has different operators for numbers and strings, Perl makes scalar values do the right thing most of the time. For example, you want to create a series of filenames like *mail_num*. The following code does this.

```
foreach my $num (1..10) {
    print "mail_" . $num . "\n";
}
```

Even though $num is a number, the string concatenation operator is able to use it as a string. Table 41-2 shows string operators, and Table 41-3 shows the numerical ones. See the perlop manpage for the full story.

Table 41-2. String operators

Operator	Example	Description
.	$saluation . " Jones"	String concatenation
eq	$foo eq $bar	String equality test
ne	$bar ne $baz	String inequality test
gt	$name gt "Bob"	True if left string comes after right in ASCII
lt	$name lt "Xavier"	True if left string comes before right in ASCII
cmp	$name cmp "Wilson"	Return −1 if left operand ASCII-sorts before the right; 0 if right and left are equal; 1 if right sorts before left
lc	lc "Bob"	Return an all-lowercase copy of the given string
uc	uc "lorrie"	Return an all-uppercase copy of the given string

Table 41-3. Numerical operators

Operator	Example	Description
+	$a + 1	Numerical addition
-	$c - 2	Numerical subtraction
*	3 * $b	Numerical multiplication
/	4/$non_zero	Numerical division
++	$a++	Autoincrement; adds one to a number
==	$a == $b	Numeric equality test
!=	$p != $q	Numeric inequality test
<	$diff < 32	Numeric less-than test
>	$sum > 64	Numeric greater-than test

Table 41-3. Numerical operators (continued)

Operator	Example	Description
<=>	$sum <=> 64	Return -1 if left is numerically less than right; 0 if left equals right; 1 if right is less than left
<=	$sum <= 64	True if left operand is numerically less than or equal to right
>=	$sum >= 64	True if left is numerally greater than or equal to right

You may have notice that some of the operators in the previous tables were described as returning true or false values. A true value in Perl is any value that isn't false, and there are only 4 kinds of false values in Perl:

- values that are numerically zero
- values that are empty strings
- values that are undef
- empty lists

Like many other languages, Perl supports Boolean operators (see Table 41-3) that return true or false values. Typically, you encounter these in if statements like the following:

```
if ($temp < 30 && $is_rainy) {
  print "I'm telecommuting today\n";
}
```

Another common use of Boolean operators is to short-circuit two expressions. This is a way to prevent the right operand from executing unless the left operand returns a desired truth value. Consider the very ordinary case of opening a filehandle for reading. A common idiom to do this is:

```
open (FH, "filename") || die "Can't open file";
```

This short-cut operation depends on the open function returning a true value if it can open the requested file. Only if it cannot is the right side of the || operator executed (die prints whatever message you provide and halts the program).

Table 41-4. Boolean operators

Operator	Example	Description
&&	$a && $b	True if both $a and $b are true
||	$a || $b	True if either $a or $b is true
!	!$a	True if $a is false
and	$a and $b	Same as &&, but with a lower precedence
or	$a or $b	Same as ||, but with a lower precedence
not	not $a	Same as !, but with a lower precedence

Looking at Table 41-4, you will notice that there appear to be redundant operators. The operators that are English words have a lower precedence that the symbolic ones. Precedence is simply the order in which Perl executes expressions. You are probably familiar with precedence rules from mathematics:

```
1 + 2 * 3 + 4 = 11
(1 + 2) * (3 + 4) = 21
```

Similarly, Perl's operators have precedence as well, as shown in Example 41-2.

Example 41-2. Precedence

```
lc $a || "BB"    # like (lc $a) || ("BB")
lc ($a || "BB")
```

Because || has a lower precedence that the lc operator, the first line of Example 41-2 is a Boolean test between two expressions. In the second line, the Boolean || operator is used to create a default argument to lc should $a be a false value.

Because Perl doesn't require parentheses around built-in operators and functions, you will often see code like:

```
open FH, "> " . "filename" or die "Can't open file";
print FH "[info]: disk write error\n";
```

Precedence ambiguities can be resolved by using parentheses where doubt occurs.

Although Perl has many special variables, the one you'll encounter most is $_. Many operators and functions, such as lc and print, will operate on $_ in the absence of an explicit parameter, as in Example 41-3.

Example 41-3. Simple echo loop

```
while(<>){
    print
}
```

In this example, every line read from standard input with the <> operator is available inside the while (41.7) loop through $_. The print function, in the absence of an explicit argument, echoes the value of $_. Note that $_ can be assigned to (e.g., $_ = "Hello, Perl") just like any other scalar.

Arrays

When you want to collect more than one value into a variable, you have two ways to go in Perl. If you need an ordered set of values, you will choose to use a Perl array. These variables start with @ and are followed by a label that follows the same convention as a scalar. Two global arrays have already been mentioned: @INC and @ARGV. Since arrays hold multiple values, getting and setting values is a little different from scalars. Here's an example of creating an array with values, looking at one, and assigning a new value to that array index.

```
@things    = ('phone', 'cat', 'hard drive');
print "The second element is: ", $things[1], "\n";

$things[1] = 'dog';
print "The second element is now: ", $things[1], "\n";
```

In the first line, the array @things is initialized with a list of three scalar values. Array indexes begin with zero, so the second element is accessed through the index value of 1. Arrays will grow as needed, so you could have added a fourth element like this:

```
$things[3] = 'DVD player';
```

Why is a $ used here and not @? Use @ only when referring to the whole array variable. Each element is a scalar whose name is $things[*index*]. This rule comes up again when dealing with hashes.

Typically you will want to iterate through all the values in an array, which is done with loops (41.7). Although there are several looping constructs, the most common idiom to examine all the values in an array sequentially is shown in Example 41-4.

Example 41-4. Using foreach to loop through an array

```
print "Paths Perl checks for modules\n";
foreach my $el (@INC) {
  print $el, "\n";
}
```

Lists are a data type that is closely related to arrays. Lists are sequences of scalar values enclosed in parentheses that are not associated with an array variable. They are used to initialize a new array variable. Common array operators are listed in Table 41-5.

```
my @primes     = (1,3,5,7,9,11);
my @empty_list = ();
```

Table 41-5. Common array operators

Name	Example	Description
pop	$last = pop @array;	Return last element of array; remove that element from array
push	push @array, @*new_elements*;	Add the contents of @*new_elements* to the end of target array
shift	$first = shift @array;	Return the first element of array; shift all elements one index lower (removing the first element)
unshift	unshift @array, @*new_elements*;	Add @*new_elements* to the beginning of target array

Hashes

Associative arrays, or hashes, are a collection of scalar values that are arranged in key-value pairs. Instead of using integers to retrieve values in a hash, strings are used. Hashes begin with %. Example 41-5 shows a hash variable in action.

Example 41-5. Using hashes

```
my %birthdays = (
                'mom'    => 'JUN 14',
                'archie' => 'JUN 12',
                'jay'    => 'JUL 11',
                );

print "Archie's birthday is: ", $birthdays{'archie'}, "\n";
$birthday{'joe'} = 'DEC 12';
print "My birthday is: ", $birthdays{'joe'}, "\n";
```

Hashes are a funny kind of list. When initializing a hash with values, it is common to arrange the list in key-value pairs. The strange-looking => operator is often called a "fat comma" because these two lines of Perl do the same thing:

```
%birthdays = ( 'jay' => 'JUL 11' );
%birthdays = ( 'jay', 'JUL 11');
```

Use the fat comma when initializing hashes since it conveys the association between the values better. As an added bonus, the fat comma makes unquoted barewords on its left into quoted strings.

Example 41-6 shows some quoting styles for hash keys.

Example 41-6. Various quoting styles for hash keys

```
my %baz = ( foo => 1,
           'bar', 2,
           'boz' => 3);
```

Unlike arrays, hashes use strings to index into the list. So to retrieve the birthday of "jay", put the key inside curly braces, like this:

```
print "Jay's birthday is: ", $birthday{'jay'}, "\n";
```

Because Perl assumes that barewords used as a key when retrieving a hash value are autoquoted, you may omit quotes between the curly braces (e.g., $birthday{jay}). Like arrays, hashes will grow as you need them to. Whenever you need to model a set or record the number of event occurrences, hashes are the variable to use.

Like arrays, you will often need to iterate over the set of key-value pairs in a hash. Two common techniques for doing this are shown in Example 41-7. Table 41-6 lists common Perl hash functions.

Example 41-7. Interating over a hash

```
my %example = (foo => 1, bar => 2, baz => 3);

while (my ($key, $value) = %example) {
   print "$key has a value of $value\n";
}

foreach my $key (keys %example) {
   print "$key has a value of $example{$key}\n";
}
```

Table 41-6. Common Perl hash functions

Name	Example	Description
delete	delete $hash{{*key*"}	Delete the key-value pair from hash that is indexed on *key*
each	($key, $value) = each %hash	Return the next key-value pair in hash; the pairs aren't usefully ordered
exists	print "key found" if exists $hash{"*key*"}	Return true if hash has *key*, even if that key's value if undefined
keys	@keys = keys %hash	Return the list of keys in the hash; not ordered
values	@values = values %hash	Return the list of values in the hash; values will be in the same order as keys fetched by keys %hash

References

As odd as it may first seem, it is sometimes necessary to have variables for variables. A funny kind of scalar, a reference is a sort of IOU that promises where the original variable's data can be found. References are primarily used in cases. First, because hashes and arrays store only scalar values, the only way to store one multivalued data type in another is to store a reference instead (see the *perldsc* manpage for more details). Second, when the size of a data structure makes a variable inefficient to pass into subroutines, a reference is passed instead. Third, because arguments passed into subroutines are really just copies of the original, there's no way to change the original values of the arguments back in the calling context. If you give a subroutine a reference as an argument, it can change that value in the caller. Consult the *perlref* and *perlreftut* manpages for more details on references.

Taking a reference to a variable is straightforward. Simply use the reference operator, \, to create a reference. For example:

```
$scalar_ref = \$bob;
$array_ref  = \@things;
$hash_ref   = \%grades;
```

You can even create references without variables:

```
$anonymous_array = [ 'Mojo Jo-Jo', 'Fuzzy Lumpkins', 'Him' ];
$anonymous_hash  = { 'pink'  => 'Blossom',
                     'green' => 'Buttercup',
                     'blue'  => 'Bubbles',
                   };
```

The square brackets return a reference to the list that they surround. The curly braces create a reference to a hash. Arrays and hashes created in this way are called *anonymous* because there is no named variable to which these references refer.

There are two ways of deferencing references (that is, getting back the original values). The first way is to use {}. For instance:

```
print "Your name is: ", ${$scalar_ref};

foreach my $el ( @{$anonymous_array} ) {
  print "Villian: $el\n";
}

while (my ($key, $value) = each %{$anonymous_hash}) {
  print "$key is associated with $value\n";
}
```

The second way, using ->, is useful only for references to collection types.

```
print "$anonymous_hash->{'pink'} likes the color pink\n"; # 'Blossom'
print "The scariest villian of all is $anonymous_array->[2]\n"; # 'Him'
```

—JJ

41.6 Perl Boot Camp, Part 3: Branching and Looping

To do any interesting stuff with data, Perl needs to be able to branch and loop. Perl supports the C-like if-then-else construct, as the following shows:

```
if ( $password eq 'secret' ) {
  print "Come on in\n";
} else {
  print "Incorrect password\n";
}
```

You can also invert simple tests that only have one statement in the then block.

```
print "Don't I know you?\n" if $user eq 'joe';
```

You can invert the logic of if by using unless:

```
print "Please supply command line arguments\n" unless @ARGV;
```

The print happens only if @ARGV is empty.

Sometimes you need to iterate through each element of a list. This can be done with the foreach loop:

```perl
foreach my $thing (@my_room) {
    print "dusting $thing\n";
    dust($thing);
}
```

A synonym for foreach is for. Bourne shell hackers (or those who don't like typing) may feel more comfortable using for rather than then foreach.

Each time through the loop, $thing is aliased to the next element in @my_room. Any change to $thing will change that element in the array, so be careful. If you don't supply a scalar variable like $thing, Perl will set $_ for you each time through the loop. The previous example could also be written:

```perl
foreach (@my_room) {
    print "dusting $_\n";
    dust($_);
}
```

Sometimes you need to continue looping while an event is happening, like reading input from standard input:

```perl
while ( my $line = <STDIN> ) {
    print "I got: $line";
}
```

Each line of input a user provides is stored in $line, including the newline at the end. When the user hits the end-of-file control key (CTRL-D), the loop exits. Like the foreach loop, you can leave off the scalar variable while reading from a filehandle,* and $_ will be set to the next line of input each time through the loop.

```perl
while (<>) {
    print "I got: $_";
}
```

Sometimes you need to interrupt the execute flow of your loop. Perl gives you three operators to do that (see Table 41-7).

Table 41-7. Loop flow-control operators

Operator	Example	Description
next	```while(<>){ next if $_ ne "continue\n"; }```	Jump to the top of the loop and iterate normally
last	```while(<>){ last if $_ eq "quit\n" }```	Jump out of the loop to the next line of the program

* STDIN is normally assumed here.

Table 41-7. Loop flow-control operators (continued)

Operator	Example	Description
redo	```for $url (@urls){ unless($content = get($url)){ print "couldn't fetch page - retrying\n"; redo; } }```	Jump to the top of the loop, but don't evaluate the loop condition

—*JJ*

41.7 Perl Boot Camp, Part 4: Pattern Matching

Perl is excellent at finding patterns in text. It does this with regular expressions, similar to the ones used by *grep* and *awk*. Any scalar can be matched against a regular expression with the matching binding operator, =~. For example:

```
if( $user =~ /jjohn/ ){
  print "I know you";
}
```

Without the matching binding operator, regular expressions match against the current value of $_. For example:

```
while (<>) {
  if (/quit/i) {
    print "Looks like you want out.\n";
    last;
  }
}
```

In this code, each line of input is examined for the character sequence quit. The /i modifier at the end of the regular expression makes the matching case-insensitive (i.e., Quit matches as well as qUIT).

As with regular expressions in other utilities, Perl attempts to find the leftmost and longest match for your pattern against a given string. Patterns are made up of characters (which normally match themselves) and special metacharacters, including those found in Table 41-8.

Table 41-8. Common Perl regular expression metacharacters

Operator	Description
^	Pattern must match at the beginning of the line.
$	Pattern must match at the end of the line.
.	Match any character (expect the newline).
pat1|*pat2*	Alternation: match the pattern on either the left or right.

Table 41-8. Common Perl regular expression metacharacters (continued)

Operator	Description
(*pattern*)	Group this pattern together as one (good for quantifiers and capturing).
[*synbols*]	Define a new character class: any of the symbols given can match one character of input (e.g. /[aeiou]/ matches a string with at least one regular vowel).
\w	Match a letter, number and underscore.
\d	Match a number.
\s	Match a whitespace character: space, tab, \n, \r.
*pattern**	Match 0 or more consecutive occurences of *pattern*.
pattern+	Match 1 or more consecutive occurrences of *pattern*.
pattern?	Optionally match *pattern*.

A very common task for which regular expressions are used is extracting specific information from a line of text. Suppose you wanted to get the first dotted quad that appears in this *ifconfig* command:

```
$ ifconfig eth0
eth0      Link encap:Ethernet  HWaddr 00:A0:76:C0:1A:E1
          inet addr:192.168.1.50  Bcast:192.168.1.255  Mask:255.255.255.0
          UP BROADCAST RUNNING MULTICAST  MTU:1500  Metric:1
          RX packets:365079 errors:0 dropped:0 overruns:0 frame:0
          TX packets:426050 errors:0 dropped:0 overruns:0 carrier:0
          collisions:3844 txqueuelen:100
          Interrupt:9 Base address:0x300
```

The output of a command can be captured into an array using the backtick operator. Each line of the command's output will be an element of the array. One way to extract the IP address from that line is with the following code:

```
my @ifconfig = `/sbin/ifconfig eth0`;
for (@ifconfig) {
  if ( /(\d+\.\d+\.\d+\.\d+)/ ) {
    print "Quad: $1\n";
    last;
  }
}
```

This regular expression looks for one or more digits (\d+) followed by a literal dot (rather than the regular expression metacharacter), followed by two more digit/dot pairs, followed by one or more digits. If this pattern is found in the current line, the part that was matched is captured (thanks to the parentheses) into the special variable $1. You can capture more patterns in a regular expression with more parentheses. Each captured text appears in a sequential higher scalar (i.e., the next paren-captured match will be $2).

Sometimes, you need to find all the matches for your pattern in a given string. This can be done with the /g regular expression modifier. If you wanted to find all the dotted quads in the *ifconfig* output, you could use the following code:

```
my @ifconfig = `/sbin/ifconfig eth0`;
for (@ifconfig) {
    while( /(\d+\.\d+\.\d+\.\d+)/g ){
        print "Quad: $1\n";
    }
}
```

Here, the *if* block is replaced with a *while* loop. This is important for /g to work as expected. If the current line has something that looks like a dotted quad, that value is capture in $1, just as before. However, the /g modifier remembers where in the string it made the last match and looks after that point for another one.

Perl's regular expression support has set the standard for other langauges. As such, it is impossible to give a comprehensive guide to Perl regular expressions here, but see O'Reilly's *Mastering Regular Expressions* or the *perlre* manpage.

—*JJ*

41.8 Perl Boot Camp, Part 5: Perl Knows Unix

There are many built-in Perl operators that mimic Unix system calls and standard utilities, as are partially listed in Table 41-9. Those that aren't hardcoded into the language are often available through modules (41.9). In fact, there are too many Unix-like operators to describe here, but this sampling should give you a good start.

Table 41-9. Perl filesystem functions

Function	Example	Description
chmod	chmod 0775, *filenames*	Change file permission on given file or list of files; same as the system command.
chown	chown *UID, GID, filenames*	Change owner and group on given list of filenames; same as the system command.
rename	rename *oldname, newname*	Change a file's name; similiar to *mv*.
unlink	unlink *filenames*	Unlink given filenames; deletes files that aren't hard linked elsewhere.
system	system(*executable*)	Create a subshell to execute an external command whose ouput isn't accessible to Perl.
qx()	@output = qc(*executable*)	Create a subshell to execute external command and return lines of output as an array to Perl; same as ` `.

One advantage Perl has over shell scripting is that Perl has filehandles. In Perl, files can only be created, edited, or read through special variables called filehandles. These variables have no funny punctuation prefixing them. It is customary to make filehandles all uppercase. The code below shows a typical way to read an existing file and echo its contents to the screen:

```perl
my $file = "your_filename";
open (IN, $file) || die "can't open $file: $!";
while (<IN>) {
    print;
}
close (IN);
```

In this simple code, the open function is used to associate the filehandle IN with whatever filename you choose. If the open fails, the expression to the right of the logical OR will execute. The die function halts the program with the string provided. Here, that string includes the special variable $!, which contains the error message from the last failed system call (which here is open). If the open succeeds, IN can be read from with the <> operator. As noted earlier, this operator populates $_ with the next line of input each time through the loop until there are no more lines to read. The print function will use $_ if no other argument is passed to it. Although Perl will free all filehandles when the script exits, it's a good habit to close all filehandles you open.

Writing to files is almost as easy as reading from them. Consider this code:

```perl
my $file = "your_filename";
open (OUT, "> ". $file) || die "can't make $file: $!";
print OUT "<html><body><h1>hello, world</h1></body></html>\n";
close(OUT);
```

This snippet starts in a familiar way, but the open call is a little different. To tell Perl you want to create a new file or overwrite an existing one, simply prefix the filename with a >. If you wanted to append to an existing file, use >> instead. Now you can print to that file by passing the filehandle to print (notice there's no comma after the filehandle). Here, a simple HTML file is being created.

You can also read directories in Perl. The following code looks in the current directory and describes each file as a directory, symbolic link, or regular file.

```perl
opendir (DIR, ".") || die "error: $!";

while (my $file = readdir(DIR)) {
    print "$file -> ";

    if ( -d $file ) {
        print "directory\n";

    } elsif ( -l $file ) {
        print "symlink\n";
```

```
        } else{
          print "file\n"
        }
    }
    closedir (DIR);
```

To read directories, use the opendir function, which has a similiar interface to open's. Unfortunately, the <> operator won't work on directory handles, so use the readdir command to iterate over each file in the directory. Perl provides file test operators, like those in the Bourne shell, to determine what kind of file its argument is. The -d operator tests whether a file is a directory, while the -l operator tests whether a file is symbolic link. Perl doesn't have a switch operator like C, but you can tack on as many elsif blocks as you need. What's not shown here is how to create a directory. Just as you would at the shell prompt, Perl provides a mkdir function that takes an octal number (which must start with zero!) and the name of the directory to create. Pretty simple.

In /etc/passwd and in password files for CVS and Apache, user passwords are stored as a string that has been passed through a one-way hashing algorithm (such as DES), usually using the system's crypt(3) system call. Perl provides access to this system call with a function of the same name. The following code prompts users for a new password for a fictional program and creates its own password file.

```
print "Username: \n";
my $user = <>;
print "Password: \n";
my $pass = <>;

chomp($user, $pass);
my $crypt = crypt($pass, substr($user, 0, 2));
open (OUT, ">>passwd") || die "error: $_";
print OUT "$user;$crypt;". localtime() . "\n";
close (OUT);
```

After collecting the username and password from the user, the chomp function removes the trailing newline from the input just collected. The crypt function expects the string to be hashed and a random two-character salt. Here, the first two characters of the username are used, via the substr function. The line written to the password file consists of a semicolon-separated list of the username, the hashed password, and a date stamp of when the account was added. Here, the localtime function call is used in scalar context because of the concatenation operator. This produces a human-readable string like Sat Mar 16 21:17:44 2002. Used in list context, localtime returns a nine element list that's not easily consumed by human eyes (see *Programming Perl*, published by O'Reilly, for more details on scalar versus list context).

This section hardly scratched the surface of using Perl as a system administration tool. Many books have been written on this very topic, including O'Reilly's *Perl for System Administration*.

—JJ

41.9 Perl Boot Camp, Part 6: Modules

Modules are Perl's way of extending functionality, in the same way C has library files. Modules can be used to encapsulate a set of related function calls (the way Data::Dumper does), implement pragmas (like use strict), or create object classes (like HTML::TokeParser). Whatever a module does, it must first be installed on your system (41.11) before you can use it.

Using a module in Perl is often straightforward. For example, the Data::Dumper module has a function called Dumper that takes a reference to a variable and deconstructs the entire structure into a printable string. This is an invaluable debugging tool. The following code shows Data::Dumper in action:

```
use Data::Dumper;
print "The current environment is: ", Dumper(\%ENV), "\n";
```

An abbreviated version of the output from this code is this:

```
The current enviroment is: $VAR1 = {
            'DISPLAY' => ':0',
            'COLORTERM' => 'gnome-terminal',
            'QTDIR' => '/usr/lib/qt-2.3.0',
            'PVM_RSH' => '/usr/bin/rsh',
            'OSTYPE' => 'linux-gnu',
            'PWD' => '/home/jjohn/docs/unix_powertools/upt',
            'EDITOR' => 'emacs -nw',
            'LOGNAME' => 'jjohn',
            'MACHTYPE' => 'i386-redhat-linux-gnu',
            'SHELL' => '/bin/bash',
            'MAIL' => '/var/spool/mail/jjohn',
            '_' => '/usr/local/bin/perl',
            'HISTSIZE' => '1000',
            'CVS_RSH' => 'ssh1',
            'HOSTNAME' => 'marian',
            'TERM' => 'xterm',
            ...
        };
```

In this code, the Data::Dumper is made available to your script with the *use* statement. You should be aware that *use* happens at the script's compile time, meaning that you can't use this statement to dynamically load modules at runtime (but this is possible; see *Programming Perl* for details). Data::Dumper automatically makes the function Dumper available to your script. Here the global hash %ENV, which contains all your shell's environment variables, is deconstructed. Dumper can take multiple variables, so when looking at a hash or array, be sure to prefix the variable with the reference operator (41.5) \. Without a passed reference, the output of Dumper won't exactly what you expect.

Many Perl modules are object oriented. Although writing object classes may not be trivial, using them is. Here, the CGI module is used to create a very simple HTML page.

```
use CGI;
$q = CGI->new;
print
    $q->header,
    $q->start_html,
    $q->h1("hello, world!"),
    $q->end_html;
```

There's no difference in how object classes are brought into your script with *use*. New objects are created through a method traditionally called new (*new* is not an operator, as it is in other languages). Sometimes, new will require arguments. Once the object ($q) is created, all method access must be made through it, using the -> operator. That's all there is too it. Of course every module is different, so you will need to use *perldoc modulename* (41.10) to the module's documentation.

Infrequently, you may need to find the module files on your system. Modules are usually files that have the extension *.pm* and are found in one of the directories listed in the @INC array. Every module should declare its own namespace, so that its variables and functions don't overwrite the ones you define in the scripts that use the modules. These namespaces are hierarchical, so so that the module Data::Dumper belongs to the Data module group.* When the Data::Dumper module is installed on your system, it is placed somewhere with the rest of your Perl modules in a directory called *Data*, in which a file called *Dumper.pm* will be copied. Generally, :: in a module name translates to a / on the filesystem. You can also use perldoc -l *modulename* to list the module's filesystem path.

There are many good reasons to learn Perl, but the ace up a Perl programmer's sleeve is the Comprehensive Perl Archive Network (41.11) (CPAN), which is the central repository for Perl modules. There are hundreds of modules on CPAN, ranging from the essential (IO::Socket) to the useful (LWP, DBI, mod_perl), to the frivolous (Acme::Buffy). The main CPAN server is accessible on the web at *http://www.cpan.org*. CPAN is mirrored all over the world, so look for a mirror near you.

—*JJ*

---

* Well, that's the theory anyway. In practice, modules that aren't written by the same group of people often have somewhat arbitrary top-level namespaces.

41.10 Perl Boot Camp, Part 7: perldoc

We all need a little help sometimes, and it's at those times that *perldoc* comes in handy. Normally, core Perl and module documentation is accessible through your system's *manpage* system, but you can also use the *perldoc* program, which has a few convenient features that you should be aware of. Like *man*, *perldoc* takes the name of a module or core Perl document as an argument.

Your system's *perl* comes bundled with hundreds of pages of very readable documentation. The top of the document tree can be accessed with either *perldoc perl* or *man perl*. This page is little more than a table of contents* for the rest of the *perl* documentation. There are over 40 documents listed there, but there are a couple that will be immediately useful to novice Perl programmers, as Table 41-10 shows.

Table 41-10. Frequently used Perl manpages

Name	Description
perlsyn	The complete guide to Perl syntax
perldata	Perl's data types explained
perlop	Perl's operators and their precedence
perlfunc	The complete guide to all of Perl's built-in functions
perlre	The complete guide to Perl's regular expressions

In many cases (such as the ones above), *perldoc* doesn't do anything *man* can't. However with *perldoc*, you can easily look up built-in Perl functions with the -f flag (-t formats any POD elements for a text console). For instance, to see the entry on print, try this:

```
$ perldoc -tf print
```

You'll get back something like the following (which has been abbreviated):

```
print FILEHANDLE LIST
print LIST
print   Prints a string or a list of strings.  Returns
        true if successful.  FILEHANDLE may be a scalar
        variable name, in which case the variable contains
        the name of or a reference to the filehandle, thus
        introducing one level of indirection.
        ...
```

Perl has quite a large FAQ. You can read each of the nine sections (*perlfaq1* through *perlfaq9*) to find the answer to your question or you can use the -q flag to keyword search all of the FAQ.

---

* There's actually a more complete table of contents available: man perltoc.

```
$ perldoc -q fork
Found in /usr/local/lib/perl5/5.6.1/pod/perlfaq8.pod
        How do I fork a daemon process?

        If by daemon process you mean one that's detached (disas-
        sociated from its tty), then the following process is
        reported to work on most Unixish systems.  Non-Unix users
        should check their Your_OS::Process module for other solu-
        tions.
        ...
```

Do take advantage of the copious documentation already on your system: you will be reward many times over.

—JJ

41.11 CPAN

The Comprehensive Perl Archive Network (CPAN), whose URL is *http://www.cpan.org*, is the place to get modules, scripts, and the Perl source code. This system is mirrored all over the world, so consult *http://www.cpan.org/SITES.html* or *http://mirror.cpan.org* for the server nearest you. There is a really complete CPAN FAQ that can be found at *http://www.cpan.org/misc/cpan-faq.html*.

This section covers obtaining and installing modules from CPAN. If your installation of Perl is up to date, module installation is trivial. If you've got a "unique" system, you may need to take matters into your own hands.

Installing Modules the Easy Way

In a fit of inspired genius (or madness), the CPAN module was created to automate the task of fetching and installing modules. If you want to install the Text::AutoFormat suite, it's as easy as becoming superuser on your system and typing:

```
# perl -MCPAN -e 'install Text::AutoFormat'
```

Perl has many command-line switches. Here, -M (equivalent to use *module*) and -e (execute the next argument as *perl* code) are used. If you've never run the CPAN module before, be prepared to answer a lot of questions about your network setup and where certain system binaries are. Luckily, you can usually accept the defaults safely. Once that's done, the CPAN module will go to the CPAN mirror you specified; find the latest version of the module you asked for; and download, unpack, configure, and install it for you with no additional typing. Now that's twenty-first-century library management! If your module depends on other modules not installed on your system, CPAN will attempt to fetch and install the missing modules. In fact, you can update the CPAN module itself with:

```
# perl -MCPAN -e 'install Bundle::CPAN'
```

The CPAN module also has an interactive shell you can access like this:

```
$ perl -MCPAN -e shell
```

Why bother with the interactive shell? Sometimes you want to install several unrelated modules at once. This is done more conveniently in the CPAN shell. Alternately, you may want only to download module archives without actualling installing them. The entire range of shell options can be found with the h command inside the shell. One of the most useful shell functions, the search function, can be used to look up available CPAN modules. For instance:

```
$ sudo perl -MCPAN -e shell

cpan shell -- CPAN exploration and modules installation (v1.59)
ReadLine support enabled

cpan> i /Text/
CPAN: Storable loaded ok
Going to read /usr/local/cpan/Metadata
Module          AddressBook::DB::Text (D/DL/DLEIGH/AddressBook-0.16.tar.gz)
Module          AnyData::Format::Text (J/JZ/JZUCKER/AnyData-0.05.tar.gz)
Module          Apache::PrettyText (C/CH/CHTHORMAN/Apache-PrettyText-1.03...
...

401 items found
cpan> quit
```

Here, we use the i command to search for the regular expression /Text/ in all the module names.

When you first run the CPAN module, you will be asked a series of configuration questions. The first question you'll be asked when configuring CPAN is to name a CPAN build and cache directory (where CPAN unpacks fetched module archives and builds them). Put this in a sensible place where you and other users can can get to it, such as /usr/local/cpan. You'll be asked to name the maximum size for the cache directory (the default is 10MB). The next question will ask when to perform size checks on the cache, atstart or never. Unless you have a compelling reason not to remove old module builds, accept the default of atstart. You then be asked whether CPAN metadata should be cached, and again, accept the default of yes.

The next question asks about what character set your terminal expects. Again, you should accept the default of yes. The configuration then asks what it should do when unfulfilled dependencies are encountered during a module installation. CPAN can automatically fetch the missing modules (follow), ask for confirmation before downloading them (ask), or do nothing (ignore). If you are on a fast Internet connection, you may want to set the policy to follow. The safest policy, and one that guards against runaway module fetching sessions, is ask.

The next several questions ask for the location of certain binaries (like *lynx*, *make*, *gzip*, etc.). Answer these appropriately. The next set of questions ask for additional *make* parameters. Again, accept the defaults. You will then be asked about your network setup. If you are behind a firewall that uses SOCKs or proxy servers for FTP and HTTP, you will need to enter those server names. CPAN will ask you to pick a CPAN mirror closest to you, by asking you for continent and country information. You'll be presented with a list of CPAN mirrors, and you can enter the numbers of the URLs in which you are interested. Generally, you'll only need to give one or two mirrors. The last question is about the WAIT system, to which you can safely accept the default. This concludes the CPAN configuration.

Installing Modules the Hard Way

Most modules on CPAN are gzipped *tar* archives that have some common files in them that makes installing them fairly simple. To install a CPAN module, unpack your archive and *cd* to the new directory that was just created. Now type:

```
$ perl Makefile.PL && make test
```

This is a similiar configure and compile idiom to the one shown in Chapter 41. If the tests all succeed, change to root and install the module with:

```
# make install
```

The module is now available to your system.

Browsing the CPAN Web Site

There's something to be said for browsing the CPAN archive with a web browser. In fact, there are all kinds of ancillary tidbits that are available only on the web site. However, CPAN's main purpose is to store and serve modules.

Modules on CPAN are arranged by author name, module name, category, and recentness. Of these, module name and category are perhaps the most useful for CPAN newbies. The full Perl documentation is linked to from CPAN, but you should have this on your system already. Of course, no serious web site these days is missing a search engine, and CPAN is no exception. In fact, the search engine has its own URL: *http://search.cpan.org*. This is an excellent resource for quickly finding modules that may solve your problem.

CPAN is an ocean of code that awaits your exploration.

—*JJ*

41.12 Make Custom grep Commands (etc.) with Perl

All of the various *grep*-like utilities perform pretty much the same function, with minor differences—they search for a specified pattern in some or all of a file and display that pattern with varying amounts of surrounding context.

As you use Unix more and more, you will find yourself wanting to do an increasing number of *grep*-like tasks, but no particular Unix utility will quite suit them all (hence the need for the various *grep* utilities discussed earlier). You'll start accumulating C programs, *awk* scripts, and shell scripts to do these different tasks, and you'll be craving one utility that can easily encompass them all so you don't have to waste the disk space for all of those binaries. That utility is Perl (41.1), the "Practical Extraction and Report Language" developed by Larry Wall. According to the documentation accompanying Perl, it is "an interpreted language optimized for scanning arbitrary text files, extracting information from those text files, and printing reports based on that information."

For example, to search for a pattern in the header of a Usenet message:

```
perl -ne 'exit if (/^$/); print if (/pattern/);' filename
```

[This works because mail and Usenet (1.21) messages always use a blank line—indicated by ^$ in regular expression syntax—to separate the header from the body of the message. —TOR]

[The -n flag tells *perl* to wrap the contents of -e into the body of a while(<>){ ... } loop. —JJ]

To do a search for a pattern and print the paragraphs in which it appears:

```
perl -ne '$/ = "\n\n"; print if (/pattern/);' filename
```

[This assumes that paragraphs are delimited by a double linefeed—that is, a blank line. You'd have to adjust this script for a *troff* or TEX document where paragraphs are separated by special codes. —TOR]

Searching through files is one of Perl's strengths, but certainly not its only strength. Perl encompasses all the functionality of *sed*, *awk*, *grep*, *find*, and other Unix utilities. Furthermore, a Perl program to do something originally done with one or more of these utilities is usually faster and easier to read than the non-Perl solution.

—JIK

41.13 Perl and the Internet

Because Perl supports Berkeley sockets, all kinds of networking tasks can be automated with Perl. Below are some common idioms to show you what is possible with Perl and a little elbow grease.

Be Your Own Web Browser with LWP

The suite of classes that handle all the aspects of HTTP are collectively known as LWP (for libwww-perl library). If your Perl installation doesn't currently have LWP, you can easily install it with the CPAN module (41.11) like this:

```
# perl -MCPAN -e 'install Bundle::LWP'
```

If you also included an X widget library such as Tk, you could create a graphic web browser in Perl (an example of this comes with the Perl Tk library). However, you don't need all of that if you simply want to grab a file from a web server:

```
use LWP::Simple;
my $url = "http://slashdot.org/slashdot.rdf";
getstore($url, "s.rdf");
```

This example grabs the Rich Site Summary file from the popular tech news portal, Slashdot, and saves it to a local file called *s.rdf*. In fact, you don't even need to bother with a full-fledged script:

```
$ perl -MLWP::Simple -e 'getstore("http://slashdot.org/slashdot.rdf", "s.rdf")'
```

Sometimes you want to process a web page to extract information from it. Here, the title of the page given by the URL given on the command line is extracted and reported:

```
use LWP::Simple;
use HTML::TokeParser;

$url = $ARGV[0] || 'http://www.oreilly.com';
$content = get($url);
die "Can't fetch page: halting\n" unless $content;

$parser = HTML::TokeParser->new(\$content);
$parser->get_tag("title");
$title = $parser->get_token;
print $title->[1], "\n" if $title;
```

After bringing in the library to fetch the web page (LWP::Simple) and the one that can parse HTML (HTML::TokeParser), the command line is inspected for a user-supplied URL. If one isn't there, a default URL is used. The get function, imported implicitly from LWP::Simple, attempts to fetch the URL. If it succeeds, the whole page is kept in memory in the scalar $content. If the fetch fails,

$content will be empty, and the script halts. If there's something to parse, a reference to the content is passed into the HTML::TokeParser object constructor. HTML::TokeParser deconstructs a page into individual HTML elements. Although this isn't the way most people think of HTML, it does make it easier for both computers and programmers to process web pages. Since nearly every web page has only one <title> tag, the parser is instructed to ignore all tokens until it finds the opening <title> tag. The actual title string is a text string and fetching that piece requires getting the next token. The method get_token returns an array reference of various sizes depending on the kind of token returned (see the HTML::TokeParse manpage for details). In this case, the desired element is the second one.

One important word of caution: these scripts are very simple web crawlers, and if you plan to be grabbing a lot of pages from a web server you don't own, you should do more research into how to build polite web robots. See O'Reilly's *Perl & LWP*.

Sending Mail with Mail::Sendmail

Often, you may find it necessary to send an email reminder from a Perl script. You could do this with sockets only, handling the whole SMTP protocol in your code, but why bother? Someone has already done this for you. In fact, there are several SMTP modules on CPAN, but the easiest one to use for simple text messages is Mail::Sendmail. Here's an example:

```perl
use Mail::Sendmail;

my %mail = (
            Subject => "About your disk quota"
            To      => "jane@hostname.com, fred@hostname.com"
            From    => "admin@hostname.com",
            Message => "You've exceeded your disk quotas",
            smtp    => "smtp-mailhost.hostname.com",
        );

sendmail(%mail) or die "error: $Mail::Sendmail::error";
print "done\a\n";
```

Since most readers will be familiar with the way email works, this module should be fairly easy to adapt to your own use. The one field that may not be immediately clear is smtp. This field should be set to the hostname or IP address of a machine that will accept SMTP relay requests from the machine on which your script is running. With the proliferation of email viruses of mass destruction, mail administrators don't usually allow their machines to be used by unknown parties. Talk to your local system administrator to find a suitable SMTP host for your needs.

CGI Teaser

What Perl chapter would be complete without some mention of CGI? The Common Gateway Interface is a standard by which web servers, like Apache, allow external programs to interact with web clients. The details of CGI can be found in O'Reilly's *CGI Programming with Perl*, but the code below uses the venerable CGI module to create a simple form and display the results after the user has hit the submit button. You will need look through your local web server's configuration files to see where such a script needs to be in order for it to work. Unfortunately, that information is very system-dependent.

```perl
use CGI;

$cgi  = CGI->new;
$name = $cgi->param("usrname");

print
  $cgi->header, $cgi->start_html,
  $cgi->h1("My First CGI Program");

if( $name ){
  print $cgi->p("Hello, $name");
}

print
  $cgi->start_form,
  $cgi->p("What's your name: "), $cgi->textfield(-name => "usrname"),
  $cgi->submit, $cgi->end_form,
  $cgi->end_html;
```

CGI scripts are unlike other scripts with which you are probably more familiar, because these programs have a notion of programming state. In other words, when the user first accesses this page, $name will be empty and a blank form with a text box will be displayed. When the user enters something into that textbox and submits the form, the user's input will be stored under the key usrname. After the user presses the form's submit button, the values of that form are available through the CGI method param. Here, the desired value is stored under the key usrname. If this value is populated, a simple message is displayed before showing the form again.

Now you have nearly all the tools necessary to create your own Internet search engine. I leave the details of creating a massive data storage and retrieval system needed to catalog millions of web pages as an exercise for the reader.

—*JJ*

42

Python

42.1 What Is Python?

Python is an interpreted scripting language, much like Perl or Tcl. Python's primary focus is on clear, concise code, and it has a feature set and wide variety of available modules designed to support this goal. In many ways, Python is an extremely scalable language; complex systems can be relatively easily built in Python without losing maintainability. From the Python home page (*http://www.python.org*):

> Python is an *interpreted, interactive, object-oriented* programming language. It is often compared to Tcl, Perl, Scheme or Java.
>
> Python combines remarkable power with very clear syntax. It has modules, classes, exceptions, very high level dynamic data types, and dynamic typing. There are interfaces to many system calls and libraries, as well as to various windowing systems (X11, Motif, Tk, Mac, MFC). New built-in modules are easily written in C or C++. Python is also usable as an extension language for applications that need a programmable interface.
>
> The Python implementation is portable: it runs on many brands of UNIX, on Windows, DOS, OS/2, Mac, Amiga... If your favorite system isn't listed here, it may still be supported, if there's a C compiler for it. Ask around on comp.lang.python—or just try compiling Python yourself.
>
> Python is copyrighted but freely usable and distributable, even for commercial use.

—*DJPH*

42.2 Installation and Distutils

python

Installing Python is generally very simple. Either install the appropriate binary package for your platform, or download the latest source from *http://www.python.org*. (Note that some Linux distributions include Python by default.) A source install is as simple as untarring the distribution, then running:

```
% ./configure
% make
% make install
```

You can run the Python interpreter interactively and find out what version you have and details about its compilation. As an example, on my laptop (which runs Windows but also has a Cygwin Unix-like environment installed), Python reports:

```
% python
Python 2.2 (#1, Dec 31 2001, 15:21:18)
[GCC 2.95.3-5 (cygwin special)] on cygwin
Type "help", "copyright", "credits" or "license" for more information.
>>>
```

To see which modules are compiled into your version of Python, examine sys.builtin_module_names:

```
>>> import sys
>>> print sys.builtin_module_names
('__builtin__', '__main__', '_socket', '_sre', '_symtable', 'exceptions',
 'gc', 'imp', 'marshal', 'new', 'posix', 'signal', 'sys', 'xxsubtype')
```

These are just the modules that are an integral part of your version of the interpreter. For a complete list of modules installed in your Python, look in all of the directories listed in sys.path:

```
>>> print sys.path
['', '/usr/lib/python2.2', '/usr/lib/python2.2/plat-cygwin',
 '/usr/lib/python2.2/lib-tk', '/usr/lib/python2.2/lib-dynload',
 '/usr/lib/python2.2/site-packages']
```

Generally, checking the documentation for the version of Python you have will tell you which modules are normally installed; the *site-packages* directory is where further packages installed on your machine will likely have been installed.

There is a large repository of modules (and other Python code resources) for Python available at the Vaults of Parnassus (*http://www.vex.net/parnassus/*), which includes a search mechanism for finding what you're looking for. Most modules will use Distutils to package their distributions.

If you download a module source distribution, you can tell pretty quickly if it was packaged and distributed with Distutils. First, the distribution's name and version number will be featured prominently in the name of the downloaded archive, for example, *foo-1.0.tar.gz* or *widget-0.9.7.zip*. Next, the archive will unpack into a similarly-named directory: *foo-1.0* or *widget-0.9.7*. Additionally, the distribution will contain a setup script, *setup.py*, and a *README*, which should explain that building and installing the module distribution is a simple matter of running:

```
% python setup.py install
```

Modules that are not packaged using the standard Distutils will generally include detailed instructions for installing them.

—DJPH

42.3 Python Basics

If you've written code in a procedural or functional language before, many parts of Python will seem familiar. Here's a quick overview of the flavor of the language. There is a lot of both reference and tutorial information available on the web (start at *http://www.python.org*) as well as in books like O'Reilly's *Programming Python*. In fact, much of the information in this chapter was gleaned or paraphrased from the official Python reference documentation.

Indentation

The number one complaint of Python detractors is almost always its use of indentation as a significant part of its syntax. Most languages use begin/end tags or curly braces ({}) to mark blocks of code and have line termination punctuation (many use the semicolon (;) as a line termination marker). In Python, indentation is used to define blocks of code, and lines are terminated with a return. The actual amount of indentation within a block is arbitrary, but it must be consistent:

```
if a:
    statement1
    statement2    # Consistent indentation
else:
    statement3
      statement4  # Inconsistent indentation (error)
```

Python assumes eight-space tab characters. If you have your editor set to four-space tabs, for example, this can bite you if there are mixed spaces and tabs. Either use eight-space tabs, or stick to spaces.

Long statements can span multiple lines by using the backslash (\) to continue the line:

```
>>> a = math.cos( 3 * ( x - n ) ) + \
...     math.sin( 3 * ( y - n ) )
```

Lines that are already grouped within triple-quotes, parentheses (...), brackets [...], or braces {...} can span multiple lines without needing to use the backslash.

Python's indentation requirements take a little getting used to, but they guarantee a certain level of readability, and editors like vim and emacs can keep track of the details for you trivially. (vim has a syntax configuration for editing Python, and emacs and xemacs both have a python-mode specifically for dealing with Python.)

Functions

Both procedural and functional languages organize programs by dividing them into smaller units called *functions*. Python's approach to functions is inspired by functional languages like Lisp and Scheme, where anonymous functions (*lambdas*) and operations like eval, apply, map, and reduce are fundamentals of the language.

Functions are defined with the def statement. To define an add function that adds together two arguments and returns the result:

```
>>> def add(a, b):
...     return a + b
```

This defines a function and attaches it to the name add in the current namespace; anything with access to this namespace can call this function by simply passing arguments to it:

```
>>> print add(3, 5)
8
```

Function arguments can be defined with default values, and variable-length argument lists and keyword arguments are also supported.

Procedural programming languages like Perl and C generally leave functions at that. Functional languages like Lisp, Scheme, and Python take functions to the next level; functions are first-class objects and can be directly manipulated and stored.

Anonymous functions, which are not automatically attached to the current namespace, are created with the lambda statement:

```
>>> add = lambda a, b: a + b
```

Lambdas are very useful for traditional functional programming tricks such as using map(). map() takes its first argument (which should be a function or lambda) and runs it over and over, passing each element of the list to the function in turn, generating a new list of the results:

```
>>> def timesThree(a):
...     return 3 * a
>>> def sum(x, y):
...     return x + y

>>> ints = [1, 2, 3, 4, 5]
>>> multiples = map(timesThree, ints)
>>> print multiples
[3, 6, 9, 12, 15]
>>> print reduce(sum, multiples)
45
```

If you use functions like map() and its cousins apply(), reduce(), and filter() a lot, your code can get pretty messy before long. Using a lambda allows you to use these functions without having to define a named function with def; instead you can just put the lambda right into the function call as an argument:

```
>>> ints = [1, 2, 3, 4, 5]
>>> multiples = map(lambda a: 3 * a, ints)
>>> print multiples
[3, 6, 9, 12, 15]
>>> print reduce(lambda x, y: x + y, multiples)
45
```

Lambdas are limited to a single expression, though that expression may be complex. Multiple statements and nonexpression statements like print and while can't be used in a lambda.

Everything's an Object

Everything in Python is an *object*. Each object has an *identity*, a *type*, and a *value*. For example, a = 42 creates an object of type integer with the value 42. You can think of the identity of an object as its address in memory; in this case, we've given the name a to that identity. Python's built-in types include fundamental building blocks such as numbers, strings, lists, dictionaries, and files, as well as structuring types like functions, modules, lambdas, and metaclasses. (Yes, a function is an object; it's just an object that implements the "function call" operator.)

Python allows the creation of new types of objects via the class statement. User-defined classes can have *class variables* and *methods*, which are shared across all *instances* of that class. In Python, methods are just functions that happen to be associated with a class (and generally take an instance of that class as the first argument). Instances can also have their own *instance variables*, specific to each instance.

Instances are created by calling the class object as if it were a function, which creates a new object and calls the __init__() method of the class (if one is defined):

```
class Account:
    "A simple example class"
    kind = "Checking"
    def __init__(self, accountHolder, startingBalance):
        self.accountHolder = accountHolder;
        self.balance = startingBalance;

>>> account = Account("Deb", 86753.09)
```

This creates a new Account object and sets the accountHolder instance variable to Deb and the balance instance variable to $86,753.09. Now, in order to be able to do anything with our Account, we need to define methods to allow manipulation of the balance:

```
class Account:
    ...
    def deposit(self, depositAmount):
        "Deposit money"
        self.balance = self.balance + depositAmount
    def withdraw(self, withdrawalAmount):
        "Withdraw money"
        self.balance = self.balance - withdrawalAmount
    def inquireBalance(self):
        "Balance inquiry"
        return self.balance

>>> account.deposit(1504.36)
>>> account.withdraw(40.00)
>>> print "Account balance is now $%.2f" % account.inquireBalance()
Account balance is now $88217.45
```

Modules and Packages

Modules and *packages* allow you to organize your code more effectively. Generally, software for Python is also distributed as a module or a package. A module groups a set of functions and classes; a package is a collection of modules and subpackages.

Any Python source file is a module, if you load it using the import statement. Importing a module creates an isolated namespace for the symbols within that file and attaches that namespace to the name of the module. It also executes the code within that module, defining variables, functions, and classes. For example, we might put our Account class in a file *account.py*, and then, in another file:

```
import account

checking = account.Account("Deb", 86753.09)
```

Note that we can't refer to Account directly; we have to refer to it through its imported name, account.Account. If, for convenience, we'd like to access the Account class directly, we can tell Python to import the class into our current namespace as well:

```
from account import Account

checking = Account("Deb", 86753.09)
```

Modules are compiled into bytecodes the first time they are imported, allowing them to run faster and be more compact.

Given that a Python module is just a file, it will probably come as no surprise that a Python package is simply a directory with modules in it. To tag a directory as a package rather than just any directory, create a file called *__init__.py* (the same name as the method to initialize an object) within that directory. Code within *__init__.py* will get run whenever any part of its package is imported. Subpackages are, of course, just subdirectories with their own *__init__.py* files.

I/O and Formatting

Dealing with input and output in Python is fairly straightforward; files are objects, and there is a set of methods for dealing with file objects that will be familiar to anyone who's ever done any Unix I/O. Files are opened with open( ), closed with close( ), and read with methods such as read( ) and readline( ).

Unix standard input, standard output and standard error are represented by file objects in the sys module: sys.stdin, sys.stdout, and sys.stderr, respectively.

The print statement prints its arguments to standard output. print can print any object by printing its string representation. Nicely formatted strings are generated using the string formatting (%) operator. % works a lot like C's sprintf( ) routine; you provide a string with special keywords in it and the objects to format and you get back a formatted string:

```
>>> print "Account balance is now $%.2f" % account.inquireBalance()
Account balance is now $86753.09
>>> print "Error:  %s(%s)." % (error, error.number)
Error:  File not found(2)
```

% takes a string and a list of arguments. (If there's only one argument, it can be any object instead of a list.) Any place that you might want to use a string, you can use the string formatting operator. For example:

```
>>> obj.name = "MyObject: %s" % name
>>> url = urlopen("%s://%s:%d/%s" % (protocol, host, port, path))
```

wxPython

Python has a couple of ways to build graphical user interfaces. The first was to use Tk, the GUI toolkit from Tcl. More recently, a Python interface to the wxWindows toolkit has been developed and has become very popular.

Extensive information about wxPython is available at *http://wxpython.org* including documentation and the wxPython distribution itself.

—DJPH

42.4 Python and the Web

Python has a number of core modules designed to deal with interacting with the web. Python can act as a web client, pulling down web resources and POSTing form results. Python has support for SSL connections in a reasonably transparent fashion. CGI scripts are easy to write in Python, and there is also an Apache module for running Python scripts within the webserver itself.

- *urllib* (42.5) provides basic functions for opening and retrieving web resources via their URLs.
- *urllib2* (42.6) provides an extended, extensible interface for accessing web resources.
- *htmllib* and *HTMLParser* (42.7) provide the ability to parse HTML.
- *cgi* (42.8) provides functions for writing CGI scripts.
- *mod_python* (42.9) is an Apache module for running Python within the Apache webserver, rather than seperately as with CGI scripts.

—*DJPH*

42.5 urllib

The application-level access to most web client activities is through modules called urllib and urllib2 (42.6). urllib is the simple web interface; it provides basic functions for opening and retrieving web resources via their URLs.

The primary functions in urllib are urlopen( ), which opens an URL and returns a file-like object, and urlretrieve( ), which retrieves the entire web resource at the given URL. The file-like object returned by urlopen supports the following methods: read( ), readline( ), readlines( ), fileno( ), close( ), info( ), and geturl( ). The first five methods work just like their file counterparts. info( ) returns a mimetools.Message object, which for HTTP requests contains the HTTP headers associated with the URL. geturl( ) returns the real URL of the resource, since the client may have been redirected by the web server before getting the actual content.

urlretrieve( ) returns a tuple (filename, info), where filename is the local file to which the web resource was copied and info is the same as the return value from urlopen's info( ) method.

If the result from either urlopen( ) or urlretrieve( ) is HTML, you can use htmllib to parse it.

urllib also provides a function `urlencode()`, which converts standard tuples or dictionaries into properly URL-encoded queries. Here is an example session that uses the GET method to retrieve a URL containing parameters:

```
>>> import urllib
>>> params = urllib.urlencode({'spam': 1, 'eggs': 2, 'bacon': 0})
>>> f = urllib.urlopen("http://www.musi-cal.com/cgi-bin/query?%s" % params)
>>> print f.read()
```

The following example performs the same query but uses the POST method instead:

```
>>> import urllib
>>> params = urllib.urlencode({'spam': 1, 'eggs': 2, 'bacon': 0})
>>> f = urllib.urlopen("http://www.musi-cal.com/cgi-bin/query", params)
>>> print f.read()
```

—DJPH

42.6 urllib2

urllib2 provides an extended, extensible interface to web resources. urllib2's application-level interface is essentially identical to urllib's `urlopen()` function (42.5). Underneath, however, urllib2 explicitly supports proxies, caching, basic and digest authentication, and so forth.

urllib2 uses an Opener, made up of a series of Handlers, to open a URL; if you know you want to use a particular set of features, you tell urllib2 which Handlers to use before you call `urlopen()`. urllib2 is extensible largely because if you need to deal with some odd set of interactions, you can write a Handler object to deal with just those interactions and incorporate it into an Opener with existing Handlers. This allows you to deal with complex behavior by just combining very simple sets of code.

For example, to retrieve a web resource that requires basic authentication over a secure socket connection:

```
>>> import urllib2
>>> authHandler = urllib2.HTTPBasicAuthHandler()
>>> authHandler.add_password("private, "https://www.domain.com/private",
...                          "user", "password")
>>> opener = urllib2.build_opener(authHandler)
>>> urllib2.install_opener(opener)
>>> resource = urllib2.urlopen("https://www.domain.com/private/foo.html")
>>> print resource.read()
```

To implement a new Handler, you simply subclass from `urllib2.BaseHandler` and implement the methods appropriate to the behavior you want to handle.

—DJPH

42.7 htmllib and HTMLParser

Python provides the htmllib module for parsing HTML content, which is often useful when dealing with web resources. Python also has an HTMLParser module, which handles both XHTML and HTML and provides a slightly lower-level view of the content. HTMLParser is also slightly simpler to use, since htmllib uses sgmllib and thus understands many of the complexities of SGML.

HTMLParser provides a class that the user subclasses from, defining methods that are called as tags are found in the input. The example below is a very basic HTML parser that uses the HTMLParser.HTMLParser class to print out tags as they are encountered:

```
from HTMLParser import HTMLParser

class MyHTMLParser(HTMLParser):
    def handle_starttag(self, tag, attrs):
        print "Encountered the beginning of a %s tag" % tag
    def handle_endtag(self, tag):
        print "Encountered the end of a %s tag" % tag
```

—*DJPH*

42.8 cgi

Python provides the cgi module for writing CGI scripts. Much of the grunt work of writing a CGI script is in dealing with parsing the parameters handed to the script by the web server. The cgi module deals with all of those details and more.

 To use the cgi module, use import cgi rather than from cgi import*. The cgi module defines a lot of symbols (many for backwards compatibility) that you don't want polluting your namespace.

When you write a new script, consider adding the line:

```
import cgitb; cgitb.enable()
```

This activates a special exception handler that will display detailed reports in the web browser if any errors occur. If you'd rather not show the guts of your program to users of your script, you can have the reports saved to files instead, with a line like this:

```
import cgitb; cgitb.enable(display=0, logdir="/tmp")
```

It's very helpful to use this feature during script development. The reports produced by cgitb provide information that can save you a lot of time tracking down bugs. You can always remove the cgitb line later when you have tested your script and are confident that it works correctly.

To get to information submitted to the CGI script, instantiate a `FieldStorage` object:

```
form = cgi.FieldStorage()
```

The FieldStorage object acts much like a dictionary of CGI information; it implements the methods has_key() and keys() and can be accessed using the [ ] operator. For instance, the following code (which assumes that the Content-Type: header and blank line have already been printed) checks that the fields name and addr are both set to a non-empty string:

```
form = cgi.FieldStorage()
if not (form.has_key("name") and form.has_key("addr")):
    print "<H1>Error</H1>"
    print "Please fill in the Name and Address fields."
    return
print "<p>Name: %s</p>" % form["name"].value
print "<p>Address: %s</p>" % form["addr"].value
...further form processing here...
```

The cgi module also supports ways to deal with multiple-selection form elements and uploaded files.

—DJPH

42.9 mod_python

mod_python is an Apache module for running Python within the Apache webserver. It's much faster than CGI scripts and generally uses less resources overall. mod_python also allows advanced functionality such as maintaining persistent database connections across web requests and access to internal Apache APIs. Information on mod_python and distributions are available at *http://www.modpython.org*.

Apache's basic methodology for handling web requests is to deal with them in phases. There is a phase for each significant element of handling the request, including authentication, content generation, and logging. Apache modules can provide a seperate handler for each phase; mod_python simply allows you to write those handlers in Python. This allows complete control over everything Apache does to process a request.

A mod_python handler is a function that takes the Request object as an argument; a Request represents a single web request and contains all the information Apache knows about that request (requested URL, method, headers, and so forth).

Each phase's handler has a specific name that Apache recognizes (and uses in its configuration file): PythonHandler, PythonAuthenHandler, PythonLogHandler and so forth. Most mod_python scripts need to implement only the main handler, PythonHandler.

mod_python finds the appropriate function to call by dropping the leading Python from the handler name, and using an all-lowercase function name. Thus, most mod_python scripts will look something like this:

```
from mod_python import apache

def handler(request):
    request.content_type = "text/plain"
    request.send_http_header()
    request.write("Hello World!")
    return apache.OK
```

This handler simply imports the apache API and then responds to every request with a plain text Hello World!. It returns apache.OK to tell Apache that the request was successful.

For more information on dealing with mod_python, read the documentation.

 One gotcha: mod_python's way of installing a mod_python handler is a little counterintuitive due to the way Apache handlers work. Make sure you understand how mod_python finds which module to import.

—DJPH

42.10 What About Perl?

Comparing languages can generate a lot of heat and very little light. However, "Why not just use Perl?" is such a common question that I'll try to provide at least a basic understanding of the relative strengths and weaknesses of Python versus Perl. Remember that you can write good code or bad code in pretty much any language, but understanding whether your tool is best at driving nails or screws is always useful.

Perl's driving motto is "There's more than one way to do it." Because of this priority and the huge archive of Perl modules on CPAN, Perl is an incredibly useful tool for building quick one-off scripts or hacking together tools in a very short time. However, it also means that it's very easy to write Perl code that will be impenetrable six months down the road. Perl provides very little assistance to someone who wants to write complex systems clearly. Features like perl -w (warnings), use strict, and Perl's module support help maintainability, but it still requires a great deal of care and discipline.

Python's support for maintainability, on the other hand, is excellent. Python's rich collection of modules and the fact that it's an interpreted language allow relatively fast development, if not quite as fast as in Perl. Generally, the more complex the system you're trying to build and the longer you expect to use it, the more potential there is for gain in using Python over Perl.

Personally, when tossing together quick one-offs or scripts that are very regular expression–heavy, I use Perl. Perl's regular expression support is so fundamental to the language that it's worth it, and its Swiss-Army-knife nature is perfect for things I don't expect to need again later. I also tend to use Perl when I want to write a very portable script, as most Unixes include Perl as part of the base system these days, whereas Python, while just as portable, tends to need to be installed seperately. When I want to build more complex scripts or larger systems, and maintainability is thus a higher priority, I use Python. I often use Python even for smaller things if I intend to keep them around for a while.

In the end, of course, it comes down to a matter of personal taste and judgment. Personally, I value being able to understand my code six months (or six years!) down the road far more than having every tool imaginable at my fingertips, so I tend to lean towards languages that help you write clear, readable code, like Python.

—DJPH

Part VIII

Communication and Connectivity

Part VIII contains the following chapters:

Redirecting Input and Output

43.1 Using Standard Input and Output

There is basically no difference between reading data from a file and reading data from a terminal.[*] Likewise, if a program's output consists entirely of alphanumeric characters and punctuation, there is no difference between writing to a file, writing to a terminal, and writing to the input of another program (as in a pipe).

The *standard I/O* facility provides some simple defaults for managing input/output. There are three default I/O streams: standard input, standard output, and standard error. By convention, standard output (abbreviated *stdout*) consists of all "normal" output from your program, while standard error (*stderr*) consists of error messages. It is often a convenience to be able to handle error messages and standard output separately. If you don't do anything special, programs will read standard input from your keyboard, and they will send standard output and standard error to your terminal's display.

Standard input (*stdin*) normally comes from your keyboard. Many programs ignore *stdin*; you name files directly on their command line—for instance, the command *cat file1 file2* never reads its standard input; it reads the files directly. But without filenames on the command line, Unix commands that need input will usually read *stdin*. Standard input normally comes from your keyboard, but the shell can redirect *stdin* from a file. This is handy for Unix commands that can't open files directly—for instance, *mail* (1.21). To mail a file to *joan*, use `< filename`—to tell the shell to attach the file, instead of your keyboard, to *mail*'s standard input:

```
% mail joan < myfile
```

[*] If a program's input consists entirely of alphanumeric characters and punctuation (i.e., ASCII data or international (non-English) characters).

The real virtue of standard I/O is that it allows you to *redirect* input or output away from your terminal to a file. As we said, Unix is file-based (1.19). Because terminals and other I/O devices are treated as files, a program doesn't even need to know* if it is sending its output to a terminal or to a file. For example, if you want to run the command *cat file1 file2*, but you want to place the output in *file3* rather than sending it to your terminal, give the command:

```
% cat file1 file2 > file3
```

This is called *redirecting* standard output to *file3*. If you give this command and look at *file3* afterward, you will find the contents of *file1*, followed by the contents of *file2*—exactly what you would have seen on your screen if you omitted the > `file3` modifier. (The Z shell takes this further with multiple-file redirection.)

One of the best-known forms of redirection in Unix is the *pipe*. The shell's vertical bar (|) operator makes a pipe. For example, to send both *file1* and *file2* together in a mail message for *joan*, type:

```
% cat file1 file2 | mail joan
```

The pipe says, "Connect the standard output of the process at the left (cat) to the standard input of the process at the right (mail)."

Article 36.15 has diagrams and more information about standard I/O and redirection. Table 43-1 shows the most common ways of redirecting standard I/O, for both the C shell and the Bourne shell, which also apply to derivatives like *tcsh* and *bash*.

Table 43-1. Common standard I/O redirections

Function	csh	sh
Send *stdout* to *file*	prog > *file*	prog > *file*
Send *stderr* to *file*		prog 2 > *file*
Send *stdout* and *stderr* to *file*	prog >& *file*	prog > *file* 2>&1
Take *stdin* from *file*	prog < *file*	prog < *file*
Send *stdout* to end of *file*	prog >> *file*	prog >> *file*
Send *stderr* to end of *file*		prog 2 >> *file*
Send *stdout* and *stderr* to end of *file*	prog >>& *file*	prog >> *file* 2>&1
Read *stdin* from keyboard until *c* (see article 27.16)	prog << *c*	prog << *c*
Pipe *stdout* to *prog2*	prog	prog2	prog	prog2
Pipe *stdout* and *stderr* to *prog2*	prog	& prog2	prog 2>&1	prog2

---

* But it can find out.

Be aware that:

- While standard I/O is a basic feature of Unix, the syntax used to redirect standard I/O depends on the shell you are using. Bourne shell syntax and C shell syntax differ, particularly when you get into the less commonly used features. The Korn shell and *bash* are the same as the Bourne shell, but with a few twists of their own. The Z shell generally understands both syntaxes (and, in its usual manner, adds even more).

- You can redirect standard input and standard output in the same command line. For example, to read from the file *input* and write to the file *output*, give the command:

  ```
  % prog < input > output
  ```

  The Bourne shell will let you go further and write *stderr* to a third file:

  ```
  $ prog < input > output 2> errors
  ```

- The C shell doesn't give you an easy way to redirect standard output without redirecting standard error. A simple trick will help you do this. To put standard output and standard error in different files, give a command like:

  ```
  % ( prog > output ) >& errors
  ```

  We'll discuss commands like this in articles 43.3 and 43.5.

- Many implementations of both shells don't care what order the redirections appear in, or even where they appear on the command line. For example, SunOS lets you type `< input > output prog`. However, clarity is a virtue that computer users have never appreciated enough. It will be easiest to understand what you are doing if you type the command name first—then redirect standard input, followed by standard output, followed by standard error.

There are some more complex forms of standard I/O redirection, particularly for the Bourne shell (**36.16**).

Of course, programs aren't restricted to standard I/O. They can open other files, define their own special-purpose pipes, and write directly to the terminal. But standard I/O is the glue that allows you to make big programs out of smaller ones, and it is therefore a crucial part of the operating system. Most Unix utilities read their data from standard input and write their output to standard output, allowing you to combine them easily. A program that creates its own special-purpose pipe may be very useful, but it cannot be used in combination with standard utilities.

Many Unix systems, and utilities such as *gawk* (**20.11**), support special filenames like */dev/stdin*, */dev/stdout*, and */dev/stderr*.* You can use these just as you'd use

---

* On Linux, at least, those are symbolic links (**10.4**) to */proc/self/fd/0*, */proc/self/fd/1*, and */proc/self/fd/2*, respectively.

other files. For instance, to have any ordinary command read from the file *afile*, then standard input (from the keyboard, for example), then the file *bfile*:

```
% somecmd afile /dev/stdin bfile
```

In the same way, a process can write to its standard output through */dev/stdout* and the standard error via */dev/stderr*.

Because reading from standard input and standard output is so common, there is a more general convention for redirecting to these two devices: using - where a program expects a filename. If the program was expecting the name of an input file, it will read from standard input instead. If it was expecting an output file, it will write to standard output. A very common place this is seen is in the unpacking of tar gzipped archives:

```
$ gzip -dc filename.tar.gz | tar -xvf -
```

Here, the -c flag tells *gzip* to stream the uncompressed file to standard output, which is then piped to *tar*. The -f flag of tar is used to specify the source tar file, which, because of the -, is standard input.

—*ML and JP*

43.2 One Argument with a cat Isn't Enough

What's wrong with this command line?

cat 12.2
```
% cat filename | tr -d '\015' > newfile
```

As Tom Christiansen wrote in a Usenet article:

> A wise man once said: if you find yourself calling *cat* with just one argument, then you're probably doing something you shouldn't.

The command line above only uses *cat* to feed the file to the standard input of *tr*. It's a lot more efficient to have the shell do the redirection for you with its < character (43.1):

```
% tr -d '\015' < filename > newfile
```

—*JP and TC*

43.3 Send (Only) Standard Error Down a Pipe

A vertical bar character (|) on a command line pipes the standard output of a process to another process. How can you pipe the standard error but not the standard output? You might want to put a long-running *cruncher* command in the background, save the output to a file, and mail yourself a copy of the errors. In the C shell, run the command in a subshell (43.7). The standard output of the command is redirected inside the subshell. All that's left outside the subshell is the standard error; the |& operator (43.5) redirects it (along with the empty standard output) to the *mail* (1.21) program:

```
% (cruncher > outputfile) |& mail yourname &
[1] 12345
```

Of course, you don't need to put that job in the background. If you want the standard output to go to your terminal instead of a text file, use */dev/tty* (36.15) as the *outputfile*.

The Bourne shell gives you a lot more flexibility and lets you do just what you need. The disadvantage is the more complicated syntax (36.16). Here's how to run your *cruncher* program, route the *stderr* through a pipe to the *mail* program, and leave *stdout* going to your screen:

```
$ (cruncher 3>&1 1>&2 2>&3 3>&-) | mail yourname &
12345
```

If this example makes your head hurt a little, you're not alone. The key to understanding this arcana is to know that programs don't refer to files by name like users do. Instead, when a program wants to read or write to a file, it must ask the operating system for a file stream that has an integer *file descriptor* associated with it. Every program has three file streams opened by default: standard input, standard output, and standard error. The file descriptors associated with standard input and standard error are 1 and 2, respectively. These file streams may be duplicated; that is, the data stream pointed by the file descriptor on the left will now go to data stream pointed to by the file descriptor on the right. If you wanted to redirect both standard error and standard output to *more*, you might do this:

```
$ command 2>&1 | more
```

To redirect *stdout* to an output file and send *stderr* down a pipe, try this:

```
$ (cruncher 3>&1 >outputfile 2>&3 3>&-) | mail yourname &
12345
```

—JP

43.4 Problems Piping to a Pager

If your window onto Unix (terminal, X window, communications program, whatever) doesn't have a way to show you the previous screenful, using a pager program like *more*, *pg*, or *less* (12.3) can be mighty handy. But piping to a pager doesn't always work the way you want it to.

Here's a *grep* command line that searches several files. What's wrong with it?

```
% grep "^set" */.cshrc | more
```

That wasn't a fair question because you can't tell what's wrong. The problem (it turns out) is that the files named *barney/.cshrc*, *edie/.cshrc*, and *gail/.cshrc* are read-protected (50.2). But as the first part of Figure 43-1 shows, the error messages scroll off your screen and the pager doesn't stop them.

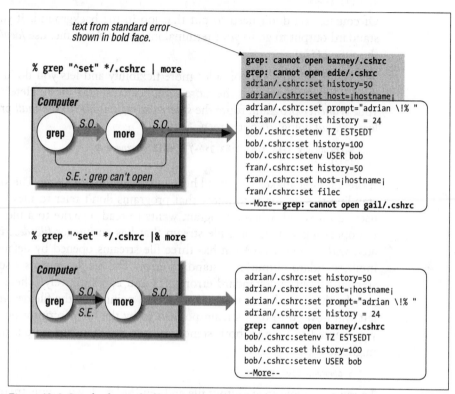

Figure 43-1. Standard error bypassing pipe, going through pipe

Unless your display is reallllly sloooowwww, the error messages are lost, and you never know they were there, or the errors are jumbled up with the "good" *grep* output. That's because you've told the shell to send only the standard output of *grep* to the pager program. And *grep* writes its errors to the standard error (36.15)! But both *stdout* and *stderr* go to the screen at once. The errors on *stderr* scroll away with the output from the pager. The pager can't count the lines of errors, so it outputs a complete screenful of *stdout* (the "good stuff"). If *grep*'s standard output (from the files it could read) is at least a screenful, as it is here, there are too many lines to fit on the screen—and some lines will scroll off.

The better way to do this is to combine *grep*'s *stdout* and *stderr* and give them both to the pager. These command lines (in *csh* and *sh*) both do that:

```
% grep "^set" */.cshrc |& more
$ grep "^set" */.cshrc 2>&1 | more
```

(The Z shell understands both.) The second part of Figure 43-1 shows how this works. Any time I pipe a command's output to a pager, I usually combine the *stdout* and *stderr* this way.

—JP

43.5 Redirection in C Shell: Capture Errors, Too?

The > (right angle bracket) operator redirects the standard output of a process to a file. It doesn't affect the standard error. If you're logged in and can see any messages written to standard error, that's okay:

```
% nroff -ms report.ms > report.out &
[1] 10316
    ...Later...
nroff: can't open file /hoem/jpeek/report.data
```

But if you log out and leave the job running, you'll never see those errors unless you use the *csh* operator >&. It redirects both standard output and standard error to a file. For example:

make **11.10**

```
% make >& make.output &
[1] 10329
% logout
    ...Later...
% cat make.output
        cc -O -c random.c
        cc -O -c output.c
"output.c", line 46: syntax error
"output.c", line 50: time_e undefined
"output.c", line 50: syntax error
    ...
```

You might also use the >& operator while you're logged in and watch the output file with *tail –f* (12.10). If you don't want the errors mixed with other output, you can split them to two files; see article 43.1.

The C shell also has a pipe operator, |&, that redirects both standard output and standard error. It's great for running a job in the background or on another computer and mailing (1.21) any output to me:

```
% make |& mailx -s "'make bigprog' output" jpeek@jpeek.com &
[1] 29182 29183
```

If I'd used plain | instead of |&, any text on the standard error wouldn't go into the mail message.

—*JP*

43.6 Safe I/O Redirection with noclobber

Have you ever destroyed a file accidentally? If you set the *noclobber* C shell variable or the *noclobber* option in *bash*, *zsh*, and *ksh*, it can help you avoid these mistakes. Setting *noclobber* prevents you from destroying a file when you are redirecting standard output (43.1).

Consider the following situation:

```
% anycommand > outputfile
```

The command above overwrites the old *outputfile*. If you have misspelled the name of your output file, or if you have forgotten that the file already exists and contains important data, or (most common) if you really meant to type >> instead of > (i.e., if you really meant to append to the end of *outputfile*, rather than start a new one), tough luck; your old data is gone.

Setting *noclobber* prevents this problem. If *noclobber* is set, the shell will not allow I/O redirection to destroy an existing file, unless you explicitly tell it to by adding an exclamation point (!) after the C shell redirect symbol or by adding a vertical bar (|) in *ksh* and *bash*. (The Z shell understands both.) Here are examples. The left column shows *csh* and *tcsh*; the right column is for *bash* (*ksh* is similar):

```
% set noclobber              $ set -o noclobber
% ls                         $ ls
filea fileb                  filea fileb
% anyprogram > fileb         $ anyprogram > fileb
fileb: File exists.          bash: fileb: Cannot clobber existing file
% anyprogram >! fileb        $ anyprogram >| fileb
%                            $
```

Be sure to put space after the !. If you don't, the C shell thinks you're making a history reference and it (usually) prints an error like fileb: Event not found.

Remember that *noclobber* is not an environment variable, so any new shells you create won't inherit it (35.9). Therefore, if you want this feature, put the *set* command (above) in your shell's setup file (3.3).

In some shells, *noclobber* will prevent you from redirecting standard output to */dev/null* (43.12) or to a terminal unless you add the !.

The *noclobber* variable has one other feature that's worth noting. Normally, shells let you append to a file that doesn't exist. If *noclobber* is set under *csh*, *tcsh*, and *zsh*, it won't; you can append only to files that already exist unless you use an exclamation point:

```
% ls
filea fileb
% anyprogram >> filec
filec: No such file or directory
% anyprogram >>! filec
%
```

—*ML and JP*

43.7 The () Subshell Operators

A useful shell trick is to use parentheses, ( ), to group commands.

Combining Several Commands

The parentheses start a subshell (24.4) that, in effect, "collects" the output of all the commands inside. (It does the same thing for the standard input and standard error.) The output of the entire group can be passed together into a single pipeline. For example:

echo 27.5

```
$ (cat file1; echo .bp; cat file2) | nroff
```

This will interpose the *nroff* .bp (break page) request between two files to be formatted.*

Parentheses are also useful in the Bourne shell if you want to put an entire sequence of commands separated by semicolons (;) (28.16) into the background. In the C shell, the command line below will go immediately into the background.

```
% nroff -ms file1; nroff -ms file2 &
```

But in the Bourne shell, the background request (&) will apply only to the second command, forcing you to wait for completion of the first job before you get back the system prompt. To get right back to work, you can type:

```
$ (nroff -ms file1; nroff -ms file2) &
```

---

* If you're using only *cat* and a single *echo*, you can use this command instead:
```
$ echo .bp | cat file1 - file2 | nroff
```
The *cat* – option tells *cat* to read its standard input (in this case, from the pipe and the *echo*) at that point. *nroff* gets exactly the same input.

Temporary Change of Directory and Environment

Commands that run between the parentheses won't affect the parent shell's environment. For instance, to run a command in another directory without changing your active shell's current directory (24.3):

```
% pwd
/home/trent
% (cd somewhere-else; nroff -ms file1 > file.out) &
[1] 22670
% pwd
/home/trent
```

The file *file.out* will be created in the *somewhere-else* directory.

—TOR and JP

43.8 Send Output Two or More Places

tee

If you're running a program and you want to send its output to a file—but you want to see the output on your screen, too, so you can stop the program if something goes wrong—you can use *tee*. The *tee* program reads its standard input and writes it to one or more files. (The web site has the GNU version.)

 A pipe may *buffer* the output of a program, collecting it in chunks and spitting it out every so often. If the program's output comes slowly and feeds *tee* through a pipe, there might be long delays before you see any output. In that case, it's better to use > to redirect output to a file, put the program into the background, and watch the output with *tail –f* (12.10). Or use a program like *script* (37.7).

Use *tee* for saving results in the middle of a long pipeline of commands. That's especially good for debugging. For example, you could type:

```
% prog | tee prog.out | sed -f sedscr | tee sed.out | ...
```

to save the output of *prog* in the file *prog.out* and also pipe it to the *sed* command, save *sed*'s output in *sed.out* and also pipe it, and so on.

Here are two other notes about *tee*. If you want to add to a file that already exists, use the *–a* option. *tee* can write to more than one file if you give all of the filenames as arguments

Z shell users usually don't need *tee* because they have the *zsh* MULTIOS option. For instance, here's how to write the pipeline above:

```
zsh% setopt multios
zsh% prog > prog.out | sed -f sedscr > sed.out | ...
```

—JP

43.9 How to tee Several Commands into One Place

The *tee* (43.8) command writes its standard input to a file and writes the same text to its standard output. You might want to collect several commands' output and *tee* them all to the same file, one after another. The obvious way to do that is with the *-a* option:

```
$ some-command | tee teefile
$ another-command | tee -a teefile
$ a-third-command | tee -a teefile
```

A more efficient way is:

> 28.12

```
$ (some-command
> another-command
> a-third-command) | tee teefile
```

The subshell operators (43.7) collect the standard output of the three commands. The output all goes to one *tee* command. This has two differences from the first method. First, you need two fewer pipes, two fewer *tee*s, and one more subshell. Second, you can pipe the output of the single *tee* command to another process—for example, to print it.

Unfortunately, the C shell doesn't make this quite as easy. If you can type all the commands on one line, you can do it this way (the same thing works in the Bourne shell):

```
% (command1; command2; command3) | tee teefile
```

Otherwise, use a semicolon and backslash (;\) at the end of each line:

```
% (some-command ;\
another-command ;\
a-third-command) | tee teefile
```

In all these examples, remember that if you don't need to see the output of the commands, you don't need *tee*. Use the subshell as above, but replace | tee teefile with > outfile or | somecommand.

—JP

43.10 Redirecting Output to More Than One Place

What if you want to use the output of a program more than once, and you don't want to deal with an intermediary file? For example, suppose I have some large, compressed PostScript files. I want to print the files, but I also want to know how many pages they are. I know that the number of pages appears on a line following %%Pages: at the end of the file. Using *bzcat* (15.6) to uncompress the file to standard output, I can type the following commands into a *for* loop (28.9) (or put them into a shell script). This loop sends each file to the printer and uses *sed* to capture the correct line:

```
for f
do
    bzcat $f | lpr
    bzcat $f | sed -n "s/^%%Pages: \([0-9][0-9]*\)/$f:    \1 pages/p"
done
```

-n 34.3

But this ends up running *bzcat* twice, which takes some time. I can expand the file with *bunzip2* first, but frankly I'm not sure I have the disk space for that.

Using process substitution and *tee* (43.8), I can do it in one line, without wasting processes and without eating disk space:

```
for f
do
  bzcat $f | tee >(lpr) | sed -n "s/^%%Pages: \([0-9][0-9]*\)/$f: \1 pages/p"
done
```

From running this script, as each file is sent to the printer I receive the following messages on my screen:

```
ch01.ps.gz: 44 pages
ch02.ps.gz: 51 pages
ch03.ps.gz: 23 pages
    ...
```

Because *tee* can write to more than one file, it can write to more than one process with process substitution. For instance, maybe you want to send the file to both a black-and-white printer and a color printer at the same time:

```
bzcat $f | tee >(lpr -Pbw) >(lpr -Pcolor) | \
    sed -n "s/^%%Pages: \([0-9][0-9]*\)/$f: \1 pages/p"
```

tpipe

If your shell doesn't have process substitution, maybe you have a shell like *bash* or *zsh* that does. (Write a shell script. Or type the shell's name at your shell prompt, then type *exit* when you're done with the temporary shell.) Otherwise, you can use *tpipe*; it's available online. *tpipe* is similar to *tee* (43.8), but instead of putting a copy of standard input in a file, it passes the input to a new pipe. Give *tpipe* the name of the command (here, *lpr*) that will read the text from its standard input:

```
bzcat $f | tpipe lpr | sed -n "s/^%%Pages: \([0-9][0-9]*\)/$f: \1 pages/p"
```

You can also simulate *tpipe* by using *awk* (20.10). Write a little *awk* script that reads each input line and writes the text both to a command and to *awk*'s standard output:

```
bzcat $f | awk "{ print | \"lpr\" ; print }" | \
    sed -n "s/^%%Pages: \([0-9][0-9]*\)/$f:    \1 pages/p"
```

This is much slower and only works on text files, but it does the job.

—*LM and JP*

43.11 Named Pipes: FIFOs

When you type a pipe symbol (|) on a command line, the two processes that communicate through the pipe must both have been started from that same shell. Newer versions of Unix have a way to let two unrelated processes (processes not started from the same parent process) communicate: a *named pipe* or FIFO (*First In First Out*).

A FIFO works like a pipe, but its interface looks like a file. It has a filename and permissions (1.17), and it's in a directory. Once you make the FIFO, one process can write to it (with the shell's > operator, or directly) and another process can read from it (the shell's < operator, or directly). Unlike a regular file, though, a FIFO doesn't "fill up" with data as a process writes to it: if there's no process waiting to read the data, the data is lost. So, when you use a FIFO between two processes, the processes still need to coordinate with each other. There are times that temporary files are better.

mkfifo

The command to make a FIFO is *mkfifo*. (The GNU version is on the CD-ROM.) Like other files, the default permission is set by your umask. There's also a *–m* option that sets the permissions—with a numeric or symbolic mode like *chmod* (50.5) uses. To remove a FIFO, use—you guessed it—*rm*.

Let's look at an example that, although it's made up, shows some important things to know about FIFOs. If you're using a window system, you'll use two terminal windows (like *xterm* (24.20)); you'll write to the FIFO from one window and read it from the other. Or if you have two terminals, you can use both of them. Otherwise, with a single terminal, you can put the writing process in the background (23.2) and run the reading process in the foreground.*

Start by making the FIFO. You can make it from any window. (The FIFO stays in the filesystem until you remove it. You can use it over and over again, though only one pair of processes can use it at any one time.) Then have a look with *ls*; the FIFO has zero size, it has a p type in the *–l* output and a | symbol from *–F*:

```
$ mkfifo /tmp/fifo
$ ls -l /tmp/fifo
prw-rw-r--    1 jpeek    jpeek        0 Dec 30 00:25 /tmp/fifo
$ ls -F /tmp/fifo
/tmp/fifo|
```

–F **8.10**

Next, start the process that reads from the FIFO. Like a program that's reading from a regular (anonymous) pipe, the process will block (sit there doing nothing) until there's something to read. For now, plain *cat* (12.2) is a good choice:

---

* This may take some juggling because your system may require you to start the reading process before the writing process. If it does, and if your system has job control (23.3), do this: start the reading process, stop it with CTRL-z, start the writing process in the background, then bring the reading process to the foreground.

```
$ cat /tmp/fifo
    ...nothing (yet)...
```

To write to the FIFO, here's a little shell script (35.1) that sends the current date and time to its standard output every three seconds. You could name it *dater*:

```
#!/bin/sh

while sleep 3
do date
done
```

while **35.15**
sleep **25.9**

In the other window or terminal, start *dater* and redirect its output to the FIFO. The process will run, writing data to the FIFO periodically:

```
$ dater > /tmp/fifo
```

In your window running *cat*, the dates should start to appear. When you kill the writing process (or it finishes by itself), the reader should terminate.

Also try reading from the FIFO with any other Unix program, like the *pr* (45.6) formatter with its *–l15* option (to make output pages 15 lines long, so you don't have to wait too long to see the next page header). This makes a nice illustration of the way that standard pipes, as well as named pipes, work: dribbling output to the reading process as the writing process makes it. (Standard pipes may be *buffered*, though, passing output in larger chunks.)

If you have a third terminal or window, and you start another reading process (like cat /tmp/fifo) there, it will block until you kill the first reading process (the previous cat /tmp/fifo).

This can be good food for thought. For instance, what output do you see when *tail* (12.8) reads from a pipe or FIFO? (Answer: nothing until the writing process dies.)

To review, though, a FIFO is useful anytime two processes need to communicate but those processes weren't started from the same parent process, so a traditional pipe can't work (because the second process can't access the open file descriptor from the first process).

—*JP*

43.12 What Can You Do with an Empty File?

It isn't a file, actually, though you can use it like one. */dev/null* is a Unix device.[*] It's not a physical device. */dev/null* is a special device that "eats" any text written to it and returns "end-of-file" (a file of length 0) when you read from it. So what the heck can you use it for?

---

[*] Well, okay. It's a *device file*.

- Empty another file. Just copy */dev/null* "on top of" the other file (15.2).

- Make another program "quiet" by redirecting its output there. For instance, if you're putting a program into the background and you don't want it to bother you, type:

  ```
  % progname > /dev/null &
  ```

  That redirects (43.1) standard output but leaves standard error hooked to your terminal, in case there is an error.

- Answer a program that asks a lot of questions—you know you'll just press RETURN at each prompt. In a lot of cases, you can redirect the program's standard input from */dev/null*:

  ```
  % progname < /dev/null
  Want the default setup? If yes, press RETURN:
  Enter filename or press RETURN for default:
      ...
  ```

  You should test that with each program, though, before you assume this trick will work. (If it doesn't work, try *yes* (14.5).)

- Where a program needs an extra filename but you don't want it to read or write an actual file. For instance, the *grep* (13.1) programs won't give the name of the file where they find a match unless there are at least two filenames on the command line. When you use a wildcard in a directory where maybe only one file will match, use */dev/null* to be sure that *grep* will always see more than one (9.21):

  ```
  % grep "whatever" * /dev/null
  ```

  You're guaranteed that *grep* won't match its regular expression in */dev/null*.

- Article 15.3 shows even more uses for */dev/null*.

Another interesting device (mostly for programmers) is */dev/zero*. When you read it, you'll get ASCII zeros (NUL characters) forever. There are no newlines either. For both of those reasons, many Unix commands have trouble reading it. If you want to play, the command below will give you a start (and *head* (12.12) will give you a stop!):*

od 12.4   `% fold -20 /dev/zero | od -c | head`

—*JP*

---

* On some Unix versions, the *head* program may not terminate after it has printed the first 10 lines. In that case, use sed 10q instead of head.

44

Devices

44.1 Quick Introduction to Hardware

Your Unix machine can likely talk to a wide collection of hardware: disk controllers and *disks* (44.4, 44.5), *CD-ROMs* (44.6), *ethernet cards* (44.8), *modems* (44.10), *sound cards* (44.13), and so on. Each device needs its own little piece of software within the kernel, called a device driver. Some device drivers are simple, and some are very complex; some cover multiple devices, and some are specific to one particular piece of hardware.

Many modern Unix platforms use loadable kernel modules for most device drivers, so that drivers can be loaded at run time rather than compiled into the kernel.

Many devices also have user-space tools to configure them, like *ifconfig* (44.8) for *network devices* (44.6, 44.7), *mount* (44.9) for disks and so forth.

In this chapter we'll give you the whirlwind overview of devices on Unix. Since there are so many devices and so many platforms, we'll gloss over a lot of details, but hopefully this will give you enough to get started with and a few hints as to where to find more information.

—*DJPH*

44.2 Reading Kernel Boot Output

As your Unix machine boots up, it will display a message for each device driver as it initializes. This is a good way to tell what devices your kernel was able to find. The exact output varies, but here is the output for hard drive controllers, hard drives, and network cards from a FreeBSD machine and a Debian Linux machine:

```
# FreeBSD
atapci0: <Intel ICH ATA66 controller> port 0xffa0-0xffaf at device 31.1 on pci0
ata0: at 0x1f0 irq 14 on atapci0
ata1: at 0x170 irq 15 on atapci0
ad0: 19569MB <ST320430A> [39761/16/63] at ata0- master UDMA66
afd0: 239MB <IOMEGA ZIP 250 ATAPI> [239/64/32] at ata0-slave using PIO3
acd0: CDROM <ATAPI CDROM> at ata1-master using PIO4
rl0: <D-Link DFE-530TX+ 10/100BaseTX> port 0xbc 00-0xbcff
     mem 0xefdfff00-0xefdfffff irq 11 at device 4.0 on pci1

# Linux
PIIX4: IDE controller on PCI bus 00 dev 39
PIIX4: not 100% native mode: will probe irqs later
     ide0: BM-DMA at 0xf000-0xf007, BIOS settings: hda:DMA, hdb:pio
     ide1: BM-DMA at 0xf008-0xf00f, BIOS settings: hdc:pio, hdd:pio
hda: WDC WD307AA-32BAA0, ATA DISK drive
ide0 at 0x1f0-0x1f7,0x3f6 on irq 14
hda: WDC WD307AA-32BAA0, 29333MB w/2048kB Cache, CHS=3739/255/63, UDMA
Partition check:
 hda: hda1 hda2 hda3
rtl8139.c:v1.07 5/6/99 Donald Becker
     http://cesdis.gsfc.nasa.gov/linux/drivers/rtl8139.html
eth0: RealTek RTL8139 Fast Ethernet at 0xd400, IRQ 11, 00:50:ba:d3:9e:14.
```

More specifically, in the line:

```
atapci0: <Intel ICH ATA66 controller> port 0xffa0-0xffaf at device 31.1 on pci0
```

atapci is the name of the device; 0 is the number of the device (devices are generally numbered sequentially with the first one probed getting the number 0); <Intel ICH ATA66 controller> is the name of the specific driver that successfully attached to this device; port 0xffa0-0xffaf at device 31.1 is physical address information about where this particular device is located; and finally, on pci0 tells us this device is attached to the first PCI bus (since pci is the device name of a PCI bus and 0 is the number assigned to the first PCI bus probed).

Note that in both FreeBSD and Linux, each line gives information about which driver is being used, hardware addresses, and options. Other platforms give similar information during boot. Often if you have a device that's not being recognized, you will see a line in the boot output telling you that a device was found but no driver for it could be found. If you would like more information, you may be able to boot your machine with *boot –v* from the bootstrap prompt—the BSDs and Solaris support *–v*. This enables verbose booting, which prints out a lot more information during device probing and may help you understand why a device driver couldn't be found. Linux doesn't have any straightforward way to get verbose information like this, but you can use *lspci* to show every device on the PCI bus, whether there's an active driver for that device or not.

—DJPH

44.3 Basic Kernel Configuration

Generally a Unix kernel is made up of some core, which handles fundamental functionality like virtual memory, and a lot of modules for various devices. A kernel configuration file is used to build a kernel and, on some platforms, a set of loadable kernel modules.

A kernel configuration file has a list of kernel options and then a list of devices and device options. The kernel build process uses this file to determine exactly what to build; this way you can have a kernel that supports exactly the hardware you have in your machine but isn't using any extra resources to support hardware you don't have.

Some example device lines from various kernel configuration files:

```
#
# FreeBSD samples
#
maxusers      128
options       INCLUDE_CONFIG_FILE
options       INET                      #InterNETworking
device        isa
device        pci
device        ata0    at isa? port IO_WD1 irq 14
device        ata
device        atadisk               # ATA disk drives
device        atapicd               # ATAPI CDROM drives
device        atapifd               # ATAPI floppy drives
device        atapist               # ATAPI tape drives
options       ATA_STATIC_ID         #Static device numbering

#
# Linux samples
#
# Loadable module support
CONFIG_MODULES=y
CONFIG_MODVERSIONS=y
# CONFIG_KMOD is not set

# General setup
CONFIG_NET=y
CONFIG_PCI=y

# Block devices
CONFIG_BLK_DEV_FD=m
CONFIG_BLK_DEV_IDE=y
# CONFIG_BLK_DEV_HD_IDE is not set
CONFIG_BLK_DEV_IDEDISK=y
CONFIG_BLK_DEV_IDECD=m
CONFIG_BLK_DEV_IDETAPE=m
CONFIG_BLK_DEV_IDEFLOPPY=m
# CONFIG_BLK_DEV_IDESCSI is not set
```

```
CONFIG_BLK_DEV_IDEPCI=y
CONFIG_BLK_DEV_IDEDMA=y
CONFIG_IDEDMA_AUTO=y
```

The kernel build process involves setting up an appropriate configuration file for your platform and then using a tool (generally *config*(8); check the manpage) to create a kernel build setup from the configuration file. Then you simply run *make* within the kernel build setup and you have a new kernel. Once the new kernel is installed, you reboot the machine, and poof, you're running on a sleek new customized kernel.

To understand how to configure the kernel on your platform, consult the documentation for that platform. Note that many platforms have tools or even GUIs for helping you configure your kernel. For the free Unixes, search the Web. There are extensive HOWTOs available describing how to configure your kernel in excruciating detail.

Linux has a very detailed HOWTO for kernel configuration at *http://www.tldp.org/HOWTO/Kernel-HOWTO.html*. The short version is that the configuration file mentioned above is stored in the *.config* file at the top of the kernel source tree (usually */usr/src/linux*). Generally you don't have to edit it directly; instead you'd use make menuconfig or make xconfig, again at the top of the kernel source tree, to use the fancy kernel configuration tools.

—DJPH

44.4 Disk Partitioning

A physical disk can be divided into smaller blocks, called *partitions*. Unix disk devices operate on partitions, where each device is a single partition. The simplest configuration is one big partition for the entire disk.

The advantage to having filesystems on separate partitions is that different parts of your operating system are somewhat protected from each other. If your users have filled up */home*, programs writing log files in */var* aren't affected if */home* and */var* are separate partitions. If your disk gets corrupted, only the corrupted partition is damaged. The disadvantage is that, in most cases, if you mistakenly allocated too little disk space for a partition, you can't steal space from your */var* to give you more room on */home* once your system is set up.

On non-PC hardware, partitioning is generally simple enough; use *format* or *disklabel* to write a partition table onto the disk. Traditionally, partitions are named with a letter following the device name, for example, */dev/ad0a*, */dev/ad0c* and so forth. By convention, partition a is for a root filesystem (*/*), b is for swap space, c represents the whole disk, and so forth. Of course, every current platform changes this in some way. Check the manpages for the various tools mentioned for more details on what to do for your specific platform.

Solaris's disk device naming scheme is */dev/dsk/c?t?d?s?*, where each ? is a number. The c is for controller, the t for target (a physical address on the controller), the d for disk, and the s for slice, another concept like partition. In this case, rather than partition c representing the whole disk, slice 2 does. This set of four numbers uniquely identifies a specific partition (slice) on a specific disk. Solaris uses *format* to manipulate partition tables.

On PC hardware, it's a bit more complicated, because the PC BIOS has a concept of partitions built into its understanding of disks. Unixes like Linux and FreeBSD that run on this hardware need to coexist with this partition table, especially if you want a machine that can dual-boot Unix and Windows. The BIOS understands no more than four *primary partitions* on each disk, due to the way it addresses partitions. To get around this limitation, one primary partition can be set to be an *extended partition*, which can then serve as a container for a different partition addressing scheme. Partitions within an extended partition are called *logical partitions* and have a few restrictions, but they aren't limited to four. The BIOS requires a primary partition to boot; it can't boot from a logical partition.

Linux names the IDE hard drives */dev/hda* through */dev/hdd* and the SCSI drives */dev/sda* through */dev/sdg*. Higher letters are possible with extra controllers. The device name itself represents the whole disk, as partition c and slice 2 did above. Linux uses the BIOS nomenclature and uses primary partitions, extended partitions and logical partitions. Primary partitions get partition numbers one through four, and thus partition two on the second IDE disk would be */dev/hdb2*. Logical partitions get numbers higher than four. Linux uses *fdisk* to manipulate partition tables.

FreeBSD calls the BIOS primary partitions *slices* and doesn't use extended or logical partitions. Its own partitions within a slice are then just called *partitions*. This has the advantage of allowing a fairly traditional a through h partitioning, which just lives in a particular slice. So the swap partition within the second BIOS slice of the first IDE drive would be */dev/ad0s2b*. FreeBSD uses *fdisk* to deal with slices and *disklabel* to manipulate partition tables.

As you can see, each platform has its own idiosyncrasies, but each unambiguously defines a scheme for uniquely referring to a particular partition on a particular disk. This lets us decide where we want our filesystems and refer to them in *mount* commands and in */etc/fstab* (44.5).

—*DJPH*

44.5 Filesystem Types and /etc/fstab

A *filesystem* is the scheme used to organize files on the disk. In the Windows world, FAT, FAT32, and NTFS are all filesystems. Various Unixes have their own filesystems with a forest of names: *ufs, ext2fs, vxfs, ffs, nfs, mfs, ISO9660* (which most CD-ROMs use) and special filesystems like *tmpfs, procfs,* and *devfs.*

Filesystems like *ufs* (Unix File System), *ffs* (Fast File System), *vxfs* (Veritas Extended File System), and *ext2fs* (Extended File System, Version 2) are simply ways of organizing inodes and bytes with various strengths and weaknesses. *nfs* (Network File System) is a filesystem for making remote files appear to be available locally. *mfs* (Memory File System) is a filesystem for ramdisks, that is, file storage in memory instead of on disk. *tmpfs* (Temporary File System) is a file system often used for /tmp which shares filespace and swap space dynamically. *procfs* (Process File System) simulates a filesystem, but with process information in it instead of files. (*procfs* on Linux is different from *procfs* on the BSDs; FreeBSD has a *linprocfs* to simulate part of Linux's *procfs.*) *devfs* is similar, but for devices instead of processes.

Standard mounts are configured using */etc/fstab* (or, on some platforms, */etc/vfstab*). *fstab* is just a list of filesystems that should be mounted, along with where they should get mounted, what type of filesystem each device contains, and any options. My FreeBSD *fstab* looks like this:

```
# Device              Mountpoint    FStype   Options      Dump    Pass#
/dev/ad0s1b           none          swap     sw           0       0
/dev/ad2s1b           none          swap     sw           0       0
/dev/ad0s1a           /             ufs      rw           1       1
/dev/ad2s1e           /home         ufs      rw           2       2
/dev/ad0s1f           /usr          ufs      rw           2       2
/dev/ad0s1e           /var          ufs      rw           2       2
/dev/acd0c            /cdrom        cd9660   ro,noauto    0       0
proc                  /proc         procfs   rw           0       0
```

I have two swap partitions, */dev/ad0s1b* and */dev/ad2s1b.* My */, /home, /usr,* and */var* are all separate *ufs* filesystems, and I have a CD-ROM that can be mounted on */cdrom* (but must be manually mounted (44.6)) and a standard *procfs.* The last two columns determine priority for backups and for being consistency checked by *fsck.* The *ufs* filesystems are all *fsck*ed, with / first; the rest of my filesystems are types that don't need to be *fsck*ed.

On other platforms, the options may be different, and the device names will certainly be different, but the basic gist of *fstab* will be the same.

Some filesystem types support "soft updates," which changes slightly the way the filesystem writes files out to the disk and can dramatically increase your effective disk speed. Consider looking at the documentation for your platform and turning on soft updates (generally this is done via *tunefs*).

—*DJPH*

44.6 Mounting and Unmounting Removable Filesystems

Removable disks are prevalent in Unix machines; CD-ROMs, DVD-ROMs, Zip disks, and floppies are all removable disks. When a Unix system boots, normal filesystems are all mounted automatically. By definition, removable filesystems may not even be in the machine at boot time, and you certainly don't want to have to reboot your machine just to change CDs.

To do this, you use *mount* and *umount*. The *–t* option allows you to specify the type of filesystem. On my FreeBSD machine, I can mount a FAT-formatted Zip disk with:

```
# mount -t msdos /dev/afd0s4 /zip
```

If I've formatted the Zip disk with a BSD *ufs* filesystem instead, I don't need the *–t* option, since *ufs* is the default on FreeBSD, and I would use the BSD partitioning scheme (*/dev/afd0c*) instead of the BIOS partitions (*/dev/afd0s4*).

If you use your removable disk regularly, you can add it to your *fstab* and make this simpler:

```
/dev/acd0c      /cdrom      cd9660   ro,noauto    0      0
/dev/afd0c      /zip        ufs      rw,noauto    0      0
/dev/afd0s4     /mszip      msdos    rw,noauto    0      0
```

Note that I've set up my fstab for both *ufs*-formatted and FAT-formatted Zip disks, and that the Zip drive and the CD-ROM are both set noauto to keep them from being automatically mounted. Having these in my *fstab* means I can just type *mount /zip* or *mount /cdrom* to mount a Zip disk or CD-ROM. Don't forget to create the directories */cdrom*, */zip*, and */mszip*!

Generally the *mount* and *umount* commands must be run as root. However, you'd often like normal users to be able to mount and unmount removable disks. Linux has an easy way to do this: just add user to the options field in */etc/fstab* and normal users will be able to mount and unmount that device. (Incidentally, Linux also has an auto filesystem type, which is very handy for removable devices, because it does its best to dynamically figure out what filesystem is on the removable media.) On other platforms, it can be a little more complex. Generally, the trick is to set the permissions on the device file properly. On FreeBSD you also need to use *sysctl* to set vfs.usermount, which will allow users to mount properly *chmod*ed devices on directories they own; similar tricks may be needed on other platforms. To set the floppy drive to allow anyone to mount it and the CD-ROM to allow anyone in the cdrom group to mount it, you'd do something like this:

```
# chmod 666 /dev/fd0
```

```
# chgrp cdrom /dev/acd0c
# chmod 640 /dev/acd0c
```

Then, as a normal user in group cdrom, you could:

```
% mkdir ~/cdrom
% mount -t cd9660 /dev/acd0c ~/cdrom
```

Solaris has a daemon, *vold*, which handles all of the messy details of removable media for you. At the time of this writing, very current versions of Linux have automount daemons and *devfsd* to handle such things; check your platform's current documentation.

—*DJPH*

44.7 Loopback Mounts

Some platforms provide the capability to mount a file as if it were a block device (like a disk partition (44.4)). This allows mounting a file as if it were a hard disk, CD-ROM, or any other physical media. The primary advantage to this is that it's a simple way to create or work with a floppy, Zip, or CD-ROM image without needing the physical device. You can mount a CD image without having to burn an actual CD or manipulate a floppy boot image. Of course, different platforms call it different things and use different tools.

Mounting file images on Linux uses the *loop device* and is called a *loop mount* or a *loopback mount*. To mount an existing image as a filesystem, use the loop option to *mount*:

```
% mount -t iso9660 -o loop image.iso /mnt
% ls /mnt
```

To create a new image, you first create an empty file of the correct size (this is effectively creating a partition (44.4))—in this case, a 100 megabyte image. You then attach the image to one of the available loop device and use *mkfs* to create a new filesystem in the image. Then you can mount the image normally. In this example, we'll release the loop device we had to allocate specifically and let the mount find an available loop device automatically.

```
% dd if=/dev/zero of=image.file bs=1k count=100000
% losetup /dev/loop image.file
% mkfs -c /dev/loop 100000
% losetup -d /dev/loop
% mount -o loop image.file /mnt
```

FreeBSD has a similar capability, called *vnode disks*, with very similar syntax, but you use */dev/vn* instead of */dev/loop* and *vnconfig* instead of *losetup*. See FreeBSD's *vnconfig*(8) manpage.

Solaris also has loop devices as of Solaris 8. The device is */dev/lofi* instead of */dev/loop*, and you use *lofiadm* to configure it. See Solaris's *lofiadm*(1M) and *lofi*(7D) manpages.

FreeBSD and Solaris don't provide an equivalent to the loop option to *mount*; instead you just use *vnconfig* or *lofiadm* to explicitly associate a particular block device with the file and mount the specific block device just like any other device.

—DJPH

44.8 Network Devices—ifconfig

ifconfig is used to configure network devices such as Ethernet cards. While booting, the kernel will find a device driver for the actual device, but it will still need to be assigned an IP address, and any protocol options need to be configured. Various platforms have different ways to store this configuration information, but most use *ifconfig* somewhere in the startup scripts to do the actual work.

The primary use of *ifconfig* is to set up a network device to use a particular IP address. *ifconfig* can also be used to set network options and aliases. To bring up an interface (in this case, rl0) on 192.168.1.1 with normal settings for a /24 network:

```
# ifconfig rl0 inet 192.168.1.1 netmask 255.255.255.0 broadcast 192.168.1.255 up
```

To temporarily bring a network interface down and then back up later, something that can be useful for maintenance:

```
# ifconfig rl0 down
# ...maintenance operations...
# ifconfig rl0 up
```

—DJPH

44.9 Mounting Network Filesystems— NFS, SMBFS

Network filesystems provide the illusion that files on a remote host are on your disk. Except for mounting and unmounting such a filesystem and but for a few low-level details, they can be treated like any local filesystem, albeit on a very slow disk. The two most common network filesystems available on Unix platforms are the Network File System (NFS) and Server Message Block File System (SMBFS).

NFS has been around for a long time and is available on every Unix system I've seen in the past ten years. Its interface is simple: an NFS server has a set of exported filesystems (usually listed in */etc/exports*), and any permitted client can mount those filesystems using a straightforward *mount* invocation. Simply specify *host:/filesystem* as the device, and tell *mount* that the filesystem is of type nfs:

```
# mount -t nfs orange:/home /orange
```

For more details on NFS on your platform, take a look at the manpages for *exports*(5) and *mount_nfs*(8) or *nfs*(5).

NFS mounts can hang up entirely if the NFS server goes down or if you lose your net connection to it. Often this can require rebooting your machine to fix. To avoid this, use the soft option when mounting NFS filesystems. soft tells the NFS client system to use timeouts, so that losing touch with the NFS server just causes I/O requests to time out instead of hanging your machine.

 NFS by itself is extremely insecure. Be aware that running NFS without any other precautions on a publicly accessible network opens you up to a wide variety of attacks. *http://nfs.sourceforge.net/ nfs-howto/security.html* addresses some of the issues involved and has links to other good information on the subject.

SMB is the primary file and printer sharing protocol used by Windows. Chapter 47 details Samba, the primary tool used to deal with SMB on Unix systems. *smbfs* is the tool used to mount SMB-shared filesystems (including Windows shared drives and the like) as if they were Unix filesystems. Much like NFS, *smbfs* allows you to use *mount*; in this case, you provide the *share name* as the device:

```
# mount -t smbfs //yellow/Public /yellow
```

smbfs is only supported on some platforms; check your installation of Samba for details.

Note that both filesystem types can be included in */etc/fstab*, just like any other filesystem:

# Device	Mountpoint	FStype	Options	Dump	Pass#
/dev/ad0s1b	none	swap	sw	0	0
/dev/ad0s1a	/	ufs	rw	1	1
/dev/acd0c	/cdrom	cd9660	ro,noauto	0	0
orange:/home	/orange	nfs	rw	0	0
//yellow/Public	/yellow	smbfs	rw	0	0

—DJPH

44.10 Win Is a Modem Not a Modem?

The word "modem" is a contraction of "modulator–demodulator." The fundamental job of a modem is to turn a digital signal into an analog signal and send that analog signal across a phone line (modulation) and to receive an analog signal from a phone line and turn it back into the original digital signal (demodulation).

Controller-based modems do all of the digital signal processing, D/A and A/D conversion, and phone-line interfacing in hardware. Generally, these modems either are external modems that plug into a serial port or have a serial port chip included and thus just look like an extra serial port to the CPU. Configuring these modems under Unix is easy; just set up whatever program uses the serial port to use the port speed and serial options you want.

Host-based modems, often called "Winmodems," provide some level of hardware support (at a minimum, the physical phone line interface) and then emulate some or all of the hardware modulation and demodulation in software. There are a variety of specifications related to "soft" modems, and current information on things like available drivers, issues, standards, and whether a modem is a hard or soft modem are available at *http://www.idir.net/~gromitkc/winmodem.html* and *http://www.linmodems.org*.

The problem that soft modems present to Unix is that the software that makes up the fundamental functionality of the modem is almost always Windows software. These modems are widely available and cheap and do have some advantages, though, so there are efforts to provide Unix software for some set of them. Unix soft-modem software is highly in flux at the time of this writing. Before you buy a modem, be sure that you check the current information on that modem and available drivers for the Unix platform you want to use before you buy. Or spend a bit more and buy a modem that doesn't have these issues.

—*DJPH*

44.11 Setting Up a Dialup PPP Session

Point-to-Point Protocol (PPP) is the way ISPs usually provide dialup access (largely because this is the default protocol Windows dialup uses). Unixes that can do dialup provide a PPP client, which you configure to call the ISP and set up a PPP connection. An established connection functions as a network connection—you can use *ifconfig* (44.8, 46.3) to examine it and packets will be routed to the PPP connection by default, and tools like *traceroute* (46.4) can be used across it.

Unixes provide two ways to run PPP: kernel PPP, where the PPP code resides in the kernel and is therefore very fast but limited in features, and user PPP, where packets have to be copied back and forth between kernel space and user space, but a wide feature set can be provided. We'll give a quick overview of both.

Kernel PPP uses *pppd* and a fairly simple set of configuration commands. You provide *pppd* with the information needed to dial your modem appropriately and with whatever login information your ISP has provided you, and it connects. Generally you then have to set up */etc/resolv.conf* to point to your ISP's DNS (46.9) server. Some implementations of *pppd* don't even know how to dial the phone, and you'll have to use something like *kermit* to dial the phone first. *pppd* must also be run as root. Look at your platform's documentation for *pppd* for details on setting up kernel PPP on that platform.

Platforms that provide a user-space PPP client are a little easier to work with. User-space PPP clients can be run by users other than root (usually limited to a specific group); they tend to configure default routes, */etc/resolv.conf*, and other details automatically; and they generally deal with PAP or CHAP authentication (which many ISPs use) a little more easily. Usually the user-space PPP client is just called *ppp*; look for its manpage to see what it requires to configure it.

—*DJPH*

44.12 USB Configuration

Many PCs support the Universal Serial Bus (USB). USB is a hot-swappable standard; devices can be plugged in and unplugged while the machine is running, and the system is supposed to recognize the new device or no longer recognize the now disconnected device.

Unixes deal with this requirement with low-level device drivers to actually interface with the devices and with a daemon, *usbd*, to monitor for changes on the fly or, on Linux, the hotplug facility (*http://linux-hotplug.sourceforge.net*).

Generally, there is very little configuration required for supported USB devices. If you have the correct kernel modules (44.3) loaded (and on many platforms they're loaded by default), just plug in the device. Check your platform's supported hardware before buying a USB device, as such devices are changing rapidly at the time of this writing and may or may not have Unix drivers implemented yet.

Specific issues you might run into include that USB disks may need to use a special filesystem type (usbdevfs) and that specific devices may require tools to actually use the device. Webcams and scanners are a good example, as the device driver provides only low-level access to the device; you still need a tool that can pull images off of the device and do something useful with them. Extensive information is available on the Web about using many USB devices on the free Unixes (*http://www.linux-usb.org* for Linux and the USB chapter in the FreeBSD handbook are places to start), and it stays fairly up to date.

—*DJPH*

44.13 Dealing with Sound Cards and Other Annoying Hardware

There are a lot of devices available for PCs that were never designed for an operating system like Unix to use. Often these devices' manufacturers simply provide Windows drivers and never expect you to need anything else. Luckily, there is a large community of developers for the various free Unixes, and they implement device drivers for many of these devices. Availability of a driver for a particular piece of hardware, however, depends entirely on whether someone happened to write a driver for it.

Sound cards are one bit of hardware that commonly has this problem. Most free Unixes have a set of drivers that support a selection of sound cards and one or two other drivers that support a lowest common denominator to get minimal functionality out of most sound cards. If you want real support for your sound card, look at the supported devices list for the OS you want to install before you buy a card, and pick one that someone's written a full driver for.

On Linux, take a look at the *sndconfig* utility, which can probably configure your sound card for you. Take a peek at *http://www.linuxheadquarters.com/howto/basic/sndconfig.shtml* for details.

Other hardware that falls into the "check your supported hardware list before buying" includes frame grabbers, multi-serial boards, AD/DA converters, X-10 controllers and any hardware that's brand new (and thus may not have had time for someone to create a Unix driver). All of the free Unixes have extensive supported hardware lists—check before you buy.

—DJPH

44.14 Decapitating Your Machine— Serial Consoles

Often server machines are placed in a rack in a colocation facility, in some back closet, or in some other out of the way place. This can make it really inconvenient to access the server's console should something go wrong or need diagnosing; hauling a monitor and keyboard into your server storage area is a real pain. If you've got your server mounted in a rack, there are devices that are essentially a flat screen monitor, keyboard, and mouse mounted in a sliding rack shelf, which work well, but they're expensive.

A simple and cheap solution is to change the console from the normal monitor/keyboard/mouse to one of the serial ports. The serial port can be hooked via null modem to a terminal server or another machine, allowing controlled access, or you can just plug your laptop into it with a null modem when you need to diagnose problems or reboot.

Linux has a howto describing details of dealing with serial consoles at *http://www.linuxdoc.org/HOWTO/Remote-Serial-Console-HOWTO/*. Essentially, you provide options to the boot loader and kernel to tell them to use your serial port as a console, and then configure *getty* to accept logins on that serial port. The HOWTO shows various potential configurations and demonstrates proper setup on each.

FreeBSD's handbook has a chapter on setting up serial consoles. Again, you have to tell the boot loader and the kernel to use the serial port, and then edit */etc/ttys* to enable *getty* on that serial port. FreeBSD can also be configured to decide whether to use a normal console or serial console based on whether or not a keyboard is plugged in. NetBSD and OpenBSD are configured similarly.

Solaris is even easier: just unplug the keyboard before you boot the machine. Solaris uses a serial console by default if no keyboard is plugged in at boot time. If you want to set it explicitly to use a serial console even if the keyboard is plugged in, just set `input-device` and `output-device` to `ttya` (or `ttyb` if you want it on the second serial port) in the boot eeprom.

—*DJPH*

45

Printing

45.1 Introduction to Printing

This chapter discusses printing, which is a surprisingly complicated subject. To understand why printing is so complicated, though, let's think a little bit about what you might want to print.

First, in the "olden days," we had line printers and their relatives: daisy-wheel printers, dot-matrix printers, and other pieces of equipment that generated typewriter-like output. Printing a simple text file was easy: you didn't need any special processing; you only needed some software to shove the file into the printer. If you wanted, you might add a banner page and do a little simple formatting, but that was really pretty trivial.

The one area of complexity in the printing system was the "spooling system," which had to do several things in addition to force-feeding the printer. Most printers were (and still are) shared devices. This means that many people can send jobs to the printer at the same time. There may also be several printers on which your file gets printed; you may care which one is used, or you may not. The spooling system needs to manage all this: receiving data from users, figuring out whether or not an appropriate printer is in use, and sending the file to the printer (if it's free) or storing the file somewhere (if the printer isn't free).

Historical note: why is this called the "spooling system"? Dave Birnbaum, a Principal Scientist at Xerox, says:

> "SPOOL (Simultaneous Printing Off and On Line)" It was written for the early IBM mainframes (of the 3-digit, i.e., 709 kind) and extended to the early 1401 machines. Output for the printer was sent to the spool system, which either printed it directly or queued it (on tape) for later printing (hence the on/off line). There was also a 2nd generation version where the 1401 would act as the printer controller for the (by then) 7094. The two were usually connected by a switchable tape drive that could be driven by either machine." [There's some controversy about exactly what the acronym means, but Dave's is as good as any I've heard. —JP]

The first few articles in this chapter, 45.2, 45.3, 45.4, and 45.5, discuss the basic Unix spooling system and how to work with it as a user.

The next few articles talk about how to format articles for printing—not the kind of fancy formatting people think of nowadays, but simpler things like pagination, margins, and so on, for text files that are to be sent to a line printer or a printer in line-printer emulation mode. Article 45.6 describes this kind of simple formatting, and article 45.7 gets a little more complicated on the same subject.

Historical note number two: why is the print spooler called *lp* or *lpr*? It typically spooled text to a line printer, a fast printer that used a wide head to print an entire line at a time. These printers are still common in data processing applications, and they can really fly!

In the mid-1970s, lots of Unix people got excited about typesetting. Some typesetters were available that could be connected to computers, most notably the C/A/T phototypesetter. Programs like *troff* and TeX were developed to format texts for phototypesetters. Typesetting tools are still with us, and still very valuable, though these days they generally work with laser printers via languages like PostScript. They're discussed in articles 45.10 through 45.17, along with the ramifications of fancy printing on Unix.

Finally, article 45.19 is about the *netpbm* package. It's a useful tool for people who deal with graphics files. *netpbm* converts between different graphics formats.

—*ML*

45.2 Introduction to Printing on Unix

Unix used a print spooler to allow many users to share a single printer long before Windows came along. A user can make a printing request at any time, even if the printer is currently busy. Requests are queued and processed in order as the printer becomes available.

Unix permits multiple printers to be connected to the same system. If there is more than one printer, one printer is set up as the default printer, and print jobs are sent there if no printer is specified.

lpr-Style Printing Commands

Many systems use the *lpr* command to queue a print job. When you use *lpr*, it spools the file for printing.

```
$ lpr notes
```

The *lpq* command tells you the status of your print jobs by showing you the print queue for a given printer.

```
$ lpq
lp is ready and printing
Rank    Owner   Job  Files                 Total Size
active  fred    876  notes                 7122 bytes
1st     alice   877  standard input        28372 bytes
2nd     john    878  afile bfile ...       985733 bytes
```

The word active in the Rank column shows the job that's currently printing. If your job does not appear at all on the listing, it means your job has finished printing or has been completely written into the printer's input buffer (or perhaps that you accidentally printed it to a different queue). If a job is not *active*, it's still in the queue.

You can remove a job with the *lprm* command. (Run *lpq* first to get the job number.)

```
$ lprm 877
dfA877host dequeued
cfA877host dequeued
```

The command *lpc status* (45.3) can be used to determine which printers are connected to your system and their names. If there is more than one printer, you can then use the –P option with *lpr*, *lpq* and *lprm* to specify a printer destination other than the default. For instance, if a laser printer is configured as *laserp*, you can enter:

```
$ lpr -Plaserp myfile
```

If you'll be using a certain printer often, put its name in the *PRINTER* environment variable (45.4).

If you're using an older system that has only *lp* (see below), or if you'd like a fancier *lpr* that supports all sorts of handy features, take a peek at *LPRng* (available at *http://www.lprng.com*). It supports everything standard *lpr* does and more, including a GUI for detailed configuration.

lp-Style Printing Commands

The System V–style print system, which Solaris uses by default, has the *lp* command to queue a print job. (Solaris also optionally includes *lpr*-style printing commands, if you install the BSD compatibility package.) When you use *lp*, it spools the file for printing and returns the request id of your print job. The request id can later be used to cancel the print job, if you decide to do so.

```
$ lp notes
request-id is lp-2354 (1 file)
```

The *lpstat* command can be used to check on the status of your print jobs. Like *lpq*, it will tell whether your job is in the queue or fully sent to the printer. Unlike *lpq*, it shows you only your own jobs by default:

```
$ lpstat
lp-2354        14519 fred    on lp
```

The message on lp indicates that the job is currently printing. If your job does not appear at all on the listing, it means your job has either finished printing or has been completely written into the printer's input buffer (or you accidentally printed it to a different queue). If the job is listed, but the on lp message does not appear, the job is still in the queue. You can see the status of all jobs in the queue with the *–u* option. You can cancel a job with the *cancel* command.

```
$ lpstat -u
lp-2354          14519 fred     on lp
lp-2355          21321 alice
lp-2356           9065 john
$ cancel lp-2356
lp-2356: cancelled
```

The *lpstat* command can be used to determine what printers are connected to your system and their names. If there is more than one printer, you can then use the *–d* option with *lp* to specify a printer destination other than the default. For instance, if a laser printer is configured as *laserp*, then you can enter:

```
$ lp -dlaserp myfile
```

If you'll be using a certain printer often, put its name in the *LPDEST* environment variable (45.4).

—DD, TOR, and JP

45.3 Printer Control with lpc

The *lpc*(8) command, for *lpr*-style printing setups, is mostly for the superuser. (You may find it in a system directory, like */usr/sbin/lpc*.) Everyone can use a few of its commands; this article covers those.

You can type *lpc* commands at the lpc> prompt; when you're done, type *exit* (or CTRL-d):

```
% lpc
lpc> help status
status          show status of daemon and queue
lpc> ...
lpc> exit
%
```

Or you can type a single *lpc* command from the shell prompt:

```
% lpc status imagen
imagen:
        queuing is enabled
        printing is enabled
        no entries
        no daemon present
%
```

The printer daemon (1.10) watches the queue for jobs that people submit with *lpr* (45.2). If queueing is disabled (usually by the system administrator), *lpr* won't accept new jobs.

lpc controls only printers on your local host. *lpc* won't control printers connected to other hosts, though you can check the queue of jobs (if any) waiting on your local computer for the remote printer.

The commands anyone can use are:

restart [printer]
> This tries to start a new printer daemon. Do this if something makes the daemon die while there are still jobs in the queue (*lpq* or *lpc status* will tell you this). It's worth trying when the system administrator is gone and the printer doesn't seem to be working. The printer name can be *all* to restart all printers. The printer name doesn't need an extra *P*. For example, to specify the *foobar* printer to *lpr*, you'd type *lpr –Pfoobar*. With *lpc*, use a command like *restart foobar*.

status [printer]
> Shows the status of daemons and queues on the local computer (see the preceding example). The printer name can be *all* to show all printers.

help [command]
> By default, gives a list of *lpc* commands, including ones for the superuser only. Give it a command name and it explains that command.

exit
> Quits from *lpc*.

—*JP*

45.4 Using Different Printers

Each printer on your system should have a name. By default, commands that send a file to a printer assume that the printer is named *lp* (a historical artifact; it stands for "Line Printer"). If you're using a single-user workstation and have a printer connected directly to your workstation, you can name your printer *lp* and forget about it.

In many environments, there are more options available: e.g., there are several printers in different locations that you can choose from. Often, only one printer will be able to print your normal documents: you may need to send your print jobs to a PostScript printer, not the line printer that the accounting department uses for billing.

There are two ways to choose a printer:

- Printing commands in the *lpr* family accept the option -P*printer*. This includes *lpr* (45.2), various scripts to format typeset documents, etc. For example, *lpr –Pps file.ps* sends the file *file.ps* to the printer named *ps*.

- Commands in the *lpr* family recognize the *PRINTER* environment variable (35.3); if *PRINTER* is defined, the command will read its value and choose a printer accordingly. So the command:

  ```
  % setenv PRINTER ps              —or
  $ PRINTER=ps ; export PRINTER
  ```

  ensures that the *lpr*-style print commands will send your documents to the printer named *ps*. The *–P* option overrides this environment variable, in case you need to send a particular print job to a different printer.

- Commands in the *lp* family use the *–d* option to select a printer. So *lp -d prfile.ps* sends *file.ps* to the printer named *pr*; it's equivalent to the previous *lpr* example.

- Commands in the *lp* family look for an environment variable named *LPDEST*, rather than *PRINTER*. So:

  ```
  % setenv LPDEST ps               —or
  $ LPDEST=ps ; export LPDEST
  ```

  ensures that the *lp*-style print commands will send your documents to the printer named *ps*. The *–d* option overrides this environment variable.

Note that Solaris and others that use *lp* can include both the *lp* and *lpr* print commands. This can make things confusing, particularly if you're using a script to process documents, and that script automatically sends your documents to the printer. Unless you know how the script works, you won't know which variable to set. I'd suggest setting both *PRINTER* and *LPDEST* for these systems.

By the way, if you have only one printer, but you've given it some name other than *lp*, the same solution works: just set *PRINTER* or *LPDEST* to the appropriate name.

—*ML*

45.5 Using Symbolic Links for Spooling

When you print a file, the file is copied to a "spooling directory." This can be a problem if you want to print a very large file: the copy operation might take a long time, or the act of copying might fill the spooling directory's filesystem.

Systems with the *lpr* family of commands provide a workaround for this problem. The *–s* option makes a symbolic link (10.4) to your file from the spooling directory.

Here's such a command:

```
% lpr -s directions
```

Rather than copying *directions*, *lpr* creates a symbolic link to *directions*. The symbolic link is much faster, and you're unlikely to get a "filesystem full" error.

Using a symbolic link has one important side effect. Because the file isn't hidden away in a special spooling directory, you can delete or modify it after you give the *lpr* command and before the printer is finished with it. This can have interesting side effects; be careful not to do it.

Of course, this warning applies only to the file that actually goes to the printer. For example, when you format a *troff* file (45.16) for a PostScript printer and then print using *-s*, you can continue to modify the *troff* file, because it's the resulting PostScript file that actually goes to the printer (thus the PostScript file, not the *troff* file, is symbolically linked).

—*ML*

45.6 Formatting Plain Text: pr

The line printer spooler (45.2) prints what you send it. If you send it a continuous stream of text (and the printer is set up to print text files rather than PostScript), that's probably just what you'll get: no page breaks, indenting, or other formatting features.

That's where *pr* comes in. It's a simple formatter that breaks its input into "pages" that will fit onto a 66-line page. (You can change that length.) It adds a header that automatically includes the date and time, the filename, and a page number. It also adds a footer that ensures that text doesn't run off the bottom of the page.

This is just what you want if you are sending program source code or other streams of unbroken text to a printer. For that matter, *pr* is often very handy for sending text to your screen. In addition to its default behavior, it has quite a few useful options. Here are a few common options:

-f

> Separate pages using formfeed character (^L) instead of a series of blank lines. (This is handy if your pages "creep" down because the printer folds some single lines onto two or three printed lines.)

-h*str*

> Replace default header with string *str*. See article 21.15.

-l*n*

> Set page length to *n* (default is 66).

-m

> Merge files, printing one in each column (can't be used with *–num* and *–a*). Text is chopped to fit. See article 21.15. This is a poor man's *paste* (21.18).

-s*c*

> Separate columns with *c* (default is a tab).

-t

> Omit the page header and trailing blank lines.

–w*num*

> Set line width for output made into columns to *num* (default is 72).

+*num*

> Begin printing at page *num* (default is 1).

–*n*

> Produce output having *n* columns (default is 1). See article 21.15.

Some versions of *pr* also support these options:

–a

> Multicolumn format; list items in rows going across.

–d

> Double-spaced format.

–e*cn*

> Set input tabs to every *n*th position (default is 8), and use *c* as field delimiter (default is a tab).

–F

> Fold input lines (avoids truncation by *–a* or *–m*).

–i*cn*

> For output, replace whitespace with field delimiter *c* (default is a tab) every *n*th position (default is 8).

–n*cn*

> Number lines with numbers *n* digits in length (default is 5), followed by field separator *c* (default is a tab). See also *nl* (12.13).

–o*n*

> Offset each line *n* spaces (default is 0).

–p

> Pause before each page. (*pr* rings the bell by writing an ALERT character to standard error and waits for a carriage-return character to be read from */dev/tty* (36.15).)

–r

> Suppress messages for files that can't be found.

Let's put this all together with a couple of examples:

- Print a side-by-side list, omitting heading and extra lines:

  `pr -m -t list.1 list.2 list.3`

- Alphabetize a list of states; number the lines in five columns.

  `sort states_50 | pr -n -5`

  If you have an old *pr* that doesn't support *–n*, you can use *cat –n* (12.13) to supply the line numbers:

  `sort states_50 | cat -n | pr -5`

—*TOR*

45.7 Formatting Plain Text: enscript

enscript is a handy program that takes your text files and turns them into Post-Script. *enscript* comes with a wide variety of formatting options. There is a GNU version available, and a few Unixes include a version by default. *enscript* is particularly useful when your main printer speaks primarily PostScript.

Detailed information on everything *enscript* can do is available in its manpage, but here are a few examples:

```
% enscript -G stuff.txt
```
Fancy ("Gaudy") headers
```
% enscript -2r stuff.txt
```
Two-up printing—two pages side-by-side on each page of paper
```
% enscript -2Gr stuff.txt
```
Two-up with fancy headers
```
% enscript -P otherps stuff.txt
```
Print to the otherps printer instead of the default
```
% enscript -d otherps stuff.txt
```
Ditto
```
% enscript -i 4 stuff.txt
```
Indent every line four spaces
```
% enscript --pretty-print=cpp Object.cc
```
Pretty print C++ source code
```
% enscript -E doit.pl
```
Pretty print doit.pl (and automagically figure out that it's Perl from the .pl suffix)

One thing to watch for: *enscript*'s default page size is A4, and in the United States most printers want letter-sized pages. You can set the default page size to letter when installing *enscript* (many U.S. pre-built binary packages do this for you), or you can use the *–M letter* or *––media=letter* option when you call *enscript*.

If you want a default set of flags to be passed to enscript, set the *ENSCRIPT* environment variable. Anything you pass on the command line will override values in *ENSCRIPT*.

—*DJPH*

45.8 Printing Over a Network

Sometimes you'd like to be able to print to a printer that's physically attached to another Unix machine. *lpd*, the print spool daemon, supports this easily.

lpd is configured using the *printcap* printer capabilities database, generally stored in */etc/printcap*. Generally, a local printer is given a line that looks something like this:

```
lp|local line printer:\
        :lp=/dev/lpt0:\
        :sd=/var/spool/output/lpd:lf=/var/log/lpd-errs:
```

The first line sets the printer name, in this case lp, and gives it a more descriptive name (local line printer) as well. The rest of the lines define various parameters for this printer using a *parameter=value* format. lp specifies the printer device—in this case, */dev/lpt0*. sd specifies the local spool directory, that is, where *lpd* will store spooled files while it's working with them. lf specifies the log file, where *lpd* will write error messages and the like for this printer.

To set up a remote printer, all you have to do is provide a remote machine (rm) and a remote printer (rp) instead of a printer device:

```
rlp|printhost|remote line printer:\
        :rm=printhost.domain.com:rp=lp:\
        :sd=/var/spool/output/printhost:lf=/var/log/lpd-errs:
```

Note that we added another name; since this is the default printer for the host *printhost*, either rlp or printhost will work as printer names. We also used a different spool directory, to keep files spooled for *printhost* separate from local files; this isn't strictly necessary, but it's handy. Don't forget to create this spool directory before trying to spool anything to this printer!

Some network connected printers have *lpd*-compatible spoolers built in. Talking to one of these printers is just as easy; just provide the printer's hostname for rm. Generally you won't have to provide rp unless the printer supports different printing modes by using different remote printer names, since the default name lp is almost always supported by these sorts of printers.

—DJPH

45.9 Printing Over Samba

Samba provides SMB networking to Unix boxes; in English, that means it allows Unix machines to share disks and printers with Windows machines and vice versa. Chapter 49 details Samba; here we'll talk a bit about tricks for printing over Samba, since it's so useful and parts of it are fairly arcane.

Printing to Unix Printers from Windows

This is the easy one. Simply configure your printer normally using *printcap*, then set this in your *smb.conf*:

```
load printers = yes
```

This tells Samba to read the *printcap* file and allow printing to any printer defined there. The default [printers] section automatically advertises all printers found and allows anyone with a valid login to print to them. You may want to make them browsable or printable by guest if you're not particularly worried about security on your network. Some Windows configurations will need guest access to browse, since they use a guest login to browse rather than your normal one; if you can't browse your Samba printers from your Windows client, try setting up guest access and see if that fixes it.

If you want to get really fancy, current versions of Samba can support downloading printer drivers to clients, just like Windows printer servers do. Take a look at the *PRINTER_DRIVER2.txt* file in the Samba distribution for more about how to do this.

Printing to Windows Printers from Unix

This one's a little more tricky. *lpd* doesn't know how to print to a Windows printer directly, or how to talk to Samba. However, *lpd* does know how to run files through a filter (45.17). So what we'll do is provide a filter that hands the file to Samba, and then send the print job right to */dev/null*:

```
laserjet:remote SMB laserjet via Samba\
    :lp=/dev/null:\
    :sd=/var/spool/lpd/laser:\
    :if=/usr/local/samba/bin/smbprint:
```

Samba comes with a sample filter called *smbprint*; it's often installed in an examples directory and will need to be moved to somewhere useful before setting this up. *smbprint* does exactly what we want; it takes the file and uses *smbclient* to send it to the right printer.

How does *smbprint* know which printer to send it to? It uses a file called *.config* in the given spool directory, which looks something like this:

```
server=WINDOWS_SERVER
service=PRINTER_SHARENAME
password="password"
```

The *smbprint* script is reasonably well documented in its comments. Look through it and tweak it to fit your own needs.

—*DJPH*

45.10 Introduction to Typesetting

Once upon a time, printers were simple. You hooked them up to your machine and dumped text out to them, and they printed the text. Nothing fancy, and not very pretty either. As printers got smarter, they became capable of more things, printing in a different font, perhaps. Printing got a bit more complex. If you wanted to use fancy features, you had to embed special characters in your text, specific to the printer.

Printers got even smarter, and could draw pictures, print images, and use all sorts of fonts. They started using complex languages (45.14) to print, which made dealing with them more complex but at least somewhat more consistent. People wrote tools to convert text (45.7) so it could be printed.

Webster defines typesetting as "the process of setting material in type or into a form to be used in printing," literally, the setting of type into a printing press. As computers have gotten more sophisticated, it has come to include the formatting of text and images to send to typesetting machines and then, later, smart printers. These days, your average printer is pretty smart and can handle everything the typesetters of old could do and more. Windows systems provide What You See Is What You Get (WYSIWYG, pronounced whiz-ee-wig) editors as a matter of course, most of which do all of their typesetting without any user intervention (and often badly, to boot).

On Unix, typesetting generally involves describing the formatting you want using a formatting language and then processing the source file to generate something that a printer can understand. There are a variety of tools and languages that do this, with various purposes, strengths, and weaknesses. Many formatting languages are markup languages, that is, they introduce formatting information by "marking up" the text you want formatted.

There is an entire science (and art) of typography that we won't try to get into here. My personal favorite books on the subject are Robert Bringhurst's *The Elements of Typographic Style* for general typography and Donald Knuth's *Digital Typography* for issues of typesetting with computers.

What we will try to cover are formatting languages (articles 45.12 and 45.13), printer languages (article 45.14), and ways to use Unix to get those formatting languages out to your printer usefully (articles 45.15 through 45.17).

Relatively recently, open source WYSIWYG tools have become available for Unix. OpenOffice, available at *http://www.openoffice.org*, is a good example. OpenOffice does its own typesetting behind the scenes and dumps out PostScript. If you don't have a PostScript printer and you're interested in using something like OpenOffice, article 45.18 might help.

—*DJPH*

45.11 A Bit of Unix Typesetting History

Unix was one of the first operating systems to provide the capability to drive a typesetter. *troff* is both a markup language and a tool for generating typesetter output.

Originally, *troff* was designed to drive a device called a C/A/T phototypesetter, and thus it generated a truly frightening collection of idiosyncratic commands. For a while, there were several version of *troff* and *troff*-related tools, including tools to translate C/A/T output into something useful, versions of *troff* that output slightly saner things than C/A/T, and so forth. It was all very confusing.

Most systems these days still have a version of *troff*, often GNU's *groff*, which outputs PostScript and other device-independent formats. Unix manpages are still written in *nroff*, a related tool that takes the same input and spits out ASCII-formatted text, using the *man* macro package. However, most people don't use *troff* and its related tools for general text formatting much any more.

So why do we care about *troff*? *The Jargon Dictionary* (Version 4.2.2) has this to say:

> *troff* /T'rof/ or /trof/ n.
>
> The gray eminence of Unix text processing; a formatting and phototypesetting program, written originally in PDP-11 assembler and then in barely-structured early C by the late Joseph Ossanna, modeled after the earlier ROFF which was in turn modeled after the Multics and CTSS program RUNOFF by Jerome Saltzer (that name came from the expression "to run off a copy"). A companion program, nroff, formats output for terminals and line printers.
>
> In 1979, Brian Kernighan modified troff so that it could drive phototypesetters other than the Graphic Systems CAT. His paper describing that work ("A Type-setter-independent troff," AT&T CSTR #97) explains troff's durability. After discussing the program's "obvious deficiencies—a rebarbative input syntax, mysterious and undocumented properties in some areas, and a voracious appetite for computer resources" and noting the ugliness and extreme hairiness of the code and internals, Kernighan concludes:
>
> > None of these remarks should be taken as denigrating Ossanna's accomplishment with TROFF. It has proven a remarkably robust tool, taking unbelievable abuse from a variety of preprocessors and being forced into uses that were never conceived of in the original design, all with considerable grace under fire.
>
> The success of TEX and desktop publishing systems have reduced troff's relative importance, but this tribute perfectly captures the strengths that secured troff a place in hacker folklore; indeed, it could be taken more generally as an indication of those qualities of good programs that, in the long run, hackers most admire.

—*DJPH*

45.12 Typesetting Manpages: nroff

The definitive documentation system for every Unix is manpages. (Much GNU software is documented fully in *info* pages instead, but manpages are so foundational that even those packages generally provide some sort of manpage.) What is a manpage, then?

A manpage is a text file, marked up with *nroff* commands, specifically using the man macro package. (Well, technically, using the *tmac.an* standard macro package—*t/nroff* takes a *–m* option to specify which *tmac.** macro package to use. Thus, *man* uses *nroff –man*.) A simple manpage (in this case, the *yes*(1) manpage from FreeBSD) looks something like this:

```
.Dd June 6, 1993
.Dt YES 1
.Os BSD 4
.Sh NAME
.Nm yes
.Nd be repetitively affirmative
.Sh SYNOPSIS
.Nm
.Op Ar expletive
.Sh DESCRIPTION
.Nm Yes
outputs
.Ar expletive ,
or, by default,
.Dq y ,
forever.
.Sh HISTORY
The
.Nm
command appeared in
.At 32v .
```

This collection of difficult-to-read *nroff* commands, when formatted by *nroff* via the *man* command on my FreeBSD machine, looks something like this:

```
YES(1)                 FreeBSD General Commands Manual              YES(1)


NAME
     yes - be repetitively affirmative

SYNOPSIS
     yes [expletive]

DESCRIPTION
     Yes outputs expletive, or, by default, "y", forever.

HISTORY
     The yes command appeared in Version 32V AT&T UNIX.

4th Berkeley Distribution       June 6, 1993                            1
```

The various *nroff/man* macros allow you to define things such as the name of the command, the short description of what it does, the list of arguments, and so forth, and formats it all into the standard look of a manpage. To write your own manpages, take a look at existing manpages for examples, and read the *man*(1) and *man*(7) manpages.

—*DJPH*

45.13 Formatting Markup Languages— troff, L^AT_EX, HTML, and So On

Article 45.12 shows an example of a simple formatting markup language; the one used by *man* via *nroff*. Don't laugh—it may seem arcane, but it is fairly simple. Like all markup languages, it attempts to abstract out certain things, to allow you to describe what you'd like the end result to look like. Manpages are simple to describe, so the markup language for them is relatively simple.

Full *troff* is somewhat more complex, both because it allows expressing far more complex ideas, and because it allows definition of macros to extend the core markup language. Similarly, TEX (pronounced "tek") is essentially a programming language for typesetting. It provides a very thorough model of typesetting and the ability to, essentially, write programs that generate the output you want.

Available on top of TEX is L^AT_EX (pronounced "lah-tek" or "lay-tek"), a complex macro package focused on general document writing. It allows you to describe the general structure of your document and let L^AT_EX (and underneath, TEX) sort out the "proper" way to typeset that structure. This sort of markup is very different to deal with than working in a WYSIWYG word processor, where you have to do all of the formatting yourself. As an example, a simple L^AT_EX document looks something like this (taken from *The Not So Short Introduction to L^AT_EX2e*):

```
\documentclass[a4paper,11pt]{article}
% define the title
\author{H.~Partl}
\title{Minimalism}
\begin{document}
% generates the title
\maketitle
% insert the table of contents
\tableofcontents
\section{Start}
Well, and here begins my lovely article.
\section{End}
\ldots{} and here it ends.
\end{document}
```

Much like the *nroff* input earlier, this describes the structure of the document by inserting commands into the text at appropriate places. The LyX editor (*http://www.lyx.org*) provides what they call What You See Is What You *Mean* (WYSIWYM, or whiz-ee-whim) editing by sitting on top of L^AT_EX. Lots of information about T_EX and L^AT_EX is available at the T_EX Users' Group web site, *http://www.tug.org*. T_EX software is available via the Comprehensive T_EX Archive Network, or CTAN, at *http://www.ctan.org*. I strongly recommend the teT_EX distribution as a simple way to get a complete installation of everything you need in one swell foop.

In contrast, while HTML is also a markup language, its markup is focused primarily on display and hypertext references rather than internal document structure. HTML is an *application* of SGML; you probably know about it already because it is the primary display markup language used on the web. The following is essentially the same as the sample L^AT_EX document, but marked up using HTML formatting:

```
<html>
<head>
<title>Minimalism</title>
</head>
<body>
<h1>Minimalism</h1>
...table of contents...
<h2>Start</h2>
<p>Well, and here begins my lovely article.</p>
<h2>End</h2>
<p>&hellip; and here it ends.</p>
</body>
</html>
```

Other markup languages common on Unixes include DocBook, which is also an application of SGML or XML, and in which a lot of Linux documentation is written, and texinfo, the source language of info pages, in which most GNU documentation is written. The manuscript for this edition of *Unix Power Tools* is written in a variant of SGML-based DocBook, in fact.

—DJPH

45.14 Printing Languages—PostScript, PCL, DVI, PDF

Printing languages, also sometimes called page description languages, are representations of exactly what needs to be on the screen or printed page. They are generally a collection of drawing commands that programs can generate, often with extra features to make drawing complex pictures or doing fancy things with text easier.

PostScript was developed by Adobe in the early 1980s to provide some sort of generic page description language. It is a fairly complete language; I've written complex PostScript programs by hand. This makes it much easier to write software that can generate PostScript output. Modern *troff*s can generate PostScript, and *ghostscript* can be used to process PostScript into printer-specific output for certain non-PostScript printers, so PostScript is a very useful output form.

Printer Command Language, or PCL, was originally developed by Hewlett-Packard, also in the early 1980s, to provide a generic printer language for their entire range of printers. Early versions were very simple, but PCL 3 was sophisticated enough that other printer manufacturers started to emulate it, and it became a de facto standard. PCL's more current incarnations are quite flexible and capable. Incidentally, *ghostscript* can turn PostScript into PCL, and most printers that can't speak PostScript can speak some form of PCL these days. My primary printer these days speaks PCL 5E, and I use it from both Windows machines and Unix machines.

DVI stands for "device independent" and is the primary output from TEX (and thus LATEX). Like PostScript, it's a generic language for describing the printed page. There are converters that convert DVI into PostScript, PCL and PDF.

PDF is Adobe's successor to PostScript. PDF has a special place on the web, because it's been promoted as a way to distribute documents on the web and have them displayed consistently in a wide variety of environments, something not possible in HTML. This consistency is possible for the same reasons any page description language can provide it: the focus of such a language is on describing exactly what the page should look like rather than being human readable or editable, like most markup languages. However, Adobe has provided Acrobat Reader free for multiple platforms and promoted PDF extensively, so it is the de facto standard for page description languages on the web these days.

—*DJPH*

45.15 Converting Text Files into a Printing Language

Article 45.7 introduced one tool that can convert plain text into PostScript for printing. In general, if your printer isn't an old text-only printer and you want to be able to print text files, you'll need some sort of filter (or filters) to convert the text into something useful.

If your printer supports PostScript, tools like *a2ps* and *enscript* (45.7) can do what you need. If your printer supports PCL or another printer language, you may want to add *ghostscript* to the mix. *ghostscript* can read PostScript and PDF and output correct representations to a variety of printers. Incidentally, *ghostscript* can also do a host of other useful things, like create PDFs from PostScript and the like.

Here's an example of using *enscript*, *ghostscript*, and *lpr* to print the *background.txt* file to my printer (an HP LaserJet 6L):

```
% enscript -2Gr background.txt -o background.ps
% gs -q -dNOPAUSE -sDEVICE=ljet4 -sOutputFile=background.lj4 background.ps -c
quit
% lpr background.lj4
% rm background.lj4 background.ps
```

–2Gr tells *enscript* that I want two-up pages with fancy headers, and *–o* sends the output to *background.ps* (remember that *enscript* generates PostScript). *–q* tells *gs* to run quietly. *–dNOPAUSE* disables *ghostscript*'s usual behaviour of pausing and prompting at the end of each page. *–sDEVICE=ljet4* says to create output for a ljet4 device. *–sOutputFile=background.lj4* redirects the output of *ghostscript* to *background.lj4*, and *–c quit* says to quit once *background.ps* is done. Then we use *lpr* to spool the now-ready output file, delete the temporary files, and we're all done.

Seems like sort of a pain, but it does show all of the steps needed to get that output to go to the printer properly. Article 45.17 shows how to arrange for most of that to be done for you by the spooler automatically.

—DJPH

45.16 Converting Typeset Files into a Printing Language

Article 45.15 showed the steps necessary to convert plain text into something printable. Generally the steps involved are similar for a typeset source file, with perhaps an extra step or two.

troff generates PostScript by default in most installations these days, or it can be made to easily enough. GNU *troff* (*groff*) can also generate PCL, DVI, and HTML by using the appropriate *–T* option.

TEX generates DVI; the teTEX package includes *dvips* to convert DVI into PostScript, *dvilj4* to convert it into PCL, *dvipdf* to convert it into PDF, and several others.

HTML can be converted into PostScript using *html2ps*.

An example of using LATEX, *dvilj4*, and *lpr* to print the *article.tex* file to my printer (an HP LaserJet 6L):

```
% latex article.tex
% dvilj4 article.dvi
% lpr article.lj
% rm article.lj article.dvi
```

This time it's slightly simpler than the example in article 45.15, because the default options all do what we want. Even so, it can be made even simpler; article 45.17 shows how.

—*DJPH*

45.17 Converting Source Files Automagically Within the Spooler

Articles 45.15 and 45.16 showed what sorts of steps are required to get files into a printable form. They seem tedious, however, and computers are really quite good at tedium, so how can we make the spooler do all this for us automatically?

There are a couple of options. One of the more well-known is *apsfilter*, which is a set of filter scripts designed to work with *lpd* to automatically convert incoming source files to an appropriate output format before dumping them to the printer. Extensive information is available at *http://www.apsfilter.org*, and *apsfilter* has its own automatic setup scripts, but I'll give a quick overview to give you an idea of what configuring *lpd*'s filters looks like.

In article 45.9, we used an input filter trick to print to a Samba printer by putting a if entry in the *printcap* for that printer. if stands for "input filter," and there are several other kinds of filters available in standard *lpd*, including a ditroff filter, a Fortran filter (!), and an output filter.

apsfilter installs itself as the input filter for any printer it manages, and looks at the source file. It decides based on a number of pieces of information what kind of source file it is, automatically processes it with the right set of programs, and poof, you have correct output coming out of your printer. There's a reason this kind of tool is called a "magic filter" (and why the title of this chapter says "Automagically"). Having a magic filter installed makes life so much easier.

If you look at your printcap once *apsfilter* is installed, you'll notice this entry (or something much like it):

```
lp|local line printer:\
    ...
    :if=/usr/local/sbin/apsfilter:\
    ...
```

That's all it takes to hook into *lpd* and tell the spooler to give *apsfilter* a shot at the text on the way through. *apsfilter* looks at the incoming file and its configuration for the printer queue and converts the source into the appropriate printer language using whatever filter or set of filters are needed.

Other magic filters include LPD-O-Matic and magicfilter. *http://www.linuxprinting.org* has all sorts of information about this and other printing subjects. Don't be fooled by the name—much of the information it provides can help you with printing on any Unix system, not just Linux.

—DJPH

45.18 The Common Unix Printing System (CUPS)

The Common Unix Printing System (CUPS) is a full network-capable printing package available for a wide variety of Unix platforms. From their web page:

> CUPS is available at:
>
> *http://www.cups.org/*
>
> CUPS provides a portable printing layer for UNIX-based operating systems. It has been developed by Easy Software Products to promote a standard printing solution for all UNIX vendors and users. CUPS provides the System V and Berkeley command-line interfaces.
>
> CUPS uses the Internet Printing Protocol ("IPP") as the basis for managing print jobs and queues. The Line Printer Daemon ("LPD") Server Message Block ("SMB"), and AppSocket (a.k.a. JetDirect) protocols are also supported with reduced functionality. CUPS adds network printer browsing and PostScript Printer Description ("PPD") based printing options to support real-world printing under UNIX.

CUPS is headed towards becoming the Linux standard for printing, and it is an easy way to configure all your printing tools at once regardless of your platform. Visit their web page for extensive information.

—DJPH

45.19 The Portable Bitmap Package

There are dozens of formats used for graphics files across the computer industry. There are *tiff* files, *PICT* files, and *gif* files. There are different formats for displaying on different hardware, different formats for printing on different printers, and then there are the internal formats used by graphics programs. This means that importing a graphics file from one platform to another (or from one program to another) can be a large undertaking, requiring a filter written specifically to convert from one format to the next.

netpbm

The *netpbm* package can be used to convert between a wide variety of graphics formats. *netpbm* evolved from the original Portable Bitmap Package, *pbmplus*, written by Jef Poskanzer. A group of *pbmplus* users on the Internet cooperated to upgrade *pbmplus*; the result was *netpbm*. *netpbm* has relatively recently seen some active development again on SourceForge, and its current home page is *http://netpbm.sourceforge.net*.

The idea behind *pbm* is to use a set of very basic graphics formats that (almost) all formats can be converted into and then converted back from. This is much simpler than having converters to and from each individual format. These formats are known as *pbm*, *pgm*, and *ppm*: the portable bitmap, graymap, and pixmap formats. (A bitmap is a two-dimensional representation of an image; a graymap has additional information encoded that gives grayscale information for each bit; a pixmap encodes color information for each bit.) The name *pnm* is a generic name for all three portable interchange formats (with the *n* standing for "*any*"), and programs that work with all three are said to be "anymap" programs.

The *netpbm* package contains well over a hundred conversion programs. There are three basic kinds of programs:

- Programs that convert a graphics file to one of the *pnm* formats. For example, if I had a *tiff* file and wanted to convert it to PostScript, I might start the process by using *tifftopnm*:

    ```
    % tifftopnm Hobbes.tiff > Hobbes.pnm
    ```

- Programs that convert from one of the *pnm* formats to another format. For example, if I wanted to convert the *Hobbes.pnm* file directly to PostScript, I could use *pnmtops*:

    ```
    % pnmtops Hobbes.pnm > Hobbes.ps
    ```

- Programs used to manipulate the image in *pnm* format. For example, if I wanted to crop the image, I could use *pnmcut* before I converted the file to PostScript and printed it:

    ```
    % tifftopnm Hobbes.tiff > Hobbes.pnm
    % pnmcut 10 10 200 200 Hobbes.pnm > Hobbes.cut
    % pnmtops Hobbes.cut > Hobbes.ps
    % lpr Hobbes.ps
    ```

    Or, on one command line (and without cluttering your disk with intermediary files):

    ```
    % tifftopnm Hobbes.tiff | pnmcut 10 10 200 200 | pnmtops | lpr
    ```

I frequently like to create X11 (1.22) bitmaps out of pictures in newspapers or magazines. The way I do this is first to scan the picture in on a Macintosh and save it as *tiff* or *PICT* format. Then I *ftp* (1.21) the file to our Unix system and convert it to *pnm* format, and then use *pbmtoxbm* to convert it to X bitmap format. If the picture is too big, I use *pnmscale* on the intermediary *pnm* file. If the picture isn't right-side-up, I can use *pnmrotate* and sometimes *pnmflip* before converting the *pnm* file to X11 bitmap format.

There are far too many programs provided with the *netpbm* package to discuss in detail, and some of these formats are ones that you've probably never even heard of. However, if you need to fiddle with image files (or, now, video files!), *netpbm* almost certainly has a converter for it. Take a peek through the documentation sometime.

—LM and JP

46

Connectivity

46.1 TCP/IP—IP Addresses and Ports

TCP/IP networking is a part of the Open Systems Interconnection (OSI) Model. Much like you can string together lots of little single-purpose Unix tools to do complex tasks, the OSI Model is made up of specific single-purpose layers that work together. Each layer builds on the layers below. Layers 1 and 2 are concerned with hardware; physical standards such as required voltages and low-level protocols like Ethernet reside there. Layers 3 and 4 are networking layers, which this article introduces. Layers 5 through 7 are application layers, where networking interfaces such as BSD sockets and applications such as web browsers, telnet clients, and diagnostic tools live.

For most Unixes, the fundamentals of networking (once you get past the network device drivers) are the Layer 3 Internet Protocol (IP) and a Layer 4 protocol on top of it, either the Transport Control Protocol (TCP), the User Datagram Protocol (UDP), or the IP Control Message Protocol (ICMP). These four protocols are so commonly treated as one unit that you'll often see them referred to together as TCP/IP.

Internet Protocol (IP)

IP's job is to get small chunks of data, called packets, from one machine to another. It is a "best effort" protocol; that is, it makes its best effort to deliver each packet to the right host, and if it can't, it simply drops the packet on the floor. It may seem like losing bits of your data would be a bad thing, but it turns out that this feature is part of what allows the Internet to route traffic around problems; higher-level protocols and applications notice that packets are being dropped and resend them, sometimes through better routes.

IP identifies machines through *IP addresses*. Every machine that wants to communicate with another machine via TCP/IP must have a unique IP address, unless it's using Network Address Translation (NAT) (46.1). When you dial up your ISP with a modem, your ISP assigns you a dynamic IP address, good for that modem session. When you have a dedicated broadband connection, often your ISP will assign you a small block of static IP addresses to use as you like. Each ISP is in turn assigned large blocks of IP addresses for them to dole out to their users, and traffic on the Internet travels from ISP to ISP based on the addresses they hold.

The current standard version of IP is Version 4 (IPv4), which uses 32-bit addresses. With the explosion of the Internet, addresses are being used up at quite an impressive rate; remember that normally every single machine connected to the Internet needs its own IP address. Version 6 (IPv6) is, at the time of this writing, a proposed standard that uses 128-bit addresses. For the purposes of this book, we'll gloss over the differences, since they mostly don't matter at this level. Our examples will use IPv4 addresses, since that's what you're most likely to be dealing with for a little while yet.

Layer 4 Protocols: TCP, UDP, and ICMP

TCP, UDP, and ICMP all "sit on top" of IP; that is, they use IP to actually deliver the packets.

TCP's job is to provide ordered and guaranteed delivery. Ordered delivery means that the application at the other end of the TCP connection reads data in the same order as it was sent. Guaranteed delivery means that TCP keeps track of which packets arrived at the other end and resends packets that were dropped. Together, these two characteristics provide a network communication mechanism that acts very much like a Unix pipe from an application's point of view; you simply write bytes in one end and they come out the other. Many common network applications sit on top of TCP and use these services, including telnet, HTTP servers and web browsers, SSH (46.6), and email (46.8).

UDP provides application access to the basic delivery mechanism of IP and adds port addressing (see below). Some applications don't need guaranteed delivery and want the lower overhead of UDP, or want the low-level control of network error recovery UDP can provide, or need to be able to do certain kinds of broadcast. Services like DNS (46.9) and DHCP (46.10) use UDP rather than TCP, as do many Internet games.

Both TCP and UDP provide addressing of their own above and beyond IP addresses; these addresses are called *ports*. Generally, simply getting a packet to a machine isn't quite enough; if you want two programs to communicate, they need a rendezvous point; there can be a lot of programs running on the destination machine, and TCP and UDP need to know to which program packets should be delivered. An IP address and a port provide the means for two programs to hook up and start talking. Every communication needs a port on each machine; one side "listens" on a well-known port and the other side "connects" to that port, generating a random port of its own.

Ports are represented by an integer number. Ports below 1024 are usually accessible only by programs running as root and are thus mostly reserved for system services and the like. /etc/services (46.2) lists most of the well-known ports used by the main system services.

Finally, ICMP provides diagnostic and traffic control messages. ICMP is primarily used by applications such as ping and traceroute (46.4) to diagnose problems, check network status, and the like. Routers can also use ICMP to control traffic.

—DJPH

46.2 /etc/services Is Your Friend

After you've been dealing with Internet services for a while, you come to remember certain well-known port numbers off of the top of your head. SMTP (46.8) is port 25, HTTP is port 80, and so on. However, unless your memory is far better than mine, you won't remember them all.

Luckily, that's part of what /etc/services is for. It's a database of well-known ports with symbolic names; any program that can take a port number should be able to take the appropriate symbolic name instead. If you want to make sure your SMTP server is up, the following two commands are equivalent:

```
% telnet localhost 25
% telnet localhost smtp
```

The definitive database of well-known ports is currently available at *http://www.iana.org/assignments/port-numbers/*. On most Unixes, /etc/services is just a snapshot taken at the time that version of that Unix was released. When installing new services, often you'll want to tweak your local copy of /etc/services to reflect the new service, if it's not already there, even if only as a reminder.

The format of the /etc/services is simple:

```
service name      port/protocol       aliases
```

Comments within the file start with a pound sign (#). As an example, a few common entries from /etc/services:

```
ftp-data     20/tcp    #File Transfer [Default Data]
ftp-data     20/udp    #File Transfer [Default Data]
ftp          21/tcp    #File Transfer [Control]
ftp          21/udp    #File Transfer [Control]
ssh          22/tcp    #Secure Shell Login
ssh          22/udp    #Secure Shell Login
telnet       23/tcp
```

```
telnet          23/udp
smtp            25/tcp      mail        #Simple Mail Transfer
smtp            25/udp      mail        #Simple Mail Transfer
```

—*DJPH*

46.3 Status and Troubleshooting

ifconfig can be used to configure network devices (44.8), but it also can be used to see the current network device configuration. *ifconfig –a* is very useful for this. Here's some sample output on a FreeBSD machine:

```
% ifconfig -a
rl0: flags=8843<UP,BROADCAST,RUNNING,SIMPLEX,MULTICAST> mtu 1500
        inet 192.168.1.1 netmask 0xffffffc0 broadcast 192.168.1.255
        inet 192.168.1.5 netmask 0xffffffff broadcast 192.168.1.255
        inet 192.168.1.6 netmask 0xffffffff broadcast 192.168.1.255
        inet 192.168.1.7 netmask 0xffffffff broadcast 192.168.1.255
        ether 0a:5c:da:a3:53:11
        media: autoselect (100baseTX <full-duplex>) status: active
        supported media: autoselect 100baseTX <full-duplex> 100baseTX 10baseT/UTP
        <full-duplex> 10baseT/UTP 100baseTX <hw-loopback>
lo0: flags=8049<UP,LOOPBACK,RUNNING,MULTICAST> mtu 16384
        inet 127.0.0.1 netmask 0xff000000
```

This shows two network devices: rl0, which is an Ethernet card, and lo0, which is the loopback device. rl0's primary IP address is 192.168.1.1, and it has aliases (that is, it also answers to) 192.168.1.5 through 192.168.1.6. This also shows me that both network devices believe that they're actively sending and receiving packets (UP) and shows various options set on each device.

The output on Linux is slightly different, but similar enough to easily find the same information. Linux also adds a few statistics to its *ifconfig* output that otherwise require a *netstat* to see. Especially useful are packets received and transmitted:

```
eth0      Link encap:Ethernet  HWaddr 0a:5c:da:a3:53:11
          inet addr:192.168.1.1  Bcast:192.168.1.255  Mask:255.255.255.0
          UP BROADCAST RUNNING MULTICAST  MTU:1500  Metric:1
          RX packets:18999386 errors:28965 dropped:0 overruns:0 frame:28965
          TX packets:33955631 errors:0 dropped:0 overruns:0 carrier:0
          collisions:29132 txqueuelen:100
          RX bytes:1496731954 (1.3 GiB)  TX bytes:2477239809 (2.3 GiB)
          Interrupt:10 Base address:0xda00

lo        Link encap:Local Loopback
          inet addr:127.0.0.1  Mask:255.0.0.0
          UP LOOPBACK RUNNING  MTU:3924  Metric:1
          RX packets:107211318 errors:0 dropped:0 overruns:0 frame:0
          TX packets:107211318 errors:0 dropped:0 overruns:0 carrier:0
          collisions:0 txqueuelen:0
          RX bytes:2880669120 (2.6 GiB)  TX bytes:2880669120 (2.6 GiB)
```

Note that on Linux 2.4 kernels, *ipconfig* and *route* (see below) are being phased out in favor of *iproute2*. See the manpage for *iproute2* if you're on a 2.4 machine and want to be up to date.

netstat can be used to get a variety of useful information. By default, *netstat* displays a list of active sockets, thus showing you what is currently connected to your machine (and what your machine is currently connected to). *netstat –r* can show your routing tables, which is particularly useful when trying to understand why your machine can't seem to talk to anything. If the interface appears to be up, and you can ping (46.4) other machines on your local network, but you can't get out, check your routing tables. It's quite possible that you don't have a default route, or your default route doesn't point to your gateway (46.11). For a private LAN running NAT (46.11), your routing table might look something like this (the *–n* option says to show IP addresses instead of attempting to resolve them into hostnames):

```
% netstat -rn
Routing tables

Internet:
Destination        Gateway          Flags    Refs    Use     Netif Expire
default            192.168.1.1      UGSc     17      543792  rl0
127.0.0.1          127.0.0.1        UH       2       2869882 lo0
192.168.1.0/24     link#1           UC       0       0       rl0 =>
```

Again, on Linux the output is slightly different but similar to interpret. The only thing to note is that 0.0.0.0 represents the default route when we use *–n*:

```
Kernel IP routing table
Destination    Gateway        Genmask        Flags  MSS Window  irtt Iface
192.168.1.0    0.0.0.0        255.255.255.0  U      0 0         0 eth0
0.0.0.0        192.168.1.1    0.0.0.0        UG     0 0         0 eth0
```

route lets you manipulate the routing table. If, for example, you didn't see the default route when you used *netstat –rn*, you could add it with:

```
% route add default 192.168.1.1
```

route allows a variety of ways to manipulate the routing table; see its manpage for details. Note that Linux's *route* has a syntax for some commands that's slightly different than any other *route*.

Finally, *dig* allows you to easily make very specific DNS (46.9) queries. For example, to find out information about *www.oreilly.com*:

```
% dig www.oreilly.com
...
;; ANSWER SECTION:
www.oreilly.com.       6H IN A      209.204.146.22

;; AUTHORITY SECTION:
oreilly.com.           6H IN NS     ns.oreilly.com.
oreilly.com.           6H IN NS     ns1.sonic.net.
...
```

This shows us the address (A) record and the nameservers (NS) that have authority over this particular address. If we want to find out the hostname for that IP address, we can do this:

```
% dig -x 209.204.146.22
;; ANSWER SECTION:
...
22.146.204.209.in-addr.arpa.  6H IN PTR  www.oreilly.com.

;; AUTHORITY SECTION:
146.204.209.in-addr.arpa.  6H IN NS  ns.oreilly.com.
146.204.209.in-addr.arpa.  6H IN NS  ns1.sonic.net.
...
```

This automatically deals with the details of reverse DNS lookups for us and shows us the pointer (PTR) record for that IP address, which tells us the canonical hostname. If we want to find out where mail should go:

```
% dig oreilly.com mx
...
;; ANSWER SECTION:
oreilly.com.          6H IN MX      20 smtp2.oreilly.com.

;; AUTHORITY SECTION:
oreilly.com.          6H IN NS      ns.oreilly.com.
oreilly.com.          6H IN NS      ns1.sonic.net.
...
```

This shows us the mail exchanger (MX) record, which is where we ought to be sending mail. Any information stored in DNS can be found out with the right *dig* query; browse the manpage to get an idea.

—*DJPH*

46.4 Where, Oh Where Did That Packet Go?

ping is a very simple tool and often the first used to diagnose a network problem. *ping* sends one or more ICMP (46.1) Echo Request messages to a particular IP address. If there is a machine at that IP address listening for ICMP messages (and no firewall filtering out packets in the middle), *ping* gets back Echo Reply messages, thus telling you that basic IP communication is functional between the two machines. If you can't *ping* something close by and you know you don't have a firewall (46.12) filtering out your packets, it's generally not worth trying anything more complex; start looking for interfaces down or routing problems (46.3) or, possibly, unplugged cables or the like.

traceroute does what you might expect from the name: it traces the route between your machine and another machine, using ICMP messages, and shows you each step of the way. Sometimes, when you can't get to another machine that's far away, you can use *traceroute* to see what's going on.

mtr stands for Matt's *traceroute* and is a more sophisticated *traceroute*. Not only does it show you each hop along the way, but it also sends multiple messages and gives you an ongoing display of latency at each hop. I use *mtr* instead of *traceroute* pretty exclusively. It's available at *http://www.bitwizard.nl/mtr/*, or your Unix may have a binary package of it available.

For serious network debugging, take a look at *tcpdump* and *ethereal*. *tcpdump* can take apart packets as they go by and show you what's going on in excruciating detail, and *ethereal* provides a nice GUI on top of *tcpdump*.

—DJPH

46.5 The Director of Operations: inetd

inetd is the primary manager of Internet services on most Unix installations. Its job is to listen on a selection of ports (46.1) and start up the appropriate server when a connection comes in. This frees servers that run under *inetd* from having to deal directly with networking issues and sockets.

inetd is configured via */etc/inetd.conf*, which lists all the ports *inetd* should manage, the server associated with each port, and any special options for that server. For specific details, read the manpage, *inetd.conf*(5). As an example, here are a few fairly standard entries from *inetd.conf* on my FreeBSD system:

```
ftp     stream tcp nowait       root   /usr/libexec/ftpd      ftpd -l
telnet  stream tcp nowait       root   /usr/libexec/telnetd   telnetd
finger  stream tcp nowait/3/10  nobody /usr/libexec/fingerd   fingerd -s
tftp    dgram  udp wait         nobody /usr/libexec/tftpd     tftpd /tftpboot
```

A common package included in many *inetd* distributions (and easily added to others) is called *tcp_wrappers*. *tcp_wrappers* allows you to create access rules to control incoming connections (generally stored in */etc/hosts.allow*) and deny connections from unauthorized hosts. This can be very handy even for machines behind a firewall (46.12), as it provides extra security by guaranteeing that certain kind of connections will not be allowed into your machine. As an example, my home firewall allows SMTP (46.8) and SSH (46.6) connections in, but my *hosts.allow* denies connections from hosts that cannot be reverse resolved (46.9), thus requiring a certain level of legitimacy before my machine will talk to a host.

—DJPH

46.6 Secure Shell (SSH)

telnet was the original application for connecting to a remote machine via the Internet. (*rsh* was developed as a quick hack because *telnet* wasn't quite ready, and so became popular enough to be included in distributions going forward, but *telnet* was always supposed to be the "real" application.) In its normal mode, *telnet* connects to an *inetd* (46.5)–managed daemon called *telnetd*, which manages the login process.

Unfortunately, the login process happens entirely in cleartext, as does all interaction with the remote shell program. Anyone tapping into the connection could get access to the user's password and thus gain illicit access to the remote system. To prevent this, Secure Shell (SSH) was developed. SSH uses Secure Sockets Layer (SSL), the same security mechanism that web browsers use. All interactions between your machine and the remote machine are encrypted, thus protecting your passwords and any other sensitive information. Its syntax is much like *rsh*'s:

```
% ssh gabriel
```
Logs into gabriel using your local username.
```
% ssh deb@bits.oreilly.com
```
Logs into bits.oreilly.com using the login name deb.
```
% ssh michael ls /tmp
```
Runs ls /tmp *on michael.*
```
% ssh deb@eli grep deb /etc/passwd
```
Runs grep deb /etc/passwd *on eli, using the login name deb.*

SSL uses public key encryption, which means that connections are protected with operations based on a public/private key pair. Information encrypted with the public key can be decoded with the private key and vice versa. A server runs *sshd*, which, much like *telnetd*, accepts connections and manages the login process. (Unlike *telnetd*, *sshd* is generally not managed by *inetd*, because *sshd*'s startup is complex and thus too slow to do every single time a connection is created. Because of this limitation, *sshd* has access rules much like *tcp_wrappers'* built in—generally by just linking with *tcp_wrappers*.) Each server has its own public/private key pair, allowing a user connecting to that server to verify its identity. This allows you to be sure that someone hasn't managed to redirect your connection to their machine instead (where they could collect your password, for example).

You can also set up your own keypair using *ssh-keygen*, which will create an identity for you. Usually this identity is stored in *$HOME/.ssh/identity* (for the private key) and *$HOME/.ssh/identity.pub* (for the public key). Some newer versions of SSH have different keytypes and so use *id_rsa/id_rsa.pub*, and *id_dsa/id_dsa.pub* instead. The advantage to having an identity set up is that you can then allow that identity to log in to other machines without a password, much like *.rhosts* allowed with *rsh*, only more securely. Simply add your public key to the *$HOME/.ssh/authorized_keys* file on the remote host.

SSH also provides a simple file copy mechanism, *scp*. Login is the same as with *ssh*; identities are used if available, or password exchanges are encrypted. *scp*'s syntax is much like *cp*'s, except that an account specification can be prepended to a filename:

```
% scp gabriel:buffoon.txt .
% scp frobnitz deb@michael:/tmp
```

The first command copies *buffoon.txt* from my home directory on *gabriel* into the current directory. The second copies *frobnitz* in the current directory into *michael*'s */tmp* directory, logging in as *deb*.

I configure my machines to disallow *telnet* and *rsh* access, and I use SSH exclusively.

—DJPH

46.7 Configuring an Anonymous FTP Server

Providing an anonymous FTP server allows anyone to anonymously download (and possibly upload) files. Normally, logging into an FTP server requires an account. Anonymous FTP creates an anonymous account and carefully limits its capabilities, so that you don't have to create a full account for everyone you might want to allow access to.

An anonymous FTP connection operates within a *chroot*, that is, an isolated area (see the manpage for *chroot*(8) and *chroot*(2) for more details on what a chroot is). A few basic things need to be provided within the chroot: a copy of *ls*, minimal versions of */etc/passwd* (sans passwords) and */etc/group* to allow *ls* to display files properly, and so forth.

Some platforms provide a simple anonymous FTP setup. RedHat has an RPM called anonftp-* that installs a proper chroot. FreeBSD's install tool can set up an anonymous FTP chroot for you. Check your platform documentation to see if it has a simple setup for you. Failing that, refer to CERT's guide on safely setting up anonymous FTP at *http://www.cert.org/tech_tips/anonymous_ftp_config.html*.

—DJPH

46.8 Mail—SMTP, POP, and IMAP

Email is one of the most well-known and commonly used Internet services. The core of Internet email is the Simple Message Transfer Protocol (SMTP), which defines a simple, extensible mechanism by which hosts can exchange mail messages. SMTP is spoken by programs known as Message Transfer Agents (MTAs);

sendmail is the most well known of these and is included with the vast majority of Unixes. *qmail*, *postfix*, and *exim* are other common MTAs (I use *qmail* on all of my systems). Configuring an MTA generally involves telling it your default domain name for outgoing email, setting up whether it allows relaying and if so, under what limits (see below), possibly setting up spam filtering, and the like. It may also involve setting up MX records (46.9) for your domain(s).

Relaying is when an MTA allows someone to connect and send an email to an email address not served by that MTA. If you want to allow someone on your local machine or local subnet to send outgoing email via your MTA, this is a very good thing. An *open relay* allows *anyone* to send outgoing email, and this allows spammers to use your machine to send their spam. As you might guess, this is a Very Bad Thing. All MTAs have ways of limiting relaying so that local users can send email but spammers can't use your machine. Check your MTA's documentation, or take a peek at *http://www.mail-abuse.org* for more information.

Mail User Agents (MUAs or just UAs) provide the interface between users and MTAs. On Unix, these include programs such as *mail*, *mailx*, *elm*, and *mutt*, all of which work directly with the filesystem. Webmail clients are also MUAs, but they run under a webserver to provide networked access to mail. Often, though, you want to be able to use a MUA on another workstation that may or may not be a Unix machine, in which case you need some sort of MUA proxy to manage the mail and communicate with the remote MUA.

Post Office Protocol (POP or POP3) and Internet Message Access Protocol (IMAP) are two different ways of providing access to remote MUAs. POP is focused on retrieving messages from a mail server and having the MUA store them, where IMAP is focused on managing mail on a mail server remotely rather than copying it to the client machine. Freely available POP servers include *qmail-pop3d* (which comes with *qmail*) and *qpopper* (the Berkeley POP3 server, now maintained by Qualcomm), along with a wide variety of others, depending what you're looking for. Freely available IMAP servers include *courier-imap* and the University of Washington IMAP server (*imap-uw*).

—*DJPH*

46.9 Domain Name Service (DNS)

Usually, when you want to refer to a machine, you want to use its *hostname*, rather than having to remember its IP address (46.1). However, IP only understands IP addresses, not hostnames, so some mapping from hostname to IP address is necessary. */etc/hosts* provides a simple mapping from hostname to IP address, but it has the disadvantage of being local to your machine. It would be impossible to maintain an */etc/hosts* file that actually reflected the constantly changing reality of the Internet. (In fact, historically, */etc/hosts* was a list of every single machine on the Internet, downloaded regularly from a central source. This system broke down when the number of hosts on the Internet surpassed a few hundred.)

The Domain Name Service (DNS) is a specification for a loosely coordinated, distributed database mapping host names to IP addresses. Generally, it's implemented by the Berkeley Internet Name Daemon (*bind*), running on hundreds of hosts. Each DNS server has authority over a small piece of the database, and coordination is accomplished through delegation. The *root servers* know which DNS servers have authority over the *top-level domains* (TLDs), such as .com, .net, .org, and so forth. Each of those DNS servers knows which DNS server has authority over each subdomain, and so on. DNS servers also cache information, so that a full, time-intensive search through the large distributed database isn't necessary every time you want to access a host's IP address.

DNS also stores other records, including Mail Exchanger (MX) records for routing mail (46.8). MTAs use MX records when resolving where to send an email by looking up MX records on the domain for which the email is destined. Typically a DNS administrator creates an address record for mail.*domain.com*, points it at a machine configured to catch mail for *domain.com*, and then adds an MX record pointing to mail.*domain.com* on each host within *domain.com*.

DNS can affect you in a few obvious ways. The first is that you might need to diagnose problems if for some reason your machine can't look up hostnames. *host* is a simple tool for making DNS queries. *host hostname.domain.com* will return the IP address for hostname.domain.com. While *host* can do slightly more complicated queries, I recommend *dig* (46.3) for anything more complicated than a quick query. *whois* can show you registration information for a domain; comparing this information to a *dig* on that domain can tell you if your DNS cache is stale (or if the root servers haven't been updated):

```
% whois oreilly.com
...
Registrant:
O'Reilly & Associates (OREILLY6-DOM)
   101 Morris Street
   Sebastopol, CA 95472
   US

   Domain Name: OREILLY.COM
...
   Record last updated on 20-Mar-2002.
   Record expires on 28-May-2003.
   Record created on 27-May-1997.
   Database last updated on 28-Mar-2002 15:33:00 EST.

   Domain servers in listed order:

   NS.OREILLY.COM          209.204.146.21
   NS1.SONIC.NET           208.201.224.11
```

```
% dig oreilly.com ns
...
;; ANSWER SECTION:
oreilly.com.              3h42m10s IN NS  ns2.sonic.net.
oreilly.com.              3h42m10s IN NS  ns.oreilly.com.
oreilly.com.              3h42m10s IN NS  ns1.sonic.net.
...
```

You might also want to set up a local DNS cache by configuring *bind* to resolve only. (You can also use *dnscache*, available at *http://cr.yp.to/djbdns.html*.) To do this, make sure you have *bind* installed and then put these lines into your *named.conf*:

```
options {
        ...
    allow-query { localnets; };
    allow-transfer { none; };
    allow-recursion { localnets; };
        ...
}
zone "." {
        type hint;
        file "named.root";
};

zone "0.0.127.IN-ADDR.ARPA" {
        type master;
        file "localhost.rev";
};
```

This allows machines on your local network to query this *bind* and will look up queries for them (which is what `allow-recursion` means). It also provides the normal basic root servers list (necessary for *bind* to do full DNS queries for its clients) and the reverse lookup for 127.0.0.1/localhost.

If you need to run your own DNS server, you'll want to configure *bind* to be authoritative for your domain or domains. An example is beyond the scope of this book, though; refer to the *bind* documentation or to O'Reilly's *DNS and Bind*.

—DJPH

46.10 Dynamic Host Configuration Protocol (DHCP)

Most servers have one or more static IP addresses, which are generally set in one of the boot configuration files. However, it's not uncommon to have one or more workstations on your network, and its often convenient to configure their addresses in a central place. DHCP allows workstations to dynamically discover their IP addresses.

If you have a cable modem, it's quite possible you get your IP address via DHCP. Your cable provider has a DHCP server, and any machine you plug into your cable modem becomes a DHCP client, automatically getting an IP address from your provider's DHCP server. Article 46.11 describes NAT, which can let you run multiple machines on your home network in a case like this.

To run your own DHCP server, you need a DHCP daemon. *isc-dhcpd* is available at *http://www.isc.org/products/DHCP/* and allows a variety of configurations. I have a variety of machines on my network at home, including servers with static IP addresses, workstations that use DHCP but always get the same IP address, and a few IP addresses dynamically allocated to random machines plugged into my network (handy for building a new machine or for friends visiting with their laptops).

Fixed dynamic addresses are extremely useful. Most of the normal workstations I have at home are configured to have fixed dynamic addresses: they get their IP addresses from the DHCP server, but the server recognizes each machine's Ethernet address (otherwise known as its MAC address) and hands out the same IP address each time. This allows me to have a centralized database of workstation addresses and makes configuration of those workstations trivial, while still giving me consistent IP addresses for all of my workstations.

—*DJPH*

46.11 Gateways and NAT

For two separate networks to communicate, a *gateway* is needed. A gateway has two network interfaces (two network cards, a network card and a modem, or so forth) and routes packets between the two networks as appropriate. Routers and cable modems both function as gateways.

Unix machines can also function as gateways. There are several reasons to use your Unix machine as your gateway: it is generally more flexible than the built-in gateways in cable modems and DSL routers; it can function as a firewall (46.12); and if you have a limited number of IP addresses, it can perform Network Address Translation (NAT) for you.

NAT allows the machines on your LAN to use *private addresses*, that is, the address ranges set out in RFC1918 as reserved for private networks. These include 192.168.0.0 with netmask 255.255.0.0 (also known as 192.168.0.0/16), 172.16.0.0 with netmask 255.240.0.0 (also known as 172.16.0.0/12), and 10.0.0.0 with netmask 255.0.0.0 (also known as 10.0.0.0/8). Within the private network, you can have as many IP addresses as you need. The gateway runs a NAT server, which translates all the private addresses into a single public address (the address of the public side of the gateway) on the way out and back into the correct private addresses on the way back in. If you use DHCP (46.10) to configure your workstations, you can easily configure your gateway and NAT server to be your DHCP server also and hand out private addresses to your LAN.

Note that you can really only use private NAT for workstations. Servers that need to be externally accessible will need public IP addresses. If you are using a private network on your internal network, you can configure your NAT server to map a particular public address to a particular private address, allowing access to your server while still keeping the server behind your gateway/firewall. However, for a straightforward setup, each server will still need its own distinct public IP address, plus the main public IP address for the gateway. At the very least, you will need one public static IP address for the gateway; it is possible to configure *natd* to direct specific ports on the gateway to ports on private servers. This way you can have a private web server and a private mail server and direct incoming port 80 (HTTP) requests to the web server and incoming port 25 (SMTP) requests to the mail server. Read the *natd* documentation for more details on how to do complex configuration like this.

In FreeBSD, enabling gatewaying is as simple as putting the line `gateway_enable="YES"` in your */etc/rc.conf*. Most Linux distributions provide a simple way to adjust the proper *sysctl* variable (`net/ipv4/ip_forward`) during startup as well. On other architectures you may need to recompile your kernel (44.3) to turn on IP forwarding, or it may be on by default.

Generally all that's required to run *natd* is to add it to your startup files and tell it which network device it should consider to be the "outside world":

```
natd -interface rl0
```

Linux doesn't use *natd* for NAT. Instead, it uses *IP masquerading*. Read the masquerading HOWTO at *http://www.linuxdoc.org/HOWTO/IP-Masquerade-HOWTO/* for more information on how to deal with NAT on Linux.

—*DJPH*

46.12 Firewalls

Gateways (46.11) route packets from one network to another. Firewalls prevent some packets from being routed, based on a set of rules. Generally these rules are based on which direction the packet is going, to which port (46.1) it is destined or from which port it came, which protocol the packet is using (TCP, UDP, or ICMP for low-level protocols, though sometimes firewalls also recognize higher-level protocols like HTTP), and so forth.

A fairly standard firewall ruleset would allow outgoing packets from all machines on the LAN, disallow incoming packets that weren't part of an established connection (which allows machines on the LAN to establish connections going out, but keeps outsiders from establishing incoming connections), and then specifically allow things like incoming connections to port 25 (the SMTP (46.8) port) on the mail server machine, ports 80 and 443 (the HTTP and HTTPS ports) on the web server machine, and port 22 (the SSH (46.6) port) on any server that should be able to receive SSH logins.

Cable modems and DSL routers generally have simple firewalls built in; a Unix machine functioning as a gateway can also firewall and often has much more complex capabilities. Firewall software varies enough that detailed configuration of a firewall is beyond the scope of this book; things to look for include the documentation for *ipfw*, *ipchains* (Linux 2.2 kernel), or *iptables* (Linux 2.4 kernel).

—*DJPH*

46.13 Gatewaying from a Personal LAN over a Modem

Often you have only dialup access but would like your home network to be able to access the Internet. A simple way to do this is to configure one Unix machine as a gateway (46.11), with one side of the gateway your LAN and the other side the modem connection. If you then set up the modem connection to dial on demand, you have a simple way to share your connection between all of the machines on the LAN.

All that's required is that you set up your PPP connection (44.11), turn on PPP's NAT (46.11) handling and then turn on gatewaying (46.11). Make sure that all your LAN machines point to the gateway as their default gateway (handing out addresses via DHCP (46.10) is an easy way to ensure this). Any attempt to access the Internet by any machine on the LAN will then cause your gateway to dial up your ISP, if the modem isn't currently connected.

Note that I said that you had to turn on NAT handling. A dialup almost always means that your dialup machine will be getting a dynamic address, and the only way to have multiple machines behind a dynamic address is NAT. Because this is so common, some PPP clients have NAT built in; no configuration is required and no separate *natd* needs to be run. NAT simply has to be enabled, generally with the *–nat* option. (Linux's *pppd* does not support NAT by itself. Read the masquerading HOWTO at *http://www.linuxdoc.org/HOWTO/IP-Masquerade-HOWTO/* for more information on how to deal with NAT on Linux.)

—*DJPH*

47

Connecting to MS Windows

47.1 Building Bridges

Too often, it seems, the discussion of operating systems devolves into accusations, recriminations, and hurt feelings. However, the reality of a heterogeneous computing environment makes cooperation among the various operating systems critically important. There are a number of ways that Unix machines can interact with and partipate in Windows networks. Many of those connections work in reverse, too, so that Windows users can begin to experience Unix without abandoning their preferred desktop. Polemics aside, operating systems are only a means to an end that is defined by your business. Fortunately, interoperability is becoming increasingly easier. The following sections will show some of the options available to you.

—*JJ*

47.2 Installing and Configuring Samba

Samba

Samba is an open source project that implements the Session Message Block (SMB) protocol, which is the core networking language of the Microsoft Windows family. Of course, the dominant networking protocol in Unix is the Transmission Control Protocol/Internet Protocol (TCP/IP). The challenge of the Samba project is to map SMB traffic onto TCP/IP networks. This is no small feat since SMB was designed for small, nonsegmented networks. Because all SMB network machine names exist in one global namespace, the practical size of an SMB network is quite limited. Although there are workgroups and NT domains (dolled-up workgroups with a domain controller), these groups don't partition a network in the same way that IP subnets do. Workgroups are simply an organizational grouping of machine names (although NT domains can also exercise some access control over the resources within their jurisdiction).

Despite these limitations, most offices these days have a very large installed base of Windows servers and workstations. With Samba, your Unix machine can participate in Windows file sharing and print services. In fact, Samba can replace Windows file and print servers in many cases. For the full reference on Samba (plus a good number of useful tips), pick up a copy of *Using Samba* from O'Reilly & Associates.

Samba consists mainly of two daemons and a host of supporting programs. The *smbd* daemon is responsible for making your machine's filesystem and printers available to a Windows network. The *nmbd* daemon handles the mapping of SMB machine names into the IP namespace and browsing other SMB resources. Some Unix systems, like Linux, are also able to mount other SMB drives onto their local filesystems using the *smbmnt* command.

Samba is available for all popular Unix platforms. The project web site, *http:// www.samba.org*, is mirrored throughout the world, so you should be able to find a server near you. The current stable release of samba will be available as a link called *samba-latest.tar.gz*. As of this writing, the latest release is 2.2.3a.

After unpacking the archive file, change into the newly created *samba* subdirectory, become the root user, and type:

```
# ./configure && make
```

This bit of shell logic simply means, "Execute the program *configure* in the current directory. It is important to run the configure as root, since there will be certain tests done that require root access. If it succeeds, run *make*." If the compilation proceeds without error, you should install the Samba components with:

```
# make install
```

Now you can configure Samba to share your system's directories and printers with your Windows neighbors.

There is only one configuration script for both Samba daemons: *smb.conf*. The Samba build process does not normally create this file for you. However, there are several example *smb.conf* files in the *examples* directory of the unpacked source code. These can be easily modified for your system. Alternatively, you may wish to use the web administration tool SWAT (47.4) to configure your installation. It is worth understanding a bit about how to configure *smb.conf* by hand.

Perhaps the best example configuration to start with is the file called *smb.conf.default*. Lines that start with a semicolon or pound sign (#) are comments and are ignored by the Samba daemons entirely. Blocks of related options begin with a line that has a label in square brackets. A special block called [global] precedes blocks that define individual shared resources. Global configuration options include what workgroup your machine is part of, what guest account to use for public shares, and which IP addresses are allowed to connect to your SMB service. For instance:

```
[global]
    workgroup      = MYGROUP
;   hosts allow    = 192.168.1. 192.168.2. 127.
    guest account  = pcguest
    log file       = /usr/local/samba/var/log.%m
    max log size   = 50
    security       = user
;   encrypt passwords = yes
```

Here, all the shares that will be described later in the configuration file will be advertised in the *MYGROUP* workgroup. Although the next line is commented out, you can use the host allow directive to permit only certain hosts or subnets access to your SMB shares. In this example, machines would have to be in either one of the two class C networks (IPs beginning with 192.168.1 and 192.168.2) or in the class A network (IPs beginning with 127) to even connect to your Samba daemons. Sometimes you will create public shares that won't require a authentication. For these shares, some real Unix account is needed. That account is specified with guest account and is usually a nonprivileged account, like *pcguest*.

A good rule of thumb when customizing your *smb.conf* is to leave the defaults in place where you don't fully understand the directive. The defaults err on the side of caution. Unless you have a good reason for changing them, leave the log file and max log size directives as is. The security and encrypt passwords directives are important and are talked about in more detail in Chapter 47. For now, keep the defaults.

Sharing one of your local directories with the SMB network is easy. For instance:

```
[tmp]
    comment    = Temporary file space
    browseable = yes
    path       = /tmp
    read only  = no
    public     = yes
```

This block describes sharing the local system's */tmp* directory with your SMB network. The comment option is a human-readable description of the share that is available to SMB browsers (like the Network Neighborhood application in Windows). The path directive indicates the local path you wish to share. The browseable option, which defaults to yes anyway, makes sure that this share appears in browse lists. The read only statement is set to no, making the share writable by SMB clients that are able to connect (47.6). When the public directive is set to yes, passwords are not required to access this resource.

There are far too many configuration options to detail here. See the Samba documemention or *Using Samba* for the full story.

After you have finished configuring the system, you are ready to run the SMB daemons. You can run these servers (as root) directly from the command line with the following:

```
# /path/to/samba/bin/smbd -D;
# /path/to/samba/bin/nmbd -D;
```

You can also have *inetd* run them. Simply add the following lines to */etc/services*:

```
netbios-ssn   139/tcp
netbios-ns    137/udp
```

Add the following lines to */etc/inetd.conf*:

```
netbios-snn stream tcp nowait root /path/to/samba/bin/smbd smbd
netbios-ns  dgram  upd wait   root /path/to/samba/bin/nmbd nmbd
```

Simply restart *inetd* to begin answering SMB requests.

To verify that your SMB services are running, use the command-line tool *smbclient* to browse yourself.

```
$ smbclient -L netbios-name
```

Your machine's NETBIOS name (that is, the name by which SMB peers are known) will be your DNS hostname or whatever you set the global directive netbios name to be. If prompted for a password, you can simply hit Enter for now. If your service is running, you should see your shares displayed in a similiar way to the following:

```
[jjohn@marian upt]$ smbclient -L marian
added interface ip=192.168.1.50 bcast=192.168.1.255 nmask=255.255.255.0
Password:
Anonymous login successful
Domain=[WORKGROUP] OS=[Unix] Server=[Samba 2.2.2]

        Sharename      Type      Comment
        ---------      ----      -------
        homes          Disk      Home Directories
        IPC$           IPC       IPC Service (Samba Server)
        ADMIN$         Disk      IPC Service (Samba Server)
        lp             Printer   hp
        tmp            Disk      Temporary file space
        Server                   Comment
        ---------                -------
        MARIAN                   Samba Server

        Workgroup                Master
        ---------                -------
        WORKGROUP                MARIAN
```

—*JJ*

47.3 Securing Samba

The topic of security under Samba falls mainly into two categories: how to make the SMB server secure and how clients authenticate with the SMB server. Since the authentication issue is the thorniest, let's talk about it first.

In the [global] section of the *smb.conf* file, there is a directive called security that can take one of four values: *share, user, server,* or *domain*. Choosing *share* means that each shared resource has a set of passwords associated with it. Users must present one of those passwords to use the resource. *User* security requires users to provide a username and password to gain access to any of the shares. Samba can ask another SMB server to authenticate user credentials, instead of using local files, by selecting the *server* security setting. If you choose this security option, you will need to provide the password server directive a space-separated list of NETBIOS machine names that will do the authentication. The last security option is *domain*. In this model, your machine joins an existing NT domain that does all the user credential authentication.

If you are new to Samba, your best bet is to use *user* security. The ugliest problem of Samba now rears its head: to use encrypted passwords or not to. The issue here is that older Windows clients (early Windows 95 and pre–SP3 NT 4.0) send user passwords over the network in clear text. The good news about clear text passwords is that Samba can use your system's */etc/passwd* to authenticate users. All real accounts on your system will use their Unix username and password to connect to your SMB shares. The problems with this approach are:

- Passwords can be easily snooped from the network.
- Every SMB user requires a real account on your system.
- Newer SMB clients will need to be patched to connect to your shares.

If the first two reasons don't scare you off using clear text passwords, the last reason is pretty daunting if you need to patch a lot of workstations. However, if you still want to go this route, you need to add the elements listed in Table 47-1 to each client's registry (using *REGEDIT.EXE*).

Table 47-1. Registry settings for clear text SMB passwords

Operating system	Registry hack
Windows 95, Windows 98, Windows Me	Create a new field called EnablePlainTextPassword with the *dword* value 1 in the registry key: \HKEY_LOCAL_MACHINE\System\CurrentControlSet\Services\VxD\VNETSUP\
Windows NT	Create a new field called EnablePlainTextPassword with a *dword* value of 1 in the registry key: HKEY_LOCAL_MACHINE\system\CurrentControlSet\Services\Rdr\Parameters\
Windows 2000	Create a new field EnablePlainTextPassword with a *dword* value of 1 in the registry key: HKEY_LOCAL_MACHINE\SYSTEM\CurrentControlSet\Services\LanmanWorkStation\Parameters\

If you're not sold on clear text passwords, you will need to create a separate password file for SMB users. Luckily, there's a utility called *smbpasswd* that can manage this file for you. Adding a new SMB user who already has a Unix account on your system is as simple as:

```
# smbpasswd username
```

You will then be prompted for a password for this account. The drawback to this approach is the added maintenance of keeping the SMB passwords in sync with the Unix passwords. See *Using Samba* for some guidance here. The hope of the near future is to use an LDAP server (either Microsoft's Active Directory or a Unix LDAP server) for all system passwords. This is the dream of single-source logins and something the Samba team is working towards supporting.

After authentication issues, the big security concerns about Samba involve access control. Some of the ways to handle access control have been shown in the configuration section of this article. Additionally, each share can use the valid users directive to limit the set of users to a space-separated list. You might also consider making the share read only and then put only a few users on the write list.

—JJ

47.4 SWAT and GUI SMB Browsers

Modern versions of Samba come bundled with a web adminstration tool called *swat*. *swat* doesn't need any web server to run, but you will need to configure your system's *inetd*. As with any new service, you'll need to define a name and a port for it in */etc/services*. For instance:

```
swat    901/tcp
```

You are now ready to make *inetd* serve *swat*. Add the following to */etc/inetd.conf*:

```
swat  stream  tcp  nowait.400 root /path/to/samba/bin/swat swat
```

Now, restart *inetd* and point your web browser to *http://localhost:901*. You will be asked for the root username and password. If all is successful, you will see a screen that has seven navigation icons: home, globals, shares, printers, status, view, and password, as shown in Figure 47-1.

swat will be on the *globals* page first. Here you can set the global directives, such as workgroup name and security type. There is online help, should an option not be immediately clear. Clicking on the *shares* icon shows you the services you are currently advertising and allows you to add more. Clicking on *printers* allows you to configure which printers you share with the SMB network. You can even restart the server from *swat*.

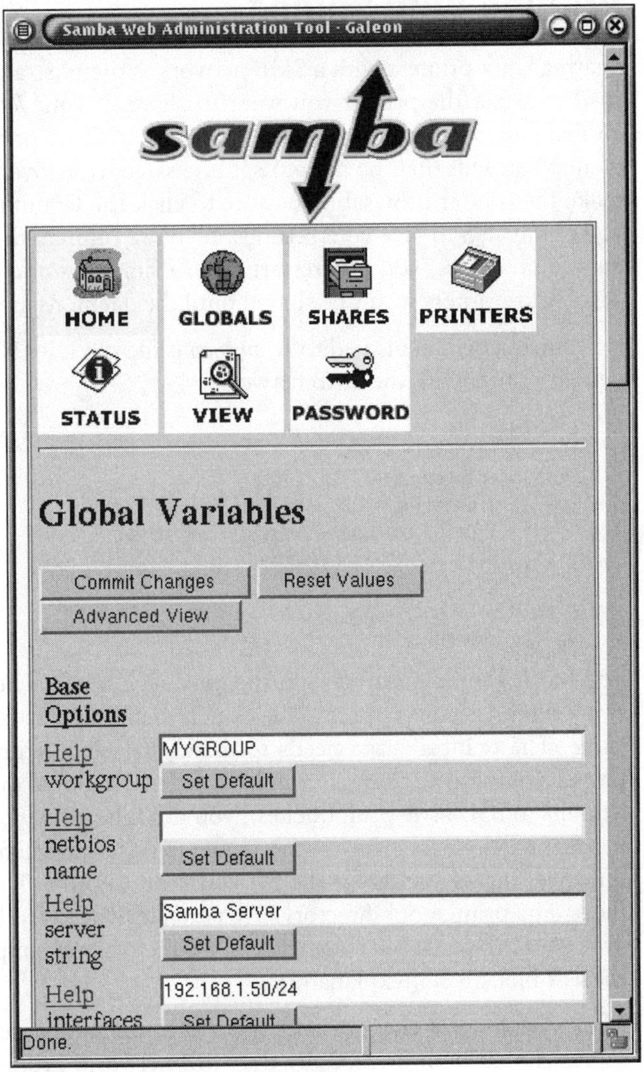

Figure 47-1. SWAT's globals page

Third-party browsing tools are also available for Samba. Some of these, like *smb2www*, are web applications that show you the local SMB neighborhood. Others, like gsnhood and xSMBrowser, are X11 programs that work somewhat like the Windows Network Neighborhood application. One of the advantages of the X11 browsers is that they can be configured to allow users to mount SMB drives (if your Unix supports the *smbfs* filesystem). You will certainly be rewarded by searching the web for third-party SMB tools.

—JJ

47.5 Printing with Samba

Sharing Unix printers with a SMB network is pretty straightforward. You can use *swat* to select the printer you want to share. If your */etc/printcap* is configured correctly, *swat* will allow you to select one of those printers from a drop-down menu. You will then be able to set access controls over that printer, as well as make the printer browsable. Be sure to click the Commit Changes button when you're finished to save your settings. If you're running the SMB daemons as standalone processes, you can restart them from the *status* section of *swat*. In any case, your printers won't be shared until the daemons are restarted.

Of course, you can also edit the *smb.conf* file directly. Here's how to share your default printer with the SMB network:

```
[lp]
        printable = Yes
        printer name = lp
        ; printing = BSD
        ; print command = /usr/bin/lpr -r %s
        path = /var/spool/samba
        guest ok = Yes
        read only = No
        comment = hp
```

The block should start off with the *lpr* queue name. The most important directive for print shares is `printable`, which identifies this block as defining a print share. The `printer name` needs to match the Unix printer queue name for the printer you wish to share. If you have defined a global directive `printing` (which defaults to BSD style print queues), you don't need to worry about explicitly telling Samba how to print to the queue. In the commented-out `print command` directive, the %s stands for the file you wish to print. The `path` directive defines the samba print spool directory. This directory needs to be writable by the *smbd* process. Both `guest ok` and `read only` directives are simple access controls. The comment block is self-explanatory.

After saving your changes and restarting the Samba servers (if needed), your shares should be browsable by the SMB network. From Unix, you can print to SMB printers with the following command:

```
$ smbclient //netbios-name/printer
smb: \> print filename-to-print
```

Here the *smbclient* program (described in more detail below) is used to connect to the SMB printer. Using the interactive shell, the *print* command will send any file you specify to the printer. On some systems, you may find a program called *smbprint* that is a Bourne shell wrapper around *smbclient*.

—JJ

47.6 Connecting to SMB Shares from Unix

From Unix, you can connect to SMB shares with the *smbclient* command. It provides an *ftp*-like interactive environment for transferring files between your Unix system and the SMB share. It also is an excellent tool for debugging your Samba setup. For instance, you can see what shares are available from an SMB host with the following:

```
$ smbclient -L //netbios-name -U SMB_username
```

The -L flag request the list of available shares from the machine specified by its NETBIOS name. You may optionally provide an SMB username name with the -U flag. If no explicit username is provided, your Unix account name is used.

Once you have found a directory share that interests you, you can "log in" to it:

```
$ smbclient //netbios-name/share -U SMB_username
smb: />
```

You will be prompted for the SMB password associated with whichever account you used. If successful, you will be at an interactive prompt. You may type ? or help to get all the options available to you. Use the *get* command to copy files from the remote host to your Unix machine and *put* to copy files in the other direction. Like *ftp*, Samba also provides the filename wildcard variants *mget* and *mput* to allow you to handle multiple files easily.

—JJ

47.7 Sharing Desktops with VNC

VNC

Virtual Network Computing (VNC) is an open source project from AT&T Labs in Cambridge, England. It is a client/server system that allows users to manipulate desktop environments remotely. There are VNC servers for Unix, Windows, and pre–MacOS X environments. The options for clients are even wider since there is a Java applet VNC client. This can be used on any system that supports a modern web browser and Java. There is also a native VNC client for Unix, Windows, and pre–MacOS X machines. VNC provides a platform-independent way to control a heterogeneous network from any client platform.

VNC provides a live picture of a desktop. When you move your mouse on the client end, the mouse also moves on the server. The VNC client gets a kind of "graphic diff" of the change on the remote desktop and applies that to its current notion of the desktop. As you might guess, VNC isn't ideal for high-performance video games, but it is very serviceable for system administration and development.

You can get either precompiled binaries or the source code at *http://www.uk.research.att.com/vnc/download.html*. If you choose to compile VNC from the source, you will need to get and unpack the tar archive from the above site. To build the source, change into the unpacked archive directory and type:

```
$ xmkmf
$ make World && cd Xvnc && make World
```

If the compile goes cleanly, change to root and install:

```
# make install
```

Connecting to a Windows VNC server

Setting up a VNC server on a Windows machine is fairly straightforward. Simply grab the appropriate binary from the VNC download page, unzip the archive, and run the *SETUP.EXE* program in the *vncserver* folder. VNC will create a folder in the Start menu in which you'll find the VNC server program. When started, this program will ask you for a password that clients will need to be able to use your Windows machine.

Connecting to any VNC server requires three things. The first is the server's hostname or IP address. The second is the *display* number of the remote desktop. Windows and Macintosh servers can only have one display (the desktop), while Unix machines can have many VNC servers active at once (just like they can have many X sessions running concurrently). Display numbers begin at zero. The last piece of information needed is the password. Be advised that this password is in no way secure, nor is the VNC network traffic encrypted.

To connect to a VNC server requires running X. From an Xterm, type the following:

```
$ vncviewer hostname:display_number
```

If the VNC server is running on that machine, you'll be prompted for a password. You should see something like Figure 47-2.

VNC desktops are also available through Java applets that can be accessed through modern web browsers. The URL for that applet is comprised of the hostname of the VNC server and a port number that is the display number plus 5800. For example, the URL for connecting to the VNC server on a Windows machine called *karl.oreilly.com* would be *http://karl.oreilly.com:5800*.

Setting up VNC on Unix

It is sometimes convenient to be able to connect to a Unix desktop remotely from a machine that isn't running X. Fortunately, setting up VNC on UNIX can be as straightforward as:

```
$ vncserver
```

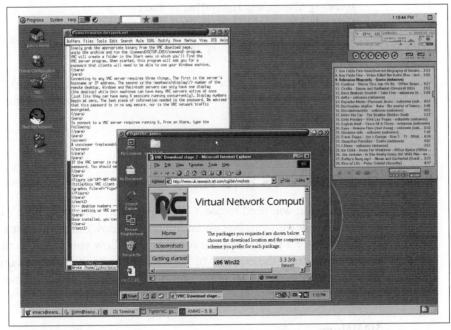

Figure 47-2. Unix VNC client connecting to a Windows server

VNC will pick the next available display number for your VNC server and report this to you.

```
New 'X' desktop is marian:1

Starting applications specified in /home/jjohn/.vnc/xstartup
Log file is /home/jjohn/.vnc/marian:1.log
```

If you haven't picked one before, you will be prompted for a password. Again, this has nothing to do with your system's */etc/passwd*. Keep in mind that the new server is running under the account that started it. The security issues are manifold, so think carefully about how you deploy this very useful service.

By default, VNC runs the very lean window manager *twm*. The fewer the needless graphic elements, the better network performance you can expected. However, you can adjust the details of that desktop by looking in your home directory for the *.vnc* directory. There, you'll find the VNC log, pid, and password files. More importantly, you'll find the *xstartup* file, which works just like *xinitrc*. You can start X programs, set the desktop color, and choose the window manager to run from this file. Here's an example of the kinds of customizations you can do:

```
#!/bin/sh
xrdb $HOME/.Xresources
xsetroot -solid gray85 &
```

```
xterm -fg blue     -bg lightyellow -g 80x25+0+0 &
xterm -fg red      -bg lightyellow -g 80x25+0-0 &
xterm -fg darkgreen  -bg lightyellow -g 80x25-0+0 &
xclock -digital -update 5 -bg lightyellow -g -0-300 &
exec twm
```

Here, three Xterms and *xclock* are arranged in a convenient way. VNC will also look in your *.twmrc*, if you're using the default window manager, for further customizations.

—JJ

47.8 Of Emulators and APIs

Sometimes you will need to use a Windows application that hasn't been ported to Unix. While you can buy an additional Windows machine just for that program, there are a few Unix solutions that will allow you access to the Windows environment from the comfort of X. While none of the solutions offered below have the performance of Windows running natively on dedicated hardware, each is worth mentioning.

VMWare

What's the next best thing to having another machine run Windows? Having a virtual machine running Windows. VMWare, Inc., has produced software called *vmware* for Intel Linux that creates a virtual i386-class machine on which Windows can be installed. All your hardware is virtualized, so the virtual machine created is a somewhat slower clone of the host. Still, the performance is adequate for Office applications and development. *vmware* creates a private network on your machine so that, with Samba (47.2), you can get to your Unix filesystem from your virtual Windows machine. You can get an evaluation copy at *http://www.vmware.com*.

Wine

If a virtual machine is overkill for your needs, you might want to look into the open source project called *wine*. A recursive acronym for Wine Is Not an Emulator, the *wine* project also runs only on Intel machines, and it tries to emulate the Windows API for Windows-native applications. This project has been under development for a long time and isn't quite ready for mission-critical applications yet. However, many Windows projects can mostly function under *wine*, including some video games, such as Blizzard's StarCraft. You will find more information about *wine* at *http://www.winehq.com*.

—JJ

47.9 Citrix: Making Windows Multiuser

Unix users needing to access Windows applications will find that VNC is not a workable solution in all instances. The reason for this is that Windows operating systems were not designed to be multiuser; they do not allow multiple concurrent user sessions. When you have more than a few users needing to run a Windows application, such as Outlook to connect to corporate email, your options are to put a Windows PC on every desk, run Windows under a virtual machine, or set up Windows Terminal Services (WTS).

WTS is the current name of the multiuser software Microsoft provides with the Windows 2000 Server product family. Its former iteration was Windows NT 4.0 Terminal Server. Similar to VNC, WTS provides a Windows 2000 desktop to a connecting client, but does it in true multiuser fashion. Dozens of users can be connected to the same machine, running different processes, all independent of the other. However, WTS is only part of the solution for Unix users. This is because Microsoft only allows connections to a WTS server via the Remote Desktop Protocol (RDP) but doesn't provide any non-Windows clients that use RDP.

On the flip side, Citrix provides a Unix client program that can connect to a WTS server, but it only uses the Independent Computing Architecture (ICA) protocol. For that client to work, a server add-on product to WTS called Citrix Metaframe must be installed. Thankfully, Metaframe provides additional features to a WTS server besides ICA connectivity that helps to justify the additional cost.

One thing to be careful of when implementing a WTS solution is licensing. Microsoft is very strict in its rules about what machines can connect under which circumstances. Like tollbooths on the highway, Microsoft wants to get paid no matter how you get on, or which vehicle you're driving. To put licensing simply, you must have a Windows 2000 Server license for each server, a Windows 2000 Server Client Access License for each machine connecting to the server, a Terminal Services License for each machine actually using WTS, and, if you are using Office, each machine that runs Office off the WTS server must have a license. These are not concurrent licenses: if 50 machines are going to use Office at some point, all 50 must have licenses, not just the 10 that are connected at any given moment. Citrix licenses are in addition to Microsoft licenses but are thankfully more friendly. Citrix allows the use of concurrent licenses, which means 20 licenses could cover the needs of 50 users, if only 20 are going to be connected at a time. Full details about Microsoft licensing in a WTS environment can be found at *http://www.microsoft.com/windows2000/server/howtobuy/pricing/tsfaq.asp*.

Citrix Metaframe

Assuming that you have a properly installed and configured Citrix Metaframe server to connect to, you should download and install the appropriate ICA client for your operating system from *http://www.citrix.com/downloads/*. Installation is very simple and adequately explained in the provided documentation.

After installation, as a user, run *wfcmgr* from program directory you installed to. This will launch the configuration program for the ICA client; see Figure 47-3.

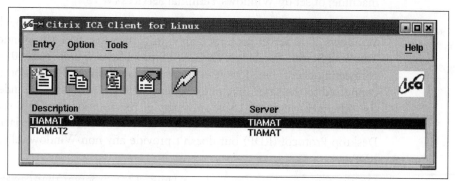

Figure 47-3. Existing entries in wfcmgr

To create a new entry, select New from the Entry menu. You will see Figure 47-4. Though all settings are important, be sure to adjust the settings pertaining to the Window properties. A good tip is to set up your screen to be 90 percent of your display size, to use a shared palette of colors, and to map drive letters to your home directory, floppy, and CD-ROM. Using full-screen mode will disable the use of multiple desktops on your Unix system, so it is not a good idea. Using a shared palette prevents odd coloring on your display. Mapping to your local devices is useful for transferring files between the WTS server and your workstation. The settings to do this are under the Option menu after you've saved the entry.

Running *wfcmgr* also creates a *.ICAClient* directory in the user's home directory. Copy this directory to */etc/skel* to insure that new users are automatically setup with default settings to access WTS. For existing users, copy the directory to their home directory and give ownership to that user.

Create a symbolic link, such as */usr/local/bin/citrix*, in your default path that points to *wfcmgr*. Give it an easy name like *citrix*. Using this link name, you can launch saved configurations in *wfcmgr* with a single command.

```
$ citrix desc description_name
```

description_name, in this instance, is the descriptive name you gave your entry in *wfcmgr* (see Figure 47-3). It is case-sensitive.

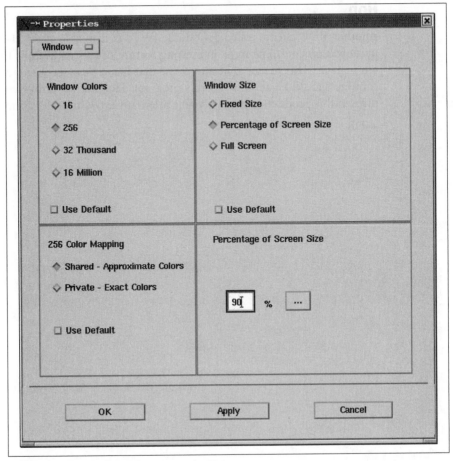

Figure 47-4. Creating a new entry in wfcmgr

Metaframe offers many additional features, such as load balancing, application publishing, automatic updates of ICA clients, and a web-based client, that may help justify its cost. Citrix even sells a Metaframe for Unix that provides Unix programs to Windows clients that don't have an X Server.

rdesktop

The fact that Microsoft has not provided an RDP client for Unix has not stopped enterprising programmers in the Open Source community from creating one. This program, called *rdesktop*, is available at *http://www.rdesktop.org*. In everyday use this program has proven to be as useful as the ICA client, though it lacks support for sound, high color depths, drive mapping, or client-side support for serial and parallel ports. If these features are important to you, you will need Metaframe; if not, this free program is an excellent alternative.

Hob

Another RDP client, called HOBLink JWT, is available from Hobsoft, *http:// www.hobsoft.com*. The most interesting feature of this program is that it is written in Java. This means that any client that has a browser with a working Java runtime should be able to run this program. Hobsoft has provided a lot of features in this product, and it is a viable alternative to Citrix Metaframe.

—*DB*

Part IX

Security

Part IX contains the following chapters:

48

Security Basics

48.1 Understanding Points of Vulnerability

Rather than being impregnable fortresses of steel, most computers are about as leaky as old wooden fishing boats. Though the press has focused primarily on Windows security violations in the last few years, Unix boxes are just as vulnerable and require as much, or more, effort to keep safe.

If your Unix box sits in your home, it is protected from unauthorized access, you live alone, and you never connect to the Internet, security probably isn't a concern for you. However, chances are your Unix box is fairly easy to access physically, and your system is most likely connected to the Internet through a modem or other network connection. In both these cases, this chapter and those that follow are of extreme interest to you.

Anytime you have a multiuser system, your account is vulnerable to others in the system and to anyone who might break into the system from outside your organization. The only way to protect accounts is to ensure that good account management practices are in place, such as removing accounts when people are no longer with the organization and using difficult-to-hack passwords, as well as making sure that sensitive data is protected by accidental or deliberate access.

For single-user systems, you'll want to make sure that someone can't accidentally or deliberately log into your machine at home or work. Chances are no one would try, but particularly if you have something such as Linux installed on a laptop, you're going to want to keep the snoops out.

More importantly, before you connect to the Internet, you have to know what you're doing with your system, particularly if you run applications such as web servers on your system. All you need is one harmful worm or virus, or to have a cracker break into your system, to have all your work and effort compromised.

The above areas of vulnerability—account, machine, and system—probably don't surprise you. But are you aware that you're vulnerable to yourself?

How many times have you accidentally deleted a file? Now, how many times have you deleted a file and not had backup in place? Security isn't just a protection against external intrusion. Used effectively, security is also an effective means to protect the system and the data and applications from internal error and blunder.

Before you install your Unix operating system and turn on your machine, you need to have a security plan in place, starting with a security checklist (48.2).

—SP

48.2 CERT Security Checklists

If you can stand the access times, one of the most valuable web sites for Unix security information is the CERT (Computer Emergency Response Team) web site at *http://www.cert.org*. At this site you'll be able to find information about the latest security alerts (48.3), where to get security patches for your operating system, and the CERT Unix Security Checklist.

The CERT Unix Security Checklist is a step-by-step overview of what security procedures you need to implement for your Unix system, regardless of the type of system you have.

There's no magic formula in the Checklist, just good common sense. First of all, keep your system up to date with the most recent security patches. Always apply the most restrictive permission (50.5) on a file: if a file only needs to be read-only, make sure its file permissions are set to read-only, and so on. Other tips are disabling Internet services you're not using and protecting your system so it can't be used to launch denial-of-service attacks (DoS) (48.5).

Above all, the Checklist emphasizes an attitude of "Go ahead, be paranoid—someone is out to break into your system." If your Unix box is connected in any way to the Internet, the Checklist is the first thing you should print out and review, one step at a time, *before* you install your Unix operating system or turn on your machine. Definitely before you connect to the Internet.

 The CERT web site has extremely slow access times. I imagine this is because it's a popular site. I can also imagine that the site is the target of every cracker in the world. Regardless of the cause of the slowness, access the site only during non-peak hours, if there is such a thing with a 24-hour-a-day Internet.

—SP

48.3 Keeping Up with Security Alerts

If you have a Microsoft Windows system, you're probably familiar with the frequent security bulletins from Microsoft's Security division. One of the nice things about Microsoft's security is that you can get security alerts emailed to you so that you're made aware of new vulnerabilities as soon as Microsoft acknowledges them.

In the Unix world, you may have to make a little more effort to keep up with the security alerts for various flavors of Unix; however, keeping up with the alerts isn't a horrendous amount of work. It's just a case of knowing where to look for them.

I've already mentioned CERT (48.2). This web site has some of the best information about new security vulnerabilities, and if you're managing a multiuser Unix system, you should check this site at least once a day. Even if you only have a single-use Unix box, you should check the site frequently. Note, though, that CERT publicizes all security vulnerabilities, not just Unix ones. On the day I wrote this, when I checked at CERT's Advisories page (at *http://www.cert.org/advisories/*), there were advisories on Oracle, the zlib Compression library, PHP, and Microsoft's Internet Explorer, to name just a few.

If you're running a Linux system, you can check Linux Security at *http://www.linuxsecurity.com* for up-to-date information on security problems related to Linux operating systems. In addition, you can read articles on Linux security and download security-related utilities. When I accessed the site, the current reported exploit was related to a vulnerability with Apache, and the most current advisory was warning about a potential buffer overflow (48.4) problem related to FreeBSD's *squid* port.

What I particularly like about Linux Security is that it shows security advisories categorized by flavor of Unix/Linux. Among the categories are Corel, Caldera, Red Hat, Slackware, Debian, FreeBSD, NetBSD, and so on. Since I run a Red Hat Linux box as well as a FreeBSD web server, it is particularly helpful for me to see what I need to be aware of in both of these environments.

O'Reilly publishes information about Unix and open source at the Linux DevCenter at the O'Reilly Network (at *http://linux.oreillynet.com*). Rather than list all vulnerabilities, this site tends to focus on specific instances and then covers each in more detail than you'll normally get at the other security sites.

—*SP*

48.4 What We Mean by Buffer Overflow

You can't run any operating system without getting security alerts related to buffer overflow vulnerabilities. Unless you're into system hacking, you're probably not aware of what this means and why buffer overflow is the base cause of so many alerts.

In a procedural language, such as the C programming language used to create Unix, functionality is broken down into separate, reusable functions. These functions are then called whenever that functionality is needed. Data is passed between the application and the function through function arguments.

Function arguments are pushed onto a section of memory called the stack. Additionally, the return point for the function—that place in the application where the function is called—is also pushed onto the stack. Finally, data internal to the function is also pushed onto the stack.

A buffer is allocated on the stack to store function parameters. If a parameter exceeds the buffer size, the data overwrites the other stack contents, including the function return call, resulting in an application failure. Many functions commonly used in C, such as scanf or strcpy, don't ensure that the buffer meets the size of the data copied, and if the application developer doesn't perform this check herself, the application will most likely fail the first time the data copied exceeds the size of the buffer.

An example of this type of problem is an application that opens and copies the contents of a file using one of the C functions that don't do buffer size checking. As long as the file contents are small enough, the application doesn't generate an error. However, if a file's contents are too large, the application will fail, abruptly, leaving application support personnel scratching their heads wondering why an application that worked to a certain point stopped working.

An application failure is not the worst that can happen in this situation. Crackers with a good understanding of how the stack works and knowledge of assembly code can exploit this vulnerability by writing code to the stack beyond the function arguments and function return address. In addition, they can rewrite the function return address to point to the address of the beginning of this malicious code. When the function finishes, the address of the new hacked code is pushed to the processor rather than the return location of the function, and the hacked code is executed, usually with disastrous results.

To prevent both application crashes and buffer-overflow vulnerabilities, boundary-checking versions of most C functions are used rather than the unsafe functions. The application developer also adds boundary checking to his or her own code, such as checking the size of the application file before processing it from our example application. Unfortunately, this doesn't always happen.

When you read about or receive an alert about buffer-overflow vulnerability in a Unix utility or application, what's happened is that crackers—or security personnel—have discovered that the application contains code that isn't testing the boundaries of the data being processed. Usually a patch that replaces the defective code accompanies this alert.

—SP

48.5 What We Mean by DoS

Another major security problem is one in which users of a Unix system can't access the functionality because access attempts are being blocked in some way. These blocking efforts are called, appropriately enough, denial-of-service attacks, usually abbreviated DoS.

CERT defines three types of DoS attacks:

- An attack that consumes all resources
- Manipulation of configuration information
- Manipulation of network components

Resources in a networked system include memory, bandwidth, Internet connections, and so on. In a DoS attack, the attacker seeks to use these resources in such a way that no one else can connect to the system. Famous examples of this type of attack involve a concept known as the distributed denial-of-service attack, DDoS.

In a DDoS attack, several machines that have not been properly secured against external control are compromised, and an application is placed on each. This application lies dormant until triggered by the attacker. When this happens, these compromised machines—known as *handlers*—direct other compromised machines—known as *agents*—to run an application that generates network packets, all of which are directed to a specific target. These packets overwhelm the available bandwidth of the victim, and they may also overwhelm routers in the path to the victim to the point where entire sections of the Internet may be negatively impacted.

Though Windows-based rather than Unix, the Code Red worm that caused so many problems in 2001 was based on the premise of DDoS.

Though disabling, DoS attacks based on overutilizing ephemeral resources such as bandwidth deny access but don't permanently damage a machine's infrastructure. However, another DoS attack is one in which an attacker gains root access to a machine and modifies configuration information such as usernames and passwords, in such a way that no one can access the network.

How simple is it to access configuration information? Accessing the password file on a system can be as easy as using TFTP (Trivial File Transfer Protocol) to download the password file unless TFTP is disabled or configured to prevent unauthorized access.

In fact, a DDoS attack is dependent on the attacker getting access to several machines in order to launch an attack. Keeping your system clean and protected not only prevents invasion of your own systems, but prevents your Unix boxes from being used to launch attacks on others.

The third type of DoS attack is based on physical attack. Literally, if someone comes after your wires with an axe, no security software is going to protect your system. However, axe-wielding intruders are beyond the scope of this book, so we'll concentrate primarily on software and system adjustments to protect against DoS attacks.

—SP

48.6 Beware of Sluggish Performance

Contrary to popular myth, systems don't just start to fail for no reason. If your system is starting to perform poorly, chances are it's because of something that's been initiated. In most cases, the cause has innocuous roots, such as a poorly designed script; however, sluggish performance could also mean an external attack. Regardless of the origin of the decreasing efficiency, you'll want to take steps to locate the problem and remove it before it takes your system down.

If you notice that your systems performance is degrading, there are several built-in utilities you can use to troubleshoot possible problems. Probably the most commonly used utility is *ps* (24.5); however, there are other utilities that can provide useful information.

Check Processes

The first check to perform if you think that you have a destructive agent running on your machine is the processes currently in operation. You'll use the basic *ps* command to do this, after first checking to make sure that *ps* itself hasn't been replaced by a bogus program (check installation date, location, and size to see if the *ps* utility has been replaced).

Running the *ps* command with the flags *—aux* shows each user's processes, the CPU and memory usage, time started and command. Here's an example of output:

```
> ps -aux

root     6910  0.0  0.1  2088   516  ??  IsJ  30Apr02   1:04.80 /usr/sbin/sshd
root     6955  0.0  0.0  2600   384  ??  IsJ  30Apr02   0:06.67 /usr/local/sbin/
xinetd -pidfile /var/run/xinetd.pid
root     6970  0.0  0.0   624     0 #C1- IWJ  -         0:00.00 /bin/sh /usr/
virtual/share/pkgs/installed/mysql-server/3.22.32/bin/
mysql    6994  0.0  0.0 11216   144 #C1- SJ   30Apr02   0:35.83 /usr/local/
libexec/mysqld --basedir=/usr/local --datadir=/var/db/my
root     7003  0.0  0.3 10028  2616  ??  SsJ  30Apr02   3:33.55 /usr/local/www/
bin/httpd -DSSL
nobody  38060  0.0  0.3 10324  3116  ??  SJ   12:01PM   0:08.60 /usr/local/www/
bin/httpd -DSSL
nobody  38061  0.0  0.3 10332  2612  ??  SJ   12:01PM   0:08.23 /usr/local/www/
bin/httpd -DSSL
nobody  38062  0.0  0.3 11212  2656  ??  SJ   12:01PM   0:08.89 /usr/local/www/
bin/httpd -DSSL
nobody  38117  0.0  0.2 10352  2580  ??  SJ   12:01PM   0:09.37 /usr/local/www/
bin/httpd -DSSL
nobody  38314  0.0  0.2 10332  2596  ??  SJ   12:03PM   0:08.98 /usr/local/www/
bin/httpd -DSSL
root    62104  0.0  0.0  2112   400  ??  SJ    9:57AM   0:00.16 sshd:
shelleyp@ttyp2 (sshd)
```

In this listing, several processes are being run by root, but all are normal processes and accounted for. In addition, several processes are being run by "nobody," which is the generic user used with HTTP web page access. Using additional *ps* flags displays additional information, including *–e* for environment and *–f* for command-line and environment information of swapped-out processes.

Checking Swap Space

If your system is under DoS attack, your swap space is a vulnerable point. This hard disk space is reserved for use by the operating system and to provide space for temporary files. If your system is sluggish and you suspect a possible DoS attack—or just a badly behaving script that results in a lot of temporary files—the first thing you should check is how much swap space you have.

The *pstat* utility can be used to check swap space when using the *–s* option on the command line:

```
pstat -s
```

The result will be a listing of swap areas by device with available and used swap space. If the percentage of used space is much higher than normal, you probably have a bad script or external interference. Additional utilities can help you determine which.

Within FreeBSD and other Unix systems, *swapinfo* returns the same information as *pstat –s*. If you're running a Mac OS X system, instead of *pstat*, you'll use the *ls* command and check the contents of */var/vm*:

```
ls -l /var/vm
-rw-------T 1 root    wheel   000000000 Jun  4 12:56 swapfile0
```

Since the system wasn't under load, the swap space didn't have any contents at the time this command was run.

Check Network Connections

Another check you can run if your system is running sluggishly and you think you might be under attack is *netstat*. This command will return activity on Unix sockets as well as all of the active Internet connections, including referrals if the connection occurs through HTTP.

Here's an example of *netstat* output:

```
Active Internet connections
Proto Recv-Q Send-Q  Local Address          Foreign Address         (state)
tcp4    0      0   burningbird.http        a25253.upc-a.che.3617   TIME_WAIT
tcp4    0      0   burningbird.http        pm66.internetsee.4301   TIME_WAIT
tcp4    0      0   burningbird.http        strider.ccs.neu..4492   TIME_WAIT
tcp4    0      0   burningbird.http        strider.ccs.neu..4491   TIME_WAIT
tcp4    0      0   burningbird.http        strider.ccs.neu..4490   TIME_WAIT
tcp4    0      0   burningbird.http        mailgate.ltsbfou.57600  FIN_WAIT_2
tcp4    0      0   burningbird.http        mailgate.ltsbfou.57595  FIN_WAIT_2
tcp4    0     20   burningbird.ssh         adsl-64-168-24-1.1076   ESTABLISHED
tcp4    0      0   burningbird.submission  *.*                     LISTEN
tcp4    0      0   burningbird.smtp        *.*                     LISTEN
tcp4    0      0   burningbird.domain      *.*                     LISTEN
tcp4    0      0   burningbird.http        *.*                     LISTEN
tcp4    0      0   burningbird.https       *.*                     LISTEN
tcp4    0      0   burningbird.pop3s       *.*                     LISTEN
tcp4    0      0   burningbird.ssh         *.*                     LISTEN
udp4    0      0   burningbird.domain      *.*
udp4    0      0   burningbird.syslog      *.*
Active UNIX domain sockets
Address  Type  Recv-Q Send-Q  Inode   Conn    Refs  Nextref Addr
e5ed4cc0 stream    0     0   e5f0cbc0    0       0       0 /tmp/mysql.sock
e5ed4d40 stream    0     0      0        0       0       0
e5e08380 dgram     0     0      0     e5ed4dc0    0 e5e083c0
e5e083c0 dgram     0     0      0     e5ed4dc0    0 e5ed4d80
e5ed4d80 dgram     0     0      0     e5ed4dc0    0       0
e5ed4dc0 dgram     0     0   e556c040    0 e5e08380    0 /var/run/log
```

Specifying *netstat* with the command line option *–s* provides a detailed report of per-protocol—TCP, UDP, IP, and so on—usage statistics.

The *netstat* program is helpful not only for determining if someone is trying to break into your system, but also for determining if your system is having basic communication problems.

Other Checks

You can use *iostat* to check I/O statistics on your various devices. For instance, to check to see what kind of activity is occurring on all devices every three seconds for nine runs, issue the following command:

```
# iostat -odICTw 2 -c 9
        tty         mlxd0              acd0              fd0              md0                 cpu
   tin tout blk xfr msps  blk xfr msps  blk xfr msps  blk xfr msps  us ni sy in id
     0    0   0   0  0.0    0   0  0.0    0   0  0.0    0   0  0.0    0  0  0  0  0
     0    0 224  12  167    0   0  0.0    0   0  0.0    0   0  0.0    0  0  0  0  0
     0    0 568  36 55.8    0   0  0.0    0   0  0.0    0   0  0.0    0  0  0  0  0
     0    0 144   5  402    0   0  0.0    0   0  0.0    0   0  0.0    0  0  0  0  0
     0    0 112   7  287    0   0  0.0    0   0  0.0    0   0  0.0    0  0  0  0  0
     0    0  48   3  670    0   0  0.0    0   0  0.0    0   0  0.0    0  0  0  0  0
     0    0 240  15  134    0   0  0.0    0   0  0.0    0   0  0.0    0  0  0  0  0
     0    0 192  12  168    0   0  0.0    0   0  0.0    0   0  0.0    0  0  0  0  0
     0    0  96   6  335    0   0  0.0    0   0  0.0    0   0  0.0    0  0  0  0  0
```

The result allows you to compare I/O over a period of time. Note that in some systems, *iostat* may be *io_stat*, instead.

Another check is *vmstat* (*vm_stat*), which displays the virtual memory statistics for a machine. As with *iostat*, running the command several times over a period of time can show if there is unusual activity within virtual memory. For instance, if the free memory unexpectedly decreases, no known user is running a process, the occurrence of the free memory use is consistent (occurring at a set time of day), and no other system processes or *cron* jobs are known to be running, you probably have an intruding application running somewhere on the system. Other tests can then be used to help you determine what the application is.

—SP

48.7 Intruder Detection

From the CERT Intruder detection checklist at *http://www.cert.org/tech_tips/ intruder_detection_checklist.html* comes a variety of helpful steps to take to determine if your system has had an intruder.

Check logfiles first, and then check for any unusual *setgid* (49.5) or *setuid* files.

A key symptom that something is wrong with your system is when something appears that doesn't belong. This includes files, directories, users, and groups. Unfortunately, these are also almost impossible to detect unless they occur in obviously incorrect locations.

You can search for modified files based on a time range using the *find* (9.1) command. For instance, the following two commands will find all files that have been changed in the last two days excluding today. The results are piped to *cat* for easier reading:

```
> find /  -mtime -2 -mtime +1 -exec ls -ld {} \; | cat
> find /  -ctime -2 -ctime +1 -exec ls -ldc {} \; | cat
```

Running these commands as root will ensure you have access to all files and directories. Note that depending on the size of your system, the command can take a considerable amount of time.

Also check for hidden files, those beginning with a period. The following command searches every directory but NFS mounted ones for files beginning with a period (.):

```
find /  -name ".*" -print -xdev | cat -v
```

In addition, review critical files such as */etc/passwd* and the *crontab* file (25.3), checking for new and unusual entries. You might want to keep off-disk copies of the files to use for comparison; online versions can also be compromised.

Check binaries for possible changes and replacements—including backups—and changes to files such as *xinetd.conf*, allowing services such as telnet that were originally disallowed.

In other words, according to CERT, knowing your system and checking for changes using built-in utilities can be the best approach to take to detect intrusion.

—SP

48.8 Importance of MOTD

If you live in the United States, and depending on which state you live in, if you include the word "welcome" within the MOTD, this can legally be construed as an invitation, which means that anyone can come into the system if they can find a username and password. And since usernames and passwords are transmitted in plain text using telnet or a similar service, you're basically leaving your system open. If someone breaks in, they may not even be prosecutable.

Avoid the use of the word "welcome" in your message; instead use a message that specifically states that only authorized personnel are allowed access to the system. In addition, you'll also want to consider removing operating system information from the MOTD: no need to tell people more about your system then they need to know.

—SP

48.9 The Linux proc Filesystem

Linux contains a */proc* filesystem with virtual files that maintain the current state of the system. You can actually access the *proc* system directly and view the command, command-line parameters, and other information.

In particular, if you have a suspicious process (detected using *ps* (49.6)), you can investigate the process more thoroughly using the Linux *proc* filesystem. For instance, if *ps –ux* returns the following procecss:

```
Root   1684   0.0   0.7   7492   3888   ?   S   13:44   0.00   rp3
```

you can change to the process directory by using the process number:

```
bash# cd /proc/1684
```

Once there, typing ls will show several entries, including ones titled *cwd*, *exe*, and *cmdline*. At that point you can use *cat* (12.2) to print out the *cmdline* entry, which will show the command, including parameters that kicked off the process:

```
bash# cat cmdline
rp3
```

Typing ls -l on *cwd* results in:

```
lrwxrwxrwx      1    root    root    9    June 4    17:44  cwd-> /root
```

Typing ls-l on *exe* results in:

```
lrwxrwxrwx      1    root    root    9    June 4    17:44  cwd-> /usr/bin/
rp3
```

The *proc* filesystem is extremely helpful, not only for security reasons, but also for general system usage.

—SP

48.10 Disabling inetd

Any remote access that takes a plain text password increases the vulnerability of your system. This includes the use of telnet and FTP.

If your flavor of Unix is running the *inet* daemon, you can disable *telnet*, *ftp*, *rlogin*, and so on by accessing *the /etc/rc.conf* file and setting the *inetd_enable* value to no:

```
inetd_enable=no
```

You can disable individual services by accessing the *inetd.conf* file and setting the associated line to no, or commenting the line out, as shown in Darwin and BSD environments such as OpenBSD or FreeBSD:

```
#telnet stream tcp  nowait  root  /usr/libexe/tcpd    telnetd
```

—SP

48.11 Disallow rlogin and rsh

The remote access tools such as *rlogin*, to login remotely, and *rsh*, to execute commands on a remote system, are handy. For instance, with *rlogin*, if your username is the same on the remote machine as it is on the local machine, you don't have to provide your username and password.

However, the very simplicity of the *rlogin* and *rsh* commands makes them security risks. If you're concerned about the security of your Unix box, you'll want to disable these.

Disable both *rlogin* and *rsh* by commenting out their entries in *inetd.conf* or *xinetd.conf*, depending on which your system is running.

—*SP*

48.12 TCP Wrappers

TCP Wrappers are programs that work with *inetd* to monitor and filter *telnet*, *ftp*, *rlogin*, and other services. In particular, TCP wrappers provide log information showing access using these services, particularly helpful if you're trying to determine if someone's attempting to break into your system.

In FreeBSD, the TCP wrapper *tcpd* (documented at *http://www.freebsddiary.org/tcpwrapper.php*) is built into the system starting with FreeBSD 3.2 release, and is configured through the */etc/syslog.conf* file. The following lines from an existing file show that TCP logging is turned on for all remote access such as *telnet*, putting the log messages into a file called *auth.log*:

```
auth.*                          /var/log/auth.log
mail.info                       /var/log/maillog
lpr.info                        /var/log/lpd-errs
```

Since I have *telnet*, *rlogin*, etc. disabled from my system, nothing shows in the log file.

The TCP wrapper is also installed by default in Mac OS X. The *tcpd* daemon is installed in place of the service—such as in place of *fingerd*—or the entry for the service is adjusted to point to *tcpd* in */etc/inetd.conf*:

```
finger stream  tcp nowait nobody /some/where/tcpd  in.fingerd
```

By default, all unprotected external sources are wrapped with the TCP wrapper.

In some systems, the TCP wrapper is controlled by the */etc/hosts.allow* and */etc/hosts.deny* files instead of within *syslog.conf*. You'll want to check *tcpd* for your system by accessing the manpage for it:

```
# man tcpd
```

The same configuration and TCP wrapper (46.5)—known as the Wietse Venema's network logger—is used with Debian (downloadable at *http://packages.debian.org/cgi-bin/download.pl*) and Linux, as well as other operating systems.

—SP

49

Root, Group, and User Management

49.1 Unix User/Group Infrastructure

Unix users are given unique usernames and also added to one or more Unix groups (49.7). Both a user and a group own all content within a system. If you list information about a file, you'll see both user and group ownership:

```
> ls -l
-rw-r--r-- 1 root      weblog.burningbi  32230 May 22 13:58 access_log
-rw-r----- 1 shelleyp  weblog.burningbi   3995 May 12 11:08 analog.cfg
-rw-r--r-- 1 root      weblog.burningbi      0 May 22 12:01 error_log
```

In this listing, the users are *root* and *shelleyp*, and the group (truncated) is *weblog.burningbird.net*.

You're assigned a primary group when you're added to a system. In addition, you can also be assigned to one or more secondary groups. Depending on the type of Unix system, you can either work with files that are owned by any one of the groups you belong to or you can work with files of your primary group only.

BSD-based Unix systems allow you to work with files from primary and secondary groups; this includes Darwin as well as the popular PC-based BSD systems, FreeBSD, and OpenBSD. System V systems restrict you to working with a primary group only.

For the majority of Unix systems, user and group membership is controlled through a couple of files, *passwd* and *group*, stored in the */etc* directory. This directory has root write access only, but read and execute access by all users.

—*SP*

49.2 When Does a User Become a User

A user is added to the system when they're given an entry in the *passwd* file, as in the following entry:

```
mike:*:1007:1007:Mike User:/usr/home/mike:/usr/local/bin/bash
```

The elements, delimited by colons that make up this record, are:

Username
> Name used to login to system

Password entry
> Encrypted password, asterisk symbolizing bad password or use of shadow file, or exclamation point (!) to signify that the password is in */etc/security/passwd* or in */etc/master.passwd* in FreeBSD systems

UID
> Unique user identifier

Primary group ID
> ID of group that will be primary group for user

Comment
> General text holding name, address, and so on

User's home directory

User's startup shell

In the example, "mike" has a UID of 1007, belongs to group 1007, has a home directory in */usr/home/mike*, and logs into a bash shell. In this FreeBSD system, the password is stored in a separate shadow file.

Usernames are usually no more than 8 characters, though this differs based on type of system. Usernames consist of alphanumeric characters and are case-sensitive. Case sensitivity also applies with passwords, which can be longer and use other characters.

The UID must be unique, as would be expected. When a new user is added, the next available UID is usually used, but there's no restriction on having gaps or using order with UIDs. However, if the Unix box is part of a network, it is essential that the person's UID be unique across the network. The same constraints apply to the group ID: in most cases a new group ID equal to the UID is assigned the person. Addition to other groups occurs after the person is added to the system.

The UID of 0 (zero) is the superuser, root. The GID of 0 (zero) is wheel, the superuser group.

The user's name, address, office location, etc. can be included in the comment field, and the default home directory (created before adding the user) and person's startup shell is added to the record.

Adding users varies widely between systems. Apple's Darwin uses a separate system called *NetInfo*, an open source application (available at *http://sourceforge.net/projects/netinfo4unix/*) to manage users, groups, directories, and so on. A daemon uses information from NetInfo to control user access; the user "flat files," as *passwd* and *group* are known in this system, are used only in single-user environments.

In Linux, Solaris, and other systems, the process of adding a user is simplified with a utility, *adduser* (or *useradd*). The simple form of the utility is:

```
# adduser username
```

The utility is called with the username of the new user. Based on the system, the user is then added with defaults or you're interactively asked for more information. Or you can specify information on the command line that's used to create the user.

In Red Hat Linux, *adduser* is an alias for *useradd*. Default values are used for each user, such as a home location of */home/username* and a default shell (*bash*), unless specified otherwise on the command line. In the following example, a new user, *testuser*, is added. Command-line options are used to override the default information:

```
# useradd -c "Test User" -d /home/local/testuser -G 501, 502 -p changepassword
  -s /bin/bash -e 2002-05-24
```

In this example, -c is used to add a username comment (the user's full name), -G specifies what groups to add the person to, -p adds a password, -s sets the person's default shell, and -e specifies that the username expires on a certain date. The person is added to their own group—503 in this example. To override this I would use the -g command-line parameter—the -G only adds the person to additional groups, it doesn't override default behavior.

Within Mac OS X, user and group management is handled through Netinfo. Find out more about Netinfo at *http://www.opensource.apple.com/projects/documentation/howto/html/netinfo.html*. The command-line utility to add a user via Netinfo is niutil. An example of its use is:

```
shelleyp% niutil-create//users/newbie
```

Use the system's manpages to see if *useradd* or *adduser* is installed and the command line parameters supported.

—*SP*

49.3 Forgetting the root Password

If a person forgets their password, it's easy for root to reset it using *passwd*, but what happens if you forget root's password?

Depending on the security implemented for a system, you can log in to single user mode and then use *passwd* to reset the root password. Or you can manually edit the password file to remove the password for root. Once you reboot and login to the system as root, you can then use *passwd* to change the password to something more restrictive.

In Redhat Linux, access single-user mode by typing linux single at the boot prompt. In Solaris, enter single-user mode by pressing STOP-a and then typing boot-s at the prompt. FreeBSD boots in this mode by booting with the –s option and then mounting the file system in read/write mode. Check your system documentation to see how to do this for your particular flavor of Unix.

This approach works only if the system doesn't password-protect single-user mode. However, if you have access to the physical machine and the installation disks, booting with the install disk will usually allow you access to the partitions. Once you have this access, edit the password file and remove the root password.

As an example, Debian requires a password in single-user mode. To reset the root password with Debian, put the installation disk into the machine and boot. Mount the /root partition and manually edit the shadow file, setting the password to a blank password. After rebooting into the system, reset the password using *passwd*.

—SP

49.4 Setting an Exact umask

You can use the *umask* command to set the default mode for newly created files. Its argument is a three-digit numeric mode that represents the access to be *inhibited*—masked out—when a file is created. Thus, the value it wants is the octal complement of the numeric file mode you want. To determine this, you simply figure out the numeric equivalent for the file mode you want and then subtract it from 777. For example, to get the mode 751 by default, compute 777–751 = 026; this is the value you give to *umask*.

```
% umask 026
```

Once this command is executed, all future files created will be given this protection automatically. System administrators can put a *umask* command in the system initialization file to set a default for all users.

You can set your own *umask* in your shell setup files to override defaults.

—AF

49.5 Group Permissions in a Directory with the setgid Bit

If you work on a Unix system with lots of users, you may be taking advantage of Unix group permissions to let users in one group write to files in a directory, but not let people in other groups write there.

How does Unix determine what group should own the files you create? There are (at least!) two ways:

1. The effective group ID of the process determines the ownership of the files you create. (Your effective GID is your *primary group membership* unless you're running a SGID program.)

2. The group that owns the directory in which you create the file owns files.

The system administrator decides which of the methods a filesystem will use for group ownership. There are other wrinkles, too. A good place to look for the gory details is your system's *open* manpage help, but it's probably easier to just create an empty new file and then check the group ownership with *ls –l* or *–lg*.

You may be able to use the directory's *set group ID* (setgid) bit to control group ownership. In those cases, if the bit is set, the rule in point 2 applies. If the bit is not set, the rule in point 1 applies. To set and remove the setgid bit, use the commands *chmod g+s* and *chmod g-s*, respectively.

```
> chmod g+s mt.pl
> ls -l mt.pl
-rwxr-sr-x  1 shelleyp  shelleyp  1939 Apr 28 22:55 mt.pl
```

You can use the *chgrp* command to change a file's group.

```
> chgrp wheel mt.pl
> ls -l mt.pl
-rwxr-xr-x  1 shelleyp  wheel  1939 Apr 28 22:55 mt.pl
```

However, you must own the file, and you must also be a member of the file's new group. If you've reset directory mode bits, it's possible to wind up with *ls –l* permissions that have an uppercase S, like drwxr-S. What's that? (It's often a mistake.) The directory's setgid bit is set, but the execute bit isn't set. If you want the directory to be group-accessible, add execute permission with *chmod g+x*. Otherwise, you may want to clear the *setgid* bit with *chmod g-s*.

—*JP, SP*

49.6 Groups and Group Ownership

Group membership is an important part of Unix security. All users are members of one or more groups, as determined by their entries in */etc/passwd* and the */etc/group* files.

To find the GID number of your primary group, *grep* your entry in */etc/passwd*:

```
> grep shelleyp /etc/passwd
shelleyp:*:1000:1000:Shelley Powers:/usr/home/shelleyp:/bin/tcsh</screen>
```

The fourth field (the second number) is your *primary group ID*. Look up this number in the */etc/group* file:

```
> grep 1000 /etc/group
> shelleyp:*:1000:
```

On my FreeBSD system, my primary group is a group of which I'm the only member, *shelleyp*. Therefore, when I log in, my group ID is set to 1000.

To see what other groups you belong to, use the *groups* command if your Unix version has it. If not, you can get *groups* from the Free Software Directory at *http://www.gnu.org/directory/index.html*. Otherwise, look for your name in */etc/group*:

```
> grep shelleyp /etc/group
wheel:*:0:root,shelleyp
webadmin:*:900:shelleyp,burningbird
ftpadmin:*:901:shelleyp,burningbird
mailadmin:*:903:shelleyp,burningbird
sysadmin:*:905:shelleyp,burningbird
pkgadmin:*:906:shelleyp,burningbird
shelleyp:*:1000:
```

In the output, you can see that I'm a member of several groups, including *wheel*, *webadmin*, and so on. These are my secondary groups. The output also shows that the user "burningbird" is also a member of several of the same groups as myself.

On BSD-derived Unix systems (OpenBSD, FreeBSD, Darwin, and so on), you're always a member of all your groups. This means that I can access files that are owned by *webadmin*, *wheel*, and so on, without doing anything in particular. Under System V Unix, you can only be "in" one group at a time, even though you can be a member of several.

Within System V and Linux, if you need to access files that are owned by another group, use the *newgrp* command to change your primary group:

```
> newgrp groupname
```

The *newgrp* command starts a subshell. When you're done, type exit to leave the subshell. *newgrp* can be important for another reason: your primary group may own any new files you create. So *newgrp* is useful on any system where you want to set your group (for creating files, for example, when you aren't using a directory that sets its own group). If you can't use *newgrp*, the *chgrp* command will change a file's group owner.

The *ls –l* command shows a file's owner (and, in many versions, the *filefs* group too; if yours doesn't, add the *–g* option). The GNU *ls –nl* option shows a file's numeric UID and GID instead of the username and group name:

```
$ ls -l
total 38
-rw-r--r--  1 root      weblog.burningbi  33922 May 23 13:52 access_log
-rw-r-----  1 shelleyp  weblog.burningbi   3995 May 12 11:08 analog.cfg
-rw-r--r--  1 root      weblog.burningbi      0 May 23 12:01 error_log
```

```
$ ls -ln
total 37
-rw-r--r--  1 0     501  32890 May 23 13:50 access_log
-rw-r-----  1 1000  501   3995 May 12 11:08 analog.cfg
-rw-r--r--  1 0     501      0 May 23 12:01 error_log
```

(System V–based Unixes even let you change to groups that you don't belong to. In this case, you have to give a group password. Group passwords are rarely used: usually the password field is filled with a *, which effectively says that there are no valid passwords for this group.)

On most systems, there are groups for major projects or departments, groups for system administration, and maybe one or two groups for visitors. BSD-based systems often have a *wheel* group; to become root, you must belong to *wheel*. Many systems make terminals writable only by the owner and a special group named *tty*; this prevents other users from sending characters to your terminal without using an approved *setgid* program like *write*.

—*JP, SP*

49.7 Add Users to a Group to Deny Permissions

Usually, Unix group access allows a group of users to access a directory or file that they couldn't otherwise access. You can turn this around, though, with groups that *deny* permission.

This trick works only on Unix systems, like BSD (FreeBSD, Darwin, OpenBSD, and so on), that let a user belong to more than one group at the same time.

For example, you might work on a computer that has some proprietary files and software that "guest" accounts shouldn't be able to use. Everyone else on the computer should have access. To do this, put the software in a directory owned by a group named something like *deny*. Then use *chmod* to deny permission to that group:

```
# chmod 705 /usr/local/somedir
# ls -lgd /usr/local/somedir
drwx---r-x  2    root   deny     512  Mar 26 12:14 /usr/local/somedir
```

Finally, add the guest accounts to the *deny* group.

Unix checks permissions in the order user-group-other. The first applicable permission is the one used, even if it denies permission rather than grant it. In this case, none of the guest accounts are root (we hope!).

They're members of the group called *deny*, however; that permission (---) is checked and the group members are shut out. Other users who aren't members of *deny* are checked for "other" access (r-x); they can get into the directory.

The same setup works for individual files (like programs). Just be careful about changing system programs that are SUID or SGID.

—JIK

49.8 Care and Feeding of SUID and SGID Scripts

Scripts may need to run within a root environment but be executed by system users other than root. To allow a nonroot user or group of users executable access of the script, its SUID or SGID bit can be set.

The SUID bit is set using the following command:

```
chmod u+s somefile
```

Running *ls –l* on the file afterwards displays the following (within FreeBSD):

```
-rwSr--r--  1 root  somegroup  7219 Oct 29  2001 somefile
```

Now, any user can execute the file, and the file runs with root permissions.

A more restricted version of SUID is SGID, set as follows:

```
-rwx-r-Sr-- 1 root somegroup 7219 Oct 29 2001 somefile
```

Users belong to the specified group, *somegroup*, can execute the file now, and it runs with root permissions.

As handy as SUID and SGID scripts are, they are also dangerous. For instance, SUID scripts are considered so dangerous that the Linux kernel won't even honor them. This is because environmental variables are easily manipulated within scripts, particularly C shell scripts, as discussed in article 50.9. And since the scripts can be run by anybody, and run as root, they represent extreme points of vulnerability.

To see where you have SUID and SGID scripts, use the following command (pulled from the Linux Security HOWTO document at *http://www.cpmc.columbia.edu/misc/docs/linux/security-howto.html*):

```
find / -type f \( -perm -04000 -o -perm -02000 \)
```

To do a thorough scan, you need to have root permissions.

You'll be surprised at the number of applications returned from the search. Among those in my FreeBSD system were:

```
/usr/virtual/share/usr/sbin/pstat
/usr/virtual/share/usr/sbin/swapinfo
/usr/virtual/share/usr/sbin/sliplogin
/usr/virtual/share/usr/sbin/timedc
/usr/virtual/share/usr/sbin/traceroute
```

However, a quick check shows that the files—sharable across different FreeBSD installations—are all SGID: not as dangerous as SUID files long as the group is restricted.

—SP

49.9 Substitute Identity with su

You don't have to login as a specific user—you can login as yourself and then issue a *su* command to login as another person.

Invoke *su* with a username and you'll be prompted for that person's password. If you invoke *su* without a username, the system logs you in as root and asks you for root's password. Without passing in any other flags, you'll be logged in with your environment variables, except for *HOME, SHELL,* and *USER.* If you want to emulate the full environment of the user—for debugging purposes or whatever—use the *–l* flag with *su:*

```
bash-2.04$ su -l
Password:
```

Using *su* to emulate another person's account is an effective debugging solution if you're trying to determine why a person is having problems accessing an application. In addition, it's also an effective way of logging into root without logging in from a console or remotely from another machine or terminal.

You exit the *su* shell by typing exit or hitting CTRL-d.

—SP, JP

49.10 Never Log In as root

The easiest way to allow a cracker into your system is to provide external root login access. In particular, if you allow root access through an unprotected and open protocol such as telnet, you're almost guaranteeing that your Unix box is going to be violated at some point.

To prevent this, most Unix systems don't allow remote login into the system as root. Instead, you log in under another username and then *su* to root once you're within the system.

Disabling root access differs between systems. If your box has an */etc/securetty* file, this lists ttys that allow root access. Removing this file or removing its contents will disable root access.

In Solaris, a line within */etc/default/login* file is commented out if remote root login is allowed:

```
#CONSOLE=/dev/console
```

Uncomment the line to allow root access through the system console. To completely disable console access, remove the *\/dev\/console* from the line:

```
CONSOLE=
```

—SP

49.11 Providing Superpowers with sudo

You may not want to give people access to the root password just to give them access to specific superuser powers. In cases such as this, you should consider using *sudo*—an application that enables specified users to execute applications that normally require root privileges.

The *sudo* application isn't installed by default on all systems, but it is available for most. You can find out if it's installed on your system by typing sudo at the command line. If it isn't installed, check online for versions that run on your machine. The application's home is at *http://www.courtesan.com/sudo/index.html*.

The *sudo* configuration file is called *sudoers* and is installed in the */etc* subdirectory. In Darwin, the default *sudoers* file has the following settings:

```
root  ALL=(ALL) ALL
%admin ALL=(ALL) ALL
```

In the file, root has open access to all applications. In addition, all members of the *admin* group (equivalent to *wheel* within Darwin) can also run all commands.

Without getting into too much detail (an online *sudoers* manual is at *http://www.courtesan.com/sudo/man/sudoers.html*), the *sudoers* file can consist of a set of aliases, used to define groups of people, commands, hosts, or run as options. It then defines rules by which specific users or group of users can run specific commands. There are four types of aliases:

User_Alias
List of specific users

Runas_Alias
List of users to emulate

Host_Alias
List of servers

Cmnd_Alias
Command list

Examples of aliases are:

```
User_Alias     SYSADMINS = shelleyp, mike, tomd
Runas_Alias    OP = root
Host_Alias     BB = burningbird
Cmnd_Alias     SU = /usr/bin/su
```

Following the aliases are override rules in reference to system defaults. For instance, warnings and "lectures" can be attached to certain commands to ensure that people are aware of the repercussions of their actions. However, people who are sysadmins shouldn't be subjected to these rules; the lectures can be turned off for them:

```
Defaults:SYSADMINS        !lecture
```

Neither aliases nor default overriding rules are required in the *sudoers* file. The only statements that are required are the command rules. In the Darwin file, the rules allowed root and *admin* access of all commands. Other rules that can be created are:

```
# sysadmins can run all commands, without password
SYSADMINS    ALL = NOPASSWD: ALL

# chris can run anything on the burningbird machine as OP (root)
chris        BB = (OP) ALL

# joe can run SU on burningbird as root
joe          BB = (root) SU
```

To edit the *sudoers* file, you use a specialized editing tool, *visudo* (see manual at *http://www.courtesan.com/sudo/man/visudo.html*), while logged in as root. The editor prevents collision between multiple authors and also verifies the correctness of the edits.

To work with *sudo* (manual at *http://www.courtesan.com/sudo/man/sudo.html*), type sudo and the command you want to exit:

```
% sudo vi test
```

Depending on your setup, you'll get a warning or a password prompt, or the command will fail or execute.

One interesting side effect of *sudo* is that if you allow root access to an application that has shell escape, such as *vi*, you are indirectly giving that person access to a root shell. Use *sudo* with caution.

—SP

49.12 Enabling Root in Darwin

The majority of Mac OS X users are never going to access the built-in Unix Terminal and never directly access the Darwin core of the operating system. Instead, they'll work within the GUI. However, Mac OS X developers and superusers will operate directly with Darwin quite extensively, and at times, they'll need to have root access.

By default, root access in Darwin is disabled. Trying to use *su* to change to root within the Terminal will fail. You have to enable root first using NetInfo.

To enable root within Mac OS X, access the Go menu option of Finder, and double-click on Applications. When the *Applications* window opens, double-click on the *Utilities* folder. In this folder, select and open NetInfo.

When NetInfo opens, select the Domain menu item and then Security. You'll need to authenticate yourself to the system first by selecting the Authenticate submenu option. Once you provide a password (and the system determines you have the authority to enable or disable root), accessing the Security menu again will show a newly enabled option: Enable Root User. Clicking on this enables root. However, you'll need to reauthenticate one more time to ensure the change goes through.

Once root is enabled for the system, it stays enabled until you disable it again. With root enabled, you'll be able to use *su* to login as root.

—*SP*

49.13 Disable logins

You can temporarily disable logins by creating an entry in */etc/nologin* (3.1) and copying a message to this location. When a user attempts to log in, he will get this message and the system will prevent entry.

—*SP*

50

File Security, Ownership, and Sharing

50.1 Introduction to File Ownership and Security

Because Unix is a multiuser system, you need some way of protecting users from one another: you don't want other users to look at the wrong files and find out compromising information about you, or raise their salaries, or something equivalently antisocial. Even if you're on a single-user system, file ownership still has value: it can often protect you from making mistakes, like deleting important executables.

In this chapter, we'll describe how file ownership works: who owns files, how to change ownership, how to specify which kinds of file access are allowed, and so on. We'll also discuss some other ways to prevent people from "prying," like clearing your screen.

In my opinion, most security breaches arise from mistakes that could easily have been avoided: someone discovers that *anyone* can read the boss's email, including the messages to his bookie. Once you've read this chapter, you'll understand how to avoid the common mistakes and protect yourself from most intruders.

—ML

50.2 Tutorial on File and Directory Permissions

Regardless of how much you think you know about file permissions, there's always something new to learn.

There are three basic attributes for plain file permissions: read, write, and execute. Read and write permission obviously let you read the data from a file or write new data to the file. When you have execute permission, you can use the file as a program or shell script. The characters used to describe these permissions are r, w, and x, for execute.

Directories use these same permissions, but they have a different meaning. If a directory has read permission, you can see what files are in the directory. Write permission means you can add, remove, or rename files in the directory. Execute allows you to use the directory name when accessing files inside that directory. (Article 10.2 has more information about what's in a directory.) Let's examine this more closely.

Suppose you have read access to a directory but don't have execute access to the files contained in it. You can still read the directory, or *inode* information for that file, as returned by the *stat*(2) system call. That is, you can see the file's name, permissions, size, access times, owner and group, and number of links. You just cannot read the contents of the file.

Write permission in a directory allows you to change the contents in it. Because the name of the file is stored in the directory and not the file, *write permission in a directory allows creation, renaming, or deletion of files.* To be specific, if someone has write permission to your home directory, they can rename or delete your *.login* file and put a new file in its place. The permissions of your *.login* file do not matter in this regard. Someone can rename a file even if they can't read the contents of a file. (See article 50.9.)

Execute permission on a directory is sometimes called search permission. If a directory gives you execute but not read permission, you can use any file in that directory; however, you *must* know the name. You cannot look inside the directory to find out the names of the files. Think of this type of directory as a black box. You can throw filenames at this directory, and sometimes you find a file, sometimes you don't. (See article 50.10.)

User, Group, and World

All files have an owner and group associated with them. There are three sets of read/write/execute permissions: one set for the user or owner of the file, one set for the group (49.6) of the file, and one set for everyone else. These permissions are determined by nine bits in the inode information and are represented by the characters rwxrwxrwx in an *ls –l* listing:[*]

```
% ls -l
drwxr-xr-x  3 jerry   books     512 Feb 14 11:31 manpages
-rw-r--r--  1 jerry   books   17233 Dec 10  2001 misc.Z
-rwxr-xr-x  1 tim     books     195 Mar 29 18:55 myhead
```

---

[*] On some Unix systems, *ls –l* produces an eight-column listing without the group name (here, books). Use *ls –lg* to get the listing format shown here.

The first character in the *ls -l* listing specifies the type of file (9.13). The first three of the nine permissions characters that follow specify the user; the middle three, the group; and the last three, the world. If the permission is not true, a dash is used to indicate lack of privilege. If you want to have a data file that you can read or write but don't want anyone else to access, the permissions would be rw-------.

An easier way to specify these nine bits is with three octal digits instead of nine characters. (Article 1.17 has diagrams of permission bits and explains how to write permissions as an octal number.) The order is the same, so the above permissions can be described by the octal number 600. The first number specifies the owner's permission. The second number specifies the group's permission. The last number specifies permission to everyone who is not the owner or not in the group of the file [although permissions don't apply to the superuser (1.18), who can do anything to any file or directory. —*JP*].

This last point is subtle. When testing for permissions, the system looks at the groups in order. If you are denied permission, Unix does not examine the next group. Consider the case of a file that is owned by user *jo*, is in the group *guests*, and has the permissions -----xrwx, or 017 in octal. This has the result that user *jo* cannot use the file, anyone in group *guests* can execute the program, and everyone else besides *jo* and *guests* can read, write, and execute the program. This is not a very common set of permissions, but some people use a similar mechanism (49.7) to deny one group of users from accessing or using a file. In the above case, *jo* cannot read or write the file she owns. She could use the *chmod* (50.5) command to grant herself permission to read the file. However, if the file was in a directory owned by someone else, and the directory did not give *jo* read or search permission, she would not be able to find the file to change its permission.

The above example is an extreme case. Most of the time permissions fall into four cases:

1. The information is personal. Many people have a directory or two in which they store information they do not wish to be public. Mail should probably be confidential, and all of your mailbox files should be in a directory with permissions of 700, denying everyone but yourself and the superuser read access to your letters. (See article 7.5.)

2. The information is not personal, yet no one should be able to modify the information. Most of my directories are set up this way, with the permissions of 755.

3. The files are managed by a team of people. This means group-write permission, or directories with the mode 775.

4. In the previous case, for confidential projects, you may want to deny access to people outside the group. In this case, make directories with mode 770.

You could just create a directory with the proper permissions and put the files inside the directory, hoping the permissions of the directory will "protect" the files in the directory. This is not adequate. Suppose you had a directory with permissions 755 and a file with permissions 666 inside the directory. Anyone could change the contents of this file because the world has search access on the directory and write access to the file.

umask.csh
umask.sh

What is needed is a mechanism to prevent any new file from having world-write access. This mechanism exists with the *umask* command. If you consider that a new directory would get permissions of 777, and that new files would get permissions of 666, the *umask* command specifies permissions to "take away" from all new files. To "subtract" world-write permission from a file, 666 must have 002 "subtracted" from the default value to get 664. To subtract group and world write, 666 must have 022 removed to leave 644 as the permissions of the file. These two values of *umask* are so common that it is useful to have some aliases (49.4) defined:

```
alias open umask 002
alias shut umask 022
```

With these two values of *umask*, new directories will have permissions of 775 or 755. Most people have a *umask* value of one of these two values.

In a friendly work group, people tend to use the *umask* of 002, which allows others in your group to make changes to your files. Someone who uses the mask of 022 will cause grief to others working on a project. Trying to compile a program is frustrating when someone else owns files that you must delete but can't. You can rename files if this is the case or ask the system administrator for help.

Members of a team who normally use a default umask of 022 should find a means to change the mask value when working on the project (or else risk flames from your fellow workers!). Besides the *open* alias above, some people have an alias that changes directories and sets the mask to group-write permission:

```
alias proj "cd /usr/projects/proj;umask 002"
```

This isn't perfect, because people forget to use aliases. You could have a special *cd* alias and a private shell file in each project directory that sets the *umask* when you *cd* there. Other people could have similar files in the project directory with different names. Article 31.13 shows how.

Still another method is to run *find* (9.1) three times a day and search for files owned by you in the project directory that have the wrong permission:

$USER 35.5
xargs 28.17
chmod 50.5

```
% find /usr/projects -user $USER ! -perm -020 -print | \
    xargs chmod g+w
```

You can use the command *crontab –e* (25.2) to define when to run this command.

Which Group is Which?

Since group-write permission is so important in a team project, you might be wondering how the group of a new file is determined. The answer depends on several factors. Before I cover these, you should note that Berkeley and AT&T-based systems would use different mechanisms to determine the default group.

Originally Unix required you to specify a new group with the *newgrp* command. If there was a password for this group in the */etc/group* file, and you were not listed as one of the members of the group, you had to type the password to change your group.

Berkeley-based versions of Unix would use the current directory to determine the group of the new file. That is, if the current directory has *cad* as the group of the directory, any file created in that directory would be in the same group. To change the default group, just change to a different directory.

Both mechanisms had their good points and bad points. The Berkeley-based mechanism made it convenient to change groups automatically. However, there is a fixed limit of groups one could belong to. SunOS 4 has a limit of 16 groups. Earlier versions had a limit of 8 groups.

SunOS and System V Release 4 support both mechanisms. The entire disk can be mounted with either the AT&T or the Berkeley mechanism. If it is necessary to control this on a directory-by-directory basis, a special bit in the file permissions is used. If a disk partition is mounted without the Berkeley group mechanism, a directory with this special bit will make new files have the same group as the directory. Without the special bit, the group of all new files depends on the current group of the user.

—*BB*

50.3 Who Will Own a New File?

If you share files with other users, it's good to be able to tell who will own each file. On many systems, this is even more important because only the superuser can change file ownership (50.14, 50.15).

1. When you create a new file, it belongs to you.

2. When you append to a file with >>*file*, the owner doesn't change because Unix doesn't have to create a new file.

3. When you rename a file with *mv*, the ownership doesn't change.

   Exception: if you use *mv* to move a file to another filesystem, the moved file will belong to you, because to move across filesystems, *mv* actually has to copy the file and delete the original.

4. When you copy a file, the copy belongs to you because you created it (50.9).

5. When you edit a file:

- With an editor like *vi* (17.2), the file keeps its original owner because a new file is never created.
- An editor like Emacs (19.1), which makes a backup copy, can be different. The backup copy could belong to you or to the original owner. If you replace the edited file with its backup, the file's ownership might have changed:

```
% emacs filea
   ...Edit a lot, then decide you don't want your changes...
% mv filea~ filea
```

If you aren't sure, use *ls –l* (50.2).

—*JP*

50.4 Protecting Files with the Sticky Bit

Unix directory access permissions specify that a person with write access to the directory can rename or remove files there—even files that don't belong to the person (see article 50.9). Many newer versions of Unix have a way to stop that. The owner of a directory can set its *sticky bit* (mode (1.17) 1000). The only people who can rename or remove any file in that directory are the file's owner, the directory's owner, and the superuser.

Here's an example: the user *jerry* makes a world-writable directory and sets the sticky bit (shown as t here):

```
jerry% mkdir share
jerry% chmod 1777 share
jerry% ls -ld share
drwxrwxrwt   2 jerry     ora          32 Nov 19 10:31 share
```

Other people create files in it. When *jennifer* tries to remove a file that belongs to *ellie*, she can't:

```
jennifer% ls -l
total 2
-rw-r--r--   1 ellie     ora         120 Nov 19 11:32 data.ellie
-rw-r--r--   1 jennifer  ora        3421 Nov 19 15:34 data.jennifer
-rw-r--r--   1 peter     ora         728 Nov 20 12:29 data.peter
jennifer% rm data.ellie
data.ellie: override 644 mode ? y
rm: data.ellie not removed.
Permission denied
```

—*JP*

50.5 Using chmod to Change File Permission

To change a file's permissions, you need to use the *chmod* command, and you must be the file's owner or root. The command's syntax is pretty simple:

```
% chmod new-mode file(s)
```

The *new-mode* describes the access permissions you want *after* the change. There are two ways to specify the mode: you can use either a *numeric mode* or some symbols that describe the changes. I generally prefer the numeric mode (because I'm strange, I suppose). To use a numeric mode, decide what permissions you want to have, express them as an octal number (1.17, 50.2), and give a command like this one:

```
% chmod 644 report.txt
```

This gives read and write access to the owner of *report.txt* and read-only access to everyone else.

Many users prefer to use the *symbolic mode* to specify permissions. A symbolic *chmod* command looks like this:

```
% chmod g-w report.txt
```

This means "take away write access for group members." The symbols used in mode specifications are shown in Table 50-1.

Table 50-1. chmod symbolic modes

Category	Mode	Description
Who	u	User (owner) of the file.
	g	Group members.
	o	Others.
	a	All (i.e., user, group, and others).
What to do	–	Take away this permission.
	+	Add this permission.
	=	Set exactly this permission (50.6).
Permissions	r	Read access.
	w	Write access.
	x	Execute access.
	X	Give (or deny) execute permission to directories, or to files that have another "execute" bit set.
	s	Set user or group ID (only valid with + or -).
	t	Set the "sticky bit" (50.4, 1.17).

(Article 50.2 explains the "Who" and "Permissions" categories.) Here are a few example symbolic modes:

o=r

>Set others access to read-only, regardless of what other bits are set.

o+r

>Add read access for others.

go-w

>Take away write access for group members and others.

a=rw

>Give everyone (user, group, and others) read-write (but not execute) access.

Remember that + and - add or delete certain permissions but leave the others untouched. The commands below show how permissions are added and sub-tracted:

```
% ls -l foo
-rwx-----x  1 mikel        0 Mar 30 11:02 foo
% chmod a+x foo
% ls -l foo
-rwx--x--x  1 mikel        0 Mar 30 11:02 foo
% chmod o-x,g+r foo
% ls -l foo
-rwxr-x---  1 mikel        0 Mar 30 11:02 foo
%
```

Note the last *chmod* command. It shows something we haven't mentioned before. With symbolic mode, you're allowed to combine two (or more) specifications, separated by commas. This command says "take away execute permission for others, and add read access for group members."

On occasion, I've wanted to change the permissions of a whole directory tree: all the files in a directory and all of its subdirectories. In this case, you want to use *chmod –R* (the R stands for recursive) or *find –exec* (9.9, 50.6). You won't need this often, but when you do, it's a real lifesaver.

—*ML*

50.6 The Handy chmod = Operator

Let's say you have a set of files. Some are writable by you; others are read-only. You want to give people in your group the same permissions you have—that is, they can write writable files but can only read the read-only files. It's easy with an underdocumented feature of *chmod*:

```
% chmod g=u *
```

That means "for all files (*), set the group permissions (g) to be the same as the owner permissions (u)." You can also use the letter o for others, which is everyone who's not the owner or in the owner's group. Article 50.2 explains these categories.

If your *chmod* has a −R (recursive) option, you can make the same change to all files and directories in your current directory and beneath. If you don't have *chmod* −R, use this *find* (9.9):

```
% find . -exec chmod g=u {} \;
```

—*JP*

50.7 Protect Important Files: Make Them Unwritable

A good way to prevent yourself from making mistakes is to make certain files read-only. If you try to delete a read-only file, you will get a warning. You will also get a warning if you try to move a file onto another file that is write-protected. If you know you want to remove or move a file, even though the file is read-only, you can use the −*f* option with *rm* or *mv* to *force* the change without warnings.

Manually changing the permissions of files all the time is counterproductive. You could create two aliases to make it easier to type:

chmod.csh
chmod.sh

```
# change mode to read only
alias -w chmod -w
# change mode to add write permission
alias +w chmod u+w
```

chmod_edit

[These are really handy! I use a script named *c−w* and *cw*, respectively, instead. For shell programming, I also added *cx* that does *chmod +x*. Article 50.8 explains the script. —*JP*] It is a good idea to remove write permission from some files. Occasionally some files contain information difficult to replace. These files might be included with other, easily replaceable files. Or you might want to protect some files that rarely change. Combined with directory permissions and the current value of *umask* (49.4), you can find some file that might be protected in this manner. You can always create a script that adds write permission, edits the file, and removes write permission:

"$@" 35.20

${..=..} 36.7

```
#!/bin/sh
# add write permission to the files
chmod u+w "$@"
# edit the files; use vi if VISUAL not defined
${VISUAL=vi} "$@"
# remove write permission
chmod -w "$@"
```

—*BB*

50.8 cx, cw, c-w: Quick File Permission Changes

Here's a short script that I use a lot. To make a new shell script executable, for example, I type:

```
% cx scriptfile
```

Using *cw* adds write permission; *c-w* takes it away. This is the single script file for all three commands:

```
#! /bin/sh
case "$0" in
*cx)  chmod +x "$@" ;;
*cw)  chmod +w "$@" ;;
*c-w) chmod -w "$@" ;;
*)    echo "$0: Help!  Shouldn't get here!" 1>&2; exit 1 ;;
esac
```

The script has three links. Put it in a file named *cx*. Then type:

```
% chmod +x cx
% ln cx cw
% ln cx c-w
```

The script tests the name it was called with, in $0, to decide which *chmod* command to run. This trick saves disk space. You can add other commands, too, by adding a line to the *case* and another link. Or you can use aliases (50.7).

—*JP*

50.9 A Loophole: Modifying Files Without Write Access

No one said that Unix is perfect (1.20), and one of its nagging problems has always been security. Here's one glitch that you should be aware of. If you don't have write access to a file, you can't modify it. However, if you have write access to the directory, you can get around this as follows:

```
% ls -l unwritable
-r--r--r-- 1 john        334 Mar 30 14:57 unwritable
% cat > unwritable
unwritable: permission denied
% cat unwritable > temp
% vi temp
   ...
% mv temp unwritable
override protection 444 for unwritable? y
% cat unwritable
John wrote this originally, and made the file read-only.
But then Mike came along and wrote:
I should not have been able to do this!!!
```

I couldn't write the file *unwritable* directly. But I was able to copy it, and then use *vi* to make whatever changes I wanted. After all, I had read access, and to copy a file, you only need to be able to read it. When I had my own copy, I could (of course) edit it to my heart's content. When I was done, I was able to *mv* the new file on top of *unwritable*. Why? Renaming a file requires only that you be able to write the file's directory. You don't need to be able to write the file itself. (Note that *cp* wouldn't work—copying requires *unwritable* to be writable, if it already exists.) This is one reason to watch directory access fairly closely.

As you can see, allowing directory-write access to others can be dangerous. If this is a problem for you, solve it by setting your *umask* (49.4) correctly and using *chmod* (50.5) to fix permissions of existing directories. Or you may be able to leave the directory writable and set the directory's sticky bit (50.4).

—ML

50.10 A Directory That People Can Access but Can't List

Do you need to let someone use a file of yours, but you don't want everyone on the system to be able to snoop around in the directory? You can give execute permission, but not read permission, to a directory. Then, if a file in the directory is accessible, a person can use the file by typing the exact filename. *ls* will say the directory is "unreadable." Wildcards won't work.

Here's an example. Let's say that your home directory has rwxr-xr-x permissions (everyone can access and list files in it). Your username is *hanna*. You have a subdirectory named *project*; you set its permissions so that everyone else on the system has execute-only permission.

```
hanna% pwd
/home/hanna
hanna% chmod 711 project
hanna% ls -ld project project/myplan
drwx--x--x  2  hanna    512  Jul 26 12:14 project
-rw-r--r--  1  hanna   9284  Jul 27 17:34 project/myplan
```

-d 8.5

Now you tell the other user, *toria*, the exact name of your file, *myplan*. Like everyone else on the system, she can access your *project* directory. She can't list it because she doesn't have read permission. Because she knows the exact filename, she can read the file because the file is readable (anyone else could read the file, too, if they knew its exact name):

```
toria% cd /home/hanna/project
toria% pwd
pwd: can't read .
toria% ls
```

```
ls: . unreadable
toria% more myplan
    ...File appears...
toria% ln myplan /home/toria/project.hanna/plan
```

(We're using the "real" *pwd* command that reads the filesystem to find your current directory. That's why it complains can't read .. If you're using the shell's shortcut *pwd*, you probably won't get the error shown above. Article 31.4 has details.)

In the example above, *toria* made a hard link (10.5) to the *myplan* file, with a different name, in her own *project.hanna* directory. (She could have copied, printed, or used any other command that reads the file.) Now, if you (*hanna*) want to, you can deny everyone's permission to your *project* directory. *toria* still has her link to the file, though. She can read it any time she wants to, follow the changes you make to it, and so on:

```
toria% cd
toria% ls -ld project.hanna project.hanna/plan
drwx------  2   toria   512  Jul 27 16:43 project.hanna
-rw-r--r--  2   hanna  9284  Jul 27 17:34 project.hanna/plan
toria% more project.hanna/plan
    ...File appears...
```

toria has protected her *project.hanna* directory so that other users can't find her link to *hanna*'s file.

If *hanna* denies permission to her directory, *toria* can still read the file through her hard link. If *toria* had made a symbolic link, though, she wouldn't be able to access the file any more. That's because a hard link keeps the file's i-number (10.2) but a symbolic link doesn't.

You might also want to give other users permission to list and access the files in a directory, but not make the directory open to all users. One way to do this is to put a fully accessible directory with an unusual name inside an unreadable directory. Users who know the exact name of the fully accessible directory can *cd* to it; other users can't find it without its name:

```
hanna% chmod 711 project
hanna% chmod 777 project/pLaN
hanna% ls -ld project project/pLaN
drwx--x--x  3   hanna   512  Jul 27 17:36 project
drwxrwxrwx  2   hanna   512  Jul 27 17:37 project/pLaN
```

Users who type cd /home/hanna/project/pLaN can list the directory's contents with *ls*. With the permissions you've set, other users can also create, delete, and rename files inside the *pLaN* directory—though you could have used more restrictive permissions like drwxr-xr-x instead.

This setup can still be a little confusing. For instance, as article 31.4 explains, the *pwd* command won't work for users in the *pLaN* directory because *pwd* can't read the *project* directory. Variables like $cwd and $PWD (35.5) will probably have the absolute pathname. If another user gets lost in a restricted directory like this, the best thing to do is *cd* to the home directory and start again.

—*JP*

50.11 Juggling Permissions

Like any security feature, Unix permissions occasionally get in your way. When you want to let people use your apartment, you have to make sure you can get them a key; and when you want to let someone into your files, you have to make sure they have read and write access.

In the ideal world, each file would have a list of users who can access it, and the file's owner could just add or delete users from that list at will. Some secure versions of Unix are configured this way, but standard Unix systems don't provide that degree of control. Instead, we have to know how to juggle Unix file permissions to achieve our ends.

For example, suppose I have a file called *ch01* that I want edited by another user, *joe*. I tell him that the file is */books/ptools/ch01*, but he reports to me that he can't access it.

```
joe % cd /books/ptools
joe % more ch01
ch01: Permission denied
```

The reason *joe* can't read the file is that it is set to be readable only by me. *joe* can check the permissions on the file using the *–l* option to the *ls* command:

```
joe % ls -l ch01
-rw------- 1 lmui     13727 Sep 21 07:43 ch01
```

joe asks me (*lmui*) to give him read and write permission on the file. Only the file owner and *root* can change permission for a file. Now, what's the best way to give *joe* access to *ch01*?

The fastest and most sure-fire way to give another user permission is to extend read and write permission to everyone:

```
lmui % chmod 666 ch01
lmui % ls -l ch01
-rw-rw-rw- 1 lmui     13727 Sep 21 07:43 ch01
```

But this is sort of like leaving your front door wide open so your cat can get in and out. It's far better to extend read and write access to a common group instead of to the entire world. I try to give *joe* access to the file by giving group read and write access:

```
lmui % chmod 660 ch01
lmui % ls -l ch01
-rw-rw----  1 lmui       13727 Sep 21 07:43 ch01
```

But *joe* reports that it still doesn't work:

```
joe % more ch01
ch01: Permission denied
```

What happened? Well, I gave read and write permission to the file's group, but *joe* doesn't belong to that group. You can find out the group a file belongs to using the *–lg* option to *ls*. (This is the default on many systems when you type ls -l. Other systems are different. For instance, the GNU *ls* command ignores *–g* and has a *–G* option for when you don't want to see the group name.)

```
joe % ls -lg ch01
-rw-rw----  1 lmui     power       13727 Sep 21 07:43 ch01
```

You can use the *groups* command (49.6) to find out what groups a user belongs to:

```
% groups joe
joe : authors ora
% groups lmui
lmui : authors power wheel ora
```

The *ch01* file belongs to group *power*. *joe* isn't a member of this group, but both *lmui* and *joe* are in the *authors* group. To give *joe* access to the file *ch01*, therefore, I need to put the file in group *authors*. To do that, I use the *chgrp* (1.17) command:

```
lmui % chgrp authors ch01
lmui % ls -lg ch01
-rw-rw----  1 lmui     authors     13727 Sep 21 07:43 ch01
```

Now *joe* can read and write the file. (On some systems, he may need to run *newgrp* (49.4) first.)

—*LM*

50.12 File Verification with md5sum

How can you know if a file has been corrupted—by accident or by a malicious user? You can check the number of characters with *ls –l* (50.2), but the corrupted file could have the same number of characters, just some *different* ones. You can check the last-modification date (8.2), but that's easy to change, to any time you want, with *touch*. And, of course, you can read through the file, unless it's a binary (nonprintable) file or it's just too long.

md5sum

The easy way is to compute a *checksum*—an electronic *fingerprint* or *message digest*—that identifies the file at a time you know it's correct. Save that checksum in a secure place (on an unwritable CD-ROM, on a filesystem with write protection disabled in hardware, or just on a piece of paper). Then, when you want to verify the file, recompute the checksum and compare it to the original. That's just what the *md5sum* utility does.

md5sum is a more secure version of the earlier Unix *sum* program, and it's also handier to use. By default, you give *md5sum* a list of pathnames; it will write checksums to its standard output. Later, use the *md5sum –c* ("check") option to compare the files to their checksums. The first command below calculates checksums for some *gzipped tar* archives and saves it in a temporary file. (If we were doing this "for real," I'd copy that temporary file someplace more secure!) The second command shows the file. The third command compares the files to their stored checksums:

```
$ md5sum *.tar.gz > /tmp/sums.out
$ cat /tmp/sums.out
018f4aee79e049095a7b16ed1e7ec925  linux-ar-40.tar.gz
52549f8e390db06f9366ee83e59f64de  nvi-1.79.tar.gz
856b4af521fdb78c978e5576f269c1c6  palinux.tar.gz
61dcb5614a61bf123e1345e869eb99d4  sp-1.3.4.tar.gz
c22bc000bee0f7d6f4845eab72a81395  ssh-1.2.27.tar.gz
e5162eb6d4a40e9e90d0523f187e615f  vmware-forlinux-103.tar.gz
       ...sometime later, maybe...
$ md5sum -c /tmp/sums.out
linux-ar-40.tar.gz: OK
nvi-1.79.tar.gz: OK
palinux.tar.gz: OK
sp-1.3.4.tar.gz: OK
ssh-1.2.27.tar.gz: OK
vmware-forlinux-103.tar.gz: OK
$ echo $?
```

$? 35.12

If all the files match, *md5sum* returns an exit status of 0. Files that don't match give a FAILED message and a nonzero exit status.

The exit status—as well as the options —*status* (no output, only return statuses) and –*w* (warn if the checksum line is improperly formatted)—can help you set up an automated checking system. Some software downloading and distribution systems, like RPM (40.11), can do this for you (although in automated systems, it's worth thinking about the integrity of the checksum: does it come from a system you can trust?). If you're a system administrator, look into Tripwire, a tool for tracking MD5 checksums of lots of files on your system.

—*JP*

50.13 Shell Scripts Must Be Readable and (Usually) Executable

Almost everyone knows that you need to make a program file executable—otherwise, Unix won't execute it. Well, that's true for directly executable binary files like C and Pascal programs, but it's not quite true for interpreted programs like shell scripts.

The Unix kernel can read an executable binary directly: if there's execute permission, the kernel is happy; it doesn't need read permission. But a shell script has to be read by a user's Unix program (a shell). To read a file, any Unix program has to have read permission. So shell scripts must be readable.

36.17

Shell scripts don't need execute permission if you start the shell and give it the script file to read:

```
% sh scriptfile
% sh < scriptfile
```

The execute permission is a sign for the kernel that it can try to execute the file when you type only the filename:

```
% scriptfile
```

So shell scripts don't need to be executable—it's just handy.

—JP

50.14 Why Can't You Change File Ownership?

This restriction is not bogus, because the system supports disk quotas (15.11). If you could give away your own files, you could do something like the following:

```
% mkdir .hide; chmod 700 .hide
% cd .hide
% create_huge_file >foo
% chown prof1 foo
% create_huge_file >bar
% chown prof2 bar
% create_huge_file >baz
% chown prof3 baz
```

All you would need do is find someone with a high quota or no quota (such as a professor) who does not often check his own usage (such as a professor) and probably does not care that the disk is 99 percent full (such as a, er, well, never mind), and then give away files as necessary to keep under your own quota. You could regain ownership of the file by copying it to another disk partition, removing the original, and copying it back.

If you need to change ownership, there is a workaround (50.15) that doesn't require root access.

—CT

50.15 How to Change File Ownership Without chown

Unix systems with disk quotas (15.11) won't let you change the owner (50.14) of a file; only the superuser can use *chown*. Here's a workaround for those systems.

1. The file's current owner should make sure that the new owner has write permission on the directory where the file is and read permission on the file itself:

-d 8.5
```
jerry% ls -dl . afile
drwxr-xr-x   2 jerry      512  Aug 10 12:20 .
-rw-r--r--   1 jerry     1934  Aug 10 09:34 afile
jerry% chmod go+w .
```

2. The new owner (logged in as herself) should rename the file, make a copy, and delete the original file. If the new owner is there at the same time, *su* (49.9) is probably the fastest way to change accounts:

```
jerry% su laura
Password:
laura% mv afile afile.tmp
laura% cp -p afile.tmp afile
laura% ls -l afile
-rw-r--r--   1 laura     1934  Aug 10 09:34 afile
laura% rm -f afile.tmp
laura% exit
jerry% chmod go-w .
```

-f 14.10

The *cp –p* (10.12) command preserves the file's original permissions and last modification time. After the new owner (*laura*) is done copying, the old owner (*jerry*) takes away the directory's write permission again. Now *laura* can edit *afile*, change its modes, and so on: she owns it.

—JP

51

SSH

51.1 Enabling Remote Access on Mac OS X

Enabling SSH (46.6) on Mac OS X is fairly simple. Access the System Preferences from the Apple menu and double-click the Sharing folder. When this opens, click the Application tab and check the box labeled "Allow remote login." Quit System Preferences, and the machine is now configured for SSH access, remotely.

To enable *telnet*, *rsh*, or *rlogin* (if you're sure you want these processes), open the Terminal window and edit the */etc/inetd.conf* file (using *sudo* (49.11) if you're logged in as a member of the administration group (49.7) or login as root). Remove the pound sign (#) from in front of whatever remote service you want to enable:

```
#ftp     stream   tcp   nowait   root   /usr/libexec/tcpd        ftpd -L
```

You'll need to restart the server, or you can restart *inetd* (46.5) by typing:

```
kill -HUP `cat /var/run/inetd.pid`
```

—*SP*

51.2 Protecting Access Through SSH

The problems associated with *telnet* and *ftp*, such as passing plain text passwords, can be overcome through the use of SSH (46.6). SSH encrypts any communication between the client and the server, preventing anyone from capturing the information in transit. You should always use SSH to connect to your system remotely.

SSH works by authenticating the client using one of several authentication schemes, including a simple authentication that looks for a client machine within */etc/hosts.equiv*. If the user on the local machine matches the username on the remote machine, they're allowed in. This isn't particularly safe, but it does provide encryption of transmitted data.

A second authentication scheme verifies that the login would normally validate with the *$HOME/.rhosts*—as with *rlogin*—and that the client can verify the host's key; if so, login is permitted. This is safer than the first authentication scheme.

However, a better method is RSA-based authentication using public-private keys. Regardless, once SSH is enabled, you can then use it to telnet or rlogin to the server machine, and all data transmitted is safe from snooping.

—*SP*

51.3 Free SSH with OpenSSH

In some systems, such as Mac OS X, SSH (46.6) is built-in. In other cases you can use commercial products, such as SecureCRT. However, there is a freely available application you can download called OpenSSH, available at *http://www.openssh.com*.

There are installation packages for OpenSSH for Linux, Solaris, FreeBSD, AIX—in fact, most versions of Unix.

OpenSSH has multiple tools, used in place of existing connectivity applications:

ssh
> Replaces *telnet* and *rlogin*

scp
> Replaces *rcp* for copying files

sftp
> Replaces *ftp*

In addition, the installation features the necessary server-side installation as well as utilities to assist in the setup and maintenance of the application.

To configure OpenSSH with FreeBSD, check the documentation page at *http://www.freebsd.org/doc/en_US.ISO8859-1/books/handbook/openssh.html*. To use OpenSSH with Redhat Linux, check the web pages at *http://www.redhat.com/docs/manuals/linux/RHL-7.3-Manual/custom-guide/ch-openssh.html*. Check your Unix system documentation for OpenSSH installation specific to your environment.

—*SP*

51.4 SSH Problems and Solutions

In the next sections, we cover a wide range of difficulties, organized by category. We list what, in our experience, are the most frequently asked of the frequently asked questions. We focus on problems that may occur in many versions of the SSH software on diverse operating systems. We don't address issues like this one, which rapidly become obsolete:

Compilation problems specific to one operating system, such as "HyperLinux beta 0.98 requires the –with-woozle flag"

In all questions, we assume you have already used debug or verbose mode (e.g., *ssh –v*) to isolate the problem. (If you haven't, you should!)

—SP

51.5 General and Authentication Problems

Q: *The commands ssh (46.6), scp, ssh-agent, ssh-keygen, etc., aren't doing what I expect. Even the help messages look weird.*

A: Maybe they are SSH2 programs when you are expecting SSH1, or vice versa. Locate the executables and do an *ls –l*. If they are plain files, they are most likely from SSH1 or OpenSSH. If they are symbolic links, check whether they point to SSH1 or SSH2 files. (SSH2 files have names ending in "2".)

Q: *When I try to connect to an SSH server, I get the error "Connection refused."*

A: No SSH server is running where you tried to connect. Double-check the hostname and TCP port number: perhaps the server is running on a port different from the default?

Q: *When I log in, the message of the day (/etc/motd) prints twice.*

A: Both *sshd* and the *login* program are printing it. Disable *sshd*'s printing by setting the serverwide configuration keyword PrintMotd to no.

Q: *When I log in, I see two messages about email, such as "No mail" or "You have mail."*

A: Both *sshd* and the *login* program are checking for mail. Prevent *sshd* from checking by setting the serverwide configuration keyword CheckMail to no.

Q: *The SSH1 server says "Permission denied" and exits.*

A: This occurs if all authentication techniques have failed. Run your client in debug mode and read the diagnostic messages, looking for clues. Also read our solutions to specific authentication problems in the rest of this section.

Q: *How do I authenticate without typing a password or passphrase?*

A: The four available authentication methods for this are:

- Public-key with *ssh-agent*
- Public-key with an unencrypted key on disk (empty passphrase)
- Trusted-host
- Kerberos (SSH1 and OpenSSH/1 only)

Automatic authentication has a number of important issues you should carefully consider before selecting from the preceding list.

Q: *I get prompted for my password or passphrase, but before I have time to respond, the SSH server closes the connection.*

A: Your server's idle timeout value may be too short. If you are a system administrator of the server machine, set IdleTimeout to a larger value in the server-wide configuration file. If you are an end user of SSH1 or OpenSSH, set an idle-timeout value in *authorized_keys*.

Q: *RequiredAuthentications doesn't work.*

A: This feature was broken in SSH2 2.0.13, causing authentication always to fail. This problem was fixed in 2.1.0.

Q: *SilentDeny doesn't seem to work for any authentication method.*

A: SilentDeny has nothing to do with authentication. It applies only to access control using AllowHosts and DenyHosts. If a connection is denied access by an AllowHosts or DenyHosts value, SilentDeny controls whether the client sees an informative failure message or not.

Q: *Password authentication isn't working.*

A: Use *ssh –v*. If the connection is being refused altogether, the SSH server is probably not running, or you are connecting to the wrong port. Port 22 is the default, but the remote system administrator might have changed it. If you see "permission denied," password authentication might be disabled in the server.

Make sure the server permits password authentication in the serverwide configuration file (PasswordAuthentication yes for SSH1 and OpenSSH, AllowedAuthentications password for SSH2). Also check your client configuration file to make sure you don't have PasswordAuthentication no.

If you are prompted for your password, but it is rejected, you might accidentally be connecting to the wrong account. Does your local username differ from the remote username? If so, you must specify the remote username when connecting:

```
$ ssh -l my_remote_username server.example.com
$ scp myfile my_remote_username@server.example.com:
```

If this still doesn't work, check your local client configuration file (*~/.ssh/config* or *~/.ssh2/ssh2_config*) to make sure you haven't accidentally set the wrong value for the User keyword. In particular, if your configuration file contains Host values with wildcards, check that your current command line (the one that isn't working) isn't matching the wrong section in the file.

One common problem on the server side involves OpenSSH and Pluggable Authentication Modules configuration. PAM is a general system for performing authentication, authorization, and accounting in an application-independent fashion. If your operating system supports PAM (as Linux and HPUX do, for example), OpenSSH will probably have been automatically compiled to use it. Unless you take the extra step of configuring PAM to support SSH, all password authentications will mysteriously fail. This is usually just a matter of copying the appropriate *sshd.pam* file from the *contrib* directory in the OpenSSH distribution, naming the copy *sshd* and placing it in the PAM configuration directory (usually */etc/pam.d*). The *contrib* directory contains several example files for different flavors of Unix. For example, on a RedHat Linux system:

```
# cp contrib/redhat/sshd.pam /etc/pam.d/sshd
# chown root.root /etc/pam.d/sshd
# chmod 644 /etc/pam.d/sshd
```

If OpenSSH isn't using PAM, and password authentication still isn't working, the compilation switches –with-md5-passwords or –without-shadow might be relevant. These make no difference if PAM support is enabled in OpenSSH, because they deal with how OpenSSH reads the Unix *passwd* map. When using PAM, the OpenSSH code doesn't read the *passwd* map directly; the PAM libraries do it instead. Without PAM, though, if your system is using MD5-hashed passwords instead of the more traditional *crypt* (DES) hash, you must use –with-md5-passwords. You can tell which hash your system is using by inspecting the */etc/passwd* and */etc/shadow* files. The hashed password is the second field in each entry; if the password field in */etc/passwd* is just "x", the real entry is in */etc/shadow* instead. MD5 hashes are much longer and contain a wider range of characters:

```
# /etc/shadow, MD5 hash
test:$1$tEMXcnZB$rDEZbQXJzUz4g2J4qYkRh.:...
# /etc/shadow, crypt hash
test:JGQfZ8DeroV22:...
```

Finally, you can try –without-shadow if you suspect OpenSSH is trying to use the shadow password file, but your system doesn't use it.

Q: *The server won't let me use an empty password.*

A: Empty passwords are insecure and should be avoided. Nevertheless, you can set PermitEmptyPasswords yes in the serverwide configuration file.

Q: *Trusted-host authentication isn't working (SSH1 RhostsRSA, SSH2 host-based).*

A: Use *ssh –v*. If everything looks right, check the following. Suppose the client user is orpheus@earth, and the target account is orpheus@hades—that is, on host *earth*, user orpheus invokes *ssh hades*.

Q: *For SSH1 and OpenSSH/1*

A: The SSH client program must be setuid root.

`RhostsRSAAuthentication` yes belongs in the server and client configurations.

The client's public host key must be in the server's known hosts list. In this case, *hades:/etc/ssh_known_hosts* must contain an entry associating the name "earth" with earth's public host key, like this:

```
earth 1024 37 71641647885140363140390131934...
```

The entry may be in the target account's known hosts file instead, i.e., in *hades:~orpheus/.ssh/known_hosts*. Take care that "earth" is the canonical name of the client host from the server's point of view. That is, if the SSH connection is coming from the address 192.168.10.1, *gethostbyname(192.168.10.1)* on hades must return "earth", not a nickname or alias for the host (e.g., if the hostname is *river.earth.net*, the lookup must not return just "river"). Note that this can involve multiple naming services, since gethostbyname can be configured to consult multiple sources to determine a translation (e.g., DNS, NIS, */etc/hosts*). See */etc/nsswitch.conf*. If your systems don't agree on canonical hostnames, you'll have no end of trouble with RhostsRSA. You can work around such problems to an extent by manually adding extra host nicknames to the known hosts file, like this:

```
earth,gaia,terra 1024 37 71641647885140363140390131934...
```

Edit *hades:/etc/shosts.equiv* or *hades:~orpheus/.shosts* to allow the login. Adding earth to *shosts.equiv* allows any nonroot user on earth to access the account by the same name on hades. Adding earth to *.shosts* allows orpheus@earth to access orpheus@hades.

Some firewalls reject outbound connections from privileged ports. This prevents RhostsRSA authentication from working, since it relies on privileged source ports. You can use *ssh –P* to get a connection to the SSH server via a nonprivileged port, but you will have to use a different kind of authentication.

Q: *For SSH2*

A: `AllowedAuthentications` hostbased in the server and client configurations.

ssh2 doesn't need to be setuid root, but *ssh-signer2* does. More precisely, it needs to be able to read the private host key, which in the normal installation means it must be setuid root.

A copy of earth's public host key in *hades:/etc/ssh2/knownhosts/earth.ssh-dss.pub* (or *hades:~orpheus:/.ssh2/knownhosts/earth.ssh-dss.pub*, if you specified "UserKnownHosts yes" on the server).

Regarding canonical hostnames, the same comments as for RhostsRSA apply.

Q: *For OpenSSH/2*

A: DSAAuthentication yes belongs in the server and client configurations.

ssh must be setuid root (or otherwise able to read the client hosts's private host key in */etc/ssh_host_dsa_key* ; it doesn't require a privileged source port).

A copy of earth's public host key in *hades:/etc/ssh_known_hosts2* (or *hades:~orpheus:/.ssh/known_hosts2*).

The same comments as for RhostsRSA apply, regarding canonical hostnames.

Q: *How do I install my public key file on the remote host the first time?*

A: Here's the general method:

1. Generate a key pair.
2. Copy the text of the public key into your computer's clipboard or other cut/paste buffer.
3. Log into the remote host via SSH with password authentication, which doesn't require any special files in your remote account.
4. Edit the appropriate authorization and key files on the remote host:
   a. For SSH1 and OpenSSH/1, append the public key to *~/.ssh/authorized_keys*.
   b. For OpenSSH/2, append the public key to *~/.ssh/authorized_keys2*.
   c. For SSH2, paste the public key into a new *.pub* file in *~/.ssh2* (say, *newkey.pub*), and append the line "Key newkey.pub" to *~/.ssh2/authorization*.
5. Log out from the remote host.
6. Log back into the remote host using public-key authentication.

When editing the remote authorization file, make sure your text editor doesn't insert line breaks into the middle of a public key. SSH1 and OpenSSH public keys are very long and must be kept on a single line.

Q: *I put my SSH public key file mykey.pub into my remote SSH directory, but public-key authentication doesn't work.*

A: Placing a valid public key file (e.g., *mykey.pub*) in your SSH directory isn't sufficient. For SSH1 and OpenSSH/1, you must append the key (i.e., the contents of *mykey.pub*) to *~/.ssh/authorized_keys*. For OpenSSH/2, append the key to *~/.ssh/authorized_keys2*. For SSH2, you must add a line of text to *~/.ssh2/authorization*, Key mykey.pub.

Q: *Public-key authentication isn't working.*

A: Invoke the client in debug mode (*ssh –v*). Make sure:

- Your local client is using the expected identity file.
- The correct public key is on the remote host in the right location.
- Your remote home directory, SSH directory, and other SSH-related files have the correct permissions.

Q: *I'm being prompted for my login password instead of my public key passphrase. Or, my connection is rejected with the error message "No further authentication methods available." (SSH2)*

A: There are several possible causes for both of these problems.

Public-key authentication must be enabled in both the client and server (SSH1/OpenSSH RSAAuthentication yes, SSH2 AllowedAuthentications publickey).

Specify your remote username with *–l* (lowercase L) if it differs from your local username, or else the SSH server will examine the wrong remote account:

```
$ ssh -l jones server.example.com
```

Check the file permissions in your server account. If certain files or directories have the wrong owner or careless access permissions, the SSH server refuses to perform public-key authentication. This is a security feature. Run *ssh* in verbose mode to reveal the problem:

```
$ ssh -v server.example.com
...
server.example.com: Remote: Bad file modes for /u/smith/.ssh
```

In your server account, make sure that the following files and directories are owned by you and aren't world writable: ~, ~/.ssh, ~/.ssh/authorized_keys, ~/.ssh2, ~/.rhosts, and ~/.shosts.

For SSH2, if you use the *–i* option to specify an identification file:

```
$ ssh2 -i my-identity server.example.com
```

check that *my-identity* is an identification file, not a private key file. (In contrast, *ssh –i* for SSH1 and OpenSSH expects a private key file.) Remember that SSH2 identification files are text files containing the names of private keys.

Q: *I'm being prompted for the passphrase of the wrong key.*

A: Make sure your desired public key is in your authorization file on the SSH server machine.

Check for SSH agent problems. Are you running an agent and trying to specify another key with *ssh –i* or the IdentityFile keyword? The presence of an agent prevents *–i* and IdentityFile from working. Terminate your agent and try again.

For SSH1 and OpenSSH, if any options are specified in *~/.ssh/authorized_keys*, check for typographical errors. A mistyped option causes the associated key line to be skipped silently. Remember that options are separated by commas, not whitespace.

Q: *After the PGP passphrase prompt, I am being prompted for my login password.*

A: If you get prompted for your PGP key, and then your password:

```
Passphrase for pgp key "mykey": ********
smith's password:
```

and you know you're typing your passphrase correctly, first make sure you're typing your PGP passphrase correctly. (For instance, encrypt a file with that public key and decrypt it.) If so, then there might be an incompatibility between the PGP implementations on your client and server machines. We've seen this behavior when the PGP key (generated on the client machine) doesn't have sufficient bits for the PGP implementation on the server machine. Generate a new key on the server machine.

Q: *I get "Invalid pgp key id number '0276C297'".*

A: You probably forgot the leading "0x" on the key ID, and SSH is trying to interpret a hexadecimal number as a decimal. Use `PgpKeyId 0x0276C297` instead.

—SP

51.6 Key and Agent Problems

Q: *I generated a key with SSH1 and tried using it with another SSH1 client, such as NiftyTelnet SSH, F-Secure SSH Client, or SecureCRT, but the client complains that the key is in an invalid format.*

A: First, make sure you generated the key using *ssh-keygen1*, not *ssh-keygen2*. SSH1 and SSH2 keys aren't compatible.

Next, make sure you transferred the key file using an appropriate file-transfer program. If you used FTP, confirm that the private key file was transferred in binary mode, or the copy will contain garbage. The public key file should be transferred in ASCII mode.

Q: *I generated an SSH1 key and tried using it with SSH2, but it didn't work. (Or vice versa.)*

A: This is normal. SSH1 and SSH2 keys aren't compatible.

Q: *I specified a key manually, using –i or IdentityFile, but it never gets used!*

A: Are you running an agent? If so, –i and `IdentityFile` don't have any effect. The first applicable key in the agent takes precedence.

Q: *Each time I run ssh-keygen, it overwrites my default identity file.*

A: Tell *ssh-keygen* to write its output to a different file. For *ssh-keygen* in SSH1 and OpenSSH, use the *–f* option. For *ssh-keygen2*, specify the filename as the last argument on the command line; no option is needed.

Q: *Can I change the passphrase for a key without regenerating the key?*

A: Yes. For *ssh-keygen* in SSH1 and OpenSSH, use the *–N* option, and for *ssh-keygen2*, use the *–p* option.

Q: *How do I generate a host key?*

A: Generate a key with an empty passphrase and install it in the correct location:

```
# SSH1, OpenSSH
$ ssh-keygen -N '' -b 1024 -f /etc/ssh_host_key
# SSH2 only
$ ssh-keygen2 -P -b 1024 /etc/ssh2/hostkey
```

Q: *Generating a key takes a long time.*

A: Yes it may, depending on the speed of your CPU and the number of bits you have requested. DSA keys tend to take longer than RSA keys.

Q: *How many bits should I make my keys?*

A: We recommend at least 1024 bits for strong security.

Q: *What does oOo.oOo.oOo.oOo mean, as printed by ssh-keygen2?*

A: The manpage calls it a "progress indicator." We think it's an ASCII representation of a sine wave. Or the sound of a chattering gorilla. You can hide it with the *–q* flag.

Q: *My ssh-agent isn't terminating after I log out.*

A: If you use the single-shell method to start an agent, this is normal. You must terminate the agent yourself, either manually (bleah) or by including appropriate lines in your shell configuration files (6.3). If you use the subshell method, the agent automatically terminates when you log out (actually, when you exit the subshell) (6.3).

Q: *When I invoke ssh-add and type my passphrase, I get the error message "Could not open a connection to your authentication agent."*

A: Follow this debugging process.

Make sure you are running an *ssh-agent* process:

```
$ /usr/bin/ps -ef | grep ssh-agent
smith 22719    1  0 23:34:44 ?        0:00 ssh-agent
```

If not, you need to run an agent before *ssh-add* will work.

Check that the agent's environment variables are set:

```
$ env | grep SSH
SSH_AUTH_SOCK=/tmp/ssh-barrett/ssh-22719-agent
SSH_AGENT_PID=22720
```

If not, you probably ran *ssh-agent* incorrectly, like this:

```
# Wrong!
$ ssh-agent
```

For the single-shell method, you must use *eval* with backquotes:

```
$ eval `ssh-agent`
```

Or, for the subshell method, you must instruct *ssh-agent* to invoke a shell:

```
$ ssh-agent $SHELL
```

Make sure the agent points to a valid socket:

```
$ ls -lF $SSH_AUTH_SOCK
prwx- - -  1 smith    0 May 14 23:37 /tmp/ssh-smith/ssh-22719-agent|
```

If not, your *SSH_AUTH_SOCK* variable might be pointing to an old socket from a previous invocation of *ssh-agent*, due to user error. Terminate and restart the agent properly.

Q: *My per-account server configuration isn't taking effect.*

A: You might be confused about which versions of SSH use which files:

> SSH1, OpenSSH/1: *~/.ssh/authorized_keys*
> SSH2: *~/.ssh2/authorization*
> OpenSSH/2: *~/.ssh/authorized_keys2* (note this isn't in *~/.ssh2*)

Remember that the *authorized_keys* and *authorized_keys2* files contains keys, whereas the SSH2 *authorization* file contains directives referring to other key files.

You might have a typographical error in one of these files. Check the spelling of options, and remember to separate SSH1 *authorized_keys* options with commas, not whitespace. For example:

```
# correct
no-x11-forwarding,no-pty 1024 35 86975112479875257848665526224505...
# INCORRECT (will silently fail)
no-x11-forwarding no-pty 1024 35 86975112479875257848665526224505...
# ALSO INCORRECT (note the extra space after "no-x11-forwarding,")
no-x11-forwarding, no-pty 1024 35 86975112479875257848665526224505...
```

—SP

51.7 Server and Client Problems

Q: *How do I get sshd to recognize a new configuration file?*

A: You can terminate and restart *sshd*, but there's quicker way: send the "hangup" signal (SIGHUP) to *sshd* with *kill –HUP*.

Q: *I changed the sshd config file and sent SIGHUP to the server. But it didn't seem to make any difference.*

A: *sshd* may have been invoked with a command-line option that overrides that keyword. Command-line options remain in force and take precedence over configuration file keywords. Try terminating and restarting *sshd.*

Q: *A feature of ssh or scp isn't working, but I'm sure I'm using it correctly.*

A: The feature might have been disabled by a system administrator, either when the SSH software was compiled (Chapter 4) or during serverwide configuration (Chapter 5). Compile-time flags cannot be checked easily, but serverwide configurations are found in the files */etc/sshd_config* (SSH1, OpenSSH) or */etc/ssh2/sshd2_config* (SSH2). Ask your system administrator for assistance.

Q: *ssh or scp is behaving unexpectedly, using features I didn't request.*

A: The program might be responding to keywords specified in your client configuration file (7.1). Remember that multiple sections of the *config* file apply if multiple Host lines match the remote machine name you specified on the command line.

Q: *My SSH1 .ssh/config file doesn't seem to work right.*

A: Remember that after the first use of a "Host" directive in the *config* file, all statements are inside some Host block, because a Host block is only terminated by the start of another Host block. The *ssh1* manpage suggests that you put defaults at the end of the *config* file, which is correct; when looking up a directive in the *config* file, *ssh1* uses the first match it finds, so defaults should go after any Host blocks. But don't let your own indentation or whitespace fool you. The end of your file might look like:

```
# last Host block
Host server.example.com
 User linda
# defaults
User smith
```

You intend that the username for logging into *server.example.com* is "linda", and the default username for hosts not explicitly listed earlier is "smith". However, the line "User smith" is still inside the "Host server.example.com" block. And since there's an earlier User statement for *server.example.com*, "User smith" doesn't ever match anything, and *ssh* appears to ignore it. The right thing to do is this:

```
# last Host block
Host server.example.com
 User linda
# defaults
Host *
 User smith
```

Q: *My .ssh2/ssh2_config file doesn't seem to work right.*

A: See our answer to the previous question for SSH1. However, SSH2 has the opposite precedence rule: if multiple configurations match your target, the *last*, not the first, prevails. Therefore your defaults go at the beginning of the file.

Q: *I want to suspend ssh with the escape sequence, but I am running more than two levels of ssh (machine to machine to machine). How do I suspend an intermediate ssh?*

A: One method is to start each *ssh* with a different escape character; otherwise, the earliest *ssh* client in the chain interprets the escape character and suspends.

Or you can be clever. Remember that if you type the escape character twice, that's the meta-escape: it allows you to send the escape character itself, circumventing its usual special function. So, if you have several chained *ssh* sessions, all using the default escape character ~, you can suspend the *n*th one by pressing the Return key, then *n* tildes, then Control-Z.

Q: *I ran an ssh command in the background on the command line, and it suspended itself, not running unless I "fg" it.*

A: Use the *–n* command-line option, which instructs *ssh* not to read from stdin (actually, it reopens stdin on */dev/null* instead of your terminal). Otherwise, the shell's job-control facility suspends the program if it reads from stdin while in the background.

Q: *ssh prints "Compression level must be from 1 (fast) to 9 (slow, best)" and exits.*

A: Your CompressionLevel is set to an illegal value for this host, probably in your *~/.ssh/config* file. It must be an integer between 1 and 9, inclusive.

Q: *ssh prints "rsh not available" and exits.*

A: Your SSH connection attempt failed, and your client was configured to fall back to an *rsh* connection. However, the server was compiled without *rsh* fallback support or with an invalid path to the *rsh* executable.

If you didn't expect your SSH connection to fail, run the client in debug mode and look for the reason. Otherwise, the SSH server is just not set up to receive *rsh* connections.

Q: *ssh1 prints "Too many identity files specified (max 100)" and exits.*

A: SSH1 has a hardcoded limit of 100 identity files (private key files) per session. Either you ran an *ssh1* command line with over 100 *–i* options, or your configuration file *~/.ssh/config* has an entry with over 100 IdentityFile keywords. You should never see this message unless your SSH command lines and/or configuration files are being generated automatically by another application, and something in that application has run amok. (Or else you're doing something *really* funky.)

Q: *ssh1 prints "Cannot fork into background without a command to execute" and exits.*

A: You used the *–f* flag of *ssh1*, didn't you? This tells the client to put itself into the background as soon as authentication completes, and then execute whatever remote command you requested. But, you didn't provide a remote command. You typed something like:

```
# This is wrong
$ ssh1 -f server.example.com
```

The *–f* flag makes sense only when you give *ssh1* a command to run after it goes into the background:

```
$ ssh1 -f server.example.com /bin/who
```

If you just want the SSH session for port-forwarding purposes, you may not want to give a command. You have to give one anyway; the SSH1 protocol requires it. Use *sleep 100000*. Don't use an infinite loop like the shell command *while true; do false; done*. This gives you the same effect, but your remote shell will eat all the spare CPU time on the remote machine, annoying the sysadmin and shortening your account's life expectancy.

Q: *ssh1 prints "Hostname or username is longer than 255 characters" and exits.*

A: *ssh1* has a static limit of 255 characters for the name of a remote host or a remote account (username). You instructed *ssh1*, either on the command line or in your configuration file, to use a hostname or username that's longer than this limit.

Q: *ssh1 prints "No host key is known for <server name> and you have requested strict checking (or 'cannot confirm operation when running in batch mode')," and exits.*

A: The client can't find the server's host key in its known-hosts list, and it is configured not to add it automatically (or is running in batch mode and so can't prompt you about adding it). You must add it manually to your per-account or systemwide known-hosts files.

Q: *ssh1 prints "Selected cipher type…not supported by server" and exits.*

A: You requested that *ssh1* use a particular encryption cipher, but the SSH1 server doesn't support it. Normally, the SSH1 client and server negotiate to determine which cipher to use, so you probably forced a particular cipher by providing the *–c* flag on the *ssh1* command line or by using the Cipher keyword in the configuration file. Either don't specify a cipher and let the client and server work it out, or select a different cipher.

Q: *ssh1 prints "channel_request_remote_forwarding: too many forwards" and exits.*

A: *ssh1* has a static limit of 100 forwardings per session, and you've requested more.

Q: *scp printed an error message: "Write failed flushing stdout buffer. write stdout: Broken pipe" or "packet too long".*

A: Your shell startup file (e.g., *~/.cshrc*, *~/.bashrc*), which is run when *scp* connects, might be writing a message on standard output. These interfere with the communication between the two *scp1* programs (or *scp2* and *sftp-server*). If you don't see any obvious output commands, look for *stty* or *tset* commands that might be printing something.

Either remove the offending statement from the startup file or suppress it for noninteractive sessions:

```
if ($?prompt) then
    echo 'Here is the message that screws up scp.'
endif
```

The latest versions of SSH2 have a new server configuration statement, `AllowCshrcSourcingWithSubsystems`, which should be set to `no` to prevent this problem.

Q: *scp printed an error message, "Not a regular file."*

A: Are you trying to copy a directory? Use the *–r* option for a recursive copy. Otherwise, you may be trying to copy a special file that it doesn't make sense to copy, such as a device node, socket, or named pipe. If you do an *ls – l* of the file in question and the first character in the file description is something other than - (for a regular file) or d (for a directory), this is probably what's happening. You didn't really want to copy that file, did you?

Q: *Why don't wildcards or shell variables work on the scp command line?*

A: Remember that wildcards and variables are expanded by the *local* shell first, not on the remote machine. This happens even before *scp* runs. So if you type:

```
$ scp server.example.com:a* .
```

the local shell attempts to find local files matching the pattern `server.example.com:a*`. This is probably not what you intended. You probably wanted files matching a* on *server.example.com* to be copied to the local machine.

Some shells, notably C shell and its derivatives, simply report "No match" and exit. Bourne shell and its derivatives (*sh*, *ksh*, *bash*), finding no match, will actually pass the string `server.example.com:a*` to the server as you'd hoped.

Similarly, if you want to copy your remote mail file to the local machine, the command:

```
$ scp server.example.com:$MAIL .
```

might not do what you intend. $MAIL is expanded locally before *scp* executes. Unless (by coincidence) $MAIL is the same on the local and remote machines, the command won't behave as expected.

Don't rely on shell quirks and coincidences to get your work done. Instead, escape your wildcards and variables so the local shell won't attempt to expand them:

```
$ scp server.example.com:a\* .
$ scp 'server.example.com:$MAIL' .
```

Q: *I used scp to copy a file from the local machine to a remote machine. It ran without errors. But when I logged into the remote machine, the file wasn't there!*

A: By any chance, did you omit a colon? Suppose you want to copy the file *myfile* from the local machine to *server.example.com*. A correct command is:

```
$ scp myfile server.example.com:
```

but if you forget the final colon:

```
# This is wrong!
$ scp myfile server.example.com
```

myfile gets copied locally to a file called *server.example.com*. Check for such a file on the local machine.

Q: *How can I give somebody access to my account by scp to copy files but not give full login permissions?*

A: Bad idea. Even if you can limit the access to *scp*, this doesn't protect your account. Your friend could run:

```
$ scp evil_authorized_keys you@your.host:.ssh/authorized_keys
```

Oops, your friend has just replaced your *authorized_keys* file, giving himself full login permissions. Maybe you can accomplish what you want with a clever forced command, limiting the set of programs your friend may run in your account.

Q: *scp -p preserves file timestamps and modes. Can it preserve file ownership?*

A: No. Ownership of remote files is determined by SSH authentication. Suppose user smith has accounts on local computer *L* and remote computer *R*. If the local smith copies a file by *scp* to the remote smith account, authenticating by SSH, the remote file is owned by the *remote* smith. If you want the file to be owned by a different remote user, *scp* must authenticate as that different user. *scp* has no other knowledge of users and uids, and besides, only root can change file ownership (on most modern Unix variants, anyway).

Q: *Okay, scp -p doesn't preserve file ownership information. But I am the superuser, and I'm trying to copy a directory hierarchy between machines (scp -r) and the files have a variety of owners. How can I preserve the ownership information in the copies?*

A: Don't use *scp* for this purpose. Use *tar* and pipe it through *ssh*. From the local machine, type:

```
# tar cpf - local_dir | (ssh remote_machine "cd remote_dir; tar xpf -")
```

Q: *sftp2 reports "Cipher <name> is not supported. Connection lost."*

A: Internally, *sftp2* invokes an *ssh2* command to contact *sftp-server*. It searches the user's PATH to locate the *ssh2* executable rather than a hardcoded location. If you have more than one version of SSH2 installed on your system, *sftp2* might invoke the wrong *ssh2* program. This can produce the error message shown.

For example, suppose you have both SSH2 and F-Secure SSH2 installed. SSH2 is installed in the usual place, under */usr/local*, whereas F-Secure is installed under */usr/local/f-secure*. You ordinarily use SSH2, so */usr/local/bin* is in your PATH, but */usr/local/f-secure* isn't. You decide to use the F-Secure version of *scp2* because you want the CAST-128 cipher, which SSH2 doesn't include. First, you confirm that the SSH server in question supports CAST-128:

```
$ /usr/local/f-secure/bin/ssh2 -v -c cast server
...
debug: c_to_s: cipher cast128-cbc, mac hmac-sha1, compression none
debug: s_to_c: cipher cast128-cbc, mac hmac-sha1, compression none
```

Satisfied, you try *scp2* and get this:

```
$ /usr/local/f-secure/bin/scp2 -c cast foo server:bar
FATAL: ssh2: Cipher cast is not supported.
Connection lost.
```

scp2 is running the wrong copy of *ssh2* from */usr/local/bin/ssh2*, rather than */usr/local/f-secure/bin/ssh2*. To fix this, simply put */usr/local/f-secure/bin* earlier in your PATH than */usr/local/bin*, or specify the alternative location of *ssh2* with *scp2 -S*.

The same problem can occur in other situations where SSH programs run other programs. We have run afoul of it using host-based authentication with both 2.1.0 and 2.2.0 installed. The later *ssh2* ran the earlier *ssh-signer2* program, and the client/signer protocol had changed, causing it to hang.

Q: *sftp2 reports "ssh_packet_wrapper_input: invalid packet received."*

A: Although this error appears mysterious, its cause is mundane. A command in the remote account's shell startup file is printing something to standard output, even though stdout isn't a terminal in this case, and *sftp2* is trying to interpret this unexpected output as part of the SFTP packet protocol. It fails and dies.

You see, *sshd* uses the shell to start the *sftp-server* subsystem. The user's shell startup file prints something, which the SFTP client tries to interpret as an SFTP protocol packet. This fails, and the client exits with the error message; the first field in a packet is the length field, which is why it's always that message.

To fix this problem, be sure your shell startup file doesn't print anything unless it's running interactively. *tcsh*, for example, sets the variable $interactive if stdin is a terminal. This problem has been addressed in SSH 2.2.0 with the AllowCshrcSourcingWithSubsystems flag, which defaults to no, instructing the shell not to run the user's startup file.

Q: *I'm trying to do port forwarding, but ssh complains: "bind: Address already in use."*

A: The port you're trying to forward is already being used by another program on the listening side (the local host if it's a *–L* forwarding or the remote host if it's a *–R*). Try using the *netstat –a* command, available on most Unix implementations and some Windows platforms. If you see an entry for your port in the LISTEN state, you know that something else is using that port. Check to see whether you've inadvertently left another *ssh* command running that's forwarding the same port. Otherwise, just choose another, unused port to forward.

This problem can occur when there doesn't appear to be any other program using your port, especially if you've been experimenting with the forwarding feature and have repeatedly used the same *ssh* to forward the same port. If the last one of these died unexpectedly (you interrupted it, or it crashed, or the connection was forcibly closed from the other side, etc.), the local TCP socket may have been left in the TIME_WAIT state (you may see this if you used the *netstat* program as described earlier). When this happens, you have to wait a few minutes for the socket to time out of this state and become free for use again. Of course, you can just choose another port number if you're impatient.

Q: *How do I secure FTP with port forwarding?*

A: This is a complex topic. FTP has two types of TCP connections, control and data. The control connection carries your login name, password, and FTP commands; it is on TCP port 21 and can be forwarded by the standard method. In two windows, run:

```
$ ssh -L2001:name.of.server.com:21 name.of.server.com
$ ftp localhost 2001
```

Your FTP client probably needs to run in passive mode (execute the passive command). FTP data connections carry the files being transferred. These connections occur on randomly selected TCP ports and can't be forwarded in general, unless you enjoy pain. If firewalls or NAT (network address translation) are involved, you may need additional steps (or it may not be possible).

Q: *X forwarding isn't working.*

A: Use *ssh –v*, and see if the output points out an obvious problem. If not, check the following.

Make sure you have X working before using SSH. Try running a simple X client such as *xlogo* or *xterm* first. Your local *DISPLAY* variable must be set, or SSH doesn't attempt X forwarding.

X forwarding must be turned on in the client and server, and not disallowed by the target account (that is, with no-X11-forwarding in the *authorized_keys* file).

sshd must be able to find the *xauth* program to run it on the remote side. If it can't, this should show up when running *ssh –v*. You can fix this on the server side with the XAuthLocation directive (SSH1, OpenSSH), or by setting a PATH (that contains *xauth*) in your remote shell startup file.

Don't set the *DISPLAY* variable yourself on the remote side. *sshd* automatically sets this value correctly for the forwarding session. If you have commands in your login or shell startup files that unconditionally set *DISPLAY*, change the code to set it only if X forwarding isn't in use.

OpenSSH sets the remote *XAUTHORITY* variable as well, placing the *xauth* credentials file under */tmp*. Make sure you haven't overridden this setting, which should look like:

```
$ echo $XAUTHORITY
/tmp/ssh-maPK4047/cookies
```

Some flavors of Unix actually have code in the standard shell startup files (e.g., */etc/bashrc, /etc/csh.login*) that unconditionally sets *XAUTHORITY* to *~/.Xauthority*. If that's the problem, you must ask the sysadmin to fix it; the startup file should set *XAUTHORITY* only if the variable is unset.

If you are using an SSH startup file (*/etc/sshrc* or *~/.ssh/rc*), *sshd* doesn't run *xauth* for you on the remote side to add the proxy key; one of these startup files must do it, receiving the proxy key type and data on standard input from *sshd*

—*SP*

Glossary

AIX

A version of Unix from the IBM Corporation.

argument

Zero or more characters passed to a program or function as a single unit. The shell breaks a command line into arguments by cutting it at unquoted whitespace.

array

An ordered collection of data items. An array has a single overall name; each item in it is called an *element* or *member*. For instance, the C shell stores its command search path in an *array* named *path*. The first array member is named $path[1], the second is $path[2], and so on. Some arrays are indexed from zero (e.g., C, Perl).

ASCII text file

Formally, a text file containing only ASCII characters. More commonly (in the U.S., at least), a file containing text that's printable, viewable, and has no "binary" (non-ASCII) characters. ASCII characters use only seven of the bits in a (8-bit) byte.

backquote

The character `. Not the same as a single quote (′). Used in pairs, does *command substitution*.

backslash

The character \. In Unix, it changes the interpretation of the next character in some way. *See also* article 27.18.

batch queue

A mechanism for sequencing large jobs. A batch queue receives job requests from users. It then executes the jobs one at a time. Batch queues go back to the earliest days of data processing. They are an extremely effective, if uncomfortable, way to manage system load.

bin directory

A directory for storing executable programs. *See also* article 7.4.

binaries, binary file

A file with nontext characters. Often, a directly executable file that can be run as a program. Binary characters use all the bits in a (8-bit) byte.

block size

The largest amount of data that a Unix filesystem will always allocate contiguously. For example, if a filesystem's block size is 8 KB, files of size up to 8 KB are always physically contiguous (i.e., in one place), rather than spread across the disk. Files that are larger than the filesystem's block size may be fragmented: 8 KB pieces of the file are located in different places on the disk. Fragmentation limits filesystem performance. Note that the filesystem block size is different from a disk's physical block size, which is almost always 512 bytes.

brain-damaged

How a program with poor design or other errors can be described.

BSD Unix

The versions of Unix developed at the University of California, Berkeley. BSD (Berkeley Software Distribution) Unix has been dominant in academia and has historically had some features more advanced than System V: BSD introduced virtual memory, TCP/IP networking, and the "fast filesystem" to the Unix community. It is also the system on which Sun OS was based. System V Release 4 and some vendors' earlier System V versions also have Berkeley features.

buffer

A temporary storage place such as a file or an area of the computer's memory. Most text editors store the file you're editing in a buffer; when you're done editing, the edited buffer is copied over (i.e., replaces) the original file.

command line

The text you type at a shell prompt. A Unix shell reads the command line, parses it to find the command name (which is usually the first word on the command line, though it can be a variable assignment), and executes the command. A command line may have more than one command joined by operators such as semicolons (;), pipes (|), or *double ampersands* (&&).

control character

A character you make by holding down the keyboard CTRL (Control) key while pressing a letter or another character key.

core file, core dump

The file made when a program terminates abnormally. The *core* file can be used for debugging. This comes from ancient "core" memory, where the contents of memory were stored in a magnetized ferrite core. *See also* article 15.4.

.cshrc file

See article 3.3.

daemon

A program that is invisible to users but provides important system services. Daemons manage everything from paging to networking to notification of incoming mail. *See also* article 1.10.

data switch

Hardware that is something like a telephone switchboard. A data switch connects many terminals to two or more computers. The user, on a terminal or through a modem, tells the data switch to which computer she wants a connection. A data switch is also called a *terminal multiplexor*. Computers without data switches usually have one terminal connected to each *tty* port; characteristics like the terminal type can be set in system files. Conversely, computers with data switches can't know in advance what sort of terminal is connected to each *tty* port.

default

In a program that gives you more than one choice, the one you get by not choosing. The default is usually the most common choice. As an example, the default file for many Unix programs is the standard input. If you don't give a filename on the command line, a program will read its standard input.

dot (.) files (.cshrc, .login, .profile)

Files that are read when you start a program (including when you log in and start a shell). These set up your environment and run any other Unix commands (for instance, *tset*). If your account uses the C shell, it will read *.cshrc* and *.login*. Accounts that use the Bourne shell and shells like it read *.profile*. *See also* article 3.6.

double quote

The " character. This isn't the same as two single quotes (' ') together. The " is used around a part of a Unix command line where the shell should do variable and command substitution (and, on the C shell, history substitution), but no other interpretation. *See also* articles 27.12 and 27.13.

escape

Using *escape* on a character or a string of characters is a way to change how it is interpreted. This can take away its special meaning, as in *shell quoting*; or it can add special meaning, as in terminal escape sequences.

flag

In programming, a *flag variable* is set to signal that some condition has been met or that something should be done. For example, a flag can be set ("raised") if the user has entered something wrong; the program can test for this flag and not continue until the problem has been fixed.

flame

A heated or irrational statement.

Free Software Foundation (FSF)

A group that develops the freely available GNU software. Their address is: 675 Massachusetts Avenue, Cambridge, MA 02139 USA.

full-duplex

Communications between a terminal and a computer where data flows in both directions at the same time. *Half-duplex* communications, where data flows in only one direction at a time, are unusual these days.

GNU

Gnu's Not Unix, a system of software planned eventually to be a freely available substitute for Unix.

gotcha

A "catch," difficulty, or surprise in the way that a program works.

hardcoded

In general, a value that can't be changed. For example, in a shell script with the command grep jane, the value jane is hardcoded; *grep* will always search for *jane*. But in the command grep $USER, the text that *grep* searches for is not hardcoded; it's a variable value.

hash table

Hashing data into the format of a hash table lets specially designed programs search for data quickly. A hash table assigns a special search code to each piece of data. For example, the C shell uses a hash table to locate commands more quickly; the *rehash* command rebuilds the hash table after you add a new command.

I/O

Input/output of text from software or hardware.

inode

A data structure that describes a file. Within any filesystem, the number of inodes, and hence the maximum number of files, is set when the filesystem is created.

i-number

A Unix file has a name (for people to identify it) and an i-number (for Unix to identify it). Each file's i-number is stored in a directory, along with the filename, to let Unix find the file that you name.

job

One Unix command. It is easy to be sloppy and use the terms job, process, and program interchangeably. I do it, and I'm sure you do, too. Within Unix documentation, though, the word "job" is usually used to mean one, and only one, command line. Note that one command line can be complex. For example:

```
pic a.ms | tbl | eqn | troff -ms
```

is one command, and hence one job, that is formed from four processes.

job number

Shells with job control assign a job number to every command that is stopped or running in the *background*. You can use job numbers to refer to your own commands or groups of commands. Job numbers are generally easier to use than process IDs; they are much smaller (typically between 1 and 10) and therefore easier to remember. The C-shell *jobs* command displays job numbers. *See also* article 23.2.

kernel

The part of the Unix operating system that provides memory management, I/O services, and all other low-level services. The kernel is the "core" or "heart" of the operating system. *See also* article 1.10.

kludge

A program or a solution to a problem that isn't written carefully, doesn't work as well as it should, doesn't use good programming style, and so on.

library function

Packages of system calls (and of other library functions) for programmers in C and other languages. In general (though not always), a library function is a "higher-level operation" than a system call.

load average

A measure of how busy the CPU is. The load average is useful, though imprecise. It is defined as the average number of jobs in the run queue plus the average number of jobs that are blocked while waiting for disk I/O. The *uptime* command shows the load average.

.login file

See the "dot (.) files (.cshrc, .login, .profile)" entry in this glossary and article 3.4.

mode

In Unix, an octal number that describes what access a file's owner, group, and others have to the file. *See also* article 1.17.

modulo

Think back to your fourth grade arithmetic. When you divide two numbers, you have a *dividend* (the number on top), a *divisor* (the number on the bottom), a *quotient* (the answer), and a *remainder* (what's left over). In computer science, this kind of division is very important. However, we're usually more interested in the remainder than in the quotient. When we're interested in the remainder, we call the operation a *modulus* (or *modulo*, or *mod*). For instance, one of the examples in your fourth grade arithmetic text might have been 13 ÷ 3 = 4 (with a remainder of 1). As computer users, we're more interested in 13 mod 3 = 1. It's really the same operation, though. *Modulo* is also used in expressions like "modulo wildcards," which means "everything but wildcards."

NFS

Network File System. NFS allows Unix systems and many non-Unix systems to share files via a TCP/IP network. Subject to certain security restrictions, systems are allowed complete access to another system's files. *See also* articles 1.21 and 44.9.

newline

The character that marks the end of a line of text in most Unix files. (This is a convention, not a requirement.) Usually expressed as "\n" or LF.

null

Empty, zero-length, with no characters—for example, a *null string*. This is *not* the same as an ASCII NUL character.

octal number

The base 8 numbering system. Octal numbers are made with the digits 0 through 7, and begin with O. For example, the decimal (base 10) number 12 is the same as the octal number 14. ASCII character codes are often shown as octal numbers.

option switch

Typed on a command line to modify the way that a Unix command works. Usually starts with a dash (-). The terms *option* and *switch* are more or less interchangeable. An option may have several settings, but a switch usually has two settings: on or off, enabled or disabled, yes or no, etc.

panic

Unix jargon for a "crash." A panic is really a special kind of a crash. Panics occur when Unix detects some irreconcilable inconsistency in one of its internal data structures. The kernel throws up its hands and shuts the system down before any damage can be done. As it is going down, it prints a "panic" message on the console.

parse

To split into pieces and interpret.

partition

A portion of a disk drive. Unix disk drives typically have eight partitions, although not all are in use.

path, search

See article 35.6.

pipe

A Unix mechanism for sending the output of one program directly to the input of another program, without using an intermediate file. All Unix systems support pipes. System V and

Sun OS also provide "named pipes," which are FIFO (first-in/first-out) buffers that have names and can be accessed via the filesystem.

portable

A program that's *portable* can be used on more than one version of Unix or with more than one version of a command.

POSIX

POSIX is not an OS, but a standard for how Unix-like OSes should behave at various levels. As an effort to counter the balkanization of Unix from vendor to vendor, POSIX defines the ways in which Unix-like OSes should expose their interfaces, from the kernel up to program- and shell-argument level.

priority

A number that determines how often the kernel will run a process. A higher-priority process will run more often—and, therefore, will finish faster—than a low-priority process.

process

A lot of the time, a process is nothing more than another name for a program that is running on the system. But there is a more formal definition: a process is a single execution thread or a single stream of computer instructions. One job may be built from many different processes. For example, a command line with pipes starts two or more processes. *See also* article 24.3.

process ID (PID)

Unix assigns every process an ID number (called a PID) when it starts. *See also* article 24. 3. This number allows you to refer to a process at a later time. If you need to *kill* a runaway program, you refer to it by its process ID. The *ps* command displays process IDs.

.profile file

See article 3.4.

prompt

How a program asks you for information: by printing a short string like Delete afile? to the terminal and waiting for a response. *See also* "shell prompt."

pseudo-code

A way to write out program text, structured like a program, without using the actual programming language. Pseudo-code usually explains a program.

read-only filesystem

Filesystems are usually set up to allow write access to users who have the proper *permissions*. The system administrator can mount a filesystem *read-only*; then no user can make changes to files there.

recursive

A program or routine that re-executes itself or repeats an action over and over. For example, the *find* program moves through a directory tree recursively, doing something in each directory.

reverse video

On a video display, reversed foreground and background colors or tones. Reverse video is used to highlight an area or to identify text to be used or modified. For instance, if text is usually shown with black letters on a white background, reverse video would have white letters on a black background.

SCSI

Small Computer Systems Interface, a standard interface for disk and tape devices now used on many Unix (and non-Unix) systems.

search path

A list of directories that the shell searches to find the program file you want to execute. *See also* articles 17.29 and 35.6.

shell

A program that reads and interprets command lines and also runs programs. *See also* article 27.3.

shell prompt

A signal from a shell (when it's used interactively) that the shell is ready to read a command line. By default, the percent sign (%) is the default C-shell prompt and the dollar sign ($) is the default Bourne-shell prompt. The default *bash*-shell prompt is also the dollar sign ($).

slash

The character /. It separates elements in a pathname. *See also* article 1.16.

single quote

The ' character. This isn't the same as a back-quote (`). The single quote is used around a part of a Unix command line where the shell should do no interpretation (except history substitution in the C shell). *See also* articles 27. 12 and 27.13.

special file

An entity in the filesystem that accesses I/O devices. There is a special file for every terminal, every network controller, every partition of every disk drive, and every possible way of accessing every tape drive. *See also* article 1.19.

string

A sequence of characters.

subdirectory

A directory within a directory. *See also* articles 1.16 and 7.7.

swapping

A technique that the Unix kernel uses to clean up physical memory. The kernel moves pages from memory to disk and then reassigns the memory to some other function. Processes that have been idle for more than a certain period of time may be removed from memory to save space. Swapping is also used to satisfy extreme memory shortages. When the system is extremely short of memory, active processes may be "swapped out."

system call

The lowest-level access to the Unix operating system. Everything else in Unix is built on system calls.

System V Unix

A version of Unix from AT&T. The most recent Release of System V is Release 4, known as V.4 or SVR4.

TCP/IP

Transmission Control Protocol/Internet Protocol. A network protocol that is commonly used for communications via an Ethernet. TCP/IP is also called the "Internet protocol." It is also common to use TCP/IP over leased lines for long-distance communications.

termcap

Stands for *term*inal *cap*abilities, an early (and still common) way to describe terminals to Unix.

terminal emulator

A program that makes a computer display emulate (act like) a terminal. For example, many terminal-emulator programs emulate the Digital Equipment Corporation VT100 terminal.

terminfo

A newer way to describe terminal capabilities to Unix.

the Net

A term for two particular networks: *Usenet and Internet.* For instance, "I read it on the Net" or "You can get that file on the Net."

timestamp

The Unix filesystem stores the times that each file was last modified, accessed, or had a change to its inode. These times—especially the modification time—are often called *time-stamps.*

truncate

To cut, to shorten—for example, "truncate a file after line 10" means to remove all lines after line 10.

uuencode, uudecode

Utilities that encode files with binary (8-bit) characters into an ASCII (7-bit) format and decode them back into the original binary format. This is used for transferring data across communications links that can't transfer binary (8-bit) data. *See also* article 39.2.

VAX/VMS

A popular computer operating system from the Digital Equipment Corporation.

wedged

A terminal or program is *wedged* when it's "frozen" or "stuck." The normal activity stops and often can't be restarted without resetting the terminal or killing the program.

whitespace

A series of one or more space or TAB characters.

word

Similar to a word in a spoken language like English, a word is a unit made up of one or more characters. But unlike English, words in Unix can contain whitespace; they can also have no characters (a *zero-length* word).

XENIX

One of the first versions of Unix to run on IBM PCs, and one of the few that will run on 80286 systems. XENIX descends from Version 7 Unix, a version developed by AT&T in the late 1970s. It has many resemblances to BSD Unix. Over time, XENIX has been rewritten as a variant of System V.2.

zombies

Dead processes that have not yet been deleted from the process table. Zombies normally disappear almost immediately. However, at times it is impossible to delete a zombie from the process table, so it remains there (and in your *ps* output) until you reboot. Aside from their slot in the process table, zombies don't require any of the system's resources. *See also* article 24.20.

Index

Symbols

& (ampersand)
  &! background operator, Z shell, 446
  &| background operator, Z shell, 446
  && (Boolean AND) operator, 216, 381, 564, 605, 718, 842, 847
  & (logical AND) operator, 763
  commands ending with, 436, 438, 454
  metacharacter in regular expressions, 677

< > (angle brackets)
  <
    << (here document) operator, 534, 560
    < (less than) operator, 385, 762, 846
    <= (less than or equal to) operator, 385, 762, 847
    <<- operator, removing tab characters, 535, 560
    < redirection character, 888
  >
    > as Bourne shell secondary prompt, 556
    > (greater than) operator, 762, 846
    >= (greater than or equal to) operator, 385, 762, 847
    > (redirection) operator, 891
    >& (redirection) operator, 891
    > tcsh shell prompt, 11
    >> (Unix redirect and append) operator, 317
  < >, enclosing event names, 132
  \< \> regular expression metacharacters, 643, 652
  <=> (comparison) operator in Perl, 847
  <-> filename wildcard, 659

* (asterisk)
  ** filename wildcard (zsh), 659
  *** filename wildcard (zsh), 659
  arithmetic operator (multiplication), 762
  executable files, denoting in ls -F listings, 164
  filename wildcard, 658, 659
  multiplication operator, 846
  regular expression metacharacter, 636, 637
    quantifier in Perl, 855
    repeating character sets with, 641
    use in Unix programs, 651
  shell metacharacter, 636
  wildcard character, 19, 189

@ (at sign)
  @ARGV array, 844
  csh built-in operator, 545
  filename wildcard, 659
  files as symbolic links, in ls -F listings, 164
  for array names, 848
  in Perl array values, 844
  @INC array, 841, 844
  kill character, 106

` (backquotes)
  \` \`, nested command substitution, 769
  arguments, reading, 565
  capturing command output in an array, 855
  command substitution operators, 96, 170, 174, 561
    excluding files from deletion, 275
    getopt, using with, 731
    nesting, 562
  expr command, running with, 764
  for loops combined with, 750
  quoting in Bourne shell, 528
  redirecting standard output, 756

We'd like to hear your suggestions for improving our indexes. Send email to *index@oreilly.com*.

success or failure of commands, indication in exit
  status, 715
sudo application, 991
SUID scripts, 989
SunOS
  groups, 998
  redirecting standard I/O, 887
superuser
  configuring, paths set by parent process
    and, 519
  file ownership, changing, 998
  killing others' processes, 471
  private directories, access to, 150
  shell prompt for, 79
  sudo application, 991
  tcsh and zsh shell prompts, 72
  UID and GID of zero, 983
susp key, 105
suspend command, 436, 455
suspending
  background jobs with stop command, 436
  current foreground job with CTRL-z
    command, 436, 438
swap space, checking for security breaches, 975
swapinfo utility, 976
swat tool, 956
  configuring smb.conf file installation, 952
  printers, selecting for sharing, 958
symbolic links, 205
  copying, 215
  directories, linking, 210
  disk space and, 280
  filenames for, showing, 212
  files as, 164
  finding for every directory owned by a
    group, 180
  finding unconnected, 169
  finding with find -type command, 184
  hard links vs., 206
  saving disk space wiwth, 279
  spooling, using for, 919
  stale, 208, 209
  syntax of, 206
  to /dev/null
    replacing log files with, 279
  to .enter and .exit files, 631
symbolic mode (chmod), 1000
symbols
  in filenames and pathnames, 725
  for keys on the keyboard (keysyms), 124
  (see also special characters; Symbols section)
symlinks (see symbolic links)
sync program, 16

synchronizing
  filesystems (rsync program), 374
  time on networks, 781
"Syntax error" error message, 777
syntax-checking program, 306
sys.stderr file object (Python), 875
sys.stdin file object (Python), 875
sys.stdout file object (Python), 875
system
  cron jobs, running on, 489
  environment variables for shells, 45
    C shells, 46
  load, checking with uptime, 506
  overloaded with background processes, 441,
    443
  password file contents, 11
  performance and profiling, 500–510
  security vulnerabilities, 969
  statistics on (/proc/stat file), 464
  time, 503
system calls, 7
  exec and fork, 452
  fork and exec, 514
  limit and ulimit (limiting file sizes), 280
  unlink( ), in Perl, 272
system command (nawk), 388
system function, 856
System V
  command version, getting, 32
  <defunct> status, 470
  echo command, shell quoting and, 540
  groups, 987
  groups (Release 4), 998
  ls command, nonprinting characters and, 166
  nice command, 509
  printing commands, 916
  priority system (Release 4), 507
  ps command
    -a option, 460
    -e option, 462
    -ef options, 458
  signals, 468
  systems derived from, rsh on, 143
  tr command
    character ranges in, 405
    -cs options, 307
    piping ww function output to, 305
system variables (awk), 382
system word file, 299
system-level key mappings, 126

T

About the Authors

Shelley Powers is an independent contractor, currently living in St. Louis, who specializes in technology architecture and software development. She's authored several computer books, including *Developing ASP Components*, *Unix Power Tools, Third Edition*, *Essential Blogging*, and *Practical RDF*. In addition, Shelley has also written several articles related primarily to web technology, many for O'Reilly.

Shelley's web site network is at *http://burningbird.net*, and her weblog is Burningbird, at *http://weblog.burningbird.net*.

Jerry Peek is a long-time user of the Unix operating system. He has acted as a Unix consultant, courseware developer, and instructor. He is one of the original authors of *Unix Power Tools* and the author of *Learning the Unix Operating System*, both by O'Reilly.

Tim O'Reilly is the founder and CEO of O'Reilly & Associates, Inc. He has written numerous books on computer topics, including *UNIX Text Processing* (with Dale Dougherty), *Managing UUCP and USENET* (with Grace Todino), and *Windows XP in a Nutshell* (with David Karp and Troy Mott). Tim is an activist for open source, open standards, and an end to bogus software patents. He received the 2001 Isaiah Thomas Award for Publishing.

Mike Loukides is an editor for O'Reilly & Associates. He is the author of *System Performance Tuning* and *UNIX for FORTRAN Programmers*. Mike's interests are system administration, networking, programming languages, and computer architecture. His academic background includes degrees in electrical engineering (B.S.) and English literature (Ph.D.).

Colophon

Our look is the result of reader comments, our own experimentation, and feedback from distribution channels. Distinctive covers complement our distinctive approach to technical topics, breathing personality and life into potentially dry subjects.

The image on the cover of *Unix Power Tools*, Third Edition, is an AC Dyno-Mite DC drill made by the Millers Falls Company, circa 1950.

Jeffrey Holcomb was the production editor for *Unix Power Tools*, Third Edition. Leanne Soylemez and Jeffrey Holcomb were the copyeditors. Mary Brady, Linley Dolby, and Claire Cloutier provided quality control. Genevieve d'Entremont, Julie Flanagan, Andrew Savikas, Brian Sawyer, and Sue Willing were the compositors. Ellen Troutman-Zaig wrote the index.

Edie Freedman designed the cover of this book. Emma Colby produced the cover layout with QuarkXPress 4.1 using Adobe's ITC Garamond font.

David Futato designed the interior layout. This book was converted to FrameMaker 5.5.6 with a format conversion tool created by Erik Ray, Jason McIntosh, Neil Walls, and Mike Sierra that uses Perl and XML technologies. The text font is Linotype Birka; the heading font is Adobe Helvetica Neue Condensed; and the code font is LucasFont's TheSans Mono Condensed. The illustrations that appear in the book were produced by Robert Romano and Jessamyn Read using Macromedia FreeHand 9 and Adobe Photoshop 6. This colophon was written by Jeffrey Holcomb.

Need in-depth answers fast?

Access over 2,000 of the newest and best technology books online

Safari Bookshelf is the premier electronic reference library for IT professionals and programmers—a must-have when you need to pinpoint exact answers in an instant.

Access over 2,000 of the top technical reference books by twelve leading publishers including O'Reilly, Addison-Wesley, Peachpit Press, Prentice Hall, and Microsoft Press. Safari provides the technical references and code samples you need to develop quality, timely solutions.

Try it today with a FREE TRIAL
Visit *www.oreilly.com/safari/max/*

For groups of five or more, set up a free, 30-day corporate trial
Contact: *corporate@oreilly.com*

What Safari Subscribers Say:

"The online books make quick research a snap. I usually keep Safari up all day and refer to it whenever I need it."

—Joe Bennett, Sr. Internet Developer

"I love how Safari allows me to access new books each month depending on my needs. The search facility is excellent and the presentation is top notch. It is one heck of an online technical library."

—Eric Winslow, Economist-System,
Administrator-Web Master-Programmer

Related Titles Available from O'Reilly

Unix Administration

CVS Pocket Reference, *2nd Edition*

DNS & BIND, *4th Edtion*

DNS & BIND Cookbook

Essential CVS

Essential System Administration, *3rd Edition*

Essential System Administration Pocket Reference

Postfix: The Definitive Guide

qmail

sendmail, *3rd Edition*

sendmail Cookbook

System Performance Tuning, *2nd Edition*

The Unix CD Bookshelf, *Version 3.0*

Unix Backup & Recovery

Unix Basics

GNU Emacs Pocket Reference

Learning GNU Emacs, *2nd Edition*

Learning the bash Shell, *2nd Edition*

Learning the Korn Shell

Learning the Unix Operating System, *5th Edition*

Learning the vi Editor, *6th Edition*

sed & awk Pocket Reference, *2nd Edition*

sed & awk, *2nd Edition*

Unix in a Nutshell, System V Edition, *3rd Edition*

Using csh & tcsh

Unix Tools

BSD Hacks

Effective awk Programming, *3rd Edition*

lex & yacc, *2nd Edition*

Managing Projects with make, *2nd Edition*

Practical PostgreSQL

The Complete FreeBSD, *4th Edition*

Writing GNU Emacs Extensions

O'REILLY®

Our books are available at most retail and online bookstores.
To order direct: 1-800-998-9938 • *order@oreilly.com* • *www.oreilly.com*
Online editions of most O'Reilly titles are available by subscription at *safari.oreilly.com*

Keep in touch with O'Reilly

1. Download examples from our books

To find example files for a book, go to:

www.oreilly.com/catalog

select the book, and follow the "Examples" link.

2. Register your O'Reilly books

Register your book at *register.oreilly.com*

Why register your books?
Once you've registered your O'Reilly books you can:

- Win O'Reilly books, T-shirts or discount coupons in our monthly drawing.
- Get special offers available only to registered O'Reilly customers.
- Get catalogs announcing new books (US and UK only).
- Get email notification of new editions of the O'Reilly books you own.

3. Join our email lists

Sign up to get topic-specific email announcements of new books and conferences, special offers, and O'Reilly Network technology newsletters at:

elists.oreilly.com

It's easy to customize your free elists subscription so you'll get exactly the O'Reilly news you want.

4. Get the latest news, tips, and tools

www.oreilly.com

- "Top 100 Sites on the Web"—PC Magazine
- CIO Magazine's Web Business 50 Awards

Our web site contains a library of comprehensive product information (including book excerpts and tables of contents), downloadable software, background articles, interviews with technology leaders, links to relevant sites, book cover art, and more.

5. Work for O'Reilly

Check out our web site for current employment opportunities:

jobs.oreilly.com

6. Contact us

O'Reilly & Associates
1005 Gravenstein Hwy North
Sebastopol, CA 95472 USA

TEL: 707-827-7000 or 800-998-9938
(6am to 5pm PST)

FAX: 707-829-0104

order@oreilly.com
For answers to problems regarding your order or our products. To place a book order online, visit:

www.oreilly.com/order_new

catalog@oreilly.com
To request a copy of our latest catalog.

booktech@oreilly.com
For book content technical questions or corrections.

corporate@oreilly.com
For educational, library, government, and corporate sales.

proposals@oreilly.com
To submit new book proposals to our editors and product managers.

international@oreilly.com
For information about our international distributors or translation queries. For a list of our distributors outside of North America check out:

international.oreilly.com/distributors.html

adoption@oreilly.com
For information about academic use of O'Reilly books, visit:

academic.oreilly.com

O'REILLY®

Our books are available at most retail and online bookstores.
To order direct: 1-800-998-9938 • *order@oreilly.com* • *www.oreilly.com*
Online editions of most O'Reilly titles are available by subscription at *safari.oreilly.com*

P 462
P 501 profiler for CPO...
504 lastcomm ?

md 5 sum
1008
1009 - snmp-Mle
to sM